ST F-DAX → F4 .

THE OXFORD HANDBOOK OF

THE HISTORY OF PHENOMENOLOGY

THE OXFORD HANDBOOK OF

THE HISTORY OF

PHENOMENOLOGY

Edited by

DAN ZAHAVI

OXFORD
UNIVERSITY PRESS

OXFORD
UNIVERSITY PRESS

Great Clarendon Street, Oxford, OX2 6DP,
United Kingdom

Oxford University Press is a department of the University of Oxford.
It furthers the University's objective of excellence in research, scholarship,
and education by publishing worldwide. Oxford is a registered trade mark of
Oxford University Press in the UK and in certain other countries

Published in the United States of America by Oxford University Press
198 Madison Avenue, New York, NY 10016, United States of America

British Library Cataloguing in Publication Data
Data available

Library of Congress Control Number: 2017959163

ISBN 978-0-19-875534-0

Printed and bound by
CPI Group (UK) Ltd, Croydon, CR0 4YY

Contents

PART III THEMES

CONTRIBUTORS

Michael D. Barber is professor of philosophy at Saint Louis University. He is the author of numerous articles and several books on the phenomenology of the social world, including *The Participating Citizen: A Biography of Alfred Schutz* (2004). With Jochen Dreher, he edited Alfred Schutz's *Schriften zur Literatur*, volume 8 of the *Alfred Schütz Werkausgabe* (2013). He is also the editor of *Schutzian Research*.

Debra Bergoffen is emerita professor of Philosophy, George Mason University where she chaired the Philosophy Department and directed the Women's Studies program. Currently the Bishop Hamilton Philosopher in Residence, American University, she has served as co-director of the Society for Existentialism and Phenomenology (SPEP). The author of *Contesting the Politics of Genocidal Rape: Affirming the Dignity of the Vulnerable Body* (2013), and *The Philosophy of Simone de Beauvoir: Gendered Phenomenologies, Erotic Generosities* (1976), and editor of several anthologies, her essays on Beauvoir, feminist theory, human rights and vulnerability can be found in numerous journals and collections.

Robert Bernasconi is Edwin Erle Sparks Professor of Philosophy and African American Studies at Penn State University. He is the author of two books on Heidegger, one on Sartre, and numerous articles in critical philosophy of race as well as on nineteenth- and twentieth-century philosophy. He is the co-editor of such volumes as *Emmanuel Levinas: Basic Philosophical Writings* (1996), *The Cambridge Companion to Levinas* (2002), and *Situating Existentialism* (2012). He is editor of the journal *Critical Philosophy of Race*.

Rudolf Bernet is Emeritus Professor of Philosophy at the University of Leuven (Belgium) and President of the Husserl Archives. He is the author of numerous articles on phenomenology, philosophical aesthetics, and psychoanalysis. His books include: *An Introduction to Husserlian Phenomenology* (with I. Kern and E. Marbach) (1993), *La vie du sujet* (1994), *Conscience et existence* (2004), *Force-Pulsion-Désir* (2013). He has prepared critical editions of Husserl's posthumous writings on time (1985, 2001) and edited (with D. Welton and G. Zavota) *Edmund Husserl: Critical Assessments of Leading Philosophers* (2005). In 2008 he was awarded the Alexander von Humboldt-Forschungspreis. He is also served as president of the German Society for Phenomenology.

Antonio Calcagno is professor of philosophy at King's University College, London, Canada. He is the author of *Giordano Bruno and the Logic of Coincidence* (1998), *Badiou* and Derrida: Politics, Events and Their Time (2007), The Philosophy of Edith Stein (2007), Lived Experience from the Inside Out: Social and Political Philosophy in Edith Stein (2014).

Steven Crowell is Joseph and Joanna Nazro Mullen Professor of Philosophy at Rice University. He has authored numerous articles on phenomenology, as well as two books: *Normativity and Phenomenology in Husserl and Heidegger* (2013) and *Husserl, Heidegger, and the Space of Meaning: Paths toward Transcendental Phenomenology* (2001). He edited *The Cambridge Companion to Existentialism* (2012) and, with Jeff Malpas, *Transcendental Heidegger* (2007). Currently he co-edits *Husserl Studies* with Sonja Rinofner-Kreidl.

Daniel O. Dahlstrom is John R. Silber Professor of Philosophy at Boston University. He is also the author of *Philosophical Legacies: Essays on the Thought of Kant, Hegel, and their Contemporaries* (2008), *The Heidegger Dictionary* (2013), and *Identity, Authenticity, and Humility* (2017). In addition to translating Heidegger's first Marburg lectures, *Introduction to Phenomenological Research* (2005), he has edited *Interpreting Heidegger: Critical Essays* (2011) and *Gatherings*, the Heidegger Circle's annual from 2010 to 2014.

Zachary Davis is an associate professor of philosophy at St. John's University. He is the author of numerous articles on phenomenology and Max Scheler, and completing the translation of Scheler's *Cognition and Work*. He is a member of the executive board for the Max Scheler Gesellschaft and president of the Max Scheler Society of North America.

Emmanuel de Saint Aubert, former student at the École Normale Supérieure, professor of philosophy and mathematics, is research director at the French National Center for Scientific Research (CNRS, École Normale Supérieure, Husserl Archives in Paris). He also educates professionals in the areas of troubled childhood and adolescence. His research bears most particularly on the work of Merleau-Ponty, rereading him through the lens of an overall knowledge of numerous unpublished writings. He published *Être et chair I* (2013), devoted to the influence of neurology, developmental psychology, and psychoanalysis on the elaboration of Merleau-Ponty's concept of Flesh.

Nicolas de Warren is associate professor at Penn State University and guest professor at KU Leuven. He is the author of numerous articles on phenomenology, aesthetics, literature, and political philosophy. He is the author of *Husserl and the Promise of Time: Subjectivity in Transcendental Phenomenology* (2009) and co-editor of *New Approaches to Neo-Kantianism* (2015). He is currently co-editor of the book series Contributions to Phenomenology.

James Dodd is associate professor of philosophy at the New School for Social Research (The New School) and director of the Husserl Archives in Memory of Alfred Schutz. Publications include *Phenomenology, Architecture and the Built World* (2017), *Phenomenology and Violence* (2009), *Crisis and Reflection. An Essay on Husserl's Crisis* *of the European Sciences* (2001), *Idealism and Corporeity: An Essay on the Problem of the Body in Husserl's Phenomenology* (1997), as well as articles on Schelling, Nietzsche, and the Czech philosopher Jan Patočka.

John J. Drummond is the Robert Southwell, S.J. Distinguished Professor in the Humanities and professor of philosophy at Fordham University in New York. He is the author of *Husserlian Intentionality and Non-Foundational Realism: Noema and Object* (1990) and *A Historical Dictionary of Husserl's Philosophy* (2008, reissued in paperback in 2010 as *The A to Z of Husserl's Philosophy*). He has edited or co-edited seven collections of articles on phenomenology, and he has published numerous articles on phenomenology, intentionality, the emotions, axiology, and ethics.

Denis Fisette is professor of philosophy at the Université du Québec à Montréal. He is the author of many papers and books on Husserl's philosophy, Brentano, the school of Brentano, and the philosophy of mind.

Thomas R. Flynn is Samuel Candler Dobbs Professor of Philosophy at Emory University. He has published numerous essays chiefly on Continental philosophy. His books include *Sartre and Marxist Existentialism: The Test Case of Collective Responsibility* (1984), *Sartre, Foucault and Historical Reason* Vol. 1: *Toward an Existentialist Theory of History* (1997), Vol. 2: *A Poststructuralist Mapping of History* (2005), *Existentialism. A Very Short Introduction* (2006), and *Sartre: A Philosophical Biography* (2014).

Christina M. Gschwandtner teaches Continental philosophy of religion at Fordham University. Her most recent books include *Postmodern Apologetics? Arguments for God in Contemporary Philosophy* (2012), *Degrees of Givenness: On Saturation in Jean-Luc Marion* (2014), and *Marion and Theology* (2016). She has also translated several books and many articles by various French phenomenologists (Marion, Henry, Lacoste, Falque, Greisch, and others).

Sara Heinämaa is academy professor of the Academy of Finland, leading a five-year research project in phenomenology of normality. Heinämaa holds a chair for philosophy at the University of Jyväskylä, Finland, and operates as the director of the interdisciplinary research community *Subjectivity, Historicity, Communality* (SHC). She is the author of numerous articles on phenomenology and of *Toward A Phenomenology of Sexual Difference* (2003) and *Birth, Death, and Femininity* (with Schott et al., 2010). She is editor of *Phenomenology and the Transcendental* (with Hartimo and Miettinen, 2014) and *New Perspectives on Aristotelianism and its Critics* (with Mäkinen and Tuominen, 2015). She is also co-founder of The Nordic Society for Phenomenology (NoSP) and has served two terms as its president.

Walter Hopp is associate professor at Boston University. He is the author of several articles on phenomenology and phenomenological philosophy, as well as *Perception and Knowledge: A Phenomenological Account* (2011). He is also co-editor, with Andreas Elpidorou and Daniel Dahlstrom, of *Philosophy of Mind and Phenomenology: Conceptual and Empirical Approaches* (2016).

Hanne Jacobs is an associate professor of philosophy at Loyola University Chicago. She is the editor of a series of Husserl's lecture courses published in the Husserliana Materialien series as *Einleitung in die Philosophie 1916–1920*. She has published articles on topics in phenomenology such as personal identity, attention, intersubjectivity, reflection, and phenomenological method.

Julia Jansen is professor of philosophy at KU Leuven. She is the author of numerous articles on Kant, Husserl, and phenomenology. She is co-editor of the *Phaenomenologica* series and editor of Husserl's *Collected Works*. She is also the co-editor of *Rediscovering Aesthetics* (2009) and of *Critical Communities and Aesthetic Practices* (2013).

Timo Kaitaro, PhD, is a neuropsychologist and adjunct professor (docent) of the history of philosophy at the University of Helsinki. His publications include *Diderot's Holism: Philosophical Anti-Reductionism and its Medical Background* (1997) and *Le Surréalisme. Pour un realisme sans rivage* (2008) and numerous articles on the French Enlightenment, the history of neurosciences, and the philosophy of surrealism. He has a long-standing interest in the history of the diverse ways in which the brain and the human body have been described and modeled in terms of technological and semiotic artefacts.

Tobias Keiling completed a PhD in philosophy at the University of Freiburg, Germany, and at Boston College, an MA, and is currently a postdoctoral researcher affiliated with the Human Dynamics Centre at the University of Würzburg, Germany. He has authored a book on the later Heidegger in German (*Seinsgeschichte und phänomenologischer Realismus*, 2015) and published articles on phenomenology and hermeneutics in English, German, and French.

Pavlos Kontos is professor of philosophy at the University of Patras. He is the author of *Aristotle's Moral Realism Reconsidered: Phenomenological Ethics* (2013), *L'action morale chez Aristote* (2002), *D'une phénoménologie de la perception chez Heidegger* (1996). He is editor of *Evil in Aristotle* (2017), *Phenomenology and the Primacy of the Political: Essays in Honor of Jacques Taminiaux* (with V. Fóti, 2017), and *Gadamer et les Grecs* (with J. C. Gens and P. Rodrigo, 2005).

Donald A. Landes is assistant professor in the Faculté de philosophie at Université Laval, Québec, where he is also the assistant director of the *Laboratoire de philosophie continentale*. He has published numerous articles on twentieth-century Continental philosophy, ethics, and the history of philosophy. He is the author of *Merleau-Ponty and the Paradoxes of Expression* (2013) and *The Merleau-Ponty Dictionary* (2013), as well as the translator of Maurice Merleau-Ponty's *Phenomenology of Perception* (2012).

Leonard Lawlor received his PhD in philosophy from Stony Brook University, NY, in 1988. He taught at the University of Memphis from 1989 to 2008 where he became Faudree-Hardin Professor of Philosophy. In 2008, he became Edwin Erle Sparks Professor of Philosophy at Penn State University, where he continues to teach and serve as director of graduate studies in philosophy. He is the author of eight books, among which are: *This Is Not Sufficient: An Essay on Animality in Derrida* and *Derrida and Husserl: The Basic Problem of Phenomenology*. His most recent book is *From Violence to Speaking Out: Apocalypse and Expression in Foucault, Derrida and Deleuze* (2016).

Sophie Loidolt is professor in the Philosophy Department of TU Darmstadt, Germany, and a member of the "Young Academy" of the Austrian Academy of Sciences (ÖAW). Her books include *Anspruch und Rechtfertigung. Eine Theorie des rechtlichen Denkens im Anschluss an die Phänomenologie Edmund Husserls* (2009), *Einführung in die Rechtsphänomenologie* (2010), and *Phenomenology of Plurality. Hannah Arendt on Political Intersubjectivity* (2017).

Sebastian Luft is professor of philosophy at Marquette University. He is the author of *Subjectivity and Lifeworld in Transcendental Phenomenology* (2011) and *The Space of Culture: Towards a Neo-Kantian Philosophy of Culture Following the Marburg School (Cohen, Natorp, and Cassirer)* (2015) and editor of *Husserliana 34* (2002, texts from the Nachlass on the phenomenological reduction) and of *The Neo-Kantian Reader* (2015) and translator of *Husserliana 7* and *8 (First Philosophy)*. He has served as visiting professor at Emory University (USA), the Universities of Graz (Austria), Freiburg i.Br., Paderborn (Germany), and San Juan (Puerto Rico).

Filip Mattens is an assistant professor at the University of Leuven. His research focuses on the relation between spatiality and the senses, images and architecture. He is the editor of *Meaning and Language: Phenomenological Perspectives* (2008) and, together with Carlo Ierna and Hanne Jacobs, *Philosophy, Phenomenology, Sciences: Essays in Commemoration of Edmund Husserl* (2010).

Karl Mertens is professor of philosophy at the Institute of Philosophy of the University of Würzburg. He is author of a monograph about Husserl's theory of knowledge (*Zwischen Letztbegründung und Skepsis. Kritische Untersuchungen zum Selbstverständnis der transzendentalen Phänomenologie Edmund Husserls*, 1996). He has published several articles on theory of action, social philosophy, theory of knowledge, philosophy of mind, and phenomenology. Since 2005 he has been co-editor of the journal *Phenomenological Studies (Phänomenologische Forschungen)*.

Dermot Moran is professor of philosophy at Boston College and president of the International Federation of Philosophical Studies/Fédération Internationale des Sociétés de Philosophie (FISP). His publications include: *The Philosophy of John Scottus Eriugena: A Study of Idealism in the Middle Ages* (1989), *Introduction to Phenomenology* (2000), *Edmund Husserl: Founder of Phenomenology* (2005), and *Husserl's Crisis of the European Sciences: An Introduction* (2012). He is founding editor of *The International Journal of Philosophical Studies* (1993) and co-editor of the book series Contributions to Phenomenology (Springer).

Komarine Romdenh-Romluc is a senior lecturer in philosophy at the University of Sheffield, UK. She is the author of the *Routledge Guide Book to Merleau-Ponty and the Phenomenology of Perception* (2011). She has also published articles on various aspects of Merleau-Ponty's philosophy, and other issues at the intersection of phenomenology and the philosophy of mind.

Hans Ruin is professor of philosophy at Södertörn university (Stockholm). He is the author of many articles on phenomenology and hermeneutics. Among his books are *Enigmatic Origins: Tracing the Theme of Historicity through Heidegger's Works* (1994), and an *Introduction to Being and Time* (in Swedish, 2005). He has co-edited around fifteen books, the latest of which is a three-volume work in the theory of history and memory in Swedish, entitled *Historiens hemvist I–III* (2016). He is also the co-editor of Nietzsche's Collected Works in Swedish and he is the co-founder and current president of the Nordic Society for Phenomenology.

Alessandro Salice is a lecturer in the Philosophy Department of University College Cork. He has published extensively on early phenomenology, philosophy of mind, and metaphysics. He is author of the entry, the "Phenomenology of the Munich and Göttingen Circles" for the *Stanford Encyclopaedia of Philosophy*. Recently he has edited *The Phenomenological Approach to Social Reality: History, Concepts, Problems* (2016), together with Hans Bernhard Schmid. He is co-editor of the *Journal of Social Ontology*.

Alexander Schnell is professor of philosophy (phenomenology and theoretical philosophy) at the University of Wuppertal. He is the author of numerous articles on phenomenology and classical German philosophy and of *Husserl et les fondements de la phénoménologie constructive* (2007) and *Wirklichkeitsbilder* (2015). He is editor of *Lire les Beiträge zur Philosophie de Heidegger* (2017) and, with Gilles Marmasse, *Comment fonder la philosophie?* (2014). He serves as director of the Institut für Transzendentalphilosophie und Phänomenologie (Wuppertal) and is editor of the *Annales de Phénoménologie*.

Andrea Staiti is Rita Levi Montalcini Professor of Philosophy at the University of Parma (Italy). He has previously held positions at Boston College and Albert-Ludwigs-Universität Freiburg, as well as a fellowship by the Alexander von Humboldt Stiftung. He has published articles and books on phenomenology, neo-Kantianism, naturalism, and the philosophy of the human sciences. Recent work includes *Husserl's Transcendental Phenomenology: Nature, Spirit, and Life* (2014); *New Approaches to Neo-Kantianism* (with Nicolas De Warren) (2015) and *Commentary on Husserl's Ideas I* (2015).

Anthony Steinbock is professor of philosophy and director of the Phenomenology Research Center, Southern Illinois University Carbondale. He works in the areas of phenomenology, social ontology, aesthetics, and religious philosophy. His books include *Moral Emotions: Reclaiming the Evidence of the Heart* (2014), *Phenomenology and Mysticism: The Verticality of Religious Experience* (2007/9), and *Home and Beyond: Generative Phenomenology after Husserl* (1995). He is editor-in-chief of the *Continental Philosophy Review* and general editor of Northwestern University Press's SPEP Series.

Peter Andras Varga is postdoctoral research fellow at the Institute of Philosophy of the Research Centre for the Humanities of the Hungarian Academy of Sciences in Budapest.

His scholarly research, based on a wide range of historical sources including unpublished documents, is dedicated to early phenomenology, the School of Brentano, and late nineteenth-century German philosophy in general (including its contemporaneous Hungarian reception), as well as to the methodology and historiography of phenomenology. He is the author of a Hungarian book on the origins of phenomenology (2013) and articles published in, for example, *Husserl Studies*, *Brentano Studien*, *Meinong Studies*, and *Phänomenologische Forschungen*.

Jonathan Webber is reader in philosophy at Cardiff University. He is the author of *The Existentialism of Jean-Paul Sartre* (2009), *Rethinking Existentialism* (forthcoming), and many articles on phenomenology and existentialism. He is the translator of the current English edition of Sartre's book *The Imaginary* (2004) and editor of *Reading Sartre* (2009). He is currently president of the UK Sartre Society.

Dan Zahavi is professor of philosophy and director of the Center for Subjectivity Research at the University of Copenhagen. In his systematic work, Zahavi has mainly been investigating the nature of selfhood, self-consciousness, intersubjectivity, and social cognition from a phenomenological perspective. He is author and editor of more than twenty-five volumes including *Husserl's Phenomenology* (2003), *Subjectivity and Selfhood* (2005), *The Phenomenological Mind* (with S. Gallagher) (2008/12), *Self and Other* (2014), and *Husserl's Legacy* (2017). He is co-editor-in-chief of the journal *Phenomenology and the Cognitive Sciences*.

INTRODUCTION

DAN ZAHAVI

AMONG its various accomplishments, phenomenology has often been praised for its incisive analyses of temporality and historicity. Like any other tradition, however, phenomenology also has its own (pre)history. Phenomenology did not emerge ready-made like Athena from Zeus' forehead, but was formed and developed in reaction to and under inspiration from various preceding and competing philosophical traditions. In addition, many of the principal figures in the movement kept refining and developing their own views over the years. Often their thinking underwent so decisive transformations that it has become customary to differentiate early and later stages in their philosophy, and to distinguish, say, the early Husserl from the later Husserl, or Heidegger before and after the turn (*Kehre*). Furthermore, as Ricœur once put it, the history of phenomenology is the history of Husserlian heresies; each generation of post-Husserlian phenomenologists took inspiration from the work of the founding figures, but kept transforming and modifying the methodology, scope, and aim of the phenomenological enterprise. As a result, many of the central concepts in phenomenology, concepts such as intentionality, embodiment, and temporality underwent important changes and revisions up through the twentieth century.

Given all these changes and transformations, does it still make sense to speak of phenomenology as a unified movement or do the differences between realist phenomenology, descriptive phenomenology, pure phenomenology, transcendental phenomenology, static phenomenology, genetic phenomenology, existential phenomenology, embodied phenomenology, hermeneutic phenomenology, material phenomenology, analytic phenomenology, etc. far outweigh what they might have in common? Is phenomenology a tradition by name only, with no stable identity, common method, or shared research program? Or are there still a set of common themes and concerns that have united and continue to unite its proponents? There are different ways to explore these questions. One might focus on the present, or on the past.

The *Oxford Handbook of Contemporary Phenomenology* from 2012 gathered systematic contributions on a variety of topics by a number of contemporary phenomenologists. Although the contributions differed widely in style and focus, they were all recognizable phenomenological research contributions, thereby putting to rest the idea that phenomenology is exclusively a tradition of the past.

To a larger extent than analytic philosophy, phenomenology has developed in continuing dialogue and conversation with its founding figures. Rather than simply being thinkers to write about, Husserl, Heidegger, Merleau-Ponty, etc., have been considered and conceived as conversation partners, as thinkers to think with. One notable feature of the collected systematic contributions, however, was the absence of any sustained engagement with historical figures. This was quite on purpose, however. During the initial discussions regarding the format and structure of the handbook, it was decided not to include scholarly essays that primarily focused on the history of phenomenology, but to reserve such essays for a subsequent complementary handbook, namely the present one.

The aim of *The Oxford Handbook of the History of Phenomenology* is to analyze and highlight historical influences, connections, and developments, thereby contributing to our comprehension and assessment of both the unity and diversity of the phenomenological tradition. How did it start? How did it develop? Where is it heading? Does it have a future?

The handbook is divided into three distinct parts:

The first part contains chapters that address the way phenomenology has been influenced by earlier periods or figures in the history of philosophy. More specifically, each of the chapters contains discussions of how various phenomenologists were influenced by ideas found in, say, Aristotle, Descartes, Kant, in German Idealism, or in the Brentano School.

The second part contains chapters targeting individual figures. Rather than simply offering a systematic analysis of specific concepts found in the work of the thinker in question, the focus is once again on historical connections. How was the philosopher affected by earlier figures, how did his or her view change over time, and what kind of influence did he or she exert on subsequent thinkers?

The contributions in the third and final part trace various core topics such as subjectivity, intersubjectivity, embodiment, spatiality, and imagination in the work of different phenomenologists, in order to explore how the notions were transformed, enriched, and expanded up through the century.

The contributors to the volume are scholars from many different parts of the world. Despite the size of the volume, however, there were inevitably many excellent contributors as well as many important topics that could not be included. This is regrettable, but also testifies to the vitality and richness of the tradition.

Let me thank the contributors for their vivid engagement in and help with this project. Special thanks are due to Steven Crowell, Dan Dahlstrom, and John Drummond who all went beyond the call of duty in their assistance during different stages of the review process. As always, many thanks to Peter Momtchiloff. Let me finally thank Patricia Meindl and Anton Thorell Steinø for having compiled the Index.

PART I

TRADITIONS

CHAPTER 1

....

ARISTOTLE *IN* PHENOMENOLOGY

....

PAVLOS KONTOS

It is not an overstatement to say that no other figure in the history of philosophy has exercised a stronger influence on phenomenology than Aristotle.[1] It suffices to recall Franz Brentano's decisive role in the genesis of phenomenology or to enumerate the Aristotelian concepts and patterns of thought that phenomenological research—from Husserl to its contemporary practitioners—has appropriated or assimilated. But the most critical element of that influence is the fact that Aristotle has served as the privileged pivot for phenomenology's own development. That is to say, phenomenology appears to evolve on the basis of prolific readings and misreadings of Aristotle.[2]

The present chapter is organized in three sections. Section 1.1 will present a brief overview of phenomenological approaches to Aristotle. Sections 1.2 and 1.3 will revisit a suggestive example of phenomenology's ambivalent stance toward Aristotle's philosophy, in particular his ethics. They will focus on two episodes in that long story, namely, on Heidegger's[3] and Gadamer's[4] interpretations of Aristotle and how they contributed to the elaboration of their conceptions of phenomenology.

---

[1] I am grateful to Panagiotis Thanassas, Dimitrios Yfantis, and the anonymous readers of OUP for their numerous and insightful comments on a penultimate draft of this chapter, and to Nicholas Pirovolachis for editing the English text.

[2] Hence it is not a coincidence that this chapter is complementary with others in the present volume and, in particular, with those on ethics, the early Heidegger, and Patočka.

[3] Unless indicated otherwise, Heidegger's works are cited according to the *Gesamtausgabe*.

[4] Unless otherwise indicated, Gadamer's works are cited according to the *Gesammelte Werke*.

1.1 A CHAIN OF PHENOMENOLOGY'S SELF-CRITICISMS

It is now widely accepted that Heidegger's early courses from 1919 to 1925 are milestones in the development of his understanding of phenomenology, and that a main source of inspiration is Aristotle's philosophy. During that early period, redefining phenomenology and returning to Aristotle represented two sides of the same coin. At times Heidegger announces a course on Aristotle, but along the way the task of explaining phenomenology completely absorbs him. Thus, the 1921–2 course with the title *Phenomenological Interpretations of Aristotle* and the subtitle *Introduction to Phenomenological Research* hardly refers to Aristotle except in its general introduction (Heidegger 1985: 1–9). At other times, the reverse is the case. The most telling example is the 1923–4 course, *Introduction to Phenomenological Research*, which offers a fairly reliable and extensive critique of Husserl's project and its Cartesian roots. Quite unexpectedly, however, one is made to realize that elucidating phenomenology will require going back to Aristotle (Heidegger 1994: 5–41). *Being and Time*, in its famous methodological section about the meaning of phenomenology (§7), will present a similar shift in direction.

No doubt Aristotle was already present in Husserl 1984 (for instance, in §§1 and 67–70 of the *Sixth Logical Investigation*). And, despite Husserl's unfamiliarity with Greek philosophy (his copies of Aristotelian texts, available in Leuven's *Husserl Archives*, readily document his lack of serious engagement with them), a number of Aristotelian themes permeate his phenomenology.[5] The central place that he ascribes to experience, for example, is reminiscent of *empeiria*; his concept of intuition has remarkable similarities with *nous* (intellect); and his notion of *phaenomenon* has affinities with *phantasma* (appearance). Likewise, one can hardly fail to recognize a certain connection— mediated by Brentano—between Husserl's and Aristotle's analyses of time. In the sphere of ethics and axiology Aristotlelian influence—again, mediated by Brentano—is also detectable: his phenomenology of will, for example, revolves around the notion of "what is feasible in action" (*Erreichbares*, i.e., the equivalent of Aristotle's *prakton*).[6] And, in our own day such an "Aristotelian Husserl" continues to stimulate insightful phenomenological inquiries of, among others, Robert Sokolowski and John Drummond.[7]

Heidegger's way of exploiting Aristotle's philosophy in order to circumvent alleged Husserlian impediments to a true or genuine phenomenology, moreover, is not the

---

[5] Husserl's aim to establish "First Philosophy" (*Erste Philosophie*) might, at first sight, seem to constitute a sort of retrieval of Aristotle's *prôtê philosophia* as defined, for example, in his *Metaphysics Epsilon* (E 1 1026^{a}16–32). Despite the distant affinity of the two projects, however, the ways in which the two philosophers understand "first" philosophy, its object and its scope, are quite different. For a thorough overview, see Sokolowski 2012.

[6] See Husserl 1988: 102–25.

[7] See, for instance, Sokolowski 1985 and Drummond 2014.

only one in the first generation of phenomenologists.[8] Jan Patočka followed the same route. His asubjective phenomenology, as a critique against Husserl's anthropocentrism, grew out of a reading of Aristotle's *Physics*, which was radically different from Heidegger's, in particular, of the definition of movement (see Patočka 2011). In the last decade, in its struggle to overcome the limits of Husserl's and of Merleau-Ponty's notion of subjectivity, a group of French phenomenologists around Renault Barbaras has been rediscovering Patočka's Aristotelianism (see Barbaras 2013).

It is well known that "Heidegger's Aristotle" provoked a number of reactions that continue up to the present time to fuel phenomenological research. To mention just three well-known examples: Hans Georg Gadamer and Hannah Arendt, notwithstanding their different objectives and their divergent views on Aristotle, each came to criticize Heidegger for his interpretation of Aristotle's practical philosophy. And Hans Jonas, recognizing in Aristotle's *De anima* the first treatise on philosophical biology, came to launch against Heidegger's Aristotle the accusation of nurturing a sort of "anthropological acosmism."[9]

The pursuit of Aristotle-inspired intra-phenomenological criticism did not come to a halt even with the second generation of phenomenologists. In France, in the 1960s, Pierre Aubenque inaugurated a tradition of Aristotle interpretation that strongly echoes phenomenological ideas, a tradition to which the more recent works by Rémi Brague and Pierre Rodrigo also belong. In Germany, Wolfgang Wieland, under the influence of Gadamer and Karl Löwith, revived the interest in Aristotle's *Physics* through a highly influential work that pairs phenomenological patterns of thought with analytico-linguistic concerns. In the 1990s, Paul Ricœur revisited Aristotle's practical philosophy and *Poetics* in order to bring to light the limits of Heidegger's fundamental ontology.[10]

In sum, Aristotle's philosophy proves to be an inexhaustible resource of phenomenological research. Why has phenomenology taken such an intense interest in it? Given the variety of the phenomenological approaches to it—approaches which aim at different objectives, thematize different aspects of it, and show a different degree of familiarity with the primary texts—one can hardly give a single answer. I would venture, however, to say that phenomenology found in Aristotle a "proto-phenomenologist," so to speak—one who firmly believed that each sort of science/knowledge should be grounded in its proper kind of experience (*empeiria*) and should adjust its method to the particularity of its subject matter (*hyle*), but who never abandoned the search for a universal (*katholou*) science.

---

[8] There is almost no phenomenologist of the first generation who has not written on Aristotle's philosophy; see for instance the analysis of Aristotle's ethics and politics in Fink 1970.

[9] Jonas 1982: 216.

[10] See, respectively, Aubenque 1962, Brague 2001, Rodrigo 1995, Wieland 1962, Ricœur 1990.

1.2 HEIDEGGER'S *NICOMACHEAN ETHICS*:
A STORY OF ADMIRATION AND CONTEMPT

Instead of continuing with a register of Aristotle's presence in phenomenology, let us now focus on a case study, that is, Heidegger's and Gadamer's confrontation with the *Nicomachean Ethics*, in order to make evident the sort of philosophical challenge that the return to Aristotle presented to each of them.[11]

The *Nicomachean Ethics* (*NE*) still provokes fierce debates, and one problem that has proved particularly intractable concerns the epistemological status of the treatise. Does it constitute a sort of science or not? If the former is the case, one should explain what sort of science it is and whether it is dependent on natural sciences like biology. Further, the question arises as to what sort of starting-points (*archai*) are proper to it. For there is no (Aristotelian) science that lacks principles. What does it take for someone to be able to write or understand the *Nicomachean Ethics*? One might think that practical wisdom (*phronêsis*) would be a sine qua non of such an undertaking. Practical wisdom, however, has to do with deliberate choice (*prohairesis*) and actions, not with science, regardless of whether the latter is practical or theoretical. Here is not the place to delve into these matters and to present the *status quaestionum* as set forth in the relevant literature.[12] It suffices to cite a passage which confirms that Aristotle was plainly aware of the need to dissociate the "philosophy of human affairs" (*NE* X 9 1181^{b}15)[13]—what one calls practical philosophy—from practical wisdom itself: "We must not let it escape notice that arguments leading *from* starting-points and arguments leading *to* starting-points are different" (*NE* I 5 1095^{a}30–2).

In this section I will argue that by elucidating Heidegger's various attempts to clear up the epistemological status of the *Nicomachean Ethics* one can shed light on the phenomenological project of *Being and Time*.[14] In order not to become lost in the translation of the imaginative terms Heidegger was experimenting with during that period, let

---

[11] One might object that the pivotal point in Heidegger's confrontation with Aristotle is not his interpretation of the *Nicomachean Ethics* but, for example, his wish to raise anew the Aristotelian question of "Being as Being" or to draw on Aristotle's notions of *logos* and *alêtheia*. It seems to me, however, that the former has, in the long term, exercised the strongest influence on the Phenomenological Movement—broadly understood to include, among others, H. G. Gadamer, Hannah Arendt (1958), Hans Jonas, Leo Strauss, Paul Ricœur. For an overview, see: Denker, Figal, Volpi, and Zaborowski 2007.

[12] See Henry and Nielsen 2015 and Reeve 2012.

[13] I use the translation by Reeve 2014.

[14] The choice to concentrate on the scientific character of the *Nicomachean Ethics* indicates that I concur with those who maintain that Heidegger does not abandon Husserl's phenomenological project in favor of pre-theoretical *phronêsis* (see Crowell 2001: 115–28). On the whole, the present approach distinguishes itself from both critics (see Taminiaux 1992) and unreserved defenders (see Brogan 2005 and McNeill 1999) of Heidegger's appropriation of Aristotle. For a critique of the thesis that *Being and Time* is a reworking of the pair *poiêsis-praxis*, see Kontos 1997.

us follow the thread of his *Phenomenological Interpretations of Aristotle*—the brief text known as *Natorp-Bericht*—which delineates the context of his whole engagement with Aristotle. Four main claims which give substance to his hermeneutics are of special interest at this juncture.

First, the exclusive object of philosophy is human life in its being-in-movement, *Leben* and *Bewegtheit*. The object of philosophical research has to be understood as "the explicit grasping of the fundamental movedness (*Bewegtheit*) of factical life" (Heidegger 2005: 348–9). Thus, for someone who is inspired by Aristotle, the *Nicomachean Ethics* and its analysis of human life (*bios*) appears to be an ideal place to start from. However, since movedness is the main trait of human life and the *Nicomachean Ethics* says nothing about that, it is Aristotle's *Physics* that must play the guiding role (Heidegger 2005: 371, 374). The plan of this philosophical itinerary, which leads from the hermeneutics of facticity to Aristotle's *Physics*, is announced in several of the courses Heidegger gave in the same period.[15] It is Aristotle's *Physics* that will remain phenomenology's first ground, not his *Nicomachean Ethics*.[16] Besides, to correctly approach the latter, one should first, "provisionally . . . disregard the ethical problematic in its specificity" (Heidegger 2005: 377).

Second, human life comprises a self-reflective moment—a pre-scientific and pre-theoretical self-understanding. In our caring about or concerning ourselves with the surrounding world, we are always aware of ourselves and of the specific modality of concern we are each time actualizing (Heidegger 2005: 349). This holds true for every single human activity, science and theoretical activities included. *Fraglichkeit* (being in question) and *Lebenssympathie* are the terms denoting this moment of self-interpreting.[17]

But, third, life also displays a tendency toward self-loss or self-forgetting and self-privation. This is due to its being absorbed in what it cares about. In *Natorp-Bericht*, Heidegger writes in terms of "a propensity (*Hang*) toward *Abfallen* . . . *Verfallen*, and *Zerfall* [alternative German words to denote fall, destruction, and degeneration]" (Heidegger 2005: 356).[18]

Fourth, life in its movedness also experiences moments of illumination and clarity that make it appear fully without losing its genuine mobility; these experiences are "bones from life's bones and flesh from life's flesh" (Heidegger 1995: 15). In *Natorp-Bericht*, the experience of death figures as an example of such self-transparency (Heidegger 2005: 359). Two years later, in *Plato: Sophist*, this state of affairs will be captured by the term *Durchsichtigkeit* (transparency),[19] which will be established as a key technical term of fundamental ontology in *Being and Time*.

---

[15] See, for instance, Heidegger 1985: 112–16; Heidegger 2002: 283–329.

[16] Aristotle's *Physics* will also be the topic of a number of seminars from 1928 to 1951–52, now available in Heidegger 2012.

[17] Heidegger 1995: 15; Heidegger 1985: 151–5; Heidegger 1987: 110.

[18] The most eloquent variation of this pattern is to be found in Heidegger's 1921–2 analysis of *Ruinanz* (ruinance, collapse) (Heidegger 1985: 131ff.).

[19] Heidegger 1992a: 50, 143, 150.

Heidegger's hermeneutical program culminates in his defining philosophy as a distinguished modality of life's self-illumination. Philosophy emerges as "the explicit and genuine actualizing of the tendency toward interpretation" or, what amounts to the same thing, as a variation of "the motion running counter to (*Gegenbewegung*) the tendency toward falling" (Heidegger 2005: 363 and 360–1).[20] Philosophy shares the deep structure of life-in-movement, in that it has to struggle against the permanent risk of concealment. It instantiates a sort of decision, an *Entscheidung*, by having "radically and clearly resolved" and "resolutely chosen" to struggle against the tendency toward ruin (Heidegger 2005: 363). Hence, philosophy should remain alert in a "constant struggle against . . . ruinance" (Heidegger 1985: 153).

This is the backdrop against which Heidegger's return to Aristotle takes place. To understand philosophy as a way of life and not as a mere natural science is fully congruent with the spirit of the *Nicomachean Ethics*. For not only does Aristotle praise contemplation (*theôria*) as the highest mode of human life but, from the outset, he also makes it clear that the very objective of the *Nicomachean Ethics* is for the student of practical philosophy to become a certain sort of human being (*NE* I 1 1103^{b}26–30). Likewise, variations of self-interpreting are omnipresent in the *Nicomachean Ethics* and Heidegger will highlight the pertinent passages of Book VI 5. Nevertheless, the type of inquiry and method that characterize the *Nicomachean Ethics* mark it out as rather resistant to the requirement of hermeneutics. And Heidegger was from the beginning aware of this. That awareness and his ensuing disappointment motivated him to make a spectacular *strategic move*: to escape from the vain attempt to adapt Aristotle's method to hermeneutical demands, he projected the features proper to his hermeneutics *not* onto practical philosophy, but onto practical wisdom itself. The result is known as the "ontologization" of *phronêsis*, that is, its transformation from a sort of ethical vigilance to a sort of ontological or "hermeneutical intuition" (Heidegger 1987: 116–17). The symptoms of such an ontologization have been extensively analyzed in the last two decades.

Disappointment at the method and at the ontological prejudices of Aristotle's ethics is explicitly confessed in *Natorp-Bericht*: Aristotle's ethics does not originate out of a positive "account of human life as such" but out of the project developed in Aristotle's *Physics*.[21] In other words, the *Nicomachean Ethics* is from the start taken to be trapped in a prior conception of Being (*Seinsvorhabe*) that conforms to the model of production (*poiêsis*) (Heidegger 2005: 373). Another way to make the same point—Heidegger adds: "and this is decisive"—is to notice that the portrait of practical wisdom is not the outcome of a "positive ontological characterization" of *praxis* but of a merely descriptive

---

[20] See also "counter-ruinant motion (*gegenruinante Bewegtheit*)" (Heidegger 1985: 153, 178) and "counter-movedness (*Gegen-Bewegtheit*)" (Heidegger 1985: 132). Elsewhere, philosophy is portrayed as an explicit tendency to render life "hard for itself" (Heidegger 2005: 349). Alternatively, Heidegger speaks of "wakefulness of Dasein for itself," *Wachsein* (Heidegger 1995: 15), and maintains that philosophy makes life and its categories "transparent" (Heidegger 2005: 364).

[21] See Heidegger 2005: 385; Heidegger 2005: 113. This is not a gratuitous assumption on Heidegger's part. There are still a good many Aristotle scholars who maintain that Aristotle's ethics is dependent on his metaphysics, physics, or biology.

comparison with other types of human activity (Heidegger 2005: 384–5). Paradoxically, though the ontological grounds of the *Ethics* are unsafe and inappropriate for a herme- neutical approach to human life, nevertheless Aristotle's analysis might prove useful to the attempt to elucidate the movedness of human life. For Heidegger, Aristotle's ethics is just a matter of this intriguing "*obwohl*" (Heidegger 2005: 46)!

Matters will not change with time. As late as 1924–5, Heidegger is still wondering about the epistemological status of the *Nicomachean Ethics*: we should finally under- stand, he says, that "The question is to what extent there can be a science of something like that [namely, an ethics concerning human life], if indeed science proper is con- cerned with beings that always are" (Heidegger 2005: 130–1). This is the question that will constantly fuel Heidegger's efforts to practice phenomenology. Let us see why.

(1) A first line of approach seemingly open to Heidegger would be to investigate the epistemological kinship between the *Ethics* and the *Physics*. For it turns out that both of them constitute a sort of science which concerns not what is eternal and unchangeable, but only what holds "for the most part." The problem for Heidegger is that he is working with the very restrictive notion of an Aristotelian science introduced in *Nicomachean Ethics* VI 3, as if the latter were only about what is eternal. He applies these same criteria to physical science, as if it were about the eternal (Heidegger 2005: 374–5). At the same time, he repeatedly remarks that science, like any other human activity, cannot but em- body in some way the movedness of human life. Be that as it may, science so understood lacks the trait that Heidegger wishes to attribute to philosophy and to the hermeneutics of human life: *Doppelung*. Thanks to a duplication of its regard (Heidegger 2005: 385), the hermeneutics of human life is expected to illuminate not only its respective object but also the movedness of hermeneutics itself as an instance of life-movedness. This was, as previously explained, the central topic of Heidegger's early courses.

Hence, at that period, Heidegger was trying to transplant, so to say, the notion of movement from Aristotle's *Physics* to his hermeneutics of facticity. The *Nicomachean Ethics* proved to be of little help in this regard and Heidegger had to exercise consider- able hermeneutical violence to make it provide evidence for the centrality of movedness in human life. To realize the price to be paid, let me make just one point. We just saw that philosophy should permanently struggle against the danger of concealment—*Kampf* was the term used by Heidegger in 1921–2 (Heidegger 1985: 153). In his *Plato: Sophist* we read: "*phronêsis* is involved in a constant struggle, *Kampf*, against a tendency of con- cealment" (Heidegger 1992a: 52). Yet, as every student of ancient ethics knows, although practical wisdom does not share the sort of freedom that is proper to theoretical wisdom (*Metaphysics*, A 2 982^{b}27), it is completely free from any such struggle, which is rather the mark of self-control and its lack (*enkrateia* and *akrasia*), in that the practically wise and virtuous person "is of one mind with himself, and desires the same things with all his soul" (*NE* IX 4 1166^{a}13–14).

What matters, however, is the philosophical exploration of the notion of movedness and not the inadequacy of Heidegger's reading of the *Nicomachean Ethics*. And the movedness of factical life will occupy a prominent place in *Being and Time* (Division II, §72), in order for Heidegger to militate against any sort of ahistorical or atemporal transcendental self. It is only by elucidating temporality (*Zeitlichkeit*) and by unfolding the limits of Aristotle's conception of time that the movedness of Dasein can be adequately described. More importantly, despite Heidegger's critique of Aristotle, it is again the *Physics*—the "foundational book of Western philosophy" (Heidegger 1976: 242)—that will accompany Heidegger in his departure from fundamental ontology. In his 1939 essay "On the Essence and the Concept of *Phusis*: Aristotle, *Physics* B 1," movedness and *phusis* will be reinterpreted in terms of "coming to presence (*Anwesung*)" (Heidegger 1976: 261), that is, in terms of Being, while the movedess of Dasein will be relegated to the rank of just an example of the essence of natural beings (Heidegger 1976: 281).

(2) In those "Supplements" that contain his notes on the *Natorp-Bericht*, and which are almost exclusively about Aristotle's *nous praktikos* (practical intellect), Heidegger emphasizes that "practical reason is at the same time, according to Aristotle, knowledge, that is, theoretical" (Heidegger 2005: 405). Thus, he touches on the epistemological question of the scientific status of Aristotle's ethics. The connection is fully warranted because practical wisdom has access to starting-points (*archai*), which is a prerequisite of any science. Heidegger devotes long comments to practical wisdom and the accessibility of principles—comments that are nicely summed up in the following note: "*phronêsis* opens onto starting-points but these are, obviously, only in the *boulê*" (Heidegger 2005: 414). *Boulê* (deliberation) crops up in this context because Heidegger envisages practical wisdom from within the perspective of deliberate choice (*prohairesis*). This is already patent in *Natorp-Bericht* (Heidegger 2005: 383) but finds its full expression in *Plato: Sophist* with its long discussion of practical *aisthêsis* (perception), which is, to my knowledge, the first time that anyone pointed out the philosophical significance of the perceptual element in practical wisdom—something that became, many decades later, the main focus of the so-called moral realism.[22] On the other hand, Heidegger is correct in presenting things as follows: practical wisdom has to do with actions and deeds that are "always something different," "something new" (Heidegger 1992a: 159, 56). For if practical wisdom has a noetic element, it is a perceptual one that captures the "last thing," that is, the ever changing circumstances of morally relevant actions, and the moment of capture occurs essentially within the perspective of deliberate choice. Hence, the starting-points (*archai*) of deliberate choice are changing too (Heidegger 1992a: 143), since they amount to the end/*telos* that on each occasion one is striving for, namely, the that-for-the-sake-of-which (*hou heneka*) that defines and motivates the various actions undertaken: "the starting-point practical wisdom has to do with is the action itself" (Heidegger 1992a: 148). This is the conclusion that anyone must reach who regards practical principles only from within the sphere of deliberation and deliberate choice and from within the perspective of the agent.[23] The correct view that, within the sphere of deliberate choice, the starting-points of action are always changing, because they embody our circumstantial ends, leads Heidegger to the incorrect conclusion

---

[22] See Kontos 2013: 9–31, 109–24.
[23] See Heidegger 1992a: 138, 163; Heidegger 2002: 145–8, 150; Heidegger 2005: 383, 419.

that "regarding the *endechomenon*" (contingent), "there is no science, but only *doxa*" (Heidegger 2002: 141). For he overlooks the fact that the *Nicomachean Ethics* provides us with non-changing principles of practical philosophy, such as the definition of happiness (I 12 1101^{b}35–1102^{a}4)—besides, he overlooks the fact that natural sciences concern the contingent too. What Heidegger fails to notice, then, is that the *Nicomachean Ethics* evokes starting-points in, at least, two different ways: (a) starting-points of practical philosophy *to* which the *Ethics* itself is meant to lead us, (b) and correct starting-points *from* which the practically wise person should reason in his deliberate choices. Heidegger is fully aware of the need to respect this very distinction between "*von wo aus*" and "*wohin*" regarding starting-points (Heidegger 2005: 382; handwritten addition). It appears, however, that the practical philosophy of the *Nicomachean Ethics* is, to him, an inappropriate context for making use of the distinction at issue.

Significantly, the above ambiguity permeates the fundamental ontology of *Being and Time* and might serve as a key to interpreting a number of perplexities stemming from the distinction between the existential and the existentiell level of analysis and their mutual dependence (*existenzial* vs. *existenziel* understanding of Dasein; see Heidegger 1986: §4). For, on the one hand, the existential-ontological traits of Dasein are revealed as equiprimordial (*gleichursprünglich*) principles to which fundamental ontology is meant to lead us. On the other hand, Dasein, in the singularity and *Jeweiligkeit* (mineness) of existence, is called to choose and undertake his/her own projects at the background of the opposition between authenticity (*Eigentlichkeit*) and inauthenticity. But the modality and the very possibility of authentic choice is to be explained only *from* the starting-points uncovered by fundamental ontology. Thus the very same difficulty that Heidegger faces in his interpretation of the *Nicomachean Ethics* reemerges in the architectonic of *Being and Time*.[24]

Let me add a further comment on points (1) and (2). The analysis we have given suggests that any simplistic hypothesis that Heidegger turned to Aristotle in order to get beyond Husserl is flawed. Although already in the Marburg courses he accuses Husserl of not having paid due attention to movedness and existential analysis, it would be misleading to say that Aristotle's views represent an antidote to Husserl's shortcomings. By contrast, so Heidegger thinks, Aristotle's concepts are themselves in need of rectification and radicalization.

(3) An alternative way of attacking our original question is to maintain that Aristotle's method in the *Nicomachean Ethics* consists in nothing but dialectic. Heidegger flirts with this option for obvious reasons: if Aristotle's analysis of practical wisdom and actions were found to have stuck for the most part to a dialectical path of argument, then the impact of the *Physics* would be mitigated. Heidegger is not the first to be attracted by the dialectical element of the *Nicomachean Ethics*; a good many Aristotle scholars,

---

[24] In a sense, this ambiguity is already traceable to Heidegger's analysis of *eudaimonia* as a starting-point: "[*Eudaimonia*] constitutes the proper being (*die Eigentlichkeit des Seins*) of human Dasein . . . This proper being is grasped in a radically ontological way so that it is as such the ontological condition of the factual concrete existence of man" (Heidegger 1992a: 172–9).

especially at the time, were attracted by it too. For Heidegger, however, this is again a knife that cuts both ways.

On the one hand, he applauds Aristotle's insistence on the *legomena* and *endoxa*, that is, on the views held by ordinary people, historians, poets, and wise men. This is precisely the way dialectic functions in the *Nicomachean Ethics*. Heidegger stresses that Aristotle's analysis of wisdom (*sophia*) in the *Metaphysics* A 1–2 as well as the distinction between craft and practical wisdom in the *Nicomachean Ethics* arise primarily within the domain of *doxa* (see, respectively, Heidegger 2005: §10 and Heidegger 1992a: 29–30). But his admiration of *endoxa* was even more eloquently expressed one semester earlier when the focus of his interpretation was on Aristotle's *Rhetoric*: "Doxa is the mode in which life (*Leben*) knows from out of itself" (Heidegger 2002: 138).[25] What is more, so Heidegger, *doxa* does not represent a mere pre-theoretical attitude toward or acquaintance with the world but constitutes the "basis" of theoretical investigation itself (Heidegger 2002: 152ff.). It is noticeable that we encounter the same praise of Aristotle's *Rhetoric* in *Being and Time* (Heidegger 1986: 138).

On the other hand, Heidegger criticizes "dialectic" as a path to genuine philosophical knowledge; one should transcend it (Heidegger 1986: 25). This move beyond dialectic is required to the extent that "*dialegesthai* . . . does not arrive at pure *noein*" (Heidegger 1992a: 197). But even as it regards *doxa* itself, what is required is not dialectic but an ontological elucidation of the existential conditions of *doxa*, that is to say, an analysis of *endoxa* in connection with the movedness proper to Dasein (Heidegger 1986: 180). The description of idle talk (*Gerede*), curiosity, and ambiguity in *Being and Time* (Division I, §§35–8) aim, among other things, at amending Aristotle's conception of *endoxa*. In the same vein, the project of "destruction of the history of ontology" (Heidegger 1986: §6) might be taken as an attempt to demonstrate that mere dialectic, without the elucidation of Dasein's historicity, is nothing but a chimera. Hence, Aristotle's conception of *endoxa* is far from serving as an antidote to the naivety regarding the historicity of philosophy that Husserl's phenomenology suffers from as well (Heidegger 1992a: 9).

(4) There is a last possible way out of the problem that offers itself. This inviting path is Aristotle's politics, and Heidegger's struggle with it is the subject of his 1924–5 courses. The analysis of justice in Book V aside, political science (*politikê*) is the direct subject matter of the *Nicomachean Ethics* in three places: in the opening section of the treatise which constitutes a sort of inquiry into method (*NE*, I 1); in the middle of Book VI where political practical wisdom is at issue (*NE*, VI 8); and in the closing section of the treatise which discusses the role of legislators (*NE*, X 9). All three passages are more or less extensively analyzed by Heidegger, but the longest analysis concerns the introductory chapter of the *Ethics*, which portrays political science as the architectonic science. Heidegger's commentary goes as follows: "The *technê*, the *methodos* . . . is *politikê*, this knowing-one's-way-around [*sich Auskennen* is here Heidegger's rendering of *technê*] in the being of human beings . . . Therefore, politics, as knowing-the-way-around the being

---

[25] See also Heidegger 1992a: 61–4, 129; Heidegger 2002: §15.

of human beings in its genuineness, is ethics . . . The *agathon* as such is encountered in *technê*, specifically in such a way that it is explicit" (Heidegger 2002: 68–70).[26] What is striking in the first place is that Heidegger—quite unexpectedly—takes for granted that craft knowledge (*technê*) gives us access to the human good (*agathon*). However, the very core of the issue is precisely that only political science and practical wisdom, not craft knowledge, have access to a genuine conception of the human good. For crafts are merely subordinate to practical wisdom. Besides, whereas the human good is meant to be the object of deliberate choice, that is, of "desiderative understanding (*dianoia orektikê*)," craft knowledge, as Aristotle conceives of it, does not involve any desire at all. Thus, a first departure becomes unavoidable: Heidegger must endow craft/science with desire (Heidegger 1992a: 39).

Heidegger makes this detour because he wants to avoid the difficulty that resides in explaining the fusion of practical science/craft and practical wisdom into one and the same sort of knowledge or intellectual virtue. The foregoing is the subject of *Nicomachean Ethics* VI 8; Heidegger touches on this text but, as the editor of the pertinent course informs us, the analysis "is not carried out further" (Heidegger 1992a: 140, editor's note). The main idea Heidegger hints at in the five lines he devotes to this crucial passage is that political science has to do with actions that take place within the polis. Thus, while he does quote line VI 8 1141^{b}25—which refers to legislative science as the architectonic one—his comment seems rather to be directed at what Aristotle calls, in the next line, the "practical and deliberative" part of politics, that is, the one that has to do with particulars. Whereas Aristotle's main concern is to distinguish these two aspects of political knowledge, Heidegger remains completely silent on the distinction.

In the face of this impasse, the two courses of 1924–5 find a single solution: "Accordingly, *politikê epistêmê* is genuine *sophia* and the *politikos* is the true *philosophos*; this is Plato's conception" (Heidegger 1992a: 136). And when the final section of the *Nicomachean Ethics* portraying legislation as a form of craft/science is at issue, Heidegger says again: "philosophers are the rightful sophists—this is what Plato wants to show in his *Sophist*" (Heidegger 2002: 135–6). One can hardly fail to notice the name that puts its stamp on both passages: Plato. And there is no doubt that in the 1930s—for example, in the 1931–2 course discussing the allegory of the cave (Heidegger 1988)—Heidegger will subscribe to Plato's ideal of philosopher-kings.

Admittedly, the "platonic sources of Heidegger's political views" are a matter of some debate.[27] If, however, the remarks above are a sufficient basis on which at least to question the reliability of the view that Plato's conception of politics become dominant only in the years of the Rectoral Address, a number of assumptions in Heidegger's hermeneutics come to light. I mean the assumptions regarding "plurality" and its access to truth. Despite the long analysis of being-with (*Mitsein*) as an existential trait of Dasein in *Being and Time* and the elucidation of Aristotle's *koinônia* in terms of being-with (Heidegger

---

[26] See also Heidegger 2002: 65, 101.

[27] I follow here the analysis by Taminiaux 2009: 133–68. For alternative views on Heidegger's politics, see Raffoul and Pettigrew 2002.

2002: §9), Heidegger does not share Aristotle's conviction that the truth proper to the political realm can be reached by men who do *not* possess scientific knowledge of political matters, on condition that they be many (*polloi*) (*Politics*, III 11). To him, from his early courses to *Being and Time*, no genuine "wakefulness" and no genuine "struggle against ruinance" can arise within Aristotle's public sphere. And there is no doubt that this same prejudice lurks behind Heidegger's analysis of *das Man* and inauthenticity throughout *Being and Time*, no matter how charitably one wishes to treat them.

To sum up, the four aspects of Heidegger's encounter with the *Nicomachean Ethics* we have explored confirm that the ambiguities that haunt Heidegger's Aristotle interpretation are nothing but a variation or a precursor of difficulties endemic to his hermeneutical phenomenology up to *Being and Time*.

1.3 GADAMER PICKS UP THE BATON

Gadamer addresses the very same problem that shaped Heidegger's interpretation of Aristotle, that is, the scientific status of practical philosophy. And there is no doubt that Heidegger's commentary on the *Nicomachean Ethics* represents for him both a source of inspiration and a target of criticism.[28]

In *Truth and Method*, he envisages Aristotle's ethics as "a kind of model regarding the problems raised by the hermeneutical task" (Gadamer 1986a: 329), perhaps even as "the unique solid model for a proper self-understanding of the human sciences" (Gadamer 1980: 319; see also Gadamer 1979). This programmatic claim, announced time and again, makes practical philosophy what enables us to explicate the sort of independence that "moral sciences" should enjoy from both natural sciences and metaphysics.[29] Thus, it is hardly a surprise that his interpretation of Aristotle revolves around the same issue.

Gadamer maintains that moral experience mirrors an essential facticity of human beings (Gadamer 1986a: 322). That is, "human beings are always already in the circle of what depends on *phronêsis*" (Gadamer 1930: 242). Correlatively, practical wisdom is not always treated as an intellectual excellence that virtuous men alone display, but as equivalent to practical reason in general—a shift that is commonly disregarded by Gadamer's readers. Hence moral experience reflects the universality of hermeneutics. What is more, moral experience, directed by its proper rationality, constitutes "the fundamental form of experience" (Gadamer 1986a: 328), since practical rationality resists control by universal rules that are determined a priori, but instead admits of a certain openness relating to particular situations and decisions.

---

[28] My reading is sympathetic to Figal 2007: 22–30 and at odds with the standard view according to which Gadamer's appropriation of *phronêsis* is fully faithful to Aristotle's text and illustrates his radical emancipation from Heidegger (see Riedel 1986: 25–7; Grondin 2001: 9; Taminiaux 2009: 169–200).

[29] See, for example, Gadamer 1978a: 302; Gadamer 1986b: 261.

The same, however, holds true in the case of practical philosophy itself, as "a science with content-laden presuppositions" (Gadamer 1980: 326). This argument concerns not only the conditions of birth of practical philosophy but also its conditions of validity (Gadamer 1998: 9). For practical philosophy is obliged to make an appeal to another source of insight which, far from hinging on a higher scientific stance of truth, is incarnated by the *phronimos* himself, since the knowledge of how to make the right decisions and act well is accessible only to him. It is no wonder that one of Gadamer's most beloved Aristotelian mottos is the one presented in *Nicomachean Ethics* II 6 1107ª1– 2: the mean is defined "by a reason and the one by which a practically wise person would define it." It should be noted, however, that the *phronimos* does not represent a source of normativity for Aristotle himself. He is the person who can *recognize* practical truth in his actions and deliberate choices, while practical truth is grounded in something other than his own knowledge and desires.

Let us take a closer look at the congruity between practical rationality and practical philosophy, since it seems that the structure of the latter mimics that of the former. Certainly, practical philosophy is theoretical. Indeed, despite certain claims which might foster the opposite impression,[30] Gadamer endorses the *theoretical* character of practical philosophy: Practical philosophy is "undoubtedly a science," "a theoretical enterprise" (Gadamer 1976: 84, 109). Being a sort of theory, it is concerned not with the particular but the universal, *das Allgemeines*: The object of practical philosophy "cannot merely be the changing situations and changing ways of conduct" (Gadamer 1998: 84; see also Gadamer 1978b: 219). Whoever deprives practical philosophy of its claim to universality equally deprives it of its theoretical status, and Gadamer is the last one who would pay this price. Furthermore, lest this universality be understood only in an extremely weak way, Gadamer makes explicit that ethics "seeks to know the starting-points (*archai*) and the causes (*aitiai*); it constitutes a research about starting-points" (Gadamer 1978a: 303).

But practical rationality itself or practical wisdom—since Gadamer equates them— imply an access to starting-points too. As a matter of fact, notwithstanding his insistence on the particularity of situations, decisions, and actions within the context of practical experience, Gadamer maintains that practical rationality, qua rationality, is not reduced to a kind of grasp of individual objects, but constitutes a *logos* which is able to apprehend the universal features of what is given in moral experience. It is not an exaggeration to say, indeed, that this very claim is the core of his practical philosophy. At least, this is what he announced in *Truth and Method*: "to rightly estimate the role that reason has to play in moral (*sittlichen*) action" (Gadamer 1986a: 317). This is also his argument against Heidegger, when he says that one should "justify the classification of practical knowledge among the intellectual excellences" (Gadamer 1998: 67). Consequently, in contrast to commonly accepted assumptions, Gadamer constantly focuses on the

---

[30] See, for example, Gadamer 1963: 186; Gadamer 1978b: 218. Berti 2004 seems to be victim of this misunderstanding. By contrast, Foster 1991: 69–78 nicely presents the issue.

universality that the object of this rationality is necessarily burdened with: practical reason "postulates universal knowledge" (Gadamer 1983: 241). The natural conclusion to draw is that universality is not a feature that can differentiate practical philosophy from practical rationality itself: "Universalization itself does not imply taking a theoretical distance, but essentially belongs to the rationality of moral experience itself" (Gadamer 1982: 212).[31]

The next step in Gadamer's reading of Aristotle is the crucial one: precisely because practical philosophy and practical rationality mimic one another, it is highly important to underline that they are *not* identical: "practical philosophy itself is not [moral] rationality" (Gadamer 1985a: 23). Aristotle's view on the matter, Gadamer thinks, is ambiguous, since Aristotle considers practical philosophy, i.e., politics, to be a science, something like "pure" philosophy (Gadamer 1998: 9).[32] This is really the nub of Gadamer's Aristotle interpretation.[33] The following quotations, coming from two of his most important works on the topic (namely, "Reason and Practical Philosophy" and *The Idea of the Good between Plato and Aristotle*) show as much: "Philosophy that has to do with praxis is not yet practical rationality and should not be understood as *phronêsis*" (1986b: 264); it "has, in any case, the character of a theory we might term *epistêmê, technê, methodos, pragmateia*, or *theôria* but not *phronêsis* (in the technical sense of the term) . . . [This is why the problem is to know] how practical philosophy is related to *phronêsis*" (Gadamer 1978b: 218). Thus, even if practical theory is admittedly not detached from the very experience it describes in the way in which natural sciences are accustomed to objectifying their subjects of study, one should not presume that practical philosophy duplicates practical wisdom: practical wisdom and practical philosophy represent *different sorts of rationality*.[34]

In what follows, I want simply to list the difficulties in which Gadamer becomes entangled in the course of explicating the scientific character of practical philosophy in its difference from practical rationality—difficulties which are in fact difficulties for all

---

[31] In other words, the problem evoked by Aristotle's ethics is the problem of application (*Anwendung*) (Gadamer 1986a: 317), that is, the fact that we cannot grasp or make sense of universal concepts, rules, etc., except in a particular and finite situation. The question then is to know whether practical rationality and practical philosophy depend on particulars in the same way.

[32] Gadamer has not departed from the question Heidegger was asking in 1922: How can "a science such as ethics with regard to human life" be possible? (Heidegger 2005: 130–1) He tries to untie the same knot: "The question is how there could be a theoretical knowledge regarding the ethical being of men and what role knowledge (that is, "logos") plays in the ethical being of men" (Gadamer 1986a: 318).

[33] As far as I know, this problem has been overlooked by Gadamer's readers. For example, Grondin 2003: 103–6 takes it for granted that "moral knowledge" is reduced to "practical wisdom" or "ethical wisdom," that is, to *phronêsis*, without suspecting that there are two kinds of rationality involved in Aristotle's *Nicomachean Ethics* and in Gadamer's appropriation of it: practical rationality *and* practical philosophy.

[34] In order to respect its subject of study, practical theory should abnegate any superiority over praxis and any intention to "usurp the place of moral consciousness" (Gadamer 1986a: 318). Inversely, a *phronimos* is not necessarily a philosopher (Gadamer 1963: 184).

Aristotelian scholars. Once again, what matters is the interpretation of the principles of practical philosophy.

In order for Gadamer to differentiate practical philosophy from practical rationality, he would need to point out a certain *difference* between the starting-points (*archai*) to which they have access. One quickly sees, however, that Gadamer assigns to both starting-points one and the same status, namely, that of a *scheme*, regardless of whether the perspective is that of practical philosophy or of practical wisdom. For, on the one hand, practical wisdom is defined, in contradistinction to technical expertise, as embedded in a hermeneutic experience. Thus universal rules are open to enrichment and rectification every time they are applied in new situations, actions, and decisions. On the other, the same words are also employed to describe practical philosophy, since practical theory is restricted to presenting fluid principles that are inseparable from their adaptation to particular situations—in clear opposition to Aristotle's starting-points, such as the definition of *eudaimonia*, which are free from fluidity. Hence, theoretical principles "merely claim the validity of schemata. They are concretized only in the concrete situation of the agent" (Gadamer 1986a: 326). Notably, every time Gadamer wants to dissociate practical philosophy from natural science,[35] the lines distinguishing practical theory from moral experience begin to crumble: "The universal, i.e., typical, which can be said only within philosophical research devoted to conceptual universality is *not essentially different* from what guides in its practical-ethical judgment the entirely nontheoretical common-average conscience of norms" (Gadamer 1963: 186; my italics).

Gadamer might instead have argued that practical philosophy and practical experience pursue different procedures, that is, he might have pointed to the difference between the "from which" and the "to which" that we encounter in the *Nicomachean Ethics*. He cannot, however, take this route either. On the one hand, he takes practical wisdom to flourish in a commonly accepted *ethos* and to reach its culmination in the context of perfect friendships, wherein genuine giving of advice is exclusively possible. On the other, practical philosophy itself is dependent on the preestablishment of a common life-world whose unity is owed to such an *ethos*.[36] By this Gadamer means not only that the "professor of ethics" is engaged in a preestablished moral and social *ethos* in the same way in which the moral agent is, but also that practical philosophy itself "is grounded in the existence of an *ethos*, of solidarity" (Gadamer 1986b: 265).

Finally, one might try to argue that while practical wisdom is engaged in practice, practical philosophy renounces any direct practical involvement. Nevertheless, this option is not open to Gadamer either. For even if he constantly maintains that practical philosophy is not a substitute for practical rationality, he decreases the distance between them by maintaining that practical philosophy is essentially involved in the context of praxis itself. *Truth and Method* speaks about the "assistance" that practical philosophy is designed to supply and, when commenting on Aristotelian ethics, he emphasizes that

---

[35] See Gadamer 1985b: 357ff.; Gadamer 1963: 184ff.
[36] I do not mean to raise the issue of relativity, since "Gadamer is not preoccupied at all by the debate between universalism and relativism" (Grondin 2003: 104).

practical philosophy "claims to assist" moral agents in accomplishing moral actions and in taking correct moral decisions (Gadamer 1998: 9).[37] Indeed, practical philosophy seems to be charged with a high mission, namely, to "direct" moral experience to the morally relevant features of the situations at stake, and to make "better known the direction to which one should turn one's sight" (Gadamer 1978b: 220). In appealing repeatedly to an oft-cited passage from the *Politics*,[38] Gadamer never doubts that practical theory constitutes a *praxis* with moral relevance (Gadamer 1963: 175, 186).[39] Thus, practical philosophy is charged with the same role as moral experience. For the accumulated moral experiences of different ethical situations and demands *and* practical philosophy both contribute to increasing the agent's capacity to detect the significant moral features of a given situation. In both cases, knowledge merely represents "an increase in pre-knowledge" (Gadamer 1930: 242) that is necessary for the application and improvisation of practical schematic rules; it aims at the clarification of the moral and social *ethos* of the community (Gadamer 1982: 201; 1985b: 364). Thus, Gadamer utilizes the same terms in order to describe practical philosophy and practical experience: "the central mission of [both] philosophical ethics and the ethical conduct [is] the concretization of the universal and its application to the occasional situation" (Gadamer 1963: 187).

Gadamer thinks, as a result, that the essential innovation introduced by Aristotle's ethics resides in the fact that he substituted *ethos* and its social connotations for the Socratic internal moral measure (*Maß*) (Gadamer 1978b: 161). Practical philosophy is indebted to the life-world from which it springs, and so is not entitled to overcome the common beliefs to which it owes its access to principles.[40] Hence, its universal claims are meant merely to clarify this *ethos* by putting certain common assumptions into question (Gadamer 1983: 241) or to render the moral agent conscious of what he shares with his fellow agents. Moral philosophy is destined to cast doubt on the limits of each particular *ethos* in order to formulate an imperative requiring the care for the realization of a "fusion of horizons" as a moral end to be universally promoted (Gadamer 1986b: 263).

Gadamer's treatment of *ethos* nicely reveals to what extent his hermeneutics departs from Aristotle's conception of starting-points. He insists on what Aristotle says about the facticity of ethical states: "for the starting point is the fact that (*hoti*) something is so; and, if this is sufficiently evident, we do not also need the explanation of why (*dioti*) it is so" (*NE* I 4 1095^{b}6–7). This Aristotelian thesis, which Gadamer uses like a slogan, only

---

[37] See also: Gadamer 1978a: 316; Gadamer 1930: 242; Gadamer 1978b: 220–1; Gadamer 1983: 240.

[38] *Politics* VII 3 1325^{b}16–21: "yet it is not necessary ... for an action-involving life to be lived in relation to other people, nor are those thoughts alone action-involving that arise for the sake of the consequences of doing an action, rather, much more so are the acts of contemplation and thought that are their own ends and are engaged in for their own sake."

[39] This is also the case for Aristotle but in a qualified sense: the practical applicability of practical philosophy requires the mediation of legislative science (*nomothetikê*), which is portrayed in the *Politics* as an amalgam, so to say, of practical and productive knowledge. This is, I suppose, the reason why Gadamer leaves it out of picture (Gadamer 1998: 9).

[40] See: Gadamer 1985b: 357; Gadamer 1963: 184; Gadamer 1982: 215; Gadamer 1978b: 219.

means that good ethical states, provided that they are already established on the basis of correct legislation and education, let us realize what good moral actions are. As a matter of fact, in the phrase just quoted, the term "starting point" simply denotes the adequate beginning of the inquiry (*arkteon*), not the starting-points *to* which the *Nicomachean Ethics* should lead us or the starting-points *from* which deliberation should start. Hence, Aristotle's text does not suggest that this is all we need to know in order either to become a practically wise person or to do practical philosophy. To Aristotle, ethical states do indeed represent a sort of starting-point, but a normative one. On the one hand, the definition ("its essence and the account that states what it is to be") of a good ethical state, that is, of virtue (*aretê*), is a starting-point of ethics (*NE* II 6 1107a6–8). On the other hand, the possession of *good* ethical states makes it possible for the moral agent to have access to the correct starting-points of action (*NE* VI 12 1144^{a}7–8), while the possession of bad ethical states blocks such an access altogether (*NE* X 9 1179^{b}23–6). By contrast, Gadamer concludes that "*ethos* is [for practical rationality itself] the *archê*, the *hoti*" (Gadamer 1978a: 315), by which he means that no other sort of principle is available either to practical rationality or to practical philosophy except for the *ethos* each individual or community happens to possess.

If the upshot of Heidegger's hermeneutics is the transmutation of practical wisdom into a sort of ontological vigilance, the upshot of Gadamer's project is the transmutation of practical philosophy and hermeneutics into a sort of practical vigilance. His encounter with Aristotle's ethics and his attempt to bring to light what Heidegger's interpretation had neglected, namely, the idiosyncrasy of practical rationality qua practical, made him believe that the *Nicomachean Ethics* could be used as a model for an assimilation of practical philosophy with *phronêsis*. I hope I have sufficiently demonstrated why this belief was not entirely accurate. It would be interesting to investigate whether this belief is one of the main factors that shaped the character of Gadamer's hermeneutics in general or just a result of it. If we take à la lettre Gadamer's claim that Aristotle's ethics is "the unique solid model for a proper self-understanding of the human sciences" as well as his autobiographical confession that Heidegger's 1924 Marburg course on Aristotle's *Nicomachean Ethics* was "unforgettable" and the "thread" to his own hermeneutics (Gadamer 2002: 229), then the former is probably the case.

The moral of this case study is that readings and misreadings of Aristotle's philosophy, the fascination it holds and the mysteries it shelters, worked as a catalyst for phenomenological research. This is a nice lesson for those who harbor the illusion that it is possible to do genuine philosophy by starting from scratch.

References

Arendt, H. (1958), *The Human Condition* (Chicago, IL: University of Chicago Press).
Aubenque, P. (1962), *Le problème de l'être chez Aristote* (Paris: Presses universitaires de France).
Barbaras, R. (2013), *Dynamique de la manifestation* (Paris: J. Vrin).

Berti, E. (2004), "The reception of Aristotle's intellectual virtues in Gadamer and the hermeneutic philosophy," in R. Pozzo (ed.), *The Impact of Aristotelianism on Modern Philosophy*
(Washington, DC: Catholic University of America Press), 285–300.

Brague, R. (2001), *Aristote et la question du monde* (Paris: Presses universitaires de France).

Brogan, W. (2005), *Heidegger and Aristotle* (Albany, NY: SUNY Press).

Crowell, S. G. (2001), *Husserl, Heidegger, and the Space of Meaning* (Evanston, IL: Northwestern
University Press).

Denker, A., Figal, G., Volpi, F., and Zaborowski H. (eds) (2007), *Heidegger und Aristoteles.
Heidegger-Jahrbuch 3* (Freiburg: Alber).

Drummond, J. (2014), "Husserl's phenomenological axiology and Aristotelian virtue ethics," in
M. Tuominen, S. Heinämaa, and V. Mäkinen (eds) *New Perspectives on Aristotelianism and
its Critics* (Leiden: Brill), 179–95.

Figal, G. (2007), *Gegenständlichkeit* (Tübingen: Mohr Siebeck).

Fink, E. (1970), *Metaphysik der Erziehung* (Frankfurt a. M.: Klostermann).

Foster, M. (1991), *Gadamer and Practical Philosophy* (Atlanta, GA: American Academy of
Religion).

Gadamer, H. G. (1930), "Praktisches Wissen," in *Gesammelte Werke 5* (Tübingen: Mohr Siebeck,
1986–95), 230–48.

Gadamer, H. G. (1963), "Über die Möglichkeit einer philosophischen Ethik," in *Gesammelte
Werke 4* (Tübingen: Mohr Siebeck, 1986–95), 175–88.

Gadamer, H. G. (1976), *Vernunft im Zeitalter der Wissenschaft* (Frankfurt a. M.: Suhrkamp).

Gadamer, H. G. (1978a), "Hermeneutik als theoretische und praktische Aufgabe," in
Gesammelte Werke 2 (Tübingen: Mohr Siebeck, 1986–95), 301–18.

Gadamer, H. G. (1978b), "Die Idee des Guten zwischen Platon und Aristoteles," in *Gesammelte
Werke 7* (Tübingen: Mohr Siebeck, 1986–95), 128–227.

Gadamer, H. G. (1979), "Practical Philosophy as a Model of the Human Sciences," *Research in
Phenomenology*, 9: 75–85.

Gadamer, H. G. (1980), "Probleme der praktischen Vernunft," in *Gesammelte Werke 2*
(Tübingen: Mohr Siebeck, 1986–95), 319–29.

Gadamer, H. G. (1982), "Wertethik und praktische Philosophie," in *Gesammelte Werke 4*
(Tübingen: Mohr Siebeck, 1986–95), 203–15.

Gadamer, H. G. (1983), "Die Idee der praktischen Philosophie," in *Gesammelte Werke 5*
(Tübingen: Mohr Siebeck, 1986–95), 238–46.

Gadamer, H. G. (1985a), "Zwischen Phänomenologie und Dialektik," in *Gesammelte Werke 2*
(Tübingen: Mohr Siebeck, 1986–95), 3–23.

Gadamer, H. G. (1985b), "Ethos und Ethik (McIntyre u.a.)," in *Gesammelte Werke 3*
(Tübingen: Mohr Siebeck, 1986–95), 333–74.

Gadamer, H. G. (1986a), *Wahrheit und Methode*, in *Gesammelte Werke 1* (Tübingen: Mohr
Siebeck, 1986–95).

Gadamer, H. G. (1986b), "Vernunft und praktische Philosophie," in *Gesammelte Werke 10*
(Tübingen: Mohr Siebeck, 1986–95), 259–66.

Gadamer, H. G. (1998), *Aristoteles. Nikomachische Ethik VI* (Frankfurt a. M.: Klostermann).

Gadamer, H. G. (2002), "Heidegger's 'theologische' Jugendschift," in M. Heidegger
Phänomenologische Interpretationen zu Aristoteles (Stuttgart: Rekclam), 76–86.

Grondin, J. (2001), *Von Heidegger zu Gadamer* (Darmstadt: Wissenschaftliche
Buchgesellschaft).

Grondin, J. (2003), *The Philosophy of Gadamer* (Chesham: Acumen).

Henry, D. and Nielsen, K. M. (eds) (2015), *Bridging the Gap between Aristotle's Science and Ethics* (Cambridge: Cambridge University Press).

Heidegger, M. (1976), "Vom Wesen und Begriff der *Phusis*. Aristoteles, *Physik* B, 1," in F.-W. von Herrmann (ed.), *Wegmarken*, Gesamtausgabe 9 (Frankfurt a. M.: Klostermann).

Heidegger, M. (1986), *Sein und Zeit* (Tübingen: Max Niemeyer Verlag).

Heidegger, M. (1987), *Zur Bestimmung der Philosophie* (1919), Gesamtausgabe 56/7 (Frankfurt a. M.: Klostermann).

Heidegger, M. (1988), *Vom Wesen der Wahrheit. Zu Platons Höhlengleichnis und Theätet* (1931/32). Gesamtausgabe 34 (Frankfurt a. M.: Klostermann).

Heidegger, M. (1992a), *Platon: Sophistes* (1924/25), Gesamtausgabe 19 (Frankfurt a. M.: Klostermann; English translation by R. Rojcewicz and A. Schuwer, Bloomington, IN: Indiana University Press, 1997).

Heidegger, M. (1992b), *Grundprobleme der Phänomenologie* (1919/20), Gesamtausgabe 58 (Frankfurt a. M.: Klostermann).

Heidegger, M. (1993), *Grundbegriffe der antiken Philosophie* (1926), Gesamtausgabe 22 (Frankfurt a. M.: Klostermann).

Heidegger, M. (1994), *Einführung in die phänomenologische Forschung* (1923/24), Gesamtausgabe 17 (Frankfurt a. M.: Klostermann; English translation by D. Dahlstrom, Bloomington, IN: Indiana University Press, 1994).

Heidegger, M. (1995), *Ontologie. Hermeneutik der Faktizität* (1923), Gesamtausgabe 63 (Frankfurt a. M.: Klosterman; English translation by J. van Buren, Bloomington, IN: Indiana University Press, 1999).

Heidegger, M. (2002), *Grundbegriffe der aristotelischen Philosophie* (1924), Gesamtausgabe 18 (Frankfurt a. M.: Klostermann; English translation by R. Metcalf and M. Tanzer, Bloomington, IN: Indiana University Press, 2009).

Heidegger, M. (2005), *Phänomenologische Interpretation ausgewählter Abhandlungen des Aristoteles zu Ontologie und Logik* (1922), Gesamtausgabe 62 (Frankfurt a. M.: Klosterman).

Heidegger, M. (2012), *Seminare: Platon—Aristoteles—Augustinus*, Gesamtausgabe 83 (Frankfurt a. M.: Klosterman).

Husserl, E. (1984), *VI. Logische Untersuchungen*, Husserliana 4, ed. U. Panzer (Berlin: Springer).

Husserl, E. (1988), *Vorlesungen über Ethik und Wertlehre (1908–1914)*, Husserliana 38, ed. U. Melle (Berlin: Springer).

Jonas, H. (1982), *The Phenomenon of Life* (Chicago, IL: University of Chicago Press).

Kontos, P. (1997), "L'éthique aristotélicienne et le chemin de Heidegger," *Revue philosophique de Louvain*, 95/1: 130–43.

Kontos, P. (2013), *Aristotle's Moral Realism Reconsidered: Phenomenological Ethics* (New York: Routledge).

McNeill, W. (1999), *The Glance of the Eye* (Albany, NY: SUNY Press).

Patočka, J. (2011), *Aristote, ses devanciers, ses successeurs*, translated by E. Abrams (Paris: J. Vrin).

Raffoul, F. and Pettigrew, D. (eds) (2002), *Heidegger and Practical Philosophy* (Albany, NY: SUNY Press).

Reeve, C. D. C. (2012), *Action, Contemplation, and Happiness* (Cambridge, MA: Harvard University Press).

Reeve, C. D. C. (2014), *Nicomachean Ethics (translated with Introduction and Notes)* (Indianapolis, IN: Hackett).

Ricœur, P. (1990), *Soi-même comme un autre* (Paris: Editions du Seuil).

Riedel, M. (1986), "Zwischen Plato und Aristoteles. Heideggers doppelte Exposition der Seinsfrage und der Ansatz von Gadamers hermeneutischer Gesprächsdialektik," *Allgemeine Zeitschrift für Philosophie*, 11/3: 1–28.

Rodrigo, P. (1995), *Aristote, l'eidétique et la phénoménologie* (Grenoble: Millon).

Sokolowski, R. (1985), *Moral Action* (Bloomington, IN: Indiana University Press).

Sokolowski, R. (2012), "How Aristotle and Husserl differ on first philosophy," in R. Breeur and U. Melle (eds), *Life, Subjectivity, and Art* (Leiden: Springer), 1–28.

Taminiaux, J. (1992), *La fille de Thrace et le penseur professionnel* (Paris: Payot; English version: *The Thracian Maid and the Professional Thinker*, edited and translated by M. Gendre, Albany: SUNY Press, 1997).

Taminiaux, J. (2009), *Maillons herméneutiques* (Paris: Presses universitaires de France).

Wieland, W. (1962), *Die aristotelische Physik* (Göttingen: Vandenhoeck und Ruprecht).

CHAPTER 2

DESCARTES' NOTION OF THE MIND–BODY UNION AND ITS PHENOMENOLOGICAL EXPOSITIONS

SARA HEINÄMAA AND TIMO KAITARO

NEUROSCIENTISTS, neurophilosophers, and experts in cognitive science often present their own research programs in opposition to a doctrine called "Cartesian dualism." According to them, this doctrine consists in the radical ontological separation of the mental and the physical, mind and body. The neurologist António Damásio is well known for such claims. In *Descartes' Error* (1994), Damásio summarizes the Cartesian misconception as follows:

> This is Descartes' error: the abyssal separation between body and mind, between sizable, dimensioned, mechanically operated infinitely divisible body stuff, on the one hand, and the unsizable, undimensional, un-pushpullable, nondivisible mind-stuff; the suggestion that reasoning, and moral judgment, and the suffering that comes from physical pain or emotional upheaval might exist separately from the body. Specifically: the separation of the most refined operations of the mind from the structure and operation of a biological organism. (Damásio 1994: 249–50; cf. Carman 2008: 15–27, 53–4)

As an alternative to "Cartesian dualism," Damásio proposes a neuroscientific account according to which the cognitive, emotive, practical, and discursive operations characteristic of human life, emerge from and supervene on biological processes of neural signaling and cerebral decoding.[1,2]

[1] We are grateful to Professor Lilli Alanen for clarifying discussions on Descartes' metaphysics, epistemology, and philosophy of passions, and to the two anonymous readers who commented on an earlier version of this chapter and offered valuable suggestions for revision.

[2] Cf. Petitot, Varela, Pachoud, and Roy 1999; Varela, Thompson, and Rosch 1991; Maturana and Varela [1987] 1992; Maturana and Varela [1972] 1980. Many contemporary philosophers who develop theories

Whatever the value of such neuroscientist and neurophilosophical theorizing may be—and we believe it to be considerable—it is philosophically crucial to see clearly how this theorization relates to the philosophy of René Descartes that it is claimed to oppose or replace.

Neuroscientific and neurophilosophical critiques of "Cartesian dualism" tend to emphasize one element of Descartes' philosophy but neglect another central factor. To be sure, Descartes made a clear *conceptual* distinction between the properties of mind and those of matter—thought and extension—but he also argued that mind and body are *in fact* connected.[3] By arguing that our mental acts, for example acts of willing and deciding, are factually always accompanied by material events in the brain, and that mental events, for example, desires and affects, are systematically connected with cerebral traces (Descartes AT XI: 407, 428; CSM I: 365, 375–6; letter to Chanut, February 1st 1647, AT IV: 600–17; CSM-K: 305–14; cf. Husserl 1952a: 288–97/302–11),[4] Descartes established a new research paradigm that later grew into the comprehensive program of modern psychophysiology and also includes contemporary inquiries into the cerebral-neural basis of mental processes. So, rather than being rejected as a metaphysical or ontological dualist, Descartes could well be celebrated as the forefather of contemporary neuroscience and neurophilosophy with their hypotheses of connectionism, embodied cognition, enactivism, and extended mind (e.g., Hutto and Myin 2013; Rietveld 2013; Noë 2004; Clark 1997).

But Descartes' hypothesis has even more far-reaching effects: his insight into the systematic correlation between mental events and physiological events, explainable by purely mechanical laws, has paradoxically also allowed the construction of purely materialist theories of the mind. His correlationistic and interactionistic insights made conceptual and theoretical space for later attempts to build materialist theories of the mind that identify the mental and the neural and purport to explain mental causation and motivation on the basis of physiological mechanisms (see Kaitaro 2007, 2004). These alternatives range from the classical non-reductionistic materialism of La Mettrie and Diderot (Kaitaro 2017) to twentieth-century reductionistic and eliminativistic approaches and further to the supervenience theories and token-identity theories developed by twentieth-century philosophers of mind (e.g., Davidson 1995: 266; Davidson 1993; Churchland P. M. 1988; Churchland P. S. 1986; Davidson [1970] 1980).

However, it is also crucial to realize that while insisting on the conceptual distinction between the mental and the material, Descartes created conceptual space for the

---

of autonomous biological organization of life or *autopoiesis* refer to Merleau-Ponty's discussion of perception and further to the work of the Estonian-German biologist Jakob von Uexküll ([1934] 2004). For Merleau-Ponty's discussion of Uexküll's conceptualization of the organism–environment relation, see his late lectures on *Nature* (1995).

[3] Cf. Merleau-Ponty [1945] 1993: 111–12/82–3.

[4] The pagination given first refers to the original source, and the pagination that follows this, after the slash, refers to the English translation. Both sources are given in one and the same entry in the list of references.

study of mental phenomena as such, that is, as experienced actions and reactions with temporal and intentional structures identifiable and describable independently of their material underpinnings. At the turn of the twentieth century, this possibility was systematically explored by Franz Brentano and his followers under the titles "descriptive psychology" and "eidetic psychology."

These two aspects of "Cartesian dualism"—the possibility to characterize the mental as such and the possibility to find systematic connections between the mental and the material—are in fact correlative and complementary aspects of Descartes' account of the human mind: they are both consequences of the conceptual distinction between mind as thought and body as extension.

Later these two approaches to the mental have been developed independently from one another and also associated with opposite metaphysical and scientific aspirations, materialism vs. idealism, objectivism vs. subjectivism, and scientism vs. humanism. In the twentieth century, we have learned to take them as alternative explanatory paradigms: scientists and science-inspired philosophers have been critical of the study of the human mind as an essentially intentional and teleological system, and mentalistic philosophers have been critical of reductionistic, materialistic, and causalistic theories of human cognition. As the French phenomenologist Maurice Merleau-Ponty so aptly put it in his late essay, "Eye and mind" (*L'Œil et l'esprit* 1964): "Our science and our philosophy are two faithful and unfaithful offshoots of Cartesianism, two monsters born of its dismemberment" (Merleau-Ponty 1964a: 58/138; cf. 1964b: 17/11, 242/188, 251/198, 288/234).

2.1 PURE MIND AND THE MIND–BODY UNION

Descartes himself was able to combine the two approaches to the mental—mind studied as such and mind studied in relation to the body—since he distinguished between three different ways of knowing and three proper objects of human knowledge. He argued that our intellection or understanding (*entendement*), when operating alone, provides us with sufficient knowledge of pure mind or mind as the thinking substance, whereas we should use both our understanding and our imagination in order to have knowledge of the nature of the extended substance or pure matter.[5] Thus, the faculties of understanding and imagination guaranteed our knowledge of the two substances. But in

---

[5] For Descartes, imagination means considering something that is not really there "as if it were present" to oneself (Descartes AT VII: 72; CSM II: 50). In distinction from understanding (*entendement*), imagination is a hybrid faculty of knowing in involving both mental and bodily components. This implies that purely mental beings (e.g., angels) cannot have the faculty of imagination, and thus this faculty is specific to the human mind. In contrast to humans, God and his angels proceed by pure intellect and will in all their thoughts.

addition to them, Descartes argued, our knowledge also includes familiarity with the union of mind and body, and the knowledge of this union depends on our sensory faculties:

> The soul is conceived only by the pure intellect; body (i.e., extension, its shapes and motions) can likewise be known by the intellect alone; but much better by the intellect aided by imagination; and finally what belongs to the union of soul and body is known only obscurely by the intellect alone or even by the intellect aided by the imagination, but it is known very clearly by the senses. (Descartes' letter to Elisabeth, June 28, 1643, AT III: 691–2; CSM-K: 227)

So, according to Descartes, the three objects of human knowledge are: first, mind as pure thought, second, body as extension, and third, the mind–body union. These are discovered and known by us thanks to three different mental faculties. Pure mind is known by understanding alone, and the extended body is best known by understanding aided by imagination. But to know the soul–body union, Descartes argues, we need to interrupt our metaphysical meditations and arrest our aptitude for calculation and imagining, and pay attention to our sensations and to our interpersonal relations.[6] In a letter to his pupil Princess Elisabeth of Bohemia, Descartes explains:

> Metaphysical thoughts, which exercise the pure intellect, help to familiarize us with the notion of the soul; and the study of mathematics, which exercises mainly imagination in the consideration of shapes and motions, accustoms us to form very distinct notions of body. But it is the ordinary course of life and conversation, and abstention from meditations and from the study of things which exercise imagination, that teaches us how to conceive the union of the soul and the body. (Descartes' letter to Elisabeth, June 28, 1643, AT III: 692; CSM-K: 227)

In his correspondence with Elisabeth, Descartes modifies and complements the dualistic account of his *Meditations on First Philosophy* by a discussion of the mind–body union. He calls this union "the third primitive notion" and argues that it is not reducible to pure mind nor to pure matter (Descartes' letter to Elisabeth, May 21, 1643, AT III: 663–8; CSM-K: 217–20; letter to Elisabeth, June 28, 1643, AT III: 690–5; CSM-K: 226–9). Further Descartes claims that it is this notion of union, and not the two notions of

---

[6] Thus, Descartes argues that while studying the extended substance we can either use our intellect independently of our imagination, imitating the thoughts of angels, or else boost the operations of our intellect with our imagination. This seems to be in tension with the explicit teaching of *Meditations*, where Descartes argues that imagination is not trustworthy as a means of representation but is deceptive in producing hallucinations and delusions. However, *Meditations* also demonstrates that free imagination has an important role in the development of human knowledge. It cannot provide certainties but it is indispensable in the production of possibilities, and some of its creations—such as the possibility of a malicious demon, summoned up by Descartes himself—promote our knowledge and deepen our understanding of its grounds (cf. Sepper 1996). Consideration of extreme possibilities is thus not merely an entertainment but is crucial to the sciences of metaphysics and mathematics.

separate substances, that allows us to conceive how our will can move our body and how external events and entities affect our sense organs and our sensibility.

Many commentators neglect the methodological implications of Descartes' discussion of the mind–body union, and present this discussion as a mere therapeutic or pedagogic supplement to his metaphysical system, intended to reconcile the insistent Princess and to advise her in her practical predicaments.[7] But Descartes is coherent in approaching the problem of the union in an epistemologically controlled manner. When he explains to Elisabeth that there are in fact three and not just two primitive notions, he insists on the fact that each of these can be known in a particular way and should not be studied in comparison with, or by reduction to, any other. Matters pertaining to the union can only be known obscurely by the understanding or intellection. Resorting to imagination does not make this notion any clearer or distincter either. What one has to realize is that the notion of the union can be known very distinctly only by the senses (Descartes' letter to Elisabeth, June 28, 1643, AT III: 691–2; CSM-K: 226–7).[8]

It is philosophically crucial to notice that the idea of conceptual distinctness that Descartes develops in *Meditations* applies not only to the notions of pure mind and pure matter, but also to the third notion, the notion of union. This implies that one should not explain the way the mind interacts with the body by the conceptual tools that are used when explaining the mutual interactions of bodies. Nor can one understand the union by merely applying concepts that are developed for the correct description of pure mind and its principal attribute of thinking. Ultimately, the result of Descartes' exchange with Elisabeth can be summed up by the epistemological and methodological thesis that the mind–body union must not be approached by the metaphysical and physical concepts developed in his *Meditations*.

The difficulty that we experience in trying to conceive of the union of mind and body results, according to Descartes, from our incapacity to distinctly conceive at the same time the three different notions: mind as pure thought, body as extension, and the union of mind and body (Descartes' letter to Elisabeth, June 28, 1643, AT III: 693; CSM-K: 227–8). In order to relieve this difficulty, Descartes suggests to Elisabeth that she should deviate from the reflective order of the *Meditations* and should feel free to attribute extension to the mind. As the Princess had remarked, this would be somewhat easier than to conceive a completely non-extensional mind as moving and as being moved by material things.

In this context, Descartes observes that attributing extension to the mind is actually identical with conceiving its union with the body. However, he feels it necessary to add not only that the extension that is attributed to thought in this manner is distinct from thought as such (*la pensée même*), but also that the extension of thought is different from the extension attributed to the body as mindless being. When extension is attributed to

---

[7] One scholar who has systematically emphasized the importance of Descartes' exchange with Elisabeth in the development of his philosophical system is Lisa Saphiro (2013, 1999). See also Saphiro and Pickavé 2012; Saphiro 2007; Alanen 2003; Tollefsen 1999.

[8] Cf. Heinämaa 2003; Garber and Wilson 1998: 835.

pure matter it is a determination of a certain place that excludes all other extensions, but this is not the case for the kind of situational extension that we need to attribute to the mind in order to conceive its union with the body (Descartes' letter to Elisabeth, June 28, 1643, AT III: 694; CSM-K: 228).

So, according to Descartes, there are actually two facts on which our knowledge of the nature of the mind depends: first, that the mind thinks, and second, that it is united with the body and acts and is acted on by it.[9] These correlate with two different conceptions of extension, extension as conceived in a system of coordinates and extension as situation (e.g., Descartes AT IXB: 47–8; CSM I: 228–9; cf. Casey 2013: 135–7, 151–2, 158–9). Descartes' main purpose in the *Meditations* was to demonstrate the conceptual distinction of mind from body, and thus he did not discuss the connectedness of mind with matter but merely mentioned the phenomenon in the sixth Meditation (Descartes' letter to Elisabeth, May 21, 1643, AT III: 664–5; CSM-K: 217–18). Consequently, there is, according to Descartes, a sphere of human knowledge which remains ambiguous to understanding and which we cannot know by the method that he devises for metaphysical inquiries.

Descartes struggles to conceptualize this ambiguous sphere of the union in correspondence with his pupils and opponents while discussing the alleged problems of his *Meditations*. Later, in *The Passions of the Soul*, he tackles the problem explicitly, trying to develop a coherent account that would do justice to the notion of the union as well as the idea of conceptual distinctness. Here he distinguishes between three types of mental phenomena that all belong to the ambiguous sphere of the mind–body union: sensations, sense perceptions, and emotions. In order to account for these phenomena, he develops a twofold description that characterizes mental states as they appear to the persons who experience them and at the same time as they can be captured in terms of the developing sciences of anatomy and physiology. Thus, he provides an account of both the representational-intentional and the causal features of sensations, sense perceptions, and emotions. On the one hand, he describes how these states (re)present their objects, specifying, for example, what value and what temporality an emotion ascribes to its objects. On the other hand, he describes the kinds of material (cerebral, neural, haematic)[10] movements that relate to such states as their causes and effects. Joy, for example, is defined by Descartes as "the soul's enjoyment of a good that impressions in the brain represent to it as its own" (Descartes AT II: 396; CSM I: 360), and desire is defined

---

[9] In a letter to Regius (January 1642), Descartes explains: "When we said that a human being is an *ens per accidens*, we meant this only in relation to its parts, the soul and the body; we meant that for each of these parts it is in a manner accidental for it to be joined to the other, because each can subsist apart, and what can be present or absent without the subject ceasing to exist is called an accident. But if a human being is considered in himself as a whole, we can of course say that he is a single *ens per se*, and not *per accidens*; because the union which joins a human body and soul to each other is not accidental to a human being, but essential, since a human being without it is not a human being" (AT III: 508; CSM-K: 209).

[10] "Haematic" means "relating to the blood."

as "an agitation of the soul caused by spirits that disposes the soul to want to have in the future the things it represents to itself as agreeable" (Descartes AT II: 392; CSM I: 358; cf. Heinämaa 2018). Both definitions operate with both representational-intentional and causal concepts. The implications of this explanatory twofoldness are equally important to our contemporary theorization as are the implications of Descartes' metaphysical theory of the two substances.

2.2 INTERACTIONISM AND HOLISM

It is crucial to notice that Descartes develops his double account of the mind–body union by means of two central metaphors.

On the one hand, he describes the mind–body relation with the concepts of interaction and mutual causal influence. The ideas of interaction and causation suggest that some part of the body functions as the principal seat of mental operation. Since organs of sensation are known to be connected to the brain by neural transmission, it seems natural to assume that the brain is the organ that primarily interacts with the mind, receiving from it the directions of the will and transmitting to it the impulses from the sense organs. However, Descartes argues even more ambitiously that our mental control of our bodies is further centralized and that a particular cerebral gland, the pineal gland, serves as the principal bodily locus in which the human mind directly "exercises its functions":

> The soul has its principal seat in the little gland which exists in the middle of the brain, from whence it radiates forth through all the remainder of the body by means of the animal spirits, nerves, and even the blood. (AT XI: 354; CSM I: 341)[11]

On the other hand, Descartes insists that the mind–body union is an inseparable whole of two principles that are comprehensively and completely "intermingled": "The whole mind is united to the whole body," he declares in a letter to his pupil Regius (Descartes' letter to Regius, January 1642, AT III: 493, cf. 508–9; CSM-K: 206, cf. 209). Moreover, in both *Meditations* and *Discourse*, he contrasts the holistic metaphors of intermingling explicitly with the traditional Platonic images of piloting and control, and argues that we cannot make sense of our sensations unless we let go of the imagery of mental piloting. In the sixth Meditation, we read:

[11] Descartes discusses the function of the pineal gland in *The Passions of the Soul* and in *Treatise of Man*, which was his first book (written before 1637, but published posthumously, first in Latin translation in 1662, and then in the original French in 1664). The topic is also debated in a number of letters written in 1640–1. For a detailed account of these discussions and their background in Greek, medieval, and Renaissance medicine, see Lokhorst 2016; Lokhorst and Kaitaro 2001.

> Nature also teaches me, by these sensations of pain, hunger, thirst and so on, that I am not merely present in my body as a sailor is present in a ship, but that I am very closely joined and, as it were, intermingled with it, so that I and the body form a unit. If this were not so, I, who am nothing but a thinking thing, would not feel pain when the body is hurt, but would perceive the damage purely by his intellect, just as a sailor perceives by sight if anything in his ship is broken. (Descartes AT VII: 81–2; CSM II: 56)

Thus, our philosophical alternatives are either (i) to identify ourselves with the intellect and free will, and fail to make philosophical sense of our sensations, or else (ii) to allow the concept of thought to cover—in its impure modes—not just the actions of the intellect and the will, but also the passions of sensation, sense perception, and emotion.[12] Descartes consistently opted for the second alternative. For him, the human mind is not merely composed of mental *acts* but also includes *passions*. In *Discourse on Method*, he summarizes his position as follows:

> I showed how it is not sufficient for [the mind] to be lodged in the human body like a helmsman in his ship . . . but that it must be more closely joined and united with the body in order to have . . . feelings and appetites like ours and so constitutes a real man. (Descartes AT VI: 59; CSM I: 141)

The metaphor of radiation used in *Passions* allows Descartes to develop this holistic intuition while at the same time entertaining the idea of an operative center in the brain. However, his characterization of sensations and sense perceptions as intrinsically mental suggests a stronger holistic view according to which sensations are not just the ultimate frontier between thought and extension but are themselves both mental and extended in the special situational sense implied by the notion of the mind–body union. This indicates that the human mind is dispersed throughout the whole human body, which undermines the hypothesis of a distinguishable bodily seat of mental activity.

In many commentaries, the twofoldness of Descartes' description of the mind–body union is explained away by suggesting that the holistic notion of the union is either a non-philosophical courtesy to the Catholic Church or else an Aristotelian relic (e.g., Garber and Wilson 1998: 834–6). Thus, Descartes' only proper thesis about the mind–body relation would be the thesis about centralized interaction (with all the problems related to interactionism).

However, in *Phenomenology of Perception*, Merleau-Ponty puts forward an alternative reading by arguing that Descartes' twofold account of embodiment anticipates later phenomenological explications of bodily forms of intentionality, originally developed by Edmund Husserl and further elaborated by himself. More precisely, Merleau-Ponty

---

[12] Thus, the mind for Descartes is not merely pure thought—acts of the will and the intellect—but includes also the passions and imagination.

maintains that we can make sense of the twofoldness of Descartes' account if we utilize phenomenological tools in our analysis of bodily experiences and experiences of bodies:

> When Descartes says that the understanding knows itself incapable of knowing the union of soul and body and leaves this knowledge for life to achieve, this means that the act of understanding presents itself as reflection on an unreflective experience which it does not absorb either in fact or in theory. (Merleau-Ponty [1945] 1993: 52–53/37)

Merleau-Ponty's *Phenomenology of Perception* thus argues that Descartes' idea of sense perception and sensation as intrinsically mental faculties can be explicated and refined by Husserl's phenomenological account of perceptual consciousness and motor intentionality. Moreover, since Husserlian phenomenology also includes an argument for the primacy of perception, i.e., an argument to the effect that perception provides a necessary foundation for conceptualization, its account of perception has important implications for our epistemological theories of conceptual knowledge (e.g., Merleau-Ponty [1945] 1993: xiii/xvi–xvii, 418–19/326–7). Eventually Merleau-Ponty's discussion of Descartes suggests that the tension between Descartes' two descriptions of the mind–body union—the interactionistic and the holistic—can be alleviated or mitigated by Husserl's distinction between different ways of conceptualizing the world and worldly relations, all veracious but valid on different conditions.

2.3 TWO-LAYERED COMPLEXES OR EXPRESSIVE WHOLES?

In the second volume of his mature work *Ideas*, Husserl distinguishes between two different attitudes and two different interests in which we can study living beings, humans and animals. On the one hand, we may want to construe a theory of such beings in order to explain and predict their behaviors, forms of behavior, or physical constitutions. On the other hand, we may need to communicate with such beings and inform them about our beliefs, emotions, aims, and needs, and correspondingly interpret their analogous intentions.

In the first case, we tend to proceed in the naturalistic attitude that conceives living beings as psychophysical systems in complex causal–functional relations to the environment and environing entities. In the second case, we usually adopt the personalistic attitude that conceives living beings as autonomous agents in intricate communicative relations with other similar beings. When we proceed in the naturalistic manner, the positions and movements of the living bodies that we study are conceptualized by us as various effects of external and internal causes, and we may want to manipulate these causes in order to produce beneficial effects. When we proceed in the personalistic manner, the very same positions and movements are understood as communicative gestures that require our responses and have sense—or occasionally lack sense—as parts of significative systems (Husserl 1952a: 183–239/192–250; cf. Stein 1917: 44–60/41–54).

According to the naturalistic paradigm, each being is either itself physical, belonging to the unified totality of physical nature, or a variable dependent on the physical, and thus at best a secondary accompaniment or adjunct. The human person is conceived as a two-layered reality, a compound system, in which a material—biological, biochemical, chemical, and physical—basis provides the foundation for the emergence of psychic or mental features. Thus understood, psychic or mental features are not properties of any types of immaterial entities—souls, agents, or persons—but are higher-order properties emergent of immensely complex physical systems, e.g., the brain or the neural network.

Husserl lays great stress on the experiential fact that we do not always, or even predominantly, grasp human bodies as two-layered unities. Rather than characterizing our everyday concern for our fellow beings, this attitude is characteristic of the scientist's explanatory interest. By default, we attend to other living beings, both humans and animals, as unitary expressive and intentional agents, and this is also our basic attitude when we encounter a novel type of being that moves in the spontaneous and reflective manner, characteristic of the living, such as a robot (cf. Husserl 1952a: 151–2/159).

Moreover, our most central human practices require that we relate to one another as expressive beings and not as complicated biochemical mechanisms. These include, not just the emotively charged practices of caring and nurturing, but also the practices of arguing, criticizing, experimenting, and testing, which are all central to the scientific enterprise itself. In order to guarantee the validity of our results, we need to subject our hypotheses, our inferences, our experimental designs, and our conceptual distinctions to the critique of other scientists, and in this essential task we cannot proceed by maintaining that our fellow beings are complicated machines manipulable by us and others. Thus, the personalistic attitude, which gives the living being as an expressive whole, is necessary both practically and epistemically (e.g., Husserl 1952a, 204ff./214ff.).

Husserl clarifies the givenness of living beings by comparing it to that of literary works (Husserl 1952a: 236ff./248ff.). The main point of the comparison is to draw attention to the way in which such entities are articulated and structured in experience. He argues that neither persons nor cultural works can be analyzed into parts in the same manner as physical and psychophysical systems can (Husserl 1952a: 134/141). Rather than having mental contents or sense contents as layers founded on a non-significative substratum, these unities are completely permeated by sense. Each part and each layer that can be disclosed by analysis is filled with sense; and no non-significative ground can be detected by analysis. Moreover, each expressive totality, and each part of such a totality, has multiple relations of sense to other expressive units (Husserl 1952a: 252–3/241, cf. 132–9/139–47).[13]

---

[13] See also Merleau-Ponty [1945] 1993: 211–12/162–3.

Thus understood, the expressive gestures of persons have a sensible substratum, but the substratum in this case is not a physical thing or a merely material object. The substratum of the smile, or a grimace, is the face that always and already is signifying and never simply there at hand as physical things are (Husserl 1952a: 239/251, cf. 246/234–5).[14]

The face and the expressive body belong to the personalistic world of communicative and motivational relations. In it, humans act as "ensouled" bodies, relating to one another and to their environments by signifying bodily movements and ways of moving (Husserl 1952a: 234ff./ 246ff., 285–6/298–9). Via such bodies, the whole environment is articulated into a system of meaningful entities that call for our attention and move us by their powers of attraction and repulsion. In *Phenomenology of Perception*, Merleau-Ponty sums up this line of thought as follows:

> This disclosure of an immanent or incipient significance in the living body extends, as we shall see, to the whole sensible world, and our gaze, prompted by the experience of our own body, will discover in all other "objects" the miracle of expression. (Merleau-Ponty [1945] 1993: 230/177)

The naturalistic and the personalistic apprehensions of the living body are not on equal footing according to Husserl's analysis. He argues that the primary way in which living bodies are given to us is personalistic and as such expressive or significative: "The question above was: is a human being [*Mensch*] a unification of two realities, is that how I see him? If I do, then I am grasping a corporeal existence. But that is not the attitude I am in when I grasp a human being. I see a human being, and in seeing him I also see his body" (Husserl 1952a: 240/251–2). We do not *perceive* living bodies as bio-mechanisms but as expressive gestures, motivated by sensations and feelings, directed by intentions and purposes, and responsive to affects and appeals. And it is perception, not understanding or pure thinking, that gives us living beings per se.

In this way, Husserl questions the alleged primacy of the naturalistic theoretical attitude and argues that this attitude depends on a more profound perceptual stance in which we do not study human beings, ourselves and others, as psychophysical complexes but experience and conceive them as unitary persons.[15] Persons are not two-layered realities with causal coherence but unified phenomena of expression. As such, the human mind is not an adjunct to an independently operating material body, but is the principle or norm according to which matter is organized into significative wholes in significative relations.

Thus, Husserlian phenomenology allows us to distinguish between two different ways of studying the mental, either as a psychophysical complex in which the psychic

---

[14] See also Merleau-Ponty [1945] 1993: 175–6/133–4, 186–7/142, 193/147–8, 215–17/165–7, 271/210.

[15] Ultimately, Husserl's thesis about the dependency of the naturalistic attitude on the personalistic attitude rests on his theory of individuation. For a discussion of this background, see the chapter on "Embodiment and Bodily Becoming" included in this volume.

is founded upon the physical, or else as an expressive whole in which matter is articulated by sense. This gives a more precise formulation to Descartes' twofold account of the mind–body union, interactionistic on the one hand, and holistic on the other. But unlike Descartes, Husserl also provides an explication of the relations of these two ways of apprehending the mind–body union. He argues that both approaches are legitimate within their own limits but that the naturalistic approach is dependent on the personalistic one in the task of individuating its research objects.

2.4 ON THE TASKS OF THE SCIENCE OF PHILOSOPHY

Husserl separates both these approaches to the human mind from his own transcendental-phenomenological inquiries that are designed to illuminate the activities of sense constitution and thus provide the foundations for both the other approaches. He argues that it is necessary to radicalize philosophical reflections in order to delineate the proper objects of the positive sciences, and their differently interested attitudes, and thus to clarify their relations of dependence and interdependence.

In his mature works, *Cartesian Meditations* (1960; (*Cartesianische Meditationen* 1929, 1931)) and *The Crisis of European Sciences and Transcendental Phenomenology* (*Die Krisis der europäischen Wissenschaften und die transzendentale Phänomenologie* 1936–7, 1954), Husserl makes clear that the main motivation of his philosophy coheres with that of Descartes: the aim is to provide rational foundations for all the sciences and for all the practical endeavors of human beings. In *Cartesian Meditations*, he characterizes his project as follows:

> Must not the only fruitful renaissance be the one that reawakens the impulse of the Cartesian *Meditations*: not to adopt their content but, in *not* doing so, to renew their spirit, the radicalness of self-responsibility, to make that radicalness true for the first time by enhancing it to the last degree, / to uncover thereby for the first time the genuine sense of the necessary regress to the ego, and consequently to overcome the hidden but already felt naïvité of earlier philosophizing. (Husserl 1950: 47–8/6; cf. 1952b: 141/408)

Husserl's first emphasis is on the fact that Descartes' *Meditations* developed in an innovative new way the idea of philosophy as a universal science. Descartes saw the importance of the unity of science and realized that this unity is not thematic or methodic but rests on the sameness of tasks and goals: each specific science—from metaphysics and geometry to quantum physics and from poetics to neuroscience— aims at providing an evidence-grounded conception of its object (Husserl 1950: 50ff./ 9ff.; 1954: 75–82/302–3). Thus, the ideas of grounding, justification, and evidence belong to the common core of all sciences. Philosophy is a foundational science in investigating the conditions of the different types of evidences by which the other sciences operate. In this context, Husserl even contends that Descartes came very close to beginning transcendental-philosophical investigations proper, and much more so than Kant. Descartes opened the way for a rigorous new philosophy but was held back by deep-seated preconceptions about the structure and method of this science (Husserl 1950: 63–4/23–5; 1954: 73ff./74ff.).

Husserl argues that Descartes' fundamental mistake was to assume that all theoretical and ideal sciences, and accordingly also philosophy, should adhere to or comply with the axiomatic-deductive model of the exact science of geometry. In the beginning of his *Cartesian Meditations*, Husserl argues:

> Obviously it was, for Descartes, a truism from the start that the all-embracing science must have the form [*Gestalt*] of a deductive system, in which the whole structure rests, *ordine geometrico*, on an axiomatic foundation that grounds the deduction absolutely. For him a role similar to that of geometrical axioms in geometry is played in the all-embracing science by the axiom of the ego's absolute certainty of himself, along with the axiomatic principles innate in the ego—only this axiomatic foundation lies deeper than that of geometry and is called on to participate in the ultimate grounding even of geometrical knowledge. None of that shall determine our thinking. As beginning philosophers we do not as yet accept any normative ideal of science; and only so far as we produce one newly for ourselves can we ever have such an ideal. (Husserl 1950: 49/8–9)

For Husserl, the geometrical idea of science is merely a historically motivated set of value judgments and goals. He argues that, proceeding in a rigorous and truly radical manner, phenomenologists must suspend this set of judgments with all others and take as their task the illumination of its constitutive basis (Husserl 1954: 83–4/81–2, 268–9/264–5).

In Husserl's reading, Descartes' methodological preconceptions restricted the radicalism of his meditations. They suggested that *ego cogito* should, and could, function as a philosophical axiom from which metaphysical truths could be deduced as theorems. This prospect led Descartes to misunderstand the nature of the newly discovered ego and its activity of thinking.

Descartes took *ego cogito* as a self-evident truth from which he purported to derive his own existence as a "thinking thing" (*res cogitans*), as a part of the psychic or mental reality. In fact, Husserl argues, *ego cogito* cannot be used in this way. For radical doubt suspends not just the belief in the reality of extended things, but also the belief in the reality of thinking things. So, the thinking ego or self is not a thinking thing but irrecoverably distinct from all thingly being and all reality, both physical and psychic. On the other hand, it is still, after the suspension of belief, inseparably related to its object: the world and its multiple beings *as given in thinking*. This means that the phenomenological *epoché* or suspension does not nullify the world but gives the world to us in a new way. It opens a new transcendental area of correlative investigation, having two distinct but inseparable poles, the egoic acts of thinking or experiencing (*ego cogito*) and the objects thought or experienced (*cogitatum*) (Husserl 1950: 60–1/21).[16] For Husserl, this is the proper subject matter of philosophy. In his reading, Descartes came close to realizing this objective but did not take the final decisive step of radically questioning the ideal model of science inherited from the Greeks (Husserl 1950: 63–4/24–5).

Thus, Husserl agrees with Descartes that philosophy can and must become a science, a "rigorous science," as he calls it (Husserl [1911] 1965). But "rigor" does not mean exactitude in the geometrical or mathematical sense of the word. It means that the inquiry is purified from the preconceptions of everyday life as well as those of the positive sciences. The phenomenologist suspends his belief in the presence of practical and theoretical objects, and the world as the totality of all objects, and turns his attention to their ways of being given and then studies how the multiple senses of objectivity are constituted in conscious experiencing and in its passive undercurrents.

There is, however, a crucial analogy between geometry and phenomenology: both are ideal sciences that aim at describing ideal objects and necessary relations between such objects. What they thus share is an attitude toward particulars. The phenomenologist is interested in particular experiences in the same way as the geometrician is interested in particular triangles and circles. He does not collect large amounts of data and then make inductive generalizations based on them. He only goes through a few particulars and studies them as concrete examples of the essence of experience. His inquiry may be advanced more by a close inspection of a fictitious case than by a survey of actual instances (Husserl 1913: 160–3/181–3).

When the philosopher studies affective experience, for example, he is not interested in describing his own sentiments or the sentiments of his fellow men. This could be the task of the psychologist or the sociologist. The philosopher aims at finding the essential features that structure all—past, present, and future—modes of emotion. Further, his inquiry is not restricted to human emotions, but allows for the possibility of nonhuman affections, the emotions of animals, for example, or those of extraterrestrial aliens.

So, there is an important similarity between the objects studied in phenomenological philosophy and those of geometry. But the disparity is equally important. Husserl argues that the ideal objects studied in phenomenology are very different in kind from the ideal objects studied in the mathematical sciences. Geometry deals with ideal space that cannot be seen or intuited but can only be extrapolated (Husserl [1939] 1985: 42–4). Its concepts are exact and they determine a closed complete whole. Phenomenology, on the other hand, deals with the essential structures of experiencing, and it discloses experience as through and through temporal. The continuum of experiences is not a closed manifold but has the character of a flow or a stream. Every singular experience

---

[16] In Husserl's analysis, the ego is not a substantial entity, or an entity of any kind, real or constructed. It is a necessary structural element of all conscious experiences and of the continuous stream of experiencing. To highlight its non-substantial, non-thingly, and non-real character, Husserl calls it a "pole," and argues that it stays constantly opposed to the other pole of experiencing, the objective one (*cogitatum*).

is unique and irrecoverable; and together experiences form an open whole (Husserl 1952a: 130–1/242, 138–9/145; 1952b: 17, 44). Thus, phenomenology cannot form a system of founding axioms and deductive steps. It is not the "mathematics of experiences" but—by necessity—a purely descriptive science (Husserl 1913: 163–74/184–93).

To find the essential features of experience, the philosopher must compare particulars that are most different from one another. He cannot contend with what is familiar or common, but has to extend his study to exceptional cases and fictitious modifications. Husserl calls the process of looking for such examples, "free variation in imagination." The philosopher starts from one particular experience and varies it in his imagination, trying to find the limit cases in which the experience transforms into some other mode of experiencing, from the perception of a human being to the perception of a dummy or an animal—and then further from perception to memory or imagination, from volition to emotion, from judgment to assumption and anticipation.

2.5 FURTHER PERSPECTIVES

We have seen that there are important connections between Descartes' discussion of the mind–body union and classical phenomenology of perception and embodiment, as developed by Husserl and Merleau-Ponty. Further, the essay has also argued that the perplexing twofoldness of Descartes' account of the mind–body union—interactionistic on the one hand, and holistic on the other—can be clarified and made coherent by phenomenological analyses of the two different attitudes in which we can study human beings: naturalistic and personalistic.

In this perspective, the main guideline that Descartes offers to contemporary theorists of the human mind is the insight that our possibilities of understanding, explaining, and predicting the behaviors of human beings depend not merely on our advanced techniques of comparing and measuring the locations, states, and functions of their bodies or body parts, but also on our capacity to converse with them and immediately perceive or intuit their presence. Phenomenologists have argued that this immediate familiarity with other conscious beings cannot be derived from any results based on comparisons and measurements since it gives such beings, not as instances of universals, but as unique individuals. Moreover, classical phenomenologists have also maintained that in order to understand our relations to other conscious beings we must be clear about the nature of our own embodiment. The chapter explicated this philosophical heritage and ended in a discussion of the most important similarities and differences between Descartes' and Husserl's conceptions of philosophy as a radical science.

These are some of the main Cartesian ingredients that can be found in classical phenomenology. Of course, the reception of Descartes and Cartesianism by twentieth-century phenomenologists is not limited to these epistemological and methodological results, and space here does not allow for a complete presentation of all the intricate debates on Descartes and Cartesianism that have evolved in phenomenology since its beginnings. However, some major tendencies and developments can, and need to be, pointed out to give a fuller picture of the reception.

In addition to Husserl's and Merleau-Ponty's constructive expositions of Cartesian insights, twentieth-century phenomenology also includes deeply critical reactions to Descartes and Cartesianism. The most influential of such approaches is Martin Heidegger's critique of all egological philosophy of consciousness and all subjectivism, starting with Descartes' own inquiries and including their radicalizations by Husserl and his epistemologically minded followers. In *Being and Time* (*Sein und Zeit* 1927), Heidegger redefines phenomenology as a hermeneutical task of disclosing the primary facticity and temporality of our being-in-the-world. This, he argues, requires a historical dismantling of the universalistic concepts of subject, consciousness, ego, and person—as well as the related concepts of body and organism—handed down to us by our modern predecessors. The fundamental ontology outlined by Heidegger in *Being and Time* depends on the results of this critical undertaking.

In a series of historical-philosophical and phenomenological inquiries, Jean-Luc Marion (1987, 1986, cf. [1975] 1993) challenges the historical starting points of Heidegger's discussion of subjectivism and argues that the ego, discovered by Descartes and discussed by Husserl, must not be assimilated with an entity of any kind—psychological, social, or metaphysical—but must be understood as a unique speaking position with a performative function and perlocutionary force (cf. Searle 1969; Austin 1975). The outcome of Marion's investigations is an original combination of Husserlian and Heideggerian insights that aims at reestablishing phenomenology as an inquiry into pure givenness or manifestation, without any thesis for the primordiality of the ego or that of Being.

There are also other alternative perspectives to Descartes' operative in phenomenology, both constructive and deconstructive. In *Totality and Infinity* (*Totalité et infini* 1961) and related works, Emmanuel Levinas builds an ethical metaphysics that draws from Descartes' philosophy of infinities and magnitudes and from Kierkegaard's philosophy of faith. A Cartesian excursion, he claims, allows us to liberate our reflections from the dominant Kantian preconception about the primacy of finiteness in respect to infinity. In *Totality and Infinity*, we read:

> For the Cartesian cogito is discovered, at the end of the Third Meditation, to be supported on the *certitude of the divine existence qua infinite*, by relation to which the finitude of the cogito . . . is posited and conceivable. This finitude could not be determined without the recourse to the infinite, as is the case in the moderns, for whom finitude is, for example, determined on the basis of the mortality of the subject. . . . This certitude [of consciousness] is due to the clarity and distinctness of the cogito, but certitude itself is sought because of the *presence of infinity* in this finite though, which without this presence would be ignorant of its own finitude. (Levinas [1961] 1971: xx/210, italics added)

Twentieth-century phenomenology also includes approaches that radically rework the intuition that led Descartes to construe his ontology as a dualism. The most influential of such dualistic approaches are Jean-Paul Sartre's existential phenomenology, which operates by the distinction between being-in-itself and being-for-itself, explicated in his *Being and Nothingness* (*L'être et le néant* 1943), and Michel Henry's phenomenological Biranism, which operates by the concepts of exteriority and interiority, as worked out in his *The Essence of Manifestation* (*L'essence de la manifestation* 1963) and *Philosophy and Phenomenology of the Body* (*Philosophie et phénoménologie du corps* 1965). Neither of these dualistic approaches establishes a dualism between mind and matter, or thought and extension. Rather, both work to redefine the concepts of subjectivity and objectivity, immanence and transcendence, in a way that corresponds to the richness of human experiencing.

All these different approaches share the core operative concepts of givenness and manifestation, and their main problematics concern the relations between the reflective self and what remains other or alien to it. In the debates between these phenomenological commentators, Descartes' work does not figure as a philosophical impasse but as a source of insight and motivation.

References

Alanen, L. (2003), *Descartes's Concept of Mind* (Cambridge, MA: Harvard University Press).

Austin, J. (1975), *How to Do Things with Words* (Oxford: Oxford University Press).

Carman, T. (2008), *Merleau-Ponty* (London: Routledge).

Casey, E. S. (2013), *The Fate of Place: A Philosophical History* (Berkeley, CA: University of California Press).

Clark, A. (1997), *Putting Brain, Body and World Together Again* (Cambridge, MA: MIT Press).

Churchland, P. M. (1988), *Matter and Consciousness*, rev. ed. (Cambridge, MA: MIT Press).

Churchland, P. S. (1986), *Neurophilosophy: Toward a Unified Science of the Mind/Brain* (Cambridge, MA: MIT Press).

Damásio, A. (1994), *Descartes' Error: Mind, Reason, and the Human Brain* (New York: Avon Books).

Davidson, D. ([1970] 1980), "Mental events," in *Essays on Actions and Events* (Oxford: Clarendon Press), 207–28.

Davidson, D. (1993), "Thinking causes," in J. Heil and A. Mele (eds), *Mental Causation* (Oxford: Clarendon Press), 3–18.

Davidson, D. (1995), "Laws and Cause," *Dialectica*, 49/2–4: 263–79.

Descartes, R. (AT) ([1964–76] 1996), *Œuvres de Descartes I–XII*, revised edition, C. Adam and P. Tannery (eds) (Paris: J. Vrin/C.N.R.S.).

Descartes, R. (CSM) (1984–91), *The Philosophical Writings of Descartes I–III*, translated by J. Cottingham, R. Stoothoff, and D. Murdoch (Cambridge: Cambridge University Press).

Garber, D. and Wilson, M. (1998), "Mind–body problems," in D. Garber and M. Ayers (eds), *History of Seventeenth-Century Philosophy, Volume I* (Cambridge: Cambridge University Press), 833–67.

Heidegger, M. ([1927] 1993), *Sein und Zeit* (Tübingen: Max Niemeyer). In English *Being and Time*, translated by J. Stambaugh (Albany, NY: SUNY Press, 1996).

Heinämaa, S. (2003), "The living body and its position in metaphysics: Merleau-Ponty's dialogue with Descartes," in D. Zahavi, S. Heinämaa, and H. Ruin (eds), *Metaphysics, Facticity, Interpretation: Phenomenology in the Nordic Countries* (The Hague: Kluwer), 23–48.

Heinämaa, S. (2018), "Love and admiration (wonder): Fundaments of the self-other relations," in J. Drummond and S. Rinofner-Kreidl (eds), *Emotional Experiences* (London: Rowman and Littlefield), 155–74.

Henry, M. (1963), *L'essence de la manifestation* (Paris: Presses universitaires de France). In English *The Essence of Manifestation*, translated by G. Etzkorn (The Hague: Martinus Nijhoff, 1973).

Henry, M. (1965), *Philosophie et phénoménologie du corps* (Paris: Presses universitaires de France). In English *Philosophy and Phenomenology of the Body*, translated by G. Etzkorn (The Hague: Martinus Nijhoff, 1975).

Husserl, E. ([1911] 1965), *Philosophie als strenge Wissenschaft* (Frankfurt: Vittorio Klostermann). In English: "Philosophy as rigorous science," in *Phenomenology and the Crisis of Philosophy*, translated by Q. Lauer (New York: Harper Torchbooks, 1965).

Husserl, E. (1913), *Ideen zu einer reinen Phänomenologie und phänomenologischen Philosophie, Erstes Buch: Allgemeine Einführung in die reine Phänomenologie*, Husserliana 3, ed. W. Biemel (The Hague: Martinus Nijhoff). In English: *Ideas: General Introduction to Pure Phenomenology*, translated by W. R. Boyce Gibson (New York: Collier, 1962).

Husserl, E. ([1939] 1985), *Erfahrung und Urteil: Untersuchungen zur Genealogie der Logik*, revised and edited by L. Landgrebe (Hamburg: Felix Mayer Verlag). In English: *Experience and Judgment: Investigations in a Genealogy of Logic*, translated by J. S. Churchill and K. Ameriks (Evanston, IL: Northwestern University Press, 1973).

Husserl, E. (1950), *Cartesianische Meditationen und pariser Vorträge*, Husserliana 1, ed. S. Strasser (The Hague: Martinus Nijhoff). In English: *Cartesian Meditations*, translated by D. Cairns (Dordrecht: Martinus Nijhoff, 1960).

Husserl, E. (1952a), *Ideen zu einer reinen Phänomenologie und phänomenologischen Philosophie, Zweites Buch: Phänomenologische Untersuchungen zur Konstitution*, Husserliana 4, ed. M. Biemel (The Hague: Martinus Nijhoff). In English: *Ideas Pertaining to a Pure Phenomenology and to a Phenomenological Philosophy, Second Book: Studies in the Phenomenological Constitution*, translated by R. Rojcewicz and A. Schuwer (Dordrecht: Kluwer Academic Publishers, 1993).

Husserl, E. (1952b), *Ideen zu einer reinen Phänomenologie und phänomenologischen Philosophie, Drittes Buch: Die Phänomenologie und die Fundamente der Wissenschaften*, Husserliana 5, ed. M. Biemel (The Hague: Martinus Nijhoff).

Husserl, E. (1954), *Die Krisis der europäischen Wissenschaften und die transzendentale Phänomenologie: Eine Einleitung in die phänomenologische Philosophie*, Husserliana 6, ed. W. Biemel (The Hague: Martinus Nijhoff). In English: *The Crisis of European Sciences and Transcendental Phenomenology: An Introduction to Phenomenological Philosophy*, translated by D. Carr (Evanston, IL: Northwestern University Press, 1988).

Hutto, D. D. and Myin, E. (2013), *Radicalizing Enactivism: Basic Minds without Content* (Cambridge, MA: MIT Press).

Kaitaro, T. (2004), "Brain-mind Identities in Dualism and Materialism—A Historical Perspective," *Studies in History and Philosophy of Biology and Biomedical Sciences*, 35/4: 627–45.

Kaitaro, T. (2007), "Technological metaphors and the anatomy of representations in eighteenth-century French materialism and dualist mechanism," in H. Whitaker, C. U. M. Smith, and S. Finger (eds), *Brain, Mind and Medicine: Essays in Eighteenth-Century Neuroscience* (Dordrecht: Springer), 335–44.

Kaitaro, T. (2017), "Eighteenth-century French Materialism Clockwise and Anticlockwise," *British Journal of the History of Philosophy* 24/5: 1022–34.

Levinas, E. ([1961] 1988), *Totalité et infini: essai sur l'extériorité* (Paris: Kluwer). In English *Totality and Infinity: An Essay on Exteriority*, translated by A. Lingis (Pittsburgh, PA: Duquesne University Press, 1969).

Lokhorst, G.-J. (2016), "Descartes and the pineal gland," in E. N. Zalta (ed.), *The Stanford Encyclopedia of Philosophy*, URL = <http://plato.stanford.edu/archives/sum2016/entries/pineal-gland/>

Lokhorst, G.-J. and Kaitaro, T. (2001), "The Originality of Descartes' Theory about the Pineal Gland," *Journal for the History of the Neurosciences*, 10: 6–18.

Marion, J.-L. ([1975] 1993), *Sur l'ontologie grise de Descartes: science cartésienne et savoir aristotélicien dans les* Regulae (Paris: J. Vrin). In English: *Descartes's Grey Ontology: Cartesian Science and Aristotelian Thought in the Regulae*, translated by S. E. Donahue (South Bend, IN: St. Augustine's Press, 2016).

Marion, J.-L. (1986), *Sur le prisme métaphysique de Descartes: constitution et limites de l'onto-théologie dans la pensée cartésienne* (Paris: Presses universitaires de France). In English: *On Descartes' Metaphysical Prism: The Constitution and the Limits of Onto-Theo-Logy in Cartesian Thought* (Chicago, IL: University of Chicago Press, 1999).

Marion, J.-L. (1987), "L'ego et le *Dasein*: Heidegger et la 'destruction' de Descartes dans *Sein und Zeit*," in *Revue de Métaphysique et de Morale* 92/1: 25–53. In English "The ego and Dasein," in *Reduction and Givenness: Investigations of Husserl, Heidegger and Phenomenology*, translated by T. A. Carlson (Evanston, IL: Northwestern University Press 1998), 77–100.

Maturana, H. R. and Varela, F. J. ([1972] 1980), *Autopoiesis and Cognition: The Realization of the Living* (Dordrecht: Reidel).

Maturana, H. R. and Varela, F. J. ([1987] 1992), *The Tree of Knowledge: The Biological Roots of Human Understanding* (Boulder, CO: Shambhala Press).

Merleau-Ponty, M. ([1945] 1993), *Phénoménologie de la perception* (Paris: Gallimard). In English *Phenomenology of Perception*, translated by C. Smith (New York: Routledge and Kegan Paul, 1979).

Merleau-Ponty, M. (1964a), *L'Œil et l'esprit* (Paris: Gallimard). In English: "Eye and mind," translated by C. Dallery, in *The Primacy of Perception and Other Essays on Phenomenological Psychology, the Philosophy of Art, History and Politics*, ed. James M. Edie (Evanston, IL: Northwestern University Press, 1964).

Merleau-Ponty, M. (1964b), *Le visible et l'invisible*, ed. C. Lefort (Paris: Gallimard). In English: *The Visible and the Invisible*, translated by A. Lingis (Evanston, IL: Northwestern University Press, 1975).

Merleau-Ponty, M. (1995), *La Nature: Notes, cours du Collège de France*, ed. D. Séglard (Paris: Seuil). In English: *Nature: Course Notes from the Collège de France*, translated by R. Vallier (Evanston, IL: Northwestern University Press, 2003).

Noë, A. (2004), *Action in Perception* (Cambridge: Cambridge University Press).

Petitot, J., Varela, F. J., Pachoud, B., and Roy, J.-M. (eds) (1999), *Naturalizing Phenomenology: Contemporary Issues in Phenomenology and Cognitive Science* (Stanford, CA: Standford University Press).

Rietveld, E. (2013), "Affordances and unreflective freedom," in R. Thybo Jensen and D. Moran (eds), *The Phenomenology of Embodied Subjectivity* (Dordrect: Springer), 21–42.

Saphiro, L. (1999), "Princess Elisabeth and Descartes: The Union of Soul and Body and the Practice of Philosophy," *British Journal for the History of Philosophy*, 7/3: 503–20.

Saphiro, L. (ed.) (2007), *The Correspondence between Elisabeth, Princess of Bohemia and Descartes* (Chicago, IL: University of Chicago Press).

Saphiro, L. (2013), "Elisabeth, Princess of Bohemia," in E. N. Zalta (ed.), *The Stanford Encyclopedia of Philosophy*, URL: http://plato.stanford.edu/archives/fall2013/entries/elisabeth-bohemia/

Saphiro, L. and Pickavé, M. (eds) (2012), *Emotion and Cognitive Life in Medieval and Early Modern Philosophy* (Oxford: Oxford University Press).

Sartre, J.-P. ([1943] 1998), *L'être et le néant: essai d'ontologie phénoménologique* (Paris: Gallimard). In English: *Being and Nothingness: A Phenomenological Essay on Ontology*, translated by H. E. Barnes (New York: Washington Square Press).

Searle, J. (1969), *Speech Acts: An Essay in the Philosophy of Language* (Cambridge: Cambridge University Press).

Sepper, D. L. (1996), *Descartes' Imagination: Proportion, Images, and the Activity of Thinking* (Berkeley, CA: University of California Press).

Stein, E. (1917), *Zum Problem der Einfühlung* (Freiburg: Herder Verlag). In English: *On the Problem of Empathy*, translated by W. Stein (The Hague: Martinus Nijhoff, 1964).

Tollefsen, D. (1999), "Princess Elisabeth and the Problem of Mind–body Interaction," *Hypatia—A Journal of Feminist Philosophy*, 14/3: 59–77.

Uexküll, J. ([1934] 2004), *Mondes animaux et monde humain suivi de Théorie de la signification*, translated by P. Müller (Paris: Pocket Agora).

Varela, F., Thompson, E., and Rosch, E. (eds) (1991), *The Embodied Mind: Cognitive Science and Human Experience* (Cambridge, MA: MIT Press).

CHAPTER 3

....

KANT, NEO-KANTIANISM, AND PHENOMENOLOGY

....

SEBASTIAN LUFT

3.1 INTRODUCTION

....

THE relation between phenomenology, Kant, and Kantian philosophizing broadly construed (historically and systematically), has been a mainstay in phenomenological research.[1] This mutual testing of both philosophies is hardly surprising given phenomenology's promise to provide a wholly novel *type* of philosophy. In the first decades of the twentieth century, if there was one "classical" form of philosophy to play off against, it was the philosophy inaugurated by Kant. Kant was the main philosopher anybody writing in German had to contend with, and since the movement promoting Kant, neo-Kantianism, was the most dominant philosophical movement at the time, this was the main sounding board for the proponents of phenomenology. If one had to choose an enemy for one's own "liberation narrative," it would have to be Kant and his successors.

A few words are in order regarding *with whom exactly* phenomenology is to be contrasted. At the time phenomenology surged, Kant was represented by neo-Kantianism, which was anything but a unified movement. Part of the methodological challenge in assessing the relation between phenomenology and Kant is to keep Kant and his representatives separated as much as possible, for the latter were innovative thinkers with original agendas. But since Kant cannot be properly assessed without a look at his self-proclaimed representatives, the neo-Kantians, too, need to be included in this account.

---

[1] See the first newer work assessing this relation, Kern's classical *Husserl und Kant* (1964), which is an excellent place to start.

This standoff that took place in the first decades of the twentieth century was not a wholesale rejection of the other's standpoint. Most phenomenologists admitted that they were able to benefit from Kant and his successors[2] and sought contact with them. In turn, some neo-Kantians appreciated aspects of the phenomenologists' writings. This *rapprochement* can partly be explained by phenomenology originally stemming from the Austrian tradition associated with Brentano, an outright critic of philosophy in a Kantian register.[3] Brentano remained an important inspiratory source; but when the Movement broadened, the ties to Brentano weakened.[4] Husserl struggled to free himself from these empiricist confines, and once he did, was surprised to see the similarities and overlaps with Kant and the neo-Kantians. Heidegger was closer to the neo-Kantians from his beginnings (being a student of Rickert). But he, too, had a knee-jerk reaction to the "idealistic" elements of Kantianism. In later years, his appreciation of Kant increased. "His" Kant is both an ingenious interpretation of Kant and an attempt at "assassinating" the neo-Kantian Kant.

Looking over into the other "camp," something like "Kant scholarship" was just developing, and would establish the main lines of interpretation the phenomenologists challenged. The influential Kant interpretations beginning in the 1870s would, by the beginning of the twentieth century, become "canonical." These readings that seem to be part of Kant's "DNA" were in fact the result of some eighty years of Kant scholarship, reaching back to the debates in the nineteenth century waged by Trendelenburg, Fischer, and Cohen.[5] As a result, the brand "neo-Kantianism" took on its own character, divorced from some of Kant's claims. This makes it even harder to assess the relationship between Kant, neo-Kantianism, and phenomenology, hardly a homogenous category itself.

As a result of this historical situation in which phenomenology evolved, many phenomenological interpretations of Kant were attempts to go back to the "true" Kant that the neo-Kantian "scholastics" had obfuscated. While some phenomenologists were attempting to establish an openly anti-Kantian philosophy in the name of phenomenology, others wanted to turn to the allegedly "real" Kant and were anti-*neo*-Kantian. In some cases, the presumed debates with Kant were really debates with the neo-Kantians, over issues that Kant would have found incomprehensible. All of these considerations make it clear that an assessment of the Kantian and neo-Kantian influence on phenomenology is tricky.

---

[2] The same goes the other way, too, as can be seen by Natorp's ringing endorsement of Husserl's *Logical Investigations* (see Natorp 2013: 257f.).

[3] Cf. Brentano's *Psychology from an Empirical Standpoint*, where Kant is a "whipping boy" for numerous wrongdoings.

[4] Brentano died in 1917 and had cut his ties with the "Phenomenological Movement." Brentano disagreed with the project of phenomenology the moment it moved from its descriptive-psychological into its philosophical register. For Husserl and his followers, leaving phenomenology at the stage of descriptive psychology rendered its main intentions moot.

[5] For a history of neo-Kantianism, see Willey 1978 and Köhnke 1991; for newer reconstructions see the recent work by Beiser 2014 and 2015.

For this reason a systematic confrontation between phenomenology and Kant/ Kantianism is impossible. Neither is the Phenomenological Movement a unified movement such that its claims could be clearly identified and neatly compared, one to one, to its "enemies." Nor is it possible to separate Kant from his interpretation in the hands of the neo-Kantians, who provided the first access to Kant for *all* contemporaries at the time.[6] While a confrontation between both traditions along the lines of main *themes* may be desirable, separating each phenomenologist's and Kant's *and* neo-Kantian's views on them would be an all-too arduous task. Instead, I have opted to present the *two main* phenomenologists', Husserl's and Heidegger's, reactions to Kant and the neo-Kantians, restricting myself to the main discussions between them. I will spend more time on Husserl than Heidegger, since I believe that Kant and the neo-Kantians were more important to Husserl than to Heidegger; though Kant was a constant companion on the latter's path of thought. Heidegger's reading of Kant is rather a matter of setting straight the record about who Kant "really" was. I believe this is the most fruitful approach for an entry path into this jungle. Other phenomenologists have dealt with Kant and the neo-Kantians, for instance Max Scheler and Eugen Fink; as well Jean-Paul Sartre, Paul Ricœur, and others in the French tradition. In confining myself to the "classical" phenomenologists, their views are representative for a first overview and apply *cum grano salis* to most phenomenologists.

3.2 HUSSERL

Husserl's relation to Kant as well as to neo-Kantianism can be summed up in his own words in a letter to Cassirer of 1925:

> In my own development, originally hostile towards Kant . . . I first started out from Descartes and from there moved to the pre-Kantian philosophy of the eighteenth century . . . However, when I, driven by the basic problem in theory of science most dear to me as a mathematician to ever new problems in a necessary consequence, made a breakthrough to the method of eidetic analysis of consciousness . . . when, with the phenomenological reduction, the realm of the fundamental sources of all cognition opened up before me, at that point I had to acknowledge that this science developing before my eyes, although in an entirely different method, encompassed the total Kantian problematic (a problematic which only now received a deeper and clearer sense), and that it confirmed Kant's main results in rigorous scientific grounding . . . After having learned to see Kant from my own perspective, I can now also—and especially in the most recent years—receive rich instructions from Kant and the true Kantians. (Husserl 1994: 4)[7]

---

[6] A collected works of Kant did not exist until the *Akademieausgabe* was begun in 1900 (with Dilthey as general editor). Later, Cassirer began his own edition of Kant's collected works.
[7] All translations from the German, unless otherwise noted, are by the author.

What is, "the total Kantian problematic" which, in Husserl's hands, has taken on a "deeper and clearer sense"? This main problematic can be divided into a few key aspects that will be considered separately. Let us turn to Kant first.

3.2.1 Kant

As Husserl mentions, he was inimical towards Kant in his early phase, but once he had established the main lines of his phenomenological "system," he sought contact with Kant and discovered that he moved, in general, in the same framework, but with some significant improvements. There are, I think, three main *substantial* moves:[8] from formal to material a priori; from sensible to categorial intuition; from deduction to reduction. I take these to be the crucial elements of Kant's philosophy, where Husserl made positive improvements over Kant. All aspects taken together result in Husserl's notion of transcendental idealism, which is not a separate topic, but the total consequence of these points.

But all of these may be prefaced by an important *methodological* difference between Kant and Husserl.

Philosophy as science: In the above quoted passage a *methodological difference* is hinted at, but can be missed easily: Husserl says that Kant's results had been confirmed by himself, but in a "rigorous scientific grounding." Put differently, Husserl accuses Kant of not being rigorous *enough*, and this is quite a reproach to someone who insists on bringing metaphysics on the path "to a science" (see Kant 2004) for the very first time. The contrast between both here may be an instructive start.

What Kant means by science in the famous formulation from *Prolegomena* is to bring philosophy on the same path to science that *natural science* had already undergone in modernity through Newton's canonization of physics under the method of mathematics. In Kant's narrative, the transition to modern science is marked by the fact that in natural science, mathematics, and not empirical induction, could be used to reach synthetic a priori results, when applying pure mathematics to empirically experienced nature. Not all of natural science is a priori, but it can be a priori to the extent that it applies a priori laws to nature: "Now we are nevertheless actually in possession of a pure natural science, which, a priori and with all of the necessity required for apodictic propositions, propounds laws to which nature is subject" (Kant 2004: 47). Hence, what Kant celebrated about modern science is that it, too (besides pure mathematics), could achieve synthetic a priori truths with respect to objects of experience (and not just

---

[8] These differences to Kant pertain to phenomenology as a theoretical discipline; hence, what is missing here are the differences between Kant and Husserl regarding *practical* philosophy. On these differences see Peucker 2007. Other differences extend to the role of the imagination (see Jansen 2010); the role of aesthetics; the importance of religion, and other aspects. Thus the above account is very restrictive.

imagined objects in geometrical space). Thus, what characterizes "science" for Kant is the possible attainment of synthetic a priori judgments.

For Kant, the upshot of this understanding of "scientific" is that philosophy, too, should be made fit to attain these kinds of truths (cf. CPR, B xviiif.). But this hopefulness has to be taken restrictively. For, metaphysics' traditional claim to provide secure truth with respect to "absolute" objects, such as God, has been forever thwarted by Kant's transcendental idealism. According to the latter, we can only speak meaningfully about, and have cognition with respect to, objects of experience. Philosophy has no privilege over the sciences in its ability to forge a special access to things in themselves. Hence, the notion that philosophy could provide judgments with respect to "metaphysical" objects in the way that other scientific disciplines cannot, is rejected. The only thing philosophy, as metaphysics, can do is to show how any talk about absolute objects is meaningless, although their transformation into ideas of reason guiding our actions is a crucial part of Kant's critique of traditional metaphysics. Philosophy cannot reach synthetic judgments a priori about *its own domain* (as a realm of possible experience), because there exists no such domain; instead, it secures the judgments made in the sciences insofar as they utilize the language of mathematics, and it justifies the legitimacy of modern science's claim to synthetic a priori cognition.

Husserl's notion of scientific as a predicate for philosophy differs vastly. Already from his 1911 essay "Philosophy as Rigorous Science," it is clear what Husserl means by "scientific," by contrast with those attempts that betray the very notion of scientificity: psychologism in logic and historicism in the human sciences. Both reduce ideal truth to either occurrences in an individual mind or to historical events. They misconstrue the notion of truth as being ideal and true-in-itself, no matter what kind of consciousness grasps it. For Husserl, philosophy *can* be a science, a rigorous (a priori) one, since it can reach truths about its own, peculiar subject matter: ideal entities that are not part of the domain of logic or mathematics.

While Kant would have rejected the very notion that philosophy has its own subject domain, a proper realm of *experience*, this is exactly what Husserl claims. If philosophy understands its task correctly, to clarify the epistemological grounds for all sciences ("first philosophy"), it must see that it can do so, or *only* do so, while maintaining that philosophy has its own subject domain where this can be achieved: this is the realm of experience on the part of the cognizing subject.[9] Hence, epistemology must become an investigation of that subject which has cognition (and besides cognition, also feelings, willings, judgments, memories, and so forth). If all scientific disciplines are by definition *worldly* disciplines—they investigate a realm in the world—then philosophy, as phenomenology, is an investigation into that realm which *has* the world as the correlate of its experience. Moreover, its investigation is scientific, *rigorously* scientific, when it understands that the truths it can furnish with respect to its subject matter,

---

[9] Hence Husserl also refers to phenomenology as "transcendental empiricism." See Husserl 2002a: 4, and Husserl 2002c: 109.

consciousness, are ideal as well. Hence we glean the notion of phenomenology as an ideal science of a subject domain wholly its own: consciousness in its *having of* the world.

From formal to material a priori: Kant claims to have redefined how cognition comes about through the two stems of cognition, sensibility and understanding. Through the understanding, the active part of the subject, the human mind is able to connect what is given in sensibility with forms of thought, categories, to make cognition possible. Hence Kant's famous statement, "thoughts without content are dumb, intuitions without concepts are blind" (Kant 1965: 94/B 75). Both need to work together to yield the conditions of the possibility for experience and hence cognition. Sensibility and concepts are the *conditions of the possibility* for cognition, and both function as forms, that, once filled with content, make possible their execution. Sensibility is the form of (possible) sensible content, while reason is the place where (possible) concepts reside that can be connected to what is given in sensibility. Both are the conditions of the possibility of any experience, hence a priori, and both are by necessity formal. They are the *forms* for possible sensible experience and *forms* of possible conceptual thought. Hence, to Kant, the status of a priori is necessarily bound up with its formality. This can also be seen in the moral law, which is the *formal* law of the categorical imperative.[10]

Husserl agrees that our access to the world must contain elements that are necessarily and universally the case for conscious agents experiencing the world. He would, however, broaden Kant's claims in two directions: these a priori elements are in place not only in the case of cognition of objects in the world (in the question, what makes synthetic judgments a priori possible?), but in *all possible* forms of experience of the world (hence asking, instead, what makes *experience* of the world in all aspects possible?). Moreover, these a priori elements pertain not only to formal aspects of experience, but also contain "material" aspects. Material elements may not be found in all regions of experience (for instance, time), but for Husserl the identification of a priori and formal is restrictive. A priori status must also be granted to non-formal, yet necessary elements in certain regions of experience. Let us take two examples.

First, take the case of external experience, which to Kant involves space and time as *forms of intuition*. Husserl would expand here; external experience of a spatiotemporal object necessarily involves a consciousness experiencing it, but a consciousness that is not merely a thinking subject but one that is, necessarily, embodied, with the capacity to walk around it, touch it, have corresponding eye movements. The body, accordingly, is more than just a physical body, but is the locus for subjectivity. The subject functions in her body, it is the organ of experience and willful actions. No external perception is possible without a body as an integral part of the experience of the physical, external world. But a body is necessarily material, it is *flesh*. Hence, the body—not in the sense of a physical body, a *Körper*, but as a lived-body, a *Leib*—is the necessary, but *material* condition of the possibility for external experience. The eidetic proof of this claim can

---

[10] Husserl is critical of the formality of the categorical imperative. In turn, he claims to have found the formal laws of feeling and willing in formal axiology and formal practology corresponding to material a priori structures in the world; see Husserl 1988: 42f.

be demonstrated in that it is also present in a phantasized permutation of experience, for instance, when I imagine myself as an animal in a jungle. Thus, even in eidetic variation of external experience, the body might be modified, but cannot be *thought away*, hence it is necessary.[11]

Second, in his ethical reflections, Husserl insists that there is also a material a priori element in moral contexts. Indeed, there are a priori elements in ethical *situations,* such that a situation I find myself in, harbors a priori the right means for action. Hence, his categorical imperative, inspired by Brentano, "do the best among the attainable *in a given situation*" (Husserl 1988: 129, italics added), implies that there is such a best course of action given the situation one finds oneself in. This is not a priori in the sense of a universalizable maxim, but in the situation itself, which demands a certain action, indeed the "best action" for a given agent. Since every situation supposedly has its options for what can be done *contained in it,* the situation is governed by material a priori laws. While the categorical imperative Husserl formulates is formal in the sense that it demands the choice of the best option among the attainable ones, its choice by necessity implies material elements that the situation itself provides, which are *necessary for the individual in it.* Hence, everybody has *her individual* categorical imperative necessary for her exclusively.

Thus, if phenomenology is an ideal science, its claims are a priori, but many of its findings are material of the sort indicated; they are necessary elements of the intentional act, but they cannot be merely formal; or put differently, what Kant specifies as a priori formalities, *can be materially "filled in"* with content, as in the case of spatial experience indicated.

From sensible to categorial intuition: One of the main claims of Kant's epistemology is the classical distinction between sensibility and the understanding. Both might stem "from a common root, which is, however, unknown to us" (CPR: B 29), but despite this "crypticism" the distinction is a firm part of Kant's epistemology. The resistance to this distinction is nearly as old as Kant's philosophy, beginning with Fichte. The notion that intuition only pertains to the senses and, conversely, that conceptuality pertains to thought alone, has been found to be critique-worthy by different thinkers in different ways, but Husserl's rejection of this distinction is germane to his idea of phenomenology. For phenomenology's impetus to get to the "things themselves" implies a wide concept of "things." Things, to phenomenology, are phenomena insofar as they give themselves to a subject with the capacity to receive them. Thus, "things" can be a visual or auditive (sensible in the broadest sense) object, but also an object of memory, a presentified object, but also a wished-for action or a loved or hated object. Thus, phenomenology's basic claim, formulated in the "principle of all principles," teaches "*that each intuition affording [something] in an originary way is a legitimate source of knowledge, that whatever presents itself to us in 'Intuition' in an originary way . . . is to be taken simply as what*

---

[11] Nuzzo (2008) has argued that there is a certain sense of embodiment in Kant as well.

it affords itself as, but only within the limitation in which it affords itself there" (Husserl 2014: 43).

Thus, intuition (*Anschauung*) is utilized by phenomenology in the broadest sense, as anything that manifests itself in consciousness in different *forms* of intuition, thereby making itself *evident* in different forms. The notion that "non-sensible" things are not evident in the same form of "in the flesh" (*leibhaftig*) as sensible phenomena is an artificial privileging of objects "given to the senses." The contents of a wish or a will or the evidence of a mathematical proof have their own form of evidence that can be equally vivid.[12] But Husserl goes even further than that. He claims that intuition pertains to categories, which, for Kant, can never be intuited but rather make all intuition possible. Hence, we find here one of Husserl's most controversial claims—that there can be such a thing as categorial intuition.

Rather than using the terminology of objects of "sensible" and "super-sensible" perception (Husserl 2001a: 673), Husserl prefers to call them "real" and "ideal" (Husserl 2001a: 674). "Ideal" intuitions are founded upon real ones, such that Husserl can say, "we can characterize the sensible or real objects as *objects of the lower levels of possible intuition, the categorial* or ideal *ones as the objects of higher levels*" (Husserl 2001a: 674). In these higher acts, the categorial character *of* the intuition becomes grasped. "In such founded acts lies the categorial character of intuition and cognition, in them the judging thinking (where it functions as expression) receives its fulfillment: the possibility of perfect adequation to such acts determines the truth of the expression as its correctness" (Husserl 2001a: 675). Thus, while the lower-level act sees a book as red, the categorial act has as its content the expression, "the book is red." They stand in a foundational relationship. "For Husserl, categorial acts are *founded* on the sensory acts of perceiving, but are not *reducible* to them" (Moran and Cohen 2012: 60). Thus, categories have their own *manner of givenness* in the form of categorical intuition. It is not important for the present context to explain what role categorial intuition plays in Husserl's theory of cognition. Suffice it to say that the very notion of an intuition of categories is a *contradictio in adiecto* to any Kantian. As a reaction to his critics, Husserl later clarified that the intuition of ideal objects and eidetic lawfulnesses—those that phenomenology develops as a science—is not a "simple" intuition like a visual perception but involves an activity he calls "eidetic variation" (cf. Husserl 1964: 410–20). This clarification only corroborates his basic idea that these ideal entities, no matter how we arrive at an experience of them (since cognition is a type of experience as well), are in some form given to consciousness, manifest in the latter, and for that reason one can say that they, too, are "intuited."

From deduction to reduction: With respect to Husserl's method of entry into transcendental phenomenology, one question that may be asked is why he uses the curious term *reduction*. While it is clear that the main meaning of the term is *re-ducere*, leading back to transcendental subjectivity, the term is still somewhat puzzling. The verbal analogy

---

[12] In this context, Husserl also rejects Brentano's distinction between "outer" and "inner" intuition (see Husserl 2001a: 760–2). They are both "of the same epistemological character given the normal conception of the terms" (Husserl 2001a: 760–2).

to Kant's central term *deduction* cannot be dismissed.[13] When it comes to the method of transcendental philosophy, reduction and deduction, respectively, can be used to term their methods. "Deduction" is Kant's crucial term for the task of justifying the knowledge claims on the part of the sciences, when intuitions are connected with concepts to bring knowledge about. The term is not meant as a deduction from highest principles, but as a justification as to why this procedure is appropriate. The term "deduction" stems from the legal language of his day, denoting a "justification" of accusations made in the courtroom. This becomes clear in the courtroom metaphor Kant uses, when he speaks of modern science putting nature on the witness stand. "Deduction" is, thus, the philosophical justification of *existing and putatively true* claims to knowledge, which the philosophical critique does not challenge; instead, the justification clarifies *how* these knowledge claims are *possible*.

To Husserl, justifying knowledge claims is a worthy enterprise, but recall that Husserl rejects the two-stem doctrine, hence justification (a term abounding in his writings) takes on a different meaning. What the phenomenologist needs to do is justify the fact of experience in general, to explain how experience becomes possible. This explanation must ensue constitutively, i.e., by showing how the objects of experience are constituted in transcendental (inter)subjectivity. Thus, if we practice the "reduction," we reduce to the world-constituting transcendental subjectivity in *all* of its forms of experience, beginning with the most primitive, up to the highest, and in its intersubjective dimensions (the world is never constituted by a single subject). From this viewpoint, a justification of knowledge claims is not wrongheaded; it comes rather late in the process of justifying subjective deeds. Thus, both methods do not form a contradiction; it is rather Husserl's claim that the task of justifying knowledge claims in the scientific register accounts only for cognition, a very small portion of our engagement with the world, although the most dignified one. An account of the world as it is experienced as a *life-world* must begin from the lowest and most primitive levels until it can connect with the Kantian question. The highest form of justification reaches beyond Kant's scope; indeed, the highest level of justification is to justify oneself and one's actions as a person and ultimately as a philosophizing subject.

Phenomenology as transcendental idealism: The sum total of what has been said can be summed up in Husserl's version of transcendental idealism. As in Kant, transcendental idealism is compatible with empirical realism insofar as the idealist is not skeptical with respect to the empirical reality of the world, but understands the latter in terms of the world as given in the natural attitude, where the world is taken to exist independently of experiencing subjectivity. But the reduction to transcendental subjectivity reveals the natural attitude as constitutively dependent on this subjectivity. If the reduction is the true way to subjectivity in its world-constitutive activity, then "it is the royal road [*Marschroute*] to transcendental idealism" (Husserl 1959: 181). This claim can be connected to Kant's Copernican Turn. The turn from objects in themselves to the

---

[13] As I have argued elsewhere (see Luft 2009).

experience of objects (as phenomena) means that we cannot get beyond phenomena, but that we must account for them and our experience and cognition of them. Husserl would agree with this, but add that this account must begin with pre-predicative levels of experience all the way up to highest experience, manifest in judgments of cognition. Thus, when phenomenology, through the reduction, lays bare the correlational a priori between our experience of the world and that which gives itself therein, Husserl claims to have carried through with the Copernican Turn in its universality. For this reason he calls Kant's thing-in-itself a "mythical" remnant. Husserl follows the move Hegel made from transcendental to absolute idealism in that the very notion of a thing-in-itself (a thing not of possible experience) is counter-sensical. Any object that can be an object at all (for us), must be an object of actual or possible experience. Husserl never called his position "absolute idealism," he prefers the notion "transcendental" idealism, which he "proves" (cf. Husserl 2003). This "proof" lies not so much in a series of arguments, but rather in the execution of the intentional analyses themselves, which demonstrate that the world constitutes itself as a world of experience, as the life-world.[14]

3.2.2 Neo-Kantianism

Neo-Kantianism was present in two different schools in Germany, the Marburg School and in Southwest Germany, at Freiburg and Heidelberg (the "Baden School"). Husserl was philosophically closer to Marburg. While Husserl had a considerable appreciation for the Marburgers, his assessment of the Southwesterners was for the most part critical. In the interest of space, I will confine myself to his relation to Marburg.

The Marburg School consisted, essentially, of Cohen and Natorp. Though they worked in unison to keep their school formation alive, they were not as close as one may have assumed. Indeed, Cohen had forged his method in his reading of Kant, the "transcendental method," which Natorp publicly endorsed. However, Natorp (secretively) promoted his own idea of a philosophical psychology, which was critical of Cohen's position, though he took pains to present both as compatible. Husserl had things to say to both of them.

The "true" transcendental method: For Cohen, Kant's crucial insight following the Copernican Turn had to be turned into a method, the "transcendental method." This method is closely tied to the defining factum of our times: mathematical, natural science. This is the factum Kant meant, Cohen argued, when he devised his transcendental turn from the objects to the cognition of objects. After this turn, the objects meant can only be the objects that science constructs:

[14] See Husserl 1959: 181: "Phenomenology in its entirety is nothing other than the first rigorous form of this idealism." Husserl also develops a "proof" for transcendental idealism around 1913 (see Husserl 2003).

> Not the stars in the heavens are the objects that this method teaches us to contem-
> plate, but the astronomical calculations; those facts of scientific reality are, as it
> were, the real that is to be accounted for, as that at which the transcendental gaze is
> directed. What is the basis of this reality that is given in such facts? Which are the
> conditions of this certitude from which visible reality derives its reality? Those facts
> of laws are the objects, not the star-objects. (Cohen 1877: 20f.)

Thus the transcendental method had to start its regressive path from the factum of the
sciences and reconstruct the logical conditions that make this factum possible. This is
a scientific restatement of Kant's question regarding the conditions of the possibility of
synthetic a priori cognition. This method had to be implemented in all "directions" of
culture, besides science, morality, and aesthetics. The net accomplishment of this investigation is a thorough critique of culture that was to supplant Kant's narrower critique of
reason's capacities. This expansion of the critique was the defining idea of the Marburg
School.

Husserl's critique of this method is not that it is altogether wrong, but that it rests on
unclarified presuppositions:

> All regressive "transcendental" methodology in the specific sense of the term—
> much-used by Kant and preferred in neo-Kantianism—operates with presuppo-
> sitions, which are never systematically sought for, never scientifically ascertained,
> and, especially, not ascertained on the purely transcendental ground. . . . All regres-
> sive methods obviously hang suspended in mid-air, as long as this ground is not given
> and prepared and as long as progressive methods of cognition have not been attained,
> of which the regressive method is in need of as positive presuppositions. (Husserl
> 1956: 370)

Phenomenology purports to provide this "positive" method, since it makes the ground
upon which the sciences stand into a theme of research. Thus, "it is clear, accordingly,
that the presupposition of the fact of science . . . has an entirely different meaning than
the presupposition of a fact that is presupposed in the realm of the natural attitude and
any natural science" (Husserl 1956: 371). Every science stands on the ground of the natural attitude. Phenomenology, on the other hand, *begins* by questioning the presupposition of the natural attitude and delves, from there, into the depths of the subjectivity
constituting it. It thereby does not render the transcendental method wrong, but
relegates it to a higher-level problem that presupposes the foundational investigation
that phenomenology provides: to study the constitution of that which makes *possible*
all activities on the ground of the natural attitude, including science. While Kant (on
this neo-Kantian reading) clarifies the conditions of the possibility of *cognition*, Husserl
clarifies the conditions of the possibility of *every possible world-experience*. It is the true
foundational discipline and in this capacity "first philosophy."

Natorp: Transcendental psychology can only be transcendental phenomenology: In
the shadow of Cohen, Natorp developed transcendental psychology. This psychology should have the inverse direction of the transcendental method and offer an

investigation into the psychological laws involved in producing culture. This project is motivated by the methodological problem all psychology faces, that to describe the mental, one interrupts the normal course of psychic life and thereby "kills" it. As Brentano says, when I am angry, I cannot describe my anger, and when I do, I am no longer angry (see Brentano 2015: 30). Hence, there lies a falsifying effect in the very notion of a self-description of the psychic. The regressive method Natorp devises in reconstructing the psychic from its normal state of affairs, its factum, is meant to solve this problem. Yet, as his contemporaries already noticed, reconstruction does not avoid being constructive and thereby falsifying.[15] Husserl knew of these issues raised by Brentano and Natorp, and his solution is his claim that a just description of psychic states are possible through a change of attitude or a splitting of the ego into a "patent" and a "latent" ego (cf. Husserl 1959: 86–92). When I reflect on myself, what happens, in effect, is a splitting of the ego into an ego that reflects on a latent ego, while the reflecting ego is patent. This could occur ad infinitum in the natural attitude; but if I break with the natural attitude and establish a new attitude, that of phenomenology, I can gain a view of the life of the ego in its totality that does not distort it. Hence Husserl's name for the phenomenologist, "unparticipating observer," who is not *uninterested* in her own life, but does not *participate* in the constitution of the world in the natural attitude.

Husserl, however, appropriates from Natorp the idea of a reconstruction of depth structures of subjectivity that are lower layers upon which current acts rest. For instance, the current seeing of an object (described in "static" phenomenology) rests on a "thick" structure of cultural habituation, sedimented meaning structures. The latter is described by "genetic" phenomenology, and it can only fully execute its task after the break with the natural attitude. What was Natorp's "great premonition" (Husserl 2002: 3) of a transcendental-reconstructive science of the psyche becomes possible only through genetic phenomenology. But one must not overlook Natorp's formative role in the development of Husserl's genetic phenomenology.[16]

3.3 HEIDEGGER

Heidegger's view on Kant is most prominently presented in his book of 1929; it is equally a critique of the neo-Kantian interpretation of Kant. While it is tempting to read *Kant and the Problem of Metaphysics* as Heidegger's definitive statement on Kant, it must not be overlooked that Heidegger dealt, prior to 1929, critically with the neo-Kantians, especially in his early Freiburg and Marburg periods (1923–8). I will mention this early treatment of the neo-Kantians before turning to the 1929 debate with Cassirer, and Heidegger's subsequent Kant interpretation in his 1929 book. The book contains

---

[15] For a summary of this discussion, see Zahavi 2003.
[16] For the reconstruction of Husserl's development of genetic phenomenology, also through the influence of Natorp, see Welton (2000, esp. ch. 9: 221–56).

Heidegger's presentation of *his* Kant vis-à-vis the alleged distortion of the neo-Kantians. I present the main disagreement between Heidegger and *Cassirer* in Davos before turning to Heidegger's treatment of Kant, which was written as a direct consequence of that debate.

3.3.1 Heidegger and the Neo-Kantians

Categories of life: As of Heidegger's earliest lectures in Freiburg (1919–23) and Marburg (1923–8), he deals critically with his contemporaries, mainly the neo-Kantians, and their predecessors in the nineteenth century. It has already been mentioned that Heidegger stemmed from the lineage of Southwest neo-Kantianism, as a protégé of Rickert's. But the Marburgers fare no better in his invectives. In his earliest years, the philosopher Heidegger is, arguably, closest to is Dilthey. It is from Dilthey that he takes his main cues in developing his early position that becomes published, as a torso, in *Being and Time*. The main strategy of his critique of the neo-Kantians is that their philosophy obfuscates what he considers (with Dilthey) the main topic of philosophy, the phenomenon of life.

Indeed, this phenomenon that Dilthey forcefully brought to the forefront of the debate in the last decade of the nineteenth century is something that goes missing in biological or psychological accounts. Though biology deals with life, *bios*, biology treats it only as a natural phenomenon, an organic feature of living creatures. Psychology, the discipline treating the soul, as it was developed in the nineteenth century, also misses the originary phenomenon of life because it treats the psyche like every other science treats its subject matter: in an objectifying way. This is exactly where Heidegger latches on to the problem of Natorp's psychology; as Heidegger acknowledges, Natorp does *recognize* the problem. For Natorp sees the problem that to *thematize* the psychic means to miss its original life beat, that all thematization is one step removed from the original *experience* of life, and hence that every psychology "kills" its very phenomenon. But although Natorp *sees* the problem, he is unable to solve it; his method of "reconstruction" does not evade the fact that it is a form of construction; Heidegger comments:

> Does the method of reconstruction achieve what it sets out to achieve? *No.* For one thing, it, too, is objectification. One must reject the notion that Natorp has made it intelligible that the meaning of *method* is different from that of objectivation [the method of the natural sciences]. . . . And it is not evident how through such a mediating thematization . . . the immediate is ever to be gained and achieved. (Heidegger 1987: 107)

Yet Husserl's method of using the individual experience from the first-person perspective as a springboard for an eidetic analysis *of* the individual consciousness is no way out either. For this method, too, no longer *lives in* the original experience. The solution can only be a method that *lets life itself speak*, without "killing" it through any scientific or philosophical method. The project of letting life speak is, in this light, an anti-philosophy. Heidegger calls it *hermeneutics of facticity*, which aims at a self-interpretation of life in its quotidian lifestyle, in "taking care of business" (*Sorge*) before any "idealizing" interpretation from above. Such an interpretation does not press this life in the Procrustean bed of artificial distinctions, such as subject–object, theory–practice, etc. (cf. Heidegger 1995: 101–4).

Heidegger unfolds this program in *Being and Time*. It is a hermeneutic laying-out of the categories of life as it is lived, as it lives itself in the creature who has an awareness of it: factical Dasein, the human being in her "thereness," thrown into the world without a choice of whence, where, and whereto. This project is the result of Heidegger's critical rejection of the neo-Kantian "logification" of everything into a systematizing account. For this reason Heidegger rejected philosophical systems and canonic distinctions within doctrinal philosophy such as epistemology and ethics.[17]

3.3.2 Heidegger and Cassirer, and Kant

The finitude of the subject: Heidegger and Cassirer were invited to the Swiss town Davos in the spring of 1929 to present their views on Kant. From the outside, this may seem like a fairly academic affair; however, within academia this event bore significance as Cassirer was considered the *eminence grise* of neo-Kantianism and Heidegger the young renegade of the new "existentialist" movement. The fact that Heidegger, only three years later, became one of the foremost thinkers of the Nazi movement and that the Jew Cassirer was forced to leave Germany, made the event auspicious in hindsight.[18] Though the discussion seems cordial and both afterwards did not attach too much weight to this meeting,[19] it was perceived as a watershed event. "All" that happened was that both presented "their" Kant and used this interpretation to highlight the main lines of their philosophies. While neither Heidegger nor Cassirer articulated any novelties, the discussion brought their positions into clear relief. The event was important enough for Heidegger to pen his *Kant und das Problem der Metaphysik* so quickly that it appeared

---

[17]   Another figure who, unfortunately, has to be passed over here and who had a significant impact on Heidegger was Emil Lask, a pupil of Windelband and Rickert, who prematurely died in the Great War. For a demonstration of this influence, see Crowell 2001.

[18]   A detailed account of Davos 1929, its prehistory and aftermath, is to be found in Gordon (2008). It reports the whole event from all angles with impressive detail.

[19]   The protocol of this dispute had already been circulated by then. One reason to quickly write the Kant book was this "uncontrolled circulation," see the letter to Jaspers quoted in the following footnote. Since the protocol continued to be circulated after the publication of the Kant book, Heidegger decided to publish it as an appendix to the edition of 1973. See Heidegger's immediate reaction to the dispute in the letter to Blochmann, from April 12, 1929: "Substantially-philosophically, I gained nothing . . . Cassirer was extremely polite in the discussion, almost too obliging. Thus I found too little resistance, which made it impossible to give the problems their proper acuity. Essentially, the questions were far too difficult for a public debate" (Heidegger/Blochmann 1989: 29f.).

in the fall of that year.[20] It has become one of the most influential, though controversial, Kant interpretations. Hence, I will work my way backward from Heidegger's discussion with Cassirer, then turn to Heidegger's treatment of Kant.[21]

The dispute quickly turns to the question of what neo-Kantianism really amounts to. Heidegger criticizes the neo-Kantian reading of Kant for reducing Kant to the "theoretician of mathematico-physical theory of natural science" (Luft 2015a: 479). Cassirer rejects this reading to be paradigmatic of neo-Kantianism: "The positioning of the mathematical sciences of nature is for me only a paradigm, not the whole of the problem" (Luft 2015a: 479). To both, there is more at stake in Kant. What is it? Cassirer suggests— ever conciliatorily—that it is the problem of freedom and its possibility (Luft 2015a: 479), but Heidegger puts the difference in a dialectical fashion: the different starting and end points of both ventures: "One could say that the *terminus ad quem* is [for Cassirer] a complete philosophy of culture in the sense of clarification of the wholeness of the form of a structure-creating consciousness. The *terminus a quo* in Cassirer is completely problematical. My position is the opposite: the *terminus a quo* is my central problematic" (Luft 2015a: 482). This starting point for Heidegger is finite Dasein in its thrownness, but this is also his *terminus ad quem*. Heidegger even asserts that "what I designate with the term Dasein cannot be translated by one of Cassirer's concepts" (Luft 2015a: 483), an interpretation with which Cassirer agrees. To Cassirer, this Dasein and its life would be philosophically trivial, were one to remain at the level of this radical individuation and not see that individual Dasein is capable of partaking in a common world of culture, something which "always already" happens (which Heidegger presupposes when committing his thoughts to paper). "The essential of the transcendental method lies in this, that it begins with a given. Thus I inquire into the possibility of the given called [e.g.] 'language.' How is it possible that we as one Dasein to another can understand each other in this medium" (Luft 2015a: 484).

For Cassirer, the Kantian problematic of inquiring into the conditions of the possibility of the given (the transcendental method) comes into its own when it is applied to all regions of culture. Accordingly, his project is a rightful extension of the critique of reason into the critique of culture. Heidegger, in turn, interprets the Kantian problematic as raising, precisely, the issue of the individual Dasein, such that "it is the essence of

---

[20] The Davos Dispute took place in March 1929. Heidegger writes to Jaspers on April 14, 1929, "I must finish the manuscript of my Kant interpretation by the end of the month" (Heidegger/Jaspers 1990: 120). Heidegger penned the manuscript in roughly six weeks.

[21] It is written mainly against the Marburg neo-Kantians, whereas it arguably has some resonance with Rickert's interpretation of Kant, see Rickert's letter to Heidegger (Heidegger/Rickert 2002: 61), where Rickert points to a passage of his book on Kant of 1921, where he writes (Rickert 1924: 153) that the "main emphasis . . . of the Critique of Pure Reason . . . lay not in the Transcendental Aesthetic or Analytic, but in the *Dialectic,* and this means: the main problem of this work is not a theory of the experiential sciences, but it is about the old, ever-recurring *problems* of metaphysics." Rickert refers Heidegger to this passage, because he feels unfairly treated in the Davos debate, since Heidegger also mentions Rickert as someone who put forward the "epistemology of science thesis." In his reply to Rickert, Heidegger does not take back his words, but expresses dissatisfaction that the protocol had been leaked, since it was in many ways "insufficient."

philosophy, as a finite affair, that it is limited within the finitude of man" (Luft 2015a: 484). Heidegger adds, God does not need philosophy; it is we humans who do. Kant as the philosopher of finitude? This is the thesis of Heidegger's "instructively idiosyncratic and challenging" (Dahlstrom 2013: 110) interpretation of Kant, to which I turn now.

Heidegger's provocative title is "Kant and the Problem of Metaphysics." What is this problem? As he writes in 1965: "The problem for metaphysics, namely, the question concerning beings as such in their totality, is what allows Metaphysics as Metaphysics to become a problem" (Heidegger 1997: xxi). "Metaphysics" is, thus, not a philosophical doctrine, but a title for the *problem, to which metaphysics is the answer.* Accordingly, Kant's *Critique of Pure Reason* is interpreted "as laying of the ground and thus of placing the problem of metaphysics before us as a fundamental ontology" (Heidegger 1997: 1). Kant's project is presented as Heidegger's *avant la lettre.* Heidegger interprets Kant's central question as to the possibility of synthetic a priori judgments as inquiring into the possibility of knowledge regarding the being of beings, of "ontological (and not merely ontic) knowledge." The latter "is hence a judging according to grounds (principles) which are not brought forth experientially" (Heidegger 1997: 9). These principles are supplied by "our faculty of knowing a priori" (Heidegger 1997: 9), pure reason. Thus, "laying the ground for metaphysics as unveiling the essence of ontology is 'Critique of Pure Reason'" (Heidegger 1997: 10). The question regarding the possibility of synthetic cognition a priori is a "derivative" problem that becomes possible once the fundamental one is clarified.[22]

What Kant achieves is an ontology that is "modeled" on the ontological makeup of the being that *does* ontology, and that is Dasein. Citing the traditional interpretation of Kant, Heidegger asserts that "the *Critique of Reason* has nothing to do with a 'theory of knowledge'" (Heidegger 1997: 11), since it is not about the possibility of "ontic knowledge (experience)" (Heidegger 1997: 11), but ontological knowledge; in Kantian terms, not about synthetic judgments a priori, but their possibility *for finite Dasein.* The fascination, allegedly for Kant, lies in the fact that finite Dasein can have access to infinity (ideality), transcending its finitude. This says nothing about infinite entities, such as mathematical axioms, but everything about Dasein. Thus, Heidegger shifts the viewpoint from the goal achieved (synthetic judgments a priori) back to the human being in its finitude. What does this say about this finitude? This is, to Heidegger, Kant's central, though concealed, question. Kant must have had an answer to it, since without one, the very project would collapse. Kant does not seem to have understood that he *had* such an answer. Only a "violent interpretation" can wrest this answer from Kant. Heidegger attempts to retrieve this question at the heart of Kant's enterprise by a "going back [needed] for carrying out the laying of the ground of metaphysics" (Heidegger 1997: 13).

This finitude is firstly to be located in our sensibility, in "finite intuition" (Heidegger 1997: 24), seen in our access merely to appearances, not "things in themselves." Moreover,

---

[22] In this point—that Kant is essentially correct but starts "too high up"—Heidegger is close to Husserl's interpretation of Kant, only that the thrust of Heidegger's interpretation targets less Kant himself than the neo-Kantian interpretation of him.

the duality of sensibility and understanding characterizes us as finite, in that we need the "detour" through sensibility to *then* append categories of the understanding to the given. Ours is an *intellectus ectypus,* not *archetypus,* as is God's, who has access to things in themselves (see B 723). Heidegger interprets Kant's two-stem doctrine as yet another "proof" for our finitude. Heidegger takes Kant's famous allusion to the "common root" of sensibility and understanding as "go[ing] into and point[ing] consciously toward the unknown" (Heidegger 1997: 26). Heidegger takes the reader on a *Holzweg* into this "unknown region."

The Transcendental Deduction becomes central to Heidegger's interpretation; to him, it is the "elucidation of finite reason as [its] basic intention" (Heidegger 1997: 50). Heidegger is among those (following Schopenhauer) expressing sympathy for the first edition of the Critique,[23] since Kant is less guarded regarding his "true" intentions, which Heidegger intends to uncover. Kant's express purpose of the Deduction—which caused him "the most effort" (A xvi)—was to give a justification for the rightful production of synthetic a priori knowledge through "pure synthesis" on the part of the understanding. Thus, "I call the explanation of the manner in which concepts a priori can refer to objects the *transcendental* deduction" (B 117). What justifies this synthesis that achieves this reference?

It is finite understanding which allows things to appear, to let them stand against . . . (*Gegen-Stand, ob-iectum,* cf. Heidegger 1997: 50–3). "For a finite creature, beings are accessible only on the grounds of a preliminary letting-stand-against" (Heidegger 1997: 54). This is achieved by a "unifying unity" (Heidegger 1997: 54), "which has already been comprehensively grasped in advance through the horizon of time, which is set forth in pure intuition" (Heidegger 1997: 54). Here, the theme of "time" is introduced, and it will become pivotal for Heidegger's interpretation. Kant is "the first and only one" (Heidegger 1996: 23) to have seen the connection between temporality and being, witnessed in Kant's observation that "all modifications of the mind . . . are subject to time . . . as that in which they must all be ordered, connected, and brought into relation with one another" (A 99, cf. Heidegger 1997: 57). What enables these modifications to "be brought in relation" is the transcendental power of imagination; Heidegger cites Kant: "We thus have a pure power of imagination as a fundamental faculty of the human soul which serves as a basis for all knowledge a priori" (A 124, cf. Heidegger 1997: 59). Thus, "the pure synthesis of the transcendental power of imagination . . . is relative to time" (Heidegger 1997: 59). How, then, does the power of imagination function?

Imagination is finite creatures' power "to make something intuitable, i.e., . . . to create a look (image) from something" (Heidegger 1997: 65). Kant discusses how this is possible in the *Schematism*-chapter. To produce a schema is to make an appearance of something general, it is the visualization of a universal. It is this capacity on the part of the human being, which lets us gain access to ideal entities through an intuition by creating a rule under which they appear. "If the concept in general is that which is in

[23] There are indications that Husserl, too, favored the first edition, see Kern 1964: 19 n. 5.

service to the rule, then conceptual representing means the giving of the rule for the possible attainment of a look in advance in the manner of its regulation" (Heidegger 1997: 67). And "such making-sensible occurs primarily in the power of the imagination" (Heidegger 1997: 68). The schema, thus, is the "possible presentation of the rule of presentation represented in the schema" (Heidegger 1997: 69), such that Kant can say that the concept "always refers immediately to the schema" (Heidegger 1997: from A 141/B 180). But how does this lead to time?

The transcendental power of imagination, as the "faculty of binding together (synthesis)" (Heidegger 1997: 91), is "productive," but not in the sense of an *intuitus originarius,* but as bringing to presence: "The productive power of imagination forms only the look of an object which is possible and which, under certain conditions, is perhaps also producible, i.e., one which can be brought to presence" (Heidegger 1997: 92). It brings into view "constant presence" (Heidegger 1997: 93). Hence, "the pure productive power of imagination . . . makes experience possible for the first time" (Heidegger 1997: 93). Thus, the transcendental power of imagination accounts for the fact that both sensibility and the understanding "necessarily hang together" (A 124). From this assessment arises Heidegger's most original interpretation of Kant, namely that it is nothing other than this transcendental power, which constitutes the root of the two stems of cognition (cf. Heidegger 1997: 97–9). It is a "ground in such a way that it lets the stems grow out of itself, lending them support and stability" (Heidegger 1997: 97). To have unveiled this ground is Kant's great achievement, and this ground is the ground of metaphysics itself. Thus, "pure thinking" is "essentially intuitive" (cf. Heidegger 1997: 108), again pointing to Dasein's main "defect": the fact that we cannot intuit originarily, which is proven in the very root of our mind, the *Gemüt,* where the transcendental power of imagination resides. This "highest principle . . . speaks of the essential constitution of the human essence in general, to the extent that it is determined as finite, pure reason" (Heidegger 1997: 112).

Heidegger's interpretation is not without drama; having glimpsed into this abyss, "Kant shrank back from [it]" (Heidegger 1997: 112); it is "thrust aside" in the second edition of the Critique. Kant suffered from "metaphysical anxiety" in the crucial moment of his thinking. Heidegger concludes, "the specific finitude of human nature is decisive for the laying of the ground for metaphysics" (Heidegger 1997: 120). But pure sensibility, as the trait of the human being, is time (see Heidegger 1997: 121), time "as the original, threefold-unifying forming of future, past, and present in general" (Heidegger 1997: 137); this is the basic thesis of Heidegger's philosophy. Only Kant's "*horror metaphysicus*" kept him from going down the path Heidegger took. Heidegger's own achievement is a "retrieval" of laying the ground for metaphysics, which leads him to term his own project a "metaphysics of Dasein" (Heidegger 1997: 153).

Heidegger's Kant has nothing to do with the philosopher of science who ponders on the possibility of synthetic a priori judgments in modern physics; he also has no relation to the "all-crusher" of traditional metaphysics as rendering questions regarding "transcendent" things unanswerable. Heidegger does not even mention the part of the Critique, which aroused most attention in Kant's day: the Transcendental Dialectics. Nor does he ponder Kant's very purpose of the critique of reason: to make freedom possible. In this "existential" interpretation, Kant is decidedly brought into the twentieth century and its concerns with individual existence. That this "twentieth-century Kant" has, perhaps, little to do with the "eighteenth-century Kant" or the Kant of the nineteenth century, is at best collateral damage for Heidegger. However, in this, Heidegger has achieved the most controversial interpretation of Kant to date, where the question of whether or not Heidegger discovered the "real Kant" has become obsolete and even naïve.

3.4 CONCLUSION: MAPPING THE TERRAIN—THEN AND NOW

Looking back upon the discussion, one may open up three categories to characterize the relationship between the Kantian and phenomenological traditions. These reflect the way in which scholarship has dealt with these figures and their mutual relations. Taken separately, none of them is entirely correct; the truth lies in the whole.

1. First there are those, mostly from the phenomenological camp, who believe that the Phenomenological Movement represents a major departure from Kant and the Kantians, in various aspects: in method, substance, main claims, and interests. They criticize the Kantian deductive method "from above," and reject many of the canonical Kantian claims, such as the fundamental distinction between sensibility and the understanding, transcendental idealism, the identification of a priori with formality. Instead, they see phenomenology's descriptive program as opening up vast arrays of investigation that were never acknowledged by the Kantians. Some Kantians, to this day, think the same of phenomenology; that its representatives never fully understood the main intentions of Kant and his followers; that there lies enough potential in Kant's philosophy to render phenomenology and its interests obsolete.

As this discussion has shown, such a reading neglects the *catalytic effect* Kant and the neo-Kantians have had on the development of phenomenology. Even in its most critical aspects, the main phenomenological import cannot be fully appreciated without a clear understanding that it was a rejection or transformation of key tenets of Kantianism. For instance, to claim that "dumb experience" is not dumb and needs to be brought to speak through an analysis of consciousness's passivity, indeed the term "passive synthesis," could only be appreciated in its pushback against Kantianism. Also, the way in which the main phenomenologists *disagreed* with Kantianism is instructive, since phenomenology's counter-claims only come into relief against the backdrop they reject. Thus, whether or not the development of phenomenology is *motivated* by Kantianism, the way in which phenomenology did *things differently* from Kant and his followers tells us a great deal about phenomenology.

2. A more radical position is that phenomenology has *nothing* to do with Kantianism. Representatives of this claim believe that the main concerns that guided Husserl,

Heidegger, and others, lay so far apart from all of what concerned Kant that to even venture into a comparison between them, misses the innovative parts of phenomenology; that the guiding intentions of phenomenology are fundamentally un-Kantian, stemming from an entirely different philosophical tradition—Brentano and his empirical psychology and his realism. Indeed, the "German" and the "Austrian" traditions lay light years apart.

This represents a questionable historical assessment, as if German and Austrian philosophies were as far apart as the Prussian and Austro-Hungarian Empires were politically. In certain philosophical decisions, both traditions might be fundamentally inimical to each other; but this should not cause us to overlook the commonalities they shared which are too important to be cast aside, such as the belief in philosophy as a science, the rejection of psychologism, and the rejection of skepticism or skeptical relativism in epistemology and ethics. Husserl's version of transcendental idealism is similar to Kant's more than just in name. Heidegger's claim that Kant discovered finite Dasein, if plausible, would also lend credibility to the commonality thesis.

3. Third, there are some who think that Kantianism and phenomenology are siblings from a common father, Kant. They believe that Husserl merely re-did, and perhaps did better, what Kant and his predecessors attempted to achieve; that Heidegger got Kant right with his insistence on the subject as a finite Dasein, that this was what Kant had attempted but was unable to do given the limitations of his philosophical vocabulary. This also goes for the neo-Kantians; the Marburg School reading of the a priori as dynamic is the only way to react, as a Kantian, to paradigm shifts in the sciences; this is what Kant *would have* said had he witnessed the paradigm shift from Newtonian to Einsteinian physics.

Yet such a reading sells their respective genuine achievements short. Phenomenology does depart significantly from many Kantian claims, justifying itself as a philosophical movement in its own right. It cannot be neatly integrated into Kantianism; nor does it simply present an *Aufhebung* of Kant. It can also not be said that phenomenology makes Kantian claims obsolete. The Kantian notion of a deductive justification of the claims of knowledge from a factum is originally Kantian and has no equivalent in phenomenology. The same goes for the neo-Kantian contributions to the theory of science, as questionable as they were from the standpoint of phenomenology. Some newer research takes the stance that the mutual relationship is constructive, that these traditions can be seen as working out (differently, but constructively) solutions to common problems, such as the nature of transcendental philosophy, the threat of skepticism, and the role of philosophy in contemporary culture.[24] Newer scholars, in the spirit of overcoming the Continental–analytic split, are thankfully no longer concerned with keeping the traditions separate, but see phenomenology and Kantianism as working on common problems that still occupy us today.

---

[24] For some newer research in these areas of overlap, see Bambach 1995, Staiti 2014, and Luft 2015b, and the essays collections edited by Makkreel and Luft (2010) and DeWarren and Staiti (2015).

Thus, all of these interpretive standpoints have their merits and must be seen as contributing their part to a fair assessment of the relation between phenomenology and Kantianism in its various guises. Acknowledging the Kantian influence on phenomenology does not sell the latter's achievements short. On the other hand, insisting on the originality of phenomenology does not necessitate the killing of one of its fathers, nor does phenomenology render all aspects of Kantianism moot. A fair and circumspect assessment of phenomenology in all of its forms and figures finds a good touchstone and starting point in Kant as well as any of the major representatives of the neo-Kantian tradition. This way of assessing the relation between Kant and his followers to phenomenology is, I would argue, true to this day.[25]

References

Bambach, C. (1995), *Heidegger, Dilthey, and the Crisis of Historicism* (Ithaca, NY: Cornell University Press).

Beiser, F. C. (2014), *After Hegel: German Philosophy, 1840–1900* (Princeton, NJ: Princeton University Press).

Beiser, F. C. (2015), *The Genesis of Neo-Kantianism, 1796–1880* (Oxford: Oxford University Press).

Brentano, F. (2015), *Psychology from an Empirical Standpoint* (London: Routledge).

Cohen, H. (1877), *Kants Begründung der Ethik* (Berlin: Dümmler).

Crowell, S. (2001), *Husserl, Heidegger, and the Space of Meaning* (Evanston, IL: Northwestern University Press).

Dahlstrom, D. (2013), *The Heidegger Dictionary* (London: Bloomsbury).

DeWarren, N. and Staiti, A. (eds) (2015), *The Legacy of Neo-Kantianism* (Cambridge: Cambridge University Press).

Gordon, P. E. (2008), *Continental Divide: Heidegger, Cassirer, Davos* (Cambridge, MA: Harvard University Press).

Heidegger, M. (1987), *Zur Bestimmung der Philosophie*, ed. B. Heimbüchel (Frankfurt a. M.: Klostermann).

Heidegger, M. (1995), *Grundprobleme der Phänomenologie*, ed. H.-H. Gander (Frankfurt a. M.: Klostermann).

Heidegger, M. (1996), *Sein und Zeit* (Tübingen: Mohr Siebeck).

Heidegger, M. (1997), *Kant and the Problem of Metaphysics*, 5th edition, translated by R. Taft (Bloomington, IN: Indiana University Press).

Heidegger, M. and Blochmann, E. (1989), *Briefwechsel 1918–1969*, ed. J. Strock (Marbach: Dt. Literaturarchiv).

Heidegger, M. and Jaspers, K. (1990), *Briefwechsel 1920–1963*, ed. W. Biemel and H. Saner (Frankfurt a. M.: Klostermann).

Heidegger, M. and Rickert, H. (2002), *Briefe 1912 bis 1933 und andere Dokumente*, ed. A. Denker (Frankfurt a. M.: Klostermann).

[25] Thanks to two anonymous readers of an earlier version of this chapter, whose suggestions I sought to include.

Husserl, E. (1956), *Erste Philosophie. Teil I. Kritische Ideengeschichte*, ed. R. Boehm (Dordrecht: Springer).

Husserl, E. (1959), *Erste Philosophie. Teil II. Theorie der phänomenologischen Reduktion*, ed. R. Boehm (Dordrecht: Springer).

Husserl, E. (1964), *Erfahrung und Urteil. Untersuchungen zur Genealogie der Logik* (Hamburg: Claassen).

Husserl, E. (1988), *Vorlesungen zur Ethik und Wertlehre (1908–1914)*, ed. U. Melle (Dordrecht: Springer).

Husserl, E. (1994), *Briefwechsel, vol. VI: Die Neukantianer*, ed. K. and E. Schuhmann (Dordrecht: Springer).

Husserl, E. (2001a), *Logical Investigations*, translated by J. N. Findlay (London: Routledge).

Husserl, E. (2001b), *Natur und Geist (Vorlesungen 1927)*, ed. M. Weiler (Dordrecht: Springer).

Husserl, E. (2002a), *Natur und Geist (Vorlesungen 1919)*, ed. M. Weiler (Dordrecht: Springer).

Husserl, E. (2002b), *Zur phänomenologischen Reduktion. Texte aus dem Nachlass (1926–1935)*, ed. S. Luft (Dordrecht: Springer).

Husserl, E. (2002c), *Einleitung in die Philosophie. Vorlesungen 1922/23*, ed. B. Goossens (Dordrecht: Springer).

Husserl, E. (2003), *Transzendentaler Idealismus. Texte aus dem Nachlass (1908–1921)*, ed. R. Sowa and R. Rollinger (Dordrecht: Springer).

Husserl, E. (2014), *Ideas for a Pure Phenomenology and Phenomenological Philosophy. First Book: General Introduction to Pure Phenomenology*, translated by D. Dahlstrom (Indianapolis, IN: Hackett).

Jansen, J. (2010), "Philosophy, imagination and interdisciplinary research," in S. Gallagher and D. Schmicking (eds), *Handbook for Phenomenology and Cognitive Science* (Dordrecht: Springer), 141–58.

Kant, I. (1956), *Kritik der reinen Vernunft* (Hamburg: Meiner).

Kant, I. (2004), *Prolegomena to Any Future Metaphysics That Will Be Able to Come Forth as Science*, tranlated and ed. G. Hatfield (Cambridge: Cambridge University Press).

Kern, I. (1964), *Husserl und Kant. Eine Untersuchung über Husserls Verhältnis zu Kant und zum Neukantianismus (Phaenomenologica 16)* (The Hague: Martinus Nijhoff).

Köhnke, K. C. (1991), *The Rise of Neo-Kantianism: German Academic Philosophy between Idealism and Positivism*, translated by R. J. Hollingdale (Cambridge: Cambridge University Press).

Luft, S. (2009), "Reduktion," in H.-H. Gander (ed.) *Husserl-Lexikon* (Darmstadt: Wissenschaftliche Buchgesellschaft), 252–7.

Luft, S. (2011), *Subjectivity and Lifeworld in Transcendental Phenomenology* (Evanston, IL: Northwestern University Press).

Luft, S. (ed.) (2015a), *The Neo-Kantian Reader* (London: Routledge).

Luft, S. (2015b), *The Space of Culture: Towards a Neo-Kantian Philosophy of Culture Following the Marburg School (Cohen, Natorp, Cassirer)* (Oxford: Oxford University Press).

Makkreel, R. A. and Luft, S. (eds) (2010), *Neo-Kantianism in Contemporary Philosophy* (Bloomington, IN: Indiana University Press).

Moran, D. and Cohen, J. (2012), *The Husserl Dictionary* (London: Continuum).

Natorp, P. (2013), *Allgemeine Psychologie nach kritischer Methode*, ed. S. Luft (Darmstadt: Wissenschaftliche Buchgesellschaft).

Nuzzo, A. (2008), *Ideal Embodiment: Kant's Theory of Sensibility* (Bloomington, IN: Indiana University Press).

Peucker, H. (2007), "Husserl's Critique of Kant's Ethics," *Journal of the History of Philosophy*, 45/2: 309–19.

Rickert, H. (1924), *Kant als Philosoph der modernen Kultur. Ein geschichtsphilosophischer Versuch* (Tübingen: Mohr Siebeck).

Staiti, A. (2014), *Husserl's Transcendental Phenomenology: Nature, Spirit, and Life* (Cambridge: Cambridge University Press).

Welton, D. (2000), *The Other Husserl: The Horizons of Transcendental Phenomenology* (Bloomington, IN: Indiana University Press).

Willey, T. (1978), *Back to Kant: The Revival of Kantianism in German Social and Historical Thought, 1860–1914* (Detroit, MI: Wayne State).

Zahavi, D. (2003), "How to Investigate Subjectivity: Natorp and Heidegger on Reflection," *Continental Philosophy Review* 36/2: 155–76.

CHAPTER 4

···

PHENOMENOLOGY AND
GERMAN IDEALISM

···

ALEXANDER SCHNELL

TRANSLATED BY MAIA NAHELE HUFF-OWEN

IN studying the connection between phenomenology and German idealism (better termed "classical German philosophy"), one might focus on the filiation between these two traditions, that is, on the relationships that phenomenologists explicitly establish with the thought that immediately follows Kant. Such an approach would allow us to determine precisely the place and role, for example, of Fichte in Husserlian phenomenology (on the theoretical as well as practical level), of Schelling in Heidegger's phenomenological ontology, or of Hegel in the phenomenology of Sartre, Merleau-Ponty, Levinas, or even in Derridean deconstruction. This approach would be valuable because, despite the fact that it has generated increasing interest for a number of years (see, for instance, Fabbianelli, Luft 2014, Artemenko, Chernavin, and Schnell 2015), nevertheless there are numerous obscure areas still left to be clarified, and on different levels.

Thus, let us begin by taking stock of the influences at work between these two traditions. On the side of the phenomenologists, I will limit myself to the two principal authors who are of concern in his chapter: Husserl and Heidegger.

In Husserl's case, one must note that his relationship to classical German philosophers was at first borrowed from the extremely critical opinion of them held by his teacher, Brentano. However, all this changed in the period after the publication of the *Logical Investigations*, where Husserl elaborated what would later be named phenomenology's "transcendental turn." We find retrospective confirmation of this in his correspondence. In fact, several months after assuming the chair in philosophy at the University of Freiburg from Heinrich Rickert (in April 1916), Husserl wrote to his predecessor:

> It was only from the moment when, climbing up paths that were for me so very daunting, I found myself, without realizing it, in the realm of idealism, that I was able to . . . grasp what is great and eternally important in German idealism. (It is Fichte,

who, logically, attracts me more and more.) Thus, for the last decade, I feel tightly bound to the main figures of the German idealist schools: we are allies in the battle against the naturalism of our era, our common adversary. (Letter to Rickert dated January 16, 1917; Husserl 1994: 178)

In concrete terms, Husserl's interest in classical German philosophy was first expressed in his *teaching*: in the summer semester of 1903, Husserl gave a course on Fichte's "The Vocation of Man," which he gave again in the summers of 1915 and 1918. Other courses that dealt with Fichte's writings were "On the Introduction to the *Wissenschaftslehre*" (summer semester, 1908) and "Fichte's Ideal of Man" (1917 and twice in 1918).[1] We also find significant references to Fichte in the courses on Ethics (1908–9, 1911, 1914, 1920, and 1924), where Husserl also refers to Hegel, in particular to the latter's critique of formalism in Kant's ethics. At the end of "Philosophy as a Rigorous Science" (1911), in *First Philosophy*, and in the *Crisis*, we find sparse references to the German Idealists, although they are numerous enough. But, although the "practical Fichte" predominates in Husserl's courses, the references remain somewhat superficial and primarily concern Fichte's "popular philosophy" elaborated in *The Vocation of Man* and *The Way toward the Blessed Life*. There is no comparison, in any case, with the very substantial critique of Kantian ethics that we find in the appendix to *Lessons on Ethics and the Theory of Value* (Husserl 1988: 381–418), and again in chapter 9—"Kantian Ethics of Pure Reason"— in the *Introduction to Ethics* written in the 1920s (Husserl 2004: 200–43). In contrast, we will see later in this chapter just how reference to "theoretical Fichte" is absolutely central to Husserlian phenomenology when the latter is understood as transcendental idealism.

Classical German philosophy's direct influence on Heidegger, however, is more pronounced. We find it first of all in multiple courses: *Der deutsche Idealismus (Fichte, Schelling, Hegel) und die philosophische Problemlage der Gegenwart* (summer semester 1929), *Schelling: Vom Wesen der menschlichen Freiheit (1809)* (summer semester 1936), *Die Metaphysik des deutschen Idealismus. Zur erneuten Auslegung von Schellings Philosophischen Untersuchungen über das Wesen der menschlichen Freiheit und den damit zusammenhängenden Gegenständen (1809)* (first trimester 1941/summer semester 1941) and *Hegels* Phänomenologie des Geistes (winter semester 1930/31). Among the essays and treatises not published during Heidegger's lifetime, we must above all refer to: *Hegel* (Heidegger 1993) and *Seminare: Hegel–Schelling* (Heidegger 2011).

The deepest development of this influence is found in the first two courses listed above. In the course he gave in the summer semester of 1929, Heidegger refers to the ensemble of the three protagonists of classical German philosophy for the first time; he primarily develops the concept of construction and its link to its German Idealist antecedents.

The 1936 course on Schelling is essential because there Heidegger shows that the relationship between being and human Dasein, seen through the prism of "evil," is set on

---

[1] I thank Roland Breuer and Thomas Vongehr at the Husserl Archives at Leuven for this information.

an entirely new foundation, identified by Schelling in the *Philosophical Inquiries into Human Freedom*, for the reason that evil is not a contingent determination of being, but is instead an essential determination (a "metaphysical" determination) precisely introduced by the human. This analysis serves Heidegger as a backdrop for his own re-configuration of the relation between "*Seyn*" and "*Da-sein*" in the 1930s (or, at the very least, it echoes it).

But, Schelling's significant role is not limited to this aspect. Quite often, Heidegger relies on sources which, though not hidden away, are nevertheless not made explicit by him. This is particularly true of Aristotle, Luther, and Kierkegaard, and to a slightly lesser degree of the Schelling of *The Ages of the World*. Indeed, numerous analyses we find in *Being and Time*, and notably also in *Fundamental Concepts of Metaphysics*, are already found in this Schelling text, without Heidegger ever explicitly evoking these "sources." This is true especially for a large number of notions that relate to time: the extase, human temporality, the "moment of vision (*Augenblick*)," the privileged status of the future with respect to *other* temporal dimensions, the entanglement of the different dimensions of time, the flattened out character of "ordinary" time, the derivative nature of eternity with respect to time, the idea that every thing has its specific time, etc.

Among the German Idealists, Hegel is by far the author most cited by Heidegger (five times as often as Fichte, and more than twice as often as Schelling). Beyond the cele-brated "Hegel's Concept of Experience" (1942/3) in *Off the Beaten Track*, and the courses already mentioned, we must especially also point out the critique of the Hegelian con-ception of the relationship between time and spirit found in §82 of *Being and Time* (Heidegger 1996), which is crucial for understanding the "ordinary" concept of time in general, which ends the published part of Heidegger's masterwork. Hegel's influence was also decisive for the first generation of French phenomenologists (Sartre, Merleau-Ponty, and Levinas, among others), in large part because of Kojève's celebrated lectures on *The Phenomenology of Spirit*, given between 1933 and 1939 at the *École pratique des hautes études* in Paris, which numerous Parisian intellectuals of the first order attended. The work of Levinas, for example, is through and through as much a discussion with Heidegger as it is with that thinker of a "totality" that Levinas critiques in the name of an "infinity" at the heart of what he sometimes called "ethics as first philosophy."

However, simply treating the relationship between "phenomenology" per se and "classical German philosophy" per se, suffers from a patent insufficiency relative to the plain variation between different projects within these two universes of thought. Therefore, here I will opt for another choice. The thesis of the present chapter consists in putting forward the idea that, from the point of view of their speculative foundation, the works of the founding fathers of phenomenology admit of a *unity*, the nature of which is clarified by certain crucial contributions from classical German philosophy. These contributions concern certain "unthought aspects" of the phenomenological method. Before directly confronting these blind spots in phenomenology, however, I would first like to state more precisely in what this unity consists.

Phenomenology—at least that of its founding fathers—rests on two bases: one epistemological and the other ontological. It advances a *correlationism* where the metaphysical tradition had always stipulated a being-*in-itself*;[2] and binds together the problematic of the radical *legitimation* of *knowledge,* expressed through this correlationist perspective, with the exposure of an *ontological substructure* of that which is known. By doing this, phenomenology abandons the cleavage between phenomenon and thing-in-itself that characterizes Kantian transcendentalism; and it returns to ontology its proud name (though it is "new") that Kant had sought to remove from all epistemological perspectives.

However, reference to the author of the *Critique of Pure Reason* is not only justified in the negative. Kant is the emblematic ancestor *both* of classical German philosophy and of phenomenology; he pointed them both in their common transcendental direction. The objective of the appeal to classical German philosophy here will be precisely to clarify, on properly phenomenological terrain, a certain reorientation with respect to the concept of the transcendental that allows for the thinking together of epistemological and ontological perspectives. In Kantian terms, this objective will be to understand that the content of the supreme principle of all synthetic judgments according to which "the conditions of the possibility of *knowledge* (the epistemological part) are at the same time the conditions of the possibility of *objects* of experience (the ontological part)."[3] (In the *Critique of Pure Reason*, Kant himself did not draw all of the consequences from the content of this principle, consequences which nonetheless ought to follow.) But first, let us document the sense of this unity of phenomenology through the following citations:

> Only someone who misunderstands either the deepest sense of intentional method, or that of transcendental reduction, or perhaps both, can attempt to separate phenomenology from transcendental idealism. (Husserl 1950: 86)[4]

> If the term idealism amounts to the understanding of the fact that Being can never be explained by beings, but is always already the "transcendental" for every being, then the sole correct possibility of a philosophical problematic lies in idealism. (Heidegger 1996: 193)

> The renewal of the very concept of the transcendental ... appears to us as an essential contribution of phenomenology. (Levinas 1998: 113)

---

[2] The first mention of this correlationism was made by Fichte, *ante litteram,* so to speak, who insisted on the fact that in terms of the "principle of the unity and disunity of consciousness and object," correlationism constitutes the essence of transcendentalism: "everyone ... can perceive that absolutely all being posits a *thinking* or *consciousness* of that being; and that therefore mere being is always only one half of a whole together with the thought of this being, and is therefore one term of an original and more general disjunction ... Thus, absolute oneness can no more reside in being than in its correlative consciousness; it can as little be posited in the thing as in the representation of the thing. Rather, it resides in the principle ... of the absolute *oneness* and *indivisibility* of both, which is equally ... the principle of their *disjunction* ... This is Kant's discovery, and is what makes him the founder of *Transcendental Philosophy*" (Fichte 2005: 25–6).

[3] This point was already glimpsed by N. Hartmann, from a point of view not directly phenomenological (Hartung and Wunsch 2014: 19–66, in particular 39–46).

[4] In the same way, Husserl wrote elsewhere that "all philosophical ontologies are transcendental-idealist ontologies" (Husserl 1959: 482).

These three claims convey the idea that, from the framework of a perspective that identifies philosophy with phenomenology, and as long as the methodological constraints of phenomenology are at least minimally respected, phenomenology must necessarily be understood as an *idealism*. Further, that idealism has a *transcendental* as much as an *ontological* dimension. This double dimension, insofar as it characterizes the phenomenological approach, amounts precisely to a *new* concept of the transcendental.

These three quotations are taken from three different universes at the heart of the phenomenological tradition: from Husserl after the "transcendental turn"; from Heidegger's "fundamental ontology";[5] and from Levinas when, for the purpose of developing his first major work (*Totality and Infinity*), he returns to the Husserlian *corpus*. It seems legitimate to me to see a unity here, and to show how this unity is built on the systematic achievements of classical German philosophy. However, this does not mean that phenomenology could be interpreted only within this particular framework. Rather, the perspective that I am here concerned to develop and display consists more in attempting to show that, if we understand phenomenology as a transcendental philosophy, or better as a "transcendental idealism," as its authors recommend in some very important passages at least, then to grasp its content and meaning, recourse to classical German philosophy is unavoidable. To this end, I shall examine the two "fundamental bases" mentioned before, which amount to an epistemological and an ontological perspective; and I shall sketch in section 4.3 how, from a perspective that draws "metaphysical" conclusions from these phenomenological analyses, these two parts can be understood as belonging to a single project. These "unthought aspects" (referring to the metaphysical conclusions) in the phenomenological project crystallize in particular around the question of the different senses of "possibility" on the one hand, and of the notion of "transcendental subjectivity" on the other. We will see which particular questions arise from this and to what extent phenomenologists benefit, in this context, from the heritage of classical German philosophy. The essential objective of this chapter will thus consist in presenting the varying dimensions contained in the concept of the transcendental in phenomenology and in showing how the latter relies in an essential way on classical transcendental idealisms.

4.1 Epistemological Perspectives

The point shared by these varying phenomenological approaches to the transcendental lies in not granting the transcendental the status of a simple "condition of possibility," but rather in valorizing a form of givenness (and of experience) that attests to this notion and legitimates it. With respect to its *attestation*, the intuitive dimension is primary

---

[5] Recall that for Heidegger *fundamentalontologisch* has the same meaning as *transzendental* (Heidegger 1978).

(here the Husserlian perspective matches that of Fichte); with respect to its legitimation, the transcendental implements "phenomenological constructions" (in both Husserl and in Fink). Finally, there is a "possibilization" (conceived of as "making possible the making-possible," as developed by Heidegger) which also echoes Fichte's first explicit development of this possibilization.

Husserlian phenomenology is ruled by "the principle of all principles," formulated in the celebrated Section 24 of *Ideas I*. This principle states that every "fact" (*Tatsache*), as it relates to our realms of knowledge, must be "founded" (*begründet*), and that "every originary presentative intuition" is a "legitimizing source" (*Rechtsquelle*) of knowledge (Husserl 1977: 51). The term "legitimizing source" (*Rechtsquelle*) here, drawn from Kant's practical philosophy, implies that the "founding" power of the "principle of all principles" is *eo ipso legitimating*. However, the Fichtean background of this characterization of the supreme principle of phenomenology is not usually sufficiently emphasized. Although Husserl does not mention or develop any further the practical dimension at the very heart of a reflection on this principle of the legitimation of knowledge (which of course already brings to mind the *Wissenschaftslehre*), it nevertheless is necessary to insist upon the proximity of the decisive role of "intuition" and of "evidence" in the work of both transcendental idealists. Before Husserl emphasized the importance of intuitive evidence for the foundation of knowledge in his phenomenology, Fichte had already done the same in the *Wissenschaftslehre,* in terms of "intuition," "light," and "seeing"— from his earliest versions (dominated by "intellectual intuition") to his late ones.[6] The idea that "intuition" or "seeing" possesses a legitimating power (beyond Kant's account of the sensitive dimension of intuition) is first a *Fichtean* idea.

How does this intuitive evidence find its legitimation? Husserl's transcendental phenomenology proceeds in two stages, on two different levels.[7] First of all, it devotes itself to the experience that the ego has of itself in a constant concordance, in a consistent accordance. All descriptive analyses—first carried out in a *non-critical* manner— of the "immanent" sphere of consciousness belong to this level. The transcendental *critique*, in the Husserlian sense (that inquires into the constitutive phenomena of appearing), is the task that the second level of phenomenological research must perform. This second level stems from the "pre-phenomenal" or "pre-immanent" sphere of consciousness.[8]

It is the exposure of *intentional implications*, which of course are implicitly contained in all intentional relations, but which are nonetheless able to be given in

---

[6] "Seeing" (*Sehen*), "insight" (*Einsicht*), and "intuition" (*Anschauung*) are central to these later versions of the *Wissenschaftslehre*. Instances illustrating this idea are too numerous to all be cited. By way of general example, we suggest the 1812 and 1813 *Science of Knowledge*.

[7] Cf. on this point see the second of the *Cartesian Meditations* (Husserl 1950).

[8] Husserl refers to a "pre-phenomenal" dimension in his 1907 course on "Ding und Raum" (in regard to the spatiality of perceived things) (Husserl 1973a) and later in a more developed way in 1913, in the last texts in Section B of Husserliana 10 (concerning the temporality below "immanent" or "phenomenal" temporality) (Husserl 1969). For more on this point, see Schnell (2007).

an intuition, that fundamentally characterizes the *first level* of intentional analysis in Husserlian transcendentalism. Even though this analysis always concerns the characteristics of actual, intentional, lived experiences first of all, grasping the object in its concrete presence, it is important to emphasize that every actuality implies its potentialities: every presence signifies the co-presence of horizontalities that are also given, though not aimed for, and every perception also refers to other non-actualized perceptions which are implicated in the past and anticipated in the future. These horizontalities are "excessive" with respect to the actual presence: that which is co-present always essentially surpasses that which is actually given to consciousness. These co-present horizons are not "empty possibilities": they are neither pure hypotheses nor fictions. Rather, they sketch out possibilities which are already realized and to be realized, that essentially characterize the effective ego. Husserl calls these intuitable possibilities "potentialities (*Potentialitäten*)" that are always the potentialities of the ego's "I can" and "I do." Every intentional relation always implies an intuitive horizon of such potentialities. This is how Husserl explains intuitivity at the level of the immanent sphere (that is, on the first level) of transcendental consciousness. But does this suffice for truly furnishing the *legitimation* of that which is thus analyzed?

Let us return once more to the formulation of the "principle of all principles" in order to see how Fichtean heritage operates at an even deeper level in the Husserlian phenomenology of the legitimation of knowledge. Husserl does not claim that *every* source of right of knowledge is originally given intuition. But in that very Section 24 of *Ideas I* he asserts that every originally given intuition is one source of right of knowledge. This implies that there could be other sources of right that do not stem from intuition—or at least not from the same kind of intuition that operates in the descriptive approach.

Although it is indeed the phenomenological reduction (which guides us to transcendental subjectivity and its intentional life) that is the "fundamental method of phenomenology" (Husserl 1950: 61), these methodological considerations are not reducible to the "uncovering" or the intuitive "laying free" (*Freilegung*) of the experiences of the ego, with their intentional implications. For the term *Freilegung* implicitly refers to certain fundamental aspects of the phenomenological method that Husserl fully appreciated only during, and especially at the end of, the 1920s. More precisely, it shows that if phenomenology's *descriptive* analysis (in the sense, of course, of an *eidetic* description) remains useful and necessary for characterizing the "real" elements of "immanent" consciousness, this analysis shows itself to be insufficient when it is—as a *transcendental* approach that is ultimately legitimating recommends—a matter of descending to the level that ultimately constitutes these immanent phenomena. In fact, these experiences of the ego are not *only* given, present, such that a description would *suffice* to uncover their structural moments (even were they given in intentional implications); they instead require the additional work of setting aside the obstacles that impede the understanding of their constitutive role—"deconstructive" work (Husserl writes of this "dismantling reduction (*Abbaureduktion*)),"[9] to which will correspond, on this same ultimately constitutive level (that is, on the second level mentioned above), a positive aspect: construction[10] that is neither speculative, nor metaphysical, but is *phenomenological*.[11] For instance: all the components of the constitution of time-consciousness (originary impressions, retentional intentionality, etc.) on the descriptive level; the phenomenological construction of the "originary process" (*Urprozess*) and its "core-structure" on the pre-immanent level (Husserl 2001). But why the need for recourse to "phenomenological constructions" at this second level (below the descriptive experience of the immanent sphere of transcendental consciousness)? It is necessary to turn to phenomenological *constructions* each time a *descriptive* intentional analysis encounters a limit. What sets these limits are all the blind spots of descriptive analysis in general.

Phenomenological construction constructs both the *factum* and the conditions of the possibility of that *factum* at once—that is, the same thing that makes it possible also "possibilizes (*ermöglicht*)" it. In constructing, the phenomenological construction follows the requirements of that which is to be constructed. But in order for phenomenological construction to be possible, far from being reduced to a purely conceptual, intellectual construction, it must possess a *specific intuition*—exactly what Fink called a "constructive intuition" in the 1930s.[12]

Moreover, this way of posing the problem corresponds precisely to Fichte's project of "genetic construction." As Fichte emphasized, in the *1804/II Wissenschaftslehre*, for example, to construct genetically amounts to starting not from *facts*, but rather from "*Tathandlung*" (a synonym for "genesis" (Fichte 2005: 106)), and to bringing to light their legitimation as stemming neither from a presupposed being, nor from a speculative principle, but instead from that whose necessity is established only through the construction itself. The kind of intuition required here is a "genetic insight,"[13] or what

---

[9] The "primordial reduction" Husserl works out in Section 44 of *Cartesian Meditations* is an apt example of such an *Abbaureduktion* (Husserl 1950). See in addition manuscript C 17 (Husserl 2006: 394ff.).

[10] On this point, Husserl writes of a "constructive complementary part (*konstruktives Ergänzungsstück*)" of the phenomenological method (Husserl 1959: 139).

[11] Cf. Sections 59 and 64 of the fifth of Husserl's *Cartesian Meditations* (Husserl 1950). One finds the concept of a "phenomenological construction" especially in certain texts from the 1930s, which are directly inspired by conversations between Husserl and Fink. To my knowledge, the first mention of the term is found in Section 39 of the *Einleitung in die Philosophie* (1922/3) (Husserl 2002: 203). The notion is thereafter explicitly used by Heidegger in paragraphs 63 and 72 of *Being and Time* (Heidegger 1996). We also find a deeper use of it in the 1929 summer semester course in which Heidegger developed his concept of a "construction" on the basis of Fichte's *Grundlage der gesammten Wissenschaftslehre* (1794/5) (Heidegger 1997). Finally, in Section 7 of the *Sixth Cartesian Meditation*, Fink grants a special place to phenomenological construction in his fundamental reflections on phenomenological method (Fink 1995).

[12] "Phenomenology is the constructive intuition" (Fink 2006: 259). In Lesson 33 of Part 2 of *First Philosophy* (Husserl 1959: 48), Husserl, too, spoke on this point of a *Herausschauen* (ejective intuiting).

[13] This term is rendered as "*Original Insight*" in Wright's translation of *The Science of Knowing*.

Fichte called *Einsicht*. There is nevertheless a significant difference between genetic construction and phenomenological construction. Fichte introduces the idea of a "genesis" of "pure knowledge" (which characterizes knowledge *as knowledge*, that which makes knowledge be knowledge) following his critique of Kant. There he charges Kant with proceeding by means of "*post factum*" syntheses (positing the unity of two disjunct terms without deducing that unity, that is, without constructing it genetically). By contrast, Husserl's phenomenological constructions are not those of such a "pure" or "absolute" knowledge. Instead, they always concern a specific *factum,* which serves as a guiding thread for the construction. Thus, the Husserlian method is not a universal one, but rather a procedure that adheres strictly to the limits displayed by particular *facta.*

If in fact Husserl at least implicitly carries out phenomenological constructions of such *facta* (in his phenomenology of time, or of intersubjectivity, for example), nowhere is there a trace of a construction of the *conditions of [the] possibility* of these *facta*. For Fichte, the (transcendental) conditions of the possibility of knowledge are legitimated by means of a reflexive "doubling," that is, by a movement establishing that that which makes possible (in this case, that which makes knowledge possible) is in turn also made possible. Fichte calls this "doubling" (Fichte 2005: 132) "possibilization" (*Ermöglichung*). It is Heidegger, in his complete reworking of the structure of intentionality, who takes advantage of the phenomenological potential of "possibilization," understanding the term to mean exactly the same thing as Fichte does. Here once again the link to the *Wissenschaftslehre* is not made on a historiographical level, but rather on a systematic one.[14]

In *Being and Time*, Heidegger gives an ontological interpretation of intentional structure that frees this structure from the limited framework of the analysis of consciousness. His interpretation replaces the concept of transcendental subjectivity with that of Dasein—"human reality" which is not analyzed anthropologically, but ontologically— which is not a being "there," *present (vorhanden)* or handy (*zuhanden*), but essentially *able-to-be*. Dasein is a being-possible—it understands itself only starting from its possibilities. Heidegger thus uses the notion of "possibility" in a horizon that not only goes beyond the framework of Husserl's analysis of intentional consciousness (because it might be related to Fichte's comprehension of it, as we will see later), but that also poses once again the question of the link between this concept and the ontological dimension of subjectivity.

Moreover, the analysis of Dasein is carried out on an ontological level—as "fundamental ontology"—which doesn't mean that Heidegger simply is opposed to the perspective of the particular sciences (such as psychology, anthropology). For him, above all it is a matter of placing the analysis into relation with the being "in its totality." This,

---

[14] To my knowledge, Heidegger does not explicitly establish this link with Fichte. It is nonetheless the case that his usage of the term in *Being and Time, Fundamental Problems of Phenomenology*, and *Fundamental Concepts of Metaphysics* is literally the same as what one finds in the *Science of Knowledge* 1804/II.

however, raises two related questions: amongst all the possibilities offered to Dasein, is there one which would have an originary and singular status? And, following that, does Dasein allow itself to be understood in its entirety?

To respond to these two questions, in Section 53 of *Being and Time* Heidegger works out a phenomenological analysis of the relation of possibility to the largest of all horizons (Heidegger 1996). He does this in order to relate all factual possibilities to an originary possibility. This latter sort of possibility is the *possibility of the impossibility of existing*, which circumscribes the possible relation to *death*.[15]

Clearly, it is a matter of understanding this relation as *a possibility*. That is, the aim is to avoid two pitfalls: on the one hand, simple abstraction (considering death by merely thinking of it), and on the other by an effective realization of it (in waiting for death, for example). The name for such a relation, which can "support" this possibility *as* possibility and uncovers it as such, is the "outstripping within possibility" (in this case, in the extreme possibility of the impossibility of existing). What is it that fundamentally characterizes this outstripping?

Heidegger specifies that the outstripping here is both a "*Seinsart*" (mode or manner of being) of Dasein and that it also constitutes a particular "understanding." In other words, with this outstripping, Heidegger is on both ontological and epistemological ground. What are the phenomenal consequences of this? Two characteristic features must be emphasized here. First, the outstripping *singularizes* Dasein. Second, and of capital importance, the factual possibilities are *freed (freigegeben)*, and are thereafter open[16] by virtue of an act of transcendence by which this extreme possibility becomes *immeasured*: "Becoming free, in anticipation, *for* one's own death frees one from one's lostness in chance possibilities urging themselves upon us, so that the factical possibilities lying before the possibility not-to-be-bypassed can first be authentically understood and chosen" (Heidegger 1996: 243ff.).

This second point demonstrates Heidegger's proximity to Fichte. Heidegger in fact questions the way in which this ultimate possibility may become *certain* for Dasein, that is, how Dasein can make it its own, can appropriate it. The answer is the idea that, on a level that exclusively concerns "'comprehending' appropriation," this ultimate being-possible doubles itself: it becomes a possibilization (*Ermöglichung*) which is the making-possible of the (being-)possible. This outstripping, then, shows itself to be the possibilization of the extreme possibility: "The disclosedness (*Erschlossenheit*) of the [ultimate] possibility is grounded in the possibilization (*Ermöglichung*) that anticipates" (Heidegger 1996: 244). Thus, just as in Fichte's work, possibilization makes

---

[15] This does not mean that Heidegger integrates anthropological elements into his fundamental ontology, but rather the reverse; namely, that a prior ontological analysis of subjectivity is confirmed by the anthropological phenomenon. On the connection between anthropology and metaphysics, see Heidegger (1997: sections 2–4).

[16] Applying this idea to the relation to the tradition in *The Fundamental Concepts of Metaphysics*, Heidegger writes, in exactly this sense: "*Liberation from the tradition is an ever new appropriation (Immerneuaneignung) of its newly recognized strength*" (Heidegger 1995: 352).

possible the self-founding of knowledge as knowledge.[17] For Heidegger, it makes possible the becoming-certain for Dasein of the extreme possibility that frees all other finite possibilities.

On a level that primarily concerns the ultimate source of right of all knowledge, a kind of "Fichtean background" to phenomenology clearly appears. At every level of legitimation—whether considering the primordial role of intuitive evidence in descriptive phenomenology or, from a still more foundational perspective, with respect to phenomenological construction and possibilization—the fundamental formulations of the *Wissenschaftslehre* echo everywhere in the work of the founding fathers of phenomenology. Let us now turn to demonstrating the link between phenomenology and classical German philosophy that likewise exists on the ontological level.

4.2 ONTOLOGICAL PERSPECTIVES

If the *epoché* and the phenomenological reduction suspend the "world-thesis" and everything that it includes, or, in other words, if the gains of phenomenology are obtained at the price of making the phenomenon ontologically insecure, the following question arises: *What sense of being* pertains to the phenomenon? Although this question can serve as a guiding thread for the clarification of the status of the meaning of being in phenomenology, in reality it governed Schelling's critique of Fichte. In order to better understand what is at stake in this debate, it is necessary here to review the fundamental meaning of the transcendental idealisms of Fichte and Schelling.

For Schelling as well as for Fichte, the task is to found and legitimize transcendental knowledge, that is, not objective knowledge (knowledge of any object), but rather knowledge *as* knowledge, i.e., what makes knowledge *knowledge*. For Fichte, this aim is only conceivable (and possible) by showing that knowledge self-justifies "from the inside"—by this he means that it is justified without any recourse to an "objective" being, to a "content," or to any "external" influence whatsoever. Only such a genetic understanding of "pure knowledge" is capable of completing Kantian transcendental idealism.

For Schelling, by contrast, the Fichtean position is an abstract "formalism" (as is clear in his correspondence with Fichte in 1800–1 (Vater and Wood 2012)). In the *System of Transcendental Idealism* (1800) (Schelling 1993), Schelling proposed a solution meant to avoid this pitfall, one which later greatly influenced Hegel and *The Phenomenology of Spirit*. This solution implemented an entirely different conception of the role of objective content in the founding of knowledge. In fact, according to this conception, the *content* of knowledge plays an integral part in understanding the Self's grasp of itself. Here, the transcendental operates at *two levels*. First, the transcendental acts at the level of the series of nature's efforts at self-reflection, thus in his *Naturphilosophie*. Second, the

---

[17]   Cf. Lecture XVII of *The Science of Knowing* (1804/II) already cited (Fichte 2005).

transcendental acts at the level of the series of self-objectivations of the Self, thus in his *Transzendentalphilosophie* proper. Each moment of the first series has a corresponding one in the second, and vice versa. The "pivot" point is the act of self-consciousness—it is the culmination of *Naturphilosophie* (the supreme power), and the starting point of *Transzendentalphilosophie*. The supreme "*power*" of the latter is that power in which the Self is posited with all the determinations which already were contained in the free and conscious act of self-consciousness. The fundamental idea is thus that the legitimation of knowledge—and even and especially of the knowledge that in turn is able to legitimate all knowledge—presupposes that the different logical and real(!) determinations of that which is known structure that very legitimation itself in a categorial way. On this view, what transcendentally constitutes is, so to speak, ontologically contaminated by that which is transcendentally constituted.

The opposition between Fichte and Schelling may be summarized thus: for Fichte, knowledge can be radically legitimated only if this legitimation precedes all determination of the objective content of knowledge—recourse to this content would remove us from the transcendental perspective and would lead to an empiricism. Schelling opposes such a "formalist" point of view, putting forth a project in which the real determinability of the transcendental refers back to the logical categoriality of the content of knowledge itself—a "referring back" to the content, in virtue of which the transcendental is constituted by content and obtains literally its "objective reality."

Moreover, Schelling's position opens up an unprecedented perspective in the transcendental philosophical tradition, one that Levinas was able to identify and make use of phenomenologically. Schelling discovers a form of transcendentalism that is characterized by a "mutual conditioning" (this idea is actually formulated explicitly by Levinas (1969)) of the constituting transcendental and the constituted. Although Schelling does not explicitly stress this, Husserl became fully aware of this new sense of the transcendental (as Levinas convincingly showed in *Discovering Existence with Husserl* (1998)). Let us now examine the meaning of this idea of "mutual conditioning."

Every critique of "idealism," of "subjectivism," or of "formalism" condemns the act of assigning the constitution of the meaning of the real to the "subjective" pole of the correlation alone. In order to avoid such a unilateral position, one must grasp very precisely the meaning of the way in which "consciousness" or "thinking" relates to its objective content. It is neither a matter of a personal appropriation, nor of a simply empirical becoming-conscious; rather, it is a question of the way in which "we" "relate" to this objective content, as well as the manner in which this content counter- contaminates the correlational structures.

One can identify three fundamental moments in the answer to this question: first, the function of the phenomenological concept of truth; second, the mutual conditioning of the constituting and the constituted in the immanent sphere, as well as in the pre-immanent sphere; third, the genetization, or the deepest genetic analysis, of this mutual conditioning. While the first two moments are developed by Husserl, we have the third thanks to Levinas in *Otherwise Than Being or Beyond Essence* (Levinas 1978).

First, we must turn to the Sixth Logical Investigation in order to assess the role of truth in clarifying the ontological substratum of intentional correlation. Husserl's thesis consists precisely in joining the legitimation of the necessity of the objectivity of appearing with the phenomenological concept of truth, prior to the concrete adequation between "mind" and "thing." Truth is what is realized when the intentional relation is "correct," is "accurate." In turn, the adequate intentional relation presupposes the object "which makes true" (the statement/utterance), while it is understood that no individual, no concrete subjectivity is involved here, but that the "transcendental" determinations have an "anonymous" status. *Truth is the a priori form of every relation to the world.* This idea is decisive for understanding the "renewal of the transcendental," which takes place on the two levels that we have already presented. For, this idea establishes that truth does not stem from the institution of a norm on the basis of a pre-given (for example), real content, but that real being and the legitimation of its necessity are mutually mediated. If, *in this respect,* Husserl's outline follows that of Schelling, it nonetheless departs from Schelling's for the reason that phenomenology does not require "deductions" of real or ideal series, but instead performs analyses in which the objective content of phenomena shows itself, phenomenologically, in intuition (whether this is intuitive or constructive). Let us deepen the ontological implications of this perspective.

In Husserl's view, the "transcendental" does not only designate that which is "brought back to a transcendental ego" (that which raises constitutive and transcendental operations to the level of a clear and distinct consciousness). Rather, as we have seen, it also designates that every presence for consciousness "implies" potentialities that do not present themselves in all clarity to consciousness. The meaning of this "renewal" of the concept of the transcendental opens up a "new ontology," as Levinas has rightly stressed: "being is posited not only as a correlate of thought, but as already founding the very thought that nonetheless constitutes it" (Levinas 1998: 116). Thinking and being, the conscious subject and the object of consciousness, are precisely in a "relation of mutual conditioning." But how can this concept of ontology be more precisely specified?

In Section 20 of the *Cartesian Meditations,* Husserl had already established (at the level of the immanent sphere of consciousness) that in every intentional relation the intending of an intended takes place, of course, but that the intended is characterized by an "excess" relative to what is explicitly intended. This means that, in this approach of transcendental phenomenology, a "horizon" opens up that sketches intentional constitution in advance, and that thereby "motivates" intentional constitution to be oriented in relation to this "excess"—which relativizes all constitution directed unilaterally and refers back to a relation of mutual dependence that concerns immanent intentional consciousness and the being of that which appears also in an immanent way. What is decisive is that a "transcendentally constituted" being that precisely "founds" in an ontological way every operation or function of consciousness blossoms at the heart of the sphere of what is opened up by the *epoché* and the reduction (in which the dogmatic concept of being is neutralized). For Levinas, "phenomenology itself" (Levinas 1998: 116) consists through and through in this relation of mutual conditioning.[18] He expresses it in the following way: "Intentionality means that all consciousness is consciousness of something, but above all *that every object calls forth and as it were gives rise to the consciousness through which its being shines and, in doing so, appears*" (Levinas 1998: 119; italics original).

But this is not all. This relation of reciprocal mediation has a still more profound sense—one that allows one to see that this "new ontology" is also at work in phenomenology at the properly transcendental constitutive level (that is, at the so-called "pre-immanent sphere"). In fact, through the *epoché* and the reduction, a "subjective terrain" opens up in yet another sense, which we may, with Husserl, term the "pre-immanent sphere" of consciousness and which is, at the same time, to return to Levinasian terms, "more objective than any objectivity" (Levinas 1998: 117). In particular, this means that the object is not simply the correlate of the subject, but that there exists a relation of mediation in virtue of which the subject is not a "pure" subject, the object is not a "pure" object (Levinas 1998: 118). The "being" in play here can no longer be considered as "being." It requires a more radical reduction. Therefore, Husserl calls it at various points in the late manuscripts—and plainly under the influence of Fink—a "pre-being."[19] From a constitutive point of view, this "pre-being" precedes to some degree the being of the world, and destroys the opposition between an epistemological perspective and an ontological perspective to the extent that it concerns both anonymous, transcendental "subjectivity" and the correlate that this subjectivity constitutes and founds.

The determination of the objective content of the real thus requires both a constitutive, subjective operation and an ontological foundation that confers an objective reality upon that which is thus constituted. And it does these in a co-originary way! Transcendental constitution is an ontological founding. Let us stress: it is only because (transcendentally constituted) being "founds" consciousness (and in this consists the "objectivity more objective" than any objectivity that is unilaterally constituted by transcendental subjectivity) that consciousness can "constitute" the being that appears. "Constitution" thus means that the object does not just serve as an abstract guideline, but that it contaminates transcendental operations or functions. Additionally, this idea parallels that of "epigenesis," as Catherine Malabou has recently worked it out, beginning with Kant (Malabou 2016). This is the idea of a genesis that is mediated by the objective content *beyond* ("epi-") the transcendental origin, which is the other side of the coin, so to speak, of a conception according to which objectivity is structured in a categorial way.

---

[18] This concept of a "reciprocal conditioning" in phenomenology's "new ontology" should not be confused with Merleau-Ponty's thoughts on "reciprocity" and "reversibility" (which also have an ontological aim) that we find, for example, in *The Visible and the Invisible* (see Merleau-Ponty 1968: 130–55). This is because Merleau-Ponty does not dig deeply enough into the question of the relation between ontological foundation and transcendental constitution.

[19] See in particular text No. 62 in the C Manuscripts (Husserl 2006: 269), as well as a note in text No. 35 in Husserliana 15 (Husserl 1973b: 613).

Finally, "mutual conditioning" may be integrated into transcendental genesis as Fichte conceived of it. This mutual conditioning, as Levinas sketched it in *Otherwise than Being*, through his concept of "diachrony," is in turn genetized (Fichte would have added: by means of (auto-)reflection). In fact, every conditioning implies a difference of level or of register that each time brings into play both a presence and a withdrawal (either of the conditioning or of the conditioned, depending on the point of view assumed). But this is not simply due to the fact (as is the case for Fichte's work when he reflects Kantian transcendentalism) that the transcendental implies an annihilation and an engendering because it admits of no possible experience (as is the case for Fichte's work when he reflects Kantian transcendentalism); when, to boot, this annihilation and engendering applies only to such-and-such a transcendental condition. Rather, here there is a leap in register encompassing the whole of the sphere prior to immanent consciousness, that puts into play an alternation between "presence" and "non-presence" ("withdrawal")—precisely in virtue of a reflexive deepening of every "conditioning." Therefore, Levinas not only identifies this double figure as the very essence of conditioning, but by evoking the "uncondition or condition"[20] numerous times in his work (Levinas 1978: 5, 117, 122, 128, 183, 184), he situates this figure "diachronically," in fact, at its origin, which assumes the form of a "principle or non-principle," one could say, or of precisely what Levinas calls "an-archy." This "leap," which is thus the fundamental meaning of genesis, is not carried out from the outside by some "spectator" (no matter how "disinterested"). Rather, it realizes, in a "reflection of reflection" (this term is once again taken from Fichte), the fundamental determination of the transcendental that consists in the characteristic doubling of possibilization.[21] That is, the determination of the transcendental consists in the fact that the true understanding of something's conditions of possibility always simultaneously exposes what in its turn makes possible those very conditions of possibility.

4.3 METAPHYSICAL CONCLUSIONS

The conclusion of this double analysis (with respect to knowledge as well as to its ontological substratum) leads to the question of knowing its implications for the status of the subject–object correlation. On this point, we affirmed from the start that this correlation constituted a fundamental aspect of phenomenology. Given the opening of the pre-immanent sphere of consciousness with its status of "pre-being," one may wonder, in particular—and I have alluded to this earlier—whether the pre-immanent sphere is an "asubjective" one, or if we can still lend it the status of some sort of "transcendental subjectivity." Fichte already answered this same question about the "absolute Self,"

---

[20] This expression refers, incidentally, to a characterization of subjectivity in terms of "place or non-place" (or, further, "place and non-place") (notably, Levinas 1978: 45).
[21] In the final part of the chapter, I will present another dimension of "possibilization."

affirming, following the passage quoted above, that the doctrine of science had consistently recognized the Self as pure only insofar as it is "engendered," and that the doctrine placed it at the apex of its deductions, not of itself, but to the extent that "the productive process will always stand *higher* than what is produced" (Fichte 2005: 106). This means that Fichte distinguishes between the "deductions" carried out by the doctrine of science and the core of the doctrine of science itself: these correspond respectively to the engendered and the engendering. We can distinguish three levels here: the empirical level, the level of that which is "engendered," and the level of the "engendering." The doctrine of science engenders its own operations, but as such it does not confuse itself with its deductions. Considered in itself and for itself, the doctrine is in fact pure engendering, genesis, pure activity, *Tathandlung*. The deduction thus does not concern the ultimate point of view of the doctrine of science because this point of view opens on a genesis that, prior to all deduction, is ruled by an "asubjective subjectivity" that is characterized by an indetermination or an irreducible contingency at the heart of which a necessity opens up. We find this same perspective once again in phenomenology.[22]

The opening of the sphere of transcendental consciousness, thanks to the *epoché* and the phenomenological reduction, raises a fundamental problem. If, on the one hand, this sphere is characterized by the correlation between consciousness and its object (which raises the question of the "reality" of the object in the transcendental regime), and if, on the other hand, prior to the immanent sphere a pre-immanent sphere of consciousness opens up (which in turn raises the question of the "reality" of this sphere), then one may wonder what constitutes the unity of this double transcendental sphere (immanent and pre-immanent). The answer to this question should take into account the "minimal" phenomenological constraint (as Jean-Toussaint Desanti would put it), which consists in holding together the return to subjectivity and its correlational structure. To phrase it in entirely different terms (given the juxtaposition of perspectives analyzed above): How is it possible to hold together, on the one hand, the epistemological demand to legitimate knowledge and, on the other hand, the ontological demand to reveal the being of all that makes up the double phenomenological sphere?

Among the sketches of an answer to this question at the heart of classical German philosophy, we here will emphasize Fichte's, since it takes into account all of the elements at issue here. In the *Wissenschaftslehre 1804/II*, Fichte ascends to the supreme level of transcendental philosophy, without troubling himself over questions of access to the transcendental sphere. A decade after writing *Grundlage der gesammten Wissenschaftslehre* in 1794/5, he no longer calls this sphere the "absolute Self," though he retains the subjective dimension of it, calling it now "light," namely, the level of "the point of unity and disjunction" of the correlation of being (object) and thinking or consciousness (subject).

---

[22] This is so first of all for Husserl, since for each of the three levels mentioned (the empirical level, the level of the engendered, and the level of engendering) we have the corresponding spheres of empirical consciousness (outside of the regime of the *epoché*), the immanent sphere, and the pre-immanent sphere of transcendental consciousness, respectively; and it is so for Heidegger, for reasons that will be presented later.

In particular, the aim is to account for the principle of the appropriation of the object of knowing, of the ontological founding of the "bearer of all reality" and of the transcendental legitimation of the supreme principle of knowledge. This brings into play the link between consciousness's self-annihilation and the "deposit" (*Absetzung*) of being, "the bearer of all reality"; and a doubling of "possibilization" (*Ermöglichung*), at the center of which Fichte locates the "As (*Als*)," as well as a giving over the self-legitimation of the conditions of possibility of knowledge.

In *The Fundamental Concepts of Metaphysics*, Heidegger returns to the notion of "possibilization," recalling in an entirely remarkable way its Fichtean sense. In the Fichte/Schelling correspondence, the incompatibility persisted between a radical transcendentalist position (centered on possibilization), and an ontologizing, as we have seen, and it seemed impossible to overcome without giving up one of the two positions. At the heart of the phenomenological tradition, between the approach of a constructive phenomenology in Husserl and a phenomenological ontology in Heidegger, this same conflict plainly erupts once again. Moreover, it is clear that in Section 76 of the 1929/30 course, an absolutely crucial text in his corpus, Heidegger seeks to think these two perspectives together. This is not simply a limited effort of thought. Rather, Heidegger specifies that it sets into motion a transformation of the human "into a more originary Dasein" (Heidegger 1995: 350). For Heidegger, it is not possible to reconcile a "subjective" dimension (which escapes dogmatic realism) with the need to renounce an analytic of consciousness unless this double perspective is explicated in terms of a "fundamental occurrence" (*Grundgeschehen*).[23]

What is the status of this "fundamental occurrence?" Its status is extremely close to the "concept–light–being schema" that governs the late Fichtean ("*Berliner*") *Wissenschaftslehren*. It concerns the principle of every relation between "thinking" and "being," mediated by a pre-subjective principle of knowledge, called "light." However, this "principle" is not a first proposition from which all others would be derived, but a configuration that is as much transcendental as metaphysical, and which presides over every subject–object and world–consciousness relation. In calling it a "fundamental occurrence," Heidegger expresses very precisely this same idea, even if its "originary structure" differs from that of the Fichtean "concept–light–being schema."

Heidegger conceives of the "unitary character" of the fundamental occurrence as an *Entwurf* (project), or more precisely, as the "possibilization of every project of sense." This "project" is characterized by a double movement:[24] a "turning away from" (*Abkehr*)

---

[23] Over the course of the 1929 summer semester (immediately prior to the course on the *Fundamental Concepts of Metaphysics*), Heidegger explicitly claims that the "object of the debate" (*Auseinandersetzung*) with Fichte and German idealism, that is, the "problem of metaphysics and the question of mankind," starts from the "fundamental occurrence (*Grundgeschehen*) of metaphysics with itself" (Heidegger 1997: 131ff.). Heidegger sees in this nothing less than the heart of the problematic situation of contemporary philosophy at the time in relation to German idealism. (Cf. the course title and Heidegger 1997: 47.)

[24] This double movement strongly recalls that of the Self emerging from itself and returning to itself of which Fichte writes in the second introduction to the *Doctrine of Knowledge* (1797).

and a "being turned toward" (*Zukehr*), a double movement that is not reflexive, but possibilizing: "what is projected in the projection compels us before what is possibly actual, i.e. the projection *binds* us—not to what is possible, nor to what is actual, but to the possibilization (Heidegger 1995: 363). The imperative and binding quality of the real—that is, its necessity—presupposes possibilization: "The object of the projection is . . . an opening for the possibilization" (Heidegger 1995: 364).

At the same time, and Heidegger's second moment is intrinsically and closely linked to the first moment, the project reveals the Being of the being (*Sein des Seienden*):[25] the fact of standing before necessity is inseparable from the upsurgence of Being. Here, Heidegger makes the explicit link to the Schelling of the *Freiheitsschrift*: "the projection is the look into the light (*Lichtblick*) of the possible-possibilizing" (Heidegger 1995: 364). It is at this point that Heidegger surpasses what he had established with respect to possibilization in Section 53 of *Being and Time*, for the perspective no longer merely concerns the "certainty" of this phenomenon. Instead, he moves even closer[26] to the Fichtean sense of "possibilization," for this term here designates exactly the same "possibilizing doubling" as in *Doctrine de la Science de 1804/II*. It is that being-open to the being has a "pre-logical" dimension that Heidegger thus explicitly relates to "possibilization" (Heidegger 1995: 351ff.).

Finally, Heidegger identifies yet a third moment of the "fundamental occurrence." For this being-open stems from a revealability (*Offenbarkeit*) that is founded in a wholeness (*Ganzes*) which Heidegger calls "world." Thus, the project is also a *Bilden* (configuring) that projects a wholeness—Heidegger even goes so far as to say that the wholeness, the world, first makes revealability possible (Heidegger 1995: 353). And at the heart of all this movement is the notion of the "As." Heidegger of course treats this notion primarily in its relation to the analysis of Aristotle's *logos apophantikos*, but it also (and especially) echoes that Fichtean "As" as the principle of possibilization—in virtue of which the assertion that "the elucidation of the essence of the 'As' goes together with the question concerning the essence of the 'is', of being" (Heidegger 1995: 334) finds its full meaning. The "common root" of the "As" and of being must be sought in possibilization, insofar as it holds together, in the case of Fichte, a principle of appropriation, being, and a principle of legitimation; or, in the case of Heidegger, necessity, being, and the prelogical configuring of a wholeness. Through this striking deepening of the relation between necessity, being, and the legitimation of knowledge, this analysis of the "fundamental occurrence" thus constitutes a culmination of the heritage of classical German philosophy in phenomenology.

Let us summarize. This chapter sought to supply arguments for the thesis that recourse to certain powerful contributions at the heart of classical German philosophy

---

[25] In the sense of the "'transcendental' for every being," indicated by Heidegger in section 43 of *Being and Time* (referred to earlier).

[26] "Even closer" because Heidegger stresses here particularly the idea of a possibilizing doubling, whereas in section 53 of *Being and Time* he insisted precisely on the way in which possibilization could be certain.

permits the clarification of some of what is "unthought" in the phenomenological method. The unthought elements concern as much the precise understanding of the transcendental as the relation between the concept (with numerous facets) of "possibility" and that of transcendental "subjectivity." Three problems oriented these reflections: How can intuitive evidence contain a legitimating power? What is the sense of being that pertains to the phenomenon under the *epoché*? How may we bring together the (epistemological) question of the "rightful sources" of knowledge and the (ontological) question of the possible attribution of an ontological substructure to that which is transcendentally constituted? The questions culminated in the question of knowing what status the field of transcendental "subjectivity" contains as opposed to a concrete "ego"—the results of the present investigations suggest that transcendental subjectivity is in fact a "field," whereas a concrete "ego" constitutes a "pole" of intentional correlation at the heart of this same field. Answers to these questions have not been provided (and could not have been) by one sole author—neither in classical German philosophy, nor in phenomenology. These answers mobilize, respectively, the concept of "construction" ("genetic" or "phenomenological"), of the "mutual conditioning" at the center of a "new ontology," and of "possibilization," that is, of the "reflection of reflection" understood as "possibilizing doubling." Schelling, and especially Fichte, thus opened the way to analyses prior to the division between epistemology and ontology, which inspired phenomenologists (notably, Husserl, Heidegger, and Levinas), and did so to some extent "behind their backs," when it comes to reflecting upon the unity of transcendental phenomenology in light of its speculative foundations.

References

Artemenko, N., Chernavin, G., and Schnell, A. (2015), "Phenomenology and Classical German Philosophy. Die Phänomenologie und die Klassische Deutsche Philosophie," *Horizon, Studies in Phenomenology* 4/2: 331.

Fabbianelli, F., and Luft, S. (2014), *Husserl und die Klassische Deutsche Philosophie* (Dordrecht: Springer).

Fichte, J. G. (2005), *J. G. Fichte's 1804 Lectures on the Wissenschaftslehre* (Albany, NY: SUNY Press).

Fink, E. (1995), *Sixth Cartesian Meditations* (Bloomington, IN: Indiana University Press).

Fink, E. (2006), *Phänomenologische Werkstatt (Vol. 3/1)* (Freiburg: Alber).

Hartung, G., and Wunsch, M. (2014), "Diesseits von idealismus und realismus," in *Nicolai Hartmann, Studien zur Neuen Ontologie und Anthropologie* (Berlin: Walter de Gruyter).

Heidegger, M. (1978), *Metaphysische Anfangsgründe der Logik im Ausgang von Leibniz* (Frankfurt am Main: Klostermann).

Heidegger, M. (1993), *Hegel* (Frankfurt am Main: Klostermann).

Heidegger, M. (1995), *The Fundamental Concepts of Metaphysics* (Bloomington, IN: Indiana University Press).

Heidegger, M. (1996), *Being and Time* (Albany, NY: SUNY Press).

Heidegger, M. (1997), *Der deutsche Idealismus (Fichte, Schelling, Hegel) und die philosophische Problemlage der Gegenwart* (Frankfurt am Main: Klostermann).

Heidegger, M. (2011), *Seminare: Hegel—Schelling* (Frankfurt am Main: Klostermann)

Husserl, E. (1950), *Cartesianische Meditationen und Pariser Vorträge* (The Hague: Martinus Nijhoff).

Husserl, E. (1959), *Erste Philosophie (1923/4)* (The Hague: Martinus Nijhoff).

Husserl, E. (1969), *Zur Phänomenologie des inneren Zeitbewusstseins (1893–1917)* (The Hague: Martinus Nijhoff).

Husserl, E. (1973a), *Ding und Raum* (The Hague: Martinus Nijhoff).

Husserl, E. (1973b), *On the Phenomenology of Intersubjectivity. Texts from the Estate. Third part. 1929–35* (The Hague: Martinus Nijhoff).

Husserl, E. (1977), *Ideen zu einer reinen Phänomenologie und phänomenologischen Philosophie* (The Hague: Martinus Nijhoff).

Husserl, E. (1988), *Vorlesungen über Ethik und Wertlehre 1908–1914* (Dordrecht: Kluwer Academic Publishers).

Husserl, E. (1994), *Briefwechsel*. Husserliana: Edmund Husserl Dokumente 3/5 (Dordrect: Kluwer Academic Publishers).

Husserl, E. (2001), *Die "Bernauer Manuskripte" über das Zeitbewußtsein (1917/18)* (Dordrecht: Kluwer Academic Publishers).

Husserl, E. (2002), *Einleitung in die Philosophie. Vorlesungen 1922/23* (Dordrecht: Kluwer Academic Publishers).

Husserl, E. (2004), *Einleitung in die Ethik. Vorlesungen Sommersemester 1920 und 1924* (Dordrecht: Kluwer Academic Publishers).

Husserl, E. (2006), *Späte Texte über Zeitkonstitution (1929–1934). Die C-Manuskripte* (Dordrecht: Springer).

Levinas, E. (1969), *Totality and Infinity* (Pittsburgh, PA: Duquesne University Press).

Levinas, E. (1978), *Otherwise Than Being or Beyond Essence* (The Hague: Martinus Nijhoff Publishers).

Levinas, E. (1998), *Discovering Existence with Husserl* (Evanston, IL: Northwestern University Press).

Malabou, C. (2016), *Before Tomorrow: Epigenesis and Rationality* (Cambridge: Polity Press).

Merleau-Ponty, M. (1968), *The Visible and the Invisible* (Evanston, IL: Northwestern University Press).

Schelling, F. W. J. (1993), *System of Transcendental Idealism* (Charlottesville, VA: University of Virginia Press).

Schnell, A. (2007), *Husserl et les fondements de la phénoménologie constructive* (Grenoble: Millon).

Vater, M. G., and Wood, D. W. (2012), *The Philosophical Rupture between Fichte and Schelling: Selected Texts and Correspondence 1800–1802* (Albany, NY: SUNY Press).

CHAPTER 5

PHENOMENOLOGY AND DESCRIPTIVE PSYCHOLOGY

Brentano, Stumpf, Husserl

DENIS FISETTE

THIS chapter is divided into five sections. Section 5.1 is about the young Husserl's years of study and his encounter with Brentano in Vienna and with Carl Stumpf in Halle. Sections 5.2 and 5.3 are meant to succinctly describe Husserl's original contribution to Brentano's philosophical program prior to the publication of his *Logical Investigations* in 1900–1. In section 5.4, I examine Husserl's criticism of Brentano's criteria in his *Psychology* for delineating the two classes of phenomena and Husserl's arguments for the delineation of his phenomenology in the first edition of his *Hauptwerk*. I will conclude on a Stumpfian note about Husserl's reasons, shortly after the publication of his *Logical Investigations*, to sharply dissociate phenomenology from descriptive psychology.

In the general introduction to the first edition of his *Logical Investigations*, Husserl (1982a: 176–7) defines phenomenology as a descriptive psychology and suggests that the choice of this term is mainly terminological in that it aims to avoid the confusion that could result from using the term psychology to refer both to empirical and descriptive psychology. This distinction corresponds to that introduced by Franz Brentano in his Vienna lectures on descriptive psychology between descriptive psychology, which he also calls *Psychognosie* or phenomenology, and genetic or physiological psychology (Brentano 1995b). Descriptive psychology's main task consists in analyzing "the experiences of presentation, judgment, and knowledge, experiences which receive a scientific probing at the hands of empirical psychology" (1982a: 166). Methodologically, the description of conscious experiences prevails over its explanation because the analysis of the *explanandum* constitutes a prior step to its explanation by genetic psychology. However, phenomenology is not confined to the role of a propaedeutic to empirical psychology, and it has nothing to expect *philosophically* from the explanations of empirical psychology, understood as a natural science (1982a: 309–20). One of the main philosophical tasks of Husserl's early phenomenology consists in the analysis and elucidation of the fundamental concepts and laws of pure logic, and this task is distinct from that of theoretical (i.e., experimental or physiological) psychology.

This chapter is about Husserl's early conception of phenomenology as descriptive psychology and his debt to Brentano's philosophical program. I begin with Husserl's remarks on the first chapter of the second book of Brentano's *Psychology* where he examines several criteria for the delimitation of the domain of psychology from that of the natural sciences, namely that of intentionality. Husserl claims that this delineation further presupposes that the criteria upon which Brentano's classification is based justify a separation between descriptive psychology, understood as the science of psychical phenomena, and natural sciences, understood as sciences of physical phenomena. The main issue is whether there is a purely descriptive criterion suitable for delineating the field of phenomenology and whether the "intentional relation" justifies Brentano's division between two classes of phenomena (Husserl 1982b: 107).

An important issue in this discussion pertains to what has been called since R. Chisholm's "Brentano's thesis," i.e., intentionality as the mark of the mental, and more recently the co-extensive character of consciousness and intentionality. This thesis is also at the heart of several contemporary debates about phenomenal consciousness, and particularly in the theories of consciousness inspired by the work of Brentano (see Fisette and Fréchette 2013: section I). Some philosophers have disputed the value and relevance of Brentano's views on consciousness by arguing that they convey traditional prejudices, which are considered a significant source of problems in cognitive sciences and philosophy of mind. The traditional debates on reflective and non-reflective consciousness as well as the more recent one in which Brentano's theory of consciousness is identified with higher-order theories of consciousness are good examples (see Fisette 2015c). Yet some philosophers argue that these prejudices and Brentano's thesis have already been refuted by the father of phenomenology, and to face the problem of consciousness, a return to Brentano is therefore misleading. One should then turn to Husserl and the tradition he has inspired in so far as his contribution to the analysis of consciousness conserves all its relevance in the context of current debates in philosophy of mind (see Zahavi 2004, 2012). There are also researchers who believe that several criticisms of Brentano's philosophy presuppose a partial and biased reading of Brentano's work and it does not entirely do justice to his true contribution to the current problem of consciousness (Fisette 2015a, 2015d). Whatever the outcome of these discussions, they raise again the issue of the true bearing of Husserl's criticisms of Brentano's descriptive psychology.

5.1 HUSSERL'S FORMATIVE YEARS
IN PHILOSOPHY

The young Husserl's formation in philosophy from his first years in Leipzig until the publication of the first volume of *Philosophy of Arithmetic* in 1891 were strongly influenced by the philosophy of Franz Brentano, which represents the heart of his philosophical training. In 1876, Husserl went to Leipzig to study astronomy, mathematics, and philosophy, and it was during this period that he met for the first time his compatriot Tomáš Masaryk, who had just returned from Vienna where, under the supervision of Brentano, he had successfully defended a dissertation on Plato.[1] In August 1877, Masaryk returned to Vienna to prepare his habilitation thesis on the statistics of suicide, again under the supervision of Brentano. He then encouraged Husserl to join him in Vienna to meet Brentano (M. Husserl 1988: 111), but Husserl remained in Leipzig until the winter semester 1877–8 and decided to study mathematics in Berlin (M. Husserl 1988: 111).

Husserl later returned to Vienna in March 1881 to prepare his dissertation with Leo Königsberger, a former student of Weierstraß, and he found his friend Masaryk, who was then privatdozent in Vienna (Husserl 1994a: 59). In January 1883, Husserl successfully defended his dissertation "Contributions to the Theory of the Calculus of Variations" and then returned to Berlin as an assistant of Weierstraß, with the intention of writing his habilitation thesis under Weierstraß' supervision. But shortly after his arrival in Berlin, he had to abandon this project because of Weierstraß' deteriorating health.

After one year of military service, he returned to Vienna in the winter semester 1884–5 with the vague intention of undertaking studies in philosophy. Masaryk, who had been in Prague since 1882 along with Stumpf, Marty, and Meinong, who was appointed that same year in Graz, were no longer in Brentano's immediate circle in Vienna. In his "Reminiscences of Franz Brentano," Husserl (1976: 47) explains that it was out of curiosity at first that he attended a lecture from Brentano, "to hear the man who was the subject of so much talk in Vienna at that time." The impression he got from this first encounter both of the man and his way of practicing philosophy confirmed the value of Masaryk's repeated recommendations and convinced him to choose philosophy as a life project (Husserl 1976: 47).

During the two years he spent with Brentano in Vienna (1884–6), Husserl attended several lectures given by Brentano (see Rollinger 1999: 17), who, as Husserl pointed out in his reminiscences, was then mainly interested in issues pertaining to descriptive psychology and psychology of sense (Husserl 1976: 49). Husserl's reminiscences further confirm that he was very close to Brentano, both academically and personally, and he even accompanied Brentano on a summer holiday in Wolfgangsee. We also know that Brentano's lectures were sometimes pursued in Brentano's house with a small circle of his students, including Husserl, C. von Ehrenfels, F. Hillebrand, E. Arleth, K. Twardowski, H. Schmidkunz, and A. Höfler. According to von Ehrenfels, Husserl did not take long to impose himself as the "new star" in Vienna (see Fabian 1986: 17).

---

[1] Masaryk attended Brentano's lectures from 1874 to 1876, including those on the Aristotle's philosophical texts, practical philosophy, and Christian philosophy in connection with Hume. In March 1876, he defended a thesis entitled *Das Wesen der Seele bei Plato. Eine kritische Studie vom empirischen Standpunkt*, which has never been published (see Capek 2001: 71).

After his studies in Vienna, Husserl moved to Halle in the fall of 1886 to complete his habilitation thesis under the supervision of Carl Stumpf, the first student of Brentano. As from 1880, Brentano was no longer entitled academically to supervise his students' research, he therefore recommended the young Husserl to Stumpf in the hope that he might also find in Georg Cantor, who was also in Halle at that time, an interlocutor for issues related to mathematics in his research project. Malvine Husserl reports that during the early period of Halle, "Stumpf was the guide, advisor, and fatherly friend" (see Schuhmann 1977: 114). Stumpf enthusiastically welcomed the young philosopher and later confirmed that Husserl "was first my student, later an instructor, and became intimately associated with me scientifically and as a friend" (Stumpf 1930: 400). This date marks the beginning of a long and fruitful relationship that lasted until Stumpf's death in 1936 (Husserl 1994b: 119).

During his first year of study in Halle, Husserl attended Stumpf's lectures on psychology in the winter semester 1886–7, and during the summer semester of 1887 he attended his lectures on logic and the encyclopaedia of philosophy. The Husserl Archives in Leuven have preserved Husserl's notes taken during these lectures, and these notes show that Husserl had already acquired a thorough knowledge of Brentano's philosophical program. In early July 1887, Husserl defended his habilitation thesis and presented seven theses, which he successfully defended. Part of his *Habilitationsschrift* was published several months later under the title "On the Concept of Number: Psychological Analysis" and it is about the psychological origin of the basic concepts of arithmetic. In his evaluation report, Stumpf emphasized Husserl's remarkable analytical skills and his important methodological contribution to Brentano's descriptive psychology in this work (Stumpf in Gerlach and Sepp 1994: 173).

5.2 Husserl on Relations

In 1891 Husserl published the first volume of *Philosophy of Arithmetic*, which he dedicated to Brentano. It bears the subtitle "Psychological and Logical Investigations," and it is a psychological analysis of the concept of number, which is strongly influenced by Brentano's philosophy (Bell 1990). One of the original contributions of this book concerns relations. In chapter 3 of his *Philosophy of Arithmetic* ("The psychological nature of the collective combination"), which reproduces almost verbatim that part of his *Habilitationsschrift* dealing with relations (Husserl 2003: 347f.), Husserl takes up Brentano's cardinal distinction in his *Psychology* between two classes of phenomena, physical phenomena (sound and color, for example) and psychical phenomena (presentations, judgments, and emotions). Relying on the work of Stumpf on space perception and on the psychology of sound, Husserl claims that Brentano's doctrine of physical phenomena is not entirely adequate because it does not account for the abstract moments of intuition, which are central in Husserl's conception of sensations (Husserl 1982b: 357). That is why Husserl proposes replacing the notion of physical phenomenon with that of "primary content," understood as "abstract moments of intuition," on which rests his own conception of sensation in the *Logical Investigations* (Husserl 2003: 71).

The criterion guiding Husserl in his classification of relations remains Brentano's concept of intentional inexistence, which, although marginally used in this work, is considered the main criterion for the division of these two classes of relations (Husserl 2003: 73). Husserl distinguishes the class of relations that has the character of primary contents from the class of relations that belong to mental acts. Every relation of this class, for example, the relation of analogy between two contents, is included non-intentionally in a presentation. In this case, Husserl says, an analogy should not be subsumed under the concept of mental phenomenon, but under that of "primary content" (Husserl 2003: 71). The same holds for relations of equality, metaphysical relations (between properties such as color and spatial extension), or logical inclusion (of the color in red). Each of these relations represents a particular kind of primary content, and in relation to that, it belongs to the same main class. The relations of this class belonging to the primary content are called "primary relations." The class of relations belonging to psychical phenomena is characterized by the use of an act (presentation, judgment, etc.) whose function is to bind together the multiplicity of elements that it unifies into a sum. The main difference between these two classes of relation is that, in the first class, "the relation is immediately given along with representing the terms, as a moment of the same representational content" (Husserl 2003: 72), whereas the presentation of a psychical relation requires "a reflective act of representing bearing upon the relating act" (Husserl 2003: 73), and it therefore belongs to a higher-order level than that of the primary contents and relations.[2]

Another original contribution of *Philosophy of Arithmetic* to descriptive psychology, which is also related to Husserl's theory of relation, concerns Husserl's figural moments, which are analogous to what C. von Ehrenfels called "Gestalt qualities." In chapter 11 of *Philosophy of Arithmetic*, the so-called figural moments designate a unitary intuition, analogous to that which we have in the perception of simple sensory qualities such as color and sound. They are called quasi-qualitative moments because they are apprehended as something unitary, in the same way as the qualitative moment of color. This immediate apprehension in a single glance of a configuration such as a constellation of stars is possible thanks to signs or marks that can be directly "read" out of the overall character of the configuration. Husserl's hypothesis is that "in the intuition of the sensible group there must be present *immediately graspable tokens (Anzeichen)* through which its character as *group* can be recognized" (Husserl 2003: 213).

---

[2] In the sketch of a letter to Anton Marty, written in 1901, Husserl explains at length the consequences of this conflation of two types of relation in the school of Brentano, and summarizes his point in this passage: "The conflation consists in the confusion of the phenomenological relation (the purely descriptive psychological) between the act-character of the apprehension and the psychical content belonging to the actual subject, whose content functions as substratum of apprehension, with the relation between the act, i.e., the mental experience, which we call presentation (*Vorstellung*), and the represented object" (Husserl 1994b: 78–9).

5.3 FROM *PHILOSOPHY OF ARITHMETIC* TO *LOGICAL INVESTIGATIONS*

In the foreword to the first volume of his *Philosophy of Arithmetic*, Husserl announced the forthcoming publication of the second volume of this work, but we know that this project was never carried out. Nevertheless, the research belonging to this project has been particularly successful not only in the field of descriptive psychology, but also in that of the foundation of logic and mathematics (see Centrone 2010).[3] It was during this period that Husserl developed the essential elements of his phenomenology in several research manuscripts, lectures, and publications (see De Boer, 1978).[4] Two of these writings deserve our attention because of their contribution to the development of Husserl's early theory of intentionality. The first was published in 1894 under the title "Psychological Studies to Elementary Logic," which Husserl considered an exercise of pure descriptive psychology (Husserl 1994a: 179). This article is composed of two studies, the first is strongly influenced by Stumpf (1873: §5) and it contains the first version of Husserl's part-whole theory, which he develops systematically in the Third Investigation. In the second study, Husserl introduces the important notions of

---

[3] Worth mentioning is Husserl's project of a *Raumbuch,* which he announces in the preface to *Philosophy of Arithmetic.* Fragments from this project which have survived (Husserl 1983) show Husserl's marked interest in the psychological issue of the origin of space perception and to the famous nativism–empiricism debate. Husserl's position in manuscripts belonging to this project, particularly in the important fragment # 10, are very close to the form of "nativism" advocated by Stumpf (1873) in his own research on space perception.

[4] It was during this period that Husserl was very much interested in James's *The Principles of Psychology*, published in 1890. In his "personal Notes" of 1906, Husserl recalls that it was in his 1891–2 lectures on psychology "which brought me to look into writings on descriptive psychology with eager anticipation. Some reading in James's Psychology—of which I was able to read only a very little—yielded a few flashes of insight. I saw how a bold and creative man was able to free himself of bondage to all tradition, and how he sought genuinely to hold onto and describe what he saw. The influence of this was, I suppose, not without significance for me, although I was able to read and understand only a very few pages. Indeed, to describe and to be faithful—that was absolutely necessary. But only after the appearance of my treatise of 1894 did I read and make excerpts from larger sections of his work" (1994a: 491). In the 1891–2 lectures, Husserl refers to the chapter of James's *Principles* on space perception, which in turn had been strongly influenced by Stumpf (1873). Recall that James went to Prague, during a trip to Europe in 1882, to meet E. Hering and E. Mach, and to discuss with Stumpf about his book on space perception. The empiricism advocated by James at that time and which he later developed systematically in his book *The Principles of Psychology*, is in many respects akin to the positions advocated by Hering, Mach, and Stumpf on sensory experience. This encounter was memorable for the young Stumpf as he confirmed in his intellectual biography on James (Stumpf 1928). Although Stumpf is very critical of James's sensualism as shown by his works on emotions, and moreover of James's later conversion to pragmatism, he has maintained a long correspondence with James that shows a close and lasting relationship between the two philosophers (see Fisette 2013). There is no doubt that Husserl's interest in James has been influenced by Stumpf and A. Marty, who was also in Prague during James's visit in 1882, and later reviewed James's *Principles* (Marty 1892). On Husserl's interests in James's notions of consciousness' halo and fringe, see Husserl 1994a: 60, 322.

intention and fulfillment together with the fundamental distinction between intuition and representation (*Repräsentation*) (Husserl 1994a: 154–5). The second writing is an important manuscript written by Husserl in 1894 under the title "Vorstellung und Gegenstand," part of which has been published under the title "Intentional Objects" (Husserl 1994a: 345–87). It contains a critical study of the immanent theory of intentionality developed by another student of Brentano, K. Twardowski (1977) in his book *On the Content and Object of Presentations* also published in 1894.[5]

The main thesis advanced by Husserl in his *Psychological Studies* is that the distinction, within the domain of presentations, between representation (as "mere intending") and intuition (as really "comprehending in itself immanent contents") in turn depends on two distinct modes of consciousness:

> (i) Those which are Representations or which have Representations as a basis and, in virtue of that basis, obtain an intentional relation to objects. Here belong, e.g., affirmation, denial, conjecture, doubt, interrogation, love, hope, courage, desire, will, and so on. (ii) Those with which this is not the case; e.g., sensuous pleasure and revulsion ("feeling tone"). These latter are, so to speak, lower modes of consciousness, and also are the genetically earlier and more primitive. (Husserl 1994a: 181)

To exemplify the distinction between these two modes of consciousness, Husserl uses the case of the perception of arabesques, in which a single sensory vehicle constitutes the basis for both an intuition and a presentation. In the transition from the mere aesthetic effect that an object initially exerts on us, to our perceiving of arabesques as symbols or signs, a significant change occurs from one mode of consciousness to another, and it depends on what Husserl calls the "act-character." It is the latter that "as it were, ensouls sense, and is, in essence, that which make us perceive this or that object . . . *Sensations*, and the acts 'interpreting' them or apperceiving them, are alike experienced, *but they do not appear as objects*, they are not seen, heard, or perceived by any sense. Objects on the other hand, appear and are perceived, but they are not *experienced*" (Husserl 1982b: 105). Arabesques acquire their sign function from the moment they are apprehended or interpreted as signs. Thereafter, they are no longer seen as a spot of ink, which was initially the object that exerted the aesthetic effect, but they are experienced as the sensory channel for the perception of the arabesque as such.[6]

---

[5] There are also two manuscripts on sense perception, which belong to the same period and provide an important contribution to Husserl's descriptive psychology. The first is entitled "Intuition and Repräsentation, Intention and Fulfilment" (Husserl 1994a: 313–44) and the second is a working manuscript on Stumpf's notion of attention dated from 1898 and it bears the title "Noten zur Lehre von Aufmerksamkeit und Interesse" (Husserl 2004: 159–89). Worth mentioning is Husserl's attempt to make the connection between the concept of intentionality and that of interest (see Schuhmann 2004).

[6] The sketch of a letter to Anton Marty, which I mentioned earlier, shows clearly that the distinction between two modes of consciousness is one of the important points, which oppose Husserl to the Brentanian orthodoxy and to the "immanent" theory of intentionality also advocated by Marty (see Husserl 1994b: 75–85).

Understood in this broad sense, the concept of intuition designates both perceptual and imaginary presentations such as "the gladiator Borghese." These intuitive
presentations have the peculiarity to "really include those objects within themselves
as their immanent contents" (Husserl 1994a: 15). Husserl opposes this class of intuitive presentations to that in which we cannot obtain an intuition, either due to a factual incapacity, or because of an "evident impossibility." Conceptual representations
that belong to the latter class such as "round square" or "iron wood," which contain
incompatibilities, are examples of representations that are directed toward something
impossible. In other words, they are mere intentions whose fulfillment is impossible.
These representations belong to what Bolzano calls the class of objectless or impossible
presentations, which is the central topic of Husserl's text "Intentional Objects." In this
remarkable piece, Husserl discards Twardowski's solution based on the assumption
of a special mode of existence of intentional objects, and he accuses Twardowski of
confusing, in his discussion with Bolzano, objective and subjective intentions. Husserl
argues that the discourse on the intentional in-existence of objects is an improper
way of speaking and disputes Twardowski's position according to which a valid affirmative existential judgment of the form "A exists" presupposes the in-existence of
an intentional object (Husserl 1994a: 355). Husserl's solution to the problem of objectless presentations in this manuscript and in the Appendix to §§11 and 20 of the
Fifth Investigation rests on the identification of intentional and valid objects (Husserl
1982b: 127), a solution which has been presumably inspired by Hermann Lotze (see
Husserl 1994a: 376–7).[7]

Now, one of the most important departures from Brentano's program occurred in the
mid 1890s when Husserl abandoned the thesis that logic is a practical discipline based
on psychology. Recall that one of the principles, which guided Husserl in his research
on the origin of the concept of number, was that all our concepts originate from experience. The formation of the basic concepts of arithmetic as of all concepts in general
was explained in terms of abstraction on counting operations or the corresponding psychical acts. Husserl abandoned this form of conceptualism soon after the publication
of the first volume of the book in favor of a form of Platonism inspired by Bolzano and
Lotze, as Husserl confirms in his correspondence with Brentano (Husserl 1994b: 39) and
in his 1903 review of M. Palagyi (Husserl 1994a: 201). As early as 1896 in his lecture on
logic, Husserl acknowledged his debt to Bolzano's *Wissenschaftslehre* with respect to the
project of a pure logic that he also conceived of in the *Logical Investigations* as a theory of
science. But Husserl also mentioned in this context Lotze's thesis formulated at the very

---

[7] The Husserl Archives in Leuven have several manuscripts in which Husserl proposes a critical
examination of Lotze great *Logic*. In addition to the notes in the margin of his copy of Lotze's *Logic*, they
own the manuscript KI 59, to which Husserl refers explicitly in his *Prolegomena to Pure Logic* and that he
intended to publish as an annex to his *Logical Investigations*. This manuscript is dated from 1895–7 and is,
essentially, a commentary of the third book of Lotze's Logic entitled "Vom Erkennen" (see Hauser 2003;
Fisette forthcoming).

beginning of his *Logic* and according to which arithmetic is merely "a piece" (*ein Stück*) of logic (Husserl 2001: 138f., 271).[8]

5.4 CRITICISM OF BRENTANO'S CRITERIA FOR THE CLASSIFICATION OF PHENOMENA

Husserl's *Hauptwerk*, published at the turn of the twentieth century and dedicated to his friend Stumpf, is the result of his research during the period at Halle. In this seminal work, Husserl publicly uses for the first time the term phenomenology to characterize his own research and it is in reference to Brentano that he defines his phenomenology as descriptive psychology (Husserl 1982a: 176–7). Much of the *Fifth Investigation* and the Appendix to the *Logical Investigations* entitled "External and internal perception; Physical and psychical phenomena" address the issue of the delimitation of the field of descriptive psychology, which Brentano conceived of in his *Psychology* as a science of mental phenomena, in contradistinction to that of natural sciences understood as sciences of physical phenomena. Husserl's starting point is here again the first chapter of the second book of Brentano's *Psychology* in which he examines several criteria to set apart the two classes of phenomena, the most important of which is intentional in-existence. The main issue for Husserl is whether there is a purely "descriptive" criterion suitable for delineating the field of phenomenology from that of empirical psychology and natural sciences as a whole. Such a criterion must satisfy at least two conditions that Husserl imposed on his phenomenology in the first edition of his *Logical Investigations*. The first is called the principle of the absence of metaphysical presupposition, while the second requires that this criterion rest on "what is truly given phenomenally" (1982a: 338). The first principle requires what I would call metaphysical neutrality, i.e., the bracketing of presuppositions about the existence and the nature of the outside world and the physical laws that underlie it. Phenomenology allows no presupposition about metaphysical realities. "Purely descriptive" means therefore that phenomenological analyses must disregard all metaphysical presuppositions related to transcendent realities. The second condition, which Brentano also had in mind when he says at the very beginning of his *Psychology* that the only guide of a truly empirical psychology is experience (Brentano 1995a: xxv), stipulates that the non-metaphysical criterion must rest on the descriptive nature of phenomena as experienced. In other words, it must rest on the primitive layer of the experience of primary contents, which in early and late phenomenology

---

[8] However, in his correspondence with Stumpf in the early 1890s, as well as in a letter to Brentano published recently (Husserl 2015), Husserl stressed the urgency for a thorough reform of logic and already envisaged the hypothesis that *arithmetica universalis* "is a segment of formal logic" (Husserl 1994a: 17). But logic was still defined as a practical science, as "a symbolic technic" and not as a purely theoretical logic or theory of science as is the case in Husserl's 1896 lecture on logic and later in his *Prolegomena*.

constitutes the ultimate tribunal. A purely descriptive criterion is therefore a criterion that satisfies both conditions.

Let us now examine Husserl's criticism of Brentano's conception of physical phenomena as objects of natural sciences. Husserl claims that by entrusting the study of sensations to the natural sciences, Brentano violates the principle of metaphysical neutrality and commits himself to a kind of metaphysics, which conveys the same kind of prejudices as classical empiricism. Husserl further accuses Brentano of confusing sensory contents and objects. The examples of physical phenomena, which we find in Brentano's *Psychology* (1995a: 61) such as "a color, a figure, a landscape which I see; a chord which I hear; warmth, cold, odor which I smell; as well as similar images which appear in the imagination," testify, according to Husserl, to the equivocal nature of this concept, insofar as it refers both to objects (landscape) and sensations, and thus conflates "sensed contents" with external objects or their phenomenal properties (Husserl 1982b: 358). This equivocation corresponds to that, in outer perception, between sensing and perceiving.[9] The source of this confusion lies in Brentano's conception of sensing as an act belonging to the class of presentation, and it obliterates, for that very reason, two modes of consciousness that are involved in sensory perception.[10] Husserl argues, instead, that sensing is not a psychical phenomenon in Brentano's sense; it is simply not an act or a mental state (Husserl 1982a: 358, 2004: 137–8) This non-act is what he calls apprehension (*Auffassung*), interpretation (*Deutung*), or the apperceptive function of consciousness, which stands out clearly in the case of arabesques, which I used earlier.

Let us now turn to Husserl's analysis of Brentano's criteria. For lack of space, I shall only consider three of these criteria. A distinctive feature of these two classes of phenomena is that mental phenomena "are only perceived in inner consciousness, while in the case of physical phenomena, only external perception is possible" (Brentano 1995a: 70). What Husserl criticizes here is the epistemic prerogative of internal perception over external perception, a prerogative that depends, in turn, on the evidence of what is internally perceived. Brentano assigns an epistemic function to internal perception, which is based on "its immediate, infallible self-evidence" (Brentano 1995a: 70). Accordingly, Brentano says of internal perception that it is literally the only perception

---

[9] It is also the main topic of Husserl's treatise *Abhandlung über Wahrnehmung von 1898*, which was intended for the second series of the *Investigations* (Husserl 2004: 123–58). Husserl's point of departure is here again the confusion in the use of the term *sensation* by psychologists and scientists of the time to distinguish between, on the one hand, content and object of perception, and on the other hand, perceiving (*Wahrnehmen*) and sensing (*Empfinden*).

[10] This is the gist of Husserl's criticism of Brentano. One can measure the importance of this distinction to Husserl's remark, in the second *Investigation,* about the form of representationalism inherited from classical empiricism and advocated by Brentano in his *Psychology* from 1874. According to Husserl, representationalism is the most stubborn and damaging prejudice which is responsible for one of the worst conceptual distortion in the history of philosophy: "To define the presentation (*Vorstellung*) of a content as the mere fact of its being experienced (*Vorgestelltsein*), and in consequence to give the name 'presentations' (*Vorstellungen*) to all experienced contents, is one of the worst conceptual distortions known to philosophy. It is without doubt responsible for an untold legion of epistemological and psychological errors" (Husserl 1982a: 276).

that deserves the name *Wahrnehmung*, i.e., literally what is taken as true. The evidence confers to internal perception an epistemic advantage over external perception in that it is the only viable source of knowledge; hence the epistemic asymmetry in Brentano's psychology between internal and external perception.

According to Husserl, one finds in Brentano's doctrine of internal perception the same kind of confusion in the percept between the perceived (secondary) object and its phenomenal content. He claims that the true distinction that Brentano was looking for with the opposition between internal and external perception corresponds, from the standpoint of Husserl's theory of knowledge, to that of adequate and inadequate perception. Understood in accordance with the distinction between phenomenal content and object, self-evidence is the adequate correspondence of the content of perception with its object, i.e., a perception in which "there are no residual intentions that must yet achieve fulfillment" (1982b: 346). Inadequate perception, on the other hand, is merely presumptive (*vermeintlich*) and is characterized by the fact that its "intention does not find fulfillment in present content, but rather goes through this to constitute the lively, but always one-sided and presumptive, presentedness of what is transcendent" (1982b: 346). It follows, first, that the only allowable self-evident and adequate perception is "the perception of one's own actual experiences" (1982b: 346) which, however, confers no privilege to internal perception over external perception since external perception may be adequate as well and constitutes, accordingly, a reliable source of knowledge. Husserl further distinguishes the epistemic function of inner perception as "a sort of intuitive knowledge" from its psychological sense proper, i.e., as consciousness.

In his discussion of Brentano's conception of feelings in §15 of the Fifth Investigation, Husserl (1982b: 107) addresses the question "as to whether the 'intentional relation' suffices to demarcate 'psychical phenomena' (the domain of psychology) or not." He criticizes the confusion in the notion of sentiment (*Gefühl*) between sense feeling (*Gefühlsempfindung*) and emotion (*Gefühlsact*), i.e., between sense feelings, in the domain of physical phenomena, and emotions, which belong to Brentano's third class of mental phenomena. The subject of the dispute is prima facie the question whether pain and bodily pleasure—feelings related to specific types of sensation such as temperature, sound, taste, color, and even aesthetic pleasure—are intentional, just as joy, sadness, anger, hope, desire, and disgust are intentional for Brentano, or whether, like for sensualists such as E. Mach and William James, they have a sensory or phenomenal nature (see Fisette 2013). Husserl argues against Brentano that phenomena such as sense feelings, which belong to a dimension of experience that he calls in his *Investigations* "*Erlebnisse*" or primary contents, do not fall under any of Brentano's two classes of phenomena (Husserl 1982b: 94). Therefore, intentionality as such cannot constitute a necessary condition for delineating the field of conscious phenomena understood broadly enough to include the field of experience as a whole. For, if we agree with Husserl that sense feelings, though falling under neither of Brentano's two classes of phenomena, nevertheless constitute an essential ingredient in a comprehensive theory of emotions (and *a fortiori* in a theory of experience as a whole), then the intentionality criterion is inadequate for this purpose, as are the other criteria associated with it in Brentano's *Psychology*.

A third criterion to which Husserl pays particular attention in his *Logical Investigations* is Brentano's principle according to which every psychical phenomenon "is either a presentation, or is founded upon presentations" (1982b: 80). Brentano claims that the class of presentations is the simplest and most universal of the three classes and is therefore relatively autonomous with respect to the remaining classes of mental phenomena, i.e., judgments and emotions. Conversely, the class of judgments like that of emotions entertain a one-sided dependency relation with the class of presentations. Husserl criticizes Brentano for conflating two senses of presentation in the formulation of this principle. Thus, the first part of the definition proposed by Brentano (every mental phenomenon is a presentation) seems to refer to what Husserl calls the quality of an act, while in the second part of the principle (it is based on a presentation), the term presentation has the meaning of the "matter" or content of an act. The quality of an act characterizes the modes through which consciousness relates to its objects, i.e., the presentational, judicative, and emotional modes of consciousness, whereas the matter is what "lent it direction to an object, which made a presentation, e.g., present *this* object and no other" (1982b: 121). Furthermore, we saw that this principle does not apply to the whole sphere of experience because Husserl unequivocally rejects Brentano's thesis that perception is a judgment, arguing that perception is always underdetermined by sensations and primary contents. Husserl maintains that the class of presentations is itself based on a more primitive *stratum* of *Erlebnisse*, namely on sensory perception, which is not as such intentional. It is not clear whether Husserl nevertheless accepted the hierarchy and the one-sided dependency relation that Brentano assumed between his three classes of acts. In any case, it is clear that this principle does not apply to sense feelings, and that acts of emotion and sense feelings belong respectively to two different types, namely psychical phenomena and primary contents (Husserl 1982b: 354).

Therefore, the criteria proposed by Brentano do not satisfy the conditions imposed by Husserl on a purely descriptive criterion because several important concepts of his *Psychology*, namely the dichotomy between internal and external perception, convey metaphysical presuppositions (Husserl 1982b: 304); and because Brentano's representationalism amounts to reducing the scope of experience to one mode of conscious experiences and he leaves something out, i.e., phenomenal experiences, which are paradigmatic for Husserl's phenomenology in the first edition of *Logical Investigations*. Brentano is therefore unable to adequately delineate the field of descriptive psychology from that of natural sciences. Husserl's main criterion for that purpose is based on primary contents and *Erlebnisse* or on what is commonly called phenomenal experience (Husserl 1982b: 90).

In a nutshell, contrary to Brentano who believed that the intentional, understood as the mark of the mental, was also the dividing line between the mental and the physical, Husserl claims that the phenomenological criterion rests on phenomena as "they are experienced by us," on "what is truly given phenomenally" (Husserl 1982b: 338). The dividing line between the phenomenological and the non-phenomenological does not pass, pace Brentano, between the intentional and the non-intentional, because there are mental states and states of mind such as moods, pains, and sense feelings, for instance, which are not intentional and do not fall, consequently, within the domain of Brentano's descriptive psychology. As for Brentano's physical phenomena, we saw that Husserl claimed that phenomena such as primary contents, which Brentano classified in the domain of natural sciences in his *Psychology*, belong to the domain of phenomenology. It follows from the broadening of the research field of phenomenology that Brentano's division of the world of phenomena into physical and psychological phenomena has to be revised and replaced by that between lived experiences (phenomenology) and what is transcendent to experience.

5.5 CONCLUSION

Husserl's debt to Brentano's descriptive psychology during the Halle period is substantial, and we saw that Husserl's research during this period can be considered a major contribution to Brentano's philosophical program. Moreover, most of the young Husserl's interlocutors in philosophy are linked directly or indirectly to the school of Brentano. Of course, Husserl is very critical of Brentano, and like philosophers such as Meinong, Twardowski, and Stumpf, for example, he significantly deviated from Brentano's teaching. However, if one conceives of Brentano's program broadly enough to include the contribution of his unorthodox students, Husserl's early phenomenology is not only a significant contribution to Brentano's program, but it is also inextricably linked to the basic principles of Brentano's philosophy. Now, Husserl's attitude toward Brentano's psychology seems to have significantly changed immediately after the publication of his *Hauptwerk*, if we are to judge by his 1903 review of T. Elsenhans (1897), in which Husserl retracted the characterization of phenomenology as psychology. This retraction is repeated in several places, namely in the second edition of *Logical Investigations* and in the first book of *Ideas* where he claims that "*that pure phenomenology . . . is not psychology and that neither accidental delimitations of its field nor its terminologies, but most radical essential grounds*, prevent its inclusion in psychology" (Husserl 1980: XVIII; 1975: 51–2). What are these essential grounds and what is the bearing of this retraction on the relationship between Husserl's phenomenology and Brentano's program?

Prima facie, the grounds to which Husserl refers in his review of Elsenhans (1897) in order to dissociate his phenomenology from explanatory and theoretical psychology are not fundamentally different from those evoked in his *Logical Investigations*. We saw that Husserl's definition of phenomenology as descriptive psychology in the first edition of *Logical Investigations* was not to be taken literally, and that this definition was primarily meant to avoid the confusion between descriptive and physiological psychology. Now, two years after the publication of this work, Husserl maintains that psychology, understood in the narrow sense of a science of facts, is not able to fulfill both conditions attached to the "purely" descriptive criterion required for the distinction between the phenomenological and the non-phenomenological, namely metaphysical neutrality and the restriction to what is given *stricto sensu*, i.e., "lived experience, just as it is in itself" (Husserl 1994a: 251). Husserl argues that a psychology remains a psychology of psychical facts, and no less than a physical science of physical facts, it presupposes pre-critical objectifications of any object that it posits "outside of the ego." These objectifications raise in turn difficulties related to the metaphysical problem of the possibility of knowledge, which are not considered problematic from the perspective of factual sciences and common sense in general (Husserl 1994a: 250–1). Methodologically, all scientific or metaphysical objectifications must remain excluded from phenomenology, which only considers what is given in experience. The difficulties related to objectifications raise the problem of transcendence, which constitutes one of the most important issues in Husserl's phenomenology of knowledge. Husserl argues that one cannot decide a priori on metaphysical issues related to transcendent realities because the problem of transcendence (and of the immanent–transcendent distinction) "is prior to all metaphysics, and lies at the very gates of the theory of knowledge: it presupposes no answers to the questions that this theory must be the first to provide" (1982b: 106).

That said, one hardly finds anything in this 1903 review that is not already in the *Logical Investigations*, including a footnote to the *Prolegomena*, where Husserl already refers to Elsenhans (1897) regarding the bearing of his critique of logical psychologism in the field of empirical psychology. When Husserl says in this review that phenomenology is not a descriptive psychology in the old sense of the term, what he criticizes is a psychology of facts ("the experiences or classes of experiences of empirical persons"), i.e., "of all conceptualization of experiences as conditions of real mental beings and, together with this, of all predications about reality in this sense" (Husserl, 1975: 51), which seems to be more akin to genetic psychology than to Brentano's descriptive psychology and therefore to his own phenomenology in the first edition of the *Logical Investigations*. Moreover, Husserl continues to claim that, methodologically, his phenomenology can take on "the character of descriptive-psychological analyses" and then functions "as the foundation for the theoretical explanations of psychology" (Husserl 1994a: 252).

Of course, one cannot disregard the transcendental turn and the major modifications that Husserl's phenomenology underwent after the publication of his groundwork. Indeed, in the introduction to *Ideas I*, Husserl repeats that "pure" phenomenology has become a science of species and laws which underlie all empirical sciences, and it has nothing to do with psychology. But the gap that he created between pure phenomenology and psychology also depends, as Stumpf pointed out in *Erkenntnislehre*, on the narrow definition of psychology as a science of matters of facts in Hume's sense. Stumpf wonders whether Husserl's arguments in *Ideas I* actually justify such a gap. For, Stumpf continues, psychology since Aristotle cannot be reduced to a science of facts dealing with the biography of, say, the "inner experiences of Johann Nepomuk Oberniedermaier born in Straubing in 1741" (see Fisette 2015b). According to Stumpf, descriptive psychology has always been defined, instead, as a regional ontology and as a science of the laws of structure of psychical life. And these laws, claims Stumpf:

> are the specific objects of descriptive psychology in the sense of Brentano, but also of Lotze and all their predecessors. This descriptive psychology is nothing but a phenomenology or regional ontology in the sense of Husserl, and he himself made a significant contribution in *Logical Investigations*. (Stumpf 1939–40: 194)

However, even if one admits with Stumpf that Brentano's descriptive psychology is not merely a science of facts, it is beyond doubt that Husserl progressively distances himself from Brentano's philosophical program that he later associated with a form of philosophical naturalism. The form of naturalism, which Husserl repeatedly criticizes in lectures, working manuscripts, and other writings (see Husserl 1977: 121f., 1975: 51, 1970: §68) seems to be related to Brentano's views on physical phenomena, to which, as we saw, Husserl never subscribed. Nevertheless, Husserl never dismissed the value of Brentano's philosophical contribution, particularly with regard to the latter's rediscovery of intentionality, which constitutes the main topic of Husserl's phenomenology after the publication of *Logical Investigations*.

References

Bell. D. (1990), *Husserl* (London: Routledge).

Brentano, F. (1995a), *Psychology from an Empirical Standpoint* (London: Routledge).

Brentano, F. (1995b), *Descriptive Psychology*, translated by B. Müller (London: Routledge).

Capek, K. (2001), *Gespräche mit Masaryk* (Munich: DVA).

Centrone, S. (2010), *Logic and Philosophy of Mathematics in the Early Husserl* (Dordrecht: Springer).

De Boer, T. (1978), *The Development of Husserl's Thought* (The Hague: Martinus Nijhoff).

Elsenhans, T. (1897), "Das Verhaltnis der Logik zur Psychologie," *Zeitschrift für Philosophie und philosophische Kritik* 109: 195–212.

Fabian, R. (ed.) (1986), *Christian von Ehrenfels: Leben und Werk* (Amsterdam: Rodopi).

Fisette, D. (forthcoming), "Hermann Lotze and the genesis of Husserl's early philosophy (1886–1901)," in N. de Warren (ed.), *From Lotze to Husserl: Psychology, Mathematics and Philosophy in Göttingen* (Berlin: Springer).

Fisette, D. (2013), "Mixed feelings," in D. Fisette and G. Fréchette (eds), *Themes from Brentano* (Amsterdam: Rodopi), 281–305.

Fisette, D. (2015a), "Reception and actuality of Carl Stumpf's philosophy," in D. Fisette and R. Martinelli (eds), *Philosophy from an Empirical Standpoint: Carl Stumpf as a Philosopher* (Amsterdam: Rodopi), 11–53.

Fisette, D. (2015b), "A phenomenology without phenomena? Stumpf's criticism of Husserl's *Ideas I*," in D. Fisette and R. Martinelli (eds), *Philosophy from an Empirical Standpoint: Carl Stumpf as a Philosopher* (Amsterdam: Rodopi), 319–56.

Fisette, D. (2015c), "Franz Brentano and Higher-Order Theories of Consciousness," Target paper of the Brazilian journal *Argumentos* 7/3: 9–29.

Fisette, D. (2015d), "Brentano's Theory of Consciousness Revisited: Reply to My Critics," *Argumentos* 7/3: 129–56.

Fisette, D. and Fréchette, G. (eds) (2013), *Themes from Brentano* (Amsterdam: Rodopi).

Gerlach, H. and Sepp, H. (eds) (1994), *Husserl in Halle* (Bern: Peter Lang).

Husserl, E. (1970), *The Crisis of European Sciences and Transcendental Phenomenology*, translated by D. Carr (Evanston, IL: Northwestern University Press).

Husserl, E. (1975), *Introduction to the Logical Investigations: A Draft of a Preface to the Logical Investigations*, translated by P. Bossert and C. Peters (The Hague: Martinus Nijhoff).

Husserl, E. (1976), "Reminiscences of Franz Brentano," translated by L. McAlister, in L. McAlister (ed.), *The Philosophy of Franz Brentano* (London: Duckworth), 47–55.

Husserl, E. (1977), *Phenomenological Psychology: Lectures, Summer Semester 1925*, ed. J. Scanlon (The Hague: Martinus Nijhoff).

Husserl, E. (1980), "Ideas pertaining to a pure phenomenology and to a phenomenological philosophy," translated by T. Klein and W. Pohl in *Collected Works*, vol. 3 (The Hague: Martinus Nijhoff).

Husserl, E. (1982a), *Logical Investigations*, vol. 1, translated by J. N. Findlay (London: Routledge).

Husserl, E. (1982b), *Logical Investigations*, vol. 2, translated by J. N. Findlay (London: Routledge).

Husserl, E. (1983), *Studien zur Arithmetik und Geometrie. Texte aus dem Nachlaß (1886–1901)*, Husserliana 21, ed. I. Strohmeyer (Berlin: Springer).

Husserl, E. (1988), *Aufsätze und Vorträge. 1922–1937*, Husserliana 27, ed. H. R. Sepp (Dordrecht: Kluwer).

Husserl, E. (1994a), *Early Writings in the Philosophy of Logic and Mathematic*, translated by D. Willard (Berlin: Springer).

Husserl, E. (1994b), *Briefwechsel. Die Brentanoschule, Bd. I*, ed. E. Schuhmann and K. Schuhmann (Dordrecht: Kluwer).

Husserl, E. (2001), *Logik. Vorlesung 1896*, Husserliana, Materialien, Bd. 1, ed. E. Schuhmann (Dordrecht: Kluwer).

Husserl, E. (2003), *Philosophy of Arithmetic*, translated by D. Willard, *Collected Works* X (Dordrecht: Kluwer).

Husserl, E. (2004), *Wahrnehmung und Aufmerksamkeit. Texte aus dem Nachlass (1893–1912)*, Husserliana 38, ed. T. Vongehr and R. Giuliani (Berlin: Springer).

Hauser, K. (2003), "Husserl and Lotze," *Archiv fur Geschichte der Philosophie* 85/2: 152–78.

Husserl, E. (2015), "A Letter from Edmund Husserl to Franz Brentano from 29 XII 1889," ed. C. Ierna, *Husserl Studies* 31/1: 65–72.

Husserl, M. (1988), "Skizze eines Lenbenbildes von E. Husserl," ed. K. Schuhmann, *Husserl Studies* 5: 105–25.

James, W. (1890), *The Principles of Psychology* (New York: Henry Holt).

Marty, A. (1892), "Anzeige von William James' Werk 'Principles of Psychology'," *Zeitschrift für Psychologie und Physiologie der Sinnesorgane* 3: 297–333.

Rollinger, R. (1999), *Husserl's Position in the School of Brentano* (Dordrecht: Kluwer).

Schuhmann, K. (1977), *Husserl-Chronik: Denk- und Lebensweg Edmund Husserls* (The Hague: Martinus Nijhoff).

Schuhmann, K. (2004), "Husserl's doppelte Vorstellungsbegriff," in C. Leijenhorst et al. (eds), *Selected Papers on Phenomenology* (Berlin: Springer), 101–17.

Stumpf, C. (1939–40), *Erkenntnislehre*, 2 vols (Leipzig: Barth).

Stumpf, C. (1928), *William James nach seinen Briefen* (Berlin: Pan Verlag).

Stumpf, C. (1930), "Autobiography," in C. Murchison (ed.), *History of Psychology in Autobiography*, vol. 1 (Worcester, MA: Clark University Press), 389–441.

Stumpf, C. (1873), *Über den psychologischen Ursprung der Raumvorstellung* (Leipzig: Hirzel).

Twardowski, K. (1977), *On the Content and Object of Presentations*, translated by R. Grossmann (The Hague: Martinus Nijhoff).

Zahavi, D. (2004), "Back to Brentano?" *Journal of Consciousness Studies* 11: 66–87.

Zahavi, D. (ed.) (2012) *The Oxford Handbook of Contemporary Phenomenology* (Oxford: Oxford University Press).

PART II

FIGURES

CHAPTER 6

HUSSERL'S EARLY PERIOD

Juvenilia and the Logical Investigations

PETER ANDRAS VARGA

6.1 BIOGRAPHY AND HISTORIOGRAPHY

EDMUND (Gustav Albrecht) Husserl was born on April 8, 1859, to a secular Jewish family of merchants whose ancestors had been living in the Moravian town of Prossnitz (Prostějov, today in the Czech Republic) since at least the seventeenth century. His future wife, Malvine née Steinschneider was similarly a descendent of a traditional, though more observant, Jewish family of Prossnitz, born in 1860 while her father served in the Transylvanian city of Klausenburg (Kolozsvár / Cluj Napoca, today in Romania) at the other end of the Habsburg Empire. Husserl's family developed strong ties to Vienna, the de facto capital of the multiethnic empire, where Husserl's mother, brothers, and sister lived and died. It was also in Vienna that he and Malvine were baptized and married. It is thus not surprising that Vienna constituted a focal point of Husserl's scientific formation.[1]

During his academic peregrination, Husserl attended the universities of Leipzig (WS 1876–WS 1877), Berlin (SS 1878–WS 1880–1), and Vienna (SS 1881–WS 1881–2). Even though the majority Husserl's studies were dedicated to mathematics and sciences (inter alia with Karl Weierstraß and Leopold Kronecker, the demigods of contemporaneous mathematics), he also attended philosophy courses given by Wilhem Wundt in Leipzig, as well as by Johann Eduard Erdmann, Moritz Lazarus, and Friedrich Paulsen in Berlin.

[1] The research of the author was supported by grant number PD105101 of the Hungarian National Scientific Fund (OTKA/NKFIH). The author is grateful to George Heffernan, Dieter Lohmar, and Dan Zahavi for their comments on draft versions of this chapter (which is, of course, not to imply that they necessarily endorse the views expounded by the author), as well as to Ullrich Melle, the director of the Husserl Archives at the K.U. Leuven for his kind permission to quote from unpublished manuscripts of Husserl.

It is worth highlighting a strange pattern in his studies that seems to suggest he was struggling to find his true vocation: during the last two semesters, Husserl turned to the study of philosophy, dedicating the whole of the second to last semester exclusively to philosophy and registering for a number of philosophy courses with Paulsen in his final semester.[2] This, however, did not immediately result in a change of Husserl's main interest, because the reason for his move to Vienna was to obtain a doctoral degree in mathematics, which he completed between November 1882 and January 1883. His highly technical unpublished doctoral dissertation, submitted in June 1882, is entitled *Beiträge zur Theorie der Variationsrechnung* (*Contributions to the Calculus of Variations*). Husserl provided simplified proofs for theorems on the extrema of integral functions, which, however, soon became obsolete due to more encompassing results. The young doctor spent the next semester in the mathematical circles of Berlin (contrary to a popular misconception, Husserl did not serve as a formal assistant of Weierstraß), and subsequently volunteered in the Austro-Hungarian army service corps.

Husserl's soul-searching was apparently not in vain, since, when he returned to Vienna in WS 1884–5, he spent the subsequent four semesters studying philosophy exclusively. His two main teachers were Robert Zimmermann, the erstwhile personal protégé of Bernard Bolzano who later turned to Herbartianism, and Franz Brentano, to whom Husserl became committed by the end of his studies.[3] Since Brentano's loss of the professorial title in 1880 prevented him from supervising habilitations, Husserl was sent to Carl Stumpf at the University of Halle-Wittenberg to obtain the habilitation degree that was a precondition for starting a career as an academic. After attending classes with Stumpf and Georg Cantor, Husserl obtained his habilitation in June 1887 and started his

---

[2] The details of Husserl's study in Berlin are not available in the usual printed sources (Schuhmann 1977: 4–10; Husserl 1994b: VIII, 222–3, 235–7). See instead: MS, Humboldt-Universität zu Berlin, Universitätsarchiv, Rektor und Senat, Universtitätsmatrikel, 68. Rektorat, Nr. 1179.

[3] Husserl's own account of his second Vienna period (1987a: 305–15; first published: Kraus 1919: 151–67) was confined to Brentano, but recent research (Varga 2015: esp. 100–1) demonstrates that Husserl attended a plethora of philosophy classes with other professors as well and his exposure to Zimmermann is quantitatively on a par with the one to Brentano. This also sheds a different light on what Brentano wrote about the alternate possibility of Husserl's allegiance to Zimmermann (Brentano and Stumpf 2014: 260), as well as on his reluctance, expressed as early as October 1886, against Husserl's obtaining a professorial appointment (see Brentano's response to the career opportunities discussed in Stumpf's reply to Brentano's letter of recommendation for Husserl, 2014: 261–3). Husserl ceased to register for Zimmermann's classes in the last semester, which seems to indicate that his special attachment to Brentano's circle developed only in late 1895–early 1896, given that Brentano famously did not tolerate divided loyalties (cf., e.g., Kraus 1919: 146). This is also consistent with the fact that the oft-cited report of Husserl's ascending to a central position within the circle around Brentano (Fabian 1986: 17) is dated February 26, 1886 (i.e., late WS 1885–6). Husserl's famous vacation with Brentano in Wolfgangsee (Schuhmann 1977: 16) also took place in the summer after his studies in Vienna. When Husserl described his university studies vis-à-vis Cantor in 1896 (see Purkert and Ilgauds 1987: 206; Cantor's letter is probably based on Husserl's own account), he mentioned *both* Brentano and Zimmermann as guides of his "most enthusiastic" study of philosophy (besides mentioning his early interest in the philosophy classes of Wundt and Paulsen). That in Husserl's Habilitation CV of 1887 the similar phrase "buried myself in philosophical studies" is confined to Brentano alone (Husserl 1994: VIII, 222) might indicate that Husserl was inclined to adopt a different tone when addressing members of the School of Brentano.

lecturing career in WS 1887–8, initiated by an inaugural lecture entitled *Über die Ziele und Aufgaben der Metaphysik* (*On the Aims and Tasks of Metaphysics*).

Husserl later claimed that his philosophical vocation had prevented him from effective forms of career building: "from publishing a lot and frequently" and "eagerly taking the audience and [the educational] government into consideration" (1994b: I, 25). Indeed, he spent twenty-six semesters as unsalaried lecturer (*Privatdozent*), relying on scholarships and family wealth. Several faculty members, most notably Stumpf and Cantor, however, continued to put their faith in him, and Husserl managed to finish his voluminous *Logische Untersuchungen* (*Logical Investigations*) in 1900–1. After a series of unsuccessful attempts, he finally secured an appointment at the University of Göttingen starting from WS 1901–2.

In Göttingen, Husserl initially had strained relationships with other philosophers in the faculty, who prevented his promotion to full professor. He was thereby drawn into the circle of mathematicians around David Hilbert. The course of history took a new turn when students of Theodor Lipps in Munich, led by Johannes Daubert, discovered the *Logische Untersuchungen* for themselves, and began flocking to Göttingen between 1903 and 1905, spreading their enthusiasm in Göttingen. The Phenomenological Movement was born and Husserl became famous almost overnight.

That the story of Husserl's philosophical formation is overshadowed by his discipleship to Brentano is far from being unintentional on the part of Husserl. Immediately after the publication of his *Logische Untersuchungen*, the wider circles of contemporary German philosophy that neither belonged to the nascent Phenomenological Movement nor directly participated in the psychologism controversy that was reignited by Husserl (see section 6.3.2) mostly situated Husserl in the context of Hermann Lotze and Bernard Bolzano (whom Husserl claimed to have thought further, respectively rediscovered), rather than the School of Brentano. This is manifested by a series of contemporaneous doctoral dissertations written on Husserl (not to mention Melchior Palagyi's implicit accusation of Husserl plagiarizing Bolzano),[4] as well as the *Ueberweg* handbook, the definitive exposition of historical and contemporaneous philosophy, which explicitly stated: "Husserl, who previously belonged to the logicians heavily influenced by Brentano . . . now repeatedly reminds us of Bolzano" (Heinze 1902: 343) and reassigned Husserl to a different headword (cf. Heinze 1897: 276 and 1902: 343).

The received view, however, underwent a sudden change due to Husserl's public oath of allegiance to Brentano, the most effective form of which was Husserl's contribution to the memorial volume edited by the orthodox disciple Oskar Kraus (Kraus 1919: 151–67, cf. Husserl 1987a: 304–15). Husserl's keen declaration that "without Brentano I would not have written a word of philosophy" (Brück 1933: 3) not only forced the origins of his philosophy into the Procrustean bed of a single influence, but was also surprising from the historical point of view, given Husserl's alienation from Brentano himself

---

[4] Dimitri Michaltschew's dissertation (1909) even went so far as to coin and frequently use the subject term "Bolzano-Husserl" (or "Husserl-Bolzano"). Concerning Husserl's reaction to the Hungarian scientist and philosopher Palagyi, see 1979: 152–61 (first published in 1903), 1994: V, 198, VI, 447.

(compare, e.g., Husserl 1994: I, 44ff. and Brentano 1946: 93), the heterodox group in Graz around Alexius Meinong, and the orthodox group of disciples in Prague, whose hostile attacks against Husserl included charges of plagiarism (not to mention the fact that Husserl's juvenilia, even when they are Brentanian, are de facto more indebted to Stumpf in their details). Nonetheless, Husserl's hagiographic recollections of Brentano were taken at their face value by a series of influential early scholars (cf. the paraphrases at Brück 1933: 3–7, Osborn 1934: 15–19, Farber 1940: 6–7), giving rise to the historio-graphic idea of a direct philosophical lineage between Brentano and Husserl. On the other hand, Husserl, despite ostensibly seeking the friendship of Paul Natorp, refused to be assimilated to the institutionalized neo-Kantianism that was already under assault (see, e.g., Husserl 1994: IV, 84), for he preferred a comparison on equal footing.

The main philosophical stake in interpreting Husserl's early philosophy is, of course, the continuity between Husserl's transcendental phenomenology and his philosoph-ical beginnings. The most pregnant exposition of the received view among Husserl's disciples was given by Oskar Becker's commemorative article, which claimed that the "fundamental principles of Husserl's logic and phenomenology," including the "prin-ciple of transcendental idealism," are, with a certain "hesitation," "present" in Husserl's juvenilia, which were nominally dedicated to the philosophy of mathematics (1930: 123). The first wave of studies dedicated to the beginning of Husserl's philosophy (Illemann 1932, Osborn 1934) followed the conspicuous signposts provided by Husserl himself, even though Osborne was more keen to diagnose ruptures in Husserl's development and was instrumental in promoting the "myth" (Embree 1998: 335) of Gottlob Frege's "devastating attack" (Osborn 1934: 50) on Husserl that is supposed to have awakened him from his psychologistic slumber (see n. 16). Moreover, the surge of postwar interest in Austrian philosophy was guided by Haller's concept of Austrian Philosophy, which sharply distinguished between the early Husserl and the Husserl of transcendental phenomenology (see already 1979: 16, 50). A sophisticated version of this caesura is exemplified by Rollinger's concept of Austrian phenomenology (2008: 2ff.).

Husserl's debut in German philosophy around 1900 was undeniably a lateral entry from the vastly different philosophical context of Austria, which underwent a different type of Kant reception, but I think it would be a foregone conclusion to assume that the difference could be narrowed down merely to Husserl's membership in the School of Brentano. At the same time, the significant discrepancy between the rich land-scape of post-Hegelian German academic philosophy and the "standard narrative" of it that emerged afterwards (Beiser 2014a: 7ff.) must also be taken into account. In sum, the study of Husserl's occasionally highly technical early philosophy is simulta-neously an investigation into the roots of phenomenology and a historical attempt at understanding phenomenology's relation to other contemporary strains of philosophy that originated in the same period. Correspondingly, the present chapter relies on a wide and modern textual basis in an attempt to provide a balanced exposition of the evolving problems that preoccupied Husserl during the early phase of his philosoph-ical career. At the same time, it intends to pay special attention to the obvious or incon-spicuous elements that connect the beginnings of Husserl's philosophy to his mature transcendental phenomenology, as well as to those roots of his philosophy that extend beyond the confines of the School of Brentano.

6.2 Juvenilia: Anticipations

6.2.1 The partial print of Husserl's habilitation thesis: A snapshot of Husserl's thinking in 1887

Husserl's *Über den Begriff der Zahl* (*On the Concept of Number*; Husserl 1887, 1970a: 289–338, English translation [hereafter: ET]: 2003a: 305–56), the first piece of text by Husserl that was printed, is a strange amalgam of what Husserl had learned during his brief apprenticeship with Brentano in Vienna and what he had acquired from other sources. In the booklet that was composed in Summer 1887 as a prerequisite to the bestowal of the *venia legendi*, Husserl essentially subscribed to Brentano's descriptive psychological research program and its Stumpfian variation, insofar as he was interested not in providing a traditional logical or modern mathematical definition of number, but rather in the "specific question" of "the content and origin [*Inhalt und Ursprung*] of the concept of number,"[5] i.e., "the psychological characterization of the phenomena upon which the abstraction of that concept is based" (Husserl 1887: 17, cf. 12–13, ET: 2003a: 318). The phenomena to which Husserl applied this methodology were, however, distinctively non-Brentanian. Stumpf, who evaluated the original manuscript of Husserl's habilitation thesis for the faculty, himself was surprised by Husserl's choice of the term "*Inbegriff*" (aggregate) over "*Collectivum*," which was more customary in the School of Brentano (Gerlach and Sepp 1994: 172). It has been readily noted (Illemann 1932: 13 n. 22) that the source of Husserl's notion of *Inbegriff* must have been Bolzano's *Paradoxien des Unendlichen* (*Paradoxes of the Infinite*), which Husserl himself reported to have encountered prior to his studies with Brentano (Husserl 2002a: 297 n. 2). What makes an aggregate special is that entirely arbitrary objects, e.g., "a few particular trees; the sun, moon, earth, and Mars," can be united to form an aggregate (Husserl 1887: 13, ET: 2003a: 315; cf. Bolzano 2012: 41). The third ingredient was the conviction shared by the "Berlin mathematical school," where Husserl studied, that "the foundation of the concept of number based on its psychological constitution" (Centrone 2010: 5) could de facto be instrumental for the "radical grounding of mathematics."[6]

---

[5] Husserl 1887: 9, ET: 2003a: 311. The "exploration of the psychological origin of a presentation" was defined by Stumpf as the "exploration [*Aufsuchung*] of the presentations from which it was formed [*sich gebildet hat*] and the modes and ways through which it was formed from them" (Stumpf 1873; in Husserl's copy this passage is marked as "N[ota] B[ene]").

[6] MS, Husserl B II 23 / 8a (also quoted by Schuhmann 1977: 7). In this unconnected retrospective note filed together with manuscripts written around 1930, Husserl contrasts the program of rational reconstruction of mathematics, he inherited from Weierstraß, with the context of discovery

The framework of Husserl's investigations is established by the thesis that he probably distilled from Brentano's discussion of various forms of wholes and parts—physical wholes and parts (e.g., an interval and its parts), metaphysical wholes and parts (e.g., a sensation and its quality), logical wholes and parts (e.g., color and red), and continua (e.g., space, time, and infinite numerical series)—namely, that "wherever we are presented with a particular class of wholes, the concept of that class has only been able to originate through reflexion upon a well-distinguished manner of combining parts [*Verbindungsweise*], one which is identical in each whole of the class in question" (Husserl 1887: 16, ET: 2003a: 317). Husserl's task was thus to identify the manner of combination that is specific to aggregates as such. He called it "collective connection" (*kollektive Verbindung*), borrowing a term that he must have encountered in Brentano's classes (see MS, Husserl Y Brentano 2 / 108). For Brentano, however, collective connections are wholes that are connected merely by virtue of "any kind of relations" (107). Husserl, in contrast, believed that collective connection is a relation *sui generis* and set out to find a "more precise characterization" of it (Husserl 1887: 33, ET: 2003a: 331).

Husserl discussed five contemporary proposals (an aggregate is constituted merely by virtue of its parts' belonging to one consciousness, or their simultaneity, temporal or spatial succession, or through the signature of their systematic differences), the authors of which included early neo-Kantians, most notably Friedrich Albert Lange, who belonged to the realist side of the debate between Kuno Fischer and Friedrich Adolf Trendelenburg (see Köhnke 1986: 257ff.). According to them, Kant's proof of the empirical reality and transcendental ideality of space and time in the *Critique of Pure Reason* did not disprove that "the a priori forms of space and time apply to things-in-themselves" as well (Beiser 2014b: 212), and this enabled them to harmonize Kant's transcendental aesthetics with modern scientific physiology and realist metaphysics. Husserl sided against this option, because, he believed, it rests on "the erroneous view that a psychic act and its" spatiotemporal object "stand to one another in the relation of pictorial resemblance" (Husserl 1887: 35, ET: 2003a: 333). At the same time, this critique enabled him to specify the nature of "synthesis" (see Husserl 1887: 33ff.) that unites the elements of an aggregate: it is neither a "'purely mental' creation[] of an inner intuition," nor a "rediscovery . . . in the external world" (Husserl 1887: 36, ET: 333).[7] The syntheses are "mental creations insofar as they are results of activities which we exercise on concrete contents." As such, they are "peculiar, relational concepts, which can only be produced again and again, but which absolutely cannot be simply found somewhere already completed" (Husserl 1887: 37, ET: 334). There is a long and venerable tradition according to which Husserl's analysis of the origins of the concept of number in *Über*

("exploratory research [*vortastende Forschung*]," 8b). This idea recurs in Husserl's justification for his habilitation thesis (Husserl 1887: 5ff.).

[7] It is precisely the clarification and rigorous exposition of the sense of this creation (*Erzeugung*) that Husserl, in retrospect, regarded as the main achievement of his *Logische Untersuchungen* and his entire phenomenology (2011b: 276).

den Begriff der Zahl, as well as in the *Philosophie der Arithmetik* already exemplifies a "phenomenological-constitutional study" of "'categorial objectivities.'"[8] I believe that this assessment could be reinforced and refined by taking into account Husserl's relationship with that broadly conceived, early neo-Kantian tradition which, by insisting on a loophole in Kant's proofs, aimed at overcoming Kant's limitations on the inner sense. The influence of this tradition is exemplified by Lange, who became the protagonist in the methodical chapter of Brentano's *Psychologie* (1874a: 13), as well as by Friedrich Ueberweg's statement of the veracity of inner perception (1882: 97ff.), to which Husserl added marginalia in his copy of Ueberweg's book.

The details of Husserl's own account of the synthesis achieved by the collective combination are difficult to decipher: "A unifying interest directed upon all the contents, plus with and in it—in that reciprocal interpenetration [*Durchdringung*] which is peculiar to psychic acts—a simultaneous act of noticing: these throw the contents into relief. And the intentional object of this act of noticing is precisely the presentation of the multiplicity or the totality of those contents" (Husserl 1887: 36, ET [modified]: 2003a: 334). "Interpenetration" (*durchdringen*) was Stumpf's technical term (see MS, Husserl Q 11 I / 129) for the entanglement of the act and its inner perception, which Brentano argued, must exhibit structural differences, lest infinite regress arises. Thus, it seems that Husserl built his account of the collective connection on the inner perception of the synthetic act itself, and, furthermore, he equated "intentional object" with the product of the inner perception. He was looking for an account that, unlike Brentano's, would be strictly independent of the actual objects unified in the aggregate.

Husserl tried to situate his account in a general theory of relations, relying on the ideas of Meinong in a way that was verging on plagiarism (Ierna 2009: 14). Husserl distinguished between physical (or contentual: *inhaltlich*) relations and psychical ones that are not connected by virtue of the contents of their *fundamenta relationis*. The collective connection, of course, belongs to the latter kind of relation, which comprises "its terms by intentionality, i.e., in that specifically determinate manner in which a 'psychical phenomenon' (an act of noticing, of willing, etc.) encompasses [*umfassen*] its content (what is noticed, willed, etc.)" (Husserl 1887: 52, ET [modified]: 2003a: 347). This passage, which contains an explicit reference by Husserl to Brentano, also makes it clear that for Husserl in 1887, intentionality was a kind of encompassing (*umfassen*), namely, that which is characteristic of inner perception, rather than a relation between acts and their objects (see Varga 2014: 105–6). At the same time, Husserl had no problems with a—phenomenologically naïve—representational relation between acts and their objects: "where we are dealing with objectively real things, these still must be represented in our consciousness by means of presentations [*Vorstellungen*]" (Husserl 1887: 13 n. 1 cf. 45, ET [mod.]: 2003a: 316 n. 10).

Husserl's own solution is essentially in alignment with what he learned from Stumpf in the previous semester, namely, that "the concept of number is based on complicated

---

[8] Husserl 1974: 91; cf., e.g., Becker 1930: 119 ff.; Biemel 1959: 194; Sokolowski 1970: 6ff.

relations, relations of higher order," i.e., "perception of relations" (MS, Husserl Q 11 II / 494). Stumpf's vague reference to inner perception might have motivated Husserl's choice of the subject of his habilitation thesis (cf. Schuhmann 2000: 80), but Stumpf's lack of descriptive resources—especially his lack of a sophisticated concept of in-tentionality (Schuhmann 2000: 65), which Husserl could not develop until 1894 (see section 6.3.1)—was also the reason for Husserl's idiosyncrasies, including his non-phenomenological use of intentionality. On the other hand, there are some scattered anticipations of Husserl's more mature phenomenological views, including the dis-tinction between the succession of presentations and the presentation of succession (1887: 20–1), which became the cornerstone of Husserl's later phenomenology of inner time consciousness.

Less attention is paid to the introductory part of Husserl's habilitation thesis, in which he elaborated on his meta-philosophical views, including Brentano's idea, which he, in turn, borrowed from Auguste Comte, that the hierarchy of sciences corresponds to the complexity chain of phenomena (cf. Brentano 1874b: 12ff.). Husserl's frequent references to metaphysics should probably be understood against the backdrop of Stumpf's Brentanian definition of metaphysics as a first-order general science: "metaphysics is the science of the general definitions and laws in the domain of inner and outer perception" (Stumpf 2015: 444).

Über den Begriff der Zahl merely constituted the first chapter of Husserl's projected book, which he struggled to realize (in 1888, e.g., Stumpf reported to Brentano that Husserl was "in need of prodding"; Brentano and Stumpf 2014: 280). Stumpf's evalu-ation of the lost habilitation manuscript, together with Husserl's lecture course in WS 1889–90 (Husserl 2005b), makes it possible to conjecture (Ierna 2005) the structural ev-olution of Husserl's draft until he managed to publish it in 1891.

6.2.2 The *Philosophie der Arithmetik* (1891) and its follow-up projects: Varieties of inauthenticity

The *Philosophie der Arithmetik* (*Philosophy of Arithmetic*; 1970a: 1–283, ET: 2003a: 299), Husserl's first printed work that became the subject of scientific discussion of the time, remained a torso, and the task of writing its projected second volume preoccupied Husserl during the great part of the 1890s.

As early as in his fifth habilitation thesis, which Husserl defended on July 1, 1887, he propounded that "one can hardly count beyond three in the authentic sense [*im eigentlichen Sinne*]" (1970a: 339, ET: 2003a: 357), and in *Über den Begriff der Zahl* he in-dicated that its scope is confined to "the very first numbers, whereas we can conceive of larger numbers only symbolically" (1887: 43, ET: 2003a: 339). Husserl came to address this issue in the *Philosophie der Arithmetik* from the point of view of arithmetical opera-tions, which are, in most cases, merely "indirect symbolizations of numbers" (1970a: 190, ET: 2003a: 200). This limitation is rooted in the finitude of our intellect. Husserl thus reversed the traditional epistemological role of arithmetic, which is, for him, precisely a sign of our imperfection ("ὁ ἄνθρωποσ ἀριθμητίζει," 1970a: 192 n. 1), while he was also in accordance with the views of experimental psychology of that time on the "extension of consciousness" (cf. Wundt 1880: 213ff.).

According to Brentano's definition, inauthentic (*uneigentliche*) presenting occurs when we "do not have an exactly corresponding presentation of something, or we cannot have such a presentation. We use a name, but we do not properly understand the name itself when we use it" (MS, Brentano EL 80, 13060). Husserl's definition of "symbolic or inauthentic" presentations (1970a: 193, ET: 2003a: 205) relies instead on Stumpf's, for whom "symbolic presentations" are "those presentations which occur only as signs for others by replacing them for the usage of judgment" (MS, Husserl Q 12 / 31 ET: Rollinger 1999: 301). The main difference between these two conceptions is that, for Brentano, inauthentic presenting is an anomaly of the use of names (e.g., the presentation of trillion, analogical presentation of God, or the presentation of colors by the visually impaired), while for Stumpf it is the pervasive normal case.[9] Stumpf himself described "the algebraical and arithmetical systems of signs" as an instance of symbolic presenting, and marvelled at our ability "to run a business with surrogates" (MS, Husserl Q 11 II / 506–7). Husserl refined Stumpf's definition by distinguishing between symbolic and general presentations (Husserl 1970a: 193 n. 1), emphasizing that number literals are general names for the corresponding aggregates, rather than singular names of abstract concepts of the corresponding numbers (Husserl 1970a: 182–3, cf. Rollinger 1993: 87–8). He relied on his proto-phenomenological understanding of the "psychical process" that originates numbers (cf. section 6.2.1) to reject Frege's definition (Husserl 1970a: 163), and developed a highly sophisticated theory of the sensuous grasp of *symbolically presented* aggregates by virtue of figural moments, which anticipates his later theory of pre-predicative constitution of collections (Lohmar 1998: 187).

The really intriguing part of Husserl's book, however, is where it failed. "I had already gone beyond it as I published it," he later remarked (1984c: 442, ET: 1994a: 490). Willard (1984: 110) maintained that "the conceptualisation which had guided [Husserl's] entire enterprise whose development is expressed in that book is in fact abandoned in its final chapter." He also pointed to Husserl's letter to Stumpf, allegedly written in early 1891 (the letter itself had already been highlighted by Biemel 1959: 195), where Husserl explicitly renounced the "opinion by which I was still guided in the elaboration of my *Habilitatonsschrift*," namely, "that the concept of cardinal number forms the foundation of general arithmetic." "By no clever devices, by no 'inauthentic presenting,' can one derive negative, rational, irrational, and the various sorts of complex numbers from the concept of the cardinal number" (1994b: I, 158, ET [mod.]: 1994a: 13). Willard's dating for the letter is historically untenable,[10] and Husserl's recognition antedated the

---

[9] This ambiguity is the source of Husserl's obscure distinction between psychological and logical symbolization (1970a: 194).

[10] Since Husserl referred to lectures by other professors (1994b: I, 163), Willard's dating (also upheld in Husserl 1994a: 12, supported by Schuhmann 1977: 29) could be refuted by the independent printed evidence of the course catalogue of the University of Halle-Wittenberg.

finalization of his book. In fact, Husserl already occupied himself with the "most general arithmetical operations" in his original habilitation manuscripts (cf. Gerlach and Sepp 1994: 173), following in the footsteps of Hermann Hankel's theory of the successive extension of the number domains, to which Husserl had already referred in his sixth habilitation thesis.[11]

Husserl's own solution was based on the notion of calculus (*Kalkül*). A calculus is, for him, a special method of symbolic derivations, namely, one which, "through an appropriate symbolization [*Signierung*] of thoughts, substitutes a calculation process— i.e., a rule-governed process of transposing and replacing signs with signs—for actual inferring; and then, by means of the assignment of symbols and thoughts set up at the outset, it derives the desired judgments from the resultant end-formulae" (1979: 21, ET [mod.]: 1994a: 69). The symbolization (*Signierung*) involved differs fundamentally from both Brentano's improper presenting and Stumpf's symbolic presentations, "for the function of the sign here absolutely is not to accompany the *thought as its expression*" (1979: 21, ET: 70).[12] The computational symbol-manipulation takes place without regard to the original assignment of thoughts, and they are only taken into account when the results are decoded at the end of the computation. Importantly, there are two different kinds of calculi, as Husserl explained in his drafts for the planned second volume of the *Philosophie der Arithmetik*, which was intended to provide the "full logical clarification [*Aufklärung*] of the true sense of general arithmetic" (1970a: 7, ET: 2003a: 7): In the first case, every computational step can be fully decoded, i.e., "there would be a direct parallelism between this algorithm and the domain of general arithmetical judgments" (1983: 28). Algorithms for the manual addition of large numbers in decimal notation, e.g., only contain intermediary steps that can be fully converted into valid arithmetic equations containing merely cardinal numbers. Husserl was more interested in calculi which do not exhibit this property: The initial assignment of the symbols in such calculi are "founded conceptually" (1983: 28), but they may contain intermediary products that "are lacking any conceptual content beyond the algorithmic" (1983: 43). In this way, Husserl was capable of accounting for the origins of "'impossible' concepts" (1994b: I, 160, ET: 1994a: 15, cf. 2011a), i.e., negative, imaginary, or fraction numbers that are lacking intuitively fulfillable conceptual content on the basis of corresponding aggregates. In the wake of the refinement of his phenomenological apparatus, Husserl called these algorithmically founded concepts objectless (1983: 56; written around 1894) and in SS 1895 he called the computational

---

[11]   1970a: 339. In Leipzig in WS 1876/77, Husserl studied at the physicist Wilhelm Gottlieb Hankel, rather than Hermann Hankel.

[12]   The distinction between semantic and non-semantic signs recurred when in 1913, during the reworking of his original theory of signs from the *First Investigation*, Husserl distinguished between categorial and non-categorial signs (so-called signals; 2005a: 52ff.).

rules "rules of the game" and the algorithmic meaning "meaning according to the game" (1983: 61 / 2001a: 310).[13]

In an occasional piece of writing from early 1891, Husserl already drew a crucial epistemological conclusion from his notion of calculus: "calculational disciplines" are capable of applying and even inventing their "algorithmical methods" independently "of insight into their essence and into the grounds of their value for knowledge" (1979: 22, ET: 1994a: 70). This is neither a superficial critique of them by philosophy, nor a manifestation of their contingent imperfection, but it is rather due to their very nature, namely, that a majority of the calculational disciplines are non-parallel algorithms only the inner nucleus of which is conceptually founded and capable of providing an insight into the "true conceptual substrates." "Thus we have the curious spectacle of a science which does not know what it is really dealing with" (1979: 22, ET: 1994a: 70).

Husserl explicitly declared that his aim was not "the formation of a new technique," but rather "the explanation and understanding of the already established technique" (1983: 40). This declaration, which is epitomized by the contrast frequently mentioned by Husserl between the roles of the "logician" and the "technician" (1979: 9, 468, 1984c: 163), clearly anticipates his later conception of transcendental phenomenology as an elucidation (*Aufklärung*) of scientific and life-world knowledge,[14] as well as his diagnosis in the *Krisis* of a "surreptitious substitution [*Unterschiebung*] of the mathematically substructed world of idealities for the only real world" (1962: 49, ET: 1970b: 48–9). Besides working on the planned second volume of the *Philosophie der Arithmetik*, Husserl also devoted his efforts to a book project dedicated to the "psychological," "logical," and "metaphysical investigations" of the presentation of space (1983: 404–5), which is another question that continued to preoccupy him during his later career.

These overlapping follow-up projects remained on Husserl's agenda until as late as 1895, but he was disrupted by two events that significantly widened his philosophical horizon: He chronicled in his diary, in November 1893, that the elaboration of his projected book on space had gotten stranded due to "difficulty" with more encompassing questions of descriptive psychology (1979: 452). A half year later, Husserl stumbled upon the habilitation thesis of Kazimierz Twardowski (1894), a later-generation heterodox disciple of Brentano, which introduced Husserl to the controversy over interpreting Brentano's notion of intentionality. Finally, in summer–fall 1896 Husserl started preparing a publication based on the manuscript of his lecture course on logic taught during the previous semester, which resulted in the *Logische Untersuchungen*.

---

[13] Husserl's more technical attempts to spell out the completeness conditions of the relation between conceptually founded inferring (semantic) and computational (syntactic) calculations, especially his attempt in 1901 in Göttingen (Husserl 2001b), made him vulnerable to objections against the Hilbert Program. This is not necessarily so, though Husserl (and others at that time) were lacking the explicit notion of metalogic that is required in order to formulate the appropriate conditions (see Hartimo 2007: esp. 289, 304ff.).

[14] As Luft has argued, Husserl's mature phenomenology exemplifies the transcendental flavor of *Aufklärungsphilosophie* (2012: 7–8, 24ff.).

6.3 The Phenomenological Breakthrough: The *Logische Untersuchungen* (1900–1) and its Incubation

6.3.1 Intentional acts and their objects

It was Alois Höfler who, probably after having independently discovered the true philosophical significance of Bolzano, ignited the debate among Brentano's later-generation heterodox Viennese disciples over an ambiguity in Brentano's notion of intentionality: The object of an intentional act is either "that which is subsisting in itself" and "at which our presenting or judging is directed" or its "psychical, more or less approximate 'image', which subsists 'in' us" (1890: 7). For Höfler, this distinction was brought to the fore by the possibility of compound presentations with incompatible parts, having empty logical extension (e.g., round square) or empty empirical extension (dirigible airship).[15] Curiously, neither Brentano nor Husserl seems to have bothered with this anomaly beforehand, insofar as they were content with either a double-object theory or the disjunctive solution (i.e., simply denying that such problematic presentations have an object at all; cf. Varga 2014: 91ff.). Husserl, e.g., wrote in early 1891: " 'Meaningless' names in the strict sense are names without a meaning—pseudo names, such as 'Abracadabra.' But 'round square' is a univocal common noun to which, however, nothing can in truth correspond" (1979: 12, ET: 1994a: 60). In a text penned in 1894 as a "reaction against Twardowski" (1994b: I, 144), Husserl is no more willing to accept such solutions, because of a "new consideration": It is "correct for us to say 'a round square' presents an object which is at the same time round and square, but there is certainly no such object" (1990: 142, ET: Rollinger 1999: 251).

Husserl's new position in the debate was based on the firm belief in the *priority of the phenomenological access* that reveals no descriptive difference between different objects: What "the sense of the apparently or really contradictory statements discussed above" implies is precisely "that it is in each case the *same* object which is presented and exists or does not exist. The same Berlin that I present also exists, and the same would no longer exist if judgment were brought down as in the case of Sodom and Gomorrha" (1990: 144, ET: Rollinger 1999: 252–3). To this extent, Husserl's involvement in the controversy in 1894 not only marks the onset of his interest in the notion of intentionality

---

[15] Höfler's latter, own example was probably a cultural reference to the failed Vienna project of the inventor Paul Haenlein (despite the technical progress in the meantime). The traces of Höfler's independent early interest in Bolzano are already visible in an educational pamphlet (Höfler 1884: 53, n.), which antedates Benno Kerry's series of articles that is usually regarded as the first reference to Bolzano by Brentano's disciples (cf., e.g., Kühne 1997: 32).

as such (Schuhmann 2004: 119–20), but it can justly be regarded as the *terminus a quo* of Husserl's mature phenomenology (simultaneously, Husserl's pre-phenomenological explanation could help to dispel the myth of Frege's alleged decisive influence on him).[16]

In a spin-off text written in 1898 during his work on the *Logische Untersuchungen*, Husserl elaborated on the above striking claim: "When a philosopher degrades the perception of an external object to an illusion, supposing . . . a thing in itself behind it, the external perception does not change into a new perception (namely that of the thing in itself), but it rather loses a significant portion of its perceptual character (. . . the perception [*Wahrnehmung*] turns into a misception [*Falschnehmung*])" and a conceptual correction becomes attached to it (2004: 129). At this point, Husserl still conceived his phenomenological priority criterion within the framework of a scientific-realist ontology. In the printed text of the *Logische Untersuchungen*, Husserl disregarded this framework: "Nothing becomes psychologically different," he wrote, except for the "various possible assertive characters that imply [*implizieren*] the conviction of the being of what is presented."[17] In the first edition of 1900–1, when Husserl did not yet conceive of phenomenology as a full-fledged philosophical position (see, e.g., 1984a: 401; cf. section 6.4), his solution might simply rest on the conviction that it is an *irreducible, but descriptively accessible* feature of certain experiences to present an object: If such an "experience is present, in its concrete psychical fullness, then, *eo ipso* [= by that very act], the intentional 'relation' to an object is achieved, and an object is, *eo ipso*, 'intentionally present.' "[18] In the second edition of 1913, Husserl then changed "psychologically"

[16] Since Frege's infamous letter to Husserl in 1891 (Husserl 1994b: 107–10) is an acknowledgement of receiving from Husserl, amongst others, the occasional writing in which the above disjunctive analysis was propounded, it is beyond question that Husserl arrived at the "distinction between meaning and object of an expression" "independently of Frege" (Mohanty 1982: 2; see also Ortiz Hill and Rosado Haddock 2000: 32–3). It must also be noted that the mere distinction between content (*Inhalt*) and extension (*Umfang*) of (conceptual) presentations—including, e.g., the possibility of special presentations (*Wechselvorstellungen*) having different content but sharing the same extension (e.g., Bolzano 1837: I, 445ff.; annotated by Husserl)—was a commonplace in post-Hegelian philosophical logic (on the Herbartian logic to which Husserl had already been exposed in secondary school, see Varga 2015: 105ff.). Furthermore, Frege's critique in his review of Husserl's *Philosophie der Arithmetik* that Husserl cleanses "the objects of their particularities" "in a psychological wash-tub," resulting in a property-less "wraith" that blurs the "boundary between the subjective and the objective" (1894: 316–17, ET: 1972: 323–5), definitely overlooked Husserl's deeper intentions (see section 2.1), even if it could be supported by certain passages (e.g., Husserl 1970a: 80). On the other hand, it must be admitted that Husserl failed to recognize the mathematical-philosophical innovations of Frege, e.g, that Frege's "introduction of the function-argument structure to analyse the content of a judgement provided a unique alternative to the whole traditional approach, also Husserl's, in terms of a subject and a predicate" (Atten 2005: 146). This requires a certain qualification, insofar as Husserl, when he later developed a comparable theory, explicitly related it to Frege (see 1996: 180). But Husserl believed that he had superseded Frege in this respect; and, furthermore, Husserl obviously remained committed to traditional (non-functional) logic. Subsequently, Frege's possible relevance for him receded into oblivion, and in 1936 he remembered Frege as a "fruitless oddball both as a philosopher and a mathematician" (1994b: VI, 369).

[17] Husserl 1984a: 387 (variant of the first edition), ET (mod.): 2001c: II, 99, 353.

[18] Husserl 1984a: 386 (variant of the first edition), ET (mod.): 2001c: II, 98.

to "phenomenologically" and "imply" to "constitute [*ausmachen*]," mirroring his transition from descriptive psychology to transcendental-phenomenological idealism that allowed him to build up a full-fledged transcendental-philosophical position around the constitutive achievements of intentionality. At each stage, however, Husserl's claim of the lack of phenomenological "difference between a veridical perception and a non-veridical perception"—"one of the striking features of Husserl's analysis of intentionality in *Logical Investigations*" (Zahavi 2002: 106)—helps to designate phenomenology's position vis-à-vis other theories of mind: intentionality cannot be explained away by reducing it to a real relation either between two immanent parts of a conscious experience or between the consciousness and a real thing (cf. Zahavi 1992: 62ff.). In other words, any difference between the intentional givenness of the real object and that of the non-real object must exhibit itself phenomenologically in the course of the perception and other intentional achievements. This phenomenological criterion itself remained constant during the development of Husserl's thinking, but initially it was conceived as a descriptive psychological feature compatible with the external framework of a scientific ontology, while later it became embedded into a transcendental-phenomenological philosophy that assumed the function of grounding every scientific and life-world ontology.

The *pars destruens* of Husserl's 1894 treatise against Twardowski already contains a series of further demarcations which lay the groundwork for Husserl's mature phenomenology of intentional acts (cf. 1984a: 436ff.). Initially, in his juvenilia, Husserl had subscribed to a phenomenologically naïve account (see section 6.2.1), and even Höfler's above distinction is plagued by a pictorial theory of representation. By 1894, Husserl argued that such theories are not only inconsistent with the phenomena ("I would like to know," Husserl commented on this popular position with irony, "what 'mental pictures' supposedly inhere in the concepts 'art,' 'literature,' 'science,' and the like," 1990: 143, ET: Rollinger 1999: 252), but they also beg the question: "One overlooks that the [pictorial] phantasy content must first become the representative image of something, and that this pointing-beyond-itself of the image" is already a higher-level intentional achievement that presupposes the basic case of intentional directedness (1990: 144, ET: 253). Husserl believes that the notion of immanent objects, as proposed by other heterodox disciples, suffers from the same "false duplication" (1990: 146, ET: 255); though he undeniably misunderstood them (cf. 1979: 458), especially their leaning toward Meinong's *Gegenstandstheorie*, the aim of which was precisely to create a rich but consistent ontology.

Husserl's positive solution in the text of 1894—the identity of the object is an identity "under hypothesis [*unter einer Hypothese*]" (1990: 151), i.e., the presentation of Zeus is implicitly conditional upon the validity of Greek mythology—provoked a plethora of diverse interpretations, exemplifying the various general attitudes toward Husserl's early philosophy (cf. section 6.1): It was praised for not "succumbing to immanentism, Platonism, or (what is worse) transcendentalism" (Rollinger 1999: 208, cf. 151ff.). For Schuhmann, Husserl anticipated Kuhn's notion of paradigms (2004: 127), for Künne, the "story operator approach" (2011: 88). Rang, on the other hand, saw a continuity with

Husserl's philosophy in the 1930s (Husserl 1979: xli). Heffernan (2015: 81) rightly pointed to the subtle evolution in Husserl's thinking on intentional objects between 1894 and the *Logische Untersuchungen*. Historically, Husserl's proposal is closely aligned with the prevalent Herbartian notion, first encountered by Husserl during secondary school (Lindner 1872: 40; cf. Varga 2015), according to which categorial judgments about non-existing objects are actually hypothetical judgments (rather than existential judgments with an improper presentation, as Brentano preferred: 1874a: 286–8, n.). Besides its affinity with Lotze's understanding of the mode of being of ideal objects as a conditional validity (the influence of which—rather than Bolzano—on the *Logische Untersuchungen* Husserl repeatedly emphasized, e.g., 1979: 156, 2002a: 297), the Herbartian background and its organic connection between psychology and logic is closer to the general trajectory of Husserl's development in the 1890s: Husserl tried to establish the sphere of objective meanings besides the *already characterized* sphere of subjective acts and intentional correlates,[19] unlike the trajectory of the logical objectivism of Bolzano, whom Husserl recurrently accused of not giving "the faintest intimation that these phenomenological relationships . . . had been noticed by him" (1979: 157, cf. 1994b: I, 29, 39; VII, 98, ET: 1994a: 202).[20]

His approach enabled Husserl to develop a rich and sophisticated variant of the traditional philosophical logic and psychology in the *Logische Untersuchungen*. Instead of the Brentanian psychical phenomenon, the building block of Husserl's descriptive psychology is experience (*Erlebnis*), which is an "immanent [*reell*], constitutive part or moment in the unity of the psychical individual."[21] Intentional experiences (also called "acts") are those experiences which intend objects or states of affairs in the manner of presentations or other analogous fashion. Contrary to Brentano, Husserl thus did not confine the objectifying function to presentations alone, even though emotive and volitional acts are said to be incapable of autonomously presenting an object (the latter restriction was subsequently lifted by Husserl, which gave way to formal and material axiology and praxiology, cf. Melle 1990). Two independently variable abstract components of the act are its matter (*Materie*), which gives the act its "reference to an object"—also determining "as what it grasps it, the properties, forms, relations that it attributes to it"—and its quality (*Qualität*), which "determines whether what is already presented in definite fashion is intentionally present as wished, asked, posited in judgement etc."[22] In accordance with the aforementioned phenomenological criterion

---

[19] The changes by Husserl to his lecture text in 2001a: 44–5, e.g., nicely illustrate his objective theory of meaning *in statu nascendi*.

[20] It must also be taken into account that, despite Husserl's very early encounter with Bolzano's *mathematical* writings (see Section 6.2.1) and the mediation through the (posthumous) writings of Benno Kerry (see Rollinger 1999: 71), Husserl's discovery of Bolzano's *Wissenschaftslehre* (1837) appears to have been a *separate event by chance* (Schuhmann 1977: 463; consider Husserl's vivid memories of the pricing of Bolzano's book in second-hand bookstores: Husserl 1994b: VII, 97, 2002a: 298, n.), and, furthermore, Bolzano's book was studied by Husserl in a very unsystematic way (Husserl 2002a: 298, n.; see note 28 below).

[21] 1984a: 392; deleted from the subsequent editions.

[22] 1984a: 429–30 (variant of the first edition), ET (mod.): 2001c: II, 121–2.

laid down in 1894, "all differences in mode of reference are descriptive differences in intentional experiences" (1984a: 427, ET: 2001c: II, 120). The quality and matter of an act constitute its intentional essence (*intentionales Wesen*), or, in case of meaning-bestowing acts, its significational essence (*bedeutungsmäßiges Wesen*), the abstraction of which results in the meaning (*Bedeutung*) of the act. Acts can be compounded or nested (e.g., a judgment about a judgment), and it is possible to transform an act by modifying its matter while preserving its quality, as well as by modifying its quality only (e.g., transforming a judgment, i.e., a positing propositional act, into a merely presentative, non-positing propositional act of the same matter). The ultimate underlying acts of complex acts are, however, always "straightforward combination[s] of a simple quality with simple matter" (1984: 518, ET: 2001c: II, 169). The link between these concepts and the traditional philosophical logic has been rightly highlighted (Künne 2011: 79–80). Yet Bolzano, for example, regarded "vivacity [*Lebhaftigkeit*]" and other features of presentations as being philosophically irrelevant, which are precisely those that are going to assume a fundamental role in Husserl's reconfiguration of his descriptive analysis of acts for the purposes of the "epistemological elucidation [*Aufklärung*] of pure logic" (Husserl 1984b: 783) in the last investigation of the *Logische Untersuchungen* (see section 6.3.3).

Yet it is not only Husserl's descriptive analysis of acts that is rooted in the mid-1890s. As early as 1896, Husserl presented the outlines of the Cartesian way to the phenomenological reduction, employed to dispel epistemological scepticism (2001a: 7–8), and the first edition of the *Logische Untersuchungen* already contained a detailed, though unsatisfactory, attempt at implementation (Lohmar 2011). Similarly, his preoccupation with Lotze was also instrumental for Husserl's understanding of the self-referential character of logic and the architectonic of his mature phenomenological philosophy (Varga 2013).

6.3.2 Husserl's critique of psychologism and his academic success

The first volume of the *Logische Untersuchungen* (finished by November 1899, first published in mid 1900; 1975, ET: 2001c: I, 9–161) was called "the most convincing volume of philosophical literature" (Levinas 1998: 114), which is not at all an overstatement with regard to its influence on the German academic philosophy of the time—even though Natorp privately described it as "an already obsolete thing" that was necessary merely due to the "schools of thought prevailing in Germany" (Holzhey 1986: 261). In less than a decade, Husserl was already complaining that "the polemic against psychologism came into fashion" (Husserl 1984c: 143), and his newly found fame resulted in a one-sided public perception of his *Logische Untersuchungen* that haunted him even as late as 1929 (e.g., 1994b: VI, 311).

The core of Husserl's anti-psychologism, which simultaneously manifests its connection with the program of the second volume, was already formulated in the manuscript of a lecture in 1898: The proper founding of logic is an epistemological one that is "rooted not in empirical psychology but in the purely descriptive phenomenology of the lived experiences of thought and cognition" (2002b: 304 n. 3, ET: 305 n. 3). As early as his lecture course on logic in 1896, Husserl renounced his previous, Brentanian conception of logic as a "practical discipline (that of a technique [*Kunstlehre*] of judging correctly)" (1887: 4, ET: 2003a: 307) and opted for the early neo-Kantian understanding of logic as a second-order science (cf. Trendelenburg 1870: I, iv): It is the "science of science" or "theory of science [*Wissenschaftslehre*]," which investigates "whatever makes sciences into sciences."[23] There are, obviously, practical-technical functions of logic, but "every practical discipline relies on one or more theoretical disciplines and takes the theoretical knowledge from them that accords with its normative interests."[24] The decisive question is, then, whether these disciplines belong to empirical psychology or not, given that logic is apparently concerned with mental occurrences. Husserl believed that he had found a major loophole in the arguments of the psychologistic camp, which falsely assumed that psychology's undeniable involvement "in the founding of logic" is the same as the "psychologistic thesis that psychology alone is involved or that it provides the essential foundation of logical technique" (2002b: 312, ET: 313, cf. 1975: 71).

In 1897, Husserl reported that he "rejects both parties' arguments" (1994b: V, 52), and later, in the printed first volume, refuted hasty anti-psychologistic arguments, including the one according to which psychologism is circular, since psychology as a science presupposes logic (1975: 69–70). Husserl had good reasons to follow Bolzano (cf. 1837: I, 8) in this regard, since the establishment of full-fledged transcendental phenomenology—i.e., what Husserl in the early 1920s started to call a "system" of phenomenological philosophy (e.g., 1994: III, 20)—itself is only possible in a zigzag fashion.[25]

The backbone of the anti-psychologistic arguments that Husserl deemed conclusive is a series of *reductio ad absurdum* arguments: the laws of a logic essentially founded on empirical psychology were, akin to psychological laws themselves, vague (*vage*), probabilistic-inductive (prone to falsification) and having matter-of-fact implications. There must be a distinction made between "causal laws, according to which thought must proceed in a manner which the ideal norms of logic might justify," and those norms themselves (1975: 79, ET: 2001c: I, 50). What could render a thinking machine (*Denkmaschine*) possible, e.g., are not the causal laws of nature as such, but "the insight into the logical laws brought forward" by its constructor

[23] Husserl 1975: 27, ET: 2001c: I, 16; adopted almost verbatim from 2001a: 6 (Husserl correspondingly modified his definition of metaphysics too). It must be noted that for Bolzano, whom Husserl owned terminologically and in the details of his conception, *Wissenschaftslehre* was, as highlighted by Husserl (1975: 43), in the end, the science of presenting sciences in appropriate textbooks (Bolzano 1837: I, 7 [marked in Husserl's copy], 56–7). Bolzano, together with Friedrich Schleiermacher, was once classified by Husserl as a proponent of logic as *Kunstlehre* (2002b: 324).

[24] 2002b: 308; ET: 309; compare 1975: 59–60; in a more rudimentary form: 2001a: 36.

[25] See, e.g., 1962: 59; earlier formulations: 1984a: 22–3, 1984b: 552.

(1975: 79). Similarly, even though "the basic notions of logic" and their "purely conceptual relations" "are abstracted from psychological experience" (1975: 85, ET: 54), they
"begin with experience" but do not "arise [*entspringen*]" from it (as Husserl said in
allusion to Kant): the psychological circumstances of discovery are not necessarily the
same as the laws discovered. That Husserl's anti-psychologistic argumentation in the
end rests on a (proto)phenomenology is best demonstrated by his "direct proof" (cf.
2002b: 314): psychologistic theories of logic violate the conditions of the possibility
of theory as such, which consists in both acknowledging the objective components
of pure theory (truths, propositions, objects, properties, etc.), as well as its equally
ideal noetic components, "whose roots lie in the form of subjectivity as such, and in
its relation to knowledge" (1975: 119, ET: 2001c: I, 76). Reducing logical laws to empirical psychological ones thus amounts to a bad phenomenology that conflates real
mental occurrences with atemporal objectivities and their corresponding ideal noetic
conditions.

The one-sided focus on the first volume of Husserl's *Logische Untersuchungen* usually
went hand in hand with the question, already formulated by Leonard Nelson (Husserl's
erstwhile student and later rival in Göttingen), with regard to Husserl's descriptive
psychology that was propounded in the second volume, subtitled *Investigations in
Phenomenology and Theory of Knowledge*: "Why is it not a 'psychologism?'" (1908: 130).
This frequent objection, however, not only overlooks the aforementioned (proto)phe-
nomenological facet of the first volume but also the second volume's detailed explanation of the difference between empirical psychology and "descriptive psychology" (or
rather, "phenomenology") "which underlies the fundamental abstractions" that embody Husserl's project of elucidating logic and epistemology (1984a: 24). In the process of his transition to transcendental phenomenology as a full-fledged philosophy
(see section 6.4), Husserl was going to repeatedly revise the details of this explanation
(1979: 206–7, 1984b: 793, 1984a: 23). But, as his above references to "abstraction" illustrate, his inability to methodically account for the position that he occupied in the
Logische Untersuchungen is rooted in one particular aspect of his admitted lack of a "systematically closed theory of conceptual cognition" in 1900–1, namely, the insufficiency
of his account of the "various 'forms of universality-consciousness.'"[26] The latter gap
was not going to be filled until Husserl arrived at the theory of eidetic variation in 1912
(cf. 2012: 57).

---

[26] 1994b: I, 169. Husserl's insufficient *species* theory of meaning and its strict separation from his
theory of evidence in the *Logische Untersuchungen*, e.g., also prevented a phenomenological analysis of
the way in which meaning itself is given (see Heffernan 1983: 104–5). Furthermore, Husserl was probably
unaware of the real extent of the Brentanian theories of abstraction he criticized (see Fréchette 2015: 289).
The other side of the same coin is, however, that Brentano and Anton Marty tried to account for the
synthetic achievements of consciousness *within* the framework of their theories of abstraction (hence
their sophistications), while Husserl was arguably aiming to develop his own theory of constitution from
the ground up.

6.3.3 Husserl's theory of judgments and its background

The second volume of the *Logische Untersuchungen* (1984a, 1984b, ET: 2001c: I, 163ff.) was published only in April 1901, after a last-minute reworking of its latter part (cf. 1994b: IX, 20ff.), which probably affected the sections on Husserl's theory of judgments. Yet it was precisely this topic that captured the interest of Johannes Daubert in Munich (cf. Schuhmann 2004: 201), who was instrumental in converting Lipps' students to phenomenology and thereby initiating the Phenomenological Movement. For Daubert (2002: 362), the most instructive specific element was Husserl's distinction between states of affairs (*Sachverhalte*) as correlates of judgment acts and logical judgments (significations that are true or false in virtue of the corresponding states of affairs) as intentional contents of judgment acts. The former was, however, already anticipated by Brentano and expounded by Stumpf (as highlighted by Stumpf himself: 1907: 29–30). Furthermore, Adolf Reinach, who refined Husserl's notion of states of affairs with regard to positive–negative polarity and its applicability at optatives and volatives, believed that the above distinction had been unclear in most of the *Logische Untersuchungen* (1911: 223 n. 2); even though Husserl must be credited with having made this distinction possible by his refutation of psychologism, by his sophisticated philosophical logic (see section 6.3.1), and especially by his explicit rejection of Brentano's thesis that confined objectifying function to presentations alone (Brentano 1874a: 266).

It has been rightly emphasized (Bernet 1981: 60) that Husserl's "original contribution" was to link the justification of judgments to the synthetic process of (partial) intuitive fulfilment that takes place when epistemic acts of the same significational essence coincide (e.g., an intending by virtue of an empty linguistic sign coincides with the corresponding perception). In one of the sections in which Husserl temporarily lifted the self-imposed methodological restriction on genetic analyses, he described how the common "phenomenological roots" of these two acts are revealed in the experience of transition (*Übergangserlebnis*; 1984b: 566, anticipated at: 1984a: 421, ET: 2001c: II, 206), and later he claimed that what is experienced in self-evidence (*Evidenz*)—the correlate of which is truth (*Wahrheit*)—is precisely this agreement "of what is meant with what is given as such" (1984b: 652, ET: II, 263); yet, self-evidence is far from being an indexical feeling "contingently attaching to the act of judgment" (656, ET: II, 266).

In order to better understand this process, Husserl refined his descriptive analysis of intentional experiences by introducing the notion of *epistemic essence* (*erkenntnismäßiges Wesen*), which consists in not only the quality and the matter, but also the fulness (*Fülle*), the liveliness (*Lebendigkeit*) of the presentation. Since the representation inherent in an intentional experience is, Husserl believed at the time of writing, the result of a complex interplay of intuitive and non-intuitive act-contents, animated according to an interpretative form and sense (*Auffassungsform, Auffassungsmaterie*), the really distinct components of the epistemic essence are the quality, the matter, and the intuitively representing contents. The other kinds of contents, e.g., the partial perceptions pertaining to the reverse sides of a spatial object, were conceived by Husserl as higher-level achievements akin to the consciousness of signs. This model of intentional experiences is prone to bringing Husserl's criterion of truth into the vicinity of a total intuitive givenness (cf. Bernet 2003: 160ff.); and Husserl's conception quickly underwent a further development, motivated partly by his growing recognition of the inadequacy of the underlying model of signs (cf. 2004: 36 n. 1, 1973: 55), which, in turn, led to a more phenomenological understanding of empty intentions (*Leerintentionen*) during Husserl's reworking of the *Logische Untersuchungen* in 1913 and the following years (2002a: 91ff.). The fact that the representation rests on intuitive contents—and ultimately on self-presenting (*selbstdarstellende*) ones that are characteristic of perceptions—testifies to the phenomenological primacy of perception for Husserl's otherwise highly technical edifice of act analysis in the *Logische Untersuchungen*.

Husserl's theory implies that compound acts of predicate form are in need of intuitive fulfillment that are structured accordingly: When I say, "This paper is white," the partial perceptual intention aiming at the white "color-aspect" itself does not suffice as a fulfilling element, "a surplus of meaning remains over, a form which finds nothing in the appearance itself to confirm it. White, i.e., being-white paper [*weiß seiendes Papier*]" (1984b: 659–60, ET [mod.]: 2001c: 272–3). To this end, Husserl developed an account of the role that sensuous intuition plays in the form of categorial intuition (*kategoriale Anschauung*). Husserl's attempt was considered controversial, and he himself renounced its first implementation (cf. 1984b: 535). Yet, it is undeniably possible for such a higher-level fulfilling intuition to emerge, starting from the straightforward perception (a unitary perceptual intention, the partial intentions of which are not articulated explicitly), followed by an articulating act based on the same act-contents (e.g., the specific perception of the paper "through" its whiteness), which coincides with the continuously operating total perception. The unity constituted by the coincidental synthesis itself, however, takes on a representative role, namely, as the fulfilling element of the categorial apprehension (i.e., the paper appears as being white). It is important to note that, since the categorial fulfilling elements are rooted in the synthetic unity itself rather than in the intuitive fulfilment of its founding acts, systems of non-intuitive judgments, too, can exhibit their own form of evidence (Lohmar 1998: 202), even though they ultimately rest on sensuous intuition. Thus Husserl's phenomenology is capable of accounting for the possibility of formal sciences, adding descriptive depth to his earlier philosophical claims about them (see section 6.2.2).

The categorial intuition was once listed by Martin Heidegger as one of phenomenology's three "decisive discoveries" (1985: 27). The unsaid reverse side of such claims is that the bulk of Husserl's theory of judgments is rooted more deeply in nineteenth-century philosophical logic than usually assumed. In particular, Christoph Sigwart's theory of denominative judgments (*Benennungsurtheil*) and their twofold synthesis could have provided important building-blocks for Husserl's analysis: The basic case of denominative judgments, according to Sigwart, consists in "the simple coincidence [*Coincidenz*] between the present intuition and the remembered presentation," in which the subject presentation and the "predicate presentation, which is inwardly reproduced by the corresponding word," are "consciously unified" in "the act of judgment."[27] Husserl undeniably reconfigured and refined these building-blocks with the aid of his sophisticated act analysis; on the other hand, Sigwart's reliance of the "corresponding word" hints at a surplus knowledge resting on the linguistic sign itself, the possibility of which was explored in new material written by Husserl in spring 1914 for the planned revised second edition of the *Logische Untersuchungen* (2002a: 296ff., esp. 302). These influences and affinities further corroborate Husserl's indebtedness to nineteenth-century philosophical logic and psychology besides Bolzano and the School of Brentano.

In hindsight, Husserl complained of the one-sidedly noetic nature of his *Logische Untersuchungen*, which he ascribed to the misleading influence of Bolzano.[28] The principle of noetic–noematic correlation, together with Husserl's breakthrough to genetic phenomenology around the same time, made Husserl's phenomenological logic both more powerful and simple: The distinction in 1909–11 of a noematic sense of meaning (*Bedeutung*) besides the noetical sense of meaning *in specie*, e.g., allowed him to find simpler alternatives to the complex structural analyses developed in the Fifth Logical Investigation (cf., e.g., 1987b: 143), as illustrated by his explanation in 1910–11 of this distinction using the turn of gaze (*Blick*) from constituted objects back to the "ego and its acts" (1996: 42). The lift of the self-imposed and untenable ban on horizontal, genetic investigations—as early as in 1912–13 (cf. Sakakibara 1997: 22)—further helped him move away from the complex, static vertical investigations of consciousness, without relinquishing the transcendental-phenomenological attitude and relapsing to empirical psychology.

6.4 Outlook: Realism, Metaphysical Neutralism, and Transcendental Phenomenology

Ever since the young early phenomenologists in Göttingen, who, according to the influential and picturesque recollections of Edith Stein, were "all . . . confirmed realists," became astounded by Husserl's next book publication in 1913 (Husserl 1976), which "included some expressions which sounded very much as though their Master wished to return to idealism" (1986: 250), the controversy has been raging about whether the standpoint of transcendental-phenomenological idealism,[29] which Husserl already

---

[27] Sigwart 1889: 63, 67, cf. 70ff. (heavily annotated by Husserl). Compare, furthermore, the examples at Sigwart 1889: 26 and Husserl 2009: 34.

[28] 1976: 217ff. A research note from 1899 (2009: 138–9) recorded Husserl's difficulties in his isolated reading of Bolzano that in fact anticipate the distinction between "the specific essence of the judging process (the noetic idea) and the noematic idea correlative to the noetic idea" (1976: 218, n. 1, ET: 1982: 230, n. 38).

[29] For a concise exposition of the strong interpretation of Husserl's idealism, see Moran 2003.

demonstrably adopted in 1908 (cf. 2003b: 12ff.) and defended through the rest of his life (though with growing reservations about the label and its traditional connotations, cf. 1994b: VII, 16), amounted to Husserl's renouncing the initial realism of his *Logische Untersuchungen* or, rather, the Phenomenological Movement came into being merely due to a creative misunderstanding on the part of Husserl's readers. The appraisal of the merits of contemporaneous realist interpretations of Husserl adds a further complicating dimension to the historiographic controversies over Husserl's early phenomenology (cf. section 6.1). Lavigne (2005), e.g., believed that subjective idealism was already lurking in the *Logische Untersuchungen*; while Willard recently offered an informed defence of the thesis that, at least one possible reading suggests, Husserl "in fact never adopted idealism" (2012: 24). Zahavi rightly pointed to the way out from the dilemma: Husserl's "criticism of representationalism" in the *Logische Untersuchungen* can be seen as "a criticism of both realism and idealism" (to this extent, Husserl's early phenomenology could rightly be called metaphysically neutral); yet, "problems inherent in his descriptive phenomenology" forced Husserl "to adopt a transcendental standpoint" during the subsequent years (2002: 98, 102).[30] I believe that the relation between Husserl's philosophical beginnings and his mature transcendental phenomenology, which is ultimately at stake in reconstructing his early phenomenology (see section 6.1), could be characterized by the following three theses: (1) A realist reading of the *Logische Untersuchungen* is not consistent with Husserl's own intentions at the time of writing (as far as it is possible to establish them), even though it is compelling to read the book in such a way. (2) In the early phase of his philosophical career, Husserl *a fortiori* did not adopt a full-fledged philosophical position (as opposed to specific descriptive psychological and epistemological investigations, as Husserl described his enterprise in the bipartite subtitle of the second volume of the *Logische Untersuchungen*). As a corollary to these first two theses, Husserl's position in and around the *Logische Untersuchungen* could be called metaphysically neutral. (3) The transcendental-philosophical position he would already occupy in the latter half of the next decade represents a logically coherent, and maybe compelling, way to augment his specific investigations into a full-fledged philosophical position, i.e., to augment them with a philosophically reflected and justified methodology. This applies both to his understanding of his endeavor as a disciple that is merely characterized by its field of research and its method of research (i.e., along the lines of the famous collective announcement of the *Jahrbuch für Philosophie und phänomenologische Forschung*, see 1987a: 25), as well as to Husserl's mature attempt at establishing a system of transcendental-phenomenological philosophy.

---

[30] The historical fact that in July–August 1913 Husserl was forced to rewrite the fourth chapter of the Sixth Logical Investigation (2002a: 171ff.) in order to turn it "into an argument for a radical form of idealism regarding real being" (Melle 2002: 122) also speaks against the hypothesis that, from the outset, Husserl was committed to a full-fledged idealism (on the perspectives of the resulting flavor of transcendental idealism, see Bernet 2004). Moreover, the philological fact that Husserl started with piecemeal alterations to the old text he had believed could suffice to "raise" the *Logische Untersuchungen* "to the level of the latest stage of his philosophical thinking" (Melle 2002: 112) seems to confirm that the first edition was not yet meant to embody any full-fledged philosophical position.

Consequently, I believe that, to settle this issue in a satisfactory fashion, it is necessary to identify the elements and sources of Husserl's idea of philosophy (as opposed to his idea of mere phenomenology) and to examine the extent to which Husserl's phenomenology gradually assumed philosophical functions over time. Ultimately, it is only by virtue of the latter distinctions that the results of a historical-developmental reconstruction can be made consistent with Husserl's later autobiographical overgeneralizations about the origins of his mature phenomenology, e.g., with the following statement from 1935–6: "The first breakthrough of this universal a priori of correlation between experienced object and manners of givenness (which occurred during work on my *Logical Investigations* around 1898) affected me so deeply that my whole subsequent life-work has been dominated by the task of systematically elaborating on" it (1962: 169 n. 1, ET: 1970b: 166 n.).

References

Atten, M. van (2005), "Edmund Husserl, Logik. Vorlesung 1902/03 . . . ," *Husserl Studies* 21/2: 145–8.

Becker, O. (1930), "Die Philosophie Edmund Husserls," *Kant-Studien* 35: 119–50.

Beiser, F. C. (2014a), *After Hegel: German Philosophy 1840–1900* (Princeton, NJ: Princeton University Press).

Beiser, F. C. (2014b), *The Genesis of Neo-Kantianism, 1796–1880* (Oxford: Oxford University Press).

Bernet, R. (1981), "Logik und Phänomenologie in Husserls Lehre von der Wahrheit," *Tijdschrift voor Filosofie* 43/1: 35–89.

Bernet, R. (2003), "Desiring to Know through Intuition," *Husserl Studies* 19/2: 153–66.

Bernet, R. (2004), "Husserl's Transcendental Idealism Revisited," *New Yearbook for Phenomenology and Phenomenological Philosophy* 4: 1–20.

Biemel, W. (1959), "Die entscheidenden Phasen der Entfaltung von Husserls Philosophie," *Zeitschrift für philosophische Forschung* 13/2: 187–213.

Bolzano, B. (1837), *Wissenschaftslehre. Versuch einer ausführlichen und größtentheils neuen Darstellung der Logik mit steter Rücksicht auf deren bisherige Bearbeiter* (Sulzbach: Seidel)—In Husserl's library (BQ 46/1–4).

Bolzano, B. (2012), *Paradoxien des Unendlichen*, ed. C. Tapp (Hamburg: Meiner).

Brentano, F. (1874a), *Psychologie vom empirischen Standpunkte* (Lepzig: Duncker and Humblot)—In Husserl's library (BQ 60).

Brentano, F. (1874b), *Ueber die Gründe der Entmuthigung auf philosophischem Gebiete . . .* (Vienna: Wilhelm Braumüller).

Brentano, F. (1946), "Briefe Franz Brentanos an Hugo Bergmann," ed. H. Bergmann, in *Philosophy and Phenomenological Research* 7/1: 83–158.

Brentano, F. and Stumpf, C. (2014), *Briefwechsel 1867–1917*, ed. M. Kaiser-el-Safti (Frankfurt a. M.: Peter Lang).

Brück, M. (1933), *Über das Verhältnis Edmund Husserls zu Franz Brentano . . .* (Bonn: Rheinische Friedrich-Wilhelms-Universität Bonn).

Centrone, S. (2010), *Logic and Philosophy of Mathematics in the Early Husserl* (Dordrecht: Springer).

Daubert, J. (2002), "Bemerkungen zur Psychologie der Apperzeption und des Urteils," ed. K. Schuhmann, in *New Yearbook for Phenomenology and Phenomenological Philosophy* 2: 344–65.

Embree, L. (1998), "Phenomenological movement," in E. Craig (ed.), *Routledge Encyclopaedia of Philosophy, Vol. 7* (London: Routledge), 333–43.

Fabian, R. (1986), "Leben und Wirken von Christian v. Ehrenfels. Ein Beitrag zur intellektuellen Biographie," in R. Fabian (ed.), *Christian von Ehrenfels: Leben und Werk* (Amsterdam: Rodopi), 1–64.

Farber, M. (1940), "Edmund Husserl and the Background of his Philosophy," *Philosophy and Phenomenological Research* 1/1: 1–20.

Fréchette, G. (2015), "Stumpf on abstraction," in R. Martinelli and D. Fisette (eds), *Philosophy from an Empirical Standpoint: Essays on Carl Stumpf* (Leiden: Brill), 263–92.

Frege, G. (1894), "Dr. E. G. Husserl: Philosophie der Arithmetik . . . ," *Zeitschrift für Philosophie und philosophische Kritik* 103/2: 313–32.

Frege, G. (1972), "Review of Dr. E. Husserl's Philosophy of Arithmetic," translated by E. W. Kluge, *Mind* 81/323: 321–37.

Gerlach, H.-M. and Sepp, H. R. (eds) (1994), *Husserl in Halle. Spurensuche im Anfang der Phänomenologie* (Frankfurt a. M.: Peter Lang).

Haller, R. (1979), *Studien zur österreichischen Philosophie. Variationen über ein Thema* (Amsterdam: Rodopi).

Hartimo, M. H. (2007), "Towards Completeness: Husserl on Theories of Manifolds 1890–1901," *Synthese* 156/2: 281–310.

Heffernan, G. (1983), *Bedeutung und Evidenz. Das Verhältniss zwischen der Bedeutungs- und der Evidenztheorie in den "Logischen Untersuchungen" und der "Formalen und transzendentalen Logik". Ein Vergleich anhand der Identitätsproblematik* (Bonn: Bouvier).

Heffernan, G. (2015), "The Paradox of Objectless Presentations in Early Phenomenology: A Brief History of the Intentional Object from Bolzano to Husserl, with Concise Analyses of the Positions of Brentano, Frege, Twardowski, and Meinong," *Studia Phaenomenologica* 15: 67–91.

Heidegger, M. (1985), *History of the Concept of Time: Prolegomena*, translated by T. Kisiel (Bloomington, IN: Indiana University Press).

Heinze, M. (1897), *Friedrich Ueberwegs Grundriss der Geschichte der Philosophie der Neuzeit von dem Aufblühen der Althethumsstudien bis auf die Gegenwart. Zweiter Band: Nachkantische Systeme und Philosophie der Gegenwart*, 8th edition (Berlin: Ernst Siegfried Mittler und Sohn).

Heinze, M. (1902), *Friedrich Ueberwegs Grundriss der Geschichte der Philosophie. Vierter Theil. Das neunzehnte Jahrhundert*, 9th edition (Berlin: Ernst Siegfried Mittler und Sohn).

Höfler, A. (1884), *Zur Propädeutik-Frage* (Vienna: Verlag der Theresianischen Akademie).

Höfler, A. (1890), *Philosophische Propädeutik. Logik* (Vienna: F. Tempsky)—In Husserl's library (BQ 193).

Holzhey, H. (ed.) (1986), *Der Marburger Neukantianismus in Quellen: Zeugnisse kritischer Lektüre, Briefe der Marburger, Dokumente zur Philosophiepolitik der Schule* (Basel: Schwabe).

Husserl, E. (1887), *Über den Begriff der Zahl. Psychologische Analysen* (Halle: Heynemann).

Husserl, E. (1962), *Die Krisis der europäischen Wissenschaften und die transzendentale Phänomenologie. Eine Einleitung in die phänomenologische Philosophie*, 2nd edition, ed. W. Biemel, Husserliana 6 (The Hague: Martinus Nijhoff).

Husserl, E. (1970a), *Philosophie der Arithmetik mit ergänzenden Texten (1890–1901)*, ed. L. Eley, Husserliana 12 (The Hague: Martinus Nijhoff).

Husserl, E. (1970b), *The Crisis of European Sciences and Transcendental Phenomenology*, translated by D. Carr, Studies in Phenomenology and Existential Philosophy (Evanston, IL: Northwestern University Press).

Husserl, E. (1973), *Ding und Raum. Vorlesungen 1907*, ed. U. Claesges, Husserliana 16 (The Hague: Martinus Nijhoff).

Husserl, E. (1974), *Formale und transzendentale Logik. Versuch eine Kritik der logischen Vernunft*, ed. P. Janssen, Husserliana 17 (The Hague: Martinus Nijhoff).

Husserl, E. (1975), *Logische Untersuchungen. Erster Band: Prolegomena zur reinen Logik. Text der 1. und 2. Auflage*, ed. E. Holenstein, Husserliana 18 (The Hague: Martinus Nijhoff).

Husserl, E. (1976), *Ideen zu einer reinen Phänomenologie und phänomenologische Philosophie. Erstes Buch. Allgemeine Einführung in die reine Phänomenologie. 1. Halbband*, ed. K. Schuhmann, Husserliana 3/1 (The Hague: Martinus Nijhoff).

Husserl, E. (1979), *Aufsätze und Rezensionen (1890–1910)*, ed. B. Rang, Husserliana 22 (The Hague: Martinus Nijhoff).

Husserl, E. (1982), *Ideas Pertaining to a Pure Phenomenology and to a Phenomenological Philosophy. First Book: General Introduction to a Pure Phenomenology*, translated by F. Kersten, Edmund Husserl—Collected Works: 2 (The Hague: Martinus Nijhoff).

Husserl, E. (1983), *Studien zur Arithmetik und Geometrie: Texte aus dem Nachlass (1886–1901)*, ed. I. Strohmeyer, Husserliana 21 (The Hague: Martinus Nijhoff).

Husserl, E. (1984a), *Logische Untersuchungen. Zweiter Band. Erster Teil. Untersuchungen zur Phämenologie und Theorie der Erkenntnis*, ed. U. Panzer, Husserliana 19/1 (The Hague: Martinus Nijhoff (Kluwer)).

Husserl, E. (1984b), *Logische Untersuchungen. Zweiter Band. Zweiter Teil. Untersuchungen zur Phänomenologie und Theorie der Erkenntnis*, ed. U. Panzer, Husserliana 19/2 (The Hague: Martinus Nijhoff (Kluwer)).

Husserl, E. (1984c), *Einleitung in die Logik und Erkenntnistheorie. Vorlesungen 1906/07*, ed. U. Melle, Husserliana 24 (Dordrecht: Martinus Nijhoff (Kluwer)).

Husserl, E. (1987a), *Aufsätze und Vorträge (1911–1921)*, ed. T. Nenon and H. R. Sepp, Husserliana 25 (Dordrecht Martinus Nijhoff (Kluwer)).

Husserl, E. (1987b), *Vorlesungen über Bedeutungslehre Sommersemester 1908*, ed. U. Panzer, Husserliana 26 (Dordrecht: Martinus Nijhoff (Kluwer)).

Husserl, E. (1990), "Husserls Abhandlung 'Intentionale Gegenstände'. Edition der ursprünglichen Druckfassung," ed. K. Schuhmann in *Brentano Studien* 3: 137–76.

Husserl, E. (1994a), *Early Writings in the Philosophy of Logic and Mathematics*, ed. D. Willard, Edmund Husserl—Collected Works: 5 (Dordrecht: Kluwer).

Husserl, E. (1994b), *Briefwechsel*, ed. K. Schuhmann and E. Schuhmann, Husserliana Dokumente: 3 (Dordrecht: Kluwer).

Husserl, E. (1996), *Logik und allgemeine Wissenschaftstheorie. Vorlesungen 1917–19 mit ergänzenden Texten aus der ersten Fassung von 1910–11*, ed. U. Panzer, Husserliana 30 (Dordrecht: Kluwer).

Husserl, E. (2001a), *Logik. Vorlesung 1896*, ed. E. Schuhmann, Husserliana Materialien 1 (Dordrecht: Kluwer).

Husserl, E. (2001b), "Husserls Manuskripte zu seinem Göttinger Doppelvortrag von 1901," ed. E. Schuhmann and K. Schuhmann, in *Husserl Studies* 17/2: 87–123.

Husserl, E. (2001c), *Logical Investigations*, ed. D. Moran, translated by J. N. Findlay (London: Routledge).

Husserl, E. (2002a), *Logische Untersuchungen. Ergänzungsband. Erster Teil. Entwürfe zur Umarbeitung der VI. Untersuchung und zur Vorrede für die Neuauflage der Logischen Untersuchungen (Sommer 1913)*, ed. U. Melle, Husserliana 20/1 (Dordrecht: Kluwer).

Husserl, E. (2002b), "Über die psychologische Begründung der Logik," ed. K. Schuhmann, in *New Yearbook for Phenomenology and Phenomenological Philosophy* 2: 302–33.

Husserl, E. (2003a), *Philosophy of Arithmetic: Psychological and Logical Investigations with Supplementary Texts from 1887–1901*, ed. D. Willard, Edmund Husserl—Collected Works: 10 (Dordrecht: Kluwer).

Husserl, E. (2003b), *Transzendentaler Idealismus. Texte aus dem Nachlass (1908–1921)*, ed. R. D. Rollinger and R. Sowa, Husserliana 36 (Dordrecht: Kluwer).

Husserl, E. (2004), *Wahrnehmung und Aufmerksamkeit. Texte aus dem Nachlass (1893–1912)*, ed. T. Vongehr and R. Giuliani, Husserliana 38 (Dordrecht: Kluwer).

Husserl, E. (2005a), *Logische Untersuchungen. Ergänzungsband. Zweiter Teil. Texte für die Neufassung der VI. Untersuchung. Zur Phänomenologie des Ausdrucks und der Erkenntnis (1893/94–1921)*, ed. U. Melle, Husserliana 20/2 (Dordrecht: Kluwer).

Husserl, E. (2005b), "Vorlesung Über den Begriff der Zahl (WS 1889/90)," ed. C. Ierna, in *New Yearbook for Phenomenology and Phenomenological Philosophy* 5: 279–308.

Husserl, E. (2009), *Untersuchungen zur Urteilstheorie. Texte aus dem Nachlass (1893–1918)*, ed. R. D. Rollinger, Husserliana 40 (Dordrecht: Springer).

Husserl, E. (2011a), "Der Durchgang durch das Unmögliche: An Unpublished Manuscript from the Husserl-Archives," ed. C. Ierna, in *Husserl Studies* 27/3: 217–26.

Husserl, E. (2011b), "Einiges über Aufgabe und historische Stellung der 'Logischen Untersuchungen,'" ed. L. Landgrebe and J. Bell, in *Journal of Speculative Philosophy* 25/3: 266–304.

Husserl, E. (2012), *Zur Lehre vom Wesen und zur Methode der eidetischen Variation. Texte aus dem Nachlass (1891–1935)*, ed. D. Fonfara, Husserliana 41 (Dordrecht: Springer).

Ierna, C. (2005), "The Beginnings of Husserl's Philosophy, Part 1: From *Über den Begriff der Zahl* to *Philosophie der Arithmetik*," *New Yearbook for Phenomenology and Phenomenological Philosophy* 5: 1–56.

Ierna, C. (2009), "Relations in the Early Works of Meinong and Husserl," *Meinong Studien* 3: 7–36.

Illemann, W. (1932), *Die vor-phänomenologische Philosophie Edmund Husserls und ihre Bedeutung für die phänomenologische* (Leipzig: Universität Leipzig)—In Husserl's library (BP 103).

Köhnke, K. C. (1986), *Entstehung und Aufstieg des Neukantianismus. Die deutsche Universitätsphilosophie zwischen Idealismus und Positivismus* (Frankfurt a. M.: Suhrkamp).

Kraus, O. (1919), *Franz Brentano. Zur Kenntnis seines Lebens und seiner Lehre. Mit Beiträgen von Carl Stumpf und Edmund Husserl* (Munich: C. H. Beck).

Künne, W. (1997), "'Die Ernte wird erscheinen . . .' Die Geschichte der Bolzano-Rezeption (1849–1939)," in H. Ganthaler and O. Neumaier (eds), *Bolzano und die österreichische Geistesgeschichte* (Sankt Augustin: Academia), 9–82.

Künne, W. (2011), "'Denken ist immer Etwas Denken.' Bolzano und (der frühe) Husserl über Intentionalität," in K. Cramer and C. Beyer (eds), *Edmund Husserl 1859–2009. Beiträge aus Anlass der 150. Wiederkehr des Geburtstages des Philosophen* (Berlin: de Gruyter), 77–99.

Lavigne, J.-F. (2005), *Husserl et la naissance de la phénoménologie (1900–1913). Des "Recherches logiques" aux "Ideen": la genèse de l'idéalisme transcendantal phénoménologique* (Paris: Presses universitaires de France).

Levinas, E. (1998), *Discovering Existence with Husserl*, translated by R. A. Cohen and M. B. Smith (Evanston, IL: Northwestern University Press).

Lindner, G. A. (1872), *Lehrbuch der formalen Logik*, 3rd edition (Vienna: Carl Gerold's Sohn).

Lohmar, D. (1998), *Erfahrung und kategoriales Denken. Hume, Kant und Husserl über vorprädikative Erfahrung und prädikative Erkenntnis* (Dordrecht: Kluwer).

Lohmar, D. (2011), "Zur Vorgeschichte der transzendentalen Reduktion in den Logischen Untersuchungen. Die unbekannte 'Reduktion auf den reellen Bestand,'" *Husserl Studies* 28/1: 1–24.

Luft, S. (2012), "Von der mannigfaltigen Bedeutung der Reduktion nach Husserl. Reflexionen zur Grundbedeutung des zentralen Begriffs der transzendentalen Phänomenologie," *Phänomenologische Forschungen (N. F.)* 2012: 5–29.

Melle, U. (1990), "Objektivierende und nicht-objektivierende Akte," in S. IJsseling (ed.), *Husserl-Ausgabe und Husserl-Forschung* (Dordrecht: Springer), 35–49.

Melle, U. (2002), "Husserl's revision of the Sixth Logical Investigation," in D. Zahavi and F. Stjernfelt (eds), *One Hundred Years of Phenomenology: Husserl's Logical Investigations Revisited* (Dordrecht: Kluwer), 111–23.

Michaltschew, D. (1909), *Beiträge zur Kritik des modernen Psychologismus* (Leipzig: Wilhelm Engelmann)—In Husserl's library (BA 1180).

Mohanty, J. N. (1982), *Husserl and Frege* (Bloomington, IN: Indiana University Press).

Moran, D. (2003), "Making sense: Husserl's phenomenology as transcendental idealism," in J. Malpas (ed.), *From Kant to Davidson: Philosophy and the Idea of the Transcendental* (London: Routledge), 48–74.

Nelson, L. (1908), *Über das sogenannte Erkenntnisproblem* (Göttingen: Vandenhoeck und Ruprecht).

Ortiz Hill, C. and Rosado Haddock, G. E. (2000), *Husserl or Frege? Meaning, Objectivity, and Mathematics* (Chicago, IL: Open Court).

Osborn, A. D. (1934), *The Philosophy of Edmund Husserl: In its Development from his Mathematical Interests to his First Conception of Phenomenology in Logical Investigations* (New York: Columbia University)—In Husserl's library (BP 190).

Purkert, W. and Ilgauds, H. J. (1987), *Georg Cantor 1845–1918* (Basel: Birkhäuser).

Reinach, A. (1911), "Zur Theorie des negativen Urteils," in *Münchener Philosophische Abhandlungen. Theodor Lipps zu seinem sechzigsten Geburtstag gewidmet von früheren Schülern* (Leipzig: Barth), 196–254.

Rollinger, R. D. (1993), *Meinong and Husserl on Abstraction and Universals*: From Hume Studies I to Logical Investigations II (Amsterdam: Rodopi).

Rollinger, R. D. (1999), *Husserl's Position in the School of Brentano* (Dordrecht: Kluwer).

Rollinger, R. D. (2008), *Austrian Phenomenology: Brentano, Husserl, Meinong, and Others on Mind and Object* (Frankfurt a. M.: Ontos).

Sakakibara, T. (1997), "Das Problem des Ich und der Ursprung der genetischen Phänemologie bei Husserl," *Husserl Studies* 14/1: 21–39.

Schuhmann, K. (1977), *Husserl-Chronik. Denk- und Lebensweg Edmund Husserls*, Husserliana Dokumente: 1 (The Hague: Martinus Nijhoff).

Schuhmann, K. (2000), "Stumpfs Vorstelllungsbegriff in seiner Hallenser Zeit," *Brentano Studien* 9: 63–88.

Schuhmann, K. (2004), *Selected Papers on Phenomenology*, ed. C. Leijenhorst and P. Steenbakkers (Dordrecht: Kluwer).

Sigwart, C. (1889), *Logik. Erster Band. Die Lehre vom Urtheil, vom Begriff und vom Schluss*, 2nd edition (J. C. B. Mohr (Paul Siebeck))—In Husserl's library (BQ 439/1).

Sokolowski, R. (1970), *The Formation of Husserl's Concept of Constitution* (The Hague: Martinus Nijhoff).

Stein, E. (1986), *Life in a Jewish Family*, translated by J. Koeppel (Washington, DC: ICS Publications).

Stumpf, C. (1873), *Über den psychologischen Ursprung der Raumvorstellung* (Leipzig: S. Hirzel)—In Husserl's library (BQ 473).

Stumpf, C. (1907), *Erscheinungen und psychische Funktionen* (Berlin: Verlag der Königl. Akademie der Wissenschaften)—In Husserl's library (BQ 463).

Stumpf, C. (2015), "Metaphysik. Vorlesung," in D. Fisette et al. (eds), *Philosophy from an Empirical Standpoint: Essays on Carl Stumpf* (Leiden: Brill), 443–72.

Trendelenburg, A. (1870), *Logische Untersuchungen*, 3rd edition (Leipzig: S. Hirzel)—In Husserl's library (BQ 479/1–2).

Twardowski, K. (1894), *Zur Lehre vom Inhalt und Gegenstand der Vorstellungen. Eine psychologische Untersuchung* (Vienna: Alfred Hölder)—In Husserl's library (BQ 482).

Ueberweg, F. (1882), *System der Logik und Geschichte der logischen Lehren*, 5th edition, ed. J. Bona Meyer (Bonn: Adolph Marcus)—In Husserl's library (BQ 485).

Varga, P. A. (2013), "The Missing Chapter from the Logical Investigations: Husserl on Lotze's Formal and Real Significance of Logical Laws," *Husserl Studies* 29/3: 181–209.

Varga, P. A. (2014), "Die Einflüsse der Brentanoschen Intentionalitätskonzeptionen auf den frühen Husserl. Zur Widerlegung einer Legende," *Phänomenologische Forschungen (N.F.)* 2014: 83–116.

Varga, P. A. (2015), "Was hat Husserl in Wien außerhalb von Brentanos Philosophie gelernt? Über die Einflüsse auf den frühen Husserl jenseits von Brentano und Bolzano," *Husserl Studies* 31/2: 95–121.

Willard, D. (1984), *Logic and the Objectivity of Knowledge: A Study in Husserl's Early Philosophy* (Athens, OH: Ohio University Press).

Willard, D. (2012), "Realism Sustained? Interpreting Husserl's Progression into Idealism," *Quaestiones Disputatae* 3/1: 20–32.

Wundt, W. (1880), *Grundzüge der physiologischen Psychologie. Zweiter Band*, 2nd edition (Leipzig: Wilhelm Engelmann).

Zahavi, D. (1992), *Intentionalität und Konstitution. Eine Einführung in Husserls Logische Untersuchungen* (Copenhagen: Museum Tusculanum Press).

Zahavi, D. (2002), "Metaphysical neutrality in Logical Investigations," in D. Zahavi and F. Stjernfelt (eds), *One Hundred Years of Phenomenology: Husserl's Logical Investigations Revisited* (Dordrecht: Kluwer), 93–108.

CHAPTER 7

HUSSERL'S MIDDLE PERIOD AND THE DEVELOPMENT OF HIS ETHICS

JOHN J. DRUMMOND

7.1 INTRODUCTION

THE periodization of Husserl's thought is a thorny issue. Three periods are often identified: (1) the early Husserl of the mathematical writings and the *Logische Untersuchungen* (Husserl [1900] 1984/1970b);[1,2] (2) the middle Husserl of the transcendental turn, a period beginning somewhere around 1907 (Husserl 1973a/1999) and notable for the publication of *Ideas I* (Husserl [1913] 1976/1983) and work on the texts gathered in *Ideas II* (Husserl [1912–28] 1952/1989a); and (3) a late Husserl in which he moves beyond a purely "static" phenomenology to "genetic" phenomenology, a period during which problems centered around the genesis of sense or meaning, around time and history, intersubjectivity, and tradition received special attention (see, e.g., Sokolowski 1970; Welton 2000; Zahavi 2003). There are merits to such distinctions, but they should be balanced by what I take to be clear continuity in Husserl's development (see Drummond 2002; 2009).

What is clear is that the so-called middle period encompasses the most important shift in Husserl's thinking, namely, the transcendental turn to the phenomenological attitude that is contrasted with the natural attitude embedded in our non-philosophical experiences. This transcendental turn immediately changes the framework for considering Husserl's relation to the Kantian tradition, including how it was transmitted

---

[1] I am grateful to an anonymous referee for helpful comments.

[2] When referring to German works, I include in square brackets the date(s) of composition, if not included in the title of the work, followed by the date of publication. If an English translation exists, the reference to it, separated by a forward slash, immediately follows the reference to the German edition.

through German Idealism, and to the neo-Kantians of his day. Many questions—in particular, questions concerning the transcendental ego, the relation of the transcendental ego to the worldly ego, transcendental intersubjectivity, and the methodology of transcendental philosophy and its relation to metaphysics—come to the fore in the differing views of various neo-Kantians and Husserl. Since this volume contains chapters examining Husserl's relation to both neo-Kantianism and German Idealism, I shall not discuss those relations here.

The so-called middle period, however, also finds Husserl in *Ideas II* drawing a distinction within the natural attitude between the naturalistic and personalistic attitudes. The personalistic attitude, Husserl says, is:

> The attitude we are always in when we live with one another, talk to one another, shake hands with one another in greeting, or are related to one another in love and aversion, in disposition and action, in discourse and discussion. Likewise, we are in this attitude when we consider the things surrounding us precisely as our surroundings and not as "objective" nature, the way it is for natural science. (Husserl [1912–28]: 183/1989a: 192)

This distinction problematizes both the conception of nature (see Crowell 1996) and the conception of the ego. How are we in the light of this distinction to understand the relation between the transcendental ego and the personal ego, the person as worldly ego constitutively prior to nature?

The issue is further complicated by the fact that this middle period—centered around the Great War—also marks an important shift in Husserl's ethical thought. Undoubtedly, there are both personal and cultural reasons for the shift. Husserl's mother died in July of 1917. His older son Gerhart was seriously wounded in the war, and his younger son Wolfgang was killed in the Battle of Verdun. Husserl's letters reveal his dismay and sadness at the loss of life in the war and the serious injuries suffered by so many, not only his sons but friends, acquaintances, and students. He was greatly affected, for example, by the death in 1917 of his student Adolf Reinach, of whom he thought most highly as a teacher and phenomenologist. The war, for Husserl, was a symptom of "the dreadfully advancing sickness of the German soul" (Husserl 1994: III, 5), a crisis that the German soul could survive only by way of an ethical renewal, first of the individual and then of the nation (see Melle 1991: 117; 2002: 242).

There are, however, also fundamental philosophical reasons behind this shift. Husserl's shift from an idealized consequentialism inherited from Brentano to a personalistic ethics is roughly contemporaneous with his reflections in *Ideas II* on the nature of the person. The change in Husserl's ethical views, while motivated by ethical considerations, touches upon issues surrounding his account of the transcendental ego and its relation to the worldly, personal ego. It also raises metaphysical issues that Husserl considered late in his career, issues that are problematic in their relation to phenomenology. The change in his ethical views, therefore, provides a window through which to view some issues at the heart of Husserl's thinking, a thinking that was driven throughout by a moral urgency toward self-responsible, rational agency. This chapter will examine that change.

7.2 HUSSERL'S EARLY ETHICAL THOUGHT

Husserl devotes the fourth section of *Ideas I* to a phenomenology of reason and identifies two senses of the term "reason." The first refers to direct, intuitive evidence, that is, the direct grasp of an object that is present to a clear and attentive mind. This is what ultimately secures the truthfulness of experience: The *adequatio rei et intellectus* manifests itself as the identity between the object as emptily intended and the object as intuitively presented. This notion of reason is more basic than the second sense of "reason," i.e., reasoning construed broadly enough to include (1) making judgments, which are ultimately grounded or to be grounded in evidential reason, and (2) fashioning arguments of the sort evaluated by Husserl's various "logics." The argumentative dimension of reasoning involves, in other words, providing reasons for our beliefs, justifying a conclusion on the basis of premises (for which we have either supporting reasons or direct evidence), and thereby invoking logical rules of argumentation. We are fully rational insofar as we possess justifying reasons for our beliefs, which justifying reasons are themselves "evidenced" in the kind of intuition appropriate to the kind of experience to be evidenced (Drummond 2015).

In addition to distinguishing two *senses* of "reason," Husserl distinguishes three *kinds* of reason: cognitive/theoretical, axiological, and practical. He sees the three kinds of reason as "intertwined" and characterizes this intertwining in foundational terms drawn, although in a revised form, from Brentano (Husserl [1913] 1976: 323–24/ 1983: 335). The distinction among the different kinds of reason in conjunction with the distinction in the senses of "reason" entails that in each domain of reason there is a distinction between the evidencing reason proper to that domain and the logical structure of propositions and arguments belonging to it. And this is precisely the view that Husserl takes. He speaks, for example, of an "axiological intuition" (Husserl [1912–28] 1952: 9/1989a: 10; cf. Husserl [1913] 1976: 323/1983: 335) comparable to perception (if the value-judgment is not yet formulated) or categorial intuition (if the value-judgment is articulated).

The intertwining of the different kinds of reason is of crucial importance. We must understand how ends, actions, and agents are valued, and this is a question for axiology. But we must also understand how we make decisions to act in a particular way, and this is a matter for practical reason. Given the two senses of reason, then, we must have an account of axiological intuition as well as a formal account of axiological reasoning and its rules—a formal axiology—and an account of practical reasoning and its rules—a formal praxiology. And we must understand how our decision-making is related to our experience of value, our experience of things as good or bad. This is what we find in Husserl's early ethics.

Husserl's early lecture courses in ethics present a view of ethics as a thoroughly rational and objective discipline comparable in its rigor and universality to logic. Ethics, as he conceives it, is a pure discipline that preserves the absolute, a priori validity of moral laws. I shall briefly outline, first, his view of the experience of value and, second, his account of the disciplines of formal axiology and formal praxiology.

7.2.1 Feeling-apprehension and value

The valuable properties of things, according to Husserl, are disclosed by intentional feelings or emotions involving intentional feelings. The experience of valued things, of objects *qua* good, *qua* likable and desirable, is founded, according to Husserl, on the purely cognitive (e.g., perceptual or judgmental) experience of the natural, material, or, as Husserl calls them, "logical properties" of objects apart from any subject-relative value-attributes or functional features. Husserl believes (1) that objects can be presented in such purely cognitive experiences, and (2) that such experiences serve as the basis for intentional feeling-acts (Husserl 1988: 252–3). It is possible, he thinks, to conceive of cognitive experiences completely divorced from the emotions and feelings. I might simply notice things in the visual field, attend to their color, and register them as stones, grass, trees, or organisms. Indeed, at one extreme, the theoretical sciences pride themselves on their separation from the domain of feeling and emotion and their pursuit of a "pure" theoretical truth.[3] In ordinary experience, however, objects affect us in such a way that we value them positively or negatively (or, in some cases, neutrally). While we can strip away the affective dimension of the experience and attain something purely cognitive, we cannot strip away the cognitive and attain a "pure" intentional feeling without cognitive content. Pleasure or displeasure, for example, is always taken in something that is presented in the kind of pure cognition that Husserl calls an "objectifying act," usually a perception or a judgment (Husserl [1900] 1984: 498, 500–1/1970b: 637, 639).

It is an essential feature of our evaluative experiences, then, that the feelings and emotions combine with cognition in presenting objects *qua* valuable by virtue of having certain natural properties. The experience of the object as valuable (1) necessarily presupposes the cognitive apprehension of the object and (2) necessarily involves a moment of intentional feeling that is grounded in the cognitive experience of the object (cf. Husserl [1912–28] 1952: 8–11/1989a: 10–13). While we can say, from the perspective of the object, that the value-predicates in our attributions of value to the object are

---

[3] While such purely cognitive experiences are existential possibilities, our ordinary, everyday experiences are seldom of this unmixed, purely cognitive character. As Husserl recognizes in his descriptions of the natural attitude (Husserl [1913] 1976: 58/1983: 53) and of the personalistic attitude (Husserl [1912–28] 1952: 183/1989a: 192–3), our ordinary experiences are *from the beginning* infused with affective and practical dimensions that at least in part determine the sense of our immediately surrounding world. Indeed, even our simple perception of objects is governed by practical interests which lead us to explore the object in particular ways and to a determinate degree (Husserl 1973b: 123–38; cf. Drummond 1983: 182–3).

founded on that object's "logical" predicates, this relation is a function of the founding relation between the objectifying act and the intentional feeling.[4] The value-attributes so predicated are the correlates specifically of the moment of intentional feeling belonging to the concrete valuing act.[5]

7.2.2 Formal axiology and praxiology

When the feeling or emotion is appropriate to the non-axiological features of the object (see Drummond 2017: 154–61), the first sense of axiological reason is achieved. We have the valued object—the good that is valued—directly and truthfully present to mind. The second sense of axiological reason has to do with the rules that govern the relations and combinations of axiological senses, and the second sense of practical reason has to do with the combination of practical meanings. Husserl considers formal axiology and formal praxiology as analogous to formal logic (Husserl 1988: 36ff.). There must be something like a logical analytic that organizes these axiological and practical judgments into consistent wholes (Husserl 1988: 37).

Husserl's accounts both of valuation and of formal axiology and praxiology make evident the rationalism of his ethics. In tying evaluation to intentional feelings, he rejects purely rationalist accounts, but he also avoids the other extreme typical of British sentimentalism. The rationalist emphasis in Husserl's thought is not so much tied to the claim that reason is the *source* of our ethical judgments and their normativity as it is tied to the views (1) that our ethical judgments are tied to the intuitive (rational) *evidence* of objective, axiological and practical truths and (2) that the laws governing our axiological and ethical reasoning are a priori laws. Ethical norms are grounded in a theoretical science whose claims about the rules governing the contents of moral thinking are necessary and universal.

---

[4] I have argued elsewhere that Husserl should have abandoned the account of the foundation of feeling-acts or emotive *experiences* on cognitive *experiences* in favor of an account of the founding of an affective or evaluative *sense* on a purely cognitive *sense* (most recently, Drummond 2013). Husserl moves toward this view in his discussion of value-predicates as founded on logical predicates. However, he does not, in my view, go far enough, since he could preserve the originality of the ordinary, everyday, mixed experience while still preserving the view that an evaluative sense—something presenting itself as valuable—presupposes an object presenting itself as having a set of non-axiological properties in which the value of the object is rooted. Instead, he perseveres in the view that the cognitive *experience*, rather than the cognitive *sense*, is foundational, and that the foundation relations in the sense are a function of the founding relations in the experience.

[5] This sketch is based on Husserl's lectures on the fundamental problems of ethics from 1908–9 in Husserl 1988. Other lectures are included in the same volume, and there are many other pre-war writings on these themes, both published and unpublished. Many of the unpublished research manuscripts will appear in the forthcoming Husserliana volume *Verstand, Gemüt und Wille: Studien zur Struktur des Bewusstseins*. I have surveyed a number of these manuscripts, and, although they add much detail, I do not find anything that conflicts with this sketch. Moreover, the change on which I am focusing relates more directly to Husserl's notions of formal axiology and praxiology.

His rationalism manifests itself in another inheritance from Brentano: an idealized consequentialism. We need consider only a few of the laws of formal axiology and praxiology to recognize this. Central to Husserl's ethics from this period is what he refers to as "the highest formal principle" (Husserl 1988: 221) of formal praxiology. This principle is the categorical imperative—not the Kantian imperative, but the imperative inherited from Brentano: "Do what is best among what is achievable" (Husserl 1988: 221). This imperative differs from the Kantian one insofar as it refers both to the material content of our evaluations ("the best") and to the situation in which one is confronted by "achievable" alternatives. Husserl thinks this subjective formulation of the imperative is provisional and offers an objective restatement: "What is best among what is achievable in the entire practical sphere is not only comparatively the best, but the sole practical good" (Husserl 1988: 221). This imperative is grounded in the axiological principle that "the better is the enemy of the good" (Husserl 1988: 221). Other laws Husserl identifies also state consequentialist principles. Chief among them are:

1. Laws of the summation of goods: "the existence of a good alone is better than the simultaneous existence of a good and a bad" $[G > (G + B)]$, and "the existence of a good and a bad at the same time is better than the existence of a bad alone" $[(G + B) > B]$, and "the existence of two random goods together is better than the existence of one of them alone" $\{[(G_1 + G_2) > G_1]$ and $[(G_1 + G_2) > G_2]\}$ (Husserl 1988: 93–4), and "for every summative composite of values, the sum of goods is better than an individual good belonging to the summation or any reduction of it" [e.g., $[(G_1,G_2 \ldots G_n) > G_2]$ and $\{(G_1,G_2 \ldots G_n) > [(G_1,G_2 \ldots G_n)–G_2]\}]$ (Husserl 1988: 97), and so on; and
2. The law of absorption: "Consider a willing subject faced with a choice between practical possibilities in which the positive values G_1 and G_2 might be realized. If $G_1 < G_2$, then the decision in favor of G_1 alone is not only worse than the decision in favor of G_2 alone, but is bad in itself; putting aside what is better and preferring what is worse, taken together, are wrong, and the choice is thus to be judged as bad" (Husserl 1988: 130); "In every choice, the better absorbs the good, and the best absorbs everything else that is to be valued as a practical good in and of itself" (Husserl 1988: 136).

These laws, taken together with the Husserlian categorical imperative, clearly entail a consequentialism concerned with acting in all cases for the greatest summative good.

7.3 GEIGER'S OBJECTION AND THE CRITIQUE OF CONSEQUENTIALISM

A standard objection to consequentialism is that following a principle that requires us to achieve the highest good for the aggregate will on occasion require that we act in ways that violate our integrity, our sense of who we are and, more specifically, the commitments that define us as who we are (see Smart and Williams 1973: 82, 98–100, 108ff.). As early as 1909 (although he later remembers it as 1907), Husserl considered such an objection, raised by Geiger, against the laws of the summation of goods (Husserl 1988: 419–22). Geiger objected that not all values are comparable such that they can be summed in a simple calculation, thereby calling into question Brentano's—and Husserl's and consequentialism's—notions of a highest practical good (Husserl 1988: 419).

By 1914, Husserl had more clearly realized the force of Geiger's objection when he appeals to the example of the mother who is faced with the choice of rescuing her child or another person, even one the mother is convinced is an exceptional person. Must one not admit, he asks, that the mother has a duty to rescue her child and that she not even need ponder whether to rescue the other person before her child (Husserl 1988: 420–1)? Nevertheless, Husserl seems conflicted still. He wonders, for example, about the case in which the stranger is a person on whom the fate of entire nation might depend or, even more dramatically, the case wherein the stranger is a Christ who seems destined to redeem humankind and whose rescue would elevate all humans (Husserl 1988: 422).

By the time he delivers his lecture course titled "Introduction to Philosophy" in 1919–20, Husserl, again referring to Geiger's objection, declares, "I shall have to abandon the entire theory of the categorical imperative, or circumscribe it anew" (Husserl 2012: 132n.) and, a bit later, "It is clear that an ethics realized merely on the basis of the categorical imperative, as, following Brentano, has here been laid down as that basis, is no ethics at all" (Husserl 2012: 146n.). Husserl now distinguishes between objective value that any axiologically rational person, when presented with the same factual bases, can grasp as a value, and that same objective value considered as an "individual, subjective value of love" (Husserl 2012: 146n.). The idea is that:

> The same value can be infinitely more "significant" for one person than another. This being-more-significant is initially to be considered in relation to values associated with mere affection. One does not merely appreciate something; one has a passion for it; one irrationally "falls in love" or the like. But one will not fail also to recognize a pure and "authentic love," which is not only the taking as valuable [*Wertnehmen*] a value one beholds, but deciding—indeed, lovingly deciding—in favor of it, a decision that originates in the innermost center of the ego. One must then further say that what is loved takes on a new value-character originating from the relevant ego, which value-character evidently belongs to the objective value insofar as it can be evidently encountered by the lover, but it belongs to it only for this ego. (Husserl 2012: 146n.)

In the same vein, in a text probably from the first half of the 1920s, Husserl, alluding once again to Geiger's objection, seems to express dismay that one might hold a mother to the obligation to deliberate about the highest good when faced with the demand to rescue her child: "A mother should consider the highest practical good and first deliberate?!"

(Husserl 2013: 391). Now, however, Husserl makes the rejection of his earlier thought explicit:

> This whole ethics of the highest practical good, as derived from Brentano and accepted by me in its essentials, cannot be the last word. It requires essential limitations! Vocation and inner calling do not have their proper place therein.
>
> There is an unconditioned "you should and must" that addresses itself to a person and that, for the person experiencing this absolute affection, is neither subject to a rational explanation nor dependent on a legitimating obligation. It precedes all rational comprehension, even where such is possible. "I would betray myself if I acted differently." "I would never forgive myself"; so runs the entire justification. (Husserl 2013: 391–2)

Where does this rejection leave Husserl with respect to his earlier ethics? Certainly he has abandoned his Brentano-style consequentialism along with the formal axiological principles and the notion of the highest good entwined in it. But he does not need to abandon his view of valuation achieved in intentional feelings and of the kinds of goods that are the correlates of intentional feelings. The above quotations recognize both (1) that disinterested observers presented with the same facts will recognize an "objective" value (even if they do not feel "called" by it) and, more importantly, (2) that Husserl has come to recognize, in a way that he perhaps did not in his early ethics, the importance of the "first-person perspective" so central to phenomenology and so important to understanding evaluative experience. Our grasp of things as valuable is tied to and dependent not only upon the "facts" but also upon our physiological constitution, our experiential history, our "loves"—we can also think of these as interests, concerns, and commitment—and our circumstances. This is not to deny that value-characteristics belong to the things valued, but it is to recognize that different individuals can vary in their valuings of things, although, because values are objective, we can also recognize why others value things that we do not or in ways that we do not. In brief, these loves that are themselves valuations and that animate other valuations focus our attention on those features of the thing or situation that are evaluatively salient, and they register these features with the "sort of resonance and importance that only emotional involvement can sustain" (Sherman 1991: 47).

Geiger's critique provides a negative motivation for Husserl to abandon his idealized consequentialism. For help in elucidating a positive ethics grounded in these loves Husserl turns to Fichte. In particular, he turns to Fichte's discussions of vocations and inner callings and to Fichte's religious views as pointing toward a new notion of the highest good.

7.4 Fichtean Inheritances

Husserl, in his lectures on Fichte from 1917, recommends several of Fichte's writings, in particular, *The Vocation of Man* (1800), *The Characteristics of the Present Age* (1806),

The Way to the Blessed Life (1806), *Speeches to the German Nation* (1808), The Erlangen Lecture *On the Essence of the Scholar* (1805), and the five Berlin *Lectures on the Vocation of the Scholar* (1811) (Husserl 1987: 271/1995: 114). These writings are the sources of his Fichtean inheritances.

7.4.1 Vocation

We are daily faced with deciding among many choiceworthy goods, not all of which can be realized in our lives. This is not simply a quantitative matter; the limitation does not arise from the mere fact that there are too many goods. Rather, we decide among goods in relation to our physiological constitution, our experiential history, and, more importantly, our capacities and talents, our interests, concerns, and commitments. An agent concerned with a rationally and emotionally well-ordered life will choose from among the goods available to her some subset of goods that are more or most highly valued in relation to these subjective factors involved in her choice. These goods, which attract her as if she were "called" by them, can be characterized as the objects of her loves, loves that impose an "absolute ought" upon her. In the successful pursuit of these vocational goods, in adhering to the oughts imposed upon her, she can be said to lead a flourishing life or, as we shall later see, even a blessed life. The rational agent, in other words, chooses goods that give order, structure, and moral significance to her life (Husserl 1989b: 28).

This, to use different words, is to choose what Charles Taylor (1989: 62ff.) calls "hypergoods," goods in relation to which a person orders all her life's pursuits. To identify a hypergood or vocational good—whether being a spouse and parent, being a scientist, being a lawyer, engaging in politics, joining a religious community, attaining salvation, teaching and writing about philosophy, or, as in most, if not all, cases, some combination of such goods—is to identify what we understand as goods that (1) are the highest goods pursued by us, and (2) order all other goods under them. All goods take their place within a hierarchy of goods as more or less conducive to the overarching vocational good.

Put this way, the view seems similar to the law of absorption. However, as soon as we recall that these goods—or values, in Husserl's parlance—are the correlates of our personal constitution, our personal circumstances, and our personal interests, concerns, and commitments ("loves"), and as soon as we recall Geiger's objection, it is easy to see that these "subjective values" are not summative goods. They override "objective" values determined by the laws of the summation of value and the law of absorption (see Husserl 2012: 146n.). They absolutely and unconditionally require us to act in certain ways, whatever the "rational" or objective (consequentialist) calculation might say. Moreover, as soon as we realize that it is common for individuals to have more than one vocational good, it is easy to see that the more significant conflicts arise not between subjective and objective values but among the vocational goods themselves, and these conflicts force difficult, sometimes tragic, choices upon us.

Indeed, when Husserl speaks of the conflict among vocations, he notes the sacrifice contained in such choices. In choosing one good over the other, a person must to some degree abandon the pursuit of the other good: "An individual value—on the implicit condition that no greater value is available—is not in general simply a value whose practical possibility absorbs a lower available value. Rather, an individual value, a value that concerns exclusively the individuality of the person and the individuality of the valued, cannot actually be absorbed, but only 'sacrificed'" (Husserl 2013: 466). Moreover, in making this choice, the person runs the risk that the other good might be forever lost.

In this same passage, Husserl offers examples of potentially permanent sacrifice. The first is Abraham's choosing to sacrifice Isaac in order to be obedient to God's command. Abraham is faced—to oversimplify—with an irresolvable inner conflict between his love for Isaac and his love for God, and to choose one is to negate the other. A choice of this type yields no joy because the negation of the one good is a disvalue that weighs upon the agent for a lifetime insofar as both goods are of the type that gives meaning to the whole of a life. The same structure is seen in Husserl's examples of a parent who, in a time of great danger for the nation, must send a child off to war, or a mother who, in a time of severe famine and out of love for her child, believes herself compelled to take food from another's child in order to save her own. Victory in the war cannot compensate for the sacrifice of one's child, and saving one's own child cannot compensate for the disvalue of the harm done to another child.

7.4.2 The human as historical agent

While the notion of vocation is important to Husserl's thinking, what most attracts him to Fichte is Fichte's view of the human subject as an historical agent. Husserl summarizes Fichte's account as follows:

> The subject is thoroughly, and nothing else than, what acts. And whatever the subject has in its presence, as substrate of action, as object of its activity, must be something immanent in it, something already enacted. Therefore, being a subject and being one who acts coincide; but also being an object for the subject and being a product of acting. Prior to the acting, when we go to the origin, there is nothing. When we think, so to speak, of the history of the subject, the beginning is not a fact (*Tatsache*) but an "action" (*Tathandlung*) and we must think of this as a "history." Being a subject is *eo ipso* a history; it is having a development. Being a subject is not only acting but necessarily also progressing from action to action, from the product of acting to a new action, to new products of acting. (Husserl 1987: 275/1995: 117; translation modified)

Husserl connects the notion of vocation to this sense of agency. The agent's absolute loves are active responses to the inner calling of the vocation, a response that both values those features of the agent's circumstances that "call" her and motivates her activity. This love and its relevant vocation arise, Husserl says, from "the innermost center of the ego" (Husserl 2012: 146n.; cf. section 7.3). Absolute loves motivate the agent to adopt an ethical life-project and to undertake a course of historical actions teleologically ordered toward realizing that project. To put the matter another way, each individual agent adopts out of her absolute loves her own ethical project, a project that is "the deepest ground of [her] personal identity and individuality" (Melle 1991: 131; 2002: 243–4).

Such appeals to absolute loves, vocations, and inner callings might suggest that ethics is a largely individual matter, but that is not the case. After the horrors of the war years, Husserl was concerned that the German nation—indeed, Europe as a whole (Husserl 1989b: 10)—be renewed by revivifying the great achievements of a rational culture that Germany and Europe had exemplified. This was an urgent ethical task, for without a corresponding cultural renewal, individual renewal could not take hold. For Husserl, there is no individual renewal without social renewal, just as there can be no social renewal without individual renewal.

The view of the subject as a historical agent who renews herself via a self-critique and a cultural critique entails a teleological view of agency. Since action flows from an exercise of practical reason, the *telos* is best understood in terms of Husserl's notions of fulfillment and evidence, that is, in terms of the primary sense of reason discussed above. It belongs to the sense of any experienced object that it can be perceived and understood from a variety of perspectives. Hence, any understanding, evidenced or not, includes, implicitly or explicitly, the sense that others may have a different perspective and a different understanding. For Husserl, authentic experience is evidenced experience, which means that I must have the evidence myself; I must think *for* myself. But it is also true for Husserl that I must test my understandings against those of others by weighing what has been handed down by tradition and evaluating the claims others make against mine; I cannot think *by* myself.

Reason as evidence, in other words, is both an individual and intersubjective achievement through which rational agents achieve rational self-responsibility and self-determination. Consequently, an ethics that relies on experiencing the truth of the state of affairs an agent encounters (evidenced cognition), a truthful apprehension of goods and bads (a rational axiology), and a correct grasp of what to do (a rational praxiology) necessarily involves both individual and social renewal. The individual must put her evaluative and ethical beliefs to the test, and society must together determine the correct sense of (1) what is good and choiceworthy and (2) how to realize those goods. As Melle (2002: 242) puts it, "a community becomes an ethical community only through the ethical reflections of the individual subjects about themselves and their community and through their association in a social movement for the ethical renewal of their life in common."

Husserl's most extended discussion of individual and social renewal is found in the *Kaizo*-articles. The third article treats at length the question of individual renewal, while the fourth and fifth (unpublished) articles treat social renewal under the heading of the renewal of culture. The first sentences of the third article set the theme:

> Renewal of the human being—of the individual human and of a communal humanity—is the chief theme of all ethics. Ethical life is essentially a life consciously standing under the idea of renewal, a life intentionally formed and guided by it. Pure ethics is the science of the essence and the possible forms of such a life in a pure (a

priori) universality. Empirical-human ethics then seeks to adapt the norms of pure ethics to the empirical; it wants to become the guide of worldly humans under the given (individual, historical, national, etc.) relations. (Husserl 1989b: 20–1)

How are we to understand the pursuit of renewal and the pursuit of a vocation within a single, ethical framework? How are we to understand renewal in both the individual and the community? And how are we to understand this distinction between pure and empirical ethics? The answers to these questions are complicated by the Fichtean conception of the absolute I as an ethical agent. Husserl raises the complicating problem in the following:

> This I cannot be some sort of individual human I. Human subjects are items in the world; in the sense of idealism, they are very much mediate formations in subjectivity. The I of Fichte, the pure or absolute I, is nothing other than this subjectivity in which (according to the law-like play of actions) the phenomenal world with all its human egos first comes to be. To write the history of the I, of the absolute intelligence, is therefore to write the history of the necessary teleology in which the world as phenomenal comes to progressive creation, to creation in this intelligence. This is no object of experience but a metaphysical power. (Husserl 1987: 276/1995: 118; translation modified)

This text notes Fichte's distinction between the absolute I and the human I. The absolute I exercises its own agency, an agency distinct from any human agency and upon which the very being of the human I—indeed, all human egos—depends. This is why Husserl characterizes Fichte's absolute I as a metaphysical power. Husserl seems to adopt both the distinction between the absolute and human egos and the historical and teleologically ordered creation of a world in the activity of the absolute I:

> Because we knowing humans, on the contrary, are egos in which this absolute I has split itself, we can, through intuitive immersion into that which belongs to the pure essence of the I, of subjectivity, reconstruct the necessary sequence of teleological processes out of which the entire world and ultimately ourselves (in what for us is an unconscious exercising of absolute intelligence) are formed in teleological necessity. If we proceed so, we are philosophers. And the only genuine task of philosophy is to be found here: to comprehend the world as the teleological product of the absolute I and, in clarifying the creation of the world in the absolute I, to make evident its ultimate sense. (Husserl 1987: 276/1995: 118; translation modified)

Husserl can assimilate the Fichtean notion of an absolute I to his phenomenology only by way of the "absolute consciousness" revealed in his account of internal time-consciousness. In that account he distinguishes between the temporalized flow of conscious experiences and the absolute "flow" of consciousness, which is actually not a flow at all. It is that which allows for the self-temporalizing of the flow of conscious experiences. Husserl developed his notion of absolute consciousness without explicit reference to Fichte's work, so we cannot definitively identify it as an inheritance of Fichte's view of the absolute I and its agency. But similarities in the relation between the absolute consciousness and empirical consciousness as well as Husserl's later writings allow us to entertain the possibility. To so think of it, however, two things must be true. First, Husserl's absolute consciousness must both be constitutively prior to individual consciousnesses, and, second, absolute consciousness must pluralize itself in a multiplicity of individual consciousnesses. Both of these views are controversial, both as interpretations of Husserl and as phenomenological positions. These views also point to metaphysical concerns, and we shall now take them up in somewhat more detail.

7.5 PHENOMENOLOGY AND METAPHYSICS

Husserl's account of absolute consciousness starts from the question of how we account for the consciousness of succession. It is on pain of infinite regress that Husserl claims that the awareness of a temporal flow of experience cannot itself be temporally qualified, for, if it were, we would then need to account for our experience of this awareness as temporal. Hence, Husserl posits an experiencing consciousness that is not itself in time but which makes possible the awareness of both the inner time of our lived experiences and the objective time of worldly things and events. This absolute consciousness, however, cannot merely be the awareness of the now, for temporality would then simply be the accumulation of successive appearings of the now. That would account, in other words, only for the succession of consciousness and not our awareness of that succession. Hence, absolute consciousness must be structured such that there is an intertwining of the consciousness of what has elapsed, of what is now, and of what is yet to come. This non-temporal structure accounts for the awareness of an experience having a temporal extent. The momentary phase of absolute consciousness, in other words, is a non-temporal temporalizing of experience. Husserl characterizes this consciousness as a "flow" that constitutes both itself and the inner flow of experience.

This account of the consciousness of inner time commits him to a threefold distinction regarding time (Husserl 1966: 371/1991: 382). He distinguishes:

1. objects with their objective, worldly time;
2. the stream of immanent experiences with their subjective, phenomenal time; and
3. the absolute time-constituting consciousness.

Absolute consciousness stands to the flow of experiences as the constituting to the constituted,[6] and this, in part, underlies Husserl's unfortunate use of the language of

---

[6] For an excellent discussion of Husserl's "discovery" of absolute consciousness, cf. Brough 1972; 1989; 1991. Zahavi (1999: 70–1), in contrast to Brough, emphasizes the unity of (2) and (3), stressing the fact that the *subject's* self-aware immanent experience is not the *object* of another level of consciousness. On Zahavi's view, we can be aware of individual experiences as constituted temporal unities, as discrete experiences, only in reflection (1999: 76–7). Brough counters by noting that Husserl clearly points to a *prereflective* awareness of experiences as temporal unities.

"immanent *objects*" to characterize experiences that belong to a *subject*. Nevertheless, it is this conception of a constitutively prior absolute consciousness that resonates with the Fichtean notion of an acting, creative absolute I.

At the same time, however, Husserl claims that there is no real separation between the second and third levels. He insists that (2) and (3), although distinguishable, are inseparable such that there is only one flow of consciousness with its worldly objects (cf. Husserl 1966: 80/1991: 84). I have argued elsewhere (Drummond 2006: 213–18; cf. Zahavi 2011: 22) that the differentiation between the time-constituting absolute consciousness and the immanent flow of experiences is best considered a distinction between a form and the *concretum* it informs rather than a distinction between a constituting level and a constituted level. Indeed, Husserl explicitly makes this connection: "The fundamental *form* [my emphasis] of this universal synthesis, which makes all other syntheses of consciousness possible, is the all-encompassing consciousness of inner time" (Husserl [1938] 1963: 81/1970a: 43; translation modified). The identification of the form of the universal synthesis—a synthesis which is equivalent to the whole of a conscious life— with the consciousness of inner time both preserves the unity of the absolute and phenomenal flows and allows a distinction between the absolute time-constituting form of consciousness and the concrete flow of subjective life itself without putting them into a constituting–constituted relation.[7]

There is no doubt that Husserl was ambiguous in his discussions of the consciousness of inner time. Despite whatever confusions Husserl might have introduced into his accounts of an enormously difficult problem, I think that from a phenomenological point of view, the view that absolute consciousness is the form of a concrete experiential flow represents the best available understanding of absolute consciousness. If this is correct, however, Husserl's absolute consciousness cannot be an inheritance of the Fichtean absolute I because it does not stand in a constituting–constituted relation to the worldly ego. To reject constitutive priority, however, precludes the metaphysical or ontological priority characteristic of the Fichtean absolute I.

Nor can the view that the absolute ego pluralizes itself in a multiplicity of individual human egos be correct, for that depends on the constitutive priority of the absolute I (see Zahavi 2001: 66–77). Hence, neither of the conditions for thinking Husserl's absolute ego is an inheritance of the Fichtean absolute I are satisfied. In fairness, however, we should note that while the view of an absolute ego constitutively prior to individual egos seems a prerequisite for this Fichtean inheritance, Husserl himself does not directly appeal to his discussions of the consciousness of inner time in the development of his late ethical views. Indeed, insofar as Husserl's late ethics moves in the direction of a constitutively prior absolute ego, he is inconsistent with what I take his phenomenological views of absolute consciousness to be.

---

[7] This view, moreover, provides reason to think that Husserl did not, in the manner of Kant and the neo-Kantians, use regressive or transcendental arguments to isolate absolute consciousness that is not itself intuitable. Absolute consciousness instead appears as an intuitively discoverable universal structure within intentional experience.

Nevertheless, Husserl in his late ethics appeals consistently to the model of the absolute I as constitutively (and now, à la Fichte, metaphysically) prior to the constituted ego. Wittingly or unwittingly, doing so reflects his attraction to Fichte's metaphysical and theological ideas. We have seen that Husserl's early ethics was avowedly and insistently rational, both in its view of evidence and its view of the disciplines of formal axiology and formal praxiology. We have also seen that Husserl's later ethics is insistently rational in its continued appeal to the idea of an intentional life teleologically ordered toward evidence. He continues to think that the vocation proper both to human individuals and the human community is a rational one: to disclose insightfully the truth and to be responsible for one's cognitive, evaluative, and practical beliefs: "Be a true human being; lead a life that you can continuously justify insightfully, a life of practical reason" (Husserl 1989b: 36; cf. Drummond 2010). This is the human *telos*, one that is realized in self-responsibly realizing particular human vocations.

There are, however, two questions that seem to defy rationalist responses: (1) How can I think the world rational and meaningful when external circumstances so easily and arbitrarily lead to reversals of fortune that block the attainment of one's goals and render one's striving vain? (Husserl 2013: 526–7; cf. Peucker n.d.: 9) and (2) why is it that members of the human community and the human community are teleologically ordered in this way? Husserl has previously foreshadowed these issues: "Among the humans in my surrounding, my child is the 'closest,' and therein is an irrationality of the absolute ought" (Husserl 2013: 384; cf. Melle 1991: 134), and again, "There is an unconditioned 'you should and must' that addresses itself to a person and that, for the person experiencing this absolute affection, is neither subject to a rational explanation nor dependent on a legitimating obligation" (Husserl 2013: 392; cf. section 7.3).

We realize vocational goods through multiple and sequential actions, actions that make possible (or foreclose) other actions. Any action, in other words, has its own proper horizon of past and future actions. In our own lives and at the level of the human community, however, the fact that we invariably find arbitrary elements affecting the ability to realize some ends reveals that the goal of the genuine, rational human community is an unattainable, infinite ideal, and the fact that the inner calling or vocation introduces an apparently irrational dimension into our ethical life calls into question the entire teleological structure. Husserl reconciles the specter of arbitrariness and of irrationality with his rationalism by invoking the distinction between the absolute I and the constituted ego, claiming that there is no irrationality in the absolute love of the constitutively and ontologically prior absolute I; the ought that is not limited to human egos is a "thoroughly rational" ought (Husserl 2013: 387). Husserl identifies this absolute and transcendent I with God. In this, we see the influence of Fichte's religious views, views that are inextricably bound up with his notion of an absolute I. These views push Husserl to conceive his ontologically and constitutively prior absolute consciousness as God. The absolute ought, Husserl tells us, "has its highest, enlightening, and rational sense in a divine world (*Gotteswelt*)" (Husserl 2013: 390; cf. Melle 1991: 134). Even more explicitly, Husserl says:

> The world . . . "must" be beautiful and good; it must be governed by a universal tele-ology. It must be God-directed, a world wherein God works everywhere. More precisely and above all: all human action is free, and the person is responsible for it. Still, God is at work in everything that is. Human life, human destiny necessarily occurs with divine guidance. (Husserl 2013: 254)

At both the human and divine levels, the striving toward intentional fulfillment, toward satisfaction, and in this context, toward blessedness operates as both the form and the finality of agency. And given the relation between the human and the divine outlined here, we can say that the world and everything in it is governed by a divine entelechy, which is the "entelechy of [natural] entelechies" (Hart 1995: 150).

The arbitrariness and irrationality of the contingency of fate and circumstance, of disappointment and despair, and of death can be overcome only by participating in the divine life, by participating in the world-engendering and world-governing activity of the absolute I, of God. This means, however, that the world and my agency can make sense for me only if I believe in God who gives meaning to the world and the human egos within it (cf. Melle 2002; 2007; Peucker n.d.: 18). Husserl explicitly makes the point in several places:

> I can be blessed amidst all the suffering, misfortune, and irrationality in my surroundings only if I believe that God exists and that this world is God's world. And if I will with all the power of my soul to hold fast to the absolute ought—and this is itself an absolute willing—then I must absolutely believe that God exists. Faith is the absolute and highest requirement. (Husserl 2013: 203)

> In order to be able to believe in myself and my true I along with its development, I must believe in God; and when I do this, I experience divine governance, divine counsel, and divine exhortation in my life. (Husserl 2013: 255)

As Peucker has noted, this is reminiscent of Kant's postulates of practical reason. But, Peucker reminds us, there is an important difference. Whereas Kant postulates the existence of God so that the concept of the highest good can be thought without contradiction, Husserl, by contrast, *presupposes* the existence of God in order to think the world meaningful as a whole and to give meaning to the activities of human beings (Peucker n.d.: 10). In this respect, the positing of God's existence conflicts with Husserl's conception of phenomenology as presuppositionless.

Moreover, the Fichtean absolute I embedded in and influencing these late Husserlian positions is, as suggested above, incompatible with a properly phenomenological account of absolute consciousness. In this sense, Husserl's later ethical views are metaphysical and theological rather than phenomenological. That there is an absolute I transcending the absolute consciousness that informs each individual human consciousness cannot be decided phenomenologically. The claim that there is would have to be imported from religious beliefs in everyday experience (Hart 1995: 156). My argument here is not meant to denigrate these religious views. It is not to say that these religious and ethical views are correct or incorrect. It is not to say that Husserl's view of the divine and the divine entelechy is true or false. My argument is meant to say only that the views Husserl advances in his late ethics cannot be established by phenomenological means.

In summary, we can see the salutary effects of Geiger's critique of Husserl with its negative motivation to abandon the idealized consequentialism inherited from Brentano. But Husserl's turn to Fichte for a positive replacement yields mixed results. Taking up the notion of vocation provides Husserl with a way to focus on an ethics of individual and social renewal and fulfillment and, in the context of his religious beliefs, even individual blessedness. But Husserl's claim that human agency is the working out of the divine entelechy through human agency requires a phenomenology of absolute consciousness that is problematic, and its religious dimension traverses the bounds of his own "presuppositionless" phenomenology. As a religious matter, Husserl may very well be correct. But one can arrive at this view only through faith, not phenomenology.

7.6 CONCLUSION

The discussion of the development of Husserl's ethics reveals the degree to which central issues of Husserl's phenomenology were involved in his ethics. Most significant are the manner in which his later ethical views (1) involve questions about the relationship between the absolute ego and the worldly ego and (2) push the boundaries of phenomenology and metaphysics. My argument has suggested that we should be (1) phenomenologically modest in claims about the absolute ego, which, I have suggested, is best understood as a formal dimension of the worldly, sense-disclosing life of a person, and (2) wary of extending our phenomenological descriptions into metaphysics. This is not to preclude treatment of metaphysical problems, but it suggests, at the least, the need to provide a clearer account of the relation between our phenomenological findings and our metaphysical positions and to avoid using the latter to undergird the former.

While I have focused on the historical influence of Fichte and the contemporary criticism of Geiger, a number of Husserl's contemporaries were also interested in exploring axiological and ethical themes, and Husserl would have been aware of their work as well, just as they were aware of Husserl's work. Alexander Pfänder, a contemporary of Husserl and with connections to phenomenology, wrote an early psychological treatise on the will (*Phänomenologie des Wollens: Eine psychologische Analyse*, 1900). Another contemporary, Max Scheler ([1913, 1916] 1954/1973), and, a bit later, Nicolai Hartmann ([1925] 1962/1967), who was influenced by both Husserl and Scheler, argued for strong value-realist positions that varied somewhat from Husserl's own. Still other phenomenologists rejected foundational, axiological approaches (Heidegger [1927] 1967/2010) or, like Sartre (1943/1992) and Merleau-Ponty (1945/2012), organized their ethical thinking around the notion of freedom or, like Levinas (1961/1969), around the demand imposed on us by the face of the other. In recent years, given the resurgence of virtue ethics with its emphasis on the evaluative role of the emotions, there has been a revival of phenomenological axiology in the work of thinkers such as Michele Averchi, John Drummond,

Ingrid Vendrell Ferran, Paul Gyllenhammer, James Hart, Sara Heinämaa, Ignacio Quepons Ramírez, Sonja Rinofner-Kreidl, Anthony Steinbock, and many others, a development that makes clear the enduring influence of Husserl's axiological and ethical thought.

References

Brough, J. (1972), "The Emergence of an Absolute Consciousness in Husserl's Early Writings on Time-consciousness," *Man and World* 5: 298–324.

Brough, J. (1989), "Husserl's phenomenology of time-consciousness," in W. McKenna and J. N. Mohanty (eds), *Husserl's Phenomenology: A Textbook* (Lanham, MD: University Press of America), 249–90.

Brough. J. (1991), "Translator's introduction," in E. Husserl, *On the Phenomenology of the Consciousness of Internal Time (1893–1917)* (Dordrecht: Kluwer).

Crowell, S. (1996). "The mythical and the meaningless: Husserl and the two faces of nature," in T. Nenon and L. Embree (eds), *Issues in Husserl's Ideas II* (Dordrecht: Kluwer), 81–105.

Drummond, J. (1983), "Object's Optimal Appearances and the Immediate Awareness of Space in Vision," *Man and World* 16: 177–205.

Drummond, J. (2002), "The *Logical Investigations*: Paving the way to a transcendental logic," in D. Zahavi and F. Stjernfelt (eds), *One Hundred Years of Phenomenology* (Dordrecht: Kluwer), 31–40.

Drummond, J. (2006), "The case(s) of (self-)awareness," in U. Kriegel and K. Williford (eds), *Self-Representational Approaches to Consciousness* (Cambridge, MA: MIT Press), 199–220.

Drummond, J. (2009), "Phénoménologie et ontologie," translated by G. Fréchette, *Philosophiques* 36: 593–607.

Drummond, J. (2010), "Self-responsibility and eudamonia," in C. Ierna, H. Jacobs, and F. Mattens (eds), *Philosophy, Phenomenology, Sciences* (Dordrecht: Springer), 411–30.

Drummond, J. (2013), "The Intentional Structure of Emotions," *Logical Analysis and the History of Philosophy/Philosophiegeschichte und logische Analyse* 16: 244–63.

Drummond, J. (2015), "Intuitions," *teorema* 34: 19–36.

Drummond, J. (2017), "Having the Right Attitudes," *The New Yearbook for Phenomenology and Phenomenological Philosophy* 15: 142–63.

Hart, J. (1995), "Husserl and Fichte: With Special Regard to Husserl's Lectures on 'Fichte's Ideal of Humanity,'" *Husserl Studies* 12: 135–63.

Hartmann, N. ([1925] 1962), *Ethik*, 4th edition (Berlin: de Gruyter).

Hartmann, N. (1967), *Ethics*, translated by S. Coit (New York: Humanities Press).

Heidegger, M. ([1927] 1967), *Sein und Zeit* (Tübingen: Max Niemeyer Verlag).

Heidegger, M. (2010), *Being and Time*, translated by J. Stambaugh and D. Schmidt (Albany, NY: SUNY Press).

Husserl, E. ([1912–28] 1952), *Ideen zu einer reinen Phänomenologie und phänomenologischen Philosophie. Zweites Buch*, ed. M. Biemel (The Hague: Martinus Nijhoff).

Husserl, E. ([1938] 1963), *Cartesianische Meditationen und die Pariser Vorträge*, ed. S. Strasser (The Hague: Martinus Nijhoff).

Husserl, E. ([1893–1917] 1966), *Zur Phänomenologie des inneren Zeitbewusstseins (1893–1917)*, ed. R. Boehm (The Hague: Martinus Nijhoff).

Husserl, E. (1970a), *Cartesian Meditations*, translated by D. Cairns (The Hague: Martinus Nijhoff).

Husserl, E. (1970b), *Logical Investigations*, translated by J. N. Findlay, 2 vols (London: Routledge and Kegan Paul).

Husserl, E. ([1907] 1973a), *Die Idee der Phänomenologie*, ed. W. Biemel (The Hague: Martinus Nijhoff).

Husserl, E. (1973b), *Ding und Raum. Vorlesungen 1907*, ed. U. Claesges (The Hague: Martinus Nijhoff).

Husserl, E. ([1913] 1976) *Ideen zu einer reinen Phänomenologie und phänomenologischen Philosophie. Erstes Buch*, ed. K. Schuhmann (The Hague: Martinus Nijhoff).

Husserl, E. (1983), *Ideas for a Pure Phenomenology and Phenomenological Philosophy. First Book*, translated by F. Kersten (The Hague: Martinus Nijhoff).

Husserl, E. ([1900] 1984). *Logische Untersuchungen. Zweiter Band*, ed. U. Panzer (The Hague: Martinus Nijhoff).

Husserl, E. (1987), "Fichtes Menschheitsideal," *Aufsätze und Vorträge (1911–1921)*, ed. T. Nenon and H. R. Sepp (Dordrecht: Martinus Nijhoff), 267–93.

Husserl, E. 1988. *Vorlesungen über Ethik und Wertlehre, 1908–1914*, ed. U. Melle (Dordrecht: Kluwer).

Husserl, E. (1989a), *Ideas Pertaining to a Pure Phenomenology and to a Phenomenological Philosophy. Second Book*, translated by R. Rojcewicz and A. Schuwer (Dordrecht: Kluwer).

Husserl, E. (1989b), *Aufsätze und Vorträge (1922–1937)*, ed. T. Nenon and H. R. Sepp (Dordrecht: Kluwer).

Husserl, E. (1991), *On the Phenomenology of the Consciousness of Internal Time (1893–1917)*, translated by J. Brough (Dordrecht: Kluwer).

Husserl, E. (1994), *Briefwechsel*, ed. K. and E. Schuhmann, 10 vols (Dordrecht: Kluwer).

Husserl, E. (1995), "Fichte's Ideal of Humanity [three lectures]," translated by J. Hart, *Husserl Studies* 12: 111–33.

Husserl, E. (1999), *The Idea of Phenomenology*, translated by L. Hardy (Dordrecht: Kluwer).

Husserl, E. (2012), *Einleitung in die Philosophie. Vorlesungen 1916–1920*, ed. H. Jacobs (Dordrecht: Springer).

Husserl, E. (2013), *Grenzprobleme der Phänomenologie. Analysen des Unbewusstseins und der Instinkte. Metaphysik. Späte Ethik. Texte aus dem Nachlass (1908–1937)* (Dordrecht: Springer).

Levinas, E. (1961), *Totalité et Infini* (The Hague: Martinus Nijhoff).

Levinas, E. (1969). *Totality and Infinity*, translated by A. Lingis (Pittsburgh, PA: Duquesne University Press).

Melle, U. (1991), "The Development of Husserl's Ethics," *Études phénoménologiques* 13–14: 115–35.

Melle, U. (2002), "Edmund Husserl: From reason to love," in J. Drummond and L. Embree (eds) *Phenomenological Approaches to Moral Philosophy* (Dordrecht: Kluwer), 229–48.

Melle, U. (2007), "Husserl's Personalist Ethics," *Husserl Studies* 23: 1–15.

Merleau-Ponty, M. (1945), *Phénoménologie de la perception* (Paris: Éditions Gallimard).

Merleau-Ponty, M. (2012), *Phenomenology of Perception*, translated by D. Landes (New York: Routledge).

Peucker, H. (n.d.) "Husserl's Conception of a Highest Good in his Late Ethics." Unpublished MS.

Pfänder, A. (1900), *Phänomenologie des Wollens* (Leipzig: Barth).

Sartre, J.-P. (1943), *L'être et le néant* (Paris: Éditions Gallimard).

Sartre, J.-P. (1992), *Being and Nothingness*, translated by H. Barnes (New York: Washington Square Press).

Scheler, M. ([1913, 1916] 1954), *Der Formalismus in der Ethik und die material Wertethik* (Bern: Francke Verlag).

Scheler, M. (1973), *Formalism in Ethics and Non-Formal Ethics of Values*, translated by M. Frings and R. Funk (Evanston, IL: Northwestern University Press).

Sherman, N. (1991), *The Fabric of Character* (Oxford: Clarendon Press).

Smart, J. and Williams, B. (1973), *Utilitarianism* (Cambridge: Cambridge University Press).

Sokolowski, R. (1970), *The Formation of Husserl's Concept of Constitution* (The Hague: Martinus Nijhoff).

Taylor, C. (1989), *Sources of the Self* (Cambridge, MA: Harvard University Press).

Welton, D. (2000), *The Other Husserl* (Bloomington, IN: Indiana University Press).

Zahavi, D. (1999), *Self-Awareness and Alterity* (Evanston, IL: Northwestern University Press).

Zahavi, D. (2001), *Husserl and Transcendental Intersubjectivity* (Athens, OH: Ohio University Press).

Zahavi, D. (2003), *Husserl's Phenomenology* (Stanford, CA: Stanford University Press).

Zahavi, D. (2011), "Objects and Levels: Reflections on the Relation between Time-consciousness and Self-consciousness," *Husserl Studies* 27: 13–25.

CHAPTER 8

PRE-PREDICATIVE EXPERIENCE AND LIFE-WORLD

Two Distinct Projects in Husserl's Late Phenomenology

ANDREA STAITI

PRE-PREDICATIVE experience and its relation to the forms of predication is the central theme of Husserl's posthumous book *Experience and Judgment* (1974),[1,2] whereas the life-world and its relation to the world described by natural science is the central theme of Husserl's *The Crisis of the European Sciences and Transcendental Phenomenology* (1970),[3] an assemblage of writings from the 1930s partly published in the Serbian journal *Philosophia* in the very last years of Husserl's life. Although each theme can be neatly ascribed to one distinct work, the fundamental difference between the two projects outlined in *EJ* and *Crisis*, respectively, is often overlooked. This hardly comes as a surprise, since the introduction to *EJ* equates the inquiry into pre-predicative experience with the movement back to the pre-scientific life-world characterizing *Crisis*; however, I will argue that this *is not* and *cannot* be Husserl's view. It is not Husserl's view because the

[1] I am deeply indebted to Dieter Lohmar and to all the participants in the seminar on Husserl's *Experience and Judgment* held at the Husserl Archive in Cologne in the summer semester of 2015. Many of the ideas presented in this chapter stem from that seminar. I subsequently presented earlier versions of the chapter at the phenomenology workshop in Cologne, at the *Werkstatt Phänomenologie* in Vienna, at the Husserl Archive in Leuven, and at the Colloquium Phaenomenologicum in Freiburg. I would like to express my gratitude to Sophie Loidolt, Nicolas de Warren, and Hans-Helmuth Gander for their invitations and to all those who attended my presentations for their helpful feedback. I benefitted greatly from conversations with Robert Stefanek, Eduard Marbach, Christopher Gutland, Carmine Di Martino, Andrea Cimino, Rocco Sacconaghi, and Evan Clarke, whose input has been decisive in improving the chapter in both style and content. The research presented in this chapter was generously supported by a grant from the Alexander von Humboldt Stiftung.
[2] Henceforth *EJ*.
[3] Henceforth *Crisis*.

author of the introduction to *EJ* is actually Ludwig Landgrebe. While it has been proven that the main text of *EJ* consists almost entirely of writings stemming from Husserl's unpublished manuscripts (Lohmar 1996), the correspondence between Landgrebe and Husserl's wife Malvine confirms the hypothesis that the introduction is Landgrebe's work. In addition to this textual piece of evidence, there is also a purely philosophical reason why the equation of pre-predicative experience with the life-world *cannot* be Husserl's view. The notion of life-world is introduced in *Crisis* as a contrastive term, which Husserl counterposes to the idealized world of natural science. The movement back from the idealized world of natural science to the pre-scientific life-world is thus the counter-movement to natural scientific idealization. By contrast, the notion of pre-predicative experience is introduced in *EJ* as a comprehensive term for all the rudimentary, low-level synthetic structures of perceptual experience that are presupposed by the more complex, high-level synthetic structures of predicative judgment. The movement back from predicative judgment to pre-predicative experience is thus an attempt to shed light on the very possibility of speaking meaningfully about the things we encounter in our everyday worldly transactions, prior to and independently of any kind of consideration of natural science. The contrast between pre-predicative experience and predicative judgment is thus entirely internal to what *Crisis* calls the life-world and the grounding of predicative forms in perceptual and proto-perceptual experiences is a presupposition for the phenomenological clarification and critique of idealizing procedures in the natural sciences. In particular, the relationship between the forms of predication and the forms of pre-predicative experience can be characterized as that between a logical *Vollform* (full-fledged form) and a perceptual *Vorform* (pre-figuring form). In this relationship, there is a structural affinity between the objects encountered in perception and the higher-order, categorial objects constituted in judgment. By contrast, there is no structural affinity between the life-worldly objects of everyday experience (with their value-predicates, their perspectival appearance, their qualitative heterogeneity, etc.) and the idealized objects of natural science.

For these reasons, I will argue that Landgrebe's introduction to *EJ* lumps together the movement from predicative judgment to pre-predicative experience and the movement from the idealized world of natural science to the life-world, thus blurring the difference between the two distinct projects characterizing Husserl's late phenomenology. Considering the centrality of the introduction to *EJ* for the reception of Husserl's late phenomenology, rectifying this mistake is of paramount importance for a correct understanding of Husserl's thought. Moreover, a due distinction of the two projects opens up the possibility to reconfigure their relationship correctly. The clarification of the transition from the rudimentary forms of pre-predicative experience to the predicative forms of judgment is entirely presupposed in the project outlined in *Crisis*.

The chapter is structured as follows. Section 8.1 examines Landgrebe's introduction to *EJ* and criticizes the equation of pre-predicative experience with life-world. Section 8.2 considers the project of *EJ* in its own right as the movement from predicative judgment to pre-predicative experience. Section 8.3 considers the project of *Crisis* in its own right as the counter-movement to natural scientific idealization. Section 8.4 turns to consider two post-husserlian phenomenologists—notably, Merleau-Ponty and the early Derrida—and argues that Landgrebe's influence continues in their work, mainly due to their predominant interest in highlighting instances of one and the same movement (from pure, self-transparent consciousness to concrete, empirically conditioned subjectivity) in various venues of Husserl's phenomenology. The conclusion recapitulates briefly the interpretation proposed.

8.1 Landgrebe's *Introduction* to EJ

On June 22, 1938, upon receiving the proofs of the typescript of *EJ* just a few weeks after Husserl's death, Malvine Husserl wrote back to Ludwig Landgrebe: "At first glance, I miss your name at the end of the introduction. It seems imperative to me that your name is indicated both there and in the table of contents: either 'the editor' or the full name."[4] On the following day, Malvine wrote another letter to Landgrebe, probably wishing to make reparation for the somewhat brusque tone of her earlier writing. Her point, however, remains the same: "After a thorough reading of the 'introduction' I came to the conclusion that it is necessary, especially with regard to your characterization of the overall sense of the book, that you take responsibility for it with your signature."[5] She then recommends Landgrebe to emphasize that the "analytical investigations—e.g., those on horizons—essentially stem from Husserl's manuscripts,"[6] thereby marking a helpful distinction between the specific analyses to be found in the *Introduction,* which are Husserl's, and the characterization of the overall project, which is distinctively Landgrebe's.

Roughly ten years earlier Husserl's assistant Ludwig Landgrebe had been entrusted with the task of putting together a book manuscript tentatively entitled *Logische Studien.* Landgrebe was to draw on manuscripts and lecture notes stemming from the late 1910s and the early 1920s and weave together coherently passages that Husserl himself had selected carefully. The first draft of what would eventually become *EJ* was ready by the end of 1928, but when Husserl sat down to write the introduction he ended up writing a whole new book instead, namely, *Formal and Transcendental Logic* (Husserl 1978), which was published by the end of 1929 (see Lohmar 1996: 32–3). The appearance of *Formal and Transcendental Logic* made a substantial revision of the draft for *Logische Studien* necessary, partly in order to avoid repetitions and partly because the analyses in *Formal and Transcendental Logic* had disclosed new horizons of problems. Landgrebe

---

[4] Malvine Husserl's letter to Ludwig Landgrebe of June 22, 1938. Preserved at the Husserl Archive in Leuven.

[5] Malvine Husserl's letter to Ludwig Landgrebe of June 23, 1938. Preserved at the Husserl Archive in Leuven.

[6] Malvine Husserl's letter to Ludwig Landgrebe of June 23, 1938.

thus produced a second draft, which Husserl read and annotated; however, as always happened, he got sidetracked by other projects (such as the *Cartesian Meditations*) and set the *Logische Studien* aside. It was not until 1937 that Husserl and Landgrebe managed to get together and agree on a final version of the manuscript.[7]

The only part of the manuscript that the two could not agree upon precisely was the introduction. Husserl wanted it to be just a brief summary of *Formal and Transcendental Logic* (Lohmar 1996: 40), whereas Landgrebe clearly had a more ambitious project in mind. The introduction should sketch out a survey of Husserl's late phenomenology as a whole. Despite Landgrebe's reassurance that the introduction had been "talked over with Husserl and was approved by him in its essential content and line of thought" (Husserl 1973: 7), Malvine's intimation that he put his name under it should make us suspicious. The introduction that made it to the printer was Landgrebe's ambitious survey, rather than Husserl's desired summary. This is confirmed by Landgrebe's own remark in the editor's foreword that the introduction is "in part a free rendering of ideas taken from *Formal and Transcendental Logic* and *The Crisis of European Sciences and Transcendental Phenomenology*" (Husserl 1973: 7), rather than *Formal and Transcendental Logic* alone.

While there is nothing wrong with Landgrebe's intention to introduce readers to Husserl's late phenomenology as a whole, and while his decision not to take credit for Husserl's ideas by removing his name is admirable, the introduction to *EJ* yields mixed results at best. Some paragraphs are successful in presenting difficult ideas in a few brushstrokes. Overall, it is a readable text. But, to name just one problematic passage, what are we to make of statements like the following? "Since Aristotle, it has been held as certain that the basic schema of judgment is the *copulative* judgment, which is reducible to the basic form *S is p*" (Husserl 1973: 15). Having studied under Brentano and having read Lotze and Frege extensively, Husserl would never have embarrassed himself with a statement that betrays scant familiarity with the developments of nineteenth-century logic. As is well known, at least since Lotze's *Logik*, but more prominently with Brentano's *Psychology from an Empirical Standpoint* and Frege's *Begriffsschrift*, copulative judgment was no longer considered the basic form and was supplanted by either impersonal judgment (Lotze), existential judgment (Brentano), or by the function/argument construal of proposition (Frege).[8]

This and other passages from the introduction to *EJ* may raise doubts about Landgrebe's command of the difficult materials at issue. However, the most problematic

---

[7] For this reason, a complete account of Husserl's late phenomenology would have to consider more thoroughly the connection between the project of a phenomenological "transcendental aesthetics" as outlined in *Formal and Transcendental Logic* and its continuation in *EJ*. For reasons of space, I decided to not address this point in the present chapter. Thankfully, the connection between *Formal and Transcendental Logic* has been already discussed convincingly by other scholars, such as Bachelard 1990 and Lohmar 2000.

[8] For a more detailed account see Staiti 2015.

statement for the purpose of this chapter is found at the beginning of §12. Landgrebe writes: "These indications must suffice to understand the sense of the retrogression from predicative to pre-predicative, objectual evidence, a retrogression which coincides with the retrogression to the evidence of life-worldly experience" (Husserl 1973: 51, translation modified). The notion of *gegenständliche Evidenz* is introduced in §6 to characterize the mode of givenness of individual objects in perception prior to all judicative activity. In the following paragraphs Landgrebe proceeds to show that the self-evident givenness of individual objects is rooted in the self-evident givenness of the world as the encompassing horizon of every perceptual experience. In this context Landgrebe introduces the term "life-world" (Husserl 1974: 41) and argues that the world of pre-predicative experience coincides with the life-world, i.e., "the world in which we are always already living and which furnishes the ground for all cognitive performance and all scientific determination" (Husserl 1974: 41). However, does it make sense to characterize the world in which we always already live as pre-predicative? Landgrebe himself seems to be uncertain. On the following page he writes that "the world in which we live and in which we carry out activities of cognition and judgment . . . is always already pre-given to us as impregnated by the sediments (*Niederschlag*) of logical operations" (Husserl 1974: 42); however, how can the life-world be simultaneously pre-predicative and impregnated by the sediments of logical operations?

One could dismiss Landgrebe's characterization of the life-world in the introduction to EJ as a flat contradiction, if only it had not been so influential in the reception of Husserl's late phenomenology. So, for instance, while acknowledging the "peculiar status of this text" (Carr 1974: 212) with respect to its authorship, David Carr devotes a whole chapter to the introduction to *EJ* in his classical study *Phenomenology and the Problem of History* (Carr 1974). This leads Carr to diagnose an unresolvable tension between Husserl's characterization of the life-world as both perceptual (i.e., according to Carr, pre-predicative viz. pre-linguistic) and cultural (i.e., according to Carr, entailing products whose givenness essentially requires language). In subsequent Husserlian scholarship one often finds characterizations of the life-world as pre-predicative, pre-categorial, or even pre-linguistic (see, for instance: Carr 1977: 208; Seebohm 1997: 144–5; Yuasa 1999: 98; Paci 1972: 461; more recently Landgrebe's direct student Blumenberg 2006: 74, and, albeit in passing, Zahavi 2003: 130). Understandably, this has lead some commentators to attribute to Husserl a kind of "epistemological Rousseaunism" (Fellman 1983: 118), the dream of a primeval state of dwelling in the world prior to all language, culture, and science.

Going back to Landgrebe's introduction to *EJ*, however, we need to raise the following basic question. Why introduce the problem of the world in the first place? Does Husserl's project of leading back the structures of predication to pre-predicative experience *necessarily require* introducing the notion of world and, more specifically, the notion of life-world as opposed to the idealized world of natural science? Landgrebe's remark that the self-evident givenness of individual objects is rooted in the self-evident givenness of the world is certainly correct, but what kind of job is this remark supposed to do in the line of argument pursued here? Although he is never explicit about it, Landgrebe's argument seems to revolve around the notion that as educated Westerners we live in a world that is shot through with and partly obfuscated by the idealizations of natural science (Husserl 1974: 45). Again, this is certainly true, but does it have a direct bearing on the issue of predication and pre-predicative experience? Landgrebe believes it does: "Every return to 'pure experience' . . . remains content with nature as already idealized, which is equally true of the logician when he inquires about the empirical foundations of knowledge; . . . the logician also always sees the meaning of cognitive functions in the attainment of this 'in itself', in 'objective' knowledge, and its goal in the determination of the existence 'for everyone' and 'once and for all'" (Husserl 1973: 45). In other words, if we want to trace back the entities and relations that are encountered in logical thinking to pre-predicative experience, we need to be alert to the fact that in a world dominated by natural science what we take to be our experience is already covered over by all sorts of idealizations. However, if by "the logician" we mean a person thinking in terms of formalized logical variables and relations such as "S is p," or "~p" (negation), or "A v B" (non-exclusive disjunction), then it is not clear at all why the logician would necessarily conceive of the entities or relations expressed by her variables as idealized in the sense of the natural sciences. First, formalized logical language already existed prior to the birth of modern natural science. Medieval handbooks of logic already employ basic formalized notation to designate, for instance, different forms of syllogism. The relationship between logical formalized language and the objects encountered in experience is thus de facto independent from the relationship between the objects encountered in experience and natural-scientific idealizations. Second, even if we now live in a world where natural science holds the interpretive upper hand, it is simply not true that the forms of predication we employ in everyday speech (and that logic in Husserl's sense categorizes) invariably refer to idealized entities. If upon leaving the house I tell my wife that the car keys are on the kitchen table, the predicative form "S is p" that articulates my judgment does not refer to idealized natural-scientific entities, but simply to the keys and table we both directly experience in perception. True, in a cultural world deeply shaped by the results of natural science, upon reflection I might be tempted to devalue my perceptual experience and tell myself that actually there are no such things as car keys, tables, and wives but only aggregates of subatomic particles. From Husserl's point of view this tendency is indeed problematic because it threatens our human self-understanding and even our understanding of natural science. In order to counteract this tendency, we need a regression to the life-world (the world of cars, keys, and wives) and an appreciation of its foundational import vis-à-vis the idealized world of subatomic particles. But this problem differs from the problem of how the predicative structure "S is p" can legitimately articulate my perceptual experience of the keys being on the kitchen table. Lumping the two problems together under one heading is not helpful as we attempt to appreciate them as problems and to appraise the value of Husserl's proposed solutions.

8.2 THE REGRESSION TO PRE-PREDICATIVE EXPERIENCE IN *EJ*

EJ offers the most complete presentation of Husserl's so-called genetic phenome-nology. In keeping with Dieter Lohmar's recent formulation, the main difference be-tween Husserl's early phenomenological project (roughly from *Logical Investigations* until *Ideas I*) and his later genetic phenomenology is that "genetic analyses investi-gate the experiential history of our acts" (Lohmar 2012: 266), whereas early (so-called "static") phenomenology focuses on the essential features of "single simple or com-plex acts" (Lohmar 2012: 266). "History" in this context does not mean the biograph-ical vicissitudes of this or that particular human subject but rather the experiential dynamics that govern the unfolding of a subjective life as such. Classical examples of static phenomenological analyses are the distinction between perceptual presentation and judgment in §§27–9 of the Fifth Logical Investigation (Husserl 2001: 127–42), where Husserl establishes that simple perception and judgment differ with respect to their act-matter, rather than their act-quality alone, or the distinction between an intentional act in the broad sense and a *cogito* as an intentional act accompanied by explicit attention in §§35–7 of *Ideas I* (Husserl 2014: 60–5). By contrast, genetic phenomenology does not ask about how simple perception, attention, and judgment differ with respect to their es-sential structure, but rather if and how acts of these three distinct classes are structurally connected in the concrete life of an experiencing subject.

For instance, in §§16–19 of EJ Husserl provides painstaking analyses of how a subject (the "ego") is affected by sensory saliences (*Abgehobenheit*) coming to prominence from the subject's perceptual background (Husserl 1973: 75–6). The occurrence of a sudden noise in our acoustic field, for instance, elicits a tendency in us to turn our attention to-ward it. If the ego gives way and complies with the tendency, thereby turning its attention explicitly toward the noise, the intentional background experience turns into a *cogito*. Thus, Husserl explains, "every cogito, every explicit ego-act, is a striving, accomplished by, and arising from, the ego and capable of being worked out in various ways" (Husserl 1973: 78). The interest-driven striving that emerges from the act of turning our attention toward a sensuous salience inaugurates a teleological dynamic in consciousness. If this dynamic unfolds unimpeded, the subject turning toward a sensuous salience, thereby enacting a *cogito*, will be motivated to "explicate" the inner components of the sensuous salience (in our example: volume, duration, intensity, pitch, etc.) and finally to articu-late full-blown predicative judgments about it ("it was a crash," etc.). With this genetic analysis, therefore, Husserl has supplemented the distinction between *cogito* and back-ground experience that is developed in the aformentioned sections of *Ideas I* with a ro-bust theory about how a background perceptual experience can be transformed into a *cogito*. Moreover, as he writes in a research manuscript, if the "interest in being and being-thus" inaugurated by an act of explicit, attentional intending (*cogito*) "comes to fruition (*sich auswirken*)" without impediments, it "leads all the way up to predicative judgment and theorizing" (Husserl 2008: 366). Background perception, *cogito* (perception accompanied by attention) and judgment are thus teleologically connected. Accordingly, we can see these three types of act as standing in a genetic relationship. The tendency inherent in our turning toward the object "generates" or "brings about," as it were, the subsequent acts of explicit perception and judgment.

The genetic perspective is particularly fruitful for Husserl's project of grounding the formalized structures of logic in pre-predicative experience. The formalized structure of categorial (viz. copulative) judgment reads "S is p." Categorial judgment is thus a form of *synthesis*, one in which a subject-concept is synthetically related through the copula to a predicate-concept. How is it possible that such a highly abstract form of synthesis involving such highly abstract kinds of entities (concepts) can be about the world, in other words, that it articulates meaningfully states-of-affairs given in perception? A Kantian might answer that the structures of judgment are already involved in the very process of perceiving, that they make meaningfully structured perceptions possible in the first place. This line of answer is untenable for a phenomenologist. We have no experience whatsoever of employing judgments or concepts when we are simply perceiving some object. We certainly *can* issue a perceptual judgment while perceiving the object, but we do not judge all the time. A Kantian might reply that to say that concepts and the forms of judgment are involved in perception does not mean to say that we are judging all the time. She might then resort to the notion of "having certain capacities" as opposed to actively exercising those capacities, or else propose some notion of tacit or implicit involvement of judicative forms and concepts in perceptual experience. These are also non-starters for a phenomenologist. The appeal to hidden faculties or capacities of the human soul, let alone the appeal to unconscious workings that remain inaccessible to experience, violates the normative principle of phenomenological description: intuitive givenness in direct experience.

Husserl's strategy is different. He sets out to show that the predicative synthesis at work in "S is p" has its origin in a more rudimentary, low-level kind of perceptual synthesis that pre-figures, as it were, synthetic forms like "S is p." This low-level perceptual synthesis is called "explicative synthesis" and it governs the activity of "explicative contemplation" (Husserl 1973: 112). Explicative contemplation consists in the exploration of the object's internal horizon, i.e., in the apprehension of the object's properties while maintaining an overriding interest in the object as such (see Husserl 1973: 113–14). The unique "synthesis of overlapping" (Husserl 1973: 115) at work in this kind of consciousness, where the properties are not apprehended as items in their own right but stand in partial coincidence with the very object in which they inhere, prefigure the conceptual synthesis of two distinct items occurring in a predicative judgment attributing the property p to the subject S. Most importantly, it is precisely in the process of explicative contemplation that "the indeterminate theme S turns into the substrate of the properties which emerge, and they themselves are constituted in it as its determinations" (Husserl 1973: 114). Thus, in order to be able to connect an S to a p in a predicative judgment, the consciousness of S as the identical object-substrate of a multiplicity of p-determinations is entirely presupposed. This kind of consciousness is not generated by predicative judgment. It is a result of the activity of explicative contemplation. For this reason Husserl can state that "with this, we are at the place of origin of the first of the so-called 'logical categories'" and that "all categories and categorial forms which appear [in predicative judgment] are erected on the pre-predicative syntheses and have their origin in them" (Husserl 1973: 115).

As mentioned at the beginning of this chapter, the conceptual pair "full-fledged form (*Vollform*)/ prefiguring form (*Vorform*)" is the fundamental guiding thread of the project carried out in *EJ*. The pattern of analysis just presented with regard to explicative contemplation and categorial judgment can be found ubiquitously in *EJ*. For instance, §21 (Husserl 1973: 87–101) is devoted to the origin of negation in the pre-predicative experience of "disappointment" (Husserl 1973: 88). When, over the course of exploring an object in perception, some of our expectations regarding the properties it will display are disappointed, a retrospective modification of sense occurs, one in which the sense previously projected on the object is canceled. Retrospective cancelation of anticipated sense is thus the pre-predicative origin of logical negation, such that Husserl can write: "It thus appears that negation is not first the business of the act of predicative judgment but that in its original form it already appears in the pre-predicative sphere of receptive experience" (Husserl 1973: 90). Furthermore, tracing back logical negation to retrospective cancelation in the wake of disappointment provides a resource to take a stand on the vexed question of the correct interpretation of negation in judgment. Affirmation and negation do not stand on equal footing as modifications of the copula, but rather, negation is a derivative form, i.e., a negative stance on an originally affirmative identification. As Dominique Pradelle argues in a recent paper: "As a result, the original structure remains the affirmative predicative form 'S / is / p', the negative declination of which is the derived form 'S /not (is / p)'" (Pradelle 2012: 355).

Another instance of the same pattern of analysis is the chapter on types and empirical generalities (Husserl 1973: 321–37). Husserl shows that the origin of concepts as ideal objects involved in universal judgments ("Cats are mammals") is to be found in the constitution of empirical types, that is, low-level, malleable bundles of expectations based on foregoing experience of various types of objects. Types guide our encounters with new objects and govern our attempts to make sense of what we do not know on the basis of analogy with what we already know. Unlike concepts, types do not have a definite intension and an indefinitely large extension. A subject's type "cat" is based on the finite number of cats she has actually experienced, and it projects onto the world a set of expectations about what can legitimately count as a cat. It is only by a shift of focus from actual instances of the type to the ideal "something" that recurs as identical in all instances that we first form concepts as new kinds of entities that, unlike types, allow us to judge in the mode of "in general."

These are just sketches of Husserl's analyses in *EJ*, but they are sufficient to identify the pattern of analysis at work in the book: from (logical, predicative) *Vollform* back to (perceptual, pre-predicative) *Vorform*. Crucially, the very idea of a rudimentary structure that prefigures the full logical structure and the backward movement employed in the analysis entail a distinctive view about the nature of the *forward movement* from pre-predicative *Vorform* to logical *Vollform*. If the rudimentary form is to prefigure the full logical form, then there has to be a kind of *structural affinity* between the two. Hence, the transition from pre-predicative to predicative form has to "preserve," so to speak, the *structural affinity*. This is why Husserl characterizes the transition from explicative contemplation to predicative judgment as a kind of *reenactment* of the pre-predicative synthesis of (partial) coincidence described above. When we judge, we are guided by an active interest in registering the enrichment of the sense of S through the explication of p. If explicative contemplation passively constitutes the unity 'S_p', then "being turned toward this unity in order to apprehend it implies repeating the process in a changed attitude, making an active synthesis from a passive one" (Husserl 1973: 208). The active reenactment of a foregoing passive synthesis, however, also has a "creative" side to it. The active articulation of the object-unity via the judgment "S is p" gives rise to an object of a new kind, namely, a categorially structured object called "state-of-affairs," which becomes available for higher-level judicative activity.

If this is correct, then we have one more reason to reject Landgrebe's equation of the movement from predicative to pre-predicative forms with the movement from the idealized world of science to the life-world. The perceptual objects encountered in the life-world and the idealized objects of mathematical natural science do not stand in a *Vorform–Vollform* relationship. We cannot say that my desk as perceived is merely a rudimentary prefiguration of my desk as viewed through the lens of natural science, namely, as a conglomeration of atoms. It does not suffice to reenact the kinds of syntheses going on in my perception of the desk guided by an active theoretical interest in order to constitute the conglomeration of atoms. The relationship between life-world objects and idealized scientific entities is precisely *not* one of structural affinity. Scientific ideali-zation amounts to a thoroughgoing alteration of our notion of object and, when natural science degenerates into the worldview of naturalism, idealized objects tend to *supplant* perceived objects. A conglomeration of atoms is not merely a perceived desk as pred-icatively articulated. It is an object of a completely new kind. In order to substantiate this claim, we now have to consider the notion of idealization presented in *Crisis* in its own right.

8.3 THE REGRESSION TO THE LIFE-WORLD IN *CRISIS*

While *EJ* is still relatively little known, Husserl's *Crisis* is arguably the most widely read and influential of his late writings. Part of the book's appeal certainly has to do with Husserl's engagement with the history of philosophy, which features prominently in the narrative developed in *Crisis*. However, the most successful concept stemming from Husserl's final philosophical feat is undoubtedly the concept of life-world.

Husserl counterposes the life-world as "the everyday surrounding world of life" (Husserl 1970: 104) to the idealized world of natural science, and argues that it is only by the rehabilitating the former that the true meaning of the scientific project can be reactivated.[9] In Husserl's narrative, science has lost significance for the questions of meaning and purpose defining our human condition. This is because as natural scientific practice became habitual over the course of the centuries, scientists lost awareness of the foundational operations at the origin of their own work and of its inherence in the world of human experience, the life-world. Thus, as the natural sciences gained increasing reputation, they became the single authoritative source for our human self-understanding. In their present shape, however, they have little to offer for this purpose. In fact, the picture of the world that the sciences helped to create dramatically downplays our human aspirations. The very world in which those aspirations emerge is demoted to a mere illusion or subjective manifestation: all that there is, we are told, are impersonal atoms, molecules, forces, and the like. Human themselves are nothing but conglomerations of atoms, molecules, and forces. However, if this is the kind of picture flowing from the natural sciences, how are we supposed to become proactive, self-responsible, and future-oriented agents? Thankfully, Husserl does not believe that the findings of natural science are necessarily irreconcilable with the project of an enlightened humanity. On the contrary, he believes that we need science in order to bring that project to fulfillment. However, in order for science to be able to give a positive contribution to human self-understanding, the first thing we need is a new self-understanding of science itself. We need a *Besinnung*, a reactivation of the original sense of natural science and a rehabilitation of the life-world as the world that is constantly presupposed by natural scientific practice.

The distinctive feature of modern natural science is what Husserl calls *mathematization of nature* (Husserl 1970: 23). This means treating the world as a system of numerical relations that can be fully mastered with the aid of formulae entailing free variables. In order for the world to fit into purely mathematical formulae, however, a preliminary move is necessary. Husserl calls this move *idealization*. Idealization consists in substituting an intuitive, albeit imperfect object with a non-intuitive idea, the corresponding intuitive instances of which can be viewed as its approximations. The clearest example of idealization is offered by geometry. As Husserl argues in the famous §9 of *Crisis*, geometrical thinking does not operate with sensible shapes, which are by necessity always imperfect. There is no such thing as a perfect circle in nature. In fact, in order to be able to visualize a circle, we need to draw a circular line in our mind (or on the board). No matter how thin, the circumference of an intuitively visualizable circle will still have some width to it, whereas the circumference that geometry defines as the

---

[9] It should be noted that the concept "life-world" in Husserl has a variety of meanings and functions, only one of which is captured by the phrase "everyday surrounding world of life" and contrasted to the idealized world of science; however, for the purpose of this chapter this is the most relevant meaning of "life-world" and hence the only one I consider. Whether this is the fundamental meaning and what is its relation to other meanings is an important question, which I cannot adjudicate here.

locus of all points equidistant from a given point should, in keeping with the definition, consist exclusively of extensionless points. The idealized circle can thus be viewed
asymptotically as the limit-case of a series of circles whose circumference becomes
increasingly thin.

As the example of geometry makes clear, modern natural science did not invent idealization. Rather, the founding father of science, Galileo Galilei, found geometry as a
cultural given, and considered the idealizing procedure characterizing the geometrical
thinking habit to be "obvious" (Husserl 1970: 24). Galileo's stroke of genius consisted
in extending the idealizing procedure to the whole of nature, rather than limiting it to
the quantitative, directly measurable dimensions of natural entities.[10] Thus, for example,
from the overall "causal style" (Husserl 1970: 31) of nature, modern natural science
creates the idea of universal deterministic causality. The idea of universal deterministic
causality is the idealized version of the experienced causal style of the world, which,
unlike universal causality, has plenty of room for sheer chance. As Husserl writes in a
manuscript: "The causal style of the world entails that some things in the world are determined and some things are open-ended; some things are 'causally' dependent from
and determined by the physical circumstances and some things occur by chance. In
this context, chance does not mean unknown causality, but rather an irruption that is
not motivated by the circumstances" (Husserl 2012: 310). In the very same way in which
an ideal circle is the limit-case of an intuitive circle whose circumference becomes increasingly thin, universal deterministic causality is the limit-case of intuitive causality in
which the chance-factor progressively disappears.

The idealization of natural causality thereby accomplished goes hand in hand with the
project of idealizing the qualitative aspects of the experienced world, those aspects that
"carry," so to speak, the very experienceability of things. If so-called secondary qualities
are caught up in the universal deterministic causality of natural processes, then they,
too, must be in principle reducible to corresponding ideas. However, is this really possible? In a manuscript dated 1924 Husserl answers this question positively. He raises the
example of our experience of red, and argues that in the experience of a multiplicity of
shades of red we can experience something like an "increment" (Steigerung), a progressive approximation to an "increasingly perfect red, whereby at each stage red is more
red" (Husserl 2012: 232). This kind of experience would generate the consciousness of
a "pure red" (Husserl 2012: 232), as the limit-case of the imperfect shades of red experienced in the series. However, this description seems seriously botched, and it is no
surprise that the theory presented in Crisis is very different from the one just sketched.
As François De Gandt aptly emphasizes: "There is no such thing as the perfection of the
color blue, or a norm for the scent of jasmine, as there is a perfection for the circle or the
plane. One cannot depart from empirical and sensible gradualness in the case of colors
or smells" (De Gandt 2004: 59). Granted, it is correct to describe our experience of a

---

[10] For a more thorough discussion of Galilei and the philosophical project of Crisis see Staiti
2014: 252–63.

multiplicity of shades of the same color as entailing (at least implicitly) the experience of a common element that grounds the similarity (i.e., "the color" itself); however, this common element is *perfectly* exhibited in each of the given shades, such that "electric blue" or "ruby red" are perfectly legitimate manifestations of "blue" or "red"[11] and not merely imperfect instances of a non-intuitive "pure blue" or "pure red." By contrast, if by "pure" we merely mean "unmixed," then we can certainly rank a multiplicity of pinkish shades of color with respect to their proximity to "pure" (unmixed) red. However, in so doing we remain entirely in the field of direct intuition. We are not operating with ideas, but rather with intuitive givens. Husserl must have come to realize the fundamental difference between quantitative and qualitative aspects of experience, since his thesis in *Crisis* is that the qualitative aspects of experience can only be idealized and mathematized *indirectly*, an operation through which the whole object in the experienced fullness of its qualities (the "plenum") becomes amenable to idealization to begin with (Husserl 1970: 37–8). Total idealizability and universal applicability of mathematical formulae thus becomes the guiding "hypothesis" (Husserl 1970: 42) of natural scientific thinking. In this context, Husserl makes the famous remark that natural-scientific theories are like "a garb of ideas," through which we "take for true being what is actually a method" (Husserl 1970: 53). In so doing, we devalue our subject-related experience (which is reduced to untrue being or mere appearance) and the life-world that discloses itself in it.[12]

What the natural scientist forgets is that in order for the whole project of natural science to work, the idealized entities and mathematized formulae that she employs must be related back to the life-world that we experience. Thus, de-idealization and re-instatement of intuitive experience is as vital to natural science as idealization.[13] Natural science, however, takes this possibility for granted and thus construes the relationship between the mathematized entities of its theories and the objects of our experience as a truth versus falsehood relationship. Husserl's project in *Crisis* is to carry out the

[11] For a more comprehensive treatment of this issue, which harks back to Lotze's theory of first and second generalities, see Staiti 2016b.

[12] Note that this characterization of the relationship between life-world and scientific theories does not automatically entail a defense of either scientific realism or instrumentalism. Awareness of the idealizing character of natural science does not necessarily prevent us from accepting non-observable dimensions of being that only idealizing procedures can disclose. It would only prevent us from taking the idealizing procedures and their products to be perfect 'mirrors' such non-observable dimensions. For an informative discussion of this point see Wiltsche 2012.

[13] Incidentally, we find the very same line of thought as a critique of Marburg neo-Kantianism over twenty years before *Crisis* in a forgotten but brilliant student of Dilthey, Max Frischeisen-Köhler. In *Wissenschaft und Wirklichkeit* Frischeisen-Köhler writes: "No matter how high up to ever more general laws theory ascends in its aspiration to comprehensiveness, since they are not meant to hold for an arbitrary possible world in general but for our unique world, these laws must entail a determination that expresses this relation to our world and makes possible to revert back to appearances in this world" (Frischeisen-Köhler 1912: 47). Husserl received and read intensively Frischeisen-Köhler's book, such that a direct influence on these matters cannot be excluded. For a presentation of Frischeisen-Köhler's philosophy see Staiti 2016a.

de-idealizing movement back to intuitive life-world experience in a different key. The world of science and the world of our direct experience are not competitors. Science itself is indebted to the world of direct experience, not only because the regularities of experience are presupposed by the idealizing procedures of science, but also because the very idea of natural-scientific cognition emerges as a desirable goal *within* rather than *against* our life-world.

However, in order for the modern ideal of natural-scientific cognition to emerge in the first place, an immeasurable repository of pre-scientific, everyday cognition must be available and capitalized upon. Natural scientific theories as intersubjective, indefinitely available cultural formations presuppose a whole host of publicly communicable cognitive achievements, whose refinement via idealization and mathematization is at the origin of natural scientific truth. For this reason, the life-world cannot be characterized as pre-predicative. Nothing like natural science could be edified on a merely pre-predicative ground. The cognitive yields of everyday, life-worldly predication, with its logical forms and patterns are the *sina qua non* for the very conception of natural science. True, as David Carr repeatedly remarks in his writings on *Crisis*, Husserl often characterizes the life-world as perceptual (see for instance Carr 1974: 190–3 and Carr 1977). For precisely this reason, Carr finds it impossible to reconcile this characterization with passages where the life-world is described as historical and cultural. The difference between the life-world as perceptual and the life-world as historical-cultural would lie precisely in the presence or absence of language. However, when Husserl speaks of the life-world as perceptual he does not mean pre-predicative or pre-linguistic. "Perception" in this context is meant in a broad sense, which includes both pre-predicative experience and perceptual predication. Describing the life-world as perceptual thus is not meant to be a gesture toward a primeval, pre-linguistic (pre-predicative) dimension. Perceiving and talking about what we perceived and how it matters to us, prior to all natural-scientific theorizing, is our daily bread in the life-world. Showing that our daily bread is not an illusion, but the nourishment on which something like natural science necessarily lives, is one of the major achievements of Husserl's *Crisis*.

8.4 Pre-Predicative Experience and Life-World in Post-Husserlian Phenomenology: A Look at Merleau-Ponty and Derrida

In light of the above analyses one may wonder why the basic distinction between life-world and pre-predicative sphere has gone mostly unnoticed. One reason is certainly the authority of the introduction to *EJ*, which mistakenly equates the two notions, as I have argued above; however, in this last section I want to address a second reason, which has to do with the interpretation of Husserl's intellectual trajectory characterizing much post-Husserlian phenomenology. Let us look briefly at Maurice Merleau-Ponty and the early Jacques Derrida, whose work is largely influenced by (and largely influenced the reception of) the late Husserl.

Despite significant differences in the development of their respective philosophies, Merleau-Ponty and the early Derrida share a common perspective on Husserl's transcendental phenomenology. This perspective is best described by their identical assessment of the phenomenological reduction, Husserl's famous methodological device to trace our naïve assumption of the existence of a subject-independent world back to the constitutive dynamics of transcendental consciousness. In his preface to *Phenomenology of Perception* Merleau-Ponty writes: "The most important lesson which the reduction teaches us is the impossibility of a complete reduction" (Merleau-Ponty 2002: xv). This is because, in Merleau-Ponty's narrative, while Husserl initially presented the reduction as "the return to a transcendental consciousness before which the world is spread out" (Merleau-Ponty 2002: xii), his subsequent analyses led him to discover a series of phenomena that are not constituted *in* or *through*, but rather presupposed by transcendental consciousness and are thus recalcitrant to every reduction. Time, genesis, the pre-predicative sphere, functioning or anonymous intentionality, and life-world thus become titles for dimensions of sense that are prior to the constitutive activity of a transcendental consciousness and cannot be fully captured through a reflective-descriptive method. While the initial gesture of the phenomenological reduction was geared toward establishing a field of absolute self-transparency and self-possession prior to all worldly being, the further development of phenomenology led Husserl to the discovery of a "'primary faith' which binds us to a world as to our native land, and the being of what is perceived is the pre-predicative being towards which our whole existence is polarized" (Merleau-Ponty 2002: 375).

Derrida echoes the same reading in his 1953–4 dissertation *The Problem of Genesis in Husserl's Philosophy*: "The 'transcendental' reduction . . . is the reduction, the farewell to every historical genesis, in the classical and 'worldly' sense of the term. But after this retreat to a philosophical purity of an idealist style, there are announced a kind of return, the outlines of a movement of broad reconquest: it is the notion of transcendental genesis which [is] resistant in principle to every reduction" (Derrida 2003: xix). In Derrida's narrative, "transcendental genesis" thus becomes the catch-all title for a whole host of different phenomena whose common denominator is their irreducibility to a constituting transcendental consciousness, thus determining the crisis of Husserl's idealism. As he puts it: "The theme of transcendental genesis . . . ought to bring us close to the sphere of pre-predicative existence, of the 'life-world' (*Lebenswelt*), of primitive time, of transcendental intersubjectivity, all factors that as such are not originally freighted with a sense arising from the activity of the 'ego'" (Derrida 2003: 3). Later in his study Derrida quotes abundantly from the introduction to *EJ* (Derrida 2003: 109–17) and defines the life-world as "the locus of all pre-predicative clear evidences"

(Derrida 2003: 109, translation modified). He then denounces as ambiguous the characterization of the world as the horizon of all pre-predicative substrates of judgment
and the world as concrete life-world, rife with all the products of foregoing transcendental constitution.

Our analysis in the sections above should have made it clear that there is actually no
ambiguity or tension here. The sphere of pre-predicative experience does not coincide
with the world, let alone the life-world, but is rather a non-independent, and yet fundamental layer of constitution *within* the life-world. Thus, there is no independent notion
of world emerging from the investigation of pre-predicative experience in *EJ* that can
be set up against or contrasted to the life-world as described in *Crisis*.[14] Merleau-Ponty's
and Derrida's failure to see this point can be explained by reference to the interpretive
schema introduced above. According to their narrative concerning the reduction, the
sphere of pre-predicative experience and the life-world can be seen as two instances of
one and the same class of "genetic" phenomena that disrupt Husserl's original project
of reaching a fully self-transparent domain of absolute consciousness. The more fine-
grained distinctions between pre-predicative experience and life-world understandably
eluded the French phenomenologists' more large-scale narrative.

8.5 CONCLUSION

In this chapter I have argued that the project of *EJ* and the project of *Crisis* must be carefully distinguished. *EJ* envisions a movement back from the forms of predication to
pre-predicative experience. This kind of movement is a movement from the *Vollformen*
(full-fledged forms) of logic to the *Vorformen* (prefigurations) of perceptual experience.
Crisis envisions a movement back from the idealized world of modern natural science to
our everyday life-world. This kind of movement is one of de-idealization and rehabilitation of our intuitive experience. Unlike the level of pre-predicative experience described
in *EJ*, there is a lot of chattering going on in our everyday life-world. The predicative
achievements of life-world experience, made possible by the underlying pre-predicative
forms, are thus a presupposition for the project outlined in *Crisis*. The project outlined
in *EJ* is thus the necessary presupposition for the project outlined in *Crisis*, and, contra
Landgrebe, does not coincide with it.

---

[14]   A glance at the index of *EJ* tellingly reveals that not only the word *Lebenswelt*, but also the word
Welt occur almost exclusively (with just a few exceptions) in the introduction. One can thus legitimately
question the widely spread assumption that the sphere of pre-predicative experience in *EJ* can be
meaningfully characterized as a full-blown "world."

REFERENCES

Bachelard, S. (1990), *A Study of Husserl's Formal and Transcendental Logic* (Evanston, IL: Northwestern University Press).

Blumenberg, H. (2006), *Beschreibung des Menschen* (Frankfurt a. M.: Suhrkamp).

Carr, D. (1974), *Phenomenology and the Problem of History: A Study of Husserl's Transcendental Philosophy* (Evanston, IL: Northwestern University Press).

Carr, D. (1977), "Husserl's problematic concept of the life-world," in F. Ellison and P. McCormick (eds), *Husserl: Expositions and Appraisals* (Notre Dame, IN: Notre Dame University Press), 202–12.

De Gandt, F. (2004), *Husserl et Galilée. Sur la crise des sciences européennes* (Paris: J. Vrin).

Derrida, J. (2003), *The Problem of Genesis in Husserl's Philosophy* (Chicago, IL: University of Chicago Press).

Fellman, F. (1983), *Gelebte Philosophie in Deutschland. Denkformen der Lebenswelt-phänomenologie und der kritischen Theorie* (Freiburg: Alber).

Frischeisen-Köhler, M. (1912), *Wissenschaft und Wirklichkeit* (Leipzig: Teubner).

Husserl, E. (1970), *The Crisis of European Sciences and Transcendental Phenomenology* (Evanston, IL: Northwestern University Press).

Husserl, E. (1974), *Experience and Judgment* (Evanston, IL: Northwestern University Press).

Husserl, E. (1978), *Formal and Transcendental Logic* (The Hague: Martinus Nijhoff).

Husserl, E. (2001), *Logical Investigations*, vol. 2 (London: Routledge).

Husserl, E. (2008), *Die Lebenswelt. Auslegungen der vorgegebenen Welt und ihrer Konstitution. Texte aus dem Nachlass (1916–1937)*, Husserliana 39 (Dordrecht: Springer).

Husserl, E. (2012), *Zur Lehre vom Wesen und zur Methode der eidetischen Variation. Texte aus dem Nachlass (1891–1935)*, Husserliana 61 (Dordrecht: Springer).

Husserl, E. (2014), *Ideas for a Pure Phenomenology and Phenomenological Philosophy: First Book: General Introduction to Pure Phenomenology* (Indianapolis, IN: Hackett).

Lohmar, D. (1996), "Zu der Entstehung und den Ausgangsmaterialien von Edmund Husserls Werk *Erfahrung und Urteil*," *Husserl Studies* 13/1: 31–71.

Lohmar, D. (2000), *Edmund Husserls "Formale und transzendentale Logik"* (Darmstadt: Wissenschaftliche Buchgesellschaft).

Lohmar, D. (2012), "Genetic phenomenology," in S. Luft and S. Overgaard (eds), *The Routledge Companion to Phenomenology* (London: Routledge), 266–75.

Merleau-Ponty, M. (2002), *Phenomenology of Perception* (London: Routledge).

Paci, E. (1972), "Life-world, time, and liberty in Husserl," in L. Embree (ed.), *Life-World and Consciousness: Essays for Aron Gurwitsch* (Evanston, IL: Northwestern University Press), 461–8.

Pradelle, D. (2012), "The phenomenological foundations of predicative structure," in D. Zahavi (ed.), *The Oxford Handbook of Contemporary Phenomenology* (Oxford: Oxford University Press), 349–76.

Seebohm, T. (1997), "Individuals, identity, names: Phenomenological considerations," in B. Hopkins (ed.), *Husserl in Contemporary Context: Prospects and Projects for Phenomenology* (Dordrecht: Kluwer), 115–50.

Staiti, A. (2014), *Husserl's Transcendental Phenomenology: Nature, Spirit, and Life* (Cambridge: Cambridge University Press).

Staiti, A. (2015), "Husserl and Rickert on the Nature of Judgment," *Philosophy Compass* 10: 815–27.

Staiti, A. (2016a), "Max Frischeisen-Köhler's Vindication of the Material Component of Cognition," *Philosophia Scientiae* 20/1: 119–42.

Staiti, A. (2016b), "Lotze and Husserl on First and Second Generality," *Discipline Filosofiche* 26/1: 47–66.

Wiltsche, H. (2012), "What Is Wrong with Husserl's Scientific Anti-Realism?" *Inquiry* 55/2: 105–30.

Yuasa, S. (1999), "Certainty, the fictitious essence of philosophy," in B. Hopkins (ed.), *Phenomenology: Japanese and American Perspectives* (Dordrecht: Kluwer), 83–103.

Zahavi, D. (2003), *Husserl's Phenomenology* (Stanford, CA: Stanford University Press).

CHAPTER 9

SCHELER ON THE MORAL AND POLITICAL SIGNIFICANCE OF THE EMOTIONS

ZACHARY DAVIS AND ANTHONY STEINBOCK

MAX Scheler (1874–1928) was a central figure to the early development of phenomenology. Husserl is owed of course the distinction as the founder of the phenomenological approach, but no thinker is more responsible for testing the boundaries and opening new horizons for phenomenological investigation than Scheler. In fact, at the height of his philosophical career, he was its brightest star (Spiegelberg 1994: 268–70). Contemporaries such Martin Heidegger and Ortega Y Gasset considered Scheler to be the greatest mind in all of Europe if not the entire world. Yet, almost as quickly as Scheler came into prominence his star has dimmed. Although considered historically important, his works have never enjoyed the same attention as those of Husserl and Heidegger or the same attention as second-generation phenomenologists such as Merleau-Ponty, Levinas, and Derrida. More recently, his work has garnered more attention as accounts of religious and emotional experiences are again taken seriously as significant fabrics of social life. Nonetheless, it is difficult to imagine that Scheler's influence will ever shine as brightly as it did during his lifetime.

In his remembrance of Scheler on the centenary of his birth (1874), Hans-Georg Gadamer describes Scheler as a *Verschwender*, as a squanderer (Gadamer 1975). This quite harsh judgment by Gadamer was meant ultimately as a means by which to pay homage to the tremendous contribution Scheler had made to both the birth and development of the Phenomenological Movement. One can only squander that which one possesses. His genius consisted in opening new avenues for phenomenological investigation. In addition to his best-known work on ethics, Scheler also wrote and pioneered work on the emotions, collective social unities, religious experience, the sociology of knowledge, philosophical anthropology, epistemology, metaphysics, history, and politics. Particularly for the latter avenues of thought, Scheler was unable to complete his projects, and as a consequence we are left with the unfinished manuscripts. For Gadamer, these were squandered opportunities, due in part to the restless and undisciplined mind of Scheler. If Scheler did not commit himself fully to a single course of thought, it can be argued that this was due to the fact that he at least saw the whole into which these avenues fit. In any case, Scheler did function as a signpost, illuminating ever new paths of unchartered phenomenological territory and gaining access to some of the most significant aspects of human experience.

The intent of this chapter is to trace Scheler's novel contribution to the phenomenological tradition by examining his distinctive approach to the evidential character of the emotions and how this manner of givenness accounts for personal bonds of solidarity. Scheler accounts for distinct modes of evidence and givenness that are irreducible to one another through a phenomenological analysis of the emotions. As a consequence, he is able to describe the unique manner in which the distinctively personal dimension of experience is given. Not only does this personal dimension reveal the unique character of the relation human beings have to one another, it also reveals the irreplaceability of each and every person. In section 9.1 of the chapter, we provide a brief historical sketch of Scheler's path to phenomenology and his development of the phenomenological approach. Section 9.2 shows how Scheler's analysis of the emotions overcomes a reductive tendency in Modernity by disclosing how the emotions have their own integrity and distinct structure of evidence. Section 9.3 builds upon this analysis and demonstrates how the emotions and their unique social nature are the basis for both the solidarity amongst persons and the call to collective action. Each of these discussions call attention to the deep influence Scheler's contemporary phenomenologists such as Edmund Husserl and Adolf Reinach had on his thought and ways in which Scheler was able to use this influence to embark upon new avenues for phenomenological investigation.

9.1 SCHELER'S PATH TO PHENOMENOLOGY

The creative nature of Scheler's mind was enriched by the great diversity of thought to which Scheler was exposed as a student of philosophy. As a youth, he read extensively in the works of Nietzsche and identified himself as a social democrat and enthusiastic Marxist. Both of these thinkers would have a lasting impact on his thought. In 1895 as a university student in Berlin, he attended the lectures of Wilhelm Dilthey and Georg Simmel. The following year, Scheler moved to Jena to finish his studies under the guidance of the neo-Kantian, Rudolf Euken. Rudolf Euken was a tremendously popular philosopher of his time, winning the Nobel Prize for literature in 1908. While studying in Jena, Scheler also traveled to Heidelberg and was introduced to Max Weber.

As his earliest writings indicate (Scheler 1971), these early philosophical influences led Scheler to think critically about the nature of our ethical and social existence. From the outset, however, it was apparent that Scheler was growing increasingly frustrated with the neo-Kantian methods used by his mentor, Rudolf Euken. The frustration was rooted in the inability of these methods to provide a secure foundation. In the concluding section of his *Habilitationsschrift*, Scheler lists twelve theses regarding his investigations into the transcendental and psychological methods. His first thesis describes his frustration:

> There is (excluding the principals of formal logic) no absolutely secure, self-evident datum from which philosophy, whether as metaphysics, epistemology, ethics, or aesthetics, could proceed. Neither the axioms of mathematics and the propositions of the mathematical natural sciences, nor "experience" (in the transcendental sense), nor the momentarily given sensation, nor an intuitive, original certainty of an ethical kind could give rise to any justified claim based on the value of such datum. (Scheler 1971: 334)

Soon after the publication of his *Habilitationsschrift*, Scheler met Husserl in 1901 and soon after read Husserl's *Logical Investigations*. According to the account Scheler gives in the Preface to the second edition of his *Habilitationsschrift* (1922), Scheler discovered in Husserl's notion of "categorial intuition" the "unshakeable datum of intuition" given in all cognition (Scheler 1971: 201). In his Sixth Logical Investigation, Husserl contrasts two distinct intuitions, simple and categorial intuitions. Simple intuitions refer to what is directly or immediately given to the senses such as the greenness of the tree or the warmth of a fire. Categorial intuitions refer to the *being* of being green or being warm, or as Husserl coins it, the "ideal being" of a particular object.[1] For Scheler, this notion a categorial intuition meant that it was possible to describe the self-givenness of ideal objects such as values that are disclosed in the emotional act of love and describe the rank order of the different value types. Not only did this discovery lead Scheler to reject his earlier thesis and overcome his frustrations regarding the lack of any irrefutable foundation, but it also led Scheler to develop his own understanding of the phenomenological approach. While Husserl's phenomenology may have allowed Scheler to overcome the limits of Euken's method, Scheler was to the very end still engaged with Euken's ideas regarding the inner quest for and irreducibility of the spiritual life.[2] The notion of evidence Scheler found in Husserl allowed him to develop further Euken's pursuit of an evidential account of the spiritual and personal dimensions of human experience.

In 1906, Scheler moved with his family to Munich where he took a position of *Privatdozent*. With Theodor Lipps, Scheler established a circle of the "Munich Phenomenologists." The early group consisted of such prominent thinkers as Alexander

---

[1] See Sokolowski's essay, "Husserl's Concept of Categorial Intuition," for further clarification on this notion in Husserl (Sokolowski 1983).

[2] At the end of his life (1928), Scheler writes that more than any other question, the questions "What is the human being and the human being's place in being?" have been with him from the first awakenings of his philosophical consciousness (Scheler 1976). Undoubtedly, Euken was the teacher that brought this question to such prominence in Scheler's consciousness.

Pfänder, Moritz Geiger, Adolf Reinach, and Theodor Conrad, all of whom were students of Lipps. Those who joined the group later were Dietrich von Hildebrand, Hedwig Martius, Herbert Leyendecker, and Maximillian Beck. After losing his teaching privileges at German universities due to controversies surrounding the divorce of his first wife and reported affairs with students, Scheler joined the Göttingen circle of phenomenology. This group consisted not only of Husserl, but also some of the most promising phenomenologists such as Adolf Reinach, Roman Ingarden, Alexandre Koyré, and Edith Stein.[3]

This period in which Scheler was a member of these earlier phenomenological circles was an incredibly prolific time for Scheler; but it was also an introduction to a growing critical attitude toward Husserl's insistence upon a transcendental phenomenology. Realist phenomenologists like Reinach insisted that phenomenology ought to concern itself directly with questions of being and ontology rather than bracket such concerns, as was Husserl's early approach. Scheler's contact with these realist phenomenologists impacted his thought greatly and motivated him to open the field of phenomenological investigation to address matters directly such as the holy, metaphysics, and the so-called world-ground.

What distinguished Scheler's phenomenological approach not only from Husserl's but also the realist phenomenologists was the personal nature of Scheler's understanding of philosophy and phenomenology. Philosophy, for Scheler, is the "*loving act of participation by the core of the human being in the essence of all things*" (Scheler 1954: 68). The human being as a loving, philosophical being is not motivated to know by a sense of a lack, as is the case of eros, but rather is motivated by the abundance and surfeit of the meaning of the world (Scheler 1963: 84). As a means to reawaken a sense of wonder, Scheler called for a rehabilitation of virtue, in particular the virtues of humility and reverence (Scheler 1972: 15). The philosopher lives in reverence of the world, an astonishment in a world of inexhaustible depth and secrets (Scheler 1972: 26).

Philosophical thought attends to the core meaning of knowledge as a *Seinsverhältnis*, an ontological relation. Knowledge, according to Scheler, is a relation of participation of a being in the *Sosein*, the being thus and so, of another being (Scheler 1980: 203). It is the humble divesting of oneself that opens one up to the other (Scheler 1980: 204) and presupposes the loving willingness to be open to that which is other. Following Augustine, Scheler takes love as the foundation for knowledge, thereby taking the affective and emotional life as the precondition for the rational (Scheler 1963: 87). Before the world is known, it is first given in love. Knowledge is possible only for a loving being (Scheler 1954: 83). This love is the movement of transcendence, a going beyond oneself, an opening to ever-richer meaning.

In Husserl's notion of the categorial intuition, Scheler found a means by which to participate most deeply in the meaning of the world. Phenomenology was thus, for Scheler,

---

[3] It was also during this time in Göttingen that Scheler became co-editor, along with Husserl, Pfänder, Geiger, and Reinach, of the greatly influential journal, *Jahrbuch für Philosophie und phänomenologische Forschung.*

a means of access. For this reason, Scheler insisted from the beginning that phenomenology was not a method, but an attitude (Scheler 1957: 380). The cultivation of this
phenomenological attitude grants access to the way in which the thing gives itself, to
the "unshakeable datum of intuition." As there is no judgment concerning the world in
advance of the investigation, there is no judgment concerning what counts and what
does not count as an experience. The phenomenologist, in the cultivation of this loving
attitude, attempts only to grasp what reveals itself as itself, as self-evident. For Scheler,
a tremendous array of experiences and essences were now made available for critical
investigation. It became possible to describe the order of the heart, the experience of
loving a person, and the givenness of the absolute. This privileged access of the phenomenological also requires that phenomenology call itself into question and what it has as a
tradition taken for granted as privileged modes of access.

9.2 SCHELER ON THE EMOTIONS AND THEIR DISTINCTIVE STRUCTURE OF EVIDENCE

Scheler opened himself to the field of evidence or self-givenness in many realms of experience. Some thinkers, including many phenomenologists, tended to presuppose the
way in which linguistic meaning or perceptual sense is given; for reasons we explain
later, they either took what we can call "presentation," as the exclusive way in which
something could count as an experience, or took it paradigmatically as what could be
given. If it fell outside of this way of object-givenness, it could not be reckoned as an experience with its own integrity, and even more, it was denied the advantage of any philosophical reckoning.

There were, and indeed are, thinkers within the phenomenological tradition who implicitly and explicitly challenge this paradigm, but many of them presuppose the very
paradigm that they are trying to challenge simply by trying to expand what presentational givenness means. For example, the other person, icons, artwork, God become accessible only because now they too join the rank of "objects."

However, it goes to the originality and incisiveness of Scheler that he detected phenomenologically distinct orders of givenness. This is marked not only with a terminological and intermittent methodological considerations in his early work—distinguishing
between a religious givenness as revelation (*Offenbarung*) from perceptual or object
manifestation (*Offenbarkeit*) (Scheler 1966, 1973a); in addition, his openness to different
kinds of givenness allowed him to elaborate systematically upon the emotional dimension of the human person and what he calls the "order of the heart" or "ordo amoris." He
did this by challenging two interrelated and fundamental presuppositions concerning
a philosophical anthropology (the meaning of the human person) and the order of
givenness (specifically, the emotional sphere).

Modernity's enthusiasm for the value of individual subjectivity, freedom as autonomy, and the prominent role that rationality plays in them left in its wake certain disvalues. Having identified cognition with rationality, and rationality with the meaning of (predominately male) human beings, the emotions became the province of what is non-human, instinctual, and characteristic of women, children, animals, and the mentally impaired. From the standpoint of rational evidence, the emotions tended to be regarded as unfounded matters of instinct, and as devoid of internal evidence and meaning. If they are to be made meaningful, they must become the province of judgment; if they are not rational, they are to find a home in the psyche or become the object of psychoanalysis; if they are to be real, they are to be naturalized or able to be quantified.

Far from having any evidential import, far from being able to disclose the meaning of persons, emotions were therefore customarily regarded as irrational ruptures of objectivity, violations of human potential, and ultimately devoid of any spiritual and/or philosophical significance. They became merely subjective matters devoid of an objective or rational grounding, and thus had no legitimate bearing on the purpose or meaning of human existence. As Max Scheler observed, Modernity no longer understood the emotional sphere as having its own cognitive order or even a meaningful symbolic language; it was no longer allowed to govern the sense and meaning of our lives. Instead, emotions were regarded as blind processes running their course in nature; as such, they required a rational technology for restraining them so that we would not come to harm, and so that human activity could be truly spiritual, cognitive, and meaningful (Scheler 1957: 364–6).

As a result, we instead become very practiced in dulling our sensibilities to the emotions as providing an interpersonal social and political compass. The entire realm of the emotions were surrendered, becoming either an object of the psychology of inner perception, a matter of individual interior ethics, or the subject of intellection belonging to the province of judgment as inferential acts of thought. Yet, if logic wants to investigate the structure of interconnections and relations, or the acts through which we grasp these logical interconnections, it is a sign of unsurpassed arbitrariness, asserts Scheler, to carry out these kinds of investigations into modes of givenness and essential connections only in the case of perception and thinking, but to abandon to psychology the remaining part of the spirit (Scheler 1957: 364–6).

For Scheler, however, the emotions have their own structure, their own cognitive dimension, their own kinds of evidence without either somehow being tied to rationality in order to be meaningful, or on the contrary, being ostracized from the sphere of evidence because they are not rational. How does this become a problem phenomenologically? Phenomenological attempts to deal with the emotions must confront the following sets of issues. In traditional phenomenological terms: Do acts peculiar to the emotional sphere simply follow the coordinates of the noesis–noema structure of intentionality? This is not to ask if they have no intentional structure, but only if the noesis–noema structure is the only form of "intentionality" that could define the emotions. Do they rely on this structure to gain their integrity and evidence? That is, are the emotions *founded in* certain epistemic acts that have relations to objects in order to exist for us, or do they have a *unique structure* that is independent of such acts? Or does the emotional sphere, which concerns the person (and not simply the epistemically engaged subject), have an essentially different structure?

We find an initial and extremely clear discussion of such a problematic in Husserlian phenomenology, first in Edmund Husserl's *Logical Investigations*, and then later in his *Ideas*. Allow us first to explain what Husserl means by these kinds of acts and their relation of foundation. While Edmund Husserl is often credited for realizing that consciousness is always consciousness of something, this insight was already well prepared by Descartes, Kant, and Hegel, among others. Husserl's groundbreaking insights did not simply involve the discovery of the intentional structure of consciousness, but concerned his unique phenomenological approach that allowed him to describe the "how" of giving (sense, meaning) of what something is (the being of the object) in relation to the power and limits of subjectivity. In the *Logical Investigations*, Husserl described this relationship under the heading of "objectivating acts." An objectivating act is that intentional act which "refers" to an object in and through a certain sense. Thus, an objectivating act is that kind of act which allows there to be an intending and an intended object. This is known generally as the intentional structure, and is what Husserl also calls a process of *Gegenständlichung*, that is, the process by which something acquires the status of a *constituted* "object"; in this way the process is a kind of object-giving, it is precisely "objectivating."

An objectivating act is not only that intentional act in which an object is given as sense, but it is also such that it needs no additional, adjuncting act in order for an object to be given. A non-objectivating act is said to be an act that is "founded" on an objectivating act, requiring the latter's structure (Husserl 1968: 493–4; Sokolowski 1964; Welton 1983). The objectivating act is what allows the non-objectivating act to have this intentional structure, to have an act–sense correlation through which something is given beyond the one who executes acts. Examples of non-objectivating acts are acts of valuing, willing, and emotional acts.

Husserl's initial portrayal of the structure of objectivating acts is carried over into his discussion of the intentional relational in the *Ideas*. In brief, the intentional structure that was characterized by means of the "quality" and the "material" of the act in the *Logical Investigations* is now described in the *Ideas* (with certain qualifications) in terms of the "noesis" or intending side of the relation and the "noema" or the intended side (Husserl 1950). Furthermore, the characterization of the relationship between objectivating acts and non-objectivating acts is also carried over into Husserl's discussion of intentionality (Husserl 1950: §§94–5). The point is that emotional acts are founded in more basic essential intentional epistemic acts, giving the latter a peculiar "privilege." Accordingly, "a perceiving, phantasying, judging, or the like, founds a stratum of valuing which overlays it completely" (Husserl 1950: §95, §117).

To say that emotional acts are founded in more basic intentional acts means for Husserl that the emotions are dependent upon "objectivating" acts because they require the characteristics of the latter in order for the "non-objectivating" acts to mean something beyond themselves as presented under a certain sense. Thus, either acts have an epistemic structure (where cognition is equated with a "rational" structure) or they are—in this case—the province of mere instinct and have no cognitive value. The founded acts are called "higher" because the noeses and noemata (acts and senses) are "built" upon the founding levels, though they, too, form a distinctive, new unity of epistemic processes such that the new object-structure will have its own modes of givenness, its "characters," its manifold modes of being intended (Husserl 1950: §93).

Even though the founding and founded dimensions constitute a new "object," the founding relation is such that these "upper" levels and strata of the total phenomenon can be "abolished" without the remainder ceasing to be a concretely complete intentional experience (Husserl 1950: §95). As noted, when describing the founding-founded structure of acts and senses in the *Ideas*, Husserl initially considered examples of lived experiences such as liking or disliking, valuing, wishing, deciding, or doing. Deciding, for example, belongs to the province of volition, but in order to will something and to decide as a willing, I still have to intend or "mean" the object in some way, where the meaning given is the meaning of the object. The "analogous" point Husserl wishes to draw here is that such experiences contain manifold intentional noetic and noematic strata (Husserl 1950: §95). As intimated above, a new sense is constituted when it is founded upon, yet encompassing the founding structure. The new sense brings a new dimension of sense, for example, when we see not just the painting, but experience it as a beautiful painting, the machine as a useful machine, etc. (Husserl 1950: §116).

A valuing that is founded upon a "perceiving, imagining, judging, and the like," by virtue of its adjunct status, qualifies the founding-founded whole as, e.g., a "wishing" (for the hot coffee over there) even though the valuing dimension can be removed, leaving intact, *mutatis mutandis*, the perceiving founding stratum; or again it could be removed and leave a judicative dimension, e.g., "that the coffee is certainly hot." Here, the founding-whole can also be teased apart from the founded without damaging the underlying basic structure.

Where valuing is concerned, then, Husserl suggests that the perceptual sense of the object, the perceived as such, belongs to the perception, but in higher-order valuing, it is also integrated into the "valued" as such as a correlate to the concrete valuing, *whose* sense it (the perceptual sense) founds (Husserl 1950: §95). Accordingly, we must distinguish the objects, things, characteristics, affair-complexes that are given as valued in the valuing, and the presentings, judgings, imaginings, etc., which found the valuing, even though the whole new intending may give the object in a unique belief modality, say, as "certainly an ugly work of art," or "probably a valuable machine."

The relations of founding are multifarious, and can describe the relation of parts to wholes (Husserl 1968: Part III, §14), or the way in which the judgment (as the noematic correlate) is founded upon the perceptual sense, as the judging act is founded upon the perceiving as a being-positing process: Doubting-being, possible-being, deeming-being-likely, rejecting- or negating-being are all modifications of a basic "simple" givenness and positing of being that is given in a straightforward attitude. This is also the sense in which Husserl conceived of passive syntheses (in a "transcendental aesthetic") to be foundational for meaning constituted in active synthesis (peculiar to a "transcendental logic") (Husserl 1950: §94).[4]

Now, Husserl's notion of foundation (*Fundierung*) is not the problematic issue here. Husserl wants to stress by such a founding structure that the relation is not a causal one between, say, perceptual and emotional acts; nor even is it a "reciprocal" relation, which would presuppose an exchange of causes. Rather, the founded has to be understood as an "elaboration of" the founding beyond what could have been anticipated in advance, but to which the founding dimension gives a radically new meaning, and which it "needs" in order to be in this unique way (Merleau-Ponty 1945: 451). At issue for us is not the founding relation, then, but the fact that the emotional sphere is said to be founded in a more basic "epistemic" intentionality, meaning that the emotions are to be understood as having the same kind of intentional structure, the same kind of rational import, the same kind of givenness, evidence, etc., as the purely judicative or perceptual sort. If this were the case, then—to give just one example—trust would itself have to be either a kind of judgment, something founded in a decision to trust, or a blind belief—whereas trust is an insighting movement peculiar to the emotional sphere, or order of the heart having its own temporality, through which my freedom is realized as being bound in vulnerability to another toward a future, constituting one of the main structures of social existence.

Accordingly, we can ask if trust is really a kind of judgment, as a rational decision, or as an epistemic assessment of risk? Is hope a kind of expectation, an optimism of what might come to be, or a belief in the future? Scheler has suggested in his own way that the emotional sphere is unique and is not "founded" in the sense described above (Steinbock 2014). It is an intentionality that does not follow the "noesis–noema" structure. Not only does value guide the orientation without itself being an object. Persons, for example, can never be given as objects, since they live only in and through the execution of acts as, themselves, a dynamic orientation. Furthermore, the emotions are not such that the so-called strata could be stripped-off, leaving an integral, self-subsistent founding objectivating layer. Rather, they show themselves to be self-subsistent, as another kind of experience that has its *own style of givenness, cognition, and evidence*, and that is irreducible both to epistemic acts on the one hand and to instinct or "private feelings," on the other. In this way, they become another clue to who we are as human persons in the moral universe, and enable us to redress our contemporary place in the world.

Modernity established itself *by* dismissing the spiritual and evidentiary role of the emotions, especially interpersonal ones, by excluding them from social and political coexistence and as incapable of making any significant contribution. In a sense, the emotions were not "irrational" because they lacked reason, but because they did not conform to the "innovations" of Modern rationality. Not only was a distinctive concept of freedom instituted within what Claude Lefort calls "the era of ideology," one in which

---

[4] See also Husserl's discussion in Division I on "Modalization" of Part 2 of his *Passive Syntheses* (Husserl 2001).

freedom was closely knit to the ingenuity of Modern individualism and the individual's autonomy, to the idea of reason, and to the possibility of critique (Lefort 1978, 1979, 1981; Kosselleck 1973); at the same time, the emotions were cast aside as irrational, "internal," merely privately ethical, psychological, devoid of spiritual sense, incapable of yielding their own kind of evidence as intersubjectively revelatory, and of having any liberating potential.

Certainly, there have been attempts to deal with the permutations of Enlightenment rationality and our era of ideology by turning to aesthetics (Adorno), to a refined sense of political judgment (Arendt, Lyotard), and even to a communicative rationality (Habermas). While these attempts are not oriented toward trying to escape Modernity, while they do not long for a pre-critical social imaginary, there is still a problem that these and other figures have in common. They ignore what Modernity has ignored, namely the *role of the emotions*, especially what we have called elsewhere, the "moral" or "interpersonal" emotions, and the possibilities opened by them (Steinbock 2014). Through the moral emotions, it is possible *to retrieve what was naïvely excluded in Modernity* without trying to go back abstractly to an earlier, pre-critical social imaginary, and yet to go forward beyond our current Modern predicament and postmodern impasse by appropriating these resources.

No Modern thinker made the exclusion of the emotions more explicit than Immanuel Kant, and this is why Scheler found it necessary to begin his project through a critique of Kant's formal ethics. The guiding presupposition that led Kant to exclude the emotions from ethics was that any value given in experience, and in particular any moral value, is necessarily a relative value, a value relative to a particular need or inclination of the subject. Under such an assumption, it is in principle impossible to develop an ethics that that could be, on the one hand, universal and thus objective, and on the other, capable of providing a ground for the dignity, i.e., absolute value, of the person. At the outset of his *Formalismus*, Scheler states this mistaken assumption on the part of Kant as follows:

> Every non-formal (material) ethics makes the person a servant to his own states and to alien goods. Only formal ethics is in a position to demonstrate and found the dignity of the person. (Scheler 1966: 40, 1973b: 7)

The project that Scheler thus undertakes in the *Formalismus* is twofold. First, he seeks to illustrate that Kant's formal approach that excludes the emotions from ethics necessarily reduces the person to a formal category and consequently compromises the dignity of the person. The second and more significant project is to show that an analysis of the relation between the emotions and values reveals a non-relative, objective hierarchy of values.[5]

---

[5] It is only possible to give a brief account of both projects in this chapter. For a fuller and more sustained account of Scheler's critique of Kant see Phillip Blosser's work, *Scheler's Critique of Kant's Ethics* (1995).

There is little doubt that no thinker had more of an influence on Scheler's own moral thought than Kant. This influence is seen clearly in Scheler's appropriation of Kant's notion of the person, namely, that a person ought always be treated as an end itself and as having "an inner absolute worth" (Kant 1996b: 6:435). The question concerns how one is to ground the absolute value and dignity of the person. When Kant introduces the notion of dignity in the *Groundwork for the Metaphysics of Morals*, he does so by first speaking of the dignity of all rational beings and declares that the dignity of the rational being is found in the obedience to only those laws that the rational being gives to itself (Kant 1996a: 4:435). The human being has dignity insofar as the human being is a rational being and thus a person. Respect for the dignity of the human being relates then to the treatment of oneself and fellow human beings as a rational being. It is thus a compromise of one's absolute value as a person to act in a manner that is not rational, that is, in a way that is not perfectly free. Kant concludes his discussion of dignity in the *Groundwork* by writing that "*autonomy* is the ground of the dignity of human nature and of every rational nature" (1996a: 4:436).

Both the identification of the person as a rational being and the grounding of dignity in autonomy are, for Scheler, direct consequences of Kant's strictly formal ethics. Such a basis leads to the depersonalization of the person. By depersonalization, Scheler means the process by which a concrete individual is treated or regarded as merely a formal category. To define the person as a rational being means that "the person is basically nothing but a logical subject of rational acts, i.e., acts that follow [moral] laws" (Scheler 1966: 371, 1973b: 371). There is nothing in particular about the individual human being that makes him or her a person other than the fact the he or she is "some X or rational activity." Dignity, in Scheler's reading of Kant, refers to a particular quality or characteristic of the person, and not the concrete individual. It is not the individual qua individual that is of absolute value and deserving of respect, but the individual qua rational being. The individual person has thus been reduced to a universal category and treated as any other rational being. There is nothing unique peculiar to the individual person and is regarded merely as a member under the category of rational being; any person can take the place of any other.

Kant's turn to formalism is a symptom of Enlightenment rationality. The only form or structure that the world appears to have is one that the rational being brings to it. In order to avoid the depersonalizing tendency of a formal ethics, Scheler must show that there is an ethical a priori given in experience. Because modern thinkers like Kant have excluded the emotions from the moral sphere, they fail to recognize the integrity and objectivity of values.

The so-called subjectivity of values rests on a conflation between values and goods. Scheler is not interested in why particular things or objects have a particular value and how the same thing can have a different value for different persons. His interest is the experience of value itself or rather how values are given. For Scheler, value is our most original relation to being. By original, he means that every experience is already value latent (Scheler 1966: 35) and every object perceived or known is already of value to us (Scheler 1966: 40). Contrary to the Modern idea that only the subject is active in the constitution of meaning, the experience of value for Scheler demonstrates that the world is also active. Prior to any conscious awareness, persons are attracted and repelled by things of value in the world. The world is, as a consequence, always already given in relief. As loving persons, we are emotionally invested in the world prior to any knowledge of it.

The attracting and repelling force that objects in the world have upon us can be understood most generally as positive and negative values. Positive values attract our attention, while negative values repel. Following Franz Brentano, Scheler finds that positive and negative values have a relation to being. Positive values are given as that which ought to be and negative values are given as that which ought not to be (Scheler 1966: 100). Hence, for Scheler, the basis of the ethical imperative is not formal as is the case with Kant's categorical imperative, but given in the experience of value itself. In relation to moral values, a person is compelled to act in a manner that brings positive values into existence and negative values out of existence. For instance, when a person is demeaned and treated in a manner not in accord with her dignity, there is the experience of the imperative to act in a manner wherein the dignity of the person is restored. This ought is not relative to the person's desires or feelings, but rooted in the value given.

In addition to the distinction between positive and negative values, there are also, for Scheler, distinct value types: pleasure, utility, life, culture, and the holy. As there is an a priori preferring of positive to negative values, there is an a priori ranking between these different value types (Scheler 1966: 104). The ranking is from lower to higher, where pleasure is the lowest and the holy the highest. Which objects bare these value types is relative to the individual person and culture. What is not relative is the ranking itself. The holy ought to be preferred to the merely useful. This ranking is grounded in the peculiar quality of each value type. In the *Formalismus*, Scheler provides a sketch of how we are able to make qualitative distinctions between the different types. For instance, the higher values are experienced as having a longer duration (Scheler 1966: 108) and greater fulfillment (Scheler 1966: 113). Because Scheler distinguishes the different value types qualitatively, Bernard Waldenfels is correct to suggest that Scheler should have described the rank order in terms of depth, rather than higher or lower (Waldenfels 1997). The "lower" values are more superficial, while the "higher" are deeper. Deeper values ought to be preferred by virtue of their value depth.

Scheler's claim is that through a phenomenological analysis of the givenness of the different value types it is possible to show that this order is descriptive of the "*ordre du coeur*," to borrow a notion from Pascal. The ranking of the value types is both objective and universal. Every individual person and culture expresses this rank order differently through practices. Objects can have a different value for different cultures. There is tremendous diversity in the manner in which the rank order is lived. Nonetheless, there is no diversity in the ranking itself. The holy is and ought to be preferred above all other value types. Yet, because this objective rank order is disclosed through experience, experience serves as a means to test and affirm the qualitative distinctions that support such a ranking.

The objectivity of this rank order, however, does not mean that there are not cases of perversions in the rank order. Scheler's critique of the modern worldview rests in the claim that modernity has reversed the order of preferring between utility and life, where what is useful is taken to be of a "higher" and deeper value. It is specifically in this sense that the universal rank order of values can have a critical function. As Scheler attempts to do in respect to the modern worldview, the rank order of values can demonstrate not only that a person or culture suffers from an impoverished relation to the world, but also that a perversion in the rank order can and does lead to devastating consequences such as the degradation of all living beings for the sake of wealth and utility. The consequences of a reversal and perversion of the value types are difficult if not at times impossible to grasp intellectually, since the value structure determines what is known and of interest. Value reversal and perversion leads to a form of value blindness. For this reason, the most penetrating critical insights are inspired by what is felt at the emotional level. Moral emotions like guilt and shame in particular can reveal the poverty of our relation to the world and others. They can also reveal how we have failed in our moral responsibility and call attention to a disorder of the heart. The modern rejection of the emotional sphere necessarily deprives the emotions of their unique critical function and their ability to reveal ever deeper ways of respecting other persons and cultures.

9.3 SCHELER ON THE EMOTIONAL GROUND OF SOLIDARITY

There has been a resurgence in recent political theory that takes the moral emotions seriously as a foundational and transformative aspect of both the social and political sphere of existence (Hall 2005; Krause 2006; Kingston 2011; Fleming 2013; Nussbaum 2015). This return to the "political emotions" or "moral emotions" stands in stark contrast to the tendency in liberalism, as articulated by thinkers such as John Rawls, to sequester the emotions in order to preserve a form of ideal rational discourse in political life (Rawls 1999: 160ff.). Scheler has gained some attention in this emotional turn, but the attention has for the most part been their significance for the social and not the political (Zahavi 2014). The exclusion of not only Scheler but also the entire phenomenological tradition from these political investigations is a common tendency in twentieth-century political thought (Thompson and Embree 2000). A consequence of this tendency has been to overlook the fertile ground of political thought at the root of the Phenomenological Movement. Scheler was greatly influenced by these early political discussions, specifically the discussions that took place amongst the members of the Göttingen Circle. The purpose of this final section is to show the influence these early political discussions had for Scheler's notion of solidarity and how this notion lends insight into the sense of political responsibility that calls for genuine collective action.

Scheler provides his first systematic treatment of solidarity in the second section of his *Formalism in Ethics and Non-Formal Ethics of Value*. The context in which solidarity arises is his discussion of the collective person. Collective person is meant to refer to the deepest level of communal living and is distinguished from the other strata of communal living such as the herd, life-community, and society. It is the deepest level of coexistence because the collective person corresponds to the more profound value types such as spirit and the holy. A life-community, by contrast, concerns the vital and is constituted through shared activity as distinctively living beings. Society is the formation of collective existence through contracts and agreements for the sake of utility. As there is a rank order amongst the value types, there is a rank order amongst the different forms of coexistence. An individual can be a member of a number of different communal types at any given moment. Yet, it is only at the level of the collective person that the relation of coexistence is between individuals as persons.

The principle of solidarity assumes two distinct types of responsibility. Not only is each member fully responsible, self-responsible, for his or her acts, but also co-responsible for the community and every member in the community (Scheler 1966: 522). Genuine or irreplaceable solidarity is only found at the level of the collective person, that sphere of communal living amongst others as persons. Scheler refers to this form of solidarity as irreplaceable since no one member can take the place of another. Each and every member holds a unique position and responsibility for the community. Because a collective person is a community of persons, there is both the genuine communal living found in the life community, a communal living organically formed by acts such as co-feeling, co-living, and co-loving, and also the genuine sense of the individual found at the level of society.

Co-responsibility entailed in irreplaceable solidarity does not compromise the autonomy of the individual. Every person is fully responsible for his or her actions. For Scheler, co-responsibility is a radical form of questioning. When another person commits an act of hate or violence, the questions implied in solidarity are how such acts are possible and how I have participated in creating a world wherein such acts are possible. The act of hate committed by another person signals that I (and each member of the given community) have not loved deeply enough and that we as a community have failed to bring about a world wherein hate does not exist (Scheler 1966: 526). Solidarity assumes the manner in which we have shared our lives and feelings with one another in a community, but also the necessity for a person to act to end evil and injustice. The presence of evil in one's community demonstrates that every member ought to love more fully and act so that evil is not possible. At the level of the collective person, this call to responsibility is felt uniquely by each person, revealing the uniqueness of one's role in and for the community.

The call to act is grounded in what Scheler refers to as the necessary condition of solidarity. There are in fact two conditions of solidarity. There is a material condition. Genuine solidarity only exists amongst a group of persons who share an "empirically real connection" that gives rise to a sense and value unity distinctive of that connection (Scheler 1966: 524). The material condition is what makes solidarity possible. What makes solidarity necessary, what grants solidarity its obligatory nature is the "*essential reciprocity (Gegenseitigkeit) and equivalency (Gegenwertigkeit)* of all morally relevant behaviors and the corresponding material principles regarding the essential relations between the fundamental *kinds* of social acts" (Scheler 1966: 524).

Scheler offers relatively little to make sense of what he means by the *Gegenseitigkeit* and *Gegenwertigkeit* of acts. His use of the term "social act" is an obvious reference to Reinach, who first coined the term. In Reinach, Scheler discovers a means by which to articulate the political obligation to end injustice through an analysis of the types of intentional acts that necessarily entail the relation to others in one's community (Scheler 1966: 524). This phenomenological approach must not assume in advance a theory of justice or preserve a space for rational discourse in order to establish regulating ideals. It proceeds from the thing itself, from the peculiarity of social acts. For Scheler, Reinach was exemplary on this point.

Adolf Reinach's work on the a priori foundations of civil law investigates how legal constructs (*rechtliche Gebilde*) exhibit a necessary structure and have a being independent of positive law (Reinach 1989: 170). For Reinach, the a priori structure of legal constructs such as a claim or obligation means that we can grasp the essence of these legal constructs, essences that are presupposed in positive law. The investigation of such legal constructs such as a claim or contract quickly leads Reinach to question the origin or foundation of obligation itself. What makes a contract binding? Or how does someone come to be owed something through a claim? For Reinach, the sense of obligation that we find at the origin of law or civil rights arises from the act of promising. An examination of the act of promising allows us to understand both the meaning of a social act and the ontological connection between a social act and social obligation and commitment.

A promise is, according to Reinach, a social act. How an obligation arises through the act of promising is shown in part by the meaning of a social act. There are at least two different defining characteristics of a social act that distinguish it from other types of acts (Reinach 1989: 189–204):

1. A social act must be made known to another person and the other must comprehend the meaning of the act. It is an act that cannot in principle be completed internally. Such an act is thus other directed and takes place between at least two persons.
2. A social act must be expressed externally and at the same time be a voluntary expression. A social act must be expressed externally and be a voluntary expression. There are in fact two sides to a social act, its inner and outer side. Internally, the subject wills some future action to take place. The external side is the gestures, words, or other appearances that make this will known to others.

There are numerous different kinds of social acts. In addition to commanding and promising, there is warning, requesting, questioning, informing, and answering. Each of these acts is directed to another and need the other for their completion. The other must not just be a singular person, and a social act can be issued to many people at once. For example, I may ask a question to a large audience. Or I may promise a group of persons to fight with them for a common cause. In like manner, a social act can have many performers. A group may collectively issue a command, a class may have a question, or a people may promise to defend an individual.

The focal point for Reinach was the a priori structure of a promise, in particular what is intuitively grasped when a promise is apprehended by both the promiser and the promisee. It is in the nature of the promise that it presupposes a will directed to some action (Reinach 1989: 200). A promise assumes a particular type of obligation, the obligation to make good on one's promised action. What Scheler learns from such analysis is how an obligation to act is grounded a priori in the act itself. For Scheler, it concerns the necessary response, the *Gegenseitigkeit*, entailed in acts of devaluation, acts wherein a person is mistreated. In the devaluation or mistreatment of a person, the obligation necessarily arises to act to end the action. Negative values such as that given in the hateful treatment of a person ought not be. The existence of a negative value calls upon each member to act for the sake of the mistreated person, to act in a way that reveals the absolute value of that person. Even though I may have not committed the hateful act, I am still obligated to act for the sake of the devalued person—this person ought to be loved as the person she is.

Throughout his life, Scheler sought different resources from which to draw the call to act, resources that would inspire a cultural and political renewal (Davis 2012). His greatest political fear was political indifference (Scheler 1990: 72). Indifference leads only to despotism, he writes, and with the looming threat of fascism throughout Europe it was more important than ever for the people of Europe to act (Davis 2009). Despite a history that only knows violence and war, peace remains a possibility. In his essay on the eternal ideal of peace, Scheler writes that peace is always a future possibility, but that this eternal ideal will not realize itself on its own. The realization of peace requires direct political action that must spring collectively from each and every member (Scheler 1990: 121). Scheler's mature social and political thought demonstrates the necessity of action and the possible terror that will ensue when indifference and apathy become the cultural norm.

The call to act springs, for Scheler, from the experience of value, what ought to be. Values such as justice and goodness are disclosed originally in the deepest emotions such as love. The disclosure of these values are, however, always already particular. As the experience of value and goodness is intentionally directed to a particular being, the givenness of the good itself is personal. This means that the good in-itself is given as the good in-itself for me (Scheler 1966: 482). In other words, the good itself is not formal or universal, but singular. It is not the good itself for anyone, but for me. Value depth determines both the weight of the imposition and the singularity of the call of the good. It is not just anyone, but I who am called to act.

For Scheler, the imperative to act is issued to either an individual or to a collective unity. There are two ways in which to understand the meaning or givenness of a collective call. First, collective unities, such as the "collective person," bear the responsibility as a unity to realize the good, while eradicating evil. This responsibility is registered and carried out through the social and collective acts of the persons belonging to that unity. The unity of the state, for example, bears the responsibility to preserve its citizens' welfare and state sovereignty. A culture must see fit to deepen its historical meaning and development and each member of a culture takes up this responsibility in every cultural act.

A call for collective action also means that an individual is called uniquely as a member of a collective unity to act on behalf of the unity. As a member of a collective unity, each individual is called as a member to act in such a manner that seeks to end injustice and the mistreatment of others, but each is called in a unique manner. No member can take the place of another and thus cannot answer for anyone else but herself. At any one time, an individual is a member of a myriad of different collective unities and consequently called to act as a member of each simultaneously. Although it is often tremendously difficult to decipher "the call of the hour" and to determine the type of action one ought to take, the emotional bonds of solidarity are not a chaotic array or confusion as modernity would have us assume. The difficulty attests rather to the tremendous richness of the emotional life of human beings, a richness rooted in the great variety of our personal relations to other persons.

The call to act in solidarity with others is a singularizing and individuating event. As called to act, I come to recognize my unique responsibility for others and for my community. This recognition is not the realization of individual freedom, but the recognition of the responsibility to others. Distinctively personal emotions such as love are the acts that disclose the uniqueness and value of the other person. The call to act for the sake of the other or for others is one meant for me and me alone. I may choose to reject this call, but the call is not my choice. It is the evidential nature of this call, the givenness of the fact that I and I alone am called to act, that reveals the uniqueness of my place and being.

Goodness gives itself as that which ought to be. The imposition of the good is experienced as an imposition precisely because it imposes a distinction upon us, namely what is and what ought to be. What grounds this experience is not some insight into some other realm or into some final end of human history. Rather what ought to be is given in the depth of value. It is, in other words, the act of love that reveals that the world ought to be different than it is. "In every healthy human heart resides the ability to see the same world event from the fundamentally different height of his or her spiritual viewpoint" (Scheler 1954: 357).

In its deepest manifestations, solidarity is the felt obligation to act for others. The danger of political indifference is that it depersonalizes the bonds of solidarity and thus mutes the call to act. Scheler understood apathy and indifference to be direct consequences of a value reversal in our cultural ethos that promotes and cultivates a reduction of the irreplaceable to the replaceable, the uniqueness of each and every person to the same. This tendency of modernity to depersonalize the emotional bonds and feelings given in the forms of injustice experienced in a community succeeds in stripping action of any collective force. The challenge of solidarity is to rediscover the personal nature of one's responsibility and how one's unique responsibility is already a collective act.

9.4 CONCLUSION

Scheler came upon phenomenology after he had completed his formal education. In this respect, he was not a student of Husserl's. This is not to say that Scheler is not deeply indebted to Husserl. It is quite to the contrary. Scheler's relatively late arrival to phenomenology did grant him a different perspective by which to undertake the phenomenological task of "returning to the things themselves." A consequence of this perspective was to diversify the manner in which experience is described and what is to be considered as a meaningful experience. Scheler benefitted tremendously from the young, fertile soil from which phenomenology took root. As is the case with any phenomenological project, Scheler's remains very much unfinished, but introduces new horizons for investigation and thought.

The political project Scheler undertakes in the final years of his life was to rethink the manner in which the emotions direct the course of power in accord with the more spiritual and personal values. This is not to say that the emotions are political in the sense of reducing their meaning to this sphere of personal existence—any more than it would be to say that economic relations define interpersonal relations. However, it is to acknowledge and to underscore a fundamental dimension of personal coexistence that has been left out of account, namely, the moral emotions, and to emphasize that they have *political, social, economic, and ecological significance*, not just "internal" private, psychological, epistemic, or so-called ethical ones. And they have *religious significance* such that the dimension of the holy is evoked and is integral in our lives, *in Modernity*, without it being reducible to fundamentalism, religious fanaticism, monarchy, or theocracy. These latter are what Bergson would term forms of "static" religion that would found a "closed" morality (Bergson 1932). Trust, loving, humility, hoping, repentance, shame, guilt, pride, etc. play as much a role in collective life as communicative rationality, rhetoric, and bio-politics, and indeed play a more fundamental role where persons are concerned. They not only reveal different forms of power and critique, but provide essential, vital insights into interpersonal relations. They do not replace power and civil society, but they provide radically unique ways of living and understanding our social and political institutions.

REFERENCES

Bergson, H. (1932), *Les deux sources de la morale et de la religion* (Paris: Presses universitaire de France).

Blosser, P. (1995), *Scheler's Critique of Kant's Ethics* (Athens, OH: Ohio University Press).

Davis, Z. (2009), "A Phenomenology of Political Apathy: Scheler on the Origins of Mass Violence," *Continental Philosophy Review* 42/2: 149–69.

Davis, Z. (2012), "The Values of War and Peace: Max Scheler's Political Transformations," *Symposium* 16/2: 128–49.

Fleming, J. E. (ed.) (2013), *Passions and Emotions* (New York: New York University Press).

Gadamer, H. (1975), "Max Scheler der Verschwender," in P. Good (ed.), *Max Scheler im Gegenwartsgeschehen der Philosophie* (Bern: Francke Verlag), 11–18.

Hall, C. (2005), *The Trouble with Passion: Political Theory beyond the Reign of Reason* (London: Routledge).

Husserl, E. (1950, *Ideen zu einer reinen Phänomenologie und phänomenologischen Philosophie. Erstes Buch: Allgemeine Einführung in die reine Phänomenologie*, ed. W. Biemel, Husserliana 3 (The Hague: Martinus Nijhoff).

Husserl, E. (1968), *Logische Untersuchungen. Band II: Untersuchungen zur Phänomenologie und Theorie der Erkenntnis*, I. Teil (Tübingen: Niemeyer).

Husserl, E. (2001), *Analyses Concerning Passive and Active Synthesis: Lecture on Transcendental Logic*, translated by A. Steinbock (Dordrecht: Kluwer).

Kant, I. (1996a), "Groundwork of the metaphysics of morals," in Mary Gregor (trans. and ed.), *The Cambridge Edition of the Works of Immanuel Kant: Practical Philosophy* (Cambridge: Cambridge University Press), 37–108.

Kant, I. (1996b), "The metaphysics of morals," in Mary Gregor (trans. and ed.), *The Cambridge Edition of the Works of Immanuel Kant: Practical Philosophy* (Cambridge: Cambridge University Press), 353–604.

Kingston, R. (2011), *Public Passion; Rethinking the Grounds for Political Justice* (Quebec: McGill-Queen's University Press).

Koselleck, R. (1973), *Kritik und Krise: Eine Studie zur Pathogenese der bürgerlichen Welt* (Frankfurt a. M.: Suhrkamp).

Krause, S. (2006), *Civil Passions: Modern Sentiment and Democratic Deliberation* (Princeton, NJ: Princeton University Press).

Lefort, C. (1978), *Les formes de l'histoire* (Paris: Éditions Gallimard).

Lefort, C. (1979), *Élements d'une critique de la bureaucratie* (Paris: Éditions Gallimard).

Lefort, C. (1981), *L'invention démocratique* (Paris: Fayard).

Luther, A. (1972), *Persons in Love* (The Hague: Martinus Nijhoff).

Merleau-Ponty, M. (1945), *Phénoménologie de la perception* (Paris: Éditions Gallimard).

Nussbaum, M. (2015), *Political Emotions: Why Love Matters for Justice* (Cambridge, MA: Belknap Press).

Rawls, J. (1999), *A Theory of Justice* (Cambridge, MA: Belknap Press).

Reinach, A. (1989), "Die apriorischen Grundlagen des bürgerlichen Rechts (1913)," in K Schumann and B. Smith (eds), *Sämtliche Werke* (Munich: Philosophia Verlag).

Scheler, M. (1954), *Vom Ewigen im Menschen*, in M. Scheler (ed.), *Gesammelte Werke V* (Bern: Francke Verlag).

Scheler, M. (1957), "Phänomenologie und Erkenntnistheorie," in M. Scheler (ed.), *Schriften aus dem Nachlass, I. Zur Ethik und Erkenntnislehre, Gesammelte Werke X* (Bern: Francke Verlag), 377–430.

Scheler, M. (1963), "Liebe und Erkenntnis, Schriften zur Soziologie und Weltanschauungslehre," in M. Scheler (ed.), *Gesammelte Werke VI* (Bern: Francke Verlag), 77–98.

Scheler, M. (1966), *Formalismus in der Ethik und die Materiale Wertethik*, in M. Scheler (ed.), *Gesammelte Werke II* (Bern: Francke Verlag).

Scheler, M. (1971), *Frühe Schriften*, in M. Scheler and M. Frings (eds), *Gesammelte Werke I* (Bern: Francke Verlag).

Scheler, M. (1972), *Zur Rehabilitierung der Tugend, Vom Umsturz der Werte*, in M. Scheler (ed.), *Gesammelte Werke III* (Bern: Francke Verlag), 13–32.

Scheler, M. (1973a), *Wesen und Formen der Sympathie*, in M. Frings (ed.), *Gesammelte Werke VII* (Bern: Francke Verlag).

Scheler, M. (1973b), *Formalism in Ethics and Non-Formal Ethics of Values: A New Attempt toward the Foundation of an Ethical Personalism* , translated by M. and R. Funk (Evanston, IL: Northwestern University Press).

Scheler, M. (1976), "Die Stellung des Menschens im Kosmos," in M. Frings (ed.), *Frühe Schriften. Gesammelte Werke IX* (Bern: Francke Verlag).

Scheler, M. (1980), "Erkenntnis und Arbeit. Eine Studie über Wert und Grenzen des pragmatischen Motivs in der Erkenntnis der Welt," in M. Scheler (ed. 1st and 2nd edition), M. Frings (ed. 3rd edition) *Die Wissensformen und die Gesellschaft, Gesammelte Werke VIII* (Bern: Francke Verlag), 191–384.

Scheler, M. (1990), *Schriften aus dem Nachlass, IV. Philosophie und Geschichte*, in M. Frings (ed.), *Gesammelte Werke XIII* (Bonn: Bouvier Verlag).

Sokolowski, R. (1964), *The Formation of Husserl's Concept of Constitution* (The Hague: Martinus Nijhoff).

Sokolowski, R. (1983), "Husserl's concept of categorial intuition," in J. N. Mohanty (ed.), *Phenomenology and the Human Sciences* (Norman, OK: University of Oklahoma Press), 193–206.

Spiegelberg, H. (1994), *The Phenomenological Movement: A Historical Introduction* (Dordrecht: Kluwer).

Steinbock, A. (2014), *Moral Emotions: Reclaiming the Evidence of the Heart* (Evanston, IL: Northwestern University Press).

Thompson, K. and Embree, L. (eds) (2000), *The Phenomenology of the Political (Contributions to Phenomenology)* (Dordrecht: Kluwer).

Waldenfels, B. (1997), "Wertqualitäten oder Erfahrungsansprüche?" in G. Pafferott (ed.), *Vom Umsturz der Werte in der modernen Gesellschaft* (Bonn: Bouvier Verlag), 306–13.

Welton, D. (1983), *The Origins of Meaning: A Critical Study of the Thresholds of Husserlian Phenomenology* (The Hague: Martinus Nijhoff).

Zahavi, D. (2014), *Self and Other: Exploring Subjectivity, Empathy, and Shame* (Oxford: Oxford University Press).

CHAPTER 10

EDITH STEIN'S CHALLENGE TO SENSE-MAKING

The Role of the Lived Body, Psyche, and Spirit

ANTONIO CALCAGNO

MUCH scholarly attention has been focused on Edith Stein's later philosophical works (see, for example, Sharkey 2006, 2009; Manganaro 2002; Schulz 2008; Maskulak 2007), which were deeply influenced by her engagement with Christian thought and medieval philosophy, but the same cannot be said about her early body of phenomenological writings. Though her doctoral dissertation, *On the Problem of Empathy* (*Zum Problem der Einfühlung*) (Stein 1989 [2013]), has had a significant impact on discussions of intersubjectivity and the problem of knowing other minds (Ales Bello 2005; Gallese 2003; Zahavi 2015, 2010; Miles 2003; Sawicki 2004; Moran 2004), her other major phenomenological works, including *Philosophy of Psychology and the Humanities* (Stein 2000b),[1] *An Investigation concerning the State* (Stein 2006a),[2] and *Einführung in die Philosophie* (Stein 2004) (*Introduction to Philosophy*), remain largely understudied, although this is slowly changing. I have argued elsewhere that these four texts can be read as a systematic phenomenology of social and political objectivities (see Calcagno 2014). Here, I argue that these texts can also be read as her view of what phenomenology is and what it can

---

[1] Originally published in 1922 as *Beiträge zur philosophischen Begründung der Psychologie und der Geisteswissenschaften*, in E. Husserl (ed.), *Jahrbuch für Philosophie und phänomenologische Forschung*, vol. 5 (Halle: Max Niemeyer). Republished by Niemeyer, Tübingen, 1979. There is also a new German critical edition: Beckmann-Zöller, B. (ed.) (2010), *Edith Stein Gesamtausgabe*, vol. 6 (Freiburg: Herder).

[2] Originally published in 1925 as *Eine Untersuchung über den Staat*, in E. Husserl (ed.), *Jarhbuch für Philosophie und phänomenologische Forschung*, vol. 7 (Halle: Niemeyer), 1–123. Republished by the same publisher in 1970, but added to the text was Stein's earlier text, *Beiträge zur philosophischen Begründung der Psychologie und der Geisteswissenschaften*. The treatise on the state remained unchanged, though the pagination shifted to 285–407. A new critical edition of Stein's text on the state is: E. Stein (2006), *Eine Untersuchung über den Staat*, in Ilona Reidel-Spangenberger (ed.), *Edith Stein Gesamtausgabe*, vol. 7 (Freiburg: Herder).

uncover. Drawing upon the work of Edmund Husserl, Max Scheler, and Adolf Reinach, Stein's work in phenomenology situates meaning- or sense-making, the core operative principle of the phenomenological method, within a nexus of materially embodied psycho-spiritual personhood that is deeply informed by and that helps to constitute social and political realities. Stein viewed her work with Husserl as a project of collaboration aimed at developing and promoting phenomenology, but rather than conceiving of constitution or sense-bestowal as belonging to the elements of logic and language, as it does in Husserl's *Logical Investigations* and his transcendental structures of noesis and noema or in Reinach's early work in phenomenology (1951), Stein argued that meaning-making must be grounded in both material nature and spiritual realities. Her early work in phenomenology was not only a critique of the shortcomings of her teachers but also a constructive attempt to expand the account of how phenomenology can seize the objectivity of things themselves by showing how consciousness itself is embodied in a psycho-spiritual unity, which Stein called a person.

10.1 Stein's Place in the Phenomenological Movement

In 1917, Edith Stein (1891–1942) was only the second woman in Germany to obtain a doctorate in philosophy. An avid campaigner for women's rights, especially for access to the university, she twice attempted to habilitate in order to secure a university professorship, but was denied a chair in philosophy because of sexism and racism (MacIntyre 2006: 14–16). Initially a student of psychology at the University of Breslau, Stein studied under Wilhelm Stern, one of the founders of modern psychology and the inventor of the IQ test. She was profoundly attracted to the new experimental psychology, inspired by Wilhelm Wundt and his followers, especially his work on personality development. As modern psychology began to assert its independence from philosophy and to rely more heavily on empirical and experimental methods to justify its claims, Stein found herself dissatisfied with the inability of the new science to ask and respond to the deeper philosophical issues raised by the research being carried out. In the course of her studies, she came across Edmund Husserl's *Logical Investigations* and became very interested in his claims about the possibility of objective knowledge and the foundations of the sciences. George Moskiewicz, Stein's friend at Breslau, suggested she visit Göttingen where Husserl had assembled around himself a notable group of young assistants and students who were interested in many of the same questions that engaged Stein. Furthermore, Husserl's assistant, Adolf Reinach, had been trained in the Würzburg School of the psychology of Wundt, who shared an affinity of thought with Stern, Stein's teacher at Breslau. Reinach led a group of young philosophers—the famous Göttingen Circle—who pursued phenomenology. Stein soon transferred to Göttingen, and there she attended seminars by Reinach

and Husserl, becoming part of the inner circle of young phenomenologists that included figures such as Max Scheler, Theodor Conrad, Roman Ingarden, Hedwig
Conrad-Martius, and Dietrich von Hildebrand. It was in this incubator of the early
phenomenology of Göttingen that Stein became familiar with different models of
phenomenology, including the various methods of Husserl, Reinach, Max Scheler,
Alexander Pfänder, and Conrad-Martius. As the classic work of Herbert Spiegelberg
(1960) shows, and the more recent work of Dermot Moran (Dermot Moran et al.
2015) and Dan Zahavi (2008) clearly confirms, the phenomenologists who gathered
in, respectively, Göttingen and Munich, though sharing a common goal, did not
offer a unified account of the phenomenological method. Rejecting a philosophical
undercurrent of skepticism and the limited conclusions of positivism and psychologism, they all believed that consciousness and what presents itself in consciousness
can afford us with objective knowledge about reality. Yet, what consciousness is and
how it works to make sense of reality were much-debated questions. Indeed, much
to the chagrin of Husserl, who often complained of his students' disloyalty, each phenomenologist of this early period had a different view of how phenomenology was
to proceed. The seeming inconsistencies between phenomenologists, however, must
not be read as phenomenology's failure to secure for itself a stable methodology;
rather, one must view these phenomenologists as sharing a desire for objective understanding while debating and refining the toolkit of phenomenology. These debates
produced a rich body of philosophical material about the nature of consciousness, its
content and understanding, as well as an understanding of objective realities in the
world, including the work of art, community, the state, the psyche, the human and
cultural sciences, color, law, etc. More than a movement, early phenomenology must
be viewed as a genuine conversation in which philosophers revisited again and again
central themes and questions pertinent to their investigations of the mind's attempt
to comprehend reality as it presents itself in consciousness. Stein was integral to this
conversation, for, as one of Husserl's and Reinach's closest followers, she had unprecedented access to their unpublished writings at the time.

Stein's unique understanding of phenomenology lies between the idealism of Husserl
and the realism of Reinach, her particular view of psychology, and the personalist and
sociologically minded writings of Max Scheler. Each text of her phenomenological
quartet displays a deep commitment to the conscious mind's capability of grasping the
phenomenological essence of those things being investigated. She shared Reinach's and
Husserl's conviction about the mind's capacity to know the reality of things, especially as
it was developed in the former's *Was ist Phänomenologie?* (Reinach 1951) and the latter's
Logical Investigations (Husserl 2001). Each of her works begins with an affirmation of her
intention to present the essence of a specific phenomenon, be it empathy, the state, the
psyche, consciousness, or community. In *Einführung in die Philosophie*, she remarked,
"It is clear . . . that phenomenology itself, insofar as it is a science of essences that wishes
to work out that which necessarily and universally belongs to the diverse forms of consciousness, and given that lived experience must be considered only in itself, in its immanence, separates out from the whole the real and changing circumstances in which

this or that lived experience presents itself" (Stein 2004: 22).[3] In fact, Stein's commitment to essential description continued to develop, even into her later Christian philosophy. For example, in *Endliches und ewiges Sein*, a large portion of the text dedicated to the question of essences is marked by Stein's profound attempt to expand the question of essences to include Jean Héring's distinction between universal essences (that is, the essence of an ideal objectivity) and the particular essence of an instantiation of an ideal objectivity, what Stein and others call a *Wesenheit* (Stein 2006b: 68). Essences in Stein's phenomenology are grasped and described as the sense (*Sinn*) of a particular phenomenon. Sometimes, in English, sense is also called meaning. One follows a phenomenon as it is lived through in conscious experience, tracing its unfolding in order to grasp and describe its constituent aspects. The correspondence of a meaning intention and a meaning fulfillment allows one to understand the sense or essence of a thing.

Though Stein shared her teachers' conviction about the possibility of grasping the essential sense of things as they appear in consciousness, she believed that consciousness alone could not deliver the fullness of meaning that the painstaking analysis of conscious, lived experience requires. Consciousness is connected to and enmeshed in the materiality of the body and psyche. Stein speaks of how the ability of consciousness to grasp and seize the essential sense of an object is conditioned by an "influence" that operates and affects consciousness, what she calls "psyche" (Stein 2000b: 14). In order for consciousness to carry out its phenomenological tasks, it must become aware of the lifepower[4] of the psyche to inform its very experience of the content that appears to it. Each work of Stein's phenomenology reiterates the importance of the psyche, describing its connection to, unity with and role in the life of the conscious person as well as its connection to the lived experience of the body and the life of spirit. More will be said about the distinction between psyche and spirit when we come to the central thesis of this chapter—Stein's expansion of the concept of meaning-making or sense. Contrary to most accounts of Stein's phenomenology, in which she is considered to have broken with psychology, we view Stein as retaining a deep connection to psychology, especially as she incorporates it into phenomenology.

Another major influence on Stein's phenomenology can be found in the work of Max Scheler (Stein 2000b: 200). Visiting the Göttingen Circle, he delivered a series of lectures that Stein attended. She was very impressed with his analyses and his depth of mind and spirit, and his work on sympathy became the focus of her critique in *On the Problem of Empathy* (Stein 1989: 27–34, 68–70). Despite her criticism of Scheler's treatment of empathy and communal we-experience, Stein admitted a profound debt to his work. Scheler's rich discussion of personhood and his phenomenology of

---

[3] Translation mine.

[4] Edith Stein discusses lifepower or *Lebenskraft* (literally, the strength of the force of life in the individual person) largely in reference to the psyche and psychic life. Drawing from the vitalist tradition of thought, including the writings of Henri Bergson, Stein maintains that the force of life itself, though it conditions and influences the life of psyche and consciousness itself, is not reducible to these aspects of reality.

value become pivotal for Stein's own understanding of empathy. By the end of *On the Problem of Empathy*, Stein (1989: 91–118) concluded that empathy is not only a special act of mind that allows us to presentify[5] the mind of the other in our own consciousness, but that it also affords us an understanding of ourselves as persons who engage in the interpersonal and collective building of rich societal, communal, and state lives that are carried out in acts of spirit. Scheler's work led Stein to the founding thinkers of sociology, including Simmel and Tönnies, whose work enhanced her comprehension of how consciousness transcends the egological empathic sphere of intersubjectivity, of ego and alter ego, in order to phenomenologically grasp and construct complex social and communal worlds of shared experience and culture. For example, Stein claims that the death of a much-loved troop leader can be experienced not only by individuals, but also by a collective or group. Empathy allows one member of the troop to understand that another member is suffering grief and sadness at the death of their shared leader. But she also maintains that an individual can grasp the collective sadness of the troop as a whole as well as the sadness of its individual members. She calls this grasping of the sense of collective sadness *Gemeinschaftserlebniss*, in which one lives in the experience of others as an *Ineinandergreifen*, a seizing of the lived experience of the community in solidarity (Stein 2000b: 134–6). Scheler's idea (1973: 519, 2008: 12–13) was similar, but he situated the collective experience of grief within the context of a collective person (*Gesamtperson*), a concept Stein rejected.

10.2 Steinian Phenomenology

Having discussed the sources of Stein's phenomenology, we must ask about its uniqueness. Each of Stein's above-mentioned phenomenological texts contains an analysis of a specific phenomenon—for example, the problem of empathy—but each also includes an elaboration of what phenomenology is and how it is to operate. Each work thus fundamentally repositions phenomenology. *On the Problem of Empathy* treats the problem of grasping other minds, and though Stein acknowledges that she had heard Husserl's discussion of empathy in his lectures on nature and spirit in 1913, her treatment of the problem is uniquely her own. She even refused to revise her dissertation because she had by that time become Husserl's assistant, which gave her unprecedented access to his writings on the theme (Stein 1989: 1–2). We know from Husserl's early writings on intersubjectivity (1973b, 1973c, 1973d) that empathy was a major topic of reflection. We also know, especially from his *Cartesian Meditations*, that Husserl (2012: 89–90) was never satisfied with his account of empathy and its role in intersubjective relations. Stein and Husserl shared an understanding of empathy as a unique act of mind that can

---

[5] Stein uses the German word *vergegenwärtigen* for what I have translated as presentify, following more standard English translation of Husserl's phenomenology. Waltraut Stein, in *On the Problem of Empathy*, translates the German as represent.

analogously presentify the mind of the other to an individual ego. Husserl describes empathy as a kind of trading places and Stein views empathy as a bringing of the mind of the other into relief. Both thinkers recognized the fundamental importance of the body for empathy, although Stein understood the role of a sexed body in empathy and Husserl did not (Husserl 1973b: 75). Borrowing from Husserl's distinction between inner and outer perception, found in the first version of his *Logical Investigations*, Stein maintained that empathy can work only if we have some awareness of what we are as individuals: we know that we are capable of sensation, we experience what it is to be embodied, we have emotions and affectivity, we are capable of spiritual acts such as willing and motivational acts. An awareness of self acquired through inner and outer perception[6] allows us to be "led" by an act of empathy into the mind of the other. We modify and variegate this self-awareness in order to compare the mind of the other with our own; we do this to be able to seize what the other is experiencing. We can come to know the mind of the other only when it is compared to our self-understanding, but the mind of the other can also bring forward new content, new experiences, which we may understand though we have never experienced them. The experience of the other's mind, then, can modify our sense of who/what we are and vice versa. Ultimately, empathy allows us to grasp that both the ego and the alter ego are persons and that they share an interpersonal world. What empathy reveals, then, is that the person is a unity of body, psyche, and spirit. These three aspects of our personhood are enmeshed, and together they allow for the full functioning of empathy.

What is unique about Stein's view of empathy is her claim that it requires a deep psychic structure—what she later will call a material or natural structure—in order to function. In fact, it is this psychic structure that allows one to fundamentally grasp that one's mind is similar to or different from another's mind. The psyche intimately links the body and the spirit (the domain of freedom, will, and motivation). This point is taken up more explicitly and with greater ramifications in her second work, *Philosophy of Psychology and the Humanities*. The psyche, sometimes called the soul, has a structure that parallels that of natural causality. Certain events can be connected in a way that shows a cause and effect relationship. The psyche largely manifests itself in affectivity and/or in stimulation: a certain affect produces a certain response or a certain stimulus elicits a certain reaction. There is a lawfulness about the psyche and its cause–effect structure. For example, the reception of bad news provokes sadness. A sharp pain will cause one to wince, registering a psychic disturbance in sentience. The awareness of the if→then causal structure of the psyche allows one to analogously compare this causal relation with another's experience of it, which, in turn, allows one to understand causality in general. This understanding of causality, as given by psychic causality, serves as a means to understanding higher forms of human action and experience, which have roots in causality but also touch upon the domain of human freedom in the life

---

[6] Outer perception, according to Stein, requires that an external "flesh and blood" object be present to consciousness. In inner perception, no external object need be present: one is conscious of inner states and presentations and representations.

of the spirit. So, my free choice to do something can be understood as being rationally motivated, but an if→then structure is operating as well as freedom. My motive to act arises from my reasoning about a certain state of affairs and my judgment about the best course of action in the given circumstances. When I carry out my action, I have an understanding of motivation that I freely act upon, but this understanding also follows a causal structure: If I choose to carry out this act, this result will follow. In spiritual acts, unlike pure psychic acts, an individual is free to follow or not follow a motivation or to carry out an act of will. There is here an action–response dynamic that is analogous to that of psychic causality, but in spiritual acts of motivation, one can assent to or reject, by means of the will, the action suggested by a motivation, whereas in pure psychic causality, one simply responds or reacts without the intervention of the will. Understanding psychic causality and how it works allows one to understand how one achieves knowledge of the other's mind: I know the mind of the other when I analogously presentify the mind of the other to my own mind, and I know the content of the other's mind *because* I have an understanding of my own mind or *because* I possess relevant knowledge about states of mind in general. This "because" is the link; it allows one mind to make the link to the other mind. In order to work, empathy requires a deep understanding of causality: I can know the mind of the other *because* I can compare it with my own and vice versa. Psyche, for Stein, not only reveals the importance of causality for empathy, but also serves as an important bridge or passageway between one's experience of the lived body and the realm of spirit.

For Stein, the discovery of the role of psychic causality in empathy has serious consequences for how we understand phenomenology. In *Philosophy of Psychology and the Humanities*, she elaborates the consequences of her insight about causality for her concept of phenomenology. According to Stein, early phenomenology's insistence on consciousness and its logical operations as foundational for any phenomenological investigation is not enough. Phenomenology requires a phenomenological account of the psyche in order to better understand consciousness as well as its capacity to experience and live reality.

10.3 THE PSYCHE

Philosophy of Psychology and the Humanities was written, in part, while Stein was working with Husserl on his manuscripts. During this period, Stein put together Husserl's *Ideas II and III* (1952, 1971), his lectures on *Ding und Raum* (*Thing and Space*) (1973a) and his lectures on inner time consciousness (1966). In her extensive correspondence with Roman Ingarden (Stein 2014), she chronicled the joys and frustrations of working with Husserl. She saw her work with him as one of collaboration, but Husserl, frustrated with his own writing, would never finalize for publication any of the drafts she had prepared and would move on to other projects. For example, Stein painstakingly put together the inner time consciousness lectures from a vast collection of papers, all written in Gabelsberger shorthand. Husserl, as was his custom, began to closely read the text, but then decided to move on to another project. His inability or reluctance to finalize his work was one of the principal reasons Stein decided to stop working with him. After Heidegger published *Being and Time*, Husserl told him that he, too, had written a text on time. Heidegger read the text and urged Husserl to publish it, which he did. Although the published text was based on the version that Stein had edited, Heidegger thanked "Fräulein Stein" for her transcription and attached his name as editor to the text. Sadly, Stein's editing and correcting of Husserl's manuscripts was erased, leaving the impression that she was merely Husserl's secretary rather than his philosophical collaborator. It should be remarked that all of Husserl's other assistants, including Landgrebe and Heidegger, were recognized as philosophers in their own right, yet for a very long time, and even in some circles today, Stein has been regarded simply as Husserl's transcriber and secretary. As scholars have begun to take up her early work in phenomenology, this prejudiced impression is slowly beginning to dissipate.

In her letters to Ingarden, Stein admitted that, as she was working on *Ideas II and III*, she felt that his discussion of noesis and noema as well as his discussion of consciousness were limited by his reluctance to address the connection of consciousness to material nature. Stein wrote that she had trouble understanding the notion of constitution, especially as it was not attached to a material nature. She recounted sitting with Husserl for hours, urging him to revise his views and take seriously the need for an account of material nature, but he refused to do so during the period of their collaboration. At one point, Stein (2014: 38–42) wrote to Ingarden about her "heresy"—how she came to understand the way in which material nature and spirit work together and require one another in order to carry out the constitutive analysis promised by Husserl in his *Ideas*. The notion of Stein's "heresy" is often read as her rejection of Husserian transcendental idealism and her adherence to an eidetic phenomenology. Stein, however, remained faithful to the Husserlian insight about the mind's capacity to grasp essences and the possibility to thus understand the sense of things. In this regard, Stein is deeply rooted in early Husserlian and Reinachian phenomenology, understood as a sense-making/giving philosophy. We must acknowledge, however, that this is Stein's take on phenomenology. One will often find scholars disagreeing with Stein's view of phenomenology. The "heresy" to which she referred was about the necessity for the phenomenological account of consciousness and sense-making to include an account of how consciousness is enmeshed in a natural, material framework: The work of phenomenology—to capture the essence or sense of things—is not only the work of the spiritual life of consciousness (recall that all phenomenological investigation begins with a willed act of taking-a-stance), but is also heavily dependent upon a material body and the bridge between body and spirit—namely the psyche, which works according to laws akin to those of physical causality. More specifically, Stein's phenomenology requires a broader account of the body and the psyche. In her texts on empathy and her *Introduction to Philosophy*, we find a substantial treatment of the lived body and material nature. In the latter Stein gives us an eidetic ontology of nature, including time and space, but not a transcendental account of time and space. In *Philosophy of Psychology and the Humanities*, we find a detailed account of how the psyche is to be phenomenologically incorporated into a phenomenological view of consciousness.

In *Philosophy of Psychology and the Humanities*, Stein remarks that consciousness, understood as a flow of experiences gathered together through an association by contact, experiences an additional kind of association, which she calls an "operative influence" (Stein 2000b: 14). Consciousness can experience itself being influenced not by content but by another kind of force; it may experience itself as weary, energized, more or less alert, etc. She notes that there are shifts in consciousness that are tied to life feelings, that is, feelings that stem from our physical, material living. For example, feeling tired makes our experience of colors less vivid, makes tones ring hollow. Stein identifies this shifting influence, which arises not from consciousness itself but from the vital force of life, as a causality that comes from the psyche. The causality of the psyche is described as being akin to natural, physical causality: a certain force or impetus, much like "mechanical production," causes a reaction or produces an effect (Stein 2000b: 15). Psychic causality, like any form of causality, is marked by an origin. Here we find the ancient and medieval notion of causality as an act that has a beginning and an end; it is understood as an originating event that carries with it a certain necessity. For example, fatigue causes consciousness to become dull.

In addition to describing the psyche as marked by a certain form of causality, understood as cause–effect, stimulus–response, Stein described the psyche as being experienced as a particular form of the tying-together of experiences. Unlike the vital becoming of consciousness, the psyche ties its experiences together in a cause–effect structure, but whereas consciousness can become aware of itself as a pure experiencing, the psyche itself is never experienced or accessed as directly as consciousness. We feel the effects of the psyche operating upon consciousness, but we never see the psyche itself. Hence, Stein (2000b: 24) describes the psyche as transcendent. For Stein (2000b: 24), the psyche also manifests life and a life force (*Lebenskraft*), especially when we experience the effects of life feelings on consciousness. Finally, Stein (2000b: 23) claims that, unlike the pure ego of consciousness, the psyche has a real ego—that is, when we experience the effects of the psyche, we become aware that there is a bearer of properties and psychic states. The real ego manifests itself in immanent data, but, like the psyche itself, it never becomes manifestly immanent—that is, it never appears directly to consciousness (Stein 2000b: 23).

Stein contends that the psyche, understood as a substrate of consciousness, affects the capacity of consciousness to experience reality in varying degrees. For Stein, consciousness structurally consists of (a) the possession of content, the data of consciousness; (b) an experience of the becoming of that content; and (c) the consciousness of that experiencing, which always accomplishes it (i.e., experiencing)—in a higher or lower degree—and for whose sake the experience itself is even designated as consciousness (Stein 2000b: 16–17). The force of the psyche ultimately "influences" the very capacity of consciousness to grasp the phenomenological sense of things. Though the psyche only manifests its effects, it is consciousness that is aware of the psyche's influence as a causal relation. Phenomenal consciousness grasps the operation of the psyche as causal (Stein

2000b: 25). To the early Husserl's understanding of the logical foundational structures of phenomenology Stein adds the force and causal structure of psyche. Stein tries to introduce, against the critiques of psychology and psychologism found in the first version of the *Logical Investigations*, a place and role for psyche. It must be noted, however, that Husserl too, especially as his thought developed, thought through the role of psyche, especially in his texts on phenomenological psychology, passive synthesis, and affectivity.

10.4 THE STATE

In Stein's third major work, *An Investigation of the State*, one finds not so much an elaboration of phenomenological structures proper, but more an attempt to apply phenomenology to the study of real objectivities in the world. Written in 1919, after Germany's defeat in World War I and after Stein's service at the front as a nurse, her text applies her phenomenological insights about the nature of community to an analysis of the essence of the state. Though the text deploys phenomenological insights gained from her other works, it would be an exaggeration to claim that this work, laced as it is with Stein's own political desires and insights, is purely phenomenological (Calcagno 2014: 161–94). For example, she dismisses contractarian theories of the state as inauthentic forms of the state because of their exclusionary assumption that all members living in a state have assented to the social contract and agreed to enter into a state relationship. Stein does not investigate the essence of the contractarian state and her summary rejection of it displays a certain prejudice on her part. She does argue, however, that the state is a middle form of community, somewhere between more intimate social communal objectivities such as the family and larger ones such as humanity. Drawing from Reinach's work (1913) on a priori right, Stein argues that the essence of the state lies in its autonomy to self-legislate and rule (an essence shared with the contractarian state, a point that Stein does not analyze to any significant extent). She accepts Reinach's essential description of law, both positive and a priori. The former refers to laws made in response to particular circumstances in cultures of a certain time and space, and the latter are universal laws that are considered just without regard to the culture, the times, or particular traditions—for example, the right to live, the right to property, to movement. What is unique about Stein's treatment of law and statehood is that she lodges them firmly in her phenomenology of community. The state can only be a state if lawgivers live a meaningful sociality of community—that is, a solidarity wherein lawgivers and the followers of the law live each other's collective we-experience of law-making and law-following. For Stein, a law-making and law-following community is the essence of the state. But she recognized that, though the law-community constitutes the sense of the state, the ontic reality of the state also includes other kinds of social relations and objectivities, including society, families, peoples, etc. Communities, for Stein, are constituted by persons, who, as we saw earlier, are unities of body, psyche, and spirit. Communities are collectively capable of experiencing both psychic and spiritual realities, even though these only manifest in individual persons. In Stein's phenomenology, the state, under-stood as a community of law-givers and law-followers, must be understood as rooted in the collective lives of persons. In fact, Stein consistently maintains, in all of her work, that the human person is the foundation of phenomenology, science, politics, social interactions, and philosophy. Stein's Schelerian-inspired personalist phenomenology shifts the emphasis away from the powers of logic or (transcendental) consciousness (read Husserl and Reinach) as the ground of science and philosophical inquiry; rather, these powers reveal a ground that consists of persons who are enmeshed in interper-sonal relationships of different kinds and intensities. Steinian phenomenology moves us away from modern philosophy's view of reason and freedom as guiding human thinking to a conception that situates both reason and freedom within the subjectivity of the bearer (*Träger*), that is, the human person—a person who experiences, acts upon, and is affected by the material world of which she is part.

The last text of Stein's phenomenology proper, *Einführung in die Philosophie* (*Introduction to Philosophy*), was written over a number of years, from about 1919 to 1922, with emendations that date from the late 1920s. One should not be deceived by the title of the text, for the book is really an introduction to Steinian phenomenology. When Stein left Husserl, she returned to her hometown of Breslau and began to give private lectures in phenomenology, using the text of her *Introduction* as notes for her lectures. The book is remarkable for numerous reasons. First, it lays out Stein's systematic view of what phenomenology is and what it is supposed to do. Second, we find in it an ampli-fication of her arguments, announced in *On the Problem of Empathy* and developed in *Philosophy of Psychology and the Humanities*, about the necessity for phenomenology to provide an account of the material, natural world upon which it depends and by which it is influenced. She again takes up, and modifies, her accounts of empathy, psyche, per-sonhood, character, and personality. Third, paralleling concepts we find in Husserl's *Ideas III* as well as his discussion of regional ontologies in the *Logical Investigations*, Stein demonstrates how we are to apply phenomenology to other disciplines: In the *Introduction*, she describes what happens to the study of history when phenomenology is applied to it, especially at the methodological level. In many ways, Stein saw phe-nomenology as radically altering how we understand and view the science of history itself, and, in effect, she gave us a phenomenological historiography (González Di Pierro 2004). Finally, for those interested in Husserl's work, the *Introduction* can be read as a critique of Husserl's *Ideas II* and *III*, texts that Stein edited and assembled for Husserl. Her *Introduction* may be read as a blueprint for the direction she thought Husserl's *Ideas* and transcendental phenomenology should have taken after the publication of *Ideas I*. Finally, Stein amplifies and reworks her social ontology; for example, we find here a re-elaboration of her notions of empathy and universal human personhood.

While we cannot take up all of these remarkable features of Stein's *Introduction* be-cause of limitations of space, I would like to point out that for phenomenology proper, the most important aspect of Stein's *Introduction* lies in her expansion of the discus-sion of physical nature. In *Philosophy of Psychology and the Humanities*, she introduced physical, material nature in her treatment of the psyche. But because of her reading of Husserl's lectures on *Thing and Space* as well as Bergson, both consciousness and psyche—indeed, the life of all persons—are seen in the *Introduction* to be deeply structured and influenced by the physics of time and space. Stein claims that the natural sciences, especially the breakthroughs of non-Euclidean geometry, and those of Einstein, Mach, and Planck, radically altered our understanding of the laws (read intelligibility) of the physical universe and our place in it. Phenomenology, then, must provide an account of how time and space structure and affect our lived experience of the world. To this end, part one of the *Introduction* is devoted to the problems of the philosophy of nature (Stein 2004: 30/23). Stein investigates themes that include the intuitive togetherness of the spatial world, the limits of material "nature" in the whole of spatial objects, the structure of material nature and the exceptional position of solid bodies, space as constitutive of material things and the tasks of a theory of space; she delineates sensible qualities, the pure theory of colors, the pure theory of movement, and the pure theory of time, the relativity of movement and the relativity of space; she describes movement as a natural process, the acceleration and designation of material properties, pure change and change in nature, the space continuum and the multiplicity of magnitudes and figures, primary and secondary qualities, etc. Stein understood nature phenomenologically, as a living whole (Stein 2004: 131/53). In his *Thing and Space* lectures, Husserl examined much of the science that Stein drew upon and made a similar argument about the importance of the thing for phenomenology. In terms of her own phenomenological view, the thing, understood as that which most generally allows the content of consciousness to first appear in any determinate shape and in a certain position within consciousness, is a necessary extension of material or physical nature, which ultimately conditions the very possibility of experiencing things in general, including what both consciousness and the psyche allow to appear.

10.5 THE IMPLICATIONS OF STEIN'S DISCUSSION OF PSYCHE AND MATERIAL NATURE FOR SENSE-MAKING

I have shown what is unique about Steinian phenomenology as it unfolds over her four major early works, but if we accept her view of phenomenology, what are its implications for our understanding of sense-making, sense-bestowal, or constitution? Sense-making, sense-bestowal, or constitution marks the achievement or fulfillment of the mind's intention of a meaning and its adequation to what an object actually is. What an object is is grasped through the mind's ability to seize the essence of an object as it manifests itself in consciousness. Following Reinach's and Husserl's early work in phenomenology, Stein believed that the mind can understand what things are in reality through the very givenness or manifestation of those objects in consciousness. Knowledge or truth, according to Husserl, is achieved when an adequation between a meaning intention and a meaning fulfillment is obtained. For example, the mind understands the sense of the number 1 by searching for its possible meanings, testing and varying the possibilities of the sense of 1, and then achieving fulfillment of the meaning of 1 as a single unit of measurement, which is neither more nor less than 1, neither 2 nor 0. According to Husserl and Reinach, we can extend the same process of meaning intention and meaning fulfillment to things in the world as they manifest themselves to intentional consciousness. But these thinkers, deeply moved by the ideality of mathematics, argued, in the works that were foundational for Stein's understanding of phenomenology, that phenomenology can uncover the logical operations (for example, the structures of parts and wholes, judgment, synthesis, etc.) that make sense-making possible.

Stein never repudiated this possibility, and her phenomenology remains doggedly faithful to it (Stein 2000b: 151–7). But she pushes her beloved teachers and fellow phenomenologists to recognize the structures of consciousness and the psyche, insisting that even the performance of logical operations is subject to other structures. In fact, we saw earlier how the psyche, especially through life feelings, affects the ability of consciousness to experience reality. One of the chief tasks of phenomenology is to closely trace lived experiences, as they unfold in consciousness, in order to uncover truths about things and consciousness itself. The process of sense-making, for Stein, is enmeshed in a complex structure of body, psyche, and spirit—that is, in the deep structure of personhood.

To demonstrate the connection between embodied psyche and spirit and sense-making, Stein returns to an examination of the constitutive flow of consciousness itself. She affirms that, though the very flow of consciousness itself is not a causal association of parts, the content of the flow contains aspects of causality, for the content of one moment of the flow can lead to an association with other content (Stein 2000b: 198). Like the later Husserl, Stein admits that both passive and active synthesis are vital for meaning- or sense-making.

Stein identifies feelings as the key that shows how the coherence of meaning straddles both the embodied psyche and the motivations of spirit (Stein 2000b: 111). Stein (2000b: 107–8) offers an example of how she understands feeling to cross both the embodied psychic and spiritual realms. One is beset by a certain mood, which carries with it a certain feeling, which, in turn, affects one's conscious experience of reality. One understands that this mood causes our feelings to be influenced in a particular way. The apprehension of this causality is not given by the feelings themselves; a higher spiritual act of reason is required in order to establish this connection between feeling and consciousness itself. In this sense, that is, in terms of their capacity to express the lawfulness of causality, feelings are described as "hollow." I can become aware that my mood and the feelings it induces can color my spiritual capacities, especially my motivations. The imagery of "dragging" is pertinent here: it seems that the feelings delivered by the psyche are often the initial stages of a growing awareness that can then be understood (that is, the full sense of the lived experience can be understood) through other spiritual acts, including reason, will, and motivation. Stein's discussion of dragging is, of course, evocative of the image of the noetic being dragged by the hyletic, an image we find developed by Angela Ales Bello in her discussion of Husserl's genetic phenomenology (Ales Bello 2015: 58–9). What is curious about the analysis of passive and active synthesis in both Husserl and Stein is the timing: both philosophers began to think about the topic when they arrived at Freiburg—Husserl to take up the chair in philosophy and Stein to defend her doctoral dissertation and serve as Husserl's assistant. Undoubtedly, both philosophers recognized the importance of passive structures and the psyche, but Stein insisted that this insight must be part of phenomenological understanding. Husserl, on the other hand, referred to the passive structures in his *Cartesian Meditations*, and ultimately left many of his brilliant insights unpublished in his lifetime. It would be fair to say that, in his published works, Husserl struggled with how to incorporate his own insights about empathy, passive synthesis, and psyche into his logical and/or transcendental framework. Husserl's reluctance to make the connection between his transcendental phenomenology and the natural, material world—because he wanted to preserve the purity of the foundational transcendental sphere he had uncovered in *Ideas I*—can be seen playing out in the *Cartesian Meditations* in his discussion of passive and active synthesis. Here we can see Husserl wrestling with Stein's criticism, working hard on the psyche and passive structures like the drives, sensations, feelings, etc. Yet we can also see his reluctance to compromise the purity of the transcendental realm.

Stein concludes her treatise on psychic causality with a discussion of the coherence of sense (Stein 2000b: 115–16). The discussion of moods and feelings reveals the influence of the psyche on our understanding of the psyche itself and its influence on the ability of consciousness to experience the objectivated world in more or less intense ways. The affects of the psyche can help to motivate reason (Stein 2000b: 110). If Stein's account of the psyche is correct, then how we arrive at sense-making is not simply a process of the conscious logical operations of reason; rather, reason finds itself affected by the psyche and even motivated by what spirit reveals about the affects of the psyche. We see the intimate interaction between the life of the psyche and spirit, for example, in the description of the lived experience of community in which both the *Lebenskraft* and sensibility of the psyche join with spiritual acts of mind, including categorial reasoning, valuing, motivation and volition, in order to help constitute the very sense of community itself.

10.6 THE STEINIAN LEGACY
OF PHENOMENOLOGY

While at Freiburg with Husserl, Stein began to give seminars, much like her teacher Reinach had done, that would help prepare students to follow Husserl's work philosophy carry on the work of phenomenology. Her social ontology, especially her views on community, could be viewed as having a deep impact on Gerda Walther, one of her students. Walther came from Munich and had a deep interest in psychology. She had worked with Pfänder and other Munich phenomenologists before coming to Freiburg to work with Stein and Husserl. In her "Zur Ontologie der sozialen Gemeinschaften,"

Walther (1923) followed Stein in adapting the classic model of social relations given by the founding fathers of sociology, especially Tönnies and Simmel, to phenomenology. Like Stein, Walther (1923: 4) privileged community as the most intense and highest form of sociality, agreeing with Stein that it is the grasping of the sense or essence of lived experience that is phenomenology's primary objective. But there are also significant differences in their respective accounts. Though both thinkers agree that community is marked by a particular form of union and though both believe that such a union consists of individuals collectively living through a shared experience, Walther also maintains that there are intense forms of community in which the union is one of fusion of profound identification, a point which Stein does not accept. Walther claimed that intense forms of communities are marked by a particular form of a lived experience of community, or *Gemeinschaftserlebnis*, a term she adopted from Stein's social ontology. She described the essence (*Wesenskonstituens*) or sense of community as a oneness (*Einigung*) that possesses both inner and outer aspects (Walther 1923: 34–6). A profound resonance between Stein and Walther is seen in the discussion of the psychic and passive (inner) aspects of community. In terms of the inner aspect of the lived experience of community, Walther was aware that both passive/unconscious aspects as well as more explicitly conscious ones exist (Walther 1923: 37). She described the oneness of community as touching upon various dimensions of the mental life of human beings: affectivity (psyche), the unconscious, passive structures (habit), and consciousness (intentionality and sense). Privileging no one dimension, she recognized that they all came with varying intensities of presence or manifestation. Although Walther did not privilege a Steinian or Schelerian personalism, and though her account of community lacks the Bergsonian-like vitalism that we find in Stein's account of the "inner" aspects of communal life, her early work on community may be read as a profound dialogue with Stein.

After Stein decided to cease working for Husserl in 1919, and after converting to Roman Catholicism in 1922, she took employment in Münster as a teacher in a training college for women who wanted to teach. She taught various subjects, including German literature. It was at this time that she began to study and translate the works of key figures of Christian philosophy, including Augustine of Hippo, Thomas Aquinas, Cardinal John Henry Newman, and Duns Scotus. In the periods between her departure from Husserl, her lectures at Breslau, and her employment at Münster, Stein visited the Bergzabern Circle of phenomenologists, a group of phenomenologists who met at the farm of Theodor Conrad and Hedwig Conrad-Martius. Phenomenologists such as Alexander Koyré and Jean Héring attended meetings at Bergzabern, where the phenomenological and philosophical works of its members were discussed. The relationship between Stein and Hedwig Conrad-Martius was marked by deep friendship and philosophical exchange. Stein often drew upon Hedwig Conrad-Martius's insights, especially in her later philosophy. In her writing on the soul and being, she drew upon Conrad-Martius's writings on science as well (Conrad-Martius 1957, 1963–5). We can see Conrad-Martius's influence on Stein in *Finite and Eternal Being*, in which we find long treatments of Conrad-Martius's ideas (Stein 2002: 259–72). Conrad-Martius was deeply interested in Scholastic philosophy as well as the natural sciences, especially biology (Ales Bello

2012). It would not be an exaggeration to claim that Hedwig Conrad-Martius, Stein's godmother, was extremely important for shaping Stein's later philosophy.

Though Stein's interest in phenomenology continued throughout her life, her interest in Christian philosophy inspired her to attempt a synthesis between phenomenology and Christian philosophy. At Heidegger's request, she composed a dialogue between Husserl and Thomas Aquinas about essences in order to honor Husserl on the occasion of his seventieth birthday. Heidegger did not appreciate the dialogue form of her composition and asked her to submit a more formal essay exploring the same ideas. Both the essay and the dialogue are preserved in *Knowledge and Faith* (Stein 2000a). Though the respective philosophies of Husserl and Aquinas, according to Stein, shared a deep affinity with respect to the role of essences, there are two important differences between them. First, they positioned reality (versus ideality) in different ways. Second, the discussion of genus and species (in relation to form), which provided an important framework for Thomas, was not as central in Husserl's philosophy. In many ways, both Stein's dialogue and essay can be read as the groundwork for her larger project, which culminated in her massive work, *Finite and Eternal Being* (Stein 2002). In this late work, Stein presented her treatment of the connection between finite and infinite being. The logic of this work, though not properly phenomenological, nonetheless displays a profound attachment to the notion of meaning-making, for it allows one to grasp the various senses of finite being and ultimately to ascend to a higher sense of infinite being, namely, the Christian God. Though Stein's *magnum opus* was typeset and ready for publication, it was not published because of anti-Jewish laws that prohibited the publication of works by Jews. The text, smuggled out of Germany into Holland, was saved, though Stein's home cloister at Echt was bombed and though Stein herself was murdered in Auschwitz. She did not live to see her work published.

The English-speaking philosophical world is now turning its attention to Stein's work in phenomenology, especially as Anglo-American social ontology shares a deep interest in many of the themes that Stein explored in her early writings.[7] As more scholarly work appears, it will become clear that Stein occupied a unique place in the Phenomenological Movement. Not only a close discussant with Husserl, she also developed her own phenomenological project, beginning with empathy and an expansion of the role of the psyche and causality within the discussion of consciousness, especially in relation to sense-making, and culminating in a fuller account of phenomenology as connected to the material natural world and an account of social and political objectivities.

REFERENCES

Ales Bello, A. (2005), "L'antropologia fenomenologica di Edith Stein," *Agathos: An International Review of the Humanities and the Social Sciences* 2/2: 23–43.

[7] For example, Szanto 2015 and Moran and Szanto 2015.

Ales Bello, A. (2012), "What Is Life? The Contributions of Hedwig Conrad-Martius and Edith Stein," *Symposium: Canadian Journal of Continental Philosophy* 16/2: 20–33.

Ales Bello, A. (2015), *The Sense of Things: Toward a Phenomenological Realism*, translated by Antonio Calcagno (Dordrecht: Springer).

Calcagno, A. (2014), *Lived Experience from the Inside Out: The Social and Political Philosophy of Edith Stein* (Pittsburgh, PA: Duquesne University Press).

Conrad-Martius, H. (1957), *Das Sein* (Munich: Kösel Verlag).

Conrad-Martius, H. (1963–5), *Schriften zur Philosophie* (Munich: Kösel Verlag).

Gallese, V. (2003), "The Roots of Empathy: The Shared Manifold Hypothesis and the Neural Basis of Intersubjectivity," *Psychopathology* 36: 171–80.

González Di Pierro, E. (2004), *De la persona a la historia. Antropología fenomenológica y filosofía de la historia en Edith Stein* (Morelia: Dríada).

Husserl, E. (1952), *Ideen zu einer reinen Phänomenologie und phänomenologischen Philosophie II*, ed. von M. Biemel (The Hague: Martinus Nijhoff).

Husserl, E. (1971), *Ideen zu einer reinen Phänomenologie und phänomenologischen Philosophie III*, ed. von M. Biemel (The Hague: Martinus Nijhoff).

Husserl, E. (1973a), *Ding und Raum: Vorlesungen 1907*, ed. von U. Claesges (The Hague: Martinus Nijhoff).

Husserl, E. (1973b), *Zur Phänomenologie der Intersubjektivität. Texte aus dem Nachlaß, Erster Teil: 1905–1920*, ed. I. Kern (The Hague: Martinus Nijhoff).

Husserl, E. (1973c), *Zweiter Teil: 1921–1928*, ed. I. Kern (The Hague: Martinus Nijhoff).

Husserl, E. (1973d), *Dritter Teil: 1929–1935*, ed. I. Kern (The Hague: Martinus Nijhoff).

Husserl, E. (2001), *Logical Investigations*, 2 vols, ed. D. Moran and translated by J. N. Findlay (London: Routledge).

Husserl, E. (2012), *Cartesian Meditations: Introduction to Philosophy*, translated by D. Cairns (Dordrecht: Springer).

MacIntyre, A. (2006), *Edith Stein: A Philosophical Prologue, 1913–1922* (Lanham, MD: Rowman and Littlefield).

Manganaro, P. (2002), *Verso l'altro. L'esperienza mistica tra interiorità e trascendenza* (Rome: Città Nuova).

Maskulak, M. (2007), *Edith Stein and the Body-Soul-Spirit at the Center of Holistic Formation* (New York: Peter Lang).

Miles, J. (2003), "Other bodies and other minds in Edith Stein: Or, how to talk about empathy," in R. Feist and W. Sweet (eds), *Husserl and Edith Stein* (Washington, DC: Council of Research in Values and Philosophy), 119–26.

Moran, D. (2004), "The problem of empathy: Lipps, Scheler, Husserl and Stein," in T. A. Kelley and P. W. Rosemann (eds), *Amor Amicitiae: On the Love That Is Friendship: Essays in Medieval Thought and Beyond in Honor of the Rev. Professor James McEvoy* (Leuven: Peeters), 269–312.

Moran, D. and Parker, R. K. B. (eds) (2015), *Early Phenomenology*, special edition of *Studia Phaenomenologica: Romanian Journal for Phenomenology* 15: 11–26.

Moran, D. and Szanto, T. (eds) (2015), *Empathy and Collective Intentionality: The Social Philosophy of Edith Stein*, special volume of *Human Studies*, vol. 38, n. 4.

Reinach, A. (1913), "Die apriorischen Grundlagen des bürgerlichen Rechtes," in *Jahrbuch für Philosophie und phänomenologische Forschung*, vol. 1 (Tübingen: Niemeyer), 685–847.

Reinach, A. (1951), *Was ist Phänomenologie?* ed. H. Conrad-Martius (Munich: Kösel Verlag).

Sawicki, M. (2004), "Personal connections: The phenomenology of Edith Stein," in *Yearbook of the Irish Philosophical Society: Voices of Irish Philosophy* (Dublin: Irish Philosophical Society), 148–69.

Scheler, M. (1973), *Formalism in Ethics and Non-Formal Ethics of Values*, translated by M. Frings and R. L. Funk (Evanston, IL: Northwestern University Press).

Scheler, M. (2008), *The Nature of Sympathy*, translated by P. Heath (New Brunswick, NJ: Transaction).

Schulz, P. (2008), "Toward the Subjectivity of the Human Person: Edith Stein's Contribution to the Theory of Identity," *American Catholic Philosophical Quarterly* 82/1: 161–76.

Sharkey, S. B. (2006), "What makes you you? Edith Stein on individual form," in J. A. Berkman (ed.), *Contemplating Edith Stein* (Notre Dame, IN: University of Notre Dame Press), 283–300.

Sharkey, S. B. (2009), *Thine Own Self: Individuality in Edith Stein's Later Writings* (Washington, DC: Catholic University of America Press).

Spiegelberg, H. (1960), *The Phenomenological Movement: A Historical Introduction* (The Hague: Martinus Nijhoff).

Stein, E. (1989), *On the Problem of Empathy*, translated by W. Stein (Washington, DC: ICS Publications).

Stein, E. (2000a), *Knowledge and Faith*, translated by W. Redmond (Washington, DC: ICS Publications).

Stein, E. (2000b), *Philosophy of Psychology and the Humanities*, translated by M. C. Baseheart and M. Sawicki (Washington, DC: ICS Publications).

Stein, E. (2002), *Finite and Eternal Being*, translated by K. F. Reinhardt (Washington, DC: ICS Publications).

Stein, E. (2004), *Einführung in die Philosophie*, ed. H. B. Gerl-Falkovitz and C. M. Wulf (Freiburg-im-Breisgau: Herder).

Stein, E. (2006a), *An Investigation Concerning the State*, translated by M. Sawicki (Washington, DC: ICS Publications).

Stein, E. (2006b), *Endliches und ewiges Sein: Versuch eines Aufstiegs zum Sinn des Sein. Anhang: Martin Heideggers Existenzphilosophie. Die Seelenburg*, ed. U. Müller, in *Edith Stein Gesamtausgabe*, vols 11 and 12 (Freiburg-im-Breisgau: Herder).

Stein, E. (2013), *Zum Problem der Einfühlung*, in A. M. Sondermann (ed.), OCD, *Edith Stein Gesamtausgabe* (ESGA), vol. 5 (Freiburg-im-Breisgau: Herder).

Stein, E. (2014), *Letters to Roman Ingarden*, translated by H. C. Hunt (Washington, DC: ICS Publications).

Szanto, T. (2015), "Collective Emotions and Empathy: A Steinian Account," *Human Studies* 38/4: 503–27.

Walther, G. (1923), "Zur Ontologie der sozialen Gemeinschaften," in E. Husserl, M. Geiger, A. Pfänder, and M. Scheler (eds), *Jahrbuch für Philosophie und phänomenologische Forschung* (Halle: Niemeyer), 1–158.

Zahavi, D. (2008), "Phenomenology," in D. Moran (ed.), *The Routledge Companion to Twentieth-Century Philosophy* (London: Routledge), 661–92.

Zahavi, D. (2010), "Empathy, Embodiment and Interpersonal Understanding: From Lipps to Schutz," *Inquiry* 53/3: 285–306.

Zahavi, D. (2015), *Self and Other: Exploring Subjectivity, Empathy, and Shame* (Oxford: Oxford University Press).

CHAPTER 11

....

THE EARLY HEIDEGGER'S PHENOMENOLOGY

....

DANIEL O. DAHLSTROM

Is Heidegger a phenomenologist? Was he ever a phenomenologist? To be sure, in lecture after lecture from 1919 to 1928, he repeatedly identifies his investigations as phenomenological. At the start of his career in Freiburg, he had regular, storied conversations with Edmund Husserl, the thinker most responsible for elaborating phenomenology as a philosophical discipline in the early twentieth century. Husserl welcomed their exchanges, entrusted Heidegger with many a manuscript, and greatly facilitated Heidegger's academic career. In 1928, presumably before delving deeply into Heidegger's *Being and Time*, Husserl reportedly tells him: "You and I are phenomenology" (Cairns 1976: 9).[1]

Yet anyone coming from the study of Husserl to the early Heidegger's courses is bound to have serious doubts about Heidegger's phenomenological credentials. Although explicit and open criticism of Husserl's phenomenology is apparent in lectures only after Heidegger's move to Marburg, there is ample evidence—some of it summarized in this chapter—of his departure from Husserl's phenomenology already in his first Freiburg lectures, 1919–23.[2] So it would come at no surprise to someone attending his early lectures to hear of his remark to Jaspers, shortly before the appearance of *Being and Time*, that if it is written against anyone, it is against Husserl (Heidegger and Jaspers 1990: 62–4, 71). For his part, Husserl recognized, albeit all too late, that what Heidegger calls phenomenology is, in Husserl's view, a travesty of phenomenology and, indeed, nothing more than a version of philosophical anthropology (Husserl 1994a: 184, 1994b: 254, 476; Breuer 1994: 13). Responding to this criticism in 1930, Heidegger advises

---

[1] In a late 1926 draft of a letter to Heidegger, Husserl writes: "No one has greater faith in you than I." I am indebted to Walter Hopp for invaluable help with this chapter and to Zachary Joachim and James Kinkaid for critical readings of it.

[2] Von Herrmann (2000: 9–98), for example, reads his first Freiburg lecture as a repudiation of Husserl's "reflective" phenomenology; but see Thomas Nenon's July 28, 2014 review in *Notre Dame Philosophical Reviews*, and Zahavi 2003: 167–71.

his students to reserve the title "phenomenology" for what Husserl has achieved and will achieve (Heidegger 1997: 40). In the years that followed, Heidegger largely follows his own advice.

The advice further adds to the puzzle of what Heidegger meant in the 1920s when he designates what he is doing as "phenomenology." Indeed, to the extent that he recognizes any continuity between his early and later thought, the advice suggests that he did not regard what is of value in the early work as necessarily falling under the rubric of "phenomenology" at all.[3] To be sure, these points are less than substantive and Heidegger may not be a faithful interpreter of his development (nor, given the volume of lectures and writings, would it be reasonable to expect him to be). Nevertheless, when taken together with the sharp differences between the two thinkers, the problem raised by these considerations is patent. What in the world does Heidegger have in mind by self-styling his investigations in the 1920s as phenomenology? Is his use of the term, when read alongside Husserl's use, simply an equivocation? Does it make sense, in the end, for Heidegger to be deemed—or, for that matter, to have deemed himself—a phenomenologist? Certainly, from a Husserlian point of view, it can be hard to see how. Still, if he was not exactly a card-carrying Husserlian phenomenologist in the 1920s, what explains his characterization (or mis-characterization) of his own investigations as phenomenology?

The main objective of this chapter is to try to answer this last question. More precisely, the aim is to shed some light on Heidegger's conception of phenomenology during this time in light of its conscious departure from Husserl's phenomenology. The period in question extends from Heidegger's first Freiburg lectures in 1919 to his return to Freiburg from Marburg in the fall of 1928.

Critical engagement with Husserl's work is by no means the only source of the early Heidegger's phenomenology. In keeping with the purpose of the present volume, section 11.1 identifies major influences on his early thought. Section 11.2 returns to its main objective. After flagging the prima facie differences between Husserl's and Heidegger's phenomenological projects, I suggest how Heidegger can nonetheless plausibly lay claim to the mantle—or even a mantle—of phenomenology.

11.1 Major Influences on Early Heidegger's Phenomenology

In the early 1920s there are arguably five major influences on Heidegger's early thought: (1) Husserlian phenomenology; (2) the efforts of Dilthey and the so-called

---

[3] Despite his disavowals, Heidegger's later thinking arguably continues to exemplify transcendental phenomenology under another rubric (given the abiding role of Dasein in it). Eminent scholars (Crowell 2013, Sheehan 2016) argue that Heidegger remained a phenomenologist from beginning to end.

"Southwest" school of neo-Kantianism (Windelband, Rickert, Lask) to elaborate the distinctiveness of historical understanding and worldly experience; (3) Natorp's psychology and criticisms of Husserl's phenomenology; (4) the formal indications provided by Pauline-Augustinian religious exhortations, viewed through the lens of "the young Luther" and Kierkegaard; and (5) Aristotle's conceptions of the inherent mobility (κίνησις) of being and being-in-the-world—Aristotle's "ontology of life" (not nature) as well as his interpretation of practical understanding (φρόνησις) as a distinctive manner of uncovering things (ἀληθεύειν) (Heidegger 2002: 322–9, 2004a: 184, 2005: 382–6).[4] Another unmistakable influence becomes discernible midway through the decade, particularly as he is putting the finishing touches on *Sein und Zeit*: (6) the transcendental subject in Kant's theoretical philosophy and Marburg neo-Kantian readings of the latter (Heidegger 1977: 431; Dahlstrom 1991). No historical treatment of the early Heidegger's thinking would be complete that did not trace his critical engagement with each of these historical influences.

Thankfully, much of this territory is well trod by eminent scholars,[5] and it is not my aim to reproduce their efforts. I restrict my comments to identifying ways in which the early Heidegger adapts aspects of Husserl's phenomenology into his methodology. However, based upon the chronology of Heidegger's lectures, the impact of Dilthey and the Southwest school of neo-Kantianism, on the one hand, and Natorp's psychology, on the other, must be accorded a certain pride of place along with Husserlian phenomenology when it comes to Heidegger's initial efforts to hammer out the specific subject matter and method of his phenomenology.[6] Indeed, Heidegger's response to both Dilthey's account of historical reality and, as discussed later, Natorp's account of psychology serves as a key catalyst for his transformation of Husserl's conception of phenomenology. When, in the course of the 1920s, Heidegger shifts his attention to religious experience, sustained readings of Aristotle's texts, and the transcendental framework of Kant's theoretical philosophy, the historical turn and non-objectifying approach that inform his own distinctive phenomenology are already in place.

---

[4] See, too, Heidegger 1988: 5: "Begleiter im Suchen war der junge Luther und Vorbild Aristoteles, den jener haßte. Stöße gab Kierkegaard, und die Augen hat mir Husserl eingesetzt." Though unmentioned by Heidegger, the influence of Hegel and Nietzsche is also unmistakable (as is that of Bergson, Jaspers, Scheler, Simmel, and Spengler—all of whom he does mention).

[5] See Kisiel (1993), van Buren (1994), and Denker et al. (2004) for surveys of Heidegger's early development. For his engagement with Husserl, see the studies by Stapleton (1983), von Herrmann (2000), Crowell (2001, 2013), Gander (2004), and Overgaard (2004); on the abiding importance of Dilthey, see Scharff (2014: esp. Part III); on the influence of the Southwest school, see Bowler (2008) and Campbell (2012); on the all-important critical reception of Aristotle, see Strube (1993), Brogan (2006), and Sheehan (2015, 2016); on Heidegger's phenomenology of religion, see Crowe (2005), Campbell (2012), and McManus (2012).

[6] Heidegger explicitly addresses the Southwest School and Natorp in his first two lectures (Heidegger 1999: 29–58, 95–111, 140–203) and Natorp again in the summer semester of 1920 (Heidegger 1993: 96–174; Zahavi 2003). Both Husserl and Heidegger take on the *Wissenschaft/Weltanschauung* debate raging between the neo-Kantians (especially Rickert) and the life-philosophers (notably Dilthey). Thanks to James Kinkaid for this reminder.

11.2 THE EARLY HEIDEGGER'S ADAPTATION OF HUSSERLIAN PHENOMENOLOGY

By the early 1930s, "phenomenology" is a term invoked less and less by Heidegger to characterize his way of thinking, so much so that at one point, as already noted, he advises students to restrict the term to its Husserlian sense. Even during the 1920s, when he finds the moniker apt enough for his lectures and publications, their themes and approaches depart strikingly from those of Husserl's phenomenology. Here a sampling of three differences may suffice:[7]

(1) While consciousness and intentionality are the fundamental subjects of Husserl's phenomenological analyses, Heidegger considers them derivative phenomena (Husserl 1976: 187f.; 1984a: 355–440).[8] In Heidegger's earliest lectures, to be sure, he focuses on lived experience, a cognate of consciousness, as he is intent on developing a conception of phenomenology as a "pre-theoretical . . . primordial science" of the pre-given experience of factical life (Heidegger 1999: 96f.; 1993a: 70f., 78f.). But it is "hopeless," he observes in this connection, for any "science of consciousness" to get at life since its goal, a certain "ideal of knowledge," has torn down all the bridges to it (Heidegger 1993: 144).[9]

(2) Husserl touts phenomenology as a return to *die Sachen selbst* and what is "given" in an originary way (Husserl 1976: 42, 52). By contrast, in Heidegger's first lectures, he debunks appeals to the given, insisting that when we look at the experience of the surrounding world, we do not even find "a consciousness of givenness" (Heidegger 1999: 98).[10] The claim that the surrounding world is given to me is misguided (to put it mildly; Heidegger actually says that it is *verkehrt*), since givenness is "very much a theoretical form already . . . the initial, objectifying encroachment on" experience of the surrounding world (Heidegger 1999: 88–9). So, too, what phenomenologists have in mind when they speak of *die Sachen selbst* is typically not so much things themselves (and certainly not the quotidian experience of things within the surrounding world) as it is the subject matters already carved up by academic traditions. The implication is that

[7] See the studies by Kisiel (1993), von Herrmann (2000), Crowell (2001, 2013), Overgaard (2004), and Sheehan (2015, 2016) for more sustained, at times differing accounts of these issues.

[8] For Heidegger, intentionality is grounded in the transcending that is proper to being-here (*Da-sein*) and being-in-the-world—and not vice versa (Heidegger 1989a: 89ff., 230, 249).

[9] The shift from the study of life and lived experience to the sense of being is not abrupt; in 1922, to offset stapling (*Verklammerung*), in Cartesian fashion, ontology together with epistemology, Heidegger probes the sense of being of life ("factical life" for which death is decisive), requiring in turn the development of a formal concept of history; Heidegger 2005: 173–81.

[10] This criticism does not stop Heidegger from appealing to "the given" himself in early lectures (Heidegger 1999: 70–3; 1993a: 28, 71, 86).

the much-ballyhooed slogan of returning to the things themselves is in reality a rather pedestrian compliance with university curriculum (Heidegger 1999: 61–9, 72–6; 1993a: 150; 1993b: 7f., 45f., 75f.).[11]

(3) An argument can be made that, in Heidegger's earliest lectures at the very least, he continues to subscribe to the central role that Husserl accords intuition in the Sixth Logical Investigation and later reaffirms in the principle of all principles.[12] To be sure, while affirming the principle, Heidegger adds the qualification—with Bergsonian flourishes—that the intuition in question be "hermeneutical" or tied to understanding (Heidegger 1999: 65, 109, 117, 219).[13] Yet the intuition that corresponds to a filled intention for Husserl is intrinsically related to an empty intention, typically some meaning or opinion that can be understood or interpreted in the absence of its fulfillment. So at this structural level there appears to be little distance between the two thinkers. Yet even if for both of them there is no intuition (in the sense of a filled intention) without an understanding (a possibly empty intention), Heidegger alone insists on the constitutive role played by affectivity in the process. *Dasein* is always in some mood; there is no understanding that is not disposed; and moods are no less fundamentally disclosive (truth-bearing, if you will) than the understanding and discourse (Heidegger 1967: 134, 137–9, 142, 144, 260). Indeed, the fundamental mood of anxiety provides "the phenomenal basis for explicitly grasping Dasein's primordial totality of being" (Heidegger 1967: 182).[14]

This list provides, to be sure, only a snapshot of the differences.[15] As a snapshot, it conveys only one perspective, omitting crucial, often mitigating features of the passing

---

[11] As with "the given," Heidegger is anything but consistent when it comes to *die Sache selbst*; see e.g., Heidegger 1993a: 24, 95, 249, 1993b: 30, 1995a: 184, 2005: 178f.

[12] Husserl 1984b: 662: "Entfällt die Anschauung ganz und gar, so erkennt das Urteil nichts."

[13] See Heidegger 1993a: 138: "Anschauung und zwar Erlebnisanschauung, d.h. originäre *genuine* Erlebniserfassung ... Erfassung hat hier eine eigene nirgends sonst antreffbare Gestalt des reinen Verstehens"; see, too, 1993a: 184: "Verstehen—als Anschauung—Mitgehen mit und in der Fülle der Situation."

[14] Whereas for Husserl every intentional experience is an objectifying act or founded upon one and he identifies joy or sadness as founded acts (Husserl 1984a: 514), moods for Heidegger ground other acts (Heidegger 1967: 162, 220, 265). On Heidegger's view, perception is not prior, structurally or otherwise, to affectivity, which he primarily understands, not in the sense of phenomenal quality, but in connection with Aristotle's sense of "ὄρεξις" (I am grateful to Al and Maria Miller for stressing Heidegger's indebtedness to Aristotle in this regard). Insisting that affective acts ground valuing for Husserl and that, in his view, all our experience is of a world somehow valued does not counter this objection. Still, the differences between the two thinkers are mitigated by the role that Husserl assigns to motivation—and perhaps Heidegger's reading of the manuscript of *Ideas II*; see Hadjioannou 2015.

[15] The list could be augmented by Heidegger's insistence on the constituting (i.e., unbracketable) character of history (thrownness), the world (a unity of horizons), and time's discontinuousness. Although Husserl and Heidegger share the view that subjectivity is fundamentally temporal, i.e., that time in some sense provides the condition of possibility of intentionality and other subjective

scene and context. Nevertheless, this fragmentary list suffices to demonstrate how much Heidegger, by his own admission, departs in the 1920s from Husserl's phenomenology. But, then, once again, it bears asking: In what sense does he understand his early thinking as phenomenology at all? Or is it a misnomer? Any of the three differences glossed above might make one think so, especially since Husserl's work is the marker for what passes for phenomenology at the time.

Yet while Heidegger does not exactly take up the baton passed to him by Husserl, during the 1920s he does craft something that he deems "phenomenology" by taking his bearings from several of Husserl's central methodological insights. Both Husserl and Heidegger conceive phenomenology primarily as a method and, more specifically, as a means to metaphysics and/or ontology (indeed, even at times as its realization) (Husserl 1950: 32, 58f., 1973a: 38, 1976: 362–8, Heidegger 1967: 27, 37f., 1994a: 60). They also jointly conceive it as a way of retrieving something that is relatively hidden from normal view, i.e., the sense of things and the constitutive experience of them—the being of beings and the disclosure of them in being-here (*Da-sein*). Heidegger learns and adapts from Husserl the lesson that this retrieval requires an analysis that is at once reductive, performative, formal, and constitutive.[16] Detailing this adaptation—part emulation, part transformation—is the objective of the rest of this chapter.

11.2.1 Phenomenology as reductive analysis

Heidegger considers Husserl's understanding of intentionality the first of the decisive discoveries of his phenomenology. Husserl articulates the common tripartite structure of intentional experiences or acts, i.e., how the relation of act to object invariably includes a way that the respective object is intended. In the terminology of *Ideas I*, each

phenomena, the early Heidegger's account of the discontinuity of time points to a substantial difference between their analyses of temporality. A more fraught issue is the question of presuppositionlessness (see Husserl 1984a: 24f.; 1976: 42f.; Heidegger 1967: 150). Notably, Heidegger later distinguishes between "prehermeneutic" and hermeneutic phenomenology (Heidegger 1989b: 188).

[16] Far from occupying ordinal or exclusive positions, these different aspects of the analysis complement and often overlap with one another. The list could be expanded to (1) the *holistic* character of what is analyzed and (2) the aim of determining it in its *essentials*. (1) Just as Husserlian phenomenology analyzes a whole constituted by non-independent, inherent parts (*Momente*), so Heidegger's phenomenology analyzes being-in-the-world as a "unified phenomenon," equiprimordially constituted by *Strukturmomente*, such as worldhood, being-with, being-in, and selfhood (Heidegger 1967: 41, 53, 64, 113, 131, 180, 190). (2) Heidegger's entire enterprise in *Being and Time* is concerned, no less than Husserl's phenomenology, with the essence(s) of its subject matter. The designation "Dasein," he notes, is selected precisely to indicate that the "essence" of the entity in question consists in having to be its own being (Heidegger 1967: 12, 42). It is of the very "essence" of Dasein to have an understanding of being, to be able to be (*Seinkönnen*), to have its death before it as a defining potential, to have a conscience, and to be capable of being authentic or not (Heidegger 1967: 42f., 231, 233, 248, 262, 278, 323). His analyses focus on the essences of the respective existentials as well as the essence of truth (Heidegger 1967: 190, 214, 222, 296, 314).

act (*noesis*) is directed at an object in terms of a purported sense (*noema*) that is not to be confused with a mental image or idea of the object. When I think of the oak tree on my front lawn or when I knowingly see it, the object of my thought or cognizant perception is not an image or an idea; it is the tree itself. Yet I would not be able to think of it or knowingly see it without a sense of what it is. Indeed, even imagining the tree requires a sense of it.

Though this structure of intentionality ranges over everything that might afford itself to us, this "phenomenological field" itself is hidden.[17] It is not in plain sight; it is not immediately given. The phenomenologist has to shift her focus from the things directly intended to the way that they are intended and to her intentionality itself. This shift requires bracketing the "entire natural world" in which we normally, in our natural attitude, find ourselves as well as any appeal to sciences which presuppose this world. Set aside are not only empirical disciplines such as psychology and physiology, but even the humanities (*Geisteswissenschaften*) insofar as they study conscious states as events taking place, broadly speaking, within nature. Once the natural attitude and all the sciences within it are bracketed, the phenomenologist is in a position to attend exclusively to what presents itself to human subjectivity in the phenomenological field. If everything encompassed by the natural attitude "in an ontic respect" is thus put "out of play," as Husserl puts it, "there remains a region of being, in principle unique, which can, indeed, become the field of a new science—that of phenomenology."[18]

This description of phenomenology and its reductive method could equally be given, without the slightest alteration, to the phenomenology that Heidegger regards as the ontological method in *Being and Time*. Indeed, if one stresses the bracketing of things naturally taken up in an "ontic respect," and takes the genitive in "region of being" as an appositive or possessive rather than a partitive or objective genitive, its suitability to Heidegger's conception is even more pronounced. Heidegger, too, insists that ontic considerations of human existence, specifically in the sciences of anthropology, psychology, and biology, be set aside in an effort to unpack its ontological sense, that is to say, to provide "an ontological analysis of the subjectivity of the subject" (Heidegger 1976: 24).[19] Heidegger's project requires the exclusion of any attempt to understand what "to be" means by referring it to some being, be it God or nature, as though it were explicable in a way analogous to the way in which one being within the world is said to be explained or caused by another (Heidegger 1967: 6). By the same token, in the effort to understand being-in-the-world as such, all otherwise legitimate efforts to comprehend human beings as transcendent objects, simply on-hand within the world, must be put

---

[17] Thus, Husserl observes that consciousness, hitherto unfamiliar (*unbekannt*), has to be made accessible to us, that we live in the cogito, without consciously having the cogitatio as an object (Husserl 1976: 68, 77, 95–7).

[18] Husserl 1976: 68; see, too, 158f.: "Durch die phänomenologische Reduktion hatte sich uns das Reich des transzendentalen Bewusstseins als des in einem bestimmten Sinn 'absoluten' Seins ergeben."

[19] For other positive invocations of subjectivity to characterize Dasein, see Heidegger 1976: 106, 229, 278, 382. For first alerting me to the positive senses of "subjectivity" in SZ, contrary to Heidegger's later position, I am indebted to Klaus Düsing.

out of play. "This particular being does not have and never has the sort of being of some-thing merely on-hand [*vorhanden*] within the world" (Heidegger 1967: 43).[20]

Heidegger also imports into his own account of phenomenology the Husserlian motif, mentioned above, of retrieving the hidden:

> [The theme of phenomenology] is obviously what does *not*, initially and for the most part, show itself, what is *hidden* relative to what shows itself initially and for the most part, but at the same time is something essentially belonging to what shows itself in this way, indeed, such that it makes up its sense and ground. (Heidegger 1967: 35)

That hidden "sense and ground" is, Heidegger continues, the "being of beings," but since there can be no study of being in the abstract but only the being of a particular being, Heidegger begins with the analysis of the being of the particular being with an under-standing of being, i.e., Dasein. And its being is only availed by bracketing ontic studies, reducing what is to be analyzed (what initially shows itself) to its being.

In Heidegger's published lectures, he retains but also transforms the reduction. In the winter semester of 1919–20 he puts a positive spin on the transcendental reduc-tion. After noting how the reduction enables us to set free the "implicit relations" in factical life with the purpose of grasping, on the basis of them, the "basic sense" of the experienced domain, he adds that this sense is determined by those relations since "the phenomenological comportment (towards itself) is . . . not knowledge of an object at all" (Heidegger 1993: 249f.).[21] Instead it is a way of going along with (*Mitgehen*) or co-enacting (*Mitmachen*) the experiences themselves (Heidegger 1993a: 23, 81, 123f., 162f., 185). Heidegger concedes that the reduction can be construed as a way of withdrawing from the experience of living, but he adds that this characterization represents only "the *negative* side of the matter," one that regards all experiences as intentional and, in addition, takes its bearings from perceptions as experiences of grasping things (Heidegger 1993a: 162n. 23, 249f., 254f.).

These last remarks may already signal a difference from Husserl's use of the reduc-tion. So it is perhaps not surprising to read Heidegger, in the summer of 1925, charging that the phenomenological reduction in Husserl's hands is "fundamentally unfit to de-termine positively the being of consciousness" (Heidegger 1994: 150).[22] Two years later, in the summer of 1927, he describes the phenomenological reduction as his method of

[20] To be sure, Heidegger does not use the term "reduction" to describe this aspect of his method, but in his first Marburg lectures he attributes this very aspect to Husserl's "transcendental reduction" and contrasts the latter with Descartes' *remotio*; see Heidegger 2006: 80, 258–60.

[21] See, however, Heidegger 1993: 151, 156 where Heidegger criticizes the reduction, when performed from an "epistemological" or "foregoing transcendental standpoint." This criticism echoes his point about the negative side of the reduction, to which he counterpoises the positive side that entails his account of the three senses (content, performative, and relational); see 1993: 162 n. 23.

[22] Heidegger's remarks, in his first Marburg lectures, about the Cartesian tendencies alive in Husserl's use of first a transcendental and then an eidetic reduction anticipate this criticism (Heidegger 2002: 273f.).

redirecting attention from the comprehension of beings to the understanding of their being. But he also makes it clear that this description hooks up with a central term of Husserl's phenomenology in words only, since for Husserl it means redirecting attention to "the transcendental life of consciousness" (Heidegger 1989a: 29). Heidegger justifies his different use of the reduction with the observation that phenomenological method, like any scientific method, "grows and transforms itself" in the process of pressing ahead to the matters in question.

Heidegger's early phenomenology thus deliberately pursues a reductive analysis, albeit in a sense that just as deliberately departs from its original Husserlian sense. Heidegger even adds two distinctive twists, historical and existential, to the method of reduction as he takes it up into his phenomenology. His aim is to pose the question of the sense of being (*Sinn des Seins*) and, accordingly, as a means of exposing and thereby bracketing "the fatal prejudice" that prevents the question from being raised, he builds into his phenomenological project the task of dismantling the history of ontology (Heidegger 1967: 3–4, 21, 25). Heidegger develops the ground for this historical modification of the reduction in his early lectures by explaining the need for "phenomenological destruction."[23] In addition, the first section of *Being and Time* is nothing less than an attempt to elaborate and then bracket the inauthentic (though nonetheless telling) ways in which human beings project (intend, are related to) themselves, others, and things within the world, ways in which what "being" means for them in each case is constituted and disclosed. Only by virtue of this existential reduction can there be any assurance of disclosing what it means for humans, in the authentic sense of the term, "to be."

11.2.2 Phenomenology as performative analysis

Reflection is arguably the basic operation of Husserlian phenomenology. Despite its defeasible character (recognized by Husserl early on), any possibility of discerning the forms of intentionality immanently, i.e., on their own terms, rests on making them objects of reflection. Herein lies, too, Husserlian phenomenology's necessary recourse to the essentially first-personal character of experience. The reduction and the reflection are operations that the phenomenologist has to perform for herself to gain access to the distinctiveness of imagining, perceiving, speaking, knowing, and so on.[24] A phenomenologist can and, indeed, must reflect on her own reflections, making them in turn into

---

[23] See Heidegger 1993b: 12, 29–38; in this lecture (summer semester 1920), after explaining the sense and necessity of phenomenological destruction, Heidegger applies it to what he regards as the two main groups of philosophical problems among his contemporaries, i.e., the problem of the a priori or ultimate validation and the problem of the irrational or lived experience. There is, nonetheless, an analogous sense of destruction in *Ideas I* (Husserl 1976: 100)—and Luther! (Crowe 2005).

[24] See Husserl's reference to *einsame Selbstbesinnungen* as the genuine beginning of philosophy and the *radikale Selbstverantwortung des Philosophierenden* (Husserl 1988: 169).

objects of reflection. But typically we live through our experiences unreflectively, and it takes a phenomenological reflection to bring their essential character to light.

Critics (e.g., Natorp) have questioned the very prospect of understanding experiences by making them into objects of reflection and description. While the early Heidegger shares some of these misgivings, he is completely on board with Husserl when it comes to what motivates reflection, namely, the need to retrieve what is typically hidden from us, namely, our being itself, equipped with its own inherent understanding of being. He also shares Husserl's methodological insight into the first-person character of the method of phenomenological analysis, i.e., appreciation of the fact that no one else can do it for you.

Especially relevant in this connection is Husserl's analysis of categorial intuition, touted by Heidegger as the second major discovery (after intentionality) of Husserl's phenomenology. A "categorial intuition" is so-called because it is the act of directly grasping what traditionally falls under the "categorial," e.g., conjunctions, disjunctions, states of affairs, collectives, universals, and—not least—being! Yet, on Heidegger's reading, the act is ubiquitous, "invested in the most everyday perception and every experience" (Heidegger 1994b: 64f.). Hand-in-hand with this ubiquitousness is a more or less articulable (not necessarily verbalized) understanding, what Heidegger in his earliest lectures deemed, as noted above, "hermeneutical intuition."[25] On Heidegger's reading, phenomenology consists in reflective, categorial intuitions of pre-reflective, but no less categorial intuitions. Something similar applies to his own phenomenological attempt to understand pre-thematic understanding and experience.

One salient way that Heidegger signals the performative character of his analysis (i.e., again, akin to reflection) is by indicating it formally and thereby conveying it to others. He states that all philosophical concepts are formally indicative (Heidegger 1983: 422), but so are philosophical propositions (Heidegger 1988: 80),[26] determinations (Heidegger 1994a: 52, 1967: 114), and questions (Heidegger 1994a: 172). Philosophy itself, its definition, and its task are indicated formally (Heidegger 1994a: 19f., 32–6; 43f., 45).[27] So, too, are various themes in terms of which this task is pursued, e.g., "living," "caring," "being in a world," "existing," and so on.[28]

Formal indications provide a point of departure, direction, and certain constraints for Heidegger's phenomenology, but their full meaning requires co-enacting what is indicated. By formally indicating a theme like "caring," Heidegger is conveying to his students the need to understand something that they already do, a way of behaving that

---

[25] Heidegger 1999: 117.

[26] Whereas taking the proposition *cogito* in a formal-ontological sense (i.e., as *res cogitans*) perverts its meaning, taking it in a "formally indicative" sense opens us to its temporality and what the ego has; see Heidegger 2006: 250.

[27] Heidegger may be drawing on Husserl's remarks (in the First Logical Investigation) about indications, in contrast to expressions, and, more specifically, how speech can indicate to a listener the presence of a hidden mental act.

[28] Formal indications include "life" (Heidegger 1993b: 29); uses of "I," "is," "has" (1995a: 147); "I am" (1994a: 172ff.; 1967: 116); "caring" and "critique" (2005: 92, 183ff.); "being in a world" (1988: 80); "care"

they already have, without objectifying it, i.e., presuming some ready-made content for it. These indications are formal in the sense that they are bereft of any such content. Instead they indicate what cannot be understood from a standpoint outside a basic experience but can only be understood by enacting the experience from within and interpreting the sense of it accordingly (Heidegger 1994a: 55, 60).[29] They point, in other words, to the outstanding (reflexive) task of taking possession of our ways of behaving and their sense.[30] As such, they are also prohibitions, warning the phenomenologist to ward off preemptive meanings, not least the presumption that the phenomenologist herself is not implicated in the task at hand. Formal indications point to the necessity of retrieving the sense of a relation (*Bezug*) afforded only by a certain enactment or performance (*Vollzug*). Far from being given in advance or without further ado, the content of a formal indication is precisely the sort "whose appropriation is a concrete task of enactment of its own" (Heidegger 1994a: 32, 61, 52f.).[31] In all these ways, Heidegger's use of formal indications reprises the performative character of Husserlian reflection.

11.2.3 Phenomenology as formal analysis

Throughout the existential analysis in SZ, Heidegger explicitly develops and employs an array of "formal" structures, senses, determinations, scaffoldings, differentiations, pre-delineations, characteristics, concepts—and, of course, indications (Heidegger 1967: 5, 31, 52, 114, 155f., 159, 179, 255, 267, 269, 241, 282, 285, 319, 327, 342).[32] So, too, he notes "the formal sense of the research that gives itself the name 'phenomenology,'" "the formal sense of the constitution of the existence of Dasein," "the formal concept" and "the formal idea" of existence (Heidegger 1967: 34, 43, 53, 179, 314). He warns, to be sure, against lapses into an "'external,' formal interpretation" or formalizations at odds with the analysis (e.g., formalizing signs into a system of formal relations or time into a sequence of nows) (Heidegger 1967: 60).[33] But he also urges the importance of

(2006: 279); being-here's "fundamental determinacy" and the "constitution of its being" (1967: 114, 117); "existence" (1967: 231, 313). Similarly, the sense of certain terms can be used in a "formally indicative" manner and something can be disclosed in this way (Heidegger 1995a: 55, 63f.; 1967: 315).

[29] See Heidegger 1993a: 161: "keine Objektivierung, keine Objektsanschauung, sondern Mitgehen des Lebens in sich selbst." Heidegger 1993a: 248, 254f.

[30] On the task indicated, see Heidegger 1994a: 60; 1993b: 85; on the direction, binding point of departure, and reflexivity of the indicated behavior, see Heidegger 1994a: 31–5, 60–3, 113, 134; 1995a: 64; on being rooted in the relational, material, and—above all—enactment sense (*Vollzugssinn*) of behaving (*Verhalten*), see Heidegger 1994a: 52f.

[31] Some formal indications drawn from factical life point to basic snares within it (Heidegger 1994a: 140ff.); the performative aspect of formal indications is to offset the formal-ontological determinacy that has hitherto "completely" dominated philosophy (Heidegger 1995a: 63f.; see also Dahlstrom 1994, Streeter 1997, Overgaard 2004, Shockey 2010, Burch 2011).

[32] So, too, he formulates "formal, existential" expressions, "formally existential" ideas, and a "formally existential totality" (Heidegger 1967: 22, 54, 192, 283).

[33] On formalizing relations, see Heidegger 1967: 77f., 88, 159f., 208, 215; on formalizing time, see Heidegger 1967: 432.

formalization, for example, in the case of spelling out the idea of guilt and dissolving its connection to concepts of "a should and law" that suppose manners of being proper to what is on hand rather than to Dasein (Heidegger 1967: 283).[34]

This reliance upon formalization in *Being and Time* is an adaptation of Husserl's account of formalization. Heidegger refers to Husserl's account in a footnote, albeit in a gloss of the sort of formalization that he finds of little use to the analysis (Heidegger 1967: 77 n. 1). In 1920 he makes a similarly dismissive remark, while differentiating formal indications from formalization in Husserl's sense.[35] In his very first Freiburg lecture, however, he comes to Husserl's defense by invoking the process of formalization.

Heidegger cites Natorp's objection to Husserl's depiction of phenomenology as a descriptive science, on the grounds that descriptions, far from being innocuous, are inherently "objectifying" and generic, embedded in some implicit or explicit theoretical explanation.[36] Heidegger responds that the notion that every description expressed in words is inherently objectifying is an "unproven prejudice." So, too, is the presumption (*Vormeinung*) that the only sort of universality is the theoretical universality attaching to a genus and that the meanings of words contain only this sort of universality. While we can construe anything in more or less generic and specific terms (e.g., x is brown, what is brown is a color, what is a color is a sensation, what is a sensation is a psychological or physiological process), we can also construe it at each step more formally as something in general (e.g., what is brown is something, what is a color is something, etc.). While the former sort of theorizing is limited to a specific sphere of reality, the latter ("formal theorizing") is not, and what motivates it must be qualitatively different from the former.

Heidegger's rejoinder to Natorp, at least up to this point, merely iterates Husserl's distinction between formalization and generalization. But in an obvious extension of Husserlian formalization, Heidegger adds that there is a way of formally theorizing or objectifying that is "free" from the motivations and sources of the theoretical content or subject matters (*Sachen*) of particular sciences (Heidegger 1999: 114–17). In addition to theoretical formalizations and generalizations, there is, Heidegger submits, a purely formal mode of discerning and articulating things independently of any particular theoretical form or content. Phenomenology approaches its "object" (*Gegenstand*)[37] formally, i.e., in a way that steers a course between individual

---

[34] For another positive sense of formalization, see Heidegger 1967: 147.

[35] The "formal" character of formal indication is "more primordial" than that of formalization; moreover, in contrast to generalization and formalization, a "formal indication has nothing to do with the universal" (Heidegger 1995a: 59–62).

[36] The charge of "objectifying" is fatal, in Natorp's view, since description thus allegedly rules out a science of the subjective (Heidegger 1999: 101, 111).

[37] While *Objekt* is reserved for the theoretical sphere, "the formally objective" (*Gegenständliche*) and "[formal] objectification" (*Vergegenständlichung*) characterize a formal way of looking at things that is not bound to any theory (material or formal ontological); see Heidegger 1989a: 458. Similarly, formal indications, while providing an access to theology, are not the "ultimate understanding, that can only be given in genuine religious experience" (Heidegger 1995a: 67).

life as such (including autobiography) and universalizations of it (material or formal ontology).

11.2.4 Phenomenology as constitutive analysis

"Constitution" is a mereological word of art that Husserl employs to examine how something is constituted in or for (but not created by) consciousness, how consciousness constitutes it, and how consciousness itself is constituted.[38] In his early works, he principally conceives the constitution as a synthesis of an intentional act (e.g., an apprehension) and its content (e.g., the content apprehended).[39] Grasping, in a perception, that the tree before me is an oak consists in an act of apprehending (*Auffassung*) some sensory givens (*Inhalt*) as part of the way an oak tree presents itself. The apprehension "animates" (forms) the sensory givens (content) as the givens of an oak tree.

This synchronic, hylomorphic model of the sense-constituting consciousness supposes the constitution of the sensory givens but without offering an explanation for them. (How is it that they afford themselves to such acts of perception and judgment?) Aware of this problem early on his career (Husserl 1968: 121ff., 128; Husserl 1980: 265f.), Husserl comes to see that "not every constitution has the schema apprehension-content/apprehension" (Husserl 1969: 7n, 137–51, 1973a: 79f.). He accordingly develops a genetic model of how sensations are constituted that coincides with internal time-consciousness. A temporal constitution thus underlies and makes possible the hylomorphic account of intentionality in at least two respects. Whereas the perception that the tree before me is an oak consists in apprehending sensory contents a certain way, i.e., with a certain sense, neither the sensory contents themselves nor the ultimate level of consciousness itself is constituted by forming some material. Instead they are alike constituted by the temporal flow of conscious life (Husserl 1969: 156f., 239–48, 358–82; Zahavi 2004: 104).

Heidegger's phenomenology, too, is replete with constitutive analyses operative on multiple levels, with the genetic constitution of temporality providing the most basic sense of other levels. He contrasts *existential* with the *existentiel* understanding by noting that the latter does not require "the theoretical transparency of the ontological structure of existence." The question of the latter aims at the analysis of "what *constitutes*

---

[38] On what is constituted and the constituting acts, see Husserl 1984b: 674f.; Husserl 1976: 180, 196ff., 272–5, 335, 344, 355; see, too, Husserl 1994b: 46of. (on the constitution of personality, environment, and the life of consciousness).

[39] See the distinction between quality of an act (e.g., whether it is a question, a wish, a judgment), its sense or matter (e.g., what the act posits, which can be common to different qualities of act), and the sensory input that somehow bear the sense (Husserl 1984a: 397f., 427ff.); in *Ideas I*, what constitutes perceptual consciousness is a noetic component (an intentional act with its distinctive quality), a noematic component (the sense), and a hyletic component (certain non-intentional sensory givens); Husserl 1976: 196, 352.

existence" (italics added) and he follows up by citing "an understanding of the being of everything that is not Dasein" as a constituting feature (*Konstituens*) of the understanding of existence (Heidegger 1967: 12f.). In addition to concentrating on other constitutive features of Dasein (worldhood, being-in, and being-with), he analyzes attunement and understanding under the heading "the existential constitution of the *Da*."[40] Discourse is "constitutive" for attunement and understanding and he analyzes it in turn in terms of its "constitutive moments" (Heidegger 1967: 162, 165). Disclosedness, the sort of being that is fundamental for Dasein, is "constituted" by attunement, understanding, and discourse (Heidegger 1967: 220, 269).

In the second section of *Being and Time*, Heidegger continues to characterize his existential analyses, the analyses of the themes of dying, conscience, and resoluteness, as constitutive analyses.[41] But more importantly, for our purposes, Heidegger, echoing Husserl's genetic model of constitution, offers an analysis of how time constitutes the basic sense of these existential themes. Dasein is constituted by three "constitutive," non-independent features of care, namely, its facticity (thrownness), existence (projection), and its fallenness. By making possible the unity of these "moments," temporality "constitutes," in a primordial way, the structure of care as a whole (Heidegger 1967: 315, 324, 328, 331).

To be sure, the structural similarities between Heidegger's constitutive analyses and Husserl's should not obscure the enormous differences in content and direction. Yet it is not surprising, given the similarities, that in *Being and Time* Heidegger explicitly calls attention to Husserl's published and unpublished analyses of constitution (Heidegger 1967: 47 n. 1).

11.3 CONCLUSION: A BASIC DIFFERENCE

In the body of this chapter I have tried to demonstrate how fundamentally the early Heidegger's phenomenology improvises upon Husserl's groundbreaking development of phenomenology. Just as Heidegger gives new meaning to phenomenological reduction, formalization, and constitutive analysis, so, too, no one would mistake the enactment of what his method formally indicates for a Husserlian reflection. Yet it remains true, all the same, that Husserl's phenomenology is the *sine qua non* of Heidegger's.

But, then, how is the difference between them to be explained? Among the many plausible answers to this question, one stands out. In several places Husserl not only equates being an object with being a possible object of consciousness, but also insists that there

[40] So, too, while the world is a "constitutive" of Dasein, a referential complex "constitutes" worldhood in turn (along with what is handy), and being-in-the-world is "essentially constituted," too, by being-with; Heidegger 1967: 52f., 64, 68, 76, 78, 83, 88, 120f., 124f.

[41] Death, constitutive of Dasein in its entirety, is "ontologically constituted by mineness and existence" (Heidegger 1967: 240, 245, 252). Conscience, guilt, and resoluteness are also constitutive of Dasein (Heidegger 1967: 270, 284–6, 297).

is nothing posited on the basis of an inadequately given appearance that cannot be rendered adequate.[42] Let's call this contention (i.e., that everything can *in principle* be given adequately) "the principle of adequate givenness" (PAG).[43] The principle begs for further clarification, to be sure, particularly standing as it does for a goal (indeed, an infinite one at that) rather than an accomplishment.[44] Yet how Husserl would be able to substantiate it, at least on a straightforward reading, is beyond me. Leaving aside a divine, un-embodied mind (to which nothing, strictly speaking, *appears*, let alone inadequately), how are we (or finite, embodied minds like ours) to know that something has been rendered adequate in contrast to what was posited on the basis of an appearance inadequately given, once the appearance is over? Why *should* we suppose that there is nothing given in perception, i.e., through appearances, that cannot be given perfectly?

More importantly for our purposes is how sharply Heidegger's views contrast with this principle. Being closed off and being covered over are inherent to the facticity of being-here. Insofar as Dasein is disclosed, it is also closed off, and, to whatever extent something within the world is uncovered, it is also "concealed or obscured as something that can be encountered within the world." Disclosing being-here in one respect means closing off access to it in another; we do not uncover things in one respect without covering them up in another. In short (in Heidegger's shorthand), we are "equiprimordially" in the truth and in the untruth, the unhiddenness and hiddenness, respectively, of being (Heidegger 1967: 222).[45] Let's call Heidegger's conviction here "the principle of the hiddenness of being."[46]

---

[42] Husserl 1966: 20f.: "Ein Gegenstand der ist, aber nicht, und prinzipiell nicht Gegenstand eines Bewusstseins sein könnte, ist ein Nonsens." Husserl 1976: 319: "keine auf... einer inadäquat gebenden Erscheinung beruhende Vernunftsetztung [kann]... unüberwindlich sein." See also Husserl 1976: 100f., 321, 329; Husserl 1984b: 680.

[43] PAG is not inconsistent with Husserl's insistence that we perceive things inadequately, that they necessarily present themselves only in "profiles," "one-sidedly" (something that supposedly holds even for a divine mind) (Husserl 1976: 88, 91, 351). In *Ding und Raum,* after observing "das Ding als ganzes ist nie endgültig gegeben," Husserl notes that the relevant appearance entails the possibility of fulfillment, more precisely, a "kontinuierlich-einheitlichen Erscheinungszusammenhang, in dem ... die Bestimmtheiten zu "vollkommener" Gegebenheit kommen würden" (Husserl 1973c: 121–5). Again, PAG (which applies to essences no less than things) is not about actual adequacy but about its possibility, echoed in subjunctives about the possibility of endless progress towards adequacy.

[44] To start with, what adequate or perfect givenness in this connection means (i.e., in connection with the givenness of what is perceived) is itself puzzling.

[45] Though more pronounced in his later work, Heidegger drives home this point in 1929 by pointing out how "slipping away"—the chief characteristic of nothingness and the various forms of nihilating (the harshness of opposing, the shrillness of loathing, the painfulness of failing, the unsparing character of forbidding, and the bitterness of going without)—is inherent to the being of beings; Heidegger 2004b: 117, 120.

[46] This hiddenness includes both the hiddenness of the unhiddenness—i.e. (metonymically) the being—of beings and the hiddenness presupposed by that unhiddenness—i.e., the hiddenness without which that unhiddenness is devoid of meaning (in keeping with Heidegger's reading of the privative *alpha* in ἀ-λήθεια; see Heidegger 1967: 222).

The contrast between the two principles could not be sharper. Although Heidegger's position strikes me as far more plausible, he offers no more in the way of an argument for being's inherent hiddenness than Husserl does for the adequate givenness of things in principle. Nor is it clear to me how enacting some formally indicated operation would be sufficient to rule out the force of Husserl's principle. Perhaps the difference between these two principles reflects a philosophical impasse of the first order, where there is no common ground on which to adjudicate the conflicting intuitions in play.

This conclusion is dissatisfying, to say the least, but it helps explain the divergence between the two phenomenologies. Husserl's confidence in the prospects of philosophy as a rigorous science rests in no small measure on his commitment to the principle of adequate givenness. Heidegger, by contrast, lacks Husserl's confidence, and his conviction of being's inherent hiddenness leads him to a "fundamentally different" inquiry. As Heidegger himself puts it in 1929:

> And the difference between Husserl and me is not simply this, that Husserl develops the problem of phenomenology in a completely abstract way (that I should have further posed the problem of consciousness), but that my inquiry is a fundamentally different one. It is directed at the being of being-here at all, in order to procure the ground for metaphysics. Standing behind this [effort] is my conviction that metaphysics and philosophy in general cannot be placed on an exact foundation, that in the sense of a rigorous science they are impossible. Philosophy necessarily moves much more in an abyss that is open, to be sure, only as long as there is concrete philosophizing. (Heidegger 2011: 310; 137–8)

References

Bowler, M. (2008), *Heidegger and Aristotle* (London: Bloomsbury).

Breeur, R. (1994), "Randbemerkungen Husserls zu Heideggers *Sein und Zeit* und *Kant und das Problem der Metaphysik*," *Husserl Studies* 11: 3–61.

Brogan, W. (2006), *Heidegger and Aristotle* (Albany, NY: SUNY Press).

Burch, M. (2011), "The Existential Sources of Phenomenology: Heidegger on Formal Indication," *European Journal of Philosophy* 21/2: 258–78.

Cairns, D. (1976), *Conversations with Husserl and Fink* (The Hague: Martinus Nijhoff).

Campbell, S. (2012), *The Early Heidegger's Philosophy of Life* (New York: Fordham University Press).

Crowe, B. (2005), *Heidegger's Religious Origins* (Bloomington, IN: Indiana University Press).

Crowell, S. (2001), *Husserl, Heidegger, and the Space of Meaning* (Evanston, IL: Northwestern University Press).

Crowell, S. (2013), *Normativity and Phenomenology in Husserl and Heidegger* (Cambridge: Cambridge University Press).

Dahlstrom, D. (1991), "Heidegger's Kantian Turn," *Review of Metaphysics* 45/2: 329–61.

Dahlstrom, D. (1994), "Heidegger's Method: Philosophical Concepts as Formal Indications," *Review of Metaphysics* 47/4: 775–95.

Denker, A. et al. (2004), *Heidegger und die Anfänge seines Denkens*. Heidegger-Jahrbuch 1 (Freiburg: Alber).

Gander, H. G. (2004), "Phänomenologie im Übergang. Zu Heideggers Auseinandersetzung mit Husserl," in A. Denker et al., *Heidegger und die Anfänge seines Denkens*. Heidegger-Jahrbuch 1 (Freiburg: Alber), 294–306.

Hadjioannou, C. (2015), "The Emergence of Mood in Heidegger's Phenomenology," Dissertation, University of Sussex.

Heidegger, M. (1967), *Sein und Zeit* (Tübingen: Niemeyer).

Heidegger, M. (1977), *Phänomenologische Interpretation von Kants Kritik der reinen Vernunft*. Gesamtausgabe Band 25, ed. I. Görland (Frankfurt a. M.: Klostermann).

Heidegger, M. (1983), *Grundbegriffe der Metaphysik*. Gesamtausgabe Band 29/30, ed. F.-W. von Herrmann (Frankfurt a. M.: Klostermann).

Heidegger, M. (1988), *Ontologie—Hermeneutik der Faktizität*. Gesamtausgabe Band 63, ed. K. Bröcker-Oltmanns (Frankfurt a. M.: Klostermann).

Heidegger, M. (1989a), *Die Grundprobleme der Phänomenologie*. Gesamtausgabe Band 24, ed. F.-W. von Herrmann (Frankfurt a. M.: Klostermann).

Heidegger, M. (1989b), *Beiträge zur Philosophie (Vom Ereignis)*. Gesamtausgabe Band 65, ed. F.-W. von Herrmann) (Frankfurt a. M.: Klostermann).

Heidegger, M. (1993a), *Grundprobleme der Phänomenologie*. Gesamtausgabe Band 58, ed. H.-H. Gander (Frankfurt a. M.: Klostermann).

Heidegger, M. (1993b), *Phänomenologie der Anschauung und des Ausdruck*. Gesamtausgabe Band 59, ed. C. Strube (Frankfurt a. M.: Klostermann).

Heidegger, M. (1994a), *Phänomenologische Interpretationen zu Aristoteles*. Gesamtausgabe Band 61, ed. W. Bröcker and K. Bröcker-Oltmanns (Frankfurt a. M.: Klostermann).

Heidegger, M. (1994b), *Prolegomena zur Geschichte des Zeitbegriffs*. Gesamtausgabe Band 20, ed. P. Jaeger (Frankfurt a. M.: Klostermann).

Heidegger, M. (1995a), *Phänomenologie des religiösen Lebens*. Gesamtausgabe Band 60, ed. M. Jung, T. Regehly, C. Strube (Frankfurt a. M.: Klostermann).

Heidegger, M. (1995b), *Logik: Die Frage nach der Wahrheit*. Gesamtausgabe Band 21, ed. W. Biemel (Frankfurt a. M.: Klostermann).

Heidegger, M. (1997), *Hegels Phänomenologie des Geistes*. Gesamtausgabe Band 32, ed. I. Görland (Frankfurt a. M.: Klostermann).

Heidegger, M. (1999), *Zur Bestimmung der Philosophie*. Gesamtausgabe Band 56/57, ed. B. Heimbüchel (Frankfurt a. M.: Klostermann).

Heidegger, M. (2002), *Grundbegriffe der aristotelischen Philosophie*. Gesamtausgabe Band 18, ed. M. Michalski (Frankfurt a. M.: Klostermann).

Heidegger, M. (2004a), *Grundbegriffe der antiken Philosophie*. Gesamtausgabe Band 22, ed. F.-K. Blust (Frankfurt a. M.: Klostermann).

Heidegger, M. (2004b), *Wegmarken*. Gesamtausgabe Band 9, ed. F.-W. von Hermann (Frankfurt a. M.: Klostermann).

Heidegger, M. (2005), *Phänomenologische Interpretation ausgewählter Abhandlungen des Aristoteles zu Ontologie und Logik*. Gesamtausgabe Band 62, ed. G. Neumann (Frankfurt a. M.: Klostermann).

Heidegger, M. (2006), *Einführung in die phänomenologische Forschung*. Gesamtausgabe Band 17, ed. F.-W. von Hermann (Frankfurt a. M.: Klostermann).

Heidegger, M. (2011), *Der deutsche Idealismus (Fichte, Schelling, Hegel) und die philosophische Problemlage der Gegenwart*. Gesamtausgabe Band 28, ed. C. Strube (Frankfurt a. M.: Klostermann).

Heidegger, M. and Jaspers, K. (1990), *Briefwechsel, 1920–1963*, ed. W. Biemel and H. Saner (Frankfurt a. M.: Klostermann).

Husserl, E. (1950), *Die Idee der Phänomenologie*. Husserliana 2, ed. W. Biemel (The Hague: Martinus Nijhoff).

Husserl, E. (1966), *Analysen zur passiven Synthesis*. Husserliana 2, ed. M. Fleischer.

Husserl, E. (1968), *Briefe an Roman Ingarden*, ed. R. Ingarden. (Dordrecht: Kluwer).

Husserl, E. (1969), *Zur Phänomenologie des inneren Zeitbewusstseins (1893–1917)*. Husserliana 10, ed. R. Boehm (The Hague: Martinus Nijhoff).

Husserl, E. (1973a), *Cartesianische Meditationen*. Husserliana 1, ed. S. Strasser (The Hague: Martinus Nijhoff).

Husserl, E. (1973b), *Zur Phänomenologie der Intersubjektivität. Texte aus dem Nachlass. Dritter Teil. 1929–35*. Husserliana 15, ed. I. Kern (The Hague: Martinus Nijhoff).

Husserl, E. (1973c), *Ding und Raum*. Husserliana 16, ed. U. Claesges (The Hague: Martinus Nijhoff).

Husserl, E. (1976), *Ideen zu einer reinen Phänomenologie und phänomenologischen Philosophie. Erstes Buch*. Husserliana 3-1, ed. K. Schuhmann.

Husserl, E. (1980), *Phantasie, Bildbewußtsein, Erinnerung 1898–1925*. Husserliana 23, ed. E. Marbach (The Hague: Martinus Nijhoff).

Husserl, E. (1984a), *Logische Untersuchungen*. Husserliana 19-1, ed. U. Panzer (The Hague: Martinus Nijhoff).

Husserl, E. (1984b), *Logische Untersuchungen*. Husserliana 19-2, ed. U. Panzer (The Hague: Martinus Nijhoff).

Husserl, E. (1988), *Aufsätze und Vorträge*. Husserliana 27, ed. T. Nenon, H. Rainer Sepp (The Hague: Martinus Nijhoff).

Husserl, E. (1994a), *Briefwechsel. Husserl Dokumente, Band III/2: Die Münchener Phänomenologen*, ed. K. Schumann and E. Schuhmann (Dordrecht: Kluwer).

Husserl, E. (1994b), *Briefwechsel. Husserl Dokumente, Band III/3: Die Göttinger Schule*, ed. K. Schumann and E. Schuhmann (Dordrecht: Kluwer).

Kisiel, T. (1993), *The Genesis of Heidegger's* Being and Time (Oakland, CA: California).

McManus, D. (2012), *Heidegger and the Measure of Truth* (Oxford: Oxford University Press).

McNeill, W. (1999), *The Glance of the Eye: Heidegger, Aristotle, and the Ends of Theory* (Albany, NY: SUNY Press).

Overgaard, S. (2004), *Husserl and Heidegger on Being in the World* (Dordrecht: Kluwer).

Sandmeyer, B. (2009), *Husserl's Constitutive Phenomenology* (London: Routledge).

Scharff, R. (2014), *How History Matters to Philosophy* (London: Routledge).

Sheehan, T. (2015), *Making Sense of Heidegger* (Lanham, MD: Rowman and Littlefield).

Sheehan, T. (2016), "Phenomenology rediviva," *Philosophy Today* 60/1: 223–35.

Shockey, R. M. (2010), "What's Formal about Formal Indication? Heidegger's Method in *Sein und Zeit*," *Inquiry* 53/6: 525–39.

Stapleton, T. (1983), *Husserl and Heidegger* (New York: SUNY Press).

Streeter, R. (1997), "Heidegger's Formal Indication: A Question of Method in *Being and Time*," *Man and World* 30: 413–30.

Strube, C. (1993), *Zur Vorgeschichte der hermeneutischen Phänomenologie* (Würzburg: Königshausen and Neumann).

Van Buren, J. (1994), *The Young Heidegger* (Bloomington, IN: Indiana University Press).

von Herrmann, F. W. (2000), *Hermeneutik und Reflexion* (Frankfurt a. M.: Klostermann).

Zahavi, D. (2003), "How to Investigate Subjectivity: Natorp and Heidegger on Reflection," *Continental Philosophy Review* 36/2: 155–76.

Zahavi, D. (2004), "Time and Consciousness in the Bernau Manuscripts," *Husserl Studies* 20: 99–118.

CHAPTER 12

··

THE MIDDLE HEIDEGGER'S PHENOMENOLOGICAL METAPHYSICS

··

STEVEN CROWELL

12.1 WHAT IS THE "MIDDLE" HEIDEGGER?

AFTER *Being and Time* appeared in 1927, Heidegger's next published volume was *Kant and the Problem of Metaphysics* (1929), based on a lecture course he delivered in 1927–8, *Phenomenological Interpretation of Kant's Critique of Pure Reason*. The juxtaposition of "phenomenology" and "metaphysics" in these titles provides a framework for exploring how the "middle" Heidegger—that is, Heidegger's thinking from 1928 to about 1950—belongs to the history of phenomenology. Though Heidegger's writings exhibit phenomenological tendencies throughout this period, it is only in the years between 1928 and about 1935 that he still explicitly embraces phenomenology, which he sees as the basis for metaphysics. The "later middle" Heidegger, in contrast—in works such as *Introduction to Metaphysics* (1935), *Contributions to Philosophy* (1936), the lectures on Nietzsche (1936–40), and on Hölderlin, Heraclitus, and Parmenides (1941–2)—believes that metaphysics, including the sort of transcendental phenomenology he practiced in *Being and Time*, is nihilistic and must be overcome.[1]

For the later middle Heidegger, metaphysics focuses exclusively on the "being" of entities (*Seiendheit*, "beingness") and so is oblivious to the "truth of being" (*Sein*) itself.[2] After 1934, the miseries of the age can no longer be addressed phenomenologically

---

[1] On the vicissitudes of the transcendental in Heidegger, see Gethmann (1974), Okrent (1988), and Dahlstrom (2007).

[2] On the development of Heidegger's thinking about truth see Dahlstrom (2001) and Wrathall (2011).

but require thinking the "history of being" (*Seinsgeschichte*), in preparation for an "other" beginning that recollects what was concealed (variously labeled *Seyn*, *Lichtung*, or *Ereignis*) in the "first" beginning when Plato interpreted beingness as Idea and Aristotle reduced *logos* to logic. This narrative of the history of being never fully disappears, but the lecture "Time and Being" (1962) concludes with the injunction "to cease all overcoming, and leave metaphysics to itself" (1972: 24), and after 1950 the "late" Heidegger returns, in essays such as *Das Ding* (1951) and *Bauen Wohnen Denken* (1951), to something resembling a phenomenological approach.[3]

Heidegger did not pull the idea of a phenomenological metaphysics out of thin air; it belonged to that "today," as he put it in *Being and Time*, when "we deem it progressive to give our approval to 'metaphysics' again" (1962: 21). In the late 1920s Husserl too was working toward a phenomenological metaphysics. In *The Idea of Phenomenology* (1907), he had defined phenomenology as "theory of knowledge," the "condition of the possibility of a metaphysics" (1964: 1), and by *The Cartesian Meditations* (1931) he had made significant steps in that direction. Today, the idea of a phenomenological metaphysics has many defenders,[4] so it may be of both systematic and historical interest to examine Heidegger's version of it. Doing so also provides insight into why Heidegger's retreat from metaphysics coincides with the collapse of his Rectorship at the University of Freiburg and his political-pedagogical attempt to steer the National Socialist movement by means of a "metapolitics" of the *Volk* (Heidegger 2014: 115–16).

I will begin with some general reflections on the relation between transcendental phenomenology and metaphysics in Husserl and Heidegger (section 12.2). This brings us to Heidegger's definition of metaphysics as "metontology," and its contrast with philosophical anthropology (section 12.3). At issue in both is "world," whose analysis clearly shows the stress fractures in Heidegger's understanding of metaphysics (section 12.4). Heidegger's "Leibnizian" way of negotiating these fractures becomes evident in his reflection on the animal (section 12.5), which both informs his metapolitical understanding of the *Volk* and suggests the reasons why he abandoned metaphysics (section 12.6). Whether these reasons are peculiar to Heidegger, or have implications for phenomenological metaphysics generally, remains an open question.[5]

---

[3] For further analysis of phenomenology in this "late" period, see the chapter in this *Handbook*.

[4] See, for instance, the discussions in Haar (1999) and Gondek and Tengelyi (2011).

[5] "Metaphysics" can be understood in many ways, and so its connection with phenomenology has many dimensions. For instance, one might understand by "metaphysics" the question of whether phenomenology entails "realism" or "idealism" (Zahavi 2008). In this chapter, however, I will be concerned only with what both Husserl and Heidegger understood by "metaphysics" at this time: an inquiry into *entities* that is neither positive science nor transcendental critique of meaning.

12.2 PHENOMENOLOGICAL NEUTRALITY AND METAPHYSICS

Husserl originally conceived phenomenology as metaphysically neutral. By way of the *epoché* and phenomenological reductions, phenomenology was to be "presuppositionless," i.e., would not appeal to any scientific findings or metaphysical constructions. This neutrality can be expressed in Kantian terms: phenomenology is not an investigation into the properties of entities but a "transcendental" inquiry into the constitution of the meaning (*Sinn*) through which entities and their properties are given in experience (Husserl 1989: 411–16). Though Heidegger's relation to the *epoché* is complicated,[6] his approach shows significant overlap with Husserl's transcendental phenomenology. When Heidegger says that "only as phenomenology is ontology possible" (1962: 60), he means, in part, that ontology must eschew all "free-floating constructions and accidental findings" (1962: 50) in order to investigate the "being" (the "meaning and ground") of beings (1962: 59). Further, it must begin with our own experience as beings who inquire into what it means to be and so already understand "being" in a "pre-ontological" way (1962: 32, 62). Since phenomenology aims at an explicit understanding of the meaning of being, it must begin by making explicit what it means for me, as inquirer, to be.

Heidegger's ontology thus includes basic elements of Husserl's transcendental phenomenology: the reflective turn to first-person experience as condition for grasping the being of entities; the concern with how entities are meaningfully given rather than with factual qualities and attributes; and the refusal to start with scientific findings or metaphysical constructs. This amounts to a commitment to transcendental neutrality in the analysis of the being of the inquirer. Husserl defined "transcendental subjectivity" as the locus of meaning-constitution and so as neutral with respect to its instantiation in some "worldly" entity such as *homo sapiens*. There is no *necessary* connection between transcendental subjectivity and the natural kind, human being. Heidegger, in turn, designates "Dasein" as "the entity which each of us is" (1962: 27), without adding any sortal drawn from extra-phenomenological sources that would further specify its scope.

A lecture course from 1928 makes this explicit: "the peculiar *neutrality* of the term 'Dasein' is essential, because the interpretation of this being must be carried out prior to every factual concretion" (1984: 136). If Dasein is that being "for which, in its being, that very being is essentially an *issue*" (1962: 117, 32), then the term "Dasein" refers exclusively to the ontological structure that makes this understanding of being (*Seinsverständnis*) possible. Heidegger's description of the transcendental subject as care (*Sorge*) differs

---

[6] For some representative interpretations, see Tugendhat (1970), Taminiaux (1991), Carman (2003), and Crowell (2013).

from Husserl's focus on consciousness because Heidegger thinks that being conscious is not a sufficient condition for the constitution of meaning. "Dasein" is neutrally defined as whatever it is that exhibits those conditions.

This transcendental neutrality entails a methodological anti-naturalism that distinguishes Heidegger's metaphysics from many others in his time and ours, but, like Husserl, Heidegger recognized that we come upon these conditions in *ourselves*: "Neutral Dasein is never what exists; Dasein exists in each case only in its factical concretion," i.e., contingently, in "human beings" (1984: 137). Transcendental phenomenology may not start with the question, "What is the human being?" but it leads to it. After *Being and Time*, this connection between transcendental inquiry and its "concretion" in a worldly entity moves Heidegger toward metaphysics and a dialogue with philosophical anthropology.[7]

12.3 METONTOLOGY AND PHILOSOPHICAL ANTHROPOLOGY

The term "metaphysics" is found in *Being and Time*, but its referent is not clear. It seems to designate an inquiry distinct from the phenomenology of Dasein. After presenting his phenomenological analysis of death, for instance, Heidegger remarks that a "metaphysic of death" lies outside its scope, since it deals with questions concerning "what 'meaning' [death] can have and is to have as an evil and affliction in the totality of entities [*All des Seienden*]" (1962: 292). Nevertheless, the phenomenology of Dasein is not irrelevant to such questions since it provides the "a priori of philosophical anthropology" (1962: 170). According Max Scheler (1954: 6), philosophical anthropology seeks to counter the anti-metaphysical currents of the nineteenth century (neo-Kantian epistemology, positivism, historicism) by determining the human being's place in nature, the cosmos: the "totality of entities" that Heidegger invokes in his remark on death. What is distinctive about Heidegger's metaphysical turn can be seen by contrast with Scheler's philosophical anthropology, to which Heidegger paid close attention.

In 1927, Scheler distinguished three intellectual capacities of the human being. The first is *Verstand*, the technical-practical knowledge of the positive sciences. The second is *Vernunftswissen*, Aristotelian first-philosophy as knowledge of "the modes of being and essential structures" of all things, a capacity that opens a "window to the Absolute." Here a third capacity emerges, whereby philosophy approaches the *ens* per se, the "ground of the human being and the world" (Scheler 1954: 6). While the capacity for essential or ontological knowledge is developed phenomenologically (1954: 9), this third capacity must employ different resources.

---

[7] On philosophical anthropology, see Fischer (2009). On Heidegger's relation to philosophical anthropology see Fahrenbach (1970), and the response by Plessner (1976).

According to Scheler, Kant demonstrated that a direct approach to metaphysics is impossible, since "all objective being in the inner and outer world is relative to the human being." The "mediating discipline" of philosophical anthropology, however, allows philosophy to approach the Absolute in a refracted way through phenomenological reflection on the "acts of human spirit [*Geist*]" (1954: 12). From there, metaphysics employs a "transcendental mode of inference" to the "ground of all things," as follows:

> [Since] the being of the world itself is certainly independent of the contingent existence of human beings and their empirical consciousness, while at the same time strict *connections of essence* obtain between certain classes of mental [*geistige*] *acts* and certain regions of *being* to which we gain access through these classes of act—we *must* ascribe to the ground of all things *everything* which, in such acts and operations, gives us transitory creatures such access. (1954: 13)

Otherwise, we could not explain how "a spatially organized world existed already before the diluvial human being came into existence" (1954: 13). In Scheler's major work of philosophical anthropology, *Die Stellung des Menschen im Kosmos* (1928), to which Heidegger often refers, this leads to a "metaphysics of trans-singular *Geist.*" Philosophical anthropology thus reflects on the human being as a "microcosm" from which one can infer "the highest ground" of the "macrocosm," and ultimately provides our "access to God" (1954: 14–15).

For Scheler, then, metaphysics is not cosmology or object-metaphysics but "*metanthropology*" (1954: 14): the "person" is a kind of "presentation" of the "one and identical infinite *spirit*"—not a mere "copier" (*Nachbildner*) of an already given world but a "co-shaper" (*Mitbildner*) of the world, a "being of *decision*" whose choices contribute to the "world-process" (1954: 15). Thus the individual addresses the ground of being not by science but by means of a worldview (*Weltanschauung*). There can be no "universally valid, true" worldview but only an "individually true" one, historically conditioned and thus restricted with respect to its "perfection and adequation." Nevertheless, Scheler believes that his "transcendental inference" is the "rigorous universally valid *method*" for developing a worldview (1954: 14–15).

In turning to metaphysics Heidegger clearly had Scheler in mind,[8] but he is highly critical of Scheler's philosophical anthropology. The person is "ontologically unclarified"—an amalgam of body, soul, and spirit (1962: 73)—and provides no basis for a "transcendental inference." In place of such an inference Heidegger proposes that the neutral phenomenology of Dasein "turn back" toward the "metaphysical ontic in which it implicitly always remains" (1984: 158). This is not an ontological inquiry, concerned with the being of entities, but an ontic inquiry into the "totality" of entities. In place of metanthropology, then, Heidegger offers "metontology," a "metaphysics of existence" (1984: 157).

---

[8] See Heidegger (1984: 50–2), but there are numerous references in texts from this period.

Metontology differs from Scheler's metanthropology on the matter of phenomenological grounding. For Scheler, the human person's "transcendence," its capacity for freedom and decision, signals a kinship with the Absolute ground of what is; for Heidegger, in contrast, Dasein's freedom is "finite," and transcendence reaches beyond the "totality of entities" (*das Seiende im Ganzen*) not toward the Absolute but toward "world."[9] Finite freedom is not an anthropological concept, however, but the *phenomenlogical* basis for a metaphysical account of the human being as one entity in the totality of entities. In turning back from the neutrality of Dasein to the ontic context in which it exists concretely as "human being," metontology interprets Dasein's transcendence as a *human* capacity for "world-picturing" or "forming" (*Welt-bildung*). Metontologically, then, *Weltanschauung* is the human being's way of "*having* world" (*Welt-haben*) (1996: 344).

The concept of finite freedom ("transcendence") informs all the major themes in Heidegger's early middle period.[10] For instance, his Davos disputation with Ernst Cassirer turns on rejecting an anthropology that infers from the finite freedom evident in moral-practical life to the sort of "infinite" rational capacity characteristic of traditional humanism.[11] But the idea of metontology remains deeply puzzling. On the one hand, inquiry into the totality of entities is not positive science; nor is it a "summary ontic" or "inductive metaphysics" which gathers scientific results into an overall picture or "guide for life" (1984: 157). On the other hand, it is supposed to furnish the context in which "the question of an ethics may be properly raised" (1984: 157), where the meaning of Dasein's "dispersal" into "nature," into "bodiliness and so thus into sexuality"—in short, its ontic embeddedness—will be determined (1984: 138). In contrast to individual positive sciences, a metaphysical inquiry into entities is supposed to situate Dasein within beings as a *whole*. But how?

Kant had proscribed such inquiry into "totalities." Theoretical reason is limited to what shows itself in experience. Science explores experience in a systematic way by means of the categories of understanding. Reason's attempt to bring closure to this exploration through a "speculative" grasp of the "totality of conditions for a given conditioned" leads to antinomy and "fanaticism" (Kant 1929: 32). Kant allowed that the concept of totality could serve science as a regulative idea, but Heidegger's rejection of inductive metaphysics suggests that this is not what he had in mind for metontology.[12] Understanding what he *did* have in mind requires that we look at how metontology is supposedly demanded by the phenomenological point of departure.

---

[9] "Metaphysics is inquiry beyond or over beings that aims to recover them as such and as a whole for our grasp" (1998c: 93). "Yet the understanding of this wholeness, an understanding that in each case reaches ahead and embraces it, is a surpassing in the direction of world" (1998a: 121).

[10] Recent treatments include Guignon (2011), Golob (2014), and Schmidt (2016).

[11] See the extensive treatment in Gordon (2010), which regrettably fails to recognize the phenomenological background of Heidegger's stance.

[12] Kant also developed a metaphysics on the basis of his transcendental critique of reason, but it has more in common with what Husserl and Heidegger call "regional ontology" than it does with Heidegger's proposed turn to the totality of entities. It is this that produces the Kantian antinomy.

12.4 THE PHENOMENOLOGICAL PROBLEM OF WORLD

In *Being and Time* Heidegger argued that the "roots of the existential analytic" are ultimately "*ontical*" (1962: 34), which seems to entail that ontology "requires an *ontic* ground" (1962: 487). What sort of ground is that? In 1928, Heidegger explains the issue this way: "[B]eing is there only when Dasein understands being. In other words, the possibility that being is there in the understanding presupposes the factical existence of Dasein, and this in turn presupposes the factual extantness of nature," i.e., presupposes that "a possible totality of beings is already there" (1984: 156–7). What sort of "presupposition" or dependence is meant here; what is the "ontic ground" that metontology is supposed to thematize? It is neither the *causal* dependence studied by natural science nor the phenomenological essence-dependence thematized in a regional ontology of nature. Instead, it pertains to Dasein's "thrownness" (*Geworfenheit*), its "abandonment" to the "fundamental powers" of nature and history (1996: 393), the ontic context of its "finite projection" of "world" (1984: 138–9). Thus if "the being-problem and the world-problem in their unity make up the genuine concept of metaphysics" (1996: 324), transcendental phenomenology addresses the former while metontology addresses the latter. What, then, is the world-problem?

Husserl, too, held that transcendental phenomenology has a kind of ontic ground. Neutral inquiry into meaning is a science, but it must begin anew with each thinker; it is "the philosopher's quite personal affair" (Husserl 1969: 2), a matter of "ultimate self-responsibility" which demands of the individual a contingent decision to live life in the transcendental attitude. Such life entails a kind of double vision. On the one hand, phenomenology reveals an asymmetry between consciousness and world: since the norms that make the meaning and validity of things available depend on the intentional experiences in which things are given, the world is "transcendentally" grounded in consciousness in a way that consciousness is not grounded in the world. Ontologically, however, there is no asymmetry. The being of the world is no less certain than the being of consciousness (Husserl 2008: 243–58), though neither possesses "absolute" necessity, but only the "necessity of a fact," an *Urfaktum*.[13] Husserl's investigations into such necessity—the metaphysical (factual, ontic) symmetry between consciousness and world—allow him to conceive meaning-constitution as a "depth dimension" of the embodied, historical, and social human being, its "transcendental life" (Husserl 1970: 118, 175).

Husserl calls this metaphysical crossing of the transcendental and the empirical "the paradox of human subjectivity" (1970: 178), and he resolves the paradox through a

---

[13] On the "necessity of a fact" see Tengelyi (2014: 180–90), together with his whole analysis of Husserl's idea of "metaphysics as the science of ultimate *facta*."

phenomenological demonstration that transcendental life is "necessarily . . . constituted in the world as a human being" (1970: 186). Here "world" is the one and unique horizon of all theoretical, evaluative, and practical life, the locus of a rational teleology immanent to the movement of life itself, an "Idea in the Kantian sense." Because the world's necessity is factual, no ultimate reason for its being can be provided; still, reason is not imposed on the world but resides within it as the human being's infinite task. Transcendental life is just human life projected to its teleological limit.

Heidegger's concept of metontology involves a similar crossing or double grounding.[14] Though the transcendental phenomenology of neutral Dasein has priority in accounting for our understanding of being (the "being-problem"), metaphysically there is no such priority. Dasein, as human being, "presupposes" that a totality of entities is already there (the "world-problem"). Since Heidegger insists on the finitude of freedom, however, he cannot appeal to an infinite rational teleology within life itself to ground his metaphysical world-concept. Instead, his approach to the paradox of human subjectivity involves interpreting elements of the transcendental world-analysis from *Being and Time* in an "ontic" way, i.e., as aspects of world-forming that themselves belong to the totality of entities understood as the "play of life" (*Spiel des Lebens*).

The transcendental analysis of world in *Being and Time* appeals to two constitutive categories of Dasein, affectivity (*Befindlichkeit*) and understanding (*Verstehen*), which we will consider in turn. Seen in its character as "whole," the "primary discovery" of world is not cognitive but belongs to "bare mood" (1962: 177). World has an horizonal structure, but this horizon does not admit of progressive determination in the manner of an "Idea in the Kantian sense" because it is the *affective* way that things as a whole matter to us, the "enigma" of Dasein's thrownness (1962: 175). In a lecture course from 1928–9, Heidegger gives this transcendental characterization of world an ontic or metaphysical interpretation.

Thrownness is "abandonment" to the "overpowering" totality of entities, registered in the mood of "floundering" (*Haltlosigkeit*) or groundlessness (1996: 328, 337).[15] This mood yields two basic attitudes from which the human being "forms" a world: "sheltering" (*Bergung*) and "self-control" (*Haltung*) (1996: 357).[16] The former yields myth, while the latter yields "philosophy." Against Cassirer, who argued that the symbolic forms of myth prefigure scientific explanation, Heidegger understands myth as the way of world-forming characteristic of sheltering, in which Dasein secures a "hold" (*Halt*) in the totality of entities through submission, supplication, and ritual (1996: 360). Myth is not an incipient reason, coming into its own with the development of Greek philosophy; rather, it is *displaced* by the latter in the way self-control forms a world. Self-control

---

[14] For a critical discussion of the notion of "ground" here, see Crowell (2001: 222–43).

[15] The anthropological direction suggested by Heidegger's emphasis on our fundamental "insecurity" (*Ungeborgenheit*) (1996: 359) has been critically elaborated by Hans Blumenberg (1985).

[16] Though *Haltung* can be translated in many ways (attitude, stance, bearing, conduct), in my view the context of this lecture course requires "self-control" (*Selbstbeherrschung*), which brings out the contrast with *Bergung* and connects with Heidegger's employment here of terms like *Verhalten* and *sich verhalten*.

secures a hold by reversing the normative orientation of sheltering from the world to the self: instead of submission, stand-taking; instead of ritual, method; instead of supplication, self-responsibility, or self-assertion (1996: 360–72). To see how, we must turn to the second constitutive category of Dasein in *Being and Time*, namely, understanding.

Understanding discloses world as a "totality of significance" (1962: 120) or horizon in which things *in* the world can show up *as* something. Understanding is not a cognitive act; rather, it is self-awareness: comporting oneself (*sich verhalten*) for the sake of (*Umwillen*) some possibility for being a self (1962: 183). In acting for the sake of being a teacher, for instance—in *trying* to be one, letting the norms of succeeding or failing at it matter to me—I disclose the world of teaching, the totality of significance in which things like students, exams, pencils, chalkboards, and so on can show up *as* what they are. Of course, these things, and this world, are familiar to me in an everyday way if there are terms for them in my culture, whether or not I act for the sake of something thanks to which they become relevant. But such familiarity does not disclose the *being* of those entities to which it nevertheless allows us to refer. Only if I *commit* myself to being a teacher, bind myself to what I understand to be the normative meaning of teaching, can I tell what truly belongs to the world of teaching.[17] Though acting for the sake of being a teacher is normally accomplished in an absorbed, reflection-free way, what it means to be a teacher is always at issue, and so my comportment is something like a *decision*, a negotiation of how best to go on. In his early middle period Heidegger provides a metaphysical or "ontic" interpretation of this transcendental sense of world as well.

As a mode of human world-forming or transcendence, self-control addresses the mood of floundering through "comportment [*Verhalten*] as self-comportment . . . the for-the-sake-of-itself [*Umwillen-seiner*]" (1996: 367). The world formed in this way is normatively ordered, not by an implicit telos of reason but by freedom's capacity, as self-control, to pass beyond the totality of entities toward what is *epekeina tes ousias, ta agathon*, toward a norm or measure (*Vor-bild*) (1998a: 123–4). To act for the sake of being a teacher, for instance, involves distinguishing between what a teacher *is* (the current public role) and what it *ought* to be. The world of teaching is thus "had" only if I transcend what "is" toward what is *best* in the matter of teaching. Since transcendence is finite, however, it does not grasp this measure as something given; it is there only as in *play* or at issue in my choices. Self-control is the way of world-forming in which this orientation toward a norm comes to prominence: the human being's responsibility for its understanding of what it means to be whatever it is trying to be.

At this point, some of the fractures in Heidegger's metaphysical world-concept begin to appear. If world is understood as the affectively accessed normatively structured horizon of acting for the sake of something, then it is essentially *plural*: there are as many worlds as there are possibilities for the sake of which we can act. If these cannot be seen as exhibiting a hidden rationality, an ultimate teleological unity, what becomes of *the*

---

[17] On the ontological significance of commitment and normative "binding," see Haugeland (1998) and Haugeland (2000).

world, the one and unique world in Husserl's sense? The transcendental phenomenology of *Being and Time* could avoid this question, but Heidegger's metontology must address it since, in thematizing Dasein's "dispersal" into "human being," the metaphysical character of the "presupposed" totality of beings into which it is dispersed must be specified. That totality cannot be identified with any particular "totality of significance" tied to a specific way of acting for the sake of something. Instead, in a move that remains phenomenologically opaque, Heidegger treats "life" as a synechdoche for the presupposed totality, and the one world becomes the "play of life" (*Spiel des Lebens*).[18]

Here Heidegger generalizes a key element of the phenomenology of acting for the sake of something, namely, that the measures of such acting are always in play or at issue. Acting (*praxis*) is not measured by a particular outcome, as is making (*techne*); rather it continually adjusts to circumstances in light of a measure of success or failure, the very meaning of which appears only in acting. Play, too, involves a kind of regulation, but it does not "merely follow the rules of the game" (1996: 311). Rather, "the rules form themselves [*bilden sich*] initially in playing"; the rule is not "a fixed norm coming from who knows where, but is mutable in playing and through the playing" (1996: 312). In its norm-orientation, play "is always world-forming" (1996: 314). If the "play of life" is the the metaphysical essence of world, it becomes possible to imagine that in *human* life an explicit "having" of world is attained in the play of trying to be something. The ontic ground of ontology would thus lie in "life's" capacity for world-forming, and the paradox of human subjectivity would be resolved by showing how the worldview of self-control develops (transcendental) philosophy—acting for the sake of being a philosopher—as one of its possibilities, one in which world-forming itself is thematized as the condition for grasping the being (*truth*) of things. But matters are not so simple.

First, Heidegger provides no epistemic justification for the metaphysical conception of life as play. Because he accepts Kant's judgment that "a science of entities as a whole is essentially impossible" (1996: 219), Heidegger's thesis about life cannot be scientific. It is simply his individual attempt at world-forming, a philosophical worldview whose *dicta* concerning the metontological themes of ethics, bodiliness, sexuality, or politics are no more than *doxa*. Second, because play is normatively promiscuous—becoming normatively determinate only when I act for the sake of some *specific* way to be—the transcendental character of Dasein as responsible for truth remains mysterious. Since it is correlated to being human as such and not to some specific *way* of being, the play of life gives rise to no totality of significance. Though Heidegger suggests that "philosophizing" is the specifically "human" way to be, the absence of anything like Husserl's telos of reason embedded in life itself leaves it unclear how acting for the sake of being a philosopher connects with truth. Finally, since no explanation has been given of how the human being translates the normative promiscuity of life into "neutral"

---

[18] The phrase comes from Kant (Heidegger 1996: 308). The notion was adopted by later phenomenologists such as Eugen Fink (1960) and Hans-Georg Gadamer (1989).

Dasein's transcendental capacity for disclosing truth, that capacity will only be *contingently* connected to the world-forming essence of the human being.

Thus the world-problem leaves Heidegger with something like an abyss, *within* the "being that each of us is" (1962: 27), between the human being and truth-disclosing Dasein. Yet Heidegger believes that he can mitigate the dualism of his metaphysical picture by substituting for the telos of reason the "destiny" of the German *Volk*. The following section examines the abyss in more detail; section 12.6, then, explores Heidegger's attempt to bridge it through "metapolitics."

12.5 "THE ANIMAL IS WORLD-POOR": HEIDEGGER'S LEIBNIZIAN METAPHYSICS

Heidegger takes up the metaphysical world-problem in a lecture course from 1929–30 where, instead of starting from world as the play of life, he focuses on *animal* life (1995: 192).[19,20] The initial methodological problem of our access to animal life proves remarkably complicated. On the one hand, the investigation must draw upon the life-sciences: "We cannot separate metaphysics and positive research"; indeed, "the inner unity of science and metaphysics is a matter of *fate*" (1995: 189). On the other hand, positive science is not enough. Though vitalistic biology is right to oppose the "mechanistic" reduction of life (1995: 189), *metaphysical* vitalism and *Lebensphilosophie* fail because their appeal to "special" vital forces and "entelechies" remains within the mechanistic framework (1995: 223, 262). A metontological understanding of animal life must employ phenomenology (1995: 232), a way of "transposing" ourselves into animal experience to uncover "what it is like to be this being" (1995: 202). The problem is that though the animal "displays a sphere of transposability or, more precisely . . . itself *is* this sphere," it "*refuses any going along with*"—that is, any first-person grasp of what it is like (1995: 210–11).

Such alienness presents no problem for the life-sciences, but metaphysics, concerned with the *totality* of entities, must find a way to integrate the whole region of life into its scope. This requires a two-step method. First, animal being is approached *privatively*: "the essence of life is accessible only if we consider it in a deconstructive [*abbauende*] fashion" (1995: 255). Starting with what can be demonstrated phenomenologically in our own being, the alienness of animal experience is seen as a privative modification thereof (1995: 211). Since phenomenology shows the human being to be

---

[19] The importance of Leibniz for Heidegger's phenomenological metaphysics—noted by Greisch (2005: 116)—deserves separate treatment. Here we can only allude to it.

[20] For a more extensive treatment of these issues see McNeill (1999), Engelland (2015), and Crowell (2017).

world-forming, Heidegger describes the animal as "world-poor," admitting that this merely serves a methodological purpose: in its own terms, each animal species is "a domain which possesses a wealth of openness with which the human world may have nothing to compare" (1995: 255). This openness is a kind of intentionality: unlike the stone, animal behavior displays an "openness for . . . " (1995: 248), where the ellipsis indicates the impossibility of characterizing the intentional correlation in a first-person way. The animal encounters beings but not *as* anything, since it lacks transcendence, the world-forming capacity to act for the sake of being something. But how do we know what animal intentionality is like? Here Heiedegger's privative method yields to a scientifically informed "ontic" phenomenology drawing on the work of Jacob von Uexküll.

Heidegger's reflections on Uexküll's ecology are guided by his metaphysical "radicalization" of Leibniz's "monadological point of departure" (1996: 143) and the "new concept of reality"—namely, *vis* (drive)—it introduces (2013: 612). The animal has something "self-like" about it (1995: 237): whereas lifeless things conform to external law, the animal's "drive" (*Trieb*) is a kind of internal "prescription" by which it "is intrinsically regulative and regulates itself" (1995: 238–9)—not a "purpose" but a point of view (*apperceptio*). The animal's "capacities" evident in its "behavior" (*Benehmen*), are governed by this prescription, which functions like an autopoietic code such that the animal remains "proper [*eigen*] to itself" without any "self-consciousness" or "reflection" (1995: 233). Animal capacities govern the functioning of organs, which in turn circumscribe what the animal can be "open for . . . " Borrowing terms from Scheler, Heidegger defines the self-like character of the animal as a kind of "captivation" (*Benommenheit*) that can be "disinhibited" (*enthemmt*) by certain things according to the capacities of its organs. For instance, the bee has a proper "openness to . . . " nectar thanks to the capacities enabled by its instinct (1995: 243).

For Heidegger, the metaphysical point concerns the "Leibnizian" grounding relation between an animal's organs and its instinctual capacities. The animal does not have a capacity because it possesses an organ that functions in a certain way; rather, *because* its instinctual drive codes for a certain capacity, it can develop an organ that serves a function (1995: 227). Thus it is not the *organ* that has a capacity, but the *organism* (1995: 221). What, then, is an organism? Heidegger denies that the organism is "the morphological unity of the [animal's] body"; from an ecological point of view, "the unity of the animal's body is grounded . . . in the *unity of captivation*" (1995: 258). The unity of captivation—what Uexküll calls *Umwelt*—is not an "environment" of occurrent entities accessible to any animal at all; rather, it is the cleared space of possible disinhibition defined by the animal's instinct. To distinguish it privatively from "world" in the ontological sense, Heidegger refers to the animal's "encircling ring" (*Umring*). Animal life is "precisely the struggle to maintain [its] encircling ring" (1995: 255).

Two points of particular importance for Heidegger's metontology follow. First, an animal's *Umring* is *species-specific*; no two species occupy the same *Umring*, and they overlap only to the extent that their codes allow for such disinhibition. Between species, then, radical alterity obtains, and one cannot view the plurality of instinctual prescriptions as teleologically oriented toward the unity of one "reason" embedded in life itself. Second, if the organism is the species-specific *Umring*, then the individual animal body is an *organ* of the species, the executor of certain prescribed capacities. This holds for the human being into which Dasein is "dispersed" as well: it is an animal species with its own instinctual *Umring*. This second point thus leads Heidegger to distinguish between the human animal and "the Da-sein in man" (1995: 205).

Recall that the goal of Heidegger's phenomenology of life is the metontological one of grasping Dasein as the "human being," i.e., as ontically grounded in "the factual extantness of nature" (1984: 156). Hence metontology operates at both an ontological and an ontic level. Ontologically (i.e., the transcendental being-problem), Heidegger rejects Uexküll's view of the human being as an animal species wholly embedded in nature (1995: 263–4). Since Dasein, as finite freedom, does not "behave" but "comports itself" (*verhält sich*)—that is, does not act according to a code but for the sake of a *norm* by which it binds itself and so is a self in the proper sense (1995: 274)—it alone "has" world. Oriented not toward some species-specific *Umring* of disinhibited things, but open to beings "as such and as a whole," it is the capacity to disclose the "truth" of beings in their being (1995: 333–43). At the ontic level of the world-problem, however, Heidegger rejects Scheler's view of the human being as "the being who unites within [itself] all the levels of being"—physical, animal, and spirit (1995: 192)—and of "nature" as the "lowest rung of the ladder which the human being would ascend" to the Absolute. Rather, "living nature holds us ourselves captive as human beings . . . from out of our essence" (1995: 278). The metaphysical question concerns how this captivation (dispersal) belongs to our essence. If the human being is captivated by nature, Da-sein, as finite freedom, constitutes a *rupture* in the human being, an ontological difference between animal life and Dasein's mode of being that is not a version of the "coded" difference obtaining between animal species (1995: 264). Thus the version of the paradox of human subjectivity that appears here returns us to the question of the sort of "ground" that obtains between the human being and Dasein.

Metaphysically, the individual human animal is an organ of the species-specific capacity or organism. Ontologically, however, Dasein's finite freedom would seem to rule out conceiving an individual case of Dasein, responsible for what it is to be, as an organ of some higher metaphysical unity. Rather than follow Husserl in arguing that the meaning-constituting capacities of the transcendental subject are teleologically prefigured in the animal's captivated behavior, Heidegger allows an "abyss" (1995: 264) to open up between Dasein and the human animal. Instead of a developmental story, he offers a metontological *pedagogy*, the goal of which is "the liberation of the Da-sein *in* man" (1995: 172). It thus appears that Heidegger exacerbates the paradox into a "gnostic" dualism where *no* grounding relation between human being and Dasein obtains, but only the "presupposition" of a fall or dispersal into an alien medium.[21] However, Heidegger's Leibnizian metaphysics suggests a different way to approach the ontic ground of ontology, namely, through *history*—not as an implicit telos of reason but

---

[21] Here he is followed by Fink; see Crowell (2001: 244–63).

as one of the two "powers," along with nature, into which Dasein is dispersed. For the human being is not only an animal species; it belongs as well to an historical *Volk*.

12.6 METAPOLITICS: VOLK, HISTORY, AND STATE

That the concept of *Volk* becomes metaphysically central after 1930 is attested in the *Black Notebooks*, where the term "metontology" is replaced by "metapolitics" (2014: 115). Behind this terminological shift is a philosophical shift from *Being and Time*'s concern with the phenomenology of radical individuation to concern with the phenomenology of collective intentionality or "we-intentions." If in *Being and Time* Dasein's capacity for authenticity, its break with the anonymity of *das Man*, was privileged for transcendental reasons, metaphysics requires an emphasis on the "We" into which Dasein is already dispersed.

This move to a metaphysics of collective intentionality is prefigured in *Being and Time*. In 1936 Heidegger claimed that "his concept of historicality," analyzed in §§72–4 of *Being and Time*, "was the basis of his political 'engagement'" (Löwith 1986: 56). Some commentators have seen these sections as the key to Heidegger's entire position.[22] Carl-Friedrich Gethmann, however, argued that "from a methodological perspective . . . the concept of historicality brings nothing new;" it "has the character of an excursus" and "does not fit into the development of fundamental ontology" (Gethmann 1974: 314). In my view, Gethmann is closer to the truth (Crowell 2004). This "excursus," in which the concept of *Volk* is introduced, is rather an early instance of the turn toward metaphysics, the ontic ground of ontology.

In *Being and Time*, authentic Dasein is neutrally defined as resoluteness, i.e., being answerable for the norms at issue in the possibility for the sake of which I act. Such possibilities are not invented by me but belongs to a "heritage" which I resolutely "take over" (1962: 435). In doing so, I embrace my *"fate,"* a way to be "which [I] have inherited and yet have chosen" (1962: 435). Heidegger calls this choice-structure "historizing." Now, he continues, since Dasein is always being-with-others, "its historizing is a co-historizing and is determinative for it as *destiny*" (1962: 436). But who are these others, and how is the heritage to be described? Heidegger continues: "co-historizing" is "how we designate the historizing of the community, of the *Volk*" (1962: 436).

To identify others as the "community" leaves much open: a community of teachers, a community of physicians, of parents, of baseball fans, all share in their respective common project, and "heritage" will mean something different depending on which of these communities is at issue. For instance, when I resolutely pursue being a teacher, I exemplify an idea of what teaching ought to be, and this may or may not conform to

---

[22] See, for instance, Wolin (1990) and Fritsche (1999).

what others take teaching to be. In this sense, my historizing is a co-historizing, since my uptake of any possibility is an *Auseinandersetzung* with the heritage in which "we"—fellow-teachers—are also involved. However, to specify the community as the *Volk* transcends any such particular heritage. What manner of phenomenological evidence speaks for such an entity? *Being and Time* does not answer this question, but Heidegger's metapolitics tries to do so.

Already in 1928 Heidegger emphasizes the priority of *Mitsein* over the "I and the Thou" (1984: 187–8), and in 1934 this phenomenologically neutral characterization is repeated: the "character of Self is . . . above and prior to all I, thou, we, you" (1998b: 43). However, in the early 1930s it takes on a metaphysical aspect, thanks to Heidegger's critique of the "liberal" concept of the self as atomistic "subjectivity" (1998b: 51). Because Heidegger attributes the ontological capacities of selfhood not only to me and to you but to *us*, socialism is not mere collectivism but genuine *selfhood*. Saying "I" is ever only authentic in the context of saying "we."

To see why, we may start with the example of collective intentionality Heidegger uses with his students. "We" are students and teachers; what makes us a "we" is that we are committed to a common project here and now, have "subordinated [ourselves] to the [normative] demands of education," and this means, to the institution of the university (1998b: 56–7). As Heidegger sees it, this *institutional* involvement means that we are *also* "willing the will of a State," and the state "wills nothing else than to be the ruling will and ruling form of a *Volk*" (1998b: 57). Thus, in trying to be students and teachers, we are already "*this Volk itself*"; indeed "our selfhood is the *Volk*" (1998b: 57). Is this identification of the "we" of collective intentionality with the *Volk* phenomenologically justified? What is a *Volk*?[23]

In answering this question, Heidegger dismisses various anthropological answers that appeal to body, soul, and spirit (1998b: 65–7), but his own view entails that the *Volk* still has one foot in nature: being a *Volk* belongs to our metaphysical dispersal into *homo sapiens* such that, while we may *choose* to cooperate in projects like education, "belonging to a *Volk*" can "never be chosen" (1998b: 60). This means that for those engaged collectively in any particular project, the question on the horizon is always "Who is *this Volk*, that we ourselves are?" (1998b: 69), and this question *is* amenable to choice. While plants and animals "cannot deviate from their essence," we have "the peculiar advantage that we can wander from our essence and become untrue to it" (1998b: 69, 161). Though belonging to a *Volk* can never be chosen, the *being* of a *Volk* is "historical" in the form of a state: "the *Volk* is the [entity] that *is* in the manner of a State" (1998b: 38), and the state is something whose meaning and structure can be at issue in collective decision-making: the *Volk* must "decide for" it so that it "comes to power" and "the *Volk* does not wander from its essence" (2015: 39).[24]

---

[23] I will leave the term "Volk" untranslated, since "people" in English has very different connotations.

[24] It should be noted that the 2015 text is a translation of student protocols from a seminar Heidegger held in 1933–4, and so one must exercise caution in ascribing exact wording to Heidegger.

Here, because Heidegger ascribes the ontological characteristics of neutral Dasein to the *Volk*, the whole analysis of resoluteness from *Being and Time* is carried over to the "we," the first-person *plural* (1998b: 70–7). Heidegger follows Aristotle in defining the human being as *zoon politikon*, "a way of being in which humans are" (2015: 38), but he does not view the state as grounded in individuals who collectively pursue decisions through debate, legislation, or *praxis*.[25] Rather, just as individuals are concerned with their own being, so the *Volk*, the "being that actualizes the State in its Being," is an agent who "knows the state, cares about it, and wills it" (2015: 48). Heidegger does not explain the nature of this collective willing, saying only that "the will of the *Volk* is a complicated structure that is hard to grasp" (2015: 60).[26] But it is clear that, for Heidegger, in addition to being responsible for what it means to be a teacher, father, or friend, I am responsible for the meaning of the state, and so answerable *to* the *Volk* that we are.

The concept of *Volk*, then, belongs to the metontological dispersal of Dasein: If Dasein "presupposes" that a "totality of beings is already there" (1984: 157), this totality is now specified not only in terms of a plurality of radically alien animal species, but also in terms of an *historical* plurality of radically alien *Völker*. And just as the human being is captivated in the species-specific capacities of the human animal, so it is captivated in its *Volk*-specific destiny. The *Volk*, as the "substance" of the state, is not *merely* "race and the community of the same stock"—though it is that too[27]—but "a kind of Being that has grown under a common fate and taken distinctive shape within a *single* State" (2015: 43). For the individual, whose relation to the state is "voluntary" rather than "organic," the order of the state depends on "binding" oneself together with others to "*one* fate" and to the actualization of "*one* idea" (2015: 49). But this idea cannot be arbitrary; rather, like the prescription that governs the animal organism, the historical *Volk* is monadologically constituted by a "point of view" that belongs to it and no other.

In Heidegger's reflections on the unity of the *Volk* the categories of neutral Dasein are given a metontological interpretation. Our "exposure" to the totality of entities is accomplished in mood, which is not an inner "bodily" phenomenon, but *Bodenständigkeit*, that which roots the body in the ground (*Boden*), the soil, so that it can "be supported, sheltered, and threatened by nature" (1998b: 152). The body itself is "nothing occurrent . . . but is rather as though suspended in the power of mood" (1998b: 153). In "work" we confront this exposure and are "carried away into the manifestness of what is and its structure," thereby encountering beings "as" beings (2015: 154). But work, the "present," is in turn supported by "what has been" and by the "future." Metontologically, these neutral categories of Dasein's temporality become "consignment" (*Sendung*) and "assignment" (*Auftrag*). Thus the *Volk* is not a collective constituted by "agreements," contracts, or legislation; rather, its unity lies in a "vocation" (*Bestimmung*) that has been

[25] See Heinz (2015: 72). On Heidegger's political thinking in light of the Greek tradition, see Fried (2000).

[26] See Richard Polt and Gregory Fried's Introduction to Heidegger (2015).

[27] On the ambiguities of Heidegger's remarks on race, *Volk*, and nature in this period, see Bernasconi (2013) and (2015).

consigned to it as heritage and assigned to it as a destiny. The metapolitical upshot is that "individuals as individuals can comport themselves" *only* "on the basis of" this vocation (1998b: 157).

No matter what else an individual tries to be, then, it is authentic only if its comportment is measured in terms of the *Volk*'s "being," namely, "the empowering of the power of the State." As resolute, the individual must always be (normatively) guided by the assignment and is thus "continually exposed to the possibility of death and sacrifice" (1998b: 160). Authenticity is no longer transcendentally defined as responsibility for the measures in light of which one acts; rather, it is metaphysically defined as answerability *to* a measure that one already possesses as a birthright. Here, as Marion Heinz notes, the concept of world as the correlate of care is "narrowed down to care for being within the community of the *Volk*" (2015: 73).

The state does not exist by "a right that derives from a timeless human nature" but from the "law of historical being" that defines a *Volk*. Thus, while the state is not an organism (2015: 38), it is the *being*—an ontological order of "mastery, rank, leadership, and following" (1998: 38)—of an entity, the *Volk*, that looks very much *like* one. Heidegger himself makes the comparison: The animal does not merely occupy space as a body, but, as the organism of which the body is an organ, it "rules space over and above the body" and possesses "a being that is oriented beyond the body" (2015: 54). Though "human being in space is completely different from that of the animal," there are structural overlaps. "Every *Volk* has a space that belongs to it," a *homeland* "which is something I have on the basis of my birth" (2015: 56).[28] Thus a *Volk* must be "rooted in the soil," and because such rootedness belongs to a particular *Volk*'s vocation, it "cannot be taught; at most, it can be awakened from its slumber" (2015: 56). At the same time, the *Volk* "must work outwards into the wider expanse" by "interacting"—testing the limits of its possible "disinhibition" in encounters with other (radically alien) *Völker*—thereby determining the "borders" of its destiny, the state (2015: 55).

The *Volk* is thus understood in Leibnizian terms as the "originating unity" (*ursprünglich einigende*) (1984: 73) to which individual human beings belong as organ-like units of its capacity. The capacity of a *Volk* is prescribed by its vocation in the form of consignment and assignment. Just as animal life is the struggle to preserve its species-specific *Umring*, so the *Volk* is an entity whose historical vocation is "the preservation of its consignment and the fight for its assignment." "Socialism," then, means *national* socialism: the collective intentionality of a *Volk* as "the *care for the measures* . . . of [its] historical being" (1998b: 165).

Heidegger's primary task as an educator was to "awaken" (1995: 351) his students' sense of rootedness in the specific consignment of the German *Volk*. Because the human being is prescriptively consigned and assigned, "destined," by its historical vocation, "the will of the *Volk* is not free in the sense of the freedom of the individual will" (2015: 60). Only

---

[28] The state, the being of the *Volk*, is not the same as the homeland: The Sudeten Germans have a German homeland but are not part of the German state and so "*are deprived of their authentic way of being*" (2015: 56, my italics).

if the individual body (a mere "citizen") recognizes what it truly is by being awakened to its belonging to this historical monad can its (objectionably liberal) "free" will bind itself in the right way to the collective law of its being.

12.7 Conclusion: Heidegger's Departure from Phenomenology

Heidegger's passage from phenomenology to metaphysics arose from the perceived need to provide ontology—transcendental reflection on the meaning of being—with an ontic ground. Such a ground is neither causal nor essential; rather, it is supposed to pertain to the totality of entities in a way that situates neutral Dasein's transcendental capacity for truth, for disclosing beings "as such" (that is, in their being) and "as a whole." Philosophical anthropology is incapable of clarifying such a ground, since its ontological conception of the human being as *animale rationale* is a composite whose unifying principle remains obscure. What, then, is the relation between neutral Dasein and the human being?

For Husserl, the "paradox" of human subjectivity arose because it appeared that phenomenology was committed to the idea that the human being—a part of the world—constituted the whole world, and so also itself. He resolved the paradox by denying that the human being constituted the world: from a transcendental point of view "world," and the human being within it, are meanings constituted by transcendental subjectivity. Such constitution involves an internal telos of reason that shows itself at work in life itself but becomes self-conscious, as it were, in the human being, whose vocation is the infinite task of realizing rationality in its evaluative, practical, and theoretical life.

For Heidegger this path to resolving the paradox is blocked, since freedom (and so reason) is finite. Instead, he turns to a Leibnizian monadological conception of life in which the human animal is one of a plurality of radically alien animal species, separated from the transcendental "Da-sein in" the human being by an abyss. The ontic ground of ontology thus seems more mysterious than ever, since the human being is, like all animals, world-poor. The one world, truth in the phenomenological sense, remains out of reach.

But the human being is also the political animal, the historical animal, in the form of the *Volk*, an agent that provides the ground for something like world-forming beyond the plural "encircling rings" of animal life. By itself, however, this historical conception of the ontic ground of ontology does not solve the problem, since the various *Völker* are themselves radically alien according to the "destiny" of their monadological constitution. Thus, transcendentally viewed, their world-forming remains "world-poor," a kind of historical *Umring* separated from the Dasein in "us" by an abyss. Heidegger responds to this problem by asserting that one *Volk*, "our German Dasein," is the "metaphysical *Volk*"; *its* destiny, the inner law of its being, is to "liberate" the Dasein in us. "The

German *Volk* has not yet lost its metaphysics, because it cannot lose it. And it cannot lose its metaphysics because it does not yet possess it. We are a *Volk* that must first *gain* its metaphysics and *will* gain it—that is, we are a *Volk* who still have a *destiny*" (2010: 63). The German *Volk*, therefore, *just is* the ontic ground of ontology, and its world-having (worldview) is "world" in the eminent sense—not as an infinite task, but as an *event*, a revolution, here and now.

Heidegger's choice in 1933 was thus nominally the same as Husserl's: to accomplish the "final establishment" (*Endstiftung*) of the Greek "primal establishment" (*Urstiftung*) of philosophy. But whereas Husserl thought that this was to be accomplished by phenomenology as the ground for a rigorous science, Heidegger held the *Endstiftung* to require establishing a state whose institutions explicitly enabled the "metaphysical" destiny of the human being. On the basis of its consignment and assignment, the German *Volk* is uniquely positioned within the totality of entities to mediate between the human animal and the "Da-sein in man." It is thereby poised to fulfill the Greek promise of self-control as a way of world-forming—namely, the promise of a genuinely *philosophical* world-having. Only in such a state can "metontological" questions of ethics, of embodiment, sexuality, politics, and others having to do with Dasein's dispersal into the totality of entities be properly addressed.

Husserl's historical hopes may have rested on a phenomenologically dubious commitment to a metaphysical teleology of reason, but Heidegger's metapolitical solution lacks phenomenological warrant altogether. Heidegger's attempt to specify the ontic ground of ontology by means of a metaphysical projection of the totality of entities that draws upon Leibniz's monadology cannot be scientific, as he himself notes. But he does not heed Kant's warning that such an attempt can lead only to "fanaticism." The empirical and the transcendental do not belong together in this way, and the attempt to pass from one to the other by means of a "metaphysical ontic" is no better than Scheler's "transcendental mode of inference" at bridging the essential difference that separates them. Indeed, Heidegger's metapolitical form of passage does away with the transcendental claims of phenomenology altogether, leaving nothing in its place but a chauvinistic historical worldview that he himself will soon abandon, and with it the incoherent idea of an ontic ground of ontology.

REFERENCES

Bernasconi, R. (2013), "Heidegger, Nietzsche, and National Socialism: The place of metaphysics in the political debate of the 1930s," in F. Raffoul and E. S. Nelson (eds) *The Bloomsbury Companion to Heidegger* (London: Bloomsbury), 47–54.

Bernasconi, R. (2015), "Who belongs? Heidegger's philosophy of the *Volk* in 1933–34," in G. Fried and R. Polt (eds) *Nature, History, State 1933–34* (London: Bloomsbury), 109–26.

Blumenberg, H. (1985), *Work on Myth*, translated by R. M. Wallace (Cambridge, MA: MIT Press).

Carman, T. (2003), *Heidegger's Analytic: Interpretation, Discourse, and Authenticity in* Being and Time (Cambridge: Cambridge University Press).

Crowell, S. (2001), *Husserl, Heidegger, and the Space of Meaning: Paths toward Transcendental Phenomenology* (Evanston, IL: Northwestern University Press).

Crowell, S. (2004), "Authentic historicality," in D. Carr and C.-F. Cheung (eds) *Space, Time, and Culture* (Dordrecht: Kluwer), 57–71.

Crowell, S. (2013), *Normativity and Phenomenology in Husserl and Heidegger* (Cambridge: Cambridge University Press).

Crowell, S. (2017), "We Have Never Been Animals: Heidegger's Posthumanism," *Études Phénoménologiques / Phenomenological Studies* 1: 215–40.

Dahlstrom, D. (2001), *Heidegger's Concept of Truth* (Cambridge: Cambridge University Press).

Dahlstrom, D. (2007), "Transcendental truth and the truth that prevails," in S. Crowell and J. Malpas (eds) *Transcendental Heidegger* (Stanford, CA: Stanford University Press), 63–73.

Engelland, C. (2015), "Heidegger and the Human Difference," *Journal of the American Philosophical Association* 1/1: 175–93.

Fahrenbach, H. (1970), "Heidegger und das Problem einer 'philosophischen' Anthropologie," in *Durchblicke. Martin Heidegger zum 80. Geburtstag*, ed. V. Klostermann (Frankfurt a. M.: Klostermann), 97–131.

Fink, E. (1960), *Spiel als Weltsymbol* (Stuttgart: Kohlhammer).

Fischer, J. (2009), *Philosophische Anthropologie: Eine Denkrichtung der 20. Jahrhunderts* (Freiburg: Alber).

Fried, G. (2000), *Heiedegger's Polemos: From Being to Politics* (New Haven, CT: Yale University Press).

Fritsche, J. (1999), *Historical Destiny and National Socialism in Heidegger's* Being and Time (Berkeley, CA: University of California Press).

Gethmann, C. F. (1974), *Verstehen und Auslegung. Das Methodenproblem in der Philosophie Martin Heideggers* (Bonn: Bouvier).

Gadamer, H.-G. (1989), *Truth and Method*, translated by J. Weinsheimer and D. G. Marshall (London: Continuum).

Golob, S. (2014) *Heidegger on Concepts, Freedom and Normativity* (Cambridge: Cambridge University Press).

Gondek, H.-D. and Tengelyi, L. (2011), *Neue Phänomenologie in Frankreich* (Berlin: Suhrkamp).

Gordon, P. E. (2010), *Continental Divide: Heidegger, Cassirer, Davos* (Cambridge, MA: Harvard University Press).

Greisch, J. (2005), "Der philosophische Umbruch in den Jahren 1928–1932. Von der Fundamentalontologie zur Metaphysik des Daseins," in D. Thomä (ed.) *Heidegger Handbuch. Leben–Werk–Wirkung* (Stuttgart: Metzler), 115–27.

Guignon, C. (2011), "Heidegger's concept of freedom, 1927–1930," in D. Dahlstrom (ed.) *Interpreting Heidegger: Critical Essays* (Cambridge: Cambridge University Press), 79–105.

Haar, M. (1999), *La philosophie française entre phénoménologie et métaphysique* (Paris: Presses universitaires de France).

Haugeland, J. (1998), "Truth and rule-following," in *Having Thought: Essays in the Metaphysics of Mind* (Cambridge, MA: Harvard University Press).

Haugeland, J. (2000), "Truth and finitude: Heidegger's transcendental existentialism," in M. Wrathall and J. Malpas (eds) *Heidegger, Authenticity, and Modernity: Essays in Honor of Hubert L. Dreyfus, vol. 1* (Cambridge, MA: MIT Press), 43–77.

Heidegger, M. (1962) *Being and Time*, translated by J. Macquarrie and E. Robinson (New York: Harper and Row).

Heidegger, M. (1972), "Time and being," in *On Time and Being*, translated by J. Stambaugh (New York: Harper and Row).

Heidegger, M. (1984), *The Metaphysical Foundations of Logic*, translated by M. Heim (Bloomington, IN: Indiana University Press).

Heidegger, M. (1985), *History of the Concept of Time: Prolegomena*, translated by T. Kisiel (Bloomington, IN: Indiana University Press).

Heidegger, M. (1995), *The Fundamental Concepts of Metaphysics: World, Finitude, Solitude*, translated by W. McNeill and N. Walker (Bloomington, IN: Indiana University Press).

Heidegger, M. (1996), *Einleitung in die Philosophie*. Gesamtausgabe Band 27, ed. O. Saame and I. Samme-Speidel (Frankfurt a. M.: Klostermann).

Heidegger, M. (1998a), "On the essence of ground," in *Pathmarks*, ed. W. McNeill (Cambridge: Cambridge University Press).

Heidegger, M. (1998b), *Logik als die Frage nach dem Wesen der Sprache*. Gesamtausgabe Band 38, ed. G. Seubold (Frankfurt: Klostermann).

Heidegger, M. (2010), *Being and Truth*, translated by G. Fried and R. Polt (Bloomington, IN: Indiana University Press).

Heidegger, M. (2013), *Seminare: Kant–Leibniz–Schiller*. Gesamtausgabe Band 84-1, ed. G. Neumann (Frankfurt: Klostermann).

Heidegger, M. (2014), *Überlegungen II–VI (Schwarze Hefte 1931–38)*. Gesamtausgabe Band 94, ed. P. Trawny (Frankfurt: Klostermann).

Heidegger, M. (2015), *Nature, State, and History 1933–1934*, ed. and translated by G. Fried and R. Polt (London: Bloomsbury).

Heinz, M. (2015), "*Volk* and *Führer*: Investigations of Heidegger's seminar *On the Essence and Concept of Nature, History, and State*," in *Nature, History, State 1933–34*, ed. and translated by G. Fried and R. Polt (London: Bloomsbury), 67–84.

Husserl, E. (1964), *The Idea of Phenomenology*, translated by W. P. Alston and G. Nakhnikian (The Hague: Martinus Nijhoff).

Husserl, E. (1969), *Cartesian Meditations: An Introduction to Phenomenology*, translated by D. Cairns (The Hague: Martinus Nijhoff).

Husserl, E. (1970), *The Crisis of European Sciences and Transcendental Phenomenology*, translated by D. Carr (Evanston, IL: Northwestern University Press).

Husserl, E. (1989), "Epilogue," in *Ideas Pertaining to a Pure Phenomenology and to a Phenomenological Philosophy, Second Book: Studies in the Phenomenology of Constitution*, translated by R. Rojcewicz and A. Schuwer (Dordrecht: Kluwer), 405–30.

Husserl, E. (2008), *Die Lebenswelt. Auslegungen der vorgegebenen Welt und ihrer Konstitution. Texte aus dem Nachlass (1916–1937)*. Husserliana 39, ed. R. Sowa (Dordrecht: Springer.

Kant, I. (1968), *Critique of Pure Reason*, translated by N. K. Smith (London: Macmillan).

Löwith, K. (1986), *Mein Leben in Deutschland vor und nach 1933* (Stuttgart: Metzler).

McNeill, W. (1999), "Life beyond the organism: Animal being in Heidegger's Freiburg lectures 1929–30," in H. P. Steeves (ed.) *Animal Others: On Ethics, Ontology, and Animal Life* (Albany, NY: SUNY Press), 197–248.

Okrent, M. (1988), *Heidegger's Pragmatism. Understanding, Being, and the Critique of Metaphysics* (Ithaca, NY: Cornell University Press).

Plessner, H. (1976), "Der Aussagewert einer philosophischen Anthropologie," in *Die Frage nach der Conditio Humana. Aufsätze zur philosophischen Anthropologie* (Frankfurt: Suhrkamp).

Scheler, M. (1954), "Philosophische Weltanschauung," in *Philosophische Weltanschauung* (Bern: Franke Verlag).

Schmidt, S. (2016), *Grund und Freiheit. Eine phänomenologische Untersuchung des Freiheitsbegriffs Heideggers* (Dordrecht: Springer).

Taminiaux, J. (1991), "From one idea of phenomenology to the other," in M. Gendre (ed. and tr.) *Heidegger and the Project of Fundamental Ontology* (Albany, NY: SUNY Press), 1–54.

Tengelyi, L. (2014), *Welt und Unendlichkeit. Zum Problem phänomenologischer Metaphysik* (Freiburg: Karl Alber).

Tugendhat, E. (1970), *Der Wahrheitsbegriff bei Husserl und Heidegger* (Berlin: de Gruyter).

Wolin, R. (1990), *The Politics of Being: The Political Thought of Martin Heidegger* (New York: Columbia University Press).

Wrathall, M. (2011), *Heidegger and Unconcealment: Truth, Language, and History* (Cambridge: Cambridge University Press).

Zahavi, D. (2008), "Internalism, Externalism, and Transcendental Idealism," *Synthese* 160/3: 355–74.

....

CHAPTER 13

PHENOMENOLOGY AND ONTOLOGY IN THE LATER HEIDEGGER

....

TOBIAS KEILING

In his early period, Heidegger explicitly endorsed phenomenology and contributed to phenomenology. Whether or in what sense this is also true for his middle and late philosophy is less evident: explicit references to Husserl or other authors associated with the phenomenological tradition subside from the 1930s on, such that interpreters often take into account a greater part of Heidegger's philosophical development. Material published from the *Nachlass* continues to complicate matters, such as the following note from a draft for an introduction to Heidegger's collected works, dating circa 1973–5, near the end of Heidegger's life: " '*Phenomenology*'—rightly understood, understood in the Greek sense, is the name for what is proper to Western thought. It names . . . what is proper to thought" (Heidegger 2012a: 89). This may be a strong endorsement of phenomenology, but it is hard to grasp what is specific about it in Heidegger's view.

The same holds true for the best-known document of Heidegger's retrospective appreciation of phenomenology: the autobiographic essay "My Way to Phenomenology" (1963). After describing his early fascination with both Aristotle's and Husserl's works, Heidegger concludes by asking about the state of phenomenology in his day. While it may appear that "the time of phenomenology is over," as it is "only recorded historically along with other schools of philosophy," this is a misjudgment: "in what is most its own phenomenology is not a school. It is the possibility of thinking, at times changing and only thus persisting, of corresponding to the claim of what is to be thought" (Heidegger 1972: 82).

Like the note from the *Nachlass*, this expresses a commitment to phenomenology as the true nature and genuine measure of all philosophical thought. But again, it is difficult to say what this commitment amounts to: as phenomenological, philosophy ought to "correspond" or "respond" (*antworten*) to the genuine manifestation of what it is concerned with, thus doing justice to the "claim" (*Anspruch*) which what "is to be thought" holds over the philosopher. But the endorsement of thinking's phenomenological nature doesn't entail, for Heidegger, retaining the name it shares with the school of thought founded by Husserl. The essay closes with what Figal has called an "anonymization" (2010: 33) of phenomenology: "If phenomenology is thus experienced and retained, it can disappear as a designation in favor of the matter of thinking whose manifestness remains a mystery" (Heidegger 1972: 82). Despite its alleged pivotal and universal importance for philosophy, comments like these again give little direction with regard to how the later Heidegger conceives phenomenology and how his view relates to the philosophical movement of the same name.

The aim of this chapter is to show that this exegetical problem amounts to a dilemma characterizing the later Heidegger's comments on phenomenology. Where to set the demarcations for an "early" and "later" and possibly a "middle" system of Heidegger's thought is itself a matter disputed in the literature. For the purpose of this chapter, I will understand by "later Heidegger" the period from *Contributions to Phenomenology* (1935–6) until the end of his life. In section 13.1, I will take a brief look into the literature on this period to suggest that the controversy surrounding Heidegger's contribution to phenomenology has at its core a disagreement about the nature of phenomenological philosophy. Instead of looking for an overlap with what one understands to define phenomenology, my approach will be to focus on what I call the "dilemma of the historicity of phenomenology." Section 13.2 shows how this dilemma emerges from Heidegger's engagement with Husserl's slogan "to the things themselves!" (*Zu den Sachen selbst!*). Sections 13.3–13.5 then develop the most important context for the dilemma of the historicity of phenomenology: The question of what the matter of thinking *is* leads to what Heidegger calls the question of being (*Seinsfrage*), i.e., the question of what the meaning of "existence" or "being" (*Sein*) is. Yet this question has a very long history. In order to establish a "historical relation to history" (Heidegger 2007: 147), phenomenology is forced to engage with the history of ontology. The dilemma of the historicity of phenomenology here takes two forms: First, the dilemma emerges in the contrast between two different aims ontology can set for itself or, in Heidegger's terms, between the two ways in which the question of being can be asked; second, the dilemma also emerges in the alternative between ontological monism and a specific historical form of ontological pluralism Heidegger envisages. In conclusion, I argue in section 13.6 that Heidegger's achievement is limited to exploring different ways to understand the dilemma, exposing but not overcoming an antinomy of the historicity of phenomenology.

13.1 The Dilemma of the Historicity of Phenomenology

Whether or what the later Heidegger contributed to phenomenology is disputed in the literature. In 1963, William Richardson influentially claimed that Heidegger moved from an early engagement with Husserlian phenomenology ("Heidegger I") to a thinking that is no longer phenomenological ("Heidegger II"). Heidegger himself, however, rejected this reading, claiming his later works contributed to phenomenology as well (see Heidegger 2009: 298–304; Richardson 1962: iix–xxiii). Similar to Richardson but with different appreciation, more recent interpreters have also highlighted the discontinuity between Husserl's and early Heidegger's phenomenology on the one hand and his later thought on the other. Kisiel's claim that there has been a "phenomenological decade" (Kisiel 1993: 59) in Heidegger's work (1916–27), followed by what Crowell has called a "metaphysical decade" (Crowell 2001: 225) ranging from 1927 to 1937, captures this position. While Kisiel and Crowell appreciate the continuity with earlier authors, Carman sees Heidegger's achievement in the transgression of Husserlian phenomenology (see Carman 2003: 53–100, Carman 2006). Mitchell has recently put emphasis on Heidegger's post-war lectures, claiming they represent Heidegger's "most phenomenological thought" (Mitchell 2010: 209) because of the capacity of Heidegger's language to articulate phenomena. Sallis to the contrary complains that the later writing has lost "the descriptive precision and specificity that once characterized phenomenology" (Sallis 2012: 290) but sees Heidegger as continuously interested in intentionality as a central problem of phenomenology. Dostal (2006) makes a similar claim about the problem of time, while Held (1992) has argued that later Heidegger can be considered a phenomenologist because the discussion of the "world" positions Heidegger vis-à-vis received phenomenological treatments of the same notion.

These examples probe the different views on later Heidegger's contribution to phenomenology, though it is not at all clear what interpreters disagree about. The different appreciations rather appear to follow from the use of different criteria for what constitutes a contribution to phenomenology: an interest in certain philosophical problems, such as time or intentionality, or an at least minimal adherence to some form of descriptive philosophical method. These different criteria indicate that the dispute about later Heidegger's contribution to phenomenology has at its core an ongoing disagreement about the very nature of phenomenology.

Yet if one recalls Heidegger's comment in "My Way to Phenomenology," one may actually welcome this disagreement. As long as phenomenology is not a past school of philosophy but a living tradition, what comprises its core problems and commitments must continue to be a matter of dispute. The fact that there are so different commitments in this regard connects even more closely with Heidegger's treatment of phenomenology, as one may recognize in the ongoing disagreement on the nature of phenomenological thought a plurality of different manifestations of phenomenology. As a matter of historical fact, all the different ideas mentioned in the literature have been associated with phenomenology. If phenomenology is to get clear on its own history, the diversity of its forms is not an aspect negligible for an account of phenomenology but concerns the very core of phenomenological thinking.

If this is something Heidegger might have said to his own interpreters, it is still unclear if it can be construed as a coherent position on the inherent historicity of phenomenology. Recall the above quote from "My Way to Phenomenology": Heidegger both holds that phenomenology constitutes the very "possibility of thinking" and that this possibility is "at times changing and only thus persisting." But it is unclear how these two claims can be compatible, as they rather seem to entail the following dilemma: Either phenomenology is the condition of possibility of philosophical thinking as "corresponding to the claim of what is to be thought"; in this case, all prior realizations of this possibility, i.e., all earlier forms of philosophy, are irrelevant to it, as they have failed to respond to this claim. Or the possibility of phenomenology has indeed been actualized before; it has been alive in ancient Greek philosophy already and subsequently revealed itself as "what is proper to Western thought." In this case, phenomenology is indeed "changing and . . . thus persisting" with historical times, but it has never been a mere, unprecedented possibility.

This alternative defines the dilemma of the historicity of phenomenology. The few lines from "My Way to Phenomenology" indicate that Heidegger was unwilling to accept the alternative, as phenomenology is to be *both* the future possibility of corresponding to the matter of thinking *and* the past achievement in doing so.

13.2 THE "PRINCIPLE" OF PHENOMENOLOGY

Recall from Heidegger's statement in "My Way to Phenomenology" that phenomenology should "correspond to the claim of what is to be thought." This idea introduces a measure for phenomenology, which Heidegger in a quite formal, even tautological way only calls "what is to be thought." But this leaves open the question *what* that might be, and it is typical for Heidegger's account of thinking that he refuses to give an answer to that question. Heidegger's discussion of phenomenology is instead motivated by the idea that a first-order determination of the range of objects or problems of phenomenology is inherently problematic. This motivation emerges most clearly in the first part of "The End of Philosophy and the Task of Thinking" (1964), one of the two public lectures, along with "Time and Being" (1962), designed by Heidegger to define his philosophical legacy. These will be discussed in section 13.4.

But the problem is first developed in a manuscript from the 1950s or 1960s entitled "Concerning the Principle 'to the Things Themselves'" ("Über das Prinzip 'Zu den Sachen selbst'"). This manuscript is interesting because Heidegger here exposes the problem outside the setup and rhetoric of the later lectures. Discussing Husserl's phenomenological "principle" to return to the "things themselves," Heidegger claims that this demand is incongruent with Husserl's "principle of all principles" (Husserl 2014: 43) and its commitment to intuition as the source of phenomenological knowledge. Heidegger is unwilling to accept the conclusion that what he takes to be the guiding principle of phenomenology—"to the things themselves!"—all by itself entails the specific epistemology and ontology of Husserl's phenomenology. The principle should rather be understood in a more "formal" way, undoing any "decision" (Heidegger 1995: 7) prematurely determining the themes and problems phenomenology should be concerned with. While Husserl allegedly recognized only consciousness as the eminent matter of phenomenology, Heidegger wishes to raise the critical question as to "*what actually is the matter itself* [*Sache selbst*] for thinking, and what is it *as such*" (Heidegger 1995: 6). As long as this remains a genuine question, the matter of phenomenology must be recognized as something that is itself "a matter of dispute, dispute itself, what is disputed, that *which* is questionable and worth questioning, what is worth thinking about" (Heidegger 1995: 7). Consequently, the matter of thinking cannot be anything simple but must be inherently plural, harboring "difference" (*Differenz, Unterschied*) (Heidegger 1995: 7). To deny this contested character of the genuine matter of thinking—as Husserl supposedly did[1]—lets the principle of phenomenology "become *paralyzed* [*erstarrt*] and closed off in its possibilities" (Heidegger 1995: 7).

Nonetheless, Heidegger's account of the principle of phenomenology seems to merge two inherently conflicting ideas. Thus complying with the primary principle of phenomenology by determining the matter of thinking amounts to violating the principle one attempts to follow. Unless any determination of the subject matter of phenomenology can potentially be called into question again, phenomenology ceases to be self-critical. Although Heidegger doesn't give any explicit criteria for when that should happen, the legitimate motivation to bracket a prior answer to the question of the matter of thinking can only be that such an answer hinders returning to the things themselves in much the same way as did the "absurd theories" against which Husserl originally directed the "principle" (Husserl 2014: 43) of phenomenology. Heidegger elsewhere calls such self-critical reflection a "step back" (*Schritt zurück*) (Heidegger 1969: 50–2).

As this idea puts the demand of philosophical justification above any prior determination of a phenomenological method or of what the matter of phenomenology is, the view developed in the manuscript can be called *normative* in the broad sense Crowell (2013: 2–3) envisages for phenomenology. But it is easy to recognize in this account of the content of the "principle" of phenomenology a version of the dilemma of the historicity of phenomenology.

13.3 A "HISTORICAL RELATION TO HISTORY"

The most elaborate account of the historicity of phenomenology emerges from the later Heidegger's discussion of the relation of phenomenology to ontology. Nonetheless, it is deeply problematic. On Heidegger's view, determining what phenomenology should be concerned with is inherently ontological already because it purports to be about the *being* of the matter of thinking. Even in the manuscript about the principle of phenomenology Heidegger remarks that the disputed matter of thinking is "Being itself" (*das

---

[1] Sallis (1995: 196–209) has argued that Husserl actually shares this recognition of a "non-identity" of the things themselves.

Seyn selbst) (Heidegger 1995: 7). Ontology and phenomenology are thus both concerned with the same subject matter. This assumption, in play throughout Heidegger's works, is stated most clearly in the introduction to *Being and Time*: "With regard to the subject matter [*sachhaltig genommen*], phenomenology is the science of the being of beings— ontology" (Heidegger 2010: 35, translation modified). According to the account of *Being and Time*, phenomenology is distinct from ontology in that it provides a "phenomeno-logical method" (§7) to understand the "being of beings"; ontology is "*possible only as phenomenology*" (Heidegger 2010: 33).

This claim foreshadows the idea that phenomenology is the very possibility of thinking. But it brings out more clearly how earlier realizations of phenomenology are to be understood, namely as different forms of ontological thinking. Given what Figal has called Heidegger's "ontologization of phenomenology" (Figal 2010: 36), even sys-tems of philosophy predating the foundation of Husserl's school, such as ancient Greek philosophy, can be considered phenomenological because they make ontological claims. More specifically, philosophical systems determine the meaning of existence, which Heidegger sees as the principal task of ontology (see Heidegger 2010: §1). But by giving an account of the meaning of existence, these systems also determine the matter of thinking and fall within the scope of the principle of phenomenology. This ties phe-nomenology to the history of ontology, as the question of being already has a long his-tory. Acknowledging the historicity of phenomenology thus forces an engagement with what Heidegger calls the history of being (*Seinsgeschichte*) (see Guignon 2005).

This reasoning becomes particularly clear in one of Heidegger's last statements on Husserl. In 1969, Heidegger refers back to the idea of phenomenology as the *possibility* of ontology. In contrast to the introduction of *Being and Time*, the context is not an account of the phenomenological method of ontology but a more general discussion about the past and prospects of phenomenology. Heidegger again begins by asking the question from the manuscript discussed in the last section: "What is the subject matter [*Sache*] of philosophy? Is it consciousness?" Deciding this question, Heidegger holds, is impossible in "egological intuition" but must include "a historical relation to history [*geschichtlicher Bezug zur Geschichte*]" (Heidegger 2007: 147). This is what Husserl's phi-losophy lacks, as Heidegger states quite directly: "It seems to me that all Husserl has achieved in his lifetime in no way gives the basis to even pose the problem of history." This comment, however, is not intended as "depreciation": "I to the contrary hold that this is what is magnificent about Husserl's thinking, [Husserl] attempts, with last conse-quence and determined by the idea of truth as certainty, a final grounding of his 'system'" (Heidegger 2007: 149). Heidegger sees here the same asymmetry between Husserl's and his own understanding of phenomenology that was to be found in the manuscript on the principle of phenomenology: Husserl allegedly recognized only consciousness as the eminent theme of phenomenology. In Heidegger's reading, this fundamental deci-sion also forces phenomenology to accept a particular form of ontology requisite for studying consciousness in the way Husserl envisaged. As was to be expected from the discussion in the manuscript, Heidegger's proposal is not to focus on some other object or range of objects instead, but to readdress the question of the matter of thinking. If one assumes, as Heidegger does, that determining a particular object and mode of inquiry entails making claims about the meaning of existence, asking what the matter of thinking should be must include readdressing the question of being.

This becomes clear by how Heidegger continues his statement on the future and possibility of phenomenology. Heidegger first presents the idea of the history of thought as history of being, or more precisely as the history of the question of being: "The history of thought is not a jumble of different past opinions but it conveys to us the demand [*Anspruch*] to ever again ask the same question, the question of the being of beings" (Heidegger 2007: 147). Heidegger then describes how this fact defines the genuine task of phenomenology:

> This leads to another question to which I lay claim as a phenomenological question: If metaphysics, throughout its entire history, speaks of the being *of beings* in its different modifications—idea, energeia, actualitas, monad, objectivity, absolute spirit, absolute knowledge, will to power—then from where is the essence of *being* determined? (Heidegger 2007: 147)

Not a specific object or a particular account of existence should thus be at the center of phenomenological attention but the question of being in a form that can function as access to the different ways in which the matter of thinking has already been determined in the past.

From the perspective that the later Heidegger claims as the genuinely phenomenological one, Husserl's "system," however, remains committed to a specific ontology based on the idea that what something is, i.e., its being, is determined "in consciousness." Whether or not this is a fair reading, if this is so, Husserl's philosophy just adds another item to the above list. By contrast, a phenomenology that is critical with regard to its own history deals with the list as such. The merger of phenomenology with the history of being thus sets the standard for later Heidegger's understanding of phenomenology: If it fails to operate as a reflection of ontological commitments, it ceases to be genuine phenomenology as the possibility of ontology.

Nonetheless, Heidegger's proposal is burdened with an ambiguity between two uses of "being" reflecting the dilemma of the historicity of phenomenology. If the question of what makes up the "essence of *being*" (*Wesen des Seins*) in contrast to the "being *of beings*" (*Sein des Seienden*) is the question to which Heidegger "[lays] claim as a phenomenological question," it is necessary to make this distinction plausible and see if it can address the dilemma of the historicity of phenomenology.

13.4 Guiding Question, Basic Question

Perhaps the best way to understand what it means to ask for the "essence of being" is to focus on a central passage in *Contributions to Philosophy* (1936–8). Although not published by Heidegger, this massive manuscript is generally considered as initiating the later period of his work. According to Heidegger's plans at the time, *Contributions* was to be the first of a number of "treatises in the history of being" (*seinsgeschichtliche Abhandlungen*) (Heidegger 1997: 433–4). Drafts for these are published in the volumes of the *Gesamtausgabe* following *Contributions*, but they never took the shape of a philosophical system. Among these treatises, *Contributions* stands out for how it reengages the history of ontology and Heidegger's own earlier works in particular, which he sees as a patent failure. According to *Being and Time*, the aim of Heidegger's project in ontology has been to renew and answer the question of being; the published part of the book closes with the comment that it indeed succeeded at "*kindling*" the "conflict with respect to the interpretation of being," still having in view to "*settle*" (Heidegger 2010: 414) it eventually. But as Heidegger admits, this never happened. The project of *Contributions* and of a history of being more generally is motivated by this failure of fundamental ontology to provide an answer to the question of being (see Frede 2006). In the context of the later discussion of phenomenology, this amounts to failing to provide a positive account of the matter of phenomenology.

In one of the central passages of *Contributions*, Heidegger returns to a discussion of the structure and implicit assumptions of the being question, announcing the introduction of "an essential distinction and clarification [of] the question of being" (Heidegger 2012b: 60). In contrast to the stated aim of *Being and Time*, Heidegger now says that no such "clarification" can ever arrive at "the answer to the question of being." All that can be achieved is "the formation of the questioning" (Heidegger 2012b: 60) by way of the distinction Heidegger then makes between two types of asking about the meaning of being, the "guiding question" (*Leitfrage*) and the "basic question" (*Grundfrage*). Their correlates are the "being of beings" and the "essence of being," respectively. I will discuss them in order.

The *guiding* question is the question of being in its closed form, as it were, oriented towards giving *one* definite account of existence, *answering* the being question. It does so by assuming, in contemporary terms, that existence is a metaphysical property, the property *that* something exists. To identify this property, it looks at descriptions of what there is: The guiding question "interrogates" entities trying to establish "the common and thus what is common to every being" (Heidegger 2012b: 60); this feature must be the manifestation of existence as such. The paradigmatic form of this way of raising the being question is to be found in Aristotle's metaphysics. Initially asking, "What are entities?" (*tí tò ón*) Aristotle specifies this question by asking, in Heidegger's words, "What is *ousía* as the beingness of beings?" Already in posing the question in this way, "being means *beingness* [*Seiendheit*]" (Heidegger 2012b: 60). This prefigures the answer: "The answer to the guiding question is the *being* of beings, the determination of beingness (i.e., the providing of the 'categories' for *ousía*)" (Heidegger 2012b: 61). As emerges from the discussion, actuality (*enérgeia*) in contrast to possibility (*dynamis*) is the most important of these categories.

This account of the guiding question links up with Heidegger's account of the historicity of phenomenology. Recall the list quoted in the last section: If all the different terms

Heidegger listed—"idea, energeia, actualitas, monad, objectivity, absolute spirit, absolute knowledge, will to power"—represent different accounts of the "being of beings," we can now specify that, according to the account in *Contributions*, these represent *answers* to the *guiding* question. Heidegger lists one-word answers provided by Plato, Aristotle, Aquinas, etc., sharing the structural feature Heidegger identified in Aristotle, as all these answers identify something that makes any entity exist. This defines what Heidegger means by the expression "being *of beings*": An answer to the being question established by way of an account of entities as provided by any ontology determining existence as a metaphysical property. According to Heidegger, this has been the dominant way of doing ontology. The guiding question is called such because it has "guided the beginning of Western philosophy and its history up to its end in Nietzsche" (Heidegger 2012b: 60).

Although Heidegger doesn't concede as much, the history of the guiding question would also include at least the projected outcome of *Being and Time*. According to §2, in ontology, "beings are, so to speak, interrogated with regard to their being" in order to arrive at the meaning of existence as that which "is to be *ascertained*" (Heidegger 2010: 5). The question of being according to the early Heidegger presupposes what he labels the "ontological difference" (Heidegger 1982: 17), the essential link between being and entities allowing for a transgression from the manifestation of entities to the meaning of being. Thus by addressing the "being of beings," the fundamental ontology of *Being and Time*, too, has been guided by the guiding question. Therefore, not only "consciousness" but "Dasein" or "temporality" should also be added to the list of how the being of beings has been understood. If this is true, then the idea that phenomenology should be concerned with the basic question in contrast to the guiding question indeed constitutes a radical break with Heidegger's earlier philosophy and its account of phenomenology as ontological method. Although Heidegger doesn't make this explicit, it would submit even his own earlier work to what it sets as the measure for genuine phenomenology.

The first characteristic defining the *basic* question in contrast to the guiding question is that it refuses to *answer* the question of being. As an ongoing "elaboration" of the being question, it remains an *open* question. But the basic question also shifts away from a thematization of entities in an attempt to transgress the schema of the ontological difference. For this type of ontological questioning, "the starting point," as Heidegger writes, "is not beings, i.e., this or that given being, nor is it beings as such and as a whole" (Heidegger 2012b: 60). Rather, the basic question articulates being without the detour of entities. To mark this contrast, Heidegger not only labels the correlate of this form of the being question the "essence of being" but also uses a different spelling (*Seyn, beyng*). The further account in the passage from *Contributions* then leans heavily on notoriously difficult terms: The basic question is said to constitute "a leap into the *truth* (clearing and concealing) of beyng itself. Experienced and interrogated here at once is what essentially occurs in advance . . . namely, the *openness for essential occurrence as such*, i.e., *truth*" (Heidegger 2012b: 60). Without discussing these notions in detail, it clearly emerges that Heidegger tries to grasp being *as such* in reference to a dynamic manifestation of truth rather than by describing the manifestation of entities. In this vein, Heidegger's discussion of different aspects of truth ("clearing," "unconcealment," "concealing") replaces the register of the ontological difference.

Thus one way to understand Heidegger's insistence that the basic question is a phenomenological question is to connect these discussions of truth to phenomenology. After all, in passages like the one from *Contributions*, it appears that the basic question eventually leads to an account of what the genuine matter of thinking is, namely the manifestation of the essence of being Heidegger attempts to grasp in his account of truth. Bernet (2012), for instance, has shown how the description of clearing and concealment takes up Husserl's theory of truth and untruth. Held (1992) has similarly argued that the discussion of the "event" (*Ereignis*) transforms Husserl's theory of evidence. Figal (2010) has tried to show that the discussion of the idea of truth as *aletheia* represents an account of the possibility and nature of phenomena as such. Von Herrmann (1990: 30) has made the same claim for the so-called "open region" (*Gegnet*), which Heidegger discusses in postwar texts.

But determining the essence of being through such accounts of truth would amount to leaving behind the guiding question and with it, the history of being. Reconceiving phenomenology not as the study of consciousness but of the dynamic manifestation of truth leads to embracing the first horn of the dilemma and denying the historicity of phenomenology. This may be a valid philosophical option. But it is definitive of Heidegger's account of phenomenology that it upholds both conflicting claims. Even the passage from *Contributions* closes with a version of the dilemma of the historicity of phenomenology. First, Heidegger envisages a philosophy embracing the historical plurality of answers to the guiding question: "The guiding question, unfolded into its structure, always allows the recognition of a *basic position* [*Grundstellung*] towards beings as such, i.e., a position of the questioner (human being) on a ground which . . . is brought into the open through the basic question" (Heidegger 2012b: 61). Connecting this idea to the later discussion, one could say that phenomenology, aware of the history of being, should study such "*basic positions*" human beings take as they answer the being question.

But Heidegger in the same paragraph also anticipates that an "unfolding of the basic question" may yet provide "the ground for taking back into a more original possession the entire history of the guiding question" (Heidegger 2012b: 61). Despite the affirmation of a plurality of answers to the being question, Heidegger thus also endorses some form of final appropriation of the history of philosophy. But if Heidegger still envisages an eventual appropriation of the history of being, it is difficult to see how this would not result in another first-order determination of the matter of phenomenology such that the history of philosophy would simply lead up to phenomenology based on a definitive ontology. As emerges from *Contributions*, Heidegger wants thinking to both kindle and settle the being question and with it, the dispute as to its proper matter. And the same dilemma continues to define even his most elaborate discussions of phenomenology in the 1960s.

13.5 THE "END OF PHILOSOPHY" AND THE TASK OF PHENOMENOLOGY

Central to the last decade of Heidegger's work are the two lectures "Time and Being" and "The End of Philosophy and the Task of Thinking," dating from 1963 and 1964. These lectures in particular give a more definitive shape to the merger of phenomenology and the history of being anticipated in *Contributions*. The two lectures attempt to present Heidegger's own work, despite some necessary corrections, as a unified philosophical project to be continued after him. His aim, as he states at the beginning of "The End of Philosophy," is merely an "immanent criticism" (Heidegger 1972: 55) of the project of *Being and Time*. While the texts from the *Nachlass* revealed Heidegger as struggling with the proper understanding of phenomenology and ontology until the end of his life, the two lectures are clearly intended as Heidegger's public heritage. But despite the appearance of a perhaps arcane but definitive philosophical system, the two lectures, especially when taken together, harbor a number of serious difficulties. In particular, it is unclear whether or not Heidegger understands ontology as aiming towards a single unified account of existence qua "essence of being." As we have seen in section 13.4, this question emerges from the transformation of fundamental ontology Heidegger envisaged in *Contributions* and is directly relevant for how he understands phenomenology. I cannot give a detailed interpretation of the lectures here, but one way to access their central problem is to ask whether or in what sense Heidegger endorses *ontological pluralism*.

Ontological pluralism is the view that there are multiple irreducible ways, kinds or modes of being and consequently multiple versions of existential quantification (see McDaniel 2009). Heidegger's notion of a history of being presents a peculiar version of this view in that it assumes different ontological paradigms Heidegger calls "epochs" (*Epochen*) in the history of being, effectively reconceiving ontological pluralism as a plurality of *historical* kinds of being. Recall the list of how the "being of beings" has been understood: each term represents a particular understanding of existence—"idea, energeia, actualitas, monad, objectivity, absolute spirit, absolute knowledge, will to power"—and by listing them, Heidegger conceives phenomenology as the engagement with ontological pluralism in this peculiar form.

The most important feature of the later Heidegger's version of ontological pluralism is that the number of meanings of beings, of "epochs," is indefinite with respect to the past, present, and future of ontology. As Werner Marx has pointed out, how many and which ontological epochs Heidegger identifies varies at different occasions, and the criteria for these choices are not made explicit. At times, an epoch is attributed to a single work or author (but not to others); at times, Heidegger uses labels such as "Greek philosophy" or "medieval philosophy" the extension of which is unclear (see Marx 1971: 169). But this only highlights that Heidegger's identification of different meanings of existence is not intended as a framework for writing the history of Western thought. Epochs are not historical "ages" (*Zeitalter*) (Heidegger 1991: 55). Once the epochs of the history of being are revealed as different answers to the guiding question, the different ontological paradigms become simultaneously accessible to the philosopher. Despite the fact that epochs often follow one another in the history of ideas, their historical sequence is irrelevant for the self-reflexive phenomenology Heidegger envisages.

The simultaneity of ontological epochs is the starting point for Heidegger's discussion in the first part of "The End of Philosophy and the Task of Thinking." The end of philosophy, Heidegger holds, is not a point in time but a "place in which the whole of philosophy's history is gathered"; the end as a place is the "gathering into the ultimate possibilities of thought" (Heidegger 1972: 57, translation modified). The plural is a first indication that Heidegger here accepts a plurality of ontological paradigms as "possibilities of thought." He explicitly states: "We lack any criterion which would permit us to evaluate the perfection of an epoch of metaphysics as compared with any other epoch. The right to this kind of evaluation does not exist" (Heidegger 1972: 56). Although it is not "perfect," any epoch is "ultimate" as it achieves the ultimate ontology can achieve: Answering the guiding question or, as Heidegger says here, thinking "beings as a whole . . . with respect to being" (Heidegger 1972: 55–6, translation modified). That each of these paradigms constitutes a "possibility" makes clear that Heidegger is not interested in these as past views about being but as different options for ontological thinking. The different ontological descriptions are "bracketed" as descriptions of entities such that they become mere possibilities for phenomenology or, as Heidegger says here, for "thinking." The topological rather than chronological register expresses the idea of a simultaneous access to these possibilities. The contrast indicates that Heidegger operates on the level of theory he claims for phenomenology.[2]

In the second part of the lecture, the "task of thinking" is indeed developed in a discussion of phenomenology. Given the discussion in his contemporaneous manuscripts, one would expect Heidegger to elaborate here how phenomenology is to study the different ontological epochs. But one finds no such discussion. While the first part of the lecture embraced ontological pluralism as a plurality of ontological epochs, it is less clear whether this is true for the second part, as Heidegger now moves from (past) philosophy to (future) "thinking": The epochs of the history of being are epochs "of metaphysics," which Heidegger identifies with "philosophy" (Heidegger 1972: 55). But they are not epochs of what Heidegger envisages as "thinking," such that it is unclear whether this future form of thought is still concerned with the different ontological paradigms at all. It is easy to recognize here the very same dilemma expressed in the autobiographic essay on phenomenology: "thinking" is to be both the unprecedented possibility of future philosophy and its past realizations.

Consequently, Heidegger's discussion of phenomenology is ambivalent with respect to ontological pluralism. Heidegger's determination of the "task of thinking"

---

[2] For a fuller account of the topological character of Heidegger's later thought, see Malpas 2006 and 2012.

proceeds by asking what the matter of thinking is to be, developing in greater detail and in reference to both Hegel and Husserl the argument from the manuscripts discussed in section 13.1. But instead of returning to the plurality of ontological paradigms emerging from the history of being, Heidegger simply asks after "what remains unthought in the call 'to the thing itself'" (Heidegger 1972: 64). Yet both this question and the answer he gives are all too simple by his own standards: Each of the two phenomenological methods presents a "mode in which the matter of philosophy comes to shine forth of itself and for itself, and thus becomes presence"; such shining-forth requires "something open, something free" (Heidegger 1972: 79, translation modified). In such a way, the "clearing" is revealed as the "openness which grants a possible letting-appear" (Heidegger 1972: 80). By way of a straightforward transcendental argument, Heidegger thus determines the "clearing" as the condition of possibility of phenomena. The task of thinking is accordingly to address this clearing in relation to that which appears in it, for which Heidegger offers the general term "presence" (*Anwesenheit*). Rather than being and time, the genuine matter of thinking is therefore "clearing and presence" (Heidegger 1972: 73). The argument thus effectively collapses the account of the epochs of the history of being from the first part of the lecture into the idea that what has been "unthought" in past philosophy is now to be thought in the philosophy Heidegger sketches.

In view of Heidegger's more elaborate treatment elsewhere, this proposal is quite disappointing, as it appears to be but another first-order determination of the matter of thinking. Although it avoided the terminology of the ontological difference, Heidegger's argument similarly proceeds from a feature of entities. These are determined as having the property or quality of shining forth; from this, Heidegger proceeds to the clearing as that which allows entities to thus shine forth. If this reconstruction is sound, however, Heidegger fails to engage in asking the basic question but returns to another version of the guiding question. Rather than working from the discovery of a historical form of ontological pluralism, Heidegger falls back on an ontological monism in disguise. Despite its peculiar topological register, the lecture would thus fail to operate on the level of theory that Heidegger, against Husserl, claimed to be the only one adequate to his understanding of phenomenology. Recall my initial exposition of the dilemma of the historicity of phenomenology: Heidegger would have eventually endorsed the first horn of the dilemma, opting for a phenomenology of "clearing and presence" uninterested in its own history.

A similar worry arises in "Time and Being." At the outset of the lecture, Heidegger announces his attempt to "think being without entities." Given his account in *Contributions*, one may say that the lecture claims to engage in asking the basic question. Unless this form of the question of being is assumed there is "no longer any possibility . . . of determining the relation of man to what has been called 'being' up to now" (Heidegger 1972: 2, translation modified). Through a discussion of being and time, Heidegger proceeds to identify "the event" (*das Ereignis*) as that which "determines both, being and time in their own, that is, in their belonging together" (Heidegger 1972: 19, translation modified). Although Heidegger earlier in the lecture again listed different ontological paradigms, emphasizing the "epochal transformations" (Heidegger 1972: 9, translation modified) of being, this plurality appears irrelevant to his final account. On the contrary: when Heidegger highlights that there is a "giving" preceding the different manifestations of being, he indicates that thinking "being without entities" may well renounce its relation to the different ontological paradigms. Heidegger continues to ask: "How is the 'it' to be thought that gives being?" (Heidegger 1972: 10, translation modified), effectively severing the basic question from the guiding question and referring to a discussion of presence as an answer. Again, Heidegger thus seems to opt for the first horn of the dilemma.

13.6 A TRANSCENDENTAL DIALECTIC?

Taking the two lectures together, the resulting picture is quite confusing. Heidegger offers transcendental arguments in the attempt to identify conditions of possibility of phenomenal presence that are, to use Cassam's distinction, "world-directed" rather than "self-directed" (see Cassam 1999). Even if one doesn't takes this as a regression to the guiding question, since Heidegger avoids putting the argument in terms of the ontological difference, it is not clear which of the concepts are explanatorily basic. There are a number of notions Heidegger offers at once: clearing, event, presence, time, giving, "it," to list only those I mentioned. Marion has highlighted the category of "giving" in developing his account of phenomenology, but this emphasis clearly transgresses the framework of Heidegger's later discussion (see Marion 2002: chs 6–7). The fact that Heidegger proposes all these different notions raises the exegetical problem which of them are decisive for determining the matter of thinking. But independent of the answer to that question, the emphasis put on these notions already is evidence that Heidegger eventually envisioned phenomenology as concentrating on a specific matter of thinking overcoming its inherently disputed character.

But there are also indications to the contrary. As we've seen in the sections 13.1–13.3, not only did Heidegger struggle with the notion of phenomenology even in the last years of his life. Shortly after he lectured on "The End of Philosophy and the Task of Thinking," Heidegger's position again becomes more hesitant. Reworking the material from the earlier lectures, Heidegger in 1965 gave a presentation entitled "On the Question of Determining the Matter of Thinking" ("Zur Frage nach der Bestimmung der Sache des Denkens") (see Heidegger 1997: 620–33). His account here differs from that in the earlier version of the lecture in several ways. Most importantly, Heidegger highlights the "finitude of the matter of thinking," assigning philosophy the task "to experience this finitude," which is "more difficult than hastily beginning with an absolute" (Heidegger 1997: 632–3).

In the concluding passage, this experience of finitude is linked with the question of the matter of thinking. As Heidegger now emphasizes, taking up a point from his discussion in *Contributions*, this question is to remain *open*. Its unanswerability is what makes it the eminent phenomenological experience. Appropriately, Heidegger puts this point in a row of questions: "What if the answer to this question of thinking would only be another question? And if this state of things [*Sachverhalt*], instead of pointing towards infinite progression would indicate the finitude of thinking that is due to the finitude of its matter?" (Heidegger 1997: 633). This suggestion not only foreshadows Derrida's account of the "undecidable" as quasi-transcendental (see Doyon 2014). In the context of Heidegger's later thought, it contradicts the idea that an account of the clearing, the event, etc. is meant to simply replace a phenomenology of the history of being. Heidegger's emphasis on the "experience" of the "finitude of the matter of thinking" points to an outcome of his argument that is indeed self-directed rather than world-directed, reinstating a subject having and reflecting on such experience, a self-critical thinker.

Rather than restoring the unity of Heidegger's philosophical project, the two lectures and the surrounding publications and manuscripts thus manifest a complex aporia. Any attempt to identify a contribution of Heidegger's later thought to phenomenology would seem well advised to ignore the intimation of a phenomenology to come and recognize its problematic character instead. It is not as a positive proposal but the incoherence of Heidegger's account of phenomenology that is most interesting. Although his later philosophy mobilizes a complex account of the history of ontology, Heidegger failed at finding a way out of the dilemma of the historicity of phenomenology. This may motivate the idea that phenomenology should disentangle itself from the history of ontology in order not to burden itself with the latter. For instance, Benoist (2001: 130) has argued that phenomenology should distance itself from ontology altogether. The failure of Heidegger's identification of phenomenology and ontology may be taken as a complex demonstration of that point.

But another possible consequence would be to acknowledge the dilemma of the historicity of phenomenology and to reinstate the idea of a history of being within an account of phenomenology as transcendental philosophy. Recall Heidegger's discussion of the orientation of phenomenology towards the "things themselves": If this "principle" of phenomenology indeed has an inherently problematic, even contradictory meaning, the later Heidegger may just have found another form of transcendental dialectic. That he was unable to solve the dilemma it involves in no way diminishes the importance of his discussion. On the contrary, the longer phenomenology's own history, the more important it becomes to get clear on the problems associated with it.

References

Benoist, J. (2001), *L'idée de la phénoménologie* (Paris: Buchesne).

Bernet, R. (2012), "Phänomenologische Begriffe der Unwahrheit bei Husserl und Heidegger," in R. Bernet, A. Denker, and H. Zaborowski (eds), *Heidegger und Husserl* (Freiburg: Alber), 108–30.

Carman, T. (2003), *Heidegger's Analytic: Interpretation, Discourse and Authenticity in* Being and Time (Cambridge: Cambridge University Press).

Carman, T. (2006), "The principle of phenomenology," in C. B. Guignon (ed.), *The Cambridge Companion to Heidegger*, 2nd edition (Cambridge: Cambridge University Press), 97–119.

Cassam, Q. (1999), "Self-directed transcendental arguments," in R. Stern (ed.), *Transcendental Arguments: Problems and Prospects* (Oxford: Clarendon Press), 83–110.

Crowell, S. G. (2001), *Husserl, Heidegger, and the Space of Meaning: Paths toward Transcendental Phenomenology* (Evanston, IL: Northwestern University Press).

Crowell, S. G. (2013), *Phenomenology and Normativity in Husserl and Heidegger* (Cambridge: Cambridge University Press).

Dostal, R. J. (2006), "Time and phenomenology in Husserl and Heidegger," in C. B. Guignon (ed.), *The Cambridge Companion to Heidegger*, 2nd edition (Cambridge: Cambridge University Press), 120–48.

Doyon, M. (2014), "The transcendental claim of deconstruction," in L. Lawlor and Z. Direk (eds), *A Companion to Derrida* (Chichester: Wiley Blackwell), 132–49.

Figal, G. (2010), "Phenomenology: Heidegger after Husserl and the Greeks," in B. W. Davis (ed.), *Martin Heidegger: Key Concepts* (Durham: Acumen), 33–43.

Frede, D. (2006), "The question of being: Heidegger's project," in C. B. Guignon (ed.), *The Cambridge Companion to Heidegger*, 2nd edition (Cambridge: Cambridge University Press), 42–69.

Guignon, C. B. (2005), "The history of being," in H. L. Dreyfus and M. A. Wrathall (eds), *A Companion to Heidegger* (Malden: Blackwell Publishing), 392–406.

Heidegger, M. (1969), *Identity and Difference*, translated by J. Stambaugh (New York: Harper and Row).

Heidegger, M. (1972), *On Time and Being*, translated by J. Stambaugh (New York: Harper and Row).

Heidegger, M. (1982), *Basic Problems of Phenomenology*, translated by A. Hofstadter (Bloomington, IN: Indiana University Press).

Heidegger, M. (1991), *The Principle of Reason*, translated by R. Lilly (Bloomington, IN: Indiana University Press).

Heidegger, M. (1995), "Über das Prinzip 'Zu den Sachen selbst,'" *Heidegger Studies* 11: 5–8.

Heidegger, M. (1997), *Reden und andere Zeugnisse eines Lebenswegs*, Gesamtausgabe Band 16, ed. H. Heidegger (Frankfurt a. M.: Klostermann).

Heidegger, M. (2007), *Zur Sache des Denkens*, Gesamtausgabe Band 14, ed. F.-W. von Herrmann (Frankfurt a. M.: Klostermann).

Heidegger, M. (2009), *The Heidegger Reader*, ed. G. Figal (Bloomington, IN: Indiana University Press).

Heidegger, M. (2010), *Being and Time*, translated by J. Stambaugh and D. J. Schmidt (Albany, NY: SUNY Press).

Heidegger, M. (2012a), "Auszüge zur Phänomenologie aus dem Manuskript 'Vermächtnis der Seinsfrage,'" *Jahresgabe der Martin-Heidegger-Gesellschaft* 2011–12.

Heidegger, M. (2012b), *Contributions to Philosophy (Of the Event)* (Bloomington, IN: Indiana University Press).

Held, K. (1992), "Heidegger and the principle of phenomenology," in C. Macann (ed.) *Martin Heidegger: Critical Assessments* II (*History of Philosophy*) (London: Routledge), 303–25.

Husserl, E. (2014), *Ideas for a Pure Phenomenology and Phenomenological Philosophy. First book: General Introduction to Pure Phenomenology*, translated by D. O. Dahlstrom (Indianapolis: Hackett).

Kisiel, T. (1993), *The Genesis of Heidegger's Being and Time* (Berkeley, CA: University of California Press).

Malpas, J. E. (2006), *Heidegger's Topology: Being, Place, World* (Cambridge, MA: MIT Press).

Malpas, J. E. (2012), *Heidegger and the Thinking of Place: Explorations in the Topology of Being* (Cambridge, MA: MIT Press).

Marion, J.-L. (2002), *Being Given: Towards a Phenomenology of Givenness* (Stanford, CA: Stanford University Press).

Marx, W. (1971), *Heidegger and the Tradition*, translated by T. Kisiel and M. Greene (Evanston, IL: Northwestern University Press).

McDaniel, K. (2009), "Ways of being," in D. Chalmers, D. Manley, and R. Wassermann (eds), *Metametaphysics: New Essays on the Foundations of Ontology* (Oxford: Oxford University Press), 290–319.

Mitchell, A. J. (2010), "The fourfold," in B. W. Davis (ed.), *Martin Heidegger: Key Concepts* (Durham: Acumen), 208–18.

Richardson, W. J. (1962), *Heidegger: Through Phenomenology to Thought* (The Hague: Martinus Nijhoff).

Sallis, J. (1995), *Delimitations: Phenomenology and the End of Metaphysics*, 2nd edition (Bloomington, IN: Indiana University Press).

Sallis, J. (2012), "The import of intentionality," in R. Bernet, A. Denker, and H. Zaborowski (eds), *Heidegger und Husserl, Heidegger-Jahrbuch* 6 (Freiburg: Alber), 187–99.

Von Herrmann, F.-W. (1990), *Weg und Methode. Zur hermeneutischen Phänomenologie seinsgeschichtlichen Denkens* (Frankfurt a. M.: Klostermann).

CHAPTER 14

....

SCHUTZ AND GURWITSCH ON AGENCY

....

MICHAEL D. BARBER

In 1935 Edmund Husserl recommended to Alfred Schutz that he look up Aron Gurwitsch on one of his business trips to Paris, and he described Schutz to Gurwitsch as a banker by day and a phenomenologist by night (Schutz and Gurwitsch 1989: xv). Guwitsch emigrated from Germany in 1933 and was teaching at the Sorbonne when Schutz and his family arrived from Austria after Hitler's *Anschluss* in 1938. They shared friendship in Paris until Schutz immigrated to the United States in 1939, with Gurwitsch and his family following in 1940. Schutz became associated with the New School for Social Research, and Gurwitsch held positions at Johns Hopkins, Harvard, and Brandeis. When Schutz died in 1959, Gurwitsch was given a position at the New School—something Schutz had tried to achieve on behalf of his friend most of his time at the New School—and Gurwitsch held that position until his death in 1973. The two friends visited each other whenever possible and carried on a rich philosophical correspondence that has been published by Indiana University Press in 1989 as *Philosophers in Exile: The Correspondence of Alfred Schutz and Aron Gurwitsch, 1939–1959*.

Each thinker's work developed over time, with Schutz expanding his phenomenology of the natural attitude (*Der sinnhafte Aufbau der socialen Welt* in 1932) to include pragmatic dimensions and developing theories of multiple realities ("On Multiple Realities" in 1945) and symbolism ("Symbol, Reality, and Society" 1955) through essays that appeared in *Collected Papers 1* (Schutz 1962). Gurwitsch began with a constitutive phenomenology that focused on consciousness (in his 1937 lectures eventually published as *Esquisse de la phénoménologie constitutive* in 2002 and translated in *The Collected Works of Aron Gurwitsch (1901–1973)*, volume 1 (Gurwitsch 2009a)). He then deepened his appropriation of the insights of Gestalt and developmental psychology, contrasted the scientific and philosophical approaches to consciousness, and examined issues of egology (in his *Studies in Phenomenology and Psychology* in 1964—all of which were republished in *The Collected Works of Aron Gurwitsch (1901–1973)*, volume 2 (Gurwitsch 2009b)) en route to his magnum opus on the foundational field of consciousness (*Theorie du champ de la conscience* in 1957, which was translated and appeared along with *Marginal Consciousness* in volume 3 of the *The Collected Works of Aron Gurwitsch (1901–1973)* (Gurwitsch 2010)). In the course of their exchanges, they disagreed about the significance of being a stranger, the ontological status of multiple realities, relevances, the survivability of Husserlian phenomenology, the difference between noematic and noetic focuses, and the work of William James on conscious-ness and of Adhémar Gelb and Kurt Goldstein on linguistic disturbances. When they cite each other in their works, though, they each present the other positively, and there is no indication that either one of them changed the mind of the other. Instead, their interchanges enabled them to appreciate how their differing frameworks limited or enabled them to see differing aspects of experience, how the one brought to attention what the other neglected or overlooked, and how the overarching phenomenolog-ical framework could accommodate their different emphases. The only example of one of them yielding to the perspective of the other is to be found in the fact that after Gurwitsch read Schutz's *Der sinnhafte Aufbau der sozialen Welt*, he discontinued fur-ther work on his Habilitationschrift, *Die Mitmenschlichen Begegnung in der Milieuwelt*, which attempted to establish the basic categories of sociology, because Gurwitsch de-cided that Schutz had already said what needed to be said from the phenomenological perspective (Gurwitsch 2009a: 47; 1976).

In seeking to relate these two preeminent phenomenologists of the era when phe-nomenology first made its entrance into the United States, I have found it most instruc-tive to select a theme on which they differed and over which they extensively engaged each other and thereby to illustrate that their philosophical camaraderie was much the way Gurwitsch (Schutz and Gurwitsch 1989: 75) described it: "Myself digging a tunnel, I hear the knocking which announces the worker from the other side." Following a suggestion by Richard Grathoff (Schutz and Gurwitsch 1989: xv), who depicts their cor-respondence as a confrontation between Schutz's phenomenology of everyday action and Gurwitsch's theory of perception and science, I have selected the theme of agency as the point through which to discuss their philosophical relationship. While it is obvious that Schutz developed a phenomenological theory of action to provide a foundation for Weberian social science and that Gurwitsch was much less concerned about agency insofar as he appropriated for phenomenology the Gestalt theory of perception at the root of the natural sciences, I believe that a more subtle and revealing approach involves demonstrating how their different emphases on agency pervade their exchanges on other topics on which they disagree and in relation to which they discuss at length the issue of agency. They disagree with each other in their understanding of what the para-mount reality is and of whether the self is to be described as an ego or a non-egological consciousness—with their differing stands revealing the importance they assign to agency. In addition, I will consider briefly whether Gurwtisch's portrayal of the percep-tual object takes sufficient account of the causal functional properties of objects, which would be of importance for Schutz's understanding of working action, that is, bodily gearing into the world. While Gurwitsch pays less attention to agency, he is, to a degree, mindful of its significance, but the differences between Schutz and him have much to do,

I will argue, with the transcendental level on which he works, trying to identify the existential suppositions of provinces of meaning in general.

"Agency" for the purpose of this chapter requires clarification. Schutz (1962: 210–12) distinguishes various levels of human activity, "essentially actual experiences," such as involuntary physiological reflexes or facial expressions; "conduct," spontaneous experiences with no project in mind, such as an affective response to a situation or turning down another path when our way is blocked; and "action," based on preconceived projects that are aimed at realization. Actions can be executed in thinking (e.g., solving an intellectual problem) or in the external world, as acts of "working," which require that one gear bodily into the world, that is, that one sets one's body in motion to affect objects or persons. Working encompasses a spectrum extending from minimal physical actions, such as purposeful linguistic expressions, to more massive physical transformations of the world, such as constructing or demolishing buildings. "Agency" in Schutz's view consists paradigmatically in acts of working, but any purposive execution of a projection, even in thinking, would exhibit agency. This essay will basically follow Schutz's understanding of agency, but the term will also include notions of activity related to Schutz's meaning of the term, as when one deliberately, reflectively, and purposively takes charge of one's intendings of the world, such as beliefs and conduct, instead of just passively and unreflectively allowing them to remain as deposits within one's intentional repertoire.

14.1 THE PARAMOUNT REALITY

Gurwitsch repeatedly asserts that the perceptual world is the paramount reality (Gurwitsch 2009b: 108; 2010: 373), the fundamental stratum of reality in general (Gurwitsch 2009b: 134; 2010: 372), and the equivalent of the life-world (Gurwitsch 1974: 29). For Schutz (1962: 212, 226–7), by contrast, the paramount reality is defined in "On Multiple Realities" as the world of working involving action in the outer world based on a project to realize a state of affairs by bodily gearing into the world. However, Schutz (1962: 346; 1964: 150; Schutz and Gurwitsch1989: 226–7), in "Symbol, Reality, and Society," describes the paramount reality as simply the world of everyday life, in which working acts regularly take place, in particular, in communication with others (Schutz 1962: 294, 322). For both Gurwitsch and Schutz, the paramount reality is that fundamental reality that other realities or provinces of meaning, such as phantasy, modify.

In "On Multiple Realities," Schutz (1962: 208–29) expands the notion of working of earlier works to include a theory of action guided by projects, devised in advance, within a complex time structure, and in the pursuit of pragmatic motives and relevances, which ultimately enable one to come to terms with the fundamental anxiety about one's death. One executes such projects through a particular wide-awake tension of an undivided consciousness that experiences itself as an *ego agens*, acting in concert with others in standard time. Furthermore, from my bodily location as the 0-point of my spatiotemporal and social coordinates, I experience different strata of reality as more or less within reach for the purposes of realizing my projects. Further, I anticipate that I, as *ego agens*, will find myself empowered to repeat or reenact in previously accessible settings repertoires of action through what Edmund Husserl (1974: 195–6) described as the idealizations of "I can do it again" and "and so on"—only now understood actionally instead of in Husserl's logical terms.

The earlier characterization of Gurwitsch as construing the paramount reality as basically perceptual with Schutz conceiving it terms of action—a characterization that Schutz (Schutz and Gurwitsch 1989: 192–3) at points concurs with—perhaps oversimplifies matters. For Gurwitsch (Schutz and Gurwitsch 1989: 194) also insists that for him "the perceptual world is also the world of actions." One can find other textual support for this claim (Schutz and Gurwitsch 1989: 121, 2010: 510), and Gurwitsch repeatedly asserts that the noemata of perceived objects include functional-practical features (before one performs any "reiform" abstraction to a pure material thing) (Gurwitsch 2009a: 245; Gurwitsch and Schutz 1989: 233; Gurwitsch 1976: 120–2) and reflect the cultural and practical typifications and relevances of the perceiver (Gurwitsch 2009a: 343; 2010: 332–4). Gurwitsch (2010: 332–5, 369) is also clear that relevances define what is thematic or marginal in experience, and he readily admits that the perceptual world is a social world (Gurwitsch and Schutz 1989: 121; Gurwitsch 1974: 117). Gurwitsch (Schutz and Gurwitsch 1989: 75), at one point, even expresses his "complete agreement" with Schutz's explanation of the daily life-world as the world of working.

Nevertheless, their differences emerge clearly in Gurwitsch's treatment of the paramount reality in "Ontological Problems" in part 6 of the *Field of Consciousness* (Gurwitsch 2010: 369–402) with its counterpart in Schutz's "On Multiple Realities." According to Gurwitsch (2010: 372–3), an order of existence is unified by a specific relevancy principle that is constitutive of it and that unifies it, and objective time serves as the constitutive relevancy-principle of reality in general, which depends upon the perceptual world, the paramount reality, as its fundamental stratum. For any event to belong to the real material world, it needs to occur at a definite moment of objective standard time, in objective space, and in relationship to other things and events in the material world (Gurwitsch 2010: 376, 382). Within this paramount reality, spheres of life and activity appear, such as professional life, family life, or political activity (all of whose ontological fundamentality Schutz (Schutz and Gurwitsch 1989: 154) questions)—distinguishable contexts with specific relevancy-principles and relatively autonomous suborders, but all within the paramount order of existence that encompasses them and that they still belong to (Gurwitsch 2010: 373, 377).

In contrast to the paramount reality defined by objectivated time, the products of imagination (belonging to a quasi-world) are unified by pertaining to a quasi-time, different from the temporal order of the acts imagining them (duration)(which are in objective time), and, as such, they are not a suborder of reality (such as family life), but an entirely separate order of existence in their own right (Gurwitsch 2010: 377–80). Gurwitsch (2010: 382–3) concludes that only the paramount reality, the perceptual world, is completely and satisfactorily explained in terms of objectivated time alone, and this order of existence seems to "have little, if any, significance from either a theoretical or practical perspective" (Gurwitsch 2010: 382). Other orders of existence (e.g., phantasy), however, must be unified by specific relevancy-principles, such as having a place within the quasi-time binding together a connected series of events imagined by someone (Gurwitsch 2010: 375, 383).

This unification of the order of existence of phantasy about quasi-time reveals again precisely the differences between Gurwitsch and Schutz, for the latter of whom (Schutz 1962: 234–59) every non-working province of meaning, such as phantasy, dreaming, or scientific theory, is distinguished by the fact that in them the subject does *not* pursue pragmatic relevances and does *not* gear bodily into the world in order to transform it. In addition, in non-working provinces of meaning one experiences a relaxed tension of consciousness in contrast to working, which generally does not allow the freedom to speculate or imagine since one must restrict one's attention to realizing the project at hand. In contrast to Gurwitsch's distinguishing orders of existence on the basis of different temporal ontologies, Schutz emphasizes the role of actional pressures in the paramount reality that the other, non-pragmatic provinces of meaning react against and provide relief from.

Gurwitsch's account of his difference with Schutz (Gurwitsch 2010: 388–93) in part 6 of *The Field of Consciousness*, namely that Schutz is engaged in a phenomenological psychology and he in a constitutive phenomenology within the limits of the reduction, might conflict with Schutz's own view (Schütz 2004: 129–30) in *The Phenomenology of the Social World* that he is developing a constitutive phenomenology of the natural attitude that relies in part on the reduction. Nevertheless, Gurwitsch in part 6 correctly captures a fundamental difference between them. Gurwitsch (2010: 390) argues that the mundane actors Schutz describes accept as existent the objects with which they pragmatically engage and that no philosophical problems, which might motivate phenomenological reduction, arise concerning such existence (Gurwitsch 2010: 390). In contrast, Gurwitsch is interested in describing the existential aspect by which finite provinces of meaning are intrinsically connected and form a coherent domain. Hence, Gurwitsch claims to address the existential presuppositions that Schutz, interested in the meaning experience has for everyday day actors (who do not care about the existence of the objects they encounter), does not thematize. As a consequence, Gurwitsch (2010: 392) describes his own position as studying "orders of existence" rather than "provinces of meaning." Schutz's position is philosophical, reflective upon the finite province of everyday working and the way its actors build up their world through the meanings they give to it, and this province becomes the pre-theoretical basis from which the theoretical province is derivative. Gurwitsch, by contrast, surveying these already established orders of existence from a transcendental theoretical perspective, seeks to pinpoint all their existential suppositions, including those of everyday life that neither its actors nor Schutz reflecting upon those actors' meanings make explicit. To be sure, the existential suppositions of everyday life that Gurwitsch clarifies in terms of objective time did not completely escape Schutz, who includes as constitutive of the world of working the "vivid present" at the intersection of inner and objective time. Schutz and Gurwitsch work on different reflective planes, and it is not surprising that the theoretical plane on which Gurwitsch works has little to say about the agency that for Schutz is central to the world of working, the pre-theoretical base from which the theoretical sphere springs.

Consequently, Schutz and Gurwitsch define the paramount reality differently. Relying on his own treatment of the paramount reality, Schutz (Schutz and Gurwitsch 1989: 8, 141, 152, 154, 166, 167, 177, 192, 236) highlights precisely how different his approach is from Gurwitsch's by repeatedly pointing out what is lacking or deemphasized in Gurwitsch's account: corporeal action; the intersubjectivity of noemata; the instituting of the positional index of the noema; the basic character of the world of working; the noetic, pragmatic relevances that determine how far we penetrate into the infinite processes and horizons of perceiving a material thing; the intersubjective presuppositions of perception; the role of pragmatic relevances in determining whether the possibilities one must pursue are wide open or limited to one often in contrast with another (open and pragmatic possibilities); the horizons for motives and goals; and the distinction between seeing (e.g., lines in a letter of the alphabet) and the interpretation that orders seeing toward action (e.g., seeing the letter as contributing to meaning in order to act on that meaning).

14.2 THE EGO

Another central issue between Gurwitsch and Schutz concerns the existence of the pure ego, which Gurwitsch, in his essay "A Non-Egological Conception of Consciousness" in his *Studies in Phenomenology and Psychology* (Gurwitsch 2009b: 307), redescribes rather minimally as simply "a thoroughgoing unity of all mental states." In addition, in his essay "Phenomenology of Thematics and of the Pure Ego" in his *Studies in Phenomenology and Pyschology*, Gurwitsch (2009b: 240) demarcates his own position as favoring the non-egological conception of consciousness of Husserls' *Logical Investigations* as opposed to the later egological position presented in *Ideas 1* (Husserl 1950b: 137–8, 194–6; 1984: 356–61, 363–4, 372–6, 389–91). In this section, we will have to examine whether Gurwitsch's rejection of the ego as the source of actions and his preference instead for a view of consciousness simply as the context within which actions and other mental states occur indicates necessarily a neglect of agency. There is, however, a prior, epistemological question to be asked, namely whether the ego can be known.

Gurwitsch (2009b: 237, 238, 240, 295) repeatedly states that the ego, which needs to be descriptively legitimated, simply cannot be found. In the first place, one finds only acts in consciousness and not an ego. While predominately focused on objects, we can become reflectively aware of the acts intending such objects, but not of our ego (Gurwitsch 2009b: 322–3). Furthermore, when one engages in higher-level reflections, focused on lower-level acts and their objects, one inevitably does not reflect on these higher-level reflections and so cannot find the ego which might be inhabiting these higher-level reflective acts (Gurwitsch 2009b: 324–5). On this basis, Gurwitsch concludes that all there is in consciousness is an organized totality of acts, without any distinct entity or center or pole from which these acts issue (Gurwitsch 2009b: 320). Hence, Sartre is correct to describe what is given in experience as not "I am conscious of this chair," but "There is a consciousness of this chair" (Gurwitsch 2009b: 326; 1966: 37). In the second place, Gurwitsch (2009b: 326–8) further contends that when one in reflection seems to find an ego, one is actually producing an object that was not there prior to reflection—and this fabrication of an object contradicts the role of reflection which is to disclose and not produce. While the just past act is grasped as having existed, in reflection that act is brought into relationship with a new object, the ego, "which did not appear before the act was grasped" (Gurwitsch 2009b: 328). In addition, while the just lived act is given in reflection and to some extent deprived of its spontaneity and objectivated, the ego, according to Gurwitsch and Sartre, is super-induced as a new object (Gurwitsch 2009b: 327) and is consequently seen to be lacking in spontaneity completely. Gurwitsch (2009b: 333; Schutz and Gurwitsch 1989: 47), concurring with Sartre (1966: 13), asserts then that if the ego is given neither in acts or consciousness nor behind them, but be-fore consciousness, that is, as the noematic correlate of reflective acts, then it would be a worldly transcendent existence and would therefore be lacking in apodictic evidence.

Schutz (Schutz and Gurwitsch 1989: 53) responds to Gurwitsch's arguments by claiming that more is found than simply acts and that the ego that is grasped in those acts is not reducible to an object. Schutz (Schutz and Gurwitsch 1989: 53) insists that from the perspective of the grasping act it is possible to interrogate a lower-level grasped act regarding its acting and its actor (i.e., the ego); and, in that process, he believes that the actor can be found. Even though the ego grasped is an object for the higher-level grasping act, it was nonetheless the subject of the grasped act. Furthermore, the ego that experienced itself in action becomes visible in (higher-level) reflection, and that ego, grasped as an object, is also grasped as identical with the ego that experienced itself in action. Schutz argues that, if by making an active ego an object of reflection we somehow or other divorce it from the active character it was just experiencing, we could never accurately reflect on any kind of activity at all, since reflection would al-ways drain any activity of its spontaneity and that we would never be able to distinguish activity from passivity or appreciate spontaneity at all (Schutz and Gurwitsch 1989: 53; Husserl 1984: 372–6).

In an extensive discussion of the ego in *Ideas 2*, which Husserl had promised in *Ideas 1* and which apparently Gurwitsch had not examined carefully (Spiegelberg 1981: 110; Marbach 1974: 124; Husserl 1950b: 138), Husserl can be seen to develop a position that converges with Schutz's in that a new cogito can grasp on the basis of an earlier cogito (which is itself altered) the subject of that earlier cogito and thus the ego can grasp itself as what it is and how it functions even as it makes itself into an object, though not a ma-terial object (Husserl 1952a: 101, 104–5). Furthermore, Husserl (1952a: 100, 107–8) points to a rhythm of stepping forth and receding that is instantiated in consciousness, when, waking from a dull sleep, we bend backward our reflective gaze and grasp what has just passed by, in its dullness and egolessness, as though we had lost for a while the active ego. But, in that moment of recovery, we still experience the ego, not as having disappeared but as having sunk into latency and as being temporally continuous with the ego that emerges to grasp, think, and undergo experiences while awake. As a consequence, this ego is not an ego that was not there until reflection produced it, as Gurwitsch suggests.

Schutz and Husserl seem, in my view rightly, to afford the possibility that higher-level reflective acts can uncover the presence of an active ego in lower-level acts and that this active ego is continuous with the ego that is the object of these reflective acts, without reflection producing that ego as an object that wasn't there before (as opposed to in fact describing what was there). Reflection discloses not merely acts but those acts as acts of an active self. However, even if Gurwitsch is wrong epistemologically in denying that we could gain access to the active ego within a previous act and, as a result, in affirming a non-egological notion of consciousness, the question can nevertheless be raised about whether this non-egological conception of consciousness necessarily diminishes the importance of agency.

As a lead in to this second question, it is important to recognize that Gurwitsch would probably have opposed Husserl's view (in *Ideas 2*) that the active ego can take stock of itself as being in continuity with earlier stage of its history when it was latent. Instead, he would have suggested that there is indeed a continuity between various stages of consciousness, but only in the sense that acts follow on each other as parts of a common temporal whole, without there being any need for an organizing principle, an ego, to bind them together. Gurwitsch (2009b: 319–20) presents his non-egological notion of consciousness as being:

> Nothing other than a complex or unity of mental facts . . . If they are united into complexes, this is because of their coexistence and succession and because of the relation the facts of consciousness bear to one another, but not by virtue of a special entity distinct from the conscious facts, which would have to support these facts and institute unity among them. What is meant by the ego is nothing apart from this united complex. It derives its unity and its coherence from the very acts that enter into it and constitute it; it is nothing other than the organized totality of these acts. Hence when the subject, reflecting upon the act he experiences, ascertains that this act is his, this only means that the act in question is part of that complex and has its place within this united and organized whole.

Consistent with this understanding of a non-egological consciousness, Gurwitsch (2009b: 325) rejects any idea of the ego as standing above the flux of experiences, over against it, such that the ego and its mental states would become "two," since the pure ego *is* the stream of consciousness and nothing more. It is as if the phenomenological observer construes consciousness as simply the unfolding of events, one following another, all in one common context, and understands the identity of this consciousness, which Gurwtisch says that Schutz can call the "ego," as equivalent to the "temporally ordered sum of all experience of the stream" (Schutz/Gurwitsch 1989: 49). Gurwitsch (Schutz and Gurwitsch 1989: 49) insists that one cannot appeal to "ego" activity in this case, that this ego is not a "source point," and that it "does nothing and suffers nothing." Likewise, he (Gurwitsch 2009b: 310) avers that the only reason I can consider a mental state as "mine" is that it belongs to the context of my conscious acts as opposed to the context pertaining to another conscious being.

On the one hand, Husserl (1952a: 98, 100–1, 102–3, 107, 108; 1950b: 137), as we have mentioned, depicts the ego as stepping forth and withdrawing into latency, as "holding sway" (*waltend*) in its acts and letting go of them, as if it presided over its flux of experiences from above them. On the other hand, he (Husserl 1952a: 99–100) was quick to assert, in subsequent reflection, that these moments of insertion into acts and of withdrawal from them, with the accompanying sense in the latter case that one seems to be accomplishing no act at all, pertain to the same ego, which cannot be thought of as separated from its lived experiences, from its own ongoing "life." Like Gurwitsch, Husserl sees that the ego itself is temporally enduring, a stream of consciousness, extending from the past to the actually flowing present now.

Still, for all Husserl's stress, parallel to Gurwitsch's, on the ego as being the temporal stream of consciousness, there is still something "more" to his notion of the ego. At just the point where Husserl (1952a: 111–13) acknowledges the temporal stream of the ego, he takes up the "persistent opinions" one finds within one's stream and argues that my identity as an ego depends not only on my merely finding present previously held opinions but also in my ability to retain my position-takings and to acknowledge and assume them as mine in repeated acts, always allowing for the possibility that other motives and insights may supervene, prompting me to change my opinions and become "unfaithful" to myself (Husserl 1952a: 112, 114). After that discussion, Husserl (1952a: 114–20) then proceeds to take up memories, predicative convictions, mathematical convictions, previous "possessions," which are not just reproduced but can involve a "re-positing" or an active taking part in them. In other words, the ego for Husserl does not consist in a simply observable procession of *cogitos*, one following on another, but it takes an active stance toward those convictions, evaluating them, reaffirming them or revising them, deciding whether they can be rationally defended, participating in them or not, and creating itself in the positions it finally endorses or rejects. The ego experiences the attractions it yields to or resists (Husserl 1952a: 98; Sartre 1966: 57), freely issues fiats that set actions in motion, and experiences captivation and thrills from objects or actively penetrates them (Husserl 1952a: 98, 105). Instead of being the passive theater in which a sequence of acts unfolds, the ego of *Ideas* 2 is an agent, actively stepping forward and withdrawing, "holding sway" (*waltend*) in its mental acts and allowing them to recede into in-actuality. The expression "holding sway" is also the term used by Husserl (1950a: 146, 148) in the *Cartesian Meditations* to describe how the ego of an animate organism governs its members and marshals them into action, as an agent rather than a spectator of its own experience.

There is a way to explain how Husserl can consistently hold that the ego is identical to its stream of consciousness and yet seems to take up a stand over against the acts in the stream and to demonstrate what distinguishes Husserl's account from Gurwitsch's. The moment of the ego overlooking the stream, the moment of an apparent "two-ness," is what one experiences as one evaluates lower-level mental acts and considers whether to endorse them or not—and here one experiences oneself as eminently active, going out to one's acts or pulling back from them, fashioning a self. However, in subsequent reflection, one realizes that those moments when the ego refrains from its mental acts, evaluates them, and endorses or abandons them—all those moments are themselves acts within one's single, unified stream of consciousness. By emphasizing that the ego is identical with its stream, Gurwitsch occupies this second position, that of subsequent reflection, and he sees all mental acts as part of a unified complex. As a consequence, though, he fails to appreciate the dynamics internal to that evaluative moment when the ego experiences itself over against the stream to which subsequent reflection will show its evaluative acts belong as acts among all the others pertaining to the whole context of acts making up the stream. This means that Gurwitsch occupies a reflective stance, grasping from outside what would be given internally as the ego takes up its stance over against its own mental acts; the particularly active ego, engaged in fashioning itself by its endorsements and withdrawals, is not seen as a consequence. Had Gurwitsch recognized that active ego, he would have seen that the sense of "mineness" pertaining to mental acts in Husserl's conception of the ego would be much more robust than his own sense of "mineness" since holding sway in one's mental acts and deliberately revisiting them and positing them again (or not) gives one a much stronger sense that they are one's own than does the mere fact that they happen to belong to one's own streaming context and not someone else's.

In fairness to Gurwitsch, there is one place in which he might have accommodated such an active self. In *The Field of Consciousness* in a section entitled "Historical Continuity of Mental Development," he (Gurwitsch 2010c: 42–5) criticizes Jean Piaget's emphasis on the historical continuity of mental development insofar as it leads him to overlook how the conditions of achievement of solving a problem, such as the mastery one has already attained of a discipline, do not account for the actual achievement, in which one reorganizes what one has learned and applies it and in which, even in cases of rapid reorganization, there is a "moment of hesitation and reflection" (Gurwitsch 2009b: 43) just prior to the creative moment when application is made to a novel situation. Here Gurwitsch's non-egological consciousness exhibits a kind of active self-determination like that attributed to the ego described by Husserl. However, Gurwitsch's granting a moment of hesitation and reflection falls short of the full description of evaluation, endorsement, or retraction characterizing Husserl's account of the active ego. This lack of development is perhaps to be expected insofar as Gurwitsch in this section is concentrating not on explaining agency but on rebutting Piaget's view that mental development tends to conflate the past conditions of achievement with the present moment of actual achievement, in which one makes novel applications that cannot be predicted on the basis of one's past. Gurwitsch's preoccupation has more to do with temporality and its interruption, not agency. Furthermore, it is difficult to reconcile such a notion of the active non-egological consciousness with Gurwitsch's statements to Schutz that the temporally ordered sum of all experience of the stream involves no ego activity and does nothing (Schutz and Gurwitsch 1989: 49).

Part of Gurwisch's motivation for his support for a non-egological consciousness and his opposition to an ego depends on his opposition to the possibility of some special entity distinct from conscious facts that would support them and institute their unity. For Gurwitsch (2009b: 332–3) rejection of the ego as a substance underlying accidents (conscious acts) is fully in accord with the advance of scientific progress that took place once the notion of substance was replaced by function and relation, as he explains to Schutz (Schutz and Gurwitsch 1989: 48). Furthermore, Gurwitsch's account of non-egological consciousness parallels his idea of perception in which an object is given as a Gestalt contexture, which consists in a system of functional significances mutually dependent upon and attuned to each other, without any need for a unifying factor from outside of itself, such as an underlying substance as John Locke thought (Gurwitsch 2009a: 197–8; 2009b: 387).

But a careful reading of Husserl's extensive treatment of the ego in *Ideas* 2 reveals that finding some special substantial entity to support conscious acts and establish their unity does not play a role in his discussion of the ego. Husserl's indifference to the idea of the ego as a kind of substance is clear insofar as he (Husserl 1952a: 110) admits that the pure ego is already "numerically one and unique already with respect to 'its' stream of consciousness" (with the "its" placed in quotes as if to emphasize that the ego is its stream and does not form a substantial underpinning separate from the stream (Husserl 1952a: 111)). If the stream of consciousness already provides unity and distinctiveness and serves, as Husserl (1952a: 113) observes, as the condition of the possibility for a steadfast and persistent ego, then Husserl's notion of the ego adds something distinctive to the idea of its being the stream: It represents the capacity of the self to take a position over against its acts and to evaluate, reject, or make them its own (through acts that will appear subsequently as constituents of the stream).

However, it might be that a stronger sense of agency should be attributed to Gurwitsch's non-egological consciousness insofar as he (Gurwitsch 2009b: 321), in his essay "A Non-Egological Conception of Consciousness," affiliates his own views with Jean-Paul Sartre's treatment of consciousness in "La transcendance de l'ego." With Sartre, Gurwitsch (2009b: 326–8) affirms that the reflective turn to the past one grasps gives rise to a new object, the ego, as an object only, and in such a moment reflection exceeds what should be its limited, disclosive role to one of producing what is not given in experience. While these claims depend upon the epistemic premises discussed above, the end result for Gurwitsch and Sartre is that one ends up attributing to the ego, constructed by reflection, characteristics, such as spontaneity, which belong to (non-egological) consciousness (Gurwitsch 2009b: 332). Gurwitsch's mode of thinking here resembles the notion spelled out by Sartre in *Being and Nothingness* as "bad faith," in which one depicts the self (the empirical ego) as a determined object, thereby hiding from one's sight the spontaneous activities of one's non-egological consciousness that are ultimately responsible for the creation of the self as an unfree object. For a concrete example of such bad faith, Sartre discusses how the café waiter attributes to himself an immutable identity by which he is bound and is blind to the many spontaneous activities by which he adopts the role, sustains it, and realizes it uniquely (Sartre 1943: 98–100). Sartre in *Being and Nothingness* (Sartre 1943: 637–8) develops a dynamic view of the self's (For-Itself's) agency to the point that one's character or temperament is not a static thing-like given, but rather a matter of one's free projection of oneself, what Alain has called a vow, insofar as one chooses to sustain one's project as a certain kind of character or not or insofar as one can comply or not with how others regard oneself (e.g., as ill-tempered). Sartre's view of the agency of the For-Itself, that is, of non-egological consciousness, paradoxically converges with Husserl's view in *Ideas 2* of the ego, choosing to commit itself or not to what previous acts had affirmed or enacted—and hence it would appear that epistemological differences divide Husserl and Sartre more than their understanding of the self. Schutz (1962: 67–72), too, understood that the self is defined in terms of its system of in-order to motives, that is, those often freely chosen and ever revisable projects, to which all its sub-acts are directed.

However, other than the brief discussion mentioned earlier in *The Field of Consciousness* and the endorsement of Sartre's view of non-egological consciousness, Gurwitsch has little to say himself about the agency of non-egological consciousness, which, as Sartre's view indicates, need not be lacking in agency, despite the fact that one's espousal of it may have followed on the rejection of the egological consciousness that seems eminently active in the views of Husserl and Schutz. One can find a clue as to why Gurwitsch discusses agency so little in his essay *Marginal Consciousness*, in particular the chapters entitled "The Awareness of Embodied Existence" and "The Somatic Ego in the Perceptual World," in which he explains how the embodied existence, which accompanies all our conscious life, is often not relevant, unthematized, and marginal, especially if our focus is on a perceptual object that guides our movement (Gurwitsch 2010: 481, 482, 487–8, 508–9, 513–16). In a similar fashion, it could be that Gurwitsch's thematic interests may have consigned the actional character of non-egological consciousness to the margin of this thought. However, despite this explanation, the facts are that Gurwitsch does not discuss agency much when he deals with the topic of egology, that his explicit statements to Schutz and in his writings seem to minimize the importance of agency, and that he seems to delegate the analysis of non-egological consciousness to Sartre.

In the discussion of the ego between Gurwitsch and Schutz, the issue of agency is prominent. When Gurwitsch (Schutz and Gurwitsch 1989: 31) points out to Schutz that there is something wrong with the transcendental ego and that he opposes the "ego" and Schutz the "transcendental" component, it is telling, since the place where Schutz locates the ego is the domain that precedes any adoption of the theoretical, transcendental phenomenological reduction, the world of everyday life, the paramount reality, whose hallmark is action, in contrast to Gurwitsch's notion of the paramount reality. Moreover, Schutz (Schutz and Gurwtisch 1989: 53) points out that Gurwitch's view that there can be no epistemological access to the acting ego implies that "I can only advert to my thinking, but not to my acting"—although Gurwitsch (2009b: 322) could easily respond here that we can grasp prior actions, just not the ego that Schutz claims is given in such actions. Schutz (Schutz and Gurwitsch 1989: 151) further opposes the idea that temporality is able to be experienced only through the "flowing-into-one-another" of one theme into another, and he insists on the importance of the egological "temporalizing of time" that Husserl spoke of so much. As if such temporalizing had nothing to do with the ego, Gurwitsch (2009b: 324) finds "highly significant" Sartre's comment that in *Vorlesungen zur Phänomenologie des inneren Zeitbewusstseins* Husserl never resorts to the unifying, synthesizing power of the ego (Sartre 1966: 22). However, in line with Schutz's suggestion, when one examines Husserl's later "C-Manuscripts" (Husserl 2006: 1–3, 30–1, 37–8, 188–9) and studies the *Zeitigung der Zeit*, that is, the intricate, unfolding intertwining of past, present, and future, one finds there, as in *Ideas 2*, the ego related to its own streaming, as the subject of acts and the "completer of activity" (Husserl 2006: 348).

Given Schutz's view of the paramount reality, it is no wonder that he (Schutz and Gurwitsch 1989: 152) also raises the question of how Gurwitsch can assert that we are aware of ourselves as existing in the world and at the same time deny the ego-reference of consciousness. The implications of this criticism become clearer later in the Schutz–Gurwitsch correspondence, when Schutz disagrees with Gurwitsch's view that the ego is only a *constitutum*. Schutz (Schutz and Gurwitsch 1989: 182) observes that only the I *modo preteritis* is a *constitutum*—a point that, Schutz points out, Husserl, Scheler, and G. H. Mead agree with. The mention of Mead refers one immediately to Schutz's discussion of the world of working as the paramount reality in "On Multiple Realities" in which he (Schutz 1962: 216) describes the working self as engaging in and originating bodily actions as an "undivided total self" in *modo presenti*. The totality of the acting self, the I, in Mead's vocabulary, remains undivided in action, but goes to pieces when reflection enters in to grasp the self, which now appears as a partial self, the occupier of a role—a division of self that also occurs when one embarks upon a non-working sphere of meaning, such as phantasy, dreaming, or theory (Schutz 1962: 239, 243, 248, 254). In this argument, Schutz opposes Gurwitsch's idea that the ego is only a *constitutum* by, in effect, reminding him of the experience of the active self as undivided, as the I that, when reflectively recovered, appears as a Me according to Mead. For Schutz, this undivided self undergoes bifurcation the moment reflection intervenes insofar as one finds oneself now both the lived self and the self reflecting on that lived self; but this bifurcation does not imply that the reflection cannot maintain contact with, capture, and convey the ego as acting in acts reflected on, as Schutz already argued. Consequently, although Gurwitsch might have been able to follow Sartre in construing the non-egological consciousness more dynamically, his notion of the ego as a mere inert *constitutum* runs into opposition from Schutz who conceives the ego as dynamically undivided in its focus, in a manner that converges with the views of Husserl, who (Husserl 1952a: 104), also, by the way, characterizes the ego as "undivided" in its manifold of acts.

As in the case of the paramount reality, Gurwitsch (Schutz/Gurwitsch 1989: 147) claims that his differences with Schutz spring from methodological procedures: Gurwitsch works in the reduced sphere, in which the ego becomes a *constitutum*, and Schutz's area is the natural attitude, in which one can assume the ego just like the existence of the world—although after this explanation, Schutz (Schutz and Gurwitsch 1989: 182) continues to dispute that the ego is a *constitutum*, as if the methodological argument had no traction with him. Perhaps Gurwitsch's method-ological constraints explain, too, why he refrains from addressing a very practical notion of subjectivity, namely that of subjectivity of the moral person concerned with repentance in his or her depth and center, since such a notion of subjectivity would presuppose the concept of the "person" which might more appropriately per-tain to the empirical ego as opposed to the pure ego and hence does not belong to pure phenomenology (Gurwitsch 2009b: 311). Herbert Spiegelberg (1981: 113) won-ders why Gurwitsch in the original German version of this essay ("Phenomenology of Thematics and of the Pure Ego") had allowed for a place for the pure ego, as a per-sonal center for personal acts such as repentance, love, hatred, etc., but then omitted it in subsequent versions. Husserl (1952a: 109–20) himself distinguishes between the empirical and the pure ego, but he envisions the discussion of the pure ego as taking up and analyzing the structural features of the empirical ego, and indeed all the discussions of the active ego relating to its own "persistent opinions" takes place in terms of the pure ego, presumably within the sphere of the reduction. Similarly, Schutz's analysis in *Der sinnhafte Aufbau der sozialen Welt* (Schütz 2004: 139–210) in chapter 2, under phenomenological reduction, does address the issue of action and treats the issue of the acts taken to belong to the ego, and it is only because he wishes to avoid problems connected with intersubjectivity that he (Schütz 2004: 219–21) dispenses in chapter 3 with the reduction that he had implemented in the previous chapter. It is unclear, then, why the question of the ego and its actional character is something that lies beyond the purview of the reduced sphere and why Gurwitsch should claim that because he works under the constraints of reduction he should leave such a theme out of consideration.

In summary, it does not seem that Gurwitsch convincingly rules out epistemic access to the ego or that Gurwitsch's opposition to outdated notions of substance is telling against the ego as Husserl presents it. Further, the conception of a non-egological con-sciousness could accommodate the idea of a self-characterized by agency, as Sartre's views in *On the Transcendence of the Ego* and *Being and Nothingness* demonstrate, and such a self, paradoxically, converges with the ego described by Husserl, which is expe-rienced as holding sway in its acts of consciousness, endorsing or retracting them and thereby shaping itself. However apart from Gurwitsch's recommendation of Sartre's notion of non-egological consciousness in *The Transcendence of the Ego*, whose active nature is developed even further in *Being and Nothingness*, Gurwitsch's own comments on the agency of the self are minimal. Schutz reiterates the active nature of the ego be-cause it is located in the pragmatic paramount reality, because the ego is active in its temporalizing, because one experiences it as undivided in its concentrated acting prior to reflection and theory; and it remains unclear why the active ego must be excluded from the phenomenological reduction as Gurwitsch believes. As in the discussion of the paramount reality, Gurwitsch's discussion of the self ends up placing much less emphasis on its agency than does Sartre, who favors non-egological consciousness, or Husserl and Schutz, who opt for consciousness as egological.

14.3 THE PERCEPTUAL OBJECT

Discussing the connection between agency and the perceptual object, which is a central but highly complicated topic in Gurwitsch's thought, would require a separate chapter, but a brief presentation can highlight the linkages. Gurwitsch (2010: 112; 2009a: 141), making use of Gestalt psychology, describes the noema as a Gestalt, as unitary whole, which, by virtue of its intrinsic articulation and structure, manifests coherence and consolidation and which can be described without discussing, as the phenomenological reduction requires, its internal or external causal origins. In addition, not all the moments within a Gestalt have the same functional weight, but there is no need for some central noematic point, some indeterminate X to unify the Gestalt whose unity must be understood simply in terms of all the moments' relationships to each other (Gurwitsch 2009a: 193–4, 197–205). Gurwitsch notes, though, that the single appearance of the thing is not equivalent to the thing itself which consists in the "all inclusive systematic grouping of its appearances" (Gurwitsch 2010: 178; 2009a: 377–8). Consequently, the single perceptual appearance is, in effect, one member, one part, of the whole of all the perceptual appearances of the object, which like a Kantian idea can never be completely realized (Gurwitsch 2010: 178, 211).

John Drummond, however, raises two, in my view, telling, objections against Gurwitsch's account of the perceptual noema. First, insofar as each appearance of the thing is only a part of a whole, that is the "all inclusive systematic grouping of its appearances" (Gurwitsch 2010: 178), the experience of the object is finally deferred to an idea-whole of an infinite number of appearing parts (Drummond 1990: 98). This system of noemata which is the "equivalent correlate" of the perceptual thing (Gurwitsch 2009b: 390) amounts for Drummond (1990: 95, 97, 152) to a form of phenomenalism, an assembly of appearances substituting for a thing that is not itself given. Drummond (1990: 159–61) defends instead the Husserlian notion (Husserl 1950b: 246–9, 329–33; 1973: 88–91) that the thing is given as an identity persisting through a manifold of experiences—an entirely different paradigm than that which construes the thing as a whole consisting in parts, that is, individual noematic appearances. Whole/parts analysis applies to a static phenomenon and identity/manifold to an identity across time (Drummond 1990: 151). An object is not composed of appearances (whole/parts) but is present *in* them (identity/ manifold) (Drummond 1990: 152). An appearance in the whole/parts analysis is a part of the thing, as opposed to being a phase of its presentation in the identity/manifold paradigm (Drummond 1990: 152). In the whole/parts model, one would not see the thing until one sees all the parts (Drummond 1990: 152). In a way, Gurwitsch's neglect of the unity of the perceptual thing given across a manifold is mirrored in his rejection of Husserl's view of the ego immersing and withdrawing itself from its manifold of acts in favor of a non-egological consciousness which he often speaks of as the temporally ordered succession of individual experiences, as both J. N. Mohanty (1994: 949–50) and Robert Sokolowski (1975: 9) point out.

One can easily envision how the conception of a thing in phenomenalist terms favors the thing as series of Gestalts of sensible qualities (color, shape, etc.) anticipating a yet to be given thing as opposed to the thing given in the present as an identity across manifolds that would lend itself to a greater degree to that bodily gearing into the world that is central for agency. Drummond (1990: 156–7) extends this manifold approach even further by arguing that there are two sets of properties given in separate manifolds to be found in the inner horizons of the experience of the material thing: sensible elements that *could* be given in direct sense experience (e.g., the color of the back side of the building which one could go around to see) and properties (e.g., causal, functional, conceptual, or value properties) which cannot be given in direct sense experience and which require associations with experiences explicitly framed, such as causal judgments (and hence are apperceived rather than perceived properties). For Husserl (1973: 343–4) the distinction between these essentially different properties constitutive of a thing, with the causal properties presupposing a sensible base, makes possible a distinction between a phantom, the object of a simple sensible encounter, such as rainbow or the sky, and the material thing, such as a rock, which can engage other things (e.g., a window) within a causal network of effecting (e.g., breaking the window) and being effected (e.g., being thrown). Gurwitsch (2009b: 209–10, 231–2, 385–8), who argues that there is no essential distinction between kinds of parts within a perceptual noema since the role of moments is defined strictly in terms of the particular whole, and only that whole to which they belong, is, in the end, unable to draw an essential distinction between the sensible and causal properties of the thing. Consequently he is unable to prevent the assimilation of the causal properties to sensible ones and thus to keep separate the phantom from the material thing (Drummond 1990: 156–60)—all despite his acknowledgement of functional properties in objects. Clearly Gurwitsch's Gestalt account that leads to a phenomenalism and to a potential assimilation of causal-functional to sensible properties ventures away from the flesh-and-blood thing and its enmeshment in its causal network that are central for the bodily gearing into the world typical of Schutz's paramount reality, the world of working.

14.4 CONCLUSION: DIVERSE STRATEGIES WITHIN A COMMON PHENOMENOLOGICAL FRAMEWORK

To conclude and to retrieve Gurwitsch's comments in chapter 6 of *The Field of Consciousness*, Gurwitsch's lack of emphasis on agency in comparison with Schutz may be traced ultimately to their diverse theoretical strategies. Gurwitsch (2009b: xv), like Schutz, emulates Husserl's "uncompromising integrity and radical philosophical responsibility" and seeks to "accomplish radical and ultimate philosophical clarification concerning objects of any kind" (Gurwitsch 2009a: xvi). Hence, he (Gurwitsch 2010: 18, 352; 2009b: 136), beginning with his noematic starting point, extends his attention to the encompassing whole perceptual context of an object, clearly evident in his appropriation of Gestalt theory, to the idea of orders of existence, which encompass any objects existent within their systematic context. Objective time, then, forms the ontological supposition of everyday life, the paramount reality of the perceptual world, within which all objects and all persons and their spatial surrounds are situated and related to each other (Gurwitsch 2010: 376–7). This perceptual world underlies all the bodily activities so basic for Schutz (Gurwitsch 2010: 510). Gurwitsch (2010: 382) readily admits that this order of existence, which is based on objective time seems to have little practical or theoretical significance—as opposed to the paramount reality for Schutz in which agency is so prominent. Yet, Gurwitsch (Schutz and Gurwitsch 1989: 135) can claim to Schutz, apologizing for any possible arrogance, "I provide you with the foundation," and by such a comment he suggests to his friend a possible convergence of the separate tunnels in which they are working. In the end, they each emphasize the different interests shaping their overall life-projects (Schutz and Gurwitsch 1989: 135, 253, 255), such that Gurwitsch's undertreatment of agency may not result from a deliberate depreciation of it, but rather that the thematic focus of a life-project always consigns some themes to the margins—at least until one hears the sounds of a laborer digging away on the other side of one's tunnel.

References

Drummond, J. (1990), *Husserlian Intentionality and Non-Foundational Realism: Noema and Object* (Dordrecht: Kluwer).

Gurwitsch, A. (1974), *Phenomenology and the Theory of Science* (Evanston, IL: Northwestern University Press).

Gurwitsch, A. (1976), *Die mitmenschlichen Begegnungen in der Milieuwelt* (Berlin: de Gruyter).

Gurwitsch, A. (2009a), *Constitutive Phenomenology in Historical Perspective: The Collected Works of Aron Gurwitsch (1901–1973)*, vol. 1 (Dordrecht: Springer).

Gurwitsch, A. (2009b), *Studies in Phenomenology and Psychology: The Collected Works of Aron Gurwitsch (1901–1973)*, vol. 2 (Dordrecht: Springer).

Gurwitsch, A. (2010), *The Field of Consciousness: Theme, Thematic Field, and Margin: The Collected Works of Aron Gurwitsch (1901–1973)*, vol. 3 (Dordrecht: Springer).

Husserl, E. (1950a), *Cartesianische Meditationen und Pariser Vorträge*. Husserliana 1 (The Hague: Martinus Nijhoff).

Husserl, E. (1950b), *Ideen zu einer reinen Phänomenologie und phänomenologische Philosophie, Allgemeine Einführung in die reine Phänomenologie*, vol. 1. Husserliana 3 (The Hague: Martinus Nijhoff).

Husserl, E. (1952a), *Ideen zu einer reinen Phänomenologie und phänomenologische Philosophie, Phänomenologische Untersuchungen zur Konstitution*, vol. 2. Husserliana 4 (The Hague: Martinus Nijhoff).

Husserl, E. (1952b), *Ideen zu einer reinen Phänomenologie und phänomenologische Philosophie, Die Phänomenologie und die Fundamente der Wissenschaften*, vol. 3. Husserliana 5 (The Hague: Martinus Nijhoff).

Husserl, E. (1973), *Ding und Raum: Vorlesungen 1907*. Husserliana 16 (The Hague: Martinus Nijhoff).

Husserl, E. (1974), *Formal und Transcendentale Logik: Versuch einer Kritik der logischen Vernunft*. Husserliana 17 (The Hague: Martinus Nijoff).

Husserl, E. (1984), *Logische Untersuchungen, Untersuchungen zur Phänomenologie und Theorie der Erkenntnis*, vol. 2, first part. Husserliana 19-1 (The Hague: Martinus Nijoff).

Husserl, E. (2006), *Späte Texte über Zeitkonstitution (1929-1934), Die C-Manuskripte*. Husserliana 8 (Dordrecht: Springer).

Marbach, E. (1974), *Das Problem des Ich in der Phänomenologie Husserls. Phaenomenologica*, vol. 59 (The Hague: Martinus Nijoff).

Mohanty, J. N. (1994), "The Unity of Aron Gurwisch's Philosophy," *Social Research* 61: 937–54.

Sartre, J.-P. (1943), *L'Etre et le neant: Essai d'ontologie phénoménologique* (Paris: Librairie Gallimard).

Sartre, J.-P. (1966), *La Transcendance de l'Ego: Esquisse d'une Description Phénoménologique* (Paris: Librairie Philosophique J. Vrin).

Schutz, A. (1962), *The Problem of Social Reality: Collected Papers*, vol. 1 (The Hague: Martinus Nijhoff).

Schutz, A. (2004), *Der sinnhafte Aufbau der socialen Welt: Eine Einleitung in die verstehende Soziologie, Alfred Schütz Werkausgabe*, vol. 2 (Konstanz: UVK Verlagsgesellschaft).

Schutz, A. and Gurwitsch, A. (1989), *Philosophers in Exile: The Correspondence of Alfred Schutz and Aron Gurwitsch, 1939-1959* (Bloomington, IN: Indiana University Press).

Sokolowski, R. (1975), "The Work of Aron Gurwitsch," *Research in Phenomenology* 5: 7–10.

Spiegelberg, H. (1981). "Gurwitsch's Case against Husserl's Pure Ego," *Journal of the British Society for Phenomenology* 12/2: 104–14.

CHAPTER 15

··

SARTRE'S TRANSCENDENTAL PHENOMENOLOGY

··

JONATHAN WEBBER

In an interview toward the end of his life, Sartre describes how he came to study philosophy. In the final year of his preparation for the entrance exam for the École Normale Supérieure, a new teacher assigned some of Bergson's work for the students to read. Sartre was hooked. He had always wanted to write literary fiction and in Bergson's work he discovered that through philosophy he could study conscious experience "as a method and instrument for my literary works" (1981: 6). Although he soon came to realize that there was more to philosophy than this, the analysis of subjective experience remained central to his thought and writing throughout his life. But he never subscribed to Bergson's philosophy itself (1981: 7). It was almost a decade later that he first discovered a philosopher whose methods and descriptions of conscious experience he wanted to adopt. Aron, a friend from university and budding philosopher, introduced him to Husserl's phenomenology. Sartre was excited and arranged to spend a year in Berlin studying Husserl, but he was to be a little disappointed by this study.

Aron had convinced him that Husserl's philosophy would provide both the method he needed and the realist ontology to which he intuitively subscribed, but what Sartre found did not live up to this expectation (1981: 10, 25). Sartre's philosophical publications for the next ten years, culminating in *Being and Nothingness*, are thus marked by an apparent ambivalence toward Husserl's philosophy. In particular, Sartre seems ambivalent about the "transcendental turn" that Husserl's philosophy takes between the publication of *Logical Investigations* at the start of the century and the publication of *Ideas* just before the First World War. In the earlier work, Husserl develops a method of describing experience as it seems to the subject. His transcendental turn then consists of two innovations. One is the "phenomenological reduction," the principle that descriptions of conscious experience should not presuppose that its objects exist independently of it. The other is the use of transcendental arguments to establish factually necessary conditions of experience. Sartre does not reject Husserl's transcendental turn itself, but is critical of its philosophical results. In this chapter, we will see how this apparent ambivalence plays out across Sartre's philosophical publications until it is resolved in his own transcendental phenomenology.

15.1 THE PROBLEM OF THE TRANSCENDENTAL EGO

One of Sartre's first publications was a critical article on Husserl's transcendental philosophy published in the journal *Recherches Philosophiques* in 1936, later reissued as a book. It opens by contrasting Husserl's theories of the ego in *Logical Investigations* and in *Ideas*. In the first work, Sartre argues, Husserl understands the ego as an object of consciousness that transcends any given experience of it just as ordinary worldly objects do. The question Sartre poses is whether this is enough, or whether Husserl is right to add in *Ideas* a second ego, the transcendental ego, which is part of the structure of consciousness rather than an object of consciousness. Sartre does not disagree here with Husserl's transcendental turn itself. He accepts the methodology of the phenomenological reduction and the resulting view of consciousness as constituting the world of ordinary experience. His concern is only with whether this transcendental consciousness includes or relies on an ego (2004a: 4–5). The first part of the essay argues against this transcendental ego. The second analyzes the way the transcendent ego, the ego that is an object of consciousness, is constituted in experience. The work closes with some philosophical implications.

Our concern here is solely with the arguments of the first part, which address possible reasons for holding there to be a transcendental ego. One set argue that we have no experience of a transcendental ego. Unreflective consciousness of the world, argues Sartre, is entirely translucent. All we are aware of is our environment, with its objects and their meanings. There is no ego among these objects (2004a: 11–13). If there were an ego in the structure of the experience itself, then this experience would not be a translucent presentation of the world. For such an ego would have more to it than is presented in the experience. It would therefore be opaque, which is incompatible with it being a structure of a translucent experience (2004a: 7–9). In reflection on experience, we can glimpse an ego to which the experience is referred. This is the "I" of the "I think." But since this was not part of the experience reflected on, it is the transcendent ego constituted by reflection rather than a transcendental ego that underlies all experience (2004a: 11–15).

Whereas these arguments address the idea that phenomenology reveals a transcendental ego in experience, Sartre's second set address transcendental arguments that the transcendental ego is factually necessary for consciousness to have certain characteristics identified by phenomenology. Sartre's basic point here is that these characteristics are fully explained by features of conscious experience already identified by Husserl's phenomenology. That my experience at a given time is unified, rather than a set of discrete and disparate experiences, is explained, according to Sartre, by the intentional structure of consciousness. The various aspects of my experience are unified by being grouped around a single focal object of experience (2004a: 6). The unity of my experiences across time as a single flow of consciousness is explained, he argues, by the structure of each experience including some retention of prior experience (2004a: 6–7). The individuality of consciousness is a function of this synchronic and diachronic unity: The experiences unified in these ways form a "synthetic, individual totality, completely isolated from other totalities of the same kind" (2004a: 7). In these arguments, Sartre has reaffirmed the theory of the unity of consciousness that Husserl held before his transcendental turn (Levy 2016: 517–19).

Each of these arguments, as Sartre has presented them, stands in need of further support. Each of them can be subjected to critical scrutiny of both its phenomenological claims and the inferences drawn from those claims. But even if we were to grant these arguments, there would remain one powerful motivation for the transcendental ego. Sartre's analyses of the unity and individuality of consciousness concern the necessary conditions of experiencing my consciousness as unified and as individuated from the world and from other minds if there are any. But they do not address the necessary conditions of my experiencing these particular features of the world rather than any other, or indeed all, features of the world. Why is it that I can currently see the room from this perspective and not from other perspectives? Why do I never experience sudden discontinuities in perspective? The obvious answer would seem to be that there is a subject of experience, an entity with a particular point of perspective on the world, and that experiences belong to that subject even though it does not appear in those experiences. Thus, a transcendental argument can be formulated that identifies the transcendental subject as a factually necessary condition of the perspectival coherence and limitation of my experience.

This obvious answer might not be correct. However, what matters for our purposes is that none of Sartre's arguments against the transcendental ego even addresses this question. Why is this? It might be thought that this ontological question of why some experiences are bundled together as mine when other possible experiences are not part of that same bundle is ruled out by the phenomenological reduction. But the reduction requires only that the structures of conscious experience are described without the natural presupposition that its objects already exist independently of it. It therefore does not preclude the use of those descriptions as premises in transcendental arguments to ontological conclusions. Here we see an aspect of Sartre's ambivalence about Husserl's transcendental turn. He enthusiastically accepts the phenomenological reduction in this work and does not object to the idea of transcendental arguments (2004a: 2–5). But he is implacably opposed to the idea of a transcendental ego underlying experience, because he considers this to entail solipsism (2004a: 50). It is perhaps for this reason that he, knowingly or otherwise, ignores the obvious transcendental argument for the transcendental ego. This work therefore does not fulfill Sartre's ambition of establishing a transcendental phenomenology that repudiates the transcendental ego.

15.2 THE PUZZLE OF EMOTION

Sartre's ambivalence about Husserl's transcendental turn underlies two otherwise puzzling aspects of the phenomenological analyses of emotion and imagination that he published in the next few years. The first of these, *Sketch for a Theory of the Emotions*, appeared in 1939. As its title suggests, it is a short volume that does not attempt to offer a comprehensive theory. Instead, its introduction outlines the idea of a phenomenological clarification of the central concepts employed in empirical psychology, the first two chapters critique existing philosophical and psychoanalytic theories of emotion, and the third chapter provides phenomenological analyses of paradigm cases of emotion that are intended as preparatory work for a full phenomenological account. The puzzle concerns this third chapter. For most of this chapter, Sartre develops a single basic conception of emotion. Toward the end, he presents an example that seems to pose a problem for this conception, then argues that it does fit the conception. But it is not clear what problem he thinks this case seems to pose or why he thinks that it does not, after all, pose that problem.

According to the conception developed up to the point at which this example is introduced, an emotional experience is a response to a perceived difficulty in the world. In ordinary experience, the world appears to us as an instrumental complex, an arrangement of items governed by deterministic causal laws. In this context, we understand what we need to do in order to bring about our goals. But when this becomes too difficult, Sartre argues, when we cannot see our way to achieving a goal by the ordinary instrumental means, we may slip into the emotional attitude that treats the world as a magical realm (2002: 39–41). In this attitude, our behavior is aimed at bringing about the desired goal magically. To jump or dance with joy on hearing that a loved one will soon visit, for example, is to attempt by magical incantation to make the loved one arrive immediately, instead of having to wait (2002: 46–7). One does not reflectively choose to do this, or even notice that one is doing it, but nevertheless this is the structure of the emotional experience and behavior itself.

Sartre develops this conception through analyses of fainting in fear, fleeing in fear, becoming inactive through sadness, and bursting into tears, as well as jumping or dancing with joy (2002: 42–7). He argues that these are all essentially magical forms of behavior. But he then raises the problematic example. This conception, he argues, "does not explain the immediate reactions of horror and wonder that sometimes possess us when certain objects suddenly appear to us." In his primary example, "I am frozen with terror" when "a grimacing face suddenly appears pressed against the outside of the window" (2002: 55). Sartre goes on to argue that this is not a counterexample to the conception of emotion that he has been developing, but rather shows that there are two varieties of emotion. In his examples of fear, sadness, and joy, "it is we who constitute the magic of the world to replace a deterministic activity which cannot be realized," but in this case of terror the world "reveals itself suddenly as a magical environment" (2002: 57). This response is puzzling. Exactly how is it supposed to show that this case of terror fits the conception of emotion developed so far?

Sarah Richmond (2011, 2014) has argued that it fails to show this. On her reading, the initial conception held that emotion distorts the instrumental structure of the world by presenting it as magical rather than deterministic, but Sartre's analysis of the terror case is that here emotion reveals a magical aspect that the world does indeed possess. Richmond sees this example of the face appearing at the window as a proto-type of the theory of the "the look" that Sartre will develop a few years later in *Being and Nothingness*. The face at the window is magical, on Richmond's reading, because another consciousness is not part of the deterministic instrumental world. The other person is not simply an object that can be put to use in my pursuit of my goals. Rather, their goals structure their own experience of the world in ways that may be at odds with my experi-ence and my goals. On this reading, however, Sartre's analysis seems rather implausible. For most of us spend a large part of our waking lives in the presence of other people. We do not all spend all of that time frozen with terror, or indeed with a general background feeling of terror.

Anthony Hatzimoysis (2011: 72–7; 2014) offers a different interpretation. On his reading, Sartre uses the terror example to isolate one of the features of the conception of emotion developed so far as the essential feature. Hatzimoysis agrees with Richmond that the face at the window is immediately experienced as already having magical properties. It is experienced as threatening even though, as Sartre makes clear in his description, it is the face of someone shut outside the room and so unable to physically reach me. Hatzimoysis argues that Sartre's resulting theory holds the essence of emo-tion to be magical behavior, which can occur either in response to a difficulty in the instrumental world or in response to the appearance of some magical object. To freeze in terror, on this reading, is to attempt magically to freeze the whole world, in order to freeze the threat posed by the face at the window. But this reading too makes Sartre's theory seem implausible. For if the threat posed by the face at the window is merely a magical threat, then it would best be neutralized by affirming the ordinary instrumental attitude to the world. The resort to magically freezing the world is therefore unexplained.

15.3 THE PUZZLE OF IMAGINATION

Neither of these considerations against the interpretations offered by Richmond and Hatzimoysis seems conclusive. For it may simply be that the sketch for a theory of the emotions that Sartre offers here is deficient in one of these ways. However, important light can be shed on this puzzle by comparing it with a puzzle that arises toward the end of Sartre's next book, *The Imaginary*, in which he develops a detailed theory of imagi-nation. We will see that these two puzzles manifest Sartre's apparent ambivalence to-ward Husserl's transcendental turn at this stage of his philosophical career. Sartre opens *The Imaginary* with a characterization of the "irrealizing" structure of imagination that distinguishes it from the "realizing" structure of perception. He then presents analyses of a wide range of conscious experiences, from recognizing the person depicted in a portrait or an impersonation through to seeing images in schematic drawings or in random patterns, as forms of imagination. He articulates a common structure of these experiences and the further roles that structure plays, including in hallucinations and dreams. He maintains his initial distinction between imagination and perception throughout these analyses (see especially 2004b: 120–2). But then in the conclusion he claims that imagination is an essential aspect of perceptual experience, that "all apprehension of the real as a world implies a hidden surpassing toward the imaginary," so that there "could be no realizing consciousness," no perception, "without imaging consciousness" (2004b: 188). How should we understand this?

We need first to clarify Sartre's initial distinction. For this poses a smaller puzzle of its own. Sartre identifies four "characteristics" of imaginative experience (2004b: 5–14). First, to imagine is to have a particular kind of conscious experience intentionally directed at an object that is not itself an image in the mind. To imagine the Eiffel Tower is to have an experience intentionally directed at the Eiffel Tower, not at a mental image. Second, this kind of experience is "quasi-observation." Like observation, the object imagined is presented as from a particular perspective. Yet, unlike perception, I cannot learn about the object by changing my perspective. For imagination can only present to me aspects that I already know the object to have. Third, this kind of experience presents its object as non-existent, as absent, as existing elsewhere, or merely with no commitment to the object's existence. Perception, by contrast, presents its object as existing and present to observation. Fourth, imaginative experience includes "nonthetic" awareness of these characteristics. Although attention is focused on the object as it is imagined, this experience includes the sense that consciousness is constructing this object as it is imagined. Perceptual experience, by contrast, includes the sense that it is responding to the object of attention.

Sartre does not make clear in this passage precisely why he thinks that perception and imagination are the only two varieties of experience that present objects at all. He is clear that imagination and perception have the first and, at one level of description, the fourth characteristics in common. Both are intentional conscious experiences that include "nonthetic" awareness of their own structures. The content of this nonthetic awareness is different in the two cases only because this content is provided by the other structures of the experience, which are different in the two cases. But this seems to leave two structures of imagination that distinguish it from perception. If imagination has both of these characteristics and perception has neither, then why should there not be two more kinds of experience, a form of quasi-observation that posits its object as present and existing, and a form of observation that does not posit its object as present and existing? If there could not be such forms of conscious experience, then that must be because the second and third characteristics of imagination mutually entail one another. Sartre has not, however, given us reason to agree that they do so.

Whatever the explanation of this mutual entailment, we can now see what is so puzzling about Sartre's claims in the Conclusion that imagination is involved in all perception. For he has defined these kinds of experience in a way that seems to make them mutually incompatible. They differ not in whether their intentional object exists independently of the experience. You can imagine something that you know to exist, as when you form a mental image of the Eiffel Tower or see your brother in a photo. The difference is rather that perception tracks qualities that it finds in its object, whereas imagination specifies its object by specifying some of its qualities. This is not to say that there is no part of the world directly present in imaginative experience. It is to say only that the part of the world present in the experience is not the intentional object of the experience. When seeing the impressionist Franconay impersonate Chevalier, it is Franconay who is present in my experience, but the intentional object of my imaginative experience is Chevalier. When you see your brother in the photo, you are having an imaginative experience of your brother that rests on the presence of the photo.

Sartre uses the term "analogon" for this item present in imaginative experience without being its intentional object. This idea derives from Husserl's comments on imagination and aesthetic experience in the context of his transcendental turn, but Sartre rejects Husserl's theory that in mental imagery this role is played by subjective contents internal to the experience itself (2012: 129–42; 2004b: 29, 59; Stawarska 2013: 25–8). Sartre proposes that where one cannot switch from the imaginative attitude to perceiving the analogon, as one can switch from imagining Chevalier through Franconay's mime to simply watching Franconay, the nature of the analogon is beyond the scope of phenomenology and must be investigated empirically (2004b: 52–3). Here we find again Sartre's ambivalence about Husserl's transcendental turn: The explication of imagination cannot be completed within the confines of the phenomenological reduction, but requires an empirical psychology that embodies the natural attitude. Full justification for this must await his resolution of that ambivalence. But consideration of Sartre's view of the analogon does clarify the puzzle raised by the Conclusion of *The Imaginary*. If the intentional object of perception is present and tracked by consciousness, but the intentional object of imagination is specified by consciousness using a present object as an analogon, then how can imagination be essential to the structure of perception?

15.4 RESOLVING THE PUZZLES OF IMAGINATION AND EMOTION

One way to resolve this puzzle in *The Imaginary* is by deflationary historical explanation. For this book has its origins in a larger work that Sartre had written a few years earlier. He had been invited to write a book that would trace the history of theories of the imagination in modern philosophy and psychology, articulate the basic problems that theories of imagination need to overcome, and present some original theoretical contributions. The manuscript he submitted did not fit the publisher's brief. It was far too long and was dominated by the development of his own philosophical theory. The publisher took only the first part of the manuscript, a conceptual history of modern philosophy and psychology of the imagination, and published it as Sartre's first book, *The Imagination*, in 1936. The rest formed the majority of *The Imaginary* four years later (Beauvoir 1965: 201, 208, 212). It is tempting to infer that the conclusion to *The Imaginary* was written some time later than the rest of the book, at which point Sartre was moving toward the more sophisticated ontology of the perceived world that he later articulated in *Being and Nothingness*, and therefore does not really form part of the book's central theory at all.

However, this deflationary explanation overlooks the parallel between this puzzle at the end of *The Imaginary* and the one at the end of *Sketch for a Theory of the Emotions*, published a year earlier. Sartre ends each book arguing for a philosophical claim that seems not to fit the preceding theory. In the case of *The Imaginary*, the argument of the conclusion is of a different kind to those in the preceding work. The first part of the book employs phenomenological reflection to identify the structures of imagination. Sartre says very little about his method here (2004b: 5). But it is clear from his earlier book on imagination that he intends to deploy the phenomenological reduction in order to isolate the essential structures of imagination (2012: 125–9, 141–2). The next three parts of the book engage critically with empirical psychology to develop a full theory of imagination that enshrines this phenomenological analysis. But the conclusion then develops transcendental arguments that aim to identify structures that consciousness itself must have in order for imagination to have the structures that phenomenology has revealed it to have.

These transcendental arguments are presented very concisely and Sartre is clear that they raise further questions. Yet they do seem to form a natural part of the book. For the first of them shows that the book's grounding phenomenological theory already implicitly carries a commitment to a transcendental condition. According to that theory, imaginative acts require some part of the material world present to consciousness to function as an analogon. For consciousness to be able to imagine, therefore, requires that a material world is present to it. Imagination requires the ability to transcend the present object in order to posit the imagined object for which the present object serves as an analogon, in contrast to the perceptual attitude that focuses on the present object itself to track its characteristics (2004b: 182–4). Both attitudes require the presence of an object whose existence is independent of one's attitude toward it. The presence of a material world is therefore a transcendental condition of imagination throughout the book. Sartre has simply not drawn out this implication until the conclusion.

It is the next step that gives rise to the puzzle. Sartre argues that the shift from the perceptual attitude to the imaginative attitude is motivated by features of the perceived world. Sartre's example prefigures one of the most famous passages of *Being and Nothingness*: "For my friend Pierre to be given to me as absent, I must have been led to grasp the world as a whole such that Pierre cannot *currently* be present in it *for me*" (2004b: 185; compare 2003: 33–5). If perception were limited to tracking its objects, then it could not motivate the shift to imagination. Perception must rather reveal a world shaped by imaginative expectation or desire. Sartre here introduces one of the central concepts of his existentialism: "situation," meaning the world as perceived in light of something absent (2004b: 185). Perception is infused with imagination in the sense that an imagined goal is required to motivate perceptual exploration and classification of the features of the world (2004b: 186–7). The puzzle arises only if we mistakenly assume that this requires that imaginative and perceptual attitudes occur simultaneously, rather than that perception constitutes its world in light of prior acts of imagination (2004b: 188). (For more a more detailed explanation of this resolution of this puzzle, see Webber forthcoming-c.)

The puzzle at the end of *Sketch for a Theory of the Emotions* has a parallel structure. The main text of *The Imaginary* concerns the structure of familiar imaginative and perceptual experiences, but the conclusion is concerned with the transcendental constitution of the world. Likewise, the central theory of *Sketch* concerns the structure of familiar emotional events in response to the world as already constituted, but Sartre's analysis of the problematic example of terror at the sudden appearance of a face at the window concerns emotion as a feature of the transcendental constitution of the world. The face at the window appears suddenly and its owner's intentions are unclear. This disrupts the transcendental activity of constituting an instrumental world of deterministic relations between objects. We cannot make instrumental sense of the scene until we have some idea of that person's intentions. We therefore cannot constitute our world. So we are incapacitated and remain transfixed on the face at the window until it provides the information that allows us to understand what is happening, which is required for us to return to the instrumental attitude. (For more a more detailed explanation of this resolution of this puzzle, see Webber forthcoming-b.)

15.5 Sartre's Transcendental Turn

In his *Sketch for a Theory of the Emotions*, therefore, Sartre sketches the basic features of strong emotional events as departures from the usual instrumental attitude toward the world. He primarily sketches intense emotional events that occur when the world becomes too difficult, so that the instrumental attitude is abandoned. But he then closes by sketching the kinds of emotional event that occur when the instrumental attitude itself cannot be maintained because some part of the world cannot be subsumed into it. This turn from the phenomenological features of familiar empirical experiences of the world to a concern with the transcendental constitution of the world of ordinary perception also occurs at the end of *The Imaginary*, though there it is more explicit. The majority of this book is concerned with the structure and roles of imagination in a world that is already constituted, but the conclusion then considers the role of imagination in the transcendental constitution of that world. Why are these two books both structured in this way? Why does their turn to transcendental constitution only occur at the end? And why does Sartre only deal with this transcendental constitution so comparatively briefly?

The answer to these questions is that Sartre considers himself to have reached the proper limits of phenomenological psychology. For a theory of the transcendental constitution of the world requires an explanation of why this transcendental power is restricted in certain ways. To elaborate his idea that terror can be the manifestation of the inability to constitute the world, Sartre would need to explain how it is that the power of transcendental consciousness to constitute the world is limited in this way. Having argued that perception is not the passive absorption of information, but is rather the transcendental constitution of the perceived world, Sartre owes an explanation of how this transcendental constitution differs from the imagination's construction of its objects, and in particular of why perception is limited in ways that imagination is not. In short, once he has raised the transcendental issue, Sartre needs to turn his philosophical attention from the structures of experience to the structures of reality itself. His theories in phenomenological psychology cannot be fully elaborated without a theory that explains which features of the world are mind-dependent and which are mind-independent.

This also explains why Sartre's earlier work, *The Transcendence of the Ego*, fails to address the question of why these particular experiences are bundled together as mine. We have seen that Sartre does not even consider in that work the transcendental argument that a transcendental ego is required to explain this. He seems not even to see that there is anything here to be explained. He considers himself to have established that there is no transcendental ego within the structures of consciousness itself, as we have seen, which is to say that a transcendental ego cannot be accepted within the constraints of phenomenological psychology. The transcendental argument that a transcendental ego is nevertheless necessary for the inherent perspectival coherence and limitation of perceptual experience has its premises established by phenomenological psychology but draws an ontological conclusion about reality itself. Our resolution of the puzzles of emotion and imagination suggests that the reason Sartre ignores this transcendental argument for the transcendental ego is precisely that he does not consider such an inference legitimate in the absence of a more general consideration of the ontology of reality.

Sartre's turn from phenomenological psychology in these works to the phenomenological ontology of *Being and Nothingness*, published three years after *The Imaginary*, is therefore the completion of his own transcendental turn. In this work, he accuses Husserl of a form of ontological idealism that constitutes the world out of subjective mental items (2003: 17). He considers such a theory to be an embarrassment to philosophy, since it leaves unexplainable how it is that the world is not entirely under my control, how it is that things can resist my efforts, or, to put it another way, why there are limits to the power of transcendental consciousness to constitute the world (2003: 3–4, 17–18). Echoing his earlier rejection of Husserl's theory that mental imagery is founded on subjective contents internal to experience, Sartre traces the root of this failure to account for the objectivity of the world to Husserl's unrestricted application of his phenomenological reduction (2003: 6, 28). Sartre's earlier apparent ambivalence about Husserl's transcendental turn is resolved by this rejection of what he considers to be

Husserl's insistence that the phenomenological reduction constrain the conclusions of transcendental arguments as well as their premises.

For this rejection facilitates Sartre's "radical reversal of the idealist position" (2003: 239). Where the idealism that he ascribes to Husserl's transcendental philosophy leaves the world dependent on the mind, Sartre's own ontology construes the mind as dependent on the world. Sartre wants to establish and elaborate it through a series of transcendental arguments that aim to establish that certain mind-independent features of the world are necessary for consciousness to have the structures that it has. His first transcendental argument of this kind, which appears in the Introduction to *Being and Nothingness*, aims to establish the brute mind-independent existence of the objects of consciousness as a necessary condition of the intentional structure that phenomenology, within the constraints of the phenomenological reduction, reveals consciousness to have. This is a particularly abstruse passage and there are various ways its argument might be reconstructed. But its outline is clear: Sartre intends to establish first the phenomenological claim that intentionality is the basic structure of consciousness, then show that the being-in-itself of the objects of perceptual experience is a necessary condition of consciousness having this structure (see especially 2003: 16–19; see also 2003: 198–200).

This is a distinctively Sartrean kind of transcendental argument. The premise is not intended to be an indisputable starting point. Sartre intends rather to show that it would be accepted by anyone who attends to their own experience without theoretical prejudice (Morris 2016: 208–13; Williford 2016: 84–8). What makes it a transcendental argument is that its conclusion claims to identify a factually necessary condition of our experience having the structure described in this premise that accurately captures our experience (Eshleman 2016: 180–1). In this case, the conclusion concerns the ontological structure of reality itself as well as the ontological structure of our consciousness of reality. It asserts that "consciousness arises oriented toward a being which is not itself" (2003: 17). Perceptual experience is essentially structured, that is to say, as an intentional relation to an object whose being does not depend on its being the object of any experience. (For more a more detailed explanation of this argument and its place in Sartre's response to Husserl, see Webber forthcoming-a.)

15.6 SARTRE'S PHENOMENOLOGICAL ONTOLOGY

Sartre's basic phenomenological ontology of consciousness and being-in-itself is thus motivated, at least partly, by the need to complete his theories of phenomenological psychology. For those theories are incomplete without an account of the basic ontology underlying the transcendental constitution of the world. But we can also discern a relation of dependence in the opposite direction. Any theory of the transcendental structures that underlie our experience of the familiar world faces a methodological problem: How can we have the conceptual capacities required to adequately describe those transcendental structures? Concepts whose content is provided by empirical experience would seem to describe only that already constituted empirical reality. Concepts whose content is specifically given by the transcendental structures themselves would seem unintelligible, except perhaps to specialists able to discern those structures directly in phenomenological reflection, but such concepts might anyway be otiose for such experts. Sartre's solution is to develop phenomenological conceptualizations of emotional and imaginative experiences that should be recognizable to anyone who has those experiences, then to model the transcendental activity of consciousness using those conceptualizations. His transcendental phenomenological ontology is thus conceptually and methodologically dependent on his phenomenological psychology.

Sartre uses his conceptualization of the imagination to articulate his claim that the world of everyday experience is shaped by our projects. Upon entering the café where I expect to meet Pierre, he argues, I may suddenly be struck by his absence. It is not that I perceive all of the things that are present and then infer that Pierre is not there. Rather, in my direct unreflective experience itself, "Pierre absent haunts this café" (2003: 34). Although I experience objects that exist independently of me, chairs and tables and crockery and bodies that have their being in themselves, the sense they have for me is provided by my imagination. This is not to say that the café and its objects function as an analogon for me to imagine Pierre, but that my prior act of imagination, my expectation, motivates and organizes my perceptual experience. Likewise, the meaning that I experience when my alarm clock rings or when a sign says "keep off the grass" depends on my own projects, on the goals that I have set. Perception organizes my world in the light of something that is not, something I have imagined (2003: 61–3, 221–3, 459).

Sartre draws on his earlier conceptualization of affectivity to describe a further dimension of this transcendental constitution of the world. Negative affective reactions such as disgust, he argues, manifest a dissonance between the mind-independent reality of some aspect of the world and my projects, the goals that I have set in imagination and am pursuing. Where some object is an obstacle to my goal or in some way demonstrates the impossibility of reality matching my imagined ideal, that object has a negative affective tenor for me (2003: 631–2). Similarly, the realization that I am perceived in some way that clashes with my own preferred self-image is experienced as shame (2003: 284–6). Conversely, when some feature of my imagined ideal is confirmed, the relevant feature of the world is perceived with a positive affective tenor. If someone admires some feature of me and this is a feature I aspire to have, then I feel pride (2003: 314). This idea of affectivity deploys the conception of magic developed in *Sketch for a Theory of the Emotions*, even though he no longer uses the word "magic" to describe this (Richmond 2011: 157).

The descriptions of emotional events in *Sketch* therefore develop concepts that Sartre then uses to describe this aspect of the transcendental constitution of the world. But this role of the magical in the world as transcendentally constituted does not entail that there is any magic in reality independently of our constitution of the world. Indeed, if we can account for any apparent magical features of the experienced world as products of this transcendental constitution, then we have no reason to hold that theoretical explanations of the construction of reality or of the workings of the mind need to be incomplete. It is perhaps for this reason that Sartre redeploys the term "magic" in *Being and Nothingness* as a pejorative term to describe the explanatory inadequacy that he finds in various scientific theories. His point is that theories fail when they retain some of this magical thinking that is very naturally encouraged by the role of magic in the transcendentally constituted world. But it is therefore mistaken to read this use of the term "magic" as an early deconstructionist denial of the opposition between science and primitive magical thinking (Richmond 2011: 159).

Having argued that being in-itself is necessary for consciousness, Sartre presents further instances of his distinctive kind of transcendental argument to contend that certain essential features of conscious experience, such as space and time, are mind-independent features of being-in-itself (2003: 202–3, 205–9, 220–1, 239–41). His claim at the end of the introduction that one can say of being-in-itself only that it is, it is in-itself, and it is what it is, only amounts to a "preliminary examination" (2003: 22). These arguments later in the book concerning the structures of being-in-itself license the assumption made in *The Imaginary* that the empirical sciences can identify features of the world or of the body whose inherent articulation makes them suitable analogons for mental imagery. Likewise, they license the assumption made in *Sketch for a Theory of the Emotions* that reality can frustrate my desires or even my ability to make sense of the world because it is already structured independently of my experience of it. Finally, they allow Sartre to solve the problem he left unaddressed in *The Transcendence of the Ego*. The necessary condition of the inherent perspectivality of my experience of the world is indeed that there is an ego underlying and unifying experience, but this does not lead to the problem of solipsism because this ego, the mind's "substance and its perpetual condition of possibility" (2003: 361), is my publicly observable body (Morris 1985: 187–9).

15.7 A New Problem

The transcendental phenomenological methodology that Sartre employs in *Being and Nothingness* therefore allows him to solve the problem left unaddressed in *The Transcendence of the Ego* and to articulate fully both the idea of affectivity sketched in *Sketch for a Theory of the Emotions* and the role of imagination in perceptual experience indicated briefly at the end of *The Imaginary*. This is the method of analyzing the structures of consciousness within the constraint of the phenomenological reduction, but drawing ontological conclusions from those analyses by means of transcendental arguments that are not constrained by the phenomenological reduction. This is why *Being and Nothingness* marks the end of Sartre's explicit critical dialogue with Husserl. The ideas established in these works of phenomenological psychology and phenomenological ontology continue to develop through his publications for the rest of his life. But the ambivalence about Husserl's transcendental turn that drove the development of the phenomenology and ontology articulated in *Being and Nothingness* has been resolved in that work. The next stage of the evolution of Sartre's philosophy is driven by a new problem, one that arises from this phenomenological ontology.

For the idea that consciousness is essentially embodied seems to be in tension with the idea that consciousness is insubstantial. The claim that consciousness is essentially embodied is crucial to Sartre's rejection of the idea that a private inner self, a publicly inaccessible ego, lies behind consciousness (2003: 370–1). Yet the claim that consciousness is insubstantial forms part of Sartre's transcendental argument for the mind-independent existence of being-in-itself. Sartre argues that the experience of nothingness in the world, as when we experience the absence of Pierre in the café, is possible only because consciousness itself is a nothingness (2003: 51–2). And consciousness could be a nothingness, could have no substance of its own, only if its intentionality is a relation to an object that exists independently of it (2003: 17). This argument for the being-in-itself of the objects of consciousness, moreover, is required for the argument that the body is the unifying seat of consciousness. This apparent tension is therefore at the core of Sartre's phenomenological ontology. How could consciousness be both insubstantial and embodied? How could it be both nothingness and essentially grounded in the region of being-in-itself that makes up the body?

This problem is sharpened in Sartre's theory of the role of projects in shaping the transcendental constitution of the world. It is these goals and values that give direction to the perceptual activity of tracking the features of the regions of being-in-itself that are present in experience. The instrumental and affective structures of the world of experience, as we have seen, are determined by the relation between the present objects and the individual's projects. Yet the theory that consciousness is itself insubstantial seems to render this function of projects mysterious. For according to Sartre's theory of radical freedom, consciousness cannot be influenced by being-in-itself, or by anything else, precisely because consciousness is insubstantial (2003: 52–8). How, then, can it be influenced by the individual's projects? Sartre's view is that projects have no substance of their own. They persist only insofar as the individual continues to uphold them (2003: 54–5). They therefore have no inertia and carry no influence over consciousness that does not derive from consciousness itself. The individual can simply overthrow any existing project, or even their whole set of projects, at any time and without their projects providing any motivation to do so (2003: 497–8).

What is mysterious about this theory is that it is not at all clear what pursuing a project amounts to. Sartre is quite clear that one need not ever have explicitly formulated the goal or value at the heart of the project, need never have explicitly decided to pursue the project, since all that is required is that one orients one's activities toward this goal or value (2003: 459). But what is this spatial metaphor of orientation intended to indicate here? What is it to develop a commitment to some goal or value without explicitly thinking about it? One option offered by the idea of the embodiment of consciousness is that the pursuit of a project is a matter of the gradual sedimentation of the relevant goal or value in the neural and physiological structures of one's body. But the ultimate purpose of Sartre's claim that consciousness is insubstantial seems to be to rule out the body having this kind of influence over the individual's projects, since such influence would be incompatible with Sartre's idea of radical freedom.

Although the idea of sedimentation is usually most associated with Sartre's friend and colleague Merleau-Ponty, his book *Phenomenology of Perception* (2012) focuses on the sedimentation of various kinds of knowledge and raises the possibility of sedimented motivations only briefly and speculatively toward the end in a passage directed against Sartre's theory of freedom (2012: 461–7). It is Beauvoir rather than Merleau-Ponty who clearly affirms and thoroughly explores the idea that the goals and values at the core of an individual's projects are gradually sedimented through cognition and action (see especially 2009: 293–351, 653–80). Her theory explains what it is to pursue a project, how projects come to shape our perceptions of the world, and how a project fulfills this function even if the individual is unaware of it, but also implies that a project can continue to fulfill this function even when the individual has explicitly rejected it, so long as that rejection has not itself yet become sedimented sufficiently to displace it (Webber 2018: chs 4, 5). Beauvoir's theory fits well with Sartre's view of consciousness as essentially embodied, but is inconsistent with his theory of the insubstantiality of consciousness and its radical freedom. The development of Sartre's philosophy in the years following the publication of *Being and Nothingness* is partly driven by this problem, which is resolved only when he finally accepts Beauvoir's theory of projects (Webber 2018: ch. 7). By this point, however, the methodology of transcendental phenomenology and the resulting philosophical ontology are no longer central to his philosophical concerns.

References

Beauvoir, S. de (1965), *The Prime of Life*, translated by P. Green (Harmondsworth: Penguin).

Beauvoir, S. de (2009), *The Second Sex*, translated by C. Borde and S. Malovany-Chevalier (London: Jonathan Cape).

Eshleman, M. (2016), "A sketch of Sartre's error theory of introspection," in S. Miguens, G. Preyer, and C. Bravo Morando (eds), *Pre-Reflective Consciousness: Sartre and Contemporary Philosophy of Mind* (London: Routledge), 176–207.

Hatzimoysis, A. (2011), *The Philosophy of Sartre* (Durham: Acumen).

Hatzimoysis, A. (2014), "Consistency in Sartre's Theory of Emotion," *Analysis* 74/1: 81–3.

Levy, L. (2016), "Intentionality, Consciousness, and the Ego: The Influence of Husserl's *Logical Investigations* on Sartre's Early Work," *The European Legacy* 21: 511–24.

Merleau-Ponty, M. (2102), *Phenomenology of Perception*, translated by D. A. Landes (London: Routledge).

Morris, K. (2016), "Sartre's method: Philosophical therapy or transcendental argument?" in S. Baiasu (ed.), *Comparing Kant and Sartre* (Basingstoke: Palgrave), 197–216.

Morris, P. S. (1985), "Sartre on the Transcendence of the Ego," *Philosophy and Phenomenological Research* 46: 179–98.

Richmond, S. (2011), "Magic in Sartre's early philosophy," in J. Webber (ed.), *Reading Sartre: On Phenomenology and Existentialism* (London: Routledge), 145–60.

Richmond, S. (2014), "Inconsistency in Sartre's Theory of Emotion," *Analysis* 74/4: 612–15.

Sartre, J.-P. (1981), "An Interview with Jean-Paul Sartre: Interview by M. Rybalka, O. Pucciani, and S. Gruenheck (Paris, May 12 and 19, 1975)," translated by S. Gruenheck, in P. A. Schilpp (ed.), *The Philosophy of Jean-Paul Sartre* (La Salle: Open Court), 3–51.

Sartre, J.-P. (2002), *Sketch for a Theory of the Emotions*, translated by P. Mairet (London: Routledge).

Sartre, J.-P. (2003), *Being and Nothingness: An Essay in Phenomenological Ontology*, translated by H. Barnes, edited by A. Elkaïm-Sartre (London: Routledge. Original first published in 1943).

Sartre, J.-P. (2004a), *The Transcendence of the Ego: A Sketch for a Phenomenological Description*, translated by A. Brown (London: Routledge).

Sartre, J.-P. (2004b), *The Imaginary: A Phenomenological Psychology of the Imagination*, translated by J. Webber (London: Routledge).

Sartre, J.-P. (2012), *The Imagination*, translated by K. Williford and D. Rudrauf (London: Routledge).

Stawarska, B. (2013), "Sartre and Husserl's *Ideen*: Phenomenology and imagination," in S. Churchill and J. Reynolds (eds), *Jean-Paul Sartre: Key Concepts* (Durham: Acumen), 12–31.

Webber, J. (2018), *Rethinking Existentialism* (Oxford: Oxford University Press).

Webber, J. (forthcoming-a), "Sartre's Critique of Husserl."

Webber, J. (forthcoming-b), "Sartre's Sketch for a Theory of the Emotions."

Webber, J. (forthcoming-c), "Sartre's phenomenological psychology of the imagination," in M. Eshleman and K. Morris (eds), *The Sartrean Mind* (London: Routledge).

Williford, K. (2016), "Degrees of self-presence: Rehabilitating Sartre's accounts of pre-reflective self-consciousness and reflection," in S. Miguens, G. Preyer, and C. Bravo Morando (eds), *Pre-Reflective Consciousness: Sartre and Contemporary Philosophy of Mind* (London: Routledge), 66–100.

CHAPTER 16

....

THE LATER SARTRE

*From Phenomenology to Hermeneutics
to Dialectic and Back*

....

THOMAS R. FLYNN

WHERE do we draw the line? Is it a matter of chronology: The move from an intellectually aggressive youth, willing to risk an injection of mescaline in order to experience the world of hallucination from the "inside"? Or the young Turk who "corrected" the phenomenology of Husserl even as he sang its praises and adopted its method? Clearly the move to the "Later Sartre" must attend to the methodological shift from what Sartre called "a rationalist philosophy of consciousness" (Sartre 1974: 41; Flynn 2014: 289) to one of "praxis" (purposive human activity in its sociohistorical context). This includes the move from the individual to the group, from the psychological and the ontological to the interpersonal and the political. The shift from early to late must acknowledge the application of "existential psychoanalysis" to increasingly large "biographies" chiefly of literary figures. And any account must respect the various expressions of philosophical insight conveyed in literary and other artistic modes. Sartre was, after all, a Nobel Prize designate in Literature even if he declined the honor.

Perhaps the most prudent approach to distinguishing the "later" from the early Sartre is to follow Sartre's own assessment of the phenomenon of his life when he confesses: "I've changed like everyone: within a permanence" (Flynn 2014: 377). We are challenged to determine what would emerge as permanent in this assessment. That would include Sartre's *existentialism*, of course, as well as its related *"ethical"* dimension. Sartre was ever the moralist but (almost) never a moralizer. One of the points of his existentialist shift was to locate and assess the moral responsibility of "free organic praxes," as he insisted in the *Critique of Dialectical Reason*, whether alone or, more likely, dispersed in series or gathered in groups. Next and of equal significance to any would-be permanence is the role of *the imaginary* that permeates his thought from its robust origin in psychological works of the 1930s and its flowering in *Nausea* (1938), *Being and Nothingness* (1943), theater and literary criticism in the 1940s and 1950s to its weakening but not disappearance in his later "realist" politics while fellow-traveling with the French Communist Party from 1952 to 1956. The latter, we should note, he justified "on [his] principles, not theirs" (1968: 68).

The question that concerns us here is whether what passes as "phenomenology" belongs to what is permanent in Sartre's thought or if it has been set aside methodologically in favor of other approaches to human life that mark his reflections later in life. What I wish to exhibit and critique from this initial survey of Sartre's philosophical positions and works throughout his later years is the career of his phenomenological thought after its apparent replacement by other approaches in the ensuing years. I shall pursue these alternatives to what I take to be classical (constitutive) Husserlian phenomenology[1] in several steps that lead to its eclipse and final reappearance in full view in what could be considered his all-encompassing work, the biography of the major nineteenth-century French novelist, Gustave Flaubert, *The Family Idiot*.

Let me begin with this caveat: what we will find is not a zero-sum game. The absence of explicit phenomenological discourse and argumentation does not mean its complete repudiation. Some of the abiding values and motives of Sartrean thought have not been repudiated as his perspective changes with the search of alternative methods to resolve new problems. The "existentialist" dimension of his thought continues in his abiding interest in individual responsibility, not just causal but moral. In accord with his developing social consciousness, he does admit to his Maoist discussants later in life that the individual alone is powerless to effect social change (see Sartre, Gavi, and Victor 1974c: 171). And the new challenge is to ground a philosophy of history, one that generates a more "supple dialectic" in contrast with the mechanical causality of what he dismisses as neo-Marxist "economism."

16.1 PHENOMENOLOGY AND DIALECTIC: APPARENT CONFLICT

While phenomenology as an eidetic science originated with Husserl's critic of psychologism (the attempt to reduce logic into empirical psychology), in his *Logical Investigations* (1900–1), the various forms of phenomenology, if distinguished into realist, transcendental, existential, and hermeneutic, already appear in the 1920s. The initial appearance in Sartre's thought of conflict between phenomenological insights and dialectical promotion occurs in the only address Sartre ever gave to the French Philosophical Society (*La Société française de philosophie*, June 2, 1947). In an attempt to be irenic, he seemed to catch himself in an inconsistency: defending phenomenological apodicticity while

---

[1] I'm using the classification of phenomenologies into "realist," "constitutive," "existentialist," and "hermeneutical" (see Embree 1997: 2–5).

proposing a quasi-Hegelian "becoming truth." Agreeing that "truth is becoming," Sartre explains:

> It is necessary to arrange a synthesis of the contemplative and nondialectic consciousness of Husserl, who leads us to the contemplation of essences, with the activity of the dialectical project—but without consciousness, and hence without foundation—that we find in Heidegger, where we see on the contrary, that the first element is transcendence. (Sartre 1967: 132)

What would the locus/instrument of that synthesis be? Consciousness itself, perhaps in its prereflective or nonthetic and reflective dimensions? That would seem to award the palm to the *Cogito* or some version thereof. But could this unifying factor be the dialectic itself? That would clearly favor the conative feature of dialectical reason and invite images of F. H. Bradley's Absolute as a cave with all tracks leading in. We seem to face a dilemma not new to epistemology and perhaps an invitation to the services of the *comprehension* of hyermeneutical phenomenology which does seem to favor a certain understanding (*Verstehen*) that Sartre finds attractive in such a paradoxical situation.

Continuing his conversation with the philosophers, Sartre underscores the dichotomy:

> I believe we can have both: a becoming truth and, nevertheless, a certitude such that one can judge. And I believe that if one reintegrates temporality into the categories, that is, if one notices that the grasp of consciousness by reflection is not the grasp of consciousness of a snapshot, but of a reality which has a past and a future, then a temporal truth is possible, often probable, but it sometimes carries an apodicticity which does not depend on the totality of history or the sciences. (1965: 136)[2]

This apodicticity seems to be a quality of judgments that are not temporal but instantaneous—like the "Aha" experience or if not that, at least pragmatically necessitated. Sartre rightly raises the problem of the criterion because, if truth is becoming, it would seem to require that we would know the meaning or value of an act or event only at the end of the process. Yet, he objects, that means that we could not make secure judgments regarding Hitler's evil actions, for example, until all the evidence was gathered, which might never happen. Discounting such sophisms, Sartre "calls the question," as it were, insisting that "we need criteria both for action and for life in general. We need certitudes" (1965: 135).

Already in *Being and Nothingness* Sartre was committed to an "existentialist" phenomenology *avant la lettre* when he speaks of *Angst* and *Boredom* as "phenomena of being." These nonconceptual modes of access to Being can be seen as dramatic forms of Merleau-Ponty's noteworthy claim that a complete reduction is impossible. In effect,

---

[2] One is reminded of Sartre's remark about Foucault's "structuralist" approach to historical understanding: where history is best recounted as a moving picture Foucault offers us a slide-show.

you cannot "reduce" the reducer. So the "phenomenological reduction" that had worked in his earlier studies of emotions and imagination was not going to be adequate for *Being and Nothingness*, optimistically subtitled "An Essay on Phenomenological Ontology." In fact, he already introduced a "hermeneutic" for interpreting the phenomena of individual existence in his "Existential Psychoanalysis" (Sartre 1974: 568–9). This will grow as he speaks of "pre-ontological comprehension" (*Verstehen*) of numerous objects (Flynn 1984: 233 n. 13).

Before considering works and actions that sought to "synthesize" the various dualities that punctuate his thought, let us mark some of those dualities themselves. On the initial side of the line between early and late Sartre but permeating his writings is the ontological–metaphysical duality of being–nothingness, haunted by the duality of spontaneity–inertia. If the former is of Cartesian inspiration, the latter can be traced to Henri Bergson, the philosopher whose *Time and Free Will* reportedly inspired Sartre to choose the path of philosophy over the way of literature (without abandoning the latter, as we shall see: another duality worth consideration). Spontaneity and even inertia, appear in Sartre's vocabulary before being-in-itself and -for-itself (see Sartre 2002: 78, 84; 2004: 25, 42). Admittedly in *Being and Nothingness*, Sartre remarks: "There is nothing more incomprehensible than the principle of inertia" (1974a: lvi). Yet in the *Critique*, he grants that the *practico*-inert is "the intelligible limit to intelligibility" (2004: 94). The practico-inert replaces being-in-itself in the *Critique*, though the two terms emerge in Sartre's last great work, the Flaubert study, *The Family Idiot*. This is one of many indications of the return of phenomenology, both classical and hermeneutical, in the Flaubert book.

Another major duality that marks his writings is the means–end dichotomy that distinguishes and unites politics and ethics in Sartre's later thought. Though confessing to a certain "amoral realism" during his four years of fellow-traveling with the French Communist Party, which he never joined, Sartre was no consequentialist (which he called "Machiavellian") except in the service of revolution against an oppressive and exploitive regime. In such a case, he considered violent resistance to be "counter-violence" that was justified as a last resort. In effect, as the title of one study put it, Sartre's position on violence was "curiously ambivalent." In fact, one can find a virtual treatise on violence, usually of the Fascist sort, in Sartre's posthumously published *Notebooks for an Ethics* (*Ethics*) (1992: 170–215). Though he opposed its publication in his lifetime due to its "idealist" tendencies (presumably in the Marxian sense of downplaying socioeconomic factors as decisive in the process as well as for its individualism), *Ethics* offers the features of invitation–response and positive reciprocity among individuals that *Being and Nothingness* seemed to exclude except for two promissory footnotes (1974a: 70 n. 9, 412 n. 14).

The last of many dualities that qualifies Sartre's social ontology and its corresponding ethic and a refinement of the means–end dichotomy is *fraternity–terror* (*violence*). If violence, under at least one description, is interiorized scarcity, terror might be described as "a state of intense fright" occasioned by the threat of scarcity. But the duality assumes a sharper edge with the solemn commitment that seals the pact. The pledge that unites the members as "the same" in practical commitment is sealed by a collective action against serial dissolution: I give you the right to kill me for treachery. Hence the duality of fraternity–terror: brotherhood is mediated by violence, the risk of death psychologized by a state of terror. "But this terror, as long as unity has not been destroyed by circumstances, is a terror *which unites* rather than a terror which separates" (2004b: 434). Thus Sartre can describe terror as "self-induced fear" that serves as "self-imposed inertia" for the organized group (see Flynn 1984: 116).

This comes to a head in Sartre's discussion of the "Statutory group" in *Critique of Dialectical Reason* and the writings that followed it, culminating in his interviews with Benny Lévy. There he seems to acknowledge that he had never succeed in reconciling this duality (see 1996: 93), conceding that violence was "almost a necessary evil" (1996: 95) in such projects—not exactly a reconciliation. The model of that duality, cited in the *Critique*, is what we may call the "blood oath" sworn by the members of the National Assembly, as they called themselves in the early days of the French revolution, never to disband until a Constitution had been established. This was a commitment under pain of death for betrayal. Sartre saw the emergence of the group, even if its members were "a little bit terrorized," as he once conceded to his Maoist discussants (1974c: 171), to be a qualitative advance over the dispersed crowd, which he called the "series" and recognized as the initial ontological level of society where "otherness," not "sameness" was the rule (see Flynn 1997: 115).

16.2 MEDIATING THESE DICHOTOMIES

Louis Althusser famously referred to Sartre as a master of mediation par excellence. The harsh dichotomies of *Being and Nothingness* called for either a Kierkegaardian "choice" or a Hegelian–Marxian "synthesis" or possibly abandonment of the entire project for something else. After all, Sartre's onetime friend, Raymond Aron, the one who reportedly introduced him to Husserlian phenomenology over a cocktail glass, challenged him with the gibe: "A follower of Kierkegaard cannot at the same time be a follower of Marx" (Flynn 2014: 299). By the time that remark was made in 1946, Sartre was well on his way toward proving Aron wrong. In *Anti-Semite and Jew* (1946) he contrasted analytic from synthetic reasoning. The former is arguably the reasoning employed in *Being and Nothingness* though in the view of *Anti-Semite and Jew*, analytic reasoning is bourgeois. By that, Sartre meant that it was individualist and blind to such collective subjects as socioeconomic class. If the distinction is chiefly epistemological and metaphysical, an equally decisive mediating move was made in the *Notebooks for an Ethics*, written 1947–8 but, as we noted, was not published till 1983. There Sartre had discussed non-objectifying reciprocity in contrast with the objectifying gaze made famous in *Being and Nothingness* and in the play *No Exit*. In *Ethics,* Sartre cites the gift–appeal relationship between the artist and the public as the model for non-alienating (non-objectifying) relationships generally: "Relations among men must be based upon this model if people want to exist as freedom for one another; 1st, by the intermediary of the work (technical as well as esthetical, political, etc.); 2nd, the work always being considered a gift" (Sartre 1992: 141). In effect, the work assumes the status of a generous gift which relates to the viewer as an appeal and not a command. This builds on Sartre's discussion of the work of art in *The Imaginary* (1940). Here it is exploited for its mediating service. In fact, Sartre suggests that it be taken as the model for positive reciprocity among individuals. The ethical and political significance are exploited in a way that complements the either/or of *Being and Nothingness* and opens the door for the mediating dialectic of the *Critique*. In fact, *Search for a Method*, the small work that was used to introduce the massive *Critique*, devotes a chapter to "The Problem of Mediations." The "softness" of these relations described here may help explain why Sartre recommended a posthumous publication of the book. But when we turn to his last published interviews with Benny Lévy, insights expressed therein show a similarity to some expressed in *Ethics*. Moreover, as a kind of proof by rejoinder, we can cite the uproar occasioned by the alleged image of a weak, feeble Sartre exploited by an arrogant Benny Lévy, especially as perceived by Aron and Beauvoir, which suggests that the Sartre of these interviews might well be drawing to some degree on the repressed "gentleness" of the gift–appeal relationship sketched in *Ethics* and *The Imaginary* decades earlier.

16.3 Two Forms of Truth but One Phenomenology?

In *The Family Idiot*, Sartre remarks that "Gustave [Flaubert] suffers from a disease of the truth (*une maladie de la Vérité*); he lacks its chief categories: having neither praxis nor vision" (Sartre 1981–93: 1:156–7). These categories separated and contrasted in the address to the French Philosophical Society, are brought together in Sartre's last major work. The category of vision is characteristic of the phenomenological grasp of an essence in eidetic reduction (*Die Wesensschau*) or simply the intuitive filling, *Erfüllung*, of *empty, merely signifying intentions*. The Hegelian–Marxist view argues that knowledge is totalizing praxis (the dialectical action whereby an agent internalizes and externalizes his environment in accord with individual and collective needs and interests. The category of Praxis has its own form of truth (the Hegelian becoming truth discussed earlier), evidence, and knowledge. Elsewhere I have discussed the two distinct approaches in some detail assessing them in view of the structure/history controversy that engaged Sartre's interest in epistemology in the 1950s and 1960s (see Flynn 1976: 21–43). Sartre states his new epistemological problematic succinctly in an address to the French Philosophical Society mentioned above:

> There has to be a synthesis of Husserl's contemplative and nondialectical consciousness, which leads us only to the contemplation of essences, with the activity

of the dialectical but nonconscious and consequently unfounded project fond in Heidegger's thought, whose basic element is seen to be, in contrast, transcendence. (Sartre 1967: 132)

Of the many examples of the imaginary mediating dualities in Sartre's thought, let me cite one from the end of his existential biography of Jean Genet, *Saint Genet* (1952). I select it because this book is one of the five works for which Sartre wished to be remembered in addition to *Nausea*, his autobiographical play *The Devil and the Good Lord*, the ten volumes of essays, *Situations*, and *The Critique of Dialectical Reason* (Flynn 2014: 137n). Toward the end of this large volume, Sartre faces us with a hard choice: Should we side with the old Bolshevik Nikolay Bukharin and the social whole (the Communist Party for which he sacrificed himself by accepting the false accusation of treason) or should we follow the anarchistic individualist Genet? Briefly, each figure represents in Sartre's mind a dimension of who we are as we search for authenticity in an inauthentic world (see Flynn 2014: 275–89). Sartre insists we must choose: "Bukharin or our will to be to-gether to the point of martyrdom; Genet or our solitude carried to the point of Passion." Reading this as a contest between the subject and the object, Sartre suggests that, "be it only once and in the realm of the imaginary, we must have the courage to go to the limits of ourselves in both directions at once" (1963: 599). Admittedly, one could give this challenge a weaker interpretation and see it as a reference to Genet's collected works to which this volume was supposed to have served as the introduction. But the conti-nuity of Sartre's loyalty to his guiding ideals and his abiding respect for the imaginary throughout his career is convincing that the reference of this powerful concluding option extends far beyond a single work of literary art.

The underlying objective in turning to mediation is twofold: to reach the concrete in contrast with the abstractions of Hegelianism and Hegelian Marxism (see Sartre 1963: 42); and second, to bring into focus the morally responsible individual in a way that gives the lie to attempts to lose the individual in the collective where the excuse is that "if everyone is responsible no one is responsible" (see Flynn, 1984: 124–50). These two theses coalesce in Sartre's remark against economic determinists (economism): "It is men whom we judge and not physical forces" (1963: 47). He sees Marx as affirming that "men, their objectifications and their labors, human relations, are finally *what is the most concrete*" (1963: 50).

Some have denied that *Search for a Method* is a proper Introduction to the *Critique*, claiming that it fits more properly the methods employed in *The Family Idiot*. The work grew out of an essay on "The Situation of Existentialism in 1957," written for a Polish journal at its editor's request. It was added to the *Critique* with some additions so one should not be surprised that the fit is imperfect. A valuable addition to the text addresses the structuralist movement that was seen as forcing the existentialist off center stage in the late 1950s. With this in mind, Sartre sets the task for *Search* and for the *Critique* which is to follow when he asks: "Do we have today the *means to constitute a struc-tural, historical anthropology*?" (1963: xxxiv, emphasis added). There was some question at that time whether emerging structuralism and traditional historical studies could be reconciled. Sartre proposes to mediate this controversy with the help of what he will sometimes call "dialectical nominalism" that would assume a supple, situational approach that respected structural relations, namely his concept of the practico-inert, while acknowledging the totalizing power of dialectical reasoning. Whenever he speaks of a "decapitated" dialectic or a "dialectic with holes," Sartre is underscoring the primacy of free organic praxis in the composition of these social phenomena. We must not lose sight of this primacy as we enter into the complexities of the *Critique* or unravel the imaginary skein of the *Family Idiot*.

Sartre's prime ontological thesis and the keystone of his theory in this regard is an echo of Marx's assertion that "there are only men and *real* relations between men" (1963: 76). It is the "real" relations that bind his dialectic together but it is the concrete praxis of individuals that sustain the social phenomena that he introduces in *Search* and especially in the *Critique*. Unfortunately, Sartre fails to address his understanding of the "real relations" on which his social ontology relies. And what he calls a "dialectical nominalism" that admits the existence of "real relations" launches a typically Sartrean paradox. It joins the ontological paradox of *Being and Nothingness* and what we shall see is the ethical paradox announced in *Saint Genet* but rendered central to the dialectical ethics to be discussed shortly. But paradoxical or not, he takes from Marx labor as the model of praxis.

16.4 THE PROGRESSIVE–REGRESSIVE METHOD

Introduced by French philosopher and sociologist Henri Lefebvre, this method is precisely what Sartre was looking for in his search for a "structural historical anthropology." Sartre seems to have forgotten that he mentions briefly the progressive discipline of "pure phenomenology" and the regressive disciplines of phenomenological psychology at the close of his *Sketch for a Theory of the Emotions* (1939). Or perhaps he has now chosen to read the method as a fruitful blend of historical materialism (the Marxist theory of history in terms of economic base and ideological superstructure) and existential psychoanalysis, introduced toward the end of *Being and Nothingness* but expanded in his increasingly lengthy "biographies" primarily of French literary figures. It is commonly admitted that the two terms should be reversed: regression to basic socioeconomic phenomena and progression being the pursuit of the concrete by the totalizing dialectic of organic praxis. Thus, Flaubert's life is to be understood both in terms of the status of medical science and literary creativity in provincial France of his time and with attention to the Flaubert family's manner of absorbing the sociocultural phenomena of their day. Speaking of the various factors that conditioned Flaubert's life, Sartre remarks optimistically that it can all become clear "if we understand that everything took place in childhood," that is, in a condition radically distinct from the adult condition (1963: 59–60).[3] If the progressive–regressive method is introduced in *Sketch*, and employed in the *Critique*, it is omnipresent in the Flaubert study, *The Family Idiot*.

And lest we overlook the continued role of phenomenology in Sartre's "dialectical" reflection, it emerges at the "descriptive" level of the model of social analysis developed by Marxist social theorist, Henri Lefebvre. His "progressive–regressive method" which Sartre introduces and adopts in *Search for a Method* is employed implicitly in the *Critique of Dialectical Reason* (see 2004 revised edition, index under "Problem of Method" (*Search for a Method* in USA)) and relied on most clearly in the multivolume Flaubert study, *The Family Idiot* which we will discuss later. Sartre is so enthused about this model that he recommends it as the proper method "for all domains of anthropology" (1963: 52n). He appeals to this method to yield an understanding of the concrete individual. In a famous remark, he cites the failure of Marxist "economists" to reach the poet in his real presence and historical depth: "Valéry is a petit bourgeois intellectual, no doubt about it. But not every petit bourgeois intellectual is Valéry. The heuristic inadequacy of contemporary Marxism is contained in these two sentences. Marxism lacks any hierarchy of mediations which would permit it to grasp the process which produces the person and his product inside a class and within a given society at a given historical moment" (1963: 56). Sartre argues that existentialism, without denying Marxist principles such as the sub- and superstructure of historical materialism, can find the *mediations* that will allow the concrete person to emerge from the general background of productive forces and relations of production. He mentions Gustave Flaubert as someone whose presence could be revealed by a judicious use of this method. We shall observe Sartre following his own advice in detail with his multi-volume study of Flaubert's life and times. It bears repeating that the drive of Sartre's entire opus is arguably in search of the concrete as the focal point of his literary, ontological, ethical, and political reflections. In the second part of his life, these phenomenological inquiries broaden their scope to include historical intelligibility in the dialectical mode. Sartre has finally discovered "History" with a Hegelian "H" (see Flynn 2014: 313; Sartre 1988: 333–4).

So there is a place for phenomenology in this phase of Sartre's thought. It occurs in the "descriptive" base of the progressive–regressive method. But it is not the essential practice that uncovers the eidos of imaging consciousness as it did in *The Imaginary*. Perhaps in an accommodated sense this base resembles the numerous descriptions of characters and situations in Sartre's novels and plays could be seen as phenomenological and in that sense the descriptive "analyses" of the formation of groups or their dissolution into series *Critique* can be seen as phenomenological insights as well. But as Sartre moves from a philosopher of consciousness to one of praxis, his phenomenology changes apace. The concluding chapter of his seminal *The Imaginary*, written after he had read *Being and Time,* clearly shows the influence of Heidegger on Sartre's thought. It seems that Heidegger's specifically hermeneutical phenomenology fits well the hermeneutic of

---

[3] For a more balanced account of this claim see his 1975 interview with Michel Contat: "I don't believe that a man's history is written in his infancy. I think there are other very important periods where things are added: adolescence, youth, even maturity" (Sartre 1977: 44).

Sartre's existential psychoanalysis as applied to his "biographies." Already with the introduction of this psychoanalysis toward the end of *Being and Nothingness,* Sartre speaks of a "preontological comprehension" of human reality (1974: 561), a basic Heideggerian technique, anticipated by Dilthey and Weber. The principle of existential psychoanalysis is that "man is a totality and not a collection. Consequently, he expresses himself as a whole in even his most insignificant and superficial behavior. In other words, there is not a taste, a mannerism, or a human act that is not revealing." The task is to decipher these phenomena, that is, to undertake a "hermeneutic" in their regard (1974a: 568–9).

Where does this appear in the later Sartre? Among other places, we find it in his implicit appeal to hermeneutical phenomenology. Sartre appeals to *comprehension* (*Verstehen*) as prereflective and more basic than knowledge. In *The Family Idiot,* we observe him note that Flaubert understood more than he knew (reflectively). Sartre takes comprehension (understanding) as a cognitive form of "the lived" (*le vécu*) which is as close as Sartre comes to admitting it functions like the unconscious. The only difference, so it seems, is that Sartre's notion of the Freudian unconscious is incompatible with Sartrean creative freedom. As we remarked earlier, he reads Freudian psychoanalysis, correctly or not, as a kind of determinism.

16.5 Sartre and the Unconscious

The introduction of "lived experience" (*Erlebnis, le vécu*) into Sartre' vocabulary was as significant as that of "praxis." As he explained in an interview (1969):

> What I call *le vécu* (lived experience) is precisely the ensemble of the dialectical process of psychic life, in so far as this process is obscure to itself because it is a constant totalization, thus necessarily a totalization which cannot be conscious of what it is. Lived experience, in this sense, is perpetually susceptible to comprehension but not to knowledge. (1974b: 41)

In other words, it is "prereflective" in the words of *Being and Nothingness.* As if to clarify this point in a subsequent interview, near the end of his life (1971). Sartre remarked: "I suppose [*le vécu*] represents for me the equivalent of conscious-unconscious." Explaining this contrast, he continues: "I want to give the idea of a whole whose surface is completely conscious, while the rest is opaque to this consciousness and, without being part of the unconscious, is hidden from you." It is in this context that he cites how Flaubert, though he did not know himself, at the same time "understood himself admirably." Sartre admits that he has not theorized this concept of the lived experience (*le vécu*) but intends to do so in his Flaubert study (1977: 127–8), which, in fact, he did to a considerable extent.

In the introduction to her edition of Sartre's *La Transcendance de L'Ego* (1972), Beauvoir's adopted daughter, Sylvie Le Bon observes that the only topic introduced in this youthful work that Sartre subsequently disowned (*renierait*) was his opposition to psychoanalysis, which, she insists, he completely revised (Le Bon 1972: 8). Of greater significance is the remark of Sartre's former student and renown psychoanalyst J. B. Pontalis. He wrote the introduction to Sartre's scenario for a film on Freud's life that was directed by John Huston. Though Sartre insisted that his name be removed from the credits, his script was published as *The Freud Scenario*. Elsewhere Pontalis noted that "one day the history of Sartre's thirty-year-long relationship with psychoanalysis, an ambiguous mixture of *equally* deep attraction and repulsion, will have to be written and perhaps his work reinterpreted in the light of it" (1974b: 220). Since we have been claiming that all of Sartre's "biographies," including his own *Words*, are existential psychoanalyses subject to the procedure he sketched in *Being and Nothingness*, we will address biography as existential psychoanalysis in greater detail when we discuss *The Family Idiot*. For the moment, suffice it to repeat Pontalis' belief that "the *Freud* made the *Flaubert* possible" in the sense that "Sartre succeeded in making perceptible, hence first and foremost in making perceptible" to himself, a certain number of phenomena such as hysteria which could no longer be adequately accounted for by the notion of bad faith that he had long promoted to counter Freud (Sartre 1984b: xiv, xii).

16.6 Sartre's Social Ontology

The task Sartre implicitly set himself at the end of *Being and Nothingness*, which he once described as his "eidetic of bad faith" (Flynn 2014: 189 n. 48; Sartre, vol IV, 1964a: 196n), was to present a theory of positive reciprocity in contrast with the inauthentic, objectifying reciprocity of *Being and Nothingness* where the essence of the relations between consciousnesses was taken to be conflict. We have observed how Sartre undertook such a project in his *Ethics* where individuals can work together in a spirit of positive mutuality, generosity and the gift-appeal already introduced in the relation between the artist, the aesthetic object and the sympathetic viewer in *The Imaginary*. In *Ethics*, Sartre proposes appeal as the promise of positive reciprocity in contrast with the conflictual, negative reciprocity set forth as the norm in *Being and Nothingness* (1992: 284).

In his masterful, if prolix, construction of a sociohistorical ontology, the two volumes of *The Critque of Dialectical Reason*, Sartre introduces what may be his major contribution to social ontology. He does so with the aid of two basic concepts, the *practico-inert* and the *mediating third* [party].

The practico-inert is the functional equivalent of being-in-itself, serving as the source of its own kind of otherness in the interpersonal realm. But unlike the in-itself, it is *practico*-inert, that is, it gathers the sedimentation of previous praxes. Thus, language is practico-inert insofar as it is the product of individual acts of speech. Sartre admitted in another interview late in life that he did not produce a theory of language but that the elements of such a theory could be found among his writings. In terms of social ontology, he lists socioeconomic class and "systems" such as colonialism or capitalism among the practico-inert. Of his several descriptions of the practico-inert, his most succinct and apt one sees it as "simply the activity of others insofar as it is sustained and diverted by inorganic inertia" (2004: 556).

When reciprocity is mediated by the practico-inert, the resultant relations are "serial" in the sense that each individual is related to the rest as other to other. This is the objectifying and alienating relationship exhibited in *Being and Nothingness* but now refined by the introduction of the practico-inert. Sartre considers seriality to be the basis of sociality. We have also observed his historical examples of the counter-finality that practico-inert mediation exhibits. Perhaps the paradigm of serial relations would be the television audience who are united and separated by the social impotence they exhibit. Another such instance would be the crowd as distinct from the organized group, with which we will contrast it shortly. One could question the strength of Sartre's example, however, if the public medium were the cell-phone, which, as we shall see makes possible a kind of immediacy and commonality, if not identity, that Sartre's "serial" relations never achieve. The counter-finality of the practico-inert is the socioeconomic reflection of the Sartrean mantra that "loser wins" *qui perd gagne* which trades on counter-finality and serves as the theme of several of his literary works.

In the *Critique*, Sartre lists two basic forms of seriality: the collective (*collectif*) and the institution. The collective is the model of unity in exteriority. The collective object, whether machine tool or opinion poll, not only symbolizes our exteriority, it constitutes it (see 2004: 264). Interpersonal relations at this stage are not those of true, positive reciprocity: Imitation or contagion, not cooperation is the rule: interchangeability and numerical equivalence, not uniqueness are its features. The institution, as we shall see, is a malformation of the social group that reintroduces practico-inert mediation by means of the oath (Sartre's dramatic vison of the social contract). His understanding of this contract with its blood oath and introduction of fraternity–terror is Hobbesian in character. In this respect, it stands to the group as Hobbes to Rousseau in Sartre's political theory.

It is with the introduction of the third party (*le tiers*) that Sartre achieves positive reciprocity among praxes in the group. Sartre describes the group as the second degree of sociality. Since he equated seriality with unfreedom and what he calls "passive activity," the appearance of the group can be described as "the sudden resurrection of freedom" (2004: 401). Clearly, this is no longer "freedom as the definition of man" as he claimed in *Being and Nothingness*. It is freedom in the interpersonal situation of positive reciprocity. The mediating third party is a functional term for the group member as such. In contrast with the "alienating" third that objectifies the other, the "mediating" third is non-objectifying but constitutes a relation of positive reciprocity similar to the gift–appeal relation discussed in *Ethics*. Each mediating third becomes the same as the other members in terms of practice and interest (though not the "identical" as would be the case of a superorganism which Sartre eschews).

Sartre offers a clearly phenomenological account of the people as group-in-fusion in the storming of the Bastille, July 14, 1789.[4] In his imaginative reconstruction, the crowd is in serial flight from royal troops, when, as if by prior agreement, someone shouts "Stop!" and the command is echoed by scores of people who reverse direction even as they change their perception of the scene. This practical awareness that "we" are acting is buoyed up by the realization that "we are a hundred strong" and can storm the Bastille. This is what Sartre calls "the interiorization of multiplicity." It requires each to act *as* common individual much as Rousseau required that each person vote as citizen, judging in terms of the general will and not the merely quantitative will of all.

Joining the nascent group, individual praxis immediately acquires what Sartre dialectically speaking, calls a "synthetic enrichment." The first of such properties relevant to group membership is power. But Sartre will then list other such "societal facts" as right, duty, function, structure, violence, and self-imposed inertia (fraternity–terror) along with co-sovereignty. As he explains:

> The members of the group are third parties, which means that each of them totalizes the reciprocities of others. And the relation of one third party to another has nothing to do with alterity: since the group is the practical milieu of the relation, it must be a human relation. (1985: 374)

This free reciprocity is the effect of a twofold mediation, that of the group between thirds, and that of each third between the group and other thirds. In addition to the sworn group of French revolutionaries cited here, Sartre seems to have in mind the Communist cell of his day.

As we shall see in the conclusion of our essay, Sartre's view of the constituted group is pessimistic in the sense that, absent an external force against which to defend their unity, the "all-for-one and one-for all" generosity of the unthreatened group will interiorize their solidity by appealing to the practico-inert via the institution and its bureaucracy. Thus, we have come full circle and will continue to do so as long as material scarcity infects our history with necessary violence.

16.7 SARTRE'S SECOND AND THIRD ETHICS: PARADOX AND DIALOGUE

In fact, Sartre never gave us a complete moral philosophy. What he offered was two (and perhaps three) "sketches" for such a theory, not unlike his early *Sketch for a Theory of the Emotions* (1939), which Francis Jeanson has described as Sartre's initial glimpse at an ethics (Jeanson 1990: 890). One might designate the perspective of these sketches as

---

[4] Actually, the storming followed the Oath by several weeks (Flynn 2014: 344 n.14).

authenticity, dialectics and dialogue, respectively. The first is his characteristically existentialist approach. To live authentically, aside from avoiding self-deception, consists of learning to abandon the "God-project" and to live without an ego. The ego is seen as the distillate of bad faith; moving beyond it, he believes, gives us the utmost creative freedom that coincides with our situation. As has been frequently remarked, authenticity is the sole virtue that one can find in existentialism.[5]

As Sartre's attention moves from consciousness to praxis, his ethical theory shifts as well. Now the ideal is not authenticity but "openness" to the creative values chosen by our freedom. One can find this value supported by Beauvoir in her *Ethics of Ambiguity* (1946).[6] But the social ontology of the *Critique* lays the groundwork for the second ethics. The terms "praxis" and "need" (felt exigence) are prominent in these pages and the attendant thesis of constituting a "socialist ethic" builds on the social ontology of that work. What has been called generically Sartre's dialectical ethic's refers to the Rome lecture, "Morality and Society," delivered at a gathering of prominent Marxist theorists at the Gramsci Institute in Rome May 23, 1964, as well as to the related set of pages intended for delivery at Cornell University entitled "Morality and History" but never given, along with hundreds of pages of notes relevant to both essays that remain unpublished.

A brief summary of the May 23rd lecture focuses on components of Sartre's socialist ethic. We have seen that the existentialist Sartre was concerned with understanding the concrete. That was the aim of his existential psychoanalysis and it continues in his dialectical ethics. But here the task is to address what he calls the *ethical paradox* proper to a socialist ethic. He had already introduced the ethical paradox in *What Is Literature?* conceived as how to take advantage of oppression in order to do good (1988: 190). In his study of Genet, where the challenge was to be an authentic individual in an inauthentic society, it was expressed in the fact that an "ethics is *for us* inevitable and at the same time impossible" (1963: 186n). There the paradox is refined into achieving an ethics that is both moral and concrete. In terms of the *Critique*, the paradox is how one resolves the problem of *fraternity* and *terror* which returns in the third, dialogical ethics. But in this Rome lecture, the decisive contrast figures between our present condition as "subhuman" and the motivating value of integral humanity. It elaborates Sartre's ontological distinction in the *Critique* between the alienating function of the practico-inert in serial relations and that of the mediating third constituting group membership, itself synonymous with freedom and the ethical.

Examining several cases, Sartre lays bare what he again calls "the paradox of ethics," namely, that the ethical moment which he terms the moment of "unconditional possibility" or "invention," a defining term in Sartrean ethics since *Existentialism Is a Humanism*, is a dimension of historical praxis. Every action insofar as it is unconditional contains an "ethical moment" which is the surpassing toward an end (non-being, the correlate of creative imagination) that is human autonomy. But in that very surpassing it

---

[5] See Grene 1952.
[6] See the "open future" (Beauvoir 1975: 60, 82, 92).

reveals its historical conditioning and practico-inert destiny. This condition of uncondi-tionality, Sartre writes, "if it could fully bloom [*s'épanouir*], would make historical action and ethical action homogeneous." In effect, this would achieve a union of authentic mo-rality, integral humanity, and committed History which describes the ideal of Sartre's second sketch for an ethic. If only we can produce a "socialism of [material] abundance" to make it possible (1993: 5:171).

With the Cornell lecture, "Morality and History," Sartre continues his quasi-Hegelian connection between the abstract individual and the fully integrated concrete group member. In the *Critique*, he referred to this as the *concrete universal*. The fruit of his dia-lectical commitment, the "notion" was already employed by the early Sartre to capture the *sens* (meaning) of the Renaissance in the *Mona Lisa's* smile and of the Enlightenment in J. S. Bach's polyphony. The "concrete universal" engenders a pair of interrelated terms, namely enveloping totalization and incarnation, that further Sartre's discussion of ethics and history but assume great relevance in the multivolume discussion of Flaubert's life and times in *The Family Idiot*.[7]

In his last years, blind from a stroke and relying greatly on the aid of his personal secretary and now interlocutor, Benny Lévy, Sartre grew enthusiastic about an ethic of the "We" that consisted of a series of conversations that he and Lévy were in the pro-cess of recording. The result is a hermeneutical puzzle or even morass. Whose voice are we hearing? The "official "Sartre, the voice of *Les Temps Modernes*, familiar to Beauvoir, Aron, and the members of his life-long "family," was not recognizable at all. What they heard was a self-assured, arrogant young man leading a sick and aged Sartre toward recanting his earlier writings in favor of a quasi-Jewish messianism that Lévy had re-cently embraced.

We have noted earlier that this so-called volte-face was not so extreme as his friends had insisted. There are a number of features in these interviews, especially from the *Ethics*, that echo the "softer" voice of the younger philosopher. Even the reference to "brotherhood" among individuals is central to the *Critique*. Admittedly, it was often conjoined with the qualifiers "terror" or "violence," but these were contingent on the fact of material scarcity. True, the name of Emmanuel Levinas, famous Jewish phenom-enologist that appears a number of times in the typescript for the first set of published interviews is virtually absent from the indexes of Sartre's previous works. Benny Lévy was reported to have been devoted to the thought of Levinas and Bernard-Henri Lévy (no relative) insisted that "the later Sartre was a Levinasian obviously, indisputably and profoundly" (Lévy 2000: 654). One indication favoring this claim is Sartre's remark that "the self considering itself as self for-the-other (*soi-même pour l'autre*), having a rela-tionship with the other—that is what I call ethical conscience (*la conscience morale*)"—a distinctly Levinasian view (1996: 71). So at the end as in the beginning we are faced with change within permanence, at the very least.

---

[7] For a lengthy summary of relevant texts in English on these three manuscripts, see Flynn 1997: 286 n. 30.

What we get with the interviews published as *Hope Now*, is a set of insights into Sartre's reconsiderations of his previous stands on the questions of ethics, humanism, and politics, guided, no doubt, by Benny Lévy. Talk of conscience, obligation, inner constraint, and even the possibility of fraternity without terror—this was the kind of "standard" ethical discourse that scandalized the Sartrean "family."

16.8 *The Family Idiot*

Like many of his other major works, this is a torso, despite its five volumes in English translation and three plus in French. A massive work, he considered it the sequel to the *Imaginary* (1940), a model phenomenological text. In addition to capturing the various aspects of Sartre's phenomenological insights in a creative union of ontology, psychology, anthropology, politics, ethics, and aesthetics, the Flaubert enlists arguably the full scope of Sartre's life's work. The existential discourse of *Being and Nothingness* reappears with the terms in-itself and for-itself, and dialectic of the *Critique* held together by the regressive–progressive method that opens the door to the artist's "choice" of the imaginary ("lying to tell the truth," in a characteristically Sartrean phrase). Indeed, it exemplifies many of the Sartrean maxims such as the thesis that a person totalizes their society to the extent that they are totalized by it. In many ways this impressive accomplishment attempts to achieve just such a totalization with an existential psychoanalysis of Flaubert and the social and artistic milieu of France in the second and third quarters of the nineteenth century. Not only is it an effective key to Flaubert's life and times, it postulates an objective neurosis that is echoed by Flaubert's own illness. On Sartre's reading, Flaubert "chooses" the life of a neurotic, *l'homme imaginaire*, in order to be able to write "for his time." Such were the "bases and structures" of his choice. Such is the *totalization* that invites Sartre to undertake "committed" history that is likewise autobiographical.

Viewed in retrospect, we can now hope to have answered our initial question and completed the circle: parted company with phenomenology at midcareer, what kind of phenomenology was at issue and how clean was the break? Though he has occasionally been accused of "loose usage," it is clear that so-called "constitutive" phenomenology was the object of his separation in favor of hermeneutical phenomenology, which was more in accord with his growing interest in History with a Hegelian "H" and its dialectical turn. "Existential" phenomenology was never in question any more than was the existentialist core of his lifelong professional thought. The foregoing "steps" in Sartre's association with generic phenomenology are meant to underscore the ambiguity of his commitment. Now as if to waken us from our constitutive phenomenological slumber, Sartre speaks of "pure phenomenological description" early in the first volume of *The Family Idiot* (1:38) and affirms that a description "can be true phenomenologically, that is, on the level of *eidos*" in the last volume (5:526). It is to this book-ending move and all that it encloses that I appeal in order to confirm the return of constitutive phenomenology in

Sartre's last great work. Of course, the entire panoply of *Sartriana* is there as well: praxis and practico-inert, comprehension and *le vécu*. In an irenic moment, Sartre admits:

> Self-consciousness (*presence-á-soi*) has the basic structure of praxis. Even on the level of non-thetic consciousness, intuition is conditioned by individual history; the spiral movement of twinning can include a refusal, a futile effort to crush the two terms in the unity of the *En-soi*. (1:141)

What we discover is a kind of "chastened" phenomenology, having survived the need to accommodate a Hegelian "becoming truth" at the expense of its highly prized "apodicticity," as well as a "comprehension" that is built on praxis and an awareness that "clouds" the translucency of even prereflective consciousness that is now admittedly modified by social conditioning.

What remains amidst the ruins of his earlier "individualistic philosophy of consciousness"? Outright contradiction? That would be too antiseptic. Rather, taking a cue from his second, dialectical ethics, perhaps "paradox" is the better term. As his decades-long fascination with the life and work of Gustave Flaubert suggests, Sartre's full panoply of terms, hypotheses, and sought-for syntheses gather in a quasi-Hegelian "concrete universal" that is a human life in its dialectic with holes (*trous*). It is phenomenology in its various forms but especially its "existential" mode that not so much fills those gaps of freedom as creates and reveals them.

References

Beauvoir, S. de (1975), *The Ethics of Ambiguity* (Secaucus, NJ: Citadel Press).

Embree, L. et al. (eds) (1997), *Encyclopedia of Phenomenology* (Dordrecht: Kluwer).

Flynn, T. R. (1976), "Praxis and Vision: Elements of a Sartrean Epistemology," *The Philosophical Forum* 8: 21–43.

Flynn, T. R. (1984), *Sartre and Marxist Existentialism: The Test Case of Collective Responsibility* (Chicago, IL: University of Chicago Press).

Flynn, T. R. (1997), *Sartre, Foucault and Historical Reason, vol. 1: Toward an Existentialist Theory of History* (Chicago, IL: University of Chicago Press).

Flynn, T. R. (2005), *Sartre, Foucault, and Historical Reason, vol. 2: A Poststructuralist Mapping of History* (Chicago, IL: University of Chicago Press).

Flynn, T. R. (2014), *Sartre: A Philosophical Biography* (Cambridge: Cambridge University Press).

Grene, M. (1952), "Authenticity: An Existential Virtue," *Ethics* 62: 266–74.

Jeanson, F. (1990), "De l'aliénation morale à l'exigence éthique," *Les Temps Modernes, Temoins de Sartre* 231–3: 890.

Lévy, B.-H. (2000), *Le Siècle de Sartre* (Paris: Bernard Grasset).

Sartre, J.-P. (1963), *Saint Genet: Actor and Martyr*, translated by B. Frechtman (New York: George Braziller).

Sartre, J.-P. (1964), *The Words*, translated by B. Frechtman (New York: George Braziller).

Sartre, J.-P. (1967), "Consciousness of self and knowledge of self," in N. Lawrence and D. O'Connor (eds), *Readings in Existential Phenomenology* (Englewood Cliffs, NJ: Prentice-Hall), 113–42.

Sartre, J.-P. (1968a), *The Communists and Peace with a Reply to Claude Lefort,* translated by M. H. Fuller and P. R. Burke (New York: George Braziller).

Sartre, J.-P. (1968b), *Search for a Method,* translated by H. E. Barnes (New York: Random House).

Sartre, J.-P. (1972), *La transcendence de l'Ego* (Paris: J. Vrin).

Sartre, J.-P. (1974a), *Being and Nothingness,* translated by H. E. Barnes (New York: William Morrow).

Sartre, J.-P. (1974b), *Between Existentialism and Marxism: Essays and Interviews,* translated by J. Mathews (London: New Left Books).

Sartre, J.-P. (1974c), *On a raison de se révolter,* with P. Victor and P. Gavi (Paris: Gallimard).

Sartre J.-P. (1977), *Life/Situations: Essays Written and Spoken,* translated by P. Auster and L. Davis (New York: Pantheon Books).

Sartre, J.-P. (1981–93), *The Family Idiot: Gustave Flaubert 1821–1857,* translated by C. Cosman, 5 vols (Chicago, IL: University of Chicago Press).

Sartre, J.-P. (1984b), *The Freud Scenario,* translated by Q. Hoare, edited by J.-B. Pontalis (Chicago: University of Chicago Press).

Sartre, J.-P. (1985a), *The Critique of Dialectical Reason,* vol. 1, translated by A. Sheridan-Smith (London: Verso).

Sartre, J.-P. (1985b), *The Freud Scenario,* translated by Q. Hoare (Chicago, IL: University of Chicago Press).

Sartre, J.-P. (1988), *What Is Literature? And Other Essays* (Cambridge, MA: Harvard University Press).

Sartre, J.-P. (1992), *Notebooks for an Ethics,* translated by D. Pellauer (Chicago, IL: University of Chicago Press).

Sartre, J.-P. (1995), *Anti-Semite and Jew,* translated by G. Becker (New York: Shocken Books).

Sartre, J.-P. (1996), *Hope Now: The 1980 Interviews with Benny Lévy,* translated by A. van den Hoven (Chicago, IL: University of Chicago Press).

Sartes, J.-P. (2002), *The Transcendence of the Ego* (London: Routledge).

Sartre J.-P. (2004), *The Imaginary,* translated by J. Webber (London: Routledge).

Sartre, J.-P. (2006), *The Critique of Dialectical Reason,* vol. 2, translated by Q. Hoare (London: Verso).

Sartre, J.-P. (2007), *Existentialism Is a Humanism with A Commentary on* The Stranger, translated by C. Macomber (New Haven, CT: Yale University Press).

CHAPTER 17

SIMONE DE BEAUVOIR

Philosopher, Author, Feminist

DEBRA BERGOFFEN

17.1 TAKING PHENOMENOLOGY ACROSS GENRES AND DISCIPLINES

SIMONE de Beauvoir was always pleased to call herself a writer. Though critical of the type of thinking traditionally defined as philosophy, she readily identified herself as a philosopher in the phenomenological-existential tradition. Later in life Beauvoir took on a third name, feminist. By adopting these identities philosopher, writer, feminist, Beauvoir creates a genealogy that tells us who she was for herself and how she wished to be seen and remembered by others (us). Different as the practices of a philosopher, author, and feminist may seem, in Beauvoir's hands they share this—a commitment to the strategies and tenants of phenomenology and existentialism. Taking my direction from the names Beauvoir gave herself and the phenomenological-existential thread that ties these names together, I ask three questions: What did Beauvoir mean when she identified herself as an author? How did she understand the terms existentialism and phenomenology? What did she commit herself to by calling herself a feminist?

Addressing these questions it becomes clear that in following the paths opened by phenomenology, Beauvoir took them in new directions. She revealed what remained hidden in traditional phenomenological accounts of the perceiving subject. She reconfigured the account of intentionality. Attending to the lived body's sex, gender, and age, she challenged the privilege phenomenology attributed to the I-can body and complicated its understanding of intersubjective embodied ambiguity. Beauvoir is most famous for her analysis of the sexed and gendered oppressions of the patriarchal life-world. These radical phenomenological revelations were not arrived at suddenly. Their groundwork, as we shall see, was laid in her literary exploration of pre-reflective experience and philosophical analyses of the ethical and political implications of intentionality and intersubjectivity.

Beauvoir's 1946 essay "Literature and Metaphysics" details her unique approach to the task of the writer. Her 1945 essays "A review of *Phenomenology of Perception* by Merleau-Ponty" and "Existentialism and Popular Wisdom," and her 1947 essay "What Is Existentialism?" explicate her understanding of herself as a philosopher. Her 1976 opening remarks to the International Tribunal on Crimes against Women describe her feminist commitments. Taking up her identity as a philosopher and author, Beauvoir wrote metaphysical novels and took a unique approach to the phenomenological-existential tenants and practice of philosophy. Taking on the identity of a feminist she deployed phenomenological-existential principles in support of women's causes. Politicizing these principles she signed petitions, founded a feminist journal and took to the streets.

17.2 From Literature and Philosophy to Politics

Like her contemporaries Albert Camus and Jean-Paul Sartre, Beauvoir invoked the imaginative discourses of literature, and the argument style of the treatise to portray (literature) and explain (the philosophical essay) her existential-phenomenological positions. Though Sartre's and Camus' literary works were always seen as expressions of their philosophical concepts, prior to the 1990s Beauvoir's identity as a writer eclipsed her standing as a philosopher.[1] Today she is recognized as an important voice in the phenomenological-existential field. Her literature, like that of Sartre and Camus, is seen as integral to her philosophy. Had her 1946 essay "Literature and Metaphysics" been read carefully when it was published it would not have taken almost fifty years for this to happen, for that essay makes it clear that Beauvoir sees literature as one way of examining the metaphysical situation within which we find ourselves and that her concept of metaphysics is decidedly phenomenological.

Two of Beauvoir's works are especially rich examples of the metaphysical novel: *She Came to Stay* (1943), for the ways that it probes the question of the intersubjective other (Barnes 1998: 157–70; Heath 1998: 171–82), and *All Men Are Mortal* (1955), for its portrayal of the responsibilities of freedom in terms of the time of the other (Bergoffen 2009: 116–20). As enacted in the lives of her literary characters, these themes are formally analyzed in her discussions of the ethical responsibilities of freedom and the temporality of the subject in *The Ethics of Ambiguity*, and *The Coming of Age*, and in her invocation of the

---

[1] See Tidd (1999: 1–4) for an account of the evolution of the establishment of Beauvoir's philosophical status during the 1990s.

category of the Other, as distinct from the phenomenological-existential encounter with the intersubjective other, to signify de-subjectification in *The Second Sex*.

If we read Beauvoir's novels as she intended them to be read, as revealing the pre-reflective grounds of our thinking, the line between her literary and philosophical writings becomes clear. Like Camus in *The Myth of Sisyphus*, Beauvoir's *Ethics of Ambiguity* uses the technique of imaginative variation to create character types that clarify her abstract arguments. In *The Second Sex* and *The Coming of Age*, leaving vignettes behind to detail the realities of peoples' lives, literature, now the literature of others, remains a resource for her philosophical thinking.

The Second Sex and *The Coming of Age* develop the political implications of our pre-reflective embeddedness in an intersubjective world. They probe the ways that the world in which we find ourselves positions us within it. Where *The Ethics of Ambiguity* appealed to the ambiguities of situated freedom to keep the idea of being situated from sliding into the idea of determinism (the world defines me) and to save the idea of freedom from succumbing to the seduction of the idea of absolute freedom (immunity from the influences of my situation), *The Second Sex* and *The Coming of Age* develop the politics of the phenomenological idea of situated freedom to reject deterministic passivity and provide liberating hope. Neither dominated by its situation nor free from its influences, Beauvoir's political subject is phenomenologically ambiguous. As a being for others it is vulnerable to their power. As a being for itself it possesses agency. It can, in solidarity with others, dismantle systems of oppression. The political valences of *The Second Sex* and *The Coming of Age* may be traced to the ways that, in paying close attention to the concrete realities of the lived body, they attend to the affective horizons of our lives—the ways that our bodies as objects for others are perceived as objects of attraction (beautiful feminine bodies) or repulsion (ugly un-feminine or decrepit bodies) and treated accordingly.

17.3 THE AUTHOR AS PHENOMENOLOGIST

Beauvoir opens "Literature and Metaphysics" with a question: Is truth found in the singularity of the earthly time of literature or in the eternal universals of philosophical systems? (Beauvoir 1946: 269). Invoking one of the signatures of her thought—the phenomenological concept of ambiguity—Beauvoir rejects the question's dualist premise. The logical antithesis between time and eternity is belied by the lives depicted in the metaphysical novel. These lives show that "in its living unity and its fundamental living ambiguity this destiny that is ours . . . is inscribed in both time and eternity" (Beauvoir 1946: 276).

Tying time and eternity together in this way, Beauvoir links literature to philosophy. Both are engaged in the task of elucidating our metaphysical situation and the drama of intersubjective subjectivity. Though philosophy may be tempted to get lost in abstractions, literature pulls it back to the concrete. Thus metaphysics acquires a new meaning. Instead of being identified in terms of a system that circumscribes the meaning of the world, it is now defined in terms of a situation where one posits oneself in one's totality before the totality of the world (Beauvoir 1946: 270). Approaching metaphysics in this way, Beauvoir argues that it is "through his joys, sorrows, resignations, revolts fears and hopes [that] each man realizes a certain metaphysical situation that defines him . . . essentially" (Beauvoir 1946: 273).

Attending to the affects that define us, especially joy, is one of Beauvoir's key phenomenological innovations. *The Ethics of Ambiguity* identifies joy as a distinctive feature of the first moment of intentionality. *The Coming of Age* cites the capacity for joy as an essential feature of a meaningful life. *The Second Sex* describes erotic joy in terms of its power to dismantle the gendered subjectivities of patriarchy. Losing the capacity for joy, Fosca, the immortal protagonist of *All Men Are Mortal*, becomes alienated from himself and the world. No longer living at the intersection of time and eternity, he loses the passion for life.

Herbert Spiegelberg and John Crunickshank read Beauvoir's metaphysical novels as applications of the phenomenological method of imaginative variation (Holveck 2002: 24). Of all of her fiction, *All Men are Mortal* is the most striking example of this literary method. Creating a character who violates the defining feature of being human, mortality, and allowing us to imagine what it would be like to realize our desire for immortality, it enacts the self-destructive and world-destroying effects of the flight from finitude.

Beauvoir's philosophical writings, rooted in the finitude of the human condition, examine the becoming of the subject as it traverses the time between birth and death. *The Ethics of Ambiguity* analyzes the relationship between the time of childhood dependency and the emergence of the ethical subject. *The Coming of Age* examines the ways the weight of the past impacts the life of the "end-of time" elderly person. The matter of time lies at the heart of Beauvoir's *The Second Sex* declaration, "One is not born but becomes woman" (Beauvoir 2009: 283). Usually read as a statement that draws us into the sex–gender controversy (Butler 1986), examined through the lens of *The Ethics of Ambiguity* it should also be read in terms of the question: What sort of becoming is compatible with becoming human? for *The Second Sex* makes it clear that in the becoming imposed on her, a woman becomes an alienated human being.

This ongoing attention to the becoming of the subject seems to confirm the importance Margaret Simons attributes to Beauvoir's frequent 1927 Diary references to Bergson. According to Simons, Beauvoir was especially impressed with Bergson's idea that time, duration, and memory are constitutive of one's sense of self (Simons 1999c: 194). Though references to Bergson do not appear in Beauvoir's formal writings, when Merleau-Ponty speaks of Bergson as "seeking the profound in appearances and the absolute beneath our eyes" (Merleau-Ponty 1964b: 183) and when he says that for Bergson "time is myself . . . And from now on we are at the absolute" (Merleau-Ponty 1964b: 184) he attunes us to the Bergsonian voice in Beauvoir's descriptions of the intersection of time and eternity in her "Literature and Metaphysics" essay and to her attention to our temporal horizons in her philosophical treatises.

Whether she is writing literary or philosophical texts, Beauvoir, adopting the method of thick descriptions[2] and engaged in the practice of imaginative variation, presents lived experience as the ground of all knowledge, and challenges the priority traditional philosophy gives to the thinking subject (Beauvoir 1946: 275). Eleanor Holveck argues, that there is a nuanced difference between what Beauvoir means by pre-predicative lived experience and what other phenomenologists, Merleau-Ponty and Husserl, for example, might mean by it, for Holveck finds that for Beauvoir the singularity of pre-predicative experience as lived by the characters in her novels is the ground of all other experiences, including those of perception (Holveck 2002: 24). This challenge to the privilege traditional phenomenologists attributed to direct perception becomes clear in *The Second Sex* where being perceived as a woman is always and already pre-reflectively culturally loaded.

Beauvoir credits Søren Kierkegaard with drawing her attention to the unsystematic subject living the historical paradoxes of the human condition.[3] Reading Beauvoir's review of Merleau-Ponty's *Phenomenology of Perception*, however, reveals that her distinct understanding of the subject's historicity passed through the lens of Merleau-Ponty's phenomenology rather than the knight of faith. The review examines the differences between the phenomenologies of Merleau-Ponty and Sartre and details Beauvoir's assessment of these differences. When distinguishing Merleau-Ponty's portrayal of the subject as opaque and forever incomplete, from Sartre's concept of the subject as a transparent for-itself, it is Sartre's concept, not Merleau-Ponty's that Beauvoir finds wanting (Beauvoir 1945a: 163). Sartre cannot, she says, account for the ambiguity of an embodied being living on the horizon of an ever-open future and its inaccessible possibilities. He cannot account for the subject as a continuous process where the history and prehistory of the lived body becomes uniquely mine as I tie past, present, and future together.

Merleau-Ponty confirms the affinity between his understanding of the subject and Beauvoir's in his 1948 essay "Metaphysics and the Novel" when he approvingly cites *She Came to Stay* as an example of metaphysical literature. He credits the novel with expressing the subjective, phenomenological experience of the world and revealing the dynamics of the transcending intentionality of consciousness. He finds that in adopting the idea of ambiguity, abandoning the idea of a subject transparent to itself and rejecting the idea of a human nature that could determine our moral choices, Beauvoir lays the foundation for an existential morality. What becomes clear in Beauvoir's later literary and philosophical writings is that Beauvoir does more than lay the foundation for an ethics, she builds on it. Anchoring her ethics in the responsibilities that accompany the uncertainties of ambiguity and the dynamics of intentionality, she becomes an important voice challenging the charge that as focused on the individual, existentialism is too subjectivist and relativist to provide us with moral principles. Going on the offensive she

---

[2] A phrase coined by Clifford Geertz to distinguish descriptions that are sensitive to context, interactional details, and to the meaning of events for those participating in them from descriptions that merely record empirical facts.

[3] For a discussion of Kierkegaard's influence on Beauvoir see Heinämaa 2009

argues that adherence to such absolute principles as God, human nature, historical dialectics, or humanism is antithetical to ethical action. She insists that an existentialism grounded in the phenomenological understanding of the subject is the only secular philosophy that takes the problem of evil and ethical action seriously.

As Beauvoir develops her ethics, it becomes clear, however, that Sartre's concept of the subject, though critiqued. is not abandoned and that Merleau-Ponty's portrayal of subjectivity is not uncritically endorsed. In Beauvoir's hands Sartre's account of the threat each subject presents to another, encounters Merleau-Ponty's ideas of intersubjectivity, transcendence, and communication. Finding that the otherness of the intersubjective other is not easily tolerated, but that the possibility of an ethics demands that alterity be bridged, Beauvoir formulates the question that drives *The Ethics of Ambiguity*: Can separate existents discover and live within the parameters of an intersubjective law that binds them to each other?

17.4 FROM PHENOMENOLOGICAL DESCRIPTIONS TO EXISTENTIAL IMPERATIVES

Turning to the essays "What Is Existentialism?" and "Existentialism and Popular Wisdom," we learn that Beauvoir credited existentialism with turning phenomenological depictions of how the subject engages the world into principles for deciphering how the subject ought to engage the world. The phenomenological descriptions of intentionality as transcendence become, in Beauvoir's existentialism, an ethic of freedom as transcendence. The fact that others transcend the meanings I give them, becomes the ground of the ethical obligation to recognize the other's transcendence as a matter of freedom that must be protected. The phenomenological description of the open horizon of perception becomes the existential responsibility to provide an open future for freedom to flourish.

In giving her phenomenology an ethical-existentialist frame Beauvoir aligns the meaning of freedom with the phenomenological rejection of closed philosophical systems to critique of the idea of a fixed reality (Beauvoir 1945b: 212). Freedom, she explains, requires "questioning and refusal of the given" (Beauvoir 1945b: 217). As a phenomenologist, Beauvoir speaks of the subject as disclosing the meaning of the world, as an existentialist she speaks of the subject as being responsible for these meanings. This phenomenological-existential understanding of the subject as both disclosing the meanings of the world and bringing meanings into it is expressed in Beauvoir's distinct account of intentionality.

The Ethics of Ambiguity describes intentionality as marked by two intersecting moments, an original moment where I joyfully discover my embeddedness in a world that speaks to me but, that as transcendent, escapes my control, and an ensuing moment where

I bring my values into the world and attempt to mold its givenness (Beauvoir 1948: 12–13). In this account, intentionality is ambiguous. It speaks in two voices, that of the world and that of my will (Bergoffen 1997: 75–112). The voice of the world beckons me through the joy of encountering the wonders of the sky, the landscape, the snowfield (Beauvoir 1948: 12). In its beckoning, this moment of intentionality awakens a desire to create the world anew, the voice of the will. The world may bend to my will for a time, but ultimately I fail to subdue it and in this failure I am thrown back to the original moment of intentionality where I experience the joy of the world as given. In Beauvoir's words, "The failure is not surpassed but assumed. Existence asserts itself as an absolute which must seek its justification within itself and not suppress itself . . . To attain his truth, man must not attempt to dispel the ambiguity of his being, but . . . accept the task of realizing it" (Beauvoir 1948: 13).

The ethical import of this affect-laden account of intentionality becomes clear as Beauvoir lodges it in an account of time that attends to the ethical significance of our premature birth and prolonged childhood dependency.[4] Beauvoir describes the child's life as metaphysically privileged. Finding itself living in a world where its place is secure and clearly defined, where values and meanings are already given, the child, according to Beauvoir, does not experience the ambiguities and anxieties of freedom. As metaphysically privileged it is dominated by the situation and the others in its life. The rebellions of adolescence mark the emergence of the child from its metaphysically privileged state. This emergence is never smooth and rarely ethically successful. The ethically deprived child, more often than not, becomes an ethically depraved adult. Finding the security of a world where meaning and value are firmly grounded preferable to the ambiguity of a situation where I am responsible for securing the conditions of a livable life for myself and others, most of us, Beauvoir says, succumb to the desire to return to the metaphysically privileged condition of the child. She writes: "The misfortune which comes to man as a result of the fact that he was a child is that his freedom was first concealed from him and that all his life he will be nostalgic for the time when he did not know its exigencies" (Beauvoir 1948: 36). The child's delight in its security is innocent. The adult's nostalgia for security is not. As Beauvoir's portraits of the sub-man, the serious man, the nihilist, and the adventurer make clear, the desire to be enshrined in the world of the authoritative other is the source of the tyrant's power.

17.5 Materializing the Existential-Phenomenological Project

Beauvoir criticizes her early philosophical writings for being too abstract. By this she seems to mean that they did not pay sufficient attention to the historical, economic,

---

[4] Rousseau's *Emile* is one of the few other texts where the imprint of childhood is seen as reflected in the ethical life of the adult.

sexed, gendered conditions that impact people's lives. This changes as her thinking takes a Marxist and feminist turn. Attending to the material realities of embodiment and economic dependency her analyses of the sources of tyranny and oppression become more specific. By aligning the Marxist idea of alienated labor with the existentialist concepts of freedom and transcendence, she identifies alienated labor as labor that imprisons one in immanence.[5] Marx used the concept of alienated labor to critique the capitalist exploitation of the proletariat. Beauvoir uses it to expose the oppression of patriarchy. Gendering the existential account of alienated labor, *The Second Sex* argues that the Sisyphus-like household chores of cleaning, washing, and ironing, for example, compromise women's capacity for transcendence and that access to labor that expresses one's freedom is a necessary condition for women's liberation from their status as the second sex Other. In this gendered-existential version of Marxism, Beauvoir parts ways with strict Marxist feminists. For Beauvoir, the economic independence of women cannot be secured by receiving a salary for domestic chores, for this labor with or without pay condemns women to immanence.

As an existential-phenomenological text attentive to the power of pre-reflective experience, *The Second Sex* reframes the concept of alienation. It cannot be confined to economic labor issues. Women, Beauvoir argues, are pre-reflectively *perceived* as the sex. Being *perceived* as the sex they are *perceived* as the embodiment of immanence (Beauvoir 2009: 6). As Marx directs us to the phenomenon of alienated labor, Beauvoir directs us to the phenomenon of alienated perceptions. *The Second Sex* pays particular attention to the alienating effects of these sexed and gendered perceptions. Its concept of alienated perception has leapt from the pages of *The Second Sex* to interrogate the effects of such other-alientated perceptions as race, nationality, and ethnicity, and to delineate the ways that these culturally infected perceptions, like that of the perception of women as the sex, situate us either as privileged subject-objects in the world who can live their ambiguity with dignity, or as "othered" subject-objects available for exploitation and oppression. The concept of alienated perception prepares us for the scene where Franz Fanon is seen as "the race" by the child who exclaims, " Mama, see the Negro! I'm frightened" (Fanon 1967: 112).

Revealing the politics of perception Beauvoir transforms the project of the epoché and reconfigures the issue of the intersubjective other. The practice of bracketing is no longer a matter of searching for the invariant body behind the lived and imaginary variations of embodiment (Heinämaa 2012: 128). Anticipating Foucault, Beauvoir finds that the phenomenological idea of an archetype body can be used to support the politics of a normal/normative body. Where Foucault identifies the disciplinary practices that produce this body, Beauvoir's category of the de-subjectified Other exposes how, in becoming the measure of the human, the normalized body is used to denigrate and exploit those who don't measure up. Thus the phenomenological question: How can I account

---

[5] For a comprehensive account of the Marxist and Hegelian influences on *The Second Sex* see Lundgren-Gothlin 1996.

for my encounter with the embodied other who transcends me? becomes the political problem: How can I oppose the power of the subject who claims to embody the principle of humanity, from establishing me as the Other, the inferior, marginal, or subhuman being who can be rendered superfluous? *The Second Sex* identifies the masculine body as the norm whose othering powers transform women's sexual difference into a mark of their inferiority. In *The Coming of Age* the mature male and female body functions as the norm that others elderly bodies. In both texts, the phenomenological attention to the ambiguities of lived bodies and the dynamics of transcendence, saves philosophy from becoming an accomplice to the normative essentialisms that are used to validate some bodies at the expense of others.

The Second Sex, describing the ways that female bodies situate women in the world differently than men, and *The Coming of Age* analyzing the differences between the world of the elderly and the world of the young or mature adult reveal the difference between the perceivable world of objects available to all and a lived world of equal accessibility. As lived, life-worlds are asymmetrical. Heidegger's practical ready-to-hand world of instruments is populated with people who are instrumentalized either by being objectified as inessential (women), reduced to useful tools (slaves and colonized people), or rendered superfluous because they are used up (the elderly). Critiquing the politics that enable some bodies, but not others, to inhabit worlds that are hospitable to their existence as subjects, Beauvoir complicates Merleau-Ponty's accounts of how different physical bodies and mental states affect our grasp on the world (the phantom limb, the use of a cane, the curious psychosis of a patient who could not make abstract movement on command or point out body parts, but could react to concrete situations). The laws, taboos, and customs through which bodily differences are stigmatized and othered must also be scrutinized.

17.6 FOLLOWING THE DEMANDS OF THE EPOCHÉ TO THE CATEGORY OF THE OTHER

One way of tracing the trajectory of Beauvoir's thinking is to see it pursuing the demands of the epoché. Exposing the assumptions of our everyday attitudes, Beauvoir uncovers the ways that our taken-for-granted categories of experience are structured by the category of the Other. She describes how the natural attitude's depiction of the laws of nature (women are naturally inferior to men, colonized people are naturally incapable of rational thought) legitimates the denigration of the Other and naturalizes the politics of oppression. Philosophy is not immune from this prejudice. Read from the perspective of *The Second Sex*, it is not a matter of exploitation, but a matter of not attending to the philosophical implications of the sexual difference (Heinämaa: 2003). The natural-attitude status of woman as Other renders her either philosophically irrelevant or invisible. Hegel's master–slave dialectic, Husserl's idea of tradable places, and

Sartre's account of the Look, for example, ignore the ways that the realities of the sexual difference undermine their accounts of reciprocity and mutual recognition. Hegel, calling women the eternal irony of the community, sees nothing amiss in the fact that they are not included in the historical dialectic that will culminate in the time of mutual recognition. He does not notice that as a dialectic reserved for men, the promised mutual recognition will not be universal. Husserl does not see that though they may seem to trade perceptual places, women's here and there is never comparable to men's. Sartre assumes that a woman can return the stare of the man on the park bench without risking harassment or rape.

As Husserl described the life-world as a field of affective relations where things appear as practical and valuable objects of intersubjective use-value; as Heidegger saw our relationship to the world in terms of their practical readiness to hand; as Sartre and Merleau-Ponty placed our relationship to things in terms of their power to attract or repel us (Heinämaa 2012: 130–2); Beauvoir, saw something that none of them noticed: this world of practical and valuable objects that attract and/or repel us is not given to women and men in the same way. As the Other, as objectified hyper-visible bodies in men's world, women's lives are circumscribed by their value to men, by the usefulness of their birthing bodies, by whether they attract or repel the men upon whom their lives depend.

Inviting us to witness a scene that might be titled "Beauvoir is awakened from her dogmatic slumber" Beauvoir depicts the immediate experience that revealed these assumptions of the natural attitude. She describes conversations where she is accused of saying certain things because she is a woman. Her words are invalidated. Fully awake, Beauvoir discovers that ideas are ranked as legitimate or not according to the sex of the speaker. "A man," she writes, "is in his right by virtue of being a man; it is the woman who is in the wrong." The only way that a woman can validate her position is by abstracting herself from her subjectivity as a woman—a solution Beauvoir rejects (Beauvoir 2009: 5). Describing the hidden realities of the world that become visible once the hold of the natural attitude is broken, and following the phenomenological logic of embodied subjectivity and situated perspectives, Beauvoir argues that men's truth claims are as situated as women's, and that all claims to objective, un-situated truths, are declarations of power. Pushing the boundaries of this logic, she shows that because she is a woman, she sees what men (willfully) do not see. With these assertions the pronoun I uttered by a woman finds a respectable place in philosophical discourse. Kierkegaard adopted the strategy of pseudonyms to counter authorial authority. Beauvoir writes in her own name to establish the legitimacy of a woman's voice.

This insistence on the truth of a woman's perspective is, I think, one of the key factors in *The Second Sex*'s vault from the sphere of philosophy into the world of popular culture—to its standing as the bible of what has been called second wave feminism and to the fact that though the author of *The Second Sex* did not at the time of its writing identify herself as a feminist, she became one of the most celebrated feminists of our times. We see Beauvoir's role in legitimating women's epistemic authority in the ongoing battle to reframe the criteria of rape from what was going on in his head: I thought her no meant yes, I thought the way she dressed was an invitation to sex; to the veracity of her "no," and to the reliability of her account of what happened to her body.

If *The Second Sex*, written before its time, has found its place in ours, *The Coming of Age* has yet to resonate.[6] This may be because affirming the humanity of this Other, the elderly, entails a critique of a culture that extols work/the working body—a critique that has difficulty gaining traction in a globalized world where work is seen as the key to dignity and equality. Philosophically and phenomenologically the attention accorded to *The Second Sex* and the silence surrounding *The Coming of Age* may be due to the fact that the phenomenological privilege accorded to the "I-can" body, accepted to a certain degree in the earlier text, is rejected in the latter one. Though in *The Second Sex* enabling women's "I-can" bodies and providing these bodies with the access to meaningful work is not a sufficient condition for women's equality, it remains a necessary one (see Young 1990). The project of disabling alienated bodily habits cannot, however, become a formula for establishing the full humanity of the aged. The elderly body has not been alienated from its "I-cans" by taboos, fashions, or codes of respectability. It cannot retrieve these capacities by removing these obstacles. Its "I-cans" have been eroded by the forces of time and materiality. So long as the "I-can" body remains the signature of our worth as persons, the old will be marginalized.

In bringing old bodies into view and affirming the dignity of the frail body Beauvoir asks us to complicate our understanding of the body as the instrument through which we engage the world. Describing the inherent humanity of the older person's capacity for accessing the joys of living in the world as it is, Beauvoir may be seen as pursuing the possibilities of her turn to the erotic body in *The Second Sex* and as probing the implications of her reformulation of intentionality in *The Ethics of Ambiguity* (Bergoffen 1977). In the first case the discussions of the erotic suggest that the working body may not be the best measure of world engagement and that encountering the singularity of the other through the solidarity of common projects does not get us to the heart of intersubjective life. In the second, the priority Beauvoir accorded to the joy of the original intentional moment becomes a resource for critiquing the culture of work—the intentionality of the willful transformation of the world as given. In both cases Beauvoir's phenomenology of intentionality and lived experience affirms the dignity of the lived body, including that of the dying body, that confronts us with the humanity of our finitude (Beauvoir 1983, 1986). By turning our attention to the ways that it is as vulnerable and fragile bodies that we embody our relationship to the world and others *The Coming of Age* may be seen as a forerunner of current discussions of precariousness and vulnerability (Butler 2004; Bergoffen 2012).

---

[6] The 2014 anthology *Simone de Beauvoir's Philosophy of Age* may signal that Beauvoir's discussions of the aged and aging is beginning to get the attention it deserves.

17.7 Feminist Contestations

Though *The Second Sex* is now a celebrated text, its continued relevance remains contested. Among feminists it has been criticized for being emblematic of what was wrong with the feminism of the 1970s. Like that feminism, Beauvoir is condemned for "essentializing" the complex realities of women's lives. She is seen as assuming that certain women—privileged, middle-class, white European women—could speak for and about all women. This critique accuses Beauvoir of forgetting what awakened her from her dogmatic slumber—men's claim that they had privileged access to the truth—for her claim of epistemic authority is seen as guilty of the same error

Elizabeth Spelman (1998) and Patricia Hill Collins (1990) are among those who have critiqued this claim of privilege. They find it unsupportable and argue that it renders Beauvoir's thought inadequate, if not obsolete. As they see it, it is precisely because she is privileged that she missed the significance of the compelling and complex ways that women's identities as women cannot be disentangled from their race, class, ethnic, national, and sexual identities. Women exist. Woman does not.

Several issues are in play here: the limitations of a privileged perspective; the ways *The Second Sex* did or did not address the intersections of sex, gender, race, ethnicity, nationality, sexuality; the adequacy of the categories of *The Second Sex* for addressing the truths of women's situated lives. Margaret Simons alerts us to the complexity of these issues. She tells us that Beauvoir was schooled by Richard Wright in the realities of American racism and that seeing this racism first hand in her travels though the Southern United States taught her to see how/that racism and economic class were barriers to women identifying with each other rather than with the men of their race and class (Simons 1999b: 170). Simons notes, however, that Beauvoir's focus on female dependency and passivity reflects a class bias that is a serious problem in feminist theory and that the idea of absolute patriarchy obscures the fact that some white women have had power over minority women and men (Simons 1999a: 26–7).

Kathryn Gines, also citing Wright's influence on Beauvoir, finds that Beauvoir failed to identify the limits of the analogy between racism and sexism. Though Gines sees an affinity between Beauvoir's critique of white women's exchange of complicity for privileges and Audre Lorde's critique of white feminism and white female privilege, she finds that Beauvoir herself was not sensitive to this issue (Gines 2010:43). Arguing that we need a framework that provides a space for the distinct voices and insights of women of color, Gines credits Anna Julia Cooper with opening this space (Gines 2010: 44).

As I see it, these critiques, in questioning the continued relevance of Beauvoir's ideas for feminist theory, direct us to ask whether the limitations of *The Second Sex*, its reliance on outdated science, its problematic Eurocentric, class, and race perspectives, for example, reflect the limitations of its analytic categories or their use by Beauvoir. Beauvoir's category of the Other is a case in point. By signaling that the visible dynamics of racism, imperialism, and slavery mimic the invisible dynamics of sexism it legitimated the use of such terms as "oppression" and "subjugation" (terms that are usually associated with class, colonial, and race domination) to characterize women's situation. The analyses of contemporary feminist philosophers show that the analogy cannot be taken too far and that insofar as the category of the Other presents women as one dimensional it is inadequate. There is a danger, however, in rejecting the category of the Other per se. Though a heavy-handed use of it erases the differences in women's lives that make a difference, a nuanced use of it shows that despite these differences, women are the object of certain forms of violence, rape, and sexual assault, for example, because they are women. By directing us to interrogate the epidemic of violence against women and to probe the politics of this violence, the category of the Other remains a potent feminist tool.

17.8 THE QUESTION OF PRIVILEGE AND THE FEMINIST TURN

Taking up the case of Djamila Boupacha, Beauvoir turns the questions of the Other and privileged perspective into the question of the responsibilities of privilege (Beauvoir 1962). Boupacha's torture and rape and Beauvoir's intervention, speak to the ways that one's sexed and gendered existence cannot be disentangled from one's colonized, raced, and classed embodiment. Boupacha, accused of being a member of the Algerian resistance, was arrested, raped, and tortured by the French authorities. Her torture included rape because she was a woman. But it is not only because she was a woman that she was raped. It was because she was an Algerian, young, virgin woman who would become unmarriageable by being raped.[7]

In coming to Boupacha's defense Beauvoir was not just one woman coming to the aid of another. As a French intellectual woman of standing she knew that her privileged position would carry weight. If Beauvoir's claim of epistemological privilege has been discredited on phenomenological and feminist grounds, Beauvoir's implicit claim in defending Boupacha, that being a privileged woman carries responsibilities, has not. The question of how to assume these responsibilities remains a live feminist issue (Shelby 2006: 93–108).

Beauvoir may be seen as giving her answer to this question in her address to the International Tribunal on Crimes against Women. This People's Tribunal, modeled on the Russell Tribunal that tried the United States for its crimes in the Vietnam War, was held in Brussels from March 4–8, 1976 to publicize the medical, economic, and

---

[7] For detailed discussions of Beauvoir and the Djamila Boupacha case see Caputi (2006: 109–26) and Murphy (1995: 263–98).

political crimes committed against women. In her address to the opening of the Tribunal Beauvoir, joining with women around the world to organize the event, sees its mobilization of women as a revolutionary moment that would begin the "radical decolonization of women" (Beauvoir 1990: 5).

The Ethics of Ambiguity and *The Second Sex* compared the oppression of women to the exploitation of slavery, here Beauvoir finds women's condition more analogous to that of colonized people—not quite enslaved but certainly not free. Clarifying what she means by calling women colonized, Beauvoir shows how the category of the Other can speak to the shared situation of women without erasing their differences. She writes, "whatever regime, law, moral code, or social environment in which they find themselves, all women suffer from a specific form of oppression"—an oppression that exploits their birthing bodies and extorts the labor of their gendered bodies (Beauvoir 1990: 5). As colonized bodies, women "are the privileged objects of male aggression." The most insidious fact about this widespread violence is that it is "unanimously unrecognized and passed over in silence" (Beauvoir 1990: 5). As colonized bodies, women are dis-embodied, not in the Cartesian sense of discovering that they are first and foremost thinking things, but in the lived experience of discovering that their bodies belong to others.

This attention to the epidemic of violence against women reveals the distance between the feminist who addressed the Tribunal and the author of *The Second Sex*. The most focused discussion of violence in *The Second Sex* occurs in the section on childhood. Comparing the childhood experiences of boys and girls, Beauvoir finds that by being schooled in the lessons of violence, the boy discovers his independence. He learns to trust his body and to affirm himself in his projects. He comes to value transcendence/freedom more than life. Where boys learn to challenge the world as it is given to them, girls are taught to be careful, to please, to make themselves objects to be admired, to renounce autonomy (Beauvoir 2009: 294–5). Adopting this Hegelian master–slave paradigm of violence, where taking up the risks of violence represent a commitment to freedom and a path to liberation, Beauvoir bemoans the fact that deprived of these lessons women have not learned to value freedom more than survival.

This account of the different ways girl and boy children are introduced to their capacity for transcendence misses the role that sexual violence plays in this sexed education. Though Beauvoir notes that girls are subjected to sexual abuse by respected family men and friends, and finds that girls must endure this abuse in silence (Beauvoir 2009: 332–3), she does not understand this abuse and the refusal to acknowledge it as an essential ingredient in the structure of patriarchy. Curing society of the epidemic of violence against women is not cited as one of the necessary conditions for the emergence of the independent woman. As an organizer of the Tribunal, however, Beauvoir sees that neither economic independence, nor destroying the myth of woman will by themselves eradicate the ways that the lessons of violence have been inscribed on women's bodies and cut their tongues. She now identifies giving women back their voice as a first and essential step in liberating women from their status as the Other.

17.9 INFLUENCES ACKNOWLEDGED
AND IGNORED

Invoking the importance of the right to appear in public and to have one's words count as the key to liberation, Beauvoir co-founded the review *Nouvelles questions féministes* (*New Feminist Issues*) with Christine Delphy, a French sociologist, feminist, writer, and theorist in 1972. Identified as the voice of such feminists as Nicole Claude-Mathieu, Emmanuèle de Lesseps, Colette Guillaumin, Monique Wittig, and Paola Tabet, the journal focused on the materialist approach to gender relations. While critiquing the limitations of the Marxist concept of class, its essays analyzed the inequalities between men and women from an economic perspective. These thinkers, taking their cue from Beauvoir, identify patriarchy, not capitalism, as the source of women's exploitation. As a founder of this journal Beauvoir directs us to the materialist valences of her work. She leads us to see Monique Wittig, for example, as drawing on and drawing out the ideas of *The Second Sex*.

Reenacting the shock of Beauvoir's "One is not born but becomes woman," Wittig startles us with her announcement that "Lesbians are not women" (Wittig 1992: 32). For Wittig, that lesbians are not women is the logical consequence of the materialist frame birthed by Beauvoir. If women are habituated to live their bodies in ways that materialize the myth of woman, and if the myth of woman situates women as the object of men's desire, then refusing to live their bodies in relationship to men is the only path to freedom. As slaves exist only so long as they are owned by masters, women exist only so long as they are tethered to men. In escaping from their masters, slaves destroy the slave class (Wittig 1992: 9). In severing relationships with men, lesbians demolish the class women. Echoing Marx's anticipation of a classless society, Wittig looks forward to a sexless one (Wittig 1992: 24). Beauvoir provisionally admitted that women existed so that she might pose the question of woman (Beauvoir 2009: xii). Wittig contends that, once the question of woman is adequately posed, it is no longer necessary to admit (provisionally or otherwise) that women exist.

The hostile relationship between those feminists affiliated with *Nouvelles questions féministes* and those who founded *Psychanalyse et Politique* (known as *Psych et Po*), a journal founded in 1968 and now defunct, would seem to indicate that those who approached the question of woman/women psychoanalytically, rather than materially, and argued for a feminism of difference rather than equality, were breaking with Beauvoir's line of thought. Examining the debates over the significance of language reveals that things are more complicated. Though Wittig for example critiques those who have taken the analytic turn for reducing the misery of the oppressed "to a few figures of speech" (Wittig 1992: 21–4), she also argued that it is the materiality of language, not just the meager paycheck, that oppresses women. Rather than seeing the gender politics of these groups as incommensurable, or as a sign of their affinity or rejection of Beauvoir, we do better, I think, to see their differences as distinct ways of developing

Beauvoir's phenomenological analyses of the power of language as it functions in the myth of woman.

From this perspective Luce Irigaray (one of the founders of *Psych et Po*) in calling for an ethics of sexual difference and a politics of equity, may be read as plying the libratory possibilities of Beauvoir's reference to the unique *Mitsein* bond of the heterosexual couple. In Beauvoir's hands Heidegger's term *Mitsein* is transformed from a descriptive term into a prescriptive one. Telling us that "in sexuality [we find] . . . the tension, the anguish, the joy, the frustration, and the triumph of existence," Beauvoir declares that "when we abolish the slavery of half of humanity, together with the whole system of hypocrisy it implies, then the 'division' of humanity will reveal its genuine significance and the human couple will find its true form" (Beauvoir 2009: 731).

From Irigaray's perspective, Beauvoir is correct in recognizing the promissory *Mitsein* of the heterosexual couple. In advocating sexual equality, however, Beauvoir, according to Irigaray, does not adequately understand this promise, for in arguing for equality, she accepts the metaphysics of the One, a metaphysics grounded in the idea of an epistemological hierarchy where each truth claim is legitimated or rejected through its reference to a single absolute Truth. Challenging this metaphysics, Irigaray argues for a metaphysics of the Two of sexual difference (Irigaray 1985b). In this metaphysics no truth is authorized to silence that of the other. Each in their difference is seen as essential to, but not the equivalent of the other. Thus feminist theory and politics must advocate equity, not equality, between women and men (Irigaray 2000). The extent to which this is radically opposed to Beauvoir's argument for difference in equality is a matter of debate.[8]

Like Irigaray, Julia Kristeva turned to psychoanalysis to upend the patriarchal status quo. Unlike Irigaray who neglected her debts to Beauvoir, Kristeva, in organizing the Parisian centennial celebration of Beauvoir's birth, signals that she sees her challenges to Beauvoir, their different positions on the meaning and realities of motherhood for example (Kristeva 1997a: 301–7; 1997c 308–31), as part of Beauvoir's project of abandoning the ruts of old quarrels for new beginnings which, grounded in the alterity we embrace theoretically, endorse practices that fruitfully disrupt each other's settled positions.

Reading between Kristeva and Beauvoir, I find Kristeva translating Beauvoir's existential-phenomenological language into the discourse of psychoanalysis. This translation is not one of equivalency. Neither language can substitute for the other. They do, however, speak to each other and we, listening to their conversation, can better understand the dynamics of the ambiguities embodied in our humanity. In her account of intentionality and in her depiction of the temporality of the subject for example, Beauvoir describes us as subjects in process who in bringing meaning and value into the world also and necessarily put the meanings and values of the world into question. Kristeva also conceives of the subject as a becoming. Here, however, the becoming of the subject is described as an embodiment of the question that emerges through the negativity of the drives that reveal alternatives to the status quo. It is not just the values and meanings

---

[8] For additional explorations of the relationship between Beauvoir and Irigaray see Bergoffen 2003.

of the world that are disrupted, our current ways of structuring the subject in terms of a stable identity are also hijacked (Kristeva 1977c: 93–115).

Calling for a "herethical" ethics grounded in the concept of a subject as a process of self-formation and transformation open to the rhythms of life captured in the semiotic sounds, touches, and flows of the maternal body (Kristeva 1997b: 27–92), Kristeva may be seen as aligning Beauvoir's ethics of praxis and projects with her phenomenological accounts of joy. Translating this idea of joy into the psychoanalytic concept of *jouissance* Kristeva finds the explosive vitality of *jouissance* at the heart of the May '68 protests (Kristeva 2002: 11–44). For Kristeva, a politics motivated by and infused with this joyful *jouissance*, carries the hope of creating a world where being an-other is a mark of singular dignity, not degradation.

17.10 By Way of an Ending and an Opening

As Merleau-Ponty spoke of Husserl as a philosopher "whose venture has awakened so many echoes" (Merleau-Ponty 1964c: 159) the continued and continuing influence of Beauvoir's thinking is indicative of the ways that her writings draw us from its explicit insights to its yet-to-be-thought possibilities—as signaling the ways that her thinking invites rather than resists being taken in divergent directions. This invitation is not accidental. It is integral to an existentialism that identifies its ethics of freedom in terms of the responsibility to being open to the desires and voices of the future. It is characteristic of a phenomenology dedicated to deciphering the ambiguities of our embodied lives as they experience the wonders of the world and the joys of embracing the singularity of the other.

References

Barnes, H. (1998), "Self encounter in *She Came to Stay*," in E. Fallaize (ed.), *Simone de Beauvoir: A Critical Reader* (London: Routledge), 157–70.

Beauvoir, S. de (1943), *She Came to Stay*, translated by L. D. Drummond (New York: World, 1954).

Beauvoir, S. de (1945a), "A review of the *Phenomenology of Perception* by Maurice Merleau-Ponty," in M. A. Simons (ed.), *Simone de Beauvoir: Philosophical Writings* (Urbana, IL: University of Illinois Press, 2006), 159–64.

Beauvoir, S. de (1945b), "Existentialism and popular wisdom," in M. A. Simons (ed.), *Simone de Beauvoir: Philosophical Writings* (Urbana, IL: University of Illinois Press, 2006), 203–20.

Beauvoir, S. de (1946), "Literature and metaphysics," translated by V. Zaytzeff and F. Morrison, in M. A. Simons (ed.), *Simone de Beauvoir: Philosophical Writings* (Urbana, IL: University of Illinois Press, 2006), 269–77.

Beauvoir, S. de (1947), "What Is Existentialism?" in M. A. Simons (ed.), *Simone de Beauvoir: Philosophical Writings* (Urbana, IL: University of Illinois Press, 2006), 323–6.

Beauvoir, S. de (1948), *The Ethics of Ambiguity*, translated by B. Frechtman (New York: Philosophical Library).

Beauvoir, S. de (1955), *All Men Are Mortal*, translated by L. Friedman (New York: W. W. Norton).

Beauvoir, S. de (1962), *Djamila Boupacha: The Story of the Torture of a Young Algerian Girl which Shocked Liberal French Opinion*, translated by P. Green (New York: Macmillan).

Beauvoir, S. de (1983), *A Very Easy Death*, translated by P. O'Brian (New York: Penguin).

Beauvoir, S. de (1986), *Adieux: A Farewell to Sartre*, translated by P. O'Brian (New York: Penguin).

Beauvoir, S. de (1990), "Preface," in D. E. H. Russell and N. Van De Ven (eds), *Crimes against Women: The Proceedings of the International Criminal Tribunal on Crimes against Women* (Berkeley, CA: Russell Publications), 5–6.

Beauvoir, S. de (1996), *The Coming of Age*, translated by P. O'Brian (New York: W. W. Norton).

Beauvoir, S. de (2009), *The Second Sex*, translated by C. Borde and S. Malovany-Chevallier (New York: Alfred A. Knopf).

Bergoffen, D. (1997), *The Philosophy of Simone de Beauvoir: Gendered Phenomenologies, Erotic Generosities* (New York: SUNY Press).

Bergoffen, D. (2003), "Failed Friendship, Forgotten Genealogies: Simone de Beauvoir and Luce Irigaray," *Bulletin de la Société Américaine de Philosophie de Langue Française* 13/21: 16–31.

Bergoffen, D. (2009), "Finitude and Justice: Simone de Beauvoir's *All Men Are Mortal*," *Philosophy Today* 53(SPEP Supplement): 116–20.

Bergoffen, D. (2012), *Contesting the Politics of Genocidal Rape: Affirming the Dignity of the Vulnerable Body* (New York: Routledge).

Butler, J. (1986), "Sex and Gender in Simone de Beauvoir's Second Sex," *Yale French Studies* 72: 35–50.

Butler, J. (2004), *Precarious Life: The Powers of Mourning and Violence* (New York: Verso).

Caputi, M. (2006), "Beauvoir and the Case of Djamila Boupacha," in L. Marso and P. Moynagh (eds), *Simone de Beauvoir's Political Thinking* (Chicago, IL: University of Illinois Press), 109–26.

Collins, P. H. (1990), *Black Feminist Thought: Knowledge, Consciousness and the Politics of Empowerment* (London: HarperCollins Academic).

Fanon, F. (1967), *Black Skin, White Masks* (New York: Grove Weidenfeld).

Gines, K. T. (2010), "Sartre, Beauvoir and the race/gender analogy: A case for black feminist philosophy," in B. Guy-Sheftall and G. Yancy (eds), *Convergences: Black Feminism and Continental Philosophy* (Albany, NY: SUNY Press), 35–51.

Heath, J. (1998), "*She Came to Stay*: The phallus stikes back," in E. Fallaize (ed.), *Simone de Beauvoir: A Critical Reader* (London: Routledge), 171–82.

Heinämaa, S. (2003), *Toward a Phenomenology of Sexual Difference: Husserl, Merleau-Ponty, Beauvoir* (New York: Rowman and Littlefield).

Heinämaa, S. (2009), "Psychoanalysis of things: Objective meanings or subjective projections?" in C. Daigle and J. Golomb (eds), *Beauvoir and Sartre: The Riddle of Influence* (Bloomington, IN: Indiana University Press), 128–42.

Heinämaa, S. (2012), "Beauvoir and Husserl: An unorthodox approach to *The Second Sex*," in S. M. Mussett and W. S. Wilkerson (eds), *Beauvoir and Western Thought from Plato to Butler* (Albany, NY: SUNY Press), 125–52.

Holveck, E. (2002), *Simone de Beauvoir's Philosophy of Lived Experience* (Lantham, MD: Rowman and Littlefield).

Irigaray, L. (1985a), *Speculum of the Other Woman*, translated by G. Gill (Ithaca, NY: Cornell University Press).

Irigaray, L. (1985b), *This Sex Which Is Not On*, translated by C. Porter (Ithaca, NY: Cornell University Press).

Irigaray, L. (1993), *An Ethics of Sexual Difference*, translated by C. Burke and G. C. Gill (Ithaca, NY: Cornell University Press).

Irigaray, L. (2000), *Democracy Begins between Two*, translated by K. Anderson (New York: Routledge).

Kristeva, J. (1997a), "Motherhood according to Bellini," in K. Oliver (ed.), *The Portable Kristeva* (New York: Columbia University Press), 301–7.

Kristeva, J. (1997b), "Revolution in poetic language," in K. Oliver (ed.), *The Portable Kristeva* (New York: Columbia University Press), 27–92.

Kristeva, J. (1997c), "Stabat mater," in K. Oliver (ed.), *The Portable Kristeva* (New York: Columbia University Press), 308–31.

Kristeva, J. (1977d) "From one identity to another," in K. Oliver (ed.), *The Portable Kristeva* (New York: Columbia University Press), 93–115.

Kristeva, J. (2002), "What's left of 1968?" in *Revolt, She Said*, translated by B. O'Keeffe (New York: Semiotext(e)), 11–44.

Lundgren-Gothlin, E. (1996), *Sex and Existence: Simone de Beauvoir's* The Second Sex (Hanover, NH: Wesleyan University Press).

Merleau-Ponty, M. (1964a), "Metaphysics and the novel," in H. D. and P. A. Dreyfus (eds), *Sense and Non-Sense* (Evanston,IL: Northwestern University Press), 26–40.

Merleau-Ponty, M. (1964b), "Bergson in the making," in *Signs* (Evanston, IL: Northwestern University Press), 182–91.

Merleau-Ponty, M. (1964c), "The philosopher and his shadow," in *Signs* (Evanston, IL: Northwestern University Press), 159–81.

Murphy, J. (1995), "Beauvoir and the Algerian War: Toward a postcolonial ethics," in M. Simons (ed.), *Feminist Interpretations of Simone de Beauvoir* (University Park, PA: Pennsylvania State University Press), 263–98.

Shelby, K. (2006), "Beauvoir and ethical responsibility," in L. Marso and P. Moynagh (eds), *Simone de Beauvoir's Political Thinking* (Chicago, IL: University of Illinois Press), 93–108.

Simons, M. (1999a), "Racism and feminism: A schism in the sisterhood," in M. Simons (ed.), *Beauvoir and* The Second Sex*: Feminism, Race, and the Origins of Existentialism* (New York: Rowman and Littlefield), 23–40.

Simons, M. (1999b), "Richard Wright, Simone de Beauvoir, and *The Second Sex*," in M. Simons (ed.), *Beauvoir and* The Second Sex*: Feminism, Race, and the Origins of Existentialism* (New York: Rowman and Littlefield), 167–84.

Simons, M. (1999c), "Beauvoir's early philosophy: The 1927 Diary," in M. Simons (ed.), *Beauvoir and* The Second Sex*: Feminism, Race, and the Origins of Existentialism* (New York: Rowman and Littlefield), 185–243.

Spelman, E. (1998), *Inessential Woman: Problems of Exclusion in Feminist Thought* (Boston, MA: Beacon Press).

Stoller, S. (ed.) (2014), *Simone de Beauvoir's Philosophy of Age: Gender Ethics and Time* (Berlin: de Gruyter).

Tidd, U. (1999), *Simone de Beauvoir: Gender and Testimony* (Cambridge: Cambridge University Press).

Wittig, M. (1992), *The Straight Mind and Other Essays* (Boston, MA: Beacon Press).

Young, I. M. (1990), "Throwing like a girl," in *Throwing Like a Girl and Other Essays in Feminist Philosophy and Social Theory* (Bloomington, IN: Indiana University Press), 141–59.

CHAPTER 18

SCIENCE IN MERLEAU-PONTY'S PHENOMENOLOGY

From the Early Work to the Later Philosophy

KOMARINE ROMDENH-ROMLUC

18.1 INTRODUCTION

PHENOMENOLOGY and science, it is often claimed, are uncomfortable bedfellows.[1] On the one hand, both share an interest in the mind (amongst other things). Certain strands of contemporary cognitive science explicitly take inspiration from phenomenology. To give just one example, Andy Clark (a leading exponent of embodied approaches to cognitive science) begins *Being There* (Clark 1997) by noting that:

> This book didn't come from nowhere. The image of the mind as inextricably interwoven with the body, world, and action, already visible in Martin Heidegger's *Being and Time* (1978), found clear expression in Merleau-Ponty's *Structure of Behaviour* (1963). (Clark 1997: xvii)

He goes on to cite Dreyfus's critique of classical artificial intelligence, *What Computers Can't Do* (1979) as a further source of inspiration—a work steeped in phenomenological ideas about the mind. Similarly, many phenomenologists (notably, Merleau-Ponty—but more of this in a minute) draw on science. On the other hand, there are (at least) two significant objections to the possibility that science may use phenomenology's insights, and vice versa. First, phenomenology's method of describing experience from a first-person perspective is often (wrongly) identified with introspection, which, it is claimed, hardly counts as a method at all, and is certainly incapable of yielding anything

[1] I would like to thank Rasmus Thybo Jensen, Donald Landes, and Dan Zahavi for many helpful comments on an earlier draft of this chapter.

of interest to science. An oft-quoted remark from Dennett gives vehement expression to this thought: "First-person science of consciousness is a discipline with no methods, no data, no results, no future, no promise. It will remain a fantasy" (Dennett 2001). Second, phenomenology and science are committed to fundamentally different stances regarding subjectivity. Science, it is claimed, is committed to realism—the view that the existence and character of the universe is independent from any subjects' experiences of, or thoughts about, it. Science is also widely seen as committed to naturalism, the view that everything—including subjectivity—can be explained using the concepts of natural science, and such an account is the best that can be given. But phenomenology holds a *transcendental* view of subjectivity, which precludes a complete treatment of it in naturalistic terms. Subjectivity (partially) constitutes the world studied by science, and so cannot be a mere part of it, fully governed by—and so fully explicable in terms of—its laws, even though scientific accounts of consciousness may have some limited uses.[2]

Merleau-Ponty's work seemingly exemplifies the tension between phenomenology and science. He endorses a transcendental view of perception, and indeed, of subjectivity more generally. He writes, "perception is not an event of nature" (Merleau-Ponty 1963: 145). Again, "there can be no question of describing [perception] as one of the facts that happens in the world" (Merleau-Ponty 2012: 215). Moreover, "I cannot think of myself as a part of the world, like the simple object of biology, psychology, and sociology; I cannot enclose myself within the universe of science" (Merleau-Ponty 2012: xxii). His transcendental view of consciousness goes hand-in-hand with a critique of science. "Scientific perspectives according to which I am a moment of the world are always naïve and hypocritical" (Merleau-Ponty 2012: xxii). In a passage from *Eye and Mind* (Merleau-Ponty 1964a), Merleau-Ponty criticizes scientific investigations that "represent themselves to be autonomous," which "treat the scientist's knowledge as if it were absolute" as leading to "all sorts of vagabond endeavours" (Merleau-Ponty 1964a: 160). Yet, he makes copious use of scientific data. For instance, a great deal of *The Structure of Behaviour* (Merleau-Ponty 1963) consists in close analysis of various psychological experiments. Similarly, some of the central arguments in his *Phenomenology of Perception* (Merleau-Ponty 2012) depend on Gestalt psychology's findings. In that text, Merleau-Ponty also makes copious use of scientific case-studies—most notably, Schneider, the injured World War I veteran, whose curious disabilities were studied at length by Kurt Goldstein and Adhémar Gelb (1920). But he also relies on data from other experiments, such as George Stratton's (1896) inverted vision experiments, to give just one example. In fact, Merleau-Ponty employs the findings of science throughout his oeuvre.

In this chapter, I will consider Merleau-Ponty's conception of the relation between science and his phenomenology. I will sketch one line of thought from his work according to which, science and phenomenology are fundamentally the same sort of investigation. They may employ different concepts to characterize their data and results.

---

[2] There are many discussions of the relation between science and phenomenology. A recent collection of essays is Carel and Meacham (2013).

They may also investigate different things—a scientist may investigate the effects of climate change on our weather systems; a phenomenologist may inquire into the structure of time consciousness. Yet, even though these investigations are directed at different things, viewed at a certain level of generality, *what* it is they are discovering and *how* they are doing so, is the same. Moreover, Merleau-Ponty holds that the different concepts they employ and the different objects they investigate are not *essential* differences between science and phenomenology. Let us say, therefore, that for Merleau-Ponty, science and phenomenology are "continuous." I will not attempt to fully defend his view here. But I hope to show that it is a provocative and interesting line of thought, which is prima facie at least, able to speak to the two worries cited above: that phenomenology and science employ fundamentally different methods, and have fundamentally different commitments.

18.2 TRANSCENDENTAL SCIENCE

The remarks quoted above illustrate the generally agreed upon fact that Merleau-Ponty's position is transcendental. He writes, "the world is inseparable from the subject, but from a subject who is nothing but a project of the world; and the subject is separable from the world, but from a world that it itself projects" (Merleau-Ponty 2012: 454). He claims here that the subject and world are mutually constituting and so depend on each other. The claim that Merleau-Ponty sees science and phenomenology as continuous may thus sound surprising, since a transcendental view of subjectivity is at odds with science's alleged commitment to realism and naturalism. Merleau-Ponty also offers a sustained critique of science.

The first step in understanding his position is to see that he rejects the claim that science is *necessarily* committed to realism and naturalism. There could be a science that recognizes the transcendental status of consciousness and the anti-realism and non-naturalism this entails. Moreover, he thinks there are actual examples of such a science. One case is that of Gestalt psychology.

The Gestalt psychologists recognized that perceptual experience is always meaningful—we are never presented with a disordered mass of sense data. Gestalten are the forms that characterize our perceptions. Importantly, Gestalten are unified wholes, composed of their parts in such a way that they are irreducible to them. To see what is at stake here, consider the following example:

> If I am walking on a beach towards a boat that has run aground, and if the funnel or the mast merges with the forest that borders the dune, then there will be a moment in which these details suddenly reunite with the boat and become welded to it . . . I merely felt that the appearance of the object was about to change . . . The spectacle was suddenly reorganized, satisfying my vague expectation. (Merleau-Ponty 2012: 17–18)

The experience described here is what is often called a "Gestalt switch" Merleau-Ponty is first presented with what appear to be trees (his experience is characterized by a trees-Gestalt). It then suddenly changes so that it takes on a boat-Gestalt (he is presented with what appears to be a boat). Whilst the perceptual meaning of the experience changes, the components of the scene do not alter—there is a sense in which he sees the same arrangement of vertical items throughout, although their incorporation into different Gestalten also means that there is another sense in which they cannot be compared. The same elements can therefore be unified as, or support, different Gestalten. Merleau-Ponty takes this to show that Gestalten cannot be simply reduced to their parts. Yet at the same time, the scene's Gestalt form as either trees or boats is not something extra to its components. Take away the vertical structures, and there is no tree, mast, or funnel. Thus Gestalten are composed of their parts in such a way that they are nothing over and above them, but they cannot be reduced to them.

In *The Structure of Behaviour* (Merleau-Ponty 1963), Merleau-Ponty argues that the Gestalt psychologists did not realize the implications of what they had discovered. First, Gestalten have a peculiar ontological status, being neither fully objective, nor created by consciousness from nothing, as the following remark from a later work makes clear:

> It is the notion of an order of meaning which does not result from the application of spiritual activity to an external matter. It is, rather, a spontaneous organization beyond the distinction between activity and passivity . . . In Gestalt psychology everything bears a meaning. There is no psychic phenomenon which is not oriented towards a certain significance . . . But this sense . . . is an earthy and aboriginal sense, which constitutes itself by an organization of the so-called elements. (1964b: 77)

Gestalten are, for Merleau-Ponty, uniquely *perceptual* phenomena. They do not exist independently of consciousness, but are brought into being when the subject makes contact with the world in perception. They are the forms the world assumes in perceptual experience. Their nature as wholes that are nothing more than the sum of their parts, yet composed of them in such a way that they cannot be reduced to them points to this fact. Gestalten must be realized in some sensuous matter. The form does not exist without the matter in which it is realized because it just *is* the form this matter assumes when perceived. In this way they are nothing over and above the sum of their parts. Gestalten are not, however, reducible to the matter in which they are realized because they do not exist independently of perceiving consciousness. Yet the perceiver does not "add" Gestalten to sensuous matter from nowhere. Instead, it *discovers* a meaningful form in it. Consciousness does not create but finds form in the matter, in a way that is neither wholly active nor wholly passive.

The Gestalt psychologists used the notion of Gestalt form primarily to characterize perceptual experience. The second thing they failed to realize, according to Merleau-Ponty, is that the concept has much wider application. He argues that all orders of being—the "physical" (inorganic existence), the "vital" world of living beings, and the "human"—must be understood using the idea: "What Köhler shows with a few examples ought to be extended to all physical laws" (Merleau-Ponty 1963: 138). Since all orders of existence are characterized by Gestalten, and since Gestalt forms cannot exist independently of consciousness, it follows that the world is dependent on consciousness. But, as we have seen, the consciousness that apprehends Gestalt form is not a subject that lies wholly outside the world and constitutes it from nothing, but an "earthy" consciousness that depends on a world in which it discerns rather than imposes meaningful structure. A thoroughgoing Gestalt psychology thus leads to a transcendental understanding of the world and consciousness:

> Form is not a physical reality, but an object of perception; without it physical science would have no meaning, moreover, since it is constructed with respect to it and in order to coordinate it . . . form cannot be defined in terms of reality but in terms of knowledge, not as a thing of the perceived world but as a perceived whole. (Merleau-Ponty 1963: 143)

Merleau-Ponty's arguments in *The Structure of Behaviour* (Merleau-Ponty 1963) are usually understood as directed at the idea that Gestalt psychology leads to, or is, a nascent phenomenology. But it is possible to read this claim in the opposite direction, as it were: Insofar as Gestalt psychology is a science that implies phenomenology, it is—or has the potential to be—a transcendental science.

Gestalt psychology is not the only example of a transcendental science. In the radio lectures that were broadcast in 1948 and subsequently published in English as *The World of Perception* (Merleau-Ponty 2004), Merleau-Ponty says:

> The scientist of today, unlike his predecessor working within the classical paradigm, no longer cherishes the illusion that he is penetrating to the heart of things, to the object as it is in itself. The physics of relativity confirms that absolute and final objectivity is a mere dream by showing how *each particular observation is strictly linked to the location of observer and cannot be abstracted from this particular situation; it also rejects the notion of an absolute observer.* We can no longer flatter ourselves with the idea that, in science, the exercises of a pure and unsituated intellect can allow us to gain access to an object free of all human traces. (2004: 44–5, my italics)

Here, Merleau-Ponty speaks approvingly of the science of relativity, which takes what is observed to depend for its character on a human perceiver (although he makes clear in the lecture course *La Nature* (2003: 111–12) that this is not the *individual* subject that Einstein envisaged, but an intersubjective community).[3] Similarly, Merleau-Ponty takes quantum mechanics to demand the same transcendental ontology—it

---

[3] *La Nature* (Merleau-Ponty 2003) contains Merleau-Ponty's most extended discussion of quantum mechanics. See particularly, Part 2 of the First Course "Modern Science and Nature." Rosen (2013) offers an interpretation of Merleau-Ponty's conception of a phenomenological physics, which develops ideas from this work.

is "a physics that is no longer objectivist" (Merleau-Ponty 1968: 25). This view is in line with the Cophenhagen Interpretation of Quantum Mechanics, which also—according to many authors, such as Hooker (1972), Honner (1982), and Chevalley (1991)—implies the same form of anti-realism, whereby the nature of what is observed depends on the observer. In both cases, consciousness (the observer) therefore has a transcendental role.

Merleau-Ponty also writes:

> I did not, of course, mean to imply that [philosophy] denies the value of science, either as a means of technological advancement, or insofar as it offers an object lesson in precision and truth. If we wish to learn how to prove something, to conduct a thorough investigation or to be critical of ourselves and our preconceptions, it remains appropriate, now as then, that we turn to science ... The question which modern philosophy asks in relation to science is not intended either to contest its right to exist or to close off any particular avenue to its inquiries. Rather, the question is whether science does, or ever could, present us with a picture of the world which is complete, self-sufficient and somehow closed in upon itself, such that there could no longer be any meaningful questions outside this picture ... *it is science itself—particularly in its more recent developments—which forces us to ask this question and which encourages us to answer in the negative.* (2004: 42–3, my italics)

Here, Merleau-Ponty suggests that contemporary science recognizes its own limits—a scientific account of the world and consciousness cannot be complete—because it recognizes the transcendental nature of subjectivity.

18.3 MERLEAU-PONTY'S CRITIQUE OF SCIENCE

It follows that Merleau-Ponty's critique cannot be directed at science in general, but must be directed at science that is committed to realism and naturalism. This is so, but it is important to note that such science is not the only target of Merleau-Ponty's criticisms. His critique is directed at science that works within the framework of what he calls "objective thought," which is the name he gives to what, at the time of his writing, he took to be our usual way of thinking about consciousness, the world, and their relation. There is some debate over how to understand what Merleau-Ponty means by "objective thought." But I take it to be a characterization of the world as causally determined, and composed of its basic elements in such a way that a reductive analysis of it is possible. It encompasses two positions that both accept the basic picture of the world, but differ in their view of its ontological status, and correspondingly, the place of consciousness in the grand scheme of things. The idealist strand—"intellectualism"—takes consciousness to constitute the world, and so lie outside it. Merleau-Ponty identifies Kant's and the earlier Husserl's transcendental idealism as central examples of this position.[4] The realist strand—"empiricism"—takes consciousness to be just one of many things within the world, made of the same stuff and bound by its laws. Particular theories that adopt this framework can have leanings toward empiricism or intellectualism without being full-blown versions of these positions (Romdenh-Romluc 2011). Merleau-Ponty holds that there are both empiricist and intellectualist scientific theories. These are the targets of his critique. Some of his arguments are directed at atomism (the claim that everything in the world is reducible to its most basic components). Some are directed at realism (the claim that the existence and character of the universe is independent from any subject's experiences of, or thoughts about, it). Some are directed at naturalism (the claim that everything, including subjectivity, is amenable to explanations using the concepts of natural science, and an account in these terms is the best that can be given).

Failure to notice this complexity has led some commentators astray. Consider, e.g., Baldwin's (2013) reading of the following passage:

> In its general effort towards objectification, science inevitably comes to a conception of the human organism as a physical system in the presence of stimuli themselves defined by their physio-chemical properties, seeks to reconstitute actual perception on this basis and to close the cycle of scientific knowledge by discovering the laws according to which knowledge itself is produced, that is, by establishing an objective science of subjectivity. It is, however, also inevitable that this attempt should fail. If we think back to the objective investigations themselves, we discover first that the exterior conditions of the sensory field do not determine it part by part and only intervene by making an autochthonous organization possible—this is what Gestalt theory shows—and second, that structure in the organism depends on variables such as the biological *sense* of the situation, which are no longer physical variables, such that the whole escapes the well-known instruments of physico-mathematical analysis and opens onto another kind of intelligibility.
>
> If we now turn back, as is done here, towards perceptual experience, we observe that science succeeds in constructing only a semblance of subjectivity: It introduces sensations, as things, precisely where experience shows there to be already be meaningful wholes; it imposes categories upon the phenomenal universe that only make sense within the scientific universe. (Merleau-Ponty 2012: 10–11)

Baldwin takes this passage to reveal that "Merleau-Ponty assumes that an objective scientific account of perception requires a reductive explanation" and that "along with this assumption of reductionism, there is a further assumption that a scientific approach has to rely on atomic 'sensations' conceived as elements of perceptual states" (Baldwin 2013: 199). He takes it as sufficient to defeat these arguments that there can

---

[4] It should be noted at this point, however, that Merleau-Ponty also draws heavily on both Husserl and Kant. He takes himself to be continuing Husserls's phenomenological project (see, e.g., the preface to his *Phenomenology of Perception* (Merleau-Ponty 2013), and his essay "The Philosopher and his Shadow" (Merleau-Ponty 1964c)). Kant's Third Critique in (Kant 2000) is also something of a touchstone for Merleau-Ponty. See Matherne (2014; 2016) for discussion of this issue.

be non-reductive and non-atomistic scientific accounts of perception. In so doing, Baldwin clearly takes Merleau-Ponty's arguments to be directed at science in general. However, rather than *assuming* that all scientific accounts of perception *must* be reductive and atomistic, Merleau-Ponty is instead attacking just those accounts that *are in fact* so. This is indicated by Merleau-Ponty's appeal to Gestalt theory in making his case: Gestalt accounts of perception are scientific, whilst being neither reductive nor atomistic. It follows that Baldwin's reading of Merleau-Ponty on these points, and his subsequent criticism, is misplaced.

18.4 SCIENTIFIC AND PHENOMENOLOGICAL INVESTIGATION

So how is it that science and phenomenology, according to Merleau-Ponty, are continuous? We can begin to see this by examining the strategy that Merleau-Ponty uses to reach his transcendental position in both *The Structure of Behaviour* (Merleau-Ponty 1963) and the *Phenomenology of Perception* (Merleau-Ponty 2012).

One reading of the latter draws on various remarks where Merleau-Ponty contrasts the primacy of perception with science as the second-order expression of the perceived world. One example is this passage, where Merleau-Ponty objects to a scientific view of the world for the following reason:

> Everything that I know about the world, even through science, I know from a perspective that is my own or from an experience of the world . . . The entire universe of science is constructed upon the lived world [i.e., the world as experienced]. (Merleau-Ponty 2012: lxxii)

Remarks like this have suggested to commentators such as Baldwin (2003) that Merleau-Ponty argues for his transcendental position on the grounds that, since our knowledge of the world must be based on experience, we can only know the world-as-perceived. As it makes no sense to speak of a completely inaccessible world, talk of the world-in-itself—one that exists independently from consciousness—is illegitimate. The only world we can acknowledge is the perceived world, which is dependent on the perceiver, entailing that consciousness must be thought of as transcendental. But this is a poor argument. The mere fact that our knowledge comes via experience does not show that we cannot gain knowledge of the world-in-itself. Experience could be a perfectly accurate guide to a mind-independent world. Neither is it wholly obvious that even if we could not gain knowledge of the world-in-itself via perception, we could not form a legitimate conception of a world that existed beyond our powers to access it. Gardner (2015) also takes such remarks to indicate an argument along these lines. But unlike Baldwin, he comes to the conclusion that the argument is so poor that we should not attribute it to Merleau-Ponty. Instead, Gardner suggests that Merleau-Ponty assumes his transcendental position from the outset, taking it to have been established—at least in broad outline—by Kant.

I think an alternative reading is available. Contra Gardner, Merleau-Ponty *does* offer arguments in favor of his transcendental position; contra Baldwin, this is *not* the weak argument extracted from the text above. Merleau-Ponty's argument, as we should expect from a phenomenologist, consists in examining phenomena. He considers our experience and then offers his various phenomenological analyses as the best way to capture it (I will say more about what it is to "capture" experience in section 18.5). Certain phenomena, he argues, resist an analysis in realist terms; our analysis of them must be *anti-realist*, which implies some form of transcendental position. (These arguments partly constitute his critique of scientific theories that are committed to realism.) Merleau-Ponty then argues that these phenomena are best captured by his particular transcendental picture.

Consider, e.g., his discussion of perceptual constancy from the *Phenomenology of Perception* (Merleau-Ponty 2012): the phenomenon whereby a thing's properties appear different in different contexts, yet are also presented as constant across these contexts. A leaf in shadow looks—in a sense—a darker green to the leaf seen in bright sunlight, yet we also perceive the leaf as being the same green. Analogous points apply to all other properties we perceive. Merleau-Ponty also observes that we have an intuitive sense of when we are not in the best context for viewing an object—we are drawn to get a better look at things. I move closer to the light when trying to match the color of thread and fabric. This has become known as seeking "maximum grip" (Merleau-Ponty 2012: 316). This observation allows Merleau-Ponty to analyze perceptual constancy as follows. My experience of a property always presents me with a-property-in-a-context, and I always have a sense of whether or not that context is the best one for viewing it. Together, these give me an awareness of how that property looks in the best viewing context, i.e., they provide me with an experience of the *real* property. This explains perceptual constancy as I both experience the property as it varies with context, *and* the real property that stays constant throughout these variations. However, the real property is not presented in my experience in the same way as the property-in-a-context. The former is presented as a norm—that to which I am drawn to get a better look. My experience presents the leaf-in-shadow, and I have the sense that this deviates from the best context for viewing color. In this way, I am both presented with the dark green of the shaded leaf, and the lighter green that is its real color. But I am not presented with these two colors in the same way—they do not appear in my experience as something like paint samples that I can compare. Instead, the real color is presented as a norm from which the color-in-shadow deviates. Merleau-Ponty takes this account to have implications for what the real color is.[5] The real color is that which draws me (or a perceiver like me) to perceive it in a particular way. But this means that the real color is one pole of a force, the other pole

---

[5] I'd like to thank Will Hornett for helping me to see this point.

is that which is drawn, i.e., consciousness. This suggests that the world and consciousness are opposite poles of a system of forces. Since a force cannot exist without its poles, the world and consciousness are mutually dependent parts of one whole.[6] Perceptual constancy is just one of many phenomena that he takes to require an anti-realist analysis.

Merleau-Ponty adopts the same strategy in *The Structure of Behaviour* (Merleau-Ponty 1963). He discusses and endorses the Gestalt psychologists' experiments that led them to the discovery that perceptual experience is characterized by Gestalt form. He then considers various phenomena—which include the results of various psychological experiments conducted on dogs, chimpanzees, and insects, as well as humans, together with observations about the nature of physical laws—and argues that the best description of those phenomena is one that understands them as characterized by meaningful structures, i.e., Gestalten. As we have already seen, the nature of Gestalt forms as neither independent of consciousness nor created by it out of nothing leads directly to his transcendental claim that the world and consciousness are mutually dependent.

Once we see that his critique of realist science, and his argument in favor of his transcendental position (at least partially) rest on an examination and analysis of phenomena, an important way in which he thinks science and phenomenology are continuous comes into view.

The fundamental starting point for phenomenology is experience. For Merleau-Ponty, this does not mean some inner Cartesian content of consciousness. It means the lived world, or the world-as-experienced. This is also the fundamental starting point for science. Scientists begin with *observations*. They then explain what they have *experienced* by forming hypotheses, which yield predictions for future *observation*. Where *experience* conflicts with these predictions, the hypothesis is either modified or rejected in favor of one that can capture more of the *observed* data. Merleau-Ponty reminds us of this when he writes, "Everything that I know about the world, even through science, I know from a perspective that is my own or from an experience of the world" (Merleau-Ponty 2012: lxxii). Of course, many scientists take it for granted that the world they study is mind-independent, and that any phenomena they may encounter can be explained by scientific laws. But as I have shown, Merleau-Ponty does not see these commitments as pre-requisites for doing science. They instead form a hypothesis that is up for grabs. We should ask whether these claims are adequately supported by the available evidence. Merleau-Ponty's strategy is to show us that they are not. Instead, our observations support a transcendental view of the subject and world as mutually constituting. Thus his investigation is broadly scientific: It begins with data in the form of observations about the world. On the basis of that data, he seeks to overturn one hypothesis (objective thought), and argue for another (his phenomenological framework).

One may wonder at this point where the transcendental-phenomenological reduction—the centrepiece of phenomenology's method—fits into Merleau-Ponty's

[6] This interpretation of the perceptual constancy material is one given by Kelly (2005). He also suggested the reading of Merleau-Ponty's ontological position to me in discussion.

strategy.[7] At its heart, the transcendental-phenomenological reduction consists in suspending some attitude toward the world, in order to examine experience afresh. For the earlier Husserl, the attitude to be suspended was "the natural attitude"—an unthinking faith in the existence of the world we perceive. In the later Husserl, however, the view to be suspended is a conception of the world inspired by Galilean science where the only real things are those that can be scientifically measured. For Merleau-Ponty, at least one conception of the transcendental-phenomenological reduction we find in his work consists in suspending objective thought, in order to collect the data required to conduct phenomenological investigation. We find an allusion to this in his discussion of the constancy hypothesis—an explanation of perceptual experience from within the framework of objective thought—"in order to catch sight of the phenomena and to judge the constancy hypothesis, the latter must first be 'suspended'" (2012: 499, n. 17).[8]

I have so far described commonalities, as Merleau-Ponty sees them, between the general shape of scientific inquiry and his phenomenological investigations. However, I have not yet said anything about how exactly the scientist and the phenomenologist use the data of experience to develop their respective accounts. One might suspect that when examined more closely, there is less continuity between scientific inquiry and phenomenological investigation than I have suggested so far. Especially given what, on the face of it, appear to be quite different goals. It is a commonly claimed view that phenomenology seeks to *describe* phenomena, rather than explain or analyze them. Indeed, this is not merely a popular conception of phenomenology; it is at the heart of its method. Merleau-Ponty himself writes, "Phenomenology involves describing, and not explaining or analyzing" (2012: lxxi). Similarly, "it is the attempt to provide a direct description of our experience such as it is, and without any consideration of its psychological genesis or of the causal explanations that the scientist, historian, or sociologist might offer of that experience" (2012: lxx). Science, in contrast—as the remark above makes clear—aims at *explanation* or *analysis*. If this is right, then science and phenomenology are in fact very different sorts of investigation.

As we might expect, we should not take these remarks quite at face value. In section 18.5 I will present two of Merleau-Ponty's arguments that conclude there is a deeper sense in which science and phenomenology are continuous.

---

[7] See Heinämaa (1999) and Smith (2005) for two interpretations of Merleau-Ponty's Transcendental-Phenomenological Reduction.

[8] The Constancy Hypothesis holds that each perceivable property of an object stimulates the corresponding sense organ, to produce a sensation corresponding to that property. There is thus a one-to-one correlation between stimulus and sensation. The same stimulus always causes the same effect. Perceptual experience is composed of these sensations. Merleau-Ponty attributes the idea that suspending the Constancy Hypothesis amounts to a transcendental reduction to Gurwitsch (1966:194).

18.5 THE DISCOVERY OF ESSENCES

In "Phenomenology and the sciences of man" (Merleau-Ponty 1964b), Merleau-Ponty uses Husserlian ideas to argue that both science and phenomenology aim to uncover the *essences* of experience, which the inquirer accomplishes via a kind of insight. (This is what it is to "capture" experience.) Importantly—as noted above—"experience" for Merleau-Ponty means the world-as-experienced, or the lived world, so the essences that characterize experience are the essential structures of the world as we perceive it. I will begin by explaining what essences are and how we uncover them, before presenting two arguments Merleau-Ponty employs to show that this is the aim of both phenomenology and science.

Merleau-Ponty, following Husserl, has a specific notion of an essence. Importantly, an essence is not an ideal, universal, abstract entity of the sort championed by Plato. Instead, essences are the meaningful forms taken by the experienced world, and are inseparable from it. Husserl holds that the relation between experience and the essences that characterize it is one of "founding." Essences cannot exist without the experiences that are their foundation, but they are neither deducible from, nor reducible to, those experiences (Husserl 2001).[9] Merleau-Ponty employs the notion of the *Gestalt* to develop the notion—"Husserl was really seeking, largely unknown to himself, a notion like that of the Gestaltists—the notion of an order of meaning which does not result from the application of spiritual activity to an external matter" (1964b: 77). As we have already seen, Gestalten are composed of their parts in such a way that they are nothing over and above them but cannot be reduced to them. Merleau-Ponty extends these ideas to the discovery of essences more generally.

Consider one phenomenon studied by the human sciences: a cultural trend such as sexual harassment. It has not always been recognized as such. The following describes an episode that took place in the United States, during the mid 1970s.

> [Carmita Wood] had worked for eight years in Cornell's department of nuclear physics, advancing from lab assistant to a desk job handling administrative chores . . . a distinguished professor seemed unable to keep his hands off her . . . [T]he eminent man would jiggle his crotch when he stood near her desk . . . he'd deliberately brush against her breasts while reaching for some papers. One night as the lab workers were leaving their annual Christmas party, he cornered her in the elevator and planted some unwanted kisses on her mouth . . . Carmita Wood went out of her way to use the stairs in the lab building in order to avoid a repeat encounter, but the stress of the furtive molestations and her efforts to keep the scientist at a distance while maintaining cordial relations with his wife, whom she liked, brought on a host of physical symptoms . . . She requested a transfer to another department, and when it

---

[9] Husserl makes this claim throughout this work. A useful discussion of his conception of how essences are related to the experiences on which they are founded in Zhok (2012).

didn't come through, she quit . . . [S]he applied for unemployment insurance. When the claims investigator asked why she had left her job after eight years, Wood was at a loss to describe the hateful episodes. She was ashamed and embarrassed . . . Her claim for unemployment benefits was denied. (Brownmiller 1990: 280–1)

Up until this point, people classed behavior like the professor's as mere flirting. But around the time that Wood gave up her job, women had begun to talk to each other about their lives, and had started to identify the pattern manifest in experiences such as Wood's. The term "sexual harassment" was coined to describe it.

In Merleau-Ponty's parlance, recognition of the behavior *as* sexual harassment is to grasp its essence. Just as the boat-Gestalt is a "meaning" that unifies different elements of the perceptual scene so that they appear as parts of a single boat—the vertical structures of the masts; the wooden planks that make up the deck; the wheel; the sails; and so on, so too sexual harassment is a "meaning" that unifies prima facie disparate instances of behavior as all being manifestations of the same cultural trend. Gestalten are composed of their elements in such a way that they are nothing over and above them, yet they cannot be reduced to them. We saw how Merleau-Ponty takes this to be so for something like the boat-Gestalt. It also holds for a cultural trend like sexual harassment. The sexual harassment of women like Carmita Wood is entirely constituted by episodes such as those described in the passage above. Take them away, and no sexual harassment remains. Yet the cultural form cannot be reduced to those episodes. We can see this in the fact that Carmita Wood was initially unable to articulate what was problematic about the professor's behavior. She lived through the episodes as "hateful," but she was unable to express to herself and to others what exactly was hateful about them. Of course, this was partly because she lacked the appropriate language with which to describe them. But the lack of adequate terminology went hand-in-hand with the fact that she, and the culture at large, had not yet discerned the pattern those incidents manifested. She and the wider culture had not yet grasped the essence of the cultural phenomenon. Thus, for Merleau-Ponty, a cultural trend like sexual harassment is not simply an accumulation of certain episodes of behavior. It is a pattern that consciousness discerns in them. He writes:

> A phenomenology, therefore, has a double purpose. It will gather together all the concrete experiences of man which are found in history—not only those of knowledge but also those of life and civilization. But at the same time it must discover in this unrolling of facts a spontaneous order, a meaning, an intrinsic truth, an orientation of such a kind that the different events do not appear as a mere succession. (Merleau-Ponty 1964b: 52)

Merleau-Ponty's use of the notion of the Gestalt to illuminate Husserl's idea of an essence also points to another important feature of it. The Gestalt form of a momentary perceptual experience is grasped all at once. One cannot grasp a Gestalt merely through reason—one either sees it or one does not. On some occasions, something like reasoning may play a role—a friend points and traces the vertical structures with her finger to show me that they are part of the boat, rather than the trunks of trees. But reasoning can only ever be a prop to help me see. More generally, one cannot identify an essence by merely following a series of steps in anything like the way that one reaches the conclusion of a piece of deductive reasoning. This is not to say that uncovering an essence *never* involves reasoning. We can, for example, imagine the women who took part in those early consciousness-raising sessions reasoning about what their bosses' inappropriate behavior meant. But identifying an essence always requires the use of insight. The reasoning—like my friend tracing the masts with her finger—is merely an aid to insight. As Merleau-Ponty says, "I grasp something through this experience . . . an intelligible structure that imposes itself on me whenever I think of the intentional object in question" (1964b: 54).

Importantly, this "imposition" of a meaning on the thinker is not *causal*. Instead, the phenomenon *motivates* the observer to see it in a certain way.[10]

Merleau-Ponty's first argument for the claim that both science and phenomenology are concerned with the discovery of essences focuses particularly on disciplines such as psychology and sociology, which study the human mind and behavior. He presents this argument as a characterization of Husserlian ideas from the *Crisis* (Husserl 1970). We might initially think that although sciences such as psychology and sociology share a subject matter with phenomenology—human existence—they are very different forms of inquiry. Whilst phenomenology aims to uncover the essences of experience, laying out its meaningful structure, psychology and other similar sciences seek *causal* explanations of human phenomena. Merleau-Ponty labels this view "psychologism." He argues that it undermines itself. The phenomena for which the human sciences seek a causal explanation include beliefs. The problem is that, as many writers have argued, causes are not justifying reasons.[11] Suppose, e.g., that a stage hypnotist induces me to believe that I am a parrot. My belief is *caused* by the hypnotist's manipulation of my mind. But this in no way *justifies* my belief—it gives me no *reason* to hold I am a parrot. Thus Merleau-Ponty argues that accounts of belief that characterize them as the product of causes disconnect them from truth. The theories about the mind offered by scientists are themselves human phenomena: Their explanations are reached through reasoning leading to the formation of beliefs. It follows that scientific explanations themselves admit of causal explanation. But this means that rather than tracking the truth of the matter, they are simply the product of causal goings-on, which we have no reason to think might be true. In this way, the scientist's causal accounts of human phenomena undermine themselves.

The opposing position is what Merleau-Ponty, following Husserl, calls "logicism." It takes its cue from the fact that when we're thinking about matters of logic, our reasoning seems to possess a certainty that it lacks when we consider empirical things. One explanation of this apparent fact is that logic concerns a realm of ideal meanings,

[10] There is no space to explicate this in any detail here. See Wrathall (2005) for a discussion of this idea.

[11] Not everyone accepts this view. Davidson (1963), e.g., argues that reasons *are* causes.

with which we have the power to make contact. This capacity means that when we deal with matters of logic, our thought transcends its situation and accesses universal truths. Logicism endorses this explanation and then attempts to ground scientific thinking about human existence in logic. If successful, this would establish that the scientist's theories are universally true. But Merleau-Ponty rejects this position on the grounds that we have to acknowledge that *all* scientific thought "is not without roots" (Merleau-Ponty 1964b: 48), being the product of its time.[12] To give just one, well-used example: Kant (1999) famously claimed that space *necessarily* takes the form described by Euclidean geometry. This was supposed to be a universal truth, grounded in the necessary structure of consciousness that gives shape to the external world. As many theorists—e.g., Helmholtz (1977) and Carnap (1966)—have pointed out, the subsequent discovery of non-Euclidean geometries show that this is false.[13] Thus, we seem to be pushed back toward psychologism. To overcome this problem, we require a way to understand how thought is conditioned by the thinker's situation without construing the relation as causal.

Merleau-Ponty argues that the conception of science as aiming to discover essences provides a way to do this. An essence is a meaning inherent in a particular set of experiences. It has *some* claim to universality insofar as it is the essence of a particular phenomenon, so future experiences of that item (further instances of that phenomenon) will unfold in accordance with that form. Yet, the essence is also tied to the particular experiences on which it is founded. As more experience accumulates, the meaning we find in the experiences can undergo something akin to a Gestalt-switch. Consider a demonstration against a government's economic policies. At the time that it happens, its meaning may just be that of an isolated protest, one of a handful that happen regularly each year, to little or no effect. But in the light of subsequent events, as unrest spreads across the country, the single protest may come to appear as the start of a national movement that brought about financial reform. In a case like this, we cannot say that the first reading of the event's essence is *wrong*. When the first protest happens, the future events have not yet occurred. The demonstration might yet be an isolated incident. It may not spark further unrest eventually leading to reform. Its essence only changes in the light of those future events. In this way, the discovery of an essence is conditioned by the thinker's situation—the thinker discerns an essence examining a particular body of experience: those that have occurred so far.

It is also part and parcel of this account that people's insight into essences can sometimes be clouded, so that they fail to discern an essence correctly. A thinker's situation may mean that she is only aware of *some* of the experiences on which an essence is founded. She may only have a partial glimpse of the phenomenon, and so read its

---

[12] It should be noted at this point that Merleau-Ponty does not deny the universal validity of logic. He attempts to ground this, not in a Platonic realm of absolute truth, but in the limits of what makes sense to us. There is no space to explicate his argument here.

[13] Various people have tried to defend Kant on this point (just one example is Strawson 1966); it is unclear whether any of these defences is successful.

essence wrongly. Consider the example of sexual harassment. The professor's behavior described in the above passage was at one time deemed "flirting," but now we see it as "sexual harassment." On Merleau-Ponty's picture, both of these conceptions should be thought of as intended to capture the essence of certain sets of experiences. Crucially, the second is founded on more relevant experiences than the first because it is founded on the experience of victims like Carmita Wood, whereas the first only focuses on the experience of perpetrators. Just as Merleau-Ponty's first perception of the boat masts as part of the forest was illusory, so too, the former reading of the essence was incorrect. To see the professor's behavior as mere flirting is not just to see it *differently*, but to see it *wrongly*. The situation of earlier thinkers meant that their reading of the essence was based on too few of the relevant experiences. Cultural habits and ideas meant that certain experiences—those of the victims—were hidden from view. Thus they only had a partial glimpse of the phenomenon, which later thinkers have been able to correct.

These points also apply to the scientist's theories. These likewise seek to discern the essences of whichever phenomenon is at stake. Since the scientist's theories are founded on the set of experiences made available at a particular moment in time, they are intimately tied to those experiences. As more experience accumulates, the meaning of that experience may switch. Furthermore, the scientist's insight into essences may sometimes be clouded so that she reads an essence incorrectly. In these two ways, the scientist's theories are conditioned by her situation in the same way as the human phenomena she examines, but this influence is not causal.

Merleau-Ponty's second argument is that not only *should* scientists studying human existence aim to discover the essences of experience via a sort of insight, this is *in fact* what *all* scientists—including those studying human existence and those studying the natural world—are already doing. His argument begins with a reflection on the relation between experience and the essences that characterize it. Recall that essences are *founded* on experience, which means they cannot exist without this foundation, but they are neither deducible from, nor reducible to, experience. For Merleau-Ponty, this means an essence is not straightforwardly a component that is common to all experiences that manifest it. If it were, it would be reducible to those experiences. Of course, insofar as the essence characterizes all the perceptions that manifest it, there is a sense in which the essence features in all of them. But the essence is a meaning that unifies them, rather than something like a perceivable property they all share. The experiences themselves—considered in terms of their perceivable properties—may be completely different. Think again about Merleau-Ponty's perception of the boat. The experience is characterized by a boat-Gestalt, which is a type of essence. This form unifies certain elements of the scene. As such, those elements are perceived as parts of the boat: the masts, the deck, the hull, the sails, etc. But they are all very different—the masts are vertical wooden structures; the sail is made from canvas; the hull is a different color from the deck; etc. The parts of the boat do not belong together in virtue of any simple similarities between them. Instead, they are unified insofar as they manifest the same boat-Gestalt.

Merleau-Ponty then argues that this is so for the entities posited by science. The laws of nature are "ceteris paribus" laws—they hold "all things being equal." There are different ways to understand what it is for all things to be equal. But the salient point for our purposes is that for each law, there is no experience that unfolds in accordance with just that law. No single law of nature describes the behavior of anything we actually perceive. Thus the experiences that are all taken to manifest a single law are all very different. Just as the boat-Gestalt is a meaning that unifies disparate elements of a perceptual scene, so too a law of nature is an essence or meaning that unifies disparate experiences. Merleau-Ponty gives the example of Galileo's discovery that all freely falling bodies descend at the same rate, despite any differences in their mass. In fact, we never observe a freely falling body, because the *actual* fall of anything is also affected by such things as friction, resistance, and so on. Thus the actual speed at which things fall—what we can observe—will vary, depending on things such as the surface area of the thing concerned. A parachute, e.g., descends more slowly than a brick. It follows that Galileo's law of falling bodies does not posit an observable element that a number of cases have in common (a constant speed of descent). Instead, it is, for Merleau-Ponty, a meaning that unifies diverse cases.

The nature of scientific laws has implications for the method by which they are discovered: induction. Merleau-Ponty argues that further support for his conception of science as discovering essences comes from examining how scientists actually proceed. Induction is usually understood as a process of identifying common element(s) in a series of observed cases. If an element is found in a sufficiently large number of similar cases, it can be considered essential to cases of that sort. One can then infer that unobserved cases of the same type will also contain that element. On this conception, the more cases one observes to contain a particular element, the more robust one's conclusions will be, as the more reason one will have to think that the element will *always* be found in cases of that type. However, if one is seeking insight into a meaning that unifies cases of a particular sort, one will proceed differently. One *might* start with a number of observed cases, but one need not. An essence can be grasped in the observation of a single case. Of course, if one is trying to identify which element(s) are common to cases of a particular sort, one *could* start from a single case. But if so, then one is merely *guessing* which element(s) it has in common with other similar examples. In contrast, one may have genuine insight into an essence from a single case, although one's insight will be verified if one's reading of the essence sheds light on other examples. Consider Galileo. Since there are no free-falling bodies on our planet, Galileo could not discover his law by observing many free-falling bodies and extracting a common element. Instead, he began with a flash of insight, which led him to posit the idea of a free-falling body. He then used it to understand the empirical facts through adding conditions such as friction and resistance. Merleau-Ponty holds that there are many other such examples in the history of science, which again supports his view that all science really aims to discover essences via insight—just like phenomenology.

18.6 WHY PHENOMENOLOGY?

Merleau-Ponty's work has inspired many scientifically minded thinkers, and he drew heavily on the results of science. The legitimacy of this cross-fertilization has been questioned. First, phenomenology's method of describing experience from a first-person perspective is claimed to be mere introspection and as such, incapable of providing anything of interest to proper science. Second, it is claimed that science is committed to realism and naturalism (the theses that the world is independent from subjectivity, and that everything in it can be, and is best, explained in naturalistic terms—including subjectivity), but phenomenology provides a transcendental account of consciousness as constituting the world studied by science. I have argued here that Merleau-Ponty sees science and phenomenology as continuous. His account answers these two objections. Phenomenology, as he conceives it, is an investigation that proceeds from observed data, i.e., *experience*, which requires an accurate *description* of what is observed. The same holds for science. Moreover, both the scientist and the phenomenologist aim to uncover the essences of experience, i.e., the essential structures of the experienced world, via a sort of insight. Essences are the meaningful forms that characterize the objects of experience. They cannot exist without the experiences that are their foundation, but they are neither reducible to, nor deducible from, these experiences. It follows that it is a misunderstanding to think that Merleau-Ponty's phenomenology, in contrast to science, proceeds by way of introspection. He realizes that phenomenology's traditional starting point of experience as it is undergone from a first-person perspective means that we should begin with the *content* of perception—rather than, e.g., its underlying mechanism—but that this means the phenomenologist should start with essentially the same sort of data as the scientist: observations of the world and accounts from others of their experiences, including those who perceive the world in extraordinary ways due to illness, injury, the influence of drugs, and so on. In connection with the second objection, whilst it is true that particular scientists/theories are committed to realism and naturalism, Merleau-Ponty holds that these are in no way necessary to science. There could be a science that acknowledges the transcendental status of subjectivity.

This may lead one to wonder: What differences, if any, remain between Merleau-Ponty's phenomenology and science? If they are, indeed, essentially the same sort of investigation, then why did he insist that his work was of *philosophical* importance, and not merely psychology? Space here prevents me from answering this question in anything like sufficient detail. But it seems the answer will be something along these lines: A science that revealed the transcendental status of subjectivity would be of central philosophical interest, since it would deal directly with one of the enduring issues in philosophy—the ontological nature of the world and our relation to it. In this way, phenomenology is of philosophical importance. It differs from science as it is actually practised, as—barring a few exceptions—science has yet to repudiate the realism and naturalism that Merleau-Ponty rejects. Phenomenology, thus penetrates more deeply to the heart of things, in revealing the true nature of subjectivity and its relation to the world, but this is not knowledge that is, in principle, closed to science. As Merleau-Ponty says of phenomenology and psychology, "[they] are not kinds of knowledge, but two different degrees of clarification of the same knowledge" (1964d: 24).[14]

REFERENCES

Baldwin, T. (2003), *Maurice Merleau-Ponty: Basic Writings* (London: Routledge).

Baldwin, T. (2013), "Merleau-Ponty's Phenomenological Critique of Natural Science," *Royal Institute of Philosophy Supplement* 72: 189–219.

Brownmiller, S. (1990), *In Our Time: Memoir of a Revolution* (New York: Dial Press).

Carel, H. and Meacham, D. (eds) (2013), *Phenomenology and Naturalism: Examining the Relationship between Human Experience and Nature* (Cambridge: Cambridge University Press).

Carnap, R. (1966), *Philosophical Foundations of Physics: An Introduction to the Philosophy of Science*, ed. M. Gardner (New York: Basic Books).

Chevalley, C. (1991), "Glossaire," in N. Bohr, *Physique atomique et connaissance humaine* (Paris: Gallimard), 345–567.

Clark, A. (1997), *Being There* (Cambridge, MA: MIT Press).

Davidson, D. (1963), "Actions, Reasons, and Causes," *Journal of Philosophy* 60/23: 685–700.

Dennett, D. (2001), "The Fantasy of First-Person Science," URL" https://ase.tufts.edu/cogstud/dennett/papers/chalmersdeb3dft.htm.

Dreyfus, H. (1979), *What Computers Can't Do* (New York: Harper and Row).

Gardner, S. (2015), "Merleau-Ponty's transcendental theory of perception," in S. Gardner and M. Grist (eds) *The Transcendental Turn* (Oxford: Oxford University Press), 294–323.

Goldstein, K. and Gelb, A. (1920), *Psychologische Analysen hirnpathologischer Fälle* (Leipzig: Barth).

Gurwitsch, A. (1966), *Studies in Phenomenology and Psychology* (Evanston, IL: Northwestern University Press).

Heidegger, M. (1978), *Being and Time*, translated by J. Macquarrie and E. Robinson (Oxford: John Wiley).

Heinämaa, S. (1999), "Merleau-Ponty's Modification of Phenomenology: Cognition, Passion, and Philosophy," *Synthese* 118: 49–68.

Helmholtz, H. (1977), *Epistemological Writings*, Boston Studies in the Philosophy of Science, vol. 37. (Dordrecht: Reidel).

Honner, J. (1982), "The Transcendental Philosophy of Niels Bohr," *Studies in the History and Philosophy of Sciences* 13: 1–30.

Hooker, C. A. (1972), "The nature of quantum mechanical reality," in R. G. Colodny (ed.) *Paradigms and Paradoxes* (Pittsburgh, PA: University of Pittsburgh Press), 135–72.

Husserl, E. (1970), *Crisis of the European Sciences and Transcendental Phenomenology*, translated by D. Carr (Evanston, IL: Northwestern University Press).

Husserl, E. (2001), *Logical Investigations*, translated by J. N. Findlay (London: Routledge).

---

[14] Rouse (2005) discusses Merleau-Ponty's conception of science.

Kant, I. (1999), *Critique of Pure Reason*, translated by P. Guyer and A. W. Wood (Cambridge: Cambridge University Press).

Kant, I. (2000), *Critique of the Power Judgement*, translated by P. Guyer and E. Matthews (Cambridge: Cambridge University Press).

Kelly, S. (2005), "Seeing things in Merleau-Ponty," in T. Carman and M. Hansen (eds) *The Cambridge Companion to Merleau-Ponty* (Cambridge: Cambridge University Press), 74–110.

Matherne, S. (2014), "The Kantian Roots of Merleau-Ponty's Account of Pathology," *British Journal for the History of Philosophy* 22/1: 124–49.

Matherne, S. (2016), "Kantian Themes in Merleau-Ponty's Theory of Perception," *Archiv für Geschichte der Philosophie* 98/2: 193–230.

Merleau-Ponty, M. (1963), *The Structure of Behaviour*, translated by A. Fisher (Boston, MA: Beacon Press).

Merleau-Ponty, M. (1964a), "Eye and mind," translated by C. Dallery, in *The Primacy of Perception* (Evanston, IL: Northwestern University Press), 159–92.

Merleau-Ponty, M. (1964b), "Phenomenology and the sciences of man," translated by J. Wild, in *The Primacy of Perception* (Evanston, IL: Northwestern University Press), 43–95.

Merleau-Ponty, M. (1964c), "The philosopher and his shadow," translated by R. McCleary, in *Signs* (Evanston, IL: Northwestern University Press), 159–81.

Merleau-Ponty, M. (1964d), "The primacy of perception and its philosophical consequences," translated by J. M. Edie, in *The Primacy of Perception* (Evanston, IL: Northwestern University Press), 12–42.

Merleau-Ponty, M. (1968), *The Visible and the Invisible*, translated by A. Lingis (Evanston, IL: Northwestern University Press).

Merleau-Ponty, M. (2003), *La Nature*, translated by R. Vallier (Evanston, IL: Northwestern University Press).

Merleau-Ponty, M. (2004), *The World of Perception*, translated by O. Davis (London: Routledge).

Merleau-Ponty, M. (2012), *Phenomenology of Perception*, translated by D. Landes (London: Routledge).

Romdenh-Romluc, K. (2011), *Routledge GuideBook to Merleau-Ponty and* Phenomenology of Perception (London: Routledge).

Rosen, S. (2013), "Bridging the 'Two Cultures': Merleau-Ponty and the Crisis in Modern Physics," *Cosmos and History: The Journal of Natural and Social Philosophy* 9/2: 1–12.

Rouse, J. (2005), "Merleau-Ponty's existential conception of science," in T. Carman and M. Hansen (eds) *The Cambridge Companion to Merleau-Ponty* (Cambridge: Cambridge University Press), 265–90.

Smith, J. (2005), "Merleau-Ponty and the Phenomenological Reduction," *Inquiry* 48/6: 553–71.

Stratton, G. (1896), "Some Preliminary Experiments on Vision without Inversion of the Retinal Image," *Psychological Review* 3/6: 611–17.

Strawson, P. F. (1966), *Bounds of Sense* (London: Methuen).

Wrathall, M. (2005), "Reasons, motives and causes," in T. Carman and M. Hansen (eds) *The Cambridge Companion to Merleau-Ponty* (Cambridge: Cambridge University Press), 111–28.

Zhok, A. (2012), "The Ontological Status of Essences in Husserl's Thought," *The New Yearbook for Phenomenology and Phenomenological Philosophy* XI: 96–127.

CHAPTER 19

MERLEAU-PONTY FROM 1945 TO 1952

The Ontological Weight of Perception and the Transcendental Force of Description

DONALD A. LANDES

SCHOLARS have come to accept that Merleau-Ponty's work divides relatively neatly into three periods: a first focused on Gestalt psychology; a second marked by Husserlian transcendental phenomenology, supplemented by structuralism; and an incomplete third shaped by ontological questions. The heuristic value of this classification notwithstanding, such a way of presenting Merleau-Ponty risks being somewhat misleading. Not only does it fail to mention his continuous engagement with political theory and politics, art and literature, psychology, the philosophy of history, and the history of philosophy, the "official history" of Merleau-Ponty's three periods also risks rendering obscure the continuity of his philosophy and the radical contributions he makes. And yet, demonstrating the continuity and radicalism of Merleau-Ponty's philosophical trajectory requires more than simply noting his persistent focus on embodiment or invoking the rich (though underdeveloped) notion of "flesh" in his unfinished project; it requires, rather, an exploration of the remarkably coherent trajectory of his philosophical style. The object of study of this chapter is Merleau-Ponty's "middle" period (from the *Phenomenology of Perception* to approximately 1952), but my goal is to also demonstrate how Merleau-Ponty's philosophy is more a developing trajectory and style than a series of juxtaposed periods. I will argue that between 1945 and 1952, Merleau-Ponty discovers the *transcendental force* of phenomenological description and reveals the *ontological weight* of perception. Thus, his middle period serves as the ground for a nuanced philosophy that avoids both the errors of classical thought and the excesses of the postmodern moment.

The event that opens this period is the publication of *Phenomenology of Perception* (1945), a text that is surely a "classic" according to Merleau-Ponty's own definition.

A classic text is a crystallization in the trajectory of thought and yet is never an *isolated* or *wholly past* event: "new facts are never absolutely outside [its] competence," Merleau-Ponty explains, because they inevitably "draw forth new echoes" and "reveal new depths" (1964b: 11, modified). Thus, a classic remains "eloquent" [*parlant*]; it continues to *speak* to us and to draw us beyond its explicit propositions. It is less an identifiable object and more an "immense field of sedimented history and thoughts where one goes to practice and to learn to think" (1964b: 12). This is not to suggest that one should not read Merleau-Ponty's text *literally*, since many of its ideas and arguments remain both pertinent and essentially correct. Rather, it is to insist that this text is: (i) an important crystallization in the history of philosophy, (ii) a key moment in the trajectory of a *particular* philosopher, and (iii) an invitation to take up the trajectory it expresses toward its philosophical consequences. In this chapter, I make a modest attempt to address all three of these aspects of this classic text that opens the middle period of Merleau-Ponty's work and launches the trajectory of coherent deformations his thought undergoes in the years immediately thereafter.

To reach this goal, I begin this chapter with an analysis of the double origin of *Phenomenology of Perception* as a response both to the Cartesian philosophical traditions and to the state of the human sciences in Merleau-Ponty's day. This reveals what I call Merleau-Ponty's "vocation," the urgent call he felt to respond to a unique configuration of traditional problems and empirical developments. Section 19.2 offers a new assessment of Merleau-Ponty's accomplishments in *Phenomenology of Perception*. Rather than following scholars who focus on the *topic* of embodiment in this book, I explore the philosophical potential of his *methodology*, especially in light of what he will eventually call "philosophical interrogation" (Merleau-Ponty 1968). I argue that *Phenomenology of Perception* establishes a version of phenomenological description that carries a "transcendental force" without thereby becoming a "transcendental philosophy." Section 19.3 offers a defence of Merleau-Ponty's use of traditional philosophical terminology by making explicit his radical reinterpretation of perception *as communication* and consciousness *as trajectory*. The final section (section 19.4), sketches how Merleau-Ponty's methodology and reinterpreted concepts shape the works that immediately follow the *Phenomenology of Perception*, particularly as he places his emerging philosophical style into conversation with political theory, aesthetics, and structuralism.

19.1 SCHISMS AND SHRAPNEL: THE DOUBLE ORIGIN OF *PHENOMENOLOGY OF PERCEPTION*

The *Phenomenology of Perception* is not only an important text in the history of philosophy, but also the manifestation of its author's unique style of responding to a particular configuration of traditional problems and empirical developments that shaped his field of practice.[1] In fact, the sustained and focused nature of Merleau-Ponty's philosophical practice would make for an interesting object of study for a phenomenology of "vocation," and Merleau-Ponty himself provides numerous indications as to how we might develop this perspective on his work, many of which point to Descartes. After all, it appears the meditating Frenchman's ghost haunted Merleau-Ponty literally unto his dying day! Consider Saint Aubert's (2004) discussion of a working note that was discovered on Merleau-Ponty's desk at the time of his sudden death in 1961. In the note, which had been "read, reread, underlined, and marked by several red lines in the margin," Merleau-Ponty draws a contrast between his own philosophy and that of Descartes. He writes: "*Encroachment [empiétement]*, which is for me philosophy itself, is nothing but *confusion* for Descartes, or in other words, *nothing*" (Saint Aubert 2004: 23). As Saint Aubert argues, this note illustrates the emergence of more violent images in Merleau-Ponty's late period. And yet it also serves to reveal a striking *continuity* that characterizes Merleau-Ponty's longstanding vocation, a continuity that comes into focus in another intriguing moment of self-reflection from 1951:

> My first published works address a perennial problem in the philosophical tradition ... It is the problem of the discord between the perspective that man can adopt toward himself via reflection or consciousness and the perspective that he obtains by linking his behaviors to the external conditions upon which they clearly depend. From the first point of view, man appears to himself as absolutely free ... And yet, an entire historical and psychological science of man has been developed that takes the perspective of an outside spectator and that reveals man's utter dependence upon his physical, biological, social, and historical milieu ... It appears impossible to renounce either of these two perspectives ... We must thus try to understand how man is simultaneously subject and object, first person and third person, absolutely free and dependent. (Merleau-Ponty 2000b: 11–12)

Thus, a first origin of *Phenomenology of Perception* is found in the "genuine antinomy" between the internal perspective of philosophical reflection (intellectualism) and the external perspective of scientific realism (empiricism) (Dillon 1997: 9–34; Carman 2008a). These competing perspectives amount to a *schism* because each one claims to be self-sufficient (Bimbenet 2004: 12–16). From *The Structure of Behavior* (1942), to the final essay published during his lifetime ("Eye and Mind," 1960), Merleau-Ponty repeatedly demonstrated that "our science and our philosophy are two faithful and unfaithful offshoots of Cartesianism, two monsters born of its dismemberment" (Merleau-Ponty 1993b: 138). Throughout his career, Merleau-Ponty felt a *call* to develop a philosophy able to sustain the "ambiguity" excluded by the Cartesian traditions as the so-called nothing of lived experience.

---

[1] For a step-by-step analysis of *Phenomenology of Perception*, readers may consult: Carman 2008b; Hass 2008; Romdenh-Romluc 2011; or Landes 2012, 2013b.

Nowhere is Merleau-Ponty's vocation more explicit than in *Phenomenology of Perception*. As Barbaras observes, "every chapter is organized according to an immutable rhythm" by which Merleau-Ponty unravels the inadequacies of *both* realist and idealist presuppositions (2004: 5–6). Moreover, the identification of Merleau-Ponty's "vocation" helps to clarify a short transition section between Merleau-Ponty's analysis of the body and his analysis of the perceived world. As he writes:

> The Cartesian tradition has taught us to disentangle ourselves from the object: the reflective attitude purifies simultaneously the common notions of body and of soul by defining the body as a sum of parts without an interior and the soul as a being directly and fully present to itself. (Merleau-Ponty 2012: 204)

This passage illustrates how the Cartesian *schism* between empiricism and intellectualism results from the attempt to develop a philosophy free of the confusion of lived experience, whereas Merleau-Ponty attempts to develop a thinking *of* and *from within* entanglement and contagion, since "the experience of one's own body . . . reveals to us an ambiguous mode of existence" (2012: 204). The *Phenomenology of Perception* is designed to demonstrate how the ambiguous aspects of our existence (motricity, sexuality, liberty, language, etc.) "are taken up and implicated in a single drama" of lived experience and clarified via phenomenological description (2012: 204). For Merleau-Ponty, the body is not an object and consciousness is not a self-transparent subject. Rather, "I am my body . . . my body is something like a natural subject, or a provisional sketch of my total being," and the ambiguity of my lived experience "spreads to the perceived world in its entirety" (2012: 205).

Another "origin" of *Phenomenology of Perception* can be found in a second facet of Merleau-Ponty's vocation, namely, his felt need to respond to a perceived crisis in the *empirical* human sciences in which researchers sought explanatory models via reductive physiological or psychological accounts. According to Merleau-Ponty, developments in Gestalt psychology represented an important step in the right direction, but although this early influence continues to shape his use of key concepts in *Phenomenology of Perception* ("horizon," "physiognomy," etc.), he was in fact critical of Gestalt theory for failing to sufficiently "think according to form" (Merleau-Ponty 1963: 136–7). Nevertheless, the Gestalt approach informs Merleau-Ponty's presentation of Gelb and Goldstein's famous "Schneider Case," which helps to illustrate this second aspect of Merleau-Ponty's vocation as the need he felt to engage with and *reinterpret* the results of the best human and natural sciences of his day. Schneider's wide-ranging deficiencies were primarily attributed to a visual agnosia caused by brain damage from shrapnel in the First World War. Insisting upon a *phenomenological* reinterpretation of the analysis, Merleau-Ponty (2012) suggests that Schneider's injuries had left him " 'bound' to the actual" to a degree that he lacks a normal person's "concrete freedom that consists in the general power of placing oneself in a situation" (2012: 137). There was an *existential* injury in Schneider's lived experience that reached beyond vision and movement to sexuality and language (2012: 159, 201–2). The injury had caused his "intentional arc" of oriented and meaningful existence to "go limp" (2012: 137). Recent scholarship has begun to reassess Merleau-Ponty's phenomenological interpretation of this now largely disputed case (Carman 2008b: 117–21; Mooney 2011; Dorfman 2015), yet the example clearly illustrates his general commitment to "thinking through" empirical findings so as to draw out their implicit *philosophical* consequences. This side of Merleau-Ponty's vocation continues to inspire the more analytic reception of Merleau-Ponty's work, which embraces the conviction that careful phenomenological description promises to contribute to empirical research. A variety of Merleau-Ponty-inspired texts have sparked important developments and debates in the study of artificial intelligence (Dreyfus and Dreyfus 1986, 1992, 2005) and the role of embodiment in philosophy of mind and action (see Carman 2008b: 219–30; Varela, Thompson, and Rosch 1991; Noë 2004; Gallagher 2006, 2008; Gallagher and Zahavi 2012; and several entries in Zahavi 2012).

Before shifting to the analysis of Merleau-Ponty's phenomenological methodology, it is worth acknowledging an influential interpretation that has led some scholars to focus on the *discontinuity* between Merleau-Ponty's early and late work. This reading is arguably most explicit in Barbaras (2004), although a close reading of Barbaras's argument reveals a highly nuanced position.[2] Barbaras suggests that in order to avoid the pitfalls of the Cartesian traditions, Merleau-Ponty refuses to adopt any *positive* philosophical position in *Phenomenology of Perception*: "The rejection of every presupposition certainly allows Merleau-Ponty to open up a new theoretical space, but this space is not thought through to the end. By symmetrically dismissing realism and intellectualism ... he is still a prisoner of the terminology belonging to these two philosophies" (Barbaras 2004: 6). There are two closely related criticisms at work here: (i) Merleau-Ponty's "neither-nor" style fails to produce a positive philosophical position and (ii) the use of classical philosophical terminology ("subject-object," "consciousness," etc.) blocks Merleau-Ponty from developing a radical contribution to the history of philosophy. Add to these criticisms Merleau-Ponty's own later apparent acknowledgement that perhaps *Phenomenology of Perception* remained trapped in a "philosophy of consciousness" (Merleau-Ponty 1968: 173), and it appears that Barbaras has developed a powerful critique of the continuity thesis defended in this chapter. After all, how could Merleau-Ponty succeed in bringing out a radical rethinking of philosophy in *The Visible and the Invisible* without utterly rejecting the content and method of this apparently misguided middle period? In short, the discontinuity thesis appears to put in jeopardy the value of Merleau-Ponty's entire middle period.

Sections 19.2 and 19.3 offer an extended defense of Merleau-Ponty's middle period against the spirit of the discontinuity thesis and against the claim that *Phenomenology of Perception* fails to offer a positive and radical reinterpretation of perception and consciousness. Given Merleau-Ponty's style of phenomenological description, he need not reject his phenomenological period, nor necessarily introduce a radically new set

---

[2] Thus, although I attribute the "discontinuity thesis" to Barbaras, this perhaps captures more the *influence* of Barbaras's interpretation than the more nuanced position he actually articulates. See Barbaras 2004. See Evans and Lawlor 2000; Evans 2008; Dastur 2001: 29–31.

of concepts. In fact, despite his later infusion of new terms ("flesh," "chiasm," etc.), he always maintained a strong connection with classical philosophical concerns, such as "seeing, speaking, and even thinking" (Merleau-Ponty 1968: 130). But before developing these counterclaims, it is also worth noting two initial observations: first, Merleau-Ponty's later critical self-assessments, found in unpublished personal working notes, are far from decisive and explicitly argued self-refutations. To consider these perhaps fleeting thoughts, jotted down but never published, as indicative of a genuine total rejection would perhaps be overly hasty. And second, according to his own philosophy of expression and reading, Merleau-Ponty does not alone have the "authority" over the value and final interpretation of his own texts. Since philosophical expression involves an "unthought" *trajectory* that solicits readers to take up and reshape its meaning (Merleau-Ponty 1964e: 160; Landes 2013a: 39–40), Merleau-Ponty's *Phenomenology of Perception* remains as an open invitation for us to "draw forth new echoes" and "reveal new depths" in light of precisely such potential critiques or subsequent developments (Merleau-Ponty 1964b: 11–12).

19.2 BODY SCHEMAS AND LATENT QUESTIONS: THE "TRANSCENDENTAL FORCE" OF PHENOMENOLOGICAL DESCRIPTION

The double origin of *Phenomenology of Perception* in Merleau-Ponty's "vocation" discussed in section 19.1 illustrates his sustained critique of all versions of *"pensée de survol"*—the attempt to think from a God's-eye view or from outside all perspectives—which amounts to a failure to address the "exceptional relation between the subject and its body and its world" (Merleau-Ponty 1964a: 4–5). Merleau-Ponty's *phenomenological methodology* thus offers another way of demonstrating continuity in his thought by establishing the radical nature of his contribution as an evolving positive alternative to the *pensée de survol*. Through what I call the "transcendental force" of his phenomenological description, Merleau-Ponty reveals a "necessary" *expressive dimensionality* in human existence, without falling back into a "transcendental philosophy." The term "transcendental force" is used here to invoke the way in which a description or a disruptive experience leads us to the necessary structures of *that* experience without thereby establishing those structures as a priori structures of all possible experience.[3] He does this precisely by setting to work a philosophical questioning that aims to *gear into*[4]

---

[3] This is a key to grasping Merleau-Ponty's phenomenological rethinking of Kant's critical project. See Landes 2015: 342.

[4] The image of "gearing into," which is a translation of Merleau-Ponty's use of the French verb *s'engrener*, is deployed here and throughout my readings of Merleau-Ponty. Perhaps as a first gloss on

and *take up* the structures of existence, which are only a priori structures given certain conditions. In short, philosophical interrogation itself expresses the *ontological weight* of perception, since perception is not merely of *psychological* interest, but rather has the capacity to bring about a rethinking of ontology itself.[5] Merleau-Ponty presents philosophy *as* expression, a new approach to philosophical thought and human existence that became explicit later in the notion of "expression" (see Landes 2013a; Waldenfels 2000) or in the late concept of "philosophical interrogation" (Merleau-Ponty 1968).[6]

Invoking "phenomenological description" in this way, however, raises some legitimate questions regarding Husserl's influence on Merleau-Ponty's middle period. Though he is reported to have attended Husserl's 1929 Paris Lectures, his early 1930s research proposals suggest he had not developed a deep familiarity with Husserlian phenomenology in the years prior to working on *Phenomenology of Perception* (Toadvine 2002). At the end of *The Structure of Behavior* (completed in 1938), Merleau-Ponty announces the need to "define transcendental philosophy anew" (Merleau-Ponty 1963: 224), and Geraets is surely correct to identify 1939 as the year he appears to have discovered what he was looking for in Husserlian phenomenology. In addition to the publication of Husserl's late fragment "The Origin of Geometry," with an introduction essay by Fink, 1939 was also the year that Merleau-Ponty became the first non-Louvain scholar to consult Husserl's unpublished manuscripts (Geraets 1971: 135–49; Van Breda 1992).

Several Merleau-Ponty scholars have questioned his interpretations of Husserl (Dillon 1997; Madison 1981), and indeed it should be acknowledged that Merleau-Ponty is hardly a Husserl scholar in the standard sense—he provides comparatively little sustained study of Husserl's texts or concepts, and no systematic application of (for instance) the eidetic method. And yet, as Zahavi argues, Merleau-Ponty's reading of Husserl is in fact "visionary" insofar as it takes up the spirit of the unpublished manuscripts (Zahavi: 2002: 7), especially the ones he briefly studied in Louvain (Van Breda 1992). In short, Merleau-Ponty in 1939 caught a glimpse of the potential of Husserl's late phenomenological method and subsequently launches a brilliant and original contribution to the *Husserlian* phenomenological tradition (Landes 2012: xxxvi). This is perhaps the best illustration of what Saint Aubert (2005) calls the "Merleau-Pontian hermeneutic,"

Merleau-Ponty's later notion of reversibility, the *Phenomenology of Perception* implies that perception has a "solicitation/gearing-into" structure whereby the perceiver is solicited by the perceived, and must find the right "fit" between his or her attitude and that which is to be perceived. In short, as I will explain below, perception is a form of ongoing *communication*. See Landes 2017.

[5] See Merleau-Ponty 1964d and 1964f.

[6] The enigmatic term "philosophical interrogation" is deployed by Merleau-Ponty in *The Visible and the Invisible* as a means of identifying a philosophical practice that resists the attempt to find final answers to perennial problems in favor of developing a practice open to revision in the face of what he calls "wild Being," that which will always overflow our attempts at explanation. He calls this an "inspired exegesis," a *gearing into* that which solicits us without the pretence of capturing it once and for all (Merleau-Ponty 1968: 133). As I argue elsewhere, this would be a practice that is simultaneously *responsive* and *creative* (Landes 2013a: 161–5).

a style of reading so as to draw out what a text "says *to us*" (2005: 20–1). Such a reading might be characterized, then, as gearing into the text and taking it up into one's own unfolding trajectory, which reveals the existential aspect of interpretation by bringing into focus the role of the reader in the ongoing coherent deformation of the text's meaning and the simultaneous evolutions in the existence of the reader. In this spirit, a sketch of Merleau-Ponty's phenomenological method can be established by considering how he "takes up" two key phenomenological themes, the phenomenological reduction and the notion of "operative intentionality," even if he ultimately remains highly critical of Husserl's transcendental period.

Merleau-Ponty's interpretation of the phenomenological reduction in fact provides a first defense of *Phenomenology of Perception* against the discontinuity reading, since his analysis aims beyond the intellectualist shortcomings of Husserl's transcendental period. He begins by setting phenomenology apart from any form of intellectualism because phenomenology, at least in spirit, embraces precisely the ambiguities of lived experience purged by the Cartesian tradition. Merleau-Ponty acknowledges, however, that "the famous 'phenomenological reduction'" is at times presented by Husserl as a return to a transcendental consciousness that actively bestows sense on the matter of perception. Nevertheless, given that the problem of others remains a problem for phenomenology, the genuine orientation of Husserl's reduction is not toward a pure ego, but toward the more Heideggerian structure of "being in the world" that "eliminates all forms of idealism" (Merleau-Ponty 2012: lxxiv–lxxvii). We are literally "caught up" in our being-in-the-world via the natural attitude and thus need the reduction so as to allow these intentional relations to appear (Zahavi 2002: 7–12). Since Merleau-Ponty generally leaves aside Husserl's technical language (e.g., noesis/noema), expressing the intentional structure instead via a series of images and descriptions, the "reduction" becomes a general term for any *rupture* in the closely woven fabric of *familiarity*, any moment that leads us to stand in "wonder" before the world (Merleau-Ponty 2012: lxxvii). A "complete reduction" that would reveal transcendental consciousness itself is thus impossible for Merleau-Ponty, since unfamiliarity stands out against a background of familiarity that he names the pre-predicative unity of the perceived world (2012: lxxxii, 131, 244, 336). He insists that only an "absolute spirit" could have a complete rupture with the reality to be known; since we necessarily exist within the world and within the temporal flow, a complete rupture (and thus a complete reduction) is impossible (2012: lxxviii). As a result, Merleau-Ponty's use of "reduction" is less methodological than Husserl's, and becomes a relatively informal way of characterizing certain forms of breakdown or hesitation. Even at the level of reflection, "there is no thought that encompasses all of our thought . . . [and] the philosopher is a perpetual beginner" (2012: lxxviii). This is arguably suggestive of Merleau-Ponty's later notion of philosophy as *interrogation*, in which "[the philosopher's] entire 'work' is this absurd effort. He wrote in order to state his contact with Being; he did not state it, and could not state it, since it is silence. Then he recommences" (Merleau-Ponty 1968: 125). Merleau-Ponty's "reduction" is not an escape from existence to a "pure perspective" of an absolute spirit or constituting consciousness, but rather a hesitation *from within the world* that solicits us to begin again the "endless" task of expressing what exists. In short, the reduction reveals existence itself as the very place of our philosophical reflection.

This understanding of the reduction leads to a radically existentialist reading of the notion of "operative intentionality." In the preface to *Phenomenology of Perception*, Merleau-Ponty discusses the distinction between "act intentionality" (explicit decisions, judgments, etc.) and "operative intentionality" [*fungierende Intentionalität*] ("non-thematized . . . passive, latent, kinaesthetic, and driven intentionality" (Depraz 2002: 119)). Yet for Merleau-Ponty, operative intentionality quickly comes to characterize lived experience *generally*, the manner in which our world and our life appear to us according to a "natural and pre-predicative unity" (Merleau-Ponty 2012: lxxxii). It provides the inexhaustible "text" of our lives whose *sense* overflows any explicit definition or analysis we might give. Thus, it amounts to a description of the lived structure of *trajectory* as a taking up of a past toward an open future and an ongoing *gearing into* that which transcends us (Landes 2013a: 81, 101). Merleau-Ponty supplements operative intentionality with the Heideggerian notion of "transcendence": since *operative intentionality* becomes the active-passive synthesis by which "my present transcends itself toward an imminent future and a recent past, and touches them there" (Merleau-Ponty 2012: 441). In short, "operative intentionality" becomes for Merleau-Ponty synonymous with our existence itself, and the consequences of this are far-reaching for Merleau-Ponty's *existential* phenomenology.[7] As a general structure of existence, operative intentionality is always "already at work prior to every thesis and every judgment" (2012: 453).

Given this account of how Merleau-Ponty takes up phenomenology, the remainder of this section illustrates the "transcendental force" of Merleau-Ponty's original and creative form of phenomenological description at the multiple "sites of reduction" where familiarity breaks down or shines forth, thereby revealing the ontological weight of perception. A first site of breakdown exploited by Merleau-Ponty is in the description of "abnormal" or pathological experiences.[8] Consider Merleau-Ponty's appropriation of the term "body schema" as illustrating something essential about "normal" lived movement. In the context of early neurophysiology, "body schema" named our implicit knowledge of the location and orientation of our limbs (Merleau-Ponty 2012: 100–1), but the term remained ambiguous between psychological and physiological interpretations. Offering a *phenomenological* reinterpretation, Merleau-Ponty shows the impossibility of these two classical approaches and insists that we must ask *how* "such a phenomenon [is] possible" (2012: 100), that is, how do we "take up" our bodily presence according to its past and as oriented toward its potential actions? In short, how do we live our body as a phase in a *trajectory*? Cases that reveal disturbances in the body schema (the phantom

---

[7] This interpretation of "operative intentionality" undermines Levinas's (1969) critique of Merleau-Ponty (2012: 207). See Landes 2017.

[8] Questioning the distinction between *normal* and *abnormal* in Merleau-Ponty opens important ways of thinking beyond the limitations of his phenomenological descriptions, particularly in terms of feminism, gender theory, queer theory, and transgender studies. See Ahmed 2006; Salamon 2010; Young 1980; Weiss 1999.

limb syndrome, or Schneider's deficiencies) demonstrate that in "normal" experience the parts of my body and the relevant aspects of my milieu are "integrated according to their value for the organism's projects" (2012: 102). "'Body schema' is, in the end, a manner of expressing that my body is in and toward the world" (2012: 103), thereby giving the phenomenological interpretation a certain *transcendental force* that reveals the dimensions of "normal" experience as embodied trajectory, something of an existential reality of a certain style of being-in-the-world. The body is not merely a topic to be inserted into an otherwise complete philosophy; invoking the "transcendental force" of this method, Merleau-Ponty writes: "by re-establishing contact with the body and with the world in this way, we will also rediscover ourselves" (2012: 213).

In direct contrast with breakdown cases, Merleau-Ponty also exploits phenomenological descriptions of hyper-familiar lived experiences. Consider the example of simply walking toward a boat whose mast merges visually with the forest bordering the beach:

> There will be a moment in which these details suddenly reunite with the boat and become welded to it. As I approached . . . I merely felt that the appearance of the object was about to change, that something was imminent in this tension, as the storm is imminent in the clouds. (Merleau-Ponty 2012: 18)

The "unity" of an object in this experience is not the result of a thetic act, but rather of the unified gesture of responding to a question that was "merely latent in the landscape" (2012: 18), of finding the attitude that will allow the phenomenon to be what it was in the process of becoming. Perception involves *creatively* responding to a situation that solicits us, gearing into the sense that is taking shape, and finding the attitude that will grasp the physiognomy of the things themselves. This again is a *trajectory*—taking up our past and the world as oriented toward an emerging *sense*—and thus resonates with what I have called Merleau-Ponty's "paradoxical logic of expression."[9] After all, "the body is a natural power of expression" (Merleau-Ponty 2012: 187). As such, Merleau-Ponty's wager is that his phenomenological descriptions of the hyper-familiar (or of breakdown situations) carry a *transcendental force* because they connect with the reader's experience and thus *establish* the necessary structure of human existence as open and *expressive* trajectory.[10]

Merleau-Ponty thus deploys phenomenological description as a sort of "existential analysis," a non-reductive taking up of all of the *dimensions* of lived experience. "Must

---

[9] "The paradoxical logic of expression" is a phrase that I have thematized at length elsewhere (see Landes 2013a). I argue that Merleau-Ponty's fundamental philosophical gesture is to identify all human gestures and action as necessarily *between* pure repetition and pure creation, never reaching either extreme. As such, expression creatively takes up the past into a new situation that itself will simultaneously shift the meaning of the words uttered and reshape the future of possible utterances, rendering meaning (or better, "sense") an ongoing individuation or creative evolution. For Merleau-Ponty, I argue, human existence is characterized by the "ontological peculiarity of *being within* a structure that we institute and sustain and yet that transcends us" (Landes 2013a: 21).

[10] Additional examples of the "hyper-familiar" (by which I mean those experiences most ensconced in the natural attitude) can be seen in Merleau-Ponty's discussions of moving through a familiar apartment (2012: 131, 209) or of having a conversation (2012: 131, 370).

history," for instance, "be understood through ideology, through politics, through religion, or through the economy? . . . We must in fact understand in all of these ways at once; everything has a sense, and we uncover the same ontological structure beneath all of these relations" (Merleau-Ponty 2012: lxxxiii). Phenomenological description reveals the ontological weight of perception as the gearing into the dynamic intertwining of the dimensions of existence; it is a philosophy finally capable of thinking ambiguity without taking a "final" position that would freeze the dynamic becoming of being itself. Surely Barbaras is correct that Merleau-Ponty refuses an "explicit" positive position, but we now see that this refusal is well founded in his philosophical reflection, a result of his insistence that we think *from within* the dynamic entanglement of existence.

And yet, do the "transcendental force" of this methodology and the ontological structures of existential dimensionality it reveals inevitably leave Merleau-Ponty with a "transcendental philosophy" in the classical sense? I do not believe so. First, Merleau-Ponty rejects the idea that existential structures are a priori in the sense of necessarily outside of history and context. The a priori is, rather, a *contingent* necessity within the world and history (Merleau-Ponty 2012: 80, 90). He suggests that phenomenological reflection "amounts to giving a new definition of the *a priori*" as a "fundamental contingency" or the "making explicit of a fact" (2012: 229–30). Thus, if Merleau-Ponty's philosophy amounts to a "transcendental philosophy," it is an *open* and *expressive* transcendentalism. Second, as Merleau-Ponty explains, he aims not to establish a transcendental philosophy, but rather to initiate us into what he calls the "transcendental *field*":

> ["Transcendental field"] signifies that reflection never has the entire world and the plurality of monads spread out and objectified before its gaze, that it only ever has a partial view and a limited power . . . The center of philosophy is no longer an autonomous transcendental subjectivity, situated everywhere and nowhere, but is rather found in the perpetual beginning of reflection at that point when an individual life begins to reflect upon itself. (Merleau-Ponty 2012: 63)

With this emphasis, Merleau-Ponty establishes a positive position via the ontological weight of perception without thereby falling into the traps of classical transcendental philosophy.

19.3 Consciousness and Perception: Trajectories and Communication in *Phenomenology of Perception*

Merleau-Ponty thus established a rigorous phenomenological method while insisting upon the phenomenological and existential reinterpretation of scientific concepts and familiar lived experience. By claiming that *Phenomenology of Perception* remained mired in a "philosophy of consciousness" (Merleau-Ponty 1968: 183) and thus failed to offer an "ontology" (1968: 176), Merleau-Ponty may appear to have been too harsh a critic of his own work. Yet perhaps this self-criticism had more to do with the *reception* of *Phenomenology of Perception* than with the actual content of the book. After all, in the working notes Merleau-Ponty only acknowledges the need to bring the results "to ontological explicitation" (without actually acknowledging the absence of an ontology animating those results). Elsewhere he writes: "The thesis of a primacy of perception risks *appearing* false, *if not for me*, then at least *for the reader*" (Merleau-Ponty, cited by Saint Aubert 2006: 24, emphasis added). Even if Merleau-Ponty admitted in 1946 that he had simply not yet "said everything that it would be necessary to say on this subject" (Merleau-Ponty 1964f: 39), he continued to maintain that there is "no difference between ontology and phenomenology . . . [since] already in our manner of perceiving is implied everything that we are" (Saint Aubert 2006: 24).[11] If a hasty or uncharitable reader might fail to grasp the ontological significance and radical rethinking of Merleau-Ponty's phenomenological descriptions, how *should* one understand *Phenomenology of Perception* and its key terms? And what of the criticism that his use of classical terminology blocks him from thinking through the philosophical consequences of his work in this middle period? To answer these questions, I turn to the radical reinterpretation that Merleau-Ponty offers of two classical themes: *perception* and *consciousness*.

"Perception is not a science of the world, nor even an act or a deliberate taking of a stand; it is the background against which all acts stand out and is thus presupposed by them" (Merleau-Ponty 2012: lxxiv). As this passage illustrates, Merleau-Ponty begins with a "neither-nor" argument, but the concluding claim about perception as "background" implies a positive alternative. For instance, in his analysis of the "phenomenological field" of perception, Merleau-Ponty shows that in perception we must speak in terms of "motivations" rather than "causalities." Parts of the field solicit a certain manner of taking up sense, and perception appears to have an existential and even ontological role. Moreover, perception is demonstrated to be temporally and spatially "thick" through Merleau-Ponty's insistence on the cascading structures of *horizons*. The *subject* of perception is not a self-transparent consciousness and the *object* of perception is not an isolated object. The subject necessarily *inhabits* a space and time "surrounded by indeterminate horizons that contain other points of view" (2012: 141). Whether it be the "horizon of the village surrounding my house" (2012: 186) or the enduring effect of my childhood structuring my present personality (2012: 467), *perception* is the meaningful taking up a place within these various structures and trajectories, both figure and background, the place of play between presence and absence, since "all knowledge is established within the horizons opened up by perception" (2012: 215). Perception is not a "fact" in the world, it is the "lacuna that we are and by which the world itself comes to exist for someone" (2012: 215). In short, *perception is our existence*. This analysis suggests

---

[11] For a detailed discussion, see Saint Aubert 2006: 21–7.

that Merleau-Ponty's later emphasis on "chiasm" or "spacing" [*écart*] in the flesh of the world is perhaps nothing other than a new fleshing out of (but *not* a radical departure from) his middle period concept of perception.

If this is correct, then perception in *Phenomenology of Perception* must be understood as a form of *communication* or, in other words, a place of *intertwining* with the world that solicits my expressive gestures. As Merleau-Ponty writes:

> When I say that I have senses and that they give me access to the world, I am not the victim of a confusion . . . I merely express the truth that forces itself upon a complete reflection, namely, that I am capable (through connaturality) of finding a sense in certain aspects of being, without myself having given them this sense through a constitutive operation. (2012: 225)

I literally *communicate* with the object perceived, taking it up according to its sense by *gearing into* it via operative and expressive intentionality. An event of "sensibility" as simple as seeing a color is never merely "accomplished" by a subject; it is a taking up of "a certain field or a certain atmosphere offered to the power of my eyes and of my entire body" (2012: 218). Perception is *expressive* because my body must creatively find a solution to the problems that solicit it by taking up its past to paradoxically anticipate the attitude that will allow the event of sensibility to crystalize, and this creative taking up is the only way for the phenomenon to become what it was in the process of becoming. This is not to uncover the object "in itself," but to expressively gear into the sensible in an ongoing expressive *communication* wherein the terms do not *pre-exist* the act. As Merleau-Ponty writes, confirming this interpretation: "every perception is a communication or a communion, the taking up or the achievement by us of an alien intention or inversely the accomplishment beyond our perceptual powers and as a coupling of our body with the things" (2012: 334). Perception thus is the *paradoxical* "communication of a finite subject with an opaque being from which the subject emerges, but also in which the subject remains engaged" (2012: 228). As a result, "perception" causes us to radically rethink subjectivity itself:

> Every perception has something anonymous about it . . . because it takes up an acquisition that it does not question. The *perceiving person* is not spread out before himself in the manner that a consciousness must be: he has an historical thickness, he takes up a perceptual tradition, and he is confronted with a present. In perception, we do not think the object . . . we are directed toward the object and we merge with this [knowing] body. (Merleau-Ponty 2012: 247–8)

This passage begins to illustrate as well Merleau-Ponty's rethinking of "*consciousness*," the second phenomenological reinterpretation of a classical theme to be considered here. After all, this concept is at the heart of the criticism that *Phenomenology of Perception* remains mired in a philosophy of *consciousness*. A close reading of the text, however, reveals an alternative interpretation. Merleau-Ponty again begins from a "neither-nor" demonstration, showing that consciousness is neither a mechanical process nor a constituting power of judgment. Linking these two themes, Merleau-Ponty (1964f) declares that "all consciousness is perceptual, even the consciousness of ourselves" (1964f: 13). Or again, "consciousness can never completely cease being what it is in perception, that is, a fact, nor fully take possession of its own operations" (Merleau-Ponty 2012: 51). A new interpretation of consciousness must thus begin from the radical account of perception *as* communication above, which is why Merleau-Ponty claims that a phenomenology of perception implies an entirely new account of "reflection and a new *cogito*" (2012: 51). Thought is not the possession of an idea, but like perception the gearing into an idea as a "horizonal" structure, that is, as a structure implicated in a field of figures and grounds and never hermetically contained in-itself. This implies that the essence of thinking itself is not *thetic*, but *operative* intentionality (since it is a gearing into a horizonal structure and not the possession of an isolatable "meaning"). Given the phenomenological observation that "all consciousness is consciousness *of* something," for Merleau-Ponty the "something" in this slogan "is not necessarily an identifiable object" (2012: 5), but rather a "something" toward which "my thought tends toward rather than encompasses, just as my body orients itself and makes it way among objects in a familiar setting without my needing to represent them to myself explicitly" (2012: 387). Consciousness is a field or an orientation toward a certain set of senses and trajectories, and its essence is to keep open this field, or to *be* this open field, which is why the "life of consciousness" is the ongoing *gearing into* whereas the "death of consciousness" is the freezing of this movement in the search for a truth outside of this expressive operation (2012: 74). In short, consciousness is an open trajectory of ongoing and dynamic communication between the subject and the world. As Merleau-Ponty writes: "To be a consciousness, or rather *to be an experience*, is to have an inner communication with the world, the body, and others, to be with them rather than beside them" (2012: 99). Just as perception becomes the place of communication, consciousness becomes the trajectory of communication, the ongoing process of expression-sedimentation, the perpetual movement between personal and anonymous existence or between the spoken cogito and the tacit cogito.

To offer some support for this reading, it is worth noting that it accounts for the importance given to temporality as that which "clarifies subjectivity" in *Phenomenology of Perception* (2012: 449), since "temporality" is precisely a name for subjectivity as *trajectory*. It also suggests how Merleau-Ponty might insist on the communication with *others* while still insisting that the problem of others is irresolvable.[12] We are *in communication* with others even if we cannot fully bridge our differences because, unlike two consciousnesses, there is no problem with "two temporalities" being able to "intertwine" while remaining distinct (2012: 457). Thus, Merleau-Ponty offers an alternative to Levinas, who insists that the other is a "radical" alterity that is "neither seen nor touched" (1969: 194). Merleau-Ponty, champion of entanglement and ambiguity, need not *dissolve*

---

[12] This responds further to Barbaras (2004), who identifies Merleau-Ponty's inability to *dissolve* this problem as a reason for the discontinuity thesis.

the problem of the other nor make the other into a radical alterity, for he recognizes that we are *trajectories in communication within the world*, sometimes intertwining, sometimes diverging irrevocably. In short, his phenomenological descriptions reveal the ontological weight of perception and thus already give us the ability to think through the existential dimensionality of *inter*subjectivity. We exist as trajectories *in communication*, by gearing into the bodily gestures or expressive traces of others, but a "complete" gearing into is as impossible as a complete reduction. As Merleau-Ponty (2012) writes: "Solitude and communication . . . [are] two moments of a single phenomenon, since other people do in fact exist for me" (2012: 376) such that any "resolution" of the problem of others is prevented. There is, then, both communication *and* "a lived solipsism that cannot be transcended" (2012: 374), and this is what allows Merleau-Ponty to simultaneously include the other *within* experience and yet insist that any final totalization or interpretation of their being is forever deferred. After all, as an expressive trajectory, even my final interpretation of myself is forever deferred (2012: 361–2; see also Landes 2017).

19.4 MERLEAU-PONTY'S PHILOSOPHY AFTER *PHENOMENOLOGY OF PERCEPTION*: "A UNITY EXPOSED TO CONTINGENCY AND TIRELESSLY RECREATING ITSELF"

The texts immediately following *Phenomenology of Perception* illustrate and extend Merleau-Ponty's phenomenological interrogation, and the continuity in his philosophical style bridges the multiplication of his objects of study. For instance, two publications in 1945 carry forward the analyses of *Phenomenology of Perception* to address themes that become increasingly important for Merleau-Ponty: *politics* and *aesthetics*. Having assumed the role of "political editor" for the new journal *Les Temps modernes* (which he cofounded with Sartre and Beauvoir), Merleau-Ponty published the essay "The War Has Taken Place" (1964g), a phenomenological reflection critical of *pensée de survol* in politics. He argued that the violence and ambiguity of intersubjective history cannot be "dissolved," and thus calls for a type of "historical responsibility" able to respond to the paradoxes of lived experience in which all of us bear some responsibility for the course of events (1964g: 146). The theme of "historical responsibility" evolves throughout his subsequent political writings, from *Humanism and Terror* (2000a [1948]) via the concept of a "Marxist humanism," to an evolving Marxist notion of a "difficult humanism" in "A Note on Machiavelli" (1949), to a new "liberalism" that would maximize the possibility for dialogue and expression in *Adventures of the Dialectic* (1955).[13]

---

[13] See Kruks 1981; Coole 2008; Landes 2013a: 103–26.

Another important essay from 1945, "Cézanne's Doubt," announces an explicit shift of focus toward *expression*. It extends the material about Cézanne and painting in *Phenomenology of Perception* and attempts to illustrate how Cézanne's work is another version of the phenomenological reduction—like phenomenology, Cézanne's paintings suspend or rupture the familiar and reveal that "expressing what exists is an endless task" (Merleau-Ponty 1993a: 65–6). Merleau-Ponty reasserts that the expressed does not preexist its expression, but rather the painter gears into a "vague fever"[14] and takes up the various trajectories that crystallize in the expression itself. As such, expression is forever between pure repetition and pure creation, between determinism and freedom. Moreover, several scholars have argued that this increasing focus on "expression" characterizes Merleau-Ponty's middle period and work more generally (Waldenfels 2000; Landes 2013a). Indeed, it seems that Merleau-Ponty came to see the role of ex-pression as perhaps avoiding some of the potential misreadings discussed above. As he writes:

> The study of perception could only teach us a "bad ambiguity," a mixture of finitude and universality, of interiority and exteriority. But there is a good ambiguity in the phenomenon of expression, a spontaneity which accomplishes what appeared to be impossible when we observed only the separate elements, a spontaneity which gathers together . . . the past and the present, nature and culture into a single whole. (Merleau-Ponty 1964a: 11)

Again, here we find Merleau-Ponty as perhaps too harsh of a critic of his own work. As the above reading has emphasized, his *existential analysis* of perception and con-sciousness is already well en route toward the "good ambiguity" found in expressivity (Landes 2013a).

Between 1949 and 1951, Merleau-Ponty was Professor of Child Psychology and Pedagogy at the Sorbonne where he enriched his vocational interest in reinterpreting empirical studies. Although he lectured on a remarkable range of topics, the most sig-nificant philosophical development through this teaching position was surely his new appreciation for Saussurean linguistics and structuralism more generally (including Lacanian psychoanalysis). With a continued critique of the danger of *pensée de survol*, Merleau-Ponty came to insist that structuralism must be supplemented by a phenom-enology of *speaking* from within lived experience. He begins this comparative project in the 1951 essay "On the Phenomenology of Language," where he presents language as a "moving equilibrium," that is, a *trajectory* that we must *perceive* as such and that we must gear into according to an "incarnate logic" (Merleau-Ponty 1964d: 88). Given the reading offered above, it is striking to cite Merleau-Ponty's characterization of human

---

[14] This "vague fever" is Merleau-Ponty's name for the felt urgency of a looming expression in a particular context. It is not the "content" preexisting its expression, but rather the question imminent in the landscape that solicits the word, the brush, or the action. See Landes 2013a: 13.

existence at the end of this essay as "the trembling of a unity exposed to contingency and tirelessly recreating itself" (1964d: 97).

All of these themes intertwine in what is arguably Merleau-Ponty's most impor-tant essay during these years, "Indirect Language and the Voices of Silence" (1952), the only part of an abandoned manuscript[15] on expression that Merleau-Ponty published. What is remarkable about this essay is how the various new themes in Merleau-Ponty's post-*Phenomenology of Perception* itinerary are here reinscribed into the realm of *per-ception*. For instance, the notion of "style" shapes the discussion of expression and com-munication, but Merleau-Ponty also places "style" into the realm of gestures, going so far as to claim that "perception already *stylizes*" (1952: 91).[16] In short, *perception* is it-self expressive as communication and trajectory, and our perception itself *expresses* our manner of taking up the world both in the perceptual gestures we deploy and in the very content that interests us. Perception is not a neutral tool we all have, our manner of perceiving expresses who and what we are. This demonstrates that, for Merleau-Ponty, each new topic or each new field of knowledge solicits an ever-evolving *encounter* in the open trajectory of philosophical interrogation. Just as in painting, where the expres-sion is a "response to what the world, the past, and the painter's own completed works demanded" (1952: 96), the philosopher's response institutes a new equilibrium that will be the ground for a new creative repetition. As Merleau-Ponty writes: "All perception, all action which presupposes it, and in short every human use of the body is already *pri-mordial expression*" (1952: 104). In a phrase that invokes the themes I have emphasized in this chapter, Merleau-Ponty writes: "The sense of philosophy is the sense of a gen-esis; thus it could not possibly be totalized outside of time, and it is still *expression*" (1952: 119, modified). Merleau-Ponty's philosophy is not only a philosophy of expressive trajectories, but as this exploration of his middle period has demonstrated, it is itself a *continuous* "coherent deformation"[17] of a unity exposed to contingency and tirelessly recreating itself. Like Merleau-Ponty's own characterization of "Bergson's duration," his philosophical interrogation should thus be understood as a trajectory that is "ever new and always the same" (Merleau-Ponty 1968: 267).

REFERENCES

Ahmed, S. (2006), *Queer Phenomenology: Orientations, Objects, Others* (Durham, NC: Duke University Press).

Barbaras, R. (2004), *The Being of the Phenomenon: Merleau-Ponty's Ontology*, translated by T. Toadvine and L. Lawlor (Bloomington, IN: Indiana University Press).

---

[15] The manuscript was published posthumously: Merleau-Ponty (1973).

[16] See Singer 1993.

[17] Adapting the term "coherent deformation" from Malraux, Merleau-Ponty aims to capture a logic of trajectory, a way in which an individual or a system changes in a manner that is anticipated but not wholly predictable in advance, without thereby losing its identity across difference. See Merleau-Ponty 1993c.

Bimbenet, É. (2004), *Nature et humanité. Le problème anthropologique dans l'œuvre de Merleau-Ponty* (Paris: J. Vrin).

Carman, T. (2008a), *Merleau-Ponty* (London: Routledge).

Carman, T. (2008b). "Between empiricism and intellectualism," in R. Diprose and J. Reynolds (eds), *Merleau-Ponty: Key Concepts* (London: Acumen), 44–56.

Coole, D. (2008), *Merleau-Ponty and Modern Politics after Anti-Humanism* (Lanham, MD: Rowman and Littlefield).

Dastur, F. (2001), *Chair et langage. Essais sur Merleau-Ponty* (Paris: Encre Marine).

Depraz, N. (2002), "What about the *praxis* of reduction? Between Husserl and Merleau-Ponty," in T. Toadvine and L. Embree (eds), *Merleau-Ponty's Reading of Husserl* (Dordrecht: Kluwer), 115–25.

Dillon, M. C. (1997), *Merleau-Ponty's Ontology* (Evanston, IL: Northwestern University Press).

Dorfman, E. (2015), "The body between pathology and the everyday," in D. Meacham (ed.), *Medicine and Society: New Perspectives in Continental Philosophy* (Dordrecht: Springer), 125–38.

Dreyfus, H. (1992), *What Computers Still Can't Do* (Cambridge, MA: MIT Press).

Dreyfus, H. (2005), "Merleau-Ponty and recent cognitive science," in T. Carman and M. Hansen (eds), *The Cambridge Companion to Merleau-Ponty* (Cambridge: Cambridge University Press), 129–50.

Dreyfus, H. and Dreyfus, S. (1986), *Mind over Machine: The Power of Human Intuition and Expertise in the Era of the Computer* (New York: The Free Press).

Evans, F. (2008), "Chiasm and flesh," in R. Diprose and J. Reynolds (eds), *Merleau-Ponty: Key Concepts* (London: Acumen), 184–93.

Evans, F. and Lawlor, L. (2000), "The value of flesh: Merleau-Ponty's philosophy and the modernism/postmodernism debate," in F. Evans and L. Lawlor (eds), *Chiasms: Merleau-Ponty's Notion of Flesh* (New York: SUNY Press), 1–22.

Gallagher, S. (2006), *How the Body Shapes the Mind* (Oxford: Oxford University Press).

Gallagher, S. (2008), "Cognitive science," in R. Diprose and J. Reynolds (eds), *Merleau-Ponty: Key Concepts* (London: Acumen), 207–17.

Gallagher, S. and Zahavi, D. (2012), *The Phenomenological Mind* (London: Routledge).

Geraets, T. (1971), *Vers une nouvelle philosophie transcendentale. La genèse de la philosophie de Maurice Merleau-Ponty jusqu'à la* Phénoménologie de la perception (The Hague : Martinus Nijhoff).

Hass, L. (2008), *Merleau-Ponty's Philosophy* (Bloomington, IN: Indiana University Press).

Kruks, S. (1981), *The Political Philosophy of Merleau-Ponty* (Atlantic Highlands, NJ: Humanities Press).

Landes, D. (2012), "Translator's introduction," in M. Merleau-Ponty, *Phenomenology of Perception* (London: Routledge), xxx–li.

Landes, D. (2013a), *Merleau-Ponty and the Paradoxes of Expression* (London: Bloomsbury).

Landes, D. (2013b), *The Merleau-Ponty Dictionary* (London: Bloomsbury).

Landes, D. (2015), "Between Sensibility and Understanding: Kant and Merleau-Ponty and the Critique of Reason," *Journal of Speculative Philosophy* 29/3: 335–45.

Landes, D. (2017), "The weight of others: Social encounters and an ethics of reading," in D. Petherbridge and L. Dolezal (eds), *Body/Self/Other: The Phenomenology of Social Encounters* (New York: SUNY Press), 161–84.

Levinas, E. (1969), *Totality and Infinity*, translated by A. Lingis (Evanston, IL: Northwestern University Press).

Madison, G. (1981), *The Phenomenology of Merleau-Ponty* (Athens, OH: Ohio University Press).

Merleau-Ponty, M. (1963), *The Structure of Behavior*, translated by A. Fisher (Pittsburgh, PA: Duquesne University Press).

Merleau-Ponty, M. (1964a), "An unpublished text by Maurice Merleau-Ponty: A prospectus of his work," translated by A. Dallery, in J. Edie (ed.), *The Primacy of Perception* (Evanston, IL: Northwestern University Press), 3–11.

Merleau-Ponty, M. (1964b), "Introduction," in *Signs*, translated by R. C. McCleary (Evanston, IL: Northwestern University Press), 3–35.

Merleau-Ponty, M. (1964c), "A note on Machiavelli," in *Signs*, translated by R. C. McCleary (Evanston, IL: Northwestern University Press), 211–23.

Merleau-Ponty, M. (1964d), "On the phenomenology of language," in *Signs*, translated by R. C. McCleary (Evanston, IL: Northwestern University Press), 84–97.

Merleau-Ponty, M. (1964e), "The philosopher and his shadow," in *Signs*, translated by R. C. McCleary (Evanston, IL: Northwestern University Press), 159–81.

Merleau-Ponty, M. (1964f), "The primacy of perception and its philosophical consequences," translated by J. Edie, in J. Edie (ed.), *The Primacy of Perception* (Evanston, IL: Northwestern University Press), 12–45.

Merleau-Ponty, M. (1964g), "The war has taken place," in *Sense and Non-Sense*, translated by H. Dreyfus and P. Dreyfus (Evanston, IL: Northwestern University Press), 139–51.

Merleau-Ponty, M. (1968), *The Visible and the Invisible*, translated by A. Lingis (Evanston, IL: Northwestern University Press).

Merleau-Ponty, M. (1973), *Adventures of the Dialectic*, translated by J. Bien (Evanston, IL: Northwestern University Press).

Merleau-Ponty, M. (1993a), "Cézanne's doubt," in G. Johnson (ed.), *The Merleau-Ponty Aesthetics Reader* (Evanston, IL: Northwestern University Press), 59–75.

Merleau-Ponty, M. (1993b), "Eye and mind," in G. Johnson (ed.), *The Merleau-Ponty Aesthetics Reader* (Evanston, IL: Northwestern University Press), 121–50.

Merleau-Ponty, M. (1993c), "Indirect language and the voices of silence," in G. Johnson (ed.), *The Merleau-Ponty Aesthetics Reader* (Evanston, IL: Northwestern University Press), 76–120.

Merleau-Ponty, M. (2000a), *Humanism and Terror*, translated by J. O'Neill (Piscataway, NJ: Transaction).

Merleau-Ponty, M. (2000b), "Titres et travaux," in *Parcours deux, 1951–1961*, ed. J. Prunair (Paris: Verdier), 9–35.

Merleau-Ponty, M. (2012 [1945]), *Phenomenology of Perception*, translated by D. A. Landes (London: Routledge).

Mooney, T. (2011), "Plasticity, Motor Intentionality and Concrete Movement in Merleau-Ponty," *Continental Philosophy Review* 44/4: 359–81.

Noë, A. (2004), *Action in Perception* (Cambridge, MA: MIT Press).

Romdenh-Romluc, K. (2011), *Routledge Philosophy GuideBook to Merleau-Ponty and Phenomenology of Perception* (London: Routledge).

Saint Aubert, E. de (2004), *Du lien des êtres aux éléments de l'être. Merleau-Ponty au tournant des années 1945–1951* (Paris: J. Vrin).

Saint Aubert, E. de (2005), *Le scénario cartésien. Recherches sur la formation et la cohérence de l'intention philosophique de Merleau-Ponty* (Paris: J. Vrin).

Saint Aubert, E. de (2006), *Vers une ontologie indirecte. Sources et enjeux critiques de l'appel à l'ontologie chez Merleau-Ponty* (Paris: J. Vrin).

Salamon, G. (2010), *Assuming a Body: Transgender and Rhetorics of Materiality* (New York: Columbia University Press).

Singer, L. (1993), "Merleau-Ponty on the concept of style," in G. Johnson (ed.), *The Merleau-Ponty Aesthetics Reader* (Evanston, IL: Northwestern University Press), 233–44.

Toadvine, T. (2002), "Merleau-Ponty's reading of Husserl: A chronological overview," in T. Toadvine and L. Embree (eds), *Merleau-Ponty's Reading of Husserl* (Dordrecht: Kluwer), 227–86.

Van Breda, H. L. (1992), "Merleau-Ponty and the Husserl Archives at Louvain," in H. J. Silverman and J. Barry, Jr. (eds), *M. Merleau-Ponty, Texts and Dialogues: On Philosophy, Politics, and Culture* (Amherst, NY : Humanity Books), 150–61.

Varela, F., Thompson, E., and Rosch, E. (1991), *The Embodied Mind: Cognitive Science and Human Experience* (Cambridge, MA: MIT Press).

Waldenfels, B. (2000), "The paradox of expression," in F. Evans and L. Lawlor (eds), *Chiasms: Merleau-Ponty's Notion of Flesh* (New York: SUNY Press), 89–102.

Weiss, G. (1999), *Body Images: Embodiment as Intercorporeality* (London: Routledge).

Young, I. (1980), "Throwing Like a Girl: A Phenomenology of Feminine Body Comportment, Motility, and Spatiality," *Human Studies* 3/2: 137–56.

Zahavi, D. (2002), "Merleau-Ponty on Husserl: A reappraisal," in T. Toadvine and L. Embree (eds), *Merleau-Ponty's Reading of Husserl* (Dordrecht: Kluwer), 3–29.

Zahavi, D. (2012), *The Oxford Handbook of Contemporary Phenomenology* (Oxford: Oxford University Press).

CHAPTER 20

REREADING THE LATER MERLEAU-PONTY IN THE LIGHT OF HIS UNPUBLISHED WORK

EMMANUEL DE SAINT AUBERT

TRANSLATED BY JANICE DEARY

AMONG the greatest French phenomenologists, Merleau-Ponty is perhaps the most refined, as a writer and as a thinker, and also the most difficult, due both to the subtlety of his thought and to his rather complex intellectual situation. His philosophy, which seems to maintain a sometimes mistaken proximity to other major contemporary figures (Husserl, Heidegger, and Sartre), cannot be dissociated from its classical heritage (Montaigne, Pascal, Descartes . . .), or from the intellectual and historical context in which its author participated—the fever of French existentialism, contemporary social and political questions, the burgeoning of the human sciences, and the sketching out of structuralism. His work is singular, moreover, in its remarkable attention to modern developments in a diverse range of research areas: psychoanalysis, Gestalt psychology, child psychology, neurology, the natural sciences, linguistics, sociology, and not forgetting a continuous interest in art and literature.

This situation has not failed to provoke an equally complex reception. Initial presentations of Merleau-Ponty as an existentialist of ambiguity, then as an (overly) psychological or (overly) literary phenomenologist, have since given way to a number of diverse and incompatible portraits: the diviner of Husserl's unpublished materials, a disciple of the second Heidegger, a precursor to both structuralism and the cognitive sciences . . . Merleau-Ponty himself, it is true, has not always facilitated the interpretation of his thought. In particular, we can think of the way his thought matures in critical debate with certain figures (such as Brunschvicg and Sartre), although the faces of these internal phantoms are progressively masked over in his rewriting of certain manuscripts.

Furthermore, although his introduction of phenomenology to a larger readership can be counted as one of his achievements, it has been tempting to box Merleau-Ponty as a mere commentator on this tradition, rather than a full philosopher in his own right who maintains a relation with the thought of Husserl and Heidegger that is free, partial, and sometimes vigorously critical. Another difficulty lies in the seductive power of his metaphorical style of writing—in reality carefully crafted and rigorous—through which the later Merleau-Ponty attempts to resuscitate the descriptive power of phenomenology in leaving behind those over-used categories that think for us from the start, while at the same time trying to avoid the sort of esoteric jargon that thinks it is renewing meaning, when in fact it is only replacing words. To fully understand and benefit from this effort thus requires us to subject his work to a scientific, rather than a poetic, exegesis.

We cannot forget a final major difficulty: the brutal interruption of his work. Merleau-Ponty disappeared from the scene in 1961 at the age of 53, at the height of his creative powers, leaving behind several thousands of pages—in particular, the mature stages of a book that had been in gestation for fourteen years, intended to constitute his major work—as well as a large volume of working and reading notes, and the preparatory notes for his nine years of courses at the Collège de France. Despite some high-quality posthumous publications produced by Claude Lefort, it has nevertheless remained difficult to follow the evolution of Merleau-Ponty's thought from his first to his last writings, and to understand the status of this philosophy of the flesh as it establishes itself as ontology. Access to a large number of manuscripts, deposited at the Bibliothèque Nationale de France in 1992, has opened a new stage of interpretation, as more and more researchers have been drawn toward an exploration of this rich and illuminating resource.

20.1 THE CARTESIAN SCENARIO

Accounting for the genesis of his thought, the later Merleau-Ponty insists that his reflection is, from the start, centered on the question of the union of the soul and the body, in reaction against an intellectualist tradition he accuses of making the *unity* of the human being unthinkable, and of making the radicality of its *relations* incomprehensible. The concept of the "flesh" (*chair*) toward which all his philosophy converges, inherits this constant double worry, and is geared toward a never-abandoned methodological challenge to understand the total life of human beings, starting from his most elementary corporeal modes of expression. That is, the challenge of thinking a corporeity which is always already, in the very principle of its animation, intercorporeity.

Hence Merleau-Ponty's work is driven, from the start, by a critical reading of the Cartesian project. Through a repeated confrontation with the sixth *Meditation*, he attempts to come to grips with the "quickly mastered trembling" that Descartes would have experienced in the clutches of the various "confusions" of the flesh—the "mixture" of the soul and the body as manifested in feelings, those indistinct phenomena that can themselves only be thought about in an ambiguous way. This confusion with three faces—ontological (this incomprehensible that we *are*), phenomenological (the disturbing world of perception and desire), and epistemological (the inability to think clearly or distinctly about this ontological mystery and its strange phenomenality)—is at the heart of Merleau-Ponty's Cartesian scenario. This scenario, which is expressed in full force in the later years (1956–61)—until it occupies the foreground of the ontological debate—must be understood as having its roots in the rebellious spirit of the 1930s.

It is in this foundational period that we also discover certain prefigurations of his future notion of the flesh, particularly in the hostile opposition of the young philosopher to the idealism of Leon Brunschvicg, under the seminal influence of Gabriel Marcel and Max Scheler.[1] Merleau-Ponty accuses the Cartesian/Kantian tradition of having abandoned precisely those major philosophical questions that deal with the bodily identity and relational radicality of the human being, in their avoidance of issues such as perceptual life, sexuality, the universe of feelings, the religious attitude, or even the arts. It is with Gabriel Marcel that Merleau-Ponty forges his first weapons against the Cartesian ontology of the object. The Marcelian problem of *incarnation* directs his philosophy toward an ontological rehabilitation of sensible experience, and his central assertion—"I am my body"—is a milestone on the way toward the concept of the flesh. The Marcelian notion of "mystery" (*mystère*) introduces him to the transgression of the face-to-face encounter constitutive of objectivism, to a thinking of depth, and writing of the encroachment of the inside on the outside, the invisible on the visible. With Max Scheler, Merleau-Ponty investigates the idealistic tradition to find what has engendered the contemporary anthropological void, which is unable to see love, trust, or hope as oriented actions, but only as affective *states*, closed and meaningless—thus missing an essential dimension of desire, its *intentional* nature.

The significance of the notion of intentionality, which Merleau-Ponty reads through the lens of Scheler's emotional intentionality, is a decisive instrument in his nascent philosophy. If the *Phenomenology of Perception* tries to think it in original but unfinished attempts, this notion tends to be erased in the last years in the wake of a description of the actual relations that form, and are formed by, the flesh. This research finds its achievement in the figure of the chiasm, borrowed from Paul Valéry's analyses of love. Inspired by the "trembling" of a Valéry himself released from intellectualism, the later Merleau-Ponty once again takes up the challenge of the Cartesian confusions, against the Cartesian ontology of the object, which he now extends to the thought of Leibniz. The chiasm of desire—the ultimate face of his relationship-focused philosophy—is

---

[1] It is thus necessary to relativize the identification, commonly assumed but hardly ever demonstrated, between the Merleau-Pontian *chair* ("flesh") and the Husserlian *Leib*. Merleau-Ponty, who never translates "*Leib*" as "*chair*," forges his own concept in the context of certain scenarios, which do not maintain a *direct* relationship with Husserl's thought, but which have a more personal philosophical objective. This objective finds its roots before his reading of the founder of phenomenology, following critical lines of thought directed primarily against Descartes and Sartre, and resting on the positive contributions made by a range of thinkers and fields—amongst which Husserl certainly holds an important place, but as do, to name only a few, Scheler, Marcel, Pascal, Maine de Biran, and not forgetting psychoanalysis, *Gestalttheorie*, or neurology.

pitched against any idea of preestablished harmony, and thus attempts to succeed where Leibniz himself seems to have failed: that is, in the description of the personal and relational unity of the human being.[2]

20.2 UNDERMINING SARTRE

If this philosophy is motivated by a challenge to recover, in the body itself, all the dimensions of our animation, there nevertheless follows a major difficulty which Merleau-Ponty gradually comes to realize: the risk of losing, along this "descent" into incarnation, certain specificities of cultural life, acts of intelligence, and language, which are irreducible to perception. The new description of perceptual life in terms of *expression* plays an important role in passing from the downward and centripetal movement of incarnation—which brought intellectualism back to the phenomenal body—toward the expansive and expressive dynamics of the flesh, which the phenomenologist thinks will lead us, without discontinuity, to language. This is the inversion entered into in 1949 (the year of the unpublished Mexico City lectures), explored in more depth in 1951 (*Man and Adversity* (1964b), *The Prose of the World* (1973)), and which comes to open the period of the Collège de France with a decisive first course (*Le monde sensible et le monde de l'expression*, 1953).

The years 1945–53 constitute a long intermediate phase between the period of the theses (1938–45) and the late writings (1953–61). During this little-known phase—of which there remain many manuscripts unfortunately ignored by most commentators—Merleau-Ponty begins to liberate himself from the traditional terminology of his first works, and looks forward to two key elements in his late thought: *flesh* and *encroachment*.[3] We find in his manuscripts an outline of these new concepts through an expeditious dispute with Kantian ethics, under the passionate climate of Beauvoirian and Sartrean existentialism. The apparent complicity of Merleau-Ponty with the latter, however, disguises the elaboration of a radical critique: The beginning of his thinking on flesh is actually oriented toward an undermining of Sartre's philosophy.[4]

For Merleau-Ponty, the late 1940s sounds the hour for a moral and political assessment of war. It also signals the discovery of modernity, which is soon to be crystallized in his original notion of encroachment. The distinctions which assured the stability of the classical world have been completely jumbled from this time onward. Incomplete and monstrous, modern man is haunted by absurdity, and his dreams of purity are ruined

---

[2] For a more in-depth outline of this direction of thought, see Saint Aubert 2005.

[3] For a more detailed account, see Saint Aubert 2004.

[4] If the disagreement with Sartre remains discreet before the publication of *Being and Nothingness*, and becomes more obvious in those pages of the *Phenomenology of Perception* devoted to the question of freedom, it is in the unpublished manuscripts of the late 1940s that we find his preparation of the severe and audacious critique that becomes more explicit from the *Adventures of the Dialectic* onwards.

forever. For him there is neither freedom nor love without encroachment on others, although this encroachment does not necessarily determine their failure; instead, it expresses the native "promiscuity" that binds me to others, carrying within its violence the very possibility, if not the springboard, for its metamorphosis into coexistence. The writings of this period therefore insist, like Sartre, on the conflict between myself and others, but so as to find there the implicit etched signs of a desire to enter into relation with others, and even the indication of a common situation. Merleau-Ponty thus delivers his own version of existentialism, which attempts to escape the pessimism and relational failure he finds in Sartre, at the same time as avoiding the optimism of any forms of pre-established harmony between me and others, or between me and myself. Seeking the permanence of deep attachments as well as the imminence of new connections in the apparent hellish impossibility of relationships, he outlines what the foreword of *Signs* calls the "secret knots" "of tragedy and of hope"—the very knots which Sartre had set out to disentangle (1964b: 28). In 1959, Merleau-Ponty persists in presenting Sartre as someone who "does not like the idea of connecting,"[5] attributing to him a major short-coming that he denounces in all philosophers from the 1930s onward: that is, the will to grasp oneself "without attachment."

It is in the midst of this new scenario that certain manuscripts begin to use the poly-semic French term *chair* ("flesh"), which appears in his drafting of what might be construed as a divergent rewriting, to the point of inverting, the Sartrean analyses of desire and the flesh. As it is introduced toward the end of *Being and Nothingness*, "flesh" is the residue of a radical process of purification that does not stop at the naked body, but continues until it withdraws any movement and power from this body, in order to reach a supposed "pure passivity." As a "web of inertia" contained in impassivity, "pure being-there" cloistered in the total exposure and impenetrability of the object, Sartre's flesh is not without a certain whiff of the Cartesian extension. With neither relief nor depth, perfectly unenveloped, this inexpressive flesh escapes, through its construction, any real logic of incorporation. Consequently, Sartrean desire is paradoxically de-erotized, and thus cannot lead to any real exchange: the meeting of flesh, in other words, cannot exceed the simple "placing against" [*poser-contre*] of two outsides without insides, two inanimate cadavers. From the Mexico City lectures (1949, unpublished) onwards, Merleau-Ponty proposes an opposite picture, and adopts straightaway the chiasmatic schematism of desire.[6] The Sartrean idea of an inexpressive flesh contributes to pushing Merleau-Ponty in the direction of a philosophy of expression centered on the eminent expressivity of the flesh.

From the end of the 1940s, the humanistic stakes of these new ideas are diffused into the first features of an ontology. Certain manuscripts of 1948–9 prefigure, in the surre-alist description of the "blood of things," the ultimate criticism of the ontology of the

---

[5] Fifth radio interview, with G. Charbonnier, 1959 (2016: 232).

[6] "In love, there is a passing of me in the other and the other in me" (1949: [143](II5)). Cf. also [163] (13). "The 'I desire', the 'I' of desire . . . seeks the inside of the outside and the outside of the inside" (BNF XVII: [85](3)).

object (1957–61). Things are "wounded" by our perceptual and desiring openness—even "the objects bleed," and thus resist their reduction to a Cartesian status. In a noteworthy complicity with the "psychoanalysis" of Bachelard, Merleau-Ponty starts working with his own ontological elements, at the antipodes of the Sartrean imagination. Against the existential psychoanalysis of *Being and Nothingness*, against the mollusc-man-made-of-stone of *L'homme et les choses*, against the isolation of the real in *The Imaginary*, Merleau-Ponty turns toward a description of "the imaginary texture of the real" (1964a: 165), which constitutes one of the essential horizons of his ontology.[7]

20.3 BODY SCHEMA AND INTERCORPOREITY

Merleau-Ponty's conception of the flesh is extended beyond its critical constitution (turned against Descartes and Sartre), along the lines of a positive relationship with a diverse range of non-philosophical fields. In the early 1950s—notably in the 1953 course *Le monde sensible et le monde de l'expression*—Merleau-Ponty revives his phenomenological research on perception (mostly in the background since 1945), which is now nourished by a remarkable attention to work being done in neurology (Lhermitte, Head, Ajuriaguerra, and especially Schilder), child psychology (Piaget, Wallon), and psychoanalysis (Freud, Klein, Lagache, Lacan).[8] He finds a major support for his philosophy in the theories of body schema and body image, found at the intersection of these three disciplines: phenomenology, neurology, psychology and psychoanalysis. This conjunction is embodied in a vital reference found in the course of 1953: Paul Schilder. The *primary* authority on the question of body schema and body image, Schilder is the first to introduce phenomenological and psychoanalytical insights to the issue.[9]

"Before being reason," Merleau-Ponty writes, "humanity is another corporeity. The concern is to grasp humanity first as another manner of being a body" (2003: 208). It is precisely in this "manner of being a body," this style that makes the flesh, that the modern notion of body schema contributes a fundamental opening for Merleau-Ponty. Initiated by the neurologists Pierre Bonnier and Henry Head, body schema theory

---

[7] Cf. Saint Aubert 2004: section B.

[8] Although Merleau-Ponty is known for his constant interest in psychoanalysis, and his remarkable knowledge of the most recent theoretical contributions—his first major text on the flesh ("Man and Adversity," 1951 [1964b]) introduces this concept in association with the novelty of certain revolutions carried out by psychoanalytical anthropology—the importance he gives to child psychology is often overlooked. It should be remembered that, before reaching the *Collège de France*, Merleau-Ponty occupied, from 1949 to 1952, the Chair of Child Psychology, and was succeeded by Piaget himself. These years are not merely a parenthesis in his career—that is, no more than the existentialist years. Merleau-Ponty integrated child psychology into his philosophical efforts from the time of his first thesis projects, and even the later manuscripts of the ontological project *Être et Monde* give a surprising amount of space to the debate with Piaget.

[9] For more on Schilder's body schema and body image, and Merleau-Ponty's understanding of body schema, see Saint Aubert 2013: section A.

emphasizes the analogical unity of the body, notably its "systems of (inter-sensorial and inter-modal) equivalences." It takes into consideration the original form of infra-representational knowledge that the body has of its own situation and its competences, thus paving the way for a subtle proximity between perception and non-perception, perceptive consciousness and the unconscious. Schilder, significantly extending the work of his predecessors, clarifies the intercorporeal and relational nature of the body image, including the way in which its dynamics are fundamentally structured by incorporation, animated by a desire to enter into relation with other body images. As the architectonics of a corporeity which itself structures the world, the body schema can only forge its unity within a relational fabric where body, world, and others serve as a symbolic matrix. This issue thus responds directly to Merleau-Ponty's philosophical objectives, and contributes toward the development of his philosophy of the flesh, both in its critical power against intellectualism, as in its free assimilation and alteration of psychoanalysis.[10]

In contrast to Sartre, Merleau-Ponty insists on the *passive–active* complexity of the flesh, starting from the intimate relations of perception and body motility. Aggressive and desiring, the flesh prevents my fusion with others—by its resistance, its thickness, and its opacity—although it is also, at the same time, the very *medium* of our communion. In arresting my gaze and my gestures at the margins of the invisible and the intangible, it also perpetually revives perception. Foreign to the total illusory presence delivered by the pure externality of the object, the flesh delivers itself within the relativity of the inexhaustible, toward the promise of an inside that calls to and hollows out our own depth. The late writings describe this "system of equivalences between the inside and the outside" (1988: 197), "through which desires are synchronized" (BNF XVII: [85](3)): the flesh thus carries and deploys the chiasm of desiring incorporation—making itself the enveloping-enveloped, "the outside of its inside and the inside of its outside" (1968: 144).

This figure of the enveloping-enveloped, which sums up Merleau-Ponty's description of the body's own spatiality, is at the heart of his carnal anthropology as much as his pre-objective ontology. After the long reign of the imaginary of extension, *partes extra partes*, that underlies the Cartesian ontology of the object, the flesh requires its own spatial structures. Not a new *mathesis*, of course, but a schematism and a renewed imaginary espousing the unstable spatiality of animality—the logic of a constantly

---

[10] Merleau-Ponty subjects psychoanalysis to the pressure of two simultaneous movements, in directing it both toward a more radical recognition of corporeity and intercorporeity, and toward an evaluation of desire as openness to being, foreign to the Freudian conception of the "drive" (*pulsion*). He wants to release psychoanalysis from the yoke of positivism that weighed on its first formulations, while also protecting it from the idealistic drift which, in his eyes, threatens its more recent developments. The "Freudian philosophy" announced in the later writings wants to look at this field from the perspective of perception and desire, starting from the flesh, by strongly dissociating it from the "everything is language" of Lacan, at the same time as trying to counter, one last time, the "existential psychoanalysis" of Sartre through the development of a mysterious "ontological psychoanalysis." For more on this direction, see Saint Aubert 2013.

restructured body image, living in and through the intercorporeity at the unconscious depths of our openness to the world. Merleau-Ponty begins to respond to this require-ment toward the end of the 1940s, as we find in the awakening of his more figurative style of writing, and in the outlining of a phenomenological ontology turned toward the imaginary texture of the real. Schilder's descriptions of the spatiality of the body image, and Melanie Klein's insistence on the exchanges of the inside and the outside in incor-poration, prepare him to discover, in Piaget's work on the structuring of space, the sig-nificance of the structures of mathematical *topology*. Merleau-Ponty can then feel more confident in the project he has already begun: the construction of an ontology based on a topology of the flesh, through a phenomenological writing increasingly centered on the figures of the flesh, which are also, at the same time, the figures of that which animate the flesh—desire—and that which the flesh expresses—being.[11]

20.4 FROM THE GENERALITY OF THE BODY TO THE FLESH OF THE WORLD

In the course of his prolonged study of the body schema, Merleau-Ponty begins an orig-inal reflection on what he calls "the generality of the body," an insight that will play a major role in the ontological horizons of his late conception of the flesh. The gener-ality of the body begins with the analogicity of the body schema—in other words, the power of transposition of each of its competences in different situations. This gener-ality ends by designating its overall capacity, through the logic of incorporation that animates it, to lend its own structure to the world and to others: to access their gen-erality by generalizing itself. The identity of the perceived thing is experienced as a manner of being that my body takes up in being configured toward it, in adopting its style through its own manner of being. The unity of the thing is thus the same in kind as that of body (see Merleau-Ponty 2012: 191): "The body schema is also a certain structure of the perceived world, and the latter has its roots in the former" (2011: 144). These ideas form the basis of the freedom Merleau-Ponty assumes in daring such limit-concepts as "flesh of the thing," "flesh of the sensible," and "flesh of the world" in his later work. The thing, the world, and even being itself are explicitly described, like the body, as systems of equivalences (BNF VIb: [149]v(4), [178]v(IV), [228](1), 1968: 205, 247). This compre-hension of the "generality of the body" leads, furthermore, to a logical generalization, of the second degree, of the concept of the flesh itself. The body "flows over into a world whose schema it bears in itself" (1973: 78): body and world are mutually transfigured in configuring each other, to the point of being a "general system of symbols" (2012: lxi) of each other. Hence the world, under the effect of the analogicity of the flesh, becomes carnal, while being, under the effect of the flesh, becomes analogical.

[11] For more on this Merleau-Pontian interpretation of topology, see Saint Aubert 2006: ch. 6.

It is through Merleau-Ponty's notion of "generality" that the logic of *incorporation* comes to replace that of *abstraction*, and the reciprocity that defines this incorporation assigns to the flesh an irreducible circularity. This happens in such a way, though, that this topological ontology of the enveloping-enveloped seems to be threatened by an all-consuming monism: The concept of the *flesh of the world* is extended so comprehensively, one might wonder in what ways it can be differentiated from being itself? Does Merleau-Ponty not risk giving up the world and being, the visible and the invisible, in the system of the *Ineinander* of the flesh, which ends up merging my face with that of the other to the point of anonymity? Certain commentators have even suspected a fusional regression in some of the late writings, which seem to be subjected to a maternal imaginary where the cognitive plenitude of representation, so intensely criticized, finally yields only to the emotional plenitude of the relational connection, thus illusorily erasing any negativity.

It seems that the critical constitution of the concept of the flesh, as anti-Cartesian and anti-Sartrean, might thus take Merleau-Ponty too far. His reactions against the face-to-face encounter of consciousness and extension, against Sartre's overly distinct dichotomies, and against a mineral imaginary where separations are so exaggerated that one can no longer think the force of ours relations at all, might in fact lead the philosopher of the flesh to a counter excess. In other words, this leads him to the excess of a generalized encroachment, the meaningful power and violence of which are dissolved by this itself, for lack of boundaries to transgress. Or to the excess of an ontology of the maternal flesh of the world where all relationality is contained within a pregnancy too generalized to emerge into true birth, the separation without which beings could not achieve their own identity. Or, finally, to the excess of a thought of ambiguity that, in its battle against the univocity of the Cartesian and Sartrean conceptual universes, nevertheless risks falling into an equally problematic equivocity and confusion of its own.

20.5 BEYOND BEING AND NOTHINGNESS: NATURE

It is impossible to respond adequately to these objections, given that the philosopher's work remains unfinished. It seems, however, that we can discern a totally different direction emerging in the unpublished manuscripts, one perhaps more faithful to the continuity of Merleau-Ponty's objectives. Through its insistence on the motifs of depth, the inexhaustible, the invisible, and incompletion, we find a philosophy on its way toward an original sense of *negativity*, which affects its conception of both man and being.

To better understand this direction, we should clarify Merleau-Ponty's decision to start his ontology from the concept of "Nature." The manuscript *La Nature ou le monde du silence*,[12] responds precisely to this question. It attempts a synthesis of his principal critical scenarios (the Cartesian and the Sartrean), through a denunciation of all those philosophies that admit no starting point other than the *cogito* or *freedom*. Although these starting points seem to ensure the solidity of the philosophical endeavor—in separating the human being from Nature, in protecting him from the illusions of the sensible and the imaginary, in giving him his own power—it is precisely here, for Merleau-Ponty, that we find the real illusion: this isolation of man, once established, is irreversible, and it stops philosophical enquiry in its tracks, leading to "a desperate wisdom" that "authorizes all madness" (see Merleau-Ponty BNF VIa: [26](3), [50](3), [53]). Free, rational man and, hence, philosophy itself, are constructed in confrontation with an *outside*; an outside that is neutralized in advance if we begin with the cogito or freedom.

Far from being locked up in a form of regressive immanence, Merleau-Ponty's ontology wants to think a confrontation with the "true outside." That is, an "outside" not played out in a face-to-face encounter that can only end with the annihilation of one of the terms (followed inexorably by the other)—i.e., the institution of a pure subject and pure object, whose roles will be substituted ad infinitum, through an alternation of giving and withdrawing without return, where nothing is ever really exchanged (see Merleau-Ponty BNF VIa: [51](6)). The true outside is not the extension, an externality without mystery, but an "externality with encroachment," a depth where we always already are (BNF VIa: [103](2)(A) et [119](11)). Not constructed, but natural, it is part of our internal fabric before we are even capable of recognizing it as "other." Thus the true outside, starting with others, is always already an inside that haunts us—and it is for this reason that we try to exorcize it through the construction of the object.

Sartre, in his understanding of freedom as a power of rupture and absolute beginning (see Merleau-Ponty BNF VIa: [77]), congeals being into being-presented by me (BNF VIa: [135]v). He thus effectively takes away freedom's very mainspring, and it is precisely this that Merleau-Ponty attempts to restore through his highlighting of both that which supports and resists freedom from the outside, and that which challenges it from the inside—the adversity without which it is nothing but a useless passion that plunges into the vertigo of the purely possible. It is both with and against being that freedom finds its bearings and affirms itself, that it finds a foundation that thrives, not on the absence of struggle, but on the obstinate fidelity of reality. The first purpose of the concept of *Nature*, then, is to illustrate this dimension of being. At the same time familiar and strange, inviting and opposing, Nature, in the end, provokes us by always slipping out of our grasp, by resisting the total mastery that is the dream of the Cartesian subject. Nature therefore interests Merleau-Ponty "as resistance to freedom or [to] subjectivity" (BNF VIa: [131]), "as an index of that which in things resists the operation of free subjectivity and as concrete access to the ontological problem" (BNF VIa: [28](7)).

---

[12] Probably written at the end of 1957, but classified later among the files of the vast project *Être et Monde* (which is actually indissociable from the *Visible and the Invisible* (1968)).

Through the concept of Nature, Merleau-Ponty also attempts to present an ontology that no longer attributes to being such absolute plenitude and density that keeps it outside all communication with my own flesh. It is a matter, rather, of drawing the consistency and vulnerability of being, the power of a Nature which is at the same time a Nature "in rags" (BNF XV: [154]v(179)): a being both strong and wounded, which raises me in restraining me, and which hollows out in front of me the openness and desire of its depth, thus attracting me by its own incompletion. The question of relationships, which has always occupied Merleau-Ponty, thus remains at the heart of his ontology. In Nature, we are introduced to a being that "holds all things together" (BNF VIa: [27]v(6)), a being one can no longer approach with the categorial separation of substance and relation which protects it from any negativity. Merleau-Ponty's ontology is interested in being as it exchanges with nothingness, and in nothingness as it exchanges with being, a double relation that defines negativity. This exchange is not external to man, and man does not hold the mythological role of Nothingness: everything occurs as if this identity of being— as connection between beings—could not be accomplished without man, without being played out at the heart of his active and desiring corporeity. At the heart of his flesh.[13]

Finally, against the substantialized negation that turns Sartre into a falsifier of the dialectic, Merleau-Ponty insists on the relativity of the negation. The negation cannot serve "the absolute positivity of being," drawing on nothing but a logical inverse; its virtue must lie in its revelation of "a being which is not absolute, which is not all that it is" (BNF VIb: [64](26)). Because "the hollow belongs to Being," and the true model of its transcendence is perceptual depth (BNF VII: [167]). For a "true thought of the negative" (BNF VII: [167]), then, there is no longer any pure negation or nothingness, there is only an expressive negativity; correlatively, there is no longer pure affirmation, nor any in-itself, there is only the deep being that regenerates thought. In a strict sense, as Merleau-Ponty explains, this ontology speaks of neither Nothingness nor Being, but of the common vibration of beings in the negativity of being, of their co-nascence in its depth (BNF VIb: [64](25–6)).

In paving the way for these ideas in his late writings, Merleau-Ponty underscores a form of co-belonging of man and being which would seem to "accredit, in the eyes of those quickly inclined to annexation, the myth of an at least latent Heideggerianism in the work of someone no longer here to deny it" (Richir 1982: 125). Yet Merleau-Ponty's approach is quite different from that of Heidegger, and is actually based on a regular critique of the latter.[14] In fact, Merleau-Ponty insists on the originality of his own approach,

---

[13] The preparatory notes for the *Visible and the Invisible* stress that Sartre "does not see the junction of nothingness and being in corporeity," and that his analysis in terms of being and nothingness "only exempts him from any concrete description of the body" (BNF VII: [141]). The composed version resumes: "The analytic of Being and Nothingness is the seer who forgets that he has a body" (1968: 77). On the whole, whether through encroachment, flesh, freedom or Nature, what sets Merleau-Ponty against Sartre is a different perception of being, of man, and of their relations, as negativity.

[14] Throughout the course of the 1950s, Merleau-Ponty progressively elaborates a new scenario, perhaps less developed than the preceding ones, but nevertheless just as severe. If his ontology finds its

which is that of an "indirect ontology" concerned to elaborate a "concrete philosophy," paying constant attention to the *primitive facts*—those radical experiences which engage "the body's relationships to life as a whole" (1964b: 229)—which he sees as constituting the true modes of access to being. He never abandons the privilege given to perception, or his essential dialogue with scientific and psychological fields. And his ontological enabling of the phenomenal body in the concept of *flesh*—for which, he informs us, that there has never been a "name in any philosophy" (1968: 147)—continues to resist any intellectualist reading that one might feel inclined to make of it, such as, for example, a flesh desensitized through its placement at the summit of an ontological purism.

20.6 "THE TRUE NEGATIVITY"

It is precisely through his continual pursuit of a phenomenology of perception that Merleau-Ponty's carnal ontology proceeds in the discovery of the common negativity of human beings and the world, of myself and others. Merleau-Ponty has always been opposed to any model of consciousness that advances from one piece of evidence to the next in the fulfillment of its empty intentions. A long and continuous consultation of modern analyses of perceptual life (particularly *Gestalttheorie*) moves him away from the ambivalence between fullness and emptiness that inhabits the scheme of fulfillment, leading him to describe the more subtle logic of an incarnate intelligence which crystallizes on the inexhaustible, both in spite of, and due to, the incompletion of the perceived.

Perceptual consciousness is no longer an instance of solitary view from above, which possesses its objects in total clarity as isolated and positive beings. It does not build an ideal presence in a unilateral way, but is the result of an expressive relation between my manner of being and that of the thing; that is, as a result of the system of equivalences established between my body schema and the structure of the sensible being. Analogicity is not identification, and the proximity which it induces can never reabsorb the distance which always separates the analogues—in other words, I do not possess the perceived being as such; I resound in unison with it. I *live* its manner of being without ever *having* it: the perceived being always remains beyond the common vibration which allows me to me perceive it (see Merleau-Ponty 2011: 49, 56). The expressive relation thus prevents a fusion of beings that it nevertheless brings into connection with each other; it nourishes their relationship while perpetually opening it up to something else already palpitating at the heart of their link.[15]

roots before a genuine late reading of Heidegger, the manuscripts show that its developing importance is accompanied by a recurring and sometimes virulent criticism of the author of *Sein und Zeit*. On this subject, see Saint Aubert 2006.

[15] This analysis of perception, in the description of a coupling without possession, of the pregnancy of an included third term, anticipates that of carnal intersubjectivity.

Merleau-Ponty insists that the *sense* woven through our relation with perceived being is itself marked by a relativity and a negativity that escapes the traditional concepts of consciousness, because this sense "is practiced, rather than possessed as such," and "manifests itself more in the exceptions where it's lacking than through its own position" (2011: 49). Far from being a positive essence that imposes itself in pure visibility, it is gradually discerned in the continual adjustment of my own infrastructure to that of the perceived. Thus, in an example privileged by Merleau-Ponty—that of the perception of a circle—we are told that circularity is experienced as a typical modulation of local space, a constant deviation, experienced as such through our motor simulation of this contour. "At every moment," he says, this line changes direction, but always in the same way; it is not located at a fixed point on the plane, but recognized through in the course of "a typical activity" that assumes the particular style of its change (2011: 49–50, 57). Our body schema lives this constant "divergence" [*écart*], and accommodates itself to it so well that it resists the variations of this style of variation through regularizing the small aberrations, compensating for what is likely to deviate from the regularity of this very mode of divergence. Merleau-Ponty immediately generalizes this example: As traction and attraction more than abstraction, the tonic consciousness of a shift, perceptive consciousness is first of all that of a typical divergence. These ideas, introduced in *Le monde sensible et le monde de l'expression* (1953), thrive in his writings under the banner of a "theory of perception as divergence [*écart*]."[16]

Through and beyond several phenomenological paths—perceptual life traversed by imperception, the imaginary texture of the perceived world, perceptual recognition through crystallization of the inexhaustible—Merleau-Ponty's reflection paves the way for the ontological direction we have already evoked: Perception aims at being through its lacunae and its changes (2011: 175). Less mobilized by the fixity of norms than by the style of a divergence, it aims at a being strong in its negativity. "Theory of perception as divergence . . . Here is the true negativity. But it is a negativity that works" (BNF VIa: [143]), a "fecund" negativity (1968: 263), because the lacuna is *expressive*— expressive of something neither positively given, nor truly absent, something promised by the lacuna and anticipated by our bodily intentionality.

In this co-expression, which binds us to perceived being, the latter is always too much and too little, both incomplete and overdetermined. Its incompleteness solicits me, but as a result I give it too much, lending it what it does not have. To perceive it, I can do nothing but engage in it and inhabit it—and therefore, inevitably, express myself in it—and at the same time let it invest itself in me, finding in me that which is ready to echo, or ready to express, its own manner of being. Perception, then, is certainly not a face-to-face encounter with an object; rather, it is an investment in a piece of the world whose presence does not face me but plays alongside, inside as well as outside of myself,

---

[16] This theme can be found in many late manuscripts, notably the 1955 course on passivity, a certain number of working notes (both published and not), and, above all, in the three sequences of the impressive unpublished project, *Être et Monde*.

a fragment of being which is also always already a fragment of myself. The perceived world "speaks to me," "solicits me," wakes up a "complicity" in me; and Merleau-Ponty still speaks of "motivation," of "waiting," of "surrender" . . . This animistic description of our expressive relationship with the perceived world points toward a theme which becomes more visible in the 1955 course on passivity and in other late texts such as the 1960 course on Nature: that is, the theme of desire.

20.7 To Surrender to Depth

If the analysis of perception leads to an ontological privileging of *negativity* and an anthropological privileging of *desire*, we might question the circularity between Merleau-Ponty's description of perceptual life and his description of the relationship with the other. His thought does in fact maintain a muted analogy between successful perception (that which "crystallizes," to use the Stendhalian verb cherished in the late writings) and full communion with the other, and this recurring feature[17] is climactically disclosed in a theme particularly important to Merleau-Ponty, the ultimate analysis of which unites negativity and desire: that is, the perception of *depth*.

From the time of his thesis projects of the 1930s, until his last writings, the question of *depth* accompanies Merleau-Ponty's research as a new type of being, conceived as neither subject nor object, neither consciousness nor extension. As "the most 'existential' " (2012: 267) spatial dimension, depth escapes the geometrism of classical intelligence, the optical paradigm of the planimetric perspective—that of a Cycloptic vision eliminating the motor and temporal dimensions of perception while crushing the inside of things onto the same plane. Merleau-Ponty's analysis of this is typical of his philosophy of the flesh: an anthropology, no longer centered on projective intelligence (representation) and will to mastery (consciousness), but extended to the whole of corporeal life. The step toward a privileged state, resolution of a tension, seeking and attempting, consent and surrender: his descriptions of an "in-depth" vision return it to a regime that is, at the same time, motor and instinctive, imaginary and desiring. In the same breath as his somewhat technical proposals on perceptive logic, Merleau-Ponty weaves the most audacious analogies—for him, the most natural—between this in-depth vision and artistic inspiration, our abandonment to words in speaking, and sexual communion with the other (see e.g., Merleau-Ponty 2011: 80–1, 85–6).

Merleau-Ponty insists on the fact that we do not see depth, but see *in* depth: unobjectifiable, depth requires that we abandon ourselves to it, so that it might deliver itself as such. We need to plunge into it, to sink into it, at risk of losing ourselves.

---

[17] In the *Phenomenology of Perception* (1945), the chapter on sexuality already expresses this eloquently. This analogy becomes explicit in the Mexico lectures (1949), and afterwards haunts many of Merleau-Ponty's more personal texts, from *Man and Adversity* to the preface of *Signs*, passing through *The Prose of the World*, the courses of 1953, 1955, 1960 . . . on the way.

It invites us to open ourselves in its openness, through the exercise of a fundamental freedom more radical than the free arbitration between possible alternatives. In front of the stall of objects, I can choose one or the other, all the while maintaining the safe neutrality of rational retreat and its calculation of interest. But "in front of" depth, the situation is totally different. Because we are never only in front of it or facing it, depth always already envelops us. It overflows us and takes us within its vertiginous being, which becomes our own vertigo—so that its power of envelopment is doubled by a capacity to invest in us. That is until, through our motor skills and desires, we might sufficiently anticipate and simulate the displacement that we would have to accomplish to penetrate and traverse it, until our body schema might be configured toward it in the furtive balance of a web of schemes. Depth thus calls upon our own infrastructure, so that it might deliver itself as such. And its urgent appeal destabilizes the immobility of the detached observer, as well as the passive neutrality of the Sartrean flesh. Depth calls our body schema to straighten up on the constellations of the world, to raise ourselves up toward depth. In a word, depth animates us: It makes us flesh.

The same applies to the gaze that the other turns toward me, which is depth. I am free to choose not to deliver myself, to flee the silence of the exchange of gazes, precipitating between others and me "the ruse of speech" (1964b: 16). But if I consent to this gaze, then I am transported into the circuit of the seeing-seen that, with its eyes, engages its own invisible and, with mine, engages my own interiority. And this unites our two depths in a common negativity, our two destinies in the same life, and "sketches out what is accomplished by desire" (1964b: 17). The other, like perceptual depth, is unobjectifiable. And just as, in a strict sense, I do not *see* depth but *in* it, and *by* that which it calls in me, so I do not truly perceive the other without seeing *in* him and *by* him: without already staring at him through this interiority of expectation, which resounds in me as a result of his own interiority, conveyed through his gaze. I cannot comprehend him without accessing his depth by my own, which his depth contributes toward hollowing in me. "Love plays out like perception," Merleau-Ponty affirms in the Mexico City lectures, and "the other exists like perceived things": that is, as inexhaustible, and yet *given* as such (1949: [142–3](II5), [163](13)).

The other is thus at the summit of this world which, if not perceived, is a lost world. Like every perceived thing, albeit at the highest point, it remains an infra-object or "ultra-thing"[18]—not because it is impenetrable, or the bearer of a positive infinity, but because it is indefinite and inexhaustible. Like every perceived thing—but at the summit— its visibility radiates from its invisible regions and lacunary shores, inviting my own depth to anticipate and understand them. Our meeting is accomplished through the other's lacunae and my own, "which never cease" (1968: 77). Like perceptual crystallization, it is tied in the adjustment of my incomplete and shifting structure toward its own, in the focusing of the inexhaustible onto the inexhaustible. Just as the perceived world is recognized only in perceptual faith, escaping the raw light of Cartesian evidence that sweeps away any shadow and crushes any relief, so the other is given only in the clarity

---

[18] In the sense of Henri Wallon, cultivated in Merleau-Ponty's late ontological manuscripts.

of desire, that of an "interrogative faith" which adheres to someone beyond proof, and promises something beyond what it knows.

References

Merleau-Ponty, M. (BNF VIa), *La Nature ou le monde du silence*, and other unpublished documents, autumn 1957 (Bibliothèque Nationale de France, volume VI).

Merleau-Ponty, M. (BNF VIb), *Être et Monde* (1958–60), unpublished (Bibliothèque Nationale de France, volume VI).

Merleau-Ponty, M. (BNF VII), unpublished preparatory notes for *Le visible et l'invisible*, 1959–60 (Bibliothèque Nationale de France, volume VII).

Merleau-Ponty, M. (BNF XV), unpublished preparatory notes for the 1957 course at the Collège de France on *Le concept de Nature* (Bibliothèque Nationale de France, volume XV).

Merleau-Ponty, M. (BNF XVII), *Notes sur le corps* (1956–60), unpublished (Bibliothèque Nationale de France, volume XVII).

Merleau-Ponty, M. (1949), unpublished preparatory notes for the Conférences de Mexico, early 1949.

Merleau-Ponty, M. (1964a), "Eye and mind," translated by C. Dallery, in *The Primacy of Perception* (Evanston, IL: Northwestern University Press).

Merleau-Ponty, M. (1964b), *Signs*, translated by R. C. McCleary (Evanston, IL: Northwestern University Press).

Merleau-Ponty, M. (1968), *The Visible and the Invisible*, translated by A. Lingis (Evanston, IL: Northwestern University Press).

Merleau-Ponty, M. (1973), *The Prose of the World*, translated by J. O'Neill (Evanston, IL: Northwestern University Press).

Merleau-Ponty, M. (1988), "Themes from the lectures at the Collège de France 1952–1960," translated by J. O'Neill, in *In Praise of Philosophy and Other Essays* (Evanston, IL: Northwestern University Press), 71–199.

Merleau-Ponty, M. (2003), *Nature: Course Notes from the Collège de France*, translated by R. Vallier (Evanston, IL: Northwestern University Press).

Merleau-Ponty, M. (2011), *Le monde sensible et le monde de l'expression*, course at the Collège de France, 1953 (Geneva: MétisPresses).

Merleau-Ponty, M. (2012), *Phenomenology of Perception*, translated by D. A. Landes (London: Routledge).

Merleau-Ponty, M. (2016), *Entretiens avec Georges Charbonnier et autres dialogues, 1946–1959* (Lagrasse: Verdier).

Richir, M. (1982), "Le sens de la phénoménologie dans *Le visible et l'invisible*," *Esprit* 6: 124–45.

Saint Aubert, E. de (2004), *Du lien des êtres aux éléments de l'être. Merleau-Ponty au tournant des années 1945–1951* (Paris: J. Vrin).

Saint Aubert, E. de (2005), *Le scénario cartésien. Recherches sur la formation et la cohérence de l'intention philosophique de Merleau-Ponty* (Paris: J. Vrin).

Saint Aubert, E. de (2006), *Vers une ontologie indirecte. Sources et enjeux critiques de l'appel à l'ontologie chez Merleau-Ponty* (Paris: J. Vrin).

Saint Aubert, E. de (2013), *Être et chair I. Du corps au désir: l'habilitation ontologique de la chair* (Paris: J. Vrin).

CHAPTER 21

JAN PATOČKA'S PHILOSOPHICAL LEGACY

JAMES DODD

In a short text written a year before his death in 1977 after a series of police interrogations, Jan Patočka recounted the story of how Edmund Husserl, during the Christmas of the even darker year of 1934, presented to him the gift of an old wooden lectern, one that had been given to him in turn almost sixty years before by the Czech philosopher and first president of Czechoslovakia, Tomáš G. Masaryk. "And so I became," Patočka remarks, "the heir of a great 'tradition', of which I have never felt quite worthy" (Patočka 1999: 282). The intersection of dates, personages, events, and intellectual legacies that come together in this story of a re-gifting among friends of this iconic piece of academic life, symbolizes the complexity of Patočka's place in twentieth-century intellectual history.

The history is often tragic. By 1934 Husserl, a converted Jew born in Moravia, now retired from the university and living in Freiburg, had been banned from speaking or publishing in Germany. Patočka had just spent the winter semester of 1933–4 in what he called the "witches cauldron" of Berlin, witnessing, as he put it in these reflections some forty years later, "the beginning of the end of Europe" (Patočka 1999: 274). He would spend the years 1934 and 1935 studying with Husserl in Freiburg, eventually developing a close philosophical friendship with both the master and his assistant, Eugen Fink (Fink and Patočka 1999). He would also make the acquaintance of another of Husserl's assistants, Ludwig Landgrebe, who would soon immigrate to Prague in hopes of escaping the coming storm, but in vain.

Husserl had already met the young Czech philosopher in Paris in 1929, on the occasion of the *soutenance de thèse* of Alexandre Koyré, himself a former student of Husserl's from Freiburg (Patočka 1999: 273). During his Paris visit Husserl presented a series of lectures that would be expanded and published in French translation in 1931 under the title *Méditations cartésiennes* (see the editor's introduction to Husserl 1991). Patočka, who attended the lectures in Paris, would later orchestrate, as the Czech secretary of the recently founded *Cercle philosophique de Prague pour recherches sur l'entendement humain*, Husserl's visit to Prague in 1936. There Husserl would present a version of another series of lectures given the same year in Vienna, which would form the foundation for Part I of the *Crisis of the European Sciences* (Husserl 1970; on Patočka's work for the *Cercle* and Husserl's visit to Prague, see Patočka 1999, 176–257).

Patočka thus became intimately acquainted with Husserl in the twilight of his professional career, when he was facing growing persecution in Germany and an increasingly uncertain future, but also during one of the most remarkable periods in the philosophical development of the founder of phenomenology. The intellectual itinerary of Husserl's late period would have a lasting impact on the trajectory of Patočka's philosophical development. Defending a dissertation in 1931 on the concept of evidence (*Evidenz*) in epistemology (Patočka 1931), Patočka turned to the topic of the problem of the "natural" world, habilitating in 1936 with his *The Natural World as a Philosophical Problem* (Patočka 2016). Deeply influenced by Husserl's critique of modern science, Patočka in this text takes the first steps in what will become a lifelong project of articulating the idea of the relation of human beings to the whole as a fundamental structure of comportment, one that is distorted by the encroachment of a scientistic conception of the world that progressively replaces a meaningful sense of the whole with an ideal of instrumental rationality. The "natural" world for Patočka is accordingly the world "natural" to humans, the world essential to their manner of existence: It is the world of the cultivated *praxis* of an engaged involvement with things, or care (*Sorge*) as Heidegger would express it; it is also the world of the pre-given horizon of familiarity that supports and renders meaningful the everyday experience of human beings, or the life-world (*Lebenswelt*), to evoke Husserl's terminology of the time.

1934 was also just a year before Masaryk resigned from the Czech presidency, bringing to a close a remarkable intellectual and political career. Masaryk, a Czech representative in the Austrian *Reichsrat* during the last years of the Habsburgs, became quickly convinced after the outbreak the First World War that the cumbersome multinational system of the Austro-Hungarian Empire was fundamentally flawed, and increasingly victim to chauvinist German politics. The only solution, Masaryk concluded, was national independence for the subject peoples. In his London exile during the war, Masaryk became an influential spokesman for the breakup of the empire and the self-determination of nations. He also organized an expatriate Czech army that fought, with some notable success, alongside the Allies in the last stages of the conflict, and after the war Masaryk became the first president of the new republic of Czechs and Slovaks (see Masaryk 1969).

More than a narrow nationalism, Masaryk's plea for national self-determination was based on a fundamental commitment to humanism, which he understood to be a deeply moral perspective on the world that he considered essential to any response to the spiritual crisis of the age. Masaryk's philosophical roots lay in the positivism of August Comte, but also, in a way not without its tensions, in profound religious conviction. In his *Habilitationsthesis* (Masaryk 1970), published in German in 1881, Masaryk had tackled the question of what lessons should be drawn from the statistical surge in suicides that had taken place in turn-of-the-century Europe, given that the phenomenon occurred in countries that were relatively stable and prosperous. Similar to Émile Durkheim's later 1897 study (Durkheim 2006), Masaryk put forward a sociological argument that emphasized the retreat of the integrative force of religious community in the wake of an ever more secularized world. Unlike Durkheim, Masaryk's response was a call for a renewed spiritual humanism, guided by the recognition of what he believed to be the objective meaning of religious truth (Masaryk 1938, see also Patočka 1989: 139–56).

Masaryk died just a year before the state he helped to found was critically weakened in the Munich Agreement of 1938, a gamble for peace that was quickly scuttled by the onset of another world war even more destructive than the first, one of the immediate consequences of which was the German occupation of Czechoslovakia in 1939. Patočka thus begins his career as a philosopher at a decisive turning point. He witnessed the eclipse of the hope that had been embodied in Masaryk, in which a promising future was overwhelmed by the catastrophe of a war that would devastate much of Europe. The Second World War and its cold aftermath would have a profound effect on Patočka's philosophical and, above all, personal life; it also shaped him politically in decisive ways. Though he was an early critic of Masaryk's positivism, Patočka would always remain a defender of Masaryk's political idealism. Yet he would be a defender of this humanism only with serious reservations: Like others of Patočka's generation, such as Jean-Paul Sartre and Emmanuel Levinas, however desirable it may otherwise be, humanism would always pose more of a philosophical problem than a given set of ideals to be uncritically embraced (see Patočka 2015, also Chvatík 2015 and Declève 1986).

Patočka was also more than just the heir of Masaryk's political legacy. Masaryk was also the older friend and colleague who, in the late 1870s, had convinced the young Husserl, then studying mathematics in Leipzig and then in Berlin as an assistant to Karl Weierstraß, to pursue philosophy under the direction of the Austrian philosopher Franz Brentano in Vienna. Brentano's descriptive psychology was crucial to the development of Husserl's phenomenology. Brentano sought to carve out a methodological space for the investigation of mental phenomena that would be free from reductively naturalistic approaches in experimental psychology, but without forsaking a basic commitment to the philosophical tenants of empiricism. Husserl, on the basis of a systematic engagement with the presuppositions of Brentano's descriptive psychology in his 1900–1 *Logical Investigations* (Husserl 2013), would radicalize the unique renewal of empiricism he found in Brentano. Armed with a powerful new methodological perspective, Husserl would announce in a 1911 article in the journal *Logos* the project of a "philosophy as rigorous science," one that would secure the project of philosophy from the twin dangers of naturalism and historicism (Husserl 1965). In Husserl philosophy finally breaks from the dominant naturalistic tendencies of the late nineteenth century, not, however, by breaking away from science, but on the contrary by attempting to establish its ultimate foundations in lived experience.

Husserl in important ways distances himself from the Comtean-style positivism that had characterized Masaryk's perspective, but it is important to emphasize that all three of these thinkers—Brentano, Masaryk, Husserl—are moving in a very similar direction, namely toward the formulation of a conception of human experience that shapes for itself a coherent understanding, and with that a "world," that is in turn understood to be an accomplishment of *meaning*.

Patočka also belongs to this basic orientation, but his appropriation of this heritage is complex. Take for example the concept of intentionality, originally elaborated in Brentano's 1874 *Psychology from an Empirical Standpoint* (Brentano 2014). In Husserl's development of this key Brentanian theme, the intentionality of conscious life describes a mode of relation, namely the manner in which consciousness stands in relation to its objects, but also how these objects are given or present "in" consciousness. That the center of focus is precisely *consciousness,* or human life as a consciousness, is a point of departure that Husserl never relinquished, even if he did deepen and transform the problematic in ways that Brentano would have found unrecognizable. It is also a point of departure that, from Patočka's point of view, leads Husserl ineluctably down the path of Cartesianism: The view that the relation between the *intentio*, the noetic act of consciousness, and the *intentum*, its noematic correlate, should be grasped specifically in terms of *subjectivity*—as if the subjectivity of intentional life, the being of the *I*, exhausted the analysis of intentional being as a whole (Patočka 1996a: 87–106, Patočka 1989: 285–326).

Patočka, in many ways comparable to Fink (Fink 2005; Bruzina 2004: 114–27), resists what he sees as the subjectivization of the concept of the phenomenon in Husserl, which reaches its high point in the 1913 *Ideas I* (Husserl 2014). For Patočka, if the accomplishment of meaning in lived experience is identified with the manner in which something is given, manifest as phenomenon, then this accomplishment cannot be reduced to the intentional acts of subjective consciousness. It must instead be understood as a kind of double movement in which the constitution of the object is dependent on the being of consciousness, but also vice versa, the being of consciousness results from the constitution of the object. The "natural" world is thus still interpreted by Patočka as an accomplishment of subjective life; but any account of the being of the I must recognize its radical dependence upon the irreducible horizon of the being of the world itself (Patočka 2000: 38–115, 1996a: 57–70).

Here the existential analytic of Heidegger has an important influence on Patočka's thinking (as it had on Fink's), with its disavowal of an uncritical acceptance of consciousness as a point of departure in phenomenological investigation. Heidegger's formulation of the concept of Dasein in the opening sections of *Being and Time* (Heidegger 1962: 26–40) is meant precisely to keep *open* the question of being, or of what it is to be a human being, that seems to be decided in advance by the concept of "consciousness," traditionally saddled with the metaphysical (specifically Cartesian) associations of an intellectual substance. Heidegger is clearly an important influence on Patočka since his time in Freiburg, but it nevertheless remains the case that, despite his criticisms of the master, he never broke completely from Husserl. The intentional analyses of lived experience one finds in Husserl's writings, and the progressively complex understanding of the being of phenomenality accomplished therein, provided a fruitful philosophical basis that in many respects was as important if not more so than Heidegger's fundamental ontology (see Part Two of Patočka 1998). That being said, any appropriation of the Husserlian path—and with that the Brentanian legacy of the concept of intentionality—could for Patočka only take the form of its reformulation as an "a-subjective" phenomenology (Patočka 1991: 267–309; see Barbaras 2011: 203–22).

The problem of the "natural" world and the formulation of the tasks of an a-subjective phenomenology were never far from another important thread in the complex legacy of Masaryk and Husserl: the diagnosis of the spiritual crisis of Europe. Brentano too belongs arguably to this thread: Essential to Brentano's project of reinventing psychology was the call for a renewal of philosophy, a rediscovery of its basic problems and methods (Brentano 1926). This in part lay behind Brentano's interest in Aristotle, who for him represented an analogous period of philosophical renewal. More, this renewal was understood in turn by Brentano as having a fundamental *ethical* import: To explain ethical existence in terms that were cognate to contemporary humanity was accordingly one of the basic tasks of modern psychology (Brentano 1921). With Masaryk and Husserl, this conception of a task of renewal basic to contemporary philosophy becomes explicitly coupled with the theme of crisis, especially in the wake of the First World War (see Patočka 1989: 139–56).

In Husserl, an account of the historical reorientation of the ideal of science as technoscience became an ever more pronounced feature of his diagnosis of the crisis of the age, a perspective powerfully articulated in Part II of the *Crisis* (Husserl 1970). The central role of technology in the crisis of modern humanity, articulated with equal power in the thought of Heidegger, would also be embraced by Patočka, perhaps most poignantly in his 1973 Varna Lecture, "The Dangers of Technization in Science according to E. Husserl and the Essence of Technology as Danger according to M. Heidegger," in which he skillfully draws on the positions of both his predecessors (Patočka 1989: 327–39).

Yet unlike Husserl, and arguably even Heidegger, Patočka's mature understanding of modern science is informed by a far more intensive and comprehensive study of the history of science, which began in earnest during the war years and never abated. Patočka's *Nachlaß* contains a large number of studies, ranging from ancient Greek philosophy (in particular an important work on Aristotle recently translated into French, Patočka 2011), to Renaissance philosophy, early modern philosophy, German idealism (above all, Hegel), and nineteenth-century philosophy (for a comprehensive bibliography see Patočka 1999: 524f.). Much of this work took place when Patočka had been prevented from teaching in the university, as well as under various censorship regimes from German occupation through the worst Stalinist years to the normalization of post-1968 Czechoslovakia.

In fact, Patočka's only time teaching at the university included a brief period after the war and before the Communist takeover in 1948, then again twenty years later during the equally brief thaw of the Prague Spring and before the normalization campaign gained the upper hand. These political and professional limitations may in part explain the energy Patočka put into his studies in the history of philosophy—the guise of a historian of ideas enabled him to assume a relatively neutral stance politically, thus allowing for at least some of his work to be published (see Kohák 1989 for this argument). Chance opportunities also availed themselves and guided the course of at least some of this work: So, for example, the immediate catalyst for Patočka's important research on the seventeenth-century Czech philosopher of education Jan Amos Komenský (Comenius) (Patočka 1981) was his minor clerical job in the 1950s at the Comenius Archive in Prague. Patočka's work on Comenius and the history of philosophy and science generally is a central part of his intellectual legacy, and he is gradually becoming recognized outside of the Czech context as an important historian of ideas (see, e.g., Hagedorn and Sepp 2006, also the introduction by Bertrand Bouckaert to Patočka 2001).

During his lifetime Patočka nevertheless labored in relative obscurity, devoted to private study and his limited, if also valuable engagement with students in his informal "apartment seminars." Forced isolation would be the norm, and is an important factor in any account of the rhetorical posture that Patočka assumes in many of his writings from 1939 onwards, including the dark character of much of his later work. Yet it would be a mistake to go so far as to credit Patočka's engagement with the history of philosophy solely to the need for a refuge from the censors. The research was ultimately motivated by insights and inspirations that date well before the war, and its progressive development shaped Patočka as a philosopher, and in two key respects.

The first is the formulation, on the basis of a comprehensive reading of Aristotle and the origins of modern science, of Patočka's mature philosophical anthropology, in which the ontology of *movement* plays a central role. The theme of movement, so central to Patočka's contribution to modern phenomenology, represents both the development of the problem of the "natural" world, as well as an important step toward the fulfillment of the program of an a-subjective phenomenology. The result is a conception of human existence as the ground or site for phenomenality, for manifestation and appearance, not on the basis of an intellectual institution of the given in concepts, but on a much more fundamental level as a triple movement of disclosure. In later texts, such as his 1968–9 university lectures *Body, Community, Language, World* (Patočka 1998) and the 1967 essay "The 'Natural' World and Phenomenology" (Patočka 1989: 239–73), Patočka's account of this triple movement of disclosure frames a series of phenomenological investigations into concrete human existence, which reveal it to be at its core bodily and worldly, anchored in the given horizon of the world but also providing the space for its articulation and comprehension.

The first of these movements is one of anchoring, of the establishment of roots in the given world. Birth sets down roots, but it is also premised on the opening and acceptance on the part of the world for human life: Human existence is possible only in a world that accepts it on some basic level, that embraces it in its utter nakedness. This anchoring of life in a world that embraces it before it has even become possible is, for Patočka, in turn a primordial dimension of human community, of being with others in the given world (Patočka 1998: 143–52). Already in the description of this first movement one can discern Patočka's unique appropriation of the central phenomenological theme of meaning: The primordial acceptance of existence, its embrace that life finds in the world, is an original form of the human relation to the whole, one in which the whole is revealed as a ground for the meaningfulness or significance of things. Yet this meaning of the world is not the result of an interpretation, an idea, but belongs to concrete human existence as one of its characteristic movements, basic to what Heidegger would call its care-structure (see Heidegger 1962: 225–55). It is a movement because, as with care, it is the active opening of a possibility, the projection of a being that "is" its possibilities.

The second movement establishes as well a meaningful relation to the whole of what is, though in this case it is a relation determined by another dimension of the experience of human finitude, namely the sense of its *fragility*. Human life requires shelter, for the same world that accepts human existence also threatens it, submits it to the open possibility of death. This second movement is accordingly one of defense, of the preservation of the possibility of life. It is also the world of work, in which life encounters itself as a burden to be endured in order to survive, and the world, including that of others, as a space of both cooperation and confrontation. Each of these first two movements is described by Patočka as explicitly bound to *earth* and *body*; each stands in an equiprimordial relation with the other, the two together coupling birth and survival at the core of the irreversible rhythm of human existence (Patočka 1998: 150–9).

The third movement that Patočka argues is basic to human comportment in the world discloses, at the heart of what is given and defended, a sense of an order of things, a coherence that saturates all things that corresponds to their basic *truth*. Life in the third movement discloses an explicit whole, a unity of understanding that reveals the world as a reality that permeates all there is, thus making manifest the world as something that does not simply dissolve into a series of chance encounters or individual things and events (Patočka 1998: 159–61). Thanks to this third movement, human existence is the disclosure not only of things, but also of things in a truth that defines the horizon of their being. This also means, however, that human existence opens itself to the possibility for falsity and dissimulation: The movement of human life is the ground for phenomenality, in that it is the concrete event making possible the showing of things as what they are, but it is equally the event that makes possible the experience of their obfuscation and opacity.

Patočka is here appropriating key Aristotelian themes within an a-subjective phenomenological framework (cf. Aristotle 1987: 277–8, and the discussion in Heidegger 2005: §2d), as well as drawing on Heidegger's concept of truth as disclosure from *Being and Time* (cf. Heidegger 1962: 256–73): human life is that wherein the truth of things finds manifestation and expression, but which also equally harbors the potential for inaccessibility and loss, or falsity in the Aristotelian sense of *pseudos*. In that human movement is potentially both, it also opens the way for a choice for either. This means that with the third movement there emerges the potentiality for a genuine life in truth, an authentic life that grasps things for what they are and defends itself against falsehood. Such a life is a life oriented toward the disclosure of things in their "essence," their what-it-is-to-be (*to ti en enai*), and which thereby establishes itself as a fundamental wisdom and understanding of all that is.

This conception of a dynamic relation to truth as a movement of human existence also highlights the second essential aspect of Patočka's engagement with the history of philosophy, namely the striking development of a unique philosophy of history. Its guiding thesis is that, if human life can be understood in terms of the complex movement of disclosure just described, this implies in turn that human existence is essentially *historical*. This is because, on Patočka's account, though the three movements of human existence are equi-primordial, their interplay can take different forms, thus giving rise to diverse manners of world-experience. This is one of the core theses of one of Patočka's last works, and perhaps his most important, the 1975 *Heretical Essays in the Philosophy of History* (Patočka 1996b).

In the *Heretical Essays* Patočka draws a contrast between "prehistorical" humanity, which for him characterizes the great ancient empires such as Mycenae or Egypt, and what he takes to be the form of properly "historical" civilization, which first emerges with the Greek *polis* (Patočka 1996b: 1–52). The distinction between prehistory and history on Patočka's account does not turn on the relative availability of written documents, but rather has to do with different experiences of time, which are determined by a particular constellation of the three movements of human existence.

The time characteristic of the experience of prehistorical humans is embodied for Patočka in myths such as stories of Gilgamesh and Oedipus (Patočka 1996b: 19–26, 2002: 38–70). In myth, the present and the future are essentially experienced as the repetition of a primordial past; it is a world in which answers always seem to precede and anticipate the questions. Life for mythical humanity is revealed to itself as a basic repetition of itself, a revolution of the eternally same. This particular form of the experience of time essentially gives precedence to the meaning of life revealed in the first two movements: Life is here anchored in a world that has always already been, and is faced with burdens and tasks that have always already been given their archetypal forms by a past that provides a comprehensive sense of their meaning as a whole (see Hagedorn 2015).

Patočka argues that historical existence, by contrast, involves a fundamental shift in preference for the present, as it is and not as it was, coupled with the now open possibility of the future. Accordingly, it is now questions that take priority; possibilities are no longer determined by what has been, but take on a new, far more unstable and riskier reality for a humanity suddenly oriented toward what could be and no longer limited to what was. Here the third movement gains a relative ascendency within the dynamic of the three movements: freed from being merely a sense of a given order permeating things, one embodied in metaphorical expressions that are never fully submitted to reflection or critique, the movement of truth now takes the form of a *questioning* of the meaning of the whole. To open the horizon of understanding and action in this way to what is and could be, or to who we are and could be, means that the self-understanding of humans now takes on a decisively *problematic* tenor (Patočka 1996b: 39–41). Nevertheless the mythical, Patočka argues elsewhere (Patočka 2002: 43–4), never fully loses its hold on human beings; myth is a structure that remains forever a part of experience, for it is an irreducible element of unreflected truth that is characteristic of the "natural" world. Yet with the emergence of history the human experience of the world is profoundly shaken, inaugurating a possible mode of human comportment that grasps itself in terms of the tasks of reflection and historical becoming.

The *Heretical Essays* track the emergence of this new figure of an historical existence, one that is not only historical but has embraced its historicity, from its origin in the ancient Greek *polis* through its complex refashioning in the wake of the emergence of modern science and technology (Patočka 1996b: 79–118). Drawing also on the work of Hannah Arendt (Arendt 1958) and her account of the heritage of Greek thought, Patočka describes the beginning of history as the emergence of a form of existence that is essentially open and dependent upon initiative and resolve. This ethic of free initiative finds expression in Aristotle's definition of the citizen (*polites*) at *Politics* 1275a20 (Aristotle 1932): The citizen takes part in rule, *arche*, but also *krisis*, the necessity to choose, to make a decision in the present for the future on behalf of the *polis*, but without any guarantee of success, or even survival. Life that no longer understands itself as a repetition of the past now takes on the form of an overt *risk*. To be such a citizen meant, on Patočka's account, to understand human being as a project that is at all possible only if one cultivates an inner discipline and fortitude that allows one to withstand the shocks of a contingent world that has suddenly become ambiguous. Patočka sums up this ancient understanding of historical existence with the Socratic–Platonic formula of the "care for the soul," or the care for an existence faced with a world that has in turn been transformed into a contentious environment of struggle, or what Heraclitus called *polemos* (Patočka 1996b: 40–4, 82–3, also see Patočka 2002: 71–130 and Cajthaml 2014).

One of the many heresies in the *Heretical Essays* is Patočka's contention that, despite an apparent embrace of progress and with that of the future, the modern age in fact represents a *retreat* from historical self-understanding, and not its fulfillment. The ancient heritage of the care for the soul, and with that the authentic historical self-understanding of human beings, has been eclipsed by the rise of modern technological civilization, in which understanding has been reduced to the capacity for technical manipulation, and the ends of humanity to possession and power (Patočka 1996b: 95–118). In the darkest but perhaps most brilliant of the essays that closes the *Heretical Essays*, "The Wars of the Twentieth Century and the Twentieth Century as War," Patočka provides a powerful analysis of the ontological significance of the wars of the past century, beginning with the First World War: The meaning of these wars rests in the opening of the possibility that in the future all of the potential of human existence to disclose the world as an order of meaning has been mobilized into patterns of organization dedicated solely to the accumulation and expenditure of force. Human beings are becoming subject to an unforgiving bondage to an ever-more meaningless and empty existence, in which the sense of something higher is being progressively erased.

The last of the *Heretical Essays* holds out a faint hope, in ways reminiscent of Heidegger's later philosophy (the influence of which is evident here), that the extreme experiences of the twentieth century can nevertheless serve as a basis for the reemergence of philosophical sensibility. Patočka couches his account of this possibility in part in the traditional language of the care of the soul, but more importantly in terms of a description of the "solidarity of the shaken" (Patočka 1996b: 134–5). Unlike the care for the soul, the solidarity of the shaken is not an ideal, not even the negative ideal that Patočka had once explored, in an early essay from the mid 1950s under the title

"Negative Platonism," as a figure appropriate to modern philosophy (Patočka 1989: 175–206). There the emphasis had been on the possibility of philosophical reflection after the end of metaphysics, one based on the cultivation of an orientation to the eternal that would no longer be defined as a metaphysical hyper-reality, but "negatively," and thus coextensive with the Socratic striving for wisdom. Here, by contrast, the emphasis is on a kind of rupture, an unanticipated crack in a reality otherwise completely determined by force, and with that an experience of freedom that bonds humans together in the raw anticipation that there is something other than life as it is, that the ontological reality of the world as war is not total.

Patočka's striking formulation in the *Heretical Essays* of the solidarity of the shaken is supplemented by the lecture already cited above on the subject of the technological age that Patočka attempted to present, unsuccessfully, in 1973 at the World Philosophy Congress in Varna, Bulgaria. An important theme late in this lecture is the phenomenon of *sacrifice*, understood as a resistance to the incorporation of the meaning of human life into the logic of technological civilization, thereby revealing the limits of the latter and thus providing a powerful form of experience definitive of the present age (Patočka 1989: 327–39, also the "Séminaire sur l'ère technique," in Patočka 1990, Perryman-Holt 2015, and Učník 2011).

Patočka's evocation of sacrifice in this context is not an abstract theme. The 1969 self-immolation of Jan Palach in protest of the Soviet invasion is in the background here, but also dissidents such as Andrei Sakharov. That solidarity can arise out of the worst of war, in the wake of the experience of the complete loss of any sense of coherence or meaning of life; that sacrifice remains a potent expression of something higher in an age that seems to have no other truth than the accumulation and expenditure of resources material and human; all of this represents for Patočka essential points of departure for a possible rediscovery of a philosophical life in truth.

These themes of sacrifice and the solidarity of the shaken are also important touchstones for any discussion of Patočka's relation to the dissident movements that took place in the former Soviet Bloc in the 1970s (so for example Tava 2016, Tardivel 2007, and Tucker 2000). Here, too, Husserl's legacy makes itself felt, and on a personal level. In his 1976 reflections on Husserl referenced above, Patočka describes the way in which Husserl and Fink had set for him an important spiritual example: In times of uncertainty and public ostracization, these two thinkers continued to comport themselves as philosophers, becoming even more engrossed in and dedicated to the life of the mind (Patočka 1999: 277). It would be a model for Patočka's own years of marginalization, and arguably an inspiration for his own act of resistance the foundations of which were being prepared in the same year that he penned his remembrances of the Freiburg master.

For 1976 was the year of the Helsinki Accords, an agreement outlining principles for cooperation among member states in both East and West that was intended to secure peace and the postwar international order. One of the provisions was a commitment among signatories for the universal recognition of human rights, including freedom of speech and thought. This and similar agreements signed by the authorities presented an opening for a diverse group of intellectuals in Czechoslovakia to form the civic initiative known as Charta 77. The movement, which included the future president of post-Communist Czechoslovakia, Václav Havel, was not organized as an outright protest or direct challenge to the authority of the regime, but instead as a principled gesture of dissidence: its aim was to call attention to the fact that the very principles to which the Czechoslovak state had unambiguously committed itself were being routinely violated.

Patočka was asked to be one of the public spokesmen for the Charta, and he accepted, after some hesitation. His contribution, both in writing and in the impact he made in the few public discussions and meetings with foreigners he managed to have, was by all accounts fundamental, forming one of the political and intellectual bases for the Velvet Revolution in 1989 (Pithart 2011 and Polouš 2011). It also led to intense police harassment and persecution, and ultimately the death from a brain hemorrhage suffered by the aging, exhausted philosopher.

It would not be too much to argue that Patočka's philosophy of history played an important role in his involvement in Charta 77. It also arguably prepared him for both the times and the task. The themes of the solidarity of the shaken, the care for the soul, of political life as struggle and the risk of the future, understood from the dark perspective of the *Heretical Essays*, are clearly much closer in tone and mood to the ethos of dissidence in 1970s Czechoslovakia than, for example, the more optimistically oriented philosophy of Masaryk. The generation that faced the challenges of 1977 was very different from the one that had faced those of 1919. At the same time, one should not ignore the legacy of Masaryk, whose optimism could be said to have formed an important counterbalance to the pessimistic, even eschatological tone of Patočka's late philosophy—perhaps, above all, for Patočka himself (see Declève 1986).

Yet Patočka's enduring legacy as a thinker arguably extends significantly beyond the ramifications of his brief role as a dissident intellectual at the end of the long twilight of the Soviet Union, or even for that matter his place among the generation of phenomenologists that succeeded Husserl and Heidegger. Neither of these contributions should of course be minimized. Though the political future for the former Czechoslovakia and Eastern Europe is generally, at the writing of this article, uncertain and at times troubling, it is still the case that the hopes for a more humane and morally sound politics raised by the 1989 Velvet Revolution represent a startling revival of the legacy of the humanist founders of the early republic, such as Masaryk and the biologist and philosopher Emanuel Rádl. Likewise, Patočka's tenacious commitment to the promise of phenomenological philosophy, the hallmark of his philosophical activity right up until his death, resulted in a remarkable body of work that documents some of the most profound engagements of Patočka's generation with the foundations of phenomenological philosophy.

Though still relatively underappreciated by the broader philosophical community, interest in Patočka's philosophical legacy has been steadily increasing since his death, perhaps above all in France due to the remarkable work of Erika Abrams in making Patočka's writings available in French. Already long admired by figures such as Paul Ricœur, substantial engagements with Patočka's philosophy can be found in the writings of a range of prominent French philosophers, such as Renaud Barbaras (Barbaras 2011), Jacques

Derrida (Derrida 2008), Françoise Dastur (Dastur 2012), Nathalie Frogneux (Frogneux 2007), and Jean-Luc Marion (Marion 2015), among others. A new generation of international scholars, including Ludger Hagedorn (Hagedorn 2015), Sandra Lehmann (Lehmann 2004), and Filip Karfík (Karfik 2008), have built on the work of Klaus Nellen, Jiří Němec, and Ilja Srubar in shaping the reception in German through a series of interpretive studies of Patočka's thought and translations of his works. Though not as robust, there continues to be a presence of Patočka scholarship in English as well, beginning with Erazim Kohák's work in the late 1980s (Kohák 1989), up to the recent publication of Erika Abram's English translation of Patocka's *The Natural World and Phenomenology*, edited by Ivan Chvatík and Ĺubica Učnik (Patočka 2016, also see Mensch 2016). In the Czech context, Patočka studies continue to be an important philosophical presence, mainly through the agency of the Center of Phenomenological Research in Prague, as well the Jan Patočka Archive, also in Prague, which was founded by former students of the philosopher, and which has overseen the editing of the critical edition of Patočka's work in Czech, *Sebrané spisy Jana Patočky*.

Such contemporary engagements with Patočka's thought cover the full range of his thinking, from his conception of an a-subjective phenomenology to his philosophy of history. Nevertheless, one might argue that the aspect of Patočka's thought that will in the end prove to be the most important for the future of philosophy is the manner in which he puts consistently the problem of *Europe* at the very center of his philosophical enterprise (see Part III of Gasché 2009, also Hagedorn and Staudigl 2008). He does this through a series of provocations, none of which have lost their force or controversy in the almost forty years since his death.

One such provocation is a strong equation of philosophy with the essence of Europe. "Europe," for Patočka, is reducible neither to a political nor to a geographical concept, nor even to the complex representation of Christendom; its principal founding pillar is instead philosophy, a way of life co-equal to the historico-political form of existence inaugurated by the Greeks. Thus it is not Christianity, nor capitalism, nor the political and social legacy of the Roman Empire, nor imperialism and revolution, nor even the abstract ideas of freedom and democracy, but philosophy as a way of life, defined by the care for the soul, that forms the genuine heritage of Europe. All of the other ideas and historical developments associated with "Europe" are of significance only as refractions of the basic problems revealed by the pursuit of a philosophical existence, or of the life in truth inaugurated by the particular constellation of the three movements described above (Patočka 2002: 1–15, Patočka 1996b: 79–94). A second provocation is the historical diagnosis that, at least spiritually, Europe is essentially *dead*—overcome by the nihilism of its embrace of technological civilization and the pursuit of power and possession for their own sake (Patočka 2002: 9). A third provocation emerges as a corollary from the first two: The question for philosophy thus remains whether the end of the promise represented by Europe is thus the end as such, or whether or not something like a "post-European" philosophy is possible, and what that might look like.

Patočka's fascination with Europe, both with the Europe that was as well as the Europe that might have been, characterizes his entire intellectual career, but arguably becomes more focused in the 1970s. One element of this is the reappraisal of the role of non-mainstream, marginal spiritual legacies that nevertheless make up an important dimension of the spiritual and intellectual options at play throughout European history. This was already a theme in earlier essays such as Patočka's 1942 "Two Senses of Reason and Nature in the German Enlightenment" (Patočka 1989), as well as his 1965 Leuven lectures "On the Contribution of Bohemia to the Ideal of Modern Science" (Patočka 2001).

Nevertheless, this strand of Patočka's thinking finds its high mark in two texts from the 1970s, both composed in German: "Was Sind die Tschechen?" (Patočka 1992: Part II), based a series of letters to a German friend, and the unfinished manuscript "Europa und Nach-Europa" (Patočka 1988: Part II). The former traces the spiritual legacy of the Czechs, with a particular emphasis on the complex history of subjugation within the Holy Roman Empire in the wake of the disaster of the Thirty Years' War. Another forced incorporation, this time into the Soviet Union, in turn undermined, or threatened to, the centuries old cultural and intellectual orientation of the Czechs to Europe. The second text poses the question of the spiritual orientation to Europe more generally, now from the perspective of the history of philosophy: What could philosophy mean in a post-European world, and specifically with respect to the latter's essential philosophical heritage?

Patočka's analyses are provocative, but they are also nuanced to the point that it is difficult, without significant oversimplification, to dismiss them as narrow-mindedly "Eurocentric," or burdened by a superficial idealism that would put philosophy above all other historical phenomena in spiritual rank and value. Drawing from his philosophical anthropology, Patočka's reflections pose profound questions about a world that, at the time of their writing, had seen two global conflicts unprecedented in their destruction, followed by a cold version of the same that seemed to risk the very future of humanity itself with the threat of nuclear annihilation. Patočka's questioning also came in the wake of a period in history in which Europe as a global power was rapidly dismantled, erasing overt colonial domination even more quickly than it had been originally established. It was, and in many ways remains, a world in which the legacies, whether political, spiritual, or intellectual, associated with "Europe" need to be both defined and evaluated, a task that continues to this day to be both complicated and difficult.

It would be a mistake to argue that Patočka had the answers to these questions, or that we can find in his writings the articulation of an understanding of Europe that we can adopt in order to be able to better address the spiritual questions of our own times. His was a first, provocative attempt to pose the contemporary problem of a post-European philosophy; historically and philosophically sophisticated, it still remains very much a child of its times, even if it points in directions that are still being explored today. But it is not too much to claim that, at least among the philosophers of the twentieth century, Patočka offers one of the most sustained and nuanced reflections on the meaning of Europe, philosophy, and the human condition, proving himself to be a worthy heir of all the traditions, whether philosophical, spiritual, or personal, that crisscross symbolically in that little lectern given to him by Husserl in 1934, as the end of Europe was well underway.

References

Aristotle (1932), *Politics: Loeb Classical Library: Aristotle Volume XXI*, translated by H. Rackham (Cambridge, MA: Harvard University Press).

Aristotle (1987), *A New Aristotle Reader*, ed. J. L. Ackrill (Princeton, NJ: Princeton University Press).

Arendt, H. (1958), *The Human Condition* (Chicago, IL: University of Chicago Press).

Barbaras, R. (2011), *L'Ouverture du monde. Lecture de Jan Patočka* (Chatou: Transparence).

Brentano, F. (1921), *Vom Ursprung sittlicher Erkenntnis*, ed. O. Kraus (Leipzig: Dunker and Humblot).

Brentano, F. (1926), *Die Vier Phasen der Philosophie und ihr augenblicklicher Stand*, ed. O. Kraus (Leipzig: Meiner).

Brentano, F. (2014), *Psychology from an Empirical Standpoint*, translated by L. McAlister (London: Routledge); originally published as *Psychologie vom empirischen Standpunkt* (Leipzig: Duncker and Humblot, 1874).

Bruzina, R. (2004), *Edmund Husserl and Eugen Fink: Beginnings and Ends in Phenomenology 1928–1938* (New Haven, CT: Yale University Press).

Cajthaml, M. (2014), *Europe and the Care of the Soul: Jan Patočka's Conception of the Spiritual Foundations of Europe* (Nordhausen: Bautz).

Chvatík, I. (2015), "Jan Patočka's studies on Masaryk," in L. Hagedorn and J. Dodd (eds), *The New Yearbook for Phenomenology and Phenomenological Philosophy, vol. XIV* (London: Routledge), 136–60.

Dastur, F. (2012), "L question de la technique: le dialogue entre Patočka et Heidegger," in F. Dastur (ed.), *Jan Patočka: Liberté, existence et monde commun* (Argenteuil: Le Cercle Herméneutique Editeur).

Declève, H. (1986), "De Patočka à Masaryk. Une complexe proximité," postface to J. Patočka, *La crise du sens*, vol. 2: *Masaryk et l'action*, translated by E. Abrams (Bruxelles: Ousia), 73–195.

Derrida, J. (2008), *The Gift of Death*, translated by D. Wills (Chicago, IL: University of Chicago Press).

Durkheim, É. (2006), *On Suicide*, translated by R. Buss (London: Penguin Books).

Fink, E. (2005), *Eugen Fink Gesamtausgabe III: Phänomenologische Werkstatt. Finks Mitarbeit bei Edmund Husserl*, 4 vols, ed. R. Bruzina (Freiburg: Alber).

Fink, E. and Patočka, J. (1999), *Briefe und Dokumente 1933–1977*, ed. M. Heitz and B. Neßler (Freiburg: Alber).

Frogneux, N. (2007), "La fragilité problématique de l'humain. Une lecture du troisième movement de l'existence de Jan Patočka," in R. Barbaras (ed.), *Jan Patočka. Phénoménologie asubjective et existence* (Paris: Association Culturelle Mimesis), 165–79.

Gasché, R. (2009), *Europe, or the Infinite Task* (Stanford, CA: Stanford University Press).

Hagedorn, L. (2015), 'Christianity unthought': A reconsideration of myth, faith, and historicity," in L. Hagedorn and J. Dodd (eds), *The New Yearbook for Phenomenology and Phenomenological Philosophy, vol. XIV* (London: Routledge), 31–46.

Hagedorn, L. and Sepp, H. R. (eds) (2006), *Andere Wege in die Moderne. Forschungsbeiträge zu Patočka s Genealogie der Neuzeit* (Würzburg: Königshausen and Neumann).

Hagedorn, L. and Staudigl, M. (eds) (2008), *Über Zivilisation und Differenz. Beiträge zu einer politischen Phänomenologie Europas* (Würzburg: Königshausen and Neumann).

Heidegger, M. (1962), *Being and Time*, translated by J. Macquarrie and E. Robinson (New York: Harper and Row).

Heidegger, M. (2005), *Introduction to Phenomenological Research*, translated by D. Dahlstrom (Bloomington, IN: Indiana University Press).

Husserl, E. (1965), *Phenomenology and the Crisis of Philosophy*, translated by Q. Lauer (New York: HarperCollins).

Husserl, E. (1970), *The Crisis of European Sciences and Transcendental Phenomenology*, translated by D. Carr (Evanston, IL: Northwestern University Press).

Husserl, E. (1991), *Cartesianische Meditationen und Pariser Vorträge*. Husserliana 1, ed. S. Strasser (Dordrecht: Springer).

Husserl, E. (2013), *Logical Investigations*, 2 vols, translated by J. N. Findlay, ed. D. Moran (London: Routledge).

Husserl, E. (2014), *Ideas for a Pure Phenomenology and Phenomenological Philosophy. First Book: General Introduction to Pure Phenomenology*, translated by D. Dahlstrom (Indianapolis, IN: Hackett).

Karfík, F. (2008), *Unendlichwerden durch die Endlichkeit. Eine Lektüre der Philosophie Jan Patočkas* (Würzburg: Königshausen and Neumann).

Kohák, E. (1989), "Jan Patočka: A philosophical biography," in *Jan Patočka: Philosophy and Selected Writings*, translated and edited by Erazim Kohák (Chicago, IL: University of Chicago Press), 1–135.

Lehmann, S. (2004), *Der Horizont der Freiheit. Zum Existenzdenken Jan Patočkas* (Würzburg: Königshausen and Neumann).

Marion, J.-L. (2015), "Givenness: Dispensation of the world," in L. Hagedorn and J. Dodd (eds), *The New Yearbook for Phenomenology and Phenomenological Philosophy, vol. XIV* (London: Routledge), 273–86.

Masaryk, T. G. (1938), *Modern Man and Religion*, translated by A. Bizba and V. Beneš (London: Allen and Unwin).

Masaryk, T. G. (1969), *The Making of a State: Memoirs and Observations 1914–1918*, translated by H. W. Steed (New York: Howard Fertig).

Masaryk, T. G. (1970), *Suicide and the Meaning of Civilization*, translated by W. B. Weist and R. G. Batson (Chicago, IL: University of Chicago Press).

Mensch, J. (2016), *Patočka's Asubjective Phenomenology: Toward a New Concept of Human Rights* (Würzburg: Königshausen and Neumann).

Palouš, M. (2011), "Jan Patočka's Socratic message for the twenty-first century: Rereading Patočka's 'Charta 77 Texts' thirty years later," in I. Chvatík and E. Abrams (eds), *Jan Patočka and the Heritage of Phenomenology* (Dordrecht: Springer), 163–74.

Patočka, J. (1931), *Pojem evidence a jeho význam pro noetiku*. Dissertation, Charles University, Prague.

Patočka, J. (1981), *Jan Amos Komenský: Gesammelte Schriften zur Comeniusforschung*, ed. K. Schaller (Bochum: Ruhr-Universität).

Patočka, J. (1988), *Ausgewählte Schriften, vol. 2: Ketzerische Essais zur Philosophie der Geschichte und ergänzende Schriften*, ed. K. Nellen and J. Němec (Stuttgart: Klett-Cotta).

Patočka, J. (1989), *Jan Patočka: Philosophy and Selected Writings*, ed. and translated by E. Kohák (Chicago, IL: University of Chicago Press).

Patočka, J. (1990), *Liberté et sacrifice*, ed. and translated by E. Abrams (Grenoble: Millon).

Patočka, J. (1991), *Ausgewählte Schriften, vol. 4: Die Bewegung der menschlichen Existenz. Phänomenologische Schriften II*, ed. K. Nellen, J. Němec, and I. Srubar (Stuttgart: Klett-Cotta).

Patočka, J. (1992), *Ausgewählte Schriften, vol. 5: Schriften zur tschechischen Kultur und Geschichte*, ed. K. Nellen, P. Pithart, and M. Pojar (Stuttgart: Klett-Cotta).

Patočka, J. (1996a), *An Introduction to Husserl's Phenomenology*, translated by E. Kohák, ed. J. Dodd (Chicago, IL: Open Court).

Patočka, J. (1996b), *Heretical Essays in the Philosophy of History*, translated by E. Kohák, ed. J. Dodd (Chicago, IL: Open Court).

Patočka, J. (1998), *Body, Community, Language, World*, translated by E. Kohák, ed. J. Dodd (Chicago, IL: Open Court).

Patočka, J. (1999), *Texte–Dokumente–Bibliographie*, ed. L. Hagedorn and H. Rainer Sepp (Freiburg: Alber).

Patočka, J. (2000), *Vom Erschinem als solchem. Texte aus dem Nachlaß*, ed. H. Blaschek-Hahn and K. Novotný (Freiburg/Munich: Karl Alber).

Patočka, J. (2001), *Conférences de Louvain. Sur la contribution de la Bohême à l'idéal de la science moderne* (Paris: J. Vrin).

Patočka, J. (2002), *Plato and Europe*, translated by P. Lom (Stanford, CA: Stanford University Press).

Patočka, J. (2011), *Aristote, ses devanciers, ses successeurs*, translated by E. Abrams (Paris: J. Vrin).

Patočka, J. (2015), "On Masaryk's philosophy of religion (1977)," in L. Hagedorn and J. Dodd (eds), *The New Yearbook for Phenomenology and Phenomenological Philosophy, vol. XIV* (London: Routledge), 95–135.

Patočka, J. (2016), *The Natural World as a Philosophical Problem*, ed. I. Chvatík and Ĺ. Učnik, translated by E. Abrams (Evanston, IL: Northwestern).

Perryman-Holt, C. (2015), "Jan Patočka and the sacrificial experience," in L. Hagedorn and J. Dodd (eds), *The New Yearbook for Phenomenology and Phenomenological Philosophy, vol. XIV* (London: Routledge), 23–30.

Pithart, P. (2011), "Questioning as a prerequisite for a meaningful protest," in I. Chvatík and E. Abrams (eds), *Jan Patočka and the Heritage of Phenomenology* (Dordrecht: Springer), 155–62.

Tardivel, É (2007), "La subjectivité dissidente. Étude sur Patočka," in I. Chvatík (ed.), *Jan Patočka and the European Heritage. Studia Phaenomenologica VII* (Bucharest: Humanitas), 435–63.

Tava, F. (2016), *The Risk of Freedom: Ethics, Phenomenology, and Politics in Jan Patočka*, translated by J. Ledlie (London: Rowman and Littlefield).

Tucker, A. (2000), *The Philosophy and Politics of Czech Dissidence from Patočka to Havel* (Pittsburgh, PA: University of Pittsburgh Press).

Učník, Ĺ (2011), "Patočka on techno-power and the sacrificial victim," in I. Chvatík and E. Abrams (eds), *Jan Patočka and the Heritage of Phenomenology* (Dordrecht: Springer), 187–201.

....

CHAPTER 22

AN IMMENSE POWER

The Three Phenomenological Insights Supporting Derridean Deconstruction

....

LEONARD LAWLOR

JACQUES Derrida (1930–2004) is the founder of the method and philosophy that he called "deconstruction." He developed deconstruction from Heidegger's idea of a destruction in *Being and Time* (Heidegger 2010: 19–25, §6) and Husserl's idea of a dismantling in *Experience and Judgment* (Husserl 1973: 41–6, §10).[1] For Derrida, deconstruction's criticisms always target conceptual hierarchies, which might be classified as metaphysical or as political. In general, the hierarchies revolve around the dichotomy between life and death; presence and non-presence; speech and writing; and, more in the ethico-political domain, between nonviolence and violence (or between peace and war). In his earliest formulation of deconstruction (at the end of the 1960s), Derrida says that deconstruction consists in two phases (Derrida 1978b: 41–2). In the first phase, deconstruction attempts to show how the inferior, unprivileged, and deriva-tive term in any given hierarchy in fact makes the superior, privileged, and original term possible. Derrida wants to show that what looks to be generated and dependent—death; non-presence; writing; and violence—makes the origin or the *arche* possible. Death, non-presence, writing, and violence make life, presence, speech, and peace possible. The first phase of deconstruction is therefore a phase of reversal. The reversal always takes place by means of classical argumentation concerning presuppositions. The second phase extends the investigations into presuppositions. It attempts to determine what makes the hierarchy itself possible in the first place. It investigates what is more original than the opposition between origin and derivative. In the second phase, deconstruction goes to the very "root," as Derrida says in this early period, of the hierarchy. However, even though it is more original than the origin, this "root" is not a unified origin. It is the

---

[1] For the connection of Derridean deconstruction to Heidegger's idea of destruction, see Derrida 2013.

fundamental difference *between* the two sides of the hierarchy being deconstructed. To put the idea of this difference most simply, we can say that it is the difference of mediation. To complicate the idea, we can say that it is the difference of inseparability without unity. The two sides—again presence and non-presence, life and death, and singularity and universality—are essential necessities in the "root" or "foundation." Because the two sides are essential or structural necessities in the "foundation," and especially because non-presence is fundamental in the "foundation," the foundation cannot strictly be called "phenomenological." Nevertheless, Derrida's attempts to conceive this "foundation" derived from phenomenological insights. In particular, they derived from three insights, hence the subtitle of this essay.

The three phenomenological insights are insights into the generation of ideal objects; temporalization; and the experience of the other.[2] In fact, there are three quotations from Husserl that seem to have inspired Derrida. The first, and *the most important*, comes from Husserl's "Fifth Cartesian Meditation": "Properly speaking, neither the other Ego himself, nor his experiences or his phenomena themselves, nor anything else belonging to his own being comes to a givenness that could function as an origin" (Husserl 1977: 109, §50, translation modified). The second comes from "The Origin of Geometry": "What is lacking is the persisting existence of the 'ideal objects' . . . The important function of written, documenting linguistic expression is that it makes communications possible without immediate or mediate personal address; it is here, so to speak, communication become virtual" (Husserl 1970: 360–1). The third comes from *The Phenomenology of Internal Time-Consciousness*. Husserl says in section 16 that retention is "the opposite of perception" in which (with protention) "perception and non-perception continuously pass into one another" (Husserl 1964: 62). Perhaps, however, the following passage from *Ideas II* is the one that most inspired Derrida: "There are fingers touching fingers . . . In the case in which a part of the body becomes equally an external object of an other part, we have the double sensation" (Husserl 1989: 155). Derrida directed all of his work towards the experience of auto-affection, attempting to show that, because auto-affection is always double and therefore mediated, it is always in fact hetero-affection. Derrida has shown us that there is always an outside within auto-affection; there is always something added into it.[3]

However, as we shall see, there is a fourth insight, which concerns the endless expansion of reductions. It is this last insight of endless expansion that leads to the question with which Derrida closes his 1967 study of Husserl, *Voice and Phenomenon* (Derrida 2011: 87): What does "to infinity" mean? This question is perhaps the most basic question that Derrida asks in all of his works. The question of infinity arises for Derrida because the fundamental mediation in the root is repetition, or, more precisely, repeatability. As the title of the essay states, repeatability (or iterability) is "an immense power."

---

[2] Most commentators on Derrida's relation to Husserl and phenomenology have recognized the role of these three insights, especially, the insight into temporalization and the other. See Baring 2011: 163–81, 243–56; Dastur 2016: 13–39; Kates 2005: 115–57; Zahavi 1999: 132–4; Zahavi 2008: 69–70.

[3] For more on auto-affection, see Lawlor 2015.

We shall end with this power. In order to be able to understand the immensity of this power, we must investigate how Derrida appropriates the first three phenomenological insights. Each insight appears in one of his texts on Husserl: the generation of ideal objects in the 1962 *Introduction to Husserl's The Origin of Geometry*; temporalization in the 1967 *Voice and Phenomenon*; and the experience of the other in Derrida's later 2000 "Tangent II" in *On Touching—Jean-Luc Nancy*.[4] Although each text builds on the insight of the former—"Tangent II" complements *Voice and Phenomenon*'s investigation of inner experience in Husserl by investigating bodily or external experience—we must start with Derrida's "Violence and Metaphysics" (Derrida 1978a). Although, as its subtitle indicates, "Violence and Metaphysics" is "an Essay on the Thought of Emmanuel Levinas," "Violence and Metaphysics" shows us that deconstruction does not (and never does) abandon phenomenology. Deconstruction always remains faithful to a certain phenomenological inspiration.

22.1 THE NECESSITY OF PRESENCE: "VIOLENCE AND METAPHYSICS"

Early in his career, Derrida characterized his own thought as the deconstruction of the metaphysics of presence. Developed from Heidegger's claim that metaphysics (in all its forms) determines being as presence (Heidegger 1972: 7), the phrase "metaphysics of presence" means the thought of something permanent, an atemporal presence— most generally, a subject or substance—beyond all natural or earthly changes. If we can know permanent presence, it would be through a means of knowledge that is immediate, that is, through intuitive knowledge. So presence in Derrida also means intuitive presence or phenomenality. Even if this atemporal presence might be inaccessible for us now, the metaphysics of presence, according to Derrida, will posit it as a teleological endpoint. This teleological orientation explains why Derrida includes Husserlian phenomenology within the metaphysics of presence. In contrast, the deconstruction of the metaphysics of presence—and Derrida would ask: Is there any other?—lies in discovering something that remains non-present; therefore deconstruction strives for a sort of non-knowledge; it aims to discover something that eludes intuition and phenomenality, and something that cannot be overcome teleologically. But this non-teleological thought does not imply that deconstruction is completely non-phenomenological.

As we see clearly in "Violence and Metaphysics," Derrida's own thought of what cannot be captured by presence is based on Levinas's question of an alterity beyond sameness (Derrida 1978a: 109). Nevertheless, Derrida does not renounce

---

[4] For examinations of these three texts, and "Violence and Metaphysics," see Lawlor 2002 and Lawlor 2005. For an excellent study of Derrida and phenomenology see Marrati 2005.

sameness and phenomenality; he does not renounce presence. Thus, in "Violence and Metaphysics," Derrida presents something like a phenomenological critique of Levinas's thought. In a nutshell, the criticism is the following. When Levinas attempts to show how the other is able to escape from phenomenality, Levinas, according to Derrida, gives up the right to speak of the other. In other words, when Levinas attempts to place the other beyond phenomenality he gives up any evidence of the other, and therefore he cannot account for his own discourse. Derrida argues that the other must appear; it must be a phenomenon; it must enter into the sphere of my own experience. Only then are we able to speak of the other and develop a discourse of alterity. The phenomenalization of the other is, for Derrida, an essential necessity; sameness and presence are essential necessities. As Derrida says, "metaphysics [in Levinas's sense] . . . always supposes a phenomenology in its very critique of phenomenology" (Derrida 1978a: 118).

In effect therefore, Derrida defends Husserlian phenomenology from the charges Levinas levels against it.[5] In particular, Derrida defends Husserl from Levinas's criticisms of Husserl's "Fifth Cartesian Meditation." Levinas's main charge is that, in the "Fifth Cartesian Meditation," Husserl reduces the other to the same. Husserl makes the other be a phenomenon (Derrida 1978a: 123). However, Derrida argues that what Husserl is particularly "sensitive" to in the Fifth Meditation is the "singular and irreducible style" of evidence, phenomenon, or appearance within which the other is given (Derrida 1978a: 123). Derrida argues that the intentionality aiming at the other is "irreducibly mediate" (Derrida 1978a: 123). In fact, the phenomenological insight into the mediate experience of the other is *the most important insight* for Derrida's thinking overall, which he confirms as late as 1999 (Derrida 1999: 71–2). In any case, what Husserl calls analogical appresentation, for Derrida, implies, not an analogical and assimilatory reduction of the other to the same, but rather "the unsurpassable necessity of . . . mediations" (Derrida 1978a: 124). Analogical appresentation is therefore, for Derrida, "respect" for the fact that the other is never given to me immediately and originally in communion with my own lived-experiences. Analogical appresentation, for Derrida, implies that the other consists in an "originary non-presence," an "original non-phenomenalization" (Derrida 1978a: 123). The originality of this non-presence, which must not be confused with mere absence, is due to the fact that the interiority of others cannot be identical with my interior life. Therefore, unlike Levinas (at least Levinas up until *Totality and Infinity* (Levinas 1969)),[6] Derrida argues one cannot go beyond phenomenology without supporting oneself on phenomenology. One cannot go beyond presence without supporting oneself on presence. One cannot go beyond intuition without supporting oneself on something like an intuition. As we shall see now, what goes beyond phenomenology, presence, and intuition, for Derrida, is writing.

---

[5] In "Violence and Metaphysics," Derrida also defends Heidegger from Levinas's criticisms.

[6] For an excellent account of Levinas's thought, see Sebbah 2012.

22.2 The Phenomenological Insight into Written Documentation: *The Introduction to the Origin of Geometry*

As part of *The Crisis* texts, Husserl's "The Origin of Geometry" attempts to determine the institution of geometrical science. Husserl starts from the intuition of morphological shapes, like roundness, which then, according to Husserl, can be developed infinitely into perfect or geometrical shapes, into ideal objects (Husserl 1970: 353–78). The development of geometrical shapes passes through several transitions for Husserl, the first being the surveying of the earth. But more importantly, it develops through the embodiment of the truth of the geometrical objects first in spoken language, and then in written documentation, which makes that truth available for everyone. There could be no science of geometry unless the truth of ideal objects was made available for everyone. In 1962, Derrida translated "The Origin of Geometry," into French. Derrida wrote an introduction to the French translation that is about five times larger than Husserl's fragment. The size of the *Introduction* alone indicates that this text is Derrida's first significant publication. However, its central section 7 is the basis for Derrida's own, original thought. It concerns "the most difficult problem" of *The Origin of Geometry*: the determination of the sense of truth's disappearance due to its paradoxical bondage in and liberation through writing (Derrida 1989a: 93).

Derrida frames the problem in this way at beginning of section 7: "by itself the speaking subject, in the strict sense of the term, is incapable of absolutely grounding the ideal objectivity of sense" (Derrida 1989a: 87). Oral language only frees the ideal objectivity of sense from individual subjectivity, but leaves it bound to the institutive community. To be absolutely ideal, the object must be freed from actual subjectivity in general, freed from actual evidence for a real subject, and freed from actual circulation within a determinate community (Derrida 1989a: 87). As Derrida says, only "the possibility of *writing* will assure the absolute traditionalization of the object, its absolute ideal objectivity" (Derrida 1989a: 87, Derrida's emphasis). In other words, only by means of writing does a truth achieve "perduring presence" (Derrida 1989a: 87). Until the truth of circularity is written down, geometrical truth and its object lacks this perduring presence. To use terminology Derrida will not develop until *Voice and Phenomenon*—and Derrida does not really invent the concept of writing until his 1967 publications like *Voice and Phenomenon* and *Of Grammatology*, to which we shall turn in a moment—writing "supplements" the lack of presence at the same time as it produces this very presence or existence. The role of writing in the institution of geometrical truth implies, according to Derrida, that writing is no longer an mnemotechnical aid to truth. Written incarnation is no longer extrinsic to ideal objectivity. As Derrida says, "The act of writing is therefore the highest possibility of all 'constitution'" (Derrida 1989a: 89). The constitutive role of writing does not imply however, for Derrida, that truth's ontological sense now derives from its factual linguistic incarnations; truth does not become relative in the worst sense of the word. Indeed, that truth must still be free in regard to all linguistic facticity in order to be itself: "Paradoxically, the graphic possibility permits the ultimate freeing of ideality" (Derrida 1989a: 90).

The paradox is that the very possibility of the appearance of truth is at once the possibility of its disappearance. Writing is at once what produces the crisis and what allows the crisis to be overcome. Derrida calls this possibility and impossibility writing's "ambiguous value" (Derrida 1989a: 87 and 92). Two descriptions of the paradox in particular anticipate the argumentation of *Voice and Phenomenon*. First, the graphic possibility implies the death of all and any actual or factual subjects. If Euclid's geometry was not able to persist beyond his own life, it would never have achieved objective truth. By constituting truth as an ideal object, writing can free the ideal object from all factual or actual subjects. By being able to do without every actual or factual subject, every actual reader or writer, writing opens up the possibility of something like a transcendental subjectivity. Although writing can function without all actual subjects, it still must be related to a consciousness which assures its functioning. If writing were not related to something like consciousness in general—a general addressee—writing would be totally insignificant. Writing can do without every actual reading in general, but, "in its sense," it is also dependent upon a writer or reader in general. Writing must be "haunted by a virtual intentionality" (Derrida 1989a: 88). Second, although the written sign would be, to use Husserl's terminology, a constituted sensible body (*Körper*) but also a constituting body proper or flesh (*Leib*), Husserl wants to dissociate, according to Derrida, *Leib* from *Körper*—and disambiguate the written sign's ambiguous value (Derrida 1989a: 97). (We shall return to the problem of the constitution of the body proper (*Leib*) below, when we turn to "Tangent II.") In any case, Husserl tries to disambiguate the sign by imposing an imperative of univocity. As Derrida stresses, a univocal expression emerges completely from all change and it harbors no depth or virtual significations. As Derrida says, "[univocal language] gives everything over in order to be seen in an actual evidence . . . nothing is hidden there or nothing is announced there in the penumbra of potential intentions . . . it has mastered the whole dynamics of sense" (Derrida 1989a: 101). Univocal expression is therefore pure phenomenality, pure appearance, or *pure presence*. Univocal expression is the *logos*. But without equivocity, and therefore without change, there would be no history, no progress, and no more discoveries like non-Euclidean geometry. Therefore, for Derrida, there must be equivocity in univocity; there must be non-presence in presence; and there must be an anti-*logos* within the *logos*.

22.3 THE PHENOMENOLOGICAL INSIGHT INTO TIME: THE 1967 *VOICE AND PHENOMENON*

Derrida continues his reflections on the ambiguous value of the sign in *Voice and Phenomenon*. Unlike in the *Introduction to the Origin of Geometry*, where Derrida gives no name to his investigation, here in *Voice and Phenomenon*, Derrida calls his project explicitly a "deconstruction." Derrida engages in a deconstruction of the concept of the sign that Husserl presents in the First Logical Investigation. In particular, making use of the methodology we outlined at the beginning of our essay, Derrida focuses on Husserl's attempt to dissociate, within the general concept of the sign, two kinds of signs, expression (*Ausdruck*) and indication (*Anzeichen*).[7] According to Derrida, for Husserl, "indication takes place whenever the sense-giving act, the animating intention, the living spirituality of the meaning-intention is not fully present" (Derrida 2011: 32). In contrast, "pure expressivity will be the pure active intention (spirit, *psyche*, life, will) of a *bedeuten* that animates a discourse whose content (*Bedeutung*) will be present" (Derrida 2011: 34). What Derrida sees in Husserl's attempted separation of expression from indication is an attempt to prioritize phenomenology's intuitionism over its formalism (Derrida 2011: 22). Phenomenology's intuitionism is captured in what Husserl himself calls "the principle of all principles," which states that every assertion must be supported with intuitive evidence (Husserl 2014: 43–4, §24). Phenomenology's formalism is found when Husserl defines ideality as indefinite availability for others, and therefore as indefinite repeatability (Husserl 2014: 258–61, §13; Husserl 1977: 60–1, §27). Husserl, Derrida argues, subordinates form and therefore repeatability, mediation, distance, and non-presence to intuition, presence, proximity, immediacy, and event-ness. This subordination of non-presence corresponds to the imperative of univocity that we just saw in the *Introduction to the Origin of Geometry*. Derrida deconstructs this hierarchy by arguing that presence (or event-ness) is inseparable from non-presence (or repeatability). In short, because every present intuition contains the possibility of repetition, there is no pure presence. It is in the context of demonstrating this irreducible possibility of repetition that Derrida invents the famous concepts of *différance*, writing, and supplementarity.[8] We shall look at each concept in turn. But it is in the concept of *différance* that we shall see the phenomenological insight into time.

Différance: The concept of *différance* appears when Derrida criticizes the primary argument that Husserl provides in the First Logical Investigation for dissociating expression

---

[7]   Husserl defines indication in the following ways. First, it can be either natural or artificial; both the canals on Mars and the instruments of conventional designation are indications. Second, the unity of the indicative function is motivation; indicative signs motivate us to think of something else not present, motivates a movement from actual knowledge to in-actual knowledge; it consists in a "because." Third, Husserl restricts this general definition of the indicative function, the "because"; there is a *strict* sense of indication. The indicative "because" is an allusion (*Hinweis*) concerning non-evident and contingent links of lived-experience; these allusions are still indications even when lived-experience intends idealities and ideal objects. In contrast, the "because" of demonstration (*Beweis*) concerns the content of the lived experience, and in expression demonstration is necessary and evident.

[8]   One could question this claim since these three concepts appear in *Of Grammatology* and in *Writing and Difference*. However, it is only within the context of *Voice and Phenomenon*'s deconstruction of phenomenology that one can clearly see that these are fundamental concepts. However, we must turn to *Voice and Phenomenon* not only because it is Derrida's most comprehensive investigation of phenomenology, but also because it shows how these concepts function at the most fundamental level, the level of the absolute.

from indication. Husserl, Derrida claims, does a sort of phenomenological reduction to interior life. According to Husserl in the First Logical Investigation, when I express something to myself in interior monologue, "the acts in question [that is, expressive acts] are experienced by [me] at that very moment" (Husserl 2001: 191, §8; Derrida 2011: 41). For Husserl, the apparent immediacy of expression makes indicative signs useless in solitary, interior life. However, in phenomenology, according to Husserl himself, whether experience is solitary or communal, experience is temporal. Husserl's primary argument for the immediacy of expression and the uselessness of indication in interior life therefore concerns the experience of time.[9] The "at that very moment" argument of the First Logical Investigation for the immediacy of expression and the uselessness of indication in interior life would be valid, Derrida is arguing, if the experience of time is itself immediate. Thus Derrida turns to Husserl's *The Phenomenology of Internal Time Consciousness* (Husserl 1964).

For Derrida, the "at that very moment" of the First Logical Investigation corresponds to the actual now as the source-point of a primal impression in *The Phenomenology of Internal Time Consciousness*.[10] We shall return to this actuality since what is at stake in all three of these concepts is potentiality, an immense power. In any case, Derrida recognizes, however, that the source-point of a primal impression is not Husserl's most important discovery in *The Phenomenology of Internal Time Consciousness*. The great phenomenological insight is that "the living present" (the present as I am living it) consists in an original "spreading out" or "thickness." The original "thickness" includes, around the now-point, a primary act of memory and a primary act of anticipation. Husserl calls primary memory and primary anticipation respectively "retention" and "protention." In order to be able to support the "at that very moment" argument, Husserl would have to show that retention is entirely different from secondary memory (or memory in the usual sense), in which there is the mediation of a recalled image.[11] Secondary memory provides us, not with a presentation (*Gegenwärtigung*), but with a re-presentation (*Vergegenwärtigung*). Secondary memory therefore resembles an indicative sign. So, if there is a pure presentation in the living present, if, in other words, there is a "radical difference" between retention and secondary memory, then there is no mediation in the living present, and indeed there is no need for an indicative sign. The "at that very moment" argument of the First Logical Investigation therefore would be valid.

---

[9] Derrida notes that the First Logical Investigation reduction to solitary interior life anticipates the "Fifth Cartesian Meditation" to "the sphere of ownness" (Derrida 2011: 33). What is at stake here is not only presence but also ownness, the proper, property, and propriety.

[10] To support this claim, Derrida cites in particular section 11 of the *Lectures*, where Husserl speaks of the now-apprehension being "the nucleus of a comet's tail of retention" (Derrida 2011: 53). Derrida also cites sections 10 and 16 of the *Lectures* and section 81 of *Ideas I*, where Husserl speaks of the actual now being "a form that persists through continuous change of matter."

[11] Derrida does not investigate the role of protention. Perhaps this omission deserves to be criticized. De Warren's *Husserl and the Promise of Time* stresses the futural in Husserl's time studies. See De Warren 2009.

In order to deconstruct the "at that very moment" argument, Derrida focuses on retention. For Husserl himself, and despite the major role of the now, retention is not an accidental modification of the living present. Retention is a constitutive or essential part of the living present. In section 17 Husserl calls retention "perception." According to Derrida, Husserl's calling retention perception is part of his attempt to keep retention separate from secondary memory and within the range of presence (Derrida 2011: 55). Yet, in section 16, as Derrida stresses, Husserl says that retention is "the opposite of perception" in which (with protention) "perception and non-perception continuously pass into one another" (Husserl 1964: 62, §16; Derrida 2011: 55–6). Undoubtedly, when Husserl calls retention non-perception, he is trying to be faithful to the experience of time. Following Husserl's own example, we could not hear a melody unless we retain the previous notes; yet, the retention of those notes, which happens virtually immediately, is really previous and past. Because retention is a pastness and not now, that is, not really present, there must be a difference here between retention and the now. We must conclude, as Derrida does, that the now phase of the present, that is the present itself, "is in *continuous composition* with a non-presence and a non-perception" (Derrida 2011: 55). Derrida argues then that, because the now or presence is in continuous composition with retention as a non-perception, and because Husserl defines secondary memory as non-perception, there must be a *continuity* between retention and secondary memory. In the living present, there is continuous composition between something like *Vergegenwärtigung*, or at least the very root of *Vergegenwärtigung*—and *Gegenwärtigung*. Therefore, if re-presentation necessarily composes with presentation in the living present, if this composition is the truth of the living present, then something like indication is always already taking place in the living present. As Derrida concludes, it is not the case that indicative signs are useless in interior life; they are essential and irreducible in interior life. In every perception, in every intuitive presence, there is mediation, and therefore something like formalization and non-presence. Non-presence has always already been introduced into the self-identity of the moment.

Formalization brings us to the concept of *différance*. According to Derrida, "we must be able to say a priori that the common root [of re-tention and re-production, that is] is the possibility of re-petition in its most general form . . . the constitution of a trace in the most universal sense, is a possibility which must not only inhabit the pure actuality of the now, but also constitute the pure actuality of the now through the very movement of the *différance* that the trace introduces into it" (Derrida 2011: 56). We can see here that Derrida defines *différance* by a repetition—a form, here called "the trace," which itself contains the possibility of more repetitions—that is more fundamental than the actuality of presence. For Derrida, everything begins with repetition and repeatability (Derrida 2011: 39n). The form or trace differentiates itself from the now. There is a fundamental difference and a differentiating—*différ-ance*—between the now-point and the retention. That everything begins with repetition and difference implies that there is neither a pure origin nor a pure end (neither a pure *arche* nor a pure *telos*). The origin is always heterogeneous because repetition is already there, making the origin different and distant; the end is always heterogeneous because repetition is there too, delaying the end from appearing.[12] Repetition produces *distance—spacing*—and it produces *delays—temporalization*. Spacing and temporalization are Derrida's most general definition of *différance* in the 1968 essay of the same name (Derrida 1982: 1–26).[13]

Writing: We just mentioned the trace, which suggests writing.[14] And we have seen the paradox of writing in the *Introduction to the Origin of Geometry*. In *Voice and Phenomenon*, however, Derrida develops the concept of writing within the context of the solitary life of the soul. When Husserl makes the reduction to interior life, he describes interior expression as speaking to oneself, as soliloquy (Husserl 2001: 191, §8). Soliloquy of course is, as Derrida stresses, a form of auto-affection. But it seems to be "an absolutely unique form of auto-affection" because of the voice (Derrida 2011: 67). It seems to be absolutely unique because when I speak to myself, my voice does not pass through the exteriority of the world. When I speak to myself, my voice seems to present the content of the speaking (expression) immediately, "within the absolute proximity of [my] present," "absolutely close to me" (Derrida 2011: 65 and 66). The sphere of hearing-oneself-speak is so close that it does not even require the interior space or extension that is required when we try to experience or imagine our own body (to which we shall return below with "Tangent II") (Derrida 2011: 68). What I want to say seems to be so close to the signified that the signifier is "diaphanous" (Derrida 2011: 69). Hearing-oneself-speak seems therefore to be an absolutely pure auto-affection (Derrida 2011: 68).

However, even in its silence or its non-externalization, the voice of hearing-oneself-speak is temporal. Here Derrida rejoins the argumentation that we just saw in relation to the concept of *différance*: "The living present arises on the basis of its non-self-identity, and on the basis of the retentional trace. It is always already a trace" (Derrida 2011: 73). As we have seen, the trace implies that there is the possibility of repetition prior to any present impression. Thus, when I *hear* myself speak, the hearing is a repetition of the speaking that has already disappeared; a difference divides the hearing from the speaking. Re-presentation (*Vergegenwärtigung*) has always already intervened, and that intervention means, in a word, space. Thanks to repeatability, there is, as Derrida says, an "exiting of time to the outside of itself" (Derrida 2011: 96). The exiting occurs because the repetition contains the potentiality to go to infinity, beyond the present, the potentiality to distance itself and be different. And, as we have seen in Derrida's *Introduction to the Origin of Geometry*, this "exiting" requires writing (Derrida 2011: 69–70). When I hear myself *speak*, the speaking can go far beyond my own hearing by being written down. However, the writing with which Derrida is concerned here is not the usual sense of writing. Derrida calls the movement of the retentional trace "archi-writing" (Derrida

---

[12] For the idea of origin-heterogeneous, see Derrida 1989b: 107–8.

[13] On the side of spacing, Derrida argues that interval or distance amounts to a "polemical otherness": "Now the word *différence* (with an e) can never refer either to *différer* as temporalization or to *différends* as *polemos*. Thus the word différance (with an a) is to compensate—economically—this loss of meaning, for différance can refer simultaneously to the entire configuration of its meanings" (Derrida 1982: 8).

[14] Derrida appropriates the idea of a trace from Levinas. See Derrida 2013: 133 and 227.

2011: 73). He calls this movement "writing" because, like any text, the retentional trace has the possibility of indefinite perdurance; an indefinite number of copies can be made; or, most precisely, a piece of writing contains the possibility of indefinite repetition. Derrida calls the movement "archi" in order to indicate its originative status. "Writing" is not secondary; it is at the origin. Because of the "writing" within soliloquy, we must conclude that the immediate presence of expression is only apparent. Or at best, the immediate presence of expression is derivative from the movement of repetition, even though it looks as though immediate presence is the source of repetition, making repetition look to be supplementary.

Supplementarity: Supplementarity is a sort of synonym with writing and *différance*, yet it stresses the originative status of archi-writing. There is even, for Derrida, a logic of supplementarity (Derrida 2011: 75).[15] The logic is structured in the following way. First, as we just saw in the auto-affection of hearing-oneself-speak, a difference divides the self; the difference between speaker and hearer means that I cannot have the presence of my own self immediately; there is an impossibility of immediate self-presence; the difference is non-presence; always already, presence had started to be *deficient* in relation to itself. As we saw in the *Introduction to the Origin of Geometry*, presence lacks persisting presence. Second, since the difference in interior life is the difference of a going across from me *to* another me, from me as the speaker *to* me as the hearer, the dative dimension is the possibility of repetition. It is this potentiality of repetition that produces self-presence: I repeat something like a form of my own self in order to send it back *to* me and have thereby my own self more fully; or, as in idealization, the power of repetition produces ideal objectivity by going beyond psychological and subjective sense. My access to perduring presence therefore is always late (there is always already non-presence) and thus presence, for Derrida, always comes later, after repeatability. So, third, since there is self-presence *now*, or since there is ideal objectivity *now, later as a product*, the difference of repeatability looks to be a *mere* supplement, contingently "added on" to presence that has been in fact constituted by repetition. Now it looks as though the contamination of repeatability (or iterability) is an after-effect of presence itself. In other words, the ideal object looks to a self-identical, present unit, it looks to be something like a model, from which possible repetitions derive—when in fact the self-identical present model has been produced by repetition. Of course writing in the usual sense seems to come after the presence of speech (which seems to be writing's model, especially when writing is phonetic). But, in truth, "writing" (that is, archi-writing or repeatability) was already at the origin, making the origin heterogeneous. As the title of *Voice and Phenomenon*'s seventh chapter says, the supplement is always "originative." Similarly, in *Of Grammatology*, Derrida says that "One wants to go back up *from the supplement to the source*: one must recognize that there is *a supplement at the source*"

---

[15] For an excellent summary of Derrida's concept of supplementarity, see Bernasconi 2015.

(Derrida 1974: 304, Derrida's emphasis). As Derrida says in *Voice and Phenomenon*, "a possibility produces that to which it is said to be added onto" (Derrida 2011: 75). In supplementarity, we see not only how the phenomenological priority of presence comes to be generated; but also how the hierarchy can be reversed. Being at the source, supplementarity produces presence; and insofar as it delays complete presence, it constantly undermines presence.

We can summarize the interconnected concepts *différance*, writing, and supplementarity in the following way. The supposedly pure auto-affection of hearing-oneself-speak *seems* to include two aspects. *First*, I seem to hear myself speak at the very moment that I speak; and, *second*, I seem to hear my own self speak. This is how auto-affection seems to take place. When I engage in interior monologue, when, in short, thinking takes place—it seems as though I hear myself speak at the very moment I speak. It seems as though my interior voice is not required to pass outside of myself, as though it is not required to traverse any space. So, my interior monologue seems to be immediate, immediately present, and not to involve anyone else. Interior monologue seems therefore to be different from the experience of me speaking to another or from the experience of me touching my body. However, are we really, truly able to distinguish and separate interior monologue from external dialogue? When I speak in general, that is, with or without the intention of communication, some moment always comes prior to the speaking. The prior moment could be silence or noise, but something like a context precedes any given act of speaking. The prior context implies that the present speaking, whether it is internal or external, whether it has the purpose of communication or not, is secondary. Whenever I start to speak—to myself, to others, for the sake of any phonation whatsoever—I find that some other speaking has already taken place and elapsed. There is always some elapsed moment that has expired, that has been lost and reduced to silence, even as something of that elapsed moment has been retained, even as something of it remains, like a trace or writing. Necessarily, my speaking is not a pure first time, even though it takes place right now, even though it seems to be the origin. The secondary character of all speaking means that there is a delay between one speaking and another. This delay then functions as well in between speaking and hearing. Just as the apparent originating speaking is in truth a "second," the hearing of the speaking is not immediate. In other words, the delay in interior monologue means that interior monologue is always involved in something like a process of mediation, which is *différance*. We must therefore conclude from this description that my interior monologue in fact resembles my experience of external speech or even writing, in which a distance separates me from my hearer or reader. I cannot, it is impossible for me to hear myself *immediately*. Regardless of whether the action is hearing or speaking, the action is a response to the past. It is difficult to see that speaking is a response to the past, because eventually presence and immediacy appear to be producers of supplements. Yet, the supplement is always originative; it is always at or with the origin, making the origin heterogeneous.

22.4 THE PHENOMENOLOGICAL INSIGHT INTO ALTERITY: "TANGENT II" IN *ON TOUCHING—JEAN-LUC NANCY*

In *Voice and Phenomenon*, Derrida deconstructs the experience of auto-affection. Most basically, he tries to show that interior life, which looks to be immediate and proximate, is actually mediated and distanced, as if my relation to myself is a relation to another. Thus, as in "Violence and Metaphysics," and in *Voice and Phenomenon*, Derrida's thinking relies on Husserl's "Fifth Cartesian Meditation" insight into the experience of the other: there is no direct access to the interior life of another; there is always a "*Vergegenwärtigung*" (representation) and never a "*Gegenwärtigung*" (presentation). In "Tangent II" in *On Touching* (published in 2000), Derrida takes up the same phenomenological insight. Here however, in "Tangent II," Derrida applies the phenomenological insight into alterity to the touching-touched relation as Husserl describes it in *Ideas II* (Husserl 1989: 155–9, §37; 171–5, §45).[16] Derrida's argumentation takes place in two steps. The first concerns the hands; the second concerns the heart. Overall, we should note that, in *On Touching*, Derrida is arguing that the Western philosophical tradition has

---

[16] In *On Touching—Jean-Luc Nancy*, Derrida also examines Merleau-Ponty's description of auto-affection, the touching-touched relation (Derrida 2005a: 183–215). Merleau-Ponty's description appears in *The Visible and the Invisible* (Merleau-Ponty 1968: 141). Derrida's interpretation of Merleau-Ponty amounts to claiming that, although Merleau-Ponty stresses non-coincidence in the touching-touched relation, he nevertheless privileges coincidence since coincidence is always imminent: "What makes reading Merleau-Ponty so troublesome (for me)? It may be this, in a word: we reencounter the movement that we had evoked—this experience of coincidence *with* noncoincidence, the coincidence of coincidence *with* noncoincidence—always, in fact, and all things considered *preferring* 'coincidence' (of coincidence with noncoincidence) to 'noncoincidence' (of coincidence with noncoincidence)" (Derrida 2005a: 211, Derrida's emphasis). Although Derrida's interpretation of Merleau-Ponty (and of Husserl's *Ideas II*) might appear to be uncharitable—and indeed, Derrida seems to discount Merleau-Ponty's famous idea of the "écart" (divergence)—his claim that Merleau-Ponty prefers coincidence has some support in Merleau-Ponty's descriptions of the touching-touched experience and double sensations. In *The Visible and the Invisible*, Merleau-Ponty says, "There is a fundamental narcissism of all vision. And thus, for the same reason, the vision [the seer] exercises, he also undergoes from the things, such that . . . I feel myself looked at by the things, my activity is *identically* [*identiquement*] passivity" (Merleau-Ponty 1968: 139, translation modified, my emphasis). Later in *The Visible and the Invisible*, he says—this is where Merleau-Ponty denies the coincidence of the touching-touched relation—"To begin with we spoke summarily of a reversibility of the seeing and the visible, of the touching and the touched. It is time to emphasize that it is a reversibility always imminent and never realized in fact." "In the *Phenomenology of Perception*, Merleau-Ponty says, "By speaking of 'double sensations,' [we] mean that . . . I can *recognize* the touched hand as the *same* hand that will be soon touching [*tout à l'heure sera touchante*]; in this package of bones and muscles that is my right hand for my left hand, I glimpse *momentarily* [*in instant*] the shell or the incarnation of this other right hand, agile and living, that I send out towards object in order to explore them. The body catches itself [*se surprend*] from the outside exercising a knowledge function" (Merleau-Ponty 2012: 95, my emphasis). It is important that Merleau-Ponty describes this experience in temporal terms, which implies a non-spatial immediacy.

valorized touch over vision because touch is a sensation of immediacy and proximity. Husserl's description of double sensations in Ideas II is, as Derrida says, one of "the exemplary stories of the 'flesh.' "[17]

In *Ideas II*, section 37, Husserl tries to distinguish between the tactile realm and the visual realm. Like the entire Western metaphysical tradition, as Derrida claims, Husserl privileges touch (Derrida 2005a: 161). Husserl privileges the sense of touch, because when I touch myself (as in Husserl's example of two hands touching one another), the sensations of touching seems to appear directly or immediately on the hand (Husserl 1989: 154 §36). We have a "double sensation," in which I undergo at once, in coincidence, it seems, the sensation of touching (active) and the sensation of being touched (passive). Importantly, for Derrida's interpretation, Husserl says that "the touching sensations, however, the sensations which constantly varying, lie on the surface of the touching finger, are, such as they are lying there spread out over the surface, nothing given through adumbration" (Husserl 1989: 157 §37). As Husserl has argued throughout his career, adumbrations indicate mediation. Thus here in Husserl's analysis of double sensations in *Ideas II* implies that the touching-touched relation is at least non mediated by adumbrations or, more strongly, is at least immediate and probably a kind of coincidence. Through the lack of adumbrations, Husserl distinguishes touch from vision. With the sense of vision, we do not, according to Husserl, have the same localization of the sensation directly and immediately on the eye. I can see my eyes, but it requires the mediation of, for instance, a mirror; in vision there is no coincidence. In *Ideas II*, Husserl says:

> I do not see my self, my Body [*Leib*], the way I touch myself. What I call the seen body is not something seeing which is seen, the way my Body as touched Body is something touching which is touched. A visual appearance of an object that sees, i.e., one in which the sensation of light could be *intuited* just as it is—that is denied us. Thus what we are denied is an analogon to the touch sensation, which is actually grasped along with the touching hand. (Husserl 1989: 155–6 §37, my emphasis)

For Husserl, as Derrida is arguing, there is not even an analogous relation between seeing-seen and touching-touched. We can see here the "old concerns" of *Voice and Phenomenon* (Derrida 2005a: 180).[18] Only the touching-touched auto-affection and the sense of touch—not vision—seem to give me my own body in presence, as in an intuition.

Derrida bases his argumentation on Husserl's description of touch in general, turning the touching-touched relation into a specific case of touch. He argues that the sense of touch in general, and not just in the occasion of the two hands grasping one another, is always a double sensation (Derrida 2005a: 163). Even when my right hand does not touch my left hand, even when my hand touches anything external to my body and my

---

[17] "Exemplary Stories of the 'Flesh' " is the title of Part II of *On Touching*.
[18] The English translation renders "préoccupations anciennes" as "ancient preoccupations."

hand, my hand senses that it is touched by the thing it is touching. No matter what, the hand is both passive and active. Derrida stresses that when I touch an external thing which is not my body, the sensation, according to Husserl, involves two surfaces (Husserl 1989: 157). On the one hand, there are the sensible impressions located on the surface of the hand and inside of it; on the other, there is experience of the material extension of the thing (its roughness for example) (Husserl 1989: 157). In other words, there is a phenomenological surface and an interiority to the hand, and a surface and exteriority to the thing. Importantly, this division, as Husserl points out, allows the subject of the body to say that the touching hand is mine, while saying that the touched material thing is not mine (Husserl 1989: 157). Thus, the contact with something other than myself allows me to recognize myself. For Derrida, the division into mine and not mine implies that exteriority and mediation are necessary to the touching-touched relation (Derrida 2005a: 175). Essentially, there can be no coincidence if the sensation is really double, non-coincident and distant from itself. Essentially there is, as in vision, the heterogeneity of a spacing between the two hands touching and being touched.

Husserl seems to recognize the impurity in the two hands touching (its doubleness) when, in section 45 of *Ideas II* (Husserl 1989: 173–4, §45), he presents the feeling of one's own heart as a special example of touch, one that allows us to better understand the lived-body in its immediacy, and, as Derrida points out, in its solipsism (Derrida 2005a: 176–7). In general, below the surface of the body, there is, as Husserl says, "the localization of somatic interiority mediated by the localization of the field of touch" (Husserl 1989: 173–4). Derrida emphasizes the word "mediated," because it is clear that when I touch my body, the feeling of my interiority is not immediate. There is always the surface of my skin. However, Husserl claims that when I press the surface of my own body in the region of the heart, the heart sensation becomes stronger. This is a sensation, Husserl says, that "does not itself belong to the touched surface." But then Husserl adds that "with my touching finger, [I] 'feel through'" to the inner organ (Husserl 1989: 174). Derrida stresses this "feels through" (despite the fact that Husserl places the phrase between scare quotes). In other words, as Derrida says, "With the hand I touch the inside of my body through a surface" (Derrida 2005a: 178). And therefore, when I press my hand over my heart, it is, as Husserl says, the same as "with other bodies: I feel through to their insides." My touching through to my heart being "the same as other bodies" blurs any rigorous distinction between myself and others. Just as with others, there is mediation with my self-experience, even the experience of me feeling my heart beating. For Derrida, this sameness in mediation at work between the solipsistic experience of my own lived-body and the experience of the lived-body of another implies that the possibility of intersubjectivity has to be essential in solipsistic experience, as if my heart were always already the heart of another. Invoking the phenomenological insight of the "Fifth Cartesian Meditation," we could say that, just as I can only ever have a *Vergegenwärtigung* of the interior life of another, I can only ever have a *Vergegenwärtigung* of the interior life of my own body. And, we have stressed several times above, it is this re-presentation, or, more precisely, this repeatability that has the potentiality to go to infinity.

22.5 Conclusion: An Immense Power

As we have tried to argue here, three phenomenological insights are fundamental for Derridean deconstruction: the generation of ideal object; temporalization; and the experience of the other. Derrida makes an original contribution to phenomenological philosophy by combining and extending these three insights. As we stated at the beginning and have tried to show throughout in this chapter, the target of deconstruction is always auto-affection. He has argued that fundamentally auto-affection is necessarily hetero-affection. The structure of his argument consists in showing that the mediation of time (retentions in particular) resembles the mediation of the experience of others enough so that no rigorous distinction can be made between self and other. Whether of oneself or other, every experience is fundamentally mediated by a trace. Even when I hear my own heart beating in my chest, it is as if those beats are a letter from someone else.

The fundamental trace in auto-affection opens out onto the question with which Derrida ends *Voice and Phenomenon*: "What does 'to infinity' mean?" This question too has its inspiration in Husserlian phenomenology.[19] It is based in a *fourth phenomenological insight*. Although Derrida never cites this quotation (as far as I know), it seems to have had an effect on his thinking: "The *expansions* . . . of the phenomenological reductions . . . [are] of enormous importance" (Husserl 2014: 110–11, my emphasis). In his last published text on Husserl, "Et Cetera," Derrida says, "Deconstruction marks still an excess of fidelity, as is often the case, to a certain phenomenological inspiration . . . For Husserl, there is more than one reduction . . . The transcendental reductions themselves pluralize themselves, radicalize themselves in a sort of hyperbolic upping of the ante. At once they carry themselves off abyssally" (Derrida 2000: 296). Husserl's claim about the expansion of reductions implies that the reductions always have to be repeated. However, while Husserl seems to think that one could have a complete reduction which would bring their repetition to an end, Derrida, as he says here, ups the ante on the repetition. As we have seen, the fundamental mediation, which we located first in writing in the *Introduction to the Origin of Geometry*, is repetition. More fundamental than writing, as a sort of archi-writing, is retention in temporalization. Retention is a fundamental repetition, which makes a form available for more repetitions. Even the feeling of my own heart is a repetition, insofar as it is the same "me" that presses where the heart is and that feels the pressure. Yet, despite the repetition of "me," there is a difference between the two surfaces of my body, which opens up the possibility of indefinite or perhaps infinite repetitions. Repeatability (or iterability (Derrida 1982: 315)) is the power of endless *expansions*, as if iterability allowed us, them, anyone, and any

---

[19] The inspiration for this question also comes from Heidegger's meditations on the future and death. Unfortunately, we cannot develop the relationship of Derrida's thinking to that of Heidegger within the confines of this chapter. In order to be thoroughly explored, the relationship between Derrida and Heidegger would require a book-length study.

future ones to add more and more brackets to the form, placing it within more and more contexts, relating it to more and more ways of understanding. Iterability is the endless possibility of augmenting, of adding "and," "et cetera," "ad infinitum," and "to infinity." Iterability therefore is an immense power. But unlike what we find in phenomenology, this power is not that of the "I can" (Derrida 2005b: 84). If the "I" could say anything in regard to iterability, it would have to say "I cannot"—I cannot stop, I cannot control, I cannot bring to an end "the potencies of repetition" (Derrida 2011: 43).

References

Baring, E. (2011), *The Young Derrida and French Philosophy 1945–1968* (New York: Cambridge University Press).

Bernasconi, R. (2015), "Supplement," in C. Colebrook (ed.), *Derrida: Key Concepts* (London: Routledge), 19–22.

Dastur, F. (2016), *Déconstruction et phénoménologie* (Paris: Hermann).

Derrida, J. (1974), *Of Grammatology*, translated by G. Spivak (Baltimore, MD: Johns Hopkins University Press).

Derrida, J. (1978a), *Writing and Difference*, translated by A. Bass (Chicago, IL: University of Chicago Press).

Derrida, J. (1978b), *Positions*, translated by A. Bass (Chicago, IL: University of Chicago Press).

Derrida, J. (1982), *Margins of Philosophy*, translated by A. Bass (Chicago, IL: University of Chicago Press).

Derrida, J. (1989a), *Edmund Husserl's Origin of Geometry: An Introduction*, translated by J. P. Leavey (Lincoln, NE: University of Nebraska Press).

Derrida, J. (1989b), *Of Spirit: Heidegger and the Question*, translated by G. Bennington and R. Bowlby (Chicago, IL: University of Chicago Press).

Derrida, J. (1999), "Hospitality, justice and responsibility: A dialogue with Jacques Derrida," in R. Kearney and M. Dooley (eds), *Questioning Ethics: Contemporary Debates in Philosophy* (London: Routledge), 65–83.

Derrida, J. (2000), "Et Cetera," in N. Royle (ed.), *Deconstructions: A User's Guide* (New York: Palgrave).

Derrida, J. (2005a), *On Touching—Jean-Luc Nancy*, translated by C. Irizarry (Stanford, CA: Stanford University Press).

Derrida, J. (2005b). *Rogues: Two Essays on Reason*, translated by P.-A. Brault and M. Naas (Stanford, CA: Stanford University Press).

Derrida, J. (2011), *Voice and Phenomenon*, translated by L. Lawlor (Evanston, IL: Northwestern University Press).

Derrida, J. (2013), *Heidegger: la question de l'Être et l'Histoire. Cours de l'ENS-Ulm 1964–1965* (Paris: Galilée).

De Warren, N. (2009), *Husserl and the Promise of Time: Subjectivity in Transcendental Phenomenology* (New York: Cambridge University Press).

Heidegger, M. (1972), *On Time and Being*, translated by J. Stambaugh (New York: Harper Colophon Books).

Heidegger, M. (2011), *Being and Time*, translated by J. Stambaugh (Albany: SUNY Press).

Husserl, E. (1964), *The Phenomenology of Internal Time Consciousness* (The Hague: Martinus Nijhoff).

Husserl, E. (1970), *The Crisis of European Sciences and Transcendental Phenomenology*, translated by D. Carr (Evanston, IL: Northwestern University Press).

Husserl, E. (1973), *Experience and Judgment*, translated by J. S. Churchill and K. Ameriks (Evanston, IL: Northwestern University Press).

Husserl, E. (1977), *Cartesian Meditations*, translated by D. Cairns (The Hague: Martinus Nijhoff).

Husserl, E. (1989), *Ideas Pertaining to a Pure Phenomenology and to a Phenomenological Philosophy. Second Book: Studies in the Phenomenology of Constitution*, translated by R. Rojcewicz and A. Schuwer (Dordrecht: Kluwer).

Husserl, E. (2001), *Logical Investigations, vol. 1*, translated by J. N. Findlay (New York: Routledge).

Husserl, E. (2014), *Ideas I*, translated by D. O. Dahlstrom (Indianapolis, IN: Hackett).

Kates, J. (2005), *Essential History: Jacques Derrida and the Development of Deconstruction* (Evanston, IL: Northwestern University Press).

Lawlor, L. (2002), *Derrida and Husserl: The Basic Problem of Phenomenology* (Bloomington, IN: Indiana University Press).

Lawlor, L. (2005), "With my hand over my heart, looking you right in the eyes, I promise myself to you: Some new reflections on Derrida's interpretation of Husserl," in G. Banham (ed.), *Husserl and the Logic of Experience* (New York: Palgrave Macmillan), 255–73.

Lawlor, L. (2015), "Auto-affection," in C. Colebrook (ed.), *Jacques Derrida: Key Concepts* (New York: Routledge), 130–8.

Levinas, E. (1969), *Totality and Infinity*, translated by A. Lingis (Pittsburgh, PA: Duquesne University Press).

Marrati, P. (2005), *Genesis and Trace: Derrida Reading Husserl and Heidegger* (Stanford, CA: Stanford University Press).

Merleau-Ponty, M. (1968), *The Visible and the Invisible*, translated by A. Lingis (Evanston, IL: Northwestern University Press).

Merleau-Ponty, M. (2012), *Phenomenology of Perception*, translated by D. Landes (New York: Routledge).

Sebbah, F.-D. (2012), *Testing the Limit: Derrida, Henry, Levinas, and the Phenomenological Tradition*, translated by S. Barker (Stanford, CA: Stanford University Press).

Zahavi, D. (1999), *Self-Awareness and Alterity: A Phenomenological Investigation* (Evanston, IL: Northwestern University Press).

Zahavi, D. (2008), *Subjectivity and Selfhood: Investigating the First-Person Perspective* (Cambridge, MA: MIT Press).

CHAPTER 23

....

WHEN ALTERITY BECOMES PROXIMITY

Levinas's Path

....

ROBERT BERNASCONI

23.1 THE DUALITY OF THE SELF AND THE I

ALTHOUGH phrases like "the face-to-face relation," "the absolute Other," and "absolute alterity" owe much of their current popularity to Emmanuel Levinas's *Totality and Infinity*, they are rarely used in the contemporary philosophical literature in the same sense in which he meant them.[1] They are frequently imported into philosophical discussions in an effort to describe our everyday experience of what is often called "intersubjectivity," but whereas Levinas allowed that they describe commonplace experiences, he at the same time was insistent that they cannot be integrated into the standard logic of philosophy, a point he emphasized repeatedly throughout his writings but never more so than in his second major book, *Otherwise than Being* (Levinas 1981). It should never be forgotten that he introduced these phrases into his writings originally as part of his effort to escape the dominant conceptual framework of Western philosophy in the conviction that both its language and its logic had contributed to the rise of totalitarianism and what he called "the Nazi horror" (Levinas 1990: 291). For this reason it was not his intention to contribute directly to the time-honored debates of philosophy into which these phrases have now found themselves inserted. Indeed, if one takes seriously the motivation behind his adoption of these phrases it could be argued that the attempt to assimilate Levinas's philosophy to standard preexisting positions set out in the literature is a domestication, and perhaps even amounts to a betrayal. The closest he

---

[1] The expression "absolutely other" is one that Levinas borrowed from Vladimir Jankélévitch, but it is now more often associated with Levinas (Levinas 1987: 48).

came to addressing standard philosophical questions, at least in the form prescribed by Kant and his followers, was in his repeated engagement throughout his philosophical writings with Husserl and Heidegger. Nevertheless, even though he chose with striking regularity to begin his essays by evoking the names of these two giants of phenomenology, his aim was always to highlight their failure to think transcendence as he himself had come to understand it, not to contest their answers to traditional questions.

To be sure, Levinas believed that the quest for concretizations of transcendence was the time-honored task of philosophy and to that extent he believed that he was returning philosophy to its original vocation. He found his inspiration here not in classical phenomenology but elsewhere: He repeatedly referenced Plato's "good beyond being" and Descartes' "infinite" as offering formal structures on which he could draw to guide him in his search. Nevertheless, even if transcendence, as he understood it, lay on the hither side of phenomenology, his route to it was through phenomenology beginning in 1934 with "Some Thoughts on the Philosophy of Hitlerism." His starting point there was the phenomenology of pain, where one discovers one's enchainment to oneself (Levinas 2004: 17–18), which he would subsequently equate with "the impossibility of getting rid of oneself" (Levinas 2001a: 89). The following year he had already formulated an account of transcendence presented as "a quest for a way out." He gave it the name *excendence* and he described the need for it as arising from the experience of suffering where one must "get out of oneself," that is, "*break that most radical and unalterably binding of chains (enchaînement), the fact that the I (moi) is oneself (soi-même)*" (Levinas 2003a: 55). This sense of an enchainment that one wants to escape points to a duality of self and I. His argument was that, behind "the ancient opposition of the I (*moi*) to the world," the need to escape oneself revealed the definitiveness with which the I (*moi*) is chained or riveted to the self and so is characterized by a certain substantiality or positionality (Levinas 2001a: 81–4, 90, translation modified). The relation of the self to the I is approached in a way that is familiar to the phenomenologist and is reflected in Levinas's engagement with Husserl's account of passive synthesis, albeit there is no object to synthesized. Levinas introduced substitution as a passive, affectively charged, opening to the Other (Bergo 2014: 109). But although Husserl provided Levinas with some guidance as to how to proceed, what mattered to Levinas, as I will show, was the task of clarifying the structure of excendence as a departure from being in which one nevertheless also retained a foothold in being (Levinas 2001a: xvii; Bernasconi 2005).

Nevertheless, albeit only in passing and with very little detail, he already in 1947 in *Existence and Existents* introduced the idea that the alterity of the other human being shattered the definitiveness of the I without this relation with the other forming a new bond (*enchaînement*), such as a bond with another I (Levinas 2001a: 86). He saw this happening not only in forgiveness, but also in eros, which he considered in the context of a rare discussion of intersubjectivity under that name. In eros there is a "proximity of the other" but at the same time "the distance is wholly maintained, a distance whose pathos is made up of this proximity and this duality of beings" (Levinas 2001a: 98). Even in this elliptical formulation Levinas's brief discussion of eros in *Existence and Existents* is remarkable because it can retrospectively be seen to have anticipated the strange combination of proximity and separation that I am arguing here marks all his work. This claim challenges the temptation to see the passage from *Totality and Infinity* to *Otherwise than Being* as a passage from a discourse focused on alterity to one based in proximity. Whereas in *Totality and Infinity* separation was explicitly presented as the precondition of the ethical, in *Otherwise than Being* it is proximity and substitution that are accorded that role. The tendency to see the two books in this way is perfectly understandable as a first impression. Terms like *alterity, distance*, and *separation* dominate *Totality and Infinity* much as *proximity, intrigue,* and *substitution* dominate *Otherwise than Being*. But although this may be what a comparison between the two books shows when they are isolated from the rest of his work, when they are placed in the context of the larger trajectory that runs from "Some Thoughts on the Philosophy of Hitlerism" (Levinas 2004: 13–21) to his very last writings, then it is *Totality and Infinity* that appears somewhat anomalous, but only for the reason that it tends to dwell on the relation of the I to the world and to the Other in that world, leaving to one side for the most part the relation of the I to the self. It is this broader perspective that I intend to develop in this chapter in an effort to show that one does not need to choose between these two main books, but that they can and must be read together in spite of the apparent tension between them.

23.2 THE SELF AS THE ONE FOR THE OTHER

As Levinas explained it in *Totality and Infinity*, the face-to-face encounter with the absolute Other puts me in question and "empties me of myself" (Levinas 2003b: 30). This is possible only because the Other approaches me from a height across a distance. The idea of the infinite implies separation (Levinas 1969: 53). Separation is thus the condition of the encounter with the Other in the face: "Separation, effected in the concrete as habitation and economy, makes possible the relation with the detached, absolute exteriority" (Levinas 1969: 220). This is the account that dominates the secondary literature and leads to the emphasis both on ethical experience and on terms like "face-to-face," "alterity," and "the absolute Other." When *Otherwise than Being* is treated at all, it tends to be treated in isolation or very selectively. The aim of the present chapter is not to give an account of how *Otherwise than Being* follows on from *Totality and Infinity*. I have tried to give a provisional answer to that question elsewhere by presenting Levinas's introduction of the term *substitution* as his answer to the question of what makes it possible that in the face of the Other I can sacrifice myself for the Other, even if one must beware any suggestion that substitution is a *transcendental* condition of the face-to-face relation (Bernasconi 2005). At its simplest Levinas's claim is that I can explain my selfishness better on the basis of an original selflessness than the other way round. More precisely, *Otherwise than Being* and especially the chapter on substitution is an attempt to show what the self must be in order for the Other to be able to challenge the I and call it into question (Bernasconi 2002). His answer in short was that it was possible only if the self is what he called "the contradictory trope of the-one-for-the-other" (Levinas 1981: 100).

Levinas's method relies heavily on highlighting the concretization of formal structures. In *Existence and Existents* Levinas's identification of eros as a concrete experience of excendence is limited to only a few brief paragraphs toward the end. By contrast, this same task of identifying concretizations of the formal structure of transcendence understood dominates the structure of *Time and the Other* where death and fecundity are considered, alongside eros in an effort to solve "the problem of the preservation of the ego in transcendence" (Levinas 1987a: 77). To the question "How in the alterity of a you, can I remain I, without being absorbed or losing myself in that you?" he answered "paternity" (Levinas 1987a: 91). The face-to-face is added to the list of concretizations of transcendence long before *Totality and Infinity* (Levinas 1998a: 34), but it is still only one among many. Indeed, many commentators on Levinas still seem to miss this dimension of his work and so they tend to pass quickly over his discussion of "relations analogous to transcendence" in the second part of *Totality and Infinity* and so fail to see them as integral to the book's organization (Levinas 1969: 109), just as they frequently fail to recognize that for Levinas to say that hospitality "coincides with the Desire for the Other absolutely transcendent" is to say that he had added it to his list of examples of excendence (Levinas 1969: 172). To be sure, a certain nervousness around Levinas's account of hospitality is appropriate because of his apparent deafness to the reactionary sexual politics he invoked by his association of it with the feminine, but this account of hospitality as the concrete and initial fact of separation is accompanied by one of the clearest statements of the philosophical purpose behind his descriptions: "The method practiced here does indeed consist in seeking the condition of empirical situations, but it leaves to the developments called empirical, in which the conditioning possibility is accomplished— it leaves to the *concretization*—an ontological role that specifies the meaning of the fundamental possibility, a meaning invisible in that condition" (Levinas 1969: 111). It is in this emphasis on the concretization that Levinas is at his most phenomenological and it forms the underlying basis of his phenomenological attack on Heidegger. On Levinas's account Heidegger had opted for an extreme formalism that effaced the concrete. This was reflected in his focus on the formal or *existenzial* structures of human existence, whereas Levinas insisted that the formal only revealed its meaning in the concrete, or, in Heidegger's terms, the *existenziell* (Levinas 1996a: 5; 1981: 80). On this basis Levinas associated Heidegger with an "obedience to the insidious forms of the impersonal and the neutral" that was characteristic of what is problematic in Western philosophy (Levinas 1969: 272).

The interplay within Levinas's analyses between the formal structure of transcendence and its concretizations are frequently overlooked because of the widespread tendency to read the book in such a way as to place it in the service of what has come to be known as Levinasian ethics, but this amounts only to a further domestication of his thought. Readings of *Totality and Infinity* in this vein rely almost exclusively on the book's third section where he presented his account of the ethical experience undergone in the face of the Other (Levinas 1969: 194–212). Nevertheless, one should not turn to Levinas in expectation of an answer to the question "What ought I to do?" because Levinas explicitly said that he was not writing an ethics. He was concerned only with its meaning, its direction, although he conceded that one could try to construct an ethics on the basis of what he had written (Levinas 1985: 90). For that matter, it would equally be a domestication of Levinas's thought to read him as providing, for example, a phenomenology of mind. The label he seems to have been most comfortable with was "metaphysics," which he understood as the description of the movement of transcendence (Levinas 1969: 35), but this metaphysics was concerned with structures or modalities hidden beneath consciousness that "can be discerned by a phenomenology attentive to the horizons of consciousness" (Levinas 1994: 111). This approach is indispensable because, as he repeatedly insisted, beginning in 1947, the departure from being called for a departure from the categories that we have used to describe Being and the Other is not a phenomenon precisely because it exceeds the categories of being (Levinas 2001a: xvii, 86).

To be sure, for Levinas, already in *Totality and Infinity*, "Metaphysics is enacted in ethical relations" (Levinas 1969: 79). The ethical experience is a relation of transcendence. Like the idea of the infinite, which, according to Descartes, could not have been produced from myself alone as a finite being, the Other is not an object of my thought but thinks itself in me (Levinas 1969: 210–12). Levinas's claim is that it is not from my own impulses that I sacrifice myself for the other. My sacrifice of myself for the Other is not experienced as something I do on my own but something the Other brings about. It is my response to a summons. The definitiveness of the I is shattered. I am taken out of myself and yet I meet the Other by responding to his or her needs. That means that there is an exit from being in the sense that I have let go of my possessions and my self-possession, but I must still retain a foothold in being in order to meet the Other's material needs. However, in the fourth section of *Totality and Infinity*, Levinas presented a further concretization of the formal structure of transcendence and it seems that at that time he regarded it as closer to what he was looking for because he gave that section the title "Beyond the Face" (Levinas 1969: 249). Again, in starkly sexist terms that have been widely and properly criticized (e.g., Irigaray 2004), he found the requisite structure of transcendence in fecundity and in the way that the father both is and is not his son: "By a total transcendence, the transcendence of trans-substantiation, the I (*le moi*) is, in the child, an other" (Levinas 1969: 267).

It is important for the purpose of this chapter to understand the way that in *Totality and Infinity* the ethical seems to be subordinated to fecundity (see further Bernasconi 2012). To do so helps to make sense of the fact that when fecundity fell out of the account, as it did immediately following the book's publication, including even from a precis of the book published in the very same year (Levinas 1961), ethics not only moved to the center of the account but did so by being presented as replicating the structure of fecundity. When in *Otherwise than Being* Levinas adopted Rimbaud's formulation "*je est un autre*"—"I is an other"—to describe the one-for-the-other of responsibility, it served as a direct echo of the formulation "the I is in the child, an other" (Levinas 1981: 118). Levinas called this "a self-identification, but also a distinction within identification" (Levinas 1969: 267). But one cannot say that the shift from fecundity to ethics as the primary concretization of transcendence as excedence arose on the basis of a reexamination of the descriptions found in *Totality and Infinity*. Rather what enabled the ethical to take the place of fecundity when the latter dropped out was its redescription in the context of the question of what the self must be for it to be possible that the Other can call me radically into question, giving rise to the introduction of the self as the one-for-the-other of responsibility, or proximity.

It is striking that the language of absolute alterity never disappears from Levinas's writings but coexists alongside the language of proximity that, as we have seen, was present early on but which fell into the background within *Totality and Infinity* before coming to the fore in *Otherwise than Being*. In particular, Levinas continued to rely on the idea of alterity whenever he found himself called upon to be as accessible to his audience as possible, as in interviews. Nevertheless, there are some moments when the change in Levinas's language could not be clearer. In section 23.3, in order to prepare for the question of how much changed philosophically with the change in terminology, I will briefly introduce three places where Levinas indicated that he has not just modified his language but reversed his decision about the appropriate terms for his philosophy. In section 23.4 I will examine Levinas's various attempts to differentiate his account from that of Martin Buber. Levinas was quite explicit at times about the extent to which he saw Buber as one of his immediate predecessors (e.g., Levinas 1996a: 20). Indeed, in 1986 he said it was Buber who "pushed me to engage in a phenomenology of sociality" (Levinas 2001b: 215). To be sure, his relation to Buber was not constant and I will suggest that the change throws light on the change of emphasis in his language. Finally, in section 23.5, I will show what is at stake with these terms *separation* and *proximity* and I will address the question of the extent to which they can be integrated. It is a question of how much continuity there is across this change and what the philosophical implications of this are for an understanding of Levinas's thought.

23.3 THE NEIGHBOUR, EXPERIENCE, AND MATERNITY

Although I am emphasizing the continuity of the structure of excedence across Levinas's work and even some continuity in his language, there are places where the change in his language is unambiguous. The first of the three cases that I will examine in an attempt to assess the significance of these changes shows him promoting a term that he had previously renounced.

At a meeting of the Société Française de Philosophie early in 1962, in the immediate aftermath of the publication of *Totality and Infinity*, Levinas found himself in discussion with Eugene Minkowsi, the psychiatrist and student of Edmund Husserl. Against Levinas's opposition between the Same and the Other and his insistence on separation, Minkowski appealed to phenomenology to highlight the everyday experience of human solidarity that was reflected in such terms as *the other* (*autrui*), *the fellow human being* (*semblable*), and *the neighbor* (*prochain*), terms that, as he pointed out, diminish distance and emphasize proximity. In response Levinas did not take up this invitation to talk about proximity, but instead he insisted that "it is necessary to avoid the words *neighbor* (*prochain*) and *fellow human being* (*semblable*), which establish so many things in common with my neighbor (*voisin*) and so many similarities with my fellow human being" (Levinas 1996a: 27). He argued that transcendence is only possible when the Other (*Autrui*) is not the fellow human being or the neighbor, but the Other (*Autre*). Nevertheless, although Levinas tended to stay away from the French words *semblable* and *voisin*, the word *prochain*, which he had largely avoided in *Totality and Infinity*, became prominent in *Otherwise than Being* and displaced the emphasis on the stranger in the earlier book.

An even more striking change is in evidence in his treatment of the term *experience*. In 1976 in *God, Death and Time* he wrote: "There is no ethical experience; there is an intrigue. Ethics is the field sketched out by the paradox of an Infinite in relation, without correlation, to the finite" (Levinas 2000: 200). The second sentence would fit comfortably in *Totality and Infinity*, but the first runs entirely counter to his appeal to the face-to-face as "experience par excellence" (Levinas 1969: 196). The notion of intrigue, which is introduced here to take the place of experience, is presented as a form of belonging and so seems to depart from the proposal that separation and distance is a condition of the ethical (Levinas 1981: 25; 2000: 198).

Nevertheless, there is an even starker contrast between *Totality and Infinity* and *Otherwise than Being* and that occurs in respect of the shift from paternity to maternity. Levinas did not present this explicitly as a change but it could hardly be more noticeable. It is tempting to see this as Levinas's response to the charges of sexism leveled against his earlier work beginning with Simone de Beauvoir (Beauvoir 2010: 5), but, if it was intended in this way, it was unsuccessful. Even though the terms *fecundity* and *paternity* all but disappear, certain sexist elements of the analysis remain (Sandford 1998: 16).

A great deal has been written on maternity in Levinas (e.g., Brody 2001 and Sandford 2000: 82–110). My concern here is limited to investigating how the displacement of paternity reflects the general shift that marks the progression from *Totality and Infinity* to *Otherwise than Being*. The maternal is not introduced as something exclusively confined to women, but represents a structure: "the gestation of the other in the same" (Levinas 1981: 75). Whereas in paternity the distance between the father and the son is such that "possibilities are beyond the limits of the possible" (Levinas 1993: 46), in maternity the for-the-other takes the form of vulnerability (Levinas 1981: 71). They are both forms of self-identification where there is also distinction within identification and yet it is also clear that the emphasis between them is different. The maternal body takes the form of the hand that gives the bread from out of its mouth to pass to the other (Levinas 1981: 67). In this way maternity, unlike paternity, is presented as inherently ethical and it is for this reason that it belongs in an attempt to account for how the ego can be called into question ethically.

23.4 BUBER AND SOCIALITY

In this section I will examine how the different emphases between *Totality and Infinity* and *Otherwise than Being*—the one emphasizing separation and the other emphasizing proximity—is reflected in the change in emphasis that can be found in Levinas's various attempts to differentiate his thought from that of the philosophy of Buber, a task to which he repeatedly returned over a period of almost forty years (see Bernasconi 2004). What makes Buber an especially appropriate point of reference is that although Levinas's focus on separation and distance in his early account of the face-to-face relation genuinely arose from his understanding of the nature of radical alterity as approaching from a height, it seems that he found it necessary to emphasize it even more in an attempt to differentiate his account from that of Buber. Initially Levinas approached Buber's I–Thou relation as if it conformed with the classical model of transcendence in which one loses oneself and so does not transcend oneself (Levinas 1969: 213). Given that Levinas seemed to moderate his criticism of Buber in his later years, one has to ask whether this was simply a consequence of a shift from separation to proximity or whether it had other sources. Levinas knew that Buber explicitly rejected the idea of an encounter that arises from a condition of separation (Buber 1970: 78). Inevitably, when Levinas shifted to the emphasis on proximity the objection became less compelling. A brief study of the evolution of Levinas's relation to Buber will help guide us in our effort to understand what did and did not change as Levinas modified his language.

One indication that Levinas did modify his position as well as his language is that whereas for Buber the I–Thou relation is "a genuine original unity" (Buber 1970: 70), in 1947 Levinas, by contrast, insisted that Buber underestimated "the ineluctable character of the isolated subjectivity" (Levinas 1987a: 94). The phrase "isolated subjectivity," like the word solitude, disappears from *Otherwise than Being* to be replaced by "proximity." Buber's account was focused on relationality. Indeed, much of the originality of Buber's approach lay in his insistence on thinking of the relation in such a way that it was thought on its own terms without being reduced to the terms of the relata. This is the point of his claim in 1923 in *I and Thou*: "In the beginning is the relation" (Buber 1970: 69). By contrast, Levinas seemed to hesitate over the term *relation* whenever he used it. He said it, but it was always as if he immediately wanted to swallow the word, so that he repeatedly wrote of the face-to-face as "a relation without relation" (Levinas 1969: 80, 295). In "Hermeneutics and the Beyond," an essay from 1977, he clarified the issue insofar as he spoke of the difficulty of thinking the relation to an Other because it is a relation that does not become a correlation. He thus referred to it as "a relationship that, properly speaking, cannot be called a relationship, since even the commonality of synchrony is lacking between its terms" (Levinas 1998b: 73). It is, he wrote in the same place, a relationship and a non-relationship.

Levinas's hesitation over Buber's idea of the relation had its source in his conviction that the terms of the relation must be absolute within the relation, that is to say, absolved from it while still being in relation. He wrote: "Separation opens up between terms that are absolute and yet in relation, that absolve themselves from the relation they maintain, that do not abdicate in it in favor of a totality this relation would sketch out" (Levinas 1969: 220). This is what Buber allegedly renounced when he rejected separation, but that difference seems to disappear when one restores to Buber's text the place of God, mention of which was entirely absent from Levinas's 1959 essay: "Martin Buber and the Theory of Knowledge" (Levinas 1967). Buber in an Afterword first included in the 1957 edition of *I and Thou* explained that his critics had missed his central concern: "the close association of the relation to God with the relation one's fellow men" (Buber 1970: 171). The difference that Levinas still maintained was that for him "the illeity of God" sends me "to serve my neighbor" (Levinas 1993: 47).

The central point then is that Levinas could not find in Buber's account an indication of that asymmetry in favor of the Other that would make possible the putting in question of the I (Levinas 1996a: 18). In the absence of the relation to height that is characteristic of the relation with the absolute Other, he concluded that Buber's relation is symmetrical in the sense of being reciprocal (Levinas 1969: 68). Whereas for Buber "the *Thou* that the *I* solicits is already, in that appeal, heard as an *I* who says *thou* to me" (Levinas 1993: 43), for Levinas, by contrast, non-reciprocity lies at the heart of subjectivity: "The knot of subjectivity consists in going to the other without concerning oneself with his movement toward me" (Levinas 1981: 84). That "one step more" consists in a hyperbolic form of responsibility: "In the responsibility which we have for one another, I have always one response more to give, I have to answer for his very responsibility" (Levinas 1981: 84). Your responsibility is my responsibility, but not vice versa. It is responsibility as "responsibility for the responsibility of the other" (Levinas 1981: 117). This conception is lacking from Buber's symmetrical account and led Levinas to complain in a 1979 essay that, although Buber sometimes deployed the word responsibility, "despite its repetitions, the word seems to lack vigor, and nothing seems to make it more specific" (Levinas 1993: 17).

This criticism reflects a larger one that goes to the heart of Levinas's philosophical method of allowing the concrete and the formal to determine each other mutually. Just as he objected to Heidegger's formalism, so he complained: "the I–Thou formalism does not determine any concrete structure" (Levinas 1961: 68). It was this formalism that lay behind Buber's failure to make explicit the concrete structure of the relation with the Other, which for Levinas was ethical (Levinas 1996b: 46). As Levinas explained it in "A propos of Buber," his own manner of proceeding "inspired by phenomenology" relied on "something like a deduction of 'concrete situations' from abstract significations whose horizons or '*mise-en-scène*' are reconstituted" (Levinas 1993: 46). The objection was not that Buber lacked an ethics. That was not something Levinas provided either. The objection highlighted methodological differences between them.

On this basis, Levinas criticized the I–Thou relation as "self-sufficient and forgetful of the universe" (Levinas 1969: 213), which is similar to what he said of the relation of lovers in their exclusion of the third party (Levinas 1969: 265–6): "the I–Thou in which Buber sees the category of interhuman relationship is the relation not with the interlocutor but with feminine alterity" (Levinas 1969: 155). At the heart of Levinas's response to Buber, therefore, was his conviction that spiritual friendship was the apogee of the I–Thou relation (Levinas 1967: 148). Buber responded explicitly to Levinas that this was an error (Buber 1967: 723), but Levinas was insistent that the face cannot be approached "with empty hands and closed home" (Levinas 1969: 172). It was for this reason that in his essay "Martin Buber, Gabriel Marcel, and Philosophy" he told a story from the Talmud about the angels who complained when the Torah was taken from heaven to be given to humanity. The Eternal attempted to comfort them by saying that the Torah does not apply to them as they are not born and they do not die; they do not eat or work; they own nothing and so have nothing to sell. In the story the angels fall silent, but Levinas asked whether they did so because they were flattered by the answer. He raised the possibility that they caught a glimpse that earthly beings have the capacity to give and to exist for one another "above and beyond the understanding of the being to which pure spirits are consigned" (Levinas 1993: 39). The point was that Buber's idea of spiritual friendship was the same as "the ethereal sociality of angels" and that the for-the-other of sociality is only made concrete in giving and so presupposes things (Levinas 1993: 47). The ethical intrigue thus necessitates that we retain our foothold in being.

Nevertheless, Levinas's adoption of the language of proximity brought him close to Buber's idea of an "innate Thou," an "innate You" (Buber 1970: 78), albeit Levinas did not truly share with Buber the language of "innateness," which is rare in Levinas. Indeed, when Buber went on in that context immediately to explain that "in the relationships through which we live, the innate You is realized in the You we encounter," he seemed to be presenting something very similar to what we attribute to Levinas when we try to understand substitution as the condition of the encounter that in separation disturbs the I to the point of dispossessing it of its attachment to its possessions and even to its own life. It was his early recognition of the innate Thou in Buber (Levinas 1996b: 22) and his much later acknowledgement of the association of the relation to God with the relation to one's fellow human beings that provided the essential background for the striking statement from 1969 that Buber was also in a quest to find "the seeds of the totalitarian state." And in this context Levinas, who almost without exception attempted to differentiate the face-to-face from the I–Thou relation, made a rare concession in favor of the latter: "For the essential, after all, for him and perhaps for us, is not the Us; it is the I–Thou" (Levinas 1993: 15).

23.5 SEPARATION, PROXIMITY, AND INTRIGUE

I have shown that Levinas adopted the word *neighbor* that he had earlier refused and that he renounced the word *experience* that he had previously made central. I have also shown both that maternity came to a prominence previously occupied by paternity and that the shift in terminology from separation and alterity to proximity led him to change his verdict on Buber. But what lay behind these changes? And how could Levinas modify his assessment of Buber without withdrawing the fundamental claim on which he had insisted when establishing their differences? Levinas's claim was that whereas Buber had insisted on the priority of the relation, he himself had in *Totality and Infinity* insisted on "the priority of the orientation over the terms that are placed in it" (Levinas 1969: 215). Levinas came to concede that Buberian dialogue accorded with an ethical relation insofar as it was a "relation with the unassimilable," but he continued to complain that Buber's I–Thou relation missed the ethical inequality of "gratuitous responsibility, resembling that of a hostage" (Levinas 1993: 41, 44).

Turning back to what Levinas in 1961 said differentiated his account from that of Buber most decisively, which was that both terms of the face-to-face absolve themselves from the relation insofar as they are both absolute within it (Levinas 1969: 64, 220), his explanation for his insistence on the separation was as follows: "The alterity, the radical heterogeneity of the other, is possible only if the other is other with respect to a term whose essence is to remain at the point of departure, to serve as *entry* into the relation, to be the same not relatively but absolutely. *A term can remain absolutely at the point of departure of relationship only as I (Moi)*" (Levinas 1969: 36). That is to say, the I is a precondition of the encounter with the radical Other. But how then can the intrigue be the precondition of the I, as it is in *Otherwise than Being*, without Levinas making the relation of belonging prior to the separation of the terms thereby going back on his refusal of Buber's claim that "in the beginning is the relation"? Either the relation is primary or the terms in it must be.

Disarmingly Levinas opted quite explicitly in *Otherwise than Being* both for the relation and the absolution of the terms from that relation. He wanted it both ways. So, for example, he wrote: "It is in proximity, which is a relation and a term [of this relation], that every commitment is made" (Levinas 1981: 86). And again, proximity "constitutes a relation in which I participate as a term, but where I am more, or less, than a term" (Levinas 1981: 82). What could the one-for-the-other be if not a relation? And yet in Levinas's own mind proximity had also to be a term because otherwise it would be impossible for the one who is persecuted to say "I am responsible even for the one who persecutes me" (Levinas 1981: 166).[2] Insofar as it is me who stands accused by the other and under this accusation against me in the first-person accusative case in the French *me voici*, albeit in English it disappears in the translation: "here I am." It is in this unlimited responsibility that one finds the point where subjectivity ceases to be identified with an ego. Levinas calls this "supplementary responsibility" and it is by virtue of it that "subjectivity is not the ego, but me (*pas le Moi, mais moi*)" (Levinas 1987b: 150). It is to

---

[2] There is more to say here as Blanchot already recognized in *The Writing of the Diasater* (Blanchot 1986: 13–30; see also Davies 1991). Whether Levinas is right about this was the subject of a paper to be published soon that I delivered at a conference on relationality organized by Simone Drichel on Relationality in Dunedin, New Zealand in November 2015.

save my asymmetrical responsibility that subjectivity is a term in the relation and that is also why the word "relation" is ultimately inapplicable.

But for Levinas to want it—and to have it—both ways was not new. I have already quoted the passage from *Existence and Existents* where the distance in eros was said to be made up of this proximity and this duality of beings. Similar passages can be found in *Totality and Infinity*, even if they are not especially prominent. So, for example, we read the following in the context of the claim that the dimension of the divine is opened in the human face: "The proximity of the Other, the proximity of the neighbor, is in being an ineluctable moment of the revelation of an absolute presence (that is, disengaged from every relation), which expresses itself" (Levinas 1969: 78). What sustains this account that strains beyond breaking point our inherited conceptual resources that are ill equipped to understand a relation that, as a relation that is absolute, is disengaged from every relation, or, as Levinas liked to say, "a relation without relation"? The answer given in *Otherwise than Being* is persecution. Ultimately what sustained Levinas's account was not everyday experience, but the experience of persecution and it is for that reason that its conclusions cannot be judged from the perspective of the logic imposed by the oppressor (Bernasconi 1995). Levinas wrote of the passivity of being persecuted, "This passivity deserves the epithet of complete or absolute only if the persecuted one is liable to answer for the persecutor" (Levinas 1981: 111). In other words, the very isolation or loneliness of the one who is persecuted is fully understood only when the full extent of one's relationality as responsibility is revealed. This insight may not have fully come together for Levinas until *Otherwise than Being*, but it is the persecuted self that ultimately sustains the analysis and it is from this perspective that all of Levinas's work must be reread, *Totality and Infinity* most especially. Hence the power of Levinas's reference to "the unreal reality of men persecuted in the daily history of the world, whose dignity and meaning metaphysics has never recognized, from which philosophers turn their faces" (Levinas 1987b: 150). It was ultimately not everyday experience, but the experience of the persecuted with which Levinas was concerned. He was not arguing that everyone had access to this realm of experience. It is only the persecuted who know with an unquestionable immediacy that one's sense of responsibility extends even to those who persecute them. Others are left debating how to make sense of such an idea.

"The difference that gapes between I and self, the non-coincidence of the identical," (Levinas 2003b: 66), lay at the source of Levinas's quest for excendence, but in *Otherwise than Being* it came to be understood differently. The duality between I and self, the otherwise inextricable bond that ties me to the self, the *moi* to the *soi*, is now finally presented as broken. The self in substitution undergoes an anarchic liberation (*affranchissment*). He wrote: "Substitution frees the subject from ennui, that is, from the enchainment to itself, where the ego (*Moi*) suffocates in itself (*en Soi*) due to the tautological way of identity" (Levinas 1981: 124). This means that the "I is an other" of substitution is ultimately different from both the face-to-face and "the I is, in the child, an other" of paternity. That is to say, the self is no longer tied to the isolated subjectivity to which the self of *Existence and Existents* belongs, but is now the self as one-for-the-other. That is to say, it is a hostage, who substitutes for the other but who cannot be substituted for (Levinas 1981: 136).

Hence the self is in a relation of belonging, an intrigue, that is prior to the relata, even while it is absolved from the relation through its need to retain a foothold in being so as to answer to the Other's concrete needs.

If the I is a term irreducible to the relation there is a remainder, but in *Otherwise than Being* the remainder is now not the self of *Existence and Existents*, but a self that is the one for the other. Here the other challenges me from within: *Je est un autre*. Otherwise said, the Other is from the outset already implicated in the self in the form of the one-for-the-other: the stranger succeeded in dispossessing me because the stranger was never foreign to me but close, close to the point of contact, by virtue of my being onto-logically one-for-the-other. To make sense of this Levinas returned to the distinction between the I and the self that he had introduced already in the 1930s but which was largely absent from *Totality and Infinity*, even though, as *Otherwise than Being* shows, it presupposes that distinction. This self behind the me becomes a prominent theme once more in *Otherwise than Being* but, unlike in the earlier treatment, this self is inherently for the other. It amounts to the undoing of the movement of the self into an I, a de-positing or de-situating that reverses what was chartered in *Existence and Existents* as the positionality and substantiality of the subject (Levinas 1981: 50).

I have used this contrast between two tendencies, a tendency in favor of the stranger, separation, and paternity and a tendency in favor of the neighbor, proximity, and maternity, as a heuristic device to highlight what looks like a fundamental equivocation within Levinas's thought. If Levinas himself seems to favor one and then the other, we cannot be surprised that commentators at times seem confused. And yet it is clear that we miss what is most radical, most challenging, in his thought if we feel obliged to choose between them. Alterity is not opposed to proximity any more than the stranger is opposed to the neighbor. When Levinas wrote that "alterity becomes proximity (*l'altérité se fait proximité*)" (Levinas 1994: 110), he was not referring to a transformation in his thought but to the structure of responsibility, where the formal structure of transcendence finds itself concretized in answering the other's needs. The sentence that follows is an attempt at an explanation, but it takes the form of an attempt to say at the same time what sounds like a variety of different things, even if, when taken together, they amount to the same thing: "Not distance, the shortest through space, but initial directness, which extends as unimpeachable approach in the call of the face of the other, in which there appears, as an order, an inscription, a prescription, an awakening (as if it were a 'me'), responsibility— mine, for the other human being" (Levinas 1994: 110). Distance is now being under-stood differently from how it was when it was attributed to eros because it is now seen through the lens of the ethical intrigue. If there was no alterity there would be no ethics in Levinas's sense; there would only be me and my projects in a world organized around me. But there is ethics only because there is this me, this self, that prior to any choice takes on responsibility for the other. Just as in *Existence and Existents* the self raises itself up to be an I in each instant, so there is a movement in the instant from alterity to proximity. But whereas in the former case the I remains chained to itself, in substitution there is liberation from those chains because I discover that it is not to myself but to the other that I am captive in the sense of a hostage. Hence *separation*, the word that along with alterity dominates *Totality and Infinity* but is a rarity in *Otherwise than Being*, combines with substitution in the concrete form of responsibility. Hence he writes: "the one-for-the-other" extends "to the point of substitution, but a substitution in separation, that is, responsibility" (Levinas 1981: 54).

Finally, that Levinas did not choose between the language of the stranger or the neighbor is clear from a passage in *Otherwise than Being* that also serves as a directive as to how to reread his earlier works: "The Good assigns the subject, according to a susception that cannot be assumed, to approach the other, the neighbor. This is an assignation to a non-erotic proximity, to a desire of the non-desirable, to a desire of the stranger in the neighbor" (Levinas 1981: 122–3). To take up what cannot be taken up, to desire what cannot be desired, to find the stranger in proximity—this is what unites the two books, but it also means that neither should be read in isolation from the other.

REFERENCES

Beauvoir, S. de (2010), *The Second Sex*, translated by C. Borde (New York: Knopf).

Bergo, B. (2014), "'When I Opened He Had Gone': Levinas's Substitution as a Reading of Husserl and Heidegger," *Discipline filosofiche* 24: 97–118.

Bernasconi, R. (1995), "'Only the persecuted . . .': Language of the oppressor, language of the oppressed," in A. T. Peperzak (ed.), *Ethics as First Philosophy* (London: Routledge), 77–86.

Bernasconi, R. (2002), "To which question is substitution the answer?" in S. Critchley and R. Bernasconi (eds), *The Cambridge Companion to Levinas* (Cambridge: Cambridge University Press), 234–51.

Bernasconi, R. (2004), "'Failure of commmunication' as a surplus: Dialogue and lack of dialogue between Buber and Levinas," in P. Atterton, M. Calarco, and M. Friedman (eds), *Levinas and Buber: Dialogue and Difference* (Pittsburgh, PA: Duquesne University Press), 65–97.

Bernasconi, R. (2005), "No Exit: Levinas's Aporetic Account of Transcendence," *Research in Phenomenology* 35: 101–17.

Bernasconi, R. (2012), "Levinas's ethical critique of Levinasian ethics," in S. Davidson and D. Perpich (eds), *Totality and Infinity at 50* (Pittsburgh, PA: Duquesne University Press), 253–69 and 295–7.

Blanchot, M. (1986), *The Writing of the Disaster*, translated by A. Smock (Lincoln, NE: University of Nebraska Press).

Brody, D. (2001), "Levinas's maternal method from 'Time and the Other' through *Otherwise than Being*," in T. Chanter (ed.), *Feminist Interpretations of Emmanuel Levinas* (University Park, PA: Penn State University Press), 53–77.

Buber, M. (1967), "Replies to my critics," in P. A. Schilpp and M. S. Friedman (eds), *The Philosophy of Martin Buber* (Chicago, IL: Open Court), 689–744.

Buber, M. (1970), *I and Thou*, translated by W. Kaufmann (New York: Scribner's).

Davies, P. (1991), "A fine risk: Reading Blanchot reading Levinas" in R. Bernasconi and S. Critchley (eds), *Re-Reading Levinas* (Bloomington, IN: Indiana University Press), 201–26.

Irigaray, L. (2004), "What other are we talking about?" *Yale French Studies* 102: 67–81.

Levinas, E. (1961), "Resumé de *Totalité et Infini*," *Annales de l'Université de Paris* 31/3: 385–6.

Levinas, E. (1967), "Martin Buber and the theory of knowledge," in P. A. Schilpp and M. S. Friedman (eds), *The Philosophy of Martin Buber* (Chicago, IL: Open Court), 133–50.

Levinas, E. (1969), *Totality and Infinity*, translated by A. Lingis (Pittsburgh, PA: Duquesne University Press).

Levinas, E. (1981), *Otherwise than Being or Beyond Essence*, translated by A. Lingis (The Hague: Martinus Nijhoff).

Levinas, E. (1985), *Ethics and Infinity*, translated by R. Cohen (Pittsbugh, PA: Duquesne University Press).

Levinas, E. (1987a), *Time and the Other*, translated by R. Cohen (Pittsburgh, PA: Duquesne University Press).

Levinas, E. (1987b), *Collected Philosophical Papers*, translated by A. Lingis (The Hague: Martinus Nijhoff).

Levinas, E. (1990), *Difficult Freedom*, translated by S. Hand (Baltimore, MD: Johns Hopkins University Press).

Levinas, R. (1993), *Outside the Subject*, translated by M. B. Smith (Stanford, CA: Stanford University Press).

Levinas, E. (1994), *In the Time of the Nations*, translated by M. B. Smith (Bloomington, IN: Indiana University Press).

Levinas, E. (1996a), *Basic Philosophical Writings*, ed. A. Peperzak, S. Critchley, and R. Bernasconi (Bloomington, IN: Indiana University Press).

Levinas, E. (1996b), *Proper Names*, translated by M. B. Smith (Stanford, CA: Stanford University Press).

Levinas, E. (1998a), *Entre nous*, translated by M. B. Smith and B. Harshaw (New York: Columbia University Press).

Levinas, E. (1998b), *Of God Who Comes to Mind*, translated by B. Bergo (Stanford, CA: Stanford University Press).

Levinas, E. (2000), *God Death, and Time*, translated by B. Bergo (Stanford, CA: Stanford University Press).

Levinas, E. (2001a), *Existence and Existents*, translated by A. Lingis (Pittsburgh, PA: Duquesne University Press).

Levinas, E. (2001b), *Is it Righteous to Be?* translated by J. Robbins (Stanford, CA: Stanford University Press).

Levinas, E. (2003a), *On Escape*, translated by B. Bergo (Stanford, CA: Stanford University Press).

Levinas, E. (2003b), *Humanism of the Other*, translated by N. Poller (Champaign, IL: Illinois University Press).

Levinas, E. (2004), *Unforeseen History*, translated by N. Poller (Champaign, IL: Illinois University Press).

Standford, S. (1998), "Writing as a Man: Levinas and the Phenomenology of Eros," *Radical Philosophy* 87: 6–17.

Sandford, S. (2000), *The Metaphysics of Love* (London: Athlone).

....

CHAPTER 24

TURN TO EXCESS

The Development of Phenomenology in Late Twentieth-Century French Thought

....

CHRISTINA M. GSCHWANDTNER

FRENCH phenomenology in the late twentieth and early twenty-first century has increasingly taken on phenomena whose study would have been unacceptable or even unthinkable before. It is variously called a "phenomenology at the limit," a "radicalized" or "new" phenomenology, and a phenomenology of the "impossible," the "wholly other," or the "extraordinary" (Sebbah 2012; Kühn 2003; Jonkers and Welten 2005; Rogozinski 2011; Gondek and Tengelyi 2011; Simmons and Benson 2013; Alliez 1995; Wolf 1999; Falque 2014). Dominique Janicaud decried it as a "theological turn" (2000) or as a phenomenology that has "clashed with" or "broken out" of its boundaries, that is "wide open" (2005). The philosophers most prominently identified with this recent tendency speak of their own work as a "material" phenomenology or a phenomenology of the invisible (Michel Henry) and as a phenomenology of givenness (Jean-Luc Marion). Other thinkers, such as Emmanuel Levinas, Jacques Derrida, Jean-Louis Chrétien, Jean-Yves Lacoste, even Paul Ricœur, are also often grouped with them.[1] Although there is little consensus regarding the range of thinkers identified with such a shift in French phenomenology after 1960,[2] there is broad agreement that one of its outstanding

---

[1] Sebbah includes Derrida and Levinas but none of the others; Kühn also does but excludes Henry. Gondek and Tengelyi discuss primarily Richir, Henry, and Marion, although they include shorter treatments on Franck, Dastur, Escoubas, Chrétien, Barbaras, Depraz, and Benoist. Janicaud includes Chrétien but specifically excludes Ricœur from his indictment, despite the latter's work on biblical hermeneutics (2000: 23, 34; 2005: 5–6). Wolf includes not only Ricœur but any number of others such as Marcel, Merleau-Ponty, Gilson, and Bruaire; Jonkers and Welten discuss eight thinkers, including Girard, Ricœur, Derrida, and Lyotard. Falque treats nine thinkers, including Derrida and Merleau-Ponty, but not Ricœur.

[2] Janicaud uses this as the "turning point," because Merleau-Ponty died in 1961, the same year in which Levinas's *Totality and Infinity* was published (2000: 25). Greisch qualifies this unilateral break (2002: 360–6).

characteristics is an interest in invisible or excessive phenomena that either are not apprehended through simple perception or are so complex that they overwhelm all attempts to constitute them definitively. While these thinkers continue to engage in phenomenological description and indeed frequently reiterate the rallying cry "back to the things themselves," the "things" to which they seek to return are quite distinct from those examined by Husserl and Heidegger or even Sartre and Merleau-Ponty.

What are the kinds of phenomena contemporary French phenomenology seeks to unfold? What is this peculiar phenomenology that breaks through "traditional" phenomenological boundaries and evokes such passionate cries of trespass, betrayal, unfaithfulness, or disciplinary confusion? In this contribution I will examine the phenomenological project of late-twentieth and early twenty-first-century French philosophy and its tendency to radicalize phenomenology or open it out onto previously unexamined phenomena, focusing especially on two of the most important, earliest, and most influential representatives, Michel Henry and Jean-Luc Marion.[3] I will begin by introducing the kinds of phenomena under investigation, before turning to a closer examination of the adjustments to phenomenological method such phenomena seem to require. In that context I will especially highlight the ways in which they appropriate Husserl's and Heidegger's thought (although it is worth pointing out that for Henry Descartes, Fichte, Schelling, and Maine de Biran are also major sources and for Marion Descartes, Pascal and Levinas are probably as significant as Husserl and Heidegger). The third part of the chapter (section 24.3) will show the contribution these phenomenological projects make to two specific areas of phenomenology, namely to the examination of aesthetic and of religious phenomena, respectively.

24.1 "Unapparent" Phenomena

Janicaud's analysis is probably the most well known one and to some extent it served to introduce several of these thinkers to the English-speaking world. In his first formulation of the "theological turn," he suggests that it is Heidegger's "turn" to a "phenomenology of the unapparent" that provokes and makes possible the "theological" turn in the French thinkers of the next generation, especially Levinas, Henry, and Marion (Janicaud 2000: 28–34).[4] Jean-François Courtine had already argued that Heidegger increasingly

---

[3] Levinas may well be said to fit into this movement of excess and certainly was strongly preoccupied with the notion of the infinite, but as there is a separate chapter on him in the volume, his philosophy will not be discussed in the context of this chapter. One might also include some English-language thinkers in this group, such as Richard Kearney, John Caputo, Merold Westphal, or in a quite different sense Anthony Steinbock, but for the sake of coherence and length, the chapter will focus only on the French thinkers. I focus in more detail on Marion and Henry not only because they are probably its most significant and most well-known representatives, but also partly because they are the two most strongly criticized by Janicaud.

[4] It is striking, however, that Janicaud does not say a word about the "phenomenology of the unapparent" in his important subsequent book on the reception of Heidegger in France (2015), although

moved toward a "phenomenology of the unapparent" in his later work (1990: 381–405). The term is briefly mentioned a couple of times in the 1973 Zähringen Seminar. (While held in Germany it followed on from the Toth Seminars held in Normandy, organized by Jean Beaufret; it was attended primarily by French thinkers and was first published in French.) Courtine contends that the late Heidegger increasingly tries to think in tautological terms, developing a phenomenology of what is "unapparent" and in some ways must be kept "secret" or "hidden" rather than being revealed or brought to light (1990: 395). In Heidegger's final essays the "unapparent" becomes formulated as the "event" (*Ereignis*) of givenness, terminology that will become important especially for Marion. Although Courtine shows throughout the essay how the emphasis on the unapparent and hiddenness grows out of and is in continuity with Heidegger's earlier work, especially his writings on language, he concludes by wondering to what extent this thinking that shows nothing and gives nothing to see can still remain phenomenological or whether it has a "disastrous or catastrophic character for the very *possibility* of phenomenology" (1990: 405). Janicaud chides Heidegger more explicitly than Courtine for abandoning the Husserlian project of constitution and for rupturing with "positive phenomenology," opting instead for a pursuit of meditative silence, generous givenness, and the sacred, which he suggests are carried further by the French thinkers. Instead Janicaud seeks to recall phenomenology to its roots in *this* world and its tangible phenomena (2000: 34, 97). This Heideggerian turn provides the first step in a slippery slope away from "real" phenomena. Whether that is a valid accusation is partly what is under investigation here.

It is certainly true that the phenomena investigated by subsequent French phenomenology are not simple, everyday phenomena and are not necessarily accessible via perception in an obvious sense. First, one might say that these thinkers all investigate phenomena that are at least to some extent invisible or at least not tangible objects. In *Michel Henry*, the primary concern is with what he explicitly calls the invisible, namely the utterly interior, completely immanent, and fully material life of self-affectivity that flows within us as our very life, expressed in the pathos of joy and suffering. As we will see, his focus on invisible life also leads him to examine questions of labor, culture, ethics, and especially aesthetics, and, at the very end of his career he employs religious terminology for it, identifying it with the life of God. *Jean-Louis Chrétien* deals with similarly invisible phenomena, although he describes them in somewhat different fashion. His phenomenology is primarily concerned with what might be called phenomena of vulnerability. He speaks of body and touch, of the voice and speech, of call and response, of hope and promise, of response and responsibility, of beauty and art, of breath and air, often in highly poetic terms, which he posits as a mode better suited to such fragile phenomena. For *Jean-Luc Marion*, the primary phenomena of interest are what he calls "rich" or "saturated" phenomena, phenomena that appear to us in overwhelming

he discusses the Toth and Zähringen seminars in detail and mentions the thinkers he criticizes in the "theological turn" without accusing them of any subversion of phenomenology that could be caused by something latent in Heidegger's work.

fashion and cannot be grasped or conceptualized. While some of them can become visible, such as works of art, or at least were once visible, such as historical and cultural events, others are clearly invisible, such as the flesh (where he for the most part simply adopts Henry's analysis), the gaze of the other (which proceeds invisibly from the "emptiness" of the pupils and is informed by Levinas's phenomenology of alterity), the erotic phenomenon, and what he calls "phenomena of revelation," i.e., an experience of or encounter with the divine. In *Jean-Yves Lacoste*'s work, we are confronted with the absolute, which he is quite clear is not only invisible, but even a "non-experience" (that occurs in a "non-place" and "non-time").[5] Although Lacoste always begins with Heidegger's "Being-in-the-world" as his starting point, the confrontation with the "absolute" leads Dasein beyond the world into an optional and extraordinary encounter that constitutes a forceful rupture with ordinary experience. *Emmanuel Falque*, a student of Marion and maybe the most important—certainly the most quickly translated— figure in the youngest generation of French thinkers, has written extensively about the phenomena of suffering and death, birth and resurrection, flesh and body, marriage and sacraments. All these phenomena are experienced, but they are not necessarily visible or tangible or ordinary, "everyday" phenomena.

The emphasis on "unapparentness" or "excess" is thus not the only and not always the most obvious characteristic of the phenomena under investigation. A second noteworthy feature is that most, if not all, of these thinkers are interested in the phenomena of the body or the flesh (investigating birth, death, aging, suffering, etc.) in various ways. This is especially true of Henry, although he focuses solely on the interiority of invisible and self-affected flesh not the "external" body; but it is also the case for Chrétien, Marion, and particularly Falque, who is deeply influenced by Merleau-Ponty and seeks to address what he interprets as an excessive privileging of the flesh over the body and passivity over activity in the two previous generations of French phenomenologists (1016b; 2014: 68). Third, all these thinkers are interested in aesthetic phenomena. Henry devotes an entire book to the art of Kandinsky, but also mentions art in other places in his work. Marion frequently writes on Klee and Rothko (2002b: 54-81), or Courbet (to whom he has recently devoted an entire book), but also broadly about various aspects of the history of aesthetics (2004) and the phenomenon of the work of art (usually painting, cf. 2011). Chrétien specifically examines the crossing of beauty and body in art and creativity in two studies (1987 and 2003), but also frequently mentions art, beauty, and creativity in other investigations. Art appears as a topic also occasionally in Lacoste's work (e.g., 2000: 55–106).

Finally, all of them investigate what might be called "religious" phenomena (although most of them are not actually interested in "religion" for its own sake or even in a broad sense, that is, beyond its "Christian" or even specifically Roman Catholic instantiation). Henry's final works root his phenomenology of the flesh and affectivity in the texts of

---

[5] See especially his *Experience and the Absolute* (1994) and *Note sur le temps* (1990). Both of these books and all of Lacoste's other works (mostly collections of essays) are deeply influenced by Heidegger and presume a Heideggerian framework throughout, even when he is critical of him (most fully in 2011).

the Christian Gospels, albeit interpreted in highly idiosyncratic ways. The most intensely saturated phenomenon for Marion is a phenomenon of revelation. Depictions of religious experiences pervade all of Chrétien's work and at times seem indistinguishable from poetic or aesthetic ones. Lacoste seeks to depict our "being-before-God" as a transgression and displacement of being-in-the-world. Falque begins with what he calls "*l'homme tout court*" or the human "as such" in our mundane experiences of suffering and the chaos of our impulses and desires and only from there explores how thinking through death and resurrection might transform them without invalidating ordinary human experience. Religious experience then does become a topic in contemporary phenomenology and religious phenomena are indeed examined. Yet all of these thinkers argue that they are investigating *phenomena* that appear to us or are given to us, although probably not in the mode of the perception of objects, and that they are not making theological claims that would import a metaphysic of transcendence into philosophy.[6] They all contend that although these may well be excessive or extraordinary experiences (which might be similarly true of our encounter with a work of art or even our own flesh), they do occur, are manifested in experience, and can be meaningfully examined phenomenologically. Let me briefly present two examples of phenomena or categories of phenomena more closely: Henry's phenomenon of life and Marion's saturated phenomenon.

24.1.1 Henry: Self-affective life

Henry seeks to overcome the phenomenological obsession with appearance, which he thinks is still rooted in the modern division between appearance and reality. Instead he focuses on manifestation itself as pure phenomenality. The "essence" of manifestation is not a relation to the "outside" but the very possibility of manifestation as such. It is experienced not as something exterior that comes to me from an outside "world," instead it is utterly immediate, manifested as immanence, as self-affectivity. This material "essence" of manifestation is life itself, because only what is alive can experience and feel—and such experience precisely is what "living" means. Life is the pure self-givenness of subjectivity and alone makes pathos as affective experience possible: "Life is absolute subjectivity inasmuch as it experiences itself and is nothing other than that experience. It is the pure fact of experiencing itself and is nothing other than that experience. It is the pure fact of experiencing itself immediately and without any distance" (2008: 134). Henry consistently draws stark divisions between this interior, invisible, immanent "life" and the exterior, visible "world" with its objects: "no life can appear in the

---

[6] Only the latter two—Lacoste and Falque—actually have official degrees in theology, although Marion acquired significant (unofficial) training along the way. Falque may be the only one who explicitly seeks to bring phenomenology and theology together in his work (cf. 2015 and especially 2016a), while Lacoste keeps them rigorously apart.

appearing of the world" (2003b: 101). Life is what generates me and makes me "living"; it is the very pathos of my desires and drives. Life alone is the source of any experience, which is thus always radically immanent as experienced within itself. Therefore life as pure phenomenality is in its very essence invisible, referring to the interior and immanent experience of self. A phenomenology of objects in the world must be radicalized to an account of experiencing per se. Such experiencing is only possible within life itself.

The self-revelatory "essence" of "life" is affectivity, the pathos of the flesh where all manifestation occurs and is sensed in enjoyment and suffering. The flesh is the phenomenological condition of affectivity, the invisible materiality within which self-affectivity operates. Auto-affection is not merely an internal sense but its condition. It has the very structure of immanence. Affectivity refers to feeling without any mediation whatsoever; this is how essence receives and feels itself as manifestation (1973: 462). Feeling cannot be sensed or perceived as something separate from what is felt, but it is always utterly immediate. It does not establish a relationship between self and something exterior, but is always an expression of the self: "The ipseity of the essence, its auto-affection in the immanence of pure affectivity, this is the Being-self of the subject as affective and concrete Self, the original Self of affection which as such makes all affection possible, even sensible affection" (1973: 467). Henry repeats over and over again that "the essence of subjectivity is affectivity" (1973: 476) and that "affectivity is not a phenomenon or some thing which manifests itself, rather it is manifestation itself and its essence." It is manifested in the flesh as "precisely the pure phenomenological matter of every genuine (i.e., radically immanent) auto-affection, in which life experiences itself" through pathos (2003b: 108). Such affectivity of the flesh is expressed or apprehended in enjoyment and suffering. We cannot observe suffering as an object: "Suffering, like every modality of life, is invisible" (2003b: 103). Yet its invisible interiority does not mean it is not real. Rather it is real within its very experience not through an external representation that would abstract from it. At the same time, affectivity is the condition for action (hence both for morality and for meaningful labor or genuine economy). Henry, then, is not seeking to highlight one particular phenomenon among others, but to grapple with the very "how" of phenomenality, not with an experience of a thing "out there" but with the very condition of experiencing itself. The very possibility of experience, as self-affectivity, as our living reality, is internal and invisible but utterly immanent and fully material.

24.1.2 Marion: Saturated phenomena

While Henry focuses on *the* phenomenon that is missed by previous phenomenology and identifies it with phenomenality itself, Marion claims that there is a whole range of phenomena excluded, ignored, or misunderstood "by virtue of their excess of evidence" (2015: 204). Their shared characteristic is their richness, their intuitive abundance, their escape from any metaphysical constraints of predictability, causality, and objective categories of apprehension. He argues that such phenomena are not obscure and esoteric, but that they are indeed abundant, frequent, and ubiquitous in our experience.

In one particularly important essay (2008: 119–44), he provides examples for all five senses, contrasting "poor" phenomena (the "metaphysical" objects on which previous phenomenology focused and which he claims are "poor" in intuition)[7] with saturated ones: the colors red, yellow, and green in the experience of a traffic light, which only conveys information, versus the experience of those colors in Rothko's painting N. 212, the sound of a voice over a loudspeaker at an airport versus the experience of listening to the aria of a famous diva at the opera, the smell of gas versus the fragrance of a perfume, the taste of a poison versus the flavors of a good wine, the attempt at orientation in a dark room through the handling of objects to find a light switch versus the loving touch of the other's flesh. In the former cases, Marion claims, we can constitute the phenomenon through intentionality, understand it fully, indeed experience it primarily in terms of the information it conveys (e.g., a change of gates, the danger of a gas explosion). The later phenomena, however, defy all such simple description or constitution, but that makes them no less phenomena: they are still given to intuition; indeed, their rich intuition is one of their primary characteristics. While abundant in intuition, they cannot be constituted according to concepts.

Indeed, Marion goes back (2002a: Part IV) to Kant's parameters for the appearance of phenomena (in terms of quantity, quality, relation, and modality), in order to show how saturated phenomena *precisely do not fit* into these categories, but are experienced otherwise: A rich historical or cultural event gives us "too much," it can never be grasped in one account, always escapes any singular cause we might assign to it; it comes unpredictably and alters our phenomenal world irreversibly (such as 9/11, which he cites as an example [2017]). The encounter with a dazzling work of art gives "too intensely"; it escapes any parameters of quality that could be assigned to it; we must go to see it again and again; it is never exhausted in any seeing. My flesh is felt so intimately as the very seat of affects and emotions that I can never separate myself from it to establish any sort of "relation" to it, but it invalidates all such categories. The gaze of the other cannot be borne in any modality, it weighs on me, calls forth my response. While this is particularly obvious for the fourth kind of phenomenon, all saturated phenomena, according to Marion, eliminate the possibility of me as subject constituting them as objects and instead turn me into someone devoted to, given over to, even addicted to (*adonné à*) the phenomenon as it gives itself to me (2002a: Part V). Such phenomena still must be received and be made manifest—otherwise they would not be phenomena—but such manifestation occurs more through reception or even resistance (like a screen blocking light and hence making it visible) rather than control or straightforward constitution. Phenomenalization occurs obliquely and partially, but it does occur.

While neither Henry's phenomenon of the flesh nor some of Marion's saturated phenomena are clearly visible to us or accessible via perception in the traditional sense, they

---

[7] Occasionally he will also speak of "common" phenomena (technical objects), but in his more recent work they are often simply assimilated to "poor" phenomena, which appear as objects and can be constituted as such. See *Being Given*, §23 (2002a: 221–33) for the initial distinctions between poor, common, and saturated.

depict phenomena with which we are certainly familiar and which we have encountered or experienced. We are affected by joy and suffering and often experience it as a pathos that renders us passive and yet fully and intimately engaged. We have experienced rich cultural or aesthetic events or moments of terror, which overwhelm us and may leave us breathless or wordless, yet obviously are phenomena that call for some sort of account. The phenomena Chrétien examines—the fragility of the voice as it catches its breath, the touch of beauty as it offers us and we offer it to the world—similarly are familiar to human experience even if they have not frequently been the subject of phenomenological investigation. Why should it be a priori forbidden, on phenomenological grounds, to unfold the phenomenality of an intimate erotic experience or a complex aesthetic one? Indeed, both Henry and Marion claim that these are the phenomena that matter most fundamentally to us and reveal something of the deepest sense of who we are (Henry 2008: 6; Marion 2017). We will return to two of such types of phenomena in more detail in the final part of this chapter (section 24.3), but will for now assume that if a phenomenon is recognizable (even if not necessarily by empirical vision), that is, if it is manifested in experience in some form, there are no a priori reason for excluding it from phenomenological investigation. Yet, if such phenomena appear "differently" than the ones traditionally examined by phenomenology, if, for example, they cannot be fully constituted, then surely the manner in which they are investigated must also be adjusted. This is why we must now turn to the phenomenological method in these thinkers.

24.2 PHENOMENOLOGY WITHOUT CONSTITUTION

A concern with methodology is maybe strongest in the early thinkers, especially Henry and Marion. It is less evident in Chrétien, Lacoste, or Falque; they often employ prior investigations as a given or at least as a starting point. Both Henry and Marion justify their descriptions of phenomena through a thorough engagement with the method of phenomenology, especially as it is put forth by Husserl and Heidegger. Their phenomenologies thus emerge as critiques of these thinkers, although that should not hide the extent to which they are also highly indebted to them and seek to carry their work further. They both see themselves at least to some extent in continuity with them and there may be more significant continuity even than they themselves recognize or are willing to acknowledge.[8] I will again begin with Henry and then discuss Marion.[9]

---

[8] Greisch argues this for Henry's harsh rejection of Heidegger (Greisch 2002: 355). French philosophy always seems to progress at least to some extent via parricide. The unique nature of the French educational system may bear a large responsibility for this (Schrift 2005).

[9] One should also note that Henry and Marion have both discussed each other's phenomenological methodology (Henry 2004; Marion 2012: 95–115).

24.2.1 Henry: Radical immanence

Henry is most critical of what he diagnoses as an essential schizophrenia in Husserl: a split between phenomenon and phenomenality, between appearance and appearing. Although Husserl stressed that consciousness is always directed toward the phenomena and sought to hold what appears and how it appears closely together, Henry thinks that he does not go far enough in overcoming the subject–object split. In Husserl, and even more strongly in Heidegger, Henry criticizes a continued preoccupation with the externality of the world, with what is "out there." Their phenomenologies introduce a distinction between the invisible essence of the phenomenon and its visible manifestation in the world. Henry argues that the concept of intuition as handled by Husserl and Heidegger is ambivalent as a condition for the appearing of objects or the horizon of Being, because thought becomes representation or objectification. For Henry, phenomenology is not about phenomena as objects, but rather about phenomenality as the essence of phenomena, the "how" of appearing rather than the "what." Phenomena are not experienced "out there" in the world, but rather "in here," in the affectivity of my interior life. Henry draws stark distinctions between a mode of being "in the world" and the mode of life. The former has no access to affectivity and hence no true experience. In the self-affectivity of life phenomena are their phenomenality. Manifestation cannot be split between Being and its appearance, but being only "is" through its life, the essence of phenomenality as pure experience (1973: 685; 2008: 3). The structures of experience, including temporality, are not found in the "world" or even the body, but within the internal, immanent essence of life as self-affected flesh.

Henry is particularly critical of Heidegger's attempt to root the being of Dasein in temporality and in projection or to conceive of it as an ek-static being "ahead" or "outside" of oneself. For Heidegger, on Henry's reading, the "ek-stasis" of Dasein is a horizon of exteriority, a place where Dasein must stand in order to receive the "transcendent" manifestation of Being. Instead of the "light" of Being, Henry pursues the "night" of the invisibility of life itself (1973: 44). Manifestation, he argues, occurs not against a separate horizon but within the very activity of manifestation, in phenomenality itself. Manifestation is not about representation but about self-revelation and self-receptivity (as immanence): "The original essence of affection resides in immanence" (1973: 244); indeed, "immanence is the essence of transcendence" (1973: 249). Transcendence is not manifested in an exterior "world" but within itself in radical immanence. Yet, Henry insists that it is this very emphasis on immanence that makes his a "material" phenomenology: "To the extent that in pure givenness it thematizes and explains its own self-givenness, material phenomenology is phenomenology in a radical sense" (2008: 42). While Husserlian phenomenology merely re-creates the subject–object split on a higher level, remains "Greek" in respect to its separation of "matter" and "form," Henry's material phenomenology brings matter into the heart of manifestation itself rather than being the object or "stuff in the world" that is being manifested. The "method" of investigation must become the "path" of phenomenality itself instead of something separate from it or indifferent to it. This means that "the objects of phenomenology and its method are the same, because the former (appearing) constitutes the path that the latter (the method) need only follow (2008: 89). The method of phenomenology is only possible through the pure appearing of life in immanence and pathos. Life reveals itself in its very experience as living (2008: 95). It is not our "being-in-the-world" that we must explore, but the self-affectivity of our most intimate and most immanent experience as living.

24.2.2 Marion: Abundant givenness

Marion explicates his critique of Husserl and Heidegger most fully in *Reduction and Givenness* (1998), summarizes it again in detail in Part I of *Being Given* (2002a) and devotes a further essay (2002b: 1–29) and later book (2012) to methodological questions.[10] He first works toward his notion of a more radical reduction in *Reduction and Givenness*, where he argues that Husserl employs the reduction in order to allow the phenomenality of objects to emerge, while Heidegger uses it (less obviously) in order to permit the phenomenality of beings, especially that of Dasein, to manifest themselves.[11] While both are useful in their particular way, Marion sees a more radical reduction emerging within and behind their texts, one which they may sense but do not fully explore. This third reduction, which Marion here calls "erotic" (occasionally he will identify it as a fourth reduction instead and list Levinas's "reduction" to "ethics" as the third) is a reduction not to objects or to beings, but to givenness itself. This new reduction would be more radical, reduce even further. Just as a chemical substance reaches greater purity the more it is reduced, so phenomenological reduction serves to let the phenomenon shine more fully from itself. Marion encapsulates this in the principle that the more reduction is practiced so much more fully does givenness emerge (2002a: 14–18; 2002b: 17). He calls this an absolute principle which allows for no doubt because everything is already given. That is to say, givenness and reduction are equivalent.

---

[10] It is worth noting that Marion started out as a Descartes scholar and published extensively in that area before he began to engage phenomenology seriously. At the same time Marion conceived of his work from the start as continuing Heidegger's mission of the *Destruktion* (destruction or deconstruction) of the history of metaphysics, pushing it even further to overcome what he perceives as lingering traces of metaphysics even in Heidegger's work. For this project he takes Heidegger's definition of metaphysics as onto-theo-logy as a given and applies it in various ways, especially in his work on the Cartesian structure of metaphysics, which he argues displays a doubled (or possibly triple) onto-theo-logical structure.

[11] In this respect it is interesting that already Henry assumes that phenomenological and eidetic reduction are ultimately the same (1973: 53). Courtine shows that Heidegger does not abandon Husserl's notion of reduction, but that it can be detected in his distinction between ontic and ontological (1990: 207–47). Courtine's essay originally appeared in a collection edited by Marion. Both cite the other in their respective works.

Marion returns to the reduction as founding principle for a phenomenology of givenness in the first chapter of *In Excess*. He argues that phenomenology might become a new first—or rather last—philosophy by allowing the given to show itself fully and entirely on its own terms. This is possible only through a more radical reduction, which entirely frees the phenomenon to give itself from itself: "No givenness without reduction, no reduction that does not lead to givenness" (2002b: 18). This is the case "because the reduction eliminates from the process of appearing all that which is not given without reserve." It serves as a purifying process that eliminates anything "transcendent" and separates the "intended" from what is truly "given" on its own terms (2002b: 19). Like Henry, Marion seeks for a greater affinity and congruity between the given phenomenon and its mode of givenness, although he does not collapse phenomenality into the phenomenon quite as fully as Henry does. The (saturated) phenomenon determines and provides its own mode of manifestation, but it is not necessarily identical with it.

There is a sense in which Marion plays Husserl and Heidegger against each other in *Reduction and Givenness*. He employs Heidegger to show that for Husserl all intuition remains categorial, but utilizes Husserl to argue that intuition is realized most fundamentally as givenness. Phenomena appear as given and intuition is a mode of givenness that ought not be mediated either through (metaphysical) categories or through the horizon of Being. Marion employs the notion of the phenomenological reduction to "free" givenness from its constrictions, especially those imposed by the constituting ego or by Dasein and the horizon of objectness or beingness, respectively. In order for phenomena to give themselves entirely from themselves, they must provide their own horizon (instead of being constituted within one that is imposed on them by intentionality) and will radically reorient the phenomenological recipient, who is no longer a constituting ego or a Dasein facing and revealing Being as such. Rather, the phenomenological recipient becomes devoted or given over to the phenomenon, phenomenalizing it by receiving it, but not controlling it through the imposition of any parameters within which it ought to appear. While Marion draws the language of givenness from Husserl (albeit suggesting that Husserl does not realize its full implications), he relies on Heidegger for arguing that Husserl reduces all phenomena to objectness and does not allow for anything objectively "unapparent" to show itself. Yet, lived experience is full of phenomena that are at least initially unapparent and manifest themselves in ways other than objective visibility. At the same time, he draws on Husserl in order to argue that Heidegger's preoccupation with being is too exclusive. While Husserl already operates to some extent on the "field of the question of Being," he can be read as seeing beyond the region of beings "to a phenomenological horizon not determined by Being, properly outside of Being, in traversing without stopping in or trying to satisfy the domain of the question of Being, where Heidegger attempted to lodge—and to block—phenomenology" (1998: 161). Phenomenology is not limited either to the realm of objects (in Husserl's sense) nor to that of beings (in Heidegger's sense). Marion appeals in this context, as he does frequently, to Heidegger's claim that in phenomenology possibility stands above or is greater than actuality (1998: 168).

In *Reduction and Givenness* Marion explores the third reduction as one proceeding from the call "as such," an anonymous claim that is identified only in the process of phenomenological reception (1998: 204–5). While such a call or appeal might come from the phenomenon of an object or from Being (Heidegger's *Anspruch des Seins*) or from the other (in Levinas's sense of the appeal of the other), it could also proceed from other phenomena, such as aesthetic, cultural, or religious ones, that are not captured in these iterations. In *Being Given*, he explicates this more radical possibility, on the one hand, in terms of a work of art, which manifests neither as an object nor as a tool but as a given that has an effect or impact on us, and, on the other hand, with the notion of the gift, which is received as a gift only when it cannot be traced to a prior cause or giver. Drawing again on Husserl's notion of *Gegebenheit* and Heidegger's concept of the *es gibt*, Marion argues that phenomenality is best expressed as givenness.[12] In order to allow phenomena to give themselves fully and entirely from themselves, we must reduce, that is, overcome or set aside, the language of the horizon and of the constituting I. Intentionality exercises a sort of power over phenomena, which does not allow them to appear on their own terms. A more radical return to the things themselves would allow them to give themselves on their own terms, to flood us with their intuitive givenness rather than being constituted, constructed, defined, and limited by our intentionality.

Intentionality for Marion becomes receptivity. Phenomena give themselves and we must receive them, bear their impact, phenomenalize what is given to us as adequately as we can, while knowing full well that we cannot bear their weight, but that they give far more than we could ever manifest. In this context, Marion outlines several characteristics of givenness. It exercises anamorphosis, which means that the phenomenon ordains where and how I have to receive it. I must receive it on its terms, not on mine. Such phenomena come in unpredictable fashion; they cannot be anticipated or foreseen. Marion appropriates the language of facticity from Heidegger but applies it to the incoming phenomenon, which gives itself as a fait accompli, one that cannot be reduced to its causality. It is an event and we cannot trace back its emergence to causal or predictable origins. Rather, the event establishes the cause only in retrospect and is always more than all of its causes. At the same time the phenomenon is given as an incident or accident; it arrives suddenly and unpredictably. It surprises us, takes our breath away, implodes on our screen of consciousness, so that we only register the "radioactive fallout." Givenness, then, becomes a universal property of all phenomena, indeed it is "equivalent to the phenomenon itself" (2002b: 21). All phenomena can be unfolded in terms of their givenness.[13]

---

[12] He justifies this again more fully in regard to Husserl (Marion 2012: 11–26), Natorp, Lask, and Rickert (Marion 2012: 34–7), Meinong (Marion 2012: 37–42), and Heidegger (Marion 2012: 45–58).

[13] In *Negative Certainties*, Marion suggests that this also has epistemological implications, inasmuch as richness of these phenomena shows that we cannot comprehend them in terms of Cartesian certainty (and that we can, precisely, be entirely "certain" about this) but that they must be received or even understood in a radically different mode (2015).

For both Henry and Marion, then, phenomenological appearance or manifestation need not mean to appear as an object or even to become entirely transparent and fully visible. Yet, both maintain rigorously that the phenomena they examine are indeed manifested in (or as) experience. While such phenomena cannot necessarily be perceived as objects within the world or constituted by intentionality as they appear to consciousness and are also not necessarily manifested as revelations of Being within the *Umwelt* or *Lichtung* of Dasein, they are given or give themselves within our affective experience of life or as the rich phenomena we encounter daily around us. They are given not as tools that are *zuhanden* in the world, but as encounters with works of art or with the loving gaze or eroticized flesh of the other. While such phenomena cannot be constituted as objects or fully comprehended, they can be received and be described phenomenologically to the extent that they are manifested to their recipients who expose themselves to their givenness. At the same time this forms a response to the phenomenological focus on the subject of experience (the transcendental ego) who is rethought as a recipient of the phenomenon without exercising autonomy over it. What might this exposure to givenness or manifestation concretely look like for some of those phenomena?

24.3 AESTHETIC AND RELIGIOUS PHENOMENA

Almost all of the French phenomenologists (indeed not just the ones examined in this chapter and not just the French) are preoccupied to some extent with aesthetic phenomena or with the phenomenality of the work of art. Many of them contend that engaging fully with aesthetic phenomenality requires a broader vision of phenomenology. A similar claim is made about religious experience. It ought to be possible to depict an experience of prayer or participation in a sacrament, such as the Eucharist, phenomenologically, yet the traditional categories might have to be adjusted in order to take account of such experiences. While many of the other thinkers mentioned (especially Chrétien and Lacoste) discuss art and religion in their work, we will focus here again on Henry and Marion, because they have explored these topics the most fully and the most systematically. At the same time we will be able to see how their treatment of art and religion is consistent with their larger phenomenological claims.[14]

---

[14] It is worth noting that Janicaud comments positively on both Henry's and Marion's treatments of art, which he takes to be genuinely phenomenological (2000: 98).

24.3.1 Henry: Barbarism, Kandinsky, Christianity

In his later years Henry became increasingly critical of contemporary culture (or maybe more precisely the destruction of culture) and applied his phenomenology to it. In his provocative work *Barbarism* he strongly chides the contemporary obsession with tele-techno-science, i.e., the triple alignment of media, science, and technology, as destructive of life and culture. Science, especially as first explicated by Galileo and continued by modern biology, is out to destroy life and knows nothing about it, has no access to it. Human identity and subjectivity is rooted in our experience of life in self-affectivity, but science erases the human by seeking to objectify life, affectivity, and radical subjectivity. This logic of the world is destructive because it is indifferent to its objects and unable to confer existence (2003b: 102). In the contemporary world "life is attacked" and therefore "all of its values also falter, not only aesthetics but also ethics and the sacred—and with them, so too the possibility of living each day" (2012: 2). We have reduced life to ciphers, livings to automata, feelings to neurotransmitters, pleasure to pure simulation. This is a deceptive "culture" of death and destruction.

Henry argues that authentic life necessarily produces culture, because the self-affectivity of life seeks expression of itself. As both the subject and object of life, true culture is "an action that life exerts on itself and through which it transforms itself insofar as life is both transforming and transformed" (2012: 5). Art, in particular, seeks to manifest the invisible: "Art is an activity of sensibility, the fulfillment of its powers, whereas modern science, with the elimination of sensible qualities from nature, defines its own field and defines itself through the exclusion of sensibility" (2012: 23). Science reduces the life-world to its own peculiar world of objects, thereby erasing the immanence of affectivity and substituting for it the transcendence of technological objects. It literally makes us sick, severing our relation to meaningful labor (thus alienating us from it), destroying culture, eliminating personhood, and erasing intellectual life (2012: 72). Art instead is an expression of living subjectivity and the interior pathos of life. The painter expresses his or her unique access to life and thus enables others to participate in its manifestation. Art does this particular well because it does not create objects "out there" but instead conveys the inner sensibility and affectivity of life through the aesthetic experience. Culture becomes closed down when the affectivity of life can no longer express itself. When it can no longer manifest the invisible, phenomenality itself becomes erased. Simulacra are substituted for the genuine.

Henry follows this up with his book on Kandinsky whom he calls "one of the greatest creators of all time" who was "radically innovative" (2009: 1). Abstract art reveals the very essence of the human, our interior invisible life of pathos; thus "the content of painting, of all paintings, is the Internal, the invisible life that does not cease to be invisible and remains forever in the Dark" (2009: 10). This "profusion of life" is radical subjectivity (2009: 16). The truth of art is a transformation of life, an interior truth that begins in life and expresses the true interiority, reality, and essence of the human. Henry analyzes various aspects of painting (form, point, line, plane, etc.) and argues that they all serve the manifestation of the pathos of self-affectivity. Even color is not about representation but instead conveys the inner sensation as color is experienced. Imagination is "real and subjective" and is tantamount to life itself: "The imagination is immanent, because life experiences itself in an immediacy that is never broken and never separates from itself; it is a pathos and the plentitude of an overflowing experience lacking nothing" (2009: 107–9). Art is not about "mimesis" and it does not manufacture "objects," but it is a "mode of life . . . life's own essence is present in art." This means that art is the "growth of the self" into itself and "the experience of its own being" as "enjoyment." Art intensifies and allows us to experience life's pathos (2009: 122). Art thus is transformation, resurrection, rebirth, eternal life, the sacred. It is the true reality of the entire cosmos and also our very interiority: "Why is life sacred? Because we experience it within ourselves as something we have neither posited nor willed, as something that passes through us without ourselves as its cause—we can only be and do anything whatsoever because we are carried by it." Consequently, our pathos-filled selfhood is an expression of life's passivity as "the invisible, abstract content of eternal art and painting" (2009: 127). All this, contemporary society seeks to dismiss, erase, destroy. In his diagnosis of communism and capitalism (2014), Henry similarly bemoans the "terrifying failure" and catastrophe that has devalued the individual and ushered us into "the empire of death" through the technological-economic revolution of the contemporary world. Fascism, which for Henry applies not only to Nazism, but also to a corrupted communism and a technocized capitalism, is a "monstrous process of the self-negation of the self" (2014: 46) that results in the "factual elimination of the living individual" (2014: 92). Life is "being flouted, humiliated, theoretically devalued, and set aside," yet it "continues to live" (2014: 117). Against the West's empty and "voracious" subjectivity that replaces life with the simulacra of technology and the "sinister" and "nauseating" principle of death, we must hear anew "the cry of life" (2014: 118).

Having diagnosed this dire state in his works of the late eighties and early nineties, wondering what can still "save" us, Henry proceeds in his final works to a vision of redemption. In the first pages of *Barbarism*, Henry speaks of the contemporary cultural crisis as a revolution or overturning (*bouleversement*). That is precisely the same word that he uses over and over again in his final work (2002) to speak of Christ's effect on the humans of his day. Christ's words overturn all our previous conception about life and relationships and teach us "true" life. Already in *I am the Truth*, Christ is posited as the "one who is Living" who can "save us" from "the shadow of death that is looming over the world" (2003: 275). In these final books Henry explicates his same phenomenology of life and affectivity by drawing on explicitly Christian texts, such as the Gospels. He now argues that life is God and that it is communicated by the "Arch-Son," Christ, to all livings who are "sons within the son." This is so, on the one hand, because Life as such, Absolute Life, must be Ipseity itself. On the other hand, our life is contingent and finite; we cannot manufacture it ourselves and are not its origin. Thus, it is given to us and generated within us: "I am given to myself, but it is not me myself who gives me to me" (2003b: 104). Unlike Galilean science and Heideggerian *ek-stasis*, the "Truth" of Christianity, which is not of this world, realizes that life is complete and utter immanence, pure manifestation, and self-revelation, wherein God is revealed as the source of all life (2003a: 21–32). This manifestation of the divine life occurs through Christ's self-affectivity where Life generates itself eternally and generates all livings within it. Christianity's "revolutionary character" pertains precisely to its deeply phenomenological account of the human as living, as generated from within the divine life and experiencing itself within it. Although Christianity is here employed to develop these insights, Henry is not articulating a phenomenology of religion per se, but is appropriating biblical texts to explicate his previous insights about the essence of life and its phenomenality as self-affectivity more starkly.[15] What is maybe most novel about this account is that it explicates somewhat more fully than earlier works how this life is communicated to multiple livings who all experience themselves self-affected within life but also remain separate individuals: "Every relation from one Self to another Self requires as its point of departure not this Self itself, an I (*moi*)—my own or the other's—but their common transcendental possibility, which is nothing other than the possibility of their relation itself: absolute Life" (2014: 243). Henry grapples with this question in other places (e.g., 2008: 101–34), but his account of love of neighbor and of the mystical body in these "Christian" works probably pushes it the furthest (2003a: 130–1, 185–90, 247–58; 2014: 237–52). Henry's analysis of Christianity is of a piece with his analysis of art: both portray the invisible essence of life as self-affectivity.

24.3.2 Marion: Nihilism, painting, revelation

Marion frequently mentions works of art in making his argument about givenness, but then also applies his phenomenology of givenness in order to analyze and depict aesthetic phenomena. In *Being Given* he employs a "mediocre Dutch painting" in order to show that works of art do not appear primarily as objects or as tools (i.e., they are neither *vorhanden* nor *zuhanden*), but instead have an effect or impact on the viewer (2002a: 40–53; 2011: 159–60). He also uses the aesthetic category of "anamorphosis" in order to describe how phenomena impose their phenomenality on the recipient and in some way direct the "how" of appearing. In other texts, such as *The Crossing of the Visible*, the third chapter of *In Excess*, and the important essay "What We See and What Appears," he focuses more fully on actual phenomenological analysis of art, often making a distinction between (mere) seeing and appearance as manifestation or vision. Aesthetic phenomena are not simply seen, but they explode into visibility. Indeed, they constitute a transfer from the realm of the "unseen" (*l'invu*) into that of the visible. The artist has had a vision of the "unseen" and renders it as a visible phenomenon in the work

---

[15] Henry is quite clear in these texts that he sees himself as continuing to do phenomenology not theology. He consistently speaks of the "phenomenology" of Christianity or its "phenomenality" and its "mode of manifestation (e.g., 2003a: 84–7). It is maybe also worth pointing out that "God" is certainly mentioned in *The Essence of Manifestation*, except that there it occurs primarily in the context of an explication of Fichte and Schelling (and later Meister Eckhart).

of art, which hence "increases the phenomenality of the world" (2002b: 25; 2011: 164). The painter is "the porter who filters the unseen's access to the visible, the master of every entrée onto the scene, the guardian of the limits of appearance." Thus, "the painter grants visibility to the unseen, delivering the unseen from its anterior invisibility, its shape-lessness" (2002b: 26). The artist must bear the weight of the unseen and only truly great artists are able to bear enough of it to convey it in the dazzling brilliance of a great work of art. Truth is accomplished in the painting via this transfer (2014: 197). We encounter the unseen as excessive visibility in these works; they cannot be seen only once, but we must return to them again and again (2011: 162–3). Both visible and invisible are always at play in a painting. To a certain extent the invisible becomes phenomenalized within and through the visible without necessarily becoming visible in any straightforward fashion. In the brilliance of the visible the invisible is manifested, even when it does not appear visibly. The phenomenality of the painting hence also cannot be appropriated in a concept or in a single "viewing," but gives us more than we can bear. Thus the work of art provides its own mode of phenomenality; it unveils a way of experiencing a partic-ular group of phenomena or maybe even becomes a paradigm for phenomenality itself (2014: 158). Marion also distinguishes between different types and periods of painting, depending on how they deal with the intentionality of the viewer and how conscious-ness is at work in the experience of their phenomenality. Like Henry, he chides a decline of art in contemporary culture where the viewer seeks to be in complete control over the image and to impose a specific vision upon it.[16] A great work of art, instead, imposes its own phenomenality, it appears from itself and cannot be constituted by intentionality. As in the case of Henry, Marion's analysis of art is of a piece with his larger phenomeno-logical claims.

Again as in Henry, there are significant parallels between Marion's work on aesthetics and his writings about religion. Like the artist, the philosopher of religion has access to a realm of the "unseen" from which phenomena like "charity" are phenomenalized and hence made accessible to others (2008: 74). Marion contends that, structurally speaking, a phenomenon of revelation is even more intensely saturated than a cultural, histor-ical, or aesthetic phenomenon and that it overwhelms and dazzles the recipient even more profoundly. Despite this excess, he appeals to phenomenology's commitment to appearance, manifestation, and even revelation, as legitimation for examining what is revealed even if such revealing occurs in an intense manner. The recipient must hear the call of the phenomenon, bear its weight, and phenomenalize it as a manifestation. Revelation appears as a phenomenon, as what is given to and within experience; it does not refer to theological claims about the meaning of such a phenomenon or "prove" the

---

[16] More broadly, Marion posits most of his philosophy as a response to the nihilism of contemporary culture, not as a recovery of ethical "values," but instead as concern for the "humanity of humans, the naturalness of nature, the justice of the polis, and the truth of knowledge" against their devaluation in "the dehumanization of humans for improving humanity, the systematic bleeding of nature in order to develop the economy, injustice so as to render society more efficient, the absolute empire of information-distraction in order to escape the constraints of the true" (2008: 150–1).

occurrence of a particular historical event. Marion rigorously tries to maintain this distinction by examining only what he calls the "possibility" of a "phenomenon of revelation" as it is manifested, rather than making claims about the historical "actuality" of a particular event, such as the resurrection of Christ (2002a: 367). Although he frequently uses biblical examples, he employs them for the aspects of phenomenality that appear in the accounts (such as the particular phenomenality of sacrifice in Abraham's offering of Isaac or the dazzling phenomenality of the transfiguration accounts). Religious phenomena are characterized not only by their abundance (*l'abandon*), but especially by their abandonment (*l'abandon*) in that they give themselves even more fully than other phenomena. They come to us as gifts and we experience them as such.

Has phenomenology here turned to theology? While the inspiration and particular "flavor" of the examination of religious phenomenality certainly comes from theological sources—the biblical Gospels in the case of Henry, the wider Christian tradition in the case of Marion and Falque, spirituality and mystical poetry in the case of Chrétien, the ascetic tradition in the case of Lacoste—all examine the manifestation of such phenomena in human experience: hearing the biblical word, eating and drinking the eucharistic bread and wine, sensing a call I did not generate myself. And if the possibility of the experience of a manifestation of something sacred or even "divine" within human experience is not a priori excluded, then surely such an experience would have to be characterized by a certain kind of excess or abundance that would distinguish it from something generated by imagination or illusion (whether such distinctions can be fully described or always neatly maintained is another issue). A religious experience is felt as coming from outside me (or maybe also from deeply within me), as addressing me, as beyond my control, one I do not generate or manufacture myself. It is hence an experience marked especially by reception (rather than constitution) and by a sense of inadequacy calling for a kind of abnegation (as stressed by Lacoste and Marion). The accounts of mystics in many religious traditions bear witness to such experiences. They are open to phenomenological investigation, as long as the examination focuses entirely on the phenomena *as experienced* rather than their possible attribution to a transcendent source. It is surely not per se prohibited to examine experiences that people identify as "religious" or "sacred" for their structure and meaning, as long as such examination consists only in unfolding and describing the phenomena, without attributing them to a divine origin or engaging in any apologetic measures.[17] While such experiences, just as experiences of art or other cultural phenomena, may be more complex and may be in some ways more slippery, less readily "apparent" than our interaction with everyday objects, this complexity does not as such forbid phenomenological investigation.

---

[17] As Steinbock does in his phenomenological analyses of mysticism (2007) and of the moral emotions (2014). Although his style is quite different than that of the French thinkers on which this chapter focuses and he draws much more fully on Husserl than on Heidegger, his work shows in a different manner that such more intense phenomena, even religious ones, can be examined with phenomenological tools and phenomenological insight gained about them. The work of Natalie Depraz (especially 2008) provides a further example.

More worrisome, perhaps, is the almost exclusive focus on the religious experience of Christianity (especially Roman Catholic) in the French thinkers. Far more work needs to be done to show how such phenomena are experienced in other religious traditions and whether their phenomenological investigation would uncover similar structures and characteristics or require us to adjust the descriptions provided so far. Such comparative practices might also ensure that the examination deals not just with empirical experiences limited to particular people but is a genuinely phenomenological analysis of underlying structures and shared meaning.

24.4 CONCLUSION

Contemporary French phenomenology, then, has opened new phenomenological possibilities of examining a range of hitherto unconsidered phenomena or of pushing preliminary analyses of "unapparent" phenomena further than had previously been the case. While one might certainly quibble with various aspects of their appropriation of or adjustments to the phenomenological projects that inspire them, they present various possibilities of confronting rich and complex phenomena of life, of the life of affects and emotions, of our encounter with art and culture, of our sense of the sacred or spiritual, as they are manifested in our flesh and in our everyday experience. Such phenomena are at times experienced as invisible, often as excessive and overwhelming, but they are genuinely experienced within immanence, and hence deserve phenomenological investigation. Janicaud ends his discussion in the second book on these thinkers by advocating a minimalist phenomenology for which, ironically enough, Heidegger's notion of the "unapparent" can serve as inspiration (2005: 72–5). As long as phenomenology gives up all desire to become a new first philosophy or the whole of philosophy and instead focuses on the phenomena as they are actually given in our "dwelling" in this world, then investigating the affective, hidden, invisible, even "pathic" dimensions of the "rich" phenomena of our lives becomes the very task of phenomenology (2005: 77–80). Yet, in many ways, this is exactly what Henry, Marion, and others are trying to do. Their phenomenologies invite us to explore more fully the phenomenality and the phenomena of our lives in all their intimate and abundant richness. At the same time they help us to reconsider more fully the "how" of this manifestation, its impact on the recipient of the phenomenon, and the phenomenological structures and methodology appropriate for such depiction.

REFERENCES

Alliez, É. (1995), *De l'impossibilité de la phénoménologie. Sur la philosophie française contemporaine* (Paris: J. Vrin).

Capelle, P. (ed.) (2004), *Phénoménologie et Christianisme chez Michel Henry. Les derniers écrits de Michel Henry en débat* (Paris: Cerf).

Chrétien, J.-L. (1987), *L'effroi du beau* (Paris: Cerf).

Chrétien, J.-L. (1990), *La voix nue. Phénoménologie de la promesse* (Paris: Minuit).

Chrétien, J.-L. (2002), *The Unforgettable and the Unhoped For*, translated by J. Bloechl (New York: Fordham University Press).

Chrétien, J.-L. (2003), *Hand to Hand: Listening to the Work of Art*, translated by S. E. Lewis (New York: Fordham University Press).

Chrétien, J.-L. (2004a), *The Call and the Response*, translated by A. A. Davenport (New York: Fordham University Press).

Chrétien, J.-L. (2004b), *The Ark of Speech*, translated by A. Brown (London: Routledge).

Chrétien, J.-L. (2005), *Symbolique du Corps. La traduction chrétiennes du Cantique des Cantiques* (Paris: Presses universitaires de France).

Chrétien, J.-L. (2007), *Répondre. Figures de la réponse et de la responsabilité* (Paris: Presses universitaires de France).

Chrétien, J.-L. (2010), *Reconnaissance philosophiques* (Paris: Cerf).

Courtine, J.-F. (1990), *Heidegger et la phénoménologie* (Paris: J. Vrin).

Depraz, N. (2008), *Le corps glorieux. Phénoménologie pratique de la* Philocalie *des pères du désert et des pères de l'église* (Louvain: Peeters).

Falque, E. (1999), *Le passeur de Gethsémani. Angoisse, souffrance et mort. Lecture existentielle et phénoménologique* (Paris: Cerf).

Falque, E. (2013), *Metamorphosis of Finitude*, translated by G. Hughes (New York: Fordham University Press).

Falque, E. (2014), *Le Combat amoureux. Disputes phénoménologiques et théologiques* (Paris: Hermann).

Falque, E. (2015), *God, Flesh, and Other*, translated by W. C. Hackett (Evanston, IL: Northwestern University Press).

Falque, E. (2016a), *Crossing the Rubicon: The Borderlands of Philosophy and Theology*, translated by R. Shank (New York: Fordham University Press).

Falque, E. (2016b), *The Wedding Feast of the Lamb*, translated by G. Hughes (New York: Fordham University Press).

Gondek, H.-D. and Tengelyi, L. (2011), *Neue Phänomenologie in Frankreich* (Berlin: Suhrkamp).

Greisch, J. (2002), *Le Buisson ardent et les Lumières de la Raison. L'invention de la philosophie de la religion, vol. 2: Les approches phénoménologiques et analytiques* (Paris: Cerf).

Greisch, J. (2012), *Du "non-autre" au "tout autre": Dieu et l'absolu dans les théologies philosophiques de la modernité* (Paris: Presses universitaires de France).

Hanson, J. and Kelly, M. R. (eds) (2012), *Michel Henry: The Affects of Thought* (London: Continuum).

Heidegger, M. (2012), *Four Seminars*, translated by A. J. Mitchell and F. Raffoul (Bloomington, IN: Indiana University Press).

Henry, M. (1973), *The Essence of Manifestation*, translated by G. Etzkorn (The Hague: Martinus Nijhoff).

Henry, M. (1975), *Philosophy and Phenomenology of the Body*, translated by G. Etzkorn (The Hague: Martinus Nijhoff).

Henry, M. (1983), *Marx: A Philosophy of Human Reality*, translated by K. McLaughlin (Bloomington, IN: Indiana University Press).

Henry, M. (2002), *Paroles du Christ* (Paris: Seuil).

Henry, M. (2003a), *I Am the Truth: Toward a Philosophy of Christianity*, translated by S. Emanuel (Stanford, CA: Stanford University Press).

Henry, M. (2003b), "Phenomenology of Life," *Angelaki: Journal of the Theoretical Humanities* 8/2: 97–110.

Henry, M. (2004), "Les quatres principes de la phénoménologie," in *Phénoménologie de la vie*, t.1, *De la phénoménologie* (Paris: Presses universitaires de France), 76–104.

Henry, M. (2008), *Material Phenomenology*, translated by S. Davidson (New York: Fordham University Press).

Henry, M. (2009), *Seeing the Invisible: On Kandinsky*, translated by S. Davidson (London: Continuum).

Henry, M. (2012), *Barbarism*, translated by S. Davidson (London: Continuum).

Henry, M. (2014), *From Communism to Capitalism: Theory of a Catastrophe*, translated by S. Davidson (London: Bloomsbury).

Henry, M. (2015), *Incarnation: A Philosophy of the Flesh*, translated by K. Hefty (Evanston, IL: Northwestern University Press).

Janicaud, D. et al. (2000), *Phenomenology and the "Theological Turn"* (New York: Fordham University Press).

Janicaud, D. (2005), *Phenomenology "Wide Open": After the French Debate*, translated by C. N. Cabral (New York: Fordham University Press).

Janicaud, D. (2015), *Heidegger in France*, translated by F. Raffoul and D. Pettigrew (Bloomington, IN: Indiana University Press).

Jdey, A. and Kühn, R. (eds) (2012), *Michel Henry et l'affect de l'art. Recherches sur l'esthétique de la phénoménologie matérielle* (Leiden: Brill).

Jonkers, P. and Welten, R. (eds) (2005), *God in France: Eight Contemporary Thinkers on God* (Leuven: Peeters).

Kühn, R. (2003), *Radikalisierte Phänomenologie* (Frankfurt a.M.: Peter Lang).

Lacoste, J.-Y. (1990), *Note sur le temps. Essai sur les raisons de la mémoire et de l'espérance* (Paris: Presses universitaires de France).

Lacoste, J.-Y. (2000), *Le monde et l'absence d'œuvre* (Paris: Presses universitaires de France).

Lacoste, J.-Y. (2004), *Experience and the Absolute: Disputed Questions on the Humanity of Man*, translated by M. Raferty-Skehan (New York: Fordham University Press).

Lacoste, J.-Y. (2006), *Présence et parousie* (Paris: Ad Solem).

Lacoste, J.-Y. (2008), *La phénoménalité de Dieu* (Paris: Cerf).

Lacoste, J.-Y. (2011), *Être en danger* (Paris: Cerf).

Marion, J.-L. (1991), *God without Being*, translated by T. A. Carlson (Chicago, IL: University of Chicago Press).

Marion, J.-L. (1998), *Reduction and Givenness: Investigations of Husserl, Heidegger, and Phenomenology*, translated by T. A. Carlson (Evanston, IL: Northwestern University Press).

Marion, J.-L. (2001), *The Idol and Distance: Five Studies*, translated by T. A. Carlson (New York: Fordham University Press).

Marion, J.-L. (2002a), *Being Given: Toward a Phenomenology of Givenness*, translated by J. L. Kosky (Stanford, CA: Stanford University Press).

Marion, J.-L. (2002b), *In Excess: Studies of Saturated Phenomena*, translated by R. Horner and V. Berraud (New York: Fordham University Press).

Marion, J.-L. (2004), *The Crossing of the Visible*, translated by J. K. A. Smith (Stanford, CA: Stanford University Press).

Marion, J.-L. (2006), *The Erotic Phenomenon*, translated by S. E. Lewis (Chicago, IL: University of Chicago Press).

Marion, J.-L. (2008), *The Visible and the Revealed* (New York: Fordham University Press).

Marion, J.-L. (2011), "What we see and what appears," in J. Ellenbogen and A. Tugendhaft (eds), *Idol Anxiety* (Stanford, CA: Stanford University Press), 152–68.

Marion, J.-L. (2012), *Figures de la phénoménologie. Husserl, Heidegger, Levinas, Henry, Derrida* (Paris: J. Vrin).

Marion, J.-L. (2014), *Courbet et la peinture à l'œil* (Paris: Flammarion).

Marion, J.-L. (2015), *Negative Certainties*, translated by S. E. Lewis (Chicago, IL: University of Chicago Press).

Marion, J.-L. (2017), *The Rigor of Things: Conversations with Dan Arbib* (New York: Fordham University Press).

Rogozinski, J., ed. (2011), *Michel Henry une phénoménologie radicale. Les Cahiers philosophiques de Strasbourg* 30 (Paris: J. Vrin).

Schrift, A. D. (2005), *Twentieth-Century French Philosophy: Key Themes and Thinkers* (Oxford: Blackwell).

Sebbah, F.-D. (2012), *Testing the Limit: Derrida, Henry, Levinas, and the Phenomenological Tradition*, translated by S. Barker (Stanford, CA: Stanford University Press).

Simmons, J. A. and Benson, B. E. (2013), *The New Phenomenology: A Philosophical Introduction* (London: Bloomsbury).

Steinbock, A. (2007), *Phenomenology and Mysticism: The Verticality of Religious Experience* (Bloomington, IN: Indiana University Press).

Steinbock, A. (2014), *Moral Emotions: Reclaiming the Evidence of the Heart* (Evanston, IL: Northwestern University Press).

Welten, R. (2011), *Phénoménologie du Dieu invisible. Essais et études sur Emmanuel Levinas, Michel Henry et Jean-Luc Marion* (Paris: L'Harmattan).

Wolf, K. (1999), *Religionsphilosophie in Frankreich. Der "ganz Andere" und die personale Struktur der Welt* (Munich: Wilhelm Fink Verlag).

PART III

THEMES

CHAPTER 25

....

PHENOMENOLOGICAL
METHODOLOGY

....

KARL MERTENS

"WHAT is phenomenology?" Half a century after Edmund Husserl founded phenomenology as a new philosophical approach, Maurice Merleau-Ponty (2005: vii) asks this question right at the beginning of the preface to his *Phenomenology of Perception* (*Phénoménologie de la perception*).[1] Looking back on the Phenomenological Movement,[2] he outlines a deeply ambiguous picture of phenomenology, retracing four entanglements or even paradoxes of the phenomenological method. *First*, phenomenology focuses on essences and eidetic laws; yet, it cannot neglect aspects of existence and facticity. *Second*, as a transcendental philosophy, phenomenology suspends our natural attitude; yet, in pursuing this program, it resorts to our naïve "contact with the world." *Third*, phenomenology originally understands itself as a rigorous science, i.e., a science founding every possible science; but it eventually turns out to be a science based on the pre-given life-world. *Fourth*, despite the methodological priority attributed to description, phenomenology is forced by its own investigations to enlarge its methods and to recognize, besides description, the crucial role of genetic and even constructive reflections (Merleau-Ponty 2005: vii f.). These four remarks on the ambiguities of phenomenological method point to "the unfinished nature of phenomenology" (Merleau-Ponty 2005: xxiii). Its initial methodological self-understanding is subject to constant revisions, which sometimes even follow those paths that were initially explicitly rejected.

[1] I am very indebted to Tyler Friedman who corrected my English text. In addition, regarding linguistic and philosophical critique of an earlier version of this chapter I am deeply obliged to Jörn Müller and, particularly, Michela Summa who thoroughly commented on my chapter and gave me a lot of important hints. In addition, I thank two anonymous reviewers for their critical remarks.
[2] Cf. the apt title of Herbert Spiegelberg's famous 1960 study surveying the history of phenomenological philosophy (Spiegelberg 1982). An instructive as well as short overview about the main strands of the historical developments of phenomenology can be found in Luft/Overgaard 2012: 2ff.

The present chapter aims to flesh out these inner ambiguities of the phenomenological method and to highlight their philosophical relevance. Section 25.1 offers a short recapitulation of the Husserlian understanding of the phenomenological method. Against the background of Merleau-Ponty's four remarks, the modifications concerning the phenomenological concepts of the a priori, transcendental subjectivity, constitution, and description are discussed in sections 25.2 through 25.5. These sections show how relevant ambiguities and modifications are already found in Husserl's works and how further developments occur in the work of later phenomenologists. Section 25.6 compares the phenomenological stance with the standpoint of ordinary language philosophy in order to outline some further possible developments concerning the phenomenological method, particularly in relation to language and social experience. A short conclusion will finally address the question of the unity and continuity in the sketched modifications and revisions of phenomenological self-understanding.

25.1 STARTING POINT: HUSSERL'S INITIAL PROGRAM OF PHENOMENOLOGY

Everyone who is—even only marginally—familiar with phenomenology has certainly already heard the phrase "back to the things themselves" (cf. Husserl 2006: 178, 228; 1983: 35). Yet, what does this phrase mean, besides its programmatic, and even somehow naïve, flavor? I wish to argue that Husserl's demand to return to the things themselves is strictly tied to his understanding of the phenomenological method, and particularly to four main features of such a method: (1) the appeal to evidence and intuition, (2) the first-person approach to experience, (3) the priority of description, and (4) the discovery of the intentional correlation.

First, the methodical interpretation of the things themselves is joined with the program of elucidating how the different types of objects we are interested in are originarily experienced. For Husserl, the turn to originary experience is connected with the programmatic idea that every meaning and claim to validity needs to be traced back to what he calls "evidence." In contrast to mere intention, evidence indicates the original givenness or self-givenness of something. For example, if we talk about the backside of a desk without perceiving or visualizing it, the backside is merely intended. Evidence, however, is reached if we walk around the desk and take a look at it from behind. Similarly, and beyond the sphere of perception, there is a difference between merely intending that, for instance, "$3^7 = 2187$," and bringing this statement to evidence by following the mathematical calculation. In both cases, we are confronted with the distinction between a merely signitive or symbolic intention, and a fulfilled intention. Only when the intention is fulfilled can we claim to have reached an insight into the intended state of affairs, or into how things are in themselves. Thus, in general terms the phenomenological method aims at re-establishing a genuine sense of intuition, precisely based on this idea of self-givenness, and to apply it to the different layers of experience.[3] This is emphatically pointed out in Husserl's well-known "principle of all principles," which claims "*that every originary presentive intuition is a legitimizing source of cognition, that everything originarily* (so to speak, in its 'personal' actuality) *offered to us in 'intuition' is to be accepted simply as what it is presented as being,* but also *only within the limits in which it is presented there*" (Husserl 1983: 44; see also Husserl 2006: 178, 228).

Second, any discourse about "originary experience," "self-givenness," or "intuition" already entails reference to a subject of experience, givenness, or intuition. Phenomenological display is necessarily a display *for* someone. And since the primal and direct experience I have of something is *my own* experience, another characteristic feature of the phenomenological method is the focus on such for-me-ness. For this reason, phenomenological investigations can be defined by the assumption of a *first-person perspective*: the inquiries into perception, judgment, feeling, or action are not accomplished from an external and detached point of view, but rather from the point of view of the experiencing subject, who reflects on his/her experiencing. Yet, it should be emphasized that such a first-person account does not turn phenomenology into an analysis of mere private experience and awareness. On the contrary, first-person experiences are taken as the basis for clarifying how specific kinds of experiencing (such as perception, judgment, feeling, and acting) are structured in general.

Third, phenomenology is often characterized negatively as an enterprise that brackets all unexamined presuppositions and prejudices stemming from both everyday assumptions and scientific theories. It is on account of such an idea of presuppositionless philosophy that Husserl understands phenomenology primarily as a descriptive enterprise. Without neglecting the validity and usefulness of scientific models, for instance those aimed at the prediction of future events, phenomenology questions their epistemic foundations and foundational claims. A genuine foundation of knowledge, for instance, cannot be provided by resorting to scientific or metaphysical constructions, but rather requires intuition- and evidence-based descriptions. By taking the phenomenological stance, we will thus revise fundamental prejudices stemming from the traditional account of the concept of knowledge, and particularly those regarding the skeptical challenges concerning the possibility of justifying knowledge *in general*. Yet, such challenges are embedded in a conception of knowledge based on the insuperable gap between the subject and the world which, in consequence, prevents us from making valid distinctions between, for example, hallucinations, dreams, etc., on the one hand, and insights, perceptions, etc., referring to the real world, on the other hand. Only if we assume such a concept of knowledge we will need a legitimation for the "bridge" between subjective experience and its objects. Instead, bracketing that assumption and following an inquiry based on description and evidence, we would bypass such a challenge from the very beginning.

---

[3] Concerning this broad meaning of intuition, Husserl turns also to an analysis of what he calls "categorial intuition" (cf. Husserl 2006: 271ff.).

Fourth, such a view only finds its justification if we stick to the crucial structure of intentionality as aboutness.[4] As has been emphasized (e.g., Sokolowski 1999; Moran 2000) this requires us to investigate the structures of both the object and the subject of experience as the "'dative' element in the experience, a 'to whom' of experience" (Moran 2000: 11), and to always consider them in correlation. Therefore, phenomenological inquiries investigate the originary experience *of* something. To give some simple examples: Perceiving is intentional because we perceive something. Similarly, in knowing we know something, in remembering we remember something, in imagining we imagine something, in doing we do something, in loving we love someone, etc. Moreover, considering that singular acts are always interconnected with other acts and experiences in the stream of consciousness, we can say that the experience disclosed by the phenomenological method includes every content we are aware of, that is, eventually, the whole world. Therefore, analysis of the intentional structure of consciousness has to be articulated by a twofold research focusing on the correlation between the process of consciousness and its intentional contents.

25.2 PHENOMENOLOGY AS AN EIDETIC SCIENCE AND THE PROBLEM OF FACTICITY: THE TRANSFORMATION OF THE A PRIORI

On Husserl's understanding, phenomenological descriptions are "structural" or "eidetic" descriptions aiming to deliver a priori insights. As opposed to "*a science of matters of fact*," phenomenology is for him "*a science of essences*," "an '*eidetic*' science." For instance, the phenomenological analysis of visual perception is not concerned with how human beings see a thing here and now, but rather with the general structures of seeing, which hold for every possible seeing subject. As far as cognition is concerned, phenomenology aims to shed light on the universal conditions justifying claims of truth or validity and to highlight how these conditions are grounded on universal structures of experience. Husserl's eidetic reduction is precisely supposed to respond to the quest for universal validity based on experiential givenness. The "reduction to the eidos," in other words, should allow us to focus on the general, necessary, unchangeable, and not spatiotemporally bound structures of the investigated phenomena (see Husserl 1983: xx, 7ff.; 1971: 142).

If we take a closer look at Husserl's concept of the a priori and its developments, however, we can see how the strict opposition between essences and matters of fact is

---

[4] Husserl took this central topic from Franz Brentano, who, for his part, picked it up from the medieval tradition, but gave it a new feature in the context of his phenomenological philosophy.

more subtle than the dichotomies "contingent/necessary," "temporal/supratemporal," "changeable/unchangeable," etc. might indicate. Already the introduction of the "material a priori" in the Third Logical Investigation (cf. Husserl 2006: 19ff.) shows that the meaning of eidetic laws concerning experience is always established in relation to some given content, which we can certainly vary, but never totally exclude from the analysis of experience.[5] In the analysis of "ideational abstraction" (*ideierende Abstraktion*) in the Second and Sixth Logical Investigations (cf. Husserl 2008: 235ff.; Husserl 2006: 292ff.), it becomes clear that not only individual facts require a related essence, but also essences presuppose facts (see also Husserl 1983: 7f.): As a founded act, indeed, ideational abstraction presupposes individual intuitions as the basis for grasping what is general. The concept of ideational abstraction, particularly in accounts preceding *Logical Investigations*, implies that essences are bound to the contingency of given intentional contents: An individual sensual intuition is required and functions as the basis of ideation in order to single out an aspect of the whole individual intuition in its universality. The concrete individual instance, thus, serves as an example of the essence.[6] In contrast, Husserl's later account of "eidetic variation" (*eidetische Variation*) relieves the intuition of essences from the dependency of a contingent individual intuition. Eidetic variation rather shows how essential insights can only be obtained by a series of free phantasy-modifications of what is given (cf., e.g., Husserl 1973a: 339ff.; 1969: 245ff.; 1999a: 69ff.). Thereby, what is factually given is merely assumed as an exemplification of the essence: Essences, thus, are determined by the scope of possible modifications of an exemplarily given. Thus, the synthesis of phantasy-variations is to be understood as the invariant structure of the intuition in question. The process of eidetic variation, however, is confronted with a methodical problem. Being unlimited and in principle endless, it is also open to revision. Therefore, insights into essential structures can be basically modified and revised in future variations. In this sense, we can say that facticity pervades (but not destroys) the claim for a priori insights of Husserl's phenomenological science.

The deep entanglement of eidetics and facticity comes to the fore if we consider Husserl's later account of the teleology of evidence. Emphasizing the horizonal structure of consciousness and focusing on the temporal and historical processes that underlie the formation of all sense and meaning, the later Husserl admits that evidence should not be restricted to single acts, but should rather embrace the totality of the stream of consciousness. Yet, if this is the case, self-evidence can only be taken as a (regulative) idea. As Husserl states: "Thus *evidence is a universal mode of intentionality, related to the whole life of consciousness*. Thanks to evidence, the life of consciousness has an *all-pervasive teleological structure*, a pointedness toward 'reason' and even a pervasive tendency toward it—that is: toward the discovery of correctness . . . and toward the cancelling of

---

[5] Husserl distinguishes a formal a priori from the material a priori. In both cases the analysis goes back to a pre-given individual. This is expressed in Husserl 1969: 212ff.

[6] As Rizzoli (2008: 58ff.) convincingly has shown in her subtle investigation, Husserl tries to get rid of the empiristic context of these considerations in his *Logical Investigations*, however, without being successful in every respect. Cf. Mertens 1996: 247ff.

incorrectnesses" (Husserl 1969: 160). Accordingly, evidence is not so much the starting point of phenomenological description as its task. In his *Cartesian Meditations* Husserl requires "*a first methodological principle*" as "our normative principle of evidence, which we shall apply consistently from now on" (Husserl 1999a: 13f.): "I must at all times reflect on the pertinent evidence; I must examine its 'range' and make evident to myself *how far* that evidence, how far its 'perfection', *the actual giving of the affairs themselves*, extends. Where this is still wanting, I must not claim any final validity, but must account my judgment as, at best, a possible intermediate stage on the way to final validity" (Husserl 1999a: 13). Therefore, gaining evident insights is not something that can be accomplished at a single blow, but rather something that requires the continuation of phenomenological investigation, which can never be finished.

At this point it should be also emphasized that the concepts of "fact" and "facticity" are not univocally understood by Husserl. On the one hand, we can understand facticity as the reference to mere accidental and contingent facts that may be otherwise and which are opposed to essences. Regarding this meaning of fact Husserl normally uses the terminological concept of matter of fact (*Tatsache*) (e.g., Husserl 1983: 10f.). On the other hand, however, we can also speak of a fact as something which is pregiven and cannot be further clarified, even in the essential analysis (cf., e.g., Husserl 1983: 346). This meaning of facticity can be understood as factual necessity or necessity of a *Faktum*.[7] The latter designates the kind of necessity pertaining to something that is not explicable by referring to the universal laws of reason, like the existence of the world (Husserl 1983: 102f.) or the inner structure of sensible contents focused in investigations of their material a priori. The former, however, comes into play when it is admitted that the process of phenomenological analysis itself is bound to a factual process of shaping the a priori that can be modified and revised in future investigations. Both meanings of facticity pervade the phenomenological analysis of essential structures and cannot be rejected.[8] All these considerations seem to substantiate Merleau-Ponty's first remark concerning the entanglement of eidetic inquiries and the facticity of experience. As he emphasizes, "phenomenology is the study of essences," but "is also a philosophy which puts essences back into existence" (Merleau-Ponty 2006: vii).[9]

---

[7] On this differentiation between "*Tatsache*" and "*Faktum*" as well as to the following explanation, cf. Summa 2014: 81f.; 317ff. (here the context of her investigation is summarized). In order to elucidate a fundamental problem in Hussserl's essential analysis this terminological distinction is very helpful. However, Husserl's use of these concepts, at least regarding the term *Faktum*, is unsteady (cf., e.g., Husserl 1983: 346). Regarding the two concepts of facticity pervading Husserl's analysis of essences see also Mertens 1996: 252ff.

[8] Though the formal and the material a priori both presuppose individual objects, the dependency of the essential analysis from the facticity (in both readings) has a greater impact to the material a priori. While the formal a priori takes recourse on an individual as "*anything whatever*," the material *a prori* "demands a return to *intuition* of individual examples—that is: to '*possible*' *experience*" (Husserl 1969: 213) which is more fundamentally affected by the problems of pregiven and contingent facticity.

[9] The claim to go beyond our usual experience to its necessary and essential conditions and the impossibility of getting rid of aspects of facticity is also reflected in Heidegger's connection between the concept of "the a priori" with the idea of a "genuine philosophical 'empiricism'" (Heidegger 2010: 49 n. 10).

25.3 Phenomenology as Transcendental Philosophy and the Natural Attitude: The Transformation of Transcendental Subjectivity

One of the crucial, and most debated, developments in Husserl's phenomenology concerns the turn from the act-oriented account of consciousness in the *Logical Investigations* to the transcendental reframing of the problem of phenomenological constitution in the texts written after the introduction of the transcendental reduction from around 1907 (see Husserl 1999b; 1983). Such a turn was explicitly criticized by several of Husserl's scholars, particularly coming from the Munich and the Göttingen "realist" circles.

Whereas the eidetic reduction, the suspension of existential position-taking (*epoché*), and the bracketing of both everyday and scientific prejudices were (more or less explicitly) already at play in the *Logical Investigations*, introducing the transcendental reduction leads Husserl to reframe the question of constitution. He does so by introducing the noetic-noematic correlation—i.e., roughly, the correlation between the real (*reell*) and the non-real or intentional components of intentional experience—and by emphasizing the accomplishments of pure or transcendental subjectivity. In a nutshell, the task of the transcendental reduction is to trace every transcendent meaning back to its givenness for pure consciousness, as a "believing in being" (*Seinsglaube*) or "supposing" (*Vermeinen*) of transcendent being (cf., e.g., Husserl 1983: 33f., 57ff., 63ff.). As Husserl says in commenting on the "residuum" of the reduction: "Strictly speaking, we have not lost anything but rather have gained the whole of absolute being which, rightly understood, contains within itself, 'constitutes' within itself, all worldly transcendencies" (Husserl 1983: 113).

On the basis of this turn to subjective constitution, phenomenology is also characterized as transcendental idealism, i.e., a theory that investigates every objectivity by going back to its sources in the subjectivity. The idea that transcendental subjectivity essentially "contains" the whole world as its intentional correlate seems to express the core of the phenomenological concept of intentionality.[10] It should be emphasized, however, that the leading question of this paradigm (mostly defended in *Ideas I*) is the epistemic question of validity and its foundation. In his later works, and somehow in parallel to the previously sketched increasing relevance of facticity in the essential analysis, Husserl seems to adopt the concept with a larger meaning,

---

[10] Regarding this point Sartre has emphasized Husserl's idea of an inclusion of the world (Sartre 1947).

embracing the different facets of our experience of the life-world.[11] Thereby, Husserl turns to the fundamental meaning of historical and cultural structures of the world shaped in our practical and social life. The concept of life-world is essentially connected with the aspects of "'merely subjective-relative' intuition(s)" (Husserl 1970: 125) or "everyday practical situational truths" which is, in contrast to "scientific truths," "exactly what praxis, in its particular projects, seeks and needs" (Husserl 1970: 132).[12] Despite this turn to situation and relativity, however, Husserl does not relinquish his claim for phenomenology as an ultimate science.[13] In addition, though he emphasizes the fundamental practical and social dimension of our life-world, this does not imply any dismissal of the cognitive priorities of transcendental philosophy. This becomes evident, for instance, in the projected order of analysis of the life-world as outlined in his *Crisis*. Here, Husserl primarily sketches "what is formal and general, what remains invariant in the life-world throughout all alterations of the relative" as "the universe of things, which are distributed within the world-form of space-time and are 'positional' . . . according to spatial position and temporal position" (Husserl 1970: 142; cf. 1970: 157). In the continuation of this research Husserl later turns to the fields of "kinesthetic processes," "*alteration of validity*," "*living with one another*," "reciprocal understanding," etc. (cf. 1970: 161ff.). Obviously, the guiding model of this analysis of the life-world is the experiencing subject who at first becomes aware of the world of things and, thereupon, becomes attentive to structures joined with its practical and social interests. Yet, with his phenomenological account of the experience of the life-world, Husserl somehow paves the way for phenomenological accounts that eventually deny the priority of the epistemic questions, like Heidegger's and Merleau-Ponty's.

Although Martin Heidegger, in *Being and Time* (*Sein und Zeit*) and later texts, explicitly drops the concepts of subjectivity and intentionality, substituting them with "Dasein" and "being-in-the-world" (*In-der-Welt-sein*), it is certainly not audacious to claim that his considerations pursue the phenomenological idea of intentionality as the essential structure of the self. In framing his inquiry on the basis of the threefold nature of all questioning (cf. Heidegger 2010: 4ff.), Heidegger contends that his investigation asks about being (*das Gefragte*) in order to find out the meaning of being as "what is to be *ascertained*" (*das Erfragte*). And, to this end, he argues that it is necessary to interrogate Dasein (*das Befragte*) as that particular being that is concerned with its own being, and thus with the question of being in general. Accordingly, Heidegger aims to answer his question of being (*Seinsfrage*) by stressing that we ourselves are characterized by the essential possibility of shaping an understanding of being (2010: 11).

---

[11] Heidegger had already used the term "life-world" in his early Freiburg lectures from 1921/2 before the concept was prominently introduced by Husserl in the *Crisis* (cf., for instance, Heidegger 1985: 96, 115, 172).

[12] Heidegger also emphasizes the connection between "life-world" and its situational and factual character (cf. Heidegger 1985: 172, 96).

[13] This point is a topic of section 25.4.

To what extent does Dasein have an understanding of being? It can be argued that an understanding of the meaning of being is implicit in any utterance containing a copula, such as "Peter is a schemer," and even in utterances making less explicit existential claims, such as "the dilapidated house collapses." Yet, not only linguistic utterances entail some understanding of a meaning of being. For Heidegger, the implicit understanding of being underlies our handling things and acting with others. Using a hammer, we have already implicitly understood "the *what-for* [*Wozu*] of the hammer" (2010: 69). Such a practically oriented meaning of being is the existential structure of a "useful thing" (*Zeug*), which Heidegger designates as "ready-to-hand" or "handiness" (*Zuhandenheit*). Similarly, while dealing with others, Dasein is guided by a particular understanding of being called "being-with" (*Mitsein*). If we take a look at such characterizations of our primary understanding of being it becomes evident that Heidegger is geared to the field of our behaving and acting with things and others. In both cases, this understanding is prior to the one expressed by the pure theoretical stance, focused on what is "present-to-hand" or "objective presence" (*vorhanden/Vorhandenheit*), which, according to Heidegger, expresses a derivative understanding of being. As engaged with things and others, Dasein is fundamentally being-in-the-world: any attempt to separate Dasein from the world, or any account of "pure" consciousness is doomed to failure: "The clarification of being-in-the-world showed that a mere subject without a world 'is' not initially and is also never given. And, thus, an isolated I without the others is in the end just as far from being given initially" (2010: 113).

Merleau-Ponty's concept of "*être au monde*" (being toward the world)[14] may be seen as an attempt to continue Husserl's phenomenology of the life-world by taking up Heidegger's essential insight into the necessity of what could be called a practical turn. However, Merleau-Ponty does not follow Heidegger in his final claim "that Dasein is initially and for the most part *together with* the 'world' that it takes care" which characterizes the existential structure of "falling" (*Verfallen*) (Heidegger 2010: 169). According to Heidegger, falling is the reason why our usual and everyday life prevents the possibility of an authentic understanding of being. Whereas, due to the sketched structure of "inauthenticity" (*Uneigentlichkeit*) (see, e.g., 2010: 169), Heidegger's philosophical enterprise is directed to overcome our everyday understanding of being, Merleau-Ponty's philosophical enterprise is not aimed at opposing authenticity to inauthenticity, but rather consists in the theoretical reevaluation of our practical understanding of being in everyday life. Above all, Merleau-Ponty's original contribution consists in the emphasis on the bodily character of consciousness and subjectivity.

Tying in with Husserl's reflections on the living body (and in contrast to Heidegger), Merleau-Ponty thoroughly investigates the bodily dimension of our being toward the world as a third dimension between pure subjectivity and mere objectivity. In so doing, he aims to overcome the complementary objectivating assumptions of both materialism

---

[14] Cf., for instance, Merleau-Ponty 2005: XII, 94; cf. 2012: 84. The translators, Colin Smith and Donald A. Landes, here unfortunately use the Heideggerian term "being in the world." However, Landes also translates with being "in and toward the world" (Merleau-Ponty 2012: xxiv).

and intellectualism. As opposed to both lines of thought, Merleau-Ponty suggests that an adequate account of the living body needs to pinpoint the particular intentionality of bodily experience in the context of our practical life.[15] In consequence, every analysis of consciousness and subjectivity needs to take seriously the fact that bodily agents and perceivers are essentially situated in a pre-given context, that they are practically interested in answering the challenges of their situation. This becomes clear if we consider Merleau-Ponty's analysis of our experience of spatiality. Here he stresses that, for example, a glass of water does not stand 156 or 45 cm away from an agent who wants to drink it. Rather, the glass is too far, too near or optimally distant vis-à-vis the bodily structure of the practically interested individual. In contradistinction to the "*spatiality of position*" (*spatialité de position*), which is based on the objective measure of distances, the spatiality that frames the possibility of action and affection of a bodily subject is the "*spatiality of situation*" (*spatialité de situation*) (Merleau-Ponty 2005: 115).

We can now elucidate the second tension identified by Merleau-Ponty: transcendental phenomenology is certainly not engaged with the usual—i.e., everyday or scientific—judgements about being. However, phenomenology intends to clarify the sense of our natural and naïve attitude disclosing the presuppositions of our everyday experience, which mostly operate on the practical level. Given that our experience is in principle open, that it can in principle proceed further and further in an unlimited way, transcendental analysis itself is turned into an enterprise that cannot be fully accomplished once and for all. Therefore, Husserl can speak of his investigations as addressing "transcendental experience." In consequence, because transcendental subjectivity is the constitutional source of all worldly experience, Heidegger and Merleau-Ponty can turn to the phenomenological subject as "being-in-the-world" or "being toward the world."

25.4 PHENOMENOLOGY AS RIGOROUS SCIENCE AND THE PROBLEM OF LIFE-WORLD: THE TRANSFORMATION OF THE PHENOMENOLOGICAL CONCEPT OF CONSTITUTION

In a famous article, published in "Logos" in 1911, Husserl outlines his program of philosophy as a rigorous science (Husserl 1987: 3ff.). Rigorous science does not mean exact science. It rather means a science in *sensu stricto*, i.e., a science which has to legitimate

---

[15] Taking recourse to the bodily character of our existence may be seen as the basic insight of recent attempts to bring phenomenology into dialogue with philosophy of mind and cognitive science. See, for instance, Petitot, Varela, Pachoud, and Roy 1999; Gallagher and Zahavi 2008; Schmicking and Gallagher 2010.

and ground all other sciences (cf., 1987: 57; Husserl 1970: 197). Husserl never dismisses such a view. This is also the case when he, as mentioned above, in his later works progressively reframes phenomenology as a science of the life-world. Both aims—philosophy as an ultimate science and as investigation of life-world—should rather be considered as connected. Hence, the task of transcendental phenomenology is ultimately to trace back the life-world to its constitutional grounds in transcendental subjectivity, i.e., to clarify the subjective conditions of possibility of every meaning relevant in our everyday life as well as in science. By this, phenomenology is developed as a transcendental philosophy "which, in opposition to prescientific and scientific objectivism, goes back to knowing subjectivity as the primal locus of all objective formations of sense and ontic validities, undertakes to understand the existing world as a structure of sense and validity" (Husserl 1970: 99). While Husserl in his static phenomenology analyzes how the respective sense appears in acts of consciousness and how it is presented (e.g., Husserl 1983: 94), "harmoniously 'made known', 'legitimated', 'rationally' determined" (1983: 207) in the subjective experience, in his later philosophy the concept of constitution is connected with the idea that every sense formation traces back to "meaning-conferring accomplishment(s)" (*sinngebende Leistungen*) (e.g., Husserl 1970: 206) of a temporal genesis, i.e., a specific history of consciousness.[16] However, independent of these developments and modifications, Husserl adheres to a clear unidirectional order of transcendental constitution, according to which the field of subjective experience is the source of every objective meaning.

While attempting to achieve this program, however, Husserl is confronted with a fundamental difficulty, which becomes manifest if we consider an essential ambiguity in Husserl's concept of the life-world. As just mentioned, for Husserl, the inquiry into the life-world refers back to the inquiry into transcendental subjectivity. Accordingly, transcendental subjectivity is the constitutional ground of the life-world. However, the assumption of such a linear foundation relation oscillates when Husserl—somehow paradoxically—tries to consider how the accomplishments of transcendental subjectivity *bring about* the life-world as a *pre-given* world. Thereby he speaks of "the universal accomplishing life in which the world comes to be as existing for us constantly in flowing particularity, constantly 'pregiven' to us" (Husserl 1970: 145). Thus, the life-world turns out to be both the pre-given ground for the constitution of our daily experiences and scientific practices as well as a result of transcendental constitution.

This tension ties in with the development of some concrete problems in Husserl's phenomenology. Thinking about perception, for example, Husserl tries to show how the experience of tridimensional objects is only possible thanks to the kinesthetic experience of a bodily subject. In doing so, he needs to already presuppose the living body and its spatial movements and orientations, and to include them into his analysis of transcendental constitution. Yet, this is in clear tension with the constitutional order, from which we should also take the body as a product of constitution (Husserl 1997: 129ff.). Similar

---

[16] To a clear and short overview about genetic phenomenology cf. Lohmar 2012.

problems challenge Husserl's theory of intersubjectivity: The egological approach in the Fifth Cartesian Meditation (Husserl 1999a: 89ff.) turns out to prevent an adequate analysis of intersubjectivity; this forces Husserl to consider reciprocal constitutional lines between ego and other egos from the very beginning.

Despite recognizing the temporality of consciousness, the constitutive role of the body (cf. Husserl 1989), and intersubjectivity as the true source of constitution (cf. Husserl 1973b), in his later phenomenology Husserl shies away from the methodologically required consideration, i.e., from evaluating whether and how constitutive consciousness itself must be understood as determined by its constitutional results.[17] On the one hand, Husserl does not admit that subjectivity itself is also determined by worldly facticity (for instance, by our bodily or social existence). Following this line, the program of tracing every formation of sense or validity back to subjective sources must at least be completed, or otherwise corrected, by the idea of a mutual constitutional direction between subject and object, subjective experience and worldly existence, consciousness and facticity, etc. On the other hand, Husserl does not draw the consequence that the factual, and even the situational and relative character distinctive of our life-world as a practical and social world affects the claim concerning the validity of the constitutional analyses. However, this would be the case if transcendental constitution is also grounded on facts in the previously sketched double meaning as necessary pregiven *Fakta* as well as *Tatsachen* that could be otherwise. The decisive step is taken later by Husserl's successors, again particularly by Heidegger and Merleau-Ponty.

Heidegger refers to Dasein as being-in-the-world by abandoning the constitutional linearity Husserl pursued in his transcendental phenomenology. If being-in-the-world characterizes Dasein, there is no reason to establish any asymmetry between *constituens* and *constitutum*. The structures of Dasein are determined by the world and vice versa. Similarly, assuming bodily existence as the starting point of his phenomenology, Merleau-Ponty primarily addresses those experiences that in Husserl tend to be obscured by the emphasis on transcendental constitution. Consequently, he stresses how the practical orientation of bodily subjectivity turns out to be tied to intercorporality, and how this makes bodily experience social through and through.

Against this background, the third tension mentioned by Merleau-Ponty can now be elucidated. It points out the ambiguity between the phenomenological self-understanding as a rigorous science and its interests in the life-world as the ground for all possible experience and cognition. On the one hand, clarifying the origins of knowledge in subjectivity as originary experience, phenomenology can neither pick up any concept of positive sciences, nor make use of the concepts available in our everyday life. In consequence, transcendental phenomenology must be realized by investigations of how objective meanings and validities of science as well as of our life-world are shaped in consciousness. On the other hand, if we understand the life-world as the sphere of

---

[17] In contrast with this assessment, Merleau-Ponty interprets Husserl's reflection in his *Ideas II* as a fundamental change in Husserl's concept of transcendental phenomenology (Merleau-Ponty 1964).

originary experience, i.e., as the basis of both everyday and scientific knowledge, phenomenology just becomes a rigorous science by going back to the constitutional accomplishments of our life-world experience. This means that we have to analyze how facticities of our life-world are sources of objective meanings and validities too.

25.5 Phenomenology between Description and Construction: The Transformation of the Concept of Phenomenological Reflection

In addition, the idea of a phenomenological reflection claiming to provide a direct and impartial description of the structures of consciousness gradually turns out to be problematic.[18] This again becomes clear if we compare Husserl's earlier and later considerations about reflection. In his *Ideas I* Husserl writes: "The kind of being belonging to mental processes is such that a seeing regard of perception can be directed quite immediately to any actual mental process as an originary living present. This occurs in the form of '*reflection*,' which has the remarkable property that what is seized upon perceptually in reflection is characterized fundamentally not only as something which exists and endures while it is being regarded perceptually but also as something which *already existed before* this regard was turned to it" (Husserl 1983: 98). Reflection, thus, does not essentially change the reflected consciousness.

In fact, Husserl weakens this optimistic view by conceding that there is an unavoidable difference between reflecting and reflected consciousness or subjectivity. He admits that reflecting is essentially performed as a recollection of the experience in question, always coming too late and somehow reifying or even modifying the primary consciousness: "Natural reflection alters the previously naïve subjective process quite essentially; this process loses its original mode, 'straightforward', by the very fact that reflection makes an object out of what was previously a subjective process but not objective" (Husserl 1999a: 34). However, this concession does not elicit a fundamental self-critique: Although we cannot gain direct access to the reflecting subject as the source of every reflection, we can demonstrate the identity of the reflecting and the reflected subject by an iterative continuation of higher-order reflections. What is thematically captured in a higher-order reflection is just the structure of the non-thematic consciousness of the lower-order reflection (cf. Husserl 1959: 89ff.).

---

[18] The following considerations are developed in a slightly different context in Mertens 2012: 170ff.

This conciliatory conclusion can be questioned. This becomes evident by looking at a further revision of the phenomenological method, which can take two directions, leading to what may be called a (1) hermeneutic or (2) constructive phenomenology.

(1) The leading idea in the hermeneutic transformation of phenomenology is outlined in the famous §7 of Heidegger's *Being and Time*. Here, Heidegger explicitly takes up the program of phenomenology as a reflection "'to the things themselves!'" (Heidegger 2010: 26). Yet, different from Husserl, for Heidegger this phrase should be reassessed on the basis of what resonates in the two parts of the concept "phenomeno-logy." Initially referring to the rather unproblematic meaning of "phenomenon" as what shows itself (2010: 27), Heidegger soon emphasizes that phenomenon (or what appears) might be taken to be opposed to what truly is. "Appearing," indeed, also means *seeming*; "manifestation" can also imply concealment. The possibility of concealing or covering-up, in other words, is grounded in the meaning of *phenomenon* (2010: 27). Regarding the suggested "possibility of covering up" (*Möglichkeit des Verdeckens*) (2010: 32), particularly in the form of "'dissimulation'" (*Verstellung*) (2010: 34), Heidegger argues that the task of phenomenology is "to let what shows itself be seen from itself, just as it shows itself from itself" (2010: 32). Elaborating on this, Heidegger arrives at his hermeneutic turn of the phenomenological method. This is mirrored in his understanding of the second half of the word "phenomeno-logy": the concept of "logos," which Heidegger interprets by conjoining *aphophansis* with "letting something be seen." Given the possibility of concealment, the task of phenomenology is obviously dependent on a particular activity which goes behind the appearing phenomena. Therefore, phenomenology cannot just describe what we find in our everyday life but is based on particular efforts of understanding which allow a description of what can be seen. Based on this double understanding, phenomenology is considered as an interpretation (*Auslegung*).

However, since in this context misunderstanding is always possible and cannot be excluded from the beginning, the problem arises of how we are able to differentiate between understanding and misunderstanding, adequate interpretation and inadequate interpretation. Heidegger picks up this problem in his distinction between inauthentic and authentic understanding. According to him, we cannot avoid beginning the analysis with our usual implicit understanding of everyday life. Assuming this tension, and in view of the possibility of dissimulation, the methodological path from the usual to the final (phenomenological or ontological) understanding takes a negative character. Therefore, the understanding of Dasein Heidegger is looking for essentially consists in avoiding our usual self-interpretation. Criterion for this difference between a self-understanding which must be avoided and the desired one is the answer to the question as to whether Dasein is following the tendency of falling (Verfallen) like in everyday understanding or capturing the own existence in its character of mineness or "*always-being-my-own-being*" (*Jemeinigkeit*) (2010: 42). Since the initial everyday understanding does not show the things themselves as they are, the understanding sought for, which grounds the initial understanding, has to be stressed against the tendencies of typical inauthentic understanding.

Heidegger's hermeneutic turn of phenomenology was further developed by Hans-Georg Gadamer in his *Truth and Method* (*Wahrheit und Methode*). The starting point of Gadamer's systematic reflection is the circularity of understanding, which was already stressed by Heidegger.[19] Like Heidegger, Gadamer holds that every understanding is guided by prejudices, i.e., by implicit contexts and horizons. Rather than being a *circulus vitiosus*, the circularity should be understood as the process of back and forth between the parts and the totality, which is the only process apt to reach understanding. Yet, Gadamer departs from Heidegger in the explication of the structure of the intended progress of understanding. Taking up a Husserlian concept, Gadamer speaks about understanding as a process of probation (*Bewährung*).[20] "Probation" is a pragmatic category not aiming at truth or falsity, authenticity or inauthenticity, but rather at success, fertility, appropriateness, etc. Understanding has to start with prejudices concerning the meaning of the whole topic in question. However, the guiding ideas or schemes of understanding can be reviewed by grasping the meaning of its parts. In consequence, the initial understanding may be confirmed or corrected on the basis of pragmatic reasons. Gadamer mentions two prominent possibilities of such a correction, particularly of texts: the examination of the matter in question and the openness to other opinions (cf. Gadamer 1991: 268f.). Considering that every understanding refers to a topic and that the process of understanding is engaged in a social context, this structure may be easily transferred to other kinds of understanding. Although we cannot reach any ultimate understanding, the issue-related and social references offer instances that may function as criteria for confirmations, modifications, and revisions in the process of understanding.[21]

(2) Another way to answer the problem of phenomenological reflection consists in picking up constructive aspects in the phenomenological description. This is precisely the topic of Merleau-Ponty's fourth remark: phenomenological reflection cannot avoid reifying and therefore altering reflecting subjectivity.[22] In contrast to Husserl, Merleau-Ponty rejects the possibility of grasping the unreflected appearance of consciousness by phenomenological reflection. He emphasizes rather the productive and constructive character of phenomenological reflection: "it appears to itself in the light of a truly

---

[19] Regarding the following, see Gadamer 1991: 265ff.

[20] The English translation uses the term "confirmation" which corresponds to the German *Bestätigung* (cf. Gadamer 1991: 267).

[21] The hermeneutic modifications of phenomenology are not limited to understanding texts or cognitive positions but concern above all our behaving and acting existence. The explicative power of hermeneutics in this field is demonstrated, for instance, by Ricœur's (1966) reflection on the practical sphere in his early work *The Voluntary and the Involuntary* (*Le volontaire et l'involontaire*).

[22] In *The Transcendence of the Ego* (*La transcendence de l'Ego*) Sartre takes up the classical problem of phenomenological reflection and comes to the negative conclusion that the reflecting consciousness cannot reach the unreflected thinking without modification (Sartre 2004: 11). The ego merely arises as an object in reflection, being a transcendent object amongst others, more precisely a psychic or psychophysic ego (2004: 4f.). However, Sartre tries to overcome the problem of reflection, namely of how it is possible to grasp the reflecting structure itself, by having recourse to an unreflected, absolute, non-positional, and non-egological consciousness.

creative act (*une véritable création*), of a changed structure of consciousness" (Merleau-Ponty 2005: xi). What is disclosed by reflection cannot simply coincide with pre-reflective consciousness. This consideration lies at the heart of the idea that thematizing subjectivity is the creation of subjectivity.

However, Merleau-Ponty recognizes that, from a phenomenological point of view, a certain understanding of construction should be criticized. "The real has to be described, not constructed or formed" (2005: xi). Therefore, he is confronted with the task of making intelligible to what extent constructive reflection may also be called descriptive. The creative aspect of reflective constitution must be distinguished from scientific construction, which is *merely* evaluated by its explanatory power, independent of the question whether the *explanans* is also understandable from the perspective of a participant in the investigated process. Take, for instance, the explanation of phenomena of warmth and cold by going back to the concept of molecular movements: In this context, there is no possibility of a meaningful speech from the point of view of a perceiving subject as a participant. Instead, phenomenological construction must be both evaluated by its explanatory power, *and* understandable from the standpoint of the reflecting subject involved in the analyzed experience. However, following the sketched critique, this is only possible insofar as phenomenological reflection uncovers the involved subject in its finally endless effort to reflectively capture unreflected consciousness: "Reflection is truly reflection only if it is not carried outside itself, only if it knows itself as reflection-on-an-unreflective-experience, and consequently as a change in structure of our existence" (2005: 72).

The reason for this reciprocal modification of the descriptive and the constructive character of phenomenological reflection is that reflecting subjects are embodied and engaged in their world. This follows from the above-mentioned problem of constitution, the unity of *constituens* and *constitutum* which leads to a fundamental dependency of the transcendental subject's accomplishments from its worldly existence. In consequence, self-reflection is always bound to a given situation and changes if it takes place in a new situation, which also implies that there cannot be any ultimate end to the reflective process. All reflection is possibly subject to corrections, modifications, and revisions. Following Husserl, Merleau-Ponty therefore highlights that phenomenology is "a dialogue or infinite meditation, and, insofar as it remains faithful to its intention, never knowing where it is going" (2005: xxiii).

Although some references to constructive phenomenology can be found in Husserl's later thought (cf., for instance, Husserl 1959: 456, 504), there is no doubt that, even here, Husserl remains committed to the fundamental relevance of description as the decisive method of phenomenology. Therefore, Merleau-Ponty traces the provocative speech of "constructive phenomenology" not to Husserlian phenomenology but rather to Fink's Sixth Cartesian Meditation (Merleau-Ponty 2005: viii, n. 2). But independently of the question of historical forerunners, the reception of the concept of construction is suggested by the systematical problems of phenomenological reflection.

25.6. Phenomenology between Pre-linguistic and Linguistic Analysis: The Transformation of the Phenomenological Concept of Originary Experience

Let me finally turn to some remarks concerning phenomenology and analytic philosophy, particularly the philosophy of ordinary language. Although these traditions are often regarded as methodological antagonists, mainly due to the opposition between a linguistic turn in analytic philosophy and the inquiry into pre-linguistic experience in phenomenology, there are crucial affinities and methodological complementarities between them.

In general, the linguistic turn is associated with an account of the publicity of language. Phenomenology, at least in its Husserlian formulation, is instead bound to the subjective stance, even when the discussion of language is concerned. Thus, in *Experience and Judgement* and *Formal and Transcendental Logic*, Husserl pursues the idea of a phenomenological foundation of predicative judgments by going back to its sources in the sphere of a pre-predicative, i.e., non-linguistic, experience.

However, if we maintain the inseparable relation of *constituens* and *constitutum*, this clear phenomenological positioning shatters, being instead itself also affected by the constituted phenomena, language is not merely constituted in a pre-linguistic subjective experience but becomes a dimension of the originary subjective experience. Therefore, assuming that the constitutional analysis is concerned with constituted intentionality, it is unavoidable for the phenomenological investigation to take into account from the beginning both the linguistic and the public character of originary experience. This may be shown already in relation to some aspects of Husserl's thought. In his program the relation between the analysis of consciousness and linguistic expression initially appears to be one-sided: starting with the sphere of pre-linguistic consciousness, phenomenology aims at clarifying our linguistically expressed judgements. However, it is the problem of metaphorical speech in particular that motivates a critical rethinking of this rough concept. Even if Husserl tends to preserve the fundamental dependency of language on consciousness, there are a few remarkable passages that possibly undermine this picture. To take an example, in a manuscript written in the context of the revision of the Sixth Logical Investigation, Husserl critically reflects on locutions designating "the linguistic expression" as "a linguistic dress for the associated thought" and—this is worth mentioning—he characterizes this view as a "prejudice" which must be avoided. In contrast, he sketches the program of a phenomenological analysis starting with a "linguistic analysis" (*Sprachanalyse*) that proceeds as an analysis of thinking and of its intuitional sources (Husserl 2005: 20ff., my translation). Without abandoning his program of the fundamental meaning of pre-linguistic intentional evidence, Husserl obviously concedes that linguistic expressions have their own power.

The distinct avowal of the priority of the intuitional account begins to totter in the philosophy of Merleau-Ponty. In the chapter "The Body as Expression, and Speech" (Merleau-Ponty 2005: 202ff.) he stresses the interdependency of the intuitional and linguistic account. It is Merleau-Ponty's decisive thesis that speech is in itself meaningful. Moreover, like gestural behavior, speaking is bodily anchored in a social world expressing and communicating to others an attitude toward a situation we are confronted with.[23] In this context, Merleau-Ponty also emphasizes the productivity of speech. In speaking we are able to find and shape our thoughts. "Thus speech, in the speaker, does not translate ready-made thought, but accomplishes it" (Merleau-Ponty 2005: 207). In addition, speech does not simply merge into thinking; for thinking exceeds speaking too. This may be noticed when we try to express a new idea for the first time. In this case, we usually are able to distinguish between adequate and inadequate attempts to express the idea. This could not be the case if speaking entirely shaped our thinking. In short, there is a difference between saying and thinking that cannot be eliminated.

The twofold relation between pre-linguistic and linguistic experience may be seen as an essential structure of a *linguistically reflected phenomenological account*. However, if a philosophical account claims that every meaning and sense is *exclusively* and *entirely* determined by language, this enterprise may not be called phenomenological anymore. For, even if all human experience was permeated by language, from a phenomenological point of view the requirement to go back to *subjective* experience is only meaningful as long as there are at least aspects in our experience which cannot be *completely* understood in linguistic terms. This may be briefly sketched by taking a look at Jacques Derrida. In his intensive reflection on Husserl's supplement to the *Crisis* about the origin of geometry, Derrida, similar to Merleau-Ponty, reflects on the bodily character of speech and writing: "As the process of that essential and constitutive capacity for embodiment, language is also where every absolutely ideal object (i.e., where truth) is factually and contingently embodied" (Derrida 1989: 92). Rather than being independent of the world, meaning is bound to the factual world. In such considerations Derrida's path to his later philosophy, which emphasizes the constitutive role of signs,[24] is prepared by the idea of "the possibility of truth's disappearance" (1989: 93). However, in contrast to his later philosophy of "*différance*," which rejects the possibility of taking recourse to primary presence, in his commentary on Husserl's manuscript, Derrida preserves the phenomenological idea of primary presence maintaining that "alterity of the absolute origin

---

[23] In his later work Merleau-Ponty stresses the priority of language even more. Since we cannot go behind language it is not a medium but something like a being in which thinking takes place (see Merleau-Ponty 1960: 54).

[24] See, for example, Derrida 1973. Such considerations are decisive for Michel Foucault's (1972) post-phenomenological reflections regarding the order of discourse.

structurally appears in *my Living Present*" and that "it can appear and be recognized only in the primordiality of something like *my Living Present*" (cf. 1989: 150ff.; esp. 153).

Taking into account the constitutional role of language is essentially joined with a turn to the public sphere because linguistic understanding presupposes social communication. Therefore, the linguistic turn requires the methodological transition from the first-person singular to the first-person plural, from the I to the We. This may be seen as a fundamental opening to a social account in phenomenology. Again, the origins of this development can be traced to Husserl's methodological considerations. Without giving up his egological understanding of consciousness, in a supplement to the second part of his *Lectures on First Philosophy* (1923–4), Husserl clearly dismisses the psychological and solipsistic interpretation of transcendental subjectivity as a dangerous prejudice (Husserl 1959: 432ff.). Phenomenology does not claim to be an ingenious conception of only one philosopher, which is finished once and forever. In contrast, phenomenology is conceived as an in principle uncompletable "working philosophy" (*Arbeitsphilosophie*) that is open to continuation on the individual as well as on the social level.

On such a basis, the affinities between the phenomenological project and the project of ordinary language philosophers should become clearer. Both philosophical enterprises are interested in an analysis of general features that are part of our public or intersubjective experience. Regarding our common experiences, they use our public language and reflect upon it. Thus, even in taking the subjective or the first-person attitude, phenomenology relies on the public stance, grammatically expressed by using the first-person plural in phenomenological analysis or by taking the first-person singular in an exemplary meaning. Following this line, the programmatic self-understanding of prominent representatives of ordinary language philosophy is not directed against an adequate self-understanding of the phenomenological enterprise. In contrast, just as phenomenologists may base their considerations on reflections about our use of language,[25] analytical philosophers may use linguistic analysis in order to sharpen our awareness of phenomena. Regarding the latter, John L. Austin has characterized his enterprise of linguistic analysis also as a " 'linguistic phenomenology' " (Austin 1979: 182).

These remarks on the intersubjective and common background of phenomenological inquiries are to be understood in a rather general way, indicating a socially shared atmosphere. This general approach changes if we pick up the bodily dimension as the fundamental character of subjectivity. With this move phenomenological analysis turns to take into account both the social accessibility and the individual diversification of our experience and understanding. On the one hand, since bodily existence is always already embedded in a social atmosphere, the problem of solipsism vanishes (Merleau-Ponty 2005: 408f.). On the other hand, however, social understanding remains confronted with a fundamental opacity apparent in the possibilities

---

[25] Beside passages such as Husserl's aforementioned reflection, a prominent example may be found in Heidegger's analysis of the use of the German term "*man*" ("they") (Heidegger 2010: 122ff.).

of misunderstanding and deception. Such opacity is also bound to bodily existence, that of others as well as my own. Considering this consequence of the embodiment of consciousness there is no priority of my subjectivity compared to the subjectivity of others (cf. 2005: 411). In such a duality, social experience can only be characterized as an essentially communicative experience, obtaining its meaning through reciprocal understanding and misunderstanding.[26]

* * *

Looking back at the analysis developed in this chapter, it seems extremely difficult to define a genuinely phenomenological methodological account. Considering the outlined methodological ambiguities it seems impossible to characterize the phenomenological enterprise. However, if we follow the *fil rouge* in the sketched movements within the phenomenological method, there is a central circuit in all variations: the claim to go back to our originary experience in its double aspect. On the one hand, by referring to our *experience* the phenomenological method requires us to take what we are familiar with (e.g., in terms of practical, social, perceptual, or aesthetic experience) into account. While doing phenomenology, nobody will discover unknown objects like hitherto unknown organisms, atoms, stars, or far-flung structures of our existence. If phenomenology cannot be traced back to what we encounter in our everyday life, there must be something wrong. On the other hand, phenomenology does not simply tell us what everybody already knows. Going back to *originary* experience is not simply referring to everyday experience. Therefore, phenomenology is quite an arduous enterprise demanding—after all—a specific training in taking a quite artificial attitude to our usual experience. Husserl thus is right in stressing the unnatural character of phenomenological experience when he says: "The source of all such difficulties lies in the unnatural direction of intuition and thought which phenomenological analysis requires" (Husserl 2008: 170).

Hans Blumenberg convincingly expressed this twofold structure of phenomenology by pointing out that philosophy, and particularly phenomenology, cannot astonish us but rather aims at an "increase and focusing of attention." "What it would have to bring about is a gentle forbearance with someone who does not tell us anything beyond what we largely could have said ourselves, if not mentioned as already said once. It also concedes forbearance to itself if it has just overlooked what could have been seen by a little bit more effort because it was seen some other time." Following this line, according to Blumenberg, it is the particular task of phenomenology "to save the phenomena from being overlooked and forgotten, from being despised and explained away as irrelevant" (Blumenberg 2002: 190, my translation).

---

[26] The mediation of the analytic and phenomenological tradition has become a topic of increasing relevance in recent decades. Cf., as paradigmatical, e.g., recent publications like Bell, Cutrofello, and Livingston (2016) and Rinofner-Kreidl and Wiltsche (2016).

References

Austin, J. L. (1979), *Philosophical Papers*, ed. by J. O. Urmson and G. J. Warnock, 3rd edition (Oxford: Oxford University Press).

Bell, J. A., Cutrofello, A., and Livingston P. M. (eds) (2016), *Beyond the Analytic–Continental Divide: Pluralist Philosophy in the Twenty-First Century* (New York: Routledge).

Blumenberg, H. (2002), *Zu den Sachen und zurück*, ed. by M. Sommer (Frankfurt a.M.: Suhrkamp).

Derrida, J. (1973), *Speech and Phenomena and Other Essays on Husserl's Theory of Signs*, translated by D. B. Allison (Evanston, IL: Northwestern University Press).

Derrida, J. (1989), *Edmund Husserl's Origin of Geometry: An Introduction*, translated, with a preface and afterword, by J. P. Leavey, Jr. (Lincoln, NE: University of Nebraska Press).

Foucault, M. (1972), *L'ordre du discours* (Paris: Gallimard).

Gadamer, H.-G. (1991), *Truth and Method*, translated and revised by J. Weinsheimer and D. G. Marshall, 2nd, revised edition (New York: Crossroad Publishing).

Gallagher, S. and Zahavi, D. (2008), *The Phenomenological Mind: An Introduction to Philosophy of Mind and Cognitive Science* (London: Routledge).

Heidegger, M. (1985), *Phänomenologische Interpretationen zu Aristoteles. Einführung in die phänomenologische Forschung*. Gesamtausgabe Band 61 (Frankfurt a. M.: Klostermann).

Heidegger, M. (2010), *Being and Time*, translated by J. Stambaugh, revised and with a foreword by D. J. Schmidt (Albany, NY: SUNY Press).

Husserl, E. (1959), *Erste Philosophie (1923/24). Zweiter Teil: Theorie der phänomenologischen Reduktion*, Husserliana 8, ed. R. Boehm (The Hague: Martinus Nijhoff).

Husserl, E. (1969), *Formal and Transcendental Logic*, translated by D. Cairns (The Hague: Martinus Nijhoff).

Husserl, E. (1970), *The Crisis of European Sciences and Transcendental Phenomenology: An Introduction to Phenomenological Philosophy*, translated by D. Carr (Evanston, IL: Northwestern University Press).

Husserl, E. (1971), *Ideen zu einer reinen Phänomenologie und phänomenologischen Philosophie. Drittes Buch: Die Phänomenologie und die Fundamente der Wissenschaften*, Husserliana 5, ed. by M. Biemel (The Hague: Martinus Nijhoff).

Husserl, E. (1973a), *Experience and Judgment: Investigations in a Genealogy of Logic*, translated by J. S. Churchill and K. Ameriks (London: Routledge and Kegan Paul).

Husserl, E. (1973b), *Zur Phänomenologie der Intersubjektivität: Texte aus dem Nachlaß. I–III*, Husserliana 13–15, ed. by I. Kern (The Hague: Martinus Nijhoff).

Husserl, E. (1983), *Ideas Pertaining to a Pure Phenomenology and to a Phenomenological Philosophy. First Book: General Introduction to a Pure Phenomenology*, translated by F. Kersten (The Hague: Martinus Nijhoff).

Husserl, E. (1987), *Aufsätze und Vorträge (1911–1921)*, Husserliana 25, ed. T. Nenon and H. R. Sepp (Dordrecht: Martinus Nijhoff).

Husserl, E. (1989), *Ideas Pertaining to a Pure Phenomenology and to a Phenomenological Philosophy. Second Book: Studies in the Phenomenology of Constitution*, translated by R. Rojcewicz and A. Schuwer (Dordrecht: Kluwer).

Husserl, E. (1997), *Thing and Space: Lectures of 1907*, translated by R. Rojcewicz (Dordrecht: Kluwer).

Husserl, E. (1999a), *Cartesian Meditations: An Introduction to Phenomenology*, translated by D. Cairns (Dordrecht: Kluwer).

Husserl, E. (1999b), *The Idea of Phenomenology*, translated and with an introduction by L. Hardy (Dordrecht: Kluwer).

Husserl, E. (2005), *Logische Untersuchungen. Ergänzungsband, 2. Teil: Texte für die Neufassung der VI. Untersuchung. Zur Phänomenologie des Ausdrucks und der Erkenntnis 1893/94–1921*, Husserliana 20/2, ed. by U. Melle (Dordrecht: Springer).

Husserl, E. (2006), *Logical Investigations, vol. 2*, translated by J. N. Findlay, transferred to digital printing (London: Routledge).

Husserl, E. (2008), *Logical Investigations, vol. 1*, translated by J. N. Findlay, transferred to digital printing (London: Routledge).

Lohmar, D. (2012), "Genetic phenomenology," in S. Luft and S. Overgaard (eds), *The Routledge Companion to Phenomenology* (London: Routledge), 266–75.

Luft, S. and Overgaard, S. (2012), "Introduction," in S. Luft and S. Overgaard (eds), *The Routledge Companion to Phenomenology* (London: Routledge), 1–14.

Merleau-Ponty, M. (1960), "Le langage indirect et les voix du silence," in *Signes* (Paris: Gallimard), 49–104.

Merleau-Ponty, M. (1964), "The philosopher and his shadow," in *Signs*, translated by R. C. McClearly (Evanston, IL: Northwestern University Press), 159–81.

Merleau-Ponty, M. (2005), *Phenomenology of Perception*, translated by C. Smith, transferred to digital printing (London: Routledge).

Merleau-Ponty, M. (2012), *Phenomenology of Perception*, translated by D. A. Landes (London: Routledge).

Mertens, K. (1996), *Zwischen Letztbegründung und Skepsis. Kritische Untersuchungen zum Selbstverständnis der transzendentalen Phänomenologie Edmund Husserls* (Freiburg: Verlag Karl Alber).

Mertens, K. (2012), "The subject and the self," in S. Luft and S. Overgaard (eds), *The Routledge Companion to Phenomenology* (London: Routledge), 168–79.

Moran, D. (2000), *Introduction to Phenomenology* (London: Routledge).

Petitot, J., Varela, F. J., Pachoud, B., and Roy, J.-M. (eds) (1999), *Naturalizing Phenomenology: Issues in Contemporary Phenomenology and Cognitive Science* (Stanford, CA: Stanford University Press).

Ricœur, Paul (1966), *Freedom and Nature: The Voluntary and the Involuntary*, translated, with an introduction by E. V. Kohák (Evanston, IL: Northwestern University Press).

Rinofner-Kreidl, S. and Wiltsche, H. A. (eds) (2016), *Analytical and Continental Philosophy: Methods and Perspectives* (Berlin: de Gruyter).

Rizzoli, L. (2008), *Erkenntnis und Reduktion. Die operative Entfaltung der phänomenologischen Reduktion im Denken Edmund Husserls*, Phaenomenologica 188 (Dordrecht: Springer).

Sartre, J.-P. (1947), "Une idée fondamentale de la phénoménologie de Husserl: *l'intentionnalité*," in *Situations I. Essais critiques* (Paris: Gallimard), 31–5.

Sartre, J.-P. (2004), *The Transcendence of the Ego: A Sketch for a Phenomenological Description*, translated by A. Brown, with an introduction by S. Richmond (London: Routledge).

Schmicking, D. and Gallagher, S. (2010), *Handbook of Phenomenology and Cognitive Science* (Dordrecht: Springer).

Sokolowski, R. (1999), *Introduction to Phenomenology* (Cambridge: Cambridge University Press).

Spiegelberg, H. (1982), *The Phenomenological Movement: A Historical Introduction*, 3rd revised and enlarged edition with the collaboration of K. Schuhmann, Phaenomenologica 5/6 (The Hague: Martinus Nijhoff).

Summa, M. (2014), *Spatio-temporal Intertwining: Husserl's Transcendental Aesthetic*, Phaenomenologica 213 (Dordrecht: Springer).

CHAPTER 26

SUBJECTIVITY

From Husserl to his Followers (and Back Again)

RUDOLF BERNET

26.1 INTRODUCTION

IT is commonly admitted that a fully fledged notion of human subjectivity entered the scene of philosophical thought only in modern times. Most often Descartes' *cogito* is credited with effecting this new turn. It is questionable, however, whether human subjectivity truly formed a central and direct object of Descartes' philosophical reflection. Was not his main concern rather to provide a new, solid foundation for modern science? In this, mathematics played a role that was at least as important as the self-evidence of our acts of thinking, feeling, etc. Descartes' use of both was more instrumental or operative than thematic. Subjectivity was actually of so little concern to Descartes that he didn't feel a real need to distinguish its mode of being from that of things. Symptomatically, he contented himself with referring to one's own "thinking substance" with the vague and untechnical term "*moi*" (I), used interchangeably with the traditional term "*âme*" (soul) (Descartes 1897–1913: 33).

All phenomenologists seem to make use of some notion of subjectivity. The obvious question about what they mean by "subject" should not prevent us from also asking what they need this notion for and how explicitly they reflect on it. Just as in Descartes, their recourse to subjectivity remains first and foremost operative. That is, it remains embedded in their phenomenology of how a subject perceives and imagines, remembers and expects, thinks and judges, feels and acts, undergoes influences and makes decisions, understands other persons and cultural objects, and so forth. However, unlike Descartes, most phenomenologists have also thought explicitly or thematically about the nature of human subjectivity. There are at least three reasons for such an explicit interest. The first reason relates to their common rejection of a theological foundation of phenomenology, the second to the phenomenological method, the third to the phenomenological phenomena themselves. For most phenomenologists these three reasons remain somehow related to Descartes' *cogito*.

1) All phenomenologists easily subscribe to Husserl's refusal of Descartes' appeal to God in an attempt to secure the truth of human knowledge (Husserl 1976: §58). They think that the limited power of the human mind should not be measured against God's creative intelligence but should be investigated on its own ground, i.e., the nature of human subjectivity.

2) All phenomenologists also agree with Husserl that phenomenology cannot simply borrow its understanding of subjectivity from physics or chemistry, from life-sciences or psychology, from sociology or political science, etc. From their common refusal of materialism, naturalism, psychologism, and scientific objectivism arises a new need for a closer look at the nature of human subjectivity. It is the set task of a phenomenological reduction not only to disclose new phenomenological phenomena but also to trace them back to the subject to whom they are given. How things and the world appear, is intimately related to how a subject experiences them actively and passively, how it understands their meaning and feels their value, how it is, at least implicitly, aware of its own involvement in all these intentional modes of mindfulness or behavior.

3) Phenomenologists disagree about the nature of the subject's involvement in the intentional correlation, and this serves as a further motive for phenomenologists to have a closer look at the nature of human subjectivity. While often disagreeing amongst themselves, a good number of phenomenologists still agree in their refusal of Husserl's conception of a transcendentally constituting subjectivity.

We should thus not take for granted that subjectivity must be the most fundamental, or even an independent, object of phenomenological reflection. And even when subjectivity becomes a phenomenological phenomenon of its own, it remains necessarily related to other issues and other phenomenological phenomena. This is principally so, because the subject experiences itself while and in the mode of how it experiences the world. It belongs to the subject's essential nature to be open to what appears to it as being different from its own being.

26.2 HUSSERL

Until the late twentieth century, Husserl's *Cartesian Meditations* was taken to be his most mature and most systematic account of the transcendentally constituting phenomenological subject. In this text Husserl presents his own conception of the transcendental subject or pure ego as a radicalization of Descartes' "*ego cogito cogitatum*" (Husserl 1963: 14). His radicalization essentially consists in purifying Descartes' *cogito* from all metaphysical presuppositions (as a *res*, substance) and from all worldly apperceptions (as a psycho-physical human being or as "a little portion of the world" (Husserl 1963: 9)). The act of the *cogito* that, for Descartes, was an instantaneous event without any kind of duration, becomes in Husserl a non-independent moment in the *temporal* stream of an individual consciousness. In addition, Descartes' *cogitationes* are identified with the "acts" or "mental experiences" (*Erlebnisse*) of an *intentional* consciousness that is always pre-reflectively aware of itself. Descartes' *cogito* is also granted the new power to "*constitute*" the meaning of all that it experiences: of the world no less than of things, of other subjects no less than of itself as both a spiritual and a bodily *transcendental* subject. Likewise, the "*meaning*" of the *cogitatum* that an *ego cogito* experiences as a persistent unity in a coherent series of multiple *cogitationes*, relates not only to its thatness and a whatness, but also and foremost to *how* the *cogitatum* is and appears as an intentional correlate or phenomenological phenomenon for a subject. This is to say that the transcendental relation of the *ego cogito* to its *cogitatum* concerns not only the existence, kind (real/ideal), and material properties of the intentional object, but also its mode of (partial/total, presumptive/adequate) givenness and its mode of (true/cancelled, certain/doubtful) being (*Seinssinn*).

For Husserl, the subjective transcendental constitution of the meaning of objects of experience or pure phenomena has both an epistemological and an ontological signification. Consequently, the tasks of a phenomenological theory of knowledge and of a phenomenological ontology are inseparable for him. However, Husserl's transcendental idealism inclines him to make ontological issues dependant on epistemological issues, and to give priority to the so-called "doxic" modes of being (being certain or doubtful, etc.) over the ontic modes of being (being a natural thing or a cultural object, an ideal object or a value, etc.). In Husserl's phenomenological philosophy, all modes of being of all kinds of objects ultimately relate to their being-*true for* a transcendental subject (of knowledge, but also of evaluation or of will). This is the ultimate meaning of Husserl's "radical transcendental subjectivism" (Husserl 1962: 101)—a qualification of phenomenology Husserl shares with many of his critics. Needless to say, this transcendental subjectivism is very different from all forms of empirical or psychological subjectivism and from all forms of psychologism, the latter of which Husserl had so forcefully criticized in the first volume of his *Logical Investigations* (Husserl 1975). It is the task of both the "eidetic" and the transcendental phenomenological 'reduction' to establish and maintain the difference between the two kinds of subjectivism. Unlike empirical psychology, committed to the prejudices of a naturalism and objectivism, phenomenology investigates the essential (a priori) features of intentional experiences—seized from a first-person perspective in their original mode of effectuation and as subjective phenomena purified from all empirical and metaphysical assumptions.

It is easy to foresee what, in Husserl's reworking of Descartes' *Meditations* into a transcendentally constitutive phenomenology and idealist phenomenological philosophy, would soon become problematic for his followers. They objected that not all intentional experiences are mental acts of thinking (*cogitations*), that not all intentionality is a matter of consciousness and mental representation of objects, that the way in which things present themselves to us (how and as what) does not necessarily relate to our theoretical knowledge of them, that Husserl's idealism loses sight of how things show themselves to us from themselves, that in their genuine mode of appearing things display a meaning of their own, that instead of constituting the meaning of things the subject responds to it, that our awareness of other persons—of what our self-awareness owes to them and of what we owe to them in terms of ethical responsibility—is beyond the scope of a subjective constitution of objective meaning, and so on.

Husserl was sufficiently aware of these (for him misguided) objections to hold back the publication of the original German text of his *Cartesian Meditations* and to devote a great deal of his final productive years to their (unfinished and unpublished) revision. Many of his late attempts to clarify the nature of the phenomenological transcendental subjectivity are now collected in his commentary on Eugen Fink's *VI. Cartesianische Meditation* (Fink 1988) and especially in the third volume of a posthumous publication that was given the title *Zur Phänomenologie der Intersubjektivität* (Husserl 1973c) by the editor Iso Kern. With the publication of these new rich materials, Husserl's pretended "departure from Cartesianism" (Landgrebe 1962) and his renouncing of the dream that philosophy should become a rigorous science proved to be wrong. Today, more than ever, Husserl's relation to Descartes is in need of a serious reevaluation. For too long phenomenologists have uncritically repeated Heidegger's interpretation of Descartes and his characterization of Husserl's phenomenology as a belated form of Cartesianism (Heidegger 1994).

It is certainly not by mere chance that Husserl's renewed meditations on the nature of subjectivity belong to the context of his growing interest in *intersubjectivity* and in different forms of social life and of social institutions. Rewriting his *Cartesian Meditations*—where he had moved from a phenomenologically transformed *cogito* to the experience of an *alter ego*—Husserl now works his way back to an analysis of subjectivity that incorporates his new views on social, ethical, and religious life. In such a perspective, the former insight into the necessary mediation of a transcendental subject's experience of the other by means of the other's body could not fail to prompt a new reflection on how the pure ego itself must have a body and be able relate to it. His development from a static to a genetic phenomenology had already helped him to take into account how a transcendental subject can be passively affected by things and how passive syntheses enter into the process of its constitution of their meaning. However, it is only with his phenomenology of intersubjectivity that Husserl's meditations on the role passivity plays in the constitution of the meaning of subjectivity itself reach their full depth. Much the same can be said of other fundamental ingredients of Husserl's phenomenology of transcendental subjectivity such as temporality and historicity, spatiality and corporeality, ethical responsibility and communal life, science and life-world, and so on. On the way, the meagre pure ego gains more flesh, concreteness, and individuality.

This development involves no real break, however. Much of Husserl's *Cartesian Meditations* (1929) (Husserl 1963) can be read as a renewed presentation of insights and arguments that mostly go back to his *Ideas* (1913) (Husserl 1976). While the Fifth Logical Investigation (1901) had still seen no need for a pure ego to explain the unity of the stream of consciousness (Husserl 1984: 374 (§8)), the *Ideas* (Husserl 1976: §37, §80) publically proclaimed Husserl's somewhat earlier (1910–11) (Husserl 1973a: 111–94) conversion to the egological nature of a transcendental phenomenological consciousness. Neo-Kantian philosophers, such as Natorp, were enthusiastic about this change and expressed their full agreement with Husserl's characterization of the transcendental subject as the ego-pole (*Ichpol*) in all acts of intentional consciousness (Natorp 1917–18). They also eagerly subscribed to Husserl's distinction between a transcendental or pure ego and a factual or empirical ego. Neo-Kantians were under the impression that Husserl's understanding of the transcendental subject as the expansive source of intentional acts of knowledge rather than as a self-centered mode of self-awareness was not essentially different from their own conception of the ego as the ultimate principle of the possibility of the unity of all objects of experience.

Neo-Kantians tended to overlook, however, the fact that Husserl was as much a disciple of Descartes as of Kant. For Husserl's phenomenology the "transcendental subjectivity" constitutes "its exclusively proper field of experience" (Husserl 1952b: 141). This means that rather than being a merely formal-logical condition of the possibility of unitary objects of experience, Husserl's transcendental subjectivity is itself an object of experience. The transcendental ego is no less experienced than its objects, and in virtue of the intentional correlation between the *cogito* and its *cogitata*, subject and object are moments in one and the same encompassing experience. For the phenomenologist—who reflects on the intentional subjective life and who (in virtue of the phenomenological reduction) "brackets" all belief in the real existence of the intentional objects—these objects become pure phenomenological phenomena. He considers intentional objects exclusively with regard to how they are "meant" and how they are given as objective correlates (*noema*) of an intentional act (*noesis*) of perception, judgment, and so on. Taking into account the transcendentally constitutive character of the ego-pole of intentional consciousness, Husserl is then led to claim that transcendent objects—as pure phenomena, the meaning of which is constituted by transcendental subjectivity—belong into an (enlarged) sphere of pure immanence: "Transcendence is an immanent mode of being that constitutes itself within the ego. Every meaning and every being one can think of (*jeder erdenkliche Sinn, jedes erdenkliche Sein*), be it called immanent or transcendent, falls in the domain of the transcendental subjectivity. An outside (*Außerhalb*) of the latter is nonsense (*Widersinn*), transcendental subjectivity is the universal and absolute concrete (*die universale, absolute Konkretion*)" (Husserl 1963: 32).

Though for different reasons, many phenomenologists were just as puzzled by Husserl's "radical transcendental subjectivism" (Husserl 1962: 101) (and "transcendental idealism" (Husserl 1963: 33)) as were most neo-Kantians. But what good reasons can a phenomenologist have to object to Husserl's view that the subject, who experiences the things and the world in its intentional consciousness, also simultaneously experiences its own experience of them? Of course, one needs then to distinguish between the pre-reflective and the reflective self-awareness a subject has of its own intentional acts. Further, on what grounds can a phenomenologist disagree with Husserl's claim that transcendental subjectivity, as it operates *incognito* in natural life (Husserl 1959: 427), is in need of a philosophical self-uncovering and self-explanation (*Selbstenthüllung*) (Husserl 1959: 448)? Of course, the event of such an un-concealment of one's proper transcendental, meaning-constituting life may require other means than an objectifying reflection. Finally, shouldn't Husserl rather be praised for holding an appealing middle position between the phenomenologists who (like Sartre and Heidegger) put all the emphasis on the self-transcending movement of human existence, and the phenomenologist who (like Henry) restrict the subject's self-awareness to the narrow sphere of affective immanence? In Husserl's transcendental phenomenology there is room for both: the sphere of intentional immanence that comprehends the phenomenon of things or of the world, and the sphere of real (*reell*) immanence that comprehends the acts of the *cogito* as well as non-intentional sensations of a self-affection. With his phenomenology of inner time-consciousness, of different sorts and modes of (bodily) active and passive affects, of the dynamism of drives, of feelings and moods, Husserl does not fail to explore the infinite richness of a subject's inner life for its own sake. It is true that Husserl claims that many of these restrictively immanent subjective experiences enter into the composition of intentional acts that concern themselves with the givenness of transcendent things and of the encompassing horizon of the world. But how can one seriously object to his attempt to relate the subject's experience of its own inner life to that other side of its life by which it is oriented toward the world?

Husserl usually accounts for the relation between different forms or layers of subjective life in terms of an essential dependency or "foundation." According to this scheme, transcending transcendental life is founded on inner transcendental life. However, this holds only as long as one restricts oneself to the consideration of what an individual subject experiences (of itself, of the world and even of other subjects) by its own means, this is to say by its own active and passive potentiality. Husserl was quick to realize that such a closed sphere of a subject's ownness (*Eigenheitssphäre*) (Husserl 1959: 176; Husserl 1963: §44) cannot render justice to a *genetic* development of the *full* life of a *concrete* and *individual* transcendental subject. For this, one needs to give up the (fictional but methodologically useful) "abstraction" from what the life of a subject owes to other individual subjects or to the higher-order personality of social institutions (Husserl 1963: §49; Husserl 1959: 176ff.).

Taking into account how other subjects are involved in the self-constitution of a concrete transcendental subject, monad, or person opens up the new perspective of reciprocal or chiastic foundational relations. The inner life of a transcendental subject that grounds its world-oriented life and its apprehension of others, is at the same time co-determined and co-constituted by a meaning that it receives from other transcendental subjects. There exists thus, after all, an "outside (*Außerhalb*)" of an individual, concrete transcendentally constituting subject. It is true that the things and the world a transcendental subject can possibly experience exist so little "outside" of it (Husserl 1963: 32) that one is rather tempted to claim (with Heidegger and Sartre) that the subject exists "in" them. But it is no less true that foreign individual subjects exist "outside" of a transcendental ego, i.e., outside of what the latter can fully experience and constitute by itself.[1] It is also true that different transcendental subjects can so effectively share the meaning of things and of the world that it is most often *together*, as an intersubjective community, that they constitute this meaning (Husserl 1963: §48, §55). But it is no less true that different transcendental subjects can never fully share the experience each of them has of its own life. It is true, finally, that the transcendentally constituting life of another subject remains in its "original self-presence (*Urpräsenz*)" inaccessible to me (Husserl 1952a: 163). But it is no less true that I can perfectly experience how this foreign life co-constitutes the meaning of my own subjective life. The self-constitution of a *concrete* transcendental subject is thus always, to some extent, grounded on a ground that it cannot provide itself by itself alone.

This is not to say that there is no *self*-constitution of an individual transcendental subject at all. In the *Cartesian Meditations* and especially in his later attempts to completely rewrite them, Husserl analyzes at length how a transcendental ego constitutes itself by itself as an individual "monad" or as a "transcendental person" (Husserl 1963: 26ff.). There is no transcendental ego that would not also be a transcendental person—although, depending on the kind of experience, the same individual transcendental subject can alternatively function as a mere ego-pole or as fully fledged person. All self-constitution of the ego as a person is ultimately and with necessity grounded in the temporal nature of a pure consciousness. Inner time-consciousness makes it so that an identical ego (although it is not completely immersed in the temporal stream of its mental states) retains its former experiences and acquires habitual anticipations of future experiences. Experiences stick to the identical ego and make it an individual and unique person. The person is what the ego has become in the course of its life and personal history (Husserl 1973b: 34ff.). The manner in which a transcendental person (co-)constitutes the meaning of things and of the world is anchored and determined by its (equally transcendental) facticity or factuality.[2]

Gaining a personal content, the identical ego-pole (which phenomenology can treat as a general essence (Husserl 1963: 28)) becomes someone, an individual transcendental person with his particular style of experience, his personal characteristics, his habits and lasting convictions, his individual character, and his surrounding world (*Umwelt*) (Husserl 2002: 198ff.; Husserl 1963: §32, §33, §57; Husserl 1952a: 182, 185, 270; Husserl 1968: §42). The person the ego has become also determines what an individual subject will be and what it wants to make of itself. Much of this self-constitution of the transcendental individual subject or person is the work of merely *passive* syntheses, of retention, association, and sedimentation. Husserl insists on the fact, however, that we need to *actively* evaluate what our life has made of us. The core-business of a transcendental person is thus the activity of a position-taking (*Stellungnahme*)—especially in relation to the course, orientation, and meaning of its own life. Factual personal characteristics

---

[1] Husserl 1963: 137: "Accordingly the intrinsically first foreign other (*das an sich erste Fremde*) (the first not-I (*das erste Nicht-Ich*)) is the other I."

[2] Husserl 2014: 123: "The apodicticity of the 'I am' is, however, not an empty apodicticity of an empty ego-pole, but of myself, as I factually (*faktisch*) am: with all that is apodictically contained in my being."

and a habitual style of life must be evaluated and re-formed in respect of one's individual vocation, deliberately chosen goals, and universal rational values. What a transcendental person consistently values, determines its own value. There is something in us— the spiritual core of our individual personality—that cannot die (Husserl 1973c: 609; Husserl 2014: 1ff.).

However, a human person is not made of spiritual stuff alone. It has a body with individual qualities and potentialities. It engages itself in the world and thereby becomes (not only for others, but also for itself) a part of the (perceptual, social, and historical) human life-world. This is to say that the transcendental pure ego has the capacity to constitute itself—in a process of humanization (*Vermenschlichung*) and of enworlding (*Verweltlichung*)—as a human being that exists toward and in the world: "But then one must also clarify how the humanization (*Vermenschlichung*) that results from a transcendental self-apperception, entails with necessity that the ego that humanizes itself therewith also humanizes all its transcendental achievements (*Leistungen*) and bestows on everything that it finds (*vorfindet*) in itself the apperceptive meaning of worldliness (*den apperzeptiven Sinn der Weltlichkeit auferlegt*)" (Husserl 2002: 289; cf. also Husserl 1963: §45; Husserl 2002: 200, 323f.).

The context of the quotation makes clear that the main motive for such a self-humanization and self-enworlding of the transcendental subject is its experience of *other subjects* as worldly human beings: "As soon as I say: 'I, the human being (*Mensch*)', I already have myself in a valid meaning (*habe ich schon mich mit einem Sinn in Geltung*) that includes the valid meaning also of other human beings and thus of the world in general (*der andere Menschen und so die Welt überhaupt in Mitgeltung hat*)" (Husserl 2002: 288). Much the same can be said about the self-constitution of the transcendental subject as a monad or as a transcendental person. While it cannot be, for Husserl, that the other *constitutes* me—for myself!—as a monad, as a person or as a bodily human being in the world, I nevertheless immediately *apprehend* myself as being such a monad, person, or psycho-physical subject *for-the-other*. Chronologically speaking, the first monad, person, or psycho-physical human being I encounter, is the other and not myself. I also experience the other as such a psycho-physical human being, individual monad, factual person before I can experience her as a transcendental *alter ego* sharing with me a same egological essence. In the temporal order of experience, the other is given to me as the first human being, and I am given to myself as the first transcendental ego. It is only in the transcendental order of foundation and essential necessity that the self-constitution of a transcendental person has a priority over its co-constitution by other transcendental persons.

26.3 HUSSERL'S FOLLOWERS

It is often because of their ignorance of the full range and richness of Husserl's analyses that many of his followers have *criticized* his idea of subjectivity. Their criticisms and claims to originality thus need to be examined and critically evaluated in light of the wealth of posthumously published material. I shall limit myself here to another task, that is to dress a short and incomplete list of the areas where later phenomenologists have made *positive* contributions to a reassessment of Husserl's understanding of subjectivity.

26.3.1 Comportment vs. consciousness

We have seen that for Husserl, in the wake of Descartes more than of Kant, to be a subject means to be consciously aware of itself as well as of appearing things and persons, intentional horizons and the world. Husserl gives the term "*consciousness*" an unprecedentedly large meaning. It covers not only the intentional awareness of things, persons, and other objective phenomena but also the self-awareness of non-intentional bodily sensations and kinaesthetic potentialities. Whether intentional or non-intentional, Husserl's consciousness can further be explicit or unthematic, actual or asleep, active or passive, present or past, egological or anonymous, mine or somebody else's. Intentional mental phenomena can take the form of perceptions no less than judgments, mere phantasies no less than true memories, background experiences no less than attentive apprehensions.

Yet, many phenomenologists (with the notable exception of Sartre, Henry, and—to some extent—Levinas) accept Heidegger's criticism of Husserl's understanding of the *subject* of consciousness. Overlooking Husserl's profound reformation of Descartes' *ego cogito cogitatum*, they often identify Husserl's understanding of subjectivity with a *mental* subject, the main *activity* of which consists in *theoretically representing to itself or inspecting objects* that it posits in front of itself. They also claim that Husserl takes these intentional objects to be presently given (*vorhanden*) in a neutral or objective mode for which the subject's personal and possibly practical concerns are of no relevance. Needless to say that they were wrong about this.

The same phenomenologists were right, however, to emphasize that intentionality is more often a matter of a (possibly bodily and also practical) *comportment* (*Verhalten*) toward things and persons than of a *distanced* mental representation *of* objects. They were also right to stress that the meaning of objective phenomena varies with the kind and mode of accomplishment (*Vollzugssinn*) of such a subjective comportment. None of this is incompatible with Husserl's analyses of an intentional consciousness in which theoretical concerns cohabit with a practical engagement in the world and with a subject's affinity for, and commitment to, values. It is true, however, that Husserl's creative followers considerably enlarged and enriched the picture of the phenomenological consciousness and of its subject. Henry's analysis of affectivity and of a self-conscious subject that affectively experiences itself as belonging to the larger dynamism of a universal life must be credited for having further explored the dimension of a non-intentional phenomenological consciousness (Henry 1990). Sartre must be praised for having introduced the fundamental dimension of negativity into Husserl's conception of the subject of intentional consciousness (Sartre 1947). And no other phenomenologist equals Merleau-Ponty in his exploration of the bodily dimension of all intentional comportments and of a chiastic reversibility that binds subjective comportments and the correlative phenomena into such a tight knot that the role of the agent and the patient (the touching and the touched) are continually redistributed (Merleau-Ponty 1945 and Merleau-Ponty 1964; cf. Bernet 1993).

To get a better view of Heidegger's contribution to a renewal and even a radical reformation of Husserl's conception of the phenomenological subject, we need to enlarge our perspective.

26.3.2 Transcendence vs. intentionality and facticity vs. essence

In his Marburg lectures Heidegger often repeats that, instead of painstakingly exploring intentional consciousness in all its forms and modes, Husserl would have done better to think more about "the being of the intentional" (Heidegger 1979: §12). For the early Heidegger, what intentionality is and how it genuinely expresses itself, depends on the mode of being of the bearer or agent of its accomplishment (*Vollzug*). Even before accounting for the human being's (Dasein) being in terms of "care (*Sorge*)" (Heidegger 1927: §41 *passim*), Heidegger had already consistently used the term "transcendence" to characterize the being of a subject that is involved in intentional relations. This made him say that, although we first come to apprehend ("*ratio cognoscendi*") the nature of transcendence through intentionality, it is transcendence that constitutes the true ontological ground ("*ratio essendi*") of intentionality as a subjective comportment (Heidegger 1975: 91; cf. Bernet 1990). Transcendence means that the subject of intentionality essentially and with necessity stands or steps outside of itself. Such an ecstatic subject, that is not only related to things and to the world but intimately connected with them, has always already crossed the border of the immanence of its own stream of consciousness. As an expression of the subject's transcendence, intentionality is for Heidegger (and Sartre) a matter of how one *loses oneself* in the things and in the world rather than of how one represents them *to oneself*. To gain an explicit relation to one's own self, one needs to turn away from the things and the world. One needs to break the spell that they operate on oneself.

What then is the nature of a self that, rather than being in full possession of itself before it turns its attention to the things, is originally oblivious of itself? It cannot be any kind of intentional object, entity, or thing. Being not a thing, it must be some kind of no-thing. *Sartre* most fully embraced this conclusion and identified the subject's transcendence with its being nothing and therefore being absolutely free. The early Heidegger hesitated to go quite so far, and the later Heidegger reserved the use of nothing (*Nichts*) to characterize the being of being rather than the being of Dasein. For the early Heidegger, when Dasein is called back to itself from its dispersion (*Zerstreuung*) in daily concerns, it discovers its own mode of *being* that is totally, properly, and individually its own. For

Sartre, the being of the subject consists in its free activity of negation; the subject negates not only the independent being of the objects intended by it, but also its own being, i.e., all that it has been or that it is said to be by others.

Looked at from a Heideggerian perspective, Sartre credits the subject with too much *spontaneity* and too much *active power*. For Heidegger, when Dasein is called back from its dispersion and self-loss, what it *finds*, is its *powerless* and *factual* self. Dasein *is* its own being-born and its own being-toward-death—not by negating this past and future being, but by positively assuming it in the existential mode of *facticity* and of *impossibility*. What Dasein truly lacks, is not its own being, but the ability to be a stable and autonomous *ground* of its own being. Likewise, what Dasein desires is not to be its own ground or *causa sui* (as in Sartre (Sartre 1943: 133ff., 717 *passim*)). Dasein's care for its own ungrounded and uncertain being can only have the form of an open *question*. The openness of this question concerning the meaning of its own being is precisely what constitutes Dasein's most authentic mode of being as transcendence.

Between Sartre for whom the true subject is the anonymous force or drive of a negating consciousness (Bernet 2002), and Husserl's transcendentally constituting ego, Heidegger chooses a middle way. Against Sartre, he claims that Dasein has or is a (paradoxical) *determined being*. Against Husserl, he claims that Dasein has no identical essence, or rather that its essence consists in nothing other than in the factual and groundless mode of its individual existence in ever-changing worldly situations.

26.3.3 Subjectivity and world

We have seen that Husserl's Cartesianism doesn't prevent him from accounting for the transcendental subject's essential relatedness to the world. Against Fink (Fink 1988), he emphasizes that the phenomenologist as a spectator of the constitution of the world does not, therefore, lack any interest in the meaning of the world and in its possible improvement. It is also only for methodological reasons that phenomenology can abstract from the fact that the transcendentally constituting ego is at the same time a person in the world and a worldly psycho-physical human being. The transcendental subject's enworlding and humanization have always already taken place before this subject gains an insight into its pure phenomenological essence.

If it cannot be the wordlessness of Husserl's transcendental subject that Heidegger and his followers are right to criticize, what is it then? We have already suggested that it is the *immanence* of Husserl's transcendental *consciousness* that gets in the way of recognizing the subject's radical transcendence and the subject's being not only *toward* the world, but *with* or *in* the world—in the world more than in itself. Characterizing the transcendence of the world as a transcendence in the immanence of the transcendental ego, Husserl leads the external world back to the inner sphere of a subjectivity that has no true "outside." Heidegger, on the contrary, sets the transcendental subject out in the world, because its very being consists in its transcendence or its being outside of itself. To be-in-the-world is more than being intentionally related to the world (Heidegger

1979: 221ff.; Heidegger 1927: §§12f. *passim*). Consequently, Heidegger can claim that in Dasein's return to its most genuine mode of existence and to an optimal understanding of its proper being, the phenomenon of the world (possibly of a world that has lost all its familiar meaning in anxiety (Heidegger (1927): §40)) is never abolished. It is in the name and for the sake of what one might call the transcendental status of the world, that Heidegger and his followers object to Husserl's transcendental-phenomenological idealism. It is not, therefore, in the name and for the sake of any kind of straightforward metaphysical realism. In their reading, Husserl's phenomenological idealism is still of a metaphysical kind when it claims that the (relative or even contingent) being of the world depends (or is founded) on the (absolute and necessary) being of the transcendentally constituting subject.

The emphasis on the transcendental subject's inherence in the world grants phenomenology an access to new phenomena and realms of investigation that Husserl, to his own and sincere regret, discovered only late in his philosophical career. A good illustration of this is Merleau-Ponty's taking advantage of new developments in empirical psychology, physics, and the life sciences to promote a new phenomenology of the life of human and animal bodies. The same is true for his appeal to social sciences in his political phenomenology and to linguistics in his phenomenology of literature. Turning the transcendental subject into *a subject under influence* (Bernet 1993), exposing the subject to what it can never fully comprehend, introducing a gaping distance or deviation (*écart*) in the very core of subjectivity, accounting for the creation of new meaning in terms of "coherent deformation" (Merleau-Ponty (2000): 339) instead of subjective constitution, radically changes the face and the style of a phenomenological philosophy. It also forces phenomenology to reconsider the difference and relatedness between an empirical and an a priori approach to phenomenological phenomena. Phenomenology's departure from psychologism and naturalism are then also in need of serious reconsideration.

26.3.4 Response vs. constitution

No Husserlian concept has been more under fire recently than his idea of a subjective transcendental *constitution* of the sense of all objects of experience (including the subject itself). Constitution is supposedly responsible for Husserl's awkward subjectivism and phenomenological idealism. For many, constitution is a condensed expression of Husserl's metaphysics of presence and his constraining of phenomenology to the field of a theoretical philosophy and, more particularly, a theory of scientific knowledge. It is said that the doctrine of a subjective constitution of the meaning of all objects stands in the way of a genuine phenomenology of events and gifts. Constitution is also blamed for reducing other persons to mere intentional objects, the being of which coincides with the meaning a transcendental subject bestows on them. The refusal of Husserl's conception of constitution logically leads to a repudiation of phenomenology as a *transcendental* philosophy.

One could object that these criticisms do not pay sufficient attention to Husserl's sensibility for intersubjective and social forms of constitution, for pre-given (*vorgegeben*) instead of self-constituted meanings, for a renewed institution (*Nachstiftung*) instead of a primal institution (*Urstiftung*) of historically transmitted meanings, for forms of constitution resulting from affection and passive synthesis, for background intentionality and the constituting effect of sedimented life-worldly meanings, for meanings in written texts that have not explicitly been constituted by the author, for old meanings gaining a new meaning in other contexts, for meanings that come as a surprise rather than as the fulfillment of a subject's anticipations, for a promised or mysterious meaning that requires an infinite investigation, and so forth.

This is not to say that nothing can be positively learned from Husserl's critical followers and their phenomenological reflections on the status of *subjectivity*. Heidegger's famous turn (*Kehre*) is as much a turn away from the transcendental subject as a turn toward the event of an un-concealment of the truth of being. After the turn, it is not any longer Dasein that, when well disposed, raises the question concerning the meaning of being, it is rather the display of the problematic meaning of being itself that calls for Dasein's *response*.

Husserl was far from ignoring the fact that most of a subject's activity comes as a response to a passive affection or motivation. He would also have been open to the idea that a subject can experience the givenness of some phenomena as a gift, as a question, as a demand, or as a mystery. What remained foreign to Husserl, however, was the status of a subject whose response to such phenomena is not any longer located in the realm of meanings or that is, at least, taken up in a fabric of meanings that it can never fully appropriate to itself or constitute by itself. More radically, Husserl's conception of a transcendentally constituting subject couldn't do justice to an externally forced instead of an internally and freely chosen subjective response, position-taking (*Stellungnahme*), or responsibility. Such a phenomenon involves an entirely new idea of subjectivity, for which phenomenology is more indebted to Levinas than to Heidegger. The way in which Levinas characterizes the appeal of the other that holds me hostage, breaks with an established phenomenological tradition that had understood the difference between the empirical and the transcendental subject in terms of an opposition between determinism and freedom, force and meaning, natural causality and self-determination, heteronomy and autonomy.

26.3.5 The self vs. the ego

For Levinas, the ethical subject that is held hostage by the external appeal of the other cannot be called an ego. It is, at best, an I in the "*accusative*" (Levinas 1978: 107), a "*me*." Interrupting all egoistic self-enjoyment, the other reduces the subject to a me or to a self that is accused of snatching the bread from the other's mouth, of breathing her air, using her for its own sake. The subject is no longer a "for-itself," it is entirely for-the-other and with-the-other. When responding to the call of the other, the thus transformed or turned-inside-out ("like a glove") subject can at best say: Here I am for you (*me voici*)! To be entirely honest, it must say: Here I am for you, despite (*malgré*) myself (Levinas 1978: 65, 71 *passim*). It goes without saying that when I experience myself as *a self despite myself* rather than as an ego, I can no longer *constitute* the other as *my alter ego*. When the other is a miserable suffering person instead of another autonomous transcendental ego, and when I am a radically passive self, coerced to respond responsibly (Levinas 1978: 63ff.) to the other's commanding needs, then all egoism is annihilated and no ego is left. This is why Levinas accounts for the nature of the ethical subject—a subject that is not only beyond transcendental phenomenology but also beyond all ontology: a subject that is neither constituting the other nor justified in its own being—in terms of a self instead of an ego. After Levinas, French phenomenologists have become used to clearly distinguishing between an (active) ego-subject (*égoïté*) and a (passive) self-subject (*ipséité*).

Sartre had already made the distinction between one's own *self* and oneself as *ego* or *moi*—albeit for entirely different reasons (Sartre 1966; 1943: 118ff.). We have already seen that for Sartre the true nature of the subject is to be a negating intentional consciousness (Sartre 1947; 1943: 24ff. *passim*). A human subject's power to negate is absolute, it is originally in no way limited by, or dependant on, what it negates. Unlike Husserl's transcendentally constituting person or monad, Sartre's subject owes its absolute active power or spontaneity, and its freedom, to the fact that it is totally undetermined, that it has no content or properties, that it is *not* somebody or something. Pure transcendence in itself and ("ecstatically") standing outside of itself, it must also be nothing for itself. The subject's force or drive (Bernet 2002) to negate is absolute, because it is unbound and anonymous.

For Sartre, as soon as the negating consciousness gains a truly subjective content and personal determination, it loses most of its freedom and power. The more that a subject gains in content, the more it loses its true self. To become somebody means *alienation*: the self becomes an other. Such alienation is no accident, it follows from the fact that pure consciousness, precisely because of its intrinsic lack of determination, remains haunted or fascinated by that which fully is what it is in-itself. There is the *self-chosen* alienation or "bad faith" when a waiter, instead of efficiently waiting, plays waiting, polishes his image as a perfect waiter, *identifies* himself (his own self) with his public character and role as a waiter (Sartre 1943: 98f.). There is *imposed and suffered* alienation when the negating subject (the for-itself or *pour-soi*) is made—by the gaze, the expectations, or the sexual desire of others—into some kind of object, into something (an in-itself or *en-soi*) (Sartre 1943: 310ff.; Bernet 2001). In both forms of alienation an indeterminate self becomes a person or an ego that is foreign to its true essence. Becoming a *transcendent* object and losing thereby its original *transcendence* and freedom: This is what Sartre means by his "transcendence of the ego." Yet, like any other object, this transcendent ego can again be negated and overcome by the true self that thereby regains its genuine freedom.

While, for Levinas, there can be an ethical subject or self that is neither an ego nor a person, and while, for Sartre, becoming a person involves a loss of one's true self, Husserl believes that it is the concept of a transcendental person instead of an ego or alter ego that best does justice to the concrete and especially ethical life of the self. In this, Husserl is in complete agreement with *Scheler* who famously built his entire phenomenological ethics on the analysis of the intimate relation that an individual person entertains with transpersonal values. This was not without consequence for Scheler's phenomenological anthropology where it is again the person rather than the ego or "I" that is said to be the true subject of intentional acts and feelings. The ego as agent in the *constitution* of meaning comes second to the person as an individual, spiritual, value-centered, and unitary self that *expresses* and *realizes* itself in what it does and feels (Scheler 1966: 370ff.). It is only in matters of theoretical knowledge that the subject as ego preserves its philosophical relevance. For Scheler, the ego belongs to the realm of abstract theoretical considerations concerning the opposition between me and my body, between me and you, between me and the external world.

Scheler's conception of the unity and individuality of the person has thus much in common with Heidegger's analysis of Dasein. Both Scheler's and the early Heidegger's understanding of subjectivity owe finally more to the tradition of a spiritualistic vitalism than to Husserl's transcendental phenomenology. This is not entirely to their advantage. Husserl may be accused of intellectualism, but this does not commit him to a one-sided spiritualistic view on human life. Quite to the contrary, he always maintained that to gain a full understanding of human subjectivity, one must approach it from both sides: the side of spirit and the side of nature. This is also the conviction that presides over his original conception of the human body as a legitimate naturalization of consciousness (Bernet 2013)—a conception that is without equivalent in Heidegger or Scheler.

26.4 CONCLUSION

Looking back to Husserl from his followers, one can see more continuity than disruption. This is so because even when they criticize Husserl, they still participate in his effort to reform the traditional concept of subjectivity. The history of the phenomenological understanding of subjectivity can be understood, *negatively*, as the history of a progressive turning away from a metaphysical conception of the human subject. It is, *positively*, also the history of a continuous *broadening* of the scope of subjectivity. In both its positive and negative side, it is less the history of the *meaning* that one ascribes to the concept of subjectivity than of the description and philosophical analysis of the subject's indispensable *function* in the human experience of all kinds of different phenomena. Some phenomenologists, like Heidegger, have also given the critical reflection on the metaphysical concept of an absolutely grounding subject a new orientation by drawing attention to the harmful role it plays in the present-day imperialism of technology, i.e., the metaphysics of our times (Heidegger 1977: 111).

In all its diverse forms, the phenomenological *destruction* of the metaphysical concept of subjectivity concerns mainly a *subject-substance*. We have seen that, in Husserl, this takes the form of a criticism of the Cartesian *res cogitans* as "a little portion of the world" (Husserl 1963: 9). Despite this, for many of his followers, Husserl's conception of a transcendentally constituting pure ego remains too indebted to the metaphysical tradition. They criticize the transcendental subject's role as a first and absolute principle, as a foundational ground or *hypokeimenon* for Husserl's entire philosophical project. They blame Husserl for having granted the transcendental subject too much active and voluntary power in the constitution of meaning, too much solipsistic autonomy, too much self-sufficiency, and too much transparent self-presence. In their view, it is this inflated absolute ego that is responsible for Husserl's questionable idealism, immanentism, solipsism, intellectualism, metaphysics of presence, and so forth. For Heidegger, most problems in Husserl come from his failing to seriously investigate the *being* of the pure ego or "the subjectivity of the subject" (Heidegger 1927: §6, 24; §44c, 229). Other phenomenologists point to the shortcomings in Husserl's account either of the immanence and self-presence of the subject or of the subject's self-transcendence: Henry asks for a radical material phenomenology of the immanent content of a non-intentional consciousness, Sartre strips intentional consciousness of all immanent contents in order to do justice to its radical transcendence. In the later Heidegger and in Levinas, the criticism of the metaphysical heritage of Husserl's concept of subjectivity is pushed so far that, eventually, little remains of a first-person phenomenological subject.

While Husserl's phenomenological analysis of subjectivity is certainly far from being monolithic, he never departed from his "radical transcendental subjectivism" (Husserl 1962: 101), i.e., from his conception of the transcendental subject as the *absolute ground* of his entire philosophy. Insofar as "grounding" or "founding" are metaphysical endeavors, then Husserl's conception of subjectivity must have remained metaphysical. But insofar as "spontaneous activity" and "unlimited power," egoistic "solipsism" and "self-sufficiency," "mentalism," and "presence" are metaphysical concepts, then Husserl must be credited with having gradually and steadily moved away from a metaphysical understanding of subjectivity. The significance of Husserl's move from a static to a genetic transcendental phenomenology cannot be reduced to his increasing awareness of the importance of passive syntheses or of subjective activities prompted by passive affections (*Reiz*). Husserl's genetic phenomenology also opens the entirely new perspectives of the *genesis of the transcendental subject* itself and of its subsequent *enworlding*. In addition, the consideration of *new phenomena* that push phenomenology to its limit (the so-called *Grenzprobleme*) (Husserl 2014) force Husserl to *broaden* the scope of a phenomenological philosophy and to reconsider the nature of transcendental subjectivity. The transcendental ego becomes less metaphysical when one considers its incarnation and bodily instincts, its personal characteristics and habitual styles of behavior, its depending on other transcendental subjects, its social and ethical life, its immersion in the world and in the history of humanity, its birth and death, and so on.

Broadening the field of phenomenological investigations, welcoming new phenomena, and, correlatively, opening new possibilities for subjective life, also creates new concerns. First, what sort of a phenomenological subject is involved in these diverse phenomena? Second, what sort of phenomena require an explicit consideration of subjectivity, and what sort of phenomena can do without it? We have addressed the first question but have mostly left the second open.

Dealing with the first question, we have failed, however, to make a clear distinction between the phenomenological phenomena that *essentially involve* subjectivity in their manifestation and meaning, and other phenomenological phenomena that so dramatically or tragically threaten the existence of a subject that they *imperatively require* a subjective response of self-affirmation. All *traumatic* experiences belong to the latter kind (Bernet 2000). Traumatic experiences cannot be accommodated by a metaphysical conception of the subject, for the simple reason that they concern events that destroy all characteristics ascribed to subjectivity by traditional metaphysics.

The second question points in a different direction. It involves a reflection on those phenomenological phenomena, the analysis of which seems to be in need of *no reference at all to subjectivity*. It is true that such phenomena can hardly be called phenomenological. But it is no less true that a radical questioning of the nature of human subjectivity entails a testing of the limits of phenomenological phenomena and thus also of a phenomenological philosophy. Among the phenomenologists we have met, the later Heidegger and Levinas have shown the greatest sensibility for these limits. They emphasize the phenomenon of an external call that *requires* some kind of responsive subject. But they also stress that phenomena can manifest themselves under the guise of a concealment or even of an explicit resistance to all subjective grasp. Phenomena that necessarily *elude* or even *exclude* the subject, belong to the sphere of the subject's encounter with the being in-itself (*Ansich*) of things or of foreign persons. For most phenomenologists, not the least for Sartre and Husserl, it goes without saying that there can be no phenomenology of what exists entirely in-itself, i.e., without manifesting itself for someone or being given to somebody. Is this insight due to a Kantian prejudice or rather to their clear-sighted modesty? Is it due to their lucidity about the violence of a being in-itself that deliberately cuts itself off from all relation with human beings? Phenomena that show not only their independence vis-à-vis the life of subjects but a total indifference to all human concerns, certainly represent the biggest challenge—not only for a (idealistic) phenomenological philosophy, but also for a meaningful and secure human life. It is difficult to deny that such inhuman phenomena exist, not least in our contemporary life-world.

References

Bernet, R. (1990), "Husserl and Heidegger on Intentionality and Being," *The Journal of the British Society for Phenomenology* 21/2: 136–52.

Bernet, R. (1993), "The subject in nature: Reflections on Merleau-Ponty's *Phenomenology of Perception*," in P. Burke and J. Van der Veken (eds), *Merleau-Ponty in Contemporary Perspective* (Dordrecht: Kluwer), 53–68.

Bernet, R. (2000), "The Traumatized Subject," *Research in Phenomenology* XXX: 160–79.

Bernet, R. (2001), "L'un-pour-l'autre chez Sartre et Lévinas," in J.-F. Mattéi (ed.), *Philosopher en français. Langue de la philosophie et langue nationale* (Paris: Presses universitaires de France), 83–94.

Bernet, R. (2002), "Sartre's 'Consciousness' as Drive and Desire," *The Journal of the British Society for Phenomenology* 33/1: 4–21.

Bernet, R. (2013), "The body as a 'legitimate naturalization of consciousness,'" in H. Carel and D. Meacham (eds), *Phenomenology and Naturalism: Examining the Relationship between Human Experience and Nature* (Cambridge: Cambridge University Press), 43–65.

Descartes, R. (1897–1913), *Discours de la méthode*, in C. Adam and P. Tannerey (eds), *Oeuvres de Descartes, vol. 6* (Paris: Léopold Cerf).

Fink, E. (1988), *VI. Cartesianische Meditation. Teil 1: Die Idee einer transzendentalen Methodenlehre*, Husserliana-Dokumente 2/1, ed. H. Ebeling, J. Holl, and G. Van Kerckhoven (Dordrecht: Kluwer).

Heidegger, M. (1927), *Sein und Zeit* (Tübingen: Max Niemeyer).

Heidegger, M. (1975), *Die Grundprobleme der Phänomenologie (Sommersemester 1927)*. Gesamtausgabe Band 2/24, ed. F.-W. von Herrmann (Frankfurt a. M.: Klostermann).

Heidegger, M. (1977), *Holzwege (1935–1946)*. Gesamtausgabe Band 1/5, ed. F.-W. von Herrmann (Frankfurt a. M.: Klostermann).

Heidegger, M. (1979), *Prolegomena zur Geschichte des Zeitbegriffs (Sommersemester 1925)*. Gesamtausgabe Band 2/20, ed. P. Jaeger (Frankfurt a. M.: Klostermann).

Heidegger, M. (1994), *Einführung in die phänomenologische Forschung (Wintersemester 1923/24)*. Gesamtausgabe Band 2/17, ed. F.-W. von Herrmann (Frankfurt a. M.: Klostermann).

Henry, M. (1990), *Phénoménologie matérielle* (Paris: Presses universitaires de France).

Husserl, E. (1952a), *Ideen zu einer reinen Phänomenologie und phänomenologischen Philosophie. Zweites Buch: Phänomenologische Untersuchungen zur Konstitution*, Husserliana 4, ed. M. Biemel (The Hague: Martinus Nijhoff).

Husserl, E. (1952b), *Ideen zu einer reinen Phänomenologie und phänomenologischen Philosophie. Drittes Buch: Die Phänomenologie und die Fundamente der Wissenschaften*, Husserliana 5, ed. M. Biemel (The Hague: Martinus Nijhoff).

Husserl, E. (1959), *Erste Philosophie (1923/24). Zweiter Teil: Theorie der phänomenologischen Reduktion*, Husserliana 8, ed. R. Boehm (The Hague: Martinus Nijhoff).

Husserl, E. (1962), *Die Krisis der europäischen Wissenschaften und die transzendentale Phänomenologie. Eine Einleitung in die phänomenologische Philosophie*, Husserliana 6, ed. W. Biemel (The Hague: Martinus Nijhoff).

Husserl, E. (1963), *Cartesianische Meditationen und Pariser Vorträge*, Husserliana 1, ed. S. Strasser (The Hague: Martinus Nijhoff).

Husserl, E. (1968), *Phänomenologische Psychologie. Vorlesungen Sommersemester 1925*, Husserliana 9, ed. W. Biemel (The Hague: Martinus Nijhoff).

Husserl, E. (1973a), *Zur Phänomenologie der Intersubjektivität. Texte aus dem Nachlass. Erster Teil: 1905–1920*, Husserliana 13, ed. I. Kern (The Hague: Martinus Nijhoff).

Husserl, E. (1973b), *Zur Phänomenologie der Intersubjektivität. Texte aus dem Nachlass. Zweiter Teil: 1921–1928*, Husserliana 14, ed. I. Kern (The Hague: Martinus Nijhoff).

Husserl, E. (1973c), *Zur Phänomenologie der Intersubjektivität. Texte aus dem Nachlass. Dritter Teil: 1929–1935*, Husserliana 15, ed. I. Kern (The Hague: Martinus Nijhoff).

Husserl, E. (1975), *Logische Untersuchungen. Erster Band: Prolegomena zur reinen Logik*, Husserliana 18, ed. E. Holenstein (The Hague: Martinus Nijhoff).

Husserl, E. (1976), *Ideen zu einer reinen Phänomenologie und phänomenologischen Philosophie, Erstes Buch: Allgemeine Einführung in die reine Phänomenologie*, Husserliana 3/1, ed. K. Schuhmann (The Hague: Martinus Nijhoff).

Husserl, E. (1984), *Logische Untersuchungen. Zweiter Band, Erster Teil: Untersuchungen zur Phänomenologie und Theorie der Erkenntnis*, Husserliana 19/1, ed. U. Panzer (The Hague: Martinus Nijhoff).

Husserl, E. (2002), *Zur phänomenologischen Reduktion. Texte aus dem Nachlass (1926–1935)*, Husserliana 34, ed. S. Luft (Dordrecht: Kluwer).

Husserl, E. (2014), *Grenzprobleme der Phänomenologie. Analysen des Unbewussten und der Instinkte. Metaphysik. Späte Ethik. Texte aus dem Nachlass (1908–1937)*, Husserliana 42, ed. S. Sowa and T. Vongehr (Dordrecht: Springer).

Landgrebe, L. (1962), "Husserls Abschied vom Cartesianismus," *Philosophische Rundschau* 9: 133–77.

Levinas, E. (1978), *Autrement qu'être ou au-delà de l'essence* (The Hague: Martinus Nijhoff).

Merleau-Ponty, M. (1945), *Phénoménologie de la perception* (Paris: Gallimard).

Merleau-Ponty, M. (1964), *Le visible et l'invisible* (Paris: Gallimard).

Merleau-Ponty, M. (2000), *Parcours deux, 1951–1961* (Paris: Verdier).

Natorp, P. (1917–18), "Edmund Husserls 'Ideen zu einer reinen Phänomenologie,'" *Logos* 7: 224–6.

Sartre, J.-P. (1943), *L'être et le néant* (Paris: Gallimard).

Sartre, J.-P. (1947), "Une idée fondamentale de la phénoménologie de Husserl: l'intentionnalité," in *Situations I. Essais critiques* (Paris: Gallimard), 29–32.

Sartre, J.-P. (1966), *La transcendance de l'ego. Esquisse d'une description phénoménologique* (Paris: J. Vrin).

Scheler, M. (1966), *Der Formalismus in der Ethik und die materiale Wertethik. Neuer Versuch der Grundlegung eines ethischen Personalismus*, Gesammelte Werke vol. 2 (Bern: Francke).

CHAPTER 27

....

THE INQUIETUDE OF TIME AND THE INSTANCE OF ETERNITY

Husserl, Heidegger, and Levinas

....

NICOLAS DE WARREN

27.1 INTRODUCTION

....

PHENOMENOLOGICAL philosophy is commonly associated with the elevation of time to an essential and encompassing philosophical concern. This prominence of time is apparent from the frequency of references to time in the titles of phenomenology's most influential works (*Being and Time, Time and the Other, Lectures on the Phenomenology of Inner Time-Consciousness*), but equally from key phenomenological concepts (*retention, original presentation, and protention, ecstatic temporality, diachronic time*) which have since become ubiquitous in contemporary philosophical discourse. Rather than speak of one uniform way in which time has been understood as a phenomenological problem, it is more appropriate to recognize different senses in which time features as an essential concern for phenomenological thinkers, often testing or surpassing the limits of their respective conceptions of phenomenology itself. This diversity of time's problem reflects in turn the different ways in which phenomenological thinkers laid claim to philosophy *through* the problem of time. Whether in the form of transcendental idealism, fundamental ontology, or ethics as first philosophy, the problem of time figures crucially in these instances of how phenomenology variously contests the answer to the question "What is philosophy?"

An overview of the development of the problem of time within phenomenology is thus a complex undertaking. Although it is common to speak of the Phenomenological Movement as either a progressive "radicalization" of a basic tendency or thrust ("critique of mind and world dualism"), a series of ruptures or "heresies" issuing from an original breach ("Husserl's discovery of intentionality," "Husserl's discovery of categorical intuition," etc.), or a narrative of "overcoming" ("overcoming transcendentalism," "overcoming ontology"), what most revealingly characterizes the enduring presence of time within phenomenological thought is the productivity of its inquietude as a problem. As I shall explore in this chapter, this inquietude of time (the sense in which how to think about time within phenomenology cannot be taken for granted) plays itself out along different vectors of questioning in Husserl, Heidegger, and Levinas (the three representative authors discussed in this chapter).[1]

This inscription of time's inquietude into the very fabric of its phenomenological questioning represents one of the more original ways in which phenomenological thinking rediscovers the original inquietude of time as a philosophical question. Ever since Aristotle's *Physics*, the question of time, in its inaugural form "What is time?" has remained haunted by the instability of its own questioning: Does time belong to those things that have being at all? If time is composed of different parts, each of which is marked by non-being (the past that is no longer, the future that is not yet, and the present that is so as not to be), how can there be a question *about* that which is no longer, not yet, or just about nothing at all?

To this inquietude of time's questionability in Aristotle, Augustine in his *Confessions* opened a further dimension that transformed the problem of time into an issue of subjectivity. In Augustine's widely quoted perplexity (*si nemo ex me quaerat, scio; si quaerenti explicare velim, nescio*), the entanglement of two essential questions comes into profile. To pose the question "What is time?" is to pose in the same breath the question "Who am I?" (who is the subject of time?). Each implies the other as the mirror for the sense of its own questioning such that the inquietude of time bespeaks the disquiet of the subject with regard to its own existence—an existence essentially subject to time. Within the three phenomenological thinkers discussed in this chapter, this disquietude of subjectivity is manifest not only in the stress placed on the intrinsic temporality of subjectivity, but as significantly, with the challenge of how to problematize an understanding of subjectivity in terms of its inescapable temporality.

This mutual implication of time and subjectivity is traversed in the *Confessions* by yet another dimension of meaning. The disquiet of the subject who exists in time gravitates around the question of what in truth comes to pass, or fruition, in time. The time of subjectivity is not merely a passing; it is a passage, or transcendence, of time. There is no sense of time's transience without a sense of time's transcendence toward a temporality other than time, the instance of eternity. Time is thus configured around a twofold sense of temporal difference: between past, present, and future times within time; between time and eternity. With Augustine's seminal inflection of the question of time with the question of subjectivity, time becomes a question of different senses of time

---

[1] Although the problem of time is also central for other phenomenological thinkers (Merleau-Ponty, Sartre, Derrida, Ricœur), the constellation of these three figures is both exemplary of the richness of the problem of time within phenomenology and well suited to illustrate the complexity of influence that structures the development of phenomenological thinking.

for a subjectivity defined by transcendence in transience. As explored in this chapter, these three interlocking themes—the inquietude of time's questioning, the disquiet of subjectivity's temporality, and the instance of eternity—are configured in different ways in the respective phenomenological approaches of Husserl, Heidegger, and Levinas. Each is commonly concerned with developing a phenomenological account that speaks to this constellation of time, subjectivity, and the instance of eternity.

27.2 THE LIVING PRESENT

The fundamental significance of time for Husserl's phenomenological enterprise was neither apparent nor envisioned with his self-characterized "breakthrough work" of the *Logical Investigations*. As Husserl discovered after the *Logical Investigations*, the problem of time, or, in its phenomenological recasting, the problem of time-consciousness, came to represent "the most difficult of all phenomenological problems." Beginning with his 1904–5 lectures "Towards a Phenomenology of Inner Time-Consciousness," Husserl's phenomenological thinking tirelessly measured itself on the question of time-consciousness.[2] The inquietude posed by "this most difficult of all phenomenological problems" is evident from the conspicious absence of any systematic treatment of time-consciousness in either Husserl's published works or in his lecture courses (with the exception of the early 1904–5 lectures). Instead, his reflections on time-consciousness occurred in the experimental confines of his research manuscripts, hidden from the published and public presentation of his phenomenological project. This inquietude of time-consciousness is equally evident from Husserl's emphatic statements about its fundamental significance. In *Ideen I*, Husserl's inaugural exposition of his transcendental enterprise, Husserl admits that the "absolute" of transcendental consciousness discovered by the phenomenological reduction of *Ideen I* does *not* in fact represent the most fundamental, and hence "absolute," form of consciousness. The noetic-noematic structure of intentionality explored in the hefty pages of *Ideen I* must in turn be situated within the constitution of *inner time-consciousness*, which Husserl, however, excludes, from *Ideen I*. In a curious footnote, Husserl refers to his *earlier* 1904–5 lectures on time-consciousness with the optimistic remark, "fortunately, these problems have been solved," when in truth, as Husserl frequently recognizes in his research manuscripts well into the 1930s, the fundamental questions for his transcendental thinking raised by inner time-consciousness remained unsettled. It is as if the defining restlessness of Husserl's thinking manifested itself most crisply in his analyses of time-consciousness, as if time-consciousness offered a moving and *telling* image of his own thought.

---

[2] Husserl's writings on time fall into three major groupings: the 1904–5 lectures and manuscripts until roughly 1911 (Husserliana 10); the Bernau Manuscripts from 1917–18; and the "C-Manuscripts" from the 1930s.

Husserl first comes to the problem of time in terms of the psychological issue of the perception of temporal succession. Toward the end of the nineteenth century, the perception of time attracted widespread interest in experimental psychology and philosophical psychology, and centered on two basic questions. How do we perceive temporal succession as a unified phenomenon? How does the consciousness of temporal succession emerge from the temporal succession of consciousness itself? What distinguishes Husserl's approach is less his proposed solutions to these problems, but rather his transposition of these problems into a phenomenological framework in which the transcendental promise of time-consciousness emerges. As Husserl remarks with regard to his approach: "We are reminded here of the long-familiar problems concerning the *psychological origin* of the 'idea of space,' the 'idea of time,' the 'idea of a physical thing,' and so forth. In phenomenology such problems present themselves as transcendental and, naturally, as *problems of intentionality*" (Husserl 1969: 76). In its mature expression, Husserl's phenomenological approach displaces the problem of time from a primarily ontological reference (*What* is time?) or psychological mooring (the *perception* of time) to a genuinely transcendental form of reflection, where time and consciousness are essentially welded together in the primordial achievement of constitution which characterizes transcendental subjectivity as "inner time-consciousness."

Without delving into the intricacies of Husserl's conception of intentionality (nor employing here his technical vocabulary or tracking its permutations), consciousness is both other-relating (directed toward a transcendent object) and self-relating (aware of itself as experiencing). This general structure of intentionality formulates Husserl's principal insight into consciousness as "transcendence in immanence." Consciousness is also an activity of synthesis, where the meaning of "activity" entails both passive and active dimensions, static and genetic layers of constitution, and where "activity" refers to the intentionality of objects as grounded in (objectifying) *acts* of consciousness (perceptual acts, imagining acts, etc.) on the basis of immanent and non-intentional *affects* in which consciousness senses itself as experiencing. Following in the footsteps of Kant, for whom time is both the form of objectivity as well as the form of "inner sense" (the form of how subjectivity is manifest for itself as consciousness), Husserl's identification of "inner time-consciousness" as the fundamental constituting structure of possible experience deepens not only his understanding of transcendental subjectivity, but as significantly, his conception of the world as temporally constituted.

Methodologically, Husserl's analysis of time-consciousness begins with the "suspension" or "neutralization" of any assumption concerning the existence of time as well as the neutralization of a merely psychological account of time's perception (Husserl 1966: 5). In this manner, Husserl broaches the question of how time is *given* in experience, and this emphasis on the *givenness* of time broadens to encompass time-consciousness as the fundamental constitutive form of how experience as such is possible. The guiding clue for Husserl is the perception of time, albeit understood from the standpoint of intentionality in a transcendental register of analysis (i.e., within the reduction). As with any form of consciousness, the perception of time is understood by Husserl as a form of intentionality, as a consciousness of time. Whereas Kant held that time is a pure form of appearance (but not an appearance itself) and Aristotle's definition of time as the number of motions with regard to the before and after rests on a noetic judgment (time is not a phenomenon since time is not to be conflated with movement), Husserl seeks a more fundamental form of temporal experience, to whit, an intuitive experience of time itself. This question of *how* time-consciousness becomes a theme of phenomenological inquiry is further compounded by Husserl's transcendental discovery that time-consciousness is not merely a *specific* form of consciousness, and hence, a particular form of intentionality, but a *fundamental* form of consciousness that operates behind the scenes, as it were, within *every* form of experience, insofar as every form of intentionality, as the consciousness of objectivity, is the synthetic unity of a manifold.

An analysis of time-consciousness must begin with time as an object of consciousness, or what Husserl dubs a "time-object" (Husserl 1966: 24). In what sense, however, can we speak of time as the "object" of consciousness, or, in other words, as a phenomenon? The meaning of "time-object" serves a dual purpose in Husserl's reflections. In its narrower meaning, it designates an object of experience with an intrinsic temporal extension, as with a musical melody. In its broader meaning, it exemplifies "objecthood" as such, insofar as any possible object of experience is a temporal unity, or synthetic manifold. On Husserl's argument, the chronological notion of time as a linear order of mathematical now-points must be based on the constitution of objects in time, or, in other words, "time-objects." Objective time is thus based on the intuitive apprehension of things in time, which, in turn, depends on the experience of time's passage in which things endure. The unity of an object is not constituted for consciousness *despite* temporal passage, but *through and in* temporal passage.

A melody of three notes is an object of experience in which each note must succeed the other. Three notes must be distinctly heard together in a temporal relation of before-and-after. If three notes were heard simultaneously, we would hear a chord. By contrast, if three notes were heard entirely separately, we would not hear a melody, but three disjointed notes. On a traditional account, which Husserl understands as extending from Aristotle to Kant to Brentano, the perceptual apprehension of a three-note melody would involve an argument about how consciousness perceives the second note as now while simultaneously holding in memory the first note as just-now while also anticipating the third note as not yet now. Such an account suffers from two debilitating problems: if an unified consciousness of the now in temporal conjunction with the just-now depends on the interplay between perception and memory, where memory is considered a species of imagination (i.e., the capacity to represent what is not present), this would imply that the first note must have already elapsed in order to be remembered as having just been: to remember is to make present *again* what once was present. Such an account either begs the question in presupposing that the note has passed away (and hence: had been perceived as passing away) or resorts to an imagined representation of the just-now. In both cases, the consciousness of a time-object is reduced to the pointillism of the now without any duration, or passing away. Such an account assumes, moreover, a temporally undifferentiated and self-present act of perception. Perception can only perceive the present, and such perceptual presence in turn presupposes the self-presence of consciousness: I can only perceive something as present on the basis of myself presently perceiving.

Rather than account for the constitution of a time-object in terms of three *distinct* faculties or powers of the soul (memory, perception, and anticipation), Husserl discovers *within* the perceptual act of consciousness a temporally differentiated form of apprehension. On Husserl's phenomenological account, in hearing a melody, I perceive in the form of what Husserl terms a "traverse-intentionality" the temporal extension of three notes as a unified time-object. Each note *of* the melody is apprehended in the temporal sequence of before and after *on the basis* of the temporal distention *of* consciousness in the form of what Husserl calls "length-intentionality," by which he means an intentionality that runs the length of the *consciousness* of time-object (Husserl 1966: 80). Both forms of intentionality are structurally inseparable from each other. The temporal phases of the melody (the three notes as just-now, now, and not yet), as forming a time-object, are the intentional correlates of an act of consciousness, which is itself temporally differentiated: Consciousness itself elapses in hearing the temporal progression of a melody. What is significant here is that both the form of objective experience (i.e., melody) and the form of subjectivity as temporally distended consciousness are structured in relation to each other in terms of this "double-intentionality" of time-consciousness.

Within this "double-intentionality," Husserl argues that the "traverse intentionality" directed toward the transcendent time-object is founded on the "length intentionality" of the temporal distension of consciousness itself. This argument does not reduce the temporal form of objects to a subjective form of time; on the contrary, Husserl's robust conception of intentionality here argues that the temporal objectivity of experience is constituted through this difference between "other-directed" and "self-directed" forms of temporal experience. Husserl characterizes the distension of time-consciousness in terms of an immanent "stream" or "flux" in which the transcendence of objects is constituted. This "stream" of *inner* time-consciousness is not to be conflated with an objective flow of time or with the psychological flow of ideas and perceptions in the mind. In its phenomenological meaning, this metaphor of streaming characterizes the temporal distension of consciousness as an "activity" of constitution, where the distinction between "activity" and "passivity" is blurred. Consciousness is not *in* the stream as a boat is in water nor is time *in* consciousness as water in a container. Consciousness *is* the stream as the constitutive temporalization of objects of experience *as well as* of consciousness itself. As Husserl is at pains to describe, the temporal extension of time-objects possesses a distinct (though not separate) form of time from the temporality of consciousness in which time-objects are constituted. A perceptual act is composed of three non-independent modes of apprehension, or what Husserl calls "retention, original presentation, and protention" (Husserl 2001: 14).[3] This threefold

---

[3] In the 1904–5 lectures on time-consciousness and research manuscripts until around 1911, Husserl speaks of "original or primal impression" (Husserl 1966: 30, 70, 106). Husserl adopts the expression "original presentation" in his Bernau Manuscripts.

form of apprehension constitutes the unity of the living present (*lebendige Gegenwart*) in which a time-object is constituted in its duration; it is how consciousness fundamentally *experiences* the world and itself temporally. Retention, original presentation, and protention are analogous to a concatenation of temporal perspectives. Much as a spatial object is apprehended through a plurality of perspectives (I see the front while also seeing the sides of the table), a time-object is likewise apprehended in an unified array of temporal profiles: as just-now (first note), now (second note), and not yet (third note).

The living present of a perceptual act of consciousness is structured in terms of retention, original presentation, and protention. Every original presentation, or, consciousness of the now-phase of an elapsing time-object, is necessarily modified through a retention, or retentional consciousness; every now must necessarily pass away into the immediate past as just-now. Likewise, every original presentation is framed by a protention, or protentional consciousness, that leans toward the not-yet now. Whereas traditional accounts are beholden to Aristotle's view that perception can only perceive what is present, Husserl discovers that perceptual consciousness perceives what is present *as well as* absent, as the threefold declension just-now, now, and not-yet. Temporal absence is integral to temporal presence. While hearing the second note as now, the first note is retained in consciousness as no longer present. Retention, for Husserl, is not a form of memory or imagination, but an intuitive sensing of the now as *no longer present* (Husserl 1966: 84). Husserl's genial insight is to argue that the *passage of the now, or the passing away of the now*, cannot be assumed, and must itself be constituted in consciousness. Husserl thus speaks of retention as a "de-presentification" (*Entgegenwärtigung*) and "emptying" of an original presentation. By contrast, an original presentation is characterized by Husserl as "novelty," or "the new," in the sense of a fulfillment of a protention: Each now represents the renewal of presence, but rather than understand this renewal as the repetition of "the same" now, each original presentation is characterized as a renewed *self-differentiation* of time into past, present, and future.[4] The now eternally returns not as itself, but as differentiated from every other now in relation to its *own* past and future. This eternal recurrence of difference is the perpetual renewal (*Erneuerung*) of time-consciousness itself. This differentiation does not fracture presence, but constitutes its veritable texture as a transience in which identity *can* appear. In every instant, time and consciousness become renewed, that is, *opened once again* to possible experience. The transcendence of the world occurs once again in every instant of its experience.

Composed as it is of a threefold "streaming" of retention, original presentation, and protention, inner time-consciousness is neither circular (i.e., the eternal recurrence of the same) nor linear (i.e., succession of discrete nows). Husserl thus breaks with two historically entrenched metaphors of time: the line and cyclical motion. As Husserl

---

[4] To put it more precisely: the now is constituted in its duration in terms of the threefold apprehension of retention, original presentation, and protention. Strictly speaking, an original presentation is itself not the now, but the anchoring phase in the elapsing of the now.

develops in the Bernau Manuscripts, retentional consciousness implicates ("contains") a protentional dimension. The past remains unsettled as long as there is a future that still awaits us: what we have been is yet to be entirely settled. Likewise, a protentional consciousness implicates ("contains") a retentional dimension (Husserl 2001: 14). The future is anticipated from what has already passed; we become what we have been. Inner time-consciousness is *ahead of itself* and *behind itself*, yet always gravitating around the zero-point of an original presentation. This weave of retentions within protentions and protentions within retentions "spirals through" the perpetual renewal of an original presentation that *both* throws time ahead of itself and returns time back to itself. Although each original presentation motivates the expectation of yet another original presentation to come, the arrival of each novel original presentation, as the fulfillment of a protentional consciousness, arrives from elsewhere than where we had expected it. With each renewed original presentation, we return to the necessary experience of the world in the form of the present, but not from *when* we first began. Time-consciousness is both "streaming" and "standing." Although we perpetually experience the world in the form of presence, this form of presence is always temporally differentiated, or "textured," by the histories of what has been and the anticipations for what might be. Time-consciousness is indeed a stream in which we can only step but once, but must repeatedly step into, since once doesn't count.

Husserl's phenomenological discovery of inner time-consciousness, as an immanent temporality of consciousness on the basis of which consciousness transcends itself toward the world, introduces a fundamental question mark concerning the meaning of "immanence," or "interiority," as the presumptive essential form of consciousness in its self-presence. In this manner, Husserl deepens and transforms our understanding of subjectivity as "other-constituting" and "self-constituting." A first question concerns the threat of infinite regress implied by the insight that an immanent act of consciousness is intrinsically temporally differentiated. Would this not imply that an act of consciousness is itself a kind of inner "time-object" for which another act of consciousness would be needed in order to constitute its temporality? What is the structural relation between inner time-consciousness and self-consciousness? A second question circles around the meaning of transcendental *constitution* with this discovery of inner time-consciousness as "self-temporalization" or, in other words, as self-constituting. Consciousness is here not *in* time nor is time *in* consciousness: Consciousness *is* time just as time *is* consciousness. Inner time-consciousness is, in this sense, absolute, or self-constituting. But, what is the meaning of "is" here?

Both questions provoked extensive reflections in Husserl's Bernau Manuscripts and C-Manuscripts. Arguably, Husserl never arrived at a conclusive view with regard to either question. With respect to the first question, Husserl proposes to avoid any threat of infinite regress and the so-called "reflection-model" of self-consciousness through a characterization of self-consciousness as pre-reflexive along its "lengthwise intentionality." In Husserl's argument, retentional consciousness not only retains the just-now phase of a time-object along the axis of "traverse-intentionality." Given the double-intentionality of time-consciousness, retentional consciousness in a non-thematic and pre-reflective manner retains *itself* as having just experienced the just-now phase (Husserl 1966: 370). In having just heard the first note of a melody, consciousness retains itself as having just heard, and this self-retention is a "manifestation" of consciousness for itself, albeit in a different or "delayed" manner. Likewise, along the protentional horizon along the "length intentionality," consciousness implicitly "anticipates" itself and, in this sense, "manifests itself" as a futural self-consciousness, as the consciousness that anticipates finds itself again as the consciousness that I have already been, and am, in the future. With respect to the second question, Husserl oscillates between the alternatives of temporality *belonging* to consciousness, in which case, consciousness, in the form of an ego, constitutes its own temporality *for itself*, and consciousness as *belonging* to temporality, in which case consciousness becomes constituted for itself through a temporality without any form of an ego, or, as Husserl proposed, in the form of a primal-ego (*Urich*): a primordial "mineness," or *me*, awaiting the identity of *I*. All of these questions (including other themes concerning the birth and death of consciousness) circle around the question that Heidegger would forcefully, if mostly obliquely, direct at Husserl's novel conception of transcendental subjectivity as inner time-consciousness: What sense of "to be" is presupposed in this configuration of time *and* consciousness?

27.3 THE INSTANT OF VISION (*AUGENBLICK*)

The philosophical relation of philosophers to each other, what commonly passes under the designation of influence, is hardly ever straightforward, even in apparently the most straightforward of circumstances. At first glance, Heidegger's relation to Husserl on the issue of time would seem direct. A few years after *Being and Time*, Heidegger published in Husserl's *Jahrbuch für Philosophie und phänomenologische Forschung* an edition of Husserl's 1904–5 lectures "Towards a Phenomenology of Inner Time-Consciousness."[5] Along with Edith Stein, Heidegger belonged to a select few who had access to Husserl's research manuscripts on time-consciousness, including, in all likelihood, the 1917–18 Bernau Manuscripts. Despite Husserl's investigations being present at hand, Heidegger's critical engagement with Husserlian phenomenology during the 1920s and his later pronouncements concerning Husserl's thinking are marked by the conspicuous absence of any explicit confrontation with Husserl's analysis of time-consciousness. In his 1925 lecture course *The History of the Concept of Time*, Heidegger discusses "the three original discoveries" of Husserl's phenomenology (intentionality, the a priori, and categorial intuition) without any inclusion of time-consciousness (arguably, a fourth original discovery). Mention is made, however, of Husserl's analysis of time-consciousness in the 1928 lecture course *Metaphysical Foundations of Logic*, where Heidegger

---

[5] Edith Stein first worked on editing Husserl's lectures before entrusting their publication to Heidegger. Although the published lectures bear the title "1904–1905 Lectures," a sizeable portion of the edited text is composed from Husserl's manuscripts after 1904–5.

acknowledges: "That which Husserl still calls time-consciousness, i.e., consciousness of time, is precisely time itself, in the primordial sense" (Heidegger 1984: 204). While Heidegger mirrors Husserl's recognition that time-consciousness poses "the most difficult of all phenomenological problems," in the same breath he insists that "with regard to the problem of time, everything remains as it was" (Heidegger 1984: 263). As Heidegger remarks with regard to the 1904–5 time-consciousness lectures: "even today this expression [*intentionality*] does not name a solution but serves as the title for a central problem."

This central problem for Heidegger does not center on the configuration of time and consciousness, but on being and time, as announced in the title of his *magnum opus* dedicated to Husserl "in friendship and admiration." In its basic form, Heidegger's approach to the problem of time during the 1920s gravitates around the question: "What is the essence of time such that Being is grounded upon it and that in such an horizon the question of Being, as the guiding problem of metaphysics, can and must necessarily be elaborated?" (Heidegger 1982: 116). If the problem of time is addressed by Husserl in terms of the intentionality of inner time-consciousness, where "inner" designates the transcendental bond between the temporality of consciousness (immanence) *and* consciousness as the temporal horizon for the possibility of experience (transcendence), for Heidegger, as he remarks in *Kant and the Problem of Metaphysics*, it is the "and" of the title *Being and Time* that "conceals the central problem."

In *Being and Time*, Heidegger proposes to retrieve the question of being from its historical oblivion on the basis of a recovery of a more fundamental understanding of human subjectivity as Dasein. As Heidegger states: "Time needs to be explicated primordially as the horizon for the understanding of Being, and in terms of temporality as the Being of Dasein, which understands Being" (Heidegger 1982: 12). Rather than operate with the question "*What* is time?" Heidegger engages the more fundamental question "*Who* is time?" where the meaning of "who" refers to Dasein, whose basic structure of existence, as what Heidegger calls "care" (*Sorge*), is grounded in temporality. The possibility of understanding being defines the essence of human existence as that being for whom the sense of being at all is an issue, and who is itself in question in questioning being. "Who is Dasein?" provides the guiding question for the question of being; it is the question that underpins the "and" in the question of being *and* time.

According to Heidegger, Western metaphysical thinking distinguishes different senses of being in terms of different senses of temporal presence: beings that have beginnings and endings, beings that have neither beginnings nor endings, beings that are created, etc. Ever since Greek thought, the fundamental sense of being remains understood as "to be present." Yet, it is precisely this unquestioned compact between "to be" (being) and "being present" (time) that Heidegger questions through a fundamental ontology based on Dasein's understanding of being. Recalling Husserl's insight in the Bernau Manuscripts, different forms of objectivity are essentially constituted as different forms of temporality. These different forms of temporality, as different forms of intentionality, are grounded in "absolute time-consciousness" and its double-intentionality of "other-consciousness" and "self-consciousness," or transcendence in immanence.

Absolute time-consciousness characterizes the self-temporalization of subjectivity in which different forms of manifestation, including subjectivity's own self-manifestation, are constituted. In Heidegger's thinking, Dasein displaces Husserl's absolute time-consciousness; different ontic senses of "to be" are keyed to different senses of time, and thus, on Heidegger's argument, presuppose an horizon of temporality identified with Dasein's primordial understanding of being, which cannot be understood in terms of subjectivity as either "soul" or "consciousness." As Heidegger develops in *Being and Time*, "care" (*Sorge*) is the fundamental structure of Dasein's being in the world. This fundamental structure of care is in turn grounded in an originary threefold "ecstatic" temporality in which Dasein "temporalizes itself" as a whole. In Heidegger's vocabulary, the three temporal ecstasies of future (*Zukunft*), having-been (*Gewesenheit*), and the present are not organized in a linear manner of succession. As indicated with the term "ecstasis" (from *ekstatikon*, "to stand out" or "to jump out"), each temporal horizon (future, having-been, and present) is "equally original" and yet implicated in each other. Rather than consider, as did Husserl, that the worldly transcendence of consciousness is constituted through the immanent unity of retention, original presentation, and protention, Heidegger argues that each temporal *ecstasis* marks an original form of transcendence. While having, in this manner, broken with a linear conception of temporality based on the primacy of the present and any conception of consciousness as "transcendence in immanence," Heidegger argues that the unity of Dasein's originary temporality is achieved, or rendered "authentic," through a projection toward the future horizon of its finitude, or death, in terms of which the "having-been" and "present" of Dasein's existence becomes taken up as one's own. Rather than exist dispersed in the "inauthentic" time of the world, as structured by the linear form of succession, Dasein comes to bear its own existence as a possibility for being and non-being for which it is singularly responsible and destined.[6]

Even though *Being and Time* would thus seem to be the most direct locus for a confrontation with Husserl's phenomenology of time-consciousness, in a substantial footnote recapitulating the history of the concept of time, Heidegger refers to Aristotle, Hegel, and Bergson without any mention of Husserl (§82). Three years after *Being and Time*, however, Heidegger offered a more transparent confrontation with Husserl's time-consciousness in his 1929–30 lecture course *The Fundamental Concepts of Metaphysics: World, Finitude, Solitude*. The extended analysis of boredom and time in these lectures presents an exemplary phenomenological investigation that *inter alia* mounts a rejection of Husserl's phenomenological analysis of time-consciousness. As with *Being and Time*, Heidegger's interest in these lectures resides with retrieving the

---

[6] In the further development of *Being and Time*, Heidegger proceeds to relate his analysis of Dasein's ecstatic temporality to the constitution of Dasein's historicity (*Geschichtlichkeit*). A consideration of this connection between temporality and historicity in Heidegger (but as well in Husserl and Levinas) would, however, exceed the scope of this chapter. Likewise, the progression of Heidegger's thinking on time and being after the abandonment of his project of *Being and Time* and "metaphysics of Dasein" will not be considered here.

question of being through a "metaphysics of Dasein." Such an undertaking requires the awakening of a fundamental attunement in which the guiding question "Who is Dasein?" can emerge along with the fundamental question of being. The urgency to reawaken this twofold question is dictated by the historical crisis of the time. The popular appeal of a cultural diagnosis of this historical crisis suggests to Heidegger that contemporary Dasein (i.e., human existence) is affected by a profound *boredom*, and thus that it is boredom, as a fundamental attunement, that must be awoken, or reflected upon, in order to motivate the question of being anew. This fundamental attunement is both transparent and veiled. In Heidegger's metaphor: "Profound boredom draws back and forth like a silent fog in the abysses of Dasein" (Heidegger 1995: 77). This image of boredom as ebbing back and forth recasts the metaphor of time as a stream into an image of time's atmospheric inquietude while at the same time telegraphing Heidegger's insight into Dasein's existential temporalization as both self-obscuring and self-revealing.

Heidegger's analysis progresses through different types of boredom: being bored by things, being bored with ourselves, and "it is boring for one." With the first type, boredom is an experience of passing the time away: bored while waiting for a train, we seek to kill time in any which way we can. We compulsively glance at the station's clock, we pace back and forth on the platform, we mindlessly flip through magazines at a store. We are at pains to drive boredom away, and this attempt to drive off boredom further drags time onwards. This experience of boredom cannot be reduced to either impatience or unfulfilled anticipation. In finding ourselves bored *by* the station, we are primarily oriented toward the present, and not toward the future (the train's expected arrival). Boredom is here an experience of things around us leaving us empty. When we are bored by things, they are neither present at hand nor ready to hand; they are there without being there for anything. As Heidegger asks: "Can the trees outside [*the train station*] that we enumerate in our boredom do anything other than stand alongside the streets and grow toward the sky" (Heidegger 1995: 102). Boredom is a time that holds us in limbo while dragging us along to the point of exposing "our ownmost ground of Dasein." In waiting for the train, we are dying of boredom.

Heidegger's repeated reference to clocks in this description of boredom indicates how boredom here sets into relief "world-time," or chronological time, as datable, public, and belonging to the world. As Heidegger presented in *Being and Time*, this everyday notion of "clock-time" defines time as an ordering of things in relation to the before and after of numerically distinct now-points. This so-called "inauthentic" form of time represents the manner in which Dasein exists as dispersed and absorbed by the world of its daily cares and concerns. Heidegger here envisions not only an historically entrenched linear conception of time stemming from Aristotle (time as the number of motion with regard to the before and after), but also subsumes within this "inauthentic" form of time the cyclical time of nature. The basic form of world-time is to be present in the now. As the experience of compulsively checking our watches when bored makes plain, this notion of chronological time is couched within the fundamental structure of Dasein's being in the world as care. We look to our watches because we are *concerned* with the world. This concern with time, in this type of boredom, is determined by boringness. We find things in the train station boring, and most explicitly, the ticking of the clock, in light of a boringness which ebbs and flows, "like a silent fog." "Boringness" is strictly speaking not an intentional object of consciousness, but a characterizing horizon in terms of which we discover things (the train station, the trees, etc.) to be boring. And yet, as Heidegger stresses, it is the very things of our surroundings that we find boring. Intentionality—the ways in which I am directed toward the clock, the trees, etc.—is itself situated within an orientation toward the world that determines not just how I have the world in view (i.e., intentionality), but how I *am* in this world in terms of Dasein's concern for its own being in the world.

Heidegger argues in this manner that boringness is *neither* exclusively a property of objects nor a subjective lived experience. As he writes: "The characteristic of 'boring' thus *belongs to the object* and is at the same time *related to the subject*" (Heidegger 1995: 84). In fact, this type of boredom functions tacitly as an *inverse* phenomenological reduction which, as a counterpoise to Husserl's reduction of experience *to* consciousness, reduces consciousness in its lived experience *to* an understanding of being-in-the-world in terms of Dasein. Heidegger has effectively introduced an *ontological* reduction of transcendental consciousness to its presupposed and more originary manner of existence as "care." Time is neither an "object" of consciousness nor a constituting act of consciousness; original temporality slips, as it were, between this distinction and the structure of intentionality. The distinction between time as *either* belonging to the object or constituted by the subject is suspended in the concrete experience of boredom. As Heidegger argues transparently against Husserl:

> We must therefore take careful note that the conception of man as consciousness, as subject, as person, as a rational being, and our *concept* of each of these: of consciousness, subject, I, and person, must be put into question . . . it is not a matter of concocting a region of lived experiences, of working our way into a stratum of interrelations of consciousness. We must precisely avoid losing ourselves in some particular sphere which has been artificially prepared or forced upon us by traditional perspectives that have ossified, instead of preserving and maintaining the immediacy of everyday *Dasein*. (Heidegger 1995: 134/91)

This questioning of "Who is the subject?" is deepened with Heidegger's analysis of being bored with ourselves. As with the first type, Heidegger anchors his description in an example: "We have been invited out somewhere for the evening. We do not need to go along. Still, we have been tense all day, and we have time in the evening. So we go along" (Heidegger 1995: 109). All things considered, the evening was enjoyable: charming conversation, friendly people, and nice atmosphere. Upon returning home, we suddenly realize that we had been bored all along. It is not that we were implicitly bored by the evening, nor even with ourselves, and only come to this realization in hindsight. On the contrary, as Heidegger underlines, the evening *was* thoroughly enjoyable. Nonetheless: we have been bored.

This disclosure of *having-been* bored does not take the form of an intentionality (recollection) directed toward an object of experience. It is not a past experience that *was* once present, but a *having-been* that only now comes to presence. Heidegger offers the example of smoking as an illustration. While smoking, we are chatting away with people and taking an interest in the party's banter. We are not attentive to our smoking, but attending to the present conversation. The casualness of our smoking characterizes our detachment from our own passing in time in passing the time away in the banter and pleasantness of the world. The wisps of smoke mark the passing of time and with it, our own passing. As Heidegger writes: "This being bored is precisely there while we are smoking, and smoking, as an occupation, itself becomes entirely part of the course of the conversation and the other activities. This sheds some initial light on the situation. It is not smoking as an isolated occupation, but our *entire comportment and behaviour* that is *passing the time*—the whole evening of the invitation itself" (Heidegger 1995: 112). Smoking functions on many levels in Heidegger's description: as a metaphor for the temporalization of time's passing; as a metonym for the whole of Dasein's temporalized existence; and as a formal indication for what is difficult to isolate as a phenomenon in this kind of boredom, namely, what comes to pass in time's passing.

Unlike the first type of boredom, time is here not experienced as "dragging" or "in limbo." In fact, time is here not noticed at all—we did not constantly eye the clock at the party, but were happily present in the moment. Although we were present to the world, *it* had nonetheless been boring, where "it" hangs without any specifiable reference. Whereas the being-left-empty of the first type of boredom profiled chronological world-time (inauthentic time), this second type of boredom reveals the *disquiet* of Dasein's existence in the form of a dislocation between Dasein's manner of being present to the world and what Heidegger terms the "resolute openness (*Entschlossenheit*) of our whole Dasein." We come to the realization that something essential about *who* we are had been absent in our being present to the world.

As Heidegger argued in *Being and Time*, Dasein *is* time in the existential manner of "temporalization." Dasein "temporalizes itself" in a manner that is both "self-revealing" *and* "self-obscuring." In its inauthentic form, Dasein loses itself, or "falls," in world-time; in its authentic form, Dasein reveals its own existence as its ownmost possibility to be and not to be. Dasein renders itself present to the world in giving of itself (literally: its own time) to the world: in finding things of the world interesting and "caring for itself" in the world, Dasein "temporalizes" itself as "present to itself in the world." In an ingenious turn of argument, Heidegger recasts the image of temporality as the standing-streaming of consciousness—Husserl's primordial temporality—into an existential manner in which Dasein has left itself behind in its own temporal self-manifestation as present to the world. Dasein has strung itself along in the time of the world, and exists in a "stretched now" (the now of the evening) that passes along without Dasein taking any notice of itself in its temporal existence (i.e., smoking). In dispersing itself in the world, Dasein is made to stand on par with the things of the world in the form of presence. Within the transience of Dasein's standing in the world, what, or better: *who,* is essential about Dasein's temporal existence is transcended. The possibility of being that Dasein "is" transcends the transience of Dasein's existence. Dasein's "stretched out" or dis-tended existence, in terms of which Dasein takes on an enduring identity, covers over and obscures Dasein's authentic temporality. *Who* Dasein is only becomes revealed in the third type of boredom. This ontologically more revelatory boredom is encapsulated in the statement: "It is boring for one. It—for one—not for me as me, not for you as you, not for us as us, but *for one*" (Heidegger 1995: 135).

What characterizes this type of boredom is its illuminating and self-transformative *instantaneousness*. All at once, without any rhyme or reason, I am struck by a profound and encompassing sense of indifference. The "whole of beings" recedes into indefinite-ness. In Heidegger's intricate German: Beings as a whole refuse to speak (*das sich im Ganzen versagende Seiende*) (Heidegger 1995: 139). The world becomes mute, and in this muteness in which the world is not longer addressable by me (nor am I address-able to the world), something is nonetheless bespoken in this silence, as this silence. Dasein is called back from dispersed standing in the world and "impelled toward the originary making-possible of Dasein as such" (Heidegger 1995: 144). Dasein becomes opened to the "there is" of its own existence—to the "there," or "instance" (*Da*), of its own being (*Sein*), in terms of its very possibility to be. Dasein's possibility of being is tex-tured with possibilities still unclaimed and unexploited, and thus by the possibility of its own possibilities. It is this transcendence of Dasein's ownmost possibility to be (the pos-sibility of being-possible itself) that is left essentially behind in the transience of Dasein's presence to the world. This realization of my existence as possibility for possibilities for which I am absolutely responsible is the depth of time, as the possibility of resolutely seizing upon my singular existence in manner that is more profound than any identity, and as instant of vision in which I come to grasp my existence as a whole in the form of the question: Who am I?

As voiced in Pink Floyd's classic song "Time," we are seized suddenly with the realiza-tion that perhaps our life has not really happened, that we have *missed* ourselves in the life that we have thus far chosen, and *had*, that life has passed us by in the very passing away of our life.[7] The point of this question concerning the point of life is not that there is an "answer." The point is the question itself. This point is understood by Heidegger as an instance of vision (*Augenblick*) that can return over the course of having a life and in this return, perforate and amplify existence to its ownmost possibility of being. As Heidegger writes: "Dasein's being impelled into the extremity (Spitze) of that which properly makes possible is a being impelled through entrancing time into that time it-self, into its proper essence, i.e., toward the moment of vision (Augenblick) as the fun-damental possibility of Dasein's proper existence" (Heidegger 1995: 149). This instance of vision is the instance of eternity, not, however, as a *nunc stans* or unending presence, but as a repetition and renewal in which Dasein's entire existence becomes amplified, as it were, and condensed into self-transforming vision of itself. In Heidegger's

---

[7] "And then one day you find ten years have got behind you | No one told you when to run, you missed the starting gun" (Pink Floyd 1973).

formulation: "Time entrances Dasein, not as the time which has remained standing as distinct from flowing, but rather the *time beyond such flowing and its standing*, the time which in each case Dasein *itself as a whole is*" (Heidegger 1995: 147). This "time beyond flowing and standing" is marked by Heidegger's German term *Augenblick* as an "instance of vision" that apprehends Dasein's existence as a whole from the perspective *sub specie aeternitatis*, but not, however, as the eternity of either an endless or standing now, but as the momentary elevation and amplification (*Spitze*) of Dasein's existence to its ownmost possibility of existence. Looking back to the originary temporality of *Being and Time*, the unity of this threefold ecstatic temporality becomes *lived* in the instant of vision in which Dasein resolutely *decides* to take over itself and own up, so to speak, to its own being. This instance is neither the now-point nor the threefold unity as such, but the transformative renewal of Dasein's authentic existence as a whole. Much as with Nietzsche's thought of the eternal recurrence, Dasein must resolutely chose its singular existence as a whole. As Heidegger notes: "It is not some now-point that we simply ascertain, but is the look of Dasein in the three perspectival directions we are already acquainted with, namely, present, future, and past. The moment of vision is a look of a unique kind, which we call the look of resolute disclosedness for action in the specific situation in which Dasein finds itself disposed in each case" (Heidegger 1995: 151). Dasein thus breaks free from the boredom in which it could only rediscover and renew itself in the proper amplitude of its existence for itself.

27.4 THE FUTURE INFINITE

In a preface written in 1979 for the republication of his 1946–7 lectures *Time and the Other*, Levinas remarks that the "way of examining time" in these lectures "still seems to me today to be the vital problem" (Levinas 1987: 30). Although the evolution of Levinas's thinking since these lectures immediately after the Second World War passed through two major works and numerous essays, "the vital problem" of time first explored there would become the theme of Levinas's final lecture courses at the Sorbonne once again in 1975–6, *God, Death, and Time*. In retrospect, these lectures from 1946–7, as Levinas observes in 1979, remain "at best preparatory," and precisely in the sense that the Other, as alterity "beyond being," has yet to be developed toward the alterity of the Infinite, or God. As Levinas formulates his basic understanding of the question of time: "Is time the very limitation of finite being or is it the relationship of finite being to God?" (Levinas 1987: 30). Even though the invocation of God remains wanting and waiting in *Time and the Other*, Levinas still insists upon the significance of this first effort to develop "a phenomenology of alterity and transcendence," and which would be taken up once more thirty-years later in *God, Death, and Time*.

With its very title, *Time and the Other* gives notice of the fundamental displacement of the problem of time from the phenomenological configurations of either "time and consciousness" or "being and time." With an evident play on Heidegger's *Being and*

Time, this shift in orientation from "being" to "the Other" belies the audacity of Levinas's proposal to break with an ontological meaning to the question of time. As Heidegger observes in his 1962 lecture *Time and Being*: "From the beginning of Western thought until today, Being has meant the same as being present . . . According to this usual conception, the present characterizes time with the past and the future. Being is determined by time as presence. This relationship alone could suffice to bring thought to a ceaseless unrest. This unrest increases as soon as we decide to reflect upon the extent to which this determination of Being by time is given" (Heidegger 2002: 1). Despite Heidegger's critique of metaphysical notions of time and their shared adherence to an unquestioned primacy of "being-present," this ontological meaning of the problem of time remains decisive for Heidegger's thinking. Against this entire philosophical tradition, the thrust of Levinas's thinking seeks to break the compact between time *and* being. As Levinas announces in *God, Death, and Time*, his aim is to understand what he terms *la durée du temps*, where the term *durée* translates the German *Zeitigung* (temporalization), so, in other words, the "temporalization of time" (Levinas 2000: 63). This doubling of "temporalizaton" (*durée*) and "time" (*temps*) is meant to underscore Levinas's intention of displacing the *sense* of the question of time from any sense of questioning determined by the question of being. In speaking of "the temporalization of time," Levinas carries over a phenomenological concern for time to the fundamental dimension of an ethics without any ontological foundation. This dislocation of the problem of temporality from the horizon of the problem of being is announced in the title *God, Death, and Time*: the *sense* of God, death, and time are no longer framed by the question of the sense of being. The audacity of Levinas's thinking thus consists in arguing that the proper manner of the temporalization of time—time in its authentic sense—is distorted in any attempt to first understand time within the horizon of the question of being. Heidegger's notion of authentic temporality as the ecstatic unity of Dasein's care for itself in its being in the world is argued to represent an inauthentic form of temporality in contrast to the authentic temporality of an ethical relation to the Other. Indeed, as Levinas argues, to even begin with either the Aristotelian question "Does time belong to things that have being?" or the Heideggerian question of time and being is to have already failed to understand the proper orientation toward the problem of time as well as the problem orientation of time itself toward the Infinite "beyond being."

The argument of *Time and the Other* rests on this reversal of the primacy of "being and time" or "time and consciousness." As Levinas states, his aim is neither to understand time "as the ontological horizon of beings" nor as the transcendental achievement of subjectivity, but as a transcendence "beyond being" in relation to the Other, whose alterity remains irreducible to any mode of presence, or being-present (Levinas 1987: 39). The configurations of "time and consciousness" and "being and time" both assume that time is the achievement of the solitary subject, either in its Husserlian form as "absolute time-consciousness" or in its Heideggerian form as Dasein.[8] Both of these approaches

---

[8] Levinas's insistence that both Husserl and Heidegger are beholden to a "solitary subject" does not fail to recognize the importance of intersubjectivity for their respective thinking. Instead, Levinas's

are wedded to two different senses of questioning time: either in terms of the transcendental question of the possibility of experience or in terms of the question of the sense of being. These two different senses of questioning time in turn reflect two different senses of subjectivity: either as inner time-consciousness, where subjectivity is essentially the power of constitution, or as Dasein, where subjectivity is essentially an understanding of being. If, for Heidegger, the traditional question "What is time?" was displaced by the fundamental ontological ground of the question "Who is Dasein?" (and likewise for Husserl, to the question "Who is transcendental subjectivity?"), the approach to time in *Time and the Other* upends the unquestioned primacy of the solitary subject in shifting the axis of questioning to the question, *Who are you, the Other?* Time in this manner becomes revealed as the inquietude of the Other for my own being. That reversal from "Who is the (solitary) subject?" to "Who is the other?" structures Levinas's argument in *Time and the Other*. Throughout its development, Levinas's thinking tacitly moves back and forth between Husserl and Heidegger, critically canvassing *both* conceptions of time as the achievement of the "solitary subject."

Given the audacity of Levinas's proposal to consider the meaning of temporality beyond the primary meaning of being, his vocabulary presents a challenge for any understanding trained in the habitual ways of beginning with the question "What" or "Who" is time? The form of Levinas's argument is, however, clear in *Time and the Other* in its movement from a critique of an ontological conception of time and subjectivity to an ethical conception of time and the Other. This movement of rupturing the ontological hold on the question of time begins with a phenomenological analysis of an experience of time: insomnia. For Levinas, insomnia is an experience of the present without beginning or end. It is an experience of the present as dislocated from any possibility of renewal. Rather than consider insomnia as a moment or experience in time, Levinas describes insomnia as the suspension of temporalization. The angst-ridden boredom of insomnia represents an unending original presentation that is neither modified, or temporalized, through retention or protention. It is also an instant that does not transform existence, but dispossesses consciousness of any lived temporality. In Levinas's formulation, insomnia suspends the distinction between sleep and wakefulness, temporal self-absence and self-presence (Levinas 1987: 48). Insomnia is an experience of consciousness *reduced* to the absurdity of its existence: It is there, mute and unblinking, without a self (*sans soi*) in an unending moment with neither promise nor transcendence. This phenomenological description of insomnia is further developed with another image for what Levinas calls the "there is" (*il y a*) that underlies the subject's solitary existence: It is like a river in which one cannot bathe once. This image refers to Heraclitus' celebrated metaphor, but unlike its more common form, in which the Heraclitean stream is a stream in which one cannot bathe *twice*, Levinas's cites the version recounted by Cratylus as a river in which one cannot even bathe *once* (Levinas 1987: 49).

---

critique here identifies the *primacy* of the solitary subject (whether the existential analysis of Dasein or inner time-consciousness) over the alterity of the Other in the constitution of time.

This Levinasian characterization of the solitary subject as reduced to its absurd facticity (the absolute of its existence as the "there is") is meant to offer a critique of any conception of the subject as self-constituting or self-temporalizing. In this manner, Levinas provides a critique of both a Husserlian conception of transcendental subjectivity *and* Heidegger's conception of Dasein. Without entering into the details of Levinas's sophisticated double-critique, the thrust of his objection centers on identifying both conceptions of subjectivity (Husserlian and Heideggerian) as beholden to an idea of the subject as "mastery over its own being (or 'existing')." Rather than define the identity of the subject (the "who" of the subject) either in terms of self-consciousness or authentic resolution, the subject is here understood as essentially enchained to itself: To be a subject is to be enchained or "riveted" to one's own existence as a subject. To be a subject is to be attached to oneself and to affirm a justification or meaning for one's existence; it is to give meaning to one's own absurd existence at the expense of accepting one's own contingency of being.

Levinas's characterization of the subject as the mastery over *one's own existence* tacitly evokes in a critical register Heidegger's Dasein as *care*. To be a subject is to care for one's own being. This existential sense in which the subject is enchained to itself (as care for oneself) is reinterpreted in terms of the manner in which the subject is a burden for itself. To care for oneself is to be bound to oneself and the world in terms of materiality (the body, desires, etc.). The materiality of the subject forms essentially the circuit of its solitude: I must perpetually feed myself, take care of my existence, and generally be concerned with my existence. It is a burden that I alone am for myself. This materiality of the subject's existence is also the misery of its being (Levinas 1987: 58). And yet, this solitude of the subject (as materiality and misery) is not without a world: I am not alone without a world, but alone in a world toward which I am directed. Even if others are there to assist me in caring for my own materiality (the burden of my existence), that burden is mine alone to carry. While, on the one hand, Levinas reinterprets Dasein's structure of care as the materiality of its burdensome existence, on the other hand, he reinterprets Husserl's structure of intentionality in terms of *desire* as the need for material satisfaction, i.e., satisfaction for the needs of our materiality. Nourishment and enjoyment are here exemplary (Levinas 1987: 62). The subject in its self-enchainment does not fully coincide with itself: It is constituted through the interval between itself and the world. Nourishment is the temporary suppression of the interval within the subject through the temporary suppression of the interval between itself and the world: to eat is literally to take something from the world and internalize it within my existence so as to lessen the burden of my own materiality, namely, that I need to eat to survive. This need is, however, forever unsatisfied, even if it finds temporary satisfaction. Likewise, enjoyment (*jouissance*) represents for Levinas the manner in which the world becomes *absorbed* by the subject: In deriving aesthetic pleasure from the world, the subject *experiences* itself in satisfaction. In a more theoretical vein, the desire to know is equally understood by Levinas as the desire to absorb the otherness of the world through the light of the subject's own self-presence in the world. As Levinas states: "Subjectivity is itself the objectivity of light. Every object can be spoken of in terms of consciousness—that is, can be brought back to light" (Levinas 1987: 66).

Levinas's ontological conception of the solitary subject is meant *inter alia* to re-verse the entrenched assumption in both Husserl and Heidegger, and, indeed, within the Western tradition since Augustine, that subjectivity is essentially a form of time, or temporality. This reversal stands behind the statement that "solitude is the absence of time" (Levinas 1987: 57). Although this is not to deny that nourishment and enjoyment (different modes of being in the world) are inscribed within a certain form of time, it is revealing that Levinas operates with a Bergsonian distinction between "spatialized time" and genuine temporality (*durée*): the time of the subject in its being in the world is formed in terms of a cyclical movement of departure and return *from the subject* in which the discontinuity of alterity is never encountered. The ontological form time, as the structure of the subject's transcendence toward the world, is considered to be inau-thentic, or, in other words, to be essentially "spatial" in the sense in which the disruption of the world in a moment of alterity is never genuinely experienced. To whit, the subject is essentially a *conatus*, or drive, to absorb alterity into itself. This perpetual movement toward the world in order to return to the subject is the *tragedy of solitude*. The subject is inscribed within an eternal recurrence of its inability to shake off and disburden itself of its own materiality and misery. The subject cannot exist by bread alone even as it seeks to exist from bread alone.

These descriptions of the tragedy of solitude introduce the principal axis for Levinas passage from "who is the subject?" to "who is the Other," from the absence of time (or inauthentic time) to temporality, from ontology to ethics. This axis turns on the opposi-tion between "satisfaction" and "salvation," as expressed in the biblical narrative of Jacob and Esau (Levinas 1987: 61). The distinction between inauthentic and authentic time in Heidegger (or objective time and subjective temporality in Husserl) becomes radically re-construed into the *ethical* significance of the time of satisfaction and the temporality of salvation. Beholden to a care *for itself*, the subject is caught within an eternal recur-rence of itself in terms of which it seeks satisfaction in vain for its misery of existence. It is only through a *disruption* of the solitary subject's self-attachment and enchainment that "salvation" for its existence is possible; it is only in a relation to the Other called tem-porality that the subject's own existence becomes redeemed.

In the argument of *Time and the Other*, this disruption and salvation of the solitary subject occurs in the hour of death, not of its own, but of the Other. Against Heidegger's view of death in *Being and Time*, where *Dasein* authentically assumes its ownmost pos-sibility of being in resolutely *facing* its own possibility of impossibility, death marks for Levinas the impossibility of possibility as such. The approach of death, as the horizon of the future, undoes the "virility" and "power" of the subject. In the face of death, the sub-ject experiences itself in absolute passivity as the inability to be able: The power of con-stitution that defined transcendental subjectivity as well as *Dasein*'s projection of its own possibilities are interrupted and reversed. Death undoes the heroism of the subject. In this respect, as Levinas remarks, the tragic hero does not assume his death; he is seized by an impending death that always arrives too soon, yet in this arrival of his own death, something *other* is revealed, a transcendence beyond his own being, and being as such (Levinas 1987: 73).

The impending arrival of death breaks the subject's attachment to itself and the world of its nourishments and enjoyments. Rather than consider the resolute embrace of death as the authentic consolidation of the subject's finitude, Levinas recasts this primacy of the future into the ethical significance of *hope*. The finitude of the subject is ruptured through the transcendence of hope. Yet, this time of hope does not prevent or save the subject from its own death. It is not the promise of an unending life or life after death, in which case, hope would be fantasy of a future without end as the continuation of my own solitude, or self-presence. The transcendence of hope decenters the subject from itself. This decentering of the subject opens the subject to a relation with alterity and the genuine temporality of the infinite, or "what is to come" (*à venir*). My death becomes *bearable*, not because I am saved from death, nor because someone else might take my place, but because in the transcendence of hope, the primacy of the question of "to be or not to be" becomes displaced: I recognize that the question of *my* being or not being is no longer the first question or concern asked of me. The question that determines me is no longer the question of my being ("Who am I?"), but the question, "Who is the Other?" The question of the Other is not a question I pose to the Other, but a question-ability of my own existence posed by the Other. In Levinas's construal of this moment of transformation, the solitary subject is placed into question and comes to define itself in relationship to an infinite responsibility for the death of the Other. Time is this entrusting of the death of the Other into my hands without thereby being able to possess or take mastery over the Other.

In an unambiguous departure from any phenomenological orientation or ontological horizon of thinking, Levinas speaks of this transcendence of hope in *God, Death, and Time* as the irruption of the Infinite within the finitude of the solitary subject. Hope is an instance of disruption, or "diachronic temporality," that separates the subject from herself *and* from the world (i.e., attachment to beings) by opening an infinite form of responsibility for the other called love (Levinas 2000: 147). Love, as the redemptive force of time, is stronger than death, but does not triumph over death. The future opened in love exceeds death, but does not surpass it. There is no heroism of death in love. This messianic future "to come" redeems the subject's existence in its tragic paradox. "We want both to die and to be"—we want both to be relieved of the misery of our existence *and* to insist upon our own self-attachment. Only a relation of time to the Other promises an answer to the question "to be or not to be," "to die and to be," not directly, but obliquely, through the promise of a future beyond being—neither mine nor yours— in which an ethical responsibility for the time of our lives becomes absolute. Whose future is this future that is neither mine or yours? *Who* is this anarchic Infinite of the future to come? Only time can tell. It is in this sense that for Levinas time is essentially the patience of God and the patience for God. It is an eternal patience not without its own profound inquietude.

27.5 CONCLUSION

This exploration of Husserl, Heidegger, and Levinas has revealed the complex ways in which these three major figures within the Phenomenological Movement (broadly conceived) each aspired to rethink fundamentally the sense in which time becomes a concern for philosophical reflection. This questioning of time cannot be undertaken without inquiring into the fundamental sense in which the question of time implicates the question of subjectivity, but likewise, the sense in which time cannot be thought of without multiple temporalities. Time is thus not only configured around the differentiation of past, present, and future. It is just as significantly configured around a difference between inauthentic and authentic time, and a time other than the temporality of this difference. As significantly, as each of these three figures represent, the struggle to understand time in its multiplications is part and parcel of the struggle to understand the question of philosophy itself in its multiplications, as transcendental, ontological, or ethical. In each register of analysis, the question "What is time?" can neither be taken for granted nor divorced from the question "who" is the subject of time. In this regard, phenomenological philosophy's elevation of time to an essential and encompassing philosophical concern is just as much the amplification of time's inquietude for the subject of philosophical thought.

REFERENCES

Heidegger, M. (2002), *Time and Being* (Chicago, IL: University of Chicago Press).
Heidegger, M. (1995), *The Fundamental Concepts of Metaphysics* (Bloomington, IN: Indiana University Press).
Heidegger, M. (1984), *Metaphysical Foundations of Logic* (Bloomington, IN: Indiana University Press).
Heidegger, M. (1982), *Vom Wesen der menschlichen Freiheit. Einleitung in die Philosophie (Summer Semester 1930)* (Frankfurt a. M.: Klostermann).
Heidegger, M. (1962), *Being and Time* (New York: Harper and Row).
Husserl, E. (2006), *Späte Texte über Zeitkonstitution (1929–1934)*, Husserliana 8 (Dordrecht: Springer).
Husserl, E. (2001), *Die Bernauer Manuskripte Über das Zeitbewußtseins (1917/1918)*, Husserliana 33 (Dordrecht: Springer).
Husserl, E. (1969), *Cartesian Meditations*, translated by D. Cairns (The Hague: Martinus Nijhoff).
Husserl, E. (1966), *Vorlesungen zur Phänomenologie des inneren Zeitbewußtseins*, Husserliana 10 (Dordrecht: Springer).
Levinas, E. (2000), *God, Death, and Time* (Stanford, CA: Stanford University Press).
Levinas, E. (1987), *Time and the Other* (Pittsburgh, PA: Duquesne University Press).
Pink Floyd (1973), "Time," on *The Dark Dide of the Moon* (London: Harvest Records).

CHAPTER 28

EMBODIMENT AND BODILY BECOMING

SARA HEINÄMAA

ONE of the strengths of contemporary phenomenology is the rich conceptual arsenal that it offers for the analysis of the bodily aspects of human experience. The base of this conceptual arsenal is in the methodology that Edmund Husserl developed at the beginning of the last century for the analysis of sense constitution and then applied with his pupils in the inquiry of many different sorts of experiences, including bodily experiences and experiences of different types of bodies. Even though several pupils and collaborators, most importantly Edith Stein, Eugen Fink, and Martin Heidegger, later departed from the strictly Husserlian methodology and engaged in philosophical projects of different types, their discussions of human bodies remained indebted to the original account outlined by Husserl during the first decades of the century.

In addition to Husserlian sources, contemporary phenomenology of embodiment also draws heavily from the subsequent inquiries that French phenomenologists, e.g., Emmanuel Levinas, Jean-Paul Sartre, Maurice Merleau-Ponty, Michel Henry, and Jean-Luc Marion, have conducted on the basis of Husserl's groundbreaking studies, starting in the 1940s. These inquiries were influenced by French history of philosophy and science, most importantly by new readings of Descartes, Pascal, Maine de Biran, Kant, Hegel, and Kierkegaard. Thus, we find a mixture in which phenomenological inquiries are combined with insights into the tradition of modern philosophy.

The main Husserlian result here is the thesis that the living body has several related but different senses in our experience and that some of these senses are crucial to the constitution of intersubjectivity and everything that depends on intersubjectivity. Living bodies do not just appear to us as biological organisms but are also given as practical tools, as communicative means, as emotive expressions and as our very means of perceiving and acting on environing things.

When a medical surgeon, for example, works to remove an opaque lens in the eye of a patient with a cataract, she needs to relate to human bodies in several different ways or intend human bodies in several different senses (cf. Merleau-Ponty [1945]

1993: 111/82).[1] On the one hand, she must be able to regard her patient as a physiological organism composed of purely material elements, such as the epithelium, nerves, connective tissues, chemical compounds, and electrical currents, and manipulable by the very same means as other material things. On the other hand, she needs to relate to her team members as free and responsible agents motivatable by requests, questions, and arguments. This requires that she apprehends their bodies as expressive and communicative units. Moreover, in order to perform her operation, she may need to pose questions or give orders to the person she is operating on. For this end, she has to be able to relate to the patient, a bodily person, in the same communicative and motivating manner as to her team members. Finally, her relation to her own body is different from all her relations to environing bodies. She does not need to enter any communicative or manipulative stance in order to move her fingers, to alter their directions and speed in case of emergency; what is needed is merely her decision and determination to cut deeper or faster.

So, several different ways of intending living bodies are integral to our communal and social lives. The bodies of human beings are not just given to us as material things but also operate as instrumental and communicative means and as our very way of perceiving and handling things. This insight is summarized in contemporary phenomenology by stating that human bodies are not just perceptual things or observational objects, but also (i) expressive wholes, (ii) conditions of action and will, (iii) zero-points (*Nullpunkt*) of spatial orientation, and (iv) original modes of intending perceptual things (e.g., Behnke 2011, cf. Taipale 2014; Welton 1999; Dodd 1997).[2] These different senses contribute in different ways to the constitution of intersubjectivity and objective reality.

Similar distinctions also figure in our relations with animals. In order to ride a horse, for example, we must be able to motivate the animal and this requires that we apprehend it, not as a biochemical unit, but as a perceiving, desiring, and feeling individual. Or to use an example discussed by Husserl himself: Our habitual ways of dealing with hunting dogs imply that we consider these animals intrinsically as sensing perceiving beings and, even more, as subjects that have better sensory capacities than we ourselves and thus are comparable to us.[3] Thus, the equivocation of the sense of a living body is not specific to human life but also characterizes our experiences and conceptions of animals.

---

[1] The pagination given first refers to the original source, and the pagination that follows this, after the slash, refers to the English translation. Both sources are given in one and the same entry in the list of references below.

[2] For classical accounts, see, e.g., Husserl 1952: §38–41; 1973a: 75–7, 90; Stein 1917; Merleau-Ponty [1945] 1993: Part I.

[3] In his studies on intersubjectivity (Husserliana15), Husserl contends: "One might object [to Husserls' arguments about animals as non-constituting others] that in the case where animals are considered as relating themselves to the world, to the same as ours, they might sometimes contribute to the constitution [*mitkonstituierend*] of the world as world. When one understands a dog sensing the hunt, the dog as it were teaches us something we did not already know. The dog enlarges the world of our experience" (Husserl 1973b: 167; cf. Husserl 1954: 230/227; 1973a: 114–20, 126, 133–4; 1973b: 625–6).

These distinctions between different senses of bodiliness can effectively be explicated and clarified by phenomenological methods.[4] The explications do not just contribute to philosophical anthropology or philosophy of life; they also help to clarify the structure and organization of the perceivable world,[5] contribute to epistemological debates on other minds and our "access to them," and advance our ethical and political discussions on freedom, justice and responsibility. Ultimately, phenomenological accounts of embodiment touch on fundamental ontological and metaphysical debates that concern the sense and the type of being that we are ourselves are.

This chapter will clarify Husserl's philosophical approach to embodiment by first explicating a set of basic analytical concepts and transcendental arguments (sections 28.1–28.2). It demonstrates that Husserlian phenomenology does not establish any simple opposition between naturalistic and phenomenological inquiries but instead offers a comprehensive account of the many senses of embodiment and the body operative in human practices, including those of the natural and the human sciences. The second part of the chapter discusses recent applications of Husserlian philosophy of embodiment in the investigation of human plurality (sections 28.3–28.5). The focus here is in the phenomena of sexuality and sexual difference, but the main interest is to show, by a study of these exemplary phenomena, that the phenomenological concepts of style and stylistic unity can serve investigations into human plurality and diversity more broadly.

28.1 CORE PHENOMENA: TWO-LAYERED REALITY AND EXPRESSIVE UNITY

The main results of the phenomenology of embodiment are often reduced to a simple opposition between body as the subject of experience and body as an object of knowledge, informed by the epistemological distinction between subjective and objective qualities of things and the ontological distinction between subjective and objective being. Another dominant contrast is that between the lived body (*Leib*), invested with psychic powers, and the mere material thing (*Körper*), dominated by efficient causality. These oppositional senses serve many argumentative ends in contemporary theorization.

---

[4] Thus, the term "embodiment," when used in a phenomenological context, does not refer to any ontological thesis according to which human brains or animal brains (or neural systems) *are parts of larger organic and non-organic systems* (e.g., the organism-environment system or the eco-system). In other words, the idea of embodiment in phenomenology is not devised to counter any skeptical brains-in-the-vat scenarios. Nor does the term refer to the methodological stance according to which human brains or animal brains *must be studied* as parts of such larger systems. What is meant by "embodiment" in phenomenology is the constitutive process in which an egoic subject of experiencing is constituted as a worldly being and as a bodily person in a world, i.e., a process in which the ego receives the senses of object and experienceable reality.

[5] Cf. Jacob's chapter (ch. 33) in this volume.

However, if their constitutional conditions and the complexity of their mutual relations are bypassed, they may obstruct philosophical progress instead of opening up new avenues. Thus, it is crucial to retrace the explication of these distinctions in Husserl's original exposition.

Husserl's main teaching in the second volume of *Ideas* is that both human beings and animals can be apprehended in two alternative ways: either as psycho-physical compounds comprised of two types of processes, physical and psycho-physical, or as expressive wholes in which the spiritual and the material are comprehensively intertwined.[6] In the first case, we have a two-layered entity: The psychic is layered upon the physical and causally dependent on it. In the second case, no layers can be distinguished: Spiritual sense permeates matter through and through and no non-spiritual layer or part stands out. In *Ideas II*, Husserl characterizes the latter phenomenon as follows:

> I hear the other speaking, see his facial gestures, attribute to him such and such conscious lived experiences and acts, and let myself be motivated by them in this or that way. The facial gestures are seen facial gestures, and they are immediately bearers of sense for the other's consciousness, e.g., his will, which, in empathy, is characterized as the actual will of this person and as a will which addresses me in communication. (Husserl 1952: 235/247; cf. 1973a: 77–9)

Husserl calls the first type of apprehension "naturalistic" and the second "personalistic," and argues that the naturalistic apprehension grounds modern scientific psychology and related disciplines, while the personalistic apprehension grounds all our communicative dealings with other living beings, including the scientific practice itself as an intersubjective enterprise. The main question of *Ideas II* then concerns the relations between these two types of apprehensions which both have a central role in our worldly dealings and our pursuit of knowledge (cf. Melle 1996).

Thus, the naturalistic-causalistic account of the human body and the animal body is not abandoned or rejected by Husserl in favor of the personalistic account, as is sometimes claimed. Rather, since both crucially belong to our conscious lives and to our scientific dealings, the task of the phenomenologist is to chart their limits and to study their conditions of possibility and mutual relations.

So, *Ideas II* distinguishes between two very different types of wholes: the living being as a psycho-physical compound and the living being as an expressive unity of spirit

---

[6] *Ideas II* (1952) was heavily edited by Husserl's two assistants, Edith Stein and Ludwig Landgrebe. Stein and Landgrebe used Husserl's original manuscript from 1916 as the starting point of the composition of the volume, but made corrections and additions on the basis of their discussions with Husserl and their own investigations supervised by Husserl (e.g., Stein 1917). This means that *Ideas II* (1952) is ultimately a text with several authors, and contemporary Husserl scholarship is still struggling to separate Husserl's own position from the insights of Stein and Landgrebe. However, a new critical edition, based on Husserl's own original manuscript versions, has been prepared by Dirk Fonfara and is now ready for publication.

and sensible matter. Consequently, we can apprehend the body of a human being in two different ways. Either the living body is conceived as the physical foundation that sustains psychic states, processes and dispositions and determines their courses, or else the body is grasped as an expressive whole that carries spiritual sense in all its parts and parcels. In the former case, there is a basic layer of purely material (physical, electro-chemical) being that operates independently of the mental organization characteristic of the higher layer(s); in the second case, no purely material elements or constituents can be distinguished in the spiritual organization of the whole (cf. Soffer 1996).

Husserl characterizes the personalistic apprehension of the human body by comparing it to the way in which we grasp the units of written and spoken languages, such as words and texts:

> The imprinted page or the spoken lecture is not a connected duality of word-sound and sense, but rather each word has its sense . . . Exactly the same holds for the unity, man. It is not that the living body is an undifferentiated physical unity, undifferenti-ated from the standpoint of its "sense," from the standpoint of the spirit. Rather, the physical unity of the living body there . . . is multiply *articulated* . . . And the articu-lation is that of *sense*, which means it is not of a kind that is to be found within the physical attitude. (Husserl 1952: 240–1/253; cf. Merleau-Ponty [1945] 1993: 186–7/142, 271–2/210)

And a few pages later Husserl explicates his main insight according to which the mental life that we capture in the bodily gestures and postures of living beings is not originally given to us as an appendix to physical being but as an organizing power:

> The spiritual is not a second something, is not an appendix, but is precisely animating; and the unity is not a connection of two, but on the contrary, one and only one is there. Physical being can be grasped for itself (carrying out the existen-tial thesis), by means of the natural attitude, as natural being, as thingly being . . . But what we have here is not a surplus which would be posited on top of the physical, but rather this is spiritual being which essentially includes the sensuous but which, once again, does not include it as part, the way one physical thing is part of another. (Husserl 1952: 239/251; cf. 1973a: 86–8)

While distinguishing between these two different senses of the lived body—the natu-ralistic sense of the body as a psycho-physical compound and the personalistic sense of the body as a signifying expression—Husserl also argues that the former sense is consti-tutionally dependent on the latter. According to him, the naturalistic apprehension of living beings, their psychic and physiological properties, is not a self-sufficient forma-tion but is dependent on the more profound personalistic attitude. In the second volume of *Ideas*, the thesis is formulated by the concepts of attitude, as follows:

> Upon closer scrutiny, it will even appear that there are not here two attitudes with equal rights and of the same order, or two perfectly equal apperceptions which at

once penetrate one another, but that the naturalistic attitude is in fact subordinated to the personalistic, and that the former only acquires by means of an abstraction or, rather, by means of a kind of self-forgetfulness of the personal ego, a certain autonomy—whereby it proceeds illegitimately to absolutize its world, i.e., nature. (Husserl 1952: 183–4/193; 1954: 244–5/297)

This argument seems to be in direct opposition to the natural scientific paradigm according to which our psychic, mental, and spiritual life, however it is organized as such, results from and remains dependent on the purely physical processes of the human brain or the neural make-up of the human organism. The opposition, however, is merely seeming since the dependency relations discussed by Husserl and the natural scientists are different in kind: Whereas Husserl studies dependency relations between different *senses* of bodily being, the natural scientific conception concerns relations of determination between two different types of *real properties*, the mental properties of veracity, aboutness, and phenomenality, on the one hand, and the physical properties of location, electric charge, intensity, length, etc., on the other.

However, on the basis of the natural scientific paradigm of explanation one can put forward a comprehensive ontological or metaphysical theory according to which all being—and consequently also all psychic, mental, and spiritual being—depends on the fundamental being of purely physical entities and forces. This is not the natural scientific position but is the ontological position of modern physicalism. In its conception, the mental is either identical with the physical or else merely an epiphenomenal and emergent property of the physical, without any power to determine the latter.

Against this, Husserl argues that all physicalistic arguments take for granted the possibility of individuating physical being (entities, events, processes) independently of any reference to individual minds. This, he claims, is a groundless prospect. In his analysis, physical individuation in terms of position in objective space-time and in terms of causal role remains dependent on individuation by the "here" and the "now," and these in turn refer back to subjective individuation, i.e., individuation of experiences and experiencing subjects, and ultimately to the individuation of streams of pure consciousness.

In *Ideas II*, this argument about the primacy of subjective individuation in respect to objective spatial-temporal individuation is compressed as follows:

What distinguishes two things that are alike is the real–causal nexus, which presupposes the here and the now. And with that we are led back necessarily to an individual subjectivity, whether solitary or an intersubjective one, with respect to which alone determinateness is constituted in the position of location and of time. *No thing has its individuality in itself.* (Husserl 1952: 299/313)[7]

---

[7] And even more explicitly a few pages below: "Objective thinghood is determined physicalistically but is determined as a this [*als Dies*] only in relation to consciousness and the conscious subject. All determination refers back to a here and now and consequently to some subject or nexus of subjects" (Husserl 1952: 301/315; 1954: 222/218, 633/230; 1973a: 99, 150).

Husserl's treatment here rests on his account of the constitution of the unity of the stream of consciousness and of immanent time as its basic structure (see, Summa 2013; Salanskis 1999; cf. Boublil 2014). In his account, all individuation of things, events, processes, and other types of realities in objective unified space-time rests on the primary individuation of subjects, and these in turn are grounded in the fundamental individuation of streams of consciousness with their egoic poles. Or, to put it more technically: Subjectivity alone is independently individual, and all spatiotemporal individuality is only non-independently individual, i.e., it necessarily presupposes the intrinsic individuality of consciousnesses. The main point here is the conceptualization of the stream as a dynamic and open continuum in which new hyletic data is constantly incorporated in the structure of "retention-primal impression-protention." The stream is irreversible, and its moments unique and unrepeatable.

The main implication of this theory of individuation to the philosophy of embodiment is the insight that bodily persons are not primarily individuated by their positions in objective space-time or in causal nexuses but are individuated by their subjective modes of responding to what is given in experience and of yielding to or withstanding from what draws them. Rather than being differentiated by physical and psychophysical properties, substances, or essences, bodily subjects are distinguished by the unique ways or styles in which they intentionally relate to constantly altering environing circumstances in their gesturing and acting, and to themselves as constantly developing sources of intending (cf. Husserl 1973a: 67–8). As subjective expressions, our bodies are not distinguished from one another by the positions that they hold in space and time or by the properties that they entertain, but are distinguished by their unique ways of moving, gesturing and acting in respect to what is given in their intentional environment.

> Every man has . . . his style of life in affection and action, with regard to the way he has of being motivated by such and such circumstances. And it is not that he merely had this up to now; the style is rather something permanent, at least, relatively so in the various stages of life, and then, when it changes, it does so again, in general, in a characteristic way, such that, consequently upon these changes, a unitary style manifests itself once more. (Husserl 1952: 270/238; 1973a: 36–7; cf. Merleau-Ponty 1969: 79/56)

Even though our intentional bodily relations to the environment change and develop dynamically, even though they sediment one upon another, confirming or canceling one another, drawing materials from earlier relations for new formations and thus creating new materials, all this fluctuation constantly exhibits an individually unique style of relating. In other words, despite the constant change and development of the relations, a distinctive style of relating manifests itself in this dynamism. Moreover, this stylistic unity has a recursive "fractal" character: Whenever it changes, as it does due to the dynamic character of intentionality, each change has the same stylistic form (cf. Merleau-Ponty [1945] 1993: 229–30/177). Thus, we can say that as an intentional whole our bodily existence—the whole of our bodily actions and passions—has the permanence and unity of a style, despite its fluid and fluctuating character.[8]

We have seen that in Husserl's account, embodiment is not one phenomenon but involves two core phenomena, the body as a natural organism on the one hand, and the body as an expressive unity on the other. These two phenomena have their own grounds, regions, and principles. We have also clarified the relations between the two phenomena and seen that instead of rejecting the naturalistic explication of the living body, as some commentators suggest, Husserl works to specify the conditions of possibility of this account and to chart its limits. He does not dismiss the naturalistic explication as false, misleading, or invalid. He merely argues that it is not self-sustaining but remains one-sidedly dependent on the personalistic apprehension of the living body in one crucial respect, i.e., in respect to the task of individuation.

This clarification allows us to avoid simple oppositions between the naturalistic philosophy of mind on the one hand, and Husserlian phenomenology on the other, but at the same time it also allows us to see that these two philosophies are not completely interchangeable or complementary, as has been argued (cf. Roy, Petitot, Pachoud, and Varela 1999: 43ff.). There is a strong critical potential in Husserlian legacy for the inspection of the transcendental conditions of naturalistic philosophies of mind and all philosophical projects that depend on them—be they epistemological, ethical, or political.

28.2 CONSTITUTIONAL RELATIONS: OWN AND ALIEN

Husserl's analysis of embodiment also harbors another crucial distinction. This is the distinction between the givenness of one's own body and the givenness of the other living body. Like the distinction between the naturalistic and personalistic apprehensions of living bodies, this distinction is also sometimes simplified as a crude opposition. It is argued, for example, that in his early works, most importantly in *Ideas*, Husserl put forward a solipsistic or egocentric account of embodiment but then later distanced himself

---

[8] A comparison with artistic work may help to illuminate this analysis by showing concretely how the ideas of dynamic change and stylistic unity can combine—and must combine if we aim to make sense of the dynamism of selfhood and personhood. The French artist Paul Cézanne is well known for comprehensive changes in his painting, both in his practice of painting and in the resulting works. Cézanne started as a Post-Impressionist but went through phases of Cubism, Fauvism, and Expressionism, constantly combining naturalistic and non-naturalistic influences. His oeuvre is a rich and dynamic multiplicity, but through all the paintings, a unique Cézannean style can be recognized. So when Merleau-Ponty in *Phenomenology of Perception* states that the unity of subjective life is like the unity of artwork (e.g., Merleau-Ponty [1945] 1993: 177/134), this is not a superficial metaphor but points to a deep analogy between artistic work and the human person: both are open-ended stylistic unities and as such their permanence and identity is found in their manner of changing.

from this early account and developed a more relational or dialogical understanding of human embodiment (e.g., Mensch 2001; Ricœur 1967).

In order to see what is involved in this second distinction, it is necessary to study somewhat closer the order in which the different senses of a living body are constituted according to Husserl.

Effectively, Husserl argues in both *Ideas* and in *Cartesian Meditations* that all sense of living bodiliness (*Leiblichkeit*), both naturalistically and personalistically apprehended, depends on the primary sense of my *own living body* and on the empathetic sense of another living body which is grounded on the fundamental sense of living that one originally constitutes in one's own case (Husserl 1950: 126–49/95–120, 1952: 80–2/85–7).

On this ground, Husserl's account of the ultimate foundations of the sense of embodiment can be characterized as "individualistic" and even "solipisistic." However, one should be careful with such characterizations, since by sense-foundation Husserl does not mean any axiom from which other senses can be derived but means a necessary starting point on the basis of which further constitutive steps are able to produce new senses. So his argument is that our concrete everyday experiences as well as our scientific, philosophical, and aesthetic understandings of living beings involve several senses of bodily being that all enrich and develop the primitive sense of self-embodiment.

Both tactile and kinesthetic sensations are needed for the constitution of the primitive sense of my own living body. The former provide a pre-objective primitive spatiality and the latter provide the sense of spontaneous movement. Both are necessary for the constitution of sense organs and the body as an organ of movement and action.

On the basis of these two types of sensations, our bodies are constituted primarily as double beings, both sensing and sensible, perceiving and perceivable:

> Touching my left hand, I have touch appearances, that is to say, I do not just sense [softness], but I perceive and have appearances of a soft, smooth hand, with such a form. The indicational sensations of movement and the representational sensations of touch which are objectified as features of the thing, "left hand," belong in fact to my right hand. But when I touch the left I also find in it, too, series of touch-sensations which are "localized" in it though there are not constitutive of properties. If I speak of the physical thing, "left hand," then I am abstracting from these sensations . . . If I do include them, then it is not that the physical thing is now richer, but instead it becomes body, it senses. (Husserl 1952: 144–5/152; cf. 150: 128/97; 1973a: 75)

This means that a consciousness that would lack the sense of its own living bodiliness, could not establish the sense of another living body and thus could not experience any other being as a living being. Husserl gives an example of such a consciousness in the second volume of his *Ideas* in order to highlight the dependency of the sense of living on tactility. He proposes that we imagine a consciousness the only sense of which would be vision, i.e., a consciousness that would lack tactile sensations altogether (Husserl 1952: 150/158). Such a consciousness, he argues, could not perceive its own body as living, and in so far as the sense of one's own living bodiliness is necessary for the constitution of the sense "other living bodies," this consciousness would not have any living bodies in its field of experiencing.[9] Since elsewhere Husserl also argues that the full sense of the world depends on the empathic sense of another self and on the communal relation between such others (e.g., Husserl 1952: 167/175–6; 1954: 256–9/252–6; 1973a: 99–102), it follows that the imagined self without the capacity of touching and self-touching would neither have other selves in its experience nor the objective world in the full sense of the term (cf. Heinämaa 2014).

Husserl's argument about the constitutive primacy of the sense of one's own body is sometimes presented as an early view that he later abandoned. For these reasons it is important to study some paragraphs from Husserl's late publications. In *The Crisis of European Sciences and Transcendental Phenomenology*, we read the following:

> Everyone experiences the embodiment of souls in original fashion only in his own case. What properly and essentially makes up the character of a living body I experience only in my own living body, namely, in my constant and immediate holding-sway [over my surroundings] through this physical body alone.[10] Only it is given to me originally and meaningfully as "organ" and as articulated into particular organs . . . Obviously it is only in this way [i.e., by having sense-organs] that I have perceptions and, beyond this, other experiences of objects in the world. All other types of holding-sway, and in general all relatedness of the ego to the world, is mediated through this. (Husserl 1954: 220/217; cf. 109–10/108)[11]

[9] In Husserl's analysis, qualitative distinct localized expanses are originally constituted in touch sensation. Husserl then argues that all perception—both the constitution of perceived objectivities and the constitution of the lived body as the subject of perception—depends on such units and on kinesthetic sensations. In this way perception is dependent on touch.

[10] Husserl's argues that the primary senses of subjectivity and ego are bound to activity, to "I move" (Husserl 1954: 220–1/217, cf. 108–9/106–7, 215–16/211–12, 310–11/331–2) and "I can" (Husserl 1952: 151–3/159–60; 216–17/228, 254–7/266–9, 330–2/241–3). The sense of passive subjectivity is dependent on the sense of active subjectivity and act (Husserl 1952: 332–3/344). For him, the subjective and egological in the proper and original sense is "the ego of 'freedom'" (Husserl 1952: 213–14/224), that is "the subject of intentionality, the subject of the acts" (Husserl 1952: 214–15/226). This means that while Husserl accepts the idea of the passive subject and the passive ego, and also thematizes and discusses this ego at length, he argues that the sense of this type of subjectivity is constitutionally dependent on the sense of the active subject, i.e., the passive subject is dependent on the active one in its sense of subjectivity. Cf. Summa 2013.

[11] Earlier formulations are similar. In 1921, he wrote: "The original givenness of a living body [*Leib*] can only be the original givenness of *my* living body and no other. The apperception 'my living body' is essentially the first and the only original one. It is only when I have constituted my living body that I can apperceive living bodies as such. This [latter] apperception is necessarily a mediate one; insofar as it associates the alien living body with a co-presentation of it in inner attitude [by the other], it always requires an antecedent apperception of my living body" (Husserl 1973a: 7). In *Cartesian Meditations*, he characterizes the primacy of the sense of one's own living body (*Leib*) by an abstractive reduction to the so-called sphere of ownness as follows: "I find my animate body as uniquely singled out—namely as the only one . . . that is not just a body but precisely an animate organism: the sole object . . . to which . . . I ascribe *fields of sensation* . . . the only object 'in' which I '*rule and govern*' immediately, governing particularly in each of its 'organs'" (Husserl 1950: 128/97).

The other body is grasped as living when the primitive sense of living, as sensing, as constituted in my own case, is transferred over from my own body to another corporeal body in the environing space (Husserl 1950: 142–3/112–13; 1952: 164–6/172–4; 1973a: 97, 126). The transfer is motivated by the similarity of perceived movements. Some things that I detect and observe in space resemble my own living body and its sensory organs in their perceived movements (Husserl 1950: 141–4/112–14; 1973a: 3–4; 1973b: 183; cf. Merleau-Ponty 1960: 286/233; Ricœur 1967: 46–7). A body over there reacts to external stimulation in the same way as my own arms and hands. And when it bumps into another thing, it does not halt or bounce back but "restores" its balance and circumvents the obstacle (Husserl 1973a: 118). Moreover, without any detectable causal influence by other material elements or things, it "spontaneously" turns in this or that direction. And finally: It also manifests the type of "reflexive" movement that is familiar to me from my own case.[12]

Such behavioral similarities motivate a complex of synthesizing experiences that terminates in an act in which the sense of sensing is transferred over to a body perceived at a distance. As a result, a new type of being is given to me: a body with its own systems of sensations and appearance-systems, sensations that I cannot have or live through but that are given to me via the thing's movements and behaviors. This is not an inferential step that produces a new proposition but an associative synthesis.

The living thing detected in perception does not appear as an amalgam or compound of two separate realities, one psychic and the other physical, nor as a two-layered psycho-physical reality. Such conceptualizations belong to the psychological sciences and the life sciences, not to straightforward perception, and they depend on the goals, the methods, and the techniques of these sciences. Instead of manifesting itself as a compounded or layered structure, the living being appears as a uniform whole of governed movements, meaningful gestures and significant behaviors (Husserl 1950: 150–3/121–4; cf. 1952: 234–41/245–53).

28.3 AN EXEMPLARY APPLICATION: SEXUAL IDENTITY AS A STYLISTIC WHOLE

One of the best-known areas in which the classical Husserlian distinctions between different senses of bodily being are applied today is in the philosophy of mind, or more precisely the philosophy of perception. Starting from Husserl's and Merleau-Ponty's discussion of embodiment and the body as a sensory-motor agent, several theorists

---

[12] The terms "restore," "spontaneous," and "reflexive," used here to characterize the movements of the other, need to be put in quotation marks since prior to the empathetic transfer of the sense all terms with subjective connotations are merely applicable to my own body and since it is only the empathetic transfer of sense that allows us to extend the use of these terms to environing bodies.

have attacked the computational, formal-semantic, and internalistic approaches that dominated the theorization of the mind at the end of the last century.[13] Today, phenomenological discussions of perception are often paralleled with the models developed by externalists and enactivists and contrasted with McDowell's conceptualistic theory of perception.

Another important area of application is in the philosophy of illness and medicine. Here phenomenological analyses illuminate the bodily and intersubjective aspects of psychopathologies, e.g., anorexia, depression, schizophrenia, and dementia, but they also shed light on the paradoxical character of medical technologies, for example, life-support systems, organ transplants, and cosmetic surgery.[14] In addition, classical phenomenology offers a set of general operative concepts for the analysis of the phenomena of normality and abnormality, including the concepts of concordance, optimacy, and liminality.[15]

In addition to the philosophy of mind and the philosophy of illness, phenomenological distinctions also figure prominently in today's social and political philosophy. The phenomenologically informed concept of the body-subject, as distinct from biological organisms, provides a starting point for many approaches in gender and race studies. Some of these approaches discuss the human body as an expressive unit with ethical and political dimensions, while others emphasize the body's mediating role in practical, instrumental, and technological settings. Moreover, the phenomenological account of the body as an subject of action and experience provides a viable alternative and complement to the dominant Foucaultian mode of theorization in which the body is conceived as a social-cultural product and an inscription of discursive power.

All these areas of application are developing rapidly today and produce new conceptualizations and completely new research questions in the fields of the philosophy of mind, the philosophy of medicine, political philosophy, and social ontology. As such, each deserves its own individual discussion and assessment in comparison to competing paradigms. Such accounts are available in several recent volumes presenting the field of contemporary phenomenology.[16]

[13] Computational approaches were developed in the 1970s and 1980s most importantly by Hilary Putnam, Jerry Fodor, and Zenon Pylyshyn on the basis of Turing's groundbreaking definition of computation. The early critics of these include, for example, Hubert Dreyfus and John Haugeland, who both were influenced by Heidegger's and Merleau-Ponty's analyses of intentionality. Externalistic approaches have later been developed, for example, by Francisco Varela, Evan Thompson, and Eleanor Rosch, and most recently by Alva Noë and Daniel Hutto.

[14] This particular area of application has a long history, including authors such as Kimura Bin, Eugène Minkowski, Karl Jaspers, and Ludwig Binswanger. Contemporary contributors include Thomas Fuchs, Josef Parnas, Mathew Ratcliffe, Louis Sass, Fredrik Svenaeus, and Dan Zahavi. New dimensions have been also introduced by Lisa Käll, Dorothée Legrand, Stefano Micali, and Jenny Slatman.

[15] The concepts of normality and normativity have been clarified, most importantly, by Bernhard Waldenfels, Anthony Steinbock, and Steven Crowell; new contributions also include those by Maxime Doyon, Théo Breyer, and Maren Wehrle.

[16] Discussions of these areas of application can be found in this volume as well as in *The Oxford Handbook of Contemporary Phenomenology* (Zahavi 2015) and in *The Routledge Companion to Phenomenology* (Luft and Overgaard 2012).

In this historical-philosophical framework, I want to draw attention to one particular discussion that has developed within the intersection of the aforementioned two areas of investigation which both draw from classical phenomenology of embodiment, i.e., the philosophy of perception and political philosophy. This is the phenomenological discussion on sexual identities and sexual difference.[17] An excursion into this particular topic is especially clarifying since it demonstrates how critical and normative philosophical perspectives have been developed within phenomenology, a discipline still often assumed to be preoccupied with purely theoretical matters or else historical-exegetic problematics.

In order to see the philosophical relevance of this particular area of application, it is crucial to recall that our contemporary theoretical debates on sexual difference have long and deep roots. The philosophical discussion of sexual difference began with Aristotle's political theory of women as rational animals with non-authoritative practical reason and, through the egalitarian and ethical alternatives developed by the Stoics, it ranged to the Enlightenment discussions concerning the capacities and excellences of men and women. From its very beginnings, the discourse combined biological, medical, moral-philosophical, and metaphysical interests. In the twentieth century, it culminated in the controversy between biological determinists and social constructivists. While the former suggested that most, if not all, observable differences between women and men result from organic differences that are hardwired in their neurological makeup of the human species, the latter argued that most, if not all, such differences are cultural-historical constructs, and as such highly variable and liable to radical changes.

Here phenomenology offers an original perspective that helps to overcome the common assumptions of both biologistic and constructivistic arguments. On the basis of its elaborate concepts of embodiment it is able to bypass the late modern disputes over nature versus nurture and open new grounds for inquiries into the experiential relations between men and women. At the same time it contributes to contemporary social ontology by offering explications of the concrete meaning of being human—man or woman.

The Husserlian account of embodiment offers the possibility of conceptualizing the question of sexual identity and sexual difference in a new way. We do not need to restrict ourselves to explaining such identities and differences by empirical realities: hormones, genes, stimulus response-systems, social roles, or historical facts. More fundamentally, we can understand sexual difference by intentional and temporal concepts as a difference between two different modes or styles of intentionally relating. As types of bodily subjectivity, masculinity and femininity, manhood and womanhood, are not anchored on any particular objects, but are given as two different modes of relating to objects, acting on them and being affected by them. Sexual identities are thus constituted together or

---

[17] Phenomenology of sexual difference and gender started to develop systematically at the end of 1980s, and was advanced by the contributions of Bernhard Waldenfels, Iris Marion Young, Linda Fisher, Sara Heinämaa, Silvia Stoller, and Gail Weiss. Most recent contributors include Alia Al-Saji, Sara Ahmed, Lisa Käll, Anne Leeuwen, and Lanei Rodemeyer.

parallel with our own living bodies, those special "things," that connect us to all material things and to the world as an open totality.

When sexual identity is understood as a modal or stylistic identity, it runs through one's whole life as a way or manner in which lived experiences and acts follow each other, continue, and change. And when this manner of changing itself changes—for example, in childhood, adolescence, sickness, or old age—then "it does so in a characteristic way, such that a unitary style manifests itself once more" (Husserl 1952: 270/283; cf. 1973a: 37–8; 2002: 200).

In *Phenomenology of Perception*, Merleau-Ponty uses the Husserlian concepts of style in a comprehensive manner to characterize the individuality and the unity of dynamically evolving totalities, persons, and their works on the one hand, and the world as a whole on the other (Merleau-Ponty [1945] 1993: 377–81/293–6; cf. 100/73–4, 176/133–6, 214/164–5, 461/359, 465/361–2, 519/406; Husserl 1973a: 128–9). He also applies these concepts explicitly in his analysis of the variety of human sexuality and the difference between men and women. In a late essay "Indirect Language and the Voices of Silence," we read:

> A woman passing by ... is a certain manner of being flesh which is given entirely in her walk ... a very noticeable variation of the norm of walking, looking, touching, and speaking that I possess in my self-awareness because I am body. (Merleau-Ponty 1960: 54)

Ultimately, maleness and femaleness are, in the phenomenological account, two variations of our basic corporeal way of relating to the world; they are two general types that include uncounted individual styles of behavior.[18] Every individual creates a modification of these two principal types. Most modifications develop and amplify the duality, but some work to undo or annul it. The development of a sexual identity, in any case, is not accounted for by objectivities, but by imitation and mimicry, repetition and modification of action (and passion).[19]

This does not mean that sexual identity is a question of choice. To suggest that we decide to be men and women is to commit an intellectualistic fallacy. Sexual identities are not and cannot be determined at will, they are experienced and formed already on the level of perception and motility.

---

[18] My discussion of woman and man as two experiential and intentional *types* depends on Husserl's distinction between two different kinds of generalities—(i) types and (ii) concepts—as explicated in his *Experience and Judgment* (*Erfahrung und Urteil* 1939). The main point here is that whereas the concept *woman* includes individual women as equal and interchangeable instances, the type *woman* includes women as partially similar singulars that cannot be replaced one for the other. For a fuller account of woman and man as two types, and for its Husserlian background, see Heinämaa 2011.

[19] For a full account of the relations between the phenomenological analysis of sexual difference, on the one hand, and empirical scientific accounts of sex/gender (bio-scientific and social scientific), see Heinämaa 2010.

In order to see how this view of sexual identities emerged and developed in the twentieth century, it is important to study the debates of French existentialists after the Second World War. A central figure here was the French philosopher and novelist Simone de Beauvoir who, in her magnum opus, *The Second Sex*, based her discussion on sexual difference on the phenomenological concepts of embodiment that she found articulated in the works of her philosophical collaborators Sartre and Merleau-Ponty.[20] I have argued elsewhere that it was the Husserlian distinction between the lived body (*Leib*) and the organism (*Körper*) that allowed Beauvoir to develop her radical philosophical account of sexual relations (Heinämaa 2003; 2012). I will focus my discussion here on her understanding of sexual difference as an existential-phenomenological category that refers to two fundamentally different ways of being human. This historical excursion is crucial to contemporary phenomenology since it allows us to notice that from its very beginnings twentieth-century phenomenology discussed human existence not as a homogenous unity, but as a plurality that involves endless variations and two generative types.

28.4 A Philosophical Debate on the Existential Status of Sexual Difference

Simone de Beauvoir found herself involved in a peculiar philosophical controversy over the phenomenon of sexual difference. This involved her nearest philosophical collaborators, Sartre and Merleau-Ponty, but also their common phenomenological sources, Heidegger and Levinas. On the one hand, there was Sartre's understanding, spelled out in *Being and Nothingness* (1943), according to which Heidegger's Daseins-analysis renders maleness/femaleness and masculinity/femininity as contingent and accidental configurations without existential or transcendental relevance.[21] In Sartre's

---

[20] More precisely, Beauvoir found Husserl's distinctions discussed and developed by Sartre in *Being and Nothingness* (1943) and by Merleau-Ponty in *Phenomenology of Perception* (1945), but she also knew Levinas's doctoral dissertation *The Theory of Intuition in Husserl's Phenomenology* (*La théorie de l'intuition dans la phénoménologie de Husserl* 1930) and his innovative account of erotic intentionality in *Time and Other* (*Le temps et l'autre* 1947).

[21] Concerning this point, Sartre argues, Heidegger fails to question the philosophical tradition. His analysis repeats the ancient prejudice according to which human sexuality is merely a dimension of instinctual animal life and has nothing to do with the essence of the human psyche: "The term 'instinct' always in fact qualifies contingent formations of psychic life which have the double character of being co-extensive with all the duration of this life . . . and of nevertheless not being such that they can be deduced as belonging to the very essence of the psychic. This is why existential philosophies have not believed it necessary to concern themselves with sexuality. Heidegger in particular, does not make the slightest allusion to it in his existential analytic with the result that his 'Dasein' appears to us as asexual. Of course, one may consider that it is contingent for 'human reality' to be specified as 'masculine' or 'feminine'; of course, one may say that the problem of sexual differentiation has nothing to do with that of Existence

understanding, the difference between men and women was for Heidegger merely an ontic formation without any fundamental ontological dimensions, comparable to the difference between left-handed and right-handed human beings or that between tall and short people.

In *The Second Sex*, Beauvoir's argues that such analyses trivialize our perceptual experience and neglect our historical understanding. She pointed out, first, that human kind seems to divide itself, constantly and universally, into two different groups, not just biologically but also in terms of its activities and passivities. She then resorted to the phenomenological notion of humanity, not as a natural species, but more fundamentally, as an open-ended totality of possibilities. This suggested to her that the sexual divide is not just a biological formation or a cultural variable but more fundamentally a mode of our being and becoming. In *The Second Sex*, she articulates this insight in reference to Merleau-Ponty's *Phenomenology* as follows:

> As Merleau-Ponty very justly puts it, man is not a species: he is a historical idea. Woman is not a completed reality, but rather a becoming, and it is in her becoming that she should be compared to man; that is to say, her *possibilities* should be defined. (Beauvoir [1949] 1993: 71–3/66; cf. 19–20/19–20; [1949] 1991: 661/740)

To be sure, Heidegger's analysis gives the sexed body an ontic significance, or a role in regional ontologies, to put it in Husserlian terms. More precisely, according to Heidegger's account, the categories of femaleness/maleness and womanhood/manhood may serve several regional ontologies, for example, those of the biosciences and medicine (sex) and those of anthropology and the social sciences (gender); but despite such regional roles, the sexed body has no fundamental ontological significance. In other words, the categories of womanhood and manhood are mere empirical categories for Heidegger, and Dasein is "sexually neutral."

In the light of Beauvoir's analysis, this is an untenable view and a prejudiced notion: Sexual difference is not an empirical accident but pierces down to the very foundation of human existence. The categories of womanhood and manhood may be incidental or idle in some other existential situation than ours, and they may become obsolete to us in the future, but as we now stand here, in this particular existential-historical situation, these categories do not just serve the sciences or some particular practices (e.g., those of reproduction) but relate to the fundamental temporal structures of human *Mitsein*.[22]

Sartre's existentialism offered an alternative way to inspect the ontological dimensions of sexual difference, but the ontological distinction that Sartre introduced

---

[*Existenz*] since man and woman equally exist. These reasons are not wholly convincing. That sexual differentiation lies within the domain of facticity we accept with reservation. But does this mean that the For-itself is sexual 'accidentally', by the pure contingency of having this particular body" (Sartre [1943] 1998: 423/383). Cf. Henry 1965; but see also Henry 1963.

[22] For a more complete account, see Heinämaa 2010.

between in-itself and for-itself was problematic for Beauvoir, since its two poles were mutually exclusive and as such limited possibilities to account for our bodily being-for-others. The Sartrean concept rendered human bodies as instrumental means and as meta-instruments for the manipulation of other instruments and neglected the fundamental character of the body as an expressive unit.[23] For this reason, Beauvoir preferred Merleau-Ponty's interpretation of phenomenology that allowed her to conceptualize one's own body (*corps propre*) as the nexus of being-for-oneself and being-with-others. Her Merleau-Ponty quotation, given above, refers us to the last page of the chapter on sexuality in *Phenomenology of Perception*, where Merelau-Ponty redefines the relations between the contingencies and necessities of human life as follows:

> Human existence will force us to revise our usual notion of necessity and contingency, because it is the transformation of contingency into necessity by the act of taking in hand. All that we are, we are on the basis of a *de facto* situation which we appropriate to ourselves and which we ceaselessly transform by a sort of *escape* which is never an unconditioned freedom. There is no explanation of sexuality which reduces it to anything other than itself, for it is already something other than itself, and indeed, if we like, our whole being. (Merleau-Ponty [1945] 1993: 199/152)

In addition to this debate on the ontological significance of sexual difference between Heidegger and his existentialist followers, Beauvoir was also influenced by the discussion of femininity that she found in Levinas's early work, *Time and Other* (1947a). In this book, Levinas developed a forceful critique of Heidegger's account of the constitution of time and temporality by substituting the model of fecundity and generativity for Heidegger's paradigm of mortality and being-towards-death.[24] This led him to develop an account of the plurality of human existence.

Beauvoir sympathized with this goal, but it seemed to her that Levinas was able to shake the Heideggerian framework only at the price of a disappointing analysis of erotic intentionality (cf. Marion 2003). In a now notoriously well-known paragraph, Levinas opposed femininity to consciousness by writing: "Otherness reaches its full flowering in the feminine, a term of the same rank as consciousness but of opposite meaning" (Levinas 1947b: 81/88).

Beauvoir saw Levinas's description as a late modern version of an ancient form of thinking that mystifies women by confusing two different uses of the term "other." First, the term was used for another similar being (*semblable*). When we identify ourselves as perceivers, for example, then we use the term "other(s)" to refer to other perceivers. If we are discussing experience and consciousness more generally, then we are talking about other consciousnesses and other selves (e.g., Beauvoir [1949] 1993: 17–18/17, 120ff./100ff;

---

[23] Sartre's discussion of flesh did not extend the analytical potential of his concepts since it described flesh as a residue left after the reduction of all instrumental relations of active and potent bodies.

[24] The aim of his lectures, Levinas explained, was "to show that time is not the achievement of an isolated and lone or solitary subject, but that it is the very relationship of the subject with the Other" (Levinas 1947b: 14/39).

cf. Husserl 1973a: 94–8). However, in Levinas's discussion, the term also carried a second meaning. It was not only another experiencing self or another consciousness that was at issue, but rather what was alien to all consciousness (Beauvoir [1949] 1993: 655/265). In Beauvoir's reading, Levinas's discussion of erotic intentionality and fecundity confused these different senses, the relative sense of "other" in respect to some specific self or community of selves, and the absolute sense of "other" in respect to all selfhood. And, what is worse, it assimilated absolute otherness with femininity.

Beauvoir argued that the opposition between consciousness and femininity is based on mystifying habits of thought that associate femininity and women with animality, sensibility, and instincts, and masculinity and men with the intellect, the spirit, and pure ideas. In her reading, this associative mode of thinking impaired both classical and contemporary analyses of the human condition. She lays the basis of this argument at the beginning of *The Second Sex*, in the introductory chapter, but continues her discussion throughout the extensive first book to its final pages, where she summarizes her view as follows:

> Each can grasp in immanence only himself, alone: from this point of view the other is always a mystery . . . But in accordance with the universal rule I have stated, the categories in which men think of the world are established *from their point of view, as absolute*: they misconceive reciprocity, here as everywhere. A mystery for man, woman is considered to be mysterious in essence. (Beauvoir [1949] 1993: 653/263)

In the light of the conflicting debates of her contemporaries, Beauvoir realized that a philosophical account of sexual difference must be grounded, first, on a critical reexamination of the traditional ideas of embodiment and sensibility and, second, on a first-person account of the experience of being woman. Traditional conceptions of the human condition were in her analysis systematically biased and in need of a fundamental revision.

28.5 Toward the Understanding of the Twoness of Human Embodiment

Beauvoir could not find a reexamination of the human body in Heidegger's *Being and Time*. Heidegger offered elaborate descriptions and analyses of our being-in-the-world (*in-der-Welt-Sein*), a corporeal relation to be sure, but he refrained from thematizing and conceptualizing the living body (e.g., Heidegger [1927] 1993: 104–113/97–105). The reason for this was Heidegger's conviction that all philosophies of consciousness, spirit, soul, and person—and the related philosophies of embodiment—are fundamentally defective in building on naïve taken-for-granted notions of being (e.g., Heidegger [1927] 1993: 48/44–6, 117/110; cf. [1925] 1979: 172–3). Moreover, since Heidegger was struggling to liberate his thinking from the epistemological legacy of classical phenomenology and its analyses of intentionality, his discourse of being-in-the-world was preoccupied with the practical-instrumental relations and bypassed the aesthetic and erotic variations of existence that Beauvoir saw as more revealing for the task of articulating sexual difference.[25]

Sartre's *Being and Nothingness* and Merleau-Ponty's *Phenomenology of Perception* both offered detailed and elaborate distinctions between different senses of bodily being, informed by classical phenomenological analyses. Both works discussed human bodies as objects of natural sciences, as instruments in multiple practical settings, as expressive gestures in communication and as our very means of having the world—or our "anchorage" in the world, as Beauvoir herself formulates it in the review that she wrote on Merleau-Ponty's *Phenomenology* for *Les temps modernes* in 1945.

But in Beauvoir's reading, Sartre's account was impaired by his indebtedness to Hegelian dialectics and its idealistic metaphysics which suggested the notion that our bodies are given to us either as fully active instruments or else as viscous sensible flesh. Merleau-Ponty's analyses were free from such dualistic notions, mainly because of his interest in the philosophy of nature and the life sciences. In the aforementioned review, Beauvoir puts great emphasis on the fact that Merleau-Ponty's modification of phenomenology does not oppose consciousness with being but describes a living bond or, better, a stratification of such bonds. For Merleau-Ponty, she writes, quoting his words, the subject "is not a pure for-itself, nor a gap in being, as Hegel wrote, and Sartre repeated, but it is 'a hollow, a fold which has been made and can be unmade'" (Beauvoir 1945: 367).[26]

The tension between these divergent conceptions of subjectivity, Sartrean and Merleau-Pontyan, pervades Beauvoir's discussion of sexual difference in *The Second Sex*. She formulates her main theses with Sartrean concepts of immanence and transcendence, being-in-itself and being-for-itself, but her descriptions of the bodily experiences of women and men, and the world as experienced by these two types of subjectivities, systematically undermine the oppositional Sartrean concepts.

---

[25] E.g., Beauvoir [1949] 1991: 485/609, 501/622. But see also Heidegger 1987.

[26] The contrast with Hegel's philosophy is part of Merleau-Ponty's original text (Merleau-Ponty [1945] 1993: 249/192; see also Merleau-Ponty 1960: 249/196, 286/233), but the comment on Sartre is added by Beauvoir. Her juxtaposition suggests that our choice is between two principal notions of consciousness and subjectivity. On the one hand, we have philosophies that define consciousness in opposition to being. For Hegel, she says, consciousness was a "gap in being," for Sartre it is a nothingness, a pure activity of negating or nihilating (*néantisation*). On the other hand, we have philosophies in which consciousness is not opposed to being, but is consistently conceptualized as a dynamic relation with being. This view Beauvoir finds elaborated in Merleau-Ponty's *Phenomenology of Perception*: "While Sartre in *Being and Nothingness* emphasized from the beginning the opposition between being-for-itself and being-in-itself, the spirit's power of negation in relation to being and its absolute freedom, Merleau-Ponty, on the contrary, sticks to the description of the concrete character of the subject which for him is never a pure being-for-itself. He thinks in effect that our existence never knows itself in its nudity, but only insofar as it is expressed by our body; and this body is not shut in an instant, but involves a whole history, even a prehistory" (Beauvoir 1945: 366).

The Second Sex demonstrates that women's lived experiences (*expérience vécue*) of their own bodies and the bodies of others undermine traditional accounts of the self–other relation and the dominant notion of intersubjectivity as a relation between subjects of equal capacities and potentials. In her view, two forms of feminine experience especially attest to the complexity of the structure of human existence. These are the experiences of pregnancy and erotic desire. In both cases, women's ways of experiencing their own bodies and the bodies of others confuse the traditional account that presents living bodies as tools or instruments for well-defined ends and as neutral media of communion (Beauvoir [1949] 1993: 485/609). She ends her inquiry by arguing that sexual difference is a permanent condition of being human:

> There will always be certain differences between men and women; her eroticism, and therefore her sexual world, have a singular form of their own and therefore cannot fail to engender a singular sensuality, a singular sensitivity. Her relations to her own body, to that of the male, to the child, will never be identical with those the male bears to his own body, to the feminine body, and to the child. (Beauvoir [1949] 1991: 661/740)

Beauvoir's argument is exceptional in twentieth-century philosophy, since it rejects the idea of one homogeneous or harmonious humankind, not merely by conceptualizing an open-ended plurality, but also by theorizing a twoness.[27] For methodological reasons it is important to notice, however, that Beauvoir's work is not completely unparalleled in the field of phenomenology. Similar analyses of the twoness of the human condition were developed by early phenomenologists before the First World War and between the wars, most importantly by Edith Stein and Max Scheler.

Stein and Scheler both utilized classical Husserlian concepts of embodiment and personhood, but developed them for their own ethical and social-theoretical interests, Stein in relation to Thomistic anthropology, and Scheler in relation to neo-Kantians and Brentano.[28] Despite these differences, both Stein and Scheler presented arguments about a fundamental twoness of the human condition, analogous to the arguments that we find in Beauvoir's *The Second Sex*. In her lectures on women, Stein contends:

---

[27] The two types *woman* and *man* cut across most social groups and surpass all cultural and historical boundaries known, but they do not coincide with the chromosomal categories *XX-individual/XY-individual* and their distinction is not exclusive or predetermined. Thus, it is possible that we humans—as subjects of our intentional lives—develop in such a manner that we cannot anymore, at some point of our common time, distinguish between the two types, or are no longer motivated to do so. However, this distinction always remains part of our lives, since these lives, as intentional, are essentially intersubjective and historical (genetic and generative). So even if the distinction between the types *woman* and *man* were erased in some common future, it would still characterize us as humans: no longer as posited or re-posited, but now as erased and overcome.

[28] We also find reflections of sexual difference in Eugen Fink's philosophical anthropology (1977, 1987, 1992) but his main starting points are in Hegel's moral and political philosophy, Heidegger's fundamental ontology, and the cosmological tradition of Western philosophy, not in Husserl's reflections on bodily persons.

I am convinced . . . that the essence of human being, whose features cannot be lacking in either one ["man" and "woman"], becomes expressed in a binate way; that the entire essential structure demonstrates the specific stamp. It is not only the material body [*Körper*] that is structured differently; not only is there a difference in particular physiological functions, but the entire living-body life [*Leibesleben*] is different; the relationship of soul and living body [*Leib*] is different, and within what pertains to the soul, the relation of spirit to sensibility as well as the relation of spiritual faculties to one another, is different. (Stein 2015: 167/187)

In Scheler's "Zum Sinn der Frauenbewegung" (1913/1914), we read:

Sexual difference is *spiritual* as *originally* as it is bodily or biological . . . In general closer inquiries will show here that sexual difference pierces down to the deepest sources [*Wurzel*] of the spirit itself, that for example the womanly concept, womanly judgment, and womanly feeling of value is built in a fundamentally different way. (Scheler [1913/1914] 2007: 205)

Moreover, in "Zur Idee des Menschen," Scheler argues that the idea of an androgynous human being is a prejudiced idea, typical of the mental makeup of men: "Also the idea of a human being that includes man and woman is only a manly idea. I do not believe that this idea would have originated and developed in a culture ruled by women. Only man is so 'spiritual', so 'dualistic' and so . . . childish, to overlook the depth of the difference that is called sexual" (Scheler [1914] 2007: 195; cf. [1915] 1955: 205).

The conceptual device that allowed these reflections on the twoness of human existence was Husserl's distinction between different senses of the living body. By introducing the analysis of the body as the center of perception, action, and communication Husserl made possible a whole new set of philosophical questions concerning human bodies and their relations to the environing world, to other bodies, to human minds, and to themselves. These questions did not concern causal and functional relations between spatiotemporal worldly entities but concerned human bodies as centers and sources of meaning.

28.6 CONCLUSION

We have seen that classical Husserlian phenomenology offers powerful conceptual tools for the analysis of different senses of bodily being. These tools include (i) the conceptual distinction between the body as a material thing (*Körper*) and the body as our way of being in the world (*Leib*), (ii) the distinction between one's own body as a double structure of sensing-sensed and the other's body as an analogous structure, and (iii) the distinction between two alternative ways of apprehending bodies as environing objects: the naturalistic apprehension that articulates the human body as a two-layered reality and the personalistic apprehension that articulates it as an expressive whole. I argued that these Husserlian distinctions must not be understood as oppositions but must be seen as differentiating between mutually complementing and supplementing structures of possible experience. However, the Husserlian framework also includes a strong critical line of thought that renders the naturalistic attitude as a secondary formation, dependent on the personalistic attitude. I discussed the grounds of this argument in Husserl's theory of individuation.

My essay has also referred to several themes and topics, the treatment of which demonstrates the relevance of Husserlian concepts of embodiment to contemporary philosophy. The most important areas of application are found in the fields of philosophy of mind and perception, social ontology, philosophy of medicine, and social and political philosophy. However, attention was drawn to one contemporary area of application: the problems of sexual identity and difference. Through the discussion of sexual identities and sexual difference, we came to see that the Husserlian concepts of embodiment explicated in the chapter allow us to conceive the generality of human embodiment, not as a universal that encompasses equal instances, but as a stylistic whole that involves unique variations. Moreover, I argued that in this framework, human embodiment is not merely discussed as an open plurality but also as a generative structure that involves two main variants, the feminine and the masculine. I ended my discussion with a historical overview of the development of these ideas in post-Husserlian studies concerning the sense of human existence.

REFERENCES

Beauvoir, S. de (1945), "La phénoménologie de la perception de Maurice Merleau-Ponty," *Les temps modernes* 1/2: 363–7.

Beauvoir, S. de ([1949] 1993), *Le deuxième sexe I: les faits et les mythes* (Paris: Gallimard). In English *The Second Sex*, translated and ed. H. M. Parshley (Harmondsworth: Penguin, 1987).

Beauvoir, S. de ([1949] 1991), *Le deuxième sexe II: l'expérience vécue* (Paris: Gallimard). In English *The Second Sex*, translated and ed. H. M Parshley (Harmondsworth: Penguin, 1987).

Behnke, E. A. (2011), "Edmund Husserl: Phenomenology of Embodiment," *Internet Encyclopedia of Philosophy*, www.iep.utm.edu/husspemb/

Boublil, E. (2014), *Individuation et vision du monde: enquête sur l'héritage ontologique de la phénoménologie* (Bucharest: Zeta Books).

Dodd, J. (1997), *Idealism and Corporeity: An Essay on the Problem of the Body in Husserl's Phenomenology* (Dordrecht: Springer).

Fink, E. (1977), *Sein und Mensch: Vom Wesen der ontologischen Erfahrung*, ed. E. Schütz and F.-A. Schwarz (Freiburg: Alber).

Fink, E. (1987), *Existenz und Coexistenz: Grundprobleme der menschlichen Gemeinschaft*, ed. F.-A. Schwarz (Würtzburg: Könighausen and Neumann).

Fink, E. (1992), *Natur, Freiheit, Welt: Philosophie der Erziehung*, ed. F.-A. Schwarz (Würtzburg: Könighausen and Neumann).

Heidegger, M. ([1925] 1979), *Prolegomena zur Geschichte des Zeitbegriffs, Gesamtausgabe, II. Abteilung: Vorlesungen 1923–1944, Band 20*, ed. P. Jaeger (Frankfurt a. M.: Klostermann). In

English *History of the Concept of Time*, translated by T. Kisiel (Bloomington, IN: Indiana University Press, 1992).

Heidegger, M. ([1927] 1993), *Sein und Zeit* (Tübingen: Max Niemeyer). In English *Being and Time*, translated by J. Stambaugh (New York: SUNY, 1996).

Heidegger, M. (1987), *Zollikoner Seminare: Protokolle–Zwiegespräche–Briefe, Gesamtsausgabe 89* (Frankfurt a. M.: Klostermann). In English *Zollikon Seminars: Protocols–Conversations–Letters*, ed. M. Boss, translated by F. M. and R. Askay (Evanston, IL: Northwestern University Press, 2001).

Heinämaa, S. (2003), *Toward a Phenomenology of Sexual Difference: Husserl, Merleau-Ponty, Beauvoir* (Lanham, MD: Rowman and Littlefield).

Heinämaa, S. (2010), "Phenomenologies of mortality and generativity," in R. M. Schott (ed.), *Birth, Death, and Femininity: Philosophies of Embodiment* (Bloomington, IN: Indiana University Press), 73–156.

Heinämaa, S. (2011), "A phenomenology of sexual difference: Types, styles, and persons," in C. Witt (ed.), *Feminist Metaphysics: Explorations in the Ontology of Sex, Gender and Identity* (Dordrecht: Springer), 131–55.

Heinämaa, S. (2012), "Sex, gender and embodiment," in D. Zahavi (ed.), *The Oxford Handbook of Contemporary Phenomenology* (Oxford University Press), 216–42.

Heinämaa, S. (2014), "The animal and the infant: From embodiment and empathy to generativity," in S. Heinämaa, M. Hartimo, and T. Miettinen (eds), *Phenomenology and the Transcendental* (London: Routledge), 129–46.

Henry, M. (1963), *L'essence de la manifestation I–II* (Paris: Presses universitaires de France). In English *The Essence of Manifestation*, translated by G. Etzkorn (The Hague: Martinus Nijhoff, 1973).

Henry, M. (1965), *Philosophie et phénoménologie du corps* (Paris: Presses universitaires de France). In English *Philosophy and Phenomenology of the Body*, translated by G. Etzkorn (The Hague: Martinus Nijhoff, 1975).

Husserl, E. (1950), *Cartesianische Meditationen und pariser Vorträge*, Husserliana 1, ed. S. Strasser (The Hague: Martinus Nijhoff). In English *Cartesian Meditations*, translated by D. Cairns (The Hague: Martinus Nijhoff, 1960). Originally published in French in 1931.

Husserl, E. (1952), *Ideen zu einer reinen Phänomenologie und phänomenologischen Philosophie, Zweites Buch: Phänomenologische Untersuchungen zur Konstitution*, Husserliana 4, ed. M. Bimel (The Hague: Martinus Nijhoff). In English *Ideas Pertaining to a Pure Phenomenology and to a Phenomenological Philosophy, Second Book: Studies in the Phenomenological Constitution*, translated by R. Rojcewicz and A. Schuwer (Dordrecht: Kluwer, 1993).

Husserl, E. (1954), *Die Krisis der europäischen Wissenschaften und die transzendentale Phänomenologie: Eine Einleitung in die phänomenologischen Philosophie*, Husserliana 6, ed. W. Biemel (The Hague: Martinus Nijhoff). In English *The Crisis of European Sciences and Transcendental Phenomenology: An Introduction to Phenomenological Philosophy*, translated by D. Carr (Evanston, IL: Northwestern University, 1988).

Husserl, E. (1973a): *Zur Phänomenologie der Intersubjektivität: Texte aus dem Nachlass, Dritter Teil: 1929–1935*, Husserliana 14, ed. I. Kern (The Hague: Martinus Nijhoff).

Husserl, E. (1973b), *Zur Phänomenologie der Intersubjektivität: Texte aus dem Nachlass, Dritter Teil: 1929–1935*, Husserliana 15, ed. I. Kern (The Hague: Martinus Nijhoff).

Husserl, E. (2002), *Zur phänomenologischen Reduktion: Texte aus dem Nachlass (1926-1935)*, Husserliana 34, ed. S. Luft (Dordrecht: Kluwer).

Levinas, E. (1947a), *Le temps et l'autre* (Paris: Quadrige/Presses universitaires de France). In English *Time and Other*, translated by R. A. Cohen (Pittsburgh, PA: Duquesne University Press, 1987).

Levinas, E. (1947b), *De l'existence à l'existant* (Paris: J. Vrin). In English *Existence and Existents*, translated by A. Lingis (The Hague: Martinus Nijhoff, 1978).

Luft, S. and S. Overgaard (eds) (2001), *The Routledge Companion to Phenomenology* (London: Routledge).

Marion, J.-L. (2003), *Le phénomène érotique: six méditations sur sur l'amour* (Paris: Grasset and Fasquelle). In English *The Erotic Phenomenon*, translated by S. E. Lewis (Chicago, IL: University of Chicago Press, 2006).

Melle, U. (1996), "Nature and spirit," in T. Nenon and L. Embree (eds), *Issues in Husserl's* Ideas II (Dordrecht: Springer), 15–36.

Mensch, J. R. (2001), *Postfoundational Phenomenology: Husserlian Reflections on Presence and Embodiment* (University Park, PA: Penn State University Press).

Merleau-Ponty, M. ([1945] 1993), *Phénoménologie de la perception* (Paris: Gallimard). In English *Phenomenology of Perception*, translated by C. Smith (London: Routledge, 1995).

Merleau-Ponty, M. (1960), *Signes* (Paris: Gallimard). In English *Signs*, translated by R. C. McCleary (Evanston, IL: Northwestern University Press, 1964).

Merleau-Ponty, M. (1969), *La prose du monde* (Paris: Gallimard). In English *The Prose of the World*, translated by J. O'Neill (Evanston, IL: Northwestern University Press, 1973).

Ricœur, P. (1967), *Husserl: An Analysis of his Phenomenology*, translated by E. G. Ballard and L. E. Embree (Evanston, IL: Northwestern University Press).

Roy, J.-M., J. Petitot, B. Pachoud, and F. J. Varela (1999), "Beyond the gap: An introduction to *Naturalizing Phenomenology*," in J. Petitot, F. J. Varela, B. Pachoud, and J.-M. Roy (eds), *Naturalizing Phenomenology: Issues in Contemporary Phenomenology and Cognitive Science* (Stanford, CA: Stanford University Press), 1–80.

Salanskis, J.-M. (1999), "Sense and continuum in Husserl," translated by G. Collins, in J. Petitot, F. J. Varela, B. Pachoud, and J.-M. Roy (eds), *Naturalizing Phenomenology: Issues in Contemporary Phenomenology and Cognitive Science* (Stanford, CA: Stanford University Press), 491–507.

Sartre, J.-P. ([1943] 1998), *L'être et le néant: essai d'ontologie phénoménologique* (Paris: Gallimard). In English *Being and Nothingness: A Phenomenological Essay on Ontology*, translated by H. E. Barnes (New York: Washington Square Press).

Scheler, M. ([1913/1914] 2007), "Zum Sinn der Frauenbewegung," in M. Scheler (ed.), *Gesammelte Werke III: Vom Umsturz der Werte, Abhandlungen und Aufsätze* (Bonn: Bouvier).

Scheler, M. ([1914] 2007), "Zur Idee des Menschen," in M. Scheler (ed.), *Gesammelte Werke III: Vom Umsturz der Werte, Abhandlungen und Aufsätze* (Bonn: Bouvier).

Soffer, G. (1996), "Perception and its causes, " in T. Nenon and L. Embree (eds), *Issues in Husserl's* Ideas II (Dordrecht: Springer), 37–56.

Stein, E. (1917), *Zum Problem der Einfühlung* (Halle). In English *On the Problem of Empathy*, translated by W. Stein (The Hague: Martinus Nijhoff, 1964).

Stein, E. (2015), *Die Frau: Fragestellungen und Reflexionen, Gesamtausgabe, Band 13* (Freiburg: Herder).

Summa, M. (2013), "Process and Relation: Husserl's Theory of Individuation Revisited," *New Yearbook for Phenomenology and Phenomenological Philosophy*, 12: 109–35.

Taipale, J. (2014), *Phenomenology and Embodiment: Husserl and the Constitution of Subjectivity* (Evanston, IL: Northwestern University Press).

Welton, D. (1999), "Soft, smooth hands: Husserl's phenomenology of the lived-body," in D. Welton (ed.), *The Body* (Malden, MA: Blackwell), 38–56.

Zahavi, D. (ed.) (2015), *The Oxford Handbook of Contemporary Phenomenology* (Oxford: Oxford University Press).

CHAPTER 29

FROM THE ORIGIN OF SPATIALITY TO A VARIETY OF SPACES

FILIP MATTENS

WHILE the distinctive feature of worldly entities is extension, "the Soul," Descartes stated, "is of such a nature that it has no relation to extension" (1649: I30). The resulting heterogeneity of mind and world, however, inspired various forms of skepticism concerning the very possibility of the mind's access to the outer world. In an attempt to fend off the idea that reality lies underneath the world as we perceive it, George Berkeley sought to demonstrate that a world existing independently of any perceiving mind is simply inconceivable. To promote this counterintuitive suggestion, he first published his short *Essay towards a New Theory of Vision* (1709). While its metaphysical message hardly gathered a following, its account of spatial perception became highly influential. By first reminding us that the retinal image cannot contain information about the distance of objects from the viewer, Berkeley suggests he needs no further proof that the visually appearing is not really out there where it seems to be. The visual *as such* cannot exist outside the mind; hence, we must accept that it is essentially non-spatial. Berkeley then explains that we nonetheless seem to see a spatial world because certain visual phenomena are associated with truly spatial perceptions acquired through moving and touching. Even though this proposal is empirically untenable, the idea that visual experience acquires spatial content through tactual interpretation convinced many philosophers up to the twentieth century. However, in the early nineteenth century the empirical investigation of the nervous system had already altered the problem, for it is unclear how a stimulus—be it visual or tactile—can report about its original location on the retina or on the skin when reaching the brain. This triggered a renewed interest among German psychologists and philosophers in the fundamental problem of a non-extended soul's experience of an extended world. Setting aside the Kantian suggestion that space is an a priori representation underlying all outer perception, Herbart demands in his 1825 *Psychologie als Wissenschaft* an answer to the question: How did we acquire the ability of spatial perception given that our presentations (*Vorstellungen*) are exclusively a matter of intensity? The assumption is that the "psychological event of spatial presentation is something entirely non-spatial" (1825: 124). Even the spatial organization within the retinal image disintegrates when it enters the soul. The soul must thus somehow reconstruct all spatial relations *ex novo*.

Herbart argued that spatiality emerges *in the presented* due to the orderly manner in which a manifold of presentations fuses (*verschmelzen*). An eye (or finger) at rest does not perceive space, Herbart observes, but when the eye (or finger) moves forward, the first presentations gradate (*abstufen*) as they sink away and thus fuse less and less with the following presentations; when the eye (or finger) returns, the series is reversed. In this process, each presentation obtains its relative position. Even though Herbart is credited with having reformulated the problem, Lotze (1846) objected that a series of tones can be played back without spatiality being generated. Lotze therefore proposed that another intensive element is connected with each presentation. He was particularly interested in explaining how two dots of color can simultaneously occur in different places. Lotze argued that each peripheral visual stimulus elicits a motor tendency to draw the stimulus in the center of the retina where eyesight is clearest. The feeling of this motor tendency is associated with the stimulation of a given point on the retina and thus attaches a certain spatial value—which Lotze later called a "local-sign"—to a stimulus occurring there. While Helmholtz rejected these local-signs as unobservable, Stumpf objected that they cannot be fine enough to explain the precision of visual localization. Stumpf himself was convinced that extension is not somehow added to the experience of color qualities since it is impossible to present a specific color to oneself without at the same time having a certain presentation of extension and vice versa. From this it follows "that space is as originally and immediately perceived as is the quality; for they constitute one inseparable content" (1873: 115). In this way, Stumpf believed to have undercut the most radical formulation of the problem, according to which only qualitative sensations are originally experienced.

This chapter will focus on two moments at which the problem of the origin of our spatial presentations steered the development of phenomenology. To begin with, this debate played a role in the emergence of phenomenology. During his doctoral exam in 1887, the young Husserl was interrogated by Stumpf on the history of theories of space, in particular on Lotze's hypothesis of "local-signs" (Schuhmann 1977: 19). Through his intensive study of Stumpf's *Über den Ursprung der Raumvorstellung* (1873), which critically reviews all existing proposals, Husserl was well informed about the elements with which philosophers and scientists sought to solve the puzzle of spatial perception. In the first part of this chapter, I will show how Husserl borrows several elements from various researchers and combines them with his own characterization of the intentional structure of external perception. It is in this phenomenological reconsideration of the problem of the origin of spatiality that the subject of perception comes to be understood as a subject of bodily capacities, involved in a peculiar form of praxis. In section 29.2, I focus on Erwin Straus's radical rejection of the classical problem itself. By focusing on auditory experience, which is generally neglected in the classical treatment of spatial perception, Straus seeks to upend the dominance of the praxis-oriented understanding of spatiality and reveals different "forms of spatiality" originating in the affective dimension of sense-perception. In section 29.3, I juxtapose the merits of Husserl's approach with Straus's reconception of sensation as an originary manner of spatially relating to the external world.

29.1 FROM COLOR TO PRACTICAL POSSIBILITIES: DISCLOSING OBJECTIVE SPACE WITH HUSSERL

In his early work on arithmetic, Husserl had observed that, while small number concepts stand for quantities that we can intuitively present, large number concepts stand for quantities that we cannot properly present. For this reason, Husserl distinguished between "proper presentations" and "improper presentations"; the object of the latter is not intuitively given. In the years following the publication of his *Philosophy of Arithmetic* (1891), Husserl compiled several preliminary outlines for a book on space—which he referred to as his *Raumbuch*—comprising geometrical and metaphysical issues as well as a descriptive and genetic inquiry into the psychological origin of our spatial perceptual presentations and concepts (Schuhmann 1977: 36–7). However, shortly after starting work on his *Raumbuch*, Husserl put this project on hold as he realized that the topic of perceptual space requires a further elaboration of the distinction between proper and improper presentations (Husserl 1979: 254). For, we cannot intuit the spatial world nor even a single spatial thing in its entirety; we have a proper presentation of the side of the thing facing us, but the reverse side is merely intended or as Husserl put it, "emptily" intended. Such empty intentions can be "fulfilled" if the perceiver moves so that the hidden sides are brought into view. Husserl's early reflections thus describe perception as a dynamic process driven by a desire for intuitive presence (see Wehrle 2015; Bernet 2003).

The crucial insight, however, consists in Husserl's descriptive analysis of the internal structure of the act of perception. When I look at a tomato, the intentional object of my perception is not the surface facing me; the object of my perception is the tomato. It is only because the actually appearing segment is encircled by empty intentions directed at the rest of it, that the properly present can be the side *of a thing*. Thus, an act of perception *necessarily* is a compound of intuitive presentation and empty intentions directed at what is not currently given of the thing; it always intends more than what is actually present. This insight into the essentially compound nature of perceptual acts entails at once a phenomenological clarification of the sense of "thing": the object of external perception is something that cannot be exhausted by any given episode of perception.

The idea that perception is a temporally extended, dynamic play of empty intentions and proper presentations will remain central to Husserl's reflections. However, it is first after the introduction of the phenomenological reduction that Husserl will return to the radical problem of the presentation of a spatial world to a non-spatial consciousness, namely in a lecture course from 1907, which Husserl referred to as his "Thing-lectures" (*Dingvorlesung*) (Husserl 1997). The phenomenological reduction frees conscious experiences from all references to transcendent entities; what remains are "pure phenomena." Arguably, as Claesges (1973: xxiv) suggests, Husserl tackles the problem of space immediately following the discovery of the reduction, since it allows him to invoke bodily movements as pure phenomena. While the experience of movements had been introduced in the debate on the origin of space as "movement sensations" or "muscle feelings,"[1] these terms are based on physiological knowledge and invoke transcendent entities (muscles make the body move; movement is a change of position in space). Therefore, Husserl prefers using the foreign term "kinaesthetic sensations" to denote the purely phenomenological datum of the *lived experience* of self-moving. Thus, within a phenomenological analysis, the phrase "when I make a bodily movement" means "when I enact (*inszeniere*) a certain kinaesthetic sequence" (1997: 239). Kinaesthesis, as Husserl later says, stands for "the inner 'I move'" and as such, kinaestheses have no spatial significance whatsoever (1973: 268). Yet they will be crucial for elucidating how a spatial world can appear to consciousness.

So, the task of a phenomenological approach to the problem of space is to elucidate how spatiality comes to givenness *while* exclusively relying on what can be found within conscious experience (and this includes the experienced *as such*).[2] Let us now consider the essential steps in the constitution of perceptual space. Husserl starts from the most elementary conscious phenomena in external perception, namely various sorts of sensations (visual, tactile, olfactory . . .). Such sensory material is not perceived, but sensed—or "lived" (*erlebt*). In a first step, Husserl relies on Stumpf's observation that one cannot present to oneself a specific color or texture without picturing it as spread out over a certain expanse.[3] A specific shade of red can only be what it is for us *as* the qualitative filling of some expanse. Somehow, color-sensations seem to be inextricably

---

[1] In his discussion of Herbart, Lotze used the terms "*Bewegungstendenz*" and "*Muskelgefühle*" (1846: 176).

[2] Arguably, the phenomenological project with its methodological abstraction from all reference to transcendent entities radicalizes the classical problem. In his *Ideas*, Husserl writes: "The problem of the '*origin of the presentation of space*,' whose profoundest, phenomenological sense has never been apprehended, reduces to the phenomenological analysis of the *essence* of all the noematic (or respectively noetic) phenomena in which space displays itself intuitively and 'constitutes' itself as the unity of appearances, the unity of the descriptive manners of displaying the spatial" (1983: 362).

[3] Only color-sensations and texture-sensations are intrinsically related with extension. As a consequence, only visual and tactual experience are capable of constituting the extended surfaces that define spatial bodies. As Husserl points out, colors and textures cover and fill the surface of objects whereas sounds and odours don't. Rather than properly showing things, they are attributed to things by us. Therefore, Husserl will distinguish between properties that are involved in the constitution of things as spatial bodies and merely "appended" properties, like a thing's smell, sonic qualities, weight.

related to extension. Because they are intrinsically related to extension, color-sensations can fuse into a sense-field. This visually lived sense-field, however, is not pre-given but is itself constituted by a system of possible kinaestheses in two directions: It is an oculomotoric field of color-expanses. However, insofar as color-sensations are immanent to consciousness, such a lived expanse of color-sensations cannot be equated with the extendedness of the colored surface of the object existing in space. To avoid the suggestion that "colored surfaces" are simply implied in "lived color-sensations," Husserl refers to the extension inherent in color-sensations as "pre-empirical extension" (1997: 57ff.; 135). The question, then, is how a pre-empirical expanse of *sensed* redness can come to function the way it always already does in perception, namely as the redness of, say, the tomato's surface that I see *over there*?

At this point, Husserl observes a connection between visual sensations and kinaesthetic sensations. This connection is not a form of mere association (as, e.g., for example in Berkeley's account), but concerns a peculiar interplay. This interplay is possible because visual and kinaesthetic sensations are *functionally* different: Whereas color-sensations feature in the visual manifestation of external objects, kinaesthetic sensations do not. Rather, kinaesthetic sequences run off in parallel with modifications in the visual sense-material and, crucially, this happens in a regulated manner: When I turn my gaze in one sense, the pre-empirical color-expanses in the visual field will be modified in a specific manner; if I undo my movement, this will restore their initial arrangement. I can thus expect specific patterns of modification when initiating a certain kinaesthetic sequence. Therefore, Husserl says, the kinaesthetic sequences "motivate" apparent changes in the visual field (1997: 158). Now, a given pre-empirical expanse of, say, redness standing out from the surrounding whiteness in the oculomotoric field can be run through—criss-crossed, so to speak—in an open number of different kinaesthetic sequences. As these kinaesthetic sequences motivate the concurrent modifications of the color-expanse in the field, the visually lived series of modifications become manifestations *of* something, the same "something" unfolds differently in each individual series of lived color experiences. In this process, consciousness comes to intend something that transcends the sensory contents of any individual experience. In this way, the interplay between presentational sensations and kinaesthetic sequences generates experiences with spatial significance, in which the *sensed* redness (which reflection discerns as a moment in the stream of consciousness) is "used up" in the presentation of the redness that covers the tomato's surface.

Husserl's approach combines two equally essential principles. On the one hand, Husserl seems to adopt Helmholtz's suggestion that our ability to perceive a spatial world draws on recognizing the lawlike dependence of sensations on one's own movements.[4] On the other hand, Husserl falls back on his own insights into the phenomenological

---

[4] Although today authors often downplay Helmholtz's pioneering work by exclusively citing his suggestion that we do not directly perceive the world, Helmholtz is also the first to have explicitly formulated the sensori–motor interplay as the key to spatial perception. He did so in his *Tatsachen in der Wahrnehmung* (*Facts in Perception*), a text discussed in Stumpf's seminar in 1885, attended by the young Husserl (Schuhmann 1977: 15): "When we perceive before us the objects distributed in space, this

structure of acts of external perception, according to which their object is intended as something that always and necessarily allows for further presentations. The combination of these two principles pervades the various levels of Husserl's constitutive analyses of spatial objects.

Already the thing's side that is facing me is essentially the product of the interplay of sensory experience and self-movement. As my gaze moves while I inspect the side facing me, the visual presentation of this surface gets modified with every eye-movement; yet, these varying presentations are synthesized in the manifestation of the one identical thing-surface (1989: 135–6). Hence, referring to the profile of the thing that I actually see from my current point of view, Husserl speaks of the "oculomotor 'side'" (1997: 170). In this way, the side facing me is itself "constituted" as a unity, something that is not exhausted by its current manifestation. Just as the side facing me appears with a horizon of further profiles beyond the currently given, the current presentation of the front side itself allows for different perspectives, each of which would present the same side differently, revealing previously unseen features.

The same combination of principles elucidates the constitution of things, understood as three-dimensional bodies. When I move with respect to a thing, at each moment different thing-profiles come into view; however, since the flow of profiles is motivated by the immediate awareness of the way in which I am moving, the manifold of appearances is absorbed into a synthetic unity while an intention runs through this flow of appearances directed at the identical thing that manifests itself in them. Even though I never get anything in view other than thing-profiles, I perceptually intend the thing itself. Hence, I do not perceive "profiles," but a thing. On the other hand, when I stand still looking at a thing, its front side appears to me with a halo of empty intentions directed at currently hidden segments of its surface, which I could bring into appearance by moving. Whatever appears in external perception is thus given perspectivally; its current appearance is pervaded with possibilities for further perception. The fact that perception is necessarily perspectival also means that each appearance of a spatial object implies a reference to the perceiver's current point of view. Whatever appears to me, appears with respect to me; my body is necessarily co-present in all perception as the "zero-point" of orientation: everything appears to my left hand, above me, etc. (1989: 166). A thing's *orientation* thus correlates with the perceiver's bodily position and posture, phenomenologically speaking, with its current kinaesthetic *situation*.

In these analyses—proceeding from pre-empirical expanses to three-dimensional bodies—constitution stands for a principle recurring at each level: Due to kinaestheses sensory variations are generated; because these variations in sensory presentations are "motivated" by kinaestheses, the manifold of presentations is in the same move absorbed into the constitution of an identical unity. Hence, despite these variations, a steady entity is intended, namely an entity that does not coincide with any single series

perception is the acknowledgement of a lawlike connection between our movements and the therewith occurring sensations" (Helmholtz 1977 [1878]: 138).

of appearances and, thus, cannot be exhausted by any single perceptual sequence. Time and again, a manifold of phenomena gets absorbed into the *bringing into appearance* of a new intentional unity, and this unity is something of a higher level, differing in nature from the multiple phenomena used up in its constitution.

To recap, neither color-sensations nor the inner experience of self-movement are themselves spatial; yet their combination allows for experiences in which the spatial appears as such. The suggestion is not, however, that the spatial meaning of movements is somehow added to visual experiences. Rather, the peculiar interplay between the experience of movements and the lived experience of colors generates the appearance of objective extension. Starting from the most fundamental constitutive achievements of the oculomotoric system, Husserl will systematically examine how further kinaesthetic systems allow for the constitution of phenomenal entities, which gradually approach "the thing" as three-dimensional body in space. First, the kinaestheses of the cephalomotoric system extend the oculomotoric field into a Riemannian space (comparable to a spherical surface seen from its center); this, however, remains a two-dimensional manifold of positions—devoid of objective depth— in which oculomotorically constituted unities flow into one another (rather than appearing as entities moving behind one another). It is only when locomotion is taken into account that new modifications in the field can be apperceived as rotation and occlusion, so that visual entities appear as bodies defined by closed surfaces situated at different distances from me.[5]

The constitution of spatial things goes hand in hand with the constitution of an ego-centrically arranged environment, which is further articulated into a near-space—in which I can haptically intervene—and a far-space. A final step in the constitution of space implies the "degradation" of the visual, oriented space to a mere *appearance* of objective space (1997: 283). At first, Husserl suggests that locomotion enables me to reach, in principle, the position of any visual object and that, hence, space is apperceived as an open, three-dimensional system of positions (*Ortssystem*) in which my body is itself positioned (1997: 283). But Husserl will repeatedly return to this issue to correct and refine his analysis (1973: 263; 659–60). In an appendix to a 1916 essay on the constitution of space, Husserl explains that "the spatial form of the designated visual space is Euclidean." What is meant by Euclidean space here is "a formal schema for all possible corporeality . . . All bodies are equal . . . and movement and rest in the geometrical sense are of the same type for every body presenting itself in any 'accidental' orientation" (1997: 371). This, however, applies to all visually given objects, but not to my own body (1973: 239). The constitution of objective space thus requires that the body is apperceived as a thing occupying a position *in space*. The final constitutive level is reached in the apperception of one's own bodily movements "as equivalent to any movement of other bodies" (1997: 371). But Husserl continues to remind us that we

---

[5] For detailed discussions, see Claesges (1964), Drummond (1979), Pradelle (2000), Giorello and Sinigaglia (2007). For influences and confrontations beyond phenomenology, see Holenstein (1999 [1972]), Scheerer (1986), Dokic (2001), Overgaard and Grünbaum (2007), Laasik (2011).

cannot take such bodily self-objectivation for granted, precisely because I am bound to my body as a zero-point with respect to which everything else appears, apart from my own body. My own bodily locomotion is never given to me as "a real change of position of my body in space" and, "correlatively, the space of external objects is not yet real space" (1973: 280). Ultimately, what enables the apperception of the lived-body as a mere physical body is a peculiar nexus of experiences, in which I pick up an object and carry it with me, so that it no longer appears at rest or in motion, near or far, but instead becomes, as it were, a member of my body; and, conversely, in which I jump on and off a moving vehicle, so that my body moves along with the vehicle as if it had become a part of it (1973: 281). This reflection, however, is performed "in primordial abstraction," that is without taking into account other constituting subjects (1973: 266). "The full constitution of my lived-body as a body equal to all bodies first occurs through the other," namely in the awareness that the other perceives my body from over there in the same way as I see hers from over here, that is as physical body *and* as a bodily subject, holding sway in its lived-body (1973: 655). I can imagine that I would be over there and picture my body appearing in varying perspectival presentations like any other physical body (1973: 662).

It is first in the context of the question of how spatiality comes to appearance that Husserl invokes the sensations accompanying bodily movements. Yet it is not so much as *sensations*, as in their specific *function of motivating* presentational modifications that kinaesthetic sequences are key to the constitution of spatiality. Series of presentational sensations run off in parallel to kinaesthetic sequences, but it is only because I am aware that I enact these sequences that they can come to *motivate* the modifications in presentational sensations. This is not supposed to mean that I must explicitly decide to carry them out, which is mostly not the case; nonetheless, in order to fulfill their motivational role, kinaesthetic sequences cannot be something that merely overcomes me. What is crucial to the motivational interplay, simply stated, is not that I *feel* myself moving, but the implicit awareness of me *doing* it.[6] To mark this point, Husserl comes to speak of "free sequences": "this freedom" is "an essential part of the constitution of spatiality" (1989: 58). Due to the peculiar interplay between kinaesthetic and presentational sensations, both components are aware in a different manner: Since I expect presentational modifications of a certain *form* (when enacting certain kinaesthetic sequences), anticipatory intentions run through all spatial perception; as regards the other component, since I initiate—or interrupt—kinaesthetic sequences *at will*, kinaestheses are aware as possibilities which I can realize (*I can* direct myself over there or return to any previous posture). Each kinaesthesis can thus be seen as a "practical possibility" within

---

[6] In his critical discussion of Herbart's proposal that running back and forth through a series of presentations would generate spatiality, Lotze argues that the association of a series of presentations *dcba* and their corresponding muscle feelings would not by itself occur as the reversal of *abcd*; there would have to be "someone else" to tell the soul that it is the same train of presentations backwards (1846: 177). This is precisely what the subjective power of self-movement adds to the mere receptive experience of muscle sensations.

"the system of my kinaesthetic 'I can'" (1989: 330; see also Husserl 2001: 50).[7] Around 1920, Husserl explains that kinaestheses fuse into a "practical system," however, not in the capacity of "mere immanent data, but as practical abilities (*praktische Vermögen*)" (2008: 12). In this way, kinaestheses come to be characterized in terms of praxis.

However, perceptual activity is not praxis in the proper sense of intervening in the physical world. Husserl distinguishes between the truly "*practically functioning of kinaestheses*," which generates changes in the world, and "*unpractically functioning*" or "merely perceptual" kinaestheses (2008: 396–8). In the merely perceptual seeing and touching a field of *res extensae* is constituted; this "still unpractical" touching *may* become practical through the application of force, so that objects get displaced, grasped, deformed . . . (2008: 399). This distinction underscores that, for Husserl, the constitution of spatiality is purely a matter of the interplay between sensations and subjective movement. Even if kinaestheses ultimately, as Husserl recognizes, have their origin in instinctive drives, and are acquired through exercise, the key principle of the constitution of space itself is not affected by the origin or factual nature of one's bodily movements.

Husserl will, nonetheless, characterize perceptual activity as a primal form of praxis, "*Urpraxis*," that is *foundational* for all "real praxis" in that it brings about the appearance of the thing-world in which we can then intervene (2008: 383). In a certain sense, perception can be seen as a proper form of action since perceptual activities seek to "produce" (*erzeugen*) the (ever-richer) self-manifestation of the object. In this sense, perceiving an object is "actively being engaged with it" (*Handelnd-mit-ihm-Beschäftigtsein*) (2008: 380). Characteristic of all praxis is an implicit awareness of the range of one's abilities in relation to what one wants to reach: "practically I am directed toward a goal as the end of a practical path (*Ende eines praktischen Weges*)" (2008: 367). What I want to perceptually reach is underlying each phase of perception. And, Husserl explains, "even when I look around aimlessly (*ziellos*), I have 'goals' (*Ziele*)," though these are only briefly picked up and dropped again. Thus, perception does not merely involve bodily activity; perception is an aiming for (*abzielen*), which is structured, like all other forms of praxis, as a "path" toward an "end," something to be achieved (*erzielen*): perceiving is being directed at an object, producing its self-manifestation (*Erzeugend-auf-ihn-Gerichtetsein*) (2008: 380).

The idea that spatial perception is constitutively related to bodily action is widely associated with the phenomenological tradition. However, it is precisely in an early attempt to upend the dominance of the praxis-oriented understanding of spatial perception that we find the inspiration for a novel motif in the phenomenological reflection on spatiality, namely the plurality of spaces.

---

[7] Once Husserl understands kinaesthesis as practical abilities, the *sensations* accompanying bodily movements are no longer seen as central to the constitution of spatiality but considered in their capacity of fusing the lived-body and the body as organ of the will.

29.2 FROM SOUND BACK TO PURPOSELESS MOVEMENT: DISCLOSING SYMBOLIC SPATIALITY WITH STRAUS

Straus's intriguing approach to spatiality is developed in an early essay "The Forms of Spatiality" (*"Die Formen des Räumlichen"*) (1966 [1930]), published in the Berlin journal *Der Nervenarzt* (neurologist), of which Straus was one of the founders. Philosophically, the ambition of Straus's essay is to show that all perceptual experiences consist of two moments: the "gnostic moment," which refers to perception's capacity to present objects, provides the basis for our cognitive and practical relation with things; the "pathic moment" refers to an affective dimension implied in all perceptual presentation, which flows from the specific sensory mode in which the object is presented. Prior to judging and evaluating, or even recognizing the object, I am already affected by its sensory manifestation; the pathic moment thus constitutes a most "immediate communication" with our surroundings (1966: 11).

What is remarkable, at first sight, is that Straus seeks to accomplish this ambition by means of an inquiry into *spatiality*; that he does so only underscores from the start that this "pathic moment" does not stand for an internal feeling, but for a form of intentionality besides perceptual presentation. Conversely, considered within the history of the philosophical reflection on space, it is remarkable that his essay focuses on the *auditory* in an attempt, even more surprisingly, to steer clear of bodily action as a model for spatial perception.

Straus is clearly aware of the methodological difficulties of his undertaking; an attempt at capturing our most intimate experience of things in concepts may seem doomed to kill what it wishes to apprehend. Therefore, he continually reminds us that his examples of movement remain within the domain of empirical observation, while the phenomena in these examples cannot be fully explained without recognizing a primal affective relation with the world. Let us begin by considering the following puzzling phenomenon, which I will then unpack.

Walking backward is a movement that people find uncomfortable; they feel the urge to look over their shoulder, even when they know there are no obstacles behind them. Turning around, or being turned around, is another type of movement that people experience as disturbing and unpleasant. Yet, when dancing, people spontaneously move backwards and they enjoy turning around over and over again. What can explain this difference *qua* experience given that the individual movements and proprioceptive sensations are identical?

To understand this difference, we must bring together a variety of observations concerning the structural features of sensory experience and the phenomenal world. Let us begin with the uncontroversial fact that people do not start longing for music when they are dancing but, conversely, start performing specific movements when they hear rhythmic sounds. To say that such movements are a quasi-automatic manner of copying the intervals of the rhythm only triggers the question why people do not respond in a similar way to visually perceived rhythms. Straus claims that this difference cannot be explained physiologically but only starting from the phenomenal structure of sound.

Sounds do not, to use Husserl's terminology, fill the surfaces of objects like colors and textures do. Sounds do not present corporeal entities but seem to come from a source. Whereas colors are seen *over there*, where the colored object is, the sounds that we hear have reached us and continue behind us. Moreover, whereas a color is found *right there*, where we direct our gaze, a sound surrounds us. In this way, sounds do not appear over against us, but approach us, flow around us, and pervade the space in which we find ourselves. The phenomenal structure of sound is such that, as Husserl observed (1997: 56), sound *seems* to fill space. Now, in so doing, Straus adds, sound "homogenizes" space (1966: 7). The homogenizing effect of sound is strongest whenever the respective sounds lose their connection with specific objects. When a dog is barking behind me or an engine is running next to me, I hear *a dog* or *an engine*. In such cases, our auditory experience is still tightly related to a specific object and thus directed at something spatially situated. However, when sounds get dissociated from the objects that produce them, they acquire a certain phenomenal autonomy. Music is such that we *can* relatively easily listen to the tones themselves letting the instruments that produce these sounds recede into the background.

Straus further examines our sensory relation to the acoustical by comparing the nature of hearing and seeing. The above-mentioned differences in the mode of appearance of colors and sounds correlate to differences in the perceiver's relation to its object. The fact that a color appears "right there" implies that "to experience the color, we must turn toward it, look at it, actively master it" (1966: 15). By contrast, because sounds pervade the space in which we find ourselves and thus surround us, we cannot turn away from them; even when we walk away from a sound source, we remain subject to the sound while doing so. Although we spatially relate to the sound source in the same way we relate to any perceptually given object, sound itself is not something that appears over against us. Whereas it is largely up to us whether our gaze grasps and keeps hold of something, we are "at the mercy" of sound (*ihm ausgeliefert*) (1966: 16). The distinctive quality of the pathic moment in sight and in hearing, then, can be summarized, Straus contends, as the opposition of *taking* and *being taken*.[8] Moreover, once sounds acquire phenomenal autonomy, their temporal articulation is experienced as such—this in contrast with optically perceived intervals, which always remain *changes* in something, taking place over there. The fact that certain sounds—in particular musical tones—appear detached from any object, and thus suffuse space and modulate time, explains why we are so easily moved by music. Then Straus turns to bodily movements that are aroused by music, like

---

[8] Indeed, we also say that a visual stimulus "grabs" my attention. However, even when we are subject to the captivating force of visual objects, the object and I remain in a state of spatial opposition, over against each other, so that I am solicited to react.

the spontaneous bodily responses to rhythmic music (to which I will refer, for the sake of convenience, as dancing).[9]

When we consider the external appearance of someone who is spontaneously moving in response to music, it is evident that these movements differ from the movements involved in everyday practices. While purposeful actions are often directed to objects, such dance movements seem to lack any relation of directedness toward a goal, be it a distant point or a point of completion. Instead, the external appearance of dance movements, Straus contends, evokes outward expansion, from the body into the surroundings, not in any particular direction but all round; an unrestrained dancer moves back and forth, up and down, sideward and obliquely, spinning and swinging her arms and legs in every direction. Straus observes that, in contrast to a subject walking toward something, a dancing person's trunk is set in motion, which makes her movements unlike, and even inapt for, purposeful action or object-manipulation. At the same time, this affects the manner in which one's own movements are *experienced*, since the increase in motility of the trunk appears to go hand in hand with a repositioning of the center of activity with respect to the body schema. Invoking a phrase from Balzac, Straus adds that the "I" sinks from the level of the eyes down into the trunk (1966: 26). Both the external form and the mode of experience indicate a rupture with the modes of moving characteristic of a goal-directed subject.

The reason for this rupture, according to Straus, is that the dancing subject is no longer focused on ego-centrically located objects. If a dancer's movements appear to be *expansive* in all directions, this is so because they contrast with the targeted conduct of a subject *concentrated* on a visual object. If it is true that a visual perceiver's relation to the world tends to be dominated by the gnostic moment in perception (because our gaze naturally grasps items by singling them out from their context, thus incessantly putting us over against objects of possible interest), then it is understandable that, as musical tones detach themselves from objects to form a pulsating soundscape in which we find ourselves immersed, the gnostic moment recedes into the background while the pathic moment comes to the fore.

A noteworthy fact, which seems to have escaped Straus's attention but only adds to the evidence, is that dancers are sometimes inclined to close their eyes, while in other circumstances people are reluctant to move around eyes closed. Closing one's eyes may be a spontaneous manner of preventing the optical world from breaking the ascent of the pathic moment. The pathic, as Straus defines it, is characterized by the melting away of the subject–object tension that typifies the gnostic moment, which tends to be dominant in visual perception; the optical is characterized by the confrontation with things over against us, which solicit thoughts and decisions (relating to knowledge and action). Hence, in vision, as in haptics, the gnostic tends to override the pathic. Closing one's

---

[9] Straus's reflections are clearly not meant to describe all dance forms; he is not providing a theory of dance. Even though he was led to these insights by the avant-gardist experiments of "absolute dance" (performed *without* music), the movements Straus refers to are those of an individual's spontaneous dancing to music rather than of contemporary choreography or even of dances that need to be learned.

eyes may be an attempt at submerging oneself in the immediate communication with things, as we *sense* them prior to any purposeful interaction suggested by the analytic gaze.[10]

What is true for the phenomenal structure of sound also applies to sounds that we produce ourselves. However, whereas the sounds occurring in our environment phenomenally embrace us, our own voice cannot in the same way seize us. Rather, in the act of speaking, we *direct* ourselves to someone else. We are aware that our voice *goes out to* and must *reach* the addressee; when we shout toward a distant person, we not only articulate but also put strength into our voice, applying force just as when we try to hit a distant target with a stone. This directedness and relation to distance, I believe, is absent when people are drawn into singing along with a song or with other singers. They do not raise their voice *in order to* reach further or to reach anyone at all. Spontaneously singing along is similar to being induced to move in accord with music. Singing out loud—not seldom while closing one's eyes—one is not doing or accomplishing something, but expressing. Characteristic of bodily expressions is that they relate not to practical but to symbolic spatial qualities, as is clear from the fact that a person who expresses pride or victory by lifting her head or throwing her arms into the air is not literally reaching higher. Similarly, the raising of one's voice is not meant to bridge a distance, but is an entirely different way of spatially relating oneself to the world. The spontaneous increase in the "volume" of one's voice, here, is akin to the expansive tendency observed in certain spontaneous bodily responses to music. It is an elated subject's way of according with symbolic spatial qualities like wideness and openness. Addressing someone over there and shouting to a distant person are *originally* spatial in nature; being induced to sing along or sing out loud are vocal doings of a spatially *different* nature.

To return to Straus, the example that he uses is the way in which marching music changes the movements and bodily posture of a troop of tired soldiers. As soon as the music begins, the soldiers raise their gaze toward the horizon and their pace revives. They no longer proceed—one step after another—from their point of departure toward their destination; now they march: they *experience* their vital doing. This transformation of the purposeful, goal-directed activity of walking into the music-induced vitality of marching initiates a different relation to spatiality: "direction and distance are

---

[10] In his 1933 study, *Le temps vécu*, Minkowski makes a similar remark in his discussion of "lived space." Minkowski, too, starts from visual space in which objects occur "in front of me" and then turns to the night, which "I no longer have . . . *before* me; instead it covers me completely, it penetrates my whole being, it touches me in a much more intimate way than the clarity of visual space." He thus opposes "clear space" to the "dark night" and then adds: "we discover the same situation when we listen to a piece of music and close our eyes, the better to abstract ourselves from what we see and from what we know of things in order to plunge into the world of sound. Here, too, auditory space envelops me and penetrates me like black space" (1970: 405–6). In a footnote to this passage, Minkowski refers back to Straus's paper. Straus had already noted that the night, which veils the boundaries that otherwise separate things, has "effects" on us similar to those of sound, since both fill and homogenize space (1966: 17). Music and twilight *affect* us, since the pathic moment rises as the usually dominant gnostic moment of perceptual experience recedes into the background.

replaced by symbolic space qualities; the stretch extending into the distance is replaced by the wide, open space ahead" (1966: 22).

It may be clear by now that pathicity, as Straus wants it to be understood, does not consist in the presence or prominence of bodily feelings. It is not that a dancer experiences her own body more intensely than, say, someone playing tennis or climbing the stairs. Rather, the dancer experiences her bodily relatedness to the world *differently*. And in dancing we find a case in which a change in the pathic moment occurring when a subject is embraced by musical tones results in a different sense of spatiality; the nature of a dancer's movements are a tangible indication of a differently articulated space. We can now return to our initial question: Walking backward is a type of movement that *feels* "contrarious," so to speak. But contrarious to what? To an optically structured space.

The fact that all movements involved in the activity of seeing relate to items that are situated with respect to oneself structures the surroundings of an optical perceiver *in a specific way*. Even though this relation is itself dynamic as the "here" of the subject's viewpoint moves around with its body, this roaming zero-point of orientation imposes its order onto the surroundings: Wherever I am, everything appears with respect to me, or in Husserl's words: "Every there is ordered around a here" (Manuscript D12/62a). Even the relations *among objects* initially appear from my point of view (e.g., I see the tree left of the house, beyond the creek). It is my space in that everything refers back to me: where I am, what I can do from here, and how I can get over there. Every "over there" is thus spatially valued with respect to my potentiality for action. Here, movement is subservient to purposive action, be it the *Urpraxis* of perception or proper praxis of physical intervention (cf. section 29.1); all movements become segments of *directed* interactions with the world.[11]

Now, walking backward feels unnatural—just as much as closing one's eyes while walking forward—because it is a type of movement that goes against the grain of a spatial order deriving from purposive actions solicited by a world of objects. It *feels* unnatural because this spatial order *is* the manner in which we spatially inhabit the world as ocular subjects. This "manner in which" however can vary (e.g., when we are affected as aural subjects) and this, Straus contends, explains why going backwards does not feel contrarious during dancing: The dancer moves about in a differently structured space, a space freed from direction. This explains why spinning around is appreciated differently during dance; for a subject engaged in practical action repeated rotation is

[11] In *Das Raumproblem in der Psychopathologie*, Binswanger (1994 [1933]) praises Straus for addressing the lived experience of movement. Straus's discussion of the pathic and dance movements features prominently in Binswanger's development of the notion "tuned space" (*gestimmter Raum*) in opposition to "oriented space," which is characterized mainly in Husserlian terms. In line with Straus's observations concerning patients who have difficulty moving forwards, but can much more easily move backwards or dance (1966: 36), Binswanger cites many cases of pathologies that reveal a relation to a spatiality different from oriented space (1994: 162ff.). World and I, according to Binswanger, always form a dialectic unity; while in oriented space the meanings upon which the system of references is built are "vital" and "purposive," in tuned space they are of an "existential nature" (1994: 149).

disturbing because one's sense of orientation is lost, while a dancing subject experiences the whirling effect of the same movements as a joyful thrill because they accord with the soundscape. Due to the phenomenal nature of sound, the autonomous tones of music appear to have the power to grasp a subject, override its optical, object-directed relation to its surroundings, and wipe out the I-centered articulation of its surrounding space thereby voiding its positional values. Obviously, a dancing person is active, yet not engaged in purposive interactions with things. Hence, the sort of spatial concerns that come with purposive actions have become completely insignificant. As a consequence, in the eyes of a bystander, an elated dancer may appear to be reckless or even careless, having lost all sense of circumspection regarding the things in her surroundings.

Mostly people move *with respect to* ego-centrically perceived items of interest; when hearing dance music, people are induced to move *in accord with* the music. Instead of being focused *on* something, one is embraced *by* the music; instead of aiming *for* a result, one is absorbed *in* the moment. While music is obviously temporal in nature, and traditionally opposed to architecture as the art of space, the absence of goal-directedness makes it so that spontaneous movements aroused by music are, as Straus puts it, "presentic" (1966: 34). Accordingly, whereas the space of purposive action is articulated by the "historical" nature of a course of events, which defines "forward" and "backward" following "after" and "before," the space structured by music is freed from destination and hence from the temporal order of succession. The spontaneous dance, the one prompted by music, has no beginning and no end; the formal features of its movements reflect the phenomenal structure of sound.

By now we understand why, according to Straus, a serial projection of lights or colors does not arouse rhythmic movements or a desire to dance. Nonetheless, a couple of decades after Straus wrote his essay, rhythmic illumination and rotating spotlights became a common accompaniment of musical performances and dance floors. In other circumstances, however, people find this type of lighting uncomfortable. Assembling a ping-pong table and playing a game under a rotating disco-ball would be a dizzying challenge. Besides confusing motion and stability, the disco-ball spreads out a field of light patches, which homogenizes the environment by fusing objects (as camouflage does). Optically, it sets the surrounding space itself in motion and we are induced to move along with it. This is also the power Straus ascribes to music, which was not meant metaphorically. The dancer moves about differently because she inhabits a differently articulated space. Much like the tones of dance music, the types of lighting that we find on dance floors are man-made sensorial phenomena that evidently don't physically change the environment, but are meant to phenomenally absorb the environment of things into one peculiar *form of spatiality*.

Conversely, a silent dance floor, well lit and empty, is not in any way inviting to dance; it appears as a pointless zone amidst an otherwise practically arranged environment. The space of dance itself, however, is not a segment of the optically directed, chromatically delineated, and historically defined environment of practical engagement, in which positions are reached and distances covered. The spatiality evoked by music, Straus concludes, is "a symbolic part of the world"; the frame of reference to which dancing relates is constituted of symbolic spatial qualities, like *wideness, openness, grandness,* and *depth* (1966: 35). Wideness and depth are neither here or there, nor are they the measurable stretch in between here and there; they are *qualitative* characteristics of perceptual space. The pathic moment, present in all perceptual experience, is ultimately responsible for our susceptibility to symbolic spatial qualities; the transition from living in optical space to moving about in acoustical space happens by virtue of an alternation in the mutual relation of dominance between the gnostic and pathic, not through the replacement of one cognitive representation of space with another.

29.3 EXTENSION OR DEPTH?

By centering his analyses of spatiality on sound, Straus breaks with a long-standing tradition. Straus does not so much want to defend the spatial abilities of auditory perception, but rather refuses to accept that auditory—or any other sort of—sensory impressions can be entirely devoid of spatial character. The idea that perception starts from entirely non-spatial sensory impressions is an unfortunate, and in itself problematic, side-effect of the Cartesian opposition between a subject that is defined as intellective spontaneity and a world characterized—in opposition to this subject—by its distinctive feature of extension. By "entering" the realm of the mental, sensory stimuli lose all worldly extension; but "coming from" the world, sensory impressions remain alien to the pure spontaneity of the intellect. In this picture, sensations are situated, as Renaud Barbaras summarizes, "at the intersection of a double negation" (Barbaras 2004: 217). Sensations are thus seen as passive entities available to this intellect; materials out of which the intellect can try to reconstruct the properties of their sources in the world, starting with their spatial configuration. This understanding of sensory impressions goes hand in hand with the positing of a subject that exists, as mental activity, prior to any encounter with the world. This idea of a mind that resides outside the world—which Straus refers to as the presupposition of the "extra-mundaneity" of the subject (1935 [1963]: 10, 337ff.)— entails the very problem of the origin of space: An unworldly mind must find a way to relate itself—out of nowhere—to the spatial objects that constitute its surroundings. Solving this problem must proceed from the mind's sensory contents which are at once defined as occurrences in the mental realm yet known to be originating in the world. It is because we—thinkers acquainted with the world—know that sonic qualities are not capable of presenting the spatial features of tables, trees, or stones that we deny auditory sensations any original spatial character. Straus, however, refuses to follow this line of thought for several reasons.

Besides the fact that an extramundane subject is a questionable construct, this idea is responsible for our impoverished understanding of sensory experience. Because the *cogito* posits itself as a *thinking* substance, we—heirs of Cartesianism—are inclined to adjust our understanding of *perceiving* to *knowing*. This implies that the only role we attribute to sensory impressions is to provide us with the material to get to *know* extra-mental objects. Straus refers to the famous picture in Descartes' *Traité de l'homme* that shows how a configuration of points is projected onto the retina and then transferred to some place in the head where this configuration is passed on to the mind (1963: 343). To transfer features of external objects is all that visual impressions are supposed to do; there is no room in this schema for the idea that enjoying visual impressions might already be a way of relating to the world. For Straus, however, all perceptual experiences are both a matter of sensing and of perceiving. Whereas perceiving stands for a form of knowing what is in one's surroundings, sensing is the way in which the subject experiences itself in its surroundings. Consider the following situation. Imagine you are in a pitch-black basement. When your hand reaches the wall, you feel that a wall is there. If instead you switch on a torch-light, you see the wall. In each case, you perceive the same surface, but it is clear that feeling or seeing its texture affects *you* in a different way. And there is no reason to maintain that this affection is some sort of *inner* state; your encounter *with the wall* is sensed differently.

Since all sensing is an immediate "communication" with the world, the idea of an extramundane subject having entirely unworldly sensations is a theoretical construct. Consequently, all solutions to the question of the origin of space are theoretical fictions. Ultimately, Straus fights for the recognition of sensing as a primordial relation to the world, arguing that we tend to ignore this dimension of perceptual experience because we approach perception primarily as a matter of knowing. A strategic starting point for Straus's crusade is the way in which philosophers, from Berkeley to Husserl or Strawson, treat auditory experience. Philosophers end up considering vision and touch as the only viable routes to spatiality[12] because they already have a specific, epistemic conception of space in mind when broaching the problem of the origin of perceptual space: What the senses *must* do is enable the subject to correctly apperceive the relative position and intrinsic spatial features of appearing bodies in accordance with a specific conception of space, to wit the schema of a homogenous three-dimensional system of positions that can be occupied by bodies, which can also move through it without therefore undergoing changes.[13] Since Straus sees no reason to start from an unworldly subject, there is no reason to say that the spatial nature of auditory experience would be inferior to that of vision or touch. Straus admits that one won't develop the Pythagorean theorem from sounds, but the lack of mathematical rationality cannot be an objection against the

[12] In his *New Theory of Vision* Berkeley argues that only touch has access to spatial features since visual appearances are variable (while the features of tangible objects are not). Visual appearances acquire spatial meaning through association with tactual perception and bodily movements. Husserl, however, does not fall back on the intrinsic spatiality of moving and touching bodily parts to explain spatial experience; for Husserl, perspectival appearances are not *associated* with the spatial meaning of objective bodily movements, but the inner "I move" *motivates* the course of visual appearances, thus generating spatial appearances. Hence, no less than touch, vision is capable of constituting a spatial object-world.

[13] The *Thing-lectures* are guided by a certain idea of the space that is to be constituted, "which is 'our' Euclidean space" (1997: 240), though without using it in the constitutive analyses. Also, with respect to the entities at the different stages in the constitution of space-things, Husserl remarks that they are "not yet" Euclidean space (1997: 353–4; 372).

original spatial character of sound; it would be, Straus adds, if spatiality meant nothing but mathematical space (1963: 342).

Although I value Straus's intention, I don't think this last argument is pertinent. The decisive difference between hearing and sight or touch is not a matter of mathematical rationality but concerns the fact that hearing is by itself not capable of constituting things, since surfaces (which define corporeal entities) do not appear sonically. Straus avoids this issue. He insists on the fact that we always experience a sound as coming toward us from somewhere, and that processing direction from binaural stimuli only makes sense if experiencing sounds is somehow spatial (1966: 5). To imagine a situation in which sounds do not have any original spatial character would be to *invent* sonic sensations in an extramundane mental realm. Even if this does not imply a logical contradiction, there is no reason to see this situation as a real problem in need of a solution. In reality, enjoying sensory impressions is experiencing *oneself in an environment*. When you softly blow in the face of a newborn baby, the baby does not thereby *know* what distance is; but what could be the point in maintaining that the baby's "sensation" is therefore extra-worldly? All sensory experience relates *us* to our surroundings; waking up to a breeze in your face, a tickling feeling on your cheek, or a shrieking sound are each immediate experiences of oneself in relation to one's surroundings, prior to knowing any spatial objects involved.[14] Hence, no sensory experience is entirely devoid of spatial character. One could, however, just as well insist on the opposite point, namely that objects—and hence *extension*—must somehow be perceived if one is to have an environment at all—spatiality without things isn't a world. We are thus left with a chicken-or-egg situation: Should we posit the interplay between presentational and kinaesthetic sensations as a principle constitutive of spatial extension or should we say that a subject having sensory impressions is always already in a basal spatial relation to its surroundings simply by sensing such impressions? Straus radically chooses for the second option. Compared to rationalism's mirage of an extramundane intellect, this may seem the most reasonable thing to do. Husserl's theory of the constitution of space, then, would be another "historical curiosity"—as Binswanger called Lotze's theory of local-signs (1994 [1933]: 135)—in a long tradition, which can only have value within the confines of a theoretical fiction.[15] However, while Husserl indeed addresses the question in its radical form, it is not the case that Husserl first posits a full-fledged thinking subject, or bodiless intellect, that thereupon must try to connect with the world; rather, as Husserl already says in his 1907 *Thing-lectures*, the constitution of a thing-world is "intertwined" with the constitution of the bodily subject (*Ich-Leib*) to whom this world

[14]   Straus's term "communication" captures the two-way aspect of the pathic as experiencing oneself in the world. Upon feeling a cold breeze, one may just as well say "I'm cold" as "it's cold out here."

[15]   At the beginning of his lecture, Binswanger states that we must not ask what "space" is nor consider the question of the "origin of our spatial presentations." Instead we should acknowledge that every "space" is merely a particular form of spatiality. And in doing so, we must bear in mind, Binswanger concludes, mentioning the name of Heidegger, that space can only be understood from the world and *In-der-Welt-Sein* (1994: 124–5).

appears (1997: 137).[16] So Husserl does start from non-spatial sensory experiences (devoid of all reference to the human body *as* a spatial object), but the process that the constitutive analysis of thing-constitution lays bare implies the concurrent constitution of a subject of bodily capacities.

In any case, Straus's rejection of the traditional way of treating the problem of space led him to consider different *forms of space*. In the wake of Straus, Binswanger, Minkowski, and Merleau-Ponty (2002 [1945]) will also recognize a variety of spaces.[17] Merleau-Ponty cites Straus's distinction between "landscape" and "geographical space" (2002: 398), and takes over his analysis of the spatiality of dance (2002: 335)[18] and, through Minkowski, of the spatiality of the night (2002: 330)—twilight and darkness entail the visual equivalent of acoustical space, precisely because darkness swallows the contours that define the objects toward which we direct ourselves during action, and in so doing, puts us in a relation to the symbolic dimensions of space, like wideness and depth. Straus was, however, most radical in his recognition of this plurality. Consider one last time the different attitudes toward sound in Husserl and Straus. While Husserl's constitutive analyses show that auditory experience cannot constitute things because sonic sensations are not intrinsically fused with extension the way visual and tactile sensations are, Husserl nonetheless emphasizes, like Heidegger (1977: 151), that what we hear is not a sonic substitute of, say, a singer; we hear *the singer herself*. Straus, however, is interested in musical tones precisely because they phenomenally detach themselves from concrete things! It is only in so doing that they acquire the power to put us in a relation to a unique form of spatiality *besides* the space of practical engagement with things. In an attempt to remind us that mathematical notions of space are abstractions derived from our concrete relation with the surrounding world, phenomenologists often invoke our bodily engagement with the world. However, acoustical space is *not* subordinated to the general perceptual space of a body that is practically attuned to the world. While later phenomenologists see the plurality of spaces against the background of the one, bodily perceptual space (Vetö 2008: 412), Straus's acoustical space is a fundamentally different form of spatiality, which is evident from the fact that we accord to it through a separate repertoire of bodily movements, movements that do *not* derive from an agreement between the body and a world of things. Straus's recognition of acoustical space as

---

[16]   Or as Husserl puts it elsewhere, "Nature" and the body, and in its intertwinement with the latter, the soul, constitute themselves at once and together in a reciprocal relatedness to each other (1971: 124).

[17]   Merleau-Ponty does not cite Straus's early essay but only his 1935 *Vom Sinn der Sinne*, in which a number of these themes are briefly mentioned. In any case, Merleau-Ponty repeatedly cites Binswanger's *Das Raumproblem in der Psychopathologie*, in which Binswanger offers a lengthy summary of Straus's essay on spatiality.

[18]   While Bollnow (1963), who praises Straus's analyses of dance, was critical of the connotations that come with his notion "historical" in relation to optical space, Merleau-Ponty follows this suggestion: "One might show that . . . the dance evolves in an aimless and unorientated space, that it is a suspension of our history, that in the dance the subject and his world are no longer in opposition" (2002: 35).

a form of spatiality in its own right breaks the binary opposition of the abstract space of science and the concrete space of embodied engagement and human life.[19]

References

Barbaras, R. (2004), "Affectivity and Movement: The Sense of Sensing in Erwin Straus," *Phenomenology and the Cognitive Sciences* 3: 215–28.

Bernet, R. (2003), "Desiring to Know through Intuition," *Husserl Studies* 19: 153–66.

Binswanger, L. (1994 [1933]), "Das Raumproblem in der Psychopathologie," in *Ausgewählte Werke 3* (Heidelberg: Asanger), 123–78.

Bollnow, O. F. (1963), *Mensch und Raum* (Stuttgart: Kohlhammer).

Claesges, U. (1964), *Husserls Theorie der Raumkonstitution* (The Hague: Martinus Nijhoff).

Claesges, U. (1973), "Einleitung des Herausgebers," in E. Husserl, *Ding und Raum. Vorlesungen 1907,* Husserliana 16 (The Hague: Martinus Nijhoff), i–xxviii.

Descartes, R. (1649 [1984]), "Passions of the soul," in J. Cottingham, R. Stoothoff, and D. Murdoch (eds), *The Philosophical Writings of Descartes,* 2 vols (Cambridge: Cambridge University Press).

Dokic, J. (2001), "Perception visuelle et kinesthésie," in J.-P. Cometti and K. Mulligan (eds), *La philosophie autrichienne de Bolzano à Musil* (Paris: J. Vrin).

Drummond, J. (1979), "On Seeing a Material Thing in Space," *Philosophy and Phenomenological Research* 40: 19–23.

Giorello, G. and Sinigaglia, C. (2007), "Space and movement," in L. Boi et al. (eds), *Rediscovering Phenomenology* (Dordrecht: Springer), 103–23.

Heidegger, M. (1977). "The Origin of the Work of Art," ed. D. F. Krell, *Basic Writings* (San Francisco: Collins).

Helmholtz, H. von (1977), *Epistemological Writings,* ed. R. Cohen (Boston: Reidel).

Herbart, J. F. (1825), *Psychologie als Wissenschaft, neu gegründet auf Erfahrung, Metaphysik, und Mathematik. Zweyter Theil* (Königsberg: Unzer).

Holenstein, E. (1999 [1972]), "The zero-point of orientation," in D. Welton (ed.), *The Body: Classic and Contemporary Readings* (Oxford: Blackwell), 57–94.

Husserl, E. (1971), *Ideen zu einer reinen Phänomenologie und phänomenologischen Philosophie. Drittes Buch,* Husserliana 5, ed. M. Biemel (The Hague: Martinus Nijhoff).

Husserl, E. (1973), *Zur Phänomenologie der Intersubjektivität III,* Husserliana 15, ed. I. Kern (The Hague: Martinus Nijhoff).

Husserl, E. (1979), *Aufsätze und Resenzionen (1890–1910),* Husserliana 22, ed. I. Strohmeyer (The Hague: Martinus Nijhoff).

Husserl, E. (1989), *Ideas Pertaining to a Pure Phenomenology and Phenomenological Philosophy, Second Book* (Dordrecht: Kluwer).

Husserl, E. (1997), *Thing and Space: Lectures of 1907* (Dordrecht: Springer).

Husserl, E. (2001), *Analyses concerning Active and Passive Synthesis* (Dordrecht: Springer).

---

[19] Straus's opposition between the "space of the landscape" and the "space of geography" (1935) thus should not be reduced to the mere opposition of a human relation to the world and a scientific mindset. What is at stake concerns a much richer philosophical inquiry into experience.

Husserl, E. (2008), *Die Lebenswelt. Auslegungen der vorgegebenen Welt und ihrer Konstitution*, Husserliana 39, ed. R. Sowa (Dordrecht: Springer).

Laasik, K. (2011), "On Perceptual Presence," *Phenomenology and Cognitive Sciences* 10: 439–59.

Lotze, H. R. (1846), "Seele und Seelenleben," *Handwörterbuch der Physiologie, vol 3*, ed. R. Wagner (Braunschweig: Vieweg).

Merleau-Ponty, M. (2002 [1945]), *Phenomenology of Perception* (London: Routledge).

Minkowski, E. (1970 [1933]), *Lived Space: Phenomenological and Psychopathological Studies*, translated by N. Metzel (Evanston, IL: Northwestern University Press).

Overgaard, S. and Grünbaum, T. (2007), "What Do Weather Watchers See?" *Cognitive Semiotics* 1: 8–32.

Pradelle, D. (2000), *L'archéologie du monde* (Dordrecht: Kluwer).

Scheerer, E. (1986), "The Constitution of Space Perception," *Acta Psychologica* 63: 157–73.

Schuhmann, K. (1977), *Husserl Chronik: Denk- und Lebensweg Edmund Husserls* (The Hague: Martinus Nijhoff).

Straus, E. (1963 [1935]), *The Primary World of Senses* (London: Macmillan).

Straus, E. (1966 [1930]), "The forms of spatiality," in *Phenomenological Psychology* (New York: Basic Books), 3–37.

Stumpf, C. (1873), *Über den psychologischen Ursprung der Raumvorstellung* (Leipzig: Hirzel).

Vetö, M. (2008), "L'eidétique de l'espace chez Merleau-Ponty," *Archives de philosophie* 71: 407–37.

Wehrle, M. (2015), "Feelings as the Motor of Perception?" *Husserl Studies* 31: 45–64.

CHAPTER 30

INTENTIONALITY

Lived Experience, Bodily Comportment, and the Horizon of the World

DERMOT MORAN

30.1 INTENTIONALITY AS THE MAIN THEME OF PHENOMENOLOGY

INTENTIONALITY (*Intentionalität, Gerichtetsein*), "directedness," or "aboutness," is central to the phenomenological tradition. Husserl calls it the "principal theme" (*Hauptthema*) of phenomenology (Husserl 2014: 161). Phenomenology treats intentionality not narrowly as a relation between a mental act and its object, and especially not as a kind of *representation* of the outer world in the inner mind (Stich and Warfield 1994; Drummond 2012). Rather, intentionality is a claim about the *sensefulness* of experience based on the irreducible inter-relatedness between embodied consciousness and the surrounding world of significance. Intentionality, for phenomenology, involves both *sense-giving*—whereby consciousness confers sense on what it encounters—and *sense-explication*—whereby consciousness articulates preexisting objectual and worldly significance. Both are normally intertwined. Sense, moreover, is broader than linguistic meaning. Husserl distinguished between "sense" (*Sinn*) (e.g., of non-linguistic perceptions) and "meaning" (*Bedeutung*), which requires linguistic expression. Perceptions, feelings, moods, and emotions already have "sense" prior to articulation.

Phenomenologists generally reject immanent, representationalist ("in the head"), causal, and naturalist accounts of intentionality and instead consider conscious states as having "sense" primarily through embodied "comportment" (*Verhalten*) and intersubjective "interaction" (*Ineinandersein*) in a pre-given world already charged with significance.

Intentionality was reintroduced into modern philosophy by Franz Brentano in 1874 (Brentano 1995), who himself drew on medieval thought (Black 2010).[1] In his effort to define the domain of psychological science, Brentano proposed that intentionality was the defining characteristic of all and only mental phenomena. Edmund Husserl expanded this insight to make intentionality the meaning-endowing character of all lived experiences.

In the Brentanian tradition, largely developed within twentieth-century philosophy of mind following Roderick Chisholm, intentionality is construed quite narrowly as the "aboutness" or "directedness" of individual conscious episodes (Forrai 2005), but Husserl and his followers speak more expansively of the "consciousness-of" (*Bewusstsein-von*) of all "lived" experiences (*Erlebnisse*), including not just perceptual and cognitive but also emotional (Vendrell Ferran 2015), volitional, bodily, and habitual states, and emphasize intentionality as a fundamental openness to the sense and meaningfulness of the world. Iris Marion Young, building on Merleau-Ponty's and Husserl's discussion of the self's sense of governing in its body—expressed as Husserl's "I can" (*Ich kann*)—adds a new dimension by highlighting how gendered, bodily intentionality and, in particular, women's "inhibited intentionality" (Young 2005), emerges in response to prevailing cultural norms.

Although intentionality is interpreted in radically different ways (Heidegger rejects the very term), nevertheless, there is, I argue, a clear continuity in the phenomenological tradition, such that Husserl's account is radicalized by Heidegger and, furthermore, informs Merleau-Ponty's analysis of embodied, habitual, and practical intentionality. My stress on this continuity challenges Hubert L. Dreyfus (2000; 1991) and others (Carman 2003), who interpret Heidegger's emphasis on non-cognitive, practical engagement as antithetical to Husserl's (and Searle's) more Cartesian-style concern with the structures of pure consciousness.

Phenomenology, starting with Husserl's *Ideas I* (Husserl 2014), furthermore, defends an explicitly *transcendental* approach towards intentionality that continues in the tradition. Since subjectivity must be presumed in all cognition, it cannot simply be treated as a natural fact. Both the suspension of the "natural attitude" and the phenomenological reduction aim to remove naïve prejudices in order to allow the essential structures of intentional consciousness to be exhibited. The "spell of the naturalistic attitude," for Husserl, blocks the true understanding of consciousness (Moran 2008). Thus he explicitly opposes the "naturalization of consciousness" (Husserl 2002: 254; Zahavi 2004) as *countersensical*, since it presupposes norms and laws and other ideal entities that it cannot explain. Intentional, "sense-giving" subjectivity is involved in the very "constitution" (*Konstitution*) of the world; hence consciousness is not a residue item or "tag-end" (Husserl 1960: 24)

---

[1] The Latin term *intentionalitas* (from *intendo*, "I stretch toward," "I aim at") already appears in the debate about first and second intentions (Perler 2004; 2001). Indeed, the concept can be traced to Aristotle (Chrudzimski 2013; Caston 1998; Sorabji 1991), the Arabic tradition of Avicenna and Averroes (Black 2010), and Aquinas (Breton 1955), among others.

in the world, but constitutes the entire *sense* of the world. For Husserl, subjectivity is not simply "in the world," but is, as he puts it in the *Crisis*, "for the world" (Husserl 1970: 181).

Heidegger similarly adopts an explicitly transcendental attitude in *Being and Time* (Heidegger 1962; Crowell and Malpas 2007; Moran 2014, 2013b, 2000a; Zahavi 2013), albeit replacing the term "intentionality" with a more radical account of ecstatic transcendence and practical human "involvement" (*Bewandtnis*) in the world, through engagement with things and others in concern, solicitude (*Fürsorge*), and, ultimately, "care" (*Sorge*). Finally, Merleau-Ponty, while emphasizing bodily comportment, defends a transcendental-phenomenological approach—although his transcendental subjectivity is also, paradoxically, incarnate. Merleau-Ponty speaks of a "transcendental field" (Merleau-Ponty 1960: 177), and of the "circularity" of persons and nature. The natural and the transcendental attitudes are interwoven and interdependent. For Merleau-Ponty, intentional human existence is a *transcendence towards* the world, but an *ambiguous* transcendence, since human beings are finite, embodied, and embedded in the world. Intentionality, he claims, is the antecedent bond "that establishes the natural and prepredicative unity of the world and of our life" (Merleau-Ponty 2012: lxxxii).

Husserl's phenomenology uncovers the necessary, essential ("eidetic") structures of intentional states (termed "noeses"), e.g., perception, memory, imagination, and their intended objects ("noemata"). The focus is not just on perceptions and cognitions, but also on the specific intentionality of emotions, moods, time-consciousness, the "apprehension of value" (*Wertnehmung*), and the apprehension of other living subjects through a *sui generis* original form of intentional apprehension, "empathy" (*Einfühlung*). In the mature Husserl, Heidegger, and Merleau-Ponty, there is a deeper focus on intentionality as pervading the whole of human existence, including the apprehension of backgrounds, contexts, "horizons," and indeed the whole vague but genuine experience of "world" that outruns all possible experience (Husserl's "worldhood" (*Weltheit*); Heidegger's "being-in-the-world" (*In-der-Welt-sein*, Heidegger 1962); Merleau-Ponty's; *être-au-monde*, (Merleau-Ponty 2012)). Object-intentionality is complemented by horizon-intentionality.

Inspired especially by Husserl's *Ideas II*, Martin Heidegger and Maurice Merleau-Ponty expanded intentionality further by focusing especially on pre-theoretical, habitual, practical behavior in an environment of already given significance. Both also emphasized, as we shall see, the essential *transcendence* of human beings in relation to the world in part because of the temporally dispersed, projective, and spatially dislocated character of human existence.

Following Heidegger, some phenomenologists (e.g., Levinas, Henry) criticized Husserlian phenomenology as being too cognitivist and as privileging objectual intentionality, and proposed to move *beyond* intentionality, but I argue, however, that Husserlian phenomenology already explored this non-cognitive, practical, and other-oriented responsivity in ways that are close to those advocated by Emmanuel Levinas (1983) and Michel Henry (Calcagno 2008). It is a distortion to portray Husserl's intentionality largely as a perceptual or cognitive relation to objects. Beginning from *Ideas* (Husserl 2014), Husserl investigated "horizonal intentionality," that examines specifically non-objectified phenomena, including the contexts and horizons of objectual experiences, within the totality of temporally streaming conscious life.

It is a mistake, moreover, to think of intentionality primarily as a willed or active directing of attention or deliberate positing of sense driven by an ego. Phenomenology also explores intentionality as a non-willed openness and *responsiveness* to others (Waldenfels 2004) and to the world, often involving passive, but nonetheless constituted, pre-conscious syntheses, harmonies, and attunement. From the outset, moreover, phenomenology investigated not just individual but also collective or group intentionality (Salice and Schmid 2016; Szanto 2014; Schmid 2009; Chant et al. 2014), including anonymous public shared intentionality to the historical past and to one's culture. A particularly original feature of phenomenology is its concern to show how the "always already" pre-given *sense* of a common, stable, enduring, shared world of objects and other subjects is established by subjects co-operating together.

30.2 Brentano: Intentionality as the Mark of the Mental

Franz Brentano (1838–1917) revived the notion of intentionality from late Scholasticism (Spiegelberg 1969), but did not elaborate it in a thematic way in his writings; what he discussed in a few pages has inspired a whole tradition of commentary. In his 1874 *Psychology from an Empirical Standpoint* (Brentano 1995), he divided psychology into two domains: genetic psychology that studied the physiological underpinnings of psychic events, and descriptive psychology that documented the "fundamental classes" of mental phenomena through careful, a priori description (Brentano 1995: xxv). Descriptive psychology was later named "phenomenology" by Brentano (Brentano 1995a), thereby inspiring Husserl.

Brentano proposed intentionality as the essential characteristic of "mental" (*das Psychische*) as opposed to "physical phenomena." All and only mental phenomena can be said to be intentional; intentionality is *the* criterion for the mental.

Brentano's descriptive psychology had undoubted metaphysical commitments. He thought we are primarily acquainted with our own presentations, thoughts, and emotions. The objects of perception are not directly apprehended, but only indirectly inferred (Brentano 1995: vii), and have only "intentional existence" (Brentano 1995: 94), whereas psychical or mental phenomena possess "actual existence" (*wirkliche Existenz*); "our mental phenomena are the things which are most our own" (Brentano 1995: 20). The occurrent psychic act has an immanent content that *is* its intentional object (according to his student Twardowski, Brentano confused "content" and "object," Twardowski 1974). *Physical* phenomena are the *contents* of psychic experiences, not extra-mental objects.

In his effort to define mental phenomena, Brentano, having excluded various traditional ways of identifying them, e.g., spatial versus non-spatial, eventually settles on a positive criterion: intentionality. He writes:

Every mental phenomenon is characterized by what the Scholastics of the Middle Ages called the intentional (or mental) inexistence of an object [*die intentionale (auch wohl mentale) Inexistenz eines Gegenstandes*], and what we might call, though not wholly unambiguously, reference to a content, direction towards an object [*die Beziehung auf einen Inhalt, die Richtung auf ein Objekt*] (which is not to be understood here as meaning a thing), or immanent objectivity. Every mental phenomenon includes something as object within itself, although they do not all do so in the same way. In presentation something is presented, in judgment something is affirmed or denied, in love loved, in hate hated, in desire desired, and so on. (Brentano 1995: 88)

Brentano's terminology—"relation" (*Beziehung*), "directedness" (*Richtung*), "object" (*Objekt*), "intentional inexistence" (*intentionale Inexistenz*), and "immanent objectivity"—generated problems for his followers. The formulations, "intentional or mental inexistence of the object" (*intentionale, mentale Inexistenz*) and "immanent objectivity" (*immanente Gegenständlichkeit*), suggest that Brentano held an immanentist account of the intentional object (Jacquette 2015; Brandl 2005; Zoeller 1992). Brentano's "inexistence" (*Inexistenz*) caused further confusion (Moran 1996). He uses it in the Scholastic sense of *inesse* (the Aristotelian sense in which knowledge is "in" the knower). In a footnote in *Psychology from an Empirical Standpoint*, Brentano explicates "inexistence" (*in-esse*), referring to Aristotle, Philo, Anselm, and Aquinas (Moran 2013a; Spruit 1994), as the "indwelling" (*Einwohnen*) of the intentional object in the act (Brentano 1995: 88). As a result Brentano was suspected of psychologism.

In a partial second edition (1911) of *Psychology from an Empirical Standpoint*, Brentano revised his earlier conception in a reist direction. Intentionality is now a "quasi-relation" [*etwas Relativliches*] (Brentano 1995: 272) *within* the subject; since there are not two relata but only one thinker. Only *the thinker* can be said to exist; the intentional object is a modification of the thinker. Brentano's later view may be characterized as *adverbial*: to think of an object is for the subject to be modified in a specific manner (Kriegel 2016). Brentano bequeathed a portfolio of problems concerning intentional content, object, and relation, to his students, including Meinong, Twardowski (Betti 2013; Rollinger 1996; Albertazzi et al. 1996) and Husserl, and these problems entered analytic philosophy of mind through Roderick Chisholm (1955–6).

30.3 EDMUND HUSSERL: FROM OBJECT-INTENTIONALITY TO HORIZON-INTENTIONALITY

Husserl always credited Brentano for awakening him to intentionality; nevertheless, from the beginning, he was critical of almost every aspect of Brentano's account and especially of his failure to defend the objectivity of ideal objects. In *Logical Investigations* (1900–1) Husserl already lists his "deviations" from Brentano (Husserl 2001 II: 353 n. 1), his "departures" (*Abweichungen*) from his master's "convictions" and his technical "vocabulary" (Varga 2015). In the Sixth Investigation, he separates "what is indubitably significant in Brentano's thought-motivation from what is erroneous in its elaboration" (Husserl 2001 II: 340). The mature Husserl claimed that Brentano was blind to his own discovery: "The proper problems of intentionality never dawned on him. He [Brentano] even failed to see that no given experience of consciousness can be described without a description of appertaining an 'intentional object as such' (for example, that this perception of the desk can only be described, when I describe this desk as *what* and *just as* it is perceived). Brentano had no inkling of intentional implication, of intentional modifications, of problems of constitution, etc. . . . " (Husserl, letter to Marvin Farber, June 18, 1937; Cho 1990: 37). Husserl remarked in 1929 that Brentano's discovery of intentionality "never led to seeing in it a complex of performances, which are included as *sedimented history* in the currently constituted intentional unity and its current manners of givenness—a history *that one can always uncover following a strict method*" (Husserl 1969: 245).

Already in early essays, e.g., his 1894 review of Twardowski's *On the Concept and Object of Presentations* (Husserl 1994: 388–95) and his unfinished 1894–8 essay "Intentional Objects" (Husserl 1994: 345–87), Husserl offered a more complex account of the "being of the intentional object," specifically addressing the problem of so-called objectless presentations, i.e., presentations to which no existing object corresponds, e.g., "centaur," "round square," "the present King of France," originally discussed by Bolzano in his *Wissenschaftslehre* [*Theory of Science*], and subsequently taken up by Twardowski, Meinong, Russell, among others (Jacquette 2015). In 1894, the mathematician Gottlob Frege reviewed Husserl's *Philosophy of Arithmetic* and accused him, perhaps unfairly, of psychologism (Mohanty 1982). Husserl's response was his extended critique of psychologism in *Prolegomena to Pure Logic* (1900), the first volume of his *Logical Investigations*, where he defends the "logical objectivism" of Bolzano, according to which mental judgments track objective "propositions in themselves" or "states of affairs" (*Sachverhalte*). Following Bolzano, for Husserl, logical and mathematical objects are *ideal* objects that stand apart from the minds contemplating them, and remain identical in repeated apprehensions of them, have "existence-in-themselves," and the states of affairs in which they are embedded can be said to "hold" (*bestehen*) or be "valid" (*gelten*). Husserl insists that psychological acts of perceiving and judging have contents, but that the intentional objects are distinct from these contents although apprehended through them.

In *Logical Investigations* Husserl states that the central feature of consciousness is *intending* (*Vermeinen, Intention,* Husserl 2001 I: 384–5). But he offers a much more complex account than Brentano, distinguishing between the immanent *real* (*reelle*), psychological "content" of the act (a temporal slice of the act), the intentional object, and the *ideal* content tokened or instantiated in the act. Husserl distinguishes between the *ideal* intentional structure of the conscious experience and its various "real" components, such as sensational content or temporal duration. In an act of speaking, the spoken sound has "real" components and other abstract parts that can be analyzed by "descriptive psychology" quite distinct from the physical sound elements, for instance the vibrations, parts of the ear, and so on. Besides both the physical and descriptive psychological elements, there is also the "ideal sense" consisting of what the word means and what it names (Husserl 2001 II: 112).

Husserl further distinguishes between the "act quality" and "matter" (Husserl 2001 II: 119). Acts of different quality (judging, willing, perceiving) may have the same matter, i.e., the state of affairs judged, willed, or perceived (e.g., *that it is raining*). The "matter"— not to be identified with the sensory content of the experience—is the content that gives the intention its reference to its specific object (Husserl 2001 II: 121).

Husserl specifically rejects Brentano's immanentist understanding of "intentional inexistence." Already in the Fifth Logical Investigation, Husserl says that, in thinking of the God Jupiter, the god is not found *inside* the thought as a real component. Husserl also challenges Brentano's account of the intentional "relation": It is not a relation between two actual entities, a consciousness and a thing; nor is it a psycho-physical relation. Later, in *Ideas I* §36, Husserl reiterates that intentionality is neither a real relation with an existent object nor a "psychological" relation between consciousness and its internal "content," but rather that intentionality is inherently disclosive of objects that transcend consciousness. In fact, for Husserl, all objects of thought, including apparently immanent objects of fantasy and memory, are *mind-transcendent*. He states in *Ideas* (1913):

> As a matter of absolutely unconditional universality or necessity, a thing cannot be given in any possible perception, in any possible consciousness at all as immanent to it in a real [*reell*] manner. (Husserl 2014: 73–4)

The intentional object is never a component piece of a lived experience; rather lived experiences are essentially self-transcending, i.e., pointing beyond themselves.

A major contribution to intentionality is Husserl's description of the specific intentional features of perceptions, memories, fantasies, acts of willing (Husserl 2001, 2014; see also Pfänder 1967), and acts of judgment. He focuses on both the structure of the intending act and the peculiar "modes of givenness" (*Gegebenheitsweise*) of objects in various acts. Objects in perception are experienced as "bodily" (*leibhaftig*) present; objects in fantasy appear detached from the subject's spatiotemporal surroundings; memories are experienced as "no longer" bodily present; photographs have a double character: appearing as physical objects (shiny paper) but also displaying a "subject" (*Sujet*) or theme, that must be *seen into* them.

Husserl offers an interesting analysis of empty intentions, where objects are not grasped as present-in-the-flesh as in perception but are apprehended in a very general way (usually through signs). Most thinking involves empty intentions, only some of which are ever fulfilled in perceptual or categorial intuitions. Scientific thinking, e.g., in formal mathematics, is a primary example of such empty, signitive intending (the square root of minus 1 can never be intuited fully in a perceptual manner, but could have its own kind of evidential fulfillment, which may require following a proof).

A conscious act takes place in objective time and may have a specific sensuous character, but its intentional structure and object are not to be identified with its sensory, real nature. The intentional object (e.g., "my dog") is intended through the "psychological" content in the occurrent experience (e.g., "I hear the dog's bark"), but the mental reference is to the actual dog and not to the occurrent sensory component or "content" (the barking sound). For Husserl, sensations belong to the "real" components of intentional acts *experienced* by the subject, but are not in themselves intended. As Husserl puts it: "Objects on the other hand appear and are perceived, but they are not *experienced*" (Husserl 2001 II: 105).

Husserl denied *all* conscious experiences were intentional; sensations such as pains are not in themselves *about* anything, but are simply undergone as experiences; nevertheless, they play a key role as the "sensuous" content of more complex intentional states, mediating the appearance of the object. A felt *sensation of smoothness* in the fingertips is not the same as an objective property of *being smooth,* but announces it. One could, of course, attend to the touch sensation itself as an intentional object. It requires however, a shift of focus to pay attention to the sensory material character of the act—what Husserl will later call "hyletic data" (Husserl 2014: 194), the putative pure contents of sensation. Normal experience is world-directed.

Husserl also distinguishes between *the object that is intended* and *the manner in which it is intended* (a variation of Frege's distinction between sense and reference). One can think of the person *Napoleon* under different descriptions, e.g., the "victor of Jena," or "the vanquished at Waterloo." It is this feature of intentionality that leads to non-substitutivitiy in different contexts while preserving truth (as discussed by Chisholm), underpinning intensionality. Husserl, however, developed it into his account of the intentional object and noema, which we discuss later.

For Husserl, the objects of intention are multiple. For instance, one can perceive objects and their properties, but also processes, relations, and complexes that Husserl calls "states of affairs" (*Sachverhalte,* Husserl 2001 II: 155). It is important to distinguish between the direct perception of an object or event and the various linguistic expressions or mental judgments that may accompany the perception or, later, replace it. Even perceptual judgments are complex, multilayered acts—my actual perception can found and motivate linguistic utterances that pick out aspects of the overall perceived state of affairs (I can say that I see *the blackbird, the blackbird flying,* that *the bird is startled,* etc.). In the Sixth Logical Investigation, Husserl's expands intentionality with his account of "categorial intuition" (*kategoriale Anschauung*), a higher-order intuition of complexes founded on sensory intuition that apprehends states of affairs and other non-sensory features of objects. Categorial acts, such as "if . . . then," "and," "or," and so on, have no correlates in the perceived objects but are *founded* on sensuous perceptions and are apprehended intuitively.

Perceptual intentionality, furthermore, always carries an "excess" or superfluity of sense that escapes full articulation in any pronouncement. Perception in that sense has a filled character that provides the intuitive basis for true judgments. Thus, crucially, for Husserl, the paradigm case of a successful intentional act is an act where the meaning is fulfilled by the *presence* in intuition of the intended object with full "bodily presence" (*Leibhaftigkeit*). Actual perception is the paradigm case of *fulfilled* intuition (albeit that the object always presents in profiles or shadings, *Abschattungen*). The perceived object is directly presented as a whole—even if it is really presented as possessing an indefinite number of further profiles that can be brought into view.

Perception is the primal or "originary" form of intuiting, whereas memory and imagination are reproductive modifications of perception. Memory is a form of "calling to mind" or "re-presenting" (*Vergegenwärtigung*) that no longer has the distinctive bodily presence that characterizes perception. Imagining is yet another form of presenting which posits an object somewhat detached from perceptual surroundings. Empty or "signitive" intendings, for Husserl, constitute the largest class of our conscious acts, and have a particular relevance in mathematics and scientific discourse where signs are manipulated in an empty way but ultimately, for Husserl, must be grounded in fulfilled intuitions. Some (Kelly 2002) interpret Husserl's empty intentions as non-sensory hypotheses or postulations, e.g., the perceiver theorizes about what the backside of the house looks like from seeing the front-side directly. But Husserl (and, following him, Merleau-Ponty) denies such empty intentions are cognitive projections. They are non-cognitive intuitions not filled with sensory content (Hopp 2015) but pregnant with determinable possibilities that are in part given through embodied potential for action and movement (drawing nearer, moving behind, etc.). Husserl conceives of the structure of intentionality as essentially a dynamic movement of empty intentions towards fulfillment. Furthermore, there are different degrees of fulfillment. Husserl also connects intentionality with the manner that objectivities have "self-givenness" (*Selbstgegebenheit*) in experience, a phenomenon he often calls "self-evidence" (*Evidenz*), and which he strongly distinguished from psychological feelings of certainty. Husserl sees intentionality and evidence as essentially correlated:

> The concept of any intentionality whatever—any life-process of consciousness-of something or other—and the concept of evidence, the intentionality that is the giving of something-itself [*Selbstgebung*] are essentially correlative. (FTL §60, p. 160)

Perfect evidence, for Husserl, involves the grasping of the object in full givenness and with the clarity and distinctness appropriate to it.

The mature Husserl, after *Ideas I*, expanded his account of intentionality to include the manner in which the object-intending involves contexts ("horizons") that manifest themselves in the temporal flow of a unified "nexus of consciousness" (*Bewusstseinszusammenhang*, Husserl 1969: 159). In *Ideas I* also, he introduced a novel language for intentionality, namely, the "fundamental correlation between noesis and noema" (Husserl 2014: 181). The terminology is Greek: *noesis*, "thought," and *noema*, "that which is thought." The "noesis" is "the concretely complete intentional experience, designated with the emphasis on its noetic components" (Husserl 2014: 192), e.g., perceiving, remembering, and so on; whereas noema means the object (a perceptual thing, quality, relation, or a state-of-affairs) of a conscious intention precisely *as it is apprehended* in the noetic act. *Ideas I* also introduces the notions of the "natural attitude" (*die natürliche Einstellung*), the phenomenological *epoché*, with its concept of "bracketing" or "parenthesis" meant to bring noetic-noematic structures into view:

> Not to be overlooked thereby is the phenomenological reduction [*die phänomen-ologische Reduktion*] that requires us "to bracket" ["*einzuklammern*"] [the actual process of] making the judgment, insofar as we want to obtain just the pure noema of the experience of judgment. (Husserl 2014: 187)

From *Ideas* Husserl's inquiry into intentionality is carried out in "the transcendental attitude" (Husserl 2014: 172), suspending the existential belief-component (*Seinsglaube*), to allow the constituting (noetic-noematic) structures to become visible undistorted by naturalistic assumptions. Lived experiences are to be considered solely in their "mode of givenness" (*Gegebenheitsweise*), i.e., the manner they are displayed to the experiencing subject, purified of everything transcendent or "worldly." "The real relation that actually obtains between perception and what is perceived is suspended" (Husserl 2014: 175), allowing Husserl to focus on the " 'objectivity meant as such', the objectivity in quotation marks" (Husserl 2014: 185). Husserl speaks of apprehending the "transcendental stream of experience in pure immanence" (Husserl 2014: 175), i.e., in its experiential character without imposition of mundane assumptions and presuppositions drawn from natural life, from science, and specifically from psychology.

Every conscious experience is a "real" psychic event, one that takes place primarily in worldly time, with its own specific "real" parts and temporal phases. On the other hand, after all reference to this natural and psychological world is suspended, there remains a structured, intentional experience that aims at or is *about something*, an intentional object that is not a *real* part of the intending act. I perceive this *blooming apple tree*, and not just the side-profile that it currently presents. The apple tree, moreover, has the "sense" of being an external or "transcendent" thing, an enduring spatiotemporal physical entity. The noema "tree" means the intentional object in the reduced experience, i.e., the tree as seen through the window. It is always possible, through a disciplined shift of focus, to move from the "really obtaining components" of the intentional experience (the current actual glimpse of the tree that presents itself) and it is also possible to shift focus in the other direction to the "intentional object"—*the seen tree as such* (Husserl 2014: 198). The intentional object is still distinct from the actual tree. When I remember the tree in the garden, *the remembered tree* is not identical to the physical tree. As Husserl puts it, the actual tree can burn up whereas the "remembered tree" cannot. Husserl uses the term "noema" to pick out the intentional object as it is intended, but he also acknowledges that there must be some noematic core (a "determinable X") that allows the remembered tree and the seen tree to be about the *same* tree.

Husserl recognized that all objects that occupy space are apprehended in "profiles" or "adumbrations" (*Abschattungen*), and their essence is never exhausted by these profiles. An object is always further determinable and portends ever-new contexts in which these prefigured experiences can be fulfilled. Physical objects present with an "excess" (*Überschuss*), whereby their determinate features are supplemented with a horizon of indeterminacy of features that can be explored in further perceptions (Hopp 2011). Husserl speaks of "modes of indeterminate suggestion and non-intuitive co-presence" (Husserl 2014: 183) that are wrapped up in the experience.

Husserl also maintained, following Brentano and the Cartesian tradition, that mental experiences themselves are presented not in profiles but as they are; their *esse* is *percipi*. On this account, experiences in themselves are incorrigible; one has first-person authority over them, although what is disclosed may contain hidden depth dimensions (such as the a priori temporal structures of the experiences) that require further phenomenological unpacking.

Husserl's noema is a rich but somewhat ambiguous and underdeveloped notion. One popular position is that the noema is an abstract, ideal entity (similar to a Fregean sense) that acts to determine the reference of a thought whose only relation to the actuality is that the latter instantiates it (Føllesdal 1978; 1990, followed by Dreyfus), what has been called an "ontological" characterization of the noema. While Husserl agrees that the ideal sense (*Sinn*) is one component of the full noema, viz. its "noematic core" (*Kern*), which guarantees sameness of reference across different thoughts of the same entity, this identical sense is not identical with the noema but is at best one "layer" (*Schicht*) of the noema (Drummond and Embree 1992). Husserl writes:

> A noematic sense "inhabits" each of these experiences, and however much this sense may be related in the diverse experiences, indeed, however essentially alike it may be in terms of its core composition [*Kernbestand*], in experiences of different kinds it is a noematic sense of a different kind in each case. (Husserl 2014: 181)

There are further dimensions of the noema that make it not exactly equivalent to a Fregean sense. The noema is a particular "this," whereas a sense is universal. A noema includes essentially the various possible modes of apprehension of the object. On this basis, Aron Gurwitsch (in Drummond and Embree 1992) argued that the noema consists of the series of possible apprehensions or appearances of the intentional object (and Sartre follows Gurwitsch here). On this account, the noema simply is the object as understood in a certain way, and no new ontological entity is being postulated. Sokolowski (1984) and Drummond (1990) propose a more nuanced account according to which noema and its intentional object are a unity in a manifold.

From around 1908, Husserl develops an original transcendental idealism that asserts that all "sense and being" is the outcome of intentional constitution of transcendental subjectivity (Husserl 1970: 204). Thus, in *Cartesian Meditations*, he claims that "phenomenology is eo ipso 'transcendental idealism', though in a fundamentally and essentially new sense" (Husserl 1960: 86). He elaborates:

> *The proof of this idealism is therefore phenomenology itself.* Only someone who misunderstands either the deepest sense of intentional method, or that of transcendental reduction, or perhaps both, can attempt to separate phenomenology from transcendental idealism. (Husserl 1960: 86)

The intentional method *is* transcendental. Husserl regularly portrays Descartes as the original discoverer of intentionality "which makes up the essence of egological life" (Husserl 1970: 82), even though, Husserl maintains, Descartes in fact lost sight of the true significance of intentionality by retreating into metaphysical dogmatism. Nevertheless, Husserl adopts the Cartesian-style construction, *ego-cogitatio-cogitatum*, to express the structure of intentionality or "having something consciously" [*etwas bewussthaben*]' (Husserl 1970: 82).

For Husserl, a physical object, apprehended phenomenologically, supports a potentially indefinite number of possible modes of access to it. Hence Husserl speaks of the intended object as "an idea in the Kantian sense" (Husserl 2014: 284). Intentional objects already contain the possible modes of approach to them as a series of lawfully related noemata. The aspectual shapes or modes of approach to the object can be visualized as "windows" or avenues of approach to the object, set up in an essentially predetermined way. Thus, in the *Amsterdam Lectures*, Husserl describes the noema of a house in a house-perception as opening onto an infinite horizon of other possible profiles of the house:

> The question immediately arises as to how come it is evident that this pointing-ahead belongs to the phenomenon-in-consciousness? How come this horizon-consciousness refers us in fact to further actually unexperienced traits of the same "phenomenon"? Certainly this is already an interpretation which goes beyond the moment of experiencing, which we have called the "horizon-consciousness," which is, indeed, as is easily determined, completely non-intuitive and thus in and of itself empty. (Husserl 1997: 226–7)

In his mature works, Husserl expands his earlier analyses of the specific features of intentional objects to consider the non-objectual intentionality of horizons, fringes, and ultimately of the life-world (*Lebenswelt*) that is "always already there" but can never be objectified. In *Ideas I* Husserl defines the "horizon" as "'what is co-given' but not genuinely" (Husserl 2014: 77) and, in *Experience and Judgment*, he speaks of "the horizon of typical pre-acquaintance in which every object in pregiven" (Husserl 1973: 150). Husserl believed he has made a genuine breakthrough with his concept of horizonal-intentionality (*Horizont-Intentionalität*), originally inspired by William James. Husserl's "horizon-intentionality" is later taken up by Gurwitsch and Merleau-Ponty (Walton 2003), to explicate the complex manners in which experiences are framed by temporal and other horizons that have their own vague but real significance.

In *Crisis of European Sciences* Husserl claimed his real philosophical breakthrough came in 1898 when he realized that there was a "universal a priori of correlation between experienced object and manners of givenness" (Husserl 1970: 166n). Every object must be understood not solely as it is "in itself" but in necessary relation to the subjective acts that disclose it. Anything that is—whatever its meaning and to whatever region it belongs—is "an index of a subjective system of correlations" (Husserl 1970: 165). This "correlationism" accounts for the whole manner of human being in the world (including the temporality of experience with its horizons of past and future). Intentionality covers

the whole of conscious life; everything is an achievement or accomplishment of intentional consciousness: "nothing exists for me otherwise than by virtue of the *actual
and potential performance of my own consciousness [Bewusstseinsleistung]*" (Husserl
1969: 234). Life is *intentional, "accomplishing" life* with its potentially infinite horizons of
intentional implication, uniting together into the collective experience known as *spirit*.
As Husserl writes in the *Crisis*:

> Conscious life is through and through an intentionally accomplishing life [*inten-
> tional leistendes Leben*] through which the life-world . . . in part attains anew and
> in part has already attained its meaning and validity. All real mundane objectivity
> is constituted accomplishment in this sense, including that of men and animals.
> (Husserl 1970: 204)

Moreover, sense-giving should not be understood as a solipsistic, individualist form
of meaning-loading, carried out by isolated Cartesian egos that are not in communion
with one another, but rather as an interactive, collective, social, historically embedded
experience, an experience of interconnecting subjects operating within the horizon of
the life-world. Husserl speaks of the "interweaving" (*Ineinandersein*) of human intentional existence, a conception subsequently taken up by Merleau-Ponty (Moran 2015).
Subjectivity exists within a nexus of other intentional subjects:

> But each soul also stands in community [*Vergemeinschaftung*] with others which are
> intentionally interrelated, that is, in a purely intentional, internally and essentially
> closed nexus [*Zusammenhang*], that of intersubjectivity. (Husserl 1970: 238)

There is, for Husserl, a network of interacting subjects or agents adding up to a "we-
subjectivity" or "we-community" (*Wir-Gemeinschaft*, Husserl 1954: 416). Husserl speaks
of an "intersubjective harmony [*intersubjective Einstimmigkeit*] of validity" (Husserl
1970: 163). Indeed, as Husserl will insist, the very idea of *objectivity* as such, of a common
objective world—including and perhaps most especially scientific objectivity—is not
a given brute fact of experience but a unique and particular achievement of subjects
cooperating together. Naïve experience does not *even raise the issue* of objectivity.
It simply lives in its experiences with an originary primal belief, an "acceptance character" (*Urglaube*). It is the task of transcendental phenomenology to uncover the hidden
intentionalities at work in the constitution of normal experiential life.

30.4 MARTIN HEIDEGGER: INTENTIONALITY RECONFIGURED AS CARE AND TRANSCENDENCE

In his lectures Martin Heidegger (1985; 1982) offered a sustained critique of the Cartesian
metaphysical presuppositions he claimed underpinned Husserlian intentionality,

leading him, in *Being and Time*, to abandon the term "intentionality" in favor of talking of the "transcendence" of human existence (Dasein) and its caring manner of "being-in-the-world" (Heidegger 1962). As Heidegger puts it, because of its uninterrogated metaphysical baggage, "intentionality" is the very last word that should be used as a phenomenological slogan. In *Being and Time* (Heidegger 1962), Heidegger avoids key Husserlian formulations, e.g., intentionality, epoché, noesis-noema, consciousness, *ego-cogito-cogitatum*, and instead proposes a new way of describing human existence (Dasein) as "care" (*Sorge*), running-ahead of itself, and "transcendence."

In his 1927 *Basic Problems of Phenomenology* lectures, Heidegger sees the "enigmatic phenomenon of intentionality" (Heidegger 1982: 58) as designating a problem rather than a solution (see also Heidegger 1984: 134). Heidegger rejects as "Cartesian" the framing of the key question of intentionality as the problem of representation: "How can this ego with its intentional experiences get outside of its sphere of experience and assume a relation to an extant world?" (Heidegger 1982: 61). Heidegger implicates Husserl in this representationalist form of intentionality. Heidegger also claims, essentially repeating Husserl's critique of Brentano, that the nature of the intentional relation has been misconstrued either as a *real* relation between two extant things, or, as in Brentano, as an *immanent* relation between the mind and its private contents, replicating the inherent representationalism of modern philosophy since Descartes. Husserl, according to Heidegger, lacks an ontological characterization of conscious intentional life:

> It is not intentionality as such that is metaphysically dogmatic but what is built under its structure [*Struktur*], or is left at this level because of a traditional tendency not to question that of which it is presumably the structure, and what this sense of structure itself means. (Heidegger 1985: 46–7)

Heidegger claims that Husserl failed to interrogate the "being of the intentional" (*Sein des Intentionalen*, Heidegger 1982: 161). In his 1928 lectures, Heidegger proclaims: "The intentional relation must be founded on the 'being-with' or 'being-by' of Dasein" (*Sein-bei*, Heidegger 1984: 134). Intentionality is a form of "ontic" transcendence that can only be understood if Dasein's more basic "ontological" transcendence is understood (Heidegger 1984: 135); and in 1927: "Intentionality is the *ratio cognoscendi* of transcendence. Transcendence is the *ratio essendi* of intentionality in its diverse modes" (Heidegger 1982: 65). Human existence is self-transcending: "Dasein is itself the passage across [*Überschritt*]" (Heidegger 1984: 165), and "transcendence means surpassing" (*Transzendenz bedeutet Überstieg*). Heidegger concedes that Husserl also conceived of intentionality in terms of transcendence but he rejects Husserl's subjectivist orientation. Heidegger recasts the problem of intentionality as: How does Dasein encounter entities within its world? (Heidegger 1962: 417–18). This leads Heidegger to a fundamental interrogation of Dasein's "being-in-the-world" (Heidegger 1982: 164). As Heidegger writes in "On the Essence of Ground":

We name *world* that *towards which* Dasein as such transcends, and shall now determine transcendence as *being-in-the-world*. (Heidegger 1998: 109)

Heidegger rejects the model of detached knowing as the primary mode of human engagement with the world. He claims that Husserl prioritized the disinterested, perceptual, or theoretical inspection of a thing as the primary mode of being-in-the-world, whereas Heidegger contends that priority must be given to the pragmatic, interested, goal-oriented engagement with things. Things manifest themselves as *tools* or *equipment* to accomplish specific goals in a set of "in-order-to's." The hammer's essence is exhibited in utilizing it correctly—not by sitting back and looking at it. Detached "theoretical" inspection is secondary and derivative to the original, concerned involvement. This pragmatic account of concerned involvement—combined with a reading of Merleau-Ponty's motor intentionality—inspired Hubert L. Dreyfus's concept of "skillful coping" (Dreyfus 1991), although Dreyfus somewhat unfairly contrasts Heideggerian copying with Husserl's representationalism and cognitivism. Dreyfus downplays Husserl's own account of habitual, pragmatic, "operative" intentionality in *Ideas II*. Merleau-Ponty, as we shall see, more accurately incorporated Husserl's account of practical lived engagement with the world in his account of embodied, habitual, motor intentionality.

30.5 Maurice Merleau-Ponty's Motor Intentionality and the "Intentional Arc"

French phenomenology—Jean-Paul Sartre and Maurice Merleau-Ponty—continued to affirm intentionality as central to human existence. Sartre stressed that Husserl's doctrine of intentionality, in opposition to Kantian epistemology, restores consciousness's direct contact with the world: "Husserl has restored to things their horror and their charm" (Sartre 1970). Sartre rejects a representationalist, immanentist account of intentionality; intentionality is precisely transcendence toward the world, even in imagining what is imagined transcends consciousness: "Consciousness has no inside" (Sartre 1970: 5); it is a "nothingness" that is always oriented to what-it-is-not.

Merleau-Ponty criticized any intellectualism that "treats the experience of the world as a pure act of constituting consciousness" (Merleau-Ponty 2012: 253), but he claims Husserl has a different account:

Husserl's originality lies beyond the notion of intentionality; rather, it is found in the elaboration of this notion and in the discovery, beneath the intentionality of representations, of a more profound intentionality, which others have called existence. (Merleau-Ponty 2012: 520 n. 57)

In *Phenomenology of Perception* (Merleau-Ponty 2012), Merleau-Ponty develops his notion of "operative intentionality" (*l'intentionnalité opérante*), based on Husserl's "functioning intentionality" (*fungeriende Intentionalität*) (Husserl 1969, 234; and Husserl 1973: 48), where Husserl talks of a hidden intentionality buried in "sedimentations." Merleau-Ponty develops the non-objectifying, lived-body intentionality expressed in Husserl's "I can" or "I do." Merleau-Ponty says that "consciousness is originarily not an 'I think that' but rather an 'I can'" (Merleau-Ponty 2012: 139), taking up Husserl's *Formal and Transcendental Logic* §98, where he speaks of an "accomplishing" (*leistende*) subjectivity that is more than the purely actual; it also consists of "abilities" (*Vermögen*)—"I can" (*ich kann*) and "I do" (*ich tue*, Husserl 1969: 246).

Merleau-Ponty correctly identified Husserl's advance beyond objectifying intentionality in the discovery of "operative intentionality" (Husserl's *fungierende Intentionalität*), characterized by anonymity and passivity. Operative intentionality is a pre-conscious intentionality that presents the world in which we find ourselves as something already there (Husserl's "*Geradehineinleben*"). Merleau-Ponty dubs this unreflective, habitual, bodily intentionality "motor intentionality" (*intentionnalité motrice*, Merleau-Ponty 2012: 113). Motor intentionality is a pervasive structure of life, achieved by the functioning, active body in its capacity for self-movements (kinaestheses).

The *locus classicus* for Merleau-Ponty's concept of pre-conscious motor intentionality is his famous analysis of the case of Schneider, where he critiques the Gestalt psychologists Gelb and Goldstein's interpretation of their patient (see Mooney 2011; Jensen 2009; Kelly 2000). Schneider's case illustrates how pathological conditions indicate breakdown in the circuit of operative intentionality. Gelb and Goldstein thought Schneider could carry out *habitual* but not spontaneous actions and concluded that habitual movements enjoy a privileged position in the schema of possible bodily movements. Merleau-Ponty argues, in contrast, that Schneider's capacity for habitual activity was *as impaired as* his capacity for spontaneous activity because his entire being-in-the-world is disrupted.

Merleau-Ponty distinguishes between the intentionality of *pointing* and that of *grasping*. Schneider cannot accomplish pointing but can scratch where a mosquito bites him. Grasping is already *with* the object, Merleau-Ponty says, whereas pointing requires separation between hand and object. Pointing is a kind of prefiguration of more cognitive intentionality, which intends an absent object; grasping is embodied practical engagement with the lived environment. This skillful unreflective bodily intentionality is what Dreyfus calls "coping"—"situation-specific skillful coping" (Dreyfus 2007: 352), "everyday skillful coping" (Dreyfus 1991: 67). As Dreyfus elucidates: "Merleau-Ponty understands motor-intentionality as *the way the body tends* toward an optimal grip of its object" (Dreyfus 2007: 63).

Merleau-Ponty rejects a purely active or intellectualist account of intentionality and argues that not all intentional activity can be construed as "constitution": "The world is not an object whose law of constitution I have in my possession" (Merleau-Ponty 2012: lxxiv). The body knows the world better than I do, he claims.

In *Phenomenology of Perception*, Merleau-Ponty employs the phrase "intentional arc," borrowed from the German psychologist Franz Fischer who, in analyzing the experience of space and time among schizophrenic patients (Fischer 1930), speaks of an "intentional arc" (*intentionaler Bogen*) binding them to the world. For Merleau-Ponty, the life of consciousness "is underpinned by an 'intentional arc' [*arc intentionnel*] that projects around us our past, our future, our human milieu, our physical situation, our ideological situation and our moral situation, or rather, that ensures that we are situated within all of these relationships" (Merleau-Ponty 2012: 137). This "intentional arc" is an overarching framework that connects the subject to the world and unifies its life, holding everything together in a coherent, meaningful way. Dreyfus links the "intentional arc" to J. J. Gibson's ideas of the "solicitations" and "affordances" in the environment (Gibson 1979). Dreyfus says Merleau-Ponty's "intentional arc" names the "tight connection between the agent and the world . . . as the agent acquires skills, these skills are 'stored', not as representations in the mind but as dispositions to respond to the solicitations of situations in the world" (Dreyfus 2007: 367). Dreyfus writes:

> The idea of an intentional arc is meant to capture the idea that all past experience is projected back into the world. The best representation of the world is thus the world itself. (Dreyfus 2007: 373)

Drawing on Husserl's *Ideas II*, for Merleau-Ponty, bodily movement ("motricity") is an integral aspect of all perception and there is an inextricable intertwining between bodily perception and the sensuous way the world appears:

> My mobile body makes a difference in the visible world, being a part of it; that is why I can steer it through the visible. Conversely it is just as true that vision is attached to movement. We see only what we look at. What would vision be without eye movement? (Merleau-Ponty 1964: 162)

Merleau-Ponty's account of embodied perception has provided a paradigm for cognitive scientists wishing to move away from predominantly cognitivist accounts towards enactive accounts of perception. Merleau-Ponty has also inspired the "naturalized phenomenology" of Francesco Varela (Petitot, Varela et al. 1999; Zahavi 2010) and Evan Thompson (2007).

30.6 THE FEMINIST CRITIQUE: IRIS MARION YOUNG ON INHIBITED INTENTIONALITY

Merleau-Ponty's discussion of Schneider, and especially of his supposedly damaged relationship to his sexuality (e.g., he no longer is aroused by pornography or experiences kisses as sexual), has been criticized by Judith Butler (1989), who commends Merleau-Ponty for situating sexuality centrally as a "current of existence" that pervades life and is intentional "in the sense that it modalises a relationship between an embodied subject and a concrete situation" (Butler 1989), but criticizes his "tacit normative assumption about the heterosexual character of sexuality" and especially the characterization of male sexuality as a disembodied gaze towards a decontextualized female body. Iris Marion Young develops this relationship between intentionality and gender in her classic 1979 paper "Throwing Like a Girl" (Young 2005), influenced by Merleau-Ponty's and Simone de Beauvoir's discussions of situated embodiment. Young writes:

> There is no situation, however, without embodied location and interaction. Conversely, the body as lived is always layered with social and historical meaning and is not some primitive matter prior to or underlying economic and political relations or cultural meanings. (Young 2005: 7)

Young starts from a critical reading of Erwin Straus' "The Upright Posture" (Straus 1966). She claims—against Straus, who assumes women and men exhibit innately different bodily styles—that women's "inhibited" bodily intentionality has been constituted through cultural norms. Applying Husserl's conception of the lived body as experienced in a series of "I can's," Young claims that there is a parallel series of "I cannot's" that have culturally been imposed on women:

> For any lived body, the world appears as the system of possibilities that are correlative to its intentions. For any lived body, moreover, the world also appears to be populated with opacities and resistances correlative to its own limits and frustrations. For any bodily existence, that is, an "I cannot" may appear to set limits to the "I can." To the extent that feminine bodily existence is an inhibited intentionality, however, the same set of possibilities that appears to be correlative to its intentions also appears to be a system of frustrations correlative to its hesitancies. (Young 2005: 37)

Young maintains that women's "inhibited intentionality" is based on the cultural norms of a particular society. As a result, woman, she claims, retains "a distance from her body as transcending movement and from engagement in the world's possibilities" (Young 2005: 39). Young's account of the intentional constitution of gender and bodily style is an interesting development of the phenomenological approach to intentionality that has led to phenomenological explorations of gender, race, and vulnerability.

30.7 CONCLUSION

Phenomenology's discussions of intentionality begin within the Brentanian framework, featuring problems concerning the intentional relation, the intentional object, and the overall scope of intentionality as the supposed "mark of the mental." Husserl elevated intentionality to a central position in all conscious life and made breakthrough contributions with his essential descriptions of perception, memory, imagining, time-consciousness, as well as the functioning intentionality of practical embodied capacities. Heidegger emphasized the ecstatic, transcendental character of temporalized being-in-the-world, with a powerful account of *moods* as essentially world-disclosing. Husserl, Heidegger, Sartre, and Merleau-Ponty all characterize human intentional existence as *transcendence towards the world*, presenting subjectivity as essentially running beyond itself, world-disclosing, and sense-giving. Finally, the manner of embodied being-in-the-world raises issues about the experiences of sex and gender insofar as they are constituted socially and historically, issues that analytic philosophers are now beginning to explore.

The analytic philosophical tradition has tended to develop intentionality largely from Brentano rather than Husserl. Roderick M. Chisholm (1967; 1989), interpreting Brentano, recast intentionality in a primarily linguistic formulation ("sentences about believing," Chisholm 1955–6). For Chisholm, intentionality is a set of specific logical and semantic features (failure of substitutivity; existential generalization, intensionality) of sentences containing "psychological" verbs designating mental acts. For Chisholm, the resistance of these logical features to a purely extensionalist treatment demonstrated the ineliminability of intentionality. This led to the distinction between intentionality (as a mental phenomenon) and intensionality-with-an-s, a logical or semantic feature referring to the non-substitutability of a term across contexts (Guttenplan 1994; Jacob 2014).

Chisholm's linguistic version of intentionality influenced Willard van Orman Quine (1960), Daniel C. Dennett (1987), with his heuristic notion of the "intentional stance," as a user interface for predicting behavior, ultimately eliminable in favor of a physicalist account, and John Searle (1983) who argues that intentionality is an ineliminable "groundfloor" property of the mind (Moran 2013a). Dennett's and Searle's accounts of intentionality reproduce many features found in Husserlian phenomenology, e.g., intentionality as an attitude, the recognition of "aspectual shape," and the "background" of skills and capacities—although both deny any direct influence (Searle 2005). Searle's distinction between "background" (bodily capacities) and "network" (framework of beliefs) roughly reproduces Husserl's own distinctions between bodily habitual functioning intentionality and horizon-intentionality, although Searle considers background to be non-intentional whereas for Husserl it is a prepredicative intentionality.

A decisive difference remains, however. Whereas Searle and Dennett want to naturalize intentionality, phenomenological approaches to intentionality offer compelling alternatives to theories of intentionality wedded to representationalism and naturalism. Representation, for phenomenology, is simply one or several ways in which objects are intended. Imagining something, depicting it, and so on, are distinct modes of representing. Not all intentionality reduces to representation. Embodied habitual intentional actions, for instance, are primarily non-representational, and touch is a good example of non-representational, intentional sensuous perception. The focus on embodied and embedded "being-in-the-world" is a particular feature of the phenomenological tradition, although it is now reemerging in the enactivist approach to cognition (Evan Thompson 2007; Noë 2005). Entirely original in phenomenology is the focus on non-objectifying forms of intentionality, e.g., on the phenomenology of "horizons" and "saturated" phenomena such as laughter or love which are meaning-laden without being object-directed in a narrow sense (Marion 2002). Phenomenology has a unique interest in the experience of "world" that is encountered as "always already" "pre-given" in a harmonious manner and as outrunning all possible intentional objec-tification. Phenomenology considers intentionality to be essential for understanding the philosophical issues clustered around conscious subjectivity, lived embodiment (Husserl 1989), the experience of "otherness" or "alterity" (*Fremderfahrung*), and the apprehension of other human subjects in empathy (*Einfühlung*), leading to wider meditations on intersubjectivity, sociality, historicality, and worldhood. As Husserl boldly proclaims: "Intentionality is the title which stands for the only actual and gen-uine way of explaining, making intelligible. To go back to the intentional origins and unities of the formation of meaning is to proceed toward a comprehension which, once achieved (which is, of course, an ideal case), would leave no meaningful question unan-swered" (Husserl 1970: 168).

REFERENCES

Albertazzi, L., Libardi, M., and Poli, R. (eds) (1996), *The School of Franz Brentano* (Dordrecht: Kluwer).

Betti, A. (2013), "We owe it to Sigwart! A new look at the content/object distinction in early phenomenological theories of judgment from Brentano to Twardowski," in M. Textor (ed.) *Judgement and Truth in Early Analytic Philosophy and Phenomenology* (London: Palgrave Macmillan), 74–96.

Black, D. L. (2010), "Intentionality in Medieval Arabic Philosophy," *Quaestio* 10/1: 65–81.

Brandl, J. (2005), "The immanence theory of intentionality," in D. W. Smith and A. L. Thomasson (eds), *Phenomenology and Philosophy of Mind* (Oxford: Clarendon), 167–82.

Brentano, F. C. ([1874] 1995), *Psychology from an Empirical Standpoint*, translated by A. C. Rancurello, D. B. Terrell, and L. L. McAlister (London: Routledge).

Brentano, F. C. (1995a), *Descriptive Psychology*, ed. R. M. Chisholm and W. Baumgartner, translated by B. Müller (London: Routledge).

Breton, S. (1955), "Conscience et intentionnalité d'après saint Thomas et Brentano," *Archives de Philosophie* 19: 63–87.

Butler, J. (1989), "Sexual ideology and phenomenological description: A feminist critique of Merleau-Ponty's *Phenomenology of Perception*," in J. Allen and M. Young (eds), *The Thinking Muse: Feminism and Modern French Philosophy* (Bloomington, IN: Indiana University Press), 85–100.

Calcagno, A. (2008), "Michel Henry's Non-Intentionality Thesis and Husserlian Phenomen-ology," *Journal of the British Society for Phenomenology* 39/2: 117–29.

Carman, T. (2003), *Heidegger's Analytic: Interpretation, Discourse and Authenticity in Being and Time* (New York: Cambridge University Press).

Caston, V. (1998), "Aristotle and the Problem of Intentionality," *Philosophy and Phenomenological Research* 58/2: 249–98.

Chant, S. R., Hindriks, F., and Preyer, G. (eds) (2014), *From Individual to Collective Intentionality: New Essays* (New York: Oxford University Press).

Chisholm, R. M. (1955-6), "Sentences about Believing," *Proceedings of the Aristotelian Society* 56: 125–48.

Chisholm, R. M. (1967), "Brentano on descriptive psychology and the intentional," in E. N. Lee and M. Mandelbaum (eds), *Phenomenology and Existentialism* (Baltimore, MD: Johns Hopkins University Press).

Chisholm, R. M. (1989), "The Formal Structure of the Intentional: A Metaphysical Study," *Brentano Studien* 1: 11–18.

Cho, K. K. (1990), "Phenomenology as Cooperative Task: Husserl–Farber Correspondence during 1936–37," *Philosophy and Phenomenological Research* 50: 36–43.

Chrudzimski, A. (2013), "Brentano and Aristotle on the ontology of intentionality," in D. Fisette and G. Fréchette (eds), *Themes from Brentano* (Amsterdam: Rodopi).

Crowell, S. and Malpas, J. (eds) (2007), *Transcendental Heidegger* (Stanford, CA: Stanford University Press).

Dennett, D. (1987), *The Intentional Stance* (Cambridge, MA: MIT Press).

Dreyfus, H. L. (1991), *Being-in-the-World. A Commentary on Heidegger's* Being and Time, *Division One* (Cambridge: MIT Press).

Dreyfus, H. L. (2000), "A Merleau-Pontyian Critique of Husserl's and Searle's Representationalist Accounts of Action," *Proceedings of the Aristotelian Society* 100/1: 287–302.

Dreyfus, H. L. (2007), "Intelligence without Representation—Merleau-Ponty's Critique of Mental Representation: The Relevance of Phenomenology to Scientific Explanation," *Phenomenology and the Cognitive Sciences* 1: 367–83.

Drummond, J. (1990), *Husserlian Intentionality and Non-foundational Realism: Noema and Object* (Dordrecht: Springer).

Drummond, J. J. (2012), "Intentionality without representationalism," in D. Zahavi (ed.), *The Oxford Handbook of Contemporary Phenomenology* (Oxford: Oxford University Press), 115–33.

Drummond, J. J. and Embree, L. E. (eds) (1992), *The Phenomenology of the Noema* (Dordrecht: Springer).

Fischer, F. (1930), "Raum-Zeit-Struktur und Denkstörung in der Schizophrenie II. Mitteilung," *Zeitschrift für die gesamte Neurologie und Psychiatrie* 124/1: 241–56.

Føllesdal, D. (1978), "Brentano and Husserl on Intentional Objects and Perception," *Grazer Philosophische Studien* 5: 83–94.

Føllesdal, D. (1990), "Noema and Meaning in Husserl," *Philosophy and Phenomenological Research* 50: 263–71.

Forrai, G. (ed.) (2005), *Intentionality: Past and Future*. Value Inquiry Book Series, vol. 173 (New York: Rodopi).

Gibson, J. J. (1979), *The Ecological Approach to Visual Perception* (London: Houghton Mifflin).

Guttenplan, S. (1994), "Intensional," in S. Guttenplan (ed.), *A Companion to the Philosophy of Mind* (Oxford: Basil Blackwell), 374–5.

Heidegger, M. (1962), *Being and Time*, translated by J. Macquarrie and E. Robinson (Oxford: Basil Blackwell).

Heidegger, M. (1982), *Basic Problems of Phenomenology*, translated by A. Hofstadter (Bloomington, IN: Indiana University Press).

Heidegger, M. (1984), *The Metaphysical Foundations of Logic*, translated by M. Heim (Bloomington, IN: Indiana University Press).

Heidegger, M. (1985), *History of the Concept of Time: Prolegomena*, translated by T. Kisiel (Bloomington, IN: Indiana University Press).

Heidegger, M. (1998), "On the essence of ground," in *Pathmarks*, translated by W. McNeill (Cambridge: Cambridge University Press), 97–135.

Hopp, W. (2011), *Perception and Knowledge: A Phenomenological Account* (Cambridge: Cambridge University Press).

Hopp, W. (2015), "Empty intentions and phenomenological character: A defense of inclusivism," in T. Breyer and C. Gutland (eds), *Phenomenology of Thinking: Philosophical Investigations in the Character of Cognitive Experiences* (London: Routledge), 44–61.

Husserl, E. (1954), *Die Krisis der europäischen Wissenschaften und die transzendentale Phänomenologie. Eine Einleitung in die phänomenologische Philosophie*, Husserliana 6, ed. W. Biemel (The Hague: Martinus Nijhoff).

Husserl, E. (1960), *Cartesian Meditations: An Introduction to Phenomenology*, translated by D. Cairns (The Hague: Martinus Nijhoff).

Husserl, E. (1969), *Formal and Transcendental Logic*, translated by D. Cairns (The Hague: Martinus Nijhoff).

Husserl, E. (1970), *The Crisis of European Sciences and Transcendental Phenomenology: An Introduction to Phenomenological Philosophy*, translated by D. Carr (Evanston, IL: Northwestern University Press).

Husserl, E. (1973), *Experience and Judgment: Investigations in a Genealogy of Logic*. Revised and ed. L. Landgrebe, translated by J. S. Churchill and K. Ameriks (London: Routledge and Kegan Paul).

Husserl, E. (1989), *Ideas Pertaining to a Pure Phenomenology and to a Phenomenological Philosophy. Second Book: Studies in the Phenomenology of Constitution*, translated by R. Rojcewicz and A. Schuwer (Dordrecht: Kluwer).

Husserl, E. (1994), *Early Writings in the Philosophy of Logic and Mathematics*, translated by D. Willard, Collected Works V (Dordrecht: Kluwer).

Husserl, E. (1997), *Psychological and Transcendental Phenomenology and the Confrontation with Heidegger (1927–31)*, *The Encyclopaedia Britannica Article, The Amsterdam Lectures "Phenomenology and Anthropology" and Husserl's Marginal Note in* Being and Time, *and* Kant on the Problem of Metaphysics, translated by T. Sheehan and R. E. Palmer Collected Works VI (Dordrecht: Kluwer).

Husserl, E. (2001), *Logical Investigations*, 2 vols, translated by J. N. Findlay, ed. with a new introduction by D. Moran and new preface by M. Dummett (London: Routledge).

Husserl, E. (2002), "Philosophy as rigorous science," translated by M. Brainard, *The New Yearbook for Phenomenology and Phenomenological Philosophy* 2: 249–95.

Husserl, E. (2014), *Ideas for a Pure Phenomenology and Phenomenological Philosophy. First Book: General Introduction to Pure Phenomenology*, translated by D. O. Dahlstrom (Indianapolis, IN: Hackett).

Jacob, P. (2014), "Intentionality," *The Stanford Encyclopedia of Philosophy* (Winter 2014 edition), Edward N. Zalta (ed.), URL https://plato.stanford.edu/archives/win2014/entries/intentionality/.

Jacquette, D. (2015), "Origins of *Gegenstandstheorie*: Immanent and transcendent intended objects in Brentano, Twardowski, and Meinong," in *Alexius Meinong, the Shepherd of Non-Being* (Dordrecht: Springer), 25–40.

Jensen, R. T. (2009), "Motor Intentionality and the case of Schneider," *Phenomenology and the Cognitive Sciences* 8/3: 371–88.

Kelly, S. D. (2000), "Grasping at straws: Motor intentionality and the cognitive science of skilled behaviour," in M. Wrathall and Jeff Malpas (eds), *Heidegger, Coping and the Cognitive Sciences: Essays in Honor of Hubert L. Dreyfus*, vol. 2 (Cambridge, MA: MIT Press), 161–77.

Kelly, S. D. (2002), "Merleau-Ponty on the body," *Ratio* 15: 376–91.

Kriegel, U. (2016), "Brentano's Mature Theory of Intentionality," *Journal of the History of Analytical Philosophy* 4/2: 1–15.

Levinas, E. (1983), "Beyond intentionality," in A. Montefiore (ed.), *Philosophy in France Today* (Cambridge: Cambridge University Press), 100–15.

Marion, J.-L. (2002), *Being Given: Toward a Phenomenology of Givenness* (Stanford, CA: Stanford University Press).

Merleau-Ponty, M. (1960), "The philosopher and his shadow," in *Signs* (Evanston, IL: Northwestern University Press).

Merleau-Ponty, M. (1964), *The Primacy of Perception*, ed. J. Edie (Evanston, IL: Northwestern University Press).

Merleau-Ponty, M. (2012), *The Phenomenology of Perception*, translated by D. A. Landes (London: Routledge).

Mohanty, J. N. (1982), *Husserl and Frege* (Bloomington, IN: Indiana University Press).

Mooney, T. (2011), "Plasticity, Motor Intentionality and Concrete Movement in Merleau-Ponty," *Continental Philosophy Review* 44/4: 359–81.

Moran, D. (1996), "Brentano's Thesis," *Proceedings of the Aristotelian Society* 70: 1–27.

Moran, D. (2000a), "Heidegger's Critique of Husserl's and Brentano's Accounts of Intentionality," *Inquiry* 43/1: 39–65.

Moran, D. (2008), "Husserl's Transcendental Philosophy and the Critique of Naturalism," *Continental Philosophy Review* 41/4: 401–25.

Moran, D. (2013a), "Intentionality: Some Lessons from the History of the Problem from Brentano to the Present," *International Journal of Philosophical Studies* 21/3: 317–58.

Moran, D. (2013b), "'Let's Look at It Objectively': Why Phenomenology Cannot be Naturalized," *Phenomenology and Naturalism*, Royal Institute of Philosophy Supplement 72: 89–115.

Moran, D. (2014), "What Does Heidegger Mean by the Transcendence of Dasein?" *International Journal of Philosophical Studies* 22/4: 491–514.

Moran, D. (2015), "*Ineinandersein* and *l'interlacs*: The constitution of the social world or 'we-world' (*Wir-Welt*) in Edmund Husserl and Maurice Merleau-Ponty," in D. Moran and T. Szanto (eds), *Discovering the We: The Phenomenology of Sociality* (London: Routledge), 107–26.

Noë, A. (2005), *Action in Perception* (Cambridge, MA: MIT Press).

Perler, D. (2001), *Ancient and Medieval Theories of Intentionality*, Volume 76 of Studien und Texte zur Geistesgeschichte des Mittelalters. (Leiden: Brill).

Perler, D. (2004), *Theorien der Intentionalität im Mittelalter* (Frankfurt a. M.: Klostermann).

Petitot, J., Varela, F. J., Pacoud, B., and Roy, J.-M. (eds) (1999), *Naturalizing Phenomenology* (Stanford, CA: Stanford University Press).

Pfänder, A. (1967), *Phenomenology of Willing and Other Phaenomenologica*, translated by H. Spiegelberg (Evanston, IL: Northwestern University Press).

Quine, W. V. O. (1960), *Word and Object* (Cambridge, MA: MIT Press).

Rollinger, R. (1996), *Husserl's Position in the School of Brentano* (Utrecht: Utrecht University Press).

Salice, A. and Schmid, H. B. (eds) (2016), *The Phenomenological Approach to Social Reality* (Dordrecht: Springer).

Sartre, J.-P. (1970), "Intentionality: A Fundamental Idea in Husserl's Philosophy," translated by J. P. Fell, *Journal of the British Society for Phenomenology* 1/2: 4–5.

Schmid, H. B. (2009), *Plural Action: Essays in Philosophy and Social Science*. Contributions to Phenomenology, vol. 58 (Dordrecht: Springer).

Searle, J. R. (1983), *Intentionality* (New York: Oxford University Press).

Searle, J. R. (2005), "The phenomenological illusion," in M. E. Reicher and J. C. Marek (eds), *Experience and Analysis. Erfahrung und Analyse*. Proceedings of the 27th International Wittgenstein Symposium, Kirchberg, Austria, August 8–14, 2004 (Vienna), 317–36.

Sokolowski, R. (1984), "Intentional Analysis and the Noema," *Dialectica* 38/2–3: 113–29.

Sorabji, R. (1991), "From Aristotle to Brentano: The Development of the Concept of Intentionality," *Oxford Studies in Ancient Philosophy* 9: 227–59.

Spiegelberg, H. (1969), "'Intention' und 'Intentionalität' in der Scholastik, bei Brentano und Husserl," *Studia Philosophica* 29: 189–216.

Spruit, L. (1994), *Species intelligibilis: From Perception to Knowledge*, 2 vols (Leiden: Brill).

Stich, S. and Warfield, T. (eds) (1994), *Mental Representation* (Oxford: Blackwell).

Straus, E. W. (1966), "The upright posture," in *Phenomenological Psychology* (New York: Basic Books), 137–65.

Szanto, T. (2014), "Social Phenomenology: Husserl, Intersubjectivity, and Collective Intentionality," *International Journal of Philosophical Studies* 22/2: 296–301.

Thompson, E. (2007), *Mind in Life: Biology, Phenomenology, and the Sciences of Mind* (Cambridge, MA: Harvard University Press).

Twardowski, K. ([1894] 1977), *On the Content and Object of Presentations: A Psychological Investigation*, translated by R. Grossmann (The Hague: Martinus Nijhoff).

Varga, P. A. (2015), "Die Einflüsse der Brentano'schen Intentionalitätskonzeptionen auf den frühen Husserl. Zur Widerlegung einer Legende" in K.-H. Lembeck, K. Mertens, and E. W. Orth (eds), *Phänomenologische Forschungen* (Hamburg: Felix Meiner).

Vendrell Ferran, I. (2015), "The Emotions in Early Phenomenology," *Studia Phaenomenolgica* 15: 349–74.

Waldenfels, B. (2004), "Bodily Experience between Selfhood and Otherness," *Phenomenology and the Cognitive Sciences* 3/3: 235–48.

Walton, R. J. (2003), "On the Manifold Senses of Horizonedness: The Theories of E. Husserl and A. Gurwitsch," *Husserl Studies* 19/1: 1–24.

Young, I. M. (2005), *On Female Bodily Experience: "Throwing Like a Girl," and Other Essays* (Oxford: Oxford University Press).

Zahavi, D. (2004), "Phenomenology and the Project of Naturalization," *Phenomenology and the Cognitive Sciences* 3: 331–47.

Zahavi, D. (2010), "Naturalized phenomenology," in S. Gallagher and D. Schmicking (eds), *Handbook of Phenomenology and Cognitive Science* (Dordrecht: Springer), 2–19.

Zahavi, D. (2013), "Naturalized phenomenology: A desideratum or a category mistake?" in H. Carel and D. Meacham (eds), *Phenomenology and Naturalism*, Royal Institute of Philosophy Supplement 72: 23–42.

Zoeller, Guenter (1992), "The Austrian way of ideas: Contents and objects of presentation in the Brentano School," in P. D. Cummins and G. Zoeller (eds), *Minds, Ideas, and Objects: Essays in the Theory of Representation in Modern Philosophy* (Atascadero: Ridgeview Publishing).

CHAPTER 31

PRACTICAL INTENTIONALITY

From Brentano to the Phenomenology of the Munich and Göttingen Circles

ALESSANDRO SALICE

31.1 INTRODUCTION

INTENTIONALITY—understood as a specific property which, if instantiated, makes minds *of* or *about* objects and facts—is a topic that is almost inextricable from phenomenology itself. However, this specific understanding of "intentionality" captures just *one* meaning of that abstract term. Given that "intentionality" is the nominalization of the predicate "intentional," there is a second and much more common usage of this predicate within ordinary English—one that first and foremost relates to actions: "A schoolteacher may ask a child who has spilled the ink in class: 'Did you do that *intentionally?*'" (Austin 1970: 274, my emphasis). Now, what property is intentionality in this *second* sense? As a first approximation, it can be said that an action is *intentional* if it is prompted and steered by a conative state. For instance, to spill ink intentionally somehow requires the agent to have a state of a kind similar to that of desires, volitions, wishes, intentions, etc. Put another way, it is at least partly because the agent has the desire or will or intention to spill ink that her action qualifies as intentional—in the more ordinary sense of this predicate.[1]

One interesting aspect of such conative states is that, however they are to be described, they too seem to be *of* something or directed *towards* something—a state of affairs or

---

[1] A preliminary version of this chapter was presented at the Workshops "Phenomenology in Action" (Munich, February 10–12, 2016) and "Intentionality and Normativity" (Dublin, February 19–20, 2016) where I received much appreciated feedback. I also wish to express my gratitude to Christopher Erhard, Uriah Kriegel, Kevin Mulligan, and Genki Uemura, who read and commented on previous drafts of this chapter. The author's work on this chapter has been supported by a fellowship of the Fritz Thyssen Foundation (Az. 10.13.1.015).

fact or event that the agent intends to bring about. Accordingly, one can ascertain a certain overlap between the two meanings of "intentionality"—for an action to be intentional in the *second* sense, the subject must have an adequate conative state that, being about a goal, is intentional in the *first* sense. This makes the conditions for an action to be *intentional* different from—and yet not unrelated to—the conditions for a mental state to be *of* something.

This practical dimension of intentionality has not escaped the attention of phenomenologists either. Quite the contrary. One segment within the history of this philosophical movement, which is especially relevant for the topic at issue, stretches from the end of the nineteenth to the first decades of the twentieth century. During this period of time, one can observe a fairly definite line of research that originates with Brentano's considerations about the specific topic of intentional action and is developed further by the phenomenological circles of Munich and Göttingen (on the phenomenology of these two circles, see Salice 2015a). In the turn of not even five years (from around 1910 to *c.* 1915), early phenomenologists have all made the notion of intentional action the target of a proper battery of investigations. Here, I am mainly referring to the relevant publications of Alexander Pfänder (1900, 1911), Adolf Reinach (1912/13), Max Scheler (1913/16), and Dietrich von Hildebrand (1916—this is the revised text of Hildebrand's dissertation submitted in 1912).[2] These contributions take all their first steps exactly from the intuition that there are intentional experiences of a conative kind, which trigger and accompany our actions, but they diverge on how exactly to account for these experiences and for their relation to action. In a recent paper, Uriah Kriegel associates the French philosophy of the 1940s with "the golden decade of conative phenomenology" (Kriegel 2013: 538)—but the considerations put forward in this article suggest that conation had already become the subject of lively research interest within early phenomenology.

This chapter claims that phenomenological contributions to the theory of action are highly relevant for at least two orders of reasons. The first is mainly historical: They indicate that phenomenological reflection on intentionality has, from its very beginning, taken into account and accommodated both senses of the term "intentionality."[3] The

---

[2] In this narrative, a fundamental role is played by Edmund Husserl. First, in Vienna, Husserl attends Brentano's courses on ethics in 1884/5 and 1886 (Schuhmann 1977: 13, 15) where Brentano develops important ideas about his theory of action (see Brentano 1954). Second, Husserl's *Logical Investigations* of 1900–1 exert a forceful influence on the work of early phenomenologists (see Salice 2012). Third, Husserl's lectures on *Ethics and the Theory of Values* given in Göttingen in the academic years 1908/9, 1911, and 1914 present ideas about volition and action that are developed in the same period of time and stand in close relation to those discussed in this chapter (see Husserl 1988). This notwithstanding, this article is not in a position to address Husserl's view in any detail (on Husserl's treatment of action in the first two decades of 1900, see Melle 1997, Mertens 1998, Rinofner-Kreidl 2014, Uemura 2015). Other important contributions to the topic at stake, which again will remain neglected in this chapter, are provided by Theodor Lipps (see 1902, 1909)—the teacher of many early phenomenologists in Munich and an equally profound source of inspiration.

[3] This clearly counteracts a widely received view in the literature according to which the first extensive account of actions or activities has to be credited to Martin Heidegger (see Dreyfus 1991). Moreover, it should not be neglected that early phenomenological investigations go much further than merely taking

second reason is grounded in systematic considerations: These contributions are second to none when it comes to the wealth of insights they secure. In particular, they uncover that intentions are mental states of a *sui generis* kind, to be distinguished from desires, wishes, willing, and other kinds of conative states, and that intentions play an indispensable role for planning, deliberation, and, ultimately, action. Early phenomenological theory about practical intentionality hence bears striking similarities to the theory of intentions later developed by Searle (1983) and Bratman (1987), as will be shown.

Against this background, the present chapter is an attempt to mine, present, and evaluate main aspects of the development of phenomenological theory about *practical intentions*. To reach this goal, hereafter the chapter is organized into three sections. In section 31.2, the notion of intention as a conative state of a genuine kind is briefly introduced by illustrating the shift that occurred within contemporary theory of action from the belief-desire (BD) to the belief-desire-intention (BDI) model of practical intentionality. Section 31.3 illustrates Brentano's view about action and presents it as a variant of the BD-account. Finally, section 31.4 reconstructs the substantial revision that Brentano's ideas underwent in early phenomenology. It is argued that early phenomenology had already accomplished a turn from a BD to a BDI account of intentional agency and that it operated with a notion of an intention that, in many respects, is more fertile than the one at the core of current debate.

31.2 THE BELIEF-DESIRE-INTENTION MODEL OF PRACTICAL INTENTIONALITY

What makes an action intentional? The answer that used to dominate the philosophical debate on action is that an action is intentional if it enters into an adequate relation with the beliefs and the desires of the agent. For instance, assuming that I am thirsty, if I wish *not* to be thirsty and if I believe that having a drink will extinguish my thirst, then the action of drinking can be considered as intentional. Philosophers diverge on how to cash out the notion of an "appropriate relation," and especially on whether this is a motivational (cf. Anscombe (2000)) or a causal relation (cf. Davidson (2002a) and Goldman (1970)), but the agreement upon the explanatory function of beliefs and desires for the notion of intentional action licenses the umbrella term "belief-desire [BD] model" to qualify this account.

In the last decades, the BD-model of intentional action has encountered growing resistance. And this is mainly because its explanatory power seems to fall too short (cf.

conation into consideration. They are not limited to pure descriptions of practical intentionality, but enter the normative dimension by crucially touching upon the ethical and legal bearing of intentional actions. (Although important and interesting, an exploration of ethical and legal aspects of actions would exceed the purposes of this chapter.)

Bratman 1987). On the BD understanding, "intentionality" is first and foremost a property that applies to actions in the sense that an action qualifies as intentional if it is done *with* an intention. And it is done *with* an intention, if the agent has the relevant beliefs and desires. But this means: the BD model does not leave space for intentions as *specific conative states of the mind*. Put another way, according to this approach, intentions are nothing other than suitably aggregated complexes of beliefs and desires (see Davidson 2002b).

Yet, it seems that there are good reasons for hosting genuine practical intentions in our mental repertoire. In particular, prior or future-directed intentions (what are also called "decisions") are difficult to accommodate within the BD framework. To see why, consider the following example. Imagine that you decide at time *t* to make mayonnaise at a later time *t'*. How should this fact, i.e., *your decision*, be described? It is certainly something related to your future action, but it is also, and crucially, formed *before* the action's onset—to be sure, there are circumstances in which actions immediately follow decisions, but this does not necessarily have to be the case. Consequently, it seems plausible to characterize (practical) intentionality as something that, when it comes to future-directed intentions especially, qualifies the mind primarily and actions secondarily. Against this background, however, one could argue that to form a decision is nothing else than to have a desire with peaking intensity. Indeed, it appears that desires or wishes occur with different degrees of intensity. Still, there are other considerations that may be able to block this interpretation.

Firstly, desires are volatile—they wax and wane over time depending on the contexts, emotions, moods of the agent, etc. Intentions, by contrast, enhance stability in one's conduct. They do so because they generate *commitments* (cf. Bratman 1987: 15ff.). If you have decided to make mayonnaise at *t'*, you will then tend to discard alternative options— that is, you will tend *not* to revise your intention: e.g., the option of making a dressing of some other kind becomes less attractive. To be sure, the commitments at stake here are intrapersonal; they are mere "creatures of the will," as Margaret Gilbert puts it (2006: 6), meaning that they can be reneged by the agent herself alone and, thus, have a limited binding force. This force is limited especially if it is compared with that of interpersonal commitments, such as those brought about by promises or other speech acts, which can be rescinded only in accordance with their addressees (as Reinach highlights, in his 2012). And, yet, intrapersonal commitments *are* commitments and, consequently, they commit the agent to the conduct she has decided upon, making it costly to retract the original intention.

Second, if one makes a decision, one puts oneself under the demand of forming at least a rough plan of how to reach the goal set by the intention (Bratman 2014: 15ff.). Intentions, in other words, are *plan states* for they involve planning and the design of a (however vague) project or plan or strategy towards the goal. That is, intentions create a pressure to settle on means and to respect the norms of instrumental rationality. If you have decided to make mayonnaise, you are already in the thick of it: You have an idea of how to make it (or of where to look for the recipe), and you structure consequent actions in light of that intention. By contrast, one can entertain desires without any pressure to settle on the means that should lead the agent to fulfill the contents of that desire. That opens the possibility for a subject to have contrasting, i.e., mutually incompatible, desires, but impedes her from having contrasting intentions, at pain of irrationality. In other words, you can have the two desires to make mayonnaise and to make Béarnaise sauce—but you can decide in favor of only *one* of the two lines of actions.

Thirdly, intentions are causally self-referential states (see Searle 1983: 86ff.). To understand what is meant by causal self-referentiality, suppose you intend to φ (for instance, you intend to become rich). Given that intentions are intentional states, they have intentional contents—the intentional content being the element of a mental state that identifies its conditions of satisfaction. Intentions are causally self-referential attitudes because their content prescribes that the state of affairs φ has to be caused by the very intention to φ. Hence, in order to satisfy your intention of becoming rich, becoming rich is something that has to be brought about by your very intention. Desires, by contrast, do not need to be causally self-referential. If you have the desire of becoming rich, your desire would be satisfied even if you become rich because, e.g., you inherit a fortune from an unknown relative.

Considered altogether, these thoughts recommend a revision of the BD-model, one that takes seriously the role of intentions as conative states of a genuine kind in our thought and agency (the "BDI"-account). One particularly interesting remark with respect to this argumentative move is made by Bratman in his *Intention, Plans, and Practical Reason* (1987). Though only in passing, Bratman claims there that the BDI-account he so convincingly advanced is supposed to be developed in accordance with commonsense psychology (Bratman 1987: 9). One way to read this remark is that everyday mentalistic talk is imbued with references to intentions and that the BDI-account is in a position to refine our commonsensical notion of an intention.

This may be correct, but it is far from clear why the BDI model has to seek congruence with commonsense psychology—for it is not the task of folk psychology to produce accurate descriptions of our mental states. Yet, and arguably, this is exactly (one of) phenomenology's task(s). And, if so, then perhaps advocates of the BDI-account may be better advised to start with accurate descriptions of our mental states, rather than with laymen's opinions—and that just means starting with phenomenology, rather than with folk psychology (see Gallagher and Zahavi 2012: 10). But then, the question arises as to whether phenomenologists do have a salient notion of intention. Sections 31.3 and 31.4 formulate an answer to this question.

31.3 BRENTANO ON WILLING

The place Brentano reserves for action and volition in his work is rather limited, especially if this is compared with his treatment of other topics within his descriptive psychology. Yet, if one reads the relevant passages against the background of the general framework of his psychology, they can be easily contextualized and can allow for a number of conclusions that enable the emergence of a coherent view about his theory of action. Hence, it is fruitful to begin by outlining some core ideas of his general framework before entering into the details of conation.

In his *Psychology from an Empirical Standpoint* (1995a), Brentano claims that mental states ("*psychische Phänomene*") fall into three, and only three, kinds: mental states are presentations, judgments, or what he calls "*Gemütsbewegungen*"—generally translated as "emotional states," or, perhaps better, "affective" states. These three kinds of mental states ("phenomena" or "acts" in Brentano's terminology) are in a hierarchical order. Presentations are the most basic states in the sense that they are always presupposed by judgments and affects. Accordingly, Brentano also qualifies the latter acts as "superposed acts" (Brentano 1995b: 90). To present an example: If a subject judges that this particular rose is red, then the judgmental act can be said to be "superposed" on a presentation of the red rose, in the sense that the former act could not exist without the latter. Similarly, if a subject hates something or someone, then a presentation of that thing or person underlies the emotion of hatred.

Superposition, according to Brentano, entails identity of the intentional object: If an act is superposed on another act, both acts have the same object. This means that the difference between superposed acts and presentations cannot be accounted for in terms of a difference in their objects. Rather, what distinguishes these mental phenomena is the very kind of intentional relation in which their subject is involved: More specifically, all superposed acts come either in a positive or in a negative form. For instance, in affects, one is directed towards an object with inclination or disinclination (love or hate, pleasure or displeasure). Similarly, judgments are characterized by the fact that the subject, when judging, adopts either a positive or a negative stance (either belief or disbelief) towards the object. By contrast, no corresponding opposition is observable in presentations (Brentano 2009: 17).

As said, judgments and affects belong to different classes of mental states. Brentano develops several arguments for distinguishing these two classes of mental acts, but one is crucial for the purposes of this chapter (but cf. Brentano 1995a: 225 for other interesting arguments): Brentano argues that, given the presentation of an object, there is only *one* correct judgment that a subject can make about that object. This is a positive judgment if the presentation targets the object (expressible by a sentence of the form "the object x exists") and a negative one if the presentation is empty or misfires (expressible by a sentence of the form "the object x does not exist"). Put differently, judgments come either in a positive or in a negative quality and, given the presentation of an object x, only *one* of these two judgmental stances can be *correctly* adopted by the subject towards object x. Things are different in the case of affects: Given the presentation of an object x, Brentano claims, the subject can adopt different affects, which can both be credited as correct with respect to that object x. For instance, suppose that you love a given object x and that, at some point, an object y presents itself to you as more valuable than object x. In this situation it seems legitimate to say that you *correctly* love x, but that you *also* correctly love x *less* than you love y.

However, this is not a faithful description of this mental scenario, Brentano contends, for "it would imply that for each instance of rejoicing only a certain amount of joy is appropriate" (Brentano 2009: 15). But loving *x* less than *y* does not necessitate that the subject is prevented from loving *x* with the greatest love possible. To put this differently, one can fully enjoy *x* and yet *prefer y* to *x*. Hence, a more accurate description is that loving *x less* than loving *y* just means *preferring* object *y* to object *x* (cf. Brentano 1954: 147). The mental state of "preference [*vorziehen, bevorzugen*]" is portrayed by Brentano as a *sui generis* affect that puts two (or more) objects into a relation: Accordingly, when a subject prefers something to something else, she is directed not to one, but to two (or more) objects. Furthermore, since *y* is more valuable than *x*, the preference of *y* over *x* is *correct* (on the axiological relations that correlate to correct preferences, cf. Chisholm 1977). This leads to the idea that judgments and affects belong to two distinct kinds of mental states. They are different because a subject can adopt two *different* yet both *correct* affects towards one and the same object—but it is impossible for her to adopt two correct judgments, but with different qualities, towards one and the same object. In other words, one can love (or hate) some things or persons more or less than others (depending on one's preferences), but one cannot judge some things "more or less" than others.

Brentano's framework accommodates conations in his *third* class of mental states. One of the reasons for this classification is that the same observations made above with respect to the emotions of love and hate can also be made about desires (*Wünsche, Begehrungen*).[4] Most importantly, what conative experiences share with emotions is the fact that desires, just like emotions, can enter into a relation *with an act of preference* (1995a: 225). But how is the act of preference to be described within the conative dimension?

Suppose a hungry and thirsty donkey is located at an equal distance from a stack of hay and a pail of water. The donkey has two contrasting and opposite desires, but it is only if the donkey has a greater desire to, say, eat rather than to drink, that it won't starve. This scenario, according to Brentano, is analogous to the one described above with respect to emotions. It is analogous because, to survive, the donkey has to realize a specific act of *preference* to the effect that, ultimately, one of the two things is preferred to the other. When a preference occurs between contrasting desires, the subject has made what in ordinary language is called a "choice." However, since the concept of preference is not confined to conation, as we saw above, "preference" can be considered to be the more general concept, while "choosing [*wählen*]" is the more specific. There are two conditions that, if fulfilled, turn a preference into a choice.

The *first* is that choosing has to entail an act of "deciding [*Entscheiden*]." Decision, again, is not an act that is confined to the sphere of *action*. To illustrate this, Brentano

---

[4] Another reason put forward is Brentano's "transition argument"—to use an expression employed by Michelle Montague (Montague 2017); this argument relies upon a certain phenomenological continuity in the quality of affects which, according to Brentano, makes it impossible to neatly distinguish volitions from emotions (Brentano 1995a: 184, but cf. Anscombe 1978 for a critical response to the transition argument).

shows that affects in general can enter into an exclusive or non-exclusive relation. For instance, one can have two affects of love, both of which are compatible with each other (non-exclusive), e.g., the love of mathematics and the love of poetry (cf. Brentano 1954: 219). But, in certain cases, affects are in an exclusive relation to each other—e.g., the desire that the sun will be shining tomorrow is not compatible with the desire that it rains tomorrow. In the latter case, the subject may be forced to *decide*. Now, not all decisions are volitions (the decision in favor of the desire that the sun will shine tomorrow is not a volition), and yet all volitions are decisions—to use Brentano's wording: "All willing is deciding" (cf. Brentano 1954: 219, my trans.).

But then, what characterizes volition or the phenomenon of willing in contradistinction to desires? What, in other words, is the *second* condition that transforms a preference into a choice? This has to do with certain *beliefs* of the subject: A decision is a volition if and only if the subject *believes* that the content of her desire can be realized through her actions. Once this element is in play, Brentano concludes:

> We can thus define the will as a decisional desire [*entscheidendes Wünschen*], which has as its object something, which can be brought about by ourselves and which is expected with conviction to be an effect of our desire. In other words, this is a desire, in whose favor we have decided and in whose realisability through our actions we believe. (Brentano 1954: 219, my translation; see also 1995a: 193, 2009: 102).

On the basis of this definition, it is just a small step to infer that "the willing is not a primitive [*elementares*] phenomenon" (1954: 219)—it is not, because it can be traced back to a desire standing in an appropriate relation to certain beliefs of the subject. More precisely, willing is always choosing in the sense that it is a decision between two or more desires and that this decision is based upon beliefs about the realizability of the desire's content. This reconstruction[5] credits the view that suitable aggregations of beliefs and desires are the horse that pulls the cart in Brentano's explanation of practical intentionality.[6] To put this differently, Brentano seems to embrace a BD model of intentional agency.

---

[5] However, these are certainly not the only beliefs that seem to accompany willing—for instance, the donkey should also have a belief about the fact that eating decreases hunger. This might lead to an objection against the above reconstruction: given that, for Brentano, all mental states are conscious, if action has to be traced back to desires and beliefs, all the agent's beliefs involved in agency should be conscious. But this is highly implausible. To resist this objection, one could invoke Brentano's notion of "habitual dispositions": these are physiological entities, which—although existent—are not mental phenomena, because they are not conscious (1995a: 45). If this is correct, then an intentional action is one that is linked not to a belief–desire pair *sic et simpliciter*, but also to habitual dispositions. (This suggestion goes back to an exchange I had with Uriah Kriegel about these issues. I am thankful to Uriah for his essential contribution, though I am solely responsible for every possible mistake made here.)

[6] It should not go unmentioned that there is another way of reading Brentano on volition—one which does not emphasize the link between desire and the belief about the desire's realizability through the subject's actions. In fact, in some passages, Brentano equates willing with decision *tout court* rather than with choice: "It should be noted that I can thus want or desire a thing without at all believing it to be something I can bring about myself. I can want or desire that the weather be good tomorrow, but I have no *choice* in the matter" (Brentano 2009: 102; see also 2009: 77). This second, and more general, sense

31.4 EARLY PHENOMENOLOGISTS
ON MOTIVATION AND DELIBERATION

Brentano's considerations on volition initiate a series of investigations that directly connect to early phenomenology. One way to read early phenomenologists is by emphasizing an important distinction that remains underdetermined in Brentano's account—this is the distinction between motivation and deliberation. Whereas, for Brentano, intentional actions can be traced back to the will and the will to a suitable combination of desires and beliefs, early phenomenologists hold, *first*, that the will belongs to a specific kind of experience and, *second*, that the will itself has to be discerned from intentions. Within the phenomenon of agency, volitions are confined to the dimension of *motivation*, whereas intentions identify the dimension of *deliberation*.

This conceptual distinction is argued for in at least *four* conceptual steps. *First*, early phenomenologists contrast the attempt to characterize willing by starting with desire— they vindicate the phenomenological credentials of willing, and some of them attempt to define desire in terms of willing. *Second*, they locate willing at the level of *motivation*, which may or may not lead the subject to form a *decision* or an *intention*. *Third*, they accommodate intentions as acts of a primitive kind, disclosing the whole dimension of deliberation. And *fourth*, they define intentional action or action *tout court* (*Handlung*) in terms of an activity that is performed upon an intention.

In this section, these argumentative steps are reconstructed and put in relation to those authors that have developed them most extensively. Steps one and two comprise the focus of subsection 31.4.1, while steps three and four comprise that of subsection 31.4.2. At this juncture it is important to note that it is not the aim of this chapter to argue that early phenomenologists articulated a *unitary* theory of intentional agency. But instead of focusing on the divergences between their ideas, the leading thread of this chapter is that their insights are largely compatible with one another's and that, if suitably combined, they license an account of intentions and actions that shows systematic relevance.

31.4.1 Willing

As seen in section 31.3, Brentano claims that desires turn into volitions if (among other conditions) they are accompanied by certain beliefs regarding the possibility of realizing the contents of those very desires. Exactly the opposite view is adopted by Scheler. According to him, willing is the most fundamental conative experience such that it is

---

of "willing" is at the core of Kriegel's reconstruction of Brentano's conative phenomenology, see Kriegel 2018: ch. 7.

the notion of desire that has to be defined through willing and not the other way around (Scheler 1973: 124). Many of Scheler's insights about intentional agency will be developed further by other phenomenologists, but the core idea seems to be that willing is, first and foremost, a striving (*Streben*), the content of which is given to the subject as something *to be realized* ("*als ein zu realisierender*," 1973: 123—the normative meaning conveyed by this formulation will be addressed in 31.4.2). Under this characterization, one could say that a child may genuinely *want* "that a star fall into his lap" (Scheler 1973: 123). And this also explains why many human beings to this day can still think that the will can make it rain or make the sun shine or even why "an educated person feels something like 'guilt' if something which he had 'willed' to happen occurs accidentally, e.g., the death of a person" (Scheler 1973: 124).

In particular, the two former cases show that individuals literally need to *learn* that for any content of the will to be realized, the will has to be complemented by a further attitude, which Scheler labels "will-to-do [*Tunwollen*]." A will-to-do is a *specific* form of will in the sense that its *contents* are more specific—for the will-to-do is, indeed, the will *to do* something (whilst "will" *tout court*, as highlighted above, is not subject to that restriction). The difference in content between these experiences is tackled in 31.4.2, but a word is first needed on how Scheler's considerations hark back to the notion of desire. According to Scheler, the will-to-do closely correlates with a third experience—the experience of *being-able-to-do* (*Tunkönnen*); the two are closely tied because the will-to-do has to be accredited, as it were, by an experience of being-able-to-do. Without the first experience, the second cannot occur for it is only if one has a sense of being able to do something that one can want to do that.

Once these two mental states (the will-to-do and the being-able-to-do) are in place, in the sense that the subject at some point in her mental life has experienced them, desires can make their appearance on the mental scene. More precisely, a volition acquires a desire character (*Wunschcharakter*) for a subject, when she forms a will that lies beyond the sphere of the *being-able-to-do*. The notion of desire, in other words, does not pick out a genuine kind of mental state, but is just an experiential coloring that the will assumes once it becomes transparent to the subject that that state cannot be accompanied by a will-to-do (and this because it is not possible for the subject to be in a state of being-able-to-do about the content of that volition).[7] If considered from this perspective, even the desire "that something should happen 'through' me remains a 'desire' and does not become a 'will'" (Scheler 1973: 124, translation modified, on this difference, see also Mulligan 2012: 65). Similarly, "willing is not wishing; even a willing that, in certain

---

[7] It seems plausible to argue that Scheler's "desire character" is a phenomenal nuance that accompanies the volition and not a qualification that the subject assigns to her volition on the basis of *inferences* grounded in beliefs about what one can and cannot do. In fact, being-able-to-do is described by Scheler as an experience (*Erlebnis*) rather than as a *belief* or *knowledge* about one's agentive possibilities (1973: 129).

circumstances, is futile, devious, impossible, is not a wishing for this very reason" (Löwenstein 1933: 167, my translation).[8]

Forming a volition is not an event that occurs out of the blue in one's mind, as it were—this experience enters into important relations with other experiences. To see this, it might be important to first look into some of the general traits of the will, which especially Hildebrand's investigations contribute to laying bare. Hildebrand describes the will as a stance or position-taking (*Stellungnahme*) of the conative kind (see also Reiner 1927: 74).[9] There are two ideas that one can find packed in the single claim of willing being a stance. The first is that the will is the subject's *response* to a correlate and the second is that it requires a *founding* experience.

The will is a response in roughly the same sense in which emotional stances, like love, enthusiasm, blame, hate, disgust, etc., can be described as *responses*: In all these states, the subject does not passively represent an object or a state of affairs, but she rather adopts a given stance towards it. More precisely, she responds to what nowadays is called the correlate's "formal object" (see Kenny 2003: 134)—in Hildebrand's terminology: She responds to the mind-independent "values" of the correlate or to the mind-dependent preferences that she associates with that correlate.[10] Put differently, volitive and emotional stances enter into relations with formal objects: If one appreciates a work of art, one appreciates it because of, say, its beauty; and if one wants something, one is responding to the goodness of the correlate or to its importance for the subject.

On the one hand, the formal object specifies the criteria of adequacy for the stance vis-à-vis its correlate—the stance is adequate if it is elicited towards suitable values or preferences. On the other hand, however, the formal object is not in a position to *exact* a response on the side of the subject. To put the last point differently, it is possible for the subject to be aware of the correlate's formal object without eliciting a corresponding response. It is possible, e.g., for a subject to be aware of an artwork's value without this awareness' giving rise to an emotion of admiration. Or it is possible for a subject to be aware of the value of a certain action (e.g., to help someone in need) without this awareness leading the subject to a will to help (on this, see also Pfänder 1967: 28).

---

[8] While insisting on the unbridgeable difference between wishing and willing, Löwenstein argues in favor of the idea that wishing is a primitive kind of mental state with its own distinctive phenomenology, see Löwenstein 1933: 177ff.

[9] Interestingly, while Brentano distinguishes between beliefs and affects, early phenomenologists tend to conceive of them as belonging to the same kind of mental state (beliefs, emotions, and volitions are stances). This is mainly due to the fact that, unlike Brentano, they distinguish belief (or conviction) from assertion (*Behauptung*) within the notion of judgment. As illustrated in 31.4.2, just like intentions, assertions are mental acts that, indeed, cannot be described as stances, but rather as spontaneous *actions* of the subject.

[10] In contrast to Scheler's theory, Hildebrand's theory of volition radically distinguishes between cases in which the will responds to values and cases in which it responds to the subject's preferences (Crosby 2002). Exploring this distinction, which bears importantly on ethical issues, would exceed the purposes of this chapter. Yet, it should suffice to say that, just like values, preferences set adequacy criteria for stances. Put differently, subjects can be mistaken about their own preferences, see Reinach 1989b: 298.

These considerations suggest that stances do not coincide with the apprehension of the correlate's formal object. And this leads to the *second* claim that early phenomenologists connect to the idea of willing as a stance: Whenever a volition occurs, this stance is based on or founded by a further act, which is supposed to grasp the correlate's formal object (see Mulligan 2010). That is to say, volitional stances are in-need-of-being-founded, given that their existence is grounded in the existence of other states that provide access to the correlate's formal object. According to Hildebrand, the routes that lead a subject to form a volition are manifold: One can be acquainted with values directly by means of an experience of feeling (*Fühlen*, cf. also Scheler 253ff., Reinach 1989b: 295). Or one can cognize that a given action has a value, or one can know (in a non-intuitive way) of a given action that it has a certain value. All these states (feeling, cognizing a state of affairs, or non-intuitive knowledge) can ground volitions (in a morally significant way, see Salice 2015b).[11]

But if the will is not *exacted* by those underlying states, what is the relation between them? Phenomenologists argue that this is a relation of *motivation*. Willing, in other words, relies on motives—*not on causes*—as Pfänder claims (1967: 33f.). More precisely, motivation requires the subject to be open to the facts and objects in the world in the sense that, given the worldly circumstances that perceptions, feelings etc. present to the subject, she is confronted with the question "what shall I do?" (Pfänder 1967: 28; Reinach 1989b: 291, 298).

This question triggers a process of reflection on the part of the subject. In this process, the subject is attentive to the demands (*Forderungen*) that the world is raising. If, e.g., I enter a room and I feel cold in the room, the perceived chill can invite me to consider the question "What shall I do?" Obviously, this question does not need to be explicitly stated, but it induces the subject to "listen to [*hinhören*]" the demands that the situation is raising. In Pfänder's example, such listening can put the subject in a position to "perceive" or, more literally, "hear [*vernehmen*]" the demand to leave the room. However, hearing the demand and acknowledging [*anerkennen*] its validity does not yet mean that one is moved to leave the room (just as perceiving the value of helping someone in need does not yet comprise the will to help him or her). It is only if the subject wants to leave the room *on the ground of* (*auf Grund*)—or *by relying on* (*sich stützend auf*)—the demand that her decision is *motivated* by the demand (on the motivational process of listening/hearing/relying to, see Pfänder 1967: 28f., and also Reinach 1989b: 290–303).

---

[11] Note that the acts grasping values can miss their targets. When the act misfires, it presents the subject with what could be called a "perfect impostor," i.e., a phenomenal element that merely emulates a value or a preference. If the subject elicits a response in this case, then this has to be the correct response with respect to the impostor. In other words, what is at fault here is primarily the act that presented the alleged formal object to the stance, while the stance itself is only indirectly at fault. Hildebrand formulates this point as follows: "concerning the phenomenal value which is *given* to me, the value-response [*Wertantwort*], if any, can only be the correct one" (Hildebrand 1969: 40, my translation).

31.4.2 Practical intentions

At this stage, a further distinction has to be drawn. Volitions, it has been said, are motivated by other states, but they can also motivate. They are motivating because they motivate actions—*via* intentions. Just as one and the same volition can be triggered by different acts, so can one and the same decision be motivated by different volitions. For instance, I can decide to go to the pub because I want to meet a friend, or because I want to have a pint, or because I am in a low mood and want to partake in the pub's jolly atmosphere, etc.

But then, what are intentions—in contradistinction to volitions? Terminologically, early phenomenologists employ the juridical term *Vorsatz*, but also the more collo-quial *Entschluss* (and sometimes the technical terms *Willensakt, Willensentschluss, Willensvorsatz*, etc.), to name these states.[12] Both terms could be translated as "res-olution" or "decision" and are used in combination with the reflexive verbs *sich entschließen, sich vornehmen* (literally, "to decide," viz. "to resolve" to do something—though the reflexivity of the verbs gets lost in the English translation). Conceptually, there are at least five different, and yet not unconnected, aspects that seem to univocally qualify intentions: (i) Intentions are mental actions of the subject; (ii) they are acts of self-determination; (iii) they generate commitments; (iv) their contents come with an instrumental structure built in (they are *projects*); and (v) they secure a unique, first-personal, perspective towards the action itself.[13] With that, it is now time to turn to the level of deliberation.

The first element is that intentions have to be described as mental acts—understood in the sense of mental *actions*: "a doing of the self [*ein Tun des Ichs*] and thereby a sponta-neous act" (Reinach 2012: 18). They are actions because the subject is active in a specific sense—she is the "phenomenal originator [*phänomenaler Urheber*]" of the act (Reinach 2012: 18). To see this, consider the difference between having a belief that *p* and asserting *p*. Assertion, though grounded in the belief that *p*, is a linguistic action that is spontane-ously performed by the subject; it exists at a given *point* in time, and does not have a tem-poral extension. By contrast, beliefs do not seem to be under the control of a subject and show a dispositional nature—they can last for years and do not need to be linguistically articulated (cf. Reinach 1989a). Similar considerations hold for the distinction between willing and intention. The willing assumes a dispositional form ("I *always* wanted to visit Copenhagen, but I never found the time"), but it can also ground a decision ("I *now*

---

[12] Interestingly, the more straightforward German equivalent of "intention," i.e., *Absicht*, is not used frequently by early phenomenologists. An exception is Scheler, who employs this term to refer to the will-to-do: "A will 'to do something specific', however, is called an 'intention [*Absicht*]'" (1973: 137). Yet, intention *in this* sense, according to Scheler, is not the same as a decision or resolution (*Vorsatz*), see 1973: 124, 138. It is the latter notion, not the former, that I use as co-extensive with "intention" in this chapter.

[13] To this list, one could also add that, whereas willing comes in a polar form ("she wants to tango, he doesn't," to use Mulligan's example), intentions do not, see Stein 1970: 311, Mulligan 2013: 108.

decide: I will fly to Copenhagen next month"), in which case we face a spontaneous and punctual action of a subject (Hildebrand 1969: 36; Pfänder 1967: 21; Reinach 2012: 18f.).[14]

But what sort of action is that? Phenomenologists tend to portray it as a case of self-determination (see Pfänder 1967: 23; Heller 1932: 254f.): Among other things, making a decision also means determining oneself to do something—in other words, the very self is at stake in intentions to the effect that "immediate self-consciousness" always belongs to these acts (see Pfänder 1967: 23).[15] Characterizing intentions as self-determining acts has two important consequences—the first is that the content of the decision has to range over actions of the self. After all, self-determination is determination of one's conduct, and I cannot decide on things that are not under my control. The second is that the perspective that a subject has towards her actions is unique and comes with a unique phenomenology. Let us approach these consequences step by step.

In the case of willing, the content of the experience—to put this in Scheler's parlance—is just something *to be realized*. No reference needs to be made to the agent in the content of willing. By contrast, intentions can only be intentions of their subjects *to do something*, meaning that the subject has to be adequately involved in the process of bringing about the state of affairs that satisfies the intention. This implies that the content of willing differs from the content of an intention, for the latter content, not the former, must include a reference to the agent.

But once this conceptual result is achieved, one is allowed to take a further step: We have seen that, according to Scheler, the content of willing is framed as something that *is to be brought about*. Such a normative perspective is inherited by the intention, as it were. It is because I want a given state of affairs to exist or obtain, that I decide to do something to bring about that state of affairs—just like the content of willing, so is the content of the intention also framed as something that shall be brought about. But given that the intention's content is about an action of the agent, the normative perspective adopted by the subject in intending to do something now puts *the very subject of this intention* under a commitment to realize the action. This is nicely formulated by Hildebrand:

> An ought-relation [*Soll-Beziehung*] with the realization is already given in willing. *But only the intention [das Vorsetzen] makes this relation committal [festlegen]*, insofar as it assigns a determined form to this relation. If the stance [i.e., the willing, A.S.] applies only to the state of affairs, then the resolution [*das Sichvornehmen*] is

---

[14] While holding that intentions are actions and, hence, aligning them with forgiving, praising, blaming, asserting, questioning, commanding, etc. (which are not stances), Reinach also maintains, somehow ambiguously, that making a resolution (*Vorsatzfassen*) is a stance, see Reinach 1913: 294.

[15] This is an idea that is captured by the reflexivity of the corresponding German verbs pointed out above, but which is not mapped onto the locution "I intend to φ." In this sentence, the infinitive clause hides the fact that it is I who am supposed to be the subject of φing. One way to make this transparent is by reformulating the dependent clause as a that-clause: "I intend *that* I φ." Despite the awkwardness of this construction, see Williamson (2017) for arguments in favor of the equivalence between these two formulations.

already directed towards the realization of the state of affairs. (1969: 34, my translation and emphasis, cf. also Reiner 1927: 71)

Accordingly, the sentence "I intend to φ" can be interpreted in two different senses. According to the *first* interpretation, this sentence is nothing other than an instance of a theoretical proposition of the form "there is an *x* such that this *x* intends to φ," where *x* refers to the utterer. But according to the *second* interpretation, which in Pfänder's[16] view is the correct one (see 1967: 21f.), that sentence does *not* express a theoretical proposition, but rather an *intent*—a logical meaning of an altogether different kind. The proposition does not posit a state of affairs; it *proposes* it (the function at stake is not one of *Setzung*, but *Vorsetzung*). And, indeed, it is the latter proposition (not the former) that is semantically equivalent with the proposition "φ should be done" (cf. Pfänder 1982: 310— and given all that was said above, one could perhaps add: "φ should be done—*by me*").

However, what is it that the agent commits herself to, when she makes a decision? Certainly, this is a given action of the subject, but early phenomenologists further specify this: They claim that the correlate of an intention is a *project* (*Projekt*, cf. Pfänder 1967: 22; Hildebrand 1969: 43; Reinach 1989b: 291)—and, in doing so, they signal that this correlate comes with an instrumental structure, even if such a structure may be articulated only *in nuce*. Put another way, the agent commits herself to bringing about a given state of affairs by means of a given strategy—a strategy that involves means and ends and that, therefore, is subject to the norms of instrumental rationality. Indeed, the process of settling on means and reflecting upon the best strategy towards a goal is one that has its own phenomenology, as Reinach highlights. He calls the epistemic agency that a subject engages in when she has to determine "how" to reach the goal an "intellectual-practical reflection" (1912–13: 304). This form of reflection is not purely practical because it is not concerned with the ultimate goal of an action (this being the object of a merely *practical* reflection, like the one outlined at the end of 31.4.1). But this is also not purely intellectual because it aims at solving a problem, which is immediately related to an action and to the identification of the best strategy to achieve a goal.

A *second* consequence of introducing intentions into the architecture of intentional agency is assigning the agent a privileged perspective towards her action. The decision being made, the agent starts engaging in the actual action the moment a further experience is formed—this is the experience of *realization* or *performance* (Reinach 1912–13: 305f.; Scheler 1973: 121f.), which can be further characterized either as a doing or as an omitting (Hildebrand 1969: 64).[17] Such an experience is always relative to and dependent

---

[16] To be more precise, Pfänder's example is "I will φ"; however, this sentence is taken to express a *Vorsatz*, hence, a resolution or an intention. The interpretation of *Vorsatz* developed in this chapter would license the reformulation of Pfänder's sentence into "I intend to φ."

[17] In addition, Hildebrand postulates a further act, an "triggering act" (*Inangriffnahme*), which is supposed to initiate the realization proper (Hildebrand 1969: 36f.). Reiner criticizes this idea by arguing that the triggering act is nothing other than the phenomenally salient initial part of the realization (Reiner 1927: 76ff.). I am thankful to Christopher Erhard who drew my attention to Reiner's criticism of Hildebrand.

on an intention—for realization is the realization *of* the content of an intention. But this means that certain bodily movements are conceived of by an agent as a genuine action only when these movements are experienced as the realization of an intention. This fact bestows the agent with unique epistemic authority: Actions are always actions from an agent's perspective, for only the agent can access her action from within, as it were.

To employ Anscombe's expression, the agent is granted non-observational knowledge about her actions, since it is her intention, and her intention alone, that determines whether certain movements or activities are experiences of realization (of that very intention) or not. This gives the agent the last word about her actions, as it were. Certainly, third parties might be in a better position to describe the bodily movements and the consequences of an action. However, bodily movements and consequences taken per se are *not* actions for they do not display the correct mind-dependence or, perhaps more precisely, the correct *intention*-dependence. That is why the very notion of an intentional action (*Handlung*) is restricted to those activities of a subject that are experienced as realizing or fulfilling an *intention* (see Hildebrand 1969: 65ff.).

31.5 Conclusion

Phenomenological investigations into practical intentionality are diverse, rich, and articulated, but they all rest upon two basic pillars. First, actions are motivated by volitions—volitions are complex attitudes: They are stances, which rely on a different stratum of experiences. Second, volitions support deliberation. The deliberative moment of action is exemplified by intentions, which play an essential role in agency. Deliberation is essential because it puts the agent and her actions under the yoke of practical rationality and grounds a unique form of practical knowledge.

Two general conclusions can be drawn. The first is that, from the very beginning, practical intentionality represented a core interest for phenomenology. Most crucially, phenomenology secured a series of insights into intentional agency that developed out of a sophisticated theory of intentionality—now in the sense of *aboutness*. But all this becomes especially visible once the focus on such historical considerations is enlarged and early phenomenologists and their works are paid the careful consideration they deserve.[18]

The second and perhaps more important conclusion one could draw from this reconstruction, is that, when it comes to the topic of intentionality in general and to that of

[18] Early phenomenologists appear to have influenced further reflection on these topics within the broader Phenomenological Movement. For instance, Stein's notion of motives (roughly corresponding to Pfänder's concept, see Stein 1970: 53f.) is explicitly endorsed by Merleau-Ponty (2002: 36) and his ideas on practical intentionality resonates with Scheler's views (2002: 508). Also, the importance of Pfänder's reflection on volition has been explicitly recognized by Ricœur (Ricœur 1982). However, the full extent of this influence remains to be ascertained.

practical intentionality more specifically, one is well advised to develop theories that are conducive to and in accordance with phenomenological descriptions—and not, or at least not primarily, folk psychology. A look at early phenomenology not only highlights all the striking convergences between the phenomenological account of practical intentionality and the current BDI model, but it can also pave the way to systematic investigations in which the wealth and fruitfulness of phenomenological distinctions and descriptions are brought to bear on the issue.

References

Anscombe, E. (1978), "Will and Emotion," *Grazer Philosophischen Studien* 5: 139–48.

Anscombe, E. (2000), *Intention* (Cambridge, MA: Harvard University Press).

Austin, J. L. (1970), "Three ways of spilling ink," in J. O. Urmson and G. J. Warnock (eds), *John L. Austin Philosophical Papers* (London: Oxford University Press), 272–88.

Bratman, M. E. (1987), *Intention, Plans, and Practical Reason* (Stanford, CA: CSLI Publications).

Bratman, M. E. (2014), *Shared Agency. A Planning Theory of Acting Together* (Oxford: Oxford University Press).

Brentano, F. (1954), *Grundlegung und Aufbau der Ethik*, ed. F. Mayer-Hillebrand (Bern: Francke).

Brentano, F. C. (1995a), *Psychology from Empirical Standpoint*, translated by A. C. Rancurello, D. B. Terrell, and L. L. McAlister (London: Routledge).

Brentano, F. C. (1995b), *Descriptive Psychology*, ed. R. M. Chisholm and W. Baumgartner, translated by B. Müller (London: Routledge).

Brentano, F. C. (2009), *The Origin of our Knowledge of Right and Wrong* (London: Routledge).

Chisholm R. (1977), "Brentano's theory of correct and incorrect emotion," in L. L. McAlister (ed.), *The Philosophy of Brentano* (Atlantic Highlands, NJ: Humanities Press), 160–75.

Crosby, J. (2002), "Dietrich von Hildebrand: Master of phenomenological value-ethics," in J. Drummond and L. Embree (eds), *Phenomenological Approaches to Moral Philosophy* (Dordrecht: Kluwer), 475–96.

Davidson, D. (2002a), "Actions, reasons, and causes," in *Essays on Actions and Events* (Oxford: Clarendon Press), 3–20.

Davidson, D. (2002b), "Intending," in *Essays on Actions and Events* (Oxford: Clarendon Press), 83–102.

Dreyfus, H. (1991), *Being-in-the-World. A Commentary on Heidegger's* Being and Time, *Division I* (Cambridge, MA: MIT Press).

Gallagher S. and Zahavi, D. (2012), *The Phenomenological Mind*, 2nd edition (London: Routledge).

Gilbert, M. (2006), "Rationality in Collective Action," *Philosophy of the Social Sciences* 36/1: 3–17.

Goldman, A. (1970), *A Theory of Human Action* (Englewood Cliffs, NJ: Prentice-Hall).

Husserl, E. (1988), *Vorlesungen über Ethik und Wertlehre 1908–1914*. Husserliana 28, ed. by U. Melle (Dordrecht: Kluwer).

Heller, E. (1933), "Über die Willenshandlung" in E. Heller and F. Löw (eds), *Neue Münchener Philosophische Abhandlungen: Alexander Pfänder zu seinem sechzigsten Geburtstag gewindet von Freunden und Schülern* (Leipzig: Barth), 250–9.

Kenny, A. (2003), *Action, Emotion and Will* (London: Routledge).

Kriegel, U. (2013), "Understanding Conative Phenomenology: Lessons from Ricœur," *Phenomenology and the Cognitive Sciences* 12: 537–57.

Kriegel, U. (2018), *Mind and Reality in Brentano's Philosophical System* (Oxford: Oxford University Press).

Lipps T. (1902), *Vom Fühlen, Wollen und Denken. Eine Psychologische Skizze* (Leipzig: Barth).

Lipps T. (1909), *Leitfaden der Psychologie. Dritte Teilweise Umgearbeitete Auflage* (Leipzig: Engelmann).

Löwenstein, K. (1933), "Wunsch und Wünschen," in E. Heller, F. Löw (eds), *Neue Münchener Philosophische Abhandlungen: Alexander Pfänder zu seinem sechzigsten Geburtstag gewindet von Freunden und Schülern* (Leipzig: Barth), 165–200.

Melle, U. (1997), "Husserl's phenomenology of willing," in J. G. Hart and L. Embree (eds), *Phenomenology of Values and Valuing* (Dordrecht: Kluwer), 169–92.

Merleau-Ponty (2002), *Phenomenology of Perception* (London: Routledge).

Mertens, K. (1998), "Husserl's phenomenology of will in his reflections on ethics," in N. Depraz, D. Zahavi (eds), *Alterity and Facticity* (Dordrecht: Kluwer), 121–38.

Montague, M. (2017), "Brentano on emotion and the will," in U. Kriegel (ed.), *Routledge Handbook of Brentano and the Brentano School* (London: Routledge), 110–23.

Mulligan, K. (2010), "Husserls Herz," in M. Frank and N. Weidtmann (eds), *Husserl und die Philosophie des Geistes* (Frankfurt a. M.: Suhrkamp), 209–38.

Mulligan, K. (2012), *Wittgenstein et la Philosophie Austro-Allemande* (Paris: J. Vrin).

Mulligan, K. (2013), "Acceptance, acknowledgment, affirmation, agreement, assertion, belief, certainty, conviction, denial, judgment, refusal and rejection," in M. Textor (ed.), *Judgement and Truth in Early Analytic Philosophy and Phenomenology* (London: Palgrave Macmillan), 97–137.

Pfänder A. (1900), *Phänomenologie des Wollens. Eine psychologische Analyse* (Leipzig: Barth).

Pfänder A. (1967 [1911]), "Motives and Motivation" in H. Spiegelberg (ed.), *Phenomenology of Willing and Motivation and Other Phaenomenologica* (Evanston, IL: Northwestern University Press), 12–40.

Pfänder A. (1982 [1909]), "Imperativenlehre," in H. Spiegelberg and E. Avé-Lallement (eds), *Pfänder-Studien* (The Hague: Martinus Nijhoff), 287–324.

Reinach, A. (1989a [1911]), "Zur Theorie des negativen Urteils," in K. Schuhmann and B. Smith (eds), *Adolf Reinach. Sämtliche Werke. Textkritische Ausgabe in 2 Bänden, Band I. Die Werke* (Munich: Philosophia), 95–140.

Reinach, A. (1989b [1912/13]), "Die Überlegung: ihre ethische und rechtliche Bedeutung," in K. Schuhmann and B. Smith (eds), *Adolf Reinach. Sämtliche Werke. Textkritische Ausgabe in 2 Bänden, Band I. Die Werke* (Munich: Philosophia), 279–311.

Reinach, A. (2012 [1913]), "The a priori foundations of the civil law," in J. Crosby (ed.), *The A Priori Foundations of the Civil Law. Along with the lecture "Concerning Phenomenology"* with an introduction by A. McIntyre (Berlin: de Gruyter), 1–142.

Reiner, H. (1927), *Freiheit, Wollen und Aktivität. Phänomenologische Untersuchungen in Richtung auf das Problem der Willensfreiheit* (Halle: Niemeyer).

Ricœur, P. (1982), "Phénomenologie du vouloir et approche par le language ordinaire," in H. Spiegelberg and E. Avé-Lallement (eds), *Pfänders Studien* (The Hague: Martinus Nijhoff), 79–96.

Rinofner-Kreidl, S. (2014), "Motive, Gründe und Entscheidungen in Husserls intentionaler Handlungstheorie," in V. Mayer, C. Erhard, and M. Scherini (eds), *Die Aktualität Husserls* (Freiburg: Alber), 232–77.

Salice, A. (2012), "Phänomenologische Variationen: Intention and fulfillment in early phenomenology," in A. Salice (ed.), *Intentionality: Historical and Systematic Perspectives* (Munich: Philosophia), 203–42.

Salice, A. (2015a), "The phenomenology of the Munich and Göttingen circles," in E. N. Zalta (ed.), *The Stanford Encyclopedia of Philosophy*, URL http://plato.stanford.edu/archives/win2015/entries/phenomenology-mg/

Salice, A. (2015b), "Actions, Values and States of Affairs in Hildebrand and Reinach," *Studia Phenomenologica* 15: 259–80.

Scheler, M. (1973 [1913/16]), *Formalism in the Ethics and Non-Formal Ethics of Values: A New Attempt toward the Foundation of an Ethical Personalism*, translated by M. S. Frings and R. L. Funk (Evanston, IL: Northwestern University Press).

Schuhmann, K. (1977), *Husserl Chronik: Denk und Lebensweg Edmund Husserls* (The Hague: Martinus Nijhoff).

Searle, J. (1983), *Intentionality: An Essay in the Philosophy of Mind* (Cambridge: Cambridge University Press).

Stein, E. (1970), "Beiträge zur philosophischen Begründung der Psychologie und der Geisteswissenschaften," in *Beiträge zur philosophischen Begründung der Psychologie und der Geisteswissenschaften—Eine Untersuchung über den Staat* (Tübingen: Niemeyer), 2–284.

von Hildebrand, D. (1969 [1916]), "Die Idee der sittlichen Handlung," in K. Mertens (ed.), *Die Idee der sittlichen Handlung. Sittlichkeit und Werterkenntnis* (Darmstadt: Wissenschaftliche Buchgesellschaft), 1–126.

Uemura, G. (2015), "Husserl's conception of cognition as an action: An inquiry into its prehistory," in M. Ubiali and M. Wehrle (eds), *Feeling and Value, Willing and Action: Essays in the Context of a Phenomenological Psychology* (Dordrecht: Springer), 119–40.

Williamson, T. (2017), "Acting on knowledge," in J. A. Carter, E. Gordon, and B. Jarvis (eds), *Knowledge First: Approaches in Epistemology and Mind* (Oxford: Oxford University Press), 163–81.

CHAPTER 32

....

IDEAL VERIFICATIONISM
AND PERCEPTUAL FAITH

Husserl and Merleau-Ponty on Perceptual Knowledge

....

WALTER HOPP

FROM at least the "breakthrough" work of the *Logical Investigations* onwards, Husserl maintains that there is an essential relationship between consciousness and being.[1] Understanding the details of that relationship—both in general and with respect to specific sorts of beings—is one of the principal tasks of Husserl's phenomenology, both before and after his transcendental turn. A. D. Smith characterizes Husserl's position as "ideal verificationism," according to which "There is nothing, no possible entity, that is not in principle experienceable"—and, therefore, knowable on the basis of experience.[2]

In what follows, I will lay out Husserl's principal argument for ideal verificationism. More specifically, I will discuss Husserl's views on the relationships among truth and being, truth and evidence, and evidence and consciousness.[3] I will then discuss Husserl's view that it is at least ideally possible that any object could be intuited adequately or completely. I then turn to Merleau-Ponty's argument against that view. Finally, I examine Merleau-Ponty's account of perception and perceptual faith, and argue that a version of Husserl's ideal verificationism is compatible with Merleau-Ponty's position.

[1] I would like to thank Steven Crowell, Zach Joachim, Jacob Rump, Charles Siewert, and Judson Webb for helpful discussions on these topics. I am especially indebted to Colin Cmiel, Daniel Dahlstrom, David Kasmier, Dan Zahavi, and two anonymous referees for their insights, criticism, and assistance.

[2] A. D. Smith 2003: 186. Also see Hardy 2013: 92 and 100.

[3] Or, in Husserl's words, the "essential relations that combine the *idea of what truly is* with the ideas of truth, reason, and consciousness" (Husserl 2014: §142, 283).

32.1 HUSSERL'S OVERALL POSITION

When it comes to a tidy summary of Husserl's position concerning the relationships among being, truth, evidence, and consciousness, one cannot ask for a more perspicuous statement than the following:

> Every possible object is, speaking in logical-formal universality, the subject of certain predicates. To each belongs an ideally closed body of true propositions in which what the object is is thought. To the possibility of each true proposition belongs *a priori* the possibility of a demonstration, and this requires an originary giving intuition of the intended state of affairs and therefore also of the object-about-which, i.e., the object to be determined. An object is without doubt possible without me or anyone else actually thinking of it . . . But an object is in principle unthinkable that would lack the ideal possibility of being experienced, and with it also the possibility of a subject experiencing it.[4]

All of the elements of our correlation are present here. There is a necessary connection between objects and their "predicates" or properties, on the one hand, and a body of true propositions about them, on the other. Every true proposition, in turn, is in principle such that it can be verified by means of an originary intuition of its object. Such originary intuitions and the corresponding verifications that they permit can only be carried out in the experiential life of conscious subjects. And so there is an essential link between objects and consciousness: Every real object is the object of a possible originary intuition carried out in the conscious life of some subject. Let us investigate each of these correlations in turn.

32.2 TRUTH AND BEING

In §39 of the Sixth Logical Investigation, Husserl conducts a rather confusing discussion of (at least) four different concepts of truth. The fourth, which is the clearest and best corresponds to what contemporary philosophers understand by "truth," is "truth as the *rightness of our intention* (and especially that of our judgment), its adequacy to its true object" (Husserl 1970: §39, 766). This is the sense of "truth" under consideration in this section. Of the essential relations under consideration, that between truth, in this sense, and being is probably the least controversial. If anything exists, there is some body of truths concerning it. And their being true, correspondingly, entails that the corresponding object exists. As Husserl puts it, discussing the "interconnection of truths" and the "interconnection of things" that jointly constitute the objective side of

---

[4] Husserl 2003: 142. Thanks to Daniel O. Dahlstrom for assistance in translating this passage.

any science, "These two things are given together a priori, and are mutually inseparable. Nothing can be without being thus or thus determined, and that it is, and that it is thus and thus determined, is the self-subsistent truth which is the necessary correlate of the self-subsistent being" (Husserl 1970: Prol., §62, 225–6).

As the passage above suggests, Husserl's position is a version of the "correspondence" theory of truth:

> Corresponding to a proposition is a state of affairs, precisely the one that is posited in it as obtaining. If the proposition is true, then the state of affairs actually obtains (and the object-about-which actually exists), and it does not obtain if the proposition is false.[5]

To use an example of Husserl's, consider the proposition <The knife is on the table>. This proposition is about the knife, but its "full and entire object" is the state of affairs of the knife's being on the table.[6] Despite their essential relationship, the proposition and the state of affairs are distinct. The state of affairs is partly composed of a knife and a table, and it is not about or directed toward anything. The proposition contains no knife or table, but is composed of the *concept of* a knife and the *concept of* a table, both of which, along with the proposition they help constitute, *are* about something. This proposition is true just in case its "corresponding" state of affairs—that is, its object—"obtains" or exists. "The proposition 'directs' itself to the thing itself, it says that it is so, and it really is so" (Husserl 1970: 6, §39, 766).

Propositions and meanings, for Husserl, are ideal, non-temporal objects. Not only must they be sharply distinguished from the objects and states of affairs that they represent, they are also distinct from mental acts. Despite some appearances to the contrary, I am not persuaded that Husserl ever abandons this view. In his later work Husserl claims that "*Judgments as senses . . . have a sense-genesis*" (Husserl 1969: §85, 207)—that is, they are "constituted" in consciousness (Husserl 1969: §85, 208). But he says this after stating, "that there are indeed truths in themselves, which one can seek, and also find, by avenues already predelineated in themselves, is surely one of life's unquestioned truisms" (Husserl 1969: §80, 198). He assures us shortly thereafter that "We do not intend to give up any of these truisms; they surely rank as evidences" (Husserl 1969: §80, 199). That "judgments as senses" are "constituted," then, appears to be compatible with the contention that they are "in themselves." But granted that *something* is true if, and only if, the knife is on the table, why should we think that it is a *proposition* or any other sort of ideal meaning? Intentional experiences might also seem to be plausible candidates, especially if some version of global metaphysical idealism is true. So it is worth asking why ideal

---

[5] Husserl 2008: §14, 52. Also see Willard 1984: 189: "For Husserl, truth is agreement between a propositional meaning and the correlative state of affairs."

[6] Husserl 1970: 5, §17, 579. Also see Smith and McIntyre 1982: 6–9. Here and in what follows, references to the *Logical Investigations* will include the investigation number, the section number, and the page number. In this case it is Investigation 5, section 17, p. 579.

meanings, rather than experiences or mental acts, are considered by Husserl to be the primary bearers of truth—those entities whose truth is metaphysically necessary and sufficient for the existence of their corresponding objects. There are a couple of reasons.

One reason is that there are true propositions which we do not and cannot grasp. After characterizing the sphere of meanings as, like numbers, "an ideally closed set of general objects, to which being thought or being expressed are alike contingent," Husserl writes that "There are therefore countless meanings which . . . are never expressed, and since they can, owing to the limits of man's cognitive powers, never be expressed" (Husserl 1970: 1, §35, 333). But among this "countless" array of humanly ungraspable meanings, some must be true. If a proposition P is graspable and expressible by us, so is its negation not-P. So if not-P is ungraspable by us, P must also be ungraspable by us, and one of those two must be true.

The argument from humanly ungraspable propositions falls short of showing that propositions are the primary bearers of truth, however. That a proposition is ungraspable by humans does not entail that it is ungraspable, or even not actually grasped, by a non-human subject. What the argument shows is that, at least with respect to at least *some* truths, the intentional acts of *humans* are not the primary bearers of truth.

Husserl does have an additional argument, however. Consider a case in which many people judge that the knife is on the table. In such a case, writes Husserl, "There is a single truth, which corresponds to the multitude of individual acts of knowledge having the same content, which is just their ideally identical content" (Husserl 1970: Prol., §66, 234). The "ideally identical content" in question is, in this case, a proposition. We believe the *same thing*; what we believe is distinct from what our beliefs are about (the corresponding state of affairs), and it is what we believe that is primarily true.[7] And it is this one thing which stands in such logical relations as entailment, contrariety, and so on with other truth-value-bearers. As is well known, Husserl in the *Investigations* holds that the relation between meanings (concepts, propositions, and so on), on the one hand, and intentional experiences, on the other, is that of instantiation (Willard 1984: 184). "The manifold singulars for the ideal unity Meaning are naturally the corresponding act-moments of meaning, the meaning-intentions" (Husserl 1970: 2, §32, 330). Concepts and propositions are "more-or-less complex intentional properties of more-or-less complex mental acts."[8] And just as the multiplication of red objects does not count as a multiplication of colors, so "Multiplication of persons and acts does not multiply propositional

---

[7] As Crane (2013: 7), following Prior (1971: 111), notes, there is a difference between "*what we think*" and "what we think *about*." Also see Davis 2003: 317. To think a proposition is not to think about that proposition.

[8] Willard 1984: 178. By this Willard means that they are the properties of acts in virtue of which they are directed upon their objects in the manner that they are. They are wholly shareable, and therefore not parts of acts. Thanks to an anonymous referee for helping me clarify this point. Note that the matter and quality of an act *are* real moments or parts—they are the property-instances of such things as propositions. "We can mean by 'content' . . . its meaning as an ideal unity . . . To this corresponds, as a real (*reelles*) moment in the real (*reellen*) content of the presentative act, the intentional essence with its . . . quality and matter" (Husserl 1970: 5, §45, 657).

meanings; the judgment in the ideal, logical sense remains single."[9] It is, finally, because mental acts instantiate such properties that "logical laws also apply informatively and normatively to particular acts, and do so precisely because they are about the characters of such acts" (Willard 1984: 185).

32.3 TRUTH AND EVIDENCE

Now we turn to the relationship between truth and evidence. Husserl's conviction that there was such a connection predates his turn to transcendental idealism, and indeed one of the main arguments for it is located in the *Logical Investigations*.[10] There he goes so far as to claim that evidence is the "experience of truth."[11] This claim, however, does not secure the link between truth and evidence that we are trying to establish. The reason is that evidence is not the experience of *truth as correspondence*. Rather, it is an experience of truth in quite another sense of "truth," namely truth in the sense of "being" (see Husserl 1970: 6, §39). As he says, "inner evidence is called a seeing, a grasping of the self-given (true) state of affairs, or, as we say with tempting equivocation, of the truth" (Husserl 1970: Prol., §51, 195). *Truth as correspondence* can be grasped in evidence too, but only in reflective acts trained upon acts in which first-order acts of evidence—the consciousness of *being*—has already occurred.[12] We must, then, look elsewhere for Husserl's argument for the essential connection between evidence and truth.

Husserl characterizes the "epistemologically pregnant sense of self-evidence [Evidenz]" as the "*most perfect synthesis of fulfillment*" (Husserl 1970: 6, §38, 765). In such an act, "The object is not merely meant, but in the strictest sense given, and given as it is meant" (Husserl 1970: 6, §38, 765). Any such experience is, or involves, an act of "primal givenness" or "adequate perception" (Husserl 1970: 6, §38, 765). In such acts, Husserl writes, a thing is not "merely meant in some manner or other: it is a thing primarily given in our act, and as what we meant, i.e., as itself given and grasped without residue" (Husserl 1970: Prol., §51, 195).

Husserl here admits that there is a "looser" sense of evidence according to which it permits of degrees. For our purposes, the most important distinction is between adequate and inadequate evidence. Evidence "is either *adequate*, i.e., intrinsically incapable of being 'strengthened' or 'weakened' any more and thus *devoid of any gradations of weight*, or it is *inadequate* and thus *capable of increase and decrease*" (Husserl 2014: §138,

---

[9] Husserl 1970: 1, §31, 329. Also see Husserl 2008: §30b, 140–1.

[10] See Heffernan (1997 and 1998) for extremely nuanced and philosophically rich treatments of Husserl's account of evidence and its modifications over the span of his writings.

[11] Husserl 1970: Prol. §51, 194; also see Husserl 1970: 6, §39, 766.

[12] Husserl 1970: 6, §39, 767. Also see Dahlstrom 2001: 67. See Crowell 2016 for a rich discussion of the "experience of truth" as against the experience of objects, and why it is and must be phenomenally conscious.

276). In all cases, however, evidence amounts to the *givenness* of things in *intuitive* acts, and specifically those which present their objects "*in an originary way*" (Husserl 2014: §1, 9). Evidence is "the giving of something itself" (Husserl 1969: §59, 156), the "mode of consciousness . . . that offers its intentional objectivity in the mode belonging to the original 'it itself.' "[13]

In the case of some objects, adequate givenness is unattainable. When an intuition is adequate to its object, its object is completely given, with no hidden features or sides, and with no indeterminacy in its mode of givenness. In adequate or "self-posing" intuitions, "the identity of the object and the identity of the perception are one and the same; I mean different perceptions have different objects" (Husserl 1997: §10, 22). There is no possible intuition of any physical object with this character; each physical object has multiple ways of appearing in and through *veridical* experiences of it. "Inadequate modes of givenness belong essentially to the spatial structure of things; any other way of givenness is simply absurd" (Husserl 2001: 58). This is true even of the properties and features of physical objects, "whether it be called a primary or a secondary quality" (Husserl 2014: §41, 72). An experience of a color which is fully in view, for instance, is not adequate or self-posing, since the color "appears but while it appears, the appearance can and must continuously change in the course of ostensive experience of it" (Husserl 2014: §41, 72). As Alva Noë says, "There is no quality that is so simple that it is ever given to us all at once, completely and fully."[14] Despite their incompleteness, however, perceptual experiences are primary sources of evidence. They are *originary* (Husserl 2014: §1, 9) without being *adequate*.

The relation between evidence, understood as originary givenness, and truth is what Husserl's account of fulfillment is largely devoted to explicating. Despite Husserl's occasional identification of evidence with fulfillment, evidence is a genus which includes both fulfillment and intuition as species.[15] Fulfillment is a more complicated act than intuition. It is an act in which "the object is seen as being exactly the same as it is thought of" (Husserl 1970: 6, §8, 696), which mandates that it be both "seen" and thought of, and that the two acts be unified or synthesized. Dallas Willard nicely brings out the complexity involved in fulfillment when he characterizes it as a "union of the conceptualizing act with the object, on the basis of a corresponding intuition of that object together with a recognition of the identity of the object of the concept and of the perception" (Willard 1995: 152). While Husserl is not always entirely clear on the distinction between intuition and fulfillment in the *Investigations*, he is aware that they are distinct, and aware that he uses "evidence" to cover both sorts of acts.[16] Of these

---

[13] Husserl 1969: §63, 168; also see Husserl 1999: §24, 57 and Hardy 2013: 85.

[14] Noë 2004: 193. Also see Jansen (2015: 62) and A. D. Smith (2008: 324).

[15] See Hardy 2013: 86–7 for a helpful discussion.

[16] He writes, "I often used 'evidence' in a sense equivalent to the givenness of something itself. But surely we must distinguish: evidence as insight that belongs to judgment, <to the> judgment that <something> is there itself that exists and that is given again <as> that—and, on the other hand, the being-given itself" (Husserl 2005: 305).

two species of evidential acts, acts of intuition are primary insofar as they are proper parts of the more complicated acts of fulfillment. (This does not, however, entail that they are primary genetically. It could be—though I myself do not think this is so—that intuitions always occur together with appropriate acts of conceptualization, and can only be isolated in reflection and analysis.)

Conceptual thinking and acts of meaning, familiarly, often occur with no intuitive fulfillment. I can think that my shirt is in the dryer with or without seeing that it is. Many conceptual acts are, nevertheless, capable of being fulfilled. Indeed, Husserl maintains that anything that can be intuited can also be thought about "emptily."[17] The converse, however, is not true. Many meanings refer to impossible objects or states of affairs, and these have no possibility of fulfillment. That is, they have, as a matter of necessity, no "fulfilling sense," where the fulfilling sense of a meaning is the totality of possible experiences which intuitively present what it represents.[18] These are the impossible meanings. A possible meaning, by contrast, is one with a fulfilling sense (Husserl 1970: 6, §30, 749). That a meaning is possible does not mean that anyone has or ever will actually undergo an experience in which the relevant meaning has been fulfilled. Rather, these claims concern "ideal possibilities" (Husserl 1970: 6, §30, 749). Just as meanings are ideal, so it is with fulfilling senses and the complicated relations, including fulfillment, that hold among them and other contents of intentional acts. Evidence is an "ideal relationship which obtains in the unity of coincidence . . . among the epistemic essences of the coinciding acts."[19]

If Husserl is right, we now have an argument connecting truth with evidence. Corresponding to any true meaning, there is a fulfilling sense. And the fulfilling sense of a meaning is the body of contents in which that meaning's object is intended intuitively or with evidence. Therefore, corresponding to every possibly true proposition, there is a body of evidence associated with it. To put it simply: To every possibly true proposition, there is the possibility of its being fulfilled.[20] Given bivalence,

---

[17] "There are empty presentations of all possible objects in all subjective modes of inner givenness; in other words, corresponding to every mode of intuition is a possible mode of empty presentation" (Husserl 2001: 113). "To every intuitive intention there pertains, in the sense of an ideal possibility, a signitive intention precisely accommodated to its material (*Materie*)" (Husserl 1970: 6, §21, 728).

[18] See Husserl 1970: 1, §14. Later, Husserl claims that corresponding to the meaning of a word—that is, to a concept—is "an ideally delimited manifold of possible intuitions, each of which could serve as the basis for an act of recognitive naming endowed with the same sense" (Husserl 1970: 6, §7, 692). Also see his discussion of an object's "manifold," which is comprised of the "possible noetic occurrences," or experiences, of that object (Husserl 2014: §135, 268; also see Smith and McIntyre 1982: 244).

[19] Husserl 1970: 6, §39, 766; also see Willard 1984: 232.

[20] In *Ideas III*, Husserl writes that no matter how we acquired the ability to use words, "the word-significations can be valid as logical essences only if according to ideal possibility the 'logical thinking' actualizing them in itself is adaptable to a 'corresponding intuition,' if there is as corresponding noema a corresponding essence that is graspable through *Intuition* and that finds its true 'expression' through the logical concept" (Husserl 1980: §7, 23).

every proposition is verifiable in principle, since either it or its negation can be fulfilled.[21]

32.4 CONSCIOUSNESS AND EVIDENCE

We can now establish an essential correlation between consciousness and evidence. As we have seen, ideal meanings are properties whose possible instances are mental acts. The same is true of their fulfilling senses; in their case, their instances are conscious experiences in which an object is given with evidence. The existence of these ideal entities—meanings, fulfilling senses, and the relations of fulfillment among them—entails that they have possible instances.[22] Therefore, such mental acts possibly exist. Not only is there, eidetically speaking, a fulfilling sense for every possibly true proposition, but there is also a possible conscious evidential experience in which that fulfilling sense is realized.

The role of evidence in the life of consciousness on Husserl's account cannot be overemphasized. From what we have said, it follows that:

> To every region and category of alleged objects there corresponds not only a basic kind of senses or posits but also a basic kind of consciousness originally affording such senses and, inherent to it, a basic type of originary evidence, that is essentially motivated by the originary givenness of the specified kind.[23]

But even this does not sufficiently state the centrality of evidence in Husserl's account of intentionality. Evidence is not just one possibility of consciousness alongside the others. It is the "quite preeminent mode of consciousness" (Husserl 1969: §59, 158), one which "precedes all other[s]" (Husserl 1969: §86, 209). It is the possibility in virtue of which the others are possible at all, upon which all other intentional achievements are even thinkable:

> *What things are*—the only things that we make assertions about, the only things whose being or nonbeing, whose being in a certain way or being otherwise we dispute and can rationally decide—*they are as things of experience.* (Husserl 2014: §47, 85)

---

[21] Because of this correlation, Husserl maintains that every logical law has an equivalent but non-identical formulation couched in terms of evidence. See, for instance, Husserl 1970: Prol., §50 and Husserl 1969: §77.

[22] I owe this point to David Kasmier (conversation). As Dorion Cairns puts it, "Any eidetic fact corresponds to a universal fact about possible instances of the essences in which the eidetic fact is founded" (Cairns 2013: 253). See also Husserl 1970: Prol., §66 B., 235.

[23] Husserl 2014: §138, 276. Also see Husserl 1969: §60, 161.

More specifically, they are what they are as actual or possible objects of *intuitive* experience. And it is in virtue of actual and possible experiences of this sort that empty intentions—including virtually all of the "propositional attitudes"—are possible (Benoist 2003: 22). As Husserl says:

> In fact, we would not be able to speak at all of empty presentations and to attribute to them the character of having a relation to an object if it did not belong essentially to each empty presentation that it admit . . . of a disclosing, of a clarification, or a manifestation of its objectlike character, i.e., that it could enter into a synthesis with a corresponding intuition. (Husserl 2001: 113)

And Husserl, far from finding intuition or givenness "weird" or "mysterious" in contrast to acts of thinking and other "propositional attitudes"—as many philosophers do—holds that exactly the opposite is the case.[24] Intentional acts are oriented towards beings, and understanding what those beings *are* is bound up with some sort of understanding of how they do or would *manifest* themselves to consciousness.[25] And this in turn is dependent upon at least some of those entities actually manifesting themselves to consciousness. Evidence, then, does not just ground the structure of knowledge. It grounds the whole structure of intentionality. It is what nourishes signitive meanings with sense and provides a teleological orientation for conscious life.[26]

32.5 CONSCIOUSNESS AND BEING

So, then, according to Husserl:

(1) An object O exists if and only if it is the subject matter of some true proposition or set of true propositions about it.

(2) If P is a true proposition, it has a fulfilling sense FS.

(3) A fulfilling sense FS exists if and only if there is a possible experience or set of experiences with FS as its content.

---

[24] "Alles Rätselhafte, alles Problematische liegt auf seiten des blossen Meinens. Das schauende Selbsterfassen, Selbsthaben, als ein Rätsel behandeln wollen, das heisst selbst nicht verstehen, es heisst von oben her über Evidenz philosophieren statt sich die Evidenz selbst anzusehen, sie sich selbst zur Evidenz bringen" (Husserl 1996: 326–7). I first encountered this passage in Heffernan 1998: 2.

[25] See Willard 1984: 206 and Kasmier 2015. For an excellent discussion of the critical role of "presence" in grounding intentionality—and of the inadequacy of most contemporary naturalistic accounts of intentionality—see Fasching 2012.

[26] "Any consciousness, without exception, either is itself already characterized as evidence . . . or else has an essential tendency toward conversion into givings of its object originaliter" (Husserl 1977: §24, 58; also see Husserl 1969: §60, 160). Also see Bernet 2003 and Willard 1984: 227. For a good discussion of the "entelechic character" of consciousness, see Dahlstrom 2001: 60ff.

(4) If an experience has a fulfilling sense FS as its content, then it is an evidential experience of that fulfilling sense's object.

(5) So, if O exists, there is a possible evidential experience or set of experiences of O.[27]

Here is an argument for the correlation between consciousness and being, one grounded in the essences of what it is to be an object, truth, meaning, fulfillment, evidence, and the types of experiences in which these can become actualized (see Willard 1984: 232). I take this to constitute one of the central planks of Husserl's mature philosophical thinking.

It is worth mentioning in passing the connection between ideal verificationism and idealism. There is considerable evidence that Husserl endorses metaphysical idealism in addition to ideal verificationism.[28] Ideal verificationism does not, however, entail idealism, nor does it exclude metaphysical realism. Metaphysical realism with respect to some class of entities is the position that they exist, and that their existence is not grounded in their being the actual or possible objects of thought, experience, or discourse.[29] If ideal verificationism is correct, then a necessary condition of every object's existence is that it is ideally knowable on the basis of an originary intuition of it. Any possible object essentially has an *appearance*, a manner in which "it is known or apprehended" (D.W. Smith 2004: 17), or could be so known, and a *full* understanding of any object requires specifying this (Sokolowski 1964: 219). That, however, does not by

---

[27] Kasmier (2015) presents two related and similar reconstructions of Dallas Willard's argument—much of it based on Husserl's work—for the thesis that if something is real, it is a possible object of knowledge. I am deeply indebted to his work and to our conversations on the topic.

[28] The strongest case of which I am aware occurs in A. D. Smith 2003, especially chapter 4. Husserliana 36 is brimming with pronouncements that real objects require the *actual* existence of subjects—including embodied subjects (Husserl 2003: 132)—to whom they could possibly appear (see, for instance, Husserl 2003: 139–40). This is not true of ideal objects, however (Husserl 2003: 74). Jeff Yoshimi's arguments in Yoshimi 2015 seem to me to attack Husserl's ideal verificationism more directly than his idealism, and therefore to constitute a more serious threat to Husserl's position.

[29] I borrow this characterization from Dallas Willard's definition of "epistemic realism," according to which "the objects of veridical thought and perception both exist and have the characteristics they are therein discovered to have without regard to whether or not they are in any way actually present to any mind of any type" (Willard 2002: 69; also see Willard 2003: 163). Epistemic realism, as here defined, is metaphysical realism with respect to the objects of true thought and veridical perception. Note that this is *not* the view that what is metaphysically real exists independently of minds. This is not an apt characterization of metaphysical realism. As Vinueza (2001: 51–2) and Khlentzos (2011: §1) note, it entails that whatever is ontologically dependent upon the mind is not metaphysically real. But minds and their states are widely regarded to be metaphysically real, despite their obvious dependence on minds. Antirealism about minds and their states or properties is not the view that minds and their states depend on minds. Ideal verificationism does appear incompatible with the brand of metaphysical realism Dan Zahavi critically discusses, according to which "If we want to know true reality, we should aim at describing the way the world is, independently of all the ways in which it happens to present itself to us human beings, that is, we should aim for a description where all traces of ourselves have been removed" (Zahavi 2010: 85). Not all brands of metaphysical realism are committed to such an aim, however.

itself entail that there is any grounding relation between existence and intuitability, or, if there is, the direction in which that grounding relation runs.[30]

Consider an example.[31] Any house can, in principle, be photographed. This is true even if there are no actual photographs or photographic processes—before there were photographic processes, houses were such that they could possibly be photographed. But a house's existence and nature is not grounded in its capacity to be photographed. Rather, the latter capacity is grounded in its existence and its nature as a house—its photographability is part of its "consequential" rather than its "constitutive" essence, to use Fine's terminology (Fine 1995: 276). Or, otherwise stated, what enables houses and photographic processes to enter into relations with one another is the intrinsic natures of each: That they can relate to one another is grounded in what each of them is, but neither the nature or existence of each of them is grounded in their actually or possibly entering into such a relation. The case may be similar with respect to consciousness and its objects. For example, because of what consciousness is and what clumps of mud are, it is ideally possible for conscious subjects and clumps of mud to enter into relations with one another. It does not follow from this that the intrinsic nature or existence of either is grounded in its ability to relate to the other. Neither the realist nor the idealist would likely maintain that either the existence or nature of consciousness is grounded in the existence or nature of clumps of mud, despite its being an essential feature of consciousness that it can, under the right conditions, be directed upon clumps of mud. The realist would simply add that it is equally implausible to hold that the nature or existence of clumps of mud is grounded in the existence or nature of consciousness, despite, again, the fact that a clump of mud is essentially such that it can enter into relations with consciousness. Because ideal verificationism is silent on such issues of grounding, it leaves it open that it is the existence and intrinsic natures of objects that ground their ability to enter into relations with consciousness, and that the activity of bringing something to conscious awareness may, far from creating or grounding that object, be "guided by the object itself" (Drummond 1990: 270).

32.6 ADEQUACY AS AN IDEAL

Now we turn to a rather surprising consequence of Husserl's position. In §142 of *Ideas I*, Husserl claims that to be an object and to be "posited in a rational way" are "equivalent correlates" (Husserl 2014: §142, 283). He adds that the rational positing in question must be "an original, perfect rational thesis," one in which "the object would not be given incompletely" or "one-sidedly," but would be "completely determined, finished off"

---

[30] The literature on grounding or "ontological dependence" has grown vast, but for the present purposes I think the discussions in Kit Fine's now classic pieces (Fine 1994 and 1995) suffice.

[31] I am grateful to an anonymous referee for insisting on clarification regarding the compatibility of metaphysical realism and ideal verificationism.

(Husserl 2014: §142, 283). This leads Husserl to propose what Daniel Dahlstrom calls the "principle of adequate givenness" (Dahlstrom, p. 634, this volume):

> To each object "that truly is," there corresponds in principle . . . the idea of a possible consciousness in which the object itself can be apprehended *in an originary* and thereby *perfectly adequate manner.* (Husserl 2014: §142, 283).

This principle is not a consequence of the view that every object can be intuited *originarily.* The reason is that an originary presentation of an object need not be adequate. It is, nevertheless, a consequence of the argument for ideal verificationism presented above. Each proposition about an object has associated with it a fulfilling sense or manifold, which in turn is the content of some possible consciousness. But if the complete fulfilling sense associated with (a proposition about) an object were the content of a conscious experience or series thereof, the object in question would be given adequately. Therefore, corresponding to each object is not only the possibility of an originary experience of it, but, ideally, of an adequate experience of it.

   An immediate problem presents itself: It would seem that if this is true, no physical objects could exist. For, as we have seen, Husserl maintains that while such objects can be given in an originary way, they cannot be given adequately. Husserl sees the "semblance of a contradiction" here, and responds: "In principle, we said, the only objects are those that appear inadequately . . . Yet our added qualifying remark should not be overlooked. 'Those that cannot be perceived adequately *in an isolated experience,*' we said."[32] An "isolated" experience is any "finite, merely transient act" (Husserl 2014: §143, 285), not an unchanging or static experience of just one side or part of an object. Even the fastidious examination of all the details of a postage stamp for ten hours, or ten years, would constitute an "isolated experience" in this sense. Husserl's way out of the seeming contradiction is to show that "*the perfect givenness is nonetheless prefigured as an 'idea'* (in the Kantian sense)."[33] What is prefigured, on the side of the experience of an object, is an "infinite, ideal manifold of noetic experiences" of it (Husserl 2014: §135, 268) and the ideal possibility of having the object given with increasing adequacy through the pursuit of "any arbitrary *line*" of that manifold (Husserl 2014: §143, 285). No complete realization of this infinite manifold is possible in any finite act or series of acts. "Nonetheless, the idea of this continuum and the idea of the perfect givenness exemplified by it are *patently discernible*" (Husserl 2014: §143, 285). As he puts it later, "every incomplete givenness . . . contains in itself a rule for the ideal possibility of its perfection" (Husserl 2014: §149, 297).

   The idea here seems plain enough. Objects cannot be given adequately because they are just *too large.* Not necessarily spatially, of course, but in terms of their possible ways of appearing, on the noematic side, and the density of their corresponding experiential

---

[32] Husserl 2014: §143, 284. Daniel Dahlstrom, to whom I am grateful for calling my attention to these passages, has a helpful discussion in Dahlstrom 2015: 282.
[33] Husserl 2014: §143, 285; also see Husserl 1969: 62 n. 1.

manifolds, on the noetic side (see Husserl 2014: §135, 268). Their adequate givenness is out of reach, an ideal limit. But it can be approached, or we can at least entertain the idea of such an approach, through the progressive realization of any "line" of the object's manifold, in and through which "empty places of the foregoing appearances are filled and the indeterminacies are determined in more detail," and by virtue of which we experience a *"thoroughly coherent repleteness [or fulfillment] with a constantly mounting rational power"* (Husserl 2014: §138, 275).

32.7 MERLEAU-PONTY ON THE IMPOSSIBILITY OF ADEQUACY

In the *Phenomenology of Perception*, Merleau-Ponty pursues a line of thought which, if correct, entails that the principle of adequacy is false. The house I see, Merleau-Ponty begins, is not identical with any of its appearances. Perhaps, as Leibniz held, it is the *"geometrical plan* that includes these perspectives and all possible perspectives"; it is the "house seen from nowhere" (Merleau-Ponty 2012: 69). But this cannot be right: A house must be seen from somewhere. To make sense of vision, we must see how it "can come about from somewhere without thereby being locked within its perspective."[34] This is accomplished by means of horizons. The house appears in a world of other things, and to see it is to see it as showing other sides of itself to those things. "The back of my lamp," he writes, "is merely the face that it 'shows' to the fireplace" (Merleau-Ponty 2012: 71), and were I where the fireplace is, I would then see the back of the lamp. And so the house is better thought of as "seen from everywhere." It is "translucent, it is shot through from all sides by an infinity of present gazes intersecting in its depth and leaving nothing there hidden" (Merleau-Ponty 2012: 71).

According to Sean Kelly, Merleau-Ponty regards this "view from everywhere" as "the norm of seeing things" (Kelly 2004: 90). "It should be clear," writes Kelly, "that the view from everywhere is not a view that *I* can have." But, he continues, it is "nevertheless an ideal from which I can sense myself deviating" (Kelly 2004: 91). I think, though, that Merleau-Ponty regards the view from everywhere as every bit as absurd as the view from nowhere, and intends to discredit both this ideal and the related Husserlian ideal of adequate givenness in one blow. Here Merleau-Ponty reminds us of our situation:

> But again, my human gaze never *posits* more than one side of the object, even if by means of horizons it intends all the others. My gaze can only be compared with

[34] Merleau-Ponty 2012: 69. Alva Noë notes that "When you perceive an object, you never take it in from all sides at once. And yet you have a sense of the presence of the object as a whole at a moment in time." This "perceptual presence," according to Noë, "is *the* problem for the theory of perception" (Noë 2012: 74).

previous acts of seeing or with the acts of seeing accomplished by others through the intermediary of time and language. If I imagine, taking my own gaze as a model, the gazes that scour the house from all directions and define the house itself, I still have but a concordant and indefinite series of points of view upon the object, I do not have the object in its fullness. In the same way, even though my present condenses within itself the time gone by and the time to come, it only possesses them in intention. And if, for example, the consciousness that I now have of my past appears to me to match precisely what it was, this past that I claim to take hold of again is not itself the past in person; it is my past such as I now see it, and I have perhaps altered it . . . Thus the synthesis of horizons is but a presumptive synthesis, it only operates with certainty and precision within the object's immediate surroundings. (Merleau-Ponty 2012: 72)

There is much here that Husserl would endorse. Of course only one side of the object is at any time "posited," if by that we mean "originarily given." Of course it is only by means of "intentions" or empty "horizons" that the rest of the object and the other pos- sible gazes on it are included in our consciousness of the object. But Merleau-Ponty's statements, if true, show that the adequate givenness of an object is an incoherent ideal (see Pietersma 2000: 140).

Let's turn to some examples. As I encounter my kitchen table at t1, I have an intuitive presentation of its brown color on the front side. I emptily intend that it is this same color on the other side. I can fulfill this empty intention by walking around to the other side of the table. Doing so at t2, I discover that it too is brown. Let us assume, in this ex- ample, that the front of the table, and my experience of it, are still retained within the ho- rizon of time consciousness at t2. That is, I don't simply remember, at t2, that the table is brown. I *retain* it. I have an originary consciousness of the just-past, not a non-originary, reproductive recollection of it.[35]

Here we have a clear case of an increase in the adequacy of my experience of the table. But what, exactly, lies within the scope of originariness here? Do I have originarily given to me at t2 that the table is brown in the front and the back? Not exactly. What I have originarily given to me is that the table's back is brown at t2, and that its front *was* brown at t1. Whether the front is brown *at* t2 is not given to me at t2. This is not to deny that I have very strong evidence that it still is brown at t2. But that evidence should not be confused with originary givenness.

Consider another example that makes this point more clearly. Suppose I am indoors during a hailstorm. I look at my front windows at t1 to determine if any have broken, and see that they have not. I run to the back of the house, arriving there at t2, to check those windows. They're also fine. Assuming, again, that my experience at t1 is still retained at t2, do I now, at t2, know that none of the windows are broken on the basis of an originary intuition? No, since a front window might easily have broken in the interim. What I have

---

[35] See Husserl 1991: 42–3 for a good discussion, where Husserl contrasts "primary memory" or retention and recollection. "For only in primary memory do we see what is past, only in it does the past become constituted—and constituted presentatively, not re-presentatively" (1991: 43).

given to me originarily at t2 is that no back window is broken at t2, and no front window *was* broken at t1. How those front windows fare at t2, however, is an open question.

If this is right, what is originarily given to me is not the relevant objects as they exist at t2. It is how one portion was at t1, and how another portion is at t2. And that is not a case of my getting an increasingly adequate *originary* consciousness of the condition of the table or the windows as they are at t2, but an increasingly adequate originary consciousness of different aspects of theirs from t1–t2. I can go back to the front of the table, or the front of the house, and see how they are at t3. Seeing the front of the table to be brown, or the front windows to be intact, at t3 provides me with incredibly strong evidence that they were brown, or intact, at t2. But again, that should not be confused with the claim that I have ever had an originary evidential consciousness of how they were at t2.

These cases are, of course, quite different. I can be much more confident that the front of my table has not changed color than I can that my window has not broken in a hail-storm at t2. And that is no doubt right. But that confidence stems, in large measure, from what I already know about the conditions under which things like tables change color. Similarly with the window: That it was not broken at t2 is something I know at t3, when I discover it to be intact. But that knowledge is heavily fortified by my general knowledge of windows, not something derived solely from an originary intuition of my window at t2.

We are even further removed from adequate perception when the past fades from retentional consciousness, as it always eventually (and quickly) does. Suppose I check that my front windows are unbroken, and then go about examining my back windows for some time—a couple of minutes, say. As my original experience of the front win-dows fades, I am left to *remember* rather than *retain* how it presented things. Similarly, if I dally long enough looking at one side of the table, the experience that revealed its other side to be brown will slip out of retentional consciousness, leaving me to the mercy of my memory. The once originary experience of the past ceases to be originary any longer. What these examples show is that it is possible that each member of a series of experiences E_1–E_n be originary, without the whole sequence E_1–E_n itself being originary. In the sequence below for instance, in which E_5 occurs in the present, only E_3 and E_4 still lie in retentional consciousness, while E_1 and E_2 have slipped away.

$$E_1 \ldots E_2 \ldots E_3 \ldots E_4 \ldots E_5$$

$$t\text{-}4 \ldots t\text{-}3 \ldots t\text{-}2 \ldots t\text{-}1 \ldots t0$$

They are no longer present "in person." And the upshot of this is just as Merleau-Ponty describes: Even if what is present at E_5 appears to correspond or harmonize exactly with what I experienced at E_1, "this past that I claim to take hold of again is not itself the past in person; it is my past such as I now see it, and I have perhaps altered it" (Merleau-Ponty 2012: 72). Naturally this latter worry is not a live one much of the time. But the greater the distance between the remembered and my memory of it, or the stronger my motivations to "alter" the past, the more pressing it becomes.

These examples make it clear that the reason objects cannot be given adequately is not just, or even principally, because of their infinitely rich manifolds. Although that's sufficient for inadequacy, it is hardly necessary. There is an additional and equally insurmountable source of inadequacy: One cannot take up multiple perspectives at once, and things might change by the time I take up a new one. If I choose to inspect the table by walking around its right side, I am now barred from perceiving its left side as it is at that time. I can only perceive it earlier or later. Even if an object's manifold consisted of only two possible lines of givenness over a time, the ideal of adequate givenness would be impossible in principle.

This is not to deny that every feature of an object could be originarily given simultaneously; we can conceive of "an infinity"—or just a couple—"of different perspectives condensed into a strict coexistence" (Merleau-Ponty 2012: 72). But this cannot be the norm of perception either, because it requires multiple subjects, and neither a perceptual experience nor a unified sequence of such experiences can be distributed across multiple subjects. A friend can view the front of the table while I am busy examining the back. But while this is a case in which the front is given and the back is given at the same time, it is not a case in which *both* are given to anyone *together*. Givenness is givenness to *a* subject, and my friend and I do not constitute a subject. If I want to know how things stand with the front of the table without consulting my memory (of a previous time), I must rely on my friend's testimony; I must appeal to the "acts of seeing accomplished by others through the intermediary of time and language" (Merleau-Ponty 2012: 72). That is, when things go well, sufficient for knowledge. But it is not sufficient for originary givenness.

The argument against Husserl's position should be clear. For any object, or any proposition about an object, there is an associated fulfilling sense. This fulfilling sense comprises an immense body of possible experiential contents, not all of which could possibly be co-realized by one consciousness. This is not to deny that *each* content making up an object's fulfilling sense is the content of a possible experience. The claim, rather, is that not *all* of them could be. Each may be possible, but they are not all compossible. This is not, moreover, because of the *infinite* size of an object's manifold, but simply because the having of some experiences of an object rules out the having of others. And so premise 3 of Husserl's argument—that the fulfilling sense of every true proposition can be the content of some possible consciousness—is false.

This argument also, it seems to me, undermines Husserl's view of nature as "the correlate of consciousness" (Husserl 2014: §47, 85), and more specifically, as the correlate of possible originary conscious experiences of it. Regarding an object, or the world, as a correlate of possible evidential presentations enables us to conceive of it as something which "is fully spread out and its parts coexist while our gaze skims over them one by one; its present does not efface its past, and its future will not efface its present" (Merleau-Ponty 2012: 73). It invites us to conceive of a house as the correlate of an infinity of ideally possible harmonious, *unified* perspectives on it—as a place in which no one could hide from an ideal observer forever. And that is just what Merleau-Ponty's observations show to be incoherent. Someone *could* hide from *an* ideal observer in a house forever, provided they always managed to move to a location where that observer is not then looking.[36]

32.8 Perceptual Evidence and Perceptual Faith

In light of this, it may seem that Merleau-Ponty's position makes our epistemic situation significantly less secure than does Husserl's. If we think of perception as a process of stitching "appearances" together, and the security of our perceptual knowledge of physical objects as proportional to the amount of harmonious stitching we have accomplished, then Merleau-Ponty's reminders of just how incomplete perception is and must be will appear to threaten our knowledge of the world.

One answer to this worry is that perception is not at all like that.[37] It can, it is true, appear to be like that in a reflective attitude. Through a series of "reductions" (Merleau-Ponty 2012: 339), I might move from the die out there in the world to a die that only shows certain sides to *me*, then to something present *only* to sight, then to this reduced visible phantom's "profiles" or "projections" which can only be seen *from here*, and finally to a cluster of mere sensations. But this process of dismantling perception through analysis is not the process of constitution carried out in reverse.[38] "The experience of the thing does not go through all of these mediations" (Merleau-Ponty 2012: 339). That's a claim we can check for ourselves. When looking at the die from various angles, I see it and its *sides*—objective, transcendent parts of it—not "profiles."[39] And we are not, in general, assured of the existence or natures of things by seeing their appearances, parts, or sides unfold over time harmoniously. The existence of the other cars on the freeway is not increasingly verified as I drive alongside them and see more and more of their parts; spotting a tailpipe does not make me *more* sure that I'm dealing with an actual car. Their reality is settled beyond any but the most artificial of doubts the instant they come into view, and now it's a matter of dealing with them. The reality of the real in perception strikes us instantly, even when it is completely unexpected (Merleau-Ponty 1968: 39), and even when only a tiny fraction of an object's manifold is experienced.

---

[36] William James's example (James 1995: 17) of a squirrel circling around a tree in concert with a human on the other side, although recruited to establish a different point, nicely illustrates the possibility. Thanks to Daniel Dahlstrom for making me aware of this example.

[37] Merleau-Ponty 2012: lxxiv. See Pietersma 2000: 137–8 for a good discussion.

[38] "Reflection does not work backward along a pathway already traveled in the opposite direction by constitution" (Merleau-Ponty 2012: 253). Also see Merleau-Ponty 2012: lxxiii and Merleau-Ponty 1968: 33 and 45.

[39] "If the subject moves, these are not signs, but rather sides of the die that appear; he does not perceive projections or even profiles of the die; rather, he sees the die itself sometimes from here, and sometimes from over there" (Merleau-Ponty 2012: 339; also see 344). Scheler (1973: 55–6) makes a similar point, and Merleau-Ponty (2012: 319) mentions him in connection with a related issue.

And the unreality of the imagined clings to it no matter how adequate our conscious-ness of it may be or how well it coheres internally—or even with our apprehension of the actual world. "The least particle of the perceived incorporates itself it from the first into the 'perceived,' the most credible phantasm glances off at the surface of the world" (Merleau-Ponty 1968: 40), and the difference between perception and imagination is "not a difference of the more and the less" (Merleau-Ponty 1968: 40; also see Merleau-Ponty 2012: lxxiv). If I am unsure of the existence of a table upon the first few seconds of seeing one, an additional decade of investigation is unlikely to help. This is why a gen-uine skeptic (if one existed) would not be converted, or even brought nearer to conver-sion, by looking at things more closely or for a very long time.

A committed skeptic would be unmoved by all of this, I suspect. Since there is a tight connection between adequate perception and knowledge, a skeptic might argue, and since no conceivable augmentation of our perceptual evidence could bring us any-where near adequacy, we simply cannot have knowledge of the world. That we become thoroughly convinced of the existence of things on the basis of massively incomplete experiences of them only adds to our misfortune: Not only do we have bad evidence, but we respond to it badly as well.

If skepticism is right, then ideal verificationism is false. Therefore, anyone at all con-cerned with defending any version of ideal verificationism must address skepticism. One promising response is to criticize the skeptic for having an overly demanding standard of evidence. Unlike the "dogmatist" (Pryor 2000), the skeptic is unwilling to accept anything less than indefeasible and apodictic evidence. If only we could persuade the skeptic to relax his standards, and that even inadequate perception really does meet any reasonable standard of evidence, perhaps everything could be made right.

There is some reason to believe that a Husserlian strategy would proceed along these or similar lines.[40] One might, for instance, establish—as a "principle of all principles" (Husserl 2014: §24, 43)—that all originary intuitions provide justification for believing propositions about the objects and states of affairs that they present, and that percep-tual experiences are such intuitions. Furthermore, an answer along these lines could, if suitably developed, reconcile Husserl's ideal verificationism with Merleau-Ponty's observations regarding the ideal impossibility of adequate perception. More specifi-cally, we could simply replace the problematic premise that the *entire* fulfilling sense belonging to any existing object could, ideally, be the content of experience with the premise that *at least some* contents composing the fulfilling sense of any existing ob-ject could be the contents of experience, and that those experiences would be originary, albeit inadequate, presentations of the object in question. The conclusion—ideal verificationism of a rather weaker variety—would still follow.

Merleau-Ponty, however, has a rather different response to skepticism. The world of perception is primary in every important sense—genetically, evidentially, and concep-tually. Any philosophical attempt to undermine or vindicate it is addressed not to us

---

[40] Berghofer 2014 and 2017; Wiltsche 2015; Hopp 2013.

as embodied and situated inhabitants of the world, but to the alleged "impartial spectator that inhabits us" (Merleau-Ponty 1968: 15). Such attempts submit perception and the world for our consideration as if we, weighing the evidence, were independently equipped with the relevant concepts to understand the questions and free to affirm or deny them. But we are not. We are embodied, involved in and open to a primary "sensible" world that is "older than the universe of thought" (Merleau-Ponty 1968: 12). As a type of "reflection," any such inquiry rests "upon the perceptual faith whose tenor it claims to give us and whose measure it claims to be."[41] More importantly, our meanings, our conceptions of essences, our epistemic criteria, and our notion of what it means to be in the first place are all grounded in and derived from the world of perception. As Dillon puts it, the "to the extent that transcendental philosophy succeeds in revealing the structure of meaning constitutive of the phenomenal world, that success is measured against the standard of actual experience."[42] Any attempt to call perception into question presupposes its accomplishments and the conceptual tools that only it could provide.

The skeptic commits just this error. The skeptic asks whether the world of perception might be a dream world, but "does not elucidate the mental existence it substitutes for it, which in fact it conceives as a weakened or degraded real existence" (Merleau-Ponty 1968: 95). But the concept and criteria of real existence are acquired in perception. The problem with the skeptical argument is that it "makes use of that faith in the world it seems to be unsettling: We would not know even what the false is, if there were not times when we had distinguished it from the true" (Merleau-Ponty 1968: 5; also Merleau-Ponty 2012: lxxx). Skepticism is, in Marcus Sacrini's words, a "self-undermining enterprise" for Merleau-Ponty.[43]

One can hardly imagine the skeptic—or Husserl—regarding Merleau-Ponty's appeal to "perceptual faith" as an adequate response to skepticism or an adequate account of perceptual knowledge. Before deciding that issue, though, it is worth taking a closer look at what perceptual faith is. First, as Todd Cronan points out, Merleau-Ponty himself assimilates perceptual faith to Husserl's "*Urdoxa*" or "*Urglaube*," a kind of primordial passive belief that precedes all (other) reasons.[44] Our perceptual faith is an "unjustifiable certitude of a sensible world common to us" (Merleau-Ponty 1968: 11). It is a certitude in the existence of both things and other consciousnesses which is "entirely irresistible" but "absolutely obscure; we can live it, we can neither think it nor formulate it nor set it up in theses" (Merleau-Ponty 1968: 11). As one would expect from Merleau-Ponty's designation of it, perceptual faith is not a "work." It is not a decision that can be made or

---

[41] Merleau-Ponty 1968: 50. Sacrini (2013: 731) writes: "It is only in opposition to this pre-reflective insertion into the world that the voluntary project of searching for absolute rational justifications makes sense." Also see Cronan 2010: 503.

[42] Dillon 1997: 175; also see Merleau-Ponty 1968: 98 and Carmen 2008: 36–7.

[43] Sacrini 2013: 729. Sacrini presents extremely sophisticated and detailed analyses of several of Merleau-Ponty's responses to skepticism, which, he argues, achieve very different levels of success.

[44] See Cronan 2010: 497 and Merleau-Ponty 2012: 359 and 553 n. 96.

revoked, nor is it a "positing" act performed by a transcendental subject (Merleau-Ponty 2012: 336; also lxxiv). Whatever reflective attitude we take toward it, it persists as long as perception does.[45] Like my visual field, I possess it by "a gift of nature, without any effort required on my part" (Merleau-Ponty 2012: 224). And because it is a gift we do not have the power to refuse, perceptual faith is, as Bernard Flynn notes, "perhaps the very opposite of the agonized Kierkegaardian 'leap of faith.' It is a faith the commitment of which has 'always already' been made" (Flynn 2011: §7).

Merleau-Ponty was undoubtedly fully aware of the theological connotations involved in characterizing perception as a kind of "faith." Perhaps the most helpful characterization of the *faith* in perceptual faith comes from Paul, who famously characterizes faith as "the conviction of things not seen" (Hebrews 11:1). So, tellingly, does Merleau-Ponty.[46] Perception—*seeing*—is or involves a conviction of things *not* seen. And that claim, while paradoxical on its face, makes a great deal of sense. The confidence I have in the existence of the tree before me involves a confidence in its having further features, its relations to other things in the environment, and its capacity to manifest itself to others. "Perception's silent thesis is that experience, at each moment, can be coordinated with the experience of the preceding moment and with that of the following one, that my perspective can be coordinated with the perspectives of other consciousnesses" (Merleau-Ponty 1968: 54). Without that "silent thesis," perception would not be perception, and would therefore not be the disclosure of the real.

We can appreciate Merleau-Ponty's point by examining how perceptual acts and their objects are what they are only if they occupy positions within a much broader contexture of other acts (some of them merely "presumptive"), other objects (many of them unseen), other embodied subjects, and the Gestalts in which they are embedded.[47] More precisely, such acts and their objects are what they are in virtue of their place within a horizon of acts and a horizon of objects which are not thematic or thematized. In the "originary field" of perception, Merleau-Ponty writes, "Nothing here is thematized. Neither the object nor the subject is *posited*." And it is this "originary field" which is presupposed by perceptual acts: "Every perceptual act appears as taken from an overall adhesion to the world" (Merleau-Ponty 2012: 251; also see 294). Likewise, every perceived object and quality appears within a field, and ultimately within the world—the "field of all fields" (Merleau-Ponty 2012: 336). "A color," he famously writes, "is never simply a color, but rather the color of a certain object, and the blue of a rug would not be the same blue if were not a wooly blue" (Merleau-Ponty 2012: 326). He goes on to say that, "The constancy of color is merely an abstract moment of the constancy of things, and the constancy of things is established upon the primordial consciousness of the world as the horizon of all of our experiences" (Merleau-Ponty 2012: 326). That "primordial consciousness" is not a synthesis of positing acts, and the world itself is not a collection of

---

[45] "The perceived is and remains, despite all critical training, beneath the level of doubt and demonstration" (Merleau-Ponty 2012: 359).

[46] As Darian Meacham (2010: 185) points out. See Merleau-Ponty 1964: 176.

[47] See Pietersma 2000: 137–8 for a helpful discussion.

things and qualities "harmoniously" synthesized in such acts.[48] Acts, things, and qualities, on the contrary, are dependent upon the "originary" field of consciousness and the world as the outmost horizon of the field of consciousness. The world, as Komarine Romdenh-Romluc expresses it, "forms the background to all one's experiences; it is that indeterminate, massive presence against which things are seen" (Romdenh-Romluc 2011: 126).

Our confidence in the thing—and with it the experiences that would reveal it—can be misplaced. The presumptive synthesis of horizons, which helps constitute this experience as an experience of a tree, might fail to unfold; perhaps the experience will turn out to be illusory or deceptive. But if it does, that is because it is overthrown by further experiences which bear the evidential strength to perform that function. "The dis-illusion is the loss of one evidence only because it is the acquisition of *another evidence*."[49] This new experience might itself be overturned by others. But what seems incapable of being overturned is our confidence in being in touch with the world. "Each perception is mutable and only probable—it is, if one likes, only an opinion; but what is not opinion, what each perception, even if false, verifies, is the belongingness of each experience to the same world, their equal power to manifest it, as possibilities of the same world."[50]

That Merleau-Ponty speaks here of disillusion as the acquisition of *evidence* suggests that he and Husserl may share common ground. This act of perceiving the tree before me is a case in which it is presented to me with strong, albeit defeasible, evidence. Of course, he also says that each perception is "only an opinion." This may suggest that each perceptual act is a case of faith. But that hardly seems right. It is not *faith* that I have in the tree. It cannot be, since our perceptual faith cannot be overturned by evidence, while any particular act of perceiving can. And perceptual faith is faith in what is unseen, and the tree is not unseen. Perceptual faith is, rather, "our experience, *prior to every opinion*, of inhabiting the world by our body" (Merleau-Ponty 1968: 28, my emphasis). An act of explicitly seeing a tree is not itself an act of faith. It may be "opinion"—that is, fallible or defeasible evidence—but perceptual faith is not opinion. Merleau-Ponty's position, rather, is that this sort of act can only exist within a more fundamental consciousness of and confidence in what is unseen—the world. In "positing" the tree, I place it in the world, which is overwhelmingly unseen, and which could never, even in principle, be completely seen. But the world itself is not posited. It is lived in.[51] "Beneath the explicit acts by which I posit an object out in front of myself . . . beneath, then, perceptions

---

[48] "The real is coherent and probable because it is real, and not real because it is coherent" (Merleau-Ponty 1968: 40; also Merleau-Ponty 2012: lxxiv).

[49] Merleau-Ponty 1968: 40. Also see Merleau-Ponty 2012: 359–60.

[50] Merleau-Ponty 1968: 41. Elsewhere he writes: "Of course, each thing can, *après coup*, appear uncertain, but at least it is certain for us that there are things, that is, that there is a world" (Merleau-Ponty 2012: 360). Also see Sacrini 2013: 721.

[51] "Natural perception is not a science, it does not posit the things upon which it bears, and it does not step back from them in order to observe them; rather, it lives among them and is the 'opinion' or the 'originary faith' that ties us to a world as if to our homeland" (Merleau-Ponty 2012: 336).

properly so-called, there is, sustaining them, a deeper function without which perceived objects would lack the mark of reality" (Merleau-Ponty 2012: 358–9). This "deeper function," he continues, "places us in the world prior to every science and every verification through a sort of 'faith'" (Merleau-Ponty 2012: 359). That deeper function, I suggest, just is perceptual faith.

The chief differences between Husserl's and Merleau-Ponty's accounts of perceptual knowledge can now be stated rather clearly. For Husserl, the ultimate foundation of knowledge is evidence. That is, perceptual knowledge is based ultimately on positing conscious episodes, whether passive or active, in which an object is presented in an originary manner to a conscious subject. Merleau-Ponty does not deny the existence of such acts, nor their importance in the generation of knowledge. Nor does he regard *them* as acts of faith. But they are founded on a general faith in the world that is maintained by our "anonymous," bodily attachment to and engagement in it. "If . . . every perception has something anonymous about it, this is because it takes up an acquisition that it does not question" (Merleau-Ponty 2012: 247). We enjoy an attachment to the world more fundamental than evidential acts of originary intuition, without which the latter could not so much as exist. And unlike Husserl, Merleau-Ponty does not think there is any possibility, even ideally, of bringing the world-horizon to explicit consciousness through progressive fulfillments—no way, that is, to transform perceptual faith into knowledge (see Merleau-Ponty 2012: 347).

How might "the skeptic" respond at this point? It's hard to image the skeptic being persuaded at all by this. In fact, the skeptic might say, there is reason to think that we have fallen into a form of skepticism that is the very antithesis of Husserl's ideal verificationism. Even if, the skeptic might argue, adequate evidence is not required for knowledge, knowledge must be founded *ultimately* on evidence or the consciousness thereof. Since "perceptual faith," on any understanding of it, is not evidence or the consciousness thereof, Merleau-Ponty's account cannot explain our possession of knowledge.

But this, I think, is a classic case of "high-altitude thinking" (Merleau-Ponty 1968: 91). Against it, and with the phenomenological description of perception that opened this section in mind, we may respond that it is monumentally more plausible to hold that what we acquire in our perceptual interaction with objects in the world is, at least some of the time, *knowledge*. At the very least, it is strongly rationally justified belief. It is undeniable that my epistemic situation changes radically when I move from merely thinking that a car is nearby to seeing one. If it should turn out that this experience constitutively depends on a sort of confidence in the world, in what is unseen, the proper conclusion to draw is that acts grounded in such a confidence *can* confer justification on my beliefs. More generally, if, instead of reasoning about what knowledge and rational engagement with the world *must* look like we instead describe what it *does* look like, by examining paradigmatic cases on whose basis we acquired the concepts of knowledge and rationality in the first place, we realize that it would be absurd to claim that someone who sees a car on a freeway is in a comparable epistemic situation as someone merely thinking about or imagining a car on a freeway. But phenomenological inquiry shows that both perceptual knowledge and perception itself are grounded in a more fundamental engagement with the world that Merleau-Ponty calls, perhaps not wholly advisedly, "perceptual faith." To adopt Husserlian terminology, we can think of perceptual faith as constituting a distinctive field, the field of the world.[52] To show up in that field is the necessary and sufficient condition for something to appear as real, quite independently of how adequately it is perceived. This explains why inadequate and surprising perceptual experiences manage to reveal the real, while highly adequate and coherent imaginative experiences reveal nothing real at all.

There is a great deal more to be said about perceptual faith. I have characterized it as a non-thetic "conviction of things not seen"—and ultimately of the world—which, among other things, makes perceptual acts and knowledge possible. I have not, however, discussed the "paradoxes" contained in our perceptual faith, the most notable being that "perception enters into the things and that it is formed this side of the body."[53] I am not entirely convinced there is much of a paradox there. James Mensch seems to me to resolve it rather neatly: "We are not in the world in the same way that the world is in us. The sense of our being within the world is spatial–temporal, while the sense of the world's being within us involves its being within our consciousness" (Mensch 2010: 455). But whatever paradoxes perceptual faith contains, it seems clear that we can say, without paradox, that perceptual knowledge is grounded in a conscious, non-thetic, embodied engagement with reality more fundamental than any positing act of intuition.

32.9 CONCLUSION

As different as Merleau-Ponty's position is from Husserl's in some respects, his observations do not threaten the heart of Husserl's position. They do not establish that there are possible objects that cannot be given to consciousness at all. Nor do they refute Husserl's contention that there is an essential correlation between consciousness and being. To be more precise, Merleau-Ponty's arguments do not cast any doubt on Husserl's contention that corresponding to every state of affairs is a true proposition. They do not undermine his view that every true proposition has a fulfilling sense. Nor do they even undermine his view that *each* of the intuitive contents contained in a true proposition's fulfilling sense is the possible content of a conscious experience. What his arguments cast doubt upon is that *all* of the contents contained in such a fulfilling sense—even if it were finite—could be the contents of a single subject's conscious experience. The first revision we are required to make, if Merleau-Ponty's arguments hold,

[52] As Orion Edgar puts it, "The unity of the world is grounded, then, in a sense, by what Merleau-Ponty calls . . . the perceptual faith" (Edgar 2016: 23).
[53] Merleau-Ponty 2012: 8. See Mensch 2010 for an excellent discussion.

is that originary intuition not only need not be adequate, but it need not even have adequacy as its ideal limit or aim. But that only requires us to modify, not abandon, ideal verificationism.

The second revision required of Husserl's view, if Merleau-Ponty is correct, is that perceptual knowledge is not *ultimately* founded on evidence, but perceptual faith. Once we understand perceptual faith as a sort of primal, non-propositional, non-thetic confidence in and inherence in the world, rather than a *belief* we hold for no good reasons—once, that is, we see perceptual faith as the kind of thing for which no reasons could be given, rather than something which could (and should) be backed up with reasons but isn't—we can recognize it as an ontological condition for the consciousness of evidence of any variety at all. Instead of an impediment to knowledge, it is, if Merleau-Ponty is right, its necessary condition.

REFERENCES

Benoist, J. (2003), "Husserl's theory of meaning in the First Logical Investigation," in D. O. Dahlstrom (ed.), *Husserl's Logical Investigations* (Boston: Kluwer), 17–35.

Berghofer, P. (2014), "Husserl and Current Analytic Epistemology: Chudnoff, Huemer, and Pryor on a Husserlian Approach to the Question of Justification," paper delivered at the Copenhagen Summer School in Phenomenology and Philosophy of Mind.

Berghofer, P. (2017), "Why Husserl Is a Moderate Foundationalist," *Husserl Studies* Online First. DOI 10.1007/s10743-017-9213-4.

Bernet, R. (2003), "Desiring to Know through Intuition," *Husserl Studies* 19: 153–66.

Cairns, D. (2013), *The Philosophy of Edmund Husserl*, ed. L. Embree (Dordrecht: Springer).

Carmen, T. (2008), *Merleau-Ponty* (New York: Routledge).

Crane, T. (2013), *The Objects of Thought* (Oxford: Oxford University Press).

Cronan, T. (2010), "Merleau-Ponty, Santayana and the Paradoxes of Animal Faith," *British Journal for the History of Philosophy* 18: 487–506.

Crowell, S. (2016), "What is it to think?" in T. Breyer and C. Gutland (eds), *Phenomenology of Thinking: Philosophical Investigations into the Character of Cognitive Experiences* (New York: Routledge), 183–206.

Dahlstrom, D. O. (2001), *Heidegger's Concept of Truth* (Cambridge: Cambridge University Press).

Dahlstrom, D. O. (2015), "Reason and experience: The project of a phenomenology of reason," in A. Staiti (ed.), *Commentary on Husserl's Ideas I* (Berlin: de Gruyter).

Davis, W. A. (2003), *Meaning, Expression, and Thought* (Cambridge: Cambridge University Press).

Dillon, M. C. (1997), *Merleau-Ponty's Ontology*, 2nd edition (Evanston, IL: Northwestern University Press).

Drummond, J. J. (1990), *Husserlian Intentionality and Non-Foundational Realism* (Dordrecht: Kluwer).

Edgar, O. (2016), *Things Seen and Unseen: The Logic of Incarnation in Merleau-Ponty's Metaphysics of Flesh* (Eugene, OR: Cascade Books).

Fasching, W. (2012), "Intentionality and Presence: On the Intrinsic Of-ness of Consciousness from a Transcendental-Phenomenological Perspective," *Husserl Studies* 28: 121–41.

Fine, K. (1994), "Essence and Modality," *Philosophical Perspectives* 8: 1–16.

Fine, K. (1995), "Ontological Dependence," *Proceedings of the Aristotelian Society* 95: 269–90.

Flynn, B. (2011), "Maurice Merleau-Ponty," *The Stanford Encyclopedia of Philosophy* (Fall 2011 Edition), E. N. Zalta (ed.), URL <http://plato.stanford.edu/archives/fall2011/entries/merleau-ponty/>.

Hardy, L. (2013), *Nature's Suit: Husserl's Phenomenological Philosophy of the Physical Sciences* (Athens, OH: Ohio University Press).

Heffernan, G. (1997), "An Essay in Epistemic Kuklophobia: Husserl's Critique of Descartes' Conception of Evidence," *Husserl Studies* 13: 89–140.

Heffernan, G. (1998), "Miscellaneous Lucubrations on Husserl's Answer to the Question 'was die Evidenz sei': A Contribution to the Phenomenology of Evidence on the Occasion of the Publication of *Husserliana Volume XXX*," *Husserl Studies* 15: 1–75.

Hopp, W. (2013), "The (many) foundations of knowledge," in D. Zahavi (ed.), *The Oxford Handbook of Contemporary Phenomenology* (Oxford: Oxford University Press), 327–48.

Husserl, E. (1969), *Formal and Transcendental Logic*, translated by D. Cairns (The Hague: Martinus Nijhoff).

Husserl, E. (1970), *Logical Investigations*, 2 vols, translated by J. N. Findlay (London: Routledge and Kegan Paul).

Husserl, E. (1980), *Phenomenology and the Foundations of the Sciences. Third Book. Ideas Pertaining to a Pure Phenomenology and to a Phenomenological Philosophy*, translated by T. E. Klein and W. E. Pohl (The Hague: Martinus Nijhoff).

Husserl, E. (1991), *On the Phenomenology of the Consciousness of Internal Time (1893–1917)*, translated by J. B. Brough (Dordrecht: Kluwer) .

Husserl, E. (1996), *Logik und Allgemeine Erkenntnistheorie 1917/18 mit Ergänzenden Texten aus der ersten Fassung von 1910/11*, Husserliana 30, ed. U. Panzer (Dordrecht: Kluwer).

Husserl, E. (1997), *Thing and Space*, translated by R. Rojcewicz (Boston: Kluwer).

Husserl, E. (1999), *Cartesian Meditations*, translated by D. Cairns (Dordrecht: Kluwer).

Husserl, E. (2001), *Analyses concerning Passive and Active Synthesis*, translated by A. J. Steinbock (Boston: Kluwer).

Husserl, E. (2003), *Transczendentaler Idealismus: Texte aus dem Nachlass (1908–1921)*, Husserliana 36, ed. R. Rollinger and R. Sowa (Dordrecht: Kluwer).

Husserl, E. (2005), *Phantasy, Image Consciousness, and Memory*, translated by J. Brough (Dordrecht: Springer).

Husserl, E. (2008), *Introduction to Logic and Theory of Knowledge: Lectures 1906/07*, translated by C. O. Hill (Dordrecht: Springer).

Husserl, E. (2014), *Ideas I: Ideas for a Pure Phenomenology and Phenomenological Philosophy*, translated by D. Dahlstrom (Indianapolis: Hackett).

James, W. (1995), *Pragmatism* (Toronto: Dover Publications).

Jansen, J. (2015), "Transcendental Philosophy and the Problem of Necessity in a Contingent World," *Metodo: International Studies in Phenomenology and Philosophy*, Special Issue 1: 47–80.

Kasmier, D. (2015), "Knowability and Willard's Reality Hook." Presented at the Conference in Honor of Dallas Willard, Boston University, November 2016.

Kelly, S. D. (2004), "Seeing things in Merleau-Ponty," in T. Carmen and M. B. N. Hansen (eds), *The Cambridge Companion to Merleau-Ponty* (Cambridge: Cambridge University Press), 74–110.

Khlentzos, D. (2011), "Challenges to Metaphysical Realism," *The Stanford Encyclopedia of Philosophy* (Spring 2011 Edition), ed. E. N. Zalta. URL <http://plato.stanford.edu/archives/spr2011/entries/realism-sem-challenge/>.

Meacham, D. (2010), "'Faith is in things not seen': Merleau-Ponty on faith, *virtù*, and the perception of style," in K. Semonovitch and N. DeRoo (eds), *Merleau-Ponty at the Limits of Art, Religion, and Perception* (New York: Continuum), 185–206.

Mensch, J. (2010), "The Temporality of Merleau-Ponty's Intertwining," *Continental Philosophy Review* 42: 449–63.

Merleau-Ponty, M. (1964), *Sense and Non-Sense*, ed. H. L. Dreyfus and P. A. Dreyfus (Evanston, IL: Northwestern University Press).

Merleau-Ponty, M. (1968), *The Visible and the Invisible*, ed. C. Lefort, translated by A. Lingis (Evanston, IL: Northwestern University Press).

Merleau-Ponty, M. (2012), *Phenomenology of Perception*, translated by D. A. Landes (New York: Routledge).

Noë, A. (2004), *Action in Perception* (Cambridge, MA: MIT Press).

Noë, A. (2012), *The Varieties of Presence* (Cambridge, MA: Harvard University Press).

Pietersma, H. (2000), *Phenomenological Epistemology* (Oxford: Oxford University Press).

Prior, A. N. (1971), *Objects of Thought*, ed. P. T. Geach and A. J. P. Kenny (Oxford: Clarendon Press).

Pryor, J. (2000), "The Skeptic and the Dogmatist," *Noûs* 34: 517–49.

Romdenh-Romluc, K. (2011), *Routledge Philosophy Guidebook to Merleau-Ponty and Phenomenology of Perception* (New York: Routledge).

Sacrini, M. (2013), "Merleau-Ponty's Reponses to Skepticism: A Critical Appraisal," *International Journal of Philosophical Studies* 21: 713–34.

Scheler, M. (1973), *Formalism in Ethics and Non-Formal Ethics of Values*, translated by M. S. Frings and R. L. Funk (Evanston, IL: Northwestern University Press).

Smith, A. D. (2003), *Routledge Philosophy Guidebook to Husserl and the Cartesian Meditations* (New York: Routledge).

Smith, A. D. (2008), "Husserl and Externalism," *Synthese* 160: 313–33.

Smith, D. W. (2004), *Mind World* (Cambridge: Cambridge University Press).

Smith, D. W. and McIntyre, R. (1982), *Husserl and Intentionality: A Study of Mind, Meaning, and Language* (Dordrecht: Reidel).

Sokolowski, R. (1964), *The Formation of Husserl's Concept of Constitution* (The Hague: Martinus Nijhoff).

Vinueza, A. (2001), "Realism and Mind Independence," *Pacific Philosophical Quarterly* 82: 51–70.

Willard, D. (1984), *Logic and the Objectivity of Knowledge* (Athens, OH: Ohio University Press).

Willard, D. (1995), "Knowledge," in B. Smith and D. W. Smith (eds), *The Cambridge Companion to Husserl* (Cambridge: Cambridge University Press), 138–67.

Willard, D. (2002), "The world well won: Husserl's epistemic realism one hundred years later," in D. Zahavi and F. Stjernfelt (eds), *One Hundred Years of Phenomenology* (Dordrecht: Kluwer), 69–78.

Willard, D. (2003), "The theory of wholes and parts and Husserl's explication of the possibility of knowledge in the *Logical Investigations*," in D. Fisette (ed.), *Husserl's* Logical Investigations *Reconsidered* (Boston: Kluwer), 163–82.

Yoshimi, J. (2015), "The Metaphysical Neutrality of Husserlian Phenomenology," *Husserl Studies* 31: 1–15.

Wiltsche, H. (2015), "Intuitions, Seemings, and Phenomenology." *teorema* 34: 57–77.

Zahavi, D. (2010), "Husserl and the 'Absolute,'" *Phaenomenologica* 200: 71–92.

CHAPTER 33

....

HUSSERL, HEIDEGGER, AND MERLEAU-PONTY ON THE WORLD OF EXPERIENCE

....

HANNE JACOBS

THE topic of world is central in phenomenology.[1] Specifically, phenomenology thematizes the world that we straightforwardly experience in everyday life and aims to bring this experience into the philosophical purview. As Merleau-Ponty puts it, phenomenology is "a philosophy for which the world is always 'already there' prior to reflection . . . and whose entire effort is to rediscover this naïve contact with the world in order to finally raise it to a philosophical status" (Merleau-Ponty 2012: lxx). But despite this shared focus on the world of experience, authors working in the phenomenological tradition make markedly different claims about the world and our experience of it. This chapter discusses a number of divergent claims about the world that can be found in the works of Husserl, Heidegger, and Merleau-Ponty and argues that some of Husserl's claims with which the later phenomenologists take issue are motivated by one of Husserl's central philosophical preoccupations.

There is much that Husserl, Heidegger, and Merleau-Ponty agree on when it comes to the thematic of world. All three conceive of the world as phenomenon—that is, the world that and as it is disclosed in experience—and maintain that this world is nothing other than the world itself.[2] Further, they all start from our experience of the world

[1] Ferrarin (2015a and b) has recently developed how the world is already prominent in Kant's work and how both Husserl and Heidegger overlook this due to their focus on the transcendental aesthetic and analytic rather than the dialectic. As he points out, the dialectic and the world as an idea are, however, discussed by Eugen Fink. Patočka (2016: 60–3) also discusses the Kantian notion of the world as regulative idea, while placing it in a broader historical context and contrasting it to the phenomenological treatment of world.

[2] Both Overgaard (2004) and Welton (2000) provide extensive accounts of the similarities and differences between Husserl's and Heidegger's notions of the world. The literature on Husserl and Merleau-Ponty is somewhat split in that some read Merleau-Ponty as critical of Husserl and others read

with the twofold aim of describing (1) the structure of the experience in which different kinds of worldly entities and the world are disclosed and (2) the structural features of different kinds of worldly entities and the world. In this way, Husserl, Heidegger, and Merleau-Ponty all take up and modify the transcendental project inaugurated by Kant, for whom the conditions of possibility of the experience of objects are conditions of possibility of the objects of experience. Signaling this continuity and break with Kant, they all use Kantian language when characterizing their own philosophical projects— specifically, as transcendental phenomenology (Husserl), fundamental ontology or existential analytic of Dasein (Heidegger), and a phenomenology of the transcendental field (Merleau-Ponty).[3]

In order to show how a shared focus on the world and important points of agreement is compatible with different philosophical concerns that inform some striking disagreements about the world, in what follows I focus on how the early Heidegger and Merleau-Ponty criticize Husserl's account of experience and world. Specifically, after providing the general outlines of Husserl's account of experience and world, I discuss how both Heidegger's and Merleau-Ponty's accounts of our experience of the world challenge Husserl's assertion of the possibility of a worldless consciousness in the first book of *Ideas for a Pure Phenomenology and Phenomenological Philosophy*; how Heidegger's discussion of the world entails a rejection of Husserl's claim that the world is at bottom nature; and how Merleau-Ponty's brief remarks on fact and essence in *Phenomenology of Perception* put pressure on Husserl's account of the necessary structure of the world. In concluding, and as a propaedeutic to adjudicating these disputes, I aim to show why Husserl makes these contested claims. Specifically, I suggest that it is Husserl's commitment to accounting for the phenomenon of reason—that is, the first-person awareness of the difference between veridical and non-veridical experiences— that motivates him to make the claims about our experience and world with which the later phenomenologists take issue.[4]

his phenomenology as a continuation of Husserl's—especially the so-called later Husserl. The latter approach is taken by Barbaras (1998: 81–94, 124–5), Heinämaa (2002 and 2015), Smith (2004), and Zahavi (2002). Toadvine (2002) provides a very helpful chronological overview of Merleau-Ponty's engagement with Husserl's thought.

[3] There are number of recent edited volumes that focus on the ways in which phenomenology inherits and transforms Kant's transcendental project. See Crowell and Malpas (2007); Gardner and Grist (2015); and Hartimo, Heinämaa, and Miettinen (2015). Jansen (2014 and 2015), Kern (1964), Nenon (2008), and Zahavi (2015) all focus on the similarities and differences between Kant and Husserl. A discussion of the relation between Kant and Heidegger is provided by, for example, Han-Pile (2005). The relation between Kant and Merleau-Ponty is the focus of, for example, Gardner (2007) and Matherne (2016).

[4] This is just one way of characterizing the source of the disagreement between these phenomenologists. Bernet (1990) and Moran (2000) focus on the way in which Heidegger radicalizes the problematic of intentionality, and elsewhere Bernet (1988) treats the relation between Husserl and Heidegger from the perspective of the problematic of time. Crowell (2013: 64–77) focuses on the differences in subject matter and method between Husserl and Heidegger and points to Husserl's rationalism as a matter of contention (2013: 68–9). Overgaard (2004: 2) emphasizes their "differences concerning the interpretation of intra-mundane entities," which is something I consider later in this chapter. And, finally, Tugendhat (1967) focuses on how Husserl and Heidegger differ when it comes

33.1 Husserl on the Experience of the World

Husserl brings the world as phenomenon (the world that and how it is experienced) into view by means of the often-discussed method of epoché or bracketing. The phenomenological method of bracketing consists in putting out of play the validity of any scientific, philosophical, or everyday convictions about the world and ourselves within it. The first step in the bracketing, which Husserl sometimes calls the "life-world epoché" (Husserl 1970: 137), specifically consists in bracketing scientific convictions about the world. Bracketing these kinds of theories, Husserl argues that it is the world itself that appears in perception and that it is this world that is investigated and understood by natural science (e.g., Husserl 1970: 48–53, 127–32; 2012: 262–3; 2014: 94–9). In doing so, he challenges the view that the world that appears to us in everyday life is different from the "real world" that causally brings about a representation in us of this world.[5]

The aim of the method of bracketing, however, is not just to bring the world that we experience in everyday life into view; rather, it is to make possible the development of a descriptive science that Husserl calls pure phenomenology. Pure phenomenology describes the necessary structure of our experience of the world, and, as a theory of constitution, it describes *how* a world can appear in these experiences. While in our everyday life we are always already aware of the world (Husserl 1970: 144), according to Husserl, an additional methodological step is required in order to arrive at the point of view from which we can provide a phenomenological account of how this experience is possible. Concretely, after bracketing our everyday beliefs concerning the world that we experience, we are to subsequently engage in what Husserl calls a reduction from this world back to our experience of this world (Husserl 1970: 148–52) to describe how structural features of consciousness such as time-consciousness, kinesthetic awareness, association, recollection, and the awareness of others make possible the appearance of an abiding world to consciousness. What is more, this phenomenology of constitution is in turn a prelude to a phenomenology of reason, or a theory of rational constitution, which uses the phenomenological descriptions of the structure of experience as the basis for an account of the distinction between veridical and non-veridical experiences

---

to the issue of truth and the idea of critical self-responsibility. On the relation between Husserl and Merleau-Ponty, Barbaras discusses the critique of Husserl's objectivism in Merleau-Ponty's work (1998: 63–79). Smith (2007: 16–20) argues that despite pervasive agreement, Merleau-Ponty conceives of the body as an existential unity, which he diagnoses as being at the root of a number of differences.

[5] I have addressed Husserl's arguments against the distinction between the phenomenal world and the world in itself as presented in the first book of *Ideas* elsewhere (Jacobs 2015). Jansen (2014) has provided an account of Husserl's non-representationalism in relation to Kant. Patočka (2016: 6–19) places the problem of unity of the world—that is, of the natural or lifeworld and the world of science—in an even broader historical perspective.

(e.g., Husserl 1960: 56–7)—a distinction without which one cannot claim to have an experience of a mind-independent, actual (*wirkliche*) world.

Husserl's phenomenological account of how we can experience an actual world begins with an account of perception and how this perception can be veridical or not. He starts with perception and not judgment, because in his view a predicative judgment that is directed at a state of affairs spontaneously determines something that is always already available or received in perceptual experience, which is a pre-predicative experience (e.g., Husserl 1973: 87–91).[6] Further, according to Husserl our concrete perceptions are never just of things with natural properties but always of things that are afforded with evaluative and practical significance, and this evaluative and practical dimension of perception can likewise be veridical or not (e.g., Husserl 2014: 231–4).[7]

According to Husserl, our perceptual experiences are, like all other intentional acts (e.g., judgments, but also emotions and volitions), *takings* (*Stellungnahmen*), which means that they posit (*setzen*) the world being a certain way. Specifically, perceptions always afford something with a certain sense (*Sinn*), where "sense" refers to how something is intended (i.e., *as* this or that) (e.g., Husserl 2014: 173–80, 255–8), and this sense can, but need not, be propositionally articulated (e.g., Husserl 2014: 246).[8] Perceptions, insofar as they posit something and, hence, make a claim (i.e., that something is indeed how one takes it to be), can bear out (*ausweisen*) or not. A positing bears out when something manifests itself (*sich gibt*) in person or in the flesh (*leibhaft*) as being how one takes it to be.

Husserl's introduction of the notion of sense, however, immediately raises a question concerning the origin of sense. That is, what makes it possible that a world can appear to us with a certain sense in perceptual experience? Husserl's talk of "sense bestowal" (*Sinngebung*) (e.g., Husserl 1960: 106; 2014: 102, 174) might seem to suggest that he considers sense to be something actively imposed by a subject on an otherwise unorganized or meaningless manifold of sensuous impressions—hence making possible the experience of something *as* something.[9] However, as his soon-to-be published *Studien zur Struktur des Bewusstseins* show, as early as the time of the first book of *Ideas*, Husserl develops an account of how the perceptual field at any moment is already structured by a passively functioning form of association, which is presupposed for any attentive awareness of worldly things and their subsequent predicative articulation (Husserl

[6] Staiti (in this volume) elaborates pre-predicative intentionality and its relation to predicative judgment in Husserl's *Experience and Judgment*. Pradelle (2013: 366–7) describes in reverse order the way in which predicative judgment is founded on perception.

[7] Space does not permit me to further elaborate on Husserl's account of the emotions and volitions here. Drummond (2004 and 2013) and Rinofner-Kreidl (2013) provide compelling renderings of Husserl's account of the emotions. Rinofner-Kreidl (2015) and Drummond (this volume) provide an account of Husserl on reason in the cognitive, evaluative, and practical spheres.

[8] Drummond (2003) focuses on perception and categorial articulation. Moran (in this volume) introduces Husserl's distinction of the positing (or quality) and sense (or matter) of intentional acts.

[9] This is also suggested by Husserl's talk in *Logical Investigations* and other works that sensations or *hyle* are "apprehended" (*aufgefasst*). Moran (in this volume) discusses this further.

2001a: 174–221; 1973, 72–6). Further, Husserl also provides analyses of how one's present experience associatively awakens past experiences (Husserl 1973, 121–4; 2001a: 221–42) and what one has appropriated from others through language, which further accounts for how we can experience something as a certain type of thing and ultimately how we can experience a socio-historical world.[10] It is primarily because sense is afforded in passivity in these ways that it is misguided to understand *Sinngebung* as an active bestowal of sense.[11]

33.2 HUSSERL'S PHENOMENOLOGICAL ONTOLOGY OF THE WORLD

While Husserl's phenomenological description of the structures of our experience aims to account for how we can experience an actual world, he regularly declares that he also aims to develop ontologies of different kinds of worldly entities and the world itself from the point of view of his phenomenology—where this ontology would be a science of the necessary structure or essential features of different kinds of objects we experience as well as the world that is experienced. Differently stated, Husserl does not only want to provide an account of the structure of our experience of the world; he also wants to provide an account of the structure of the world of experience from the point of view of his phenomenology. As he writes: "As developed systematically and fully, transcendental phenomenology would be *ipso facto* the true and *genuine universal ontology*" (Husserl 1960: 155). And he claims that phenomenology and ontology taken together constitute the core of a *phenomenological* metaphysics, which, by providing the epistemological and ontological complement to the empirical sciences of the world, would provide a comprehensive account of this world (e.g., Husserl 1959: 367–9; 1960: 155; 2008b, 97–9, 137). That is, Husserl is of the conviction that "genuine philosophy, the idea of which is to realize the idea of absolute knowledge, is rooted in pure phenomenology" (Husserl 2014: 7).

However, and for a number of reasons, it is not immediately clear how Husserl's phenomenology could also be ontology, or how a philosophy, including ontology, could be rooted in his phenomenology. First, the idea that the development of ontology requires that we take up the phenomenological perspective might seem to be contradicted by Husserl's own explicit bracketing of all ontological considerations under the epoché

---

[10] I have discussed the way in which our current experience of the world is shaped by our socio-historical context in more detail elsewhere (Jacobs 2016a and 2016b).

[11] Hence, Dahlstrom's translation of *Sinngebung* as "affordance of sense" (Husserl 2014) is preferable to "sense bestowal." Husserl does acknowledge a specific form of activity at work in how something appears in perception insofar as we take what appears to be actual—which is an activity he calls *receptivity* to differentiate it from the passivity that characterizes the affordance of sense and the spontaneity of predicative judgment. I have developed this more fully elsewhere (Jacobs 2016a).

(Husserl 2014: 109–11). Second, the seeming contingency of association with which Husserl accounts for the genesis of sense in his account of how an experience of the world is possible might seem to pose a problem for the development of an ontology of this world, which, on Husserl's own terms, would describe not the contingent but rather the necessary structures of things and the world. Third, even if we can make sense of such an ontology of the world of experience, Husserl himself on other occasions clearly states that ontology (the science that spells out those features without which certain entities would not be what they are) is to be distinguished from phenomenology (which describes our experience of different kinds of entities) (e.g., Husserl 1980: 65–79; 2008a: 283, 692; 2008b: 428–31, 425; 2014: 308). And fourth, that phenomenology and ontology are different scientific enterprises and that we do not need phenomenology to do ontology is further suggested by the fact that a number of ontological disciplines were readily available, according to Husserl, before the development of pure phenomenology (e.g., formal ontologies such as number theory and material ontologies such as geometry).

Nevertheless, how ontology could in Husserl's view fall within the purview of phenomenology might become clearer if one recalls that for Husserl worldly objects are in principle accessible to veridical experiences of these objects (e.g., Husserl 1960: 83–8; 1970: 165–7; 2006: 54; 2014: 96). More broadly stated, the world is phenomenal for Husserl—not in the sense of being *merely* phenomenal but in the sense of being in principle accessible to consciousness. For this reason, any ontology of this world cannot but be articulated from within our experience of the world, and ontology is always a phenomenological ontology or an ontology of the world of experience (and in this sense different from the ontologies that were the target of Kant's critique). Thus, even if the development of phenomenology requires an initial bracketing of ontological considerations, phenomenology and ontology are correlative sciences in the sense that the first describes our experience of the world of which the second spells out the necessary structure. What this also means is that the necessary structures of consciousness will correlate to the necessary structures of the world that discloses itself to consciousness. So, concretely, Husserl's phenomenology of time-consciousness and kinesthetic experience describe how an abiding world can manifest itself to consciousness, and this world that is in principle accessible to a spatiotemporal experience of it is necessarily spatiotemporal (2014: 299).

This, however, leads to the second aforementioned concern: Husserl, in addition to time-consciousness and kinesthetic experience, also calls on association to account for how a world of different kinds of abiding individual entities (e.g., things, organisms, and artworks) discloses itself to us. But the very nature of association—a seemingly empirical mechanism of contingently pairing like with like—seems to be in tension with Husserl's ontological ambitions. That is, even if Husserl's ontology is an ontology of the world of experience, this ontology is not just a description of the actual world that appears but a description of the necessary structures without which a world and specific kinds of objects within it would not be what they are. In other words, for Husserl, ontology is a science of the pure essence of the world and different kinds of entities (Husserl

2014: 20–2). But this claim that the world of experience has necessary structures beyond time and space might seem to be in tension with Husserl having association play the leading role in his account of how a structured world of different kinds of abiding entities appears in experience. To understand how Husserl's claim that it is association that accounts for how a world appears in perception is compatible with his claim that there are necessary features of the world of experience, it is important to note that, in Husserl's view, association is grounded in the specificity of what appears, and this specificity allows us to understand how Husserl can claim that certain ways that the world appears are necessary.

Consider, for example, the organization of the perceptual field at a given moment. Husserl points out that in order for something in my present perceptual field to inductively associate with something that I have previously experienced, and in this way to appear as such and such, the perceptual field must already have some structure (Husserl 2001a: 166, 505). According to Husserl this structure is made possible by a more original form of association by similarity (*Ähnlichkeit*) within the present (Husserl 2001a: 175, 199, 510). Specifically, he asserts that it is due to fusion (*Verschmelzung*) and saliency (due to *Kontrast, Abhebung*, and *Sonderung*) that something in the field of perception can stand out in the first place and associate with something I have experienced in the past. The possibility of fusion and saliency is in turn grounded in the specific characteristics of what appears (e.g., the specific color of what appears allows for something to stand out against a background) (Husserl 2001a: 192, 108–9, 497–8). Now, while the specific features with which something within my perceptual field appears are contingent (e.g., this color rather than another color appears), what appears at the same time also has necessary features (e.g., something extended that appears in my field of perception necessarily appears as colored) (Husserl 2001a: 236–7; 2012: 155).[12]

More generally, Husserl identifies an "ontological a priori" (Husserl 2008a: 491), a "concrete logic" (Husserl 2012: 333), "an a priori style" (Husserl 2001c: 118), and an "a priori" of the lifeworld (Husserl 1960: 140). Correspondingly, the ontology of worldly objects and the world is a material ontology that formulates synthetic or material apriori laws (Husserl 1973: 339–40, 352–4; 1980: 29–32; 2001b: 19–22; 2014: 31–2).[13] On the one hand, the material a priori is different from the logical or formal a priori, which applies to anything whatsoever (Husserl 2001c: 103–12, 120; 2012: 42–3, 101). The formal a priori is delimited by the structure of (empty) thought (Husserl 2008b: 290, 327) and, hence, does not in itself require a consideration of the world of experience even though an inquiry into how thought arises from perception would. On the other hand, the

---

[12] Jansen (2015) provides a detailed discussion of Husserl's account of the necessary order of what appears in contrast to Kant.

[13] Benoist (1995), Drummond (1995), De Palma (2014 and 2015), and Tugendhat (1967: 163–5) discuss Husserl's notion of material a priori in more detail.

ontology of the lifeworld is also different from the material ontological sciences of the world scientifically understood that are historically available to us (e.g., geometry). Unlike geometry, the ontology of the life-world does not describe exact or mathematical essences; it describes inexact essences (Husserl 1970: 25, 139–40) and proceeds from the world of experience instead of idealizations of this world like geometry does (Husserl 1960: 24–8).[14]

Thus far I have elaborated how, for Husserl, an ontology of the world can be developed from within the experience that is described in phenomenology. However, for Husserl, the phenomenological description of our experience of the world also more positively contributes to the development of ontology. There are at least two reasons why Husserl believes that the phenomenological perspective is not just a correlate to but also a prerequisite for the development of an ontology of the world of experience. First, as I started out discussing, for Husserl the first step of the so-called epoché is to bracket our scientific understanding of reality and in this way to bring into view the world of everyday life. By bracketing our natural-scientific understanding of the world and bringing the world of experience into view, Husserl puts himself into a position to correct a certain ontological myopia that exclusively focuses on material nature (and a specific natural-scientific understanding of it at that). Indeed, the world as we experience it in everyday life is not just an extended nature but a world in which we encounter and interact with objects and individuals with evaluative and practical significance.[15] Second, Husserl believes that his phenomenological descriptions of our experience of the world of everyday life in all its concreteness can also contribute to the development of previously overlooked a priori sciences—specifically, those sciences that spell out the structure of minds and societies, hence providing psychology and the so-called human sciences with insights into their basic concepts and ontological commitments concerning the kind of object they are dealing with (Husserl 2014: 304–5). This shows that a phenomenological description of our experience of the world does indeed have bearing on questions concerning the structure of worldly entities, which is an idea that is taken up and elaborated differently in Heidegger's early writings that culminate in the publication of *Being and Time*, a work that critically targets Husserl's transcendental phenomenology, or descriptive science of our conscious experience of worldly objects and the world, and the correlated phenomenological ontology, or science of the structure of worldly objects and the world.[16]

---

[14] Sowa (2010) provides a detailed reconstruction of Husserl's ontology of the life-world.

[15] See Staiti's chapter in this volume for a more elaborate discussion of Husserl's account of the life-world.

[16] Overgaard (2004: 61–2; 68; 74–7; 79–82; 90–5; 100–3; 205–6), McManus (2012: 11–37), and Zahavi (2003: 43–66) further elaborate on the relation between phenomenology and ontology in Heidegger and/or Husserl.

33.3 HEIDEGGER AND HUSSERL
ON EXPERIENCE AND WORLD

Husserl's focus is on how a world appears for consciousness, and, insofar as it is the structures of this consciousness that make possible the appearance of a world, this consciousness can be characterized as transcendental consciousness. Further, as was discussed in section 33.2, the world that is disclosed by consciousness comes with its own structure that is described in a phenomenological ontology. Even though on Husserl's account transcendental consciousness is temporal, embodied, personal, and socio-historically embedded, and even though Husserl provides the outlines of an elaborate phenomenological ontology of a spatiotemporal socio-historical world, Heidegger objects in his early work that Husserl never sufficiently addressed the question of the being of this consciousness or the being of the world (e.g., Heidegger 1962: 150–3; 1985: 102–16).[17] Heidegger's analytic of Dasein, or his fundamental ontology, can be understood as redressing this supposed lack.[18] Specifically, Heidegger's fundamental ontology provides an account of the being that experiences the world by way of a description of the structures of Dasein (i.e., the so-called *existentialia*). In providing this account, Heidegger also aims to correct a general misconception of the world and its structure as a spatiotemporal causal nature in the history of modern philosophy up to Husserl.[19] And it is from this vantage point of an account of the structures of Dasein and world that Heidegger comes to criticize Husserl's account of both the subject that experiences the world and the structure of the world that is experienced in everyday life.

At least two of Heidegger's characterizations of Dasein can be understood as entailing criticisms of Husserl's account of consciousness and world. First, Heidegger defines Dasein as being-in-the-world (*In-der-Welt-Sein*) (Heidegger 1962: 78–90; 1985: 157–60), and, second, he contends that the fundamental mode of disclosing the world should be characterized in terms of the structure of care (*Sorge*) (Heidegger 1962: 235–44; 1985: 292–303). These claims pertaining to the kind of being that discloses a world respectively challenge Husserl's characterization of a consciousness that would conceivably not disclose a world in the first book of *Ideas* and his claim that the world of experience is at bottom nature.

Specifically, Heidegger's claim that Dasein is being-in-the-world means that it belongs to the being of Dasein to disclose a world (Heidegger 1985: 213–14), which is also why Heidegger speaks of a correlation (Heidegger 1985: 221) or "peculiar union

---

[17] I have discussed the embodied, personal, and socio-historical character of consciousness elsewhere (Jacobs 2015, 2016a, and 2016b). See, for example, Crowell (2013: 31–57), for an elaboration of a critique of Husserl from a Heideggerian perspective.

[18] Taminiaux (1991: 1–54) traces the transformation of Husserl's transcendental phenomenology of consciousness into a fundamental ontology of Dasein.

[19] There is an ongoing and complex debate in the Heidegger scholarship concerning the status of Heidegger's claims about the ontological constitution of beings. See Han-Pile (2005) for an overview.

(*Verklammerung*) of the being of the world with the being of Dasein" (Heidegger 1985: 202; see also 1962: 78, 247). Heidegger's characterization of Dasein as being-in-the-world can hence be read as directly challenging Husserl's infamous claim in section 49 of the first book of *Ideas* that, while the world is in principle accessible to consciousness, or in principle a correlate of an experience of this world, consciousness itself is not necessarily an experience of an actual world (Husserl 2014: 88–9). Instead, Husserl concedes the possibility of a consciousness for which no actual world appears—that is, for which the world is annihilated (*vernichtet*), which Husserl at times glosses as the imagined case in which we are confronted with an unorganized chaos of appearances (Husserl 1959: 48, 55, 64–7; Husserl 2008a: 227–8).

One of the things that the thought experiment of the annihilation of the world can be taken to show is that the experience of an actual world in perception amounts to more than the presence of sense-impressions or mere appearances. For a world to appear, the appearances must unfold following a regulated order (Husserl 2014: 88–9). So, for example, my kinesthetic movements would have to, in a reliable and regulated manner, be accompanied by changes in the visual field for me to experience something like an abiding spatiotemporal thing at rest. And it is these kinds of regularities that Husserl asks us to imaginatively vary in section 49, regularities that a phenomenology of our experience of the world would in turn describe. As such, the thought experiment of the annihilation of the world fits into the broader project of accounting for how a world can manifest itself in experience—which is a project that Husserl and Heidegger share. Nevertheless, Husserl's thought experiment and his characterization of the relation between consciousness and world do indeed appear problematic in a number of respects, one of which is in line with Heidegger's critique.

First, if anything, the thought experiment seems to describe a case of mental disintegration or death, or at least it appears to be indistinguishable from such cases in which even though my experience of the world has changed the world itself has remained unchanged—hence not warranting the conclusion of a worldless consciousness. At the same time, however, Husserl is adamant that what we are asked to imagine is nothing like a mental disintegration or death (Husserl 1959: 51–64; 2008a: 228; 2012: 358). Mental disintegration and death are worldly events. When considering consciousness as a worldly event, we usually consider our conscious experience to be causally brought about within the world (Husserl 2014: 94). In Husserl's view, however, this is a characterization of the relation between consciousness and world that, while perhaps empirically valid, already presupposes the validity of our positing an actual world that is intersubjectively accessible. To account for how such positing is possible and for how it can be valid, however, a transcendental approach is called for. And it is from this transcendental point of view that the thought experiment of the annihilation of the world is to be understood. Specifically, what the thought experiment asks us to imagine is a scenario in which our experience is such that the conditions for an actual world to appear do not obtain. Insofar as Heidegger himself rejects an account of Dasein as something in the world like an object is in the world (Heidegger 1962: 79; 1985: 257–8) and provides an account of how a world and worldly entities can be disclosed to Dasein, it seems that he would be in general agreement with Husserl on the distinction between an empirical and transcendental account of experience.

Another concern that one might have with the thought experiment of the annihilation of the world is that it appears to be in conflict with one of Husserl's own insights—that is, with the very idea of the aforementioned material a priori. For, if, for example, an appearing color is necessarily extended, the very idea of an *entirely* unorganized chaos of appearances would seem to be not even imaginable.[20] Further, Husserl's introduction of the conceivability of an annihilation would also seem to lend credence to understanding *Sinngebung* as an organizing activity that can be present (in the case of the awareness of a structured world) or absent (in the case of an annihilation of the world). However, this suggestion of an active sense-bestowal can be resisted if one addresses the apparent inconsistency by pointing out that one can still imagine a field of appearance that is structured but that nevertheless does not allow for our anticipations pertaining to the actual world to bear out. And this is indeed what Husserl seems to have in mind with his thought experiment, which asks us to imagine a case in which "rough formations of unity would still come to be constituted to some extent—fleeting stopovers from intuitions that would be mere analogues of intuitions of a thing, since such analogues are entirely incapable of constituting sustained 'realities,' enduring unities that 'exist in themselves, whether they are perceived or not'" (Husserl 2014: 88). That is, section 49 of the first book of *Ideas* is concerned with the existence of an actual world and with how its existence is not necessary (even if what appears happens to abide by some material a priori laws) (see also Husserl 1959: 48). And for our experience to be of an existing world, it is not enough that the field of perception appears with *some* order and regularity; it must also display the kind of order that allows us to identify and re-identify spatiotemporally enduring objects. However, understanding the thought experiment of the annihilation of the world in this way leads to another source of concern that also leads to what Heidegger is getting at with his characterization of the world.

By characterizing a situation in which no abiding objects appear as an annihilation of the *world*, Husserl appears to conflate worldly objects with the world, which is a distinction that Heidegger could not be clearer on (Heidegger 1962: 102, 246–7; 1985: 190). That is, while we might be able to imagine how our experience would fail to sustain a positing of abiding things, things whose existence would thus be nullified, it seems to make little sense to state that the world could be nullified in this way, since the world is not an object that I posit in experience in the first place. The idea that Husserl falls prey to confusing the world for a worldly object is further suggested by the way he characterizes the method of epoché. Specifically, Husserl characterizes the epoché or bracketing in terms of an inhibition of what he calls the general thesis of the world—a thesis or positing of the world as actual or existing (*wirklich*)—that undergirds all our other takings and commitments (Husserl 2014: 52–58). However, to characterize our belief in the actuality

---

[20] Majolino (2010 and 2016) discusses the limits of a variation of the world in more detail in the context of an interpretation of section 49 of the first book of *Ideas*.

of the world in this way is to suggest that this belief is on a par with the belief that is operative in our perception of or judgment concerning individual worldly objects.

Elsewhere, Husserl does, however, clearly differentiate between our experience of the world and of worldly objects respectively: Worldly things are disclosed as things within the horizon of the world, the experience of which is different in kind according to Husserl from the experience of a worldly thing (e.g., Husserl 1970: 143). Further, as Husserl at times states, while my experience of worldly objects is in principle fallible, our experience of a world is not. Specifically, as Husserl points out, while my perceptual anticipations pertaining to a worldly entity can be disappointed, such disappointment is inconceivable with regard to the world since this disappointment is only possible because of our horizonal anticipations of what more there is to be seen. Insofar as the world *is* this horizon of what more there is to be seen, however, this kind of disappointment is inconceivable with regard to the world itself (Husserl 2008a: 236, 256).[21] This way of characterizing the difference between our experience of things and our experience of the world also excludes the possibility of the illusion of a world (Husserl 2008a: 728, 730)—which would be an appearing world that is not actual but merely *appears* to be a world—because to speak of illusion only makes sense with regard to a worldly entity when our perception unfolds and shows that it is different than we took it to be.

In addition, Husserl's descriptions of the intentional implications or horizons (Husserl 1960: 46–9) that inform the sense with which something at present appears to us further indicate that Husserl does not conflate our consciousness of the world with the consciousness of an object.[22] And this account of the horizon is congenial to Heidegger's claim that the worldliness of the world demands its own analysis, apart from the account of the entities we deal with in our daily interactions, which are ready to hand (*zuhanden*) and on rare occasions become present at hand or occurrent (*vorhanden*) in attentive scrutiny (Heidegger 1962: 101).[23] That is, for Heidegger the worldliness of the world resides in the referential totality (*Verweisungsganzheit*) that makes possible that things are afforded *as* something, or with a sense (*Sinn*) (e.g., *as* a certain kind of tool) (Heidegger 1962: 189–92). More concretely, something can show up as something (e.g., as a pen) only in light of that for which (*wofür*) or to what end (*wozu*) it is used (e.g., writing) (Heidegger 1962: 97–8, 114–15; 1985: 187). Similarly, for Husserl, it is the temporal horizon of past and future as well as the inner horizon (including determinations and dimensions of the object of which I am aware but which are currently not visible) and outer horizon (including everything surrounding what I am attentively aware of and everything that falls outside my perceptual field of which I nevertheless have a

---

[21] Patočka (2016: 63–71) describes the horizon further in the context of a discussion of the phenomenological concept of world in a way that draws on elements in both Husserl's and Heidegger's analyses.

[22] Landgrebe (1963: 44–5) pointed this out.

[23] Overgaard (2004: 109–30) and Welton (2000: 347–70) both provide detailed analyses of the overlap between Husserl's descriptions of the horizon and Heidegger's account of the world.

background awareness) that determines the sense with which something is afforded in perception—the horizon that he denotes as world (Husserl 1960: 158; 2008a: 78, 129).

What Husserl's recognition of the difference of our experience of worldly things and our experience of the world means for his thought experiment of the annihilation of the world is at least that the term *Weltvernichtung* is a misnomer. Indeed, the thought experiment is about imagining a case in which the course of my experience does not warrant me positing abiding actual *things*. However, as I mentioned, this is compatible with some order in the course of experience. And for as long as some order obtains, it seems conceivable that this experience would be accompanied by horizonal anticipations—even if these anticipations would repeatedly be disappointed and the experience would, hence, not be one of actual things. In that sense, then, we would not be dealing with an annihilation of the world.

But even if we can, to some extent, neutralize the concerns that section 49 of *Ideas* raises, and if we can discern parallels between the horizon discussed by Husserl and the referential totality described by Heidegger, Heidegger's conception of world is in an important sense still different from Husserl's. That is, as commentators have not failed to point out, Heidegger's characterization of the being of Dasein as care entails a further critique of Husserl's characterization of our consciousness of the world and, importantly, of the ontological structure of the world of our everyday experience, which Husserl considers to be at bottom nature.

Heidegger considers our basic openness to the world to have the structure of care (*Sorge*). Among other things, this means that Dasein's disclosing (*erschliessen*) of something *as* something (e.g., as a pen for writing) is due to Dasein's projecting (*entwerfen*) itself into the future (e.g., as a writer), which is the for the sake of which (*Worumwillen*) of Dasein (e.g., Heidegger 1962: 182–6, 370–5, 415–16). Or, as Heidegger more generally puts it, it is our own being that is at stake in our being in the world and that is the condition of possibility of the disclosure of a world (1962: 116, 236). This means that for Heidegger the disclosure of things in a meaningful surrounding world is what he calls a founded presence. That is, "it is not something original but grounded in the presence of that which is placed under care" (Heidegger 1985: 195; see also 1962: 236). Thus, what accounts for how something can appear as something in our everyday dealings is in Heidegger's view the way we project ourselves into the future. Importantly, Heidegger immediately adds: "If this handily nearest, the handy in concern, is already a founded presence, then this applies even more so to the character of reality which we learned about earlier and which Husserl claims to be the authentic presence of the world" (Heidegger 1985: 195). That is, we can only look at something as a natural entity, and we rarely do so, because we have always already encountered it in the context of our practical activities. What Heidegger targets here and elsewhere is Husserl's view that the world is at bottom nature (Heidegger 1962: 130–1, 189–91).[24]

---

[24] Overgaard (2004: 173–83) provides a nuanced and compelling account of this critique.

Husserl thinks that the world is at bottom nature because in his view all so-called predicates of significance (*Bedeutungsprädikate*) are founded on sense (*Sinn*) (e.g., Husserl 2008a: 327, 341, 427), which in turn is accounted for by means of the afore-mentioned forms of passivity (time-consciousness and association). More concretely, according to Husserl, something can be afforded as valuable, useful, or worthwhile be-cause it is experienced with natural properties (even if only non-thematically) in virtue of which it is in turn afforded as valuable, useful, or worthwhile (e.g., Husserl 2008a: 33, 288, 291, 297; 2014: 231–4).[25] So, for example, depending on the kind of project I am en-gaged in, something can indeed afford itself as a tool for hammering or as something that has an archeological value, but not just anything can be taken in this way (e.g., a curtain or an apple respectively). That evaluative and practical properties are founded on natural properties, however, does not mean that we start out with a cognitive per-ception of these natural properties to then in turn appraise and want on the basis of this cognitive perception (e.g., Husserl 2008a: 326, 523). For, according to Husserl, to focus on nature and natural properties within the world of everyday life is always an abstrac-tion (e.g., Husserl 2008a: 264, 517, 698), and perception always already entails cognitive, emotive, and practical dimensions (Husserl 2008a: 273, 314–15) due to the way in which the past shapes how we experience something in the future.

Heidegger acknowledges that what we are practically dealing with indeed has certain natural properties (Heidegger 1962: 100; 1985: 193). However, he resists Husserl's charac-terization of the foundation of practical significance on natural properties (Heidegger 1962: 100–1, 131–2; 245–6; 1985: 198–9).[26] And this disagreement between Husserl and Heidegger ultimately comes down to a quite fundamental difference in the way they think about the ontological structure of the world. For Husserl, the world of everyday life is at bottom a world of things (e.g., Husserl 1973: 132–40), and it is only because the world is a world of things that they can be taken up in a project that affords them with a practical significance in relation to other things. Heidegger, on the contrary, seems to consider the world to be fundamentally relational, where these relations constitute things in their being such and so (Heidegger 1962: 121–2, 254–5; 1985: 186–90, 200).[27]

As I will elaborate in the conclusion to this chapter, both Husserl's thought experi-ment of the annihilation of the world and his insistence that the world is at bottom na-ture can be further understood in light of his specific and lasting concern with reason or rationality. Before doing so, however, I would like to point to an additional critical

---

[25] Drummond (in this volume) discusses this in more detail.

[26] It would take me too far afield to elaborate on the intricacies of Heidegger's own account of the relation between what he calls entities that are ready-to-hand (*zuhanden*) and those that are present-to-hand (*vorhanden*). McManus (2012) provides a book-length treatment of the issue.

[27] Pointing to the constitutive role of the horizon in Husserl's account of the constitution of objects does not change this. That is, even if my past experiences shape my perception of the practical significance of something (e.g., as a spoon for eating), this significance is founded on this object being afforded with certain natural properties that allow for this object to be taken as having a practical significance in the first place.

concern that Merleau-Ponty formulates, albeit not entirely unambiguously, concerning Husserl's account of the world of experience.

33.4 MERLEAU-PONTY AND HUSSERL ON EXPERIENCE AND WORLD

In his early work *Phenomenology of Perception*, Merleau-Ponty seems to depart from Husserl's methodological starting point in his treatment of our experience of the world as well as his characterization of the world of experience. Right at the outset of this work, Merleau-Ponty claims that there is no such thing as a complete reduction (Merleau-Ponty 2012: lxxvii). The idea of a complete reduction presupposes that everything that appears can be traced back to a constituting consciousness that is transparent to itself and, hence, fully accessible to reflection (Merleau-Ponty 2012: lxxiv, 64). Merleau-Ponty, on the contrary claims that the reduction always remains incomplete, because in his view the subject that perceives a world is a body subject, and according to him both this subject and the world that appears for this subject are in a certain sense opaque (e.g., Merleau-Ponty 2012: lxxv, 62, 228, 265, 448). It is for this reason that Merleau-Ponty characterizes the target of phenomenological description as a transcendental *field*. As Merleau-Ponty writes, "of all philosophies, only phenomenology speaks of a transcendental *field*. This word signifies that reflection never has the entire world and the plurality of monads spread out and objectified before its gaze" (Merleau-Ponty 2012: 62).

With his characterization of subject and world, Merleau-Ponty explicitly targets what he calls empiricism and intellectualism. While empiricism considers the relation between world and self in terms of causation, thereby reducing what appears to the transparency of a present stimulus or sensation (Merleau-Ponty 2012: 214), intellectualism considers consciousness to be a form of judgment, thereby making the world transparent insofar as it can be treated as something posited by a consciousness that is transparent to its own operations (Merleau-Ponty 2012: 204). Further, in Merleau-Ponty's general account, both these positions operate with a conception, or, better, a prejudice, of a determinate world, which is either posited as the cause of our perceptions or posited by consciousness (e.g., Merleau-Ponty 2012: 5, 33, 40–1, 53, 286), hence presupposing what must be accounted for—namely, how something like a consciousness of a determinate world is possible in the first place (e.g., Merleau-Ponty 2012: 33–4, 48). It is by no means clear, however, whether and to what extent the denial of a complete reduction and the emphasis on the opacity of subject and world constitutes an implicit or explicit criticism of Husserl's phenomenological philosophy.[28] While Merleau-Ponty at times

---

[28] Heinämaa (2002) and Smith (2004) provide a more in-depth discussion of the claim that the reduction remains incomplete, how this statement is tied to the way in which Merleau-Ponty conceives of the subject, and how it is not in conflict with Husserl's account of the reduction.

characterizes Husserl as an intellectualist (e.g., Merleau-Ponty 2012: 251n), there are several ways in which his critique of intellectualism does not apply to and is not directed at Husserl. One respect in which Husserl and Merleau-Ponty do part ways, however, is in their characterization of the distinction between the contingent and necessary features of the world.

According to Merleau-Ponty, intellectualism accounts for how we can experience a world by appealing to a constituting consciousness (e.g., Merleau-Ponty 2012: 148, 452), thetic or positing consciousness (e.g., Merleau-Ponty 2012: 453), objectifying function (e.g., Merleau-Ponty 2012: 141), judgment (e.g., Merleau-Ponty 2012: 34–5), intellectual consciousness (e.g., Merleau-Ponty 2012: 223), determining thought (e.g., Merleau-Ponty 2012: 95), understanding (e.g., Merleau-Ponty 2012: 48), or act of *Sinngebung* (e.g., Merleau-Ponty 2012: lxxv, 453). Merleau-Ponty's intellectualist calls on these subjective activities to account for the organization of a manifold of impressions into an experience of a world—this manifold being a presupposition that intellectualism shares with empiricism in Merleau-Ponty's view.

Against the intellectualist, Merleau-Ponty argues that our experience of an organized natural world is not the result of an activity but rather precedes and is presupposed by any such activity. This is not to say that Merleau-Ponty does not account for *how* this experience is possible. Indeed, Merleau-Ponty's description of perception is to provide this account. Merleau-Ponty characterizes our experience of the world as an original intentionality (e.g., Merleau-Ponty 2012: 139, 407), an operative intentionality (e.g., Merleau-Ponty 2012: lxxxii, 441, 453), or more generally as existence (e.g., Merleau-Ponty 2012: 334), which he characterizes as pre-personal (e.g., Merleau-Ponty 2012: 86, 216, 345, 368), anonymous (e.g., Merleau-Ponty 2012: 86, 223, 247, 265, 369), and, as previously mentioned, opaque. He calls this form of intentionality original and operative because it is presupposed by any active, egoic, or explicit forms of intentionality (such as judging in the form of a predication). This intentionality can further also be characterized as pre-personal, anonymous, and non-transparent because it is not a self-conscious I who accomplishes this organization of the field of perception. Nevertheless, Merleau-Ponty still at times himself speaks of constitution (e.g., Merleau-Ponty 2012: 33, 53, 466), *Sinngebung* (Merleau-Ponty 2012: 464), and transcendental subjectivity (Merleau-Ponty 2012: 378), which already by itself suggests that his account can still be inscribed within the transcendental tradition broadly understood (in the sense that a meaningful world manifests itself to a subject that makes possible this manifestation). However, at the same time, Merleau-Ponty uses these terms in a modified sense in that they refer to a more original intentionality than has hitherto been focused on in the transcendental tradition.

Our experience of the world is made possible, according to Merleau-Ponty, by a motor intentionality (e.g., Merleau-Ponty 2012: 113, 331). That is, in Merleau-Ponty's view, our bodies make possible that we perceive a world that is organized, and these bodies are organized wholes of parts that only receive their meaning in the context of this whole (e.g., a hand can only perform its function as a hand due to the place it has in the organization of the body as a whole) (e.g., Merleau-Ponty 2012: 100–1, 150) and as capable of a range of possible movements (e.g., Merleau-Ponty 2012: 142, 260).

In his description of the intentionality that affords a world, Merleau-Ponty at times speaks of a projecting (e.g., Merleau-Ponty 2012: 137–9, 300, 407) the world and even of an imposition of sense (Merleau-Ponty 2012: 148), which might seem to suggest that one is dealing with a one-sided organization of what appears by and for the subject—albeit a body subject. But Merleau-Ponty rejects this characterization (e.g., Merleau-Ponty 2012: 62, 275) and is clear that the world that appears has its own logic (e.g., Merleau-Ponty 2012: 50, 326, 341, 427), perceptual syntax (e.g., Merleau-Ponty 2012: 38), structure (e.g., Merleau-Ponty 2012: 58, 395), or style (e.g., Merleau-Ponty 2012: 287, 342) that is articulated and accessed by the body in the way that an answer is formulated in response to a question (e.g., Merleau-Ponty 2012: 18, 331). More concretely, the body has a take or hold on something in the field of perception (e.g., Merleau-Ponty 2012: 261, 278–9, 288, 334) by means of its movement, which, insofar as it brings an organization to articulation that is prefigured (e.g., Merleau-Ponty 2012: 32) or motivated (e.g., Merleau-Ponty 2012: 270, 275, 395), can also be characterized as a taking up (e.g., Merleau-Ponty 2012: 265, 331) or as a tracing of the borders and directions in what manifests itself (Merleau-Ponty 2012: 115). So, for example, Merleau-Ponty describes how different colors like blue and red appear to a body that takes up a certain manner of looking (Merleau-Ponty 2012: 217) or a certain attitude or bodily comportment (Merleau-Ponty 2012: 219) and how something is experienced as large when my gaze cannot envelop it (Merleau-Ponty 2012: 317). Hence, the relation between bodily self and world is one that Merleau-Ponty can characterize as communication (e.g., Merleau-Ponty 2012: 53, 95, 99, 265, 331), as inseparable (e.g., Merleau-Ponty 2012: 430), or, with a nod to Heidegger, as a structure of two abstract moments (Merleau-Ponty 2012: 455).

While it is clear that Merleau-Ponty's account of perception entails a critique of a certain Kantianism, it is not clear to what extent this also entails a critique of Husserl. A first criticism that might be taken to apply to Husserl is Merleau-Ponty's rejection of any talk of sensations (or *hyle* that are in turn apperceived or given form (*morphe*) by a constituting consciousness (e.g., Merleau-Ponty 2012: lxxv, 154, 253)—a constituting that is in the Kantian tradition mediated by the concepts that, when schematized, allow for the organization of the manifold of appearances according to a rule (Merleau-Ponty 2012: 314–15). However, it is not at all clear that this critique ultimately applies to Husserl. Indeed, as I previously elaborated, and as Merleau-Ponty himself recognizes (Merleau-Ponty 2012: 453), in Husserl's view the sensuous field is organized both contingently and necessarily.

Even so, Merleau-Ponty's characterization of the relation of body subject and world as a structure of two abstract moments would seem to directly counter Husserl's characterization of the relation of consciousness and world in section 49 of *Ideas*. However, Husserl does acknowledge that a *bodily* subject is necessarily one that affords an actual world.[29] As Husserl writes: "However I imagine myself as personal human being, I remain one that has a world and is living in the world in this structure" (Husserl

---

[29] Zahavi (2002: 12–14) has discussed this point of convergence between Husserl and Merleau-Ponty.

2008a: 246). A person or human being is a bodily self, and insofar as that person has kin-esthetic systems and capabilities it is embodied in the world. That is, what Husserl calls embodiment—which is more than the awareness of fleeting kinesthetic experiences and involves the awareness of an acquired "I can"—is not imaginable outside a spati-otemporal world of things in which kinesthetic systems are maintained and bodily capabilities are exercised in the perception of things.[30] Husserl's statement that a person always discloses and finds himself or herself in a world, however, is compatible with the possibility of an even more radical variation, where my experiences lose all regularity— which is a case in which worldly objects would not appear and bodily habits would not be maintained. In this case, the variation is not bound to what Husserl sometimes calls "the general form of being a child of the world (*Weltkindheit*)," and the variation yields "knowledge of the absolutely free variability of pure subjectivity without constraint" (Husserl 2012: 353). This pure subjectivity or consciousness is one for which no world would appear: "When I engage in such a free variation, then I immediately recognize: I am, even if a world would not be" (Husserl 2012: 352). Indeed it is the consciousness that we are to imagine in the thought experiment of the annihilation, which is a conceiva-bility that Husserl wants to leave open for reasons I return to in the conclusion to this chapter.

A final noteworthy difference between Husserl's and Merleau-Ponty's conceptions of the world of experience is that Merleau-Ponty at one point seems to propose that we give up on the distinction between contingent and necessary features of the world, or the distinction between fact and essence, specifically when he states that "there is no longer any means of distinguishing a level of a priori truths and a level of factual ones, or between what the world ought to be and what the world actually is" (Merleau-Ponty 2012: 229), which is a distinction that Husserl presupposes when he distinguishes on-tology from empirical science and for the development of an ontology of the lifeworld.[31] But *Phenomenology of Perception* also suggests that Merleau-Ponty thinks he is aligning himself with Husserl in this respect. So, for example, echoing Husserl, Merleau-Ponty speaks of a logic of the factual: "The a priori is the fact as understood, made explicit, and followed through into all of the consequences of its tacit logic; the a posteriori is the isolated and implicit fact" (Merleau-Ponty 2012: 230, my emphasis). And he later again mentions the logic of the aesthetic world, this time explicitly referencing Husserl (Merleau-Ponty 2012: 492). Further, Merleau-Ponty commends Husserl for grounding the possible on the real (Merleau-Ponty 2012: lxxxi) and then later claims on his own behalf that "it is nevertheless from the world of perception that I borrow the notion of essence" (Merleau-Ponty 2012: 407). And in a certain sense Merleau-Ponty is here in-deed in agreement with Husserl. That is, as Husserl himself puts it: "We can hence call pure eidetic concepts, such as color, also 'a posteriori'" (Husserl 2012: 101, emphasis

---

[30] I have addressed the self-constitution of the embodied perceiver in conjunction with the constitution of the world elsewhere (Jacobs 2014).

[31] Barbaras (1998: 67–71; 2004: 71–3) has developed this difference between Husserl and Merleau-Ponty in more detail.

added). As Husserl points out, only a subject that has color experiences can arrive at the kinds of examples that would in turn allow it to discern the necessities pertaining to color (e.g., it being necessarily extended).[32]

However, it would seem that Merleau-Ponty goes a step too far when he further suggests that the late Husserl breaks with his philosophy of essence (Merleau-Ponty 2012: 51n). For, Husserl always wanted to do more than express mere empirical generalities about the world of experience on the basis of induction. After all, Husserl proposes we use a method of imaginative variation when doing ontology: Necessary characteristics of something cannot be varied in the imagination without destroying the very thing one is imagining (Husserl 1973: 339–49; 2012: 292).[33] Further, as I hope to show in concluding, Husserl's commitment to and understanding of the phenomenon of reason would be in tension with giving up on the distinction between contingent and necessary features of the world.

33.5 THE PHENOMENON OF REASON

Thus far I have spelled out some similarities and differences between Husserl's and Heidegger's and Merleau-Ponty's accounts of the world. In concluding, I would like to outline how exactly Husserl's commitment to accounting for the phenomenon of reason, or the first person awareness of the difference between veridical and non-veridical experiences, motivates the three claims with which Heidegger and/or Merleau-Ponty take issue—namely, Husserl's claims concerning the relation between consciousness and world in section 49 of the first book of *Ideas*, the claim that the world is at bottom nature, and the claims pertaining to the distinction between facts and pure essences.

First, how Husserl's assertion of the possibility of a worldless consciousness is motivated by his commitment to accounting for the phenomenon of reason becomes clear when we take note of the fact that this assertion occurs in the context of a discussion of the relation between the essence of consciousness and the essence of world in the first book of *Ideas*. For Husserl, essences can be related in four different ways: mutual independence, mutual dependence, and one-sided dependence (in two ways) (Husserl 2001b: 11–13, 27–28). These different kinds of relations determine how, by necessity, the existence of one thing requires the existence of another thing or not (Husserl 2001b: 6–13). Now, in claiming that the actual world is (in principle) a correlate of a (veridical) conscious experience and that a conscious experience in which no actual world appears is conceivable, Husserl characterizes the relation between world and consciousness as

---

[32] In line with this, Tengelyi (2015: 51–2) argues for the contingency of the necessity of the structure of the world for Husserl in distinction to Kant.

[33] Smith (2004: 564–8) convincingly shows how Husserl and Merleau-Ponty part ways when Merleau-Ponty characterizes imaginative variation as induction. Of course, whether Husserl is right in insisting on the difference is an altogether different question.

one of one-sided dependence.[34] My suggestion is that Husserl characterizes the relation between consciousness and world in terms of a one-sided dependence of the world on consciousness because it is, in his view, the only way of conceiving of the relation between the essence of consciousness and the essence of world that allows for the first-person experience of reason in which we become aware that the actual world does or does not correspond to how we take the world to be in experience, and where this very awareness is indeed the mark of the success or failure of how we take the world to be.

First, thinking of the relation between the essence of consciousness and world in terms of independence would be incompatible with the phenomenon of reason because this way of conceiving the relation between consciousness and world leaves open the possibility that we could have a veridical conscious experience of the world being a certain way without the world actually being that way (e.g., my seeing that the keys are on the table could occur when these keys are in fact not on the table) because the one can exist without the other and vice versa. Second, if we conceive of the essence of consciousness as one-sidedly dependent on the essence of world, all my experiences would in fact correspond to something in the actual world, because while something could exist without there being an experience of it, an experience of something would by necessity correspond to something actually existing. If so, however, we would exclude the possibility of an experience that does not correspond to anything in the actual world, in this way also excluding the possibility of me becoming aware that my experience of something being a certain way does not in fact correspond to what the actual world is like. The same is the case for an account of the relation between consciousness and world that considers them to be mutually dependent. On this view the existence of a certain experience means that something in the world corresponds to it and vice versa, thereby doing away with the possibility of an experience in which I become aware that nothing in fact correlates to how I took it to be.

Hence, for Husserl, only one option remains—namely, the one in which an actual experience does not necessarily correlate to something in the actual world, but something in the actual world necessarily correlates to an (in principle possible actual) experience of it. As Husserl writes: "the idea of this transcendence [i.e., of things] is thus the eidetic correlate of the pure idea of this identifying (*ausweisenden*) experience" (Husserl 2014: 86). And, on the other hand: "The existence of consciousness is not relative to the existence of an actual reality. Of course, intentionality belongs to the essence of consciousness. However, it does not belong to the essence of intentionality that some transcendent intentional something 'actually exists' or, what amounts to the same, that the

---

[34] It is worth noting that the functional dependence can occur on different levels of specification. So, for example, in the case of color and extension, the functional dependence is between the species color and extension, which means that no color can exist without it being a color of an extension. However, as Husserl notes (2001b: 18), and as is implied by what follows, the functional dependence can also reign between the lowest specific differences, which would be the case for the relation between consciousness and world, where the existence of a determinate (veridical) perception (e.g., a perception of something of having this or that color) is correlated to something determinate in the actual world (e.g., having this or that color).

conscious intentions that posit reality are harmoniously fulfilled. The relativity between the real world and consciousness is hence strictly speaking not a correlativity. The being of a real world is contingent with respect to the being of a consciousness" (Husserl 2006: 79). This way of construing the relation between consciousness and world does allow for the possibility that we have actual experiences that do not correlate with how the world actually is and secures that veridical experiences in which I have evidence for the world being a certain way do—and hence for Husserl it is the only option of conceiving of the relation between the essence of consciousness and the essence of world that preserves the phenomenon of reason.

Second, Husserl's insistence that the world is at bottom nature can also be understood as motivated by his concern with the phenomenon of reason—albeit in a different way. Specifically, this claim can be understood as following from the way in which Husserl preserves the intersubjective character of reason in the practical domain. According to Husserl, if something actually exists, then it is (in principle) accessible in experience to any conscious subject. What this means is that disagreement about things and facts is and should be only provisional. And if such disagreement persists, the way to resolve this disagreement is by establishing a distinction between normalcy and abnormalcy (like we do in the cases of colorblindness and deafness).[35] Things are different in the practical realm, however, where certain forms of disagreement can be tolerated and do not need to be resolved in this way. Specifically, even if I am engaged in actions that aim to realize different goals than my fellows, we can still validate one another's practical decisions because validating the practical decisions of others does not entail that I value and decide the same (like in the case of the perception of natural properties and related perceptual judgments) (e.g., Husserl 2008a: 297, 393). This kind of disagreement is possible because part of what happens when I validate someone's practical decisions is that I (can in principle) become aware of the natural properties in virtue of which something is taken as valuable and worth realizing from a certain perspective as well as of the bodily capacities that put someone in a position to bring about what is valued. While both the natural properties and their bodily situation are facts that we should in principle agree on, the difference in our respective situations allows for a certain form of disagreement in the sense that my validating your decisions does not necessarily entail that I, in my situation, should make the same decisions. However, and this is one way of making sense of Husserl's insistence on the world being at bottom nature, if we did not have access to a shared nature, we could not validate or question another's practical decisions in the way we do—namely, by pointing out that they are mistaken about what is being valued or about their own capabilities or situation. Hence, Husserl's insistence on the world being at bottom nature can be understood as guaranteeing the intersubjective nature of practical reason, which allows for different individuals validating and questioning practical decisions of others that are not and never will be their own.[36]

---

[35] Zahavi (2003: 133–6), Staiti (2010: 137–8), and Fricke (2012) also point this out.

[36] This is not to say that a view like Heidegger's could not in a different way account for this kind of validating. Indeed, several commentators have addressed the challenge of how to think of success and

Finally, third, Husserl's concern with the intersubjective dimension of the phenomenon of reason can also be taken as motivating his insistence on the distinction between the contingent and necessary, between fact and pure essence. In Husserl's view, the world is for everyone (Husserl 1960: 92), which is to say that there is only one world (Husserl 2014: 87–8). And Husserl at several points insists that it is the necessary structure of the world that guarantees that despite radical differences in our experience of the world we still experience the same world.[37] That is, the world displays the same necessary structure, form, or style (e.g., Husserl 2008a: 57, 295, 544, 677–8, 691, 712) to different perceivers, which allows for identification of things between perceivers that might very well vastly differ when it comes to the perception of the contingent features of these things (e.g., their specific color).[38]

So, I would like to suggest, in this way the claims that the later phenomenologists take issue with can be understood as motivated by Husserl's conception and commitment to the phenomenon of reason. And, what is more, Husserl's commitment to the phenomenon of reason itself is also not unmotivated. Husserl's insistence that we are aware of the difference between veridical and non-veridical experience from the first-person perspective can be understood as following from his denial that an absolute distinction can be made between a merely phenomenally appearing world and the world itself. For, according to Husserl, once we start doubting that we can draw the distinction between veridical and unveridical experiences from within experience itself, we pave the way to distinguish the world that phenomenally appears from the world as it is in itself, which is a distinction that the three discussed phenomenologists unanimously resist. It would be an altogether different project to show why one should and how one can resist this distinction without having to commit to Husserl's three claims outlined above. I hope to have shown, though, that Husserl can be understood as making these commitments

failure or better or worse ways of disclosing the world from within Heidegger's early philosophy. Smith (2007), who traces the challenge back to Tugendhat (1976), critically considers several proposals before formulating his own according to which we are to look at the way that Dasein is beholden to itself in authenticity and resoluteness (which is in line with Crowell 2013: 191–213). Most recently, McKinney (2016) has proposed a competing interpretation arguing that we are beholden to the world itself and that authenticity is to be understood as sustaining our openness to the world. McManus (2015), then again, has elaborated how one, from a Heideggerian perspective, can call into question that the different understandings of Being are like different perspectives that can be better or worse because these different understandings are not rivals in that they are not about the same aspect of the world.

[37] Merleau-Ponty acknowledges that we need to account for how different embodied perceivers can disclose the same world (2012: 304–5). Barbaras (1998: 161–3; 169–74) elaborates this concern and how Merleau-Ponty addresses it.

[38] Further substantiating Husserl's claim would, however, require that we not only take into account how different perceivers might differ when it comes to the same modality of perception (e.g., visual perception) but also how different perceivers experience the world in different modalities of perception (e.g., some do not have visual perception, others perceive through echolocation). Husserl considers spatial extension but not color (e.g., Husserl 1989: 73–7) to be a candidate for a structure that is experienced in different modalities of perception. Hence, perceivers that do not share modalities of perception would nevertheless still experience the same spatial world—extension being indeed a necessary structure of the world.

in a way that is motivated by his concern for and specific understanding of the phenomenon of reason.

References

Barbaras, R. (1998), *Le tournant de l'expérience. Recherches sur la philosophie de Merleau-Ponty* (Paris: J. Vrin).

Barbaras, R. (2004), *The Being of the Phenomenon: Merleau-Ponty's Ontology* (Bloomington, IN: Indiana University Press).

Benoist, J. (1995), "La découverte de l'apriori synthétique matériel: au-delà du 'quelque chose,' le tous et les parties (RL III)," *Recherches Husserliennes* 3: 3–22.

Bernet, R. (1988), "Die Frage nach dem Ursprung der Zeit bei Husserl und Heidegger," *Heidegger Studies* 3/4: 89–104.

Bernet, R. (1990), "Husserl and Heidegger on Intentionality and Being," *Journal of the British Society for Phenomenology* 21/2: 136–52.

Crowell, S. (2013), *Normativity and Phenomenology in Husserl and Heidegger* (Cambridge: Cambridge University Press).

Crowell, S. and Malpas, J. (2007), *Transcendental Heidegger* (Stanford, CA: Stanford University Press).

De Palma, V. (2014), "Die Fakta leiten alle Eidetik. Zu Husserls Begriff des materialen Apriori," *Husserl Studies* 30/3: 195–223.

De Palma, V. (2015), "Der Ursprung des Akts. Husserls Begriff der genetischen Phänomenologie und die Frage nach der Weltkonstitution," *Husserl Studies* 31/3: 189–212.

Drummond, J. J. (1995), "Synthesis, Identity, and the *A Priori*," *Recherches Husserliennes* 2/4: 27–51.

Drummond, J. J. (2003), "Pure Logical Grammar: Anticipatory Categoriality and Articulated Categoriality" *International Journal of Philosophical Studies* 11/2: 125–39.

Drummond, J. J. (2004), "Cognitive Impenetrability and the Complex Intentionality of the Emotions," *Journal of Consciousness Studies* 11/10–11: 109–26.

Drummond, J. J. (2013), "The Intentional Structure of the Emotions," *Logical Analysis and the History of Philosophy/Philosophiegeschichte und logische Analyse* 16: 244–63.

Ferrarin, A. (2015a), *The Powers of Pure Reason: Kant and the Idea of Cosmic Philosophy* (Chicago, IL: University of Chicago Press).

Ferrarin, A. (2015b), "From the world to philosophy, and back," in J. Bloechl and N. de Warren (eds), *Phenomenology in a New Key: Between Analysis and History* (Dordrecht: Springer), 63–92.

Fricke, C. (2012), "Overcoming disagreement–Adam Smith and Edmund Husserl on strategies of justifying descriptive and evaluative judgments," in D. Føllesdal and C. Fricke (eds), *Intersubjectivity and Objectivity in Adam Smith and Edmund Husserl: A Collection of Essays* (Heusenstamm bei Frankfurt: Ontos Verlag), 171–242.

Gardner, S. (2007), "Merleau-Ponty's transcendental theory of perception," in S. Gardner and M. Grist (eds), *The Transcendental Turn* (Oxford: Oxford University Press), 294–323.

Gardner, S. and Grist, M. (eds) (2015), *The Transcendental Turn* (Oxford: Oxford University Press).

Han-Pile, B. (2005), "Heidegger's appropriation of Kant," in H. L. Dreyfus and M. Wrathall (eds), *The Blackwell Companion to Heidegger* (Oxford: Blackwell Publishing), 88–101.

Hartimo, M., Heinämaa, S., and Miettinen, T. (2015), *Phenomenology and the Transcendental* (London: Routledge).

Heidegger, M. (1962), *Being and Time* (Oxford: Blackwell).

Heidegger, M. (1985), *History of the Concept of Time* (Bloomington, IN: Indiana University Press).

Heinämaa, S. (2002), "From decision to passions: Merleau-Ponty's interpretation of Husserl's reduction," in L. Embree and T. Toadvine (eds), *Merleau-Ponty's Reading of Husserl* (Dordrecht: Springer), 127–46.

Heinämaa, S. (2015), "Anonymity and Personhood: Merleau-Ponty's Account of the Subject of Perception," *Continental Philosophy Review* 48: 123–42.

Husserl, E. (1959), *Erste Philosophie (1923–24). Zweiter Teil* (The Hague: Martinus Nijhoff).

Husserl, E. (1960), *Cartesian Meditations. An Introduction to Phenomenology* (The Hague: Martinus Nijhoff).

Husserl, E. (1970), *The Crisis of European Sciences and Transcendental Phenomenology: An Introduction to Phenomenological Philosophy* (Evanston, IL: Northwestern University Press).

Husserl, E. (1973), *Experience and Judgment: Investigations in a Genealogy of Logic* (Evanston, IL: Northwestern University Press).

Husserl, E. (1980), *Ideas Pertaining to a Pure Phenomenology and to a Phenomenological Philosophy. Third Book: Phenomenology and the Foundations of the Sciences* (The Hague: Martinus Nijhoff).

Husserl, E. (1989), *Ideas Pertaining to a Pure Phenomenology and to a Phenomenological Philosophy. Second Book: Studies in the Phenomenology of Constitution* (Dordrecht: Kluwer).

Husserl, E. (2001a), *Analyses Concerning Passive Synthesis and Active Synthesis: Lectures on Transcendental Logic* (Dordrecht: Kluwer).

Husserl, E. (2001b), *Logical Investigations, vol. 2* (London: Routledge).

Husserl, E. (2001c), *Natur und Geist. Vorlesungen Sommersemester 1927* (Dordrecht: Kluwer).

Husserl, E. (2006), *Transzendentaler Idealismus. Texte aus dem Nachlass (1908–1922)* (Dordrecht: Kluwer).

Husserl, E. (2008a), *Die Lebenswelt. Auslegungen der vorgegebenen Welt und ihrer Konstitution. Texte aus dem Nachlass (1916–1937)* (Dordrecht: Springer).

Husserl, E. (2008b), *Introduction to Logic and Theory of Knowledge: Lectures 1906/07* (Dordrecht: Springer).

Husserl, E. (2012), *Zur Lehre vom Wesen und zur Methode der eidetischen Variation. Texte aus dem Nachlass (1891–1935)* (Dordrecht: Springer).

Husserl, E. (2014), *Ideas for a Pure Phenomenology and Phenomenological Philosophy. First Book: General Introduction to Pure Phenomenology* (Indianapolis, IN: Hackett).

Jacobs, H. (2014), "Transcendental subjectivity and the human being," in M. Hartimo, S. Heinämaa, and T. Miettinen (eds), *Phenomenology and the Transcendental* (London: Routledge), 87–105.

Jacobs, H. (2015), "From psychology to pure phenomenology," in A. Staiti (ed.), *Commentary on Husserl's Ideas I* (Berlin: de Gruyter), 95–118.

Jacobs, H. (2016a), "Husserl on Reason, Reflection, and Attention," *Research in Phenomenology* 46/2: 257–76.

Jacobs, H. (2016b), "Socialization, reflection, and personhood," in S. Rinofner-Kreidl and H. Wiltsche (eds), *Analytic and Continental Philosophy: Methods and Perspectives. Proceedings of the 37th International Ludwig Wittgenstein Symposium* (Berlin: de Gruyter), 323–35.

Jansen, J. (2014), "Taking a transcendental stance: Anti-representationalism and direct realism in Kant and Husserl," in F. Fabianielli and S. Luft (eds), *Husserl und die klassische deutsche Philosophie* (Dordrecht: Springer), 79–92.

Jansen, J. (2015), "Transcendental Philosophy and the Problem of Necessity in a Contingent World," *Metodo: International Studies in Phenomenology and Philosophy* 1: 47–80.

Kern, I. (1964), *Husserl und Kant. Eine Untersuchung über Husserls Verhältnis zu Kant und zum Neukantianismus* (The Hague: Martinus Nijhoff).

Landgrebe, L. (1963), *Der Weg der Phänomenologie. Das Problem einer ursprünglichen Erfahrung* (Gütersloh: Gerd Mohn).

Majolino, C. (2010), "La partition du réel: Remarques sur l'eidos, la phantasia, l'effondrement du monde et l'être absolu de la conscience," in C. Ierna, H. Jacobs, and F. Mattens (eds), *Philosophy, Phenomenology, Sciences* (Dordrecht: Springer), 573–660.

Majolino, C. (2016), "Until the End of the World: Eidetic Variation and Absolute Being of Consciousness—A Reconsideration," *Research in Phenomenology* 46/2: 157–83.

Matherne, S. (2016), "Kantian Themes in Merleau-Ponty's Theory of Perception," *Archiv für Geschichte der Philosophie* 98/2: 193–230.

McKinney, T. (2016), "Objectivity and Reflection in Heidegger's Theory of Intentionality," *Journal for the American Philosophical Association* 2/1: 111–30.

McManus, D. (2012), *Heidegger and the Measure of Truth* (Oxford: Oxford University Press).

McManus, D. (2015), "Heidegger and the Supposition of a Single, Objective World," *European Journal of Philosophy* 23/2: 195–220.

Merleau-Ponty, M. (2012), *Phenomenology of Perception* (London: Routledge).

Moran, D. (2000), "Heidegger's Critique of Husserl's and Brentano's Accounts of Intentionality," *Inquiry* 43/1: 39–65.

Nenon, T. (2008), "Some Differences between Kant's and Husserl's Conception of Transcendental Philosophy," *Continental Philosophy Review* 41/4: 427–39.

Overgaard, S. (2004), *Husserl and Heidegger on Being in the World* (Dordrecht: Kluwer).

Patočka, J. (2016), *The Natural World as a Philosophical Problem* (Evanston, IL: Northwestern University Press).

Pradelle, D. (2013), "The phenomenological foundations of predicative structure," in D. Zahavi (ed.), *Oxford Handbook of Contemporary Phenomenology* (Oxford: Oxford University Press), 349–76.

Rinofner-Kreidl, S. (2013), "Husserls Fundierungsmodell als Grundlage einer intentionalen Wertungsanalyse," *Metodo* 1/2: 59–82.

Rinofner-Kreidl, S. (2015), "Husserl's analogical and teleological conception of reason," in A. Staiti (ed.), *Commentary on Husserl's 'Ideas I'* (Berlin: de Gruyter), 287–326.

Smith, A. D. (2004), "Merleau-Ponty and the Phenomenological Reduction," *Inquiry* 48/6: 553–71.

Smith, A. D. (2007), "The flesh of perception: Merleau-Ponty and Husserl," in T. Baldwin (ed.), *Reading Merleau-Ponty: On Phenomenology of Perception* (London: Routledge), 1–22.

Smith, W. H. (2007), "Why Tugendhat's Critique of Heidegger's Concept of Truth Remains a Critical Problem," *Inquiry* 50/2: 156–70.

Sowa, R. (2010), "Husserls Idee einer nicht-empirischen Wissenschaft von der Lebenswelt," *Husserl Studies* 26/1: 49–66.

Staiti, A. (2010), "Different Worlds and Tendency to Concordance," *New Yearbook for Phenomenology and Phenomenological Philosophy* 10: 127–43.

Taminiaux, J. (1991), *Heidegger and the Project of Fundamental Ontology* (Albany: SUNY).

Tengelyi, L. (2015), "Categories of experience and the transcendental," in M. Hartimo, S. Heinämaa, and T. Miettinen (eds), *Phenomenology and the Transcendental* (London: Routledge), 49–60.

Toadvine, T. (2002), "Merleau-Ponty's reading of Husserl: A chronological overview," in T. Toadvine and L. Embree (eds), *Merleau-Ponty's Reading of Husserl* (Dordrecht: Springer), 227–86.

Tugendhat, E. (1967), *Der Wahrheitsbegriff bei Husserl and Heidegger* (Berlin: de Gruyter).

Welton, D. (2000), *The Other Husserl: The Horizons of Transcendental Phenomenology* (Bloomington, IN: Indiana University Press).

Zahavi, D. (2002), "Merleau-Ponty on Husserl: A Reappraisal," in T. Toadvine and L. Embree (eds), *Merleau-Ponty's Reading of Husserl* (Dordrecht: Springer), 3–29.

Zahavi, D. (2003), *Husserl's Phenomenology* (Stanford, CA: Stanford University Press).

Zahavi, D. (2015), "Husserl and the transcendental," in S. Gardner and M. Grist (eds), *The Transcendental Turn* (Oxford: Oxford University Press), 228–43.

CHAPTER 34

IMAGINATION DE-NATURALIZED

Phantasy, the Imaginary, and Imaginative Ontology

JULIA JANSEN

THERE are several reasons why one might expect the imagination to have played a special role in the history of phenomenology. For one, phenomenologists are said to be less,
or not at all, interested in the existence, or being of objects, but only in their appearance.[1]
Taken together with an entrenched understanding of imagination as conjuring up the
"mere" appearance of non-existing, or absent objects, this makes for a strong coupling
between phenomenology and imagination. Further, the often-cited understanding of
phenomenology as a *general* "study of consciousness" also suggests the inclusion of the
imagination besides, allegedly, "more important" modes of consciousness, such as perception and cognition. Moreover, a certain kinship between the so-called phenomenological attitude, which pays specific attention to *how* objects appear, and an aesthetic
attitude, which in its own way does so too, reinforces the expectation of a special bond
between phenomenology and the (aesthetic) imagination. And even the controversial
link between specifically Husserlian phenomenology and idealism, might lead one to
suspect such a bond. After all, "transcendental" and "productive" notions of the imagination were central fixtures in post-Kantian and post-Hegelian idealisms of different
persuasions throughout the nineteenth century—so much so, in fact, that wide-spread
anti-idealist sentiments in the wake of various realist and materialist turns have, to a certain extent, hampered research on the imagination ever since. If anything, the fact that
many phenomenologists continued to make the imagination an important focus of their
research throughout the twentieth century, may have contributed to a sense, still lingering in some places, that they were hanging on to a questionable, or at least antiquated

---

[1] This view, in different guises, still fuels contemporary critiques of phenomenology as "anti-realist"
and "correlationalist."

project. Be that as it may, the history of phenomenology offers some of the most thorough investigations of the imagination in the twentieth century—investigations that tend to go beyond the treatment of specific phenomena (such as fiction, pretense, or "mind-reading") and to explore the wider significance of the imagination, including, for example, its methodological, epistemological, and ontological dimensions.

To find a specific entry on the imagination in a handbook of the history of phenomenology is therefore hardly surprising. However, many of the common assumptions, on which the thus confirmed expectation rests, reflect serious misunderstandings regarding the nature of phenomenology; and yet, they still touch upon some of its key tenets. In what follows, I therefore start by clarifying some of these misunderstandings insofar as they are directly relevant to a proper understanding of the important role the imagination has played in the history of phenomenology. I then present Husserl's groundbreaking investigations and advance my reading of the most important contribution he, in my view, made to phenomenological research on the imagination: what I call his "de-naturalization" of the imagination. In section 34.3 I detail some of the most decisive ways in which Sartre and Merleau-Ponty depart from Husserl's approach. I give an account of how both, in their distinct ways, build upon Husserl's earlier work and also reject some of its tenets. Not being able here to present more than a few facets of the rich history of phenomenological treatments of the imagination, I single out Sartre and Merleau-Ponty as the two most well-known contributors after Husserl.[2] Both of them significantly advanced phenomenological research on the imagination and radically widened its role. Their new impulses not only changed the trajectory of that history but also aided its diversification.[3]

---

[2] The fact that Sartre and Merleau-Ponty are already so well known to a wide audience, as major figures in the phenomenology of the imagination, would have also supported different choices, and different lines could have been traced. An alternative article could have paid more attention to some of Husserl's contemporaries, such as Meinong 1904; Twardowski 1977; Conrad 1908–9; Geiger 1913; or to other post-Husserlian philosophers, such as Fink 1930; Kaufmann and Heider 1947; or, with a stronger aesthetic inflection, to Dufrenne 1973; Ingarden 1973; Ricœur 1978, 1986; or, more politically, to Baudrillard 1995; or, in an arc that also would have included Sartre and Merleau-Ponty, to the strong influence Bergson 1994 has exerted on French phenomenology in particular; or to a different kind of narrative again that would have led to Richir 2004. I at least want to mention these non-actualized possibilities to underscore the historical richness and plurality of phenomenologies of the imagination. The almost complete omission of Heidegger from the one history I present here is due to the fact that Heidegger, while delivering an appropriation of Kant's notion of productive imagination, otherwise abandons the notion, which, from a Heideggerean perspective, is simply too indebted to the very subject-philosophy he attempts to overcome. For a more detailed account that connects the issue of imagination with Heidegger's later post-philosophical turn towards poetry, see Elliot 2005.

[3] Nothing forces a choice between a more Sartrean or more Merleau-Pontian approach to the imagination, but most contemporary phenomenologists working on, or making use of their work do choose. Another way to capture this point is to say that, while it is trivial that there have always been many ways of phenomenologically approaching the imagination, since Sartre's and Merleau-Ponty's contributions there have been distinct *established* ways of doing so.

34.1 IMAGINATION IN PHENOMENOLOGY: SOME PRELIMINARY CLARIFICATIONS

None of the major phenomenological thinkers of the twentieth century, not even Husserl, who is often criticized for his idealism, advance a transcendental notion of the imagination that would render the imagination part and parcel of an idealism that considers reality in its all its formal and structural elements dependent on a subject's mental, imaginative projections. At the same time, however, phenomenologists are not naïve realists either, and there is indeed a sense, with different modulations for different phenomenologists, that the imagination gives access to dimensions of reality that would be difficult to access, if not outright inaccessible, without the imagination.

By speaking of "reality," we are immediately confronted with the misunderstanding that phenomenologists are not interested in the being of objects, but only in their "mere" appearance, and that phenomenology, as the general "study of consciousness," is in fact nothing else but the study of appearances. Indeed, it is a distinctive feature of phenomenological approaches that they take seriously *all* modes of appearing, including the mode of appearing real (*real*), or actual (*wirklich*). In fact, the very understanding of "reality," not as an assumed metaphysical category, but as a particular mode of appearing, which occurs under specific conditions, has always been integral to phenomenology. To speak with Husserl, we could say that the question regarding "reality" that is of philosophical interest to the phenomenologist is how we come to "posit (*setzen*)" something as real, i.e., as being an object of possible sense-perception (Husserl 2001: VI, §43, §47); or even, with a modal inflection, how we come to posit something as actual.[4] In this understanding, "reality" is something that is "constituted" in complex webs of experiential events and processes, not something that is simply assumed to be "out there," ready to be scientifically examined, the fundamental assumption of what Husserl calls "naturalism." Thus, by contrast to empirical, or "natural" investigations into the causal relations between objects and events (which are unproblematically taken to be real as

---

[4] I am using Husserl's notion of "real (*reale*)" objects here, in line with common understanding, in contrast with illusory, fictional, or other "unreal" objects. Husserl's technical notion of "real," however, contrasts with his notion of "ideal (*ideale*)" objects, i.e., objects (such as, for example, numbers, logical and other laws, meanings) that, although they are not spatiotemporal objects of possible sense perception, are, according to Husserl, still intersubjectively determinable objects. To the extent that ideal objects are still objects in this sense (and not, for example, mere concepts or psychological ideas), they can be said to have their own, ideal "reality." Hence one can speak of a narrow and a wide sense of reality in Husserl—the former referring only to objects of possible sense perception, the latter including ideal objects. I will turn to Husserl's wider sense of reality later. Husserl's notion of "actual (*wirklich*)" is the classical modal notion and as such contrasts with "possible" or "necessary." Objects of possible sense perception are real; if sense perception occurs or has occurred, these objects are real and actual. Ideal objects may also be regarded as actual, possible, or necessary.

observably spatio-temporal objects), phenomenological investigations typically study the *conditions* under which things appear *as* real, and the conditions under which things are justifiably judged or legitimately taken, or posited to *be* real.

Following Husserl, we can call a notion of reality that starts from and simply assumes a totality of spatio-temporal objects and events that stand in causal relations, and now merely need to be explored and explained, a *natural* notion of reality. By contrast, a *phenomenological* notion of reality proceeds from the phenomenological epoché, which brackets all assumptions about what counts as real or un-real. However, the epoché is not meant to establish the phenomenologist's lack of interest in reality. On the contrary, it is meant to first of all enable the phenomenologist to investigate the very ways in which reality is constituted; for example, by reflecting on how some experiences come to stand out as experiences of something *real*, against others, which may be taken, for example, as experiences of something fictional, or illusory. Thus, reality does not "disappear" or become irrelevant for the phenomenologist, but reality first of all comes into view as a phenomenon, i.e., as something in itself worthy of philosophical attention whose very nature can be clarified. This is why Husserl always so adamantly insisted that the world is not lost, but properly "regained" by the epoché (e.g., Husserl 1960: 36, 157).

The most basic experience of something as real, and in fact actual, is the experience of its being "bodily present," i.e., the experience of perceiving it. Other experiences, for example the experience of remembering something, also contribute to the sense of its reality, but in different degrees of certainty. (The reality or actuality of something we remember is, for example, more doubtful than the reality of something that we see in front of us "in the flesh." In other words, the evidence for something's reality we gain from memory is more limited than the evidence we gain from perception.) Of course, something perceived can also "merely" appear to be real, the realization of which may transform my experience of (veridical) perceiving into an experience of illusory perceiving (as when I realize that I have been crossing the desert not towards a real oasis, but following a mirage), or into an experience of hallucinating (as when I realize that the voices that are speaking to me are not the voices of other people). However, phenomenological reflection does not test a particular mental state against an object with which it is correlated in order to then identify—based on whether that object is actually present, or real, or at least possible—that mental state as either a perception, an illusion, a memory, or a figment of the imagination. That too, is prohibited by the epoché because it would have to leave the conditions unquestioned under which we deem that very object present or absent, real or unreal, possible or impossible in the first place.[5] Rather, phenomenological reflections attend to the very acts of consciousness and to their intentional objects, which are inseparable from them. They are meant to illuminate the complex nature of those acts themselves (perceiving, imagining, etc.), and their

---

[5] This is also why, while one may of course exploit resources from the history of phenomenology for contributions to contemporary debates, such as the one concerning disjunctivism, these debates do not arise from phenomenological approaches to perceiving or imagining and often challenge the very terms of the debate (cf. Jansen 2016).

interrelations and conditions, including how they lead to specific modes of positing their objects (as perceived, imagined object, etc.); *and* vice versa, the complex nature of the objects thus posited, and their interrelations and conditions, including how they may "elicit" or "afford" specific acts.[6] As part of this, reflections on imagining (and on imagined objects) are critical to a comprehensive phenomenological understanding of the complex whole which, depending on the specific philosophical perspective taken, may be understood as, for example, "consciousness," or "being."

The emphasis on how objects appear and on the conditions of their appearance, suggests a close proximity between the phenomenological attitude and an aesthetic attitude, understood as an attitude of attention towards the *appearance* of an object's aesthetic qualities, and of "disinterest" towards its objective features (its size, its weight, its price, etc.), or towards its consumption or possession. Phenomenologists do not necessarily pay special attention to aesthetic qualities of objects, and certainly not exclusively. They rather reflect on the complex ways in which acts, engagements, and relations legitimize judgments about reality, constitute values (amongst them aesthetic values), make possible empirical and non-empirical sciences, and so forth. Nor is it the case that phenomenological reflection simply manifests in aesthetic pleasure, which is not straightforwardly enjoyed, but which itself becomes something that can be explored and understood. However, while phenomenological reflection is not aimed at aesthetic experience (or at pleasure, as many readers of Husserl's writings will confirm), it can certainly be triggered by such an experience. In analogy to Heidegger's example of the broken hammer that effects a switch from the "ready-to-hand" to the "present-at-hand" (Heidegger 2010, §§15–16), we can understand encounters with art, or aesthetic experiences more generally, as "breaks" that aid the awareness that other attitudes than the "natural," and other interests than the "ready-to-hand," are possible. However, an even stronger claim runs through the history of phenomenology, namely that aesthetic experiences, and in particular the encounter with and making of artworks, reveal aspects and dimensions of consciousness, reality, or existence, which "naturally" and "for the most part" are closed off for us. In their distinct ways, both Sartre and Merleau-Ponty, and Heidegger too (Heidegger 1971), are profoundly moved by this insight into what is at least an analogy, if not a much stronger kinship, between phenomenological and artistic practice. Even Husserl, the "rigorous scientist," admits of this close relation and acknowledges that the

> *artist*, who "observes" the world in order to gain "knowledge" of nature and man for his own purposes, relates to it in a similar way as the phenomenologist. Thus: not

---

[6] Mark Rowlands has recently pointed out how empiricist assumptions that reduce consciousness to (the phenomenal content of) mental *states*, which are themselves construed as *objects* of introspection or thought, make it impossible to conceive of consciousness in terms of mental *acts in virtue of which* we can access any objects at all. However, Rowlands does not consider the ways in which objects condition the acts. He also thinks of those acts as themselves inaccessible, whereas phenomenologists claim to access those acts as "objects" *of phenomenological reflection* (Rowlands 2016: 20–7).

as an observing natural scientist and psychologist, not as a practical observer of man . . . When he observes the world, it becomes a phenomenon for him, its existence is indifferent, just as it is to the philosopher. (Husserl 2009: 26)[7]

Although Husserl's talk of "indifference" to, or "disinterest" in the world is unacceptable to his existentialist followers, it remains a constant in the history of phenomenology that aesthetic experience, artistic engagement, and works of art are considered unique sources of insight into the nature of consciousness as well as the nature of being. The imagination is, implicitly or explicitly, associated with this aesthetic dimension—its notion thereby expanded from a merely "mental" and "private" activity to include embodied practices that deal with "material" objects. Aesthetic and artistic imagination does not merely occur "in the head," but bodily engages with and operates within different materials and different media, which both enable and constrain the productive imagination of art making.

Moreover, a phenomenological, "wide" notion of reality, which—and this is critical—is not reducible to what is "real" in the narrower sense of the word (spatio-temporal objects of possible sense experience), also gives the *products* of the imagination (of acts or practices of imagining) an ontological significance that is different, but not inferior to the significance of real objects. Even after the various "realist" and "existentialist" rejections of Husserl's idealism (which began, in Husserl's earliest works, with the claim that reality was composed also of "ideal" objects, such as logical laws, numbers, generalities, etc.), phenomenological ontologies remain inclusive and treat imagined objects as a class of objects in their own right with their own distinctive ontological features.[8] In the context of such a "wide" ontology, imagining is considered amongst those acts by which we are conscious of reality in a certain mode. The imagination here does not "lack its object," as is often said. Imagining is an act that displays an intentional structure, directed at imagined objects manifesting in it—an intentional structure that is distinct from the intentional structure of other acts, such as perceiving or remembering, but that is intentional just the same. Imagined objects *are*, only they are *as* absent, *as* non-existent, or *as* "irreal" (fictional rather than factual, possible rather than actual, etc.). The imagination, in turn, is not an epistemic liability that confuses and deceives us with "mere" fictions, illusions, and hallucinations, but it is *disclosive* of reality in the wide sense (in particular, of its possibilities) and thus has its own evidential power, whose range and limitations must be carefully determined.[9]

---

[7] For a detailed discussion of the relation between perception under the phenomenological epoché and aesthetic, or artistic modes of perception see Bernet 2012.

[8] It might be helpful here to remember that this "wide" sense of reality is coupled with a "wide" sense of object. Anything that can be thought of, or that can be the theme of a judgment, here counts as object.

[9] I am alluding here to the second half of Husserl's "principle of all principles" in which he points to the "limits" of evidential force in different kinds of intuition (Husserl 1983: §24). For example, not only perception, but also memory offers evidence for the reality of an object. However, the evidence offered by memory is more limited.

The notion of imagining as an act of disclosure radically breaks with classical modern accounts that construe the imagination as, for example, a faculty of synthesis (Kant), a supreme productive power (Fichte), or, in the empiricist tradition, a matter of faint afterimages, or of fiction (Hobbes, Locke), even when that "fiction" constitutes "reality" (Hume). Rather than inferring the nature of imagination as a faculty from certain functions ascribed to it in an overall economy of the mind, phenomenological approaches distance themselves from available philosophical "constructions" of imagination. In this regard, Brentano is an important transitional figure in the turn towards phenomenological accounts of the imagination. On the one hand, he avoids the Kantian term *Einbildungskraft*, and instead uses (inspired, as so often, by Aristotle) the term *Phantasie*, of which he attempts a "descriptive psychological" account investigating the presentations (*Vorstellungen*) that can be attributed to it. His break with the modern, and specifically Kantian tradition, his move towards a descriptive account of phantasy, and his insistence on the, more or less, "intuitive" character of phantasy presentations (*Phantasievorstellungen*) are crucial impulses for Husserl, who reportedly found Brentano's seminar on "Ausgewählte Fragen aus Psychologie und Ästhetik," which he took in the winter semester 1885–6, "unforgettable" (Marbach 1980: XLIV; cf. Marbach 1993: 142; Rollinger 2008: 29). On the other hand, also under the influence of empiricist philosophies of mind, Brentano assumes a sliding scale of presentations (*Vorstellungen*), with phantasy presentations and perceptual presentations on opposite ends of a spectrum on which phantasy presentations can only ever "approximate" the "authentic (*eigentliche*)" intuitiveness of perceptual presentations. Moreover, Brentano's notion of "original association," which effectively declares time-consciousness a product of the imagination—while paving the way for Husserl's notion of retention—is, from a Husserlian perspective, a "construction" and belongs to those aspects of Brentano's "descriptive psychology" that are still firmly locked within the "natural attitude," and that Husserl seeks to overcome in his "de-naturalized" phenomenology of imagination.[10]

34.2 THE BREAKTHROUGH: HUSSERL'S DE-NATURALIZATION OF THE IMAGINATION

The aim of this section is to demonstrate what I take to be Husserl's most important innovation for research on imagination: namely its "de-naturalization." By this I mean Husserl's groundbreaking insight that any construal of the imagination in terms of

---

[10] It has been argued that Brentano, and more generally Austrian psychology, semantics, and ontology, of that period constitutes a distinct "Austrian phenomenology" (Rollinger 2008). I do not dispute that general claim here, nor do I deny the importance of emphasizing continuities. However, with regards to imagination in particular, I believe that despite Brentano's undisputably important impulses, his account remains, in the sense of the term developed here, largely "natural."

"natural"[11] assumptions obscures the view on what is most distinctive and most interesting about it. For example, based on the assumptions that there are only real, i.e., spatio-temporal objects, and only causal relations, one can get caught up in the problem of how to explain an intuitive presentation of nothing (real), or how to account for "mental imagery" in terms of, supposedly, spatio-temporal representations causing it. By putting those assumptions out of play, one can instead pay attention to the distinct awareness of objects that is characteristic of imagining, to the various modes in which imagined objects manifest themselves to us, and to what kinds of operations and achievements this awareness and these distinct objects enable us to perform.

This insight also pushes much further Husserl's earlier critique of psychologism (Husserl 2001). In this way, it becomes part and parcel of both his development of a general critique of "naturalism," strongly asserted in his 1910 *Logos* article (Husserl 1965), and his "transcendental" transformation of phenomenology, which was beginning to take shape shortly after his 1904–5 lectures on *Phantasy, Image Consciousness, and Memory* (Husserl 2005) with his clarification of the transcendental reduction first brought to public attention in 1907 in *Thing and Space* and culminating in the first book of *Ideas* of 1913. What is especially interesting in this context is that Husserl achieves his "de-naturalized" account of the imagination only gradually in the course of his 1904–5 lectures and in further research manuscripts until it settles by 1909–12, due also in part to major new developments in his research on inner time consciousness. As Brough remarks in his translator's introduction about the lectures, Husserl here

> experiments—raising, exploring, and discarding possibilities—and concedes that the phenomena often defy his efforts to understand them and to capture them in an appropriate terminological net. He sometimes changes his mind and freely admits that something he has written is not correct. (Brough 2005: xxxi)[12]

The particular case of his work on the imagination thus affords us the opportunity to witness how much Husserl himself struggled to overcome his own "natural" assumptions.

---

[11] Husserl may be said to fight against both "natural (*natürlich*)" and "naturalist (*naturalistisch*)" assumptions. "Naturalism" refers to a view that reduces reality to what is causally explicable by the natural sciences and thus also misconstrues consciousness as something physical. In the guise of "psychologism," Husserl argues against this view in the *Logical Investigations*. His explicit turn against "naturalism" follows the *Logos* article, and is still further developed as late as in the *Crisis*. The term "natural" refers to the development of Husserl's transcendental position, which aims at overcoming the "natural attitude" (Husserl 1983: §27). Later Husserl explains naturalism as the result of a "naturalistic attitude" (Husserl 1989: §49), a "rigidification of the natural attitude" (Moran 2008: 403). In what follows I use the term "natural" in the general technical sense, which also encompasses "naturalistic" thinking, in order to emphasize how Husserl's "de-naturalization" of the imagination is an integral part of the development of his transcendental stance.

[12] After this, Husserl continues to deepen his account of imagination up until the 1920s. In fact, still in 1923, he remarks: "Determining the essence of phantasy is a great problem" (Husserl 2005: 671).

Even though Husserl rejects, already in the *Logical Investigations*, the "image theory," which claims "Outside the thing itself is there (or is at times there); in consciousness there is an image which does duty for it" (Husserl 2001: vol. 2, 125) as a "fundamental" and "well-nigh ineradicable" error, he must have had primarily perception in mind at the time. [13] For at the start of his 1904–5 lectures he takes phantasy as a kind of "image presentation (imagination)" analogous to "physical image presentation" (Husserl 2005: 18ff.). A this point, he follows the remarkably "natural" view that in phantasy only *the image* appears, but not what is imagined by means of it (Husserl 2005: 26f.). This is Husserl's early explanation for why imagining gives us objects, like images do, in the mode of "unreality" (*Unwirklichkeit*) (Husserl 2005: 49).[14] Perceiving involves a presentation (*Gegenwärtigung*), "in which the object itself appears to us in its own person, as it were, as present itself." Imagining, by contrast, involves a presentification (*Vergegenwärtigung*),[15] "in which the object appears . . . but it does not appear as present. It is only presentified (*vergegenwärtigt*); it is as though it were there, but only as though" (Husserl 2005: 18). Phantasy, as he puts it there, has "a certain mediacy" (Husserl 2005: 25), i.e., it intends its intentional objects indirectly via "another object," the phantasy image (Husserl 2005: 26). While his anti-psychologism already pushes him to reject the idea that the phantasy "image" has any "psychological existence," he does not yet seem to fully appreciate his own remark that it "truly does not exist" (Husserl 2005: 22). At the very least, there is still a "natural" "prejudice of presence" (Brough 2005: liii) at work, according to which nothing can be presented, not even imagined, unless something is ("really") present to consciousness.

However, as the lecture course progresses, Husserl's thorough reflections on *phantasmata* of 1905 also lead him to the insight that no appropriate account of imagining can be gained from introducing as it were a "secondary" real, namely *phantasmata* (or mental representations of any sort) that stand in for the "real" objects that are *absent* in imagining (Husserl 2005: 150, 161).[16] Whereas at first he construes *phantasmata* as sensory contents that (like sensations in perception) had to be "animated" by a specific mode of apprehension, Husserl's comes to understand them as integral ("non-independent") moments of the experience of imagining. They can be singled out in abstract thought for purposes of analysis, but they are not *present* "in"

---

[13] Sartre will later also exercise the same rejection of what he will call the "illusion of immanence" (Sartre 2004: 5).

[14] We need not imagine unreal, non-existent objects; we may just as well imagine objects that in fact exist. However, they will still seem "*unwirklich*" in the sense of "non-actual"; their appearance will be in conflict with what is actually (perceptually) present.

[15] I translate *Vergegenwärtigung* not as "re-presentation" (as Brough does in Husserl 2005), but as "presentification" in order to emphasize the sense of "making" present what is not "by itself" present, and in order to deemphasize the sense that this necessarily involves a re-petition, or re-collection of an earlier experience, as is the case in memory. I explain how presentification relates to "reproduction" later on.

[16] These reflections are then echoed eight years later in *Ideas I*, when Husserl states, in a passage concerning imagining, but clearly meant to have wider application, that "as long as one deals with mental processes as 'contents' or as psychical 'elements' which are still regarded as bits of things ([*Sächelchen*]) . . . there can be no improvement" (Husserl 1983: 262f.).

consciousness (Husserl 2005: 161). In a text already written in 1909, Husserl explicitly rejects his earlier "natural" model: "*On the contrary*," he declares, "'Consciousness' consists of consciousness through and through, and the sensation as well as phantasm is already 'consciousness'" (Husserl 2005: 323). There is no sheer phenomenal "matter" to be found "in" consciousness and in need of "mental form."

Now Husserl identifies imagining as a distinct and non-derivative act of consciousness that constitutes a *direct* sensory awareness (i.e., an awareness that is, like perception, unmediated by images) of objects, which are imagined of course, but not therefore any less "transcendent" in the phenomenological sense (as opposed to "immanent" to consciousness). Both perception and imagination constitute *unmediated* object consciousness in which "the intention aims . . . at an object in a direct way" (Husserl 2005: 192).[17] This insight might not look like much, but it effectively refutes (not by means of a logical argument, but based on painstakingly describing the differences between imagining something versus seeing something in an image) the "image theory" once again—now not only for perception, but also for phantasy. According to Husserl's increasingly maturing account, to imagine something is to relate to *it*, albeit in the mode of non-actuality or unreality, and *not* to a mental image that represents the object in its absence.

It is important in this context that Husserl thinks only of cases of intuitive (*anschauliche*) presentations as "genuine" cases of imagining (as opposed to, for example, cases of "mere supposing," or of "imagining that," which require no more than conceptual thinking). Presented in their intuitiveness (*Anschaulichkeit*), the imagined objects refer back to possible ways of intuiting them, which are thus implied in the act of imagining. In most cases, we imagine something as we would perceive it (under circumstances that would allow us to do so).[18] In those cases, we imagine not an image, neither merely the imagined object, but we also, often tacitly, quasi-experience *seeing*,

---

[17] "Direct" and "unmediated" here only refer to the lack of mediation by means of a third entity, such as an image, or more generally a representation. As I explain later on, there is a different sense of mediation that Husserl comes to adopt. Moreover, taking the genetic and generative dimensions of his later work into account, it is also clear that the "empirical" phantasy of any phenomenologists is never "untouched" by contexts of culture, language, etc. Husserl has a sophisticated account of the ways in which any "seeing as" is affected and conditions by those contexts—an account that, at a minimum, involves processes of "typification" (Husserl 1973) and "sedimentation" (Husserl 1970). Husserl thus even wonders "whether there is such a thing as a completely pure phantasy" since in "the realm of actual experience, every experience is bound into a nexus of actual experience" (Husserl 2005: 610). However, he still insists on at least the ideal of "pure phantasy" as what yields "pure possibility" (Husserl 2005: Text 19).

[18] This is not to say that we always imagine things *exactly* as we would perceive them if they were present. Our imagined perceptions may be, and often are, unlike any of our real ones. For example, I may in my imagination see Paris while flying over it, or hear fish have conversations with one another, or be able to touch my own heart. Still, when I visualize Paris, I necessarily visualize it from some perspective, and I cannot imagine it from all perspectives at the same time; when I hear fish talking, I cannot hear everything they say all at once; and when I imagine touching my own heart the way I imagine doing it still has to have essential features in common with experiences of actually touching something, or I would not be imagining *touching* it.

hearing, smelling, tasting, and/or *touching* it. An imagined object or scene is, in other words, imagined "as if" *being seen, heard, smelled, tasted,* and/or *touched.*[19] It is thus not the viewing of mental images that characterizes imagining, but the *simulation* of possible experiences of thus imagined objects.

The discovery of the complex structure of phantasy consciousness eventually helps Husserl to find a way to account for the "certain mediacy" (Husserl 2005: 25) that is still an undeniable aspect of imagining, even though imagining is "immediate" insofar as it does not rely on a present image to represent its absent object. Here Husserl mobilizes the profound insights into "inner consciousness" gained in the context of his intensive work on time consciousness around 1909–12. There he notes that awareness of objects is accompanied by a non-thetic awareness, a "lived experience (*Erleben*)" of the act "immanently perceived (internal consciousness), although naturally not posited, not meant" (Husserl 2005: 369; cf. Husserl 1991: 130ff.). This explains how phantasy can be both immediate and still have a "certain mediacy." While its *object* is intended "immediately" (i.e., without the mediation of a intermediary representation), the *act* of phantasy implies the "reproduction" of the act originally intending that object—of course, not "actually," but only in the modification of the "as if," as what I have called a "simulation" (Husserl 2005: 372f.).[20]

With this, a radical shift is made. Imagining is rid of the last "natural" remainders, and Husserl moves towards an account of consciousness within which we can distinguish only dynamic, inter-relational, reciprocally affecting, dependent moments of the complex whole—even in the case of phantasy consciousness alone.

Husserl's overcoming of "natural" conceptions of the imagination not only aids a "denaturalized" and complex notion of consciousness, but also corroborates the "wide" sense of reality in phenomenology. The discovery of "reproduction" in presentification here enables Husserl to account not only for actual objects (remembered, perceived, or anticipated) and non-actual objects (imagined), but also for *possible* objects. The *as if*-appearance of an *actual* object may also be grasped as an *actual* appearance of a *possible* object (Husserl 2005: 608, 633, 661f.); the *simulated* ("reproduced") act implied by the actual act of imagining may also grasped as a *possible* act or experience. By imagining, we may presentify an actuality or present a possibility (Husserl 1959: 116–19).

---

[19] Genuine imagining can thus, not using the classical German notion of "intuitive," be described as "sensory." Although perhaps less common, we can imagine not only perceiving something, but also remembering something, or anticipating something. In these cases, the acts are even more complex but still imply perception because to remember is to remember perceiving something (Husserl 2005: 367), and anticipating is to anticipate perceiving something (where remembering and anticipating are again understood in the "sensory" or "intuitive" sense).

[20] Husserl's technical term "reproduction" is, as he himself concedes (Husserl 2005: 372), misleading insofar as it suggests that imagining is confined literally to "reproducing" a former *actual* experience, which is not the case. All of these terms are attempts to approximate the sense of somehow experiencing something, as Bernet has put it, "from a distance" (Bernet 2004: 112). However, there also seems something right about the term "reproduction," namely insofar as it is plausible that we can only simulate a *type* of experience that is already available to us. This would mean that we cannot imagine a sound if we cannot hear, or a color if we cannot see.

Even though the recognition of such a possibility *as* possibility still requires a further "categorial" act (after all, we cannot take simply as possible whatever we imagine), the imagination nonetheless provides evidence for possibilities.[21]

The evidential power of the imagination, in particular with regards to pure possibilities, is of course exploited in Husserl's method of eidetic variation and thus indispensable for "eidetic analysis." Even though the imagination is not sufficient for knowledge of what is essential, the variation of different possibilities in imagination and thus the testing of the limits of such variability are necessary for the valid distinction between what is essential and what is inessential in a given case (Husserl 1983: 160; Husserl 1973: §§86–8). As Husserl puts it, it is by means of the imagination that from "every concrete actuality, and every individual trait actually experienced in it or capable of being experienced, a path stands open to the realm of ideal or pure possibility and consequently to that of a priori thinking" (Husserl 1973: 353f.). Imagining thus enables Husserlian phenomenology as "an a priori science, which confines itself to the realm of pure possibility (pure imaginableness) and, instead of judging about actualities of being (*Seinswirklichkeiten*), judges about its a priori possibilities and thus at the same time prescribes rules a priori for actualities" (Husserl 1960: 28). It is these "eidetic" and "a priori" ambitions that the existentialists Sartre and Merleau-Ponty vehemently reject. Husserl's "de-naturalization" of the imagination, on the contrary, is profoundly valuable to them both.

34.3 TRANSFORMATIVE TRAJECTORIES: SARTRE AND MERLEAU-PONTY

Sartre is evidently greatly inspired by Husserl's account of imagination. Not having access to Husserl's research manuscripts from which I have mostly cited, he relates to Husserl's early account of imagining, which emphasizes the proximity between imagining and image consciousness. Thus the "image" becomes central to Sartre's early existentialist phenomenology, a term that in the context of French philosophy also resonates with Bergson's earlier influential use of the term (Bergson 1994), although it has substantially little in common with it. While image consciousness is of interest to Husserl mainly as a contrast to imagining and in the context of his refutations of "image theory," he still provides us with one of the most insightful analyses on the topic to date. However, it is Sartre who elevates the analysis to general philosophical significance with his account of the "imaginary" (Sartre 2004).

---

[21] The correlation between what is "ideally" (not actually for any one imaginer) imaginable and what is possible only holds for what Husserl calls "pure possibilities." For further details on this point see Jansen forthcoming and Mohanty 1984.

Sartre is taken by Husserl's point regarding the "non-positing" character that image consciousness has in common with imagining. Indeed, this similarity explains why imagining is often understood by analogy with "seeing something in an image." Image consciousness involves an awareness of a perceptual image (for example a photograph, canvas or computer screen), which mediates the experience of the object that it depicts or lets us "see." In fact, looking at an image and seeing something "in it" involves, according to Husserl, three distinct moments: (1) the *physical image*, such as the patches of color distributed on the canvas, or the pixels on the screen; (2) the *image object*, i.e., the figure, which appears through a certain distribution of colors and shapes; and (3) the *image subject*, the object, person, or scene depicted or represented by the picture (Husserl 2005: 20f.). We need to perceive the physical image in order to be able to apprehend the image object and in order to "see" (or "hear," if we are listening to a musical "image") "in" it the depicted image subject.

Sartre also is as convinced as Husserl was that "images" cannot be found "in" consciousness. To make such a presupposition is, for Sartre, antithetical to the very idea of consciousness. It would be:

> Impossible to slip these material portraits into a conscious synthetic structure without destroying the structure, cutting the contacts, stopping the current, breaking the continuity. Consciousness would cease to be transparent to itself; everywhere its unity would be broken by the inassimilable, opaque screens. (Sartre 2004: 6)

However, for Husserl, the fact that image consciousness requires the perception of an actual image while imagining does not, constitutes an essential difference between two fundamentally different modes of consciousness. Sartre, on the contrary, emphasizes that both the "image object" (the image "proper," in contradistinction to its physical carrier and to the subject it pictures) and the "imagined object" are, as Husserl had already put it, "nothing," a "nullity" (Husserl 2005: 50, 51). He thus drops Husserl's strict distinction between imagining and image consciousness and instead attempts to pay equal attention to various members of the "the image family" (Sartre 2004: 17), thus opening up the field of "the imaginary"—from the most the most concrete (a photograph of Pierre) via increasingly abstract ones (portraits, caricatures, impersonations, drawings, hypnagogic images, even things seen in coffee grounds and crystal balls) to mental images. In all these cases the respective image is "no thing," but "nothing other than a relation," namely "the relation of consciousness to the object," or an "act" (Sartre 2004: 7, 9), as Sartre puts it, "that aims in its corporeality at an absent or nonexistent object, through a physical or psychic content that is given not as itself but in the capacity of 'analogical representative' of the object aimed at" (Sartre 2004: 20, 52). The "certain mediacy" that Husserl attempted to clarify by means of his notion of "reproduction" Sartre thus accounts for by means of his notion of the "analogon."

A photograph, a caricature, a mental image of Pierre:

> In the three cases, I aim at the object in the same way: it is on the ground of perception that I want to make the face of Pierre appear, I want to "make it present" to me.

> And, as I cannot make a direct perception of him spring up, I make use of a certain matter that acts as an *analogon*, as an equivalent of perception. (Sartre 2004: 18)

What at first sight might look like a relapse into a "natural" understanding that reverts to a present "matter" as a stand-in for an absent object,[22] in fact betrays both how Sartre uses Husserl's "de-naturalization" and also departs from him in an existentialist transformation of imagination. Not being tied to a "natural" understanding, Sartre can use "matter" here in the sense of Husserl's *Logical Investigations* as "that element in an act which first gives it reference to an object, and reference . . . the precise way it is meant" (Husserl 2001: vol. 2, 121). As Sartre is thus able to elucidate, the "as if" character that pertains to all images is due to the fact that their matter is somehow "insufficient" for presenting the object "in person"; we make do with it, but it is only an "analogon." Where no physical analogon is available, there is still, according to Sartre, a "psychical" one, perhaps including memories of the imagined object (Sartre 2004: 14), beliefs concerning it, or emotions, bodily sensations, and other modes of consciousness that help imagine it in "the precise way it is meant." There is, then, inherent in images a gap between their matter and what it enables us to imagine—a source of shifts, substitutions, transferences, and distortions. This very gap, on the one hand, inescapably ties consciousness to its facticity (from which it must take its *analoga*) and, on the other hand, enables consciousness to transcend it (because it never coincides with them).

Thus, at least for the early Sartre, the imagination becomes paradigmatic for consciousness as a whole and critical to his understanding of freedom. For to imagine one "must be able to deny the reality of the picture, and . . . deny this reality . . . by standing back from reality grasped in its totality. To posit an image is to constitute an object in the margin of the totality of the real, it is therefore to hold the real at a distance, to be freed from it, in a word, to deny it" (Sartre 2004: 183). It is only by being able to (imaginatively) negate and hold at bay what actually impinges on us that we become able to step back and grasp our surroundings, i.e., our world, as a whole. Only then can we understand ourselves existentially as in a particular situation to which we can respond and which we can change. For Sartre, "a *philosopher* of the imaginary," the imagination is thus "the locus of possibility, negativity and lack, articulated in creative freedom" (Flynn 2014: 76; my emphasis).

By contrast, in his provocative essay "The Philosopher and his Shadow," Merleau-Ponty points to that which *resists* the common practice of philosophy and, at the same time, refuses immediate dismissal.[23] Even the phenomenological method—itself

---

[22] This concern has been at the heart of many of criticisms against Sartre's account of imagination. See for example Hering 1947; Casey 1981; Ricœur 1981; Kearney 1991.

[23] I realize that I am here comparing the early Sartre with the late Merleau-Ponty, and I do not want to present the contrast I am drawing out in this context as a general difference between the two. I use it instead in order to emphasize two quite different ways in which the imagination has been taken in the history of phenomenology after Husserl. That said, it is also true that whereas Sartre began his own philosophizing with the imagination, Merleau-Ponty only gradually came to appreciate its significance (Mazis 2016: 75).

meant to resurrect "authentic" philosophy—has its limits: simultaneously attempting to describe the complexity of experience without being able to contain or reflect it in its entirety or ever being able to account for its source. Merleau-Ponty's task, then, is to do phenomenology by other means, by means that help us see, show, or think what cannot be spoken of philosophically, or be described phenomenologically. As he says in *Signs*, "What resists phenomenology within us—natural being, the 'barbarian' source Schelling spoke of—cannot remain outside phenomenology and should have its place within it" (Merleau-Ponty 1964a: 178). It finds, Merleau-Ponty contends, its way into phenomenology as it is practiced by Cézanne, by Klee, and by Proust. Through this admission, Merleau-Ponty's philosophy becomes, as Barbaras has put it, "a philosophy which feeds and limits the classical pretensions of philosophy—a philosophy of non-philosophy" (Barbaras 2004: 70). The inclusion of philosophy's outside also draws attention to the imagination as one of the most persistent of its "internal" pretensions. Again, it is not the philosopher, for Merleau-Ponty, but the artist who is well aware that what she imagines does not have its sole origin and cannot be contained or controlled from "within."

The imagination here attains a significant *ontological* role that is also based on Merleau-Ponty's realization that the existentialist position should not misconstrue human existence as either shackled to the real, or as finding its freedom in opposing it:

> On the basis of what I have said, one might think that I hold that man lives only in the realm of the real. But we also live in the imaginary, also in the world of ideality. Thus it is necessary to develop a theory of imaginary existence. (Merleau-Ponty 1964b: 40)

While Husserl shows us that the real emerges from a dynamic play of interrelated presences and absences, and while Sartre attempts to keep apart perception and imagination, Merleau-Ponty questions any stark contrast between the real and the imaginary. He thus shows us that what we call "the real" is not a solid, fully present totality of objects and events that stand in explicable, causal relations to one another: a fully observable, perceivable realm that can be fully accounted for by the means of natural science. Merleau-Ponty, on the contrary, reminds us of the instability of the real—of its dynamism, of its imaginary dimensions, of its oneiric qualities, which are not confined to the "other" of reality, to our reveries, our poetic and artistic creations, our feverish fantasies and pathological aberrations, or our childhood plays and dreams; but which permeate the very real itself, its fringes, its gaps, its in-surmountables, its un-emcompassables, its affects. Imagination, like perception, is "not a retreat from the world, but a way of moving further into it" (Semonovich and de Roo 2010: 160); "to imagine is to stretch out toward the real object" (Merleau-Ponty 1968: 177) in affective and motor intentionality. With this, Merleau-Ponty has transformed the imagination into an ontological element of embodied being which can only be appropriately elucidated by means of an embodied imaginative ontology.

Husserl thought, to a certain extent, that ontology should be done in this way. The famous, now perhaps trite sounding adage that "fiction is the vital element of phenomenology" (Husserl 1983: 160), is meant, I take it, to encourage us, to demand from us that we explore the ontological, in Husserl's view, "essential" linings of reality *imaginatively*.[24] With the late Merleau-Ponty, we can take this further, albeit differently, namely by thinking of imagining as a practice of "exploration of an invisible and the disclosure of a universe of ideas" (Merleau-Ponty 1968: 130). However, the imagination here is not solely anymore the activity of an individual "consciousness" (of an imagining philosopher even); and the "imaginary" is not "a mere figment of my imagination, a mental entity that I could still possess in the very absence of its object" (Dufourcq 2015: 33). Rather, the imaginative "exploration of the invisible" only expresses and responds to the "imaginal" (Mazis 2016: 175) *of the "flesh"*—a "fundamental dimension of the real" (Dufourcq 2012: 187–9), which is part and parcel of the intricate "intertwining (*entrelacs*)" of things and ideas that "institutes" being (Merleau-Ponty 1968: 262). Like "flesh" itself, the "imaginal" thus is, for Merleau-Ponty, "a 'general thing' between the individual and the idea that does not correspond to any traditional philosophical concept, but is closest to the notion of an 'element' in the classical sense" (Toadvine 2016; Merleau-Ponty 1968: 139).

With this, any description *ad distans* of "the imagination" becomes a philosophical pipe dream. Imaginative interrogation takes the place of description: reversible interrogation, in which the philosopher at times takes the lead, but in which she also must be open to be questioned; in which she is vulnerable to being summoned and exposed, and to being called to respond; an interrogation in which the philosopher concedes that she is not in control, but still free—free also to let herself be taken by the pull of being.

34.4 CONCLUSION

Husserl's *de-naturalization* opens up a distinct phenomenological approach to the imagination. Both Sartre and Merleau-Ponty, despite their disagreements with one another and with Husserl, appropriate this de-naturalized notion and take it into two very different directions: Sartre emphasizes the freedom of the imagination and its existential significance while Merleau-Ponty understands the "imaginal" ontologically as a very dimension of the real. For Sartre, the imagination thus retains its link to an imagining consciousness whereas for Merleau-Ponty it is a doing and being "of the flesh," that is, an intricate element of the very interweaving of the texture of being.

---

[24] Husserl's method of "eidetic variation" may seem like the epitome of a "disciplined" and "controlled" imagination, an imagination that is degraded, once again, to being a handmaiden to the understanding, to being a power of "mere" variation. Husserl, on the contrary, insisted on the absolute necessity that this imagination be *free*. Only then can it test and challenge the strictures of our conventional ontologies in order to help us discover, among the many inessential and arbitrary distinctions and attributions we make, those for whose essentiality we can gather some evidence (evidence, which he thought could never be infallible, but that, if right, would bear out the *logos* of being).

Thereby, Merleau-Ponty also picks up Husserl's conviction that the imagination is central for a phenomenological ontology. However, according to Merleau-Ponty, the imagination not only varies, but potentially *transforms* the ontological texture, as it were, "from within." This is one reason why Merleau-Ponty speaks of the imaginary also as a "*Stiftung* (institution) of being" (Merleau-Ponty 1968: 316). This "oneiric being" (Merleau-Ponty 2000: 281) is an anonymous imaginary field and is as such creative. It is the excess of being. We, who are *of* this excessive being, are free to modulate and change the "order of things"—exposing and reconfiguring the ambiguities, dynamics, and openness of being, thereby exploring and interrogating being and letting ourselves be explored and interrogated (Merleau-Ponty 1993: 129).

References

Barbaras, R. (2004), *The Being of the Phenomenon: Merleau-Ponty's Ontology*, translated by T. Toadvine and L. Lawlor (Bloomington, IN: Indiana University Press).

Baudrillard, J. (1995), "Illusion, desillusion, ästhetik," in Stefan Iglhaut et al. (eds), *Illusion und Simulation* (Ostfildern: Cantz), 90–101.

Bergson, H. (1994), *Matter and Memory*, translated by N. M. Paul and W. S. Palmer (New York: Zone Books).

Bernet, R. (2004), *Conscience et existence. Perspectives phénoménologiques* (Paris: Presses universitaires de France).

Bernet, R. (2012), "Phenomenological and aesthetic epoché: Painting the invisible things themselves" in D. Zahavi (ed.), *The Oxford Handbook of Contemporary Phenomenology* (Oxford: Oxford University Press), 564–82.

Braver, L. (2007), *A Thing of this World: A History of Continental Anti-Realism* (Evanston, IL: Northwestern University Press).

Brentano, F. (1995), *Descriptive Psychology*, translated by B. Müller (London: Routledge).

Brough, J. (2005), "Translator's introduction," in E. Husserl, *Phantasy, Image Consciousness and Memory (1898–1925)* (Dordrecht: Springer), xxix–lxviii.

Brough, J. (2012), "Something that is nothing but can be anything: The image and our consciousness of it," in D. Zahavi (ed.), *The Oxford Handbook of Contemporary Phenomenology* (Oxford: Oxford University Press), 545–63.

Casey, E. S. (1976), *Imagining: A Phenomenological Study* (Bloomington, IN: Indiana University Press).

Casey, E. S. (1981), "Sartre on imagination," in P. A. Schilpp (ed.), *The Philosophy of Jean-Paul Sartre* (La Salle, IL: Open Court), 139–66.

Castoriadis, C. (1994), "Radical imagination and the social instituting imaginary," in G. Robinson (ed.), *Rethinking Imagination: Culture and Creativity* (New York: Routledge), 136–54.

Conrad, W. (1908–9), "Der ästhetische Gegenstand. Eine phänomenologische Studie," *Zeitschrift für Ästhetik und allgemeine Kunstwissenschaft* 2: 71–118; 3: 469–511; 4: 400–55.

Depraz, N. (2010), "Imagination" in H. R. Sepp and L. E. Embree (eds), *Handbook of Phenomenological Aesthetics* (Dordrecht: Springer), 155–60.

Dillon, M. C. (1998), *Merleau-Ponty's Ontology* (Evanston, IL: Northwestern University Press).

Dufourcq, A. (2012), *Merleau-Ponty: Une Ontologie de l'Imaginaire* (Dordrecht: Springer).

Dufourcq, A. (2015), "The Fundamental Imaginary Dimension of the Real in Merleau-Ponty's Philosophy," *Research in Phenomenology* 45/1: 33–52.

Dufrenne, M. (1973), *The Phenomenology of Aesthetic Experience*, translated by E. Casey (Evanston, IL: Northwestern University Press).

Elliot, B. (2005), *Phenomenology and Imagination in Husserl and Heidegger* (New York: Routledge).

Fink, E. (1930), "Vergegenwärtigung und Bild," *Jahrbuch für Philosophie und phänomenologische Forschung* 11: 239–309.

Flynn, T. R. (2014), *Sartre: A Philosophical Biography* (Cambridge: Cambridge University Press).

Geiger, M. (1913), "Beiträge zur Phänomenologie des ästhetischen Genusses," *Jahrbuch für Philosophie und phänomenologische Forschung* 1: 567–684.

Heidegger, M. (1971) "The origin of the work of art," in *Poetry, Language, Thought*, translated by A. Hofstadter (New York: Harper and Row), 17–87.

Heidegger, M. (2010), *Being and Time*, translated by J. Stambaugh, revised by D. J. Schmidt (Albany, NY: SUNY Press).

Hering, J. (1947), "Concerning Image, Idea, and Dream," *Philosophy and Phenomenological Research* 8/2: 188–205.

Husserl, E. (1959), *Erste Philosophie (1923/4). Zweiter Teil: Theorie der phänomenologischen Reduktion*, Husserliana 8 (The Hague: Martinus Nijhoff).

Husserl, E. (1960), *Cartesian Meditations*, translated by D. Cairns (The Hague: Martinus Nijhoff).

Husserl, E. (1965), "Philosophy as Rigorous Science," translated and edited by Q. Lauer (ed.), *Phenomenology and the Crisis of Philosophy* (New York: Harper), 71–147.

Husserl, E. (1970), *The Crisis of European Sciences and Transcendental Phenomenology*, translated by D. Carr (Evanston, IL: Northwestern University Press).

Husserl, E. (1973), *Experience and Judgment*, translated by J. S. Churchill and K. Ameriks (Evanston, IL: Northwestern University Press).

Husserl, E. (1983), *Ideas Pertaining to a Pure Phenomenology and to a Phenomenological Philosophy, First Book*, translated by F. Kersten (Dordrecht: Martinus Nijhoff).

Husserl, E. (1989), *Ideas pertaining to a Pure Phenomenology and to a Phenomenological Philosophy, Second Book*, translated by R. Rojcewicz and A. Schuwer (Dordrecht: Kluwer).

Husserl, E. (1991), *On the Phenomenology of the Consciousness of Internal Time (1893–1917)*, translated by J. Brough (Dordrecht: Kluwer).

Husserl, E. (1997), *Thing and Space: Lectures of 1907*, translated by R. Rojcewicz (Dordecht: Kluwer).

Husserl, E. (2001), *Logical Investigations*, 2 vol., ed. D. Moran, translated by J. N. Findley, with a forward by M. Dummett (London: Routledge).

Husserl, E. (2005), *Phantasy, Image Consciousness and Memory (1898–1925)*, translated by J. Brough (Dordrecht: Springer).

Husserl, E. (2009), "Letter to Hofmannsthal (January 12, 1907), translated by S.-O. Wallenstein, *Site*, 26–27: 2.

Ingarden, R. (1973), *The Literary Work of Art*, translated by G. G. Grabowicz (Evanston, IL: Northwestern University Press).

Jansen, J. (2005), "Phantasy's systematic place in Husserl's work," in R. Bernet, D. Welton and G. Zavota (eds), *Edmund Husserl: Critical Assessments of Leading Philosophers, vol. 3.* (New York: Routledge), 221–43.

Jansen J. (2014), "Imagination: Phenomenological accounts," in M. Kelly (ed.), *Encyclopedia of Aesthetics, 2nd ed.* (Oxford: Oxford University Press), 430–4.

Jansen, J. (2015), "Imagination: Phenomenological approaches," in *Routledge Encyclopedia of Philosophy*, URL https://www.rep.routledge.com/articles/imagination-phenomenological-approaches/v-1/.

Jansen, J. (2016), "Husserl," in A. Kind (ed.), *Routledge Handbook of the Imagination* (London: Routledge), 69–81.

Jansen, J. (forthcoming), "Possibility and Its Conditions," *Husserl Studies*.

Kaufmann, F. and Heider, F. (1947), "On Imagination," *Philosophy and Phenomenological Research 7/3*: 369–75.

Kearney, R. (1991), *Poetics of Imagining* (London: Harper Collins).

Marbach, E. (1980), "Einleitung des Herausgebers" in E. Husserl, *Phantasie, Bildbewußtsein, Erinnerung*, Husserliana 23, ed. E. Marbach (The Hague: Martinus Nijhoff), xxv–lxxxii.

Marbach, E. (1993), "The phenomenology of intuitional presentation," in R. Bernet, I. Kern, and E. Marbach (eds), *An Introduction to Husserlian Phenomenology* (Evanston, IL: Northwestern University Press), 141–65.

Mazis, G. A. (2016), *Merleau-Ponty and the Face of the World: Silence, Ethics, Imagination, and Poetic Ontology* (Albany, NY: SUNY Press).

Meinong, A. (1904), *Untersuchungen zur Gegenstandstheorie und Psychologie* (Leipzig: Barth).

Merleau-Ponty, M. (1964a), "The philosopher and his shadow," in *Signs* (Evanston, IL: Northwestern University Press), 159–81.

Merleau-Ponty, M. (1964b), "The primacy of perception and its philosophical consequences," in *The Primacy of Perception*, translated by C. Dallery (Evanston, IL: Northwestern University Press).

Merleau-Ponty, M. (1968), *The Visible and the Invisible*, translated by A. Lingis (Evanston, IL: Northwestern University Press).

Merleau-Ponty, M. (1993), "Eye and mind," in G. Strawson and M. Smith (eds), *The Merleau-Ponty Aesthetics Reader* (Evanston, IL: Northwestern University Press), 121–49.

Merleau-Ponty, M. (2000), "L'Oeuvre et l'esprit de Freud" in *Parcours deux* (Lagrasse: Verdier), 276–84.

Merleau-Ponty, M. (2005), *Phenomenology of Perception*, translated by C. Smith (New York: Routledge).

Mohanty, J. N. (1984), "Husserl on 'Possibility,'" *Husserl Studies* 1: 13–29.

Moran, D. (2008), "Husserl's Transcendental Philosophy and the Critique of Naturalism," *Continental Philosophy Review* 41: 401–25.

Richir, M. (2004), *Phantasia, Imagination, Affectivité* (Grenoble: Millon).

Ricœur, P. (1978), *The Rule of Metaphor*, translated by R. Czerny with K. McLaughlin and J. Costello (Toronto: University of Toronto Press).

Ricœur, P. (1981), "Sartre and Ryle on the imagination," in P. A. Schilpp (ed.), *The Philosophy of Jean-Paul Sartre* (La Salle, IL: Open Court), 167–78.

Ricœur, P. (1986), *Lectures on Ideology and Utopia*, ed. G. H. Taylor (New York: Columbia University Press).

Rollinger, R. D. (2008), *Austrian Phenomenology* (Frankfurt: Ontos).

Rowlands, M. (2016), *Memory and the Self. Phenomenology, Science, and Autobiography* (Oxford: Oxford University Press).

Sartre, J.-P. (2004), *The Imaginary*, translated by J. Webber (New York: Routledge).

Sartre, J.-P. (2012), *The Imagination*, translated by K. Williford and D. Rudrauf (London: Routledge).

Semonovich, K. and de Roo, N. (eds) (2010), "Introduction," in *Merleau-Ponty at the Limits of Art, Religion, and Perception* (New York: Bloomsbury Continuum).

Steeves, J. B. (2004), *Imagining Bodies: Merleau-Ponty's Philosophy of Imagination* (Pittsburgh, PA: Duquesne University Press).

Toadvine, T. (2016), "Maurice Merleau-Ponty," *The Stanford Encyclopedia of Philosophy* (Winter 2016 Edition), Edward N. Zalta (ed.), URL https://plato.stanford.edu/archives/win2016/entries/merleau-ponty/.

Twardowski, K. (1977), *On the Content and Object of Presentations*, translated by R. Grossmann (The Hague: Martinus Nijhoff).

CHAPTER 35

....

VALUE, FREEDOM, RESPONSIBILITY

Central Themes in Phenomenological Ethics

....

SOPHIE LOIDOLT

35.1 PHENOMENOLOGICAL APPROACHES TO ETHICS: VALUE, FREEDOM, RESPONSIBILITY

....

IN the history of phenomenology, different sets of ethical problems and phenomena have emerged, concerning, for example, our access to values, the nature of our freedom, or the source of our ethical responsibility.[1,2] Different critical and affirmative links have been drawn to the philosophical tradition, first and foremost to Aristotelian and Kantian ethics, as well as to the Humean and utilitarian tradition by Scheler, Brentano, Husserl, and Heidegger. Further connections have been established to Kierkegaard by the existential phenomenologists, to Plato and the Bible by Levinas, and to hedonism and neo-Kantianism by Husserl—just to mention a few of the various fields of discussion. Like phenomenology itself, the different approaches do not form a unitary corpus, but instead represent a phenomenological style of addressing the topic.

Yet, the question might arise whether ethics[3] is such an important topic in the history of phenomenology after all. Three of the most important figures of the

[1] I would like to thank the anonymous reviewers and especially Steven Crowell, Andrea Staiti, Inga Römer, and Ullrich Melle for their helpful commentaries on earlier versions of this chapter.
[2] The standard publication that gives a comprehensive picture of the diversity and broadness of phenomenological positions in ethics is Drummond and Embree 2002. Cf. also Sanders/Wisnewski 2012.
[3] As for the equivocality and difference between the terms "ethics" and "morality" in different traditions, see Drummond (2002: 2f.). I will use these terms more or less interchangeably, with a preference for "ethics," here referring to the philosophical reflection on moral norms and demands.

phenomenological tradition, namely Husserl, Heidegger, and Merleau-Ponty, have either not published works on ethics during their lifetimes or have, like Heidegger (1998: 271f.), even explicitly rejected the idea of it. In the case of Heidegger, much work has been done by phenomenologists in the last decades to elaborate on the normative implications of existence in spite of this (e.g., Olafson 1998, Crowell 2015). More remains to be done after the publication of Heidegger's *Black Notebooks*, which has again made reconsideration of what his approach implies in terms of ethics and politics inevitable (Farin and Malpas 2016). Husserl's *Nachlass*, by contrast, speaks clearly for the formerly hidden importance of ethics in his broader work and his ethical writings are discussed with increasing interest today. Ethics was not only a recurring topic for Husserl's detailed phenomenological considerations, but also a major driving force for his entire project of transcendental phenomenology in the context of an enlightened ethical humanism (cf. Husserl 1989). Finally, also Merleau-Ponty's work has started to be evaluated in terms of its ethical implications (Hamrick 1987), and the posthumous publication of Sartre's *Cahiers pour une morale* (Sartre 1992b) underlines the concern for the topic shared by French existential phenomenologists.

Clearly, an engagement with phenomenological ethics only starts with mentioning these developments. The most salient and influential representatives of a phenomenological approach to ethics have gone far beyond mere implicit or unpublished ethical considerations: Max Scheler and the group of value ethicists in early phenomenology, as well as Emmanuel Levinas have written works chiefly on ethics, with Levinas even having declared ethics to be "first philosophy." However, interrelation or common discussion between these two positions scarcely occurs. Rather, they represent two different strands in phenomenological ethics: value ethics on the one hand, and alterity-ethics on the other.[4] As it stands now both strands have a strong and growing group of representatives and both are engaged in vivid discussions on issues of normativity, virtue-ethics, moral realism or anti-realism on the one hand (see Drummond 1995, 2002a; Hermberg and Gyllenhammer 2013; Hart and Embree 1997), and implications for social and political philosophy on the other (see Bernasconi 2005; Mensch 2003; Waldenfels 2012; Bedorf 2011). The general tendency of the last thirty years to cross borders between Kantian, deontological and Aristotelian, eudaimonistic approaches has also been reflected by phenomenologists: Value ethicists tackle questions concerning the ground of obligation (Drummond 2005, Steinbock 2014); Kantian influenced phenomenologists investigate the role of normativity and affectivity (Rinofner 2010, Römer 2014); and some even actively join both approaches (Ricœur 1992). Hence, ethics has not only been an important theme in the history of phenomenology; it is also a hot topic today.

In light of this, I want to look again at the systematic thread that leads through these explicit and implicit discussions of ethical issues in the works of major

---

[4] Other historical figures from the early period of phenomenology that are to be mentioned alongside Scheler are Dietrich von Hildebrand, Moritz Geiger, Nicolai Hartmann, Edith Stein, Adolf Reinach, and Herbert Spiegelberg. As for the later development of alterity-ethics further prominent representatives are Jacques Derrida, Paul Ricœur, and Bernhard Waldenfels.

phenomenological authors. What I want to undertake in this article is the rather un-common task of showing what are the crucial and connecting elements that make an approach to ethics a "phenomenological" one—even if the results might plainly differ. Usually the two lines of value ethics and alterity ethics are kept apart,[5] which prevents seeing that those diverging approaches arise from common grounds that are then subse-quently taken into different directions. Furthermore, the field must be divided not only into two, but into at least three big groups that have consecutively developed in critical reference to each other: (a) a personalistic ethics of values and feelings, (b) an existen-tialist ethics of freedom and authenticity, and (c) an ethics of alterity and responsibility.

My goal here is not to force these debates together. Rather, I want to show that there is a common thread running through the course of historical development from value ethics to an ethics of freedom and, finally, to an ethics of responsibility, where each approach discovers a new set of problems. Instead of reading this as something like a teleological development, the contemporary discussion shows that we are dealing with equally important fields. My focus here will be on the inner systematic, "phenomeno-logical" link between these fields—and the specific strength these arguments develop in ethical argumentation. I propose that this link can be recognized in the following three interconnected topics:

(1) All approaches address a certain concept of *subjectivity* that explains *how eth-ical issues can gain relevance for us in the first place*. The answers are, respectively, (a) through the feeling person; (b) through Dasein who is an issue for itself; (c) through a subjectivity that is summoned by the call of alterity.

(2) These theories of a subjectivity susceptible to ethics are respectively accompanied by different concepts of *intentionality*: (a) the intentionality of consciousness in emotive and evaluative acts; (b) Dasein's "transcendence" as a radicalized notion of intentionality; (c) intentionality as being inverted by the ethical call.

(3) Hence, phenomenological approaches to ethics deal with "ethical experience"—ranging from emotions (such as love) as a way of experiencing values, and affective experiences (such as anxiety) as a form of existential self-encounter, to experiences that exceed the realm of emotions and embrace the dimensions of speech and interaction (such as the experience of the other). Phenomenologists analyze the structure of those experiences that essentially constitute us as ethical beings and claim that normative questions can only arise in this venue.

In the second and main section, section 35.2, I spell out how these key terms of sub-jectivity, experience, and intentionality become relevant for ethical argumentation by portraying the transitions and interrelations between the three main ethical approaches.

---

[5] This manifests itself, for example, in the layout of the *Routledge Companion to Phenomenology*, where two articles on "Moral Philosophy" (Rinofner 2012) on the one hand, and "Ethics as First Philosophy" on the other, appear completely independently from one another.

In section 35.3, I examine which forms of practical reason and justification follow from this and I elaborate on the strengths of a phenomenological perspective on ethical questions.

35.2 WHY ARE WE ETHICAL BEINGS? SUBJECTIVITY, EXPERIENCE, INTENTIONALITY

Most phenomenological reflections on ethics do not directly address the issue as to how my actions and motives can be justified. Rather, they focus on the question as to how it is possible in the first place that the ethical becomes meaningful in relation to the subject; or, to put it differently, how it is possible that we are ethically affected at all. Only through this, is a field of meaning constituted wherein normative questions can gain relevance. The respective answers as to how this happens seem quite divergent at first: *Because we feel. Because we are free. Because we are responsive.* Yet, these differences can be coherently understood along the lines of the development of the notions of intentionality and subjectivity. In fact, I would like to claim that the endorsement of a certain notion of intentionality has a stronger impact on a phenomenologist's ethical conception than his or her Kantian, Aristotelian, Platonic, or Marxist convictions. Rather, the main question beyond these general orientations is whether intentionality and its "bearer" are conceived of as a person cognizing values, as a self-projecting transcendence, or as a subjectivity that is radically put into question. Accordingly, ethical experience is conceptualized as the "givenness of values," as "free self-projection," or as "responding to the other."

35.2.1 Value ethics

The first major work of phenomenological ethics, Max Scheler's (1973) *Formalism in Ethics and Non-Formal Ethics of Values*, published in 1913, positions itself prominently against Kant. It counters any type of formalistic ethics with a material ethics grounded in values. This is made possible primarily by the phenomenological notion of intentionality: Scheler's main argument against Kant is that he has degraded the sphere of sensibility to an irrational, causally induced a posteriori, precisely because he does not see its intentional character: i.e., the *givenness* of "the experienced" in an act of "experiencing," and therefore, an "openness to the world" instead of blindly caused, unfree states of a self-enclosed mind. For Kant, no material ethics can ever claim validity, since he regards affection in experience as empirical, contingent, and only leading to hedonistic principles.

Against this, Scheler argues that, first, the ethical remains inconceivable without the sphere of emotions and that, second, emotive acts of feeling and valuing do in fact possess an a priori, thanks to their intentional structure. This a priori is accessible via eidetic insight. Scheler thereby not only opens up the phenomenal field of direct and irreducible value-experience. He also claims that in it our ethical being is fundamentally grounded and our ethical judgments ground their validity. This is how intentionality becomes an ethically and meta-ethically relevant topic: It allows for the argument that we have an immediate, non-constructive, and cognitivist access to the world in its ethically relevant features.

Scheler argues that values are given directly in the intentional feeling of value-experience or value-perception/value-taking (*Wertnehmen*). They are neither deduced through judgments nor constructed through processes of practical reason—just like how the sensuous qualities of colors cannot be constructed, but instead have to be experienced. In acts of feeling, values are given to us in their distinct qualities. These qualities are not simply empirical occurrences. Rather, they display essential differences like the difference between the essences of red and blue (see Scheler 1973: 163–7). Accordingly, our ethical experience can be as diverse as the range of colors, acquainting us with the good, the noble, the beautiful, the wise, the detestable, the vile, etc. According to Scheler (1973: 260), in the experience of values not only do qualities become apparent, but also objective rankings. The latter are encountered in the acts of preferring (*Vorziehen*) and placing after (*Nachsetzen*). Along these lines, he develops a ranking of certain groups of values, starting out with sensory values (pleasant/painful) at the bottom, leading up to vital values (noble/common), cultural and spiritual values (true/false, right/wrong, beautiful/ugly), and finally holy values (profane/sacred).

Scheler combines this material a priori, cognized through emotive acts, with a strong notion of the *person*. Thereby, he dynamically interrelates value universalism with value individualism. This opens up the second relevant ethical field for phenomenology: Persons intentionally experience values, specifically through the acts of loving and hating. This characterizes the distinguished type of being that they are. Now, in addition to the order of values lying within their experienced qualities, each person has her individual "*ordo amoris*" (Scheler 1957) calling her to realize specific constellations of values. Scheler does not see a contradiction in this setup, but rather a pluralistic approach to historically, culturally, and personally specific possibilities of realizations of values without there being any need to give up on their objectivity.

The ethical "ought" for Scheler is founded in the positive value itself which calls for its realization. Importantly, moral obligation is thereby grounded primarily in insight and not in duty, like in the Kantian model. Although in the tradition of value ethics the detailed experience of values has been spelled out in different ways (first and foremost by von Hildebrand, but also by Hartmann, Geiger, Kolnai, Stein, Reinach, etc.), the general approach of Scheler, being based on cognitive emotional intentionality, unites the phenomenological value ethicists.

Husserl's early confrontation with ethics, documented in a manuscript from 1902, is—just like Scheler's approach—mainly a criticism of Kant, inspired by his teacher

Brentano. And just like Scheler, Husserl argues primarily by using the notion of intentionality (Husserl 1988: 402–17). Husserl attacks the general Kantian notion that reason as an a priori principle "forms," as it were, the empirical. For Husserl, this amounts to a nonsensical intertwining of the a priori and the factical (cf. Husserl 2004: 221). As his counter-model, he proposes that the essential structure of something has to be grasped intuitively from the factical, like the geometrician grasps the essential structure of the triangle by looking at a factically drawn triangle. All intentional correlations as well as their parts can thus be analyzed with respect to their essential structures. From his theory of intentionality, Husserl derives a clear scheme about how a phenomenological ethics must be constructed (Husserl 1988): The respective eidetic insights are to be drawn from the emotive acts (Gemütsakte) of valuing and willing as well as from their correlates. This has to be done with respect to formal and material aspects, which results in something like a "mathesis universalis" of the ethical: The formal part tells me how to value and will reasonably, i.e., consistently with respect to the inner logic of the acts themselves, but without regard to their content; the material part clarifies what actually is "the best among the attainable" in a concrete situation—i.e., Brentano's formulation of the categorical imperative, which Husserl (1988: 153) adopts.

Interestingly, Husserl, without explicitly giving up this scheme and its theoretical requirements, later moves in a different direction in order to articulate the relevance of the ethical. On the one hand, this happens because he increasingly takes seriously the individualizing ethical experience of the person; on the other hand, he faces so many difficulties spelling out the evidence of non-objectifying acts like valuing and willing that, unlike Scheler, he never actually presents a hierarchical catalogue of material values. Another contrast to Scheler lies in Husserl's argument that non-objectifying acts (valuing, willing) have to build on objectifying acts (mainly perception). Whereas Scheler (1973: 68) would not accept such a conditional structure and instead gives a certain primacy to value-perception, Husserl (1988: 255–7) argues that I can only value something if it is "given" to me. Hence, there is no such thing as value-perception that might simply be "up in the air" and not connected to anything (see Drummond 2002a: 33f.). Accordingly I can only will something if I have valued it positively. Analyzing this conditional structure of intentional acts allows for a rich description of ethical experience and makes the necessary motivational layers for actions conceivable in intentional consciousness. But—and this is also one of Husserl's main questions—does this already capture what it means to be ethically affected?

Husserl's later ethics deals with this question. On the one hand, he responds to it with his "ethics of renewal" (Husserl 1989), which has teleological and perfectionist features. But he also draws on the Kantian notion of obligation. This question arises in the context of Husserl's experiences of the First World War, which deeply shattered his belief in the ability to realize the universal telos of an "ethical mankind" (Husserl 2014: 301–13). Since this telos could now only provide a fragile motivational basis for ethics, the imperative of an "absolute ought" becomes more important (Loidolt 2012). On the other hand, Husserl develops an "ethics of love" in fragments, which, with a certain Schelerian flair, puts the person and her individual ethical love in the centre (Melle 2002, Hart 1992).

This makes Husserl shift to the view that values are no longer emotionally "cognized," but are instead experienced in an ethical call, constituting the existential task of each person, her "vocation" (Husserl 2014: 388–90). Nevertheless, these values remain experienced as something "given" and not "constructed" or "created." Rather, the person undergoes her ethical call passively, which Husserl also describes in the language of his later genetic phenomenology of passivity and affectivity.

With this brief foray into the characteristics of personalist value ethics, we can see that in earlier phenomenological approaches to ethics the specifically phenomenological answer to the question "Why is ethics relevant for us at all?" is as follows: *because we are specific beings, persons, to whom the world is opened up by our intentional feelings.* Through them, we discover values as the correlates of feeling that exceed the mere function of being relative to our subjective pleasures. Rather, intentional acts of feeling *disclose* an ethical reality beyond our mere inclinations. What we feel is *ethically* relevant for us, first, because we value it, which includes acts of preferring; second, because the positively valuable implies an "ought" to realize it and motivates the will to do so; and third, because we are persons who are called to realize certain values and thus have an ethically relevant experience of "vocation."

All of these insights are rooted in the theory of intentionality and the conception of subjectivity tied to it. Instead of globally reducing our sensibility to blind affection, the phenomenological approach allows for discernment between sensuous states (*Gefühlssinnlichkeit*) that only inform me about myself on the one hand, and intentional, world-disclosing acts of feeling on the other hand (Scheler 1973: 255–60; Husserl 1988: 424). We are originally open to values. Were it not so, there would be no ethics. Valuing and willing are certain types of intentional acts, each of which possesses a specific form of reason, called "axiological" and "practical" reason, ideally leading to the full givenness of the intended. This concept of intentionality, teleologically tending toward evidence, gives us the picture of a feeling subjectivity disclosing the ethically relevant features of a person's world by critically "feeling through" what is given. Furthermore, this subjectivity is a person who is meaningfully instituted in the ethical dimension, not only by grasping values, but by being called, which makes her the creative source of response to this vocation in the individual realization of values of love. What it means to be a person is phenomenologically also conceived through the notion of intentionality and the unique perspective it actualizes on the world. For Scheler, a person lives and is given in the "*execution of acts*" (Scheler 1973: 387), being the concrete unity in actualizing different types of acts. Unity here means a certain style of actualization and being in these acts. The person is thus present in every act but is never reducible to any of these acts.

Early phenomenology provides us with rich descriptions of different ethical experiences. Its approach allows for consideration of feelings and layers of motivation in a differentiated manner. But there are, of course, also problems. Phenomenologists typically reject all kinds of subjectivism, relativism, and scepticism, due to their concept of intentionality, in which the subjective act is clearly discerned from its intended objective entity. But in the case of ethics, the conceptually required evidence of a value in an intentional act, which vouches for its objectivity and normative validity, is much more disputed than perceptual and logical evidence—and rightly so, given the plurality of value rankings and the perpetual debates about them. Sonja Rinofner-Kreidl (2012: 420) speaks of the dilemma where phenomenologists "are either thrown back on subjective intuitions or they have to commit themselves to some version of moral realism." This poses not only questions concerning the relation between phenomenology and ontology, but also, and more importantly here, questions concerning normative obligation. Work has been done on these questions, especially in the last twenty years (Drummond 2005). With the recent rediscovery of authors from the Göttingen and Munich phenomenology circles and the resulting implications for the fields of social ontology and the phenomenology of emotions, further investigations are to be expected.

As far as the issue of historical development is concerned, however, I would like to formulate the problem in terms of an objection drawn out by Moritz Geiger, which indeed already bothered Husserl (1988: xlvi): Even an elaborated axiology and praxeology does not yet necessarily have to be an ethics. It could present a comprehensive set of essential laws of preferring, choosing, and willing. But this does not yet answer the question whether or not there is something that really obliges me and binds me, something that is urgently and normatively demanded of me as this person, in short: something that I *ought* to do. The transition from meta-ethics to normative ethics thus poses the questions of obligation and validity anew. From the viewpoint of value phenomenologists, the answer must lie in the givenness of values and how those values and their properties are obliging, combined with the obliging values of personal vocation. The phenomenological tradition, however, has also yielded new ways of addressing this question, together with new sets of ethical problems. These ways go hand in hand with a transformation of the notion of intentionality and thus of the concept of subjectivity itself, as well as with the manners of experiencing a normatively significant call.

35.2.2 Existentialist ethics

The new approach announces itself in Heidegger's famous critique of Scheler's value ethics. Crucially, Heidegger's rejection of value ethics originates from his new concept of intentionality and of the being who is intentional: Subjectivity for Heidegger is "Dasein." This opens up a novel set of issues in phenomenological ethics focused on the topics of freedom and authenticity, inspired also by the Kierkegaardian ethical concern for a truthful form of existence. This new approach is taken up in different ways by the French existential phenomenologists.

For Heidegger (1962: 132), values, as propagated by value ethicists, are entities of an ontology of the present-at-hand. This ontology misconceives the nature of Dasein's *being-in-the-world*: The world is meaningful in the first place because Dasein exists in the manner of the care structure, which means that it is "an *issue* for it" (Heidegger 1962: 32). A philosophy of values petrifies and thereby misconstrues the holistic and dynamic movement of care, suggesting instead entities with propositional predicates

(Heidegger 1962: 132). To elucidate the mode of Dasein as being ahead of itself in the world, Heidegger (1988: 162) radicalizes Husserl's original concept of intentionality and henceforth speaks of "transcendence" as a fundamental existentiale. Here, what "transcends" is Dasein itself. Its being-in-the-world is a constant temporal movement and enactment, which, as Heidegger argues, is the condition for any significance and any objectifying intentional comportment. Dasein is thus always already a project, thrown into the world and reflecting itself in the things that it takes care of.

Although Heidegger did not want to deduce an ethics from his "fundamental ontology," interpreters like Steven Crowell (2008) have shown how the structure of projection enhances experience with *normative significance* in the first place, to the extent that I can succeed or fail only with respect to a measure inherent in the projection. Beyond that, Heidegger's analyses of the "call of conscience" (Heidegger 1962: 312–48) can count as the description of an "ethical experience" par excellence, insofar as it calls me to being my true self and to reject the moral complacency of existing in the anonymous and irresponsible mode of "the one" (*das Man*). In the foundational mood of anxiety, Dasein affectively experiences its nothingness, i.e., its purely temporal and non-objective character, and thus its "*Being-free for* the freedom of choosing itself and taking hold of itself" (Heidegger 1962: 232). Seizing my possibilities in the distinctness of my existence requires that I take responsibility for my decisions. Furthermore, this can also imply care for others and their authentic being.

However, this reading might count as benevolent. It can be disputed on the grounds that Heidegger consciously embraces the problematic implication that his so conceptualized "call of conscience" is empty, even formalistic. This leaves the question of what authenticity amounts to for each and every Dasein totally open. Indeed, the call of conscience as such carries no implication of obligation in it to care about others; it does not even provide formal constraints with respect to the treatment of others. Hence, while Dasein eludes "*das Man*" by not letting itself dictate its possibilities, this responsibility undertaken toward oneself is primary to everything else. Accordingly, the Kantian "good will" becomes "the will to will oneself" in Heidegger's interpretation (2005: 193), far beyond any law demanding universalizability. This statement from a lecture course from 1930 already clearly points to the "aporias of *Mitsein*" (Römer 2018: 270) caused by resolute selves willing themselves, for which even in *Being and Time*, the common "destiny" of a "*Volk*" was the only remedy Heidegger (1962: 436) was prepared to offer. The repelling testimonials in the *Black Notebooks* (Heidegger 2016) prove even more that the ethical and political understanding of authenticity pursued by Heidegger was not only hostile to moral and cosmopolitan universalism, but resulted in the super-narrative of a "forgetting of Being," impersonated by groups of people ("the Jews," "the Catholics/ Christians," "the Americans," "the Soviets") labelled as political enemies tantamount to "enemies of Being."

Nevertheless, Heidegger has provided us with valuable phenomenological analyses of the ethical that do not necessarily lead in this direction, for example with his reinterpretation of the Aristotelian notion of *phronesis* (Heidegger 2003: 33–40), or with his phenomenological interpretation of the Kantian notion of "*respect*" as "the givenness of the moral law," disclosing not only the world but also the moral self (Heidegger 1990: 109–12). Heidegger's fundamental phenomenological orientation becomes obvious here: Dasein never projects itself in an empty space but instead has an ethical openness for the situation, which lies beyond the confining alternatives of realism and idealism/constructivism. As his later work, e.g., *The Letter on Humanism* (Heidegger 1998) spells out more clearly, Heidegger instead sees Dasein in a fundamentally responsive position (even if the call of impersonal "Being" seems always more important than that of concrete others). What he describes is neither an a priori principle imposing itself on the given and thereby preparing the situation for judgment, nor an eidetic insight into values, but an originally perceiving, differentiating, and normatively susceptible mode of Dasein through its "being ahead of itself" and its "responsiveness." The new field and set of problems Heidegger hence opens up concerns how ethical significance and obligation are only to be understood by inquiring into the Being of Dasein. That this new start has important implications but also needs more theoretical efforts to cope with its shortcomings has been proved by the works of Emmanuel Levinas, Hannah Arendt, Karl Löwith, Jacques Derrida, Jean-Luc Nancy, and many others. All of these authors have criticized in one or the other way how ethical and political significance only emerges through Dasein *in the plural* and how new forms of *Mitsein* (Being-with) have to be developed according to this insight. These critiques have transformed the Heideggerian approach and have taken it to new levels that deal with the ethical and political difficulties of his work without totally rejecting it.

A short look at Sartre makes clear that he also approaches intersubjectivity in a new, ethically relevant manner: not in the horizontal line of a with-world but in direct opposition, where subjectivities vertically break into each other's worlds (Bedorf 2011: 93). This importantly shifts the question of the source of normativity. At the same time, the free projection of the self is radicalized. Sartre places Heidegger's concept of a thrown and projecting existence in a more Cartesian context. "Creation" and "invention," also implying self-invention, are thus the keywords for Sartre's subjectivity in ethical situations. According to Sartre, our freedom is rooted in the ontology of consciousness, for which, again, its intentionality is decisive: Consciousness transparently presents the world and thus is "nothingness," i.e., nothing objective or constituted in the world; yet, it is a pre-reflective "for-itself" (Sartre 1992a: 9–17). To the extent that I am this consciousness, I am pure actualization, pure spontaneity. Every attempt to make out something like a personal core or a specific character already takes the constituted for the constituting element and therefore results in self-objectification (Sartre 1962).

Again, the ethical task would be to lead an authentic existence according to the nature of one's being: radical freedom and spontaneity. Sartre diagnoses a bad-faith flight from freedom by appropriating an ego-character ("That's who I am, I can't do anything about it"), which serves as an excuse for not facing the demand to *make something out* of what I have been *made into* (Flynn 2005: 250). Yet, not even an ethical call toward authenticity can bind this absolute freedom, let alone give it an ethical principle apart from "authenticity." Sartre (2007) tries to mitigate the contingency and decisionism of this constellation by linking my existential choice to an implicit universalization which introduces

Kant's moral law by way of a Socratic–Platonic argument: choosing is affirming, in an absolute way. My chosen form of existence is thus what I affirm to be "the good," not just for me but "the good" in general. Even though this reasoning remains unconvincing, it expresses two main principles rooted in Sartre's concept of subjectivity: First, that I am absolutely responsible for my existence and second, that the only thing that counts is what I do, not what I think. Sartre's ethics becomes more political the more he emphasizes the social and economical conditions of bad faith and alienation, but what always remains the core of his ethics is that we are "condemned to be free" (Sartre 2007: 29) and that we are therefore responsible for ourselves and our societies.

What about the freedom of others? In the *Notebooks for an Ethics*, Sartre (1992b: 139) suggests that a demand only exists through another freedom and that free existences respectively create each other by demanding their freedom from one another. This indicates a possible solution to the aporetic constellation in *Being and Nothingness*, where the encounter with the other only results in the struggle of reciprocal objectification and alienation. Yet, what can be gained from Sartre's analyses of shame, love, or hate, is that he introduces the other as gaining normative significance for my self-experience (Crowell 2015). Others are not only there as transcendental co-constituters; they are always already recognized as someone who judges me. Hence, I become "responsive to norms" through the concrete encounter with the other. Crowell (2015: 578) argues that Sartre fails in grasping the establishment of normativity correctly because he still conceptualizes the situation from an "ontological" point of view, i.e., as a symmetrical encounter of two consciousnesses—and not, like Levinas, in a strictly asymmetrical first-person perspective. This is where the next move in ethical phenomenological reflection will lead. Still, Sartre undertakes an important shift with respect to Heidegger's holistic context of Being-with by emphasizing the alterity of the other. He thus introduces an ethical verticality that manifests itself, again, in an "ethical experience" of a demand interrupting my freedom.

To conclude: In the phenomenological ethics of freedom and authentic existence the answer to the question "Why is ethics relevant for us at all?" is as follows: because our ownmost being is disclosed in affective foundational experiences like anxiety, shame, and respect, calling us to live according to what and who we are qua ontological subjectivity and qua ontic, concrete existence. To be sure, Heidegger's and Sartre's conceptions of subjectivity significantly diverge from each other. Both, however, originate from a radicalization of the concept of intentionality: In Dasein's ek-sisting enactment intentionality becomes transcendence; in its pure spontaneity, conscious being is a translucent "for-itself" that forbids any habitualization or personalization (Sartre 1962).

The ethical moment of these self-disclosive, affective experiences lies in how they tear us out of our everyday life and bring us before ourselves with the demand to exist authentically. Yet, the ethically troubling problem of these "formalisms of the authentic self" (Römer 208: 255f.) is that they essentially remain *empty* and lack the demand for universalization, a formal criterion that would take into account the freedom of others. This of course raises the question to what extent these theories can be justifiably regarded as being morally relevant at all. Another question is where and if their normativity ever goes beyond the normative scheme to fail or succeed with respect to *oneself*, which would make the voluntaristic and decisionist being of the self the only ground of obligation.

With regard to earlier material value ethics, the parameters have now apparently changed drastically: Instead of objective values that are emotionally cognized, the valuable now seems to be thoroughly dependent on the projection of a subjectivity, even if this does not in any way imply hedonistic or utilitarian principles. As Beauvoir (2010: 37) emphasizes, existentialist ethics is clearly not about happiness but about freedom. But instead of persons whose individuality is constituted in the loving response to an ethical call, we are now confronted with ontologically radical transcendences, whose respective freedoms are unfathomable and not bound to any context by obligation, except for the realization of one's own self. Sartre's (2007: 33) exclamation "You are free, so chose; in other words, invent" not only means that there is no transcendent beyond, no sky of ideas. It also means that there are no values or moral facts to be cognized in this world. Everything depends on my interpretation.

Do these approaches have anything to do with each other anymore? Certainly, one could even reinforce the contrasts by highlighting the deep rifts between a certain nihilism on the one hand and a teleology drifting toward theological implications on the other. Yet, these undisputed differences should not lead us to overlook there being a discussion at work concerning the question of how to grasp phenomenologically that we are ethically affected. While the first group holds that we become responsive to norms by an insight into values which we disclose by way of an emotional cognitivist intentionality, the second group locates the normative dimension much more in the structure of subjectivity itself than in a cognizing cor/relation to the world. This apparently voluntaristic "internalization" of the normative is soon interrupted by a new element that ruptures correlations and also "externalizes" subjectivity beyond Dasein's projections: the encounter with the other.

35.2.3 Alterity ethics

Emmanuel Levinas is known as *the* ethicist among all phenomenologists who argues for a "primacy of the ethical" and thereby reinterprets and revolutionizes key phenomenological notions. No one, for example, has formulated more explicitly that "the very node of the subjective is knotted in ethics understood as responsibility" (Levinas 1985: 95). Levinas's approach is to analyze ethical experience within the paradigm of alterity, which entails an ethical inversion of the intentionality of consciousness.

Levinas transforms phenomenological thought by exposing it to an encounter with "the other"—however, not in a Sartrean struggle, but in being "taught" by the other (Levinas 1969: 51, 67, 171) The ethical subversion of the subject's cognizing intentionality takes place in this encounter. It becomes clear that neither theory nor ontology are modes in which I could ever do justice to the other *as* other. By definition, alterity always escapes the efforts of knowledge wanting to capture and explain it and thereby reduce it to being "the same." Likewise, alterity eludes the subject's mode of need, in which "the same" strives to incorporate "the other." This is why Levinas (1969: 33) speaks of "metaphysical desire" in contrast to need as the mode in which alterity is experienced. To speak of such an experience does not state facts of being. Indeed, it can no longer be captured within the realm of ontology, since alterity is not part of its totality. Levinas's critique of ontology as "totality" and "war" and of subjects being fully describable by this ontology, is, more generally, a critique of the whole Western tradition, from Homer's figure of Ulysses up to Hegel's great philosophical "return to the self." More specifically, it is a critique of Heidegger's ontology and philosophy of immanence. Most of all, however, it is a philosophical and ethical response to the Second World War and the Holocaust.

Against all obvious annihilation and destruction, and war as the evident ontological law, Levinas testifies for a subjectivity violently opened to *ethical transcendence*. Yet, the ethical experience I make in the encounter with alterity manifests itself only as a "trace" within the totality of Being, as an irritation that keeps me awake and open, as something that does not originate in me myself but that instead permeates me like a rupture within myself. Without shifting the perspective to the "optics" (Levinas 1969: 29) of ethics, this experience thus cannot be described at all. Levinas inscribes himself in the tradition of Plato, claiming that the ought cannot be grounded in the is, in Being. Instead, it fundamentally transcends Being. But instead of articulating this as a transcendent beyond, Levinas describes it as a breaking or severe irritation of my experience that leads to an "evasion" or "escape" (Levinas 2003a) from Being. It is thus always *within the phenomenal* that a movement of withdrawal is revealed which calls upon me to follow this movement. The paradigmatic case for such an analysis that starts with the phenomenal and proceeds to the non-phenomenal is Levinas's description of the *face of the other*. Insofar as the essence of the face of the other lies in its not being present, the Levinasian "description" is not about identifying human faces as special entities which are then ascribed the essential "property" of alterity. "Description" in his sense is certainly not a depiction that results in predication. Rather, it tries to capture the *original ethical access* we have to the face, which is not a lifeless statue at which we look, but which, as Levinas (1987: 283) says, "speaks."

Thus, the only mode for appropriately encountering alterity is *responding*, to this appeal, which means fully entering into the encounter with the other and giving up the position of knowledge. For Levinas, this amounts to not being able to cease responding in a completely unreserved way, beyond oneself. In this sense, *infinite responsibility* is the central notion of Levinas's ethics, which does not aim at sketching out a normative theory, but seeks to describe the *fundamental structure of subjectivity in ethical terms* (Levinas 1985: 95). Subjectivity cannot avoid or elude its responsibility, i.e., it cannot *not* respond, since no response is also a response; neither can it actively *accept* its responsibility, since it *is* this responsibility before being an "I" who could be the author of free acts. Hence subjectivity fundamentally *is* responsibility. It is the being-called-by-another that has taken place before every possible being-a-self. The slightly different exposition of subjectivity in Levinas's two main works, *Totality and Infinity* and *Otherwise than Being*, can be explained by Levinas's adoption of a "genetic" perspective first and then a "static" one. Subjectivity in *Totality and Infinity* is first depicted in the "becoming" of an interiority which can then be ruptured by the ethical call, while in *Otherwise than Being* that event has "always already" taken place.

A genuine phenomenological characteristic of Levinas's ethics is making *subjectivity* and the first-person perspective his point of departure. With this approach, Levinas also appropriates the Husserlian notion of the "originarily inaccessible" (Husserl 1969: 114, translation modified) of the *alter ego* and radicalizes it. The experience of alterity is described in the first-person perspective and *only* from this perspective can the uncapturable moment of alterity be appropriately described. In a third-person perspective, impartially looking down on all subjects, one would quickly arrive at a relation of reciprocity. But this is precisely the abstract epistemic view, which for Levinas as well as for Husserl and Heidegger, can only be a second subsequent view, built on the originary first-person perspective of experiencing. In this sense, *the point of departure for an experience of alterity is the experience of a subjectivity*. Levinas calls this irreversibility between me and the other *asymmetry*. The ethical experience is a radical experience of asymmetry: to be in the position of the addressed, of the one being called upon, of having to respond—of being the responsible party.

This also has, as mentioned before, consequences for the notions of *experience* and *intentionality*: For Levinas, the originary inaccessibility of the other is not the "neutral" phenomenological mode of the experience of the other (as it is for Husserl)—it is an ethical call from the very beginning. Levinas (1991: 47) illustrates this with what he calls the "inversion of intentionality": In the encounter with an infinite withdrawal, thus with alterity itself, intentionality is not able to stay anymore, as it were, with itself as *being the presence of something*. Instead, the relationship with alterity exceeds this core feature of intentionality. It cannot make alterity "present." Hence, according to Levinas, intentionality is disrupted, burst apart by the encounter with alterity. The relation with the other is no "correlation" of act and object or of signifying act and the signified—it overthrows this relation. Since alterity can never be brought to full "givenness," my intentional and my bodily capabilities, my "I can" (Husserl), encounters a border. If I trace this experience further, I am finally confronted with my fundamental non-ability vis-à-vis this alterity, which causes a collapse or inversion of intentional directedness and thereby fundamentally challenges the "natural right" of my position, the position of the first person: "consciousness in question and not the consciousness of putting in question" (Levinas 1986: 353, translation modified). In this experience, I become, within my first-person experience, "second person" (Crowell 2016): the Thou who is always already addressed, who is always already in a relation with the other.

This is also the reason why an ontological perspective on the other fails to capture the ethical relation, thematizing structures of Dasein as such, or the relation between plural freedoms. Only from a first-person perspective, converted into the position of the addressed (the second person), can the appeal of the other be understood as a *command*, an *imperative* which comes "from a height" (Levinas 1969: 35, 67) and which constitutes me normatively: "Thou shalt not commit murder" (Levinas 1969: 199). Levinas (1969: 199) calls this "ethical resistance." This new constellation fundamentally calls into question the freedom of existentialism's subjectivity. Ethical resistance does not resist my freedom in the *factical* sense—I *can* kill the other—but calls it into question *normatively* and so obliges me (Crowell 2015: 578).

It is important not to conceive of this point as an irrational facticity, as if I were simply straitened by the call of the other through psychical pressure. Rather, what is described here, is the *establishment of normativity and "practical reason,"* as a faculty which institutes a different register vis-à-vis the factical and which thereby throws me into a different space of meaning than that of ontology. To this endowment, *Otherwise than Being* adds the figure of "the third" (Levinas 1991: 157–62), which clarifies that subjectivity is "always already" exposed to a *plurality* of calls, investing its reason as a distributing, weighing, and justifying faculty in order to be able to realize justice (I will come back to this issue in section 35.3).

To sum up: Since Levinas describes the encounter with the other as an invasion of transcendence, he far exceeds the conceptions of subjectivity advanced by Scheler, Husserl, and Heidegger. Instead of conceiving of subjectivity as a "loving person" or "Dasein" (who cares for its own being), i.e., primarily as a being-for-oneself, Levinas (1985: 96) conceives of subjectivity as being "initially a *for the Other*": This is why infinite responsibility is not a dissolution but a "*substitution*" (Levinas 1991: 113) that creates the very locus of the subject qua *sub-iectum*: The-one-*for*-the-other. Furthermore, the social relation is now not conceived anymore as anything that could be captured in eidetic insight or by social ontology. Rather, the new phenomenal field that Levinas opens up is that of the direct face-to-face encounter with the other, overthrowing all attitudes of theoretical distance and consuming needs, and bringing the self in a genuinely ethical relationship with the other.

This brings about the following consequences for phenomenological ethics: Freedom, which has been the paradigm of the existentialist approach, is now not only freedom that has been called in question, but it is *invested* freedom (Levinas 1969: 84f., 302). Instead of looking at the material abundance of the sphere of values, the focus is now put on the obligation emerging in subjectivity itself, as something that has been ruptured and called into question through an imperative—which has nothing to do with the self calling itself. Rather, this imperative has always already interrupted my natural egoism. Being or becoming "oneself" is now understood in the context of responding to the other: This transition from a (self-)disclosing feeling/affectivity toward speaking also indicates that, for Levinas, the paradigm of "ethical experience" occurs face-to-face in the enactment of speech.

35.3 HISTORICAL BREAKING POINTS AND COMBINED STRENGTHS OF PHENOMENOLOGICAL ETHICS

The historical events and catastrophes of the twentieth century have repeatedly challenged philosophers to rethink the world in which they live. This holds true even more for ethical considerations, given the breakdown of all traditional moral convictions and conventions. Along these lines, one could also write a history of phenomenological ethics grouped around the events of the First and Second World Wars, the ethical and political "zero hour" ("*Stunde Null*") after the Holocaust and other politically and ethically relevant events of the last century—which could include a colorful spectrum of phenomenologists' worldviews running the gamut from conservative Catholicism all the way to atheist Marxism.[6]

I would only like to point to one noticeable circumstance in this context, which seems not to be entirely coincidental: the major historical and systematic breaking points in phenomenological ethics revolve—at least to a certain extent—around the declared non-ethicist and National Socialist university rector Martin Heidegger. Heidegger was the one who declared value ethics and Enlightenment-inspired approaches like Husserl's as outmoded nineteenth-century ways to address the burning issues of his time. His critique remained so powerful that it long inhibited a further reception of Scheler and other early phenomenologists (Blosser 2002: 403f.), who are consequently barely present in the works of Levinas and other alterity-ethicists.[7] The second breaking point is of course Heidegger's own political involvement and the shadows it casts on his philosophy, until today. The disturbing question how and where exactly Heidegger's revolutionary and undeniably influential approach becomes ethically and politically problematic was immediately a concern for the phenomenological thinkers after him. It certainly motivated Levinas to break with ontology altogether. And it is evident in the debated issue of humanism, which continued to be rejected by Heidegger on ontological grounds, and which is taken up as a topic by Sartre (2007), Merleau-Ponty (1969), Arendt (1994), and Levinas (2003b) directly after the Second World War. That Heidegger's work remains an ethical and political challenge for and also beyond phenomenological ethics, is obvious if we look at the works of Derrida, Lyotard, Agamben, Badiou, Rancière, etc.

There are also *systematic* insights that can be drawn from this development. One is that phenomenology has in a fundamental sense become "ethical" or ethically sensitive, first and foremost through the work of Emmanuel Levinas. Instead of treating ethics as a "regional ontology" connected to certain types of acts, the whole phenomenological method and its key notions of intentionality, subjectivity, temporality, embodiment, sensibility, and affectivity are reinterpreted from a primarily ethical perspective. They are re-articulated as responsibility, vulnerability, and Being-for-the-other. In this sense, they have become "practical." Another tendency is that Aristotelian questions concerning the "good life" have moved to the background, while the establishment of the normative in intersubjective experience has moved to the foreground. This amounts to a transition from anti-Kantianism to a phenomenologically shaped question concerning the source of obligation. And again, this involves a radicalization of phenomenology's key notions with respect to an ethical call which not only befalls but institutes the subject.

---

[6] Michael Gubser, for example, has presented a study of this sort, in his *Ethics, Phenomenology, and the Call for Social Renewal in Twentieth-Century Central Europe* (2014).

[7] Levinas, for example, mentions Scheler only once in his two main works (Levinas 1991: 66).

Let me wrap up this account by emphasizing once again that I see the concern with ethical experience and ethically instituted subjectivity as central and uniting for *all* phenomenological approaches to ethics—despite the obvious differences and transformations. As the contemporary situation shows, the historical development is not a one-way street, as classic questions from value ethics are being taken up again in new discourses, also beyond phenomenology. Notwithstanding the mentioned historical and systematic breaking points, it therefore makes sense to consider the combined strengths of phenomenological approaches to ethics. What they all do is take into account how normative demands are bound up with *affectivity, situatedness,* and *interpersonal interrelatedness.* This makes them a strong corrective for predominantly rational and formal procedures of justification. Furthermore, they have a strong "meta-ethical" element, which in the Levinasian case expresses itself as a treatment of the "proto-normative": The question of how we can be sensitive to an ethical call at all.

Yet, this does not mean that phenomenology has nothing to say about normative principles[8] and normative justification. It rather provides an alternative angle by conceiving practical reason as emerging from experience. Levinas, again, gives us a twofold answer, concerning reason's genealogy and universality: The *normative* dimension of practical reason *opens up* in the other's interrupting imperative ("Thou shalt"), making me the addressed and responsible subjectivity in the accusative. Its *universalizing* capacity *unfolds* in answering to *plural* appeals. With the figure of the "third" (Bernasconi 2005), the cry for justice emerges and with it the need for "comparison, coexistence, contemporaneousness, assembling, order, thematization, the visibility of faces, and thus intentionality and the intellect" (Levinas 1991: 157). The moral criterion of universalization is hence *invested* by the relation of proximity to the other, and does not precede the relationship to the other. This is why, for Levinas, universalizations must constantly let themselves be disturbed and called into question, in order to resist a closure or self-immunization of reason.

Although conceptualized differently, Husserl (1989: 37) also makes clear in his essays on "renewal" that rational (self-)justification is a constant process with no final end. These rationalizations and justifications of practical reason occur in feeling and willing. They develop into a specifically disclosive mode yielding "reasons of the heart" (Scheler 1973: 255; cf. Steinbock 2014). Yet, justification, implying the constitution of objectivity, can only occur intersubjectively. Additionally, Husserl (2014: 384) claims that every other is a theme of "absolute ought" for me. Hence, the "best among the attainable," the individual standpoint, my judgment in the wake of "the third"—all that must be justifiable intersubjectively and cannot only be up to my judgment. Phenomenology's

---

[8] Phenomenology's ethical principles are gained from experience and are articulated in its analysis: *"realization of values through persons," "authentic and free existence"* and *"responsibility for the other."* These principles can also be formulated as imperatives for normative ethics: "Do the best among the attainable!" (Brentano); "Realize values of love!" (Scheler); "Remain in the process of critical renewal!" (Husserl); "Respond to the call of conscience and exist authentically!" (Heidegger); "Be free and invent!" (Sartre); "Respond to the other and do justice in wake of the third!" (Levinas).

conviction is that moral validity can only be gained in working through the specific conditions and phenomena of a specifically (inter-)personal, historical, and (multi/inter-)cultural situation. And here we would have a case where different phenomenological approaches could work together. For the process of intersubjective justification, the phenomenological criteria of the disclosive character of feelings, the individuality of the person, the necessity of an authentic projection, and the responsibility for the other and others in the plural can and should be interrelated and critically examined together.

35.4 CONCLUSION

Phenomenological approaches to ethics are committed to ethical experience, which they analyze in different ways. What they have in common is conceptualizing experience along the lines of intentionality and thereby characterizing the experiencing subjectivity. This happens in particularly ethical and meta-ethical terms: as feeling and valuing subjectivity, as freely projecting subjectivity, as responding subjectivity. In taking into account *affectivity, situatedness, and individuality*, phenomenological approaches offer strong complementary alternatives to rational procedures of moral justification. Furthermore, they deliver a differentiated picture of ethically affected subjectivity, be it in a personalistic sense or by locating the origin of our responsiveness to norms in the encounter with the other. The historical development of phenomenological ethics, notwithstanding its differences and breaks, shows the growing importance of the topic, up to the "ethical turn" of core notions and methods, leading to a phenomenological articulation of "ethics as first philosophy."

REFERENCES

Arendt, H. (1994), "What is existential philosophy?" translated by R. and R. Kimber, in *Essays in Understanding 1930–1954* (Berlin: Schocken), 163–87.

Beauvoir, S. de (2010), *The Second Sex*, translated by C. Borde and S. Malovany-Chevallier (London: Vintage).

Bedorf, T. (2011), *Andere. Eine Einführung in die Sozialphilosophie* (Bielefeld: transcript).

Bernasconi, R. (2005), "The third party: Levinas on the intersection of the ethical and the political," in C. E. Katz and L. Trout (eds), *Emmanuel Levinas: Critical Assessments of Leading Philosophers, vol. 1* (London: Routledge), 45–57.

Blosser, P. (2002), "Max Scheler: A sketch of his moral philosophy," in J. J. Drummond and L. Embree (eds), *Phenomenological Approaches to Moral Philosophy* (Dordrecht: Kluwer), 391–413.

Crowell, S. G. (2008), "Measure-Taking: Meaning and Normativity in Heidegger's Philosophy," *Continental Philosophy Review* 41/3: 261–376.

Crowell, S. G. (2015), "Why Is Ethics First Philosophy? Levinas in Phenomenological Context," *European Journal of Philosophy* 23/3: 564–88.

Crowell, S. G. (2016), "Second-person phenomenology," in T. Szanto and D. Moran (eds), *The Phenomenology of Sociality: Discovering the 'We'* (London: Routledge), 70–89.

Drummond, J. J. (1995), "Moral Objectivity: Husserl's Sentiments of the Understanding," *Husserl Studies* 12: 165–83.

Drummond, J. J. (2002), "Aristotelianism and phenomenology," in J. J. Drummond and L. Embree (eds), *Phenomenological Approaches to Moral Philosophy* (Dordrecht: Kluwer), 15–45.

Drummond, J. J. (2005), "Self, Other, and Moral Obligation," *Philosophy Today* 49 (Supplement): 39–47.

Drummond, J. J. and Embree, L. (eds) (2002), *Phenomenological Approaches to Moral Philosophy* (Dordrecht: Kluwer).

Farin, I. and Malpas, J. (eds) (2016), *Reading Heidegger's Black Notebooks 1931–1941.* (Cambridge, MA: MIT Press).

Flynn, T. (2005), *Sartre, Foucault, and Historical Reason* (Chicago, IL: University of Chicago Press).

Gubser, M. (2014), *The Far Reaches: Ethics, Phenomenology, and the Call for Social Renewal in Twentieth-Century Central Europe* (Stanford, CA: Stanford University Press).

Hamrick, W. S. (1987), *An Existential Phenomenology of Law: Maurice Merleau-Ponty* (The Hague: Martinus Nijhoff).

Hart, J. G. (1992), *The Person and the Common Life: Studies in a Husserlian Social Ethics* (Dordrecht: Kluwer).

Hart, J. G. and Embree, L. (eds) (1997). *Phenomenology of Values and Valuing* (Dordrecht: Kluwer).

Hermberg, K. and Gyllenhammer, P. (eds) (2013), *Phenomenology and Virtue Ethics* (London: Bloomsbury).

Heidegger, M. (1962), *Being and Time*, translated by J. Macquarrie and E. Robinson (Oxford: Blackwell).

Heidegger, M. (1988), *Basic Problems of Phenomenology*, translated by A. Hofstadter (Bloomington, IN: Indiana University Press).

Heidegger, M. (1990), *Kant and the Problem of Metaphysics*, translated by R. Taft (Bloomington, IN: Indiana University Press).

Heidegger, M. (1998), 'Letter on "humanism"', translated by F. A. Capuzzi, in *Pathmarks* (Cambridge: Cambridge University Press), 239–76.

Heidegger, M. (2003), *Plato's Sophist*, translated by R. Rojcewicz and A. Schuwer (Bloomington, IN: Indiana University Press).

Heidegger, M. (2005), *The Essence of Human Freedom: An Introduction to Philosophy*, translated by T. Sandler (New York: Continuum).

Heidegger, M. (2016), *Ponderings II–VI. Black Notebooks 1931–1938*, translated by R. Rojcewicz (Bloomington, IN: Indiana University Press).

Husserl, E. (1969), *Cartesian Meditations*, translated by D. Cairns (The Hague: Martinus Nijhoff).

Husserl, E. (1988), *Vorlesungen über Ethik und Wertlehre (1908–1914)*, Husserliana 28, ed. U. Melle (Dordrecht: Kluwer).

Husserl, E. (1989), *Aufsätze und Vorträge (1922–1937)*, Husserliana 27, ed. T. Nenon and H. R. Sepp (Dordrecht: Kluwer).

Husserl, E. (2004), *Einleitung in die Ethik. Vorlesungen Sommersemester 1920/1924*, Husserliana 37, ed. H. Peucker (Dordrecht: Kluwer).

Husserl, E. (2014), *Grenzprobleme der Phänomenologie. Texte aus dem Nachlass (1908–1937)*, Husserliana 42, ed. R. Sowa and T. Vongehr (Dordrecht: Springer).

Levinas, E. (1969), *Totality and Infinity*, translated by A. Lingis (Pittsburgh, PA: Duquesne University Press).

Levinas, E. (1985), *Ethics and Infinity: Conversations with Philippe Nemo*, translated by R. A. Cohen (Pittsburgh, PA: Duquesne University Press).

Levinas, E. (1986), "The trace of the other," translated by A Lingis, in M. C. Taylor (ed.), *Deconstruction in Context* (Chicago, IL: University of Chicago Press), 345–59.

Levinas, E. (1987), *Time and the Other*, translated by R. A. Cohen (Pittsburgh, PA: Duquesne University Press).

Levinas, E. (1991), *Otherwise than Being or Beyond Essence*, translated by A. Lingis (The Hague: Martinus Nijhoff).

Levinas, E. (2003a), *On Escape. De l'évasion*, translated by B. Bergo (Stanford, CA: Stanford University Press).

Levinas, E. (2003b), *Humanism of the Other*, translated by N. Poller (Carbondale, IL: Southern Illinois University Press).

Loidolt, S. (2012), "A phenomenological ethics of the absolute ought: Investigating Husserl's unpublished ethical writings," in M. Sanders and J. J. Wisnewski (eds) *Ethics and Phenomenology* (Rowman and Littlefield), 9–38.

Melle, U. (2002), "From reason to love," in J. J. Drummond and L. Embree (eds), *Phenomenological Approaches to Moral Philosophy* (Dordrecht: Kluwer), 229–48.

Mensch, J. (2003), *Ethics and Selfhood: Alterity and the Phenomenology of Obligation* (New York: SUNY Press).

Merleau-Ponty, M. (1969), *Humanism and Terror*, translated by J. O'Neill (Boston: Beacon Press).

Olafson, F. A. (1998), *Heidegger and the Ground of Ethics: A Study of Mitsein* (Cambridge: Cambridge University Press).

Ricœur, P. (1992), *Oneself as Another*, translated by K. Blamey (Chicago, IL: University of Chicago Press).

Rinofner-Kreidl, S. (2010), "Husserl's categorical imperative and his related critique of Kant," in P. Vandevelde and S. Luft (eds), *Epistemology, Archaeology, Ethics: Current Investigations of Husserl's Corpus* (New York: Continuum), 188–210.

Rinofner-Kreidl, S. (2012), "Moral philosophy," in S. Luft and S. Overgaard (eds), *The Routledge Companion to Phenomenology* (London: Routledge), 417–28.

Römer, I. (ed.) (2014), *Affektivität und Ethik bei Kant und in der Phänomenologie* (Berlin: de Gruyter).

Römer, I. (2018), *Das Begehren der reinen praktischen Vernunft. Kants Ethik in phänomenologischer Sicht* (Hamburg: Meiner).

Sanders, M. and Wisnewski, J. J. (eds) (2012), *Ethics and Phenomenology* (Rowman and Littlefield).

Sartre, J.-P. (1962), *Transcendence of the Ego*, translated by F. Williams and R. Kirkpatrick (New York: Noonday Press).

Sartre, J.-P. (1992a), *Being and Nothingness: An Essay in Phenomenological Ontology*, translated by H. E. Barnes (New York: Washington Square Press).

Sartre, J.-P. (1992b), *Notebook for an Ethics*, translated by D. Pellauer (Chicago, IL: University of Chicago Press).

Sartre, J.-P. (2007), *Existentialism Is a Humanism* (New Haven, CT: Yale University Press).

Scheler, M. (1957), "Ordo amoris," in *Schriften aus dem Nachlass* Band 1, *Gesammelte Werke* Band 10, ed. Maria Scheler (Bern: Francke), 347–76.

Scheler, M. (1973), *Formalism in Ethics and Non-formal Ethics of Values* (Evanston, IL: Northwestern University Press).

Steinbock, A. (2014), *Moral Emotions: Reclaiming the Evidence of the Heart* (Evanston, IL: Northwestern University Press).

Waldenfels, B. (2012), "Responsive ethics," in D. Zahavi (ed.), *The Oxford Handbook of Contemporary Phenomenology* (Oxford: Oxford University Press), 423–41.

CHAPTER 36

HISTORICITY AND THE HERMENEUTIC PREDICAMENT

From Yorck to Derrida

HANS RUIN

36.1 INTRODUCTION

IN one of the introductory sections of *Being and Time*, where the methodological framework for the whole enterprise is presented, Heidegger stresses that the inquiry into Being "is itself characterized by historicity" (Heidegger 2010/1927: 20). As philosophy seeks to address and think the fundamental questions of metaphysics, it is led to recognize that philosophical thinking is itself historically *situated*. This does not only refer to the fact that the thinking human being is located *within* the stream of history, but that thinking *is historical* in a particular sense that needs to be explicated, and that it has to take this predicament into consideration and act upon it accordingly if it is to be carried out in an adequate way. Later on in the book, he devotes an entire chapter to "historicity" (*Geschichtlichkeit*), as one of the basic *existentiales* of Dasein, describing it as the way in which Dasein *happens*, through a *repetition* of what has been for a future (Heidegger 2010/1927: 372–404). It is also here that he outlines the possibility of an *authentic* way of living this predicament, where the temporality of the *moment*, the *Augenblick*, captures the fullest potential of historical existence, as also a practical-ethical task of responding to its own present situation.

The concept and theme of historicity lies at the heart of the fusion of Dilthey's hermeneutics and Husserl's phenomenology that Heidegger accomplishes in *Being and Time*. When asked in 1962 by William Richardson to spell out the most important difference between Husserl's and his own version of phenomenology, he referred specifically to this theme: "Meanwhile 'phenomenology' in Husserl's sense was elaborated into a distinctive philosophical position according to a pattern set by Descartes, Kant, and Fichte. The *historicity* of thought remained completely foreign to such a position" (Richardson 1963: xv, my emphasis). The validity of this claim is something we shall return to in this chapter, in view of the fact that Husserl too, especially in his later years, moved toward a more "historical" conception of phenomenology, if in a somewhat different sense.

These latter developments in Husserl's work were at the centre of Jacques Derrida's seminal 1962 introduction to Husserl's late essay "On the Origin of Geometry." In this two-hundred page "introduction" he traced a unique but only semi-articulated understanding of the historicity of truth in Husserl's own work. It was this interpretation that, together with his appropriation of Heidegger, served as the principal inspiration for the idea of an original *difference* that from there on would result in the theoretical adventure of *deconstruction* (Derrida (1978/1962: 153, *passim*) Around the same time, Hans-Georg Gadamer published *Truth and Method*, a book that became the starting point for *philosophical hermeneutics*. At the heart of this new theoretical enterprise he too situated the theme of the "historicity of understanding," building on Heidegger's analysis, but elevating it to the status of a "hermeneutic principle" (Gadamer 1993/1960: 265ff.).

Finally, and just to highlight from the outset the extraordinarily complex and disputed legacy of this concept in and for phenomenology, it should be noted, that when asked by Karl Löwith in 1936 about the connection between his philosophy and his support for Hitler and National Socialism, Heidegger is reported to have pointed specifically to the theory of historicity of Dasein in Chapter 7 of *Being in Time* as the intellectual underpinning of his political commitment (Löwith 1986: 56). Somehow his own understanding of the political-historical situation, and what it meant to stand and act authentically from within a tradition, had convinced him that this was the right choice to make at the time.

From this brief survey, it should be obvious that an adequate understanding of the role and meaning of historicity is crucial for grasping the inner critical development of phenomenological thinking. In what follows, I will move through the trajectory thus indicated, giving a deeper context to the emergence of this theme, including some remarks on the history of the term itself. I will situate it briefly in the general space of the increased preoccupation with history in modern thinking from German idealism onward, commenting on its place in the work of Dilthey, Yorck von Wartenburg, and in Nietzsche, and then move to a more detailed discussion of Heidegger and Gadamer, and then back to Husserl, and from him to Derrida (for a more extensive survey and context, see Ruin 1994a and Cavalcante and Ruin 2005). Concerning the question of the more socio-political dimension of the topic, that also involves the critical issue of its applicability and scope and its relation to the question of universalism, objectivity, and truth, and the often-voiced criticism that historicity implies relativism, this will be addressed toward the end. There I also indicate how its underlying philosophical concerns continue to resonate in more contemporary theories of tradition and cultural inheritance, in conceptual history and in the workings of so-called collective and cultural memory.

36.2 History, Historicism, and the Hermeneutic Condition

From the second part of the eighteenth century, *history* and *the historical* gradually obtain a new and philosophically more charged significance. After having signified simply what belongs to the past and the knowledge of this past, it starts to signal both a mode of becoming and a redemptive hope of self-understanding through a proper grasp of this development. The schema is anticipated in Herder and brought to its full articulation in Hegel, whose phenomenology conveys the hope of a historically mediated self-explication of spirit. From that point onward, *history* becomes an intellectual battleground, with competing narratives of the inner logic of the historical fate of humanity, but also with competing views on the value of historical-developmental thinking as such, mirrored in the intense debates of the meaning and value of "historicism" around the turn of the nineteenth century. Against the then dominant historicist conceptions of philosophy, both the early proponents of analytical philosophy Frege and Russell, as well the early Husserl, reacted with a call for a more *systematic* and scientific way of doing philosophy. In the programmatic 1911 essay "Philosophy as Rigorous Science," Husserl explicitly spoke out against what he saw as current "historicist" tendencies in philosophy, that ultimately lead to relativism and "extreme sceptical subjectivism" (Husserl 1965: 125). Yet, even in this most explicitly anti-historicist text, it is important to see that Husserl was not principally opposed to historically informed thinking as such, he only insisted that it must be fused with the inner systematic goals of philosophy, in order to enable previous philosophies to "work on us as an inspiration," as he also writes (Husserl 1965: 146).

At the same time there were strong voices arguing for an even deeper engagement with the historical nature of thought. Husserl's essay is partly written in critical dialogue with Dilthey, who from his 1883 *Introduction to the Human Sciences* onward had sought to develop a method for the interpretative human sciences that included a sense of how the interpreting subject is always historically situated, while still seeking to avoid the threat of subjectivism and relativism. His overarching goal was to accomplish for the human sciences what Kant had done for the natural sciences. Whereas the knowledge of nature concerns the possibility of having a knowledge of what is external to the human mind, the study of humanity in its historical expressions must be understood as an inescapable self-reflexive enterprise, where "life knows life" (Dilthey 1957: 4). The problem of historicity concerns precisely this intersection, and how to conceptualize life as both a topic and condition of possibility in the study of history. Another significant voice was Nietzsche, who in his so-called second untimely meditation, *On the Use and Abuse of History for Life* (Nietzsche 1980/1874) had described life as characterized by memory and historical awareness, forcing it always to orient itself within a historically determined space, in either a *monumental*, an *antiquarian*, or a *critical* spirit. A few years later he spoke out in *Human all too Human* of the need for developing for the first time a truly historical philosophizing and of how the "lack of historical sense is the congenial defect of all philosophers" (Nietzsche 1984: 14).

Within the group gathered around Husserl these two seemingly contradictory views constituted part of the dynamism of the Phenomenological Movement. On the one hand, there was a strong commitment to the basic sense of phenomenology as a new form of foundational first philosophy that could reach deeper into the origin of experience, consciousness, and life than the different competing more epistemologically and logically oriented neo-Kantianisms (to which Frege could also be said to belong). On the other hand, the hermeneutic and critical sensibility of Dilthey, Nietzsche, and Hegel, pointed in the direction of an even more radical historical thinking. This productive tension comes out clearly in Heidegger's early Freiburg lectures, where he repeatedly returns to the issue of how to ultimately overcome the dichotomy between history and systematics altogether. In the famous so-called *Kriegsnotsemester* of 1919 he writes of the "close connection between historical and 'systematic' considerations" and of how "both must be overcome" (Heidegger 1987: 132). In the end this goal leads him to opt for a conception of philosophy as "historical knowing in a radical sense," which is the formulation he then uses in his seminal 1922 essay on the interpretation of Aristotle, often described as the blueprint for *Being and Time* (Heidegger 1989b: 249).

It is in this text that he articulates most succinctly the basic predicament of the interpreter as standing in a "hermeneutic situation," where "the past discloses itself only in proportion to the decisiveness and power of the ability to unlock that which a present has at its disposal," and to "repeat that which is understood in the sense of and for one's own situation" (Heidegger 1989: 237, 239). The model deviates in at least one important respect from the Husserlian formula of mapping historical problems onto a systematic framework. To this schema Heidegger adds that the meaning of the present and its supposedly systematic concerns can never be taken for granted. Just as the past becomes fully intelligible only by being mediated through the present, the present too becomes available to itself only as mediated through a history in which it exposes itself to a critical "destruction" of its own inherited motives. It is this circularity of the fully actualized hermeneutical situation that captures the core of what he here sees as a genuinely *historical* thinking.

With this program the basic methodological structure and organization of the existential analytic is in place. The "hermeneutic situation" brings together the essential elements of historicity, as a name for what it means to always stand in the open exposure of a tradition. History is no longer a name for what is simply *past*, but for what confronts life as both its foundation and its task to assume in interpretation and action. By 1922 Heidegger has not yet begun, however, to use the actual concept of "historicity" to designate this existential predicament. The terms only appears in his writing the following year, after he read the correspondence between Dilthey and Paul Yorck von Wartenburg, published by the latter's relative Sigrid v. d. Schulenburg that same year (Dilthey 1923).

Whereas Dilthey was much discussed in the phenomenological circle, Yorck had until then remained completely unknown. He had studied philosophy in his youth, but at the age of thirty be had become head of his family's estate with a permanent seat in the upper chamber of the parliament in Prussia. He continued his philosophical studies and writing in private, publishing nothing during his lifetime, but throughout his life he corresponded with Dilthey, to whom he showed his work and for whom he was probably the most important philosophical friend and critic. For the readers of the correspondence it immediately became clear that Yorck in some respects was a more interesting and deeper thinker than Dilthey himself, especially when it came to the problem of *history* and the *historicity* (*Geschichtlichkeit*) of human existence, a topic that Dilthey in one of the letters describes as "their shared fundamental concern" (Dilthey 1923: 185). It was the way in which Yorck in his letters spoke of "historicity" that propelled this concept into a philosopheme of the highest density from 1923 onward, as a designation for how thinking and subjectivity are historically situated and historically determined through and through. The impact of Yorck, not only on Heidegger but on the Freiburg phenomenologists at large, can be measured by the fact that in 1928 one of Husserl's students, Fritz Kaufmann, wrote his Habilitation on Yorck's scant writings. More importantly for the present context, however, was that in the central chapter on "historicity" in the second part of *Being and Time*, Heidegger chose to conclude the text with a section of long excerpts from Yorck's letters, making the hitherto almost completely unknown Prussian count into the single most quoted author in the entire book (see also Ruin 1994b).

In one passage Yorck is quoted saying: "Just as physiology cannot be studied in abstraction from physics, neither can philosophy from historicity, especially if it is critical" (Heidegger 2010/1927: 402, Dilthey 1923:29). Another important quotation concerns his criticism of the earlier school of historicists, notably Ranke, whom he accuses of having an "ocular" approach to the past as only visualized forms that "can never become realities" (Heidegger 2010/1927: 400, Dilthey 1923: 60). From that moment on the concept of "historicity" holds a place at the heart of hermeneutic-phenomenological thinking, as a designation of the inescapable historical situatedness of subjectivity, thinking, and truth, indeed of life itself, but also as the practical challenge of authentically confronting its past as possibility for a future. To the more detailed content and implications of this program we now turn.

36.3 HISTORICITY IN *BEING AND TIME*

Chapter 5 in the second part of *Being and Time* remains the most extensive attempt to develop a phenomenological description of historicity as a basic existential condition and as itself the condition of possibility of historical experience or experience of what is historical. A standard answer to what makes something "historical" is simply that it belongs to "the past." Yet, since the past is no longer present it is hard to see how the pastness of something could account for the experience of it as historical in the present. Heidegger then turns to the example of a specific artefact, as encountered in a historical museum. This is experienced as "historical," he writes, not in virtue of itself being past, since it obviously exists here and now in the present. Instead it obtains this experiential feature of *pastness* and historicity in virtue of being perceived as belonging to a *world* that once was, in other words to Daesin as "having-been." It is this projected reactivation of a world no longer there and thus of a Dasein that has-been that accounts for its historical aura. In other words, the historicity of the object does not ultimately come from the object itself, but from a type of intentionality or concern (*Sorge*) that is characteristic of human Dasein as it projects itself toward a future so as to make Dasein as having-been appear again, in the form of *repetition* (*Wiederholung*). It is this achievement or enactment of present and living Dasein that constitutes its historicity as one of its so-called existentiales. As such it also provides the existential foundation for *history* in the standard sense as a source-based account of the past.

The basic strategy that runs throughout the existential analytic of *Being and Time* is to explicate the meaning of a given phenomenon in terms of the lived and concerned futural projection of a corresponding understanding. In the central §74, that outlines the basic phenomenological constitution of historicity as repetition, Heidegger describes it as the general "event-structure" of human existence and as an *a priori* of historical existence and experience. In and through this event of repetition, Dasein discloses its own possibilities for the future in terms of a "heritage" that it takes over (Heidegger 2010/1927: 383). Since life is always also a being-with-others, this constantly projected constitution of itself through the affirmation of an inheritance is carried out in a *shared* space of meaning. In an ominous formulation, Heidegger writes that Dasein always acts and understands with its "generation" and with its "people." It is this collective overtaking of an inherited possibility in a moment of decision that he here designates as "fate" and "destiny," *Schicksal* and *Geschick* (Heidegger 2010/1927: 384).

In a foregoing chapter of *Being and Time* human existence has been defined by Heidegger in terms of the three-fold ecstatic structure of "temporality," *Zeitlichkeit*, a finite future-oriented repetition of the past for the present. According to his own assessment, this marks the deepest level of the existential analytic, and as such also a foundation for historicity. Yet, since temporal finitude does not provide life with any specific possibilities, it calls for an opening of past possibilities to enable a choice of action in the present. For this reason, Heidegger writes in the earlier chapter that temporality "reveals itself as the historicity of Dasein" (Heidegger 2010/1927: 332). When this repetition of past possibilities happens in an *authentic* way it has the temporal form of *the moment of vision*, the *Augenblick*, in and and through which living Dasein repeats the past in the form of a *response* (*Erwiderung*) for its own situation.

As can be seen already from this short summary, the more precise relation between temporality and historicity in *Being and Time* remains somewhat unclear, and in the years that follow it is renegotiated several times. The basic phenomenological, and we could say transcendental-philosophical, premise of the whole endeavor of the existential analytic, is that all possible modes of experience should in principle be possible to analyse in terms of possible projections and comportments of finite Dasein, including the structure of space and time itself, as well as the very possibility of "truth." This means the the whole domain of *the historical* should also be possible to account for in terms of certain modes of intentional comportment and enactment of individual Dasein. However, since it belongs to the very meaning of the historical that it concerns what is not present, but absent, and only indirectly available, it pushes the analysis in new directions, where it becomes a question of opening itself and preparing for the return and re-arrival of what was once actual, but which should now become actual again, but for another future.

So far we have seen how the basic structure of historicity continues to be modeled on the idea of a "hermeneutic situation" and the ideal of the authentic critic for his own time, as first explored in the early essay on Aristotle. Yet when fused with the overall question of Being the stakes become higher. Historicity then becomes the fundamental shape in which Dasein continues to *happen* (*geschehen*) as it constantly relates and responds to its inherited possibilities. As such, historicity also regulates the form in which the question of Being itself must be addressed, for there is ultimately no stepping back or behind the historical predicament of life and understanding.

36.4 Historicity in Later Heidegger

In the years that follow the publication of *Being and Time* the question of the historicity of human existence becomes the topic of much continued discussion and research in the group of phenomenologists and beyond. On this topic Herbert Marcuse (Marcuse 1987/1932), e.g., writes a thesis where he combines Dilthey and Hegel, with the help of Heidegger. Heidegger himself, however, appears to lose interest in the specific topic of the existential historicity of Dasein, as its drops from his technical vocabulary. At the same time, however, he moves toward an even more encompassing *historical* mode of thinking, opting instead for a "history of being" and speaking of the "historicity of being" as such. In the literature on Heidegger, one source of disagreement has been precisely how to view the relation between this subsequent phase of the history and historicity of Being and the theory of the historicity of Dasein in *Being and Time*. Seen from one perspective, the earlier theory was limited to the historicity of individual Dasein, whereas the latter is concerned with a very different matter, namely the historical structure and happening of being itself. Yet from another angle it is possible to see this turn toward the history of Being as issuing precisely from the discovery of historicity as the way in which Dasein always happens as also a *being-with*, in other words as a shared *fate*.

In what is sometimes referred to as Heidegger's "second major work," the *Contributions to Philosophy (of the Event)*, written in the years 1936–8 and published posthumously in 1989, this *historical* mode of thought and its inner tensions are brought to their most radical conclusions. The book is centred around one core topic, that also characterized much of Heidegger's work throughout the 1930s up until the end of the war, namely of how to secure access to philosophy as a *beginning*, an *Anfang*. He sees thinking, and culture at large as taking place and being enacted in the space of a tradition that was once constituted and set into motion but that today remains largely unthought. In response to this predicament, thinking must rise to the challenge of another or second beginning, an *anderer Anfang*. However, this second beginning can only come about through a radical engagement with the first beginning and its legacy, whereby it can aspire to repeat this beginning in a new way.

His untiring hermeneutical exercises during these years, where he explores the history and legacy of German idealism, of Nietzsche, and of Greek philosophy, especially its earliest sources, all point toward this goal, namely of reaching a point where thinking can begin *anew*, not as just another history of philosophy, but as the genuine happening of being itself. In this culminating stage, philosophical thinking should not even speak *about* anything, instead he writes that in this new mode of speaking "nothing is described explained, declared, or taught: here the saying does not stand over against what is to be said; instead it is this itself as the essencing of being" (Heidegger 1989: 4). What on one level could appear as a programmatically anti-historicist approach is then quickly countered by the declaration that what is needed is "a more original insertion into history," where thinking becomes "evermore historical" (Heidegger 1989: 451).

It is not just a question of intensifying the engagement with history and with tradition, but of developing a new and even more radical historical mode of thinking. In the *Contributions*, the *historical* now comes to function as a designation for the mode of thinking itself, its "way of being enacted," its *Vollzugsweise*. A key formulation in all of this is that here thinking recognizes its primordial *belonging* to what it simultaneously tries to articulate and understand, its *Zugehörigkeit*. The German term becomes significant here, for it opens itself to thinking this belonging is also *a listening to*, a *Hören*, that explicitly distances itself from the more *ocular* mode of thought, echoing again a theme from Yorck's critique of historicism. A radical sense of *indebtedness* runs through the entire project, where philosophy is called upon to question ideas of autonomy and objectivity, and to move beyond representational thinking altogether into the enactment of thought as an "event" of Being itself, as *Ereignis*. Throughout these long and repetitive meditations on the nature of thinking in the second beginning, Heidegger does not refer to the historicity of Dasein or thinking. Instead he speaks of an "original historicity of being itself" (Heidegger 1989: 460), a historicity that manifests itself through our critical encounter with the possibility of the other beginning.

Just as "historicity" is transposed as a designation of human Dasein to Being as such, so also is the notion of "destiny" (*Schicksal*) during these years. The lectures on Hölderlin's so-called river-poetry, "Germanien" and "Der Rhein" from 1934–5 contain the most elaborated discussion of this topic that we find in any of Heidegger's writings after *Being and Time*. He takes this word directly from Hölderlin himself as the poem "Der Rhein" recalls a *Schicksal* several times. It is a word with many different meanings, but in the end, Heidegger writes, we have no concept for what destiny truly is, nor can poetry provide us with one, for the poem itself is not just an image of destiny, but it *is* destiny in its own right (Heidegger 1980: 173). This remark sets the stage for how he will continue to elaborate this concept in the years that follow, applying it not least in his readings of ancient philosophy. "Destiny" for Heidegger is not a concept that refers to an ordained fate in a deterministic sense. Instead it becomes the word that he uses to capture the sense of a history that both encompasses us and challenges us to respond to it. As such it remains a hermeneutic category for thinking of history as an inexhaustible engagement. The *destinal* is what places us, before any possible conscious choice, in the position of having to respond, thus echoing again the idea of historicity.

Seen from a political and ideological angle this figure of thought is highly ambiguous. It has both a radical and conservative dimension, in a way that is ultimately difficult to disentangle. It stresses the need for a constant critical-destructive *engagement* with the past, since its image of history is precisely that of an ongoing challenge, namely to live up to and respond to its original possibilities in and for the present. As such it insists on holding the present *open* to its possible transformations, criticizing any conventional sense of a cultural-philosophical foundation. At the same time, it clearly contributes to propelling Heidegger's thinking in a conservative-nationalist direction, as he opts for a particular cultural legacy, the *we* of a German-Occidental destiny, claiming to know in what form this *we* is challenged by and called to respond to *its* past. Its overall program remains fixed to a limited reservoir of the same canonical texts and questions that are rehearsed over and over again. As he himself would also recognize, it is this radical-conservative sensibility that also motivates him to align his philosophical program with that of Hitler and National Socialism in 1933, as documented in his infamous Rectoral address from that year. In this text, the discursive apparatus of the historical-destinal nature of thinking is activated in the service of affirming the particular historical moment and to assume its challenge as the "fate of the German people," a phrase used repeatedly throughout the text (Heidegger 1983).

From this abyssal moment in his own career and thinking and through the very same figures of thought, Heidegger nevertheless continues his ever-deepening spirals of critical-hermeneutic engagements with the legacy of Western thinking. The same period that sees him plunging into a national-conservative and at times even anti-Semitic discourse (as documented in the so-called *Black Notebooks*) also witnesses the birth of some of his most important interpretative works, on Schelling, Hegel, Nietzsche, and early Greek thinking. It also comprises his most radical poetical-philosophical attempts to reach beyond representational thinking altogether in favor of a thought of the event (*Ereignis*). For Heidegger the *historical* mode of philosophizing, as first articulated in the early lectures and systematically explored in *Being and Time*, was never abandoned, only transformed and refigured.

36.5 GADAMER ON HISTORICITY

When Gadamer published *Truth and Method* in 1960, Heidegger is said to have voiced skepticism towards this attempt to reintroduce hermeneutics as a method for the human sciences in the style of Dilthey. By that time, he himself had long abandoned the term hermeneutics, in favor of a thought of the happening and event of Being, as he also remarks in his "Conversation with a Japanese" (Heidegger 1971: 51). Yet, through

Gadamer's seminal contribution it became possible to see once again how Heidegger's fusion of phenomenology and hermeneutics and his understanding of historicity was rooted in a larger question of trying to come to terms with the inner logic and dynamics of living within the workings of a tradition, where the tension between history and systematics and between meaning and truth, was constantly being enacted. Gadamer situated Hegel's dialectic's, Dilthey's and Yorck's philosophy of hermeneutics and life, as well as Husserl's and Heidegger's phenomenologies, within this panoramic question of thinking of the event or happening of truth as an unending process of historical mediation. This process, he argues, can not be captured in an ordinary scientific objectifying discourse, for it transgresses every limited methodology.

In *Truth and Method*, Gadamer pays particular homage to the hermeneutic transformation of phenomenology accomplished by Heidegger in *Being and Time*, and especially to his theory of historicity of existence and understanding. Whereas the latter used hermeneutics and historicity to access the question of Being, Gadamer himself instead claims to have done "justice to the historicity of understanding" through his critique of a limited scientific sense of objectivity and truth (Gadamer 1993/1960: 265). The truth brought about through a productive confrontation with tradition is never a question of sheer repetition, instead it always involves a *distance*, that enables a truth to be transmitted as both itself and something other. Here Heidegger's formula of a repetition as response, *Wiederholung* as *Erwiderung*, is given a new turn that further stresses the *openness* of tradition to new meanings, not as deficiency and loss, but as an unending potential of self-transformation through critical rehearsal and reappraisal of a past.

Gadamer's philosophical intervention brought attention to the question of truth in history and historical understanding, that resonated with the methodological disputes that reignited during the 1960s, and that have continued through the era of post-modern thinking. For him, the insistence on the historicity of life, in the sense of a finite situated temporal existence, did not imply a *skepticism* with regard to the possibility of obtaining historical truth. On the contrary he saw this existential-hermeneutic structure as the very premise for there being any kind of historical truth in the first place. But in trying to situate himself on this middle ground, he found himself the target of multiple critiques, from seemingly contrary positions. On the one hand, he was criticized by more traditional representatives of historical hermeneutics, such as Eric Hirsch, for giving up on the possibility of historical truth and of abandoning the historically oriented humanities to relativism (Hirsch 1967). On the other hand, he was criticized by Habermas and other representatives of critical theory for defending a too-conservative notion of tradition as a normative framework of truth. Finally there was also the deconstructive criticism, that he was unable to think the more radical *difference* operating within tradition itself. To some extent the theory of historicity is really at the heart of these double controversies. For it is only in virtue of being always already historically situated within a tradition that historical understanding can emerge in the first place and become a source of dispute. At the same time, it also implies that no historical truth, i.e., no interpretation of a historical event or meaning, can ever be fully identical with the original, since all historical understanding involves a productive distance as its very precondition.

36.6 HISTORICITY IN HUSSERL AND DERRIDA

Whereas Husserl had long been associated with his attack against historicism and its relativistic consequences as expressed in the 1911 essay on philosophy as rigorous science, it gradually became clear after his death to what extent he too had been engaged in trying to articulate a sense of the historicity of philosophical thinking. For Gadamer, writing in 1960, this was obvious, and he enlists Husserl together with Dilthey and Yorck as philosophers of historical life (Gadamer 1993/1960: 242ff.). He quotes Husserl from the posthumously published sixth volume of *Husserliana*, *The Crisis of the European Sciences and Transcendental Phenomenology* (Husserl 1978/1954), that showed him in his last years openly struggling with the problem of history and the historical as also a cultural-philosophical task. The overall ambition of these last writings was to critically address the consequences of the mathematization of nature in modern physics and how this leads to the gradual obfuscation of subjectivity in nature. Ultimately it was described as leading to how mathematics itself, as an ideational spiritual activity, was obscured by the result of its idealizations. It was this triple task, of criticizing the objectifying effects of modern mathematization on both nature, subjectivity, and ultimately on rational thinking itself, that gives this work its particular edge. Even though Husserl did not openly address the politics of his time, it is clear that he also had a political agenda, namely of overcoming what he saw as a *spiritual* crisis of Western modernity. This was to be done through a reawakening of a critical rationality through an historical meditation on its roots in ancient Greek culture, from where it had suffered a gradual self-alienation through cultural sedimentation and forgetfulness of its original impetus.

Some of the material from this later phase had been made available earlier, notably the essay "The Origin of Geometry" from 1936, that Eugen Fink had published separately as a journal article in 1939. The importance of this particular essay for the subsequent reception of Husserl as also a thinker of history and historicity can hardly be overstated. Here he directs his attention to the problem of the origin of geometrical knowledge and truth, not as an empirical-historical problem, but as what he calls an "intentional-historical" problem. By this he means an exploration of the inner necessary genesis of geometrical knowledge as such, how it is that it must have come about in order to have the shape and standing that it has today. Every mathematical insight must first be thought as an emergent discovery and revelation of and by *someone* at *some* point. Even ideal truths have such an origin, even though we do not, and most often cannot know where and when. Yet, in order for it to be a mathematical discovery in a full and genuine sense, it cannot remain a mere "psychic" or "personal" insight in the head of its discoverer. It is a form of knowledge to whose essence it belongs that it is there for potentially *anyone* to see and grasp. This opens the question how it is that an insight can move from the personal inner sphere to become a general and ideal transmittable truth. Husserl's answer to this question is *language*, which provides the elementary thought with a "linguistic living body (*Sprachleib*)" (Husserl 1978/1954: 357). For a full idealization to take place it is not enough, however, that there be *oral* communication. It also needs *writing*, an inscription of some kind as a virtual language through which it can be communicated. Only thus can it fulfill "the communalization of man" (Husserl 1978/1954: 360) With the production of a stable and transmittable symbolically secured ideality we have the beginning of a *tradition*, where the original meaning can be received first passively and then reactivated again in subsequent generations, and built upon in further discoveries and constructions through deductive reasoning.

Along the way of this transmittance, it does not follow automatically, however, that the entire structure is reactivated as such. Instead parts of it will naturally remain only as a "passively" received inheritance. What we then have, in Husserl's conception, is a tradition characterized by a varying degree of opacity and lack of full understanding, which eventually will result in a form of alienation, or what he speaks of here as a "non-genuine" tradition (Husserl 1978/1954: 366). It is therefore only through a proper form of *historical* reflection that the inner interconnectedness can be revealed and the "primal self-evidences" be explored. To access this basic historical premise does not require us to move back in time to the actual historical *event* of or *person* behind the discovery of this or that geometrical truth—of which we may know little or nothing—but to reflect systematically on the the principal and necessary conditions that must have obtained.

A methodological premise for his whole exploration is thus that we can reach, through reflexive variation of possibilities, into such an historical a priori as an "apodictic of the prescientific world" (Husserl 1978/1954: 373). Against the ethnological historicism of his time, with its relativization of historical life forms, Husserl argues strongly for the need to explore and articulate such a general cultural-historical theoretical framework, as the implicit prerequisite and condition for every specific history. What he presents is thus an argument for both the necessity and possibility of a kind of transcendental-philosophical hermeneutics, within which the basic structure and form of the historicity of meaning is in principle possible to retrieve, over and beyond the facticity of every specific event and discovery. In its extension it also points to what Foucault would later attempt under a similar heading (on this, see Moran 2016).

Husserl was often described as having come upon the problem of history and historicity only late in life, and perhaps more as a belated response to Heidegger's emphasis on these questions. We also saw above how Heidegger considered him to have been inattentive to these issues altogether. But a more correct assessment is that the program outlined in the *Crisis* builds on and expands Husserl's interest in so-called *genetic* phenomenological questions that stretches all the way back to his very earliest works and his critique of naturalism. To open up an awareness of how entities are not simply there but also given as a result of constitutive processes is already from the outset to have opened thinking to the experience of an *inner* temporality of meaning. In this sense, an interest in the question of the historical and genetic-generative dimension of ideality and truth as explored explicitly in the *Crisis* had already been long in the making in Husserl's thinking (see also Steinbock 1995 on this topic).

As we have seen, this was also how Gadamer read Husserl in *Truth and Method*. Even more important for the continued development of the theme of historicity, however, is that this is also how Derrida read him in his two-hundred-page commentary to his own translation of the "Origin of Geometry" that he published as his first book in 1962 (Derrida 1978/1962). For the young Derrida this late text by Husserl holds, as he states at the outset of his long commentary, an "exemplary significance." It is significant, both for what it says and argues for in terms of a uniquely elaborated theory of the possibility of trans-temporal meaning, inheritance, and communication, but even more so for the inner tensions to which it gives voice, and of which it itself seems to be only partly aware. In the end it demonstrates both the relevance and necessity of its questions, as well as the insurmountable limits of its task.

Derrida showed how it is Husserl himself who openly insists on the limitations of a Platonic or Fregean solution, according to which ideal meanings are simply there as eternal existing truths for the human intellect to grasp. For, as he states, even idealities like the eternal truths of mathematics have an (internal) historicity, a way of being constituted in their meaning for and as a living legacy. At the heart of this constitution is not just their shared spiritual and communicable essence in general, but also their inescapable connection to a material trace, in short: their *inscription*. For it is ultimately the production of a material trace that lies at the heart of the constitution of ideal meaning that can henceforth become the object of a shared tradition.

In his critical reconstruction of Husserl's argument, Derrida connects this account of the meaningful shared expression to the inner structure of subjectivity in general. It is within the "living present" of a subjective life that meaning and experience is originally generated, and within which it is reactivated as a possibility from the past for a future. However, this living present, as Husserl himself describes it, is characterized by the tripartite structure of "retention," "protention," and "making-present." Even in its elementary existential form, subjectivity is thus never fully present to itself: Its experience, of itself as well as of its world, is made possible only through a separation from itself, in a continuously re-enacted inner distance, deferral, and difference. The establishment of subjectivity and awareness, involves such a primordial deferral (*différant*). Any consciousness of meaning thus presupposes both distinction, deferral, and difference, the dimensions of a consciousness of meaning that Derrida would later combine in the neologism *différance*, with an *a*. The actual term is introduced first in his *Grammatology*, published five years later. But on the very last page of his commentary to the Geometry essay, he labels this difference as "transcendental." The inner logic of the argument that would eventually form the groundwork of Derrida's subsequent texts is thus already in place in the 1962 commentary to Husserl's essay, and it is largely driven by his particular preoccupation with the problem of historicity. With the publication in later years of Derrida's early dissertation and of his lecture courses it has also become even more clear to what extent his philosophical trajectory developed out a profound confrontation with the problem of history, historicity, and generativity in the work of both Husserl and Heidegger (see Derrida 2003 and Derrida 2016, and also Naas 2015).

On the very last page of his long introduction, Derrida asks rhetorically: "Could there be an authentic thought of Being as History, as well as an authentic historicity of thought, if the consciousness of delay could be reduced? But could there be any philosophy, if this consciousness of delay was not primordial and pure?" (Derrida 1989/1962: 153). With these questions he brings together the problem of historicity as it has been raised and articulated by both Heidegger and Husserl, and by Gadamer. At the same time, he pushes the whole problematic in a new direction. If, for Heidegger, the problem of historicity primarily concerned how situated and finite life can respond authentically and originally to its (destinal) predicament, and if for Husserl it was about securing and re-establishing a self-transparent and non-alienated sense of tradition, historicity in the hands of Derrida focuses instead on a primordial deferral and exteriority of presence, meaning, and truth. This should not, however, be taken to mean that the concept has simply been stretched beyond recognition. Throughout its transformations, there is a continuity in this trajectory, that concerns how the finitude of life is both conceptualized and made into a platform for a critical confrontation with tradition. It is only by entering and exposing oneself to the process of historical mediation that thinking can begin. And even in the more material-linguistic version of the problematic that we find in Derrida, the transcendental motive behind the whole enterprise remains operative.

36.7 HISTORICITY AND MEMORY

In this final section, I bring together a few of the many ways in which the phenomenological-hermeneutic problem of historicity is today being cultivated and developed along new trajectories, notably so in the increasing interest in the workings of *memory* as also a historical category. In the aforementioned "second untimely meditation," Nietzsche speaks interchangeably of history and memory. It is in virtue of being equipped with a *memory* that humans find themselves immersed in a history, and as having to relate to a past. The issue of memory is not one that Heidegger addresses explicitly, even while he mentions the importance of Nietzsche's essay for the problem of the historicity of Dasein. On the contrary, it is notable that among all the fundamental existential comportments that he enlisted and explored in *Being and Time*, memory is not one of them. The same tendency to downplay the role and importance of memory can be seen in the continued development of phenomenological and hermeneutic thinking, also in Gadamer, with a few notable exceptions. It is only more recently that the impact and importance of this mnemic dimension of consciousness and experience has begun to receive a more thorough attention in the phenomenological literature, notably in the last work of Ricœur (2004). The reluctance to address the question of memory in hermeneutic thinking could seem puzzling, since memory is already from Augustine onward a name for that interior space in which subjectivity retrieves itself in its historical-sensual depth. When Husserl turns to the problem of inner time consciousness it is precisely to Augustine that he refers, and the conceptual apparatus that he uses to discuss the inner dynamics of temporality is taken from the domain of memory, as he speaks of a primary and secondary recollection (*Erinnerung*). Also in the case of Heidegger, the underlying significance of memory surfaces in the way he speaks of the question of the meaning of Being, since this is seen as having undergone a "forgetting," which must be countered by a critical-destructive work of recollection. Indeed, the whole vocabulary of the dynamics of historicity can on one level be seen as processes of memory, as it works through "repetition" in the sense of "recovery" and "recollection," *Wiederholung*.

There are several reasons for why this "mnemic" dimension of the problem of historicity was not raised to a more principal level at the outset. At least in Heidegger's case, it had partly to do with wanting to avoid Platonic conceptions of memory and anamnesis as also implying a metaphysics of eternal truths. It also had to do with a wish to distance himself from the dominant psychological and psychologizing sense of "memory," where it is conceived primarily as a psychic faculty with no essential connection to the problem of history and historical awareness. But if we disregard the more limited sense of memory as just a cognitive capacity, and consider it in the longer lineage of Platonic and Augustinian thinking up through the work of Husserl, we can sense how the problem of historicity is also connected precisely to the workings of memory in the sense of how consciousness is linked to and mediated through tradition and its various means of transmission of meaning.

In the multifaceted contemporary domain of so-called cultural memory studies this connection to the hermeneutic dimension of memory is sometimes indicated, but rarely explored (see Ruin 2015). The study of cultural memory usually takes its principal theoretical starting point in the sociology of so-called collective memory, as was first developed by Durkheim's student Maurice Halbwachs. In this discipline there was no interest in a historical a priori in Husserl's or Heidegger's sense. What it sought to understand and map were the workings of collective memories as also a study of how traditions are upheld over the course of several generations and within social structures. The distinction between memory as something subjective and history as the objective past was never really questioned. Whereas the theory of historicity was partly driven by a transcendental-philosophical motive, from Dilthey up through Derrida, the study of collective memory is largely oriented by a sociological-anthropological interest in the workings of tradition and cultural inheriting. But in the field of cultural memory studies as this has been developed by the group of Jan and Aleida Assmann there is also an attempt to connect the more sociological discourse on memory to a hermeneutic-philosophical and also deconstructive legacy (Assmann 2011). When the historicity of meaning and truth is seen as essentially involving various forms of technical supplements, as in the work of Derrida, then the sense of historicity as a mode of "interiority" as opposed to an outer, objective chronological understanding of the past, is blurred. At the same time, the very idea of such an objective exterior temporal space of tradition can not even begin to make sense unless we presuppose some elemental sense of historicity as the way in which life opens itself to the happening of the past as a futural possibility. In more recent elaborations of Gadamer's hermeneutics and its understanding of historicity, the topic of *memory* also emerges as a way to capture this double edge of indebtedness and openness to the new (Risser 2012).

It is in and around this uncertain, unstable and "quasi-transcendental" space of the possibility of historical awareness and its socio-political, material, and psychic conditions, that future work on the problem of the historicity needs to be continued. But it is then important to understand that historicity is not just the name for an existential phenomenon and a domain to be studied and explored from a theoretical-sociological perspective. It is also a name for the practical situation in which thinking already finds itself, compelled to respond to a legacy and tradition, in the face of an undecided future. Heidegger's hopes for an *authentic* historicity, and also the ensuing idea of history of being as a collective *fate*, propelled him during a time into the dead end of nationalist politics. But the existential-hermeneutic understanding of how thinking and human existence at large is always intertwined with history is also what made the theory of historicity into perhaps the most compelling part of his and the phenomenological-hermeneutic legacy. Through the insistence on the situatedness and finitude of historical awareness and thinking, the problem of historicity thus points toward a continued critical questioning of the possibility of inheritance and belonging as ultimately a question of the possibility of historical awareness and historical knowing. And as a name for the critical awareness of how history is never just an object of knowledge of what is past, but also a mode in which we continue to live and respond to a pastness in ourselves, and thus to an inner difference in our relation to the present, it stands at the centre of philosophical reflection and awareness as such.

References

Assmann, J. (2011), *Cultural Memory and Early Civilization: Writing, Remembrance, and Political Imagination* (Cambridge: Cambridge University Press).

Cavalcante, M. and Ruin, H. (2005), *The Past's Presence: Essays on the Historicity of Philosophical Thinking*, Södertörn Philosophical Studies 3 (Stockholm: Södertörns Högskola).

Derrida, J. (1978 /1962), *Edmund Husserl's 'Origin of Geometry': An Introduction*, translated by J. P. Leavey (Lincoln, NE: University of Nebraska Press).

Derrida, J. (2003), *The Problem of Genesis in Husserl's Philosophy*, translated by M. Hobson (Chicago, IL: Chicago University Press).

Derrida, J. (2016), *Heidegger: The Question of Being and History*, translated by G. Bennington (Chicago, IL: Chicago University Press).

Dilthey, W. (1957), *Gesammelte Schriften*, vol. 5, ed. G. Misch (Leipzig: Teubner Verlagsgesellschaft).

Dilthey, W. (1923), *Briefwechsel zwischen Wilhelm Dilthey und dem Grafen Paul Yorck von Wartenburg 1877–1897*, ed. S. v. d. Schulenberg (Tübingen: Niemeyer).

Gadamer, H.-G. (1993/1960), *Truth and Method*, translated by J. Weinsheimer and D. Marschall (New York: Continuum).

Heidegger, M. (1971), *On the Way to Language*, translated by P. Hertz (Harper and Row).

Heidegger, M. (1980), *Hölderlins Hymnen 'Germanien' und 'Der Rhein'* (Frankfurt a. M.: Klostermann).

Heidegger, M. (1983), *Die Selbstbehauptung der deutschen Universität* (Frankfurt a. M.: Klostermann).

Heidegger, M. (1987), *Zur Bestimmung der Philosophie* (Frankfurt a. M.: Klostermann).

Heidegger, M. (1989a), *Beiträge zur Philosophie (vom Ereignis)* (Frankfurt a. M.: Klostermann).

Heidegger, M. (1989b), "Phänomenologische Interpretationen zu Aristoteles. Anzeige der hermeneutischen Situation," *Dilthey-Jahrbuch* 6: 237–69.

Heidegger, M. (2010/1927), *Being and Time*, translated by J. Stambaugh (New York: SUNY Press).

Hirsch, E. (1967), *Validity in Interpretation* (New Haven, CT: Yale University Press).

Husserl, E. (1965), *Philosophy as Rigorous Science,* translated by Q. Lauer (New York: Harper & Row).

Husserl, E. (1978/1954), *The Crisis of the European Sciences and Transcendental Phenomenology: An Introduction to Phenomenological Philosophy*, translated by D. Carr (Evanston, IL: Northwestern University Press).

Löwith, K. (1986), *Mein Leben in Deutschland* (Stuttgart: Metzler).

Marcuse, H. (1987/1932), *Hegel's Ontology and the Theory of Historicity*, translated by S. Benhabib (Cambridge, MA: MIT Press).

Moran, D. (2016), "Sinnboden der Geschichte: Foucault and Husserl on the Structural a priori of History," *Continental Philosophy Review* 49/1: 13–127.

Naas, M. (2015), "'Violence and Historicity,' Derrida's Early Readings of Heidegger," *Research in Phenomenology* 45/2: 191–213.

Nietzsche, F. (1980/1874), *On the Advantage and Disadvantage of History for Life*, translated by P. Preuss (Indianapolis, IN: Hackett).

Nietzsche, F. (1984/1878), *Human all too Human*, translated by M. Faber (Lincoln, NE: University of Nebraska Press).

Richardson, W. (1963), *Through Phenomenology to Thought* (The Hague: Martinus Nijhoff).

Ricœur, P. (2004), *Memory, History, Forgetting*, translated by K. Blamey and D. Pellauer (Chicago, IL: Chicago University Press).

Risser, J. (2012), *The Life of Understanding: A Contemporary Hermeneutics* (Bloomington, IN: Indiana University Press).

Ruin, H. (1994a), *Enigmatic Origins: Tracing the Theme of Historicity through Heidegger's Works* (Stockholm: Almqvist and Wiksell).

Ruin, H. (1994b), "Yorck von Wartenburg and the Problem of Historical Existence," *Journal of the British Society for Phenomenology* 25/21: 111–30.

Ruin, H. (2015), "Spectral phenomenology: Derrida, Heidegger, and the problem of the ancestral," in S. Kattago (ed.), *The Ashgate Research Companion to Memory Studies* (Farnham: Ashgate), 61–74.

Ruin, H. (2015), "Anamnemic Subjectivity: New Steps towards a Phenomenology of Memory," *Continental Philosophy Review* 48: 197–216.

Steinbock, A. (1995), *Home and Beyond: Generative Phenomenology after Husserl* (Evanston, IL: Northwestern University Press).

....

CHAPTER 37

INTERSUBJECTIVITY, SOCIALITY, COMMUNITY

The Contribution of the Early Phenomenologists

....

DAN ZAHAVI

WHEN discussing the history and development of phenomenological accounts of intersubjectivity, one can encounter different narratives. One narrative is that a decisive rupture exists between Husserl and other phenomenologists. According to that narrative, Husserl only started to realize the challenge of intersubjectivity fairly late. His commitment to methodological solipsism, his trenchant idealism, and his disregard of the role of embodiment, however, seriously impeded his efforts and ultimately meant that his attempt to develop a phenomenology of intersubjectivity failed. By contrast, later phenomenologists such as Heidegger, Merleau-Ponty, and Levinas all realized the significance and importance of intersubjectivity from early on. Rather than desperately trying to fit intersubjectivity into an already fossilized framework, Heidegger would argue that a basic constituent of Dasein's *being-in-the-world* is its *being-with*. And while Merleau-Ponty would insist that embodiment is crucial to both self-experience and other-experience and that the foreign body and my own body form a single whole, an *intercorporeity* by virtue of their structural similarity, Levinas would go even further and propose that ethics should serve as a new first philosophy.

I have in previous writings sought to offer a competing narrative. Not only was Husserl the first to employ and discuss the notion of intersubjectivity in a comprehensive and systematic manner, but his profound analyses also exerted a decisive (positive) influence on later phenomenologists such as Merleau-Ponty and Levinas (Zahavi 1996, 1999). In the present contribution, I will again seek to challenge the standard narrative with its privileging of post-Husserlian phenomenology, but this time by taking a closer look at some of the rich contributions to a phenomenology of sociality that can be found in the first decades of the twentith century. More specifically, I will show how various early phenomenologists by starting from an examination of empathy and other forms of dyadic interpersonal relations would develop analyses of larger social units and ultimately offer accounts of our communal being-together. Due to the comprehensiveness of these early investigations, however, it will be impossible to cover all aspects in a single chapter.[1] In the following, my focus will be on some central ideas found in Husserl, Scheler, Walther, and Gurwitsch.[2]

37.1 HUSSERL ON EMPATHY

Whereas Husserl's investigation of intentionality in *Logische Untersuchungen* (1900–1) paid scant attention to the problem of intersubjectivity, let alone to collective forms of intentionality, the situation soon changed. Within five years, Husserl was working on empathy (as shown by texts gathered in *Husserliana* 13). That Husserl took empathy to be a topic of particular importance is not only revealed by the fact that he kept working on it for the rest of his life, but also by his decision to dwell on it in his very last lecture course from the winter semester of 1928/9, which was entitled *Phänomenologie der Einfühlung in Vorlesungen und Übungen.*

Initially, Husserl's discussion of empathy was informed by his encounter with the work of Theodor Lipps, the influential philosopher and psychologist, who was also the teacher of a number of Munich phenomenologists. In various writings, Lipps had defended the view that empathy was a *sui generis* kind of knowledge, one that provided us with knowledge of other minds, and which could be explained in terms of specific mechanisms of imitation and projection (Zahavi 2010, 2014). Husserl disagreed with Lipps' explanation and in his own writings often used the term empathy (*Einfühlung*) interchangeably with the terms other-experience (*Fremderfahrung*) or other-perception (*Fremdwahrnehmung*). These terms are already suggestive of Husserl's understanding of empathy. As he writes in *Ideen II*:

> Empathy is not a mediate experience in the sense that the other would be experienced as a psychophysical annex to his corporeal body but is instead an immediate experience of the other. (Husserl 1989: 384–5, translation modified)

Along similar lines, Husserl speaks of how the other is given in his being-for-me (*Für-mich-sein*) in empathy, and how that counts as a form of perception (Husserl 1973c: 641). If I talk with another, if we see one another with our own eyes, there is an immediate contact, an immediately experienced personal relationship. We "see" the other qua

---

[1] For two recent edited volumes that also target and discuss the contributions of, for instance, Reinach, Stein, Löwith, and Hildebrand, see Szanto and Moran 2016, and Salice and Schmid 2016.

[2] I have previously written on and discussed these authors in separate publications. My discussion in the following will partially draw on material found in Zahavi 2014, Zahavi 2016, León and Zahavi 2016, and Zahavi and Salice 2017.

person, and not merely as body (Husserl 1989: 385). Indeed, when speaking of how we encounter foreign subjectivity, Husserl also writes that:

> It would be countersensical to say that it [foreign subjectivity] is inferred and not experienced when given in this original form of empathic presentation. For every hypothesis concerning a foreign subject already presupposes the "perception" of this subject as foreign, and empathy is precisely this perception. (Husserl 1973b: 352)

In some manuscripts, Husserl talks of empathy as that which permits us to encounter true transcendence, and also writes that our consciousness in empathy transcends itself and is confronted with otherness of a completely new kind (Husserl 1973b: 8–9, 442). It should consequently not come as a surprise that Husserl is critical of the suggestion that empathy involves some kind of reproduction or reduplication of oneself (Husserl 1973a: 188, 1973b: 525). To experience the other is not to engage in a kind of imaginative self-transformation, since that would only allow me to encounter myself as other and not to encounter a true other (Husserl 1973c: 314). Furthermore, although it is true that we sometimes imagine what it must be like for the other, what the other must be going through, it is simply unconvincing to claim that every act of empathy involves imagination. When we empathically understand the other, we do so immediately and often without any imaginative depiction, and in those circumstances where we do depict the other's experience imaginatively, we precisely consider this an exception (Husserl 1973a: 188).

An important feature of Husserl's analysis, one that will prove significant for what follows, is that empathic understanding normally involves co-attending to the object of the other's experience (Husserl 1973c: 427, 513). It is consequently important to emphasize that the other, rather than being given to me simply as a nucleus of experiences, is given as a center of orientation, as a perspective on the world. The other is precisely given to me as intentional, as directed at the same world as I, and the other's world, and the objects that are there for him, is given along with the other (Husserl 1973b: 140, 287, 1973a: 411, 1989: 177):

> Regardless of how one describes this experiencing-of-another . . . more precisely— whether it be called "empathy" or "comprehending experiencing" or whatever else—it remains a form of experience. We refer to this now, in order to point out that conjointly with the empathic experience of the other the following peculiarity accrues: when comprehending his experiencing, my experience normally passes through his experiencing and reaches all the way through to what he experiences. (Husserl 2008: 617)

An implication of this is that I rarely thematize the other as an object, when I empathize with him. By contrast, the primary object in sympathy (*Mitgefühl*), care and pity (*Mitleid*) is not the object of the other's distress, but the other him- or herself. The intentional object of the other's distress and the intentional object of my sympathy consequently differ. To use Husserl's own example, if the other is sad about the fact that his mother had died, I am also sad about this, and sad about the fact that he is sad. However, it is his sadness that is my primary object, and it is only subsequently and conditional upon that that the death of his mother is something that also saddens me (Husserl 1973b: 189–90). More generally speaking, Husserl was quite clear about the distinction between empathy and sympathy. We find similar, but more fine-grained distinctions in Scheler.

37.2 SCHELER ON THE VARIETY OF SOCIAL FORMATIONS

Due to his dissatisfaction with Lipps' account of empathy, Scheler rarely talked of empathy (*Einfühlung*), but preferred to use the term *Nachfühlen*, which the English translation not very helpfully renders as reproduced or vicarious feeling. This is a problematic translation, since Scheler was quite explicit in his rejection of the view that our understanding of the experiential life of others always involves some kind of reproduction of or participation in the foreign experience. Instead, he defended the view that in a number of central cases we can enjoy a basic and direct experiential recognition and grasp of the minded life of others as it is perceptually manifest in their bodily expressivity (Scheler 2008: 9–10, 218, 260). Like Husserl, Scheler also occasionally spoke of *Fremdwahrnehmung* (other-perception),[3] and for the sake of simplicity, I will in the following simply translate *Nachfühlen* as empathy.[4]

What is more important in this context, however, is the fact that Scheler goes on to distinguish empathy (*Nachfühlen*) from three other related phenomena, namely sympathy (*Mitgefühl*), emotional contagion (*Gefühlsansteckung*), and emotional sharing (*Mitfühlen* or *Miteinanderfühlen*). In order to feel sympathy for somebody who is suffering, you first need to realize or recognize that the other is indeed suffering. So for Scheler it is not through sympathy that I first learn of someone's being in pain, rather the latter's suffering must already be given in some form to me, must already be understood

[3] For a comparison of Husserl and Scheler and for a more elaborate presentation of Husserl's and Scheler's theories of interpersonal understanding, see Zahavi 2014.

[4] Schloßberger has recently insisted on the difference between *Nachfühlen* and empathy and instead proposed to translate *Nachfühlen* as "sensing." As he argues, *Nachfühlen* does not involve some (unconscious) inferential "putting oneself in another's shoes," but is rather the immediate experience of the (expressive) other as other (2016: 180–2). I agree with the latter definition, but see no reason to stay clear of the term "empathy," since other phenomenologists, in contrast to Lipps, precisely understood empathy very much in the same way as Scheler conceived of *Nachfühlen*. It is revealing that several of them, Husserl included, referred to Scheler's theory precisely as a theory of empathy (Husserl 1960: 147, Walther 1923: 17).

by me, if I am to feel sympathy for him (Scheler 2008: 8). Whereas empathy provides this prior perceptually based understanding, sympathy adds the emotional response.

Consider now, by contrast, the case of emotional contagion. You might join a carnival and be swept over by the jolly atmosphere or you might encounter a funeral procession and your mood might drop. A distinctive feature of *emotional contagion* is that you literally catch the emotion in question (Scheler 2008: 15). It is transferred to you. It becomes your own emotion. In emotional contagion, the feeling you are infected by is not phenomenally given as belonging to another, but as your own. It is only its causal origin that points to the other (Scheler 2008: 37). Indeed, when infected by the panic or the jolly mood of others you might not even be aware of them as distinct individuals. But all of this is precisely what makes emotional contagion different from empathy and sympathy. For Scheler, in both of the latter cases, the difference between self and other is preserved and upheld. It is *your* emotion that *I* perceptually grasp; it is *your* distress that *my* commiseration is directed at (Scheler 2008: 23, 64). To suggest that sympathy involves some kind of fusion with the other is, according to Scheler, to transform sympathy into a form of (supra-individual) egoism. This is also, why Scheler rejects the proposal that the existence of sympathy and compassion should ultimately testify to the metaphysical unity of all individuals (Scheler 2008: 51, 54).

A limiting case of emotional contagion is what Scheler called emotional identification (*Einsfühlung*). He discusses a variety of different examples, including totemism, hypnotism, and sexual intercourse, but also, and this is something I will return to shortly, the case of the mass or mob, where the respective members not only identify with the despotic leader, but also through various processes of contagion coalesce into a single "stream of instinct and feeling, whose pulse thereafter governs the behaviour of all . . . like leaves before a storm" (Scheler 2008: 25).

What then about the case of what Scheler terms *emotional sharing* (*Mitfühlen*):

> The father and the mother stand beside the dead body of a beloved child. They feel in common the "same" sorrow, the "same" anguish. It is not that A feels this sorrow and B feels it also, and moreover that they both know they are feeling it. No, it is a *feeling-in-common*. A's sorrow is in no way "objectual" for B here, as it is, e.g., for their friend C, who joins them, and commiserates "with them" or "upon their sorrow." On the contrary, they feel it together, in the sense that they feel and experience in common, not only the self-same value-situation, but also the same keenness of emotion in regard to it. The sorrow, as value-content, and the grief, as characterizing the functional relation thereto, are here *one and identical*. (Scheler 2008: 12–13, translation modified)

As is clear from the example, Scheler denies that emotional sharing should be understood as individual experience plus reciprocal knowledge, that is, he denies that it can be understood along the following line: independently of each other, but in parallel, individual A has a token experience of type x, individual B has a token experience of type x and, in addition, they each have knowledge of the other (Scheler 1973: 526). If this construal is rejected, however, what might a positive account of emotional sharing look like? It is clear from Scheler's description that both parents are intentionally directed at the same object and are also evaluating it in the same manner. Scheler also emphasizes, however, that the parents are feeling something *together*, i.e., that what they experience is not independent of the relation they have to each other. This makes their relation different from the situation where, say, a friend of the couple becomes sad by witnessing their grieving (Scheler 2008: 12–13, 37). In the latter case, the friend is intentionally directed at the grieving parents—and his intentional object is consequently different from theirs. Moreover, although he is sad, their grief does not become his, it is not felt by him as *ours*. As Scheler points out, in sympathy, the other's grief is first given to me as belonging to the other, and my commiseration and the other's grief are consequently phenomenologically given as two different facts. In emotional sharing, by contrast, the empathic grasp of the other's state and the emotional sharing are so intertwined that they are not experientially given as distinct (Scheler 2008: 13). In addition, Scheler is quite clear about the need for a careful distinction between 1) the phenomenon of "mutual coalescence," which he finds exemplified in fusional forms of love, where the individualities of the partners seem to dissolve and relapse into a single life-stream, and 2) a proper consciousness of "us" which is "founded on the respective self-awareness of each" (Scheler 2008: 25). Emotional sharing, experiencing an emotion as *ours*, consequently involves and requires not only a directedness to and evaluation of the very same object, but also a non-objectifying awareness of the other as co-attender and co-evaluator (which is why empathy is required rather than simply being superfluous). We are presented with a situation where the participating individuals are given as co-subjects, and where what they feel is constitutively interdependent, i.e., dependent upon the relation they have to each other.

The decisive step forward is now taken not in *Wesen und Formen der Sympathie* (1913/ 23),[5] but in *Der Formalismus in der Ethik und die materiale Wertethik* (1913/16) where Scheler suggests that the different ways of experiencing one another just outlined also constitute distinctly different social units and group formations, i.e., different ways of being together. The task of a philosophical sociology is, as he puts it, precisely to develop a theory of these different social formations (Scheler 1973: 525).

The most primitive formation, the *mass* or *horde* is constituted through processes of contagion and involuntary imitation (Scheler 1973: 526). It is characterized by the absence of individual self-consciousness and self-responsibility and does not yet amount to any real we-formation. A more sophisticated type of social unity is one that Scheler calls *life-community* (*Lebensgemeinschaft*). It is distinguished by some amount of empathy and experiential sharing, since the individual members have some understanding of and solidarity with each other, but it remains a non-objectifying understanding. It is not as if each member takes the other member(s) as his or her intentional object,

---

[5] The book was initially published in 1913 under the title *Zur Phänomenologie und Theorie der Sympathiegefühle und von Liebe und Hass*, but Scheler changed the name of the second edition, which was substantially reworked and doubled in size.

nor is this understanding one that precedes or is separate from the co-experiencing (*Miterleben*). Furthermore, according to Scheler, the mutual understanding among members of such a community is non-inferential, it requires no inference from a manifest expression to a concealed experience, nor does the formation of a common will require contracts or the making of promises (Scheler 1973: 526–7), rather a basic trust pervades the community (Scheler 1973: 529).

Although Scheler again emphasizes that experiential sharing cannot be explained in terms of parallel experiences plus reciprocal knowledge, and although he argues that there is neither a division between my experience and your experience, nor between my experience and my bodily expressivity, we are not faced with an undifferentiated fusional unity. In contrast to two further social formations, which I will discuss shortly, however, Scheler does argue that the individuality of the community members is somewhat derived. As he writes, "the experiences of an individual are given to him as single experiences, but only on the basis of a special singularizing act that clips him, as it were, out of the communal whole" (Scheler 1973: 527). Each member can, so to speak, stand in for any other member, all of them being interchangeable representatives of the same supra-individual communal unity. For that very reason, we are at this stage not yet dealing with a truly personal community, i.e., with a community of mature individuals. The members are rather defined by their communal position and function in say, the family, clan, or tribe. Indeed, at one point, Scheler emphasizes the primitiveness and immaturity of the life-community when remarking that it is made up of "people who are *not of age*" (Scheler 1973: 529).

A third social unity is what Scheler calls society (*Gesellschaft*). This is an artificial unity of individuals that lacks the primordial and organic living-with-one-another (*Miteinanderleben*) characterizing the life-community. All contact between these self-conscious and mature individuals are accomplished through specific cognitive acts, where one individual directs his or her attention towards the other. In addition, Scheler also claims that the kind of other-understanding obtained in societal contexts necessarily presupposes a separation between the bodily expressivity of the other and his or her experiences, a separation that is then bridged by analogical inference (or some similar cognitive process). The society lacks co-responsibility and true solidarity in the form of one for all and all for one, and is instead based on contractual obligations and instrumental and strategic interests. Distrust remains the basic attitude (Scheler 1973: 528–9).

The fourth and final form of social formation discussed by Scheler is the one he calls personal community (*Persongemeinschaft*). It amounts to a unity of irreplaceable individuals that together form a collective person (*Gesamtperson*). Although this (ideal) social unity is not an actual synthesis of life-community and society, essential characteristics of both are, as Scheler writes, co-given in it (Scheler 1973: 539). There is genuine and mature individuality as well as real communal unity. What we find here, are true individuals who at the same time are community members, and who experience themselves as both simultaneously. One's true individuality flourishes and comes to fruition in the social unit, which would not be the unit it is, were it not for the individuality of its members. On this level, we also encounter a new type of mutual loving solidarity, one that involves both self-responsibility and co-responsibility (Scheler 1973: 534). Whereas the natural unity of the life-community has been praised by romanticists, and whereas the rational organization of society has been applauded by liberals, both have according to Scheler been equally wrong and failed to realize how both of these social formations are subordinate to the personal community (Scheler 1973: 540).

How should one understand the relation between these different social formations? First of all, it is crucial not to interpret Scheler's distinctions as if they were supposed to describe the historical development of concretely existing social units. It is not as if *homo sapiens* first gathered in hordes, then moved on to the more developed stage of life-communities, and then after some time of maturation adopted a form of societal existence, in order finally to enter the personal-communal stage. No, the four formations are elements that occur in any concrete social unity, or as Scheler writes "at all places and at all times *all* of these forms and their corresponding ethoses have in some measure been present in various *mixtures*" (Scheler 1973: 541). This is not to deny, however, that there are founding relations obtaining between them, founding relations which furthermore mirror those obtaining between emotional contagion, empathy, sympathy, and emotional sharing (Scheler 2008: 96). As Scheler, for instance, writes apropos the relation between society and life-community:

> The basic nexus is this: there can be *no society without life-community* (though there can be life-community without society). All *possible* society is therefore *founded* through community. (Scheler 1973: 531)

As Scheler proceeds to point out, this does not mean than any societal group must necessarily also be bound together as a community. It only means that 1) individuals who enter into societal relations must previously have participated in a communal life, and 2) that any concrete societal combination of individuals is only possible if the individuals in question are at the same time communal members (though not necessarily members of the same community) (Scheler 1973: 532). Part of the argument offered for this line of reasoning is that the kind of being-with-one-another found in a life-community serves as a precondition for the kind of analogical reasoning found in society (Scheler 1973: 531). But what kind of interpersonal understanding is it that we find in life-communities? Whereas the mass is constituted and characterized by emotional contagion and identification, the society by analogical reasoning, and the personal community by experiential and emotional sharing (Scheler 1973: 520), it is somewhat more controversial what the binding principle of a life-community is. In *Der Formalismus*, Scheler highlights the role of emotional and experiential sharing for the life-community as well (Scheler 1973: 526). In *Wesen und Formen der Sympathy*, by contrast, Scheler writes that it is a fundamental principle of the evolution of feeling, be it from child to adult, from animal to man, or from savagery to civilization, that we first encounter emotional identification and later empathy. Thus, whereas we in the mass and horde find true identification, we first find empathy in the communal life of the family (Scheler 2008: 97). As Krebs has rightly pointed out, however, given that empathy for Scheler is compatible with indifference and even cruelty, this is a somewhat surprising statement and does not resonate well with Scheler's claim that the communal life is characterized by trust and basic solidarity (Krebs 2015: 130).

37.3 WALTHER AND THE FEELING OF TOGETHERNESS

In 1921, a few years after the publication of the second part of Scheler's *Formalismus* (1916), Walther defended her doctoral dissertation *Ein Beitrag zur Ontologie der sozialen Gemeinschaften*. As indicated by the title, her focus is on the nature of the social community, and as she readily acknowledges at the outset, her investigation presupposes and builds upon the analysis of empathy offered by phenomenologists such as Scheler and Stein (Walther 1923: 17).

Like Scheler (and before him Tönnies), Walther distinguishes a society from a community and argues that whereas the former designates an aggregation of individuals who decide to join forces based on purely strategic or instrumental considerations, a community is formed by individuals who understand themselves and others as members of a *we*, and who are tied together by bonds of solidarity.

What must be in place for a plurality of individuals to constitute a community? A community is distinguished by the fact that its members have something in common, there is something they share (Walther 1923: 19). However, it is certainly not enough that they merely have the same kind of intentional state and are directed at the same kind of object. Such a match could obtain even in situations where the individuals have no awareness or knowledge of each other. What must also be required is that the individuals have some knowledge of each other, and furthermore that this knowledge is of a special kind. Assume that A, B, and C are three scientists living in three different countries who are all working on the same scientific problem. The mere fact that each of the scientists knows about the existence of the other two would not as such make them into a community (Walther 1923: 20). But what if they interacted with one another? As Walther observes, such a reciprocal interaction, where each individual influences the intentional life of the other certainly brings us closer to what we are after. However, something would still be missing. Consider the case of a group of workers who are brought together to finish a construction, and who interact in order to obtain the same goal. To some extent, they work together, but they might still consider each other with suspicion or at best with indifference (Walther 1923: 31). Seen from without, they might be indistinguishable from a communal group, but they only form a society and not a community. For the latter to obtain, something more is needed. What is missing in an inner bond or connection (*innere Verbundenheit*), a feeling of togetherness (*Gefühl der Zusammengehörigkeit*), or reciprocal unification (*Wechseleinigung*). Only when the latter is present does a social formation become a community (Walther 1923: 33, 63):

> We are standing here on the same ground as those theorists . . . who consider the essential element of the community to be a *"feeling of togetherness,"* or an *inner unification* [*inneren Einigung*]. Every social configuration that exhibits such an inner unification, and only those configurations are, in our opinion, communities. Only in communities can one really speak about shared experiences, actions, goals, aspirations, desires, etc. (in contrast to similar or related experiences, actions, etc. that can be present in societal relations). (Walther 1923: 33)

In her analysis, Walther refers to and largely agrees with Scheler's distinction between experiential sharing on one hand and empathy, sympathy, and emotional contagion on the other. Empathically to grasp the experiences of the other is quite different from sharing his experiences. In empathy, I grasp the other's experiences insofar as they are expressed in words, gestures, bodily postures, facial expressions, etc. Throughout, I am aware that it is not I who am living through these experiences, but that they belong to the other, that they are the other's experiences, and that they are only given to me qua expressive phenomena (Walther 1923: 73). Even if by coincidence we were to have the same kind of experience, this would not amount to a shared experience, to an experience *we* were undergoing *together*. Despite the similarity of the two experiences, they would not be unified in the requisite manner, but would simply stand side by side as belonging to distinct individuals (Walther 1923: 74). To feel sympathy for somebody, to be happy because he is happy or sad because he is sad, also differs from being happy or sad *together* with the other (Walther 1923: 76–7). Finally, we also need to distinguish experiential sharing from emotional contagion. In the latter case, I might take over the experience of somebody else and come to experience it as my own. Insofar as that happens, however, and insofar as I then no longer have any awareness of the other's involvement, it has nothing to do with a shared experience. When an experience is shared, each partner is not only conscious of the other's experiencing, but identifies with and incorporates the other's perspective: "Communal experiences [*Gemeinschaftserlebnisse*] in our sense . . . are definitely *only* those experiences that emerge *in me* from them and *in them* from me, from *us* . . . on the basis of my unification [*Einigung*] with the others" (Walther 1923: 72). According to Walther, this peculiar belonging-to-me of the other's experience is what is distinctive and unique about communal we-experiences [*Gemeinschafts- und Wirerlebnisse*]. This is why the sense of ownership accompanying such experiences undergo a peculiar transformation. The joy is no longer simply experienced by me as *yours* and/or *mine*, but as *ours*, i.e., as co-owned, as one *we* are experiencing (Walther 1923: 75). The we in question is not, however, one that is behind, above, or independent of the participating individuals. The we is not an experiencing subject in its own right. Rather, we-experiences occur and are realized in and through the participating individuals (Walther 1923: 70).

The fact that a we-experience involves a certain unification or integration does not entail that it lacks internal complexity. For one, it is not enough that I feel an emotion as ours, you have to feel it as well. Moreover, I also have to be aware of your incorporation of my experiential perspective, just as you have to be aware of mine. Indeed, according to Walther, the following elements must be present: (1) the experience of A is directed at an object, (1a) the experience of B is directed at the same object. (2) A empathically grasps the experience of B, (2a) just as B empathically grasps the initial experience of A. (3) A unifies with the empathically grasped experience of B, just as (3a) B unifies with the empathically grasped experience of A. (4) Finally, A empathically grasps B's unification with A's experience, (4a) just as B empathically grasps A's unification with B's experience. Only once this complex structure of interlocked acts of iterative empathy is in place does an affect qualify as a shared emotion (Walther 1923: 85).[6]

According to Walther, the direct awareness of and interaction with others allows for a special kind of community, one that Walther labels purely personal communities or life communities (*rein personale Gemeinschaften* or *Lebensgemeinschaften*). In some cases, these communities are organized around the pursuit of shared external goals. In other cases, like friendships, families, and marriages, there is also a shared goal, but rather than being external, the goal is the flourishing of the community itself. Walther calls these forms of communities "reflexive communities" (*reflexive Gemeinschaften*) (Walther 1923: 67). But communal life cannot be restricted to such forms, since it cannot be a necessary feature of every community that all its members engage in reciprocal interaction (Walther 1923: 66, 68). In fact, people can experience themselves as members of a community, can identify with other members of the same community whom they have never met in person, and can have group experiences even if they are not temporally and spatially together. In such cases, shared objects, goals, rituals, conventions, norms etc. play a crucial role (Walther 1923: 49–50). Walther labels such (institutionalized) communities "objectual communities" (*gegenständliche Gemeinschaften*) (Walther 1923: 50). The more the community is centered around externalized factors (rather than being tied to the immediate interpersonal contact) the greater the spatiotemporal separation of the members can be (Walther 1923: 82), and the more replaceable these members will be. Consider, for instance, someone who converts to a new religion or acquires a new citizenship. Here one might identify with the new community before one starts to identify with particular individuals, and one's relation to such individuals might at first only be qua representative group-members rather than qua unique individuals (Walther 1923: 99–100). Given that the identification with such communities might remain unreciprocated—I can identify with a certain community, although the other community members remain unaware of my existence—it is not immediately clear how Walther's model of iterative and integrative empathy can directly elucidate the constitution of objectual communities. However, she would in all likelihood argue that the latter communities are founded upon personal communities, and to that extent indirectly depend upon a web of empathic intentionalities.

In a further step, Walther explores the question of whether members of a community must necessarily realize or recognize this membership. As she points out, there is a difference between identifying with and being united with certain other people, and

---

[6] For a more extensive discussion of Walther's rather complicated model, see León and Zahavi 2016.

knowing that one belongs to a particular community. It often happens that one lives together with others in a reciprocal unity without reflecting on this relation. But this can change, for instance, because of intergroup conflict. Thus, as Walther remarks, war can often make people aware of themselves as members of a special community (1923: 96). Only then is a community constituted as a community *for itself* in the full sense (1923: 97). Finally, Walther also discusses the case where a community isn't simply recognized as such by its own members, but also by members belonging to another community. When that happens, and especially if the out-group members in question are representatives of, and act in the name of, their own community, one might talk of a higher-order interaction between communities. Walther suggests that the community through this kind of external recognition acquires a new and more objective status (1923: 121).

37.4 HUSSERL ON RECIPROCAL EMPATHY AND SOCIAL ACTS

Whereas Husserl's engagement with the question of intersubjectivity was initially focused on the analysis of empathy, his continuing wrestling with the issue of intersubjectivity eventually led him beyond this narrow focus. It would lead beyond the confines of this chapter to engage in a more extensive analysis of Husserl's later reflections on, say, the importance of generativity, the difference between a natural and cultural community, or on the relation between homeworld and alien world as found for instance in *Husserliana* 15 and 39 (Steinbock 1995). So let me instead discuss some themes that figures prominently in two intriguing texts from 1921 and 1932 entitled *Gemeingeist I* (Husserl 1973b: 165–84), and *Phänomenologie der Mitteilungsgemeinschaft* (Husserl 1973c: 461–79) respectively, and which might be seen as elucidating further the process of identification also referred to by Walther.

Initially, Husserl discusses how we can imitate another, or love or hate another, or empathically experience another, and then writes that none of these acts amounts to truly social acts (Husserl 1973b: 165–6). Why not? Because truly social acts are acts that must be apprehended by the addressee (Reinach 1913: 705–18). They involve a special kind of reciprocity. As Husserl further argues, if we consider a situation where I directly experience another, just as he experiences me, does that then suffice for the required reciprocity? Husserl's answer is negative. Each of us could simultaneously be directed at the other without any of us being aware of the other's attention, and as long as that mutual awareness were lacking, we wouldn't have a proper primordially social (*ursozialen*) I-thou relation (Husserl 1973b: 171). In fact, even a case of reciprocal empathy that involves mutual awareness will still not suffice for the kind of social unification that the I–thou connection exemplifies, and which Husserl further insists is the condition of possibility for a we-unity. As he explains in *Erste Philosophie II* (from 1923–4):

A peculiar and very important instance of the kind of empathic experience, where the other is given to me as somebody who on his part is grasping another, is the case where I myself am co-experienced as this further subject, and where this indirect empathic experience coincides with my own self-experience. In this situation, I experience my counterpart as being experientially directed at myself. On the basis of this most fundamental form of being-there-*for-one-another*-reciprocally the most disparate *I–Thou*-acts and *We-acts* become possible. (Husserl 1959: 136–7)

Being-for-one-another (*Füreinander-dasein*) in and through reciprocal empathy, i.e., being mutually aware of being attended to by the other is only a necessary and not a sufficient condition for social communalization (*sozial Vergemeinschaftet-sein*) (Husserl 1973c: 471–2). What more is needed? The second-personal address: "What is still missing is the intention and will to intimate—the specific act of communication (of communicating oneself), the community creating act that in Latin is simply called *communicatio*" (Husserl 1973c: 473).

In *Gemeingeist I*, one can find further thoughts on this, since Husserl there talks of the I–thou relation as involving a communicative engagement. Both of us, you and I, "look each other in the eyes," you understand me, are aware of me, just as I am simultaneously aware of you. I then address you and seek to influence you. For instance, I might call your attention to a common object by pointing at it. If successful, your attention will shift from my expression to the intended object. In this way, my intention is realized in you (Husserl 1973b: 167–8). Socio-communicative acts involve reciprocity (*Wechselbeziehung*) and lead to a we-synthesis if the intentions interlock in the requisite way (*Willensverflechtung*) (Husserl 1973b: 170). What is distinctive about the I–thou relation, in short, is that I does not simply stand next to the other, rather I motivate you, just as you motivate me, and through this reciprocal interaction, through various social acts, a unity of willing is established that encompasses both subjects (Husserl 1973b: 171):

> I am not merely for myself, and the other is not standing opposed to me as an other, rather the other is my you, and speaking, listening, responding, we already form a we, that is unified and communalized in a particular manner. (Husserl 1973c: 476)

As Husserl consequently makes clear, something momentous happens the moment I turn toward and start to address the other as a you. Relating to the other not simply as an other, but as a you, is simultaneously to be aware of oneself in the accusative as attended to or addressed by the other. This is why Husserl argues that I come to attain personal self-consciousness, and become a personal subject, in the I–thou relation (Husserl 1973b: 171). *Socialization* (being constituted as full-fledged social beings) and *communalization* (being constituted as a member of a social group and a community) are for Husserl two sides of the same process, as Szanto correctly points out (Szanto 2016: 148). Why should Husserl hold such a thesis? Well, as Husserl explains in a central passage in *Ideen II*, when I take over the apprehension that others have of me, when I come to be in possession of such a socially mediated externalized self-apprehension,

"*I fit myself into the family of man,* or, rather, I create the constitutive possibility for the unity of this 'family.' It is only now that I am, in the proper sense, an Ego over against an other and can then say 'we'" (Husserl 1989: 254).

As I interpret Husserl, his guiding idea is that any we-formation, on the one hand, necessarily requires a preservation of plurality. On the other hand, if the difference between self and other is too salient, it will prevent the required sense of togetherness. To adopt a we-perspective and group-identify, to come to think of and experience oneself as *one of us,* consequently requires that the difference between self and others is somewhat downplayed. This is what happens when one comes to experience and adopt the other's perspective on oneself. It is no coincidence that Husserl occasionally describes this process as amounting to a form of self-alienation (*Selbstentfremdung*) (Husserl 1973c: 634–5).[7]

37.5 GURWITSCH ON PARTNERSHIP AND COMMUNAL MEMBERSHIP

Let me end my survey by taking a closer look at some themes in Gurwitsch's Habilitation *Die mitmenschlichen Begegnungen in der Milieuwelt* where he, on the one hand, engages with themes already explored by Scheler and Walther, but, on the other hand, also advocates what ultimately amounts to an alternative phenomenological approach to community.[8]

Like Scheler and Walther before him, Gurwitsch discusses a variety of different social formations and initially distinguishes what he calls *partnership* from (communal) *membership.* For Gurwitsch, the partnership is a kind of instrumental and strategic association (Gurwitsch 1979: 117). The relation of the partners is determined by the situation at hand, and their understanding of each other is "provided by the setting of the things" (Gurwitsch 1979: 105). The partners consequently do not encounter each other as specific individuals, but precisely as (substitutable) partners who are defined and exhausted by the role they play (Gurwitsch 1979: 104, 108, 112). Their relation is consequently somewhat external. The partners are not related to each other independently of the specific situation in which they engage and they remain, as Gurwitsch remarks, "alien to one another" (Gurwitsch 1979: 118). This detached form of interpersonal relation is then contrasted with the communal being-together which, for Gurwitsch, is characterized by a different kind of unity and belonging. His distinction consequently mirrors the distinction between society and community. But how do we get from one to the other? This is where Gurwitsch takes issue with Walther's account. As I explained above, Walther

---

[7] For a fuller development of this interpretation, see Zahavi 2016.

[8] The manuscript was completed in 1932, but due to the political circumstances, Gurwitsch was unable to actually habilitate (he left Germany in 1933) and the book was only published in German in 1976.

took the feeling of inner unification and togetherness to be the decisive ingredient that is present in community but absent in society. One difficulty with this proposal, however, is that it seems to imply that the only difference between community and society is the presence of a certain supervening positive emotional dimension. In both cases, the underlying structure remains exactly the same. Gurwitsch criticizes this proposal and argues that one should recognize not only that partnerships can sometimes occur accompanied by positive feelings, but also that a community is not necessarily threatened or undermined in cases where conflicts or feuds take the place of positive sentiments. Membership in a community can persist even when negative interpersonal emotions are present. We should consequently reject the proposal that the presence of positive feelings is constitutive of communal membership (Gurwitsch 1979: 121–2). But, if a feeling of togetherness is not what constitutes a community qua community, what is then decisive? For Gurwitsch the essential factor is the presence of a shared tradition (Gurwitsch 1979: 122).

Whereas partnerships can be voluntarily initiated and discontinued, one is born into and brought up within a community, and this communal membership is not something from which one can voluntarily dissociate oneself (Gurwitsch 1979: 124). In fact, it is quite beyond the domain of personal will and decision. This is also why, according to Gurwitsch, the being-together in the dimension of the community is not a being-together of individuals qua particular individuals, but qua community members (Gurwitsch 1979: 130). Those with whom one is communally joined have not been selected by free choice based on their personal qualities, but rather based on a shared heritage. Communalization is consequently essentially historical. Our membership in a community determines the way we understand both the world and ourselves and provides us with a deep rootedness in a context that is taken for granted. When members of a community encounter each other, this encounter is informed and shaped by their shared communal possession. This is also why the relation between members of a community is unlike the relation between partners in a work situation. In the latter case, the individuals have their identity prior to engaging in a partnership. In the former case, by contrast, the comprehensive life-context and historicality precede the actual being-together, for which reason the whole might be said to be prior to the parts (Gurwitsch 1979: 132).

Towards the end of his book, Gurwitsch also briefly explores the character of a third social formation, namely the fusional (sectarian) group, where a group of followers are gripped by a common idea and the charismatic power of their leader, and come to feel united as "one" (Gurwitsch 1979: 141–2). It is surprising though that Gurwitsch nowhere in his analysis discusses types of social formations that preserve and cherish the individuality of the members, such as friendships. As should be amply clear from what has already been said, however, Gurwitsch obviously takes issue with an idea, central to the other thinkers previously discussed, namely that bodily expressivity and dyadic face-to-face encounters play a foundational role in the constitution of sociality and community.

37.6 CONCLUSION

A feature common to Husserl, Scheler, and Walther (as well as Stein and later Schutz) is that the investigation of the dyadic empathic encounter figures prominently in their analysis of we-intentionality and experiential sharing. On their view, a proper account of our communal being-together requires an exploration of how individuals are experientially interrelated. We just saw how Gurwitsch questioned this approach. A few years earlier, however, an even more pronounced criticism had already been articulated by Heidegger. In *Sein und Zeit* as well as in lecture courses from around that period, including *Prolegomena zur Geschichte des Zeitbegriffs* (1925), *Die Grundprobleme der Phänomenologie* (1927), and *Einleitung in die Philosophie* (1928–9), Heidegger spoke out against empathy and denied its epistemological and ontological primacy. Not only did he consider the very attempt empathically to grasp the experiences of others to be an exception rather than the default mode of our being-with-others. He also took the very suggestion that a bridge or connection had to be established between two initially independent selves, an I and a thou, to involve a fundamental misunderstanding. There is no gap to be bridged by empathy, since a basic constituent of Dasein's being-in-the-world is its being-with:

> Dasein is essentially *being-with* others *as being-among* intraworldly beings. As being-in-the-world it is never first merely being among things extant within the world, then subsequently to uncover other human beings as also being among them. Instead, as being-in-the-world it is being with others, apart from whether and how others are factically there with it themselves. On the other hand, however, the Dasein is also not first merely being-with others, only then later to run up against intraworldly things in its being-with-others; instead, being-with-others means being-with other being-in-the-world—being-with-in-the-world . . . Put otherwise, being-in-the-world is with equal originality both being-with and being-among. (Heidegger 1982: 278)

As Heidegger insisted, one problem with earlier empathy theorists was that they had failed to realize to what extent the very notion of empathy (*Einfühlung*) is committed to a problematic ontological assumption. The assumption is that the I is at first at home in its own ego-sphere and must then subsequently exit that sphere and enter the sphere of the other in order to establish a connection. This is all wrong, however, since Dasein is already from the start outside, and that is also where it encounters the other (Heidegger 2001: 145). In addition, the empathy theorists had failed to grasp to what extent empathy rather than constituting our being-with is first possible on its basis (Heidegger 1996: 117), or as Heidegger writes in *Einleitung in die Philosophie*:

> The With-one-another [*Miteinander*] cannot be explained through the I–Thou relation, but rather conversely: this I–Thou relation presupposes for its inner possibility that Dasein functioning as I and also as Thou is determined as with-one-another;

indeed even more: even the self-comprehension of an I and the concept of I-ness arise only on the basis of the with-one-another, not from the I–Thou relation. (Heidegger 2001: 145–6)

In a lecture from 1934, Heidegger went on to reject the equation of self and I (Heidegger 2009: 34). Rather, selfhood is something that can also be ascribed to the we. And the very question Who are we? is in his view a timely question, since I-time, the time of liberalism, has now (i.e., in the Germany of the thirties) been replaced by we-time. There are, however, many ways in which people can come together, from a nameless and revolting mass, to a bowling team or a band of robbers (Heidegger 2009: 45). But as long as we think simply of the we as a plurality, as an "assembly of individual human beings" (Heidegger 2009: 55), or as a "multitude of separate Is" (Heidegger 2009: 34) we will definitely not have grasped what a genuine community is (Heidegger 2009: 45). A more radical investigation of who we are will make us realize that "our self-being is the *Volk*" (Heidegger 2009: 50). As Heidegger then goes on to argue, the *Volk* doesn't come about because several independent subjects agree to found a community. Rather, the *Volk* possesses an original vocational unity "that has been consigned to it as heritage and assigned to it as a destiny" (Crowell 2018: 245) and it is on its basis that individuals can come to experience themselves as individuals (Heidegger 2009: 130). Whether or not we belong to the *Volk* is consequently not up to us. Rather it is always already decided, based on our history and descent (Heidegger 2009: 50, 72). Indeed, for Heidegger the national community [*Volksgemeinschaft*] is an ethnic-cultural unity rooted in the forces of blood and soil (Heidegger 2000: 132, 151).

One might have profound concerns about the political implications of this view, just as one might question whether Heidegger's treatment of empathy does justice to the discussions of his phenomenological predecessors, but whatever the case, Heidegger's own approach was certainly not universally endorsed by subsequent phenomenologists. In *Totalité et infini*, Levinas attacks Heidegger for offering a totalizing account that fails to respect and appreciate the alterity and difference of the other (Levinas 1969: 45–6, 67–8, 89). A somewhat similar criticism can also be found in Sartre's *L'être et le néant*. Sartre argued that Heidegger's attempt to downplay the importance of the face-to-face encounter and his insistence on the extent to which our everyday being-with-one-another is characterized by anonymity and substitutability—as Heidegger famously wrote, the others are those among whom one is, but from whom "one mostly does *not* distinguish oneself" (Heidegger 1996: 111)—made Heidegger lose sight of the real nexus of intersubjectivity: the encounter and confrontation with *radical otherness* (Sartre 2003: 271–3).

As these brief references should make clear, the phenomenological debate about the foundations of sociality did not end with the contributions of Heidegger and Gurwitsch. The question of whether second-person engagement and dyadic face-to-face encounters have priority over more anonymous and communal forms of being-with-others continued up through the twentieth century. A proper treatment of the post-war discussion is a topic for another time.

References

Crowell, S. (2018), "The middle Heidegger's phenomenological metaphysics," in D. Zahavi (ed.), *The Oxford Handbook of the History of Phenomenology* (Oxford: Oxford University Press), 229–50.

Gurwitsch, A. (1979), *Human Encounters in the Social World* (Pittsburgh, PA: Duquesne University Press).

Heidegger, M. (1982), *The Basic Problems of Phenomenology*, tr. A. Hofstadter (Bloomington, IN: Indiana University Press).

Heidegger, M. (1996), *Being and Time*, tr. J. Stambaugh (Albany, NY: SUNY).

Heidegger, M. (2000), *Reden und andere Zeugnisse eines Lebensweges (1910–1976).* Gesamtausgabe Band 16 (Frankfurt a. M.: Klostermann).

Heidegger, M. (2001), *Einleitung in die Philosophie.* Gesamtausgabe Band 27 (Frankfurt am Main: Klostermann).

Heidegger, M. (2009), *Logic as the Question Concerning the Essence of Language*, tr. W. T. Gregory and Y. Unna (Albany, NY: SUNY).

Husserl, E. (1959), *Erste Philosophie (1923/24). Zweiter Teil. Theorie der phänomenologischen Reduktion*, Husserliana 8, ed. R. Boehm (The Hague: Martinus Nijhoff).

Husserl, E. (1960), *Cartesian Meditations: An Introduction to Phenomenology*, tr. D. Cairns (The Hague: Martinus Nijhoff).

Husserl, E. (1973a), *Zur Phänomenologie der Intersubjektivität I. Texte aus dem Nachlass. Erster Teil. 1905–1920*, Husserliana 13, ed. I. Kern (The Hague: Martinus Nijhoff).

Husserl, E. (1973b), *Zur Phänomenologie der Intersubjektivität II. Texte aus dem Nachlass. Zweiter Teil. 1921–28*, Husserliana 14, ed. I. Kern (The Hague: Martinus Nijhoff).

Husserl, E. (1973c), *Zur Phänomenologie der Intersubjektivität III. Texte aus dem Nachlass. Dritter Teil. 1929–35*, Husserliana 15, ed. I. Kern (The Hague: Martinus Nijhoff).

Husserl, E. (1989), *Ideas Pertaining to a Pure Phenomenology and to a Phenomenological Philosophy. Second Book: Studies in the Phenomenology of Constitution*, tr. R. Rojcewicz and A. Schuwer (Dordrecht: Kluwer Academic Publishers).

Husserl, E. (2008), *Die Lebenswelt. Auslegungen der vorgegebenen Welt und ihrer Konstitution. Texte aus dem Nachlass (1916–1937)*, Husserliana 39, ed. R. Sowa (Dordrecht: Springer).

Krebs, A. (2015), *Zwischen Ich und Du: Eine dialogische Philosophie der Liebe* (Berlin: Suhrkamp).

Levinas, E. (1969), *Totality and Infinity: An Essay on Exteriority*, tr. A. Lingis (The Hague: Martinus Nijhoff).

León, F. and Zahavi, D. (2016), "Phenomenology of experiential sharing: The contribution of Schutz and Walther," in A. Salice and H. B. Schmid (eds), *The Phenomenological Approach to Social Reality* (Dordrecht: Springer), 219–36.

Reinach, A. (1913), "Die apriorischen Grundlagen des bürgerlichen Rechtes," in E. Husserl (ed.), *Jahrbuch für Philosophie und phänomenologische Forschung I* (Halle: Max Niemeyer), 685–847.

Salice, A. and Schmid, H. B. (eds) (2016), *The Phenomenological Approach to Social Reality* (Dordrecht: Springer).

Sartre, J.-P. (2003), *Being and Nothingness: An Essay on Phenomenological Ontology*, tr. H. Barnes (London: Routledge).

Scheler, M. (1973), *Formalism in Ethics and Non-Formal Ethics of Values: A New Attempt toward the Foundation of an Ethical Personalism*, tr. M. S. Frings and R. L. Funk (Evanston, IL: Northwestern University Press).

Scheler, M. (2008), *The Nature of Sympathy*, tr. P. Heath (London: Transaction Publishers).

Schloßberger, M. (2016), "The varieties of togetherness: Scheler on collective affective intentionality," in A. Salice and H. B. Schmid (eds), *The Phenomenological Approach to Social Reality* (Dordrecht: Springer), 173–95.

Steinbock, A. (1995), *Home and Beyond: Generative Phenomenology after Husserl* (Evanston, IL: Northwestern University Press).

Szanto, T. (2016), "Husserl on collective intentionality," in A. Salice and H. B. Schmid (eds), *The Phenomenological Approach to Social Reality* (Dordrecht: Springer), 145–72.

Szanto, T., and Moran, D. (eds) (2016), *The Phenomenology of Sociality. Discovering the 'We'* (London/New York: Routledge).

Walther, G. (1923), "Zur Ontologie der sozialen Gemeinschaften," in E. Husserl (ed.), *Jahrbuch für Philosophie und phänomenologische Forschung* VI (Halle: Max Niemeyer), 1–158.

Zahavi, D. (1996), *Husserl und die transzendentale Intersubjektivität: Eine Auseinandersetzung mit der Sprachpragmatik* (Dordrecht: Kluwer).

Zahavi, D. (1999), *Self-awareness and Alterity: A Phenomenological Investigation* (Evanston, IL: Northwestern University Press).

Zahavi, D. (2010), "Empathy, Embodiment and Interpersonal Understanding: From Lipps to Schutz," *Inquiry* 53/3: 285–306.

Zahavi, D. (2014), *Self and Other: Exploring Subjectivity, Empathy, and Shame* (Oxford: Oxford University Press).

Zahavi, D. (2016), "Second-person Engagement, Self-alienation, and Group-identification," *Topoi*, doi: 10.1007/s11245-016-9444-6.

Zahavi, D., and Salice, A. (2017), "Phenomenology of the we: Stein, Walther, Gurwitsch," in J. Kiverstein (ed.), *The Routledge Handbook of Philosophy of the Social Mind* (London: Routledge), 515–27.

Index

suffering 447–50, 452
suicide 397
Summa, M. 474
supervene 25
supervenience 26
supplementarity 418, 422–3
surroundings 575
suspend 38
Svenaeus, F. 544
symbolization 116
sympathy (*Mitgefühl*) 736–9, 741, 743
synthesis 61, 112, 162
  active-passive 368
  associative 543
  coincidental 126
  passive 164, 180, 431, 498
Szanto, T. 735, 746

Tabet, P. 334
Taminiaux, J. 15, 658
Taylor, C. 143
technological civilization 407
technology 400, 506
teleological 27, 162
teleology 247
temporal 568
  passage 515
temporality 12, 40, 259, 277, 373,
    549, 722
  diachronic 531
Tengelyi, L. 235, 445, 668
terminus a quo 59
terminus ad quem 59
terror 289, 316
*The Fundamental Concepts of Metaphysics:
    World, Finitude, Solitude* 77, 84, 521
Time and the Other 433, 511, 526–8, 530
there is (*il y a*) 528
things in themselves 49
things themselves, return to the 215
thinking machine 123
Thomistic anthropology 552
Thompson, E. 544, 595
thrownness (*Geworfenheit*) 235, 236
Tidd, U. 321
time 61, 70, 75–6, 224, 253, 419–20, 549
  -object 515
  its transience 512

objective 271
  transcendence of 512
time consciousness 114, 498, 515
  absolute 520, 527
  inner 513–14, 518
  internal 223
  its inquietude 513
  stream of inner 516
Toadvine, T. 651
Tönnies, F. 197, 207, 742
tool 552
topology 387
totality 708
  of entities (*das Seiende im Ganzen*) 234,
    237, 239, 244
*Towards a Phenomenology of Inner Time
    Consciousness* 513, 519
trace 421, 427, 729
tradition 718, 748
tragedy of solitude 530
trajectory 360–1, 365, 367–9, 373–6
transcendence 41, 176, 234, 240, 431,
    433–6, 449, 453, 458, 501–2, 551, 592, 597,
    704, 736
  ambiguous 581
  in immanence 514
  of hope 531
  problem of 101
transcendent 462
transcendental 36–7, 71–4, 79, 80–3, 85,
    231, 235, 246, 263–5, 341, 342, 344–5,
    347–9, 357, 493, 503, 540, 547, 580–1, 588,
    597, 659
  aesthetics 158
  arguments 286–7, 535
  Dialectics 62
  empiricism 49
  field 370
  method 54
  power of imagination 61
  quasi- 732
transfer 543
translucent 287
transparency (*Durchsichtigkeit*) 9
Trendelenburg, F. 46, 112
truth 79, 80, 225, 259–60, 402,
    624, 718
Tugendhat, E. 652, 656, 671